Rick Steves'®

ITALY

2011

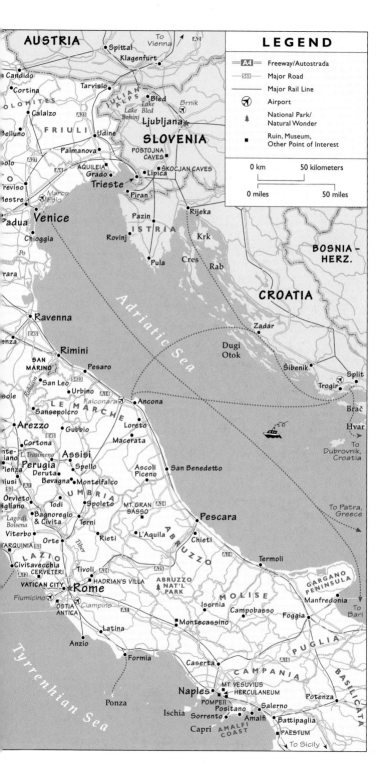

Venice

PONTE GUGLIE →

To Mestre & Mainland

SANTA LUCIA TRAIN STATION (FERROVIA)

Canal Grande

SANTA CROCE

Campo San Geremia

Campo S. Simeone Grande

Campo N. Sauro

Campo Stroppe

Giardino Papadopoli

Piazzale Roma

Campo Lavadori

S. NICOLO TOLENTINO

SAN ROCCO

SCUOLA SAN ROCCO

Campo Mosche

Campo Pantalon

Campo Santa Margherita

Campo Carmini

Campo S. Barnaba

Campo S. Trovaso

GONDOLA WORKSHOP

Zattere

SAN MARCUOLA

CASINÒ

TURKISH EXCHANGE

Campo S. Giacomo dell'Orio

Campo S. Boldo

Campo S. Stin

Campo San Polo

SAN POLO

Campo dei Frari

Campo S. Rocco

FRARI

SAN TOMA

PALAZZO BALBI

CA' FOSCARI

Campo Squellini

CA' REZZONICO

PALAZZO GRASSI

Campo S. Samuele

S. STEFANO

Campo Santo Stefano

SAN VITALE

Campo S. Vidal

Campo Pisani

ACCADEMIA BRIDGE

PEGGY GUGGENHEIM COLLECTION

ACCADEMIA GALLERY

Campo S. Vio

Campo S. Agnese

DORSODURO

Canale della Giudecca

To Giudecca

SIGHTS

1. Accademia Gallery
2. Bridge of Sighs
3. Ca' d'Oro
4. Ca' Pesaro
5. Ca' Rezzonico
6. Campanile (Bell Tower)
7. Clock Tower
8. Correr Museum
9. Doge's Palace
10. Frari Church
11. To Jewish Ghetto & Museum
12. La Fenice Opera House
13. La Salute Church
14. Palazzo Grassi
15. Palazzo Mocenigo Costume Museum
16. Peggy Guggenheim Collection
17. Punta della Dogana Museum
18. Rialto Bridge
19. San Giorgio Maggiore Church
20. San Polo Church
21. San Silvestro Church
22. San Zaccaria Church
23. Scala Contarini del Bovolo
24. To Scuola Dalmata di San Giorgio
25. Scuola San Rocco
26. St. Mark's Basilica
27. St. Mark's Square
28. Train Station
29. To Tronchetto (Main Parking Lot)
30. To Tronchetto via People Mover

CANNAREGIO

Fondamenta Nuove
To Murano,
Burano
& Torcello

Campo
S. Felice

CA' D'ORO

CA'D'
ORO

Ca
d'Oro

Campo
della
Pescheria

FISH
MKT.

Campo
d. Beccarie

Mercato
Rialto
FRUIT &
VEGETABLE
MKT.

Campo
S.Giacomo

RIALTO
BRIDGE

COIN

POST

18

Campo
S.S. Apostoli

Campo
S. Canciano

Campo
S. Maria
Nova

Campo
S. Marina

COLLEONI
STATUE

Campo
S.S. Giovanni
e Paolo

HOSPITAL

SAN
ZANIPOLO

CASTELLO

Campo di
San Silvestro

Corte
Barzizza

21

S. Silvestro

Campo
S. Salvador

SAN
ZULIAN

S. MARIA
FAVA

Campo
S. Maria
Formosa

Campo
S. Benedetto

Campo
Chiesa

Campo
S. Luca

Campo
Manin

23

SAN
MARCO

Campo
S.S. Filippo

SAN
ZACCARIA

24

Campo
S. Angelo

LA
FENICE

12

SAN MARCO

POST
WC

8

Piazza
San
Marco

CAMPANILE

6

Piazzetta
dei Leoni

7

SAN
MARCO

26

27

DOGE'S
PALACE

9

BRIDGE
OF SIGHS

To Public
Gardens

SAN
ZACCARIA

22

Campo S.
Maria

Campo
Traghetto

OSTREGHE

Corte
Barozzi

S. MOISÈ

Giardinetti
Reali

WC

COLUMNS

RIVA D.
SCHIAVONI

San
Zaccaria-
Danieli

San
Zaccaria-
Jolanda

San
Zaccaria-
M.V.E.

S. Maria
del Giglio

Salute

Campo
Salute

S. Marco-
Giardinetti

S. Marco-
Vallaresso

Bacino di San Marco

Canal Grande

C. BASTION

13

17

LA
SALUTE
CHURCH

PUNTA DELLA
DOGANA
MUSEUM
(CUSTOMS
HOUSE)

San Giorgio

SAN
GIORGIO
MAGGIORE

19

To
Giudecca

SAN
GIORGIO

LEGEND

Popular Shopping Area

■ Landmark or Point of
Interest (sight number
marks entrance)

V Vaporetto Stop

T Traghetto Crossing

G Gondola Station

A Alilaguna Stop

A To/From Airport

i Tourist Information

0   200 meters

200 yards

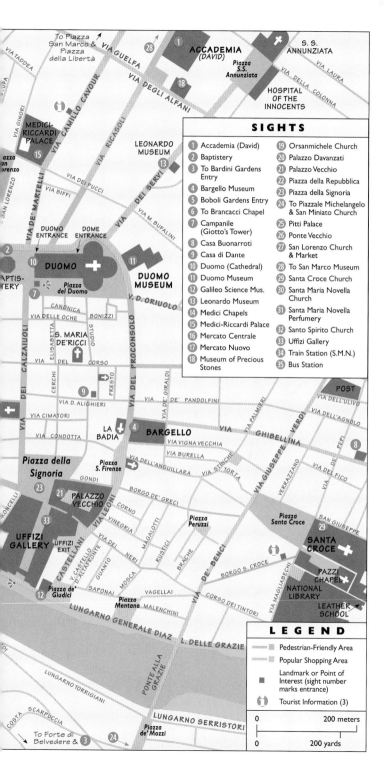

SIGHTS

1. Accademia (David)
2. Baptistery
3. To Bardini Gardens Entry
4. Bargello Museum
5. Boboli Gardens Entry
6. To Brancacci Chapel
7. Campanile (Giotto's Tower)
8. Casa Buonarroti
9. Casa di Dante
10. Duomo (Cathedral)
11. Duomo Museum
12. Galileo Science Mus.
13. Leonardo Museum
14. Medici Chapels
15. Medici-Riccardi Palace
16. Mercato Centrale
17. Mercato Nuovo
18. Museum of Precious Stones
19. Orsanmichele Church
20. Palazzo Davanzati
21. Palazzo Vecchio
22. Piazza della Repubblica
23. Piazza della Signoria
24. To Piazzale Michelangelo & San Miniato Church
25. Pitti Palace
26. Ponte Vecchio
27. San Lorenzo Church & Market
28. To San Marco Museum
29. Santa Croce Church
30. Santa Maria Novella Church
31. Santa Maria Novella Perfumery
32. Santo Spirito Church
33. Uffizi Gallery
34. Train Station (S.M.N.)
35. Bus Station

LEGEND

- Pedestrian-Friendly Area
- Popular Shopping Area
- ■ Landmark or Point of Interest (sight number marks entrance)
- ↑ Tourist Information (3)

| 0 | | 200 meters |
| 0 | | 200 yards |

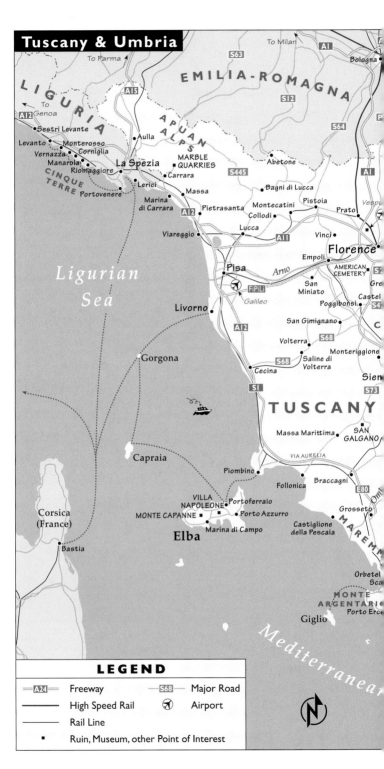

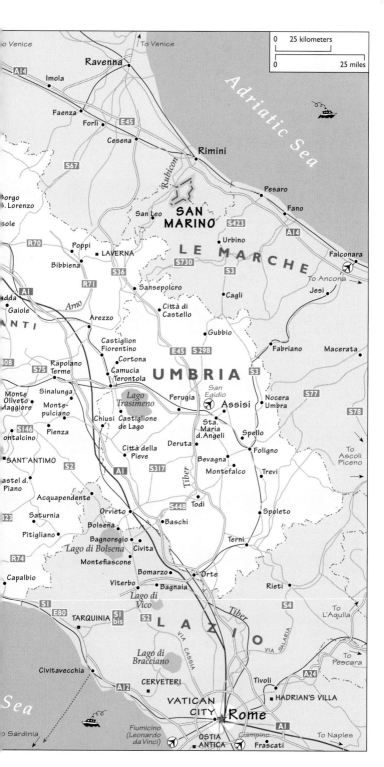

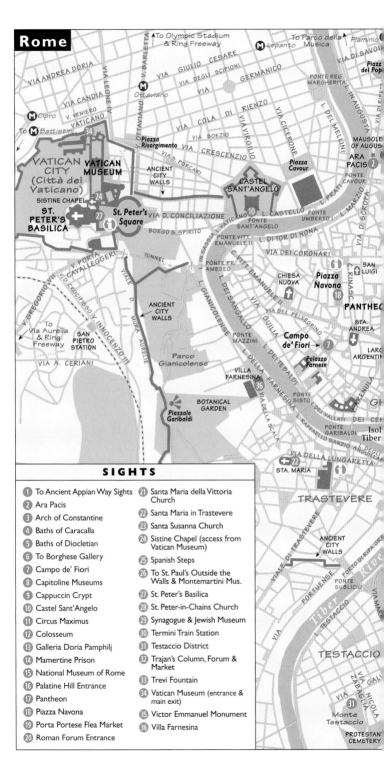

Rome

To Olympic Stadium & Ring Freeway
To Parco della Musica
Flaminio
Lepanto
To Battistini
Cipro
Ottaviano

VIA ANDREA DORIA
V. BARLETTA
VIA LEONE IV
VIA GIULIO CESARE
VIA DEGLI SCIPIONI
GERMANICO
VIA
VIA DI SAVOIA
Piazza del Popolo
PONTE REG. MARGHERITA
L. IN AUGUSTA

V. VENIERO
VATICANO
OTTAVIANO
VIA CANDIA
VIA COLA DI RIENZO
VIA BOEZIO
VIA VIRGILIO
VIA CICERONE
VIA CRESCENZIO
VIA S. PORCARI

VATICAN CITY (Città del Vaticano)
VATICAN MUSEUM
SISTINE CHAPEL
ST. PETER'S BASILICA
St. Peter's Square

Piazza Risorgimento
ANCIENT CITY WALLS
Piazza Cavour
CASTEL SANT'ANGELO

MAUSOLE OF AUGUS
ARA PACIS
PONTE CAVOUR
L. PRATI
L. MARZIO
L. DI SCROFA

VIA D. CONCILIAZIONE
BORGO S. SPIRITO
PONTE SANT'ANGELO
L. CASTELLO
PONTE UMBERTO I
VIA IN SASSIA
VIA VATICANO
PONTE VITT. EMANUELE II

VIA D. CONCILIAZIONE
VIA DEI CORONARI
PONTE PR. AMEDEO
L. DI TOR DI NONA
C. VITT. EMANUELE II

TUNNEL
V. PORTA CAVALLEGGERI
V.D. CROCIFISSO
V. GREGORIO VII
ANCIENT CITY WALLS
SAN PIETRO STATION

VIALE D. MURA AURELIE
V. INNOCENZO III

CHIESA NUOVA
Piazza Navona
SAN LUIGI
C. RINASC.
PANTHEON
STA. ANDREA
LARG ARGENTINA

VIA DEL PELLEGRINO
VIA GIULIA
Campo de' Fiori
Palazzo Farnese
PONTE MAZZINI
PONTE SISTO
L. DEI TEBALDI

To Via Aurelia & Ring Freeway
VIA A. CERIANI
Parco Gianicolense
Piazzale Garibaldi
BOTANICAL GARDEN
VILLA FARNESINA
PONTE GARIBALDI
L. DELLA FARNESINA
VIA DELLA SCALA

VIA DELLA LUNGARETTA
STA. MARIA
TRASTEVERE
VIALE DI TRASTEVERE
ANCIENT CITY WALLS

L. DEI VALLATI
L. RAFFAELLO SANZIO
Isola Tiberina
DEI CENCI

PONTE SUBLICIO
PORTO DI RIPA GR.
Tiber River
PORTUENSE
L. TESTACCIO
VIA MARM

TESTACCIO
VIA GALV
VIA NICOLA ZABAGLIA
Monte Testaccio
PROTESTANT CEMETERY

SIGHTS

1 To Ancient Appian Way Sights
2 Ara Pacis
3 Arch of Constantine
4 Baths of Caracalla
5 Baths of Diocletian
6 To Borghese Gallery
7 Campo de' Fiori
8 Capitoline Museums
9 Cappuccin Crypt
10 Castel Sant'Angelo
11 Circus Maximus
12 Colosseum
13 Galleria Doria Pamphilj
14 Mamertine Prison
15 National Museum of Rome
16 Palatine Hill Entrance
17 Pantheon
18 Piazza Navona
19 Porta Portese Flea Market
20 Roman Forum Entrance
21 Santa Maria della Vittoria Church
22 Santa Maria in Trastevere
23 Santa Susanna Church
24 Sistine Chapel (access from Vatican Museum)
25 Spanish Steps
26 To St. Paul's Outside the Walls & Montemartini Mus.
27 St. Peter's Basilica
28 St. Peter-in-Chains Church
29 Synagogue & Jewish Museum
30 Termini Train Station
31 Testaccio District
32 Trajan's Column, Forum & Market
33 Trevi Fountain
34 Vatican Museum (entrance & main exit)
35 Victor Emmanuel Monument
36 Villa Farnesina

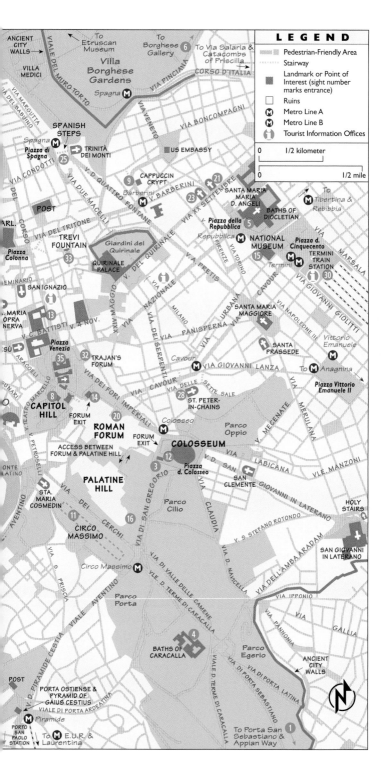

LEGEND

▨	Pedestrian-Friendly Area
⋯⋯	Stairway
■	Landmark or Point of Interest (sight number marks entrance)
□	Ruins
Ⓜ	Metro Line A
Ⓜ	Metro Line B
ⓘ	Tourist Information Offices

0   1/2 kilometer

0   1/2 mile

ANCIENT CITY WALLS

VILLA MEDICI

To Etruscan Museum

To Borghese Gallery

To Via Salaria & Catacombs of Priscilla

CORSO D'ITALIA

Villa Borghese Gardens

Spagna Ⓜ

VIA PINCIANA

VIA BONCOMPAGNI

VIA DEL MURO TORTO

VIA MARGUTTA

VIA DEI BABUINO

SPANISH STEPS

Spagna Ⓜ

Piazza di Spagna

TRINITÀ DEI MONTI

VIA VENETO

US EMBASSY

CAPPUCCIN CRYPT

Barberini

V. BARBERINI

SANTA MARIA MARIA D. ANGELI

BATHS OF DIOCLETIAN

To Tibertina & Rebibbia

VIA CONDOTTI

VIA DUE MACELLI

VIA V.D. QUATTRO FONTANE

V. XX SETTEMBRE

VIA XX SETTEMBRE

POST

VIA DEL TRITONE

TREVI FOUNTAIN

Giardini del Quirinale

Piazza della Repubblica

Repubblica

NATIONAL MUSEUM

Piazza d. Cinquecento

TERMINI TRAIN STATION

VIA MARSALA

Piazza Colonna

QUIRINALE PALACE

V. DEL QUIRINALE

VIA NAZIONALE

VIA FIRENZE

VIA TORINO

Termini

VIA GIOVANNI GIOLITTI

SEMINARIO

SAN IGNAZIO

V. A PRETIS

SANTA MARIA MAGGIORE

VIA CAVOUR

VIA NAPOLEONE II

Vittorio Emanuele Ⓜ

MARIA OPRA NERVA

V. C. BATTISTI V. 4 NOV.

Piazza Venezia

TRAJAN'S FORUM

VIA PANISPERNA

VIA URBANA

SANTA PRASSEDE

To Ⓜ Anagnina

SÙ

VIA DEI SERPENTI

Cavour Ⓜ

VIA GIOVANNI LANZA

Piazza Vittorio Emanuele II

CAPITOL HILL

FORUM EXIT

ROMAN FORUM

VIA DEI FORI IMPERIALI

VIA CAVOUR

VIA DELLE SETTE SALE

ST. PETER-IN-CHAINS

Colosseo Ⓜ

Parco Oppio

V. MECENATE

VIA MERULANA

FORUM EXIT

ACCESS BETWEEN FORUM & PALATINE HILL

PALATINE HILL

COLOSSEUM

Piazza d. Colosseo

VIA LABICANA

VLE. MANZONI

STA. MARIA COSMEDIN

VIA DEI CERCHI

CIRCO MASSIMO

VIA DI SAN GREGORIO

Parco Cilio

SAN CLEMENTE

VIA CLAUDIA

SAN GIOVANNI IN LATERANO

V. S. STEFANO ROTONDO

HOLY STAIRS

Circo Massimo Ⓜ

VIA DI VALLE DELLE CAMENE

VLE. D. TERME DI CARACALLA

VIA DELL'AMBA ARADAM

SAN GIOVANNI IN LATERANO

VIA IPPONIO

Parco Porta

Parco Egerio

ANCIENT CITY WALLS

VIA GALLIA

VIA PANNONIA

BATHS OF CARACALLA

VIALE D. TERME DI CARACALLA

VIA DI PORTA LATINA

VIA DI PORTA SEBASTIANO

POST

PORTA OSTIENSE & PYRAMID OF GAIUS CESTIUS

VIALE DI PORTA ARDEATINA

PORTO SAN PAOLO STATION

Piramide Ⓜ

To Ⓜ E.U.R. & Laurentina

To Porta San Sebastiano & Appian Way

CONTENTS

Italy

Italia

Bella Italia! Italy has Europe's richest, craziest culture. If you take Italy on its own terms, you'll experience a cultural keelhauling that actually feels good.

Some people, often with considerable effort, manage to hate this country. Italy bubbles with emotion, corruption, stray hairs, inflation, traffic jams, strikes, rallies, holidays, crowded squalor, and irate ranters shaking their fists at each other one minute and walking arm-in-arm the next. Have a talk with yourself before you cross the border. Promise yourself to relax and accept it all as a package deal.

After all, Italy is the cradle of European civilization— established by the Roman Empire and carried on by the Roman Catholic Church. As you explore Italy, you'll stand face-to-face with some of the world's most iconic images from this 2,000-year history: the Colosseum of Ancient Rome, the medieval Leaning Tower of Pisa, Michelangelo's *David* and Botticelli's *Venus* that signal the Renaissance, the playful Baroque exuberance of the Trevi Fountain...and the Italian city that preserves this legacy in a state of elegant decay: Venice.

Beyond these famous sights, though, Italy offers Europe's richest culture. Traditions still live within a country that is vibrant and fully modern. Go with an eye open to both the Italy of the past and of the present.

Italy is diverse, encompassing German-flavored Alps, Mediterranean beaches, sun-baked Sicily, romantic hill towns,

the urban jungle of Naples, the business center of Milan, and the art-drenched cities of Venice, Florence, and Rome. The country is reasonably small and laced with freeways and train lines, so you're never more than a day's journey away from any of these places. Each of Italy's 20 regions has its own distinct character, whether it's scenic Tuscany, busy Lombardy, or the place where it all mixes together—Lazio, home of the capital, Rome.

Many travelers discover that there are two Italys: The North is industrial, aggressive, and "time is money" in its outlook. The weather is temperate, and the people are more like Northern Europeans. The South is hot and sunny, crowded, poor, relaxed, farm-oriented, and traditional. Families here are very close-knit and usually live in the same house for many generations. Loyalties are to family, city, region, soccer team, and country—in that order. (For more on the two Italys, see "Rome vs. Milan: A Classic Squabble" on page 276).

Economically, Italy has had its problems, but somehow things have always worked out. Today, Italy is the world's seventh-largest industrial power, and the fourth-largest in Europe. Ferraris, Fiats, Maseratis, and Lamborghinis are world-renowned (though they're not really major exports). Tourism is big business—Italy is considered the world's fifth most-visited tourist destination.

Cronyism, which complicates my work, is an integral part of the economy. Much of Italy's business is hidden in a large "black market" unreported to government officials. Labor unions are strong, strikes are frequent, and the country today is faced with pressure to compete globally.

While most Italians are nominally Catholic, the true dominant religion is life—motor scooters, soccer, fashion, girl-watching, boy-watching, good coffee, good wine, and *il dolce far niente* (the sweetness of doing nothing). The Italian character shows itself on the streets in the skilled maniac drivers and the classy dressers who star in the ritual evening stroll, or *passeggiata*.

Italians are more social and communal than most other Europeans. In small towns, everyone knows everyone. People get out of their apartments to socialize on the main square. Young women walk hand in hand, and young teenagers shove

or punch each other playfully or hang all over each other.

Because they're so outgoing and their language is so fun, Italians are a pleasure to communicate with. Be melodramatic and talk with your hands. Hear the melody; get into the flow. Italians want to connect, and they try harder than any other Europeans. Play with them. Even in non-touristy towns,

Italy Almanac

Official Name: Repubblica Italiana (Italian Republic), or Italia for short.

Population: 58 million, comprised almost entirely of indigenous Italians who speak Italian (German and French are spoken in some Alpine regions) and are nominally Roman Catholic (90 percent).

Latitude and Longitude: 43°N and 12°E (similar to Oregon and Maine).

Area: 116,000 square miles, including the islands of Sicily, Sardinia, and others.

Geography: Italy is shaped like a boot, 850 miles long and 150 miles wide, jutting into the central Mediterranean. (By comparison, Florida is 500 miles long.) The terrain is generally mountainous or hilly, with the Alps in the north and a north-south "spine" of the Apennine Mountains. The highest point is Mont Blanc (15,771 feet), on the border with France. Outside the Alps, the highest point is Monte Cimone (7,100 feet). Italy has 5,000 miles of coastline. Major rivers include the Po (the longest at 400 miles), Arno, Adige, and Tiber. Italy has three active volcanoes: Vesuvius, Etna, and Stromboli.

Regions: Italy is divided into 20 regions (including Tuscany, Umbria, Veneto, and Lazio). Locally, there are some 8,000 "communes," each with a community council and mayor.

Major Cities: Rome (the capital, 2.6 million), Milan (1.3 million), and Naples (1 million).

Economy: The Gross Domestic Product is $1.8 trillion; the GDP per capita is $30,300. About 73 percent of the economy consists of service jobs (especially tourism), 25 percent is industry (textiles, chemicals), and 2 percent is agriculture (fruit, vegetables, olives, wine, plus fishing). There are 10,000 miles of train lines (mostly government-run) and 4,300 miles of expressway (autostrada).

Government: Italy is a republic, with three branches of government. The chief executive is three-term Prime Minister Silvio Berlusconi. The bicameral legislature is elected by (mostly) direct voting. Since World War II, the fragmented country has had 61 national governments.

Flag: Three vertical bands of green, white, and red.

Italian Inventions: Opera, cologne, thermometer, barometer, pizza, wireless telegraph, espresso machine, typewriter, batteries, nitroglycerin, yo-yos...and the ice-cream cone.

Museums: 3,000.

Average "Gio": The average Italian is 43 years old, has 1.3 kids, and will live to the ripe old age of 80 (one in five Italians is older than 65). Every day, he or she consumes two servings of pasta, a half-pound of bread, and two glasses of wine. Nearly half of all Italians use the Internet.

where English is rare and Italian is the norm, showing a little warmth lets you hop right over the language barrier.

Like most Europeans (and Americans), Italians enjoy watching TV (game shows, sitcoms, etc.), going to movies (American films are almost always dubbed, not subtitled), and listening to their homegrown pop music. Though Italy is the birthplace of opera and much classical music, it's not much more "cultured" today than America is.

Italian food, however, is a cut above. If America's specialty is fast food, Italy's is slow food: locally grown ingredients, in season, bought daily, prepared with love, and enjoyed in social circumstances with friends and family. Even in modern cities,  big supermarkets are rare. Instead, people buy their bread from the baker and their meats from the butcher, enjoying a chance to catch up on gossip with the shopkeeper. Italians buy foods in season, celebrating the arrival of fresh artichokes in the spring and porcini mushrooms in the fall.

The three-hour meal is common. For many Italians, dinner is the evening's entertainment. They eat in courses, lingering over each one. A typical meal might start with an antipasto plate of cold cuts and veggies. Next comes the pasta, then the meat dish, then a salad. No meal is complete without dessert (Italian gelato is considered the best ice cream in the world), accompanied by coffee or a dessert drink.

Wine complements each course. Italy is the world's number-one wine producer (just ahead of France). It'd be a shame to visit Italy without sampling the specialties from each region, whether it's the famous Chianti from central Italy, a white Soave from the Veneto, Bardolinos from the North, or a Lacryma Christi from the South.

Italian "bars" are not taverns, but cafés...and social watering holes. In the morning, they serve coffee, orange juice, and croissants to workers on the go. At lunch, it's sandwiches *(panini)* and mini-pizzas for university students. In the afternoon, housewives might drop in for an ice-cream bar. At night, men and women enjoy a glass of wine and watch TV while the kids play a video game in the corner.

Besides food, travelers enjoy sampling Italy's other wares. While no longer a cheap country, Italy is still a hit with shoppers. Find glassware in Venice; gold, silver, leather, and prints in Florence; and high fashion in Rome and Milan.

Italians are obsessed with sports—though not American sports. Italian sports idols are soccer players (Francesco Totti, Antonio Cassano), skiers (Giorgio Rocca), and cyclists (Paolo Savodelli). Motor racing—Formula 1/Grand Prix—is huge. And since many Italians grow up zipping through narrow streets on small Vespas, it's little wonder that motorcycle racing *(moto,* led by Valentino Rossi) is a major sport here. A favorite participant sport is bocce, played casually at parks

throughout Italy. The players take turns tossing small metal balls on a dirt court, aiming at a small wooden ball.

Italy's undisputed number-one sport is soccer (called *il calcio*). Soccer fans *(tifosi)* are passionate. Star players are paid millions and treated like movie stars. Little kids everywhere grow up pretending to score the winning goal just like them. On big game nights, bars are packed with men crowded around TV sets. After a loss, they drown their sorrows. After a victory, fans celebrate by driving through the city streets honking horns and waving team flags. Many Italians place their national, regional, and personal pride on the backs of their athletes. It's a cliché that remains true: In a Europe at peace, the football field is the battleground.

But even as Europe evolves, Italy remains a mix of old and new. Appreciate the extreme changes Italian society has gone through in just 50 years: the "economic miracle" of the 1950s, the liberal reforms of the 1960s, a wave of domestic terrorism (from the left and the right) in the 1970s and 1980s, the entry into the European Union in the 1990s, and several years ago, the Berlusconi government's unpopular support of the Iraq war. Italian politics are a reckless pendulum that swings between right- and left-wing extremes. It seems that nobody holds office for very long. But, as Berlusconi demonstrated in the 2008 elections, it's always possible to bounce back.

Italy, home of the Vatican, is still 90 percent Catholic...but not particularly devout. Most people would never think of renouncing their faith, but they don't attend church regularly. They baptize their kids at the local church (there's one every few blocks), but they hold modern opinions on social issues, often in conflict  with strict Catholic dogma. Italy is now the land of legalized abortion, the lowest birth rate in Europe, nudity on TV, socialist politics, and a society whose common language is decidedly secular.

Some traditions thrive. Italian families and communities are still more close-knit than many others in the modern world. Many Italians, especially in rural regions, still follow the traditional siesta schedule (called *reposo* in Italy). At about 1:00 p.m., shops close and people go home for a three-hour break to have lunch, socialize with friends and family, and maybe take a short nap in front of the TV. And on festival days, locals still dress up in medieval garb to paddle gondolas (Venice), race horses (Siena), battle over a bridge (Pisa), or play rugby or soccer (Florence). But these days, the traditional ways are carried on by choice. Italians are wary of the dangers of a fast-paced global lifestyle. Their history is long, and they're secure in their place in the world.

Accept Italy as Italy. Zero in on the fine points. Don't dwell on the problems. Savor your cappuccino, dangle your feet over a canal (if it smells, breathe through your mouth), and imagine what it was like centuries ago. Ramble through the rabble and rubble of Rome and mentally resurrect those ancient stones. Look into the famous sculpted eyes of Michelangelo's *David* and understand Renaissance Man's assertion of himself. Sit silently on a hilltop rooftop. Get chummy with the winds of the past. Write a poem over a glass of local wine in a sun-splashed, wave-dashed Riviera village. If you fall off your moral horse, call it a cultural experience. Italy is for romantics.

INTRODUCTION

This book will help you make the most of your trip. It breaks Italy into its top destinations—offering a balanced, comfortable mix of exciting cities and cozy towns, from brutal but *bella* Rome to *tranquillo,* traffic-free Riviera villages. It covers the predictable biggies and stirs in a healthy dose of "Back Door" intimacy. Along with marveling at Michelangelo's masterpieces, you'll enjoy a snack of *bruschetta* (fresh garlic rubbed on toast) prepared by a village boy. I've been selective, including only the most exciting sights and experiences. For example, after visiting many hill towns, I recommend just my favorites.

You'll get all the specifics and opinions necessary to wring the maximum value out of your limited time and money. If you plan a month or less in Italy, and you have a normal appetite for information, this book is all you need. If you're a travel-info fiend like me, you'll find that this book sorts through all the superlatives and provides a handy rack upon which to hang your supplemental information.

Italy is my favorite European country. Experiencing its culture, people, and natural wonders economically and hassle-free has

been my goal for three decades of traveling, tour guiding, and writing. With this book, I pass on to you the lessons I've learned, updated for 2011.

The best of Italy is, of course, only my opinion. But after spending half my adult life researching Europe, I've developed a sixth sense for what travelers enjoy.

INTRODUCTION

Top Destinations in Italy

THE LAKES

DOLOMITES

MILAN

RIVIERA TOWNS NEAR CINQUE TERRE

TOWNS NEAR VENICE

VENICE

CINQUE TERRE

FLORENCE

SIENA

PISA & LUCCA

HILL TOWNS OF CENTRAL ITALY

ASSISI

ROME

NAPLES

SORRENTO & CAPRI

AMALFI COAST & PAESTUM

DCH

About This Book

Rick Steves' Italy 2011 is a personal tour guide in your pocket. This book is organized by destination, with each one covered as a mini-vacation on its own, filled with exciting sights and comfortable, affordable places to stay. In the following chapters, you'll find these sections:

Orientation includes specifics on public transportation, helpful hints, local tour options, easy-to-read maps, and tourist information. The "Planning Your Time" section offers a suggested schedule for how to best use your limited time.

Sights describes the top attractions and includes their cost and hours.

Self-Guided Walks take you through interesting neighborhoods, with a personal tour guide in hand.

Sleeping describes my favorite hotels, from good-value deals to cushy splurges.

Key to This Book

Updates

This book is updated every year—but once you pin down Italy, it wiggles. For the latest, visit www.ricksteves.com /update. For a valuable list of reports and experiences—good and bad—from fellow travelers, check www.ricksteves.com /feedback.

Abbreviations and Times

I use the following symbols and abbreviations in this book: Sights are rated:

▲▲▲	**Don't miss**
▲▲	**Try hard to see**
▲	**Worthwhile if you can make it**
No rating	**Worth knowing about**

Tourist information offices are abbreviated as **TI,** and bathrooms are **WC**s. To categorize accommodations, I use a **Sleep Code** (described on page 20).

Like Europe, this book uses the **24-hour clock.** It's the same through 12:00 noon, then keep going: 13:00, 14:00, and so on. For anything over 12, subtract 12 and add p.m. (14:00 is 2:00 p.m.).

When giving **opening times,** I include both peak season and off-season hours if they differ. So, if a museum is listed as "May–Oct daily 9:00–16:00," it should be open from 9 a.m. until 4 p.m. from the first day of May until the last day of October (but expect exceptions).

For **transit** or **tour departures,** I first list the frequency, then the duration. So, a train connection listed as "2/hour, 1.5 hours" departs twice each hour and the journey lasts an hour and a half.

Eating serves up a range of options, from inexpensive eateries to fancy restaurants.

Connections outlines your options for traveling to destinations by plane, train, bus, and cruise ship. In car-friendly regions, I've included route tips for drivers.

Italian History gives you a helpful overview of Italy's history, art, and architecture.

The **appendix** is a traveler's tool kit, with telephone tips, transportation basics, recommended books and films, a festival list, a climate chart, a handy packing checklist, a hotel reservation form, and Italian survival phrases.

Browse through this book, choose your favorite destinations, and link them up. Then have a *buono* trip! Traveling like a temporary local, you'll get the absolute most out of every mile, minute, and euro. As you visit places I know and love, I'm happy that you'll be meeting some of my favorite Italian people.

Planning

This section will help you get started planning your trip—with advice on trip costs, when to go, and what you should know before you take off.

Travel Smart

Many people travel through Italy thinking it's a chaotic mess. They feel that any attempt at efficient travel is futile. This is dead wrong—and expensive. Italy, which seems as orderly as spilled spaghetti, actually functions quite well. Only those who understand this and travel smart can enjoy Italy on a budget.

This book can save you lots of time and money. But to have an "A" trip, you need to be an "A" student. Read it all before your trip, noting holidays, specific advice on sights, and days when sights are closed. A smart trip is a puzzle—a fun, doable, and worthwhile challenge.

Be sure to mix intense and relaxed periods in your itinerary. To maximize rootedness, minimize one-night stands. Every trip—and every traveler—needs slack time (laundry, picnics, people-watching, and so on). Pace yourself. Assume you will return.

As you travel, take advantage of the Internet and phones to make your trip run smoothly. Get online at Internet cafés or your hotel, and buy a phone card or carry a mobile phone. You can find tourist information, learn the latest on sights (special events, English tour schedule, etc.), book tickets and tours, make reservations, reconfirm hotels, research transportation connections, and keep in touch with your loved ones.

Enjoy the friendliness of the Italian people. Connect with the culture. Set up your own quest for the best piazza, bell tower, gelato, or whatever. Slow down and be open to unexpected experiences. Ask questions—most locals are eager to point you in their idea of the right direction. Keep a notepad in your pocket for organizing your thoughts. Wear your money belt, learn the currency, and figure out how to estimate prices in dollars. Those who expect to travel smart, do.

Trip Costs

Six components make up your trip costs: airfare, surface transportation, room and board, sightseeing/entertainment, shopping/miscellany, and gelato.

Airfare: A basic round-trip flight from the US to Milan or Rome should cost from $900 to $1,600, depending on where you fly from and when you go. Smaller budget airlines provide bargain service from several European capitals to many cities in Italy (see "Cheap Flights" on page 975). If your trip covers a wide area, consider saving time and money in Europe by flying "open jaw" (into one city and out of another; e.g., into Milan and out of Rome).

Surface Transportation: For a three-week whirlwind trip of all of my recommended destinations, allow $500 per person for buses and second-class trains ($700 for first-class trains). For a three-week car rental, tolls, gas, and insurance, allow $900 per person (based on two people sharing). Car rentals and leases are cheapest if arranged from the US. Train passes are normally available only outside of Europe. You may save money by simply buying tickets as you go (see "Transportation," in the appendix for more details on car rental and public transportation).

Room and Board: You can thrive in Italy in 2011 on $120 a day per person for room and board (more in big cities). This allows $15 for lunch, $25 for dinner, and $80 for lodging (based on two people splitting the cost of a $160 double room that includes breakfast). If you've got more money, I've listed great ways to spend it. Students and tightwads can enjoy Italy for as little as $60 a day ($30 for a bed, $30 for meals and snacks).

Sightseeing and Entertainment: In big cities, figure about $15–20 per major sight (museums, Colosseum), $5–10 for minor ones (climbing church towers), and $25–30 for splurge experiences (e.g., walking tours and concerts). An overall average of $35 a day works for most people. Don't skimp here. After all, this category is the driving force behind your trip—you came to sightsee, enjoy, and experience Italy.

Shopping and Miscellany: Figure $3 per postcard, coffee, soft drink, or gelato. Shopping can vary in cost from nearly nothing to a small fortune. Good budget travelers find that this category has little to do with assembling a trip full of lifelong and wonderful memories.

Sightseeing Priorities

Depending on the length of your trip, here are my recommended priorities:

4 days:	Florence, Venice
6 days, add:	Rome
8 days, add:	Cinque Terre
10 days, add:	Civita and Siena
14 days, add:	Sorrento, Naples, Pompeii, Amalfi Coast, Paestum
18 days, add:	Milan, Lake Como, Varenna, Assisi
21 days, add:	Dolomites, Verona, Padua

This includes nearly everything on the map on page 11.

Italy at a Glance

These attractions are listed (as in this book) roughly from north to south.

▲▲▲**Venice** Romantic island city, powerful in medieval times, famous for St. Mark's Basilica, the Grand Canal, and singing gondoliers.

▲**Near Venice** Several interesting towns: Padua (with Giotto's gloriously frescoed Scrovegni Chapel), Verona (Roman amphitheater plus Romeo and Juliet sights), and Ravenna (top Byzantine mosaics).

▲**The Dolomites** Italy's rugged rooftop with a Germanic flair, featuring Bolzano (home of Ötzi the Ice Man), Castelrotto (charming village), and Alpe di Siusi (alpine meadows laced with lifts and hiking trails).

▲**The Lakes** Two relaxing lakes, each with low-key resort towns and a mountainous backdrop: Lake Como, with quaint Varenna and upscale Bellagio; and Lake Maggiore, with straightforward Stresa, manicured islands, and elegant villas.

▲▲**Milan** Powerhouse city of commerce and fashion, with the prestigious La Scala opera house, Leonardo's *The Last Supper*, and two airports.

▲▲▲**The Cinque Terre** Five idyllic Riviera hamlets along a rugged coastline (and part of a national park), connected by scenic hiking trails and dotted with beaches.

Riviera Towns near the Cinque Terre More Italian Riviera fun, including the beach towns of Levanto, Sestri Levante, the larger Santa Margherita Ligure, and trendier Portofino nearby, and to the south, resorty Portovenere and workaday La Spezia (transportation hub).

When to Go

Italy's best travel months (also its busiest and most expensive) are May, June, September, and October. These months combine the convenience of peak season with pleasant weather.

The most grueling thing about travel in Italy is the summer heat in July and August, when temperatures hit the high 80s and 90s. Most mid-range hotels come with air-conditioning—a worthwhile splurge in the summer—but it's usually available only from

▲▲▲**Florence** The cradle of the Renaissance, with the world-class Uffizi Gallery, Brunelleschi's dome-topped Duomo, Michelangelo's *David,* and Italy's best gelato.

▲**Pisa and Lucca** Two classic towns: Pisa, with its famous Leaning Tower and surrounding Field of Miracles, and Lucca, with a charming walled old center.

▲▲▲**Siena** Florence's smaller and (some say) more appealing rival, with its grand Il Campo square and striking striped cathedral.

▲▲**Assisi** St. Francis' hometown, perched on a hillside, with a divinely Giotto-decorated basilica.

▲▲**Hill Towns of Central Italy** Picturesque, wine-soaked villages of Italy's heartland, including San Gimignano, Volterra, Montalcino, Pienza, Montepulciano, Cortona, Orvieto, and the adorable pocket-sized Civita di Bagnoregio.

▲▲▲**Rome** Italy's capital, the Eternal City, studded with Roman remnants (Forum, Colosseum, Pantheon), romantic floodlit-fountain squares, and the Vatican, home to one of Italy's top museums and the Sistine Chapel.

▲▲**Naples** Gritty, in-love-with-life port city featuring vibrant street life and a top archaeological museum, with the famous Pompeii ruins a day-trip away.

▲**Sorrento and Capri** The seaside resort port of Sorrento, and a short cruise away, the jet-set island getaway of Capri, with its Blue Grotto.

▲▲**Amalfi Coast and Paestum** String of seafront villages—including hilly Positano and Amalfi—tied together by a scenic mountainous coastal road, plus nearby Paestum, with its well-preserved ancient Greek temples.

June through September.

Peak season (roughly May–Sept) offers the longest hours and the most exciting slate of activities—but terrible crowds. During peak times, many resort-area hotels maximize business by requiring that guests take half-pension, which means buying a meal per day (usually dinner) in their restaurants. August, the local holiday month, isn't as bad as many make it out to be, but big cities tend to be quiet (with discounted hotel prices), and beach and mountain

Major Holidays and Weekends

Popular places are even busier on weekends...and inundated on three-day weekends. Holidays bring many businesses to a grinding halt. Plan ahead and reserve your accommodations and transportation well in advance.

In Italy, hotels get booked up for major holidays—Easter weekend (April 24-25 in 2011), Liberation Day (April 25), Labor Day (May 1), Feast of the Ascension Day (June 2 in 2011), All Saint's Day (Nov 1), Christmas (Dec 25-26), and New Year's Eve—and on Fridays and Saturdays year-round.

For more information, check "Holidays and Festivals" in the appendix. A myriad of religious and neighborhood celebrations can catch you by surprise anywhere in Italy.

resorts are jammed (with higher hotel prices). Note that Italians generally wear shorts only at beach resort towns. If you want to blend in, wear lightweight long (or Capri) pants in Italy, even in summer, except at the beach.

Between November and April, you can usually expect pleasant weather, and you'll miss most of the sweat and stress of the tourist season. Off-season, expect shorter hours, more lunchtime breaks, and fewer activities. However, spring and fall can be cool (and most hotels don't turn the heat on until winter). In the winter, it often drops to the 40s in Milan and the 50s in Rome (see the climate chart in the appendix).

Know Before You Go

Your trip is more likely to go smoothly if you plan ahead. Check this list of things to arrange while you're still at home.

You need a **passport**—but no visa or shots—to travel in Italy. You may be denied entry into certain European countries if your passport is due to expire within three to six months of your ticketed date of return. Get it renewed if you'll be cutting it close. It can take up to six weeks to get or renew a passport (for more on passports, see www.travel.state.gov). Pack a photocopy of your passport in your luggage in case the original is lost or stolen.

Book rooms in advance, particularly during peak season (roughly May–Sept). Check to see if you'll be visiting Italy during any major holidays, when rooms can cost more and get booked up quickly. (See the "Major Holidays and Weekends" sidebar, above).

Make reservations ahead of time for major sights. For **Florence's** Uffizi Gallery (Renaissance paintings), book at least a month ahead; for the Accademia (Michelangelo's *David*), a minimum of a few days is enough (make reservations for both as soon as you know when you'll be in town—see page 430). While reservations are mandatory and free for Florence's Brancacci Chapel, spots are generally available a day or two in advance (see page 453). For **Milan,** book several months ahead for Da Vinci's *Last Supper* (see page 298); for **Padua,** at least two days in advance for Giotto's Scrovegni Chapel (see page 147); and for **Rome,** up to a week ahead for the Borghese Gallery (Bernini sculptures; see page 753). The Vatican Museum now takes online reservations, and while not mandatory, these can save you substantial time in line (see page 760).

Call your **debit- and credit-card companies** to let them know the countries you'll be visiting, to ask about fees, and more (see page 14).

Do your homework if you want to buy **travel insurance.** Compare the cost of the insurance to the likelihood of your using it and your potential loss if something goes wrong. For more tips, see www.ricksteves.com/insurance.

If you're bringing an MP3 player, you can download free information from **Rick Steves Audio Europe,** featuring hours of travel interviews on Italy, audio tours of major sights, and more (at www.ricksteves.com and in iTunes; for details, see page 977).

Bring your driver's license if you're planning on **renting a car** in Italy, and consider getting an International Driving Permit from AAA (see page 970). Driving is prohibited in some places; obey the signs or risk getting fined (see page 973).

If you're taking an **overnight train** in Italy (especially to Paris), and you need a *cuccetta* (overnight bunk) or sleeper—and you must leave on a certain day—consider booking it in advance through a US travel agent, even though it may cost more than buying it in Italy. Other Italian trains, like the high-speed ES trains, require a seat reservation, but it's usually possible to make arrangements in Italy just a few days ahead. (For more on train travel, see the appendix.)

Because **airline carry-on restrictions** are always changing, visit the Transportation Security Administration's website (www.tsa.gov/travelers) for an up-to-date list of what you can bring on the plane with you...and what you have to check.

Practicalities

Emergency and Medical Help: In Italy, dial 113 for English-speaking police help. To summon an ambulance, call 118.

If you get sick, do as the Italians do and go to a pharmacist for advice. Or ask at your hotel for help; they know of the nearest medical and emergency services.

Time Zones: Italy, like most of continental Europe, is generally six/nine hours ahead of the East/West Coasts of the US. The

INTRODUCTION

Italy's Best Three-Week Trip (By Car)

Day	Plan	Sleep in
1	Arrive in Milan	Milan
2	Milan to Lake Como	Varenna
3	Lake Como	Varenna
4	To Dolomites via Verona (pick up car in Milan or Verona)	Castelrotto
5	Dolomites	Castelrotto
6	To Venice	Venice
7	Venice	Venice
8	To Florence	Florence
9	Florence	Florence
10	To Cinque Terre	Vernazza
11	Cinque Terre	Vernazza
12	To Siena via Pisa	Siena
13	Siena	Siena
14	To Assisi	Assisi
15	To Civita	Civita or Orvieto
16	To Sorrento via Pompeii	Sorrento
17	Sorrento	Sorrento
18	To Paestum via Amalfi Coast	Sorrento
19	To Rome, drop car	Rome
20	Rome	Rome
21	Rome	Rome
22	Fly home	

For Train Travelers: This trip is designed to be done by car, but works fine by rail with a few modifications. In the Dolomites, consider basing yourself in Bolzano. From Venice, go directly to the Cinque Terre, then visit Florence and Siena. A car is efficient in the hill towns of Tuscany and Umbria, but a headache elsewhere. Sorrento is a good home base for Naples and the

exceptions are the beginning and end of Daylight Saving Time: Europe "springs forward" the last Sunday in March (two weeks after most of North America), and "falls back" the last Sunday in October (one week before North America). For a handy online time converter, see www.timeanddate.com/worldclock.

Business Hours: Traditionally, Italy uses the siesta plan, where people usually work from about 9:00 to 13:00 and from 15:30 to 19:00, Monday through Saturday. However, many businesses have adopted the government's recommended 8:00 to 14:00 workday. In tourist areas, shops are open longer. Stores are usually closed on Sunday, and often on Monday, as well as for a couple of weeks around August 15. Banking hours are generally Monday

Amalfi Coast. Skip Paestum unless you love Greek ruins. To save Venice for last, start in Milan and see everything but Venice on the way south, then sleep through everything you've already seen by catching the night train from Naples to Venice. This saves you a day and gives you an early arrival in Venice. (Or consider taking a cheap flight to connect Rome and Venice—see page 975.)

through Friday from 8:30 to 13:30 and 15:30 to 16:30, but can vary wildly.

Saturdays are virtually weekdays, with earlier closing hours. Sundays have the same pros and cons as they do for travelers in the US: Sightseeing attractions are generally open, while shops and banks are closed, public transportation options are fewer (e.g., no bus service to or from the smaller hill towns), and there's no rush hour. Rowdy evenings are rare on Sundays.

Watt's Up? Europe's electrical system is different from North America's in two ways: the shape of the plug (two round prongs) and the voltage of the current (220 volts instead of 110 volts). For your North American plug to work in Europe, you'll need an adapter, sold inexpensively at travel stores in the US. As for the voltage, most newer electronics or travel appliances (such as hair dryers, laptops, and battery chargers) automatically convert the voltage—if you see a range of voltages printed on the item or its plug (such as "110–220"), it'll work in Europe. Otherwise, you can buy a converter separately in the US (about $20).

Discounts: Discounts are not listed in this book. However, children (under 18), students (with International Student Identity Cards, www.isic.org), and seniors can sometimes get discounts at sights—but only by asking. For example, Venice's city museums offer discounts to non-European youths and seniors (bring ID).

News: Americans keep in touch via the *International Herald Tribune* (published almost daily throughout Europe and online at www.iht.com). Other newsy sites are http://news.bbc.co.uk and www.europeantimes.com. Every Tuesday, the European editions of *Time* and *Newsweek* hit the stands with articles of particular interest to travelers in Europe. Sports addicts can get their daily fix online or from *USA Today*. Many hotels have CNN and BBC News television channels.

Money

This section offers advice on how to pay for purchases on your trip (including getting cash from ATMs and paying with plastic), dealing with lost or stolen cards, VAT (sales tax) refunds, and tipping.

What to Bring

Bring both a credit card and a debit card. You'll use the debit card at cash machines (ATMs) to withdraw local cash for most purchases, and the credit card to pay for larger items. Some travelers carry a third card as a backup, in case one gets demagnetized or eaten by a temperamental machine.

I also carry a few hundred dollars in hard cash as an emergency backup (in $20 bills rather than hard-to-exchange $100 bills). Don't bother changing cash before you leave home—European ATMs are easy to find and easy to use. And skip traveler's checks—they're a waste of time (long waits at slow banks) and a waste of money in fees.

Cash

Cash is just as desirable in Europe as it is at home. Small European businesses (hotels, restaurants, shops, etc.) prefer that you pay your bills with cash. Some vendors will charge you extra for using a credit card, and some won't take credit cards at all. Cash is the best—and sometimes only—way to pay for bus fare, taxis, and local guides.

Exchange Rate

1 euro (€) = about $1.25

To convert prices in euros to dollars, add about 25 percent: €20 = about $25, €50 = about $65. (Check www.oanda.com for the latest exchange rates.) Just like the dollar, one euro is broken down into 100 cents. You'll find coins ranging from €0.01 to €2, and bills ranging from €5 to €500.

Look carefully at any €2 coin you get in change. Some unscrupulous merchants are giving out similar-looking gold-rimmed old 500-lire coins (worth $0) instead of €2 coins (worth $2.80). You are now warned!

Throughout Europe, ATMs offer the best and simplest way to get local currency. To use an ATM (called a *bancomat*) to withdraw money from your account, you'll need a debit card—ideally with a Visa or MasterCard logo for maximum usability—plus a PIN code. Know your PIN code in numbers; there are only numbers—no letters—on European keypads. You could use a credit card for ATM transactions, but it's generally more expensive (because it's considered a "cash advance" rather than a "withdrawal").

When using an ATM, taking out large sums of money can reduce your per-transaction bank fees. Most ATMs in Italy allow you to take up to €250 at a time. If you need more than that, try making multiple withdrawals, either using the same ATM or another ATM operated by a different bank. It's easier to pay for purchases with smaller bills; if the ATM gives you big bills, try to break them at a bank or larger store.

To keep your cash safe, use a money belt—a pouch with a strap that you buckle around your waist like a belt, and wear under your clothes. Pickpockets target tourists. A money belt provides peace of mind, allowing you to carry lots of cash safely. Don't waste time every few days tracking down a cash machine—withdraw a week's worth of money, stuff it in your money belt, and travel!

Credit and Debit Cards

For purchases, Visa and MasterCard are more commonly accepted than American Express. While you can use either a credit card or a debit card for most transactions, credit cards offer a greater degree of fraud protection (since debit cards draw funds directly from your account).

Just like at home, credit or debit cards work easily at larger hotels, restaurants, and shops. I typically use my credit card only in a few specific situations: to book hotel reservations by phone, to make major purchases (such as car rentals, plane tickets, and long hotel stays), and to pay for things near the end of my trip (to avoid another visit to the ATM).

Ask Your Credit- or Debit-Card Company: Before your trip, contact the company that issued your debit or credit cards.

• Confirm your card will work overseas, and alert them that you'll be using it in Europe; otherwise, they may deny transactions if they perceive unusual spending patterns.

• Ask for the specifics on transaction **fees.** When you use your credit or debit card—either for purchases or ATM withdrawals— you'll often be charged additional "international transaction" fees of up to 3 percent plus $5 per transaction. If your card's fees are too high, consider getting a card just for your trip: Capital One (www .capitalone.com) and most credit unions have low-to-no international fees.

• If you plan to withdraw cash from ATMs, confirm your daily **withdrawal limit.** Some travelers prefer a high limit that allows them to take out more cash at each ATM stop, while others prefer to set a lower limit in case their card is stolen.

• Ask for your credit card's **PIN** in case you encounter Europe's "chip-and-PIN" system.

Chip and PIN: If your card is declined for a purchase in Europe, it may be because of chip and PIN, which requires cardholders to punch in a PIN instead of signing a receipt. While chip and PIN is not yet common in Italy, much of Europe is adopting it. Chip and PIN is used by some merchants, and also at automated payment machines—such as those at train and subway stations, toll roads, parking garages, luggage lockers, bike-rental kiosks, and self-serve pumps at gas stations. If you're prompted to enter your PIN (but don't know it), ask if the cashier can print a receipt for you to sign instead, or just pay cash. If you're dealing with an automated machine that won't take your card, look for a cashier nearby who can make your card work. But if the place is unstaffed and you don't have cash, you might simply be out of luck.

Dynamic Currency Conversion: If merchants offer to convert your purchase price into dollars (called dynamic currency conversion, or DCC), refuse this "service." You'll pay even more in fees for the expensive convenience of seeing your charge in dollars.

Damage Control for Lost Cards

If you lose your credit, debit, or ATM card, you can stop people from using your card by reporting the loss immediately to the respective global customer-assistance centers. Call these 24-hour US numbers collect: Visa (410/581-9994), MasterCard (636/722-7111), and American Express (623/492-8427).

At a minimum, you'll need to know the name of the financial institution that issued you the card, along with the type of card (classic, platinum, or whatever). Providing the following information will allow for a quicker cancellation of your missing card: full card number, whether you are the primary or secondary cardholder, the cardholder's name exactly as printed on the card, billing address, home phone number, circumstances of the loss or theft, and identification verification (your birth date, your mother's maiden name, or your Social Security number—memorize this, don't carry a copy). If you are the secondary cardholder, you'll also need to provide the primary cardholder's identification-verification details. You can generally receive a temporary card within two or three business days in Europe (see www.ricksteves.com/help for more).

If you promptly report your card lost or stolen, you typically won't be responsible for any unauthorized transactions on your account, although many banks charge a liability fee of $50.

Tipping

Tipping in Italy isn't as automatic and generous as it is in the US, but for special service, tips are appreciated, if not expected. As in the US, the proper amount depends on your resources, tipping philosophy, and the circumstances, but some general guidelines apply.

Restaurants: The "service" charge *(servizio)* is generally already included in your bill. Most Italians don't tip beyond this, but if you're happy with the service, it's fine to round up a euro or two. If you order at a counter rather than from waitstaff, there's no need to tip. For more on tipping at restaurants, see page 31.

Taxis: To tip the cabbie, round up. For a typical ride, round up your fare a bit (e.g., if the fare is €4.50, pay €5). If the cabbie hauls your bags and zips you to the airport to help you catch your flight, you might want to toss in a little more. But if you feel like you're being driven in circles or otherwise ripped off, skip the tip.

Special Services: Tour guides at public sights sometimes hold out their hands for tips after they give their spiel. If I've already paid for the tour, I don't tip extra, unless they've really impressed me. At hotels, if you let the porter carry your luggage, it's polite to give them a euro for each bag. I don't tip the maid, but if you do, you can leave a euro per overnight at the end of your stay.

In general, if someone in the service industry does a super job for you, a small tip (the equivalent of a euro or two) is appropriate...but not required.

When in doubt, ask. If you're not sure whether (or how much) to tip for a service, ask your hotelier or the tourist information office; they'll fill you in on how it's done on their turf.

Getting a VAT Refund

Wrapped into the purchase price of your Italian souvenirs is a Value-Added Tax (VAT) of about 20 percent. You're entitled to get most of that tax back if you purchase more than €155 (about $190) worth of goods at a store that participates in the VAT-refund scheme. Getting your refund is usually straightforward and, if you buy a substantial amount of souvenirs, well worth the hassle. If you're lucky, the merchant will subtract the tax when you make your purchase. (This is more likely to occur if the store ships the goods to your home.) Otherwise, you'll need to:

Get the paperwork. Have the merchant completely fill out the necessary refund document, called a "cheque." You'll have to present your passport.

Get your stamp at the border or airport. Process your cheque(s) at your last stop in the EU (e.g., at the airport) with the customs agent who deals with VAT refunds. It's best to keep your purchases in your carry-on for viewing, but if they're too large or dangerous to carry on (such as knives), track down the proper customs agent to inspect them before you check your bag. You're not supposed to use your purchased goods before you leave. If you show up at customs wearing your new leather shoes, officials might look the other way—or deny you a refund.

Collect your refund. You'll need to return your stamped document to the retailer or its representative. Many merchants work with a service, such as Global Refund (www.globalrefund.com) or Premier Tax Free (www.premiertaxfree.com), which have offices at major airports, ports, or border crossings. These services, which extract a 4 percent fee, can refund your money immediately in your currency of choice or credit your card (within two billing cycles). If the retailer handles VAT refunds directly, it's up to you to contact the merchant for your refund. You can mail the documents from home, or quicker, from your point of departure (using a stamped, self-addressed envelope or one that's been provided by the merchant). You'll then have to wait—it can take months.

Customs for American Shoppers

You are allowed to take home $800 worth of items per person duty-free, once every 30 days. The next $1,000 is taxed at a flat 3 percent. After that, you pay the individual item's duty rate. You can also bring in duty-free a liter of alcohol (slightly more than one standard-size bottle of wine; you must be at least 21), 200 cigarettes, and up to 100 non-Cuban cigars.

As for food, you can take home vacuum-packed cheeses; dried herbs, spices, or mushrooms; and canned fruits or vegetables, including jams and vegetable spreads. Baked goods, candy, chocolate, oil, vinegar, mustard, and honey are OK. Fresh fruits and vegetables (even that banana from your airplane breakfast) are not permitted. Meats are generally not allowed, though canned pâtés from some countries are usually permitted if made from goose, duck, or pork. Just because a duty-free shop in an airport sells a food product, that doesn't mean it will automatically pass US customs. Be prepared to lose your investment.

Note that you'll need to carefully pack any bottles of wine, jam, honey, oil, and other liquid-containing items in your checked luggage, due to the three-ounce limit on liquids in carry-on baggage. To check the latest customs rules and duty rates before you go, visit www.cbp.gov, and click on "Travel," then "Know Before You Go."

Sightseeing

Sightseeing can be hard work. Use these tips to make your visits to Italy's finest museums meaningful, fun, efficient, and painless.

Plan Ahead

Set up an itinerary that allows you to fit in all your must-see sights. For a one-stop look at opening hours, see the "At a Glance" sidebars for each major city (Venice, Milan, Florence, Siena, and Rome). Most sights keep stable hours, but you can easily confirm the latest by checking with the TI or visiting museums' websites. Or call sights in the morning and ask: "Are you open today?" (*"Aperto oggi?"*; ah-PER-toh OH-jee) and "What time do you close?" (*"A che ora chiuso?"*; ah kay OH-rah kee-OO-zoh). I've included telephone numbers for this purpose.

Sometimes you can make reservations for an entry time (for example, at Florence's Uffizi Gallery or Rome's Vatican Museum). Some cities offer museum passes for admission to several museums (e.g., Roma Pass or Venice's San Marco Museum Plus Pass) that let you skip ticket-buying lines. At some popular places (such as Rome's Colosseum or Venice's Doge's Palace), you can get in more quickly by buying your ticket or pass at a less-crowded sight. Booking a guided tour can help you avoid lines at many sights.

Don't put off visiting a must-see sight—you never know when a place will close unexpectedly for a holiday, strike, or restoration. On holidays (see list on page 981), expect shorter hours or closures. In summer, some sights stay open late, allowing easy viewing without crowds. Many museums have shorter hours off-season.

When possible, visit the major sights first thing (when your energy is best) and save other activities for the afternoon. Hit the highlights first, then go back to other things if you have the stamina and time.

Depending on the sight, there may be ways to avoid crowds.

This book offers tips on specific sights. Try visiting popular sights very early, at lunch, or very late. Evening visits are usually peaceful with fewer crowds.

Study up. To get the most out of the sight descriptions in this book, read them before you visit.

At Sights

Here's what you can typically expect:

Some important sights have metal detectors or conduct bag searches that will slow your entry, while others require you to check daypacks and coats. They'll be kept safely. If you have something you can't bear to part with, stash it in a pocket or purse. To avoid checking a small backpack, carry it under your arm like a purse as you enter. From a guard's point of view, a backpack is generally a problem while a purse is not.

Photography is normally allowed, but flashes or tripods are not. Look for signs or ask. Flashes damage oil paintings and distract others in the room. Even without a flash, a handheld camera will take a decent picture (or buy postcards or posters at the museum bookstore). If photos are permitted, video cameras generally are OK, too.

You'll likely have to pay cash for the admission fee; few sights take credit cards. Museums may have special exhibits in addition to their permanent collection. Some exhibits are included in the entry price, while others come at an extra cost (which you may have to pay even if you don't want to see the exhibit).

Expect changes—artwork can be on tour, on loan, out sick, or shifted at the whim of the curator. To adapt, pick up any available free floor plans as you enter, and ask museum staff if you can't find a particular item. Say the title or artist's name, or point to the photograph in this book and ask, *"Dov'è?"* (doh-VEH; meaning "Where is?").

Many sights rent audioguides, which offer dry-but-useful recorded descriptions in English (about $4). If you bring along your own pair of headphones and a Y-jack, you can sometimes share one audioguide with your travel partner and save money. I have produced free audio tours for the major sights in Rome, Florence, and Venice (see page 977).

Guided tours in English are most likely to be available during peak season (usually €5–15 and widely ranging in quality). Some sights also run short films about the attraction. These are generally well worth your time. I make it standard operating procedure to ask when I arrive at a sight if there is a film in English.

Know the terms. Art historians and Italians refer to the great Florentine centuries by dropping a thousand years. The Trecento (300s), Quattrocento (400s), and Cinquecento (500s) were the

1300s, 1400s, and 1500s. Also, in Italian museums, art is dated with *sec* for *secolo* (century, often indicated with Roman numerals), A.C. (for *Avanti Cristo*, or B.C.), and D.C. (for *Dopo Cristo*, or A.D.). O.K.?

Important sights may have an on-site café or cafeteria (usually a good place to rest and have a snack or light meal). The WCs at sights are free and generally clean.

Many sights sell postcards and guidebooks that highlight their attractions. Before you leave, scan the postcards and thumb through the biggest guidebook (or skim its index) to be sure that you haven't overlooked something that you'd like to see.

Most sights stop admitting people 30–60 minutes before closing time, and some rooms close early (generally about 45 minutes before the actual closing time). Guards usher people out, so don't save the best for last.

Every sight or museum offers more than what is covered in this book. Use the information in this book as an introduction—not the final word.

Find Religion

Churches offer some amazing art (usually free), a cool respite from heat, and a welcome seat.

A modest dress code (no bare shoulders or shorts for anyone, even kids) is enforced at larger churches, such as Venice's St. Mark's and the Vatican's St. Peter's, but is often overlooked elsewhere. If you are caught by surprise, you can improvise, using maps to cover your shoulders and a jacket for your knees. (I wear a super-lightweight pair of long pants rather than shorts for my hot and muggy big-city Italian sightseeing.)

Some churches have coin-operated audioboxes that describe the art and history; just set the dial on English, put in your coins, and listen. Coin boxes near a piece of art illuminate the art (and present a better photo opportunity). I pop in a coin whenever I can. It improves my experience, is a favor to other visitors trying to appreciate a great piece of art in the dark, and is a little contribution to that church and its work. Whenever possible, let there be light.

Sleeping

For hassle-free efficiency, I favor hotels and restaurants that are handy to your sightseeing activities. Rather than list hotels scattered throughout a city, I describe two or three favorite neighborhoods and recommend the best accommodations values in each, from €25 bunks to plush €300 doubles with all the comforts.

Sleeping in Italy is expensive. Cheap big-city hotels can be depressing. Tourist information services cannot give opinions

Sleep Code

(€1 = about $1.25, country code: 39)

Price Rankings

To help you easily sort through my hotel listings, I've divided the rooms into three categories based on the price for a standard double room with bath during high season:

$$$ **Higher Priced**
$$ **Moderately Priced**
$ **Lower Priced**

I always rate hostels as $, whether or not they have double rooms, because they have the cheapest beds in town. Prices can change without notice; verify the hotel's current rates online or by email. For other updates, see www.ricksteves .com/update.

Abbreviations

To pack maximum information into minimum space, I use the following code to describe accommodations in this book. Prices listed are per room, not per person. When a price range is given for a type of room (such as double rooms listing for €100–150), it means the price fluctuates with the season, size of room, or length of stay.

S = Single room (or price for one person in a double).

D = Double or Twin room. "Double beds" are often two twins sheeted together and are usually big enough for nonromantic couples.

T = Triple (generally a double bed with a single).

Q = Quad (usually two double beds).

b = Private bathroom with toilet and shower or tub.

s = Private shower or tub only (the toilet is down the hall).

According to this code, a couple staying at a "Db-€140" hotel would pay a total of €140 (about $175) for a double room with a private bathroom. Unless otherwise noted, breakfast is included, hotel staff speak basic English, and credit cards are accepted.

If I mention "Internet access" in a listing, there's a public terminal in the lobby for guests to use. If I use the terms "Wi-Fi" or "cable Internet," you can access it in your room, but only if you have your own laptop.

on quality of hotels. A major feature of this book is its extensive listing of good-value rooms. I like places that are clean, central, relatively quiet at night, reasonably priced, friendly, small enough to have a hands-on owner and stable staff, run with a respect for Italian traditions, and not listed in other guidebooks. (In Italy, for me, six out of these eight criteria means it's a keeper.)

As you look over the listings, you'll notice that some hotels promise special prices to my readers who book direct (without using a TI room-finding service or hotel-booking website, which take a commission). To get these rates, mention this book when you reserve, then show the book upon arrival. During slow times or online promos, rooms might be offered for even less than listed.

Given the economic downturn, hoteliers are willing and eager to make a deal. I'd suggest emailing several hotels to ask for their best price. Comparison-shop and make your choice.

In general, prices can soften if you do any of the following: offer to pay cash, stay at least three nights, or mention this book. You can also try asking for a cheaper room or a discount, or offer to skip breakfast. To save money off-season, consider arriving without a reservation and dropping in at the last minute. Big, fancy hotels put empty rooms on an aggressive push list, offering great prices.

If you're arriving on an early flight or an overnight train, your room probably won't be ready first thing in the morning. You should be able to safely check your bag at the hotel and dive right into Italy.

Types of Accommodations
Hotels

Double rooms listed in this book will range from about €50 (very simple, toilet and shower down the hall) to €300 (maximum plumbing and more), with most clustered around €130 (with private bathrooms). Prices are higher in big cities and heavily touristed cities, and lower off the beaten path.

Solo travelers find that the cost of a *camera singola* is often only 25 percent less than a *camera doppia*. Three or four people can economize by requesting larger rooms. (If a double room is €110, a quad would be about €150.) Most listed hotels have rooms for any party from one to five people. If there's room for an extra cot, they'll cram it in for you (charging you around €25). English works in all but the cheapest places.

The Italian word for "hotel" is *hotel,* and in smaller, nontouristy towns, *albergo*. A few places have kept the old titles *locanda* or *pensione,* indicating that they offer budget beds.

Nearly all places offer private bathrooms, but some hotels also rent rooms sans bathroom. You'll save €30 if you request a room without a shower and just use the shower down the hall. Generally

Chill Out

All but the cheapest hotels have air-conditioning. Because Europeans are generally careful with energy use, you'll find government-enforced limits on air-conditioning and heating. There's a one-month period each spring and fall when neither is allowed. Air-conditioning sometimes costs an extra per-day charge, is worth seeking out in summer (though it may be on only at certain times of the day), and is rarely available from fall through spring. Fancier hotel rooms usually include air-conditioning in the price. Conveniently, many business-class hotels drop their prices in July and August, just when the air-conditioned comfort they offer is most important.

Most hotel rooms with air conditioners come with a control stick (like a TV remote) that generally has the same symbols and features: fan icon (click to toggle through wind power, from light to gale); louver icon (choose steady airflow or waves); snowflake and sunshine icons (cold air or heat, depending on season); clock ("O" setting: run x hours before turning off; "I" setting: wait x hours to start); and the temperature control (20 or 21 degrees Celsius is comfortable).

rooms with a bath or shower also have a toilet and a bidet (which Italians use for quick sponge baths). The cord that dangles over the tub or shower is not a clothesline. You pull it when you've fallen and can't get up.

Double beds are called *matrimoniale,* even though hotels aren't interested in your marital status. Twins are *due letti singoli.* (Convents offer cheap accommodation but only *letti singoli.*) Even if a hotel doesn't list single or triple rooms, ask; they can usually accommodate your needs.

When you check in, the receptionist will normally ask for your passport and keep it for a couple of hours. Hotels are legally required to register each guest with the local police. Relax. Americans are notorious for making this chore more difficult than it needs to be.

Assume that breakfast is included in the prices I've listed, unless otherwise noted. If breakfast is optional, you may want to skip it. While convenient, it's usually expensive—€5–8 for a simple continental buffet with ham, cheese, yogurt, cereal, and unlimited *caffè latte.* A picnic in your room followed by a coffee at the corner café can be a lot cheaper.

More pillows and blankets are usually in the closet or available on request. In Italy, towels and linen aren't always replaced every day. Hang your towel up to dry. Budget hotels often use "waffle" or very thin tablecloth-type towels, which use less water and electricity to launder.

Most hotel rooms have a TV and phone, and Internet access (usually Wi-Fi) is increasingly common. Simpler places rarely have a phone. Pricier hotels usually come with a small stocked fridge called a *frigo bar* (FREE-goh bar; pay for what you use).

Hotels in resort areas will often charge you for half-pension, called *mezza pensione*, during peak season (which can run from May through mid-October for resorts). Half-pension means that you pay for one meal per day per person (lunch or dinner, though usually dinner), whether you want to or not. Wine is rarely included. If half-pension is required, you can't opt out and pay less. Some places offer half-pension as an option; it can be worth considering. If they charge you less per meal than you've been paying for an average restaurant meal on your trip, half-pension is a fine value—if the chef is good. Ask other guests about the quality or check out their restaurant yourself.

Hoteliers can be a great help and source of advice. Most know their city well, and can assist you with everything from public transit and airport connections to finding a good restaurant, the nearest launderette, or an Internet café.

Even at the best hotels, mechanical breakdowns occur: air-conditioning malfunctions, sinks leak, hot water turns cold, and toilets gurgle and smell. Report your concerns clearly and calmly at the front desk. For more complicated problems, don't expect instant results.

If you suspect night noise will be a problem, ask for a quiet room in the back or on an upper floor. To guard against theft in your room, keep valuables out of sight. Some rooms come with a safe, and other hotels have safes at the front desk. Use them if you're concerned.

Checkout can pose problems if surprise charges pop up on your bill. If you settle up your bill the night before you leave, you'll have time to discuss and address any points of contention.

Hotels near Airports: If you have an early-morning flight, I strongly suggest staying in the center of town and getting to the airport via bus, train, or taxi. You can get a taxi at any hour. Save time and money, and have a richer experience, by staying put in your downtown hotel until you fly. But if you really want a hotel near an airport for the first or last night of your trip, try www .worldairportguide.com.

Hostels

You'll pay about €25 per bed to stay at a hostel. Travelers of any age are welcome if they don't mind dorm-style accommodations or meeting other travelers. Most hostels offer kitchen facilities, Internet access, Wi-Fi, laundry (generally self-service), sometimes cheap meals, and other handy amenities. Expect youth groups in spring, crowds in the summer, snoring, and great variability in quality from one hostel to the next. Family and private rooms are sometimes available on request, but it's mostly larger bunk-bed dorms (usually divided by gender, but sometimes mixed).

There are two basic types of hostels: official and independent. **Official hostels** belong to the same parent organization, Hostelling International. They adhere to various rules (such as a 17:00 check-in, lockout during the day, and a curfew at night), making them predictable but sometimes institutional. If you plan to spend at least six nights at official HI hostels, buy a membership card before you go ($28/year, www.hihostels.com); non-members pay an extra $5 per night to sleep at HI hostels.

Independent hostels tend to be more easygoing and colorful, but not as reliably clean or organized as official hostels. Independent hostels don't require membership cards or charge extra for non-members, and generally have fewer rules. Various organizations promote independent hostels, including www.hostelworld.com, www.hostelz.com, www.hostelseurope.com, and www.hostels.com.

Private Rooms and Apartments

In small towns, there are often few hotels to choose from, but an abundance of *affitta camere*, or rental rooms. This can be anything from a set of keys and a basic bed to a cozy B&B with your own Tuscan grandmother. Local TIs can give you a list of possibilities (or try the free Ciao Italia Bed & Breakfast, which books B&Bs and hostels in Rome, Florence, and Venice at www.ciaoitalia-bb.com). These rooms are usually a good budget option, but since they vary in quality, shop around to find the best value. It's always OK to ask to see the room before you commit.

Apartment rentals, a great value for families or multiple couples traveling together, are also listed at TIs and are common in small towns. Rentals are generally by the week, with prices starting around €100 per day. A bigger place for a group of four to five rents for around €200. Apartments generally offer a couple of bedrooms, a sitting area, and a teensy *cucinetta* (kitchenette), usually stocked with dishes and flatware. After you check in, you're basically on your own. While you won't have a doorman to carry your bags or a maid to clean your room each day, you will get an inside peek at an Italian home, and you can save lots of money—especially if you take advantage of the cooking facilities—with no loss of comfort.

Agritourism

Agriturismo (agricultural tourism), or rural B&Bs, began in the 1980s as a way to encourage small farmers in the countryside to survive in a modern economy where, like in the US, so many have been run out of business by giant agricultural corporations. By renting rooms to travelers, farmers can remain on their land and continue to produce food. A peaceful home base for exploring the region, these rural Italian B&Bs are ideal for those traveling by car—especially families.

It's wise to book several months in advance for high season (May–Sept). Weeklong stays are preferred in July and August, but shorter stays are possible off-season. To sleep cheaper, avoid peak season. A farmhouse that rents for as much as $2,000 a week at peak times can go for as little as $700 in late September or October. In the winter, you might be charged extra for heat, so confirm the price ahead of time. Payment policies vary, but generally a 25 percent deposit is required (lost if you cancel), and the balance is due one month before arrival.

As the name implies, *agriturismi* are in the countryside, although some are located within a mile of town. Most are family-run. *Agriturismi* vary wildly in quality—some properties are rustic, while others are downright luxurious, offering amenities such as swimming pools and riding stables. The rooms are usually clean and comfortable. Breakfast is often included, and *mezza pensione* (half-pension, which in this case means a home-cooked dinner) might be built into the price whether you want it or not. Most places serve tasty homegrown food; some are vegetarian or organic, others are gourmet. Kitchenettes are often available to cook up your own feast. Make sure you know how to operate the appliances. To maximize your time, ask the owner for suggestions on local restaurants, sights, and activities.

To qualify officially as an *agriturismo,* the farm must still generate more money from its farm activities, thereby insuring that the land is worked and preserved. Some farmhouse B&Bs aren't actual farms, though are fine places to stay. But if you want the real thing, make sure the owners call their place an *agriturismo.*

In this book, I've listed some *agriturismi* and farmhouses under the towns that they're nearest, but there are many, many more. Local TIs can give you a list of farms in their area, and many *agriturismi* now have their own websites. For a sampling, visit www.agriturismoitaly.it or do a Web search for *agriturismo.* One booking agency among many is Farm Holidays in Tuscany (closed Sat–Sun, tel. 0564-417-418, www.byfarmholidays.com, info@byfarmholidays.com).

Phoning

To call Italy from the US or Canada, dial 011-39 and then the local number. (The 011 is our international access code, and 39 is Italy's country code.) If you're calling Italy from another European country, dial 00-39-local number. (The 00 is Europe's international access code.) To make calls within Italy, simply dial the local number. Land lines start with 0; mobile lines start with 3. For more tips on calling, see page 954.

Making Reservations

Given the quality of the accommodations I've found for this book, I'd recommend that you reserve your rooms in advance, particularly if you'll be traveling during peak season. Book several weeks ahead, or as soon as you've pinned down your travel dates. Note that some national holidays jam things up and merit your making reservations far in advance (see the "Major Holidays and Weekends" sidebar on page 8). Just like at home, holidays that fall on a Monday, Thursday, or Friday can turn the weekend into a long holiday, so book the entire weekend well in advance.

Requesting a Reservation: To reserve, contact hotels directly by email, phone, or fax. Email is the clearest and most economical way to make a reservation. Or you can go straight to the hotel website; many have secure online reservation forms and can instantly inform you of availability and any special deals. But be sure you use the hotel's official site and not a booking agency's site—otherwise you may pay higher rates than you should. If you're phoning from the US, be mindful of time zones. Most recommended hotels are accustomed to guests who speak only English.

Your hotelier needs to know these key pieces of information (also included in the sample request form in the appendix):

- number and type of rooms
- number of nights
- date of arrival
- date of departure
- any special needs (e.g., bathroom in the room or down the hall, twin beds vs. double bed, air-conditioning, quiet, view, ground floor, etc.)

When you request a room, use the European style for writing dates: day/month/year. Hoteliers need to know your arrival and departure dates. For example, for a two-night stay in July, I would request "1 double room for 2 nights, arrive 16/07/11, depart 18/07/11." (Consider carefully how long you'll stay; don't just assume you can tack on extra days once you arrive.) Mention any discounts offered (for Rick Steves readers or otherwise) when you make the reservation.

If you don't get a reply to your email or fax, it usually means the hotel is already fully booked (but you can try sending the message again, or call to follow up).

Confirming a Reservation: If the hotel's response tells you its room availability and rates, it's not a confirmation. You must tell them that you want that room at the given rate. Most hoteliers will request your credit-card number to hold the room. While you can email your credit-card information (I do), it's safer to share that personal info via phone call, fax, two successive emails, or secure online reservation form (if the hotel has one on its website).

Canceling a Reservation: If you must cancel your reservation, it's courteous to do so with as much advance notice as possible. Simply make a quick phone call or send an email. Hotels lose money if they turn away customers while holding a room for someone who doesn't show up. Understandably, many hoteliers bill no-shows for one night.

Cancellation policies can be strict: For example, you might lose a deposit if you cancel within two weeks of your reserved stay, or you might be billed for the entire visit if you leave early. Ask about cancellation policies before you book.

If canceling via email, request confirmation that your cancellation was received to avoid being accidentally billed.

Reconfirming Your Reservation: Always call to reconfirm your room reservation a few days in advance from the road. Smaller hotels and B&Bs appreciate knowing your estimated time of arrival. If you'll be arriving late (after 17:00), alert your hotelier. On the small chance that a hotel loses track of your reservation, bring along a hard copy of their confirmation.

Reserving Rooms as You Travel: If you enjoy having a flexible itinerary, you can make reservations as you travel, calling hotels a few days to a week before your visit. If everything's full, don't despair. Call a day or two in advance and fill in a cancellation. If you'd rather travel without any reservations at all, you'll have greater success snaring rooms if you arrive at your destination early in the day. When you anticipate crowds (weekends are worst), call hotels at about 9:00 on the day you plan to arrive, when the hotel clerk knows who'll be checking out and just which rooms will be available. If you encounter a language barrier, ask the fluent receptionist at your current hotel to call for you.

Eating

The Italians are masters of the art of fine living. That means eating...long and well. Lengthy, multicourse lunches and dinners and endless hours sitting in outdoor cafés are the norm. Americans eat on their way to an evening event and complain if the check is slow in coming. For Italians, the meal is an end in itself, and only rude waiters rush you. When you want the bill, mime-scribble on your raised palm or ask for it: *"Il conto?"* You may have to ask for it more than once. To save time, ask for the check when you receive the last item you order.

Even those of us who liked dorm food will find that the local cafés, cuisine, and wines become a highlight of our Italian adventure. Trust me: This is sightseeing for your palate, and even if the rest of you is sleeping in cheap hotels, your taste buds will relish an occasional first-class splurge. You can eat well without going broke. But be careful: You're just as likely to blow a small fortune on a disappointing meal as you are to dine wonderfully for €25.

Restaurants

When restaurant-hunting, choose places filled with locals, not the place with the big neon signs boasting, "We speak English and

accept credit cards." High-rent restaurants parked on famous squares must pass on their costs, and they generally serve bad food at high prices to tourists. The natives eat better at lower-rent holes-in-the-wall, which need to be good to be known. Family-run places operate without hired help and can offer cheaper meals. Good restaurants don't open for dinner before 19:00.

A *trattoria* or *osteria* (which historically meant a simple restaurant) can now be just as elegant and pricey as a *ristorante*. For unexciting but basic values, look for a *menù turistico*, a three- or four-course fixed-price *menù* (also called *menù del giorno*—menu of the day). The price includes a service charge, and there's no need to tip. While set-price meals can be cheap and easy, galloping gourmets order à la carte with the help of a menu translator. (The *Rick Steves' Italian Phrase Book & Dictionary* has a menu decoder with enough phrases for intermediate eaters.)

A full meal consists of an appetizer (antipasto, €4–6), a first course

MENU € 19,0
TURISTICO

ANTIPASTO di MARE

PRIMI PIATTI
RISOTTO alla PESCATORA
SPAGHETTI alla MARINARA
SPAGHETTI allo SCOGLIO
TRENETTE al PESTO

SECONDI PIATTI
PESCE ai FERRI
FRITTO MISTO
GRIGLIATA di CARNE

CONTORNI
PATATE FRITTE o INSALATA

Eating with the Seasons

Italian cooks love to serve you fresh produce and seafood at its tastiest. If you must have porcini mushrooms outside of October and November, they'll be frozen. Each region in Italy has its own specialties, which you'll see displayed in open-air markets. To get the freshest veggies at a fine restaurant, request *"Un piatto di verdure della stagioni, per favore"* ("A plate of seasonal veggies, please").

Here are a few examples of what's fresh when:

April–May:	Calamari, squid, green beans, asparagus, artichokes, and zucchini flowers
April–May and Sept–Oct:	Black truffles
May–June:	Mussels, asparagus, zucchini, cantaloupe, and strawberries
May–Aug:	Eggplant
Oct–Nov:	Mushrooms, white truffles, and chestnuts
Nov–Feb:	Radicchio
Fresh year-round:	Clams, meats, and cheese

(*primo piatto*, pasta or soup, €5–12), and a second course (*secondo piatto*, expensive meat and fish dishes, €10–20). Vegetables *(contorni, verdure)* may come with the *secondo* or cost extra (€4–6) as a side dish.

The euros can add up in a hurry. Light and budget eaters get a *primo piatto* each and share an antipasto. (Italians admit the *secondo* is the least interesting part of their cuisine.) Another good option is sharing an array of *antipasti*—either several specific dishes or a big plate of mixed delights assembled from a buffet. Some restaurants have self-serve *antipasti* buffets, offering a variety of cooked appetizers spread out like a salad bar. When Americans hear "buffet," we think it's a pile-the-plate-high, all-you-can-eat deal; but in Italy, an *antipasti* buffet is designed and priced as an appetizer (about €8)—locals visit the buffet once, taking a moderate amount. Watch others and imitate.

To maximize the experience and flavors, small groups can mix *antipasti* and *primi piatti* family-style (skipping *secondi*). If you do this right (e.g., under-ordering because courses are often bigger than necessary), you can eat well in better places for less than the cost of a tourist *menù* in a cheap place.

When going to an especially good restaurant with an approachable staff, I like to find out what they're eager to serve, or I'll simply say, "Make me happy" (in this case, it's just fine to set a

Italian Wines

The ancient Greeks who colonized Italy more than 2,000 years ago called it *"Oenotria"*—land of the grape. Little has changed over the centuries. Ideal conditions for grapes (warm climate, well-draining soil, and an abundance of hillsides) make the Italian peninsula a paradise for grape-growers, winemakers, and wine drinkers. Italy makes and con-sumes more wine per capita than any other country.

In almost every part of Italy you'll find wine varieties designed to go with the regional cuisine. Choosing a wine can be intimidating, but the Italian government tries to help you choose something decent, even if you're clueless. In general, wines are designated by one of four categories:

Vino da Tavola (table wine) is the lowest grade. It's inexpen-sive, but Italy's wines are so good that, for many people, a basic *vino da tavola* is just fine with a meal. Many restaurants, even modest ones, take pride in their house wine *("vino della casa")*, bottling their own or working with wineries.

Denominazione di Origine Controllata (DOC), a cut above table wine, is usually cheap, but can be surprisingly good. You'll see DOC wines all over Italy. In Tuscany, for example, many such wines come from the Chianti region, located between Florence and Siena.

Denominazione di Origine Controllata e Guarantita (DOCG) is the highest grade, and can be identified by the pink or green label on the neck and the scary price tag on the shelf. They're

price limit).

Seafood and steak may be sold by weight (priced by the kilo—1,000 grams, or just over two pounds; or by the *etto*—100 grams). The letters *s.q.* mean "according to quantity." Fish is usually served whole with the head and tail; you can't just get half a fish or a fillet unless it already comes prepared as just a fillet (*filetto,* sometimes *trancio*—slice, as in tuna or swordfish). However, you can ask your waiter to select a smaller fish for you. Sometimes, especially for steak, restaurants require a minimum order of four or five *etti*. Beware, or be shell-shocked by €50 entrées. Make sure you're really clear on the price before ordering.

Some special dishes come in large quantities meant for two people; the shorthand way of showing this on a menu is "X2" (meaning "for two people"). The price listed generally indicates the cost per person.

generally a good bet if you want a quality wine, but you don't know anything else about the winemaker.

Indicazione Geographica Tipica (IGT) is a broad group of wines that range from basic to some of Italy's best. It includes the "Super Tuscans"—wines that don't follow the strict "recipe" required for DOC or DOCG status, but that give local vintners more opportunity to be creative. Super Tuscans are made from a mix of international grapes (such as cabernet sauvignon) grown in Tuscany and aged in small oak barrels for only two years. The result is a lively full-bodied wine that dances all over your head... and is worth the steep price for aficionados.

Visit an *enoteca* (wine bar) and sample these wines side-by-side to figure out what you like—and what suits your pocketbook.

Words to Live By, or...How to Describe Wine in Italian

As you can see from many of the words listed below, adding a vowel to the English word often gets you close to the Italian one. Have some fun, gesture like a local, and you'll have no problems speaking the language of the *enoteca. Salute!*

dry	*secco*	SAY-koh
sweet	*dolce*	DOHL-chay
earthy	*terroso*	tay-ROH-zoh
tannic	*tannico*	TAH-nee-koh
young	*giovane*	JOH-vah-nay
mature	*maturo*	mah-TOO-roh
sparkling	*spumante*	spoo-MAHN-tay
fruity	*fruttoso*	froo-TOH-zoh
full-bodied	*corposo*	kor-POH-zoh
elegant	*elegante*	ay-lay-GAHN-tay

Restaurants normally pad the bill with a cover charge (*pane e coperto,* "bread and cover charge") of around €2, even if you don't eat the bread, and a service charge.

The "service" charge *(servizio)* is usually built into your bill's grand total in one of two ways: if the menu says *servizio incluso*, the listed prices already include this fee; if it says *servizio non incluso*, a fixed percentage (usually 10–15 percent of the total) will be added as a line item to the bottom of the bill. In either case, the total you pay already includes a basic tip. If you're pleased with the service, you can round up the bill by a euro or two (though most Italians rarely add this additional tip). Even if you pay your bill with a credit card, it's best to tip in cash—leave it on the table or hand it directly to your server.

Tipping is an issue only at restaurants that have waiters and waitresses. If you order your food at a counter, don't tip.

Wine Bars *(Enoteche)*

An *enoteca* (wine bar) is a popular, fast, and inexpensive option for lunch. Surrounded by the local office crowd, you can get a fancy salad, plate of meats and cheeses, and a glass of fine wine (see blackboards for the day's selection and price per glass—and go for the top end). A good *enoteca* aims to impress visitors with its wines and will generally choose excellent-quality ingredients for the simple dishes it offers with the wine. Some of my favorite Italian eating experiences have been at *enoteche*.

Bars/Cafés

Italian "bars" are not taverns, but cafés. These neighborhood hang-outs serve coffee, mini-pizzas, sandwiches, and drinks from the cooler. Many dish up plates of fried cheese and vegetables from under the glass counter, ready to reheat. This budget choice is the Italian equivalent of English pub grub.

For quick meals, bars usually have trays of cheap, pre-made sandwiches (*panini* or *tramezzini*)—some are delightful grilled. (Others have lots of mayo between crustless slices of Wonder Bread.) To save time for sightseeing and room for dinner, consider a ham-and-cheese *panino* (called *toast*) at a bar for lunch; have it grilled twice if you want it really hot. Many bars are small—if you can't find a table, you'll need to stand up to eat. To get food to go, say, *"Da portar via"* (for the road). All bars have a WC *(toilette, bagno)* in the back, and customers (and the discreet public) can use it.

Bars serve great drinks—hot, cold, sweet, caffeinated, or alcoholic. Chilled bottled water, still *(naturale)* or carbonated *(frizzante)*, is sold cheap to go.

Coffee: Take some time to learn Italian coffee lingo—the names and the rituals are a little different from those at your hometown java joint. If you ask for *"un caffè,"* you'll get espresso. If you ask for a latte, you'll get just that—a glass of hot milk. Starbucks-style mochas aren't on the menu at all.

Cappuccino is served to locals before noon and to tourists any time of day. (To an Italian, cappuccino is a breakfast drink and a travesty after eating anything with tomatoes.) Italians like their coffee only warm—to get it hot, request *"Molto caldo"* (MOHL-toh KAHL-doh; very hot) or *"Più caldo, per favore"* (pew KAHL-doh pehr fah-VOH-ray; hotter, please).

Experiment with a few of the options:
- Cappuccino: Espresso with foamed milk on top
- *Caffè latte:* Tall glass with espresso mixed with hot milk, no foam (ordering just a "latte" gets you only milk)
- *Caffè hag:* instant decaf (any coffee drink is available decaffeinated—ask for it *decaffeinato:* day-kah-fey-een-AH-toh)

- *Macchiato* (mah-kee-AH-toh): Espresso with only a little milk (*macchiato* means "marked" or "stained")
- *Latte macchiato:* Hot milk with a shot of espresso
- *Caffè americano:* Espresso diluted with water
- *Caffè freddo:* Sweet and iced espresso
- *Cappuccino freddo:* Iced cappuccino
- *Caffè Corretto:* Espresso with a shot of liqueur, usally grappa or Sambuca, but amaretto is also good.

More Hot Drinks: *Cioccolato* is hot chocolate. *Tè* is hot tea. *Tè freddo* (iced tea) is usually from a can—sweetened and flavored with lemon or peach.

Juice: *Spremuta* means freshly squeezed as far as *succo* (fruit juice) is concerned (order *una spremuta*); it's usually orange juice, and February through April it's almost always made from blood oranges. (Note: *spumante* means champagne.)

Beer: Beer on tap is *alla spina*. Get it *piccola* (33 cl, 11 oz), *media* (50 cl, about a pint), or *grande* (a liter, about two pints). Italians drink mainly lager beers. You'll find local brews (Peroni or Moretti) and imports such as Heineken as well. A *lattina* is a can and a *bottiglia* (boh-TEEL-yah) is a bottle.

Wine: To order a glass (*bicchiere;* bee-kee-AY-ree) of red *(rosso)* or white *(bianco)* wine, say, "*Un bicchiere di vino rosso/bianco.*" *Secco* is dry, *corposo* means full-bodied, and *frizzante* is fizzy. House wine *(vino della casa)* comes in a carafe: quarter-liter (8.5 oz, *un quarto*), half-liter pitcher (17 oz, *un mezzo*), or one-liter pitcher (34 oz, *un litro*). An *ombra* is the smallest glass. Trendy wines with small production (such as Brunello di Montalcino) are good but overpriced.

Other Drinks: Some restaurants make their own after-dinner alcoholic brew (called a *digestivo*), using a secret combination of herbs to aid digestion. Popular commercial brands are Fernet Branca and Montenegro. If your tastes run sweeter, try an anise-flavored liqueur called Sambuca, served *con moscha* (with three "flies"—coffee beans).

Prices: You'll notice a two- or three-tiered pricing system. It's cheapest to drink a cup of coffee while standing at the bar; you'll pay more for that same cup to sit at an indoor table, and often still more at an outdoor table. Many places have a *listino prezzi* (price list) with two columns—*al bar* and *al tavolo* (table)—posted somewhere by the bar or cash register. If you're on a budget, don't sit down without first checking out the financial consequences. Ask, "Same price if I sit or stand?" by saying, "*Costa uguale al tavolo o al banco?*" (KOH-stah oo-GWAH-lay ahl TAH-voh-loh oh ahl BAHN-koh). A cup of coffee at any bar generally costs only a euro if you stand. While coffee may cost €5 at a table, you can stand at the fanciest place in town and sip your coffee at the bar for the same price as at a basic café.

If the bar isn't busy, you can probably just order and pay when you leave. Otherwise: 1) Decide what you want; 2) find out the price by checking the price list on the wall, the prices posted near the food, or by asking the barista; 3) pay the cashier; and 4) give the receipt to the barista (whose clean fingers handle no dirty euros) and tell him or her what you want.

Budget Eating

Italy offers many budget options for hungry travelers, but beware of cheap eateries that sport big color photos of pizza and piles of different pastas. They have no kitchens and simply microwave disgusting prepackaged food.

Stop by a *rosticcería* for great cooked deli food. Self-service cafeterias (called "free flow" in Italian) offer the basics without add-on charges. *Döner kebab* places sell veal, chicken, or falafel and salad fixings wrapped in pita bread, offering a budget break from Italian food.

Pizzerias

Pizza is cheap and readily available. At take-out pizza shops, slices are sold by weight (100 grams, or *un etto*, is a hot and cheap snack; 200 grams, or *due etti*, makes a light meal).

Key pizza vocabulary: *capricciosa* (generally ham, mushrooms, olives, and artichokes), *funghi* (mushrooms), *marinara* (tomato sauce, oregano, garlic, no cheese), *quattro formaggi* (four different cheeses), and *quattro stagioni* (different toppings on each of the four quarters, for those who can't choose just one menu item). If you ask for pepperoni on your pizza, you'll get *peperoni* (green or red peppers, not sausage); request *diavola* instead (the closest thing in Italy to American pepperoni). Kids like the bland *margherita* (cheese with tomato sauce).

Tavola Caldas ("Hot Tables")

For a fast, cheap, and healthy lunch, find a *tavola calda* bar with a buffet spread of meat and vegetables, and ask for a mixed plate of vegetables with a hunk of mozzarella *(piatto misto di verdure con mozzarella)*. Don't be limited by what's displayed. If you'd like a salad with a slice of cantaloupe and a hunk of cheese, they'll whip that up for you in a snap. Belly up to the bar and, with a pointing finger and key words in the chart in this chapter, you can get a fine mixed plate of vegetables. If something's a mystery, ask for *un assaggio* (oon ah-SAH-joh) to get a little taste.

Ordering Food at Tavola Caldas

plate of mixed veggies	*piatto misto di verdure*	pee-AH-toh MEES-toh dee vehr-DOO-ray
"Heated, please."	*"Scaldare, per favore."*	skahl-DAH-ray, pehr fah-VOH-ray
"A taste, please."	*"Un assaggio, per favore."*	oon ah-SAH-joh, pehr fah-VOH-ray
artichoke	*carciofi*	kar-CHOH-fee
asparagus	*asparagi*	ah-spah-RAH-jee
beans	*fagioli*	fah-JOH-lee
breadsticks	*grissini*	gree-SEE-nee
broccoli	*broccoli*	BROH-koh-lee
cantaloupe	*melone*	may-LOH-nay
carrots	*carote*	kah-ROT-ay
green beans	*fagiolini*	fah-joh-LEE-nee
ham	*prosciutto*	proh-SHOO-toh
mushrooms	*funghi*	FOONG-ghee
potatoes	*patate*	pah-TAH-tay
rice	*riso*	REE-zoh
spinach	*spinaci*	speen-AH-chee
tomatoes	*pomodori*	poh-moh-DOH-ree
zucchini	*zucchine*	zoo-KEE-nay

(Excerpted from *Rick Steves' Italian Phrase Book & Dictionary*)

Picnics

Picnicking saves lots of euros and is a great way to sample regional specialties. In the process of assembling your meal, you get to deal with the Italians in the market scene. For a colorful experience, gather your ingredients in the morning at the produce market; you'll probably visit several small stores or market stalls to put together a complete meal, and many close around noon. While it's fun to visit the small specialty shops, an *alimentari* is your one-stop corner grocery store (most will slice and stuff your sandwich for you if you buy the ingredients there). The rare *supermercato* gives you more efficiency with less color for less cost. At busier supermarkets you'll need to take a number for deli service.

Juice-lovers can get a liter of O.J. for the price of a Coke or coffee. Look for "100% *succo*" (juice) on the label. Hang on to the half-liter mineral-water bottles (sold everywhere for about €1). Buy juice in cheap liter boxes, then drink some and store the extra in your water bottle. (Like locals, I refill my water bottle with tap

INTRODUCTION

How Was Your Trip?

Were your travels fun, smooth, and meaningful? If you'd like to share your tips, concerns, and discoveries, please fill out the survey at www.ricksteves.com/feedback. I value your feedback. Thanks in advance—it helps a lot.

water—*acqua del rubinetto*.)

Picnics can be an adventure in high cuisine. Be daring. Try the fresh mozzarella, *presto* pesto, shriveled olives, and any UFOs the locals are excited about. Shopkeepers are happy to sell small quantities of produce. They seem to enjoy giving you a taste *(un assaggio)*. It is customary to let the merchant choose the produce for you. Say *"Per oggi"* (pehr OH-jee; "For today") and he or she will grab you something ready to eat, weigh it, and make the sale. A typical picnic for two might be fresh rolls, 100 grams of cheese, 100 grams of meat *(un etto = 100 grams = about a quarter pound)*, two tomatoes, three carrots, two apples, yogurt, and a liter box of juice. Total cost: about €10.

Traveling as a Temporary Local

We travel all the way to Italy to enjoy differences—to become temporary locals. You'll experience frustrations. Certain truths that we find "God-given" or "self-evident," such as cold beer, ice in drinks, bottomless cups of coffee, hot showers, and bigger being better, are suddenly not so true. One of the benefits of travel is the eye-opening realization that there are logical, civil, and even better alternatives. A willingness to go local ensures that you'll enjoy a full dose of Italian hospitality.

Europeans generally like Americans. But if there is a negative aspect to Italians' image of Americans, it's that we are big, loud, aggressive, impolite, rich, and a bit naive. Think about the

rationale behind "crazy" Italian decisions. For instance, many hoteliers turn off the heat in early April and can't turn on air-conditioning until June. The point is to conserve energy, and it's mandated by the Italian government. You could complain about being cold or hot... or bring a sweater in winter, and in summer, be prepared to sweat a little like everyone else.

While Italians, flabbergasted by our Yankee excesses, say in disbelief, *"Mi sono cadute le braccia!"* ("I throw my arms down!"), they nearly always afford us individual travelers all the warmth that we deserve. Judging from all the happy feedback I receive from travelers who have used this book, it's safe to assume you'll enjoy a great, affordable vacation—with the finesse of an independent, experienced traveler.

Thanks, and *buon viaggio!*

Back Door Travel Philosophy
From Rick Steves' Europe Through the Back Door

Travel is intensified living—maximum thrills per minute and one of the last great sources of legal adventure. Travel is freedom. It's recess, and we need it.

Experiencing the real Europe requires catching it by surprise, going casual..."Through the Back Door."

Affording travel is a matter of priorities. (Make do with the old car.) You can travel—simply, safely, and comfortably—anywhere in Europe for $120 a day plus transportation costs. In many ways, spending more money only builds a thicker wall between you and what you came to see. Europe is a cultural carnival, and time after time, you'll find that its best acts are free and the best seats are the cheap ones.

A tight budget forces you to travel close to the ground, meeting and communicating with the people. Never sacrifice sleep, nutrition, safety, or cleanliness to save money. Simply enjoy the local-style alternatives to expensive hotels and restaurants.

Connecting with people carbonates your experience. Extroverts have more fun. If your trip is low on magic moments, kick yourself and make things happen. If you don't enjoy a place, maybe you don't know enough about it. Seek the truth. Recognize tourist traps. Give a culture the benefit of your open mind. See things as different but not better or worse. Any culture has plenty to share.

Of course, travel, like the world, is a series of hills and valleys. Be fanatically positive and militantly optimistic. If something's not to your liking, change your liking.

Travel can make you a happier American, as well as a citizen of the world. Our earth is home to six and a half billion equally precious people. It's humbling to travel and find that other people don't have the "American Dream"—they have their own dreams. Europeans like us, but, with all due respect, they wouldn't trade passports.

Thoughtful travel engages us with the world. In tough economic times, it reminds us what is truly important. By broadening perspectives, travel teaches new ways to measure quality of life.

Globetrotting destroys ethnocentricity, helping us understand and appreciate other cultures. Rather than fear the diversity on this planet, celebrate it. Among your most prized souvenirs will be the strands of different cultures you choose to knit into your own character. The world is a cultural yarn shop, and Back Door travelers are weaving the ultimate tapestry. Join in!

VENICE

Venezia

Soak all day in this puddle of elegant decay. Venice is Europe's best-preserved big city. This car-free urban wonderland of a hundred islands—laced together by 400 bridges and 2,000 alleys—survives on the artificial respirator of tourism.

Born in a lagoon 1,500 years ago as a refuge from barbarians, Venice is overloaded with tourists and is slowly sinking (unrelated facts). In the Middle Ages, the Venetians became Europe's clever middlemen for East–West trade and created a great trading empire. By smuggling in the bones of St. Mark (San Marco) in A.D. 828, Venice gained religious importance as well. With the discovery of America and new trading routes to the Orient, Venetian power ebbed. But as Venice fell, her appetite for decadence grew. Through the 17th and 18th centuries, Venice partied on the wealth accumulated through earlier centuries as a trading power.

Today, Venice is home to just over 60,000 people in its old city, down from a peak population of nearly 200,000. While there are about 500,000 in greater Venice (counting the mainland, not counting tourists), the old town has a small-town feel. Locals seem to know everyone. To see small-town Venice away from the touristic flak, escape the Rialto–San Marco tourist zone and savor the town early and late without the hordes of vacationers day-tripping in from cruise ships and nearby beach resorts. A 10-minute walk from the madness puts you in an idyllic Venice that few tourists see.

Planning Your Time

Venice is worth at least a day on even the speediest tour. Hyper-efficient train travelers take the night train in and/or out. Sleep in

VENICE

Venice Overview

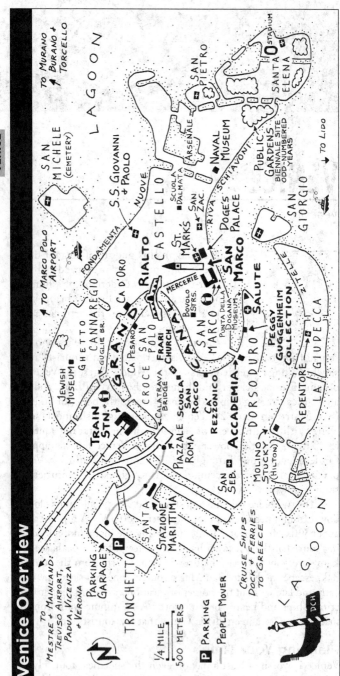

the old center to experience Venice at its best: early and late. For a one-day visit, cruise the Grand Canal, do the major sights on St. Mark's Square (the square itself, Doge's Palace, Correr Museum, and St. Mark's Basilica), see the Frari Church for art, and wander the back streets on a pub crawl. Enjoy an evening gondola ride. Venice's greatest sight is the city itself. While doable in a day, Venice is worth two. It's a medieval cookie jar, and nobody's looking. Make time to simply wander.

Take advantage of the free self-guided Rick Steves audio tours of Venice's major sights (download them from www.ricksteves.com or search for "Rick Steves Audio Tours" in iTunes); these are available for St. Mark's Basilica, St. Mark's Square, Frari Church, and the Grand Canal Cruise.

Orientation to Venice

The island city of Venice is shaped like a fish. Its major thoroughfares are canals. The Grand Canal winds through the middle of the fish, starting at the mouth where all the people and food enter, passing under the Rialto Bridge, and ending at St. Mark's Square (Piazza San Marco). Park your 21st-century perspective at the mouth and let Venice swallow you whole.

Venice is a car-less kaleidoscope of people, bridges, and odorless canals. The city has no major streets, and addresses are

hopelessly confusing. There are six districts (shown on map on page 40): San Marco (most touristy), Castello (behind San Marco), Cannaregio (from the train station to the Rialto), San Polo (other side of the Rialto), Santa Croce (the "eye" of the fish, east of the train station), and Dorsoduro (the "belly" of the fish and southernmost district of the city). Each district has about 6,000 address numbers.

To find your way, navigate by landmarks, not streets. Many street corners have a sign pointing you to *(per)* the nearest major landmark, such as San Marco, Accademia, Rialto, and Ferrovia (train station). Obedient visitors stick to the main thoroughfares as directed by these signs...and miss the charm of back-street Venice.

Beyond the city's core lie several other islands, including San Giorgio (with great views of Venice), Giudecca (more views), San Michele (old cemetery), Murano (famous for glass), Burano (lacemaking), Torcello (old church), and the skinny Lido beach.

Tourist Information

With this book, a free city map from your hotel, and the *Un Ospite di Venezia* entertainment guide (described below), there's little need to visit a tourist office in Venice. That's fortunate, because the city's TIs are crowded and clunky. If you need to check or confirm something, there are four offices: **train station** (daily 8:00–21:00), **St. Mark's Square** (daily 9:00–15:30, opposite end from church), nearby at the **San Marco–Vallaresso vaporetto stop** (daily 10:00–18:00), and at the **airport** (daily 9:00–21:00). You can save time by phoning 041-529-8711 or visiting www.turismovenezia.it.

At the TI—or at many hotels—pick up two free pamphlets: *Shows and Events* and *Un Ospite di Venezia.* Besides upcoming events and nightlife, they also list museum hours, train and vaporetto schedules, emergency telephone numbers, and so on (www.aguestinvenice.com, info@aguestinvenice.com).

For a creative travel guide written by young Venetians, consider *My Local Guide Venice,* for its neighborhood histories, self-guided walking tours, and recommendations on sights and activities (sold at TIs for €9.90).

Maps: In Venice of all places, you need a good map. Hotels give away freebies (no better than the small color one at the front of this book). The TI sells a decent €2.50 map and miniguide—but you can find a wider range at bookshops, newsstands, and postcard stands. The cheap maps are pretty bad, but if you spend €5, you'll get a map that shows you everything. Investing in a good map can be the best €5 you'll spend in Venice. Don't take street names too seriously—spellings change with the dialect. Also, keep in mind that many street names change midway.

Arrival in Venice

A two-mile-long causeway (with highway and train lines) connects Venice to the mainland. Mestre, the sprawling mainland transportation hub, has fewer crowds, cheaper hotels, and plenty of inexpensive parking lots, but zero charm. Don't stop in Mestre unless you're parking your car or transferring trains.

By Train: All trains to "Venice" stop at Venezia Mestre (on the mainland). Most continue on to Santa Lucia Station on the island of Venice itself. If your train only stops at Mestre, worry not. Shuttle trains regularly connect Mestre's station with Venice's Santa Lucia Station (6/hour, 10 minutes, €1).

Venice's **Santa Lucia train station** plops you right into the old town on the Grand Canal, an easy vaporetto ride or fascinating 40-minute walk to St. Mark's Square. Upon arrival, skip the station's crowded TI, because the two TIs at St. Mark's Square are better, and it's not worth a long wait for a minimal map (buy a good one from a newsstand or pick up a free one at your hotel).

Arrival in Venice

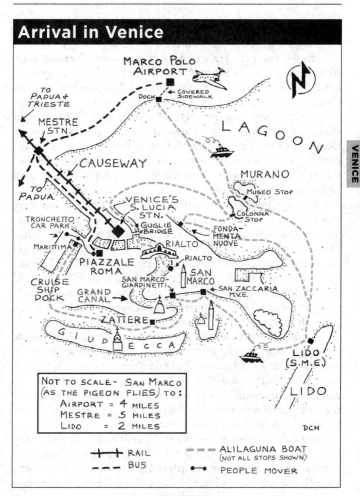

VENICE

Confirm your departure plan (stop by train info desk or just study the *partenze*/departures posters on walls).

Consider storing unnecessary heavy bags, although lines for **baggage check** may be very long (at track 1, €4/5 hours, daily 6:00–24:00, no lockers, 45-pound weight limit on bags). **WCs** are at track 1 and in the back of the big bar-cafeteria area inside the station.

Minimize your time in the station—the banks of user-friendly automated ticket machines (marked ***Biglietto Veloce/Fast Ticket***) are handy. They take euros and credit cards, display schedules, issue tickets, and even make reservations for railpass-holders. The gray-only machines are for tickets to nearby destinations such as Padua. Or you could take care of these tasks at downtown travel agencies (see page 49). For more on train travel in Italy—including your ticket-buying options—see page 962.

To get from the train station to downtown Venice, walk straight out of the station to the canal. On your left is a vaporetto ticket booth and the dock for vaporetto #2 (fast boat down Grand Canal, catch from right side of dock). To your right is the dock for *vaporetti* #1 (slow boat down Grand Canal, catch from far right dock) and #51 (goes counterclockwise around Venice, handy for Dorsoduro hotels). See the hotel listings in the "Sleeping in Venice" section to find out which boat to catch to get to your hotel. See "Getting Around Venice—By Vaporetto," on page 52 for details on vaporetto tickets and passes.

By Car: The freeway dead-ends after crossing the causeway at Venice, near several parking lots on the edge of the island. The most central and expensive lot is San Marco on Piazzale Roma. Tronchetto (across the causeway and on the right) has a bigger and cheaper multistoried garage (€20/day, tel. 041-520-7555). From there, avoid the travel agencies masquerading as TIs, and head directly for the vaporetto docks for the boat connection (#2) to the town center. Don't let water-taxi boatmen con you out of the relatively inexpensive €6.50 vaporetto ride.

Venice's new **People Mover** monorail, a shuttle train fixed to a circular cable, opened in 2010 and carries passengers from the parking lot at Tronchetto to Piazzale Roma. It costs €1, departs every few minutes, makes the half-mile trip in three minutes, is completely automated (no crew on board), and drops you a block from the Calatrava Bridge on Piazzale Roma (across the Grand Canal from Santa Lucia train station).

Parking in **Mestre** (on the mainland) is simple and cheap (open-air lots cost €8/day Mon–Fri, €10/day Sat–Sun, across from Mestre train station, easy shuttle-train connections to Venice's Santa Lucia Station—6/hour, 10 minutes, €1). There are also huge and economical lots in Verona, Padua, and Vicenza.

By Plane: For information on Venice's airport and connections into the city, see page 132.

Passes for Venice

The sights you probably care the most about (Accademia, Peggy Guggenheim Collection, Scuola San Rocco, Campanile, and the three sights within St. Mark's Basilica that charge admission) are not covered on any pass. To see the Doge's Palace, you must also pay for the less-visited Correr Museum (both on St. Mark's Square). While this €13 ticket is called a "pass" (described next), think of it as just a combo-ticket. Venice offers various other cards and passes that cover multiple sights few visitors want to see; these are generally not worth the trouble.

Doge's Palace/Correr Museum Tickets: The **San Marco Museum Plus Pass** (€13) covers admission to the Doge's Palace and Correr Museum (including two other museums within the Correr—the National Archaeological Museum and the Monumental Rooms of Marciana National Library), plus your choice of **one** of these seven museums: Ca' Rezzonico (Museum of 18th-Century Venice); Palazzo Mocenigo Costume Museum; Casa Goldoni (home of the Italian playwright); Ca' Pesaro (modern art); Museum of Natural History in the Santa Croce district; Murano's Glass Museum; or Burano's Lace Museum (www.musei civiciveneziani.it). To bypass the long line at the Doge's Palace, purchase this pass at the less-crowded Correr Museum (or any other included museum).

The San Marco Museum Plus Pass is available only from April through October. Off-season (Nov–March), it's replaced by the **Museum Card of the Museums of St. Mark's Square** (€12), which covers only the Doge's Palace and Correr Museum (includes the two museums inside the Correr).

Museum Pass: Busy sightseers may prefer the more expensive Museum Pass. This pass covers the Doge's Palace and Correr Museum, plus entry to **all** of the museums listed above for the San Marco Museum Plus Pass (€18, www.museiciviciveneziani .it). In general, this pass saves you money only if you visit five or more sights; before you buy, make sure they're sights you really want to see.

Chorus Pass: Church-lovers can get admission to 16 of Venice's churches and their art (generally €3 each)—including the Frari—for €9 (€18 for Family Pass, www.chorusvenezia.org).

Transportation Passes: Venice also sells transit-only passes covering *vaporetti* and buses that arrive on the edge of town. For a rundown on these, see "Getting Around Venice," later.

Helpful Hints

Get Lost: Accept the fact that Venice was a tourist town 400 years ago. It was, is, and always will be crowded. While 80 percent of Venice is, in fact, not touristy, 80 percent of the tourists never notice. Hit the back streets. Venice is the ideal town to explore on foot. Walk and walk to the far reaches of the town. Don't worry about getting lost. In fact, get as lost as possible. Keep reminding yourself, "I'm on an island, and I can't get off." When it comes time to find your way, just follow the directional arrows on building corners or simply ask a local, *"Dov'è San Marco?"* ("Where is St. Mark's?") People in the tourist business (that's most Venetians) speak some English. If they don't, listen politely, watch where their hands point, say, *"Grazie,"* and head off in that direction. If you're lost, refer

Daily Reminder

Sunday: While anyone is welcome to worship, most churches are closed to sightseers during Mass on Sunday morning. The Church of San Giorgio Maggiore (on an island across from St. Mark's Square) hosts a Gregorian Mass at 11:00. The Church of San Polo is closed today, and these sights are open only in the afternoon: St. Mark's Basilica (14:00–17:00, until 16:00 Nov–March), Frari Church (13:00–18:00), and the Church of San Zaccaria (16:00–18:00). Today, the Rialto open-air market consists mainly of souvenir stalls (fish and produce sections closed). It's a bad day for a pub crawl, as most pubs are closed.

Monday: All sights are open except the Rialto produce market, Ca' Pesaro, and Torcello Museum (on Torcello Island). The Accademia and Ca' d'Oro close at 14:00. Don't side-trip to Verona today, as most sights in these towns are closed.

Tuesday: All sights are open except the Peggy Guggenheim Collection, Ca' Rezzonico (Museum of 18th-Century Venice), and Punta della Dogana.

Wednesday/Thursday/Friday: All sights are open.

Saturday: All sights are open except the Jewish Museum.

Notes: The Accademia is open earlier (daily at 8:15) and closes later (19:15 Tue–Sun) than most sights in Venice. Some sights close earlier off-season (such as the Correr Museum, Campanile bell tower, and St. Mark's Basilica).

to your map, or pop into a hotel and ask for their business card—it comes with a map and a prominent "You are here."

Be Prepared to Splurge: Venice is expensive for residents as well as tourists. Demand is huge, supply is limited, and running a business is costly. Things just cost more here; everything must be shipped in and hand-trucked to its destination. Perhaps the best way to enjoy Venice is just to succumb to its charms and blow a lot of money.

Warning: The dark, late-night streets of Venice are safe. Even so, pickpockets (often elegantly dressed) work the crowded main streets, docks, and *vaporetti* (wear your money belt, zip up your valuables, and watch your purse or day bag). Your biggest risk of pickpockets is inside St. Mark's Basilica.

A handy Polizia station is on the right side of St. Mark's Square (near Caffè Florian). A service called Counter of Tourist Mediation at the Venice Complaint Office handles complaints about local crooks—including gondolier, restaurant, or hotel rip-offs (tel. 041-529-8710, fax 041-523-0399, complaint.apt@turismovenezia.it).

Immigrants selling items such as knock-off handbags on

Churches: Modest dress is recommended at churches and required at St. Mark's Basilica—no bare shoulders, shorts, or short skirts. Some churches are closed to sightseers on Sunday morning (including St. Mark's Basilica, Frari Church, Church of San Zaccaria, and after 11:00 at San Giorgio Maggiore), and many are closed from roughly 12:00 to 14:30 or 15:30 Monday through Saturday (this includes La Salute and San Giorgio Maggiore).

Crowd Control: The city is inundated with cruise-ship crowds and tours from mainland hotels daily from 10:00 to about 17:00. Crowds can be a serious problem at **St. Mark's Basilica.** Try going early or late, or even better, you can bypass the line if you have a bag to check (see page 72).

At the **Doge's Palace,** avoid the long line by purchasing your ticket at the less-crowded Correr Museum. You can also visit late in the day, buy your ticket online, or book a tour.

For the **Campanile,** ascend late (it's open until 21:00 July–Sept), or skip it entirely if you're going to the similar San Giorgio Maggiore bell tower.

For the **Accademia,** go early or late—or you can reserve a ticket in advance by phone or online.

The sights that have crowd problems get even more crowded when it rains.

VENICE

the streets are doing so illegally—if you buy goods from them, you'll risk getting a big fine.

Medical Help: Venice's S.S. Giovanni e Paolo hospital (tel. 118) is a 10-minute walk from both the Rialto and San Marco neighborhoods, located on Fondamenta dei Mendicanti toward Fondamenta Nuove. You can take vaporetto #41 from San Zaccaria–Jolanda to the Ospedale stop.

Take Breaks: Venice's endless pavement, crowds, and tight spaces are hard on the tourist. Schedule breaks in your sightseeing. Grab a cool place to sit down, relax, and recoup—meditate on a pew in an uncrowded church, or stop in a café.

Etiquette: Walk on the right and don't loiter on bridges. On St. Mark's Square, a "decorum patrol" admonishes snackers and sunbathers. Picnicking is forbidden (keep a low profile). The only place for a legal picnic is in Giardinetti Reali, the small park along the waterfront west of the Piazzetta near St. Mark's Square.

Dress Modestly: Men should keep their shirts on. When visiting St. Mark's Basilica or other major churches, men, women, and even children must cover their shoulders and knees (or risk being turned away). Remove hats when entering a church.

Public Toilets: Handy public WCs (€1.50) are near major landmarks, including: St. Mark's Square (one is behind the Correr Museum, to the left of the post office; another is at the waterfront park, Giardinetti Reali), Rialto, and at the Accademia Bridge. Use free toilets whenever you can—in a museum you're visiting or a café you're eating in. Like Mom always said, "Just try."

Best Views: While the best views of Venice may be from water level, there are several upper-altitude viewing spots: On St. Mark's Square, try the soaring Campanile, St. Mark's Basilica (specifically the balcony of the San Marco Museum, requires admission), or the St. Mark's Square clock tower (requires tour). The Rialto and Accademia bridges provide free, expansive views of the Grand Canal, along with a cooling breeze. Or get off the main island for a view of the Venetian skyline: Ascend the Church of San Giorgio Maggiore's bell tower, or venture to La Giudecca island to visit the swanky bar of the Molino Stucky Hilton Hotel (free shuttle boat from San Zaccaria-M.V.E. vaporetto stop).

Pigeon Poop: If your head is bombed by a pigeon, resist the initial response to wipe it off immediately—it'll just smear into your hair. Wait until it dries, and it should flake off cleanly. But if the poop splatters on your clothes, wipe it off immediately to avoid a stain.

Water: I carry a water bottle to refill at public fountains. Venetians pride themselves on having pure, safe, and tasty tap water piped in from the foothills of the Alps. You can actually see the mountains from Venice's bell towers on crisp, clear winter days.

Street Lingo: *Campo* means square, *campiello* is a small square, *calle* is street, *fondamenta* is the road running along a canal, *rio* is a small canal, *rio terra* is a street that was once a canal and has been filled in, and *ponte* is a bridge.

Services

Internet Access: You'll find handy, if pricey (up to €8/hour), little Internet places all over town. They are usually on back streets: Ask your hotelier for the nearest place. Most hotels provide both free Internet access and Wi-Fi for guests.

Post Office: The main P.O. is near the Rialto Bridge (on the St. Mark's side, Mon–Sat 8:30–13:00, closed Sun). Use post offices only as a last resort, as simple transactions can take 45 minutes if you get in the wrong line. You can buy stamps from tobacco shops and mail postcards at any of the red postboxes around town.

Bookstores: In keeping with its literary heritage, Venice has classy and inviting bookstores.

The following have great English-language travel sections (and stock my guidebooks): **Libreria Mondadori** is a block behind St. Mark's Square (daily May–Oct 10:00–23:00, Nov–April 10:00–20:00, 1345 Complesso del Ridotto, tel. 041-522-2193); **Libreria Studium** is a block behind St. Mark's Basilica (Mon–Sat 9:00–19:30, Sun 9:30–13:30, Calle de la Canonica, tel. 041-522-2382). **Acqua Alta** ("high water") is a funky secondhand bookstore with bargain books in English and reproduction prints of Venice. Quirky Luigi has prepared for the next "high water" by displaying his wares in a selection of vessels, including bathtubs and a gondola (daily 9:00–21:00, just beyond Campo Santa Maria Formosa at Calle Longa Santa Maria Formosa 5176, tel. 041-296-0841, mobile 340-680-0704).

Laundry: I've listed launderettes near some of my recommended hotels. For more options, ask your hotelier to direct you to one nearby.

Travel Agencies: If you need to get train tickets, make seat reservations, or arrange a *cuccetta* (koo-CHET-tah—a berth on a night train) avoid a time-consuming trip to the crowded train station by using a downtown travel agency. Most trains between Venice, Florence, and Rome require reservations, even for railpass-holders. A travel agency can also give advice on cheap flights (book at least a week in advance for the best fares).

Near St. Mark's Square, **Oltrex Change and Travel** sells train and plane tickets and books train reservations for a €3.50 fee (tickets sold daily May–Oct 9:00–18:00, Nov–April 9:00–16:30, one bridge past the Bridge of Sighs, Riva degli Schiavoni 4192, tel. 041-524-2828, Luca and Beatrice).

Near Rialto, **Kele & Teo Travel** sells train tickets for about a 10 percent service charge (Mon–Fri 9:00–18:00, Sat 9:00–12:00, closed Sun; leaving the Rialto Bridge heading for St. Mark's, it's half a block away, tucked down a side street on the right; tel. 041-520-8722).

English Church Services: The **San Zulian Church**—the only church in Venice that you can actually walk around—offers a Mass in English (generally May–Sept Mon–Fri at 9:30 and Sun at 11:30, Sun only Oct–April, 2 blocks toward Rialto off St. Mark's Square). **St. George's Anglican Church** welcomes all Christians to its English-speaking Eucharist (Sun at 10:30, located in Dorsoduro, midway between Accademia and Peggy Guggenheim Collection).

Haircuts: I've been getting my hair cut at **Coiffeur Benito** for

VENICE

Venice

TO MAINLAND

CAMPO DI GHETTO NUOVO

JEWISH GHETTO

S. LEO.

MADDA.

PONTE DI GUGLIE

S. MARCUOLA

DI SPAGNA

R. BIASIO

S. STAE

FERROVIA (TRAIN STN.)

LISTA

BARI

BEMBO

TINTOR

TO TRONCHETTO & MAINLAND

S. SIMON

LACA

CHIESA

TO TRONCHETTO

GARAGE

AMAI

CAMPO S. STIN

CAMPO S. POLO

PIAZZALE ROMA

S. ROCCO

FRARI CHURCH

S. POLO

TINT

SAION

S. TOMA

SCUOLA SAN ROCCO

GRAND

200 YARDS

200 METERS

DCH

CAMPO SANTA MARG.

FOSC

CAP.

CA' REZZ

PAL. GRASSI

S. SAM. BOT.

CAMPO S. STEF.

AVOGARIA

CAMPO SAN BARNABA

TOLETTA

CORFU

ACCADEMIA

ZATTERE PONTE LONGO

RIO TERRA FOSCARINI

AGNESE

ZATTERE SPIRITO E

T TRAGHETTO CROSSING

V VAPORETTO STOP

G GONDOLA STATION

• PEOPLE MOVER

VENICE

nearly two decades. Benito has been keeping local men and women trim for 27 years. He's an artist—actually a "hair sculptor"—and a cut here is a fun diversion from the tourist grind (about €20 for women, €18 for men, Tue–Fri 8:30–13:00 & 15:30–19:30, Sat 8:30–13:00 only, closed Sun–Mon, behind San Zulian Church near St. Mark's Square, Calle S. Zulian Già del Strazzariol 592a, tel. 041-528-6221).

Getting Around Venice

On Foot: Navigate by major landmarks. There are signs on street corners all over town pointing to *San Marco, Accademia, Ferrovia* (train station), and *Piazzale Roma* (the bus stop behind the train station). Determine whether your destination is in the direction of a major signposted landmark, then follow the signs through the maze of squares, lanes, and bridges.

By Vaporetto: The public-transit system is a fleet of motorized bus-boats called *vaporetti*. They work like city buses except that they never get a flat, the stops are docks, and if you get off between stops, you might drown.

For most travelers, only two *vaporetti* lines matter: line #1 and line #2. These lines leave every 10 minutes (less off-season) and go up and down the Grand Canal, between the "mouth" of the fish at one end and San Marco at the other. Line #1 is the slow boat, taking 45 minutes and making every stop along the way. Line #2 is the fast boat that zips down the Grand Canal in 25 minutes, stopping only at Tronchetto (parking lot), Piazzale Roma (bus station), Ferrovia (train station), San Marcuola, Rialto Bridge, San Tomà (Frari Church), Accademia Bridge, San Marco (west end of St. Mark's Square), and San Zaccaria (east end of St. Mark's Square).

Catching a vaporetto is very much like catching a city bus. Helpful charts at the docks show a map of the lines and stops. At one end of the Grand Canal are Tronchetto, Piazzale Roma (Ple. Roma), and Ferrovia. At the other end is San Marco. The sign on the dock lists the line number that stops there and which direction the boat is headed, for example: "#2—Direction San Marco." Nearby is the sign for line #2 going in the other direction, for example: "#2—Direction Tronchetto."

It's simple, but there are a few quirks. Some stops have just one dock for boats going in both directions, so make sure the boat you get on is pointing in the direction you want to go. Larger stops might have two separate docks side by side (one for each direction), while some smaller stops have docks across the canal from each other (one for each direction). Electronic reader boards on busy docks display which boats are coming next, and when.

To clear up any confusion, ask a ticket-seller or conductor (there's often one stationed on the dock to help confused tourists), or pick up the most current ACTV timetable (free at ticket booths, in English and Italian, tel. 041-2424, www.hellovenezia.com or www.actv.it).

A **single ticket** costs a whopping €6.50. (Don't worry—much cheaper passes are described below.) Tickets are good for 60 minutes in one direction; you can hop on and off at stops during that time. Technically, you're not allowed a round-trip (though in practice, a round-trip is allowed if you can complete it within a 60-minute span). Note that you'll pay only €2 for a few shorter runs, including the route from San Marco to La Salute or from San Zaccaria–Jolanda to San Giorgio Maggiore.

You can also buy a **pass** for unlimited use of *vaporetti* and ACTV buses: €16/12 hours, €18/24 hours, €23/36 hours, €28/48 hours, €33/72 hours, €50/7-day pass). Because single tickets cost a hefty €6.50 a pop, these passes can pay for themselves in a hurry. Think through your Venice itinerary before you step up to the ticket booth to pay for your first vaporetto trip. It makes sense to get a pass if you'll be taking four rides or more (e.g., to your hotel, on a Grand Canal joyride, into the lagoon and back, to the train station). And it's fun to be able to hop on and off spontaneously, and avoid long ticket lines. On the other hand, many tourists just walk and rarely use a boat.

Those settling in can ride like a local by buying the **CartaVenezia** ID card (€40, which lets you ride for about €1 per trip; see www.actv.it for details).

Buy vaporetto tickets or passes at ticket booths at main stops (such as Ferrovia, Rialto, Accademia, and San Marco–Vallaresso). You can buy individual tickets on board from a conductor (do it immediately upon boarding or you risk a €50 fine). Plan your travel so you'll have tickets or a pass handy when you need them—not all stops have ticket booths. Passes are validated and start with your first swipe. The pass system (called iMob) is electronic—just touch your card to the electronic reader on the dock to validate it.

For fun, take my Grand Canal Cruise (see page 57). Boats can be literally packed during the tourist rush hour. Morning rush hour (8:00–10:00) is headed in the direction of St. Mark's Square, as tourists and commuters arrive. Afternoon rush hour (about 17:00) is when they're headed in the other direction for the train station. Riding at night, with nearly empty boats and chandelier-lit

Handy *Vaporetti* from San Zaccaria, near St. Mark's Square

Several *vaporetti* leave from the San Zaccaria docks, located 150 yards east of St. Mark's Square. There are four separate San Zaccaria docks spaced about 70 yards apart: Danieli, Jolanda, M.V.E., and Pietà. (Note: Although I list which specific dock these lines leave from, they often change from season to season—be prepared.)

- Line #1 goes up the Grand Canal, making all the stops, including San Marco–Vallaresso, Rialto, Ferrovia (train station), and Piazzale Roma (but it does not go as far as Tronchetto). In the other direction, it goes to the Lido. Line #1 departs from the San Zaccaria–Danieli dock.
- Line #2 zips over to San Giorgio Maggiore, the island church across from St. Mark's Square (5 minutes, €2 ride). From there, it continues on to the parking lot at Tronchetto (departs from San Zaccaria–M.V.E.)
- Line #41 goes to San Michele and Murano in 45 minutes (departs from San Zaccaria–Jolanda).
- The "LN" heads to Burano (70 minutes, from San Zaccaria–Pietà dock).
- The Molino Stucky shuttle boat takes even non-guests to the Hilton Hotel, with its popular view bar (free, 20-minute ride, leaves at 0:20 past the hour from near the San Zaccaria–M.V.E. dock).
- Lines #51 and #52 are the *circulare* (cheer-koo-LAH-ray), making a loop around the perimeter of the island, with a stop at the Lido—perfect if you just like riding boats. Line #51 goes counterclockwise (departs from San Zaccaria–Danieli), and #52 goes clockwise (departs from San Zaccaria–Jolanda).
- The Alilaguna airport shuttle to and from the airport stops at the San Zaccaria–Jolanda dock.

palace interiors viewable from the Grand Canal, is an entirely different experience.

By *Traghetto:* Only four bridges cross the Grand Canal, but *traghetti* (gondolas) shuttle locals and in-the-know tourists across the Grand Canal at eight handy locations (marked on the color map of Venice at the front of this book). Venetians stand while riding, but you shouldn't (€0.50, don't tip—literally). Note that *traghetti* generally don't run in the evening.

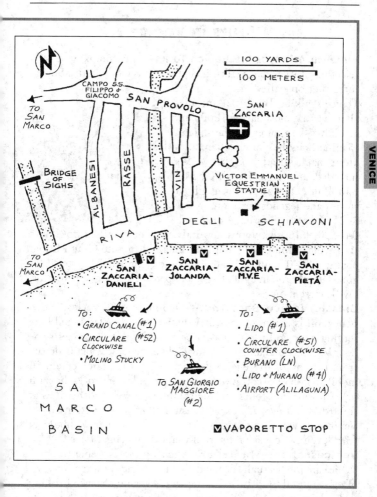

By Water Taxi: Venetian taxis, like speedboat limos, hang out at busy points along the Grand Canal. Prices, which average €65, are soft (about €70 to train station or €110 to airport for up to four people, extra fees for very early or late runs). Negotiate and settle on the price before stepping in. For travelers with lots of luggage or small groups who can split the cost, taxi-boat rides can be a worthwhile and time-saving convenience—and skipping across the lagoon in a classic wooden motorboat is a cool indulgence. For €90 an hour, you can have a private unguided taxi-boat tour.

By Gondola: To hire a gondolier for your own private cruise, see page 92.

Tours in Venice

Avventure Bellissime Venice Tours—This company offers a selection of two-hour walks, including a basic St. Mark's Square introduction called the "Original Venice Walking Tour" (€21, includes church entry, most days at 11:00, Sun at 14:00; 45 minutes on the square, 15 minutes in the church, 60 minutes along back streets). Other walks include Cannaregio/Jewish Ghetto, San Polo/Dorsoduro, and ghost stories and legends (€20, group size 8–22, English-language only, tel.  041-520-8616, see www.tours-italy.com for details, info@tours -italy.com, Monica or Jonathan). Their 70-minute Grand Canal boat tour (€40, daily at 16:30, limited to eight people) is timed for good late-afternoon light. To get a 10 percent discount on any tour, say "Rick sent me."

Classic Venice Bars Tour—Debonair guide Alessandro Schezzini is a connoisseur of Venetian *bacari*—classic old bars serving wine and traditional *cicchetti* snacks. He organizes two-hour Venetian pub tours (€30, any night on request at 18:00, depart from the top of the Rialto Bridge, reserve by phone or email, mobile 335-530-9024, www.schezzini.it, alessandro@schezzini .it). Alessandro's tours include sampling *cicchetti* with wines at three different *bacari*, plus he'll answer all of your questions about Venice. (If you think of this tour as a light dinner with a local friend, you can consider it part of your eating budget.)

Venicescapes—Michael Broderick's private theme tours of Venice are intellectually demanding and beyond the attention span of most mortal tourists. But those with a keen interest in learning and a desire to gain a solid understanding of Venice find him passionate and engaging. Rather than a "sightseeing tour," your time with Michael is more like a rolling graduate-level lecture. For a description of his various itineraries, see his website (book well in advance, tours last 4–6 hours: $275 for 2 people, $50/person after that, pay in dollars or the current euro equivalent, admissions and transportation are extra, tel. 041-520-6361, www.venicescapes.org, info@venicescapes.org).

Artviva: The Original and Best Walking Tours—This company offers a number of tours, including a Venice in One Glorious Day Special and four theme tours (Grand Canal, Venice Walk, Doge's Palace, Gondola Tour). The two-hour "Learn to Be a Gondolier" tour teaches the ancient craft of rowing Venetian-style (€80, 4 people maximum). See the tour details and Rick

Steves readers' discounts on their website (book in advance, tours run March–Nov, tel. 055-264-5033, www.italy.artviva.com, staff @artviva.com).

Local Guides—Licensed guides are carefully trained and love explaining Venice to visitors. If you organize a small group at breakfast at your hotel to split the cost (figure on roughly €70/hour with a 2-hour minimum), the fee becomes more reasonable. The following companies and guides give excellent tours to individuals, families, and small groups.

Elisabetta Morelli (€65/hour with this book in 2011, 2-hour minimum, tel. 041-526-7816, mobile 328-753-5220, bettamorelli @inwind.it).

Walks Inside Venice is a group of three women enthusiastic about teaching (€70/hour per group, 3-hour minimum; Roberta: mobile 347-253-0560; Cristina: mobile 348-341-5421; Sara: mobile 335-522-9714; www.walksinsidevenice.com, info@walksinside venice.com).

Venice with a Guide is a co-op of 10 equally good guides (www.venicewithaguide.com).

Alessandro Schezzini, mentioned earlier for his Classic Venice Bars Tour, isn't a licensed Italian guide and therefore can't take you into sights. But his relaxed two-hour back-streets "Rick Steves" tour does a great job of getting you beyond the clichés and into offbeat Venice (€15/person, book by email—alessandro @schezzini.it, mobile 335-530-9024, www.schezzini.it).

Treviso Car Service, run by Igor, offers tours beyond Venice to 16th-century villas, wine-and-cheese tastings, and the Dolomites, in addition to airport transfers (see listing on page 134, mobile 348-900-0700, www.trevisocarservice.com, tvcarservice @gmail.com).

Self-Guided Cruise

▲▲▲Welcome to Venice's Grand Canal Cruise

Take a joyride and introduce yourself to Venice by boat. Cruise the Canal Grande all the way to San Marco, starting at Ferrovia (the train station).

If it's your first trip down the Grand Canal, you might want to stow this book and just take it all in—Venice is a barrage on the senses that hardly needs a narration. But these notes give the cruise a little meaning and help orient you to this great city.

This tour is designed to be done on the slow boat #1 (which takes about 45 minutes). The express boat #2 travels the same route, but it skips many stops and takes only 25 minutes, making it hard to sightsee.

To help you enjoy the visual parade of canal wonders, I've

organized this tour by boat stop. I'll point out both what you can see from each stop, and what to look forward to as you cruise to the next stop. (For a free downloadable audio tour of this cruise, see www.ricksteves.com.)

Overview

The Grand Canal is Venice's "Main Street." At more than two miles long, nearly 150 feet wide, and nearly 15 feet deep, the Grand Canal is the city's largest, lined with its most impressive palaces. It's the remnant of a river that once spilled from the mainland into the Adriatic. The sediment it carried formed barrier islands that

cut Venice off from the sea, forming a lagoon. Venice was built on the marshy islands of the former delta, sitting on pilings driven nearly 15 feet into the clay (alder was the preferred wood). About 25 miles of canals drain the city, dumping like streams into the Grand Canal. Technically, Venice has only three canals: Grand, Giudecca, and Cannaregio. The 45 small waterways that dump into the Grand Canal are referred to as rivers (e.g., Rio Nuovo).

Venice is a city of palaces, dating from the days when it was the world's richest city. The most lavish palaces formed a grand chorus line along the Grand Canal. Once frescoed in reds and blues, with black-and-white borders and gold-leaf trim, they made Venice a city of dazzling color. This cruise is the only way to truly appreciate the palaces, approaching them at water level, where their main entrances were located. Today, strict laws prohibit any changes in these buildings, so while landowners gnash their teeth, we can enjoy Europe's best-preserved medieval city—slowly rotting. Many of the grand buildings are now vacant. Others harbor chandeliered elegance above mossy, empty (often flooded) ground floors.

The Grand Canal Cruise Begins

This tour starts at the Ferrovia vaporetto stop (at Santa Lucia train station). It also works if you board upstream from Ferrovia, either at Tronchetto (where cars arrive) or Piazzale Roma (where airport buses and the People Mover monorail from Tronchetto arrive). Just start the tour when your vaporetto reaches Ferrovia.

A few tips: You're more likely to find an empty seat if you catch the vaporetto at Piazzale Roma, which is just a short walk from Ferrovia over the Calatrava Bridge. If you start at Tronchetto, your only choice is boat #2—which really rushes this tour. Wherever

Venice's Grand Canal

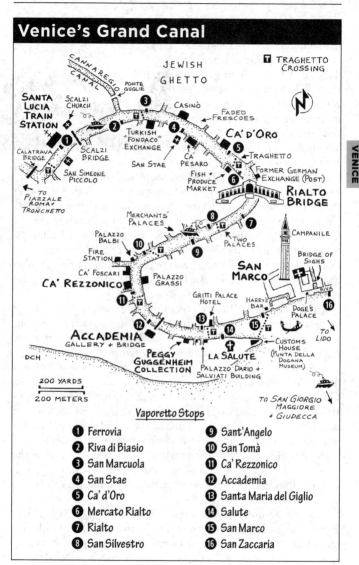

TRAGHETTO CROSSING

JEWISH GHETTO

CANNAREGIO CANAL

PONTE GUGLIE

SCALZI CHURCH

SANTA LUCIA TRAIN STATION

CASINÒ

FADED FRESCOES

CA' D'ORO

CALATRAVA BRIDGE

SCALZI BRIDGE

TURKISH "FONDACO" EXCHANGE

SAN SIMEONE PICCOLO

SAN STAE

CA' PESARO

TRAGHETTO

FORMER GERMAN EXCHANGE (POST)

FISH + PRODUCE MARKET

TO PIAZZALE ROMA + TRONCHETTO

RIALTO BRIDGE

MERCHANTS' PALACES

PALAZZO BALBI

FIRE STATION

CA' FOSCARI

CA' REZZONICO

PALAZZO GRASSI

TWO PALACES

CAMPANILE

BRIDGE OF SIGHS

SAN MARCO

RIVA

GRITTI PALACE HOTEL

HARRY'S BAR

DOGE'S PALACE

TO LIDO

ACCADEMIA GALLERY + BRIDGE

PEGGY GUGGENHEIM COLLECTION

LA SALUTE

CUSTOMS HOUSE (PUNTA DELLA DOGANA MUSEUM)

PALAZZO DARIO + SALVIATI BUILDING

DCH

200 YARDS
200 METERS

TO SAN GIORGIO MAGGIORE + GIUDECCA

VENICE

Vaporetto Stops

1. Ferrovia
2. Riva di Biasio
3. San Marcuola
4. San Stae
5. Ca' d'Oro
6. Mercato Rialto
7. Rialto
8. San Silvestro
9. Sant'Angelo
10. San Tomà
11. Ca' Rezzonico
12. Accademia
13. Santa Maria del Giglio
14. Salute
15. San Marco
16. San Zaccaria

you catch your vaporetto, confirm that you're on a boat that goes all the way to San Marco, by way of Rialto (*"San Marco via Rialto"*). If the conductor announces *"Solo Rialto!,"* the boat only goes as far as Rialto.

Ferrovia: The **Santa Lucia train station,** one of the few modern buildings in town, was built in 1954. It's been the gateway into Venice since 1860, when the first station was built. "F.S." stands for "Ferrovie dello Stato," the Italian state railway system.

More than 20,000 people a day commute in from the mainland, making this the busiest part of Venice during rush hour. To alleviate some of the congestion and make the commute easier, the new **Calatrava Bridge** spans the Grand Canal between the train station and

Piazzale Roma upstream (see page 88).

Opposite the train station, atop the green dome of **San Simeone Piccolo** church, St. Simeon waves *ciao* to whoever enters or leaves the "old" city. The pink church with the white Carrara-marble facade, just beyond the train station, is the **Church of the Scalzi** (Church of the Barefoot, named after the shoeless Carmelite monks), where the last doge (Venetian ruler) rests. It looks relatively new because it was partially rebuilt after being bombed in 1915 by Austrians aiming (poorly) at the train station.

Riva de Biasio: Venice's main thoroughfare is busy with all kinds of **boats:** taxis, police boats, garbage boats, ambulances, construction cranes, and even brown-and-white UPS boats. Somehow they all manage to share the canal in relative peace.

About 25 yards past the Riva de Biasio stop, you'll look left down the broad **Cannaregio Canal** to see what was the **Jewish Ghetto** (see page 86). The twin pale-pink six-story "skyscrapers"—the tallest buildings you'll see at this end of the canal—are reminders of how densely populated the world's original ghetto was. Set aside as the local Jewish quarter in 1516, this area became extremely crowded. This urban island developed into one of the most closely knit business and cultural quarters of all the Jewish communities in Italy, and gave us our word "ghetto" (from *geto*, the copper foundry located here).

San Marcuola: At this stop, facing a tiny square just ahead, stands the unfinished church of San Marcuola, one of only five churches fronting the Grand Canal. Centuries ago, this canal

was a commercial drag of expensive real estate in high demand by wealthy merchants. About 20 yards ahead on the right stands the stately gray **Turkish "Fondaco" Exchange,** one of the oldest houses in Venice. Its horseshoe arches and roofline of triangles and dingleballs are reminders of its Byzantine heritage. Turkish traders in turbans docked here, unloaded their goods into the warehouse on the bottom story, then went upstairs for a home-style meal and a place to sleep. Venice in the 1500s was very cosmopolitan, welcoming every religion and ethnicity, so long as they carried cash. (Today the building contains the city's newly reopened Museum of Natural History—and Venice's only dinosaur skeleton.)

Just 100 yards ahead on the left, Venice's **Casinò** is housed in the palace where German composer Richard *(The Ring)* Wagner died in 1883. See his distinct strong-jawed profile in the white plaque on the brick wall. In the 1700s, Venice was Europe's Vegas, with casinos and prostitutes everywhere. Casinòs ("little houses") have long provided Italians with a handy escape from daily life. Today they're run by the state to keep Mafia influence at bay. Notice the fancy front porch, rolling out the red carpet for high rollers arriving by taxi or hotel boat.

San Stae: The San Stae Church sports a delightful Baroque facade. Opposite the San Stae stop, look for the peeling plaster that once made up **frescoes** (scant remains on the lower floors). Imagine the facades of the Grand Canal at their finest. As colorful as the city is today, it's still only a faded, sepia-toned remnant of a long-gone era, a time of lavishly decorated, brilliantly colored palaces.

Just ahead, jutting out a bit on the right, is the ornate white facade of **Ca' Pesaro.** "*Ca'*" is short for *casa* (house). Because only the house of the doge (Venetian ruler) could be called a palace *(palazzo),* all other Venetian palaces are technically "*Ca'*."

In this city of masks, notice how the rich marble facades along the Grand Canal mask what are generally just simple, no-nonsense brick buildings. Most merchants enjoyed showing off. However, being smart businessmen, they

only decorated the side of the buildings that would be seen and appreciated. But look back as you pass Ca' Pesaro (which houses the International Gallery of Modern Art—see page 83). It's the only building you'll see with a fine side facade. Ahead, on the left, with its glorious triple-decker medieval arcade (just before the next stop) is Ca' d'Oro.

Ca' d'Oro: The lacy **Ca' d'Oro** (House of Gold) is the best example of Venetian Gothic architecture on the canal. Its three stories offer different variations on balcony design, topped with a spiny white roofline. Venetian Gothic mixes traditional Gothic

VENICE

(pointed arches and round medallions stamped with a four-leaf clover) with Byzantine styles (tall, narrow arches atop thin columns), filled in with Islamic frills. Like all the palaces, this was originally painted and gilded to make it even more glorious than it is now. Today the Ca' d'Oro is an art gallery (see page 88).

Look at the Venetian chorus line of palaces in front of the boat doing an architectural cancan. On the right is the arcade of the covered **fish market,** with the open-air **produce market** just beyond. It bustles in the morning but is quiet the rest of the day. This is a

great scene to wander through—even though European Union hygiene standards have made it cleaner, but less colorful, than it once was. Find the *traghetto* gondola ferrying shoppers—standing like Washington crossing the Delaware—back and forth. There are eight *traghetto* crossings along the Grand Canal, each one marked by a classy low-key green-and-black sign. Make a point to use them. At €0.50 a ride, they are one of the best deals in Venice.

Mercato Rialto: This stop was opened in 2007 to serve the busy market (boats only stop here from 8:00 to 20:00). The long and officious-looking building at this stop is the Venice courthouse. Straight ahead in the distance, rising above the huge post office, is the tip of the Campanile (bell tower) crowned by its golden angel at St. Mark's Square, where this tour will end. The former post office (100 yards directly ahead, on left side) will soon be a shopping center. It was once the German Exchange—the trading center for German metal merchants in the early 1500s.

You'll cruise by some trendy and beautifully situated wine bars on the right, but look ahead as you round the corner and see the impressive Rialto Bridge come into view.

A major landmark of Venice, the **Rialto Bridge** is lined with shops and tourists. Constructed in 1588, it's the third bridge built on this spot. Until the 1850s, this was the only bridge crossing the Grand Canal. With a span of 160 feet and foundations stretching 650 feet on either side, the Rialto was an impressive engineering feat in its day. Earlier Rialto Bridges could open to let big ships in, but not this one. When this new bridge was completed, much of the Grand Canal was closed to shipping and became a canal of palaces.

Rialto: Rialto, a separate town in the early days of Venice, has always been the commercial district, while San Marco was the religious and governmental center. Today, a winding street called the Mercerie connects the two, providing travelers with human traffic jams and a mesmerizing gauntlet of shopping temptations. This is the only stretch of the historic Grand Canal with landings upon which you can walk. They unloaded the city's basic necessities here: oil, wine, charcoal, iron. Today, the quay is lined with tourist-trap restaurants.

Venice's sleek, graceful black **gondolas** are a symbol of the city (for more on gondolas, see page 92). With about 500 gondoliers joyriding amid the churning *vaporetti*, there's a lot of congestion on the Grand Canal. Pay attention—this is where most of the gondola and vaporetto accidents take place. While the Rialto is the highlight of many gondola rides, gondoliers understandably prefer the quieter small canals. Watch your vaporetto driver curse the better-paid gondoliers.

Ahead 100 yards on the left, two gray-colored **palaces** stand side by side (the City Hall and the mayor's office). Their horseshoe-shaped arched windows are similar and their stories are the same height, lining up to create the effect of one long balcony.

San Silvestro: We now enter a long stretch of important **merchants' palaces,** each with proud and different facades. Because ships couldn't navigate beyond the Rialto Bridge, the biggest palaces—with the major shipping needs—line this last stretch of the navigable Grand Canal.

Palaces like these were multi-functional: ground floor for the warehouse, offices and showrooms upstairs, and the living quarters above the offices on the "noble floors" (with big windows designed to allow in maximum light). Servants lived and worked on the top floors (with the smallest windows). For fire safety reasons, the kitchens were also located on the top floors. Peek into the noble floors to catch a glimpse of their still-glorious chandeliers of Murano glass.

Sant'Angelo: Notice how many buildings have a foundation of waterproof white stone *(pietra d'Istria)* upon which the bricks sit high and dry. Many canal-level floors are abandoned as the rising water level takes its toll. The **posts**—historically painted gaily with the equivalent of family coats of arms—don't rot under water. But

Venice at a Glance

▲▲▲**St. Mark's Square** Venice's grand main square. **Hours:** Always open. See page 69.

▲▲▲**St. Mark's Basilica** Cathedral with mosaics, saint's bones, treasury, museum, and viewpoint of square. **Hours:** Basilica—Mon-Sat 9:45-17:00, Sun 14:00-17:00 (until 16:00 Nov-March); Treasury, Golden Altarpiece, and San Marco Museum close 15 minutes before church (shorter hours in winter). See page 72.

▲▲▲**Doge's Palace** Art-splashed palace of former rulers, with prison accessible through Bridge of Sighs. **Hours:** Daily April-Oct 8:30-18:30, Nov-March 9:00-18:00. See page 74.

▲▲▲**Rialto Bridge** Distinctive bridge spanning the Grand Canal, with a market nearby. **Hours:** Bridge—always open; market—souvenir stalls open daily, produce market closed Sun-Mon, fish market closed Sun. See page 83.

▲▲**Correr Museum** Venetian history and art. **Hours:** Daily April-Oct 9:00-19:00, Nov-March 9:00-17:00. See page 77.

▲▲**Accademia** Venice's top art museum. **Hours:** Mon 8:15-14:00, Tue-Sun 8:15-19:15. See page 80.

▲▲**Peggy Guggenheim Collection** Popular display of 20th-century art. **Hours:** Wed-Mon 10:00-18:00, closed Tue. See page 81.

▲▲**Frari Church** Franciscan church featuring Renaissance masters. **Hours:** Mon-Sat 9:00-18:00, Sun 13:00-18:00. See page 83.

▲▲**Scuola San Rocco** "Tintoretto's Sistine Chapel." **Hours:** Daily 9:30-17:30. See page 86.

▲**Campanile** Dramatic bell tower on St. Mark's Square with elevator to the top. **Hours:** Daily April-June and Oct 9:00-19:00, July-Sept 9:00-21:00, Nov-March 9:30-15:45, closed from Christmas to mid-Jan. See page 77.

▲**Bridge of Sighs** Famous enclosed bridge, part of Doge's Palace, near St. Mark's Square. **Hours:** Generally viewable, but covered with scaffolding during renovation. See page 79.

▲**La Salute Church** Striking church dedicated to the Virgin Mary. **Hours:** Daily 9:00-12:00 & 15:00-17:30. See page 82.

▲**Ca' Rezzonico** Posh Grand Canal palazzo with 18th-century Venetian art. **Hours:** April–Oct Wed–Mon 10:00–18:00, Nov–March Wed–Mon 10:00–17:00, closed Tue. See page 82.

▲**Punta della Dogana** Museum of contemporary art. **Hours:** Wed–Mon 10:00–19:00, closed Tue. See page 82.

▲**Ca' Pesaro** International modern art gallery in a canalside palazzo. **Hours:** Tue–Sun 10:00–17:00, closed Mon. See page 83.

▲**Scuola Dalmata di San Giorgio** Exquisite Renaissance meeting house. **Hours:** Mon 14:45–18:00, Tue–Sat 9:15–13:00 & 14:45–18:00, Sun 9:15–13:00. See page 89.

Church of San Zaccaria Final resting place of St. Zechariah (San Zaccaria), plus a Bellini altarpiece and an eerie crypt. **Hours:** Mon–Sat 10:00–12:00 & 16:00–18:00, Sun 16:00–18:00 only. See page 79.

Church of San Polo Ninth-century church with works by Tintoretto, Veronese, and Tiepolo. **Hours:** Mon–Sat 10:00–17:00, closed Sun. See page 86.

Nearby Islands
▲**San Giorgio Maggiore** Island across the lagoon featuring church with Palladio architecture, Tintoretto paintings, and fine views back on Venice. **Hours:** May–Sept Mon–Sat 9:30–12:30 & 14:30–18:00, Sun 8:30–11:00 & 14:30–18:00; Oct–April until 16:30. See page 80.

San Michele Cemetery island on the lagoon. **Hours:** Always open. See page 89.

Murano Island famous for glass factories and glassmaking museum. **Hours:** Glass museum open daily April–Oct 10:00–18:00, Nov–March 10:00–17:00. See page 89.

Burano Sleepy lacemaking island. **Hours:** Always open. See page 91.

Torcello Near-deserted island with old church, bell tower, and museum. **Hours:** Most sights open daily March–Oct 10:30–17:30, Nov–Feb 10:00–17:00, museum closed Mon. See page 91.

the wood at the waterline, where it's exposed to oxygen, does. On the smallest canals, little blue gondola signs indicate that these docks are for gondolas only (no taxis or motor boats).

San Tomà: Fifty yards ahead, on the right side (with twin obelisks on the rooftop) stands **Palazzo Balbi,** the palace of an early-17th-century captain general of the sea. These Venetian equivalents of five-star admirals were honored with twin obelisks decorating their palaces. This palace, like so many in the city, flies three flags: Italy (green-white-red), the European Union (blue with ring of stars), and Venice (a lion on a field of red and gold). Today it houses the administrative headquarters of the regional government.

Just past the admiral's palace, look immediately to the right, down a side canal. On the right side of that canal, before the bridge, see the traffic light and the **fire station** (with four arches hiding fireboats parked and ready to go).

The impressive **Ca' Foscari,** with a classic Venetian facade (on the corner, across from the fire station), dominates the bend in the canal. This is the main building of the University of Venice, which has about 25,000 students. Notice the elegant lamp on the corner.

The grand heavy white **Ca' Rezzonico,** just before the Ca' Rezzonico stop, houses the Museum of 18th-Century Venice (see page 82). Across the canal is the cleaner and leaner **Palazzo Grassi,** the last major palace built on the canal, erected in the late 1700s. It was recently purchased by a French tycoon and now displays his contemporary art collection.

Ca' Rezzonico: Up ahead, the Accademia Bridge leads over the Grand Canal to the **Accademia Gallery** (right side), filled with the best Venetian paintings. The bridge was put up in 1934 as a temporary structure. Locals liked it, so it stayed.

Accademia: From here, look through the graceful bridge and way ahead to enjoy a classic view of **La Salute Church,** topped by a crown-shaped dome supported by scrolls (see page 82). This Church of Saint Mary of Good Health was built to thank God for delivering Venetians from the devastating plague of 1630 (which had killed about a third of the city's population).

The low white building among greenery (100 yards ahead, on the right, between the Accademia Bridge and the church) is the **Peggy Guggenheim Collection.** The American heiress "retired" here, sprucing up a palace that had been abandoned in mid-construction. Peggy willed the city her fine collection of modern art (described on page 81).

As you approach the next stop, notice on the right how the fine line of higgledy-piggledy palaces evokes old-time Venice. Two doors past the Guggenheim, Palazzo Dario has a great set of characteristic **funnel-shaped chimneys.** These forced embers through a loop-the-loop channel until they were dead—required in the days when stone palaces were surrounded by humble wooden buildings, and a live spark could make a merchant's workforce homeless. Notice this early Renaissance building's flat-feeling facade with "pasted-on" Renaissance motifs. Three doors later is the **Salviati building** (with the fine mosaics), which was once a glassworks.

Santa Maria del Giglio: Back on the left stands the fancy Gritti Palace hotel. Hemingway and Woody Allen both stayed here (but not together).

Take a deep whiff of Venice. What's all this nonsense about stinky canals? All I smell is my shirt. By the way, how's your captain? Smooth dockings? To get to know him, stand up in the bow and block his view.

Salute: The huge La Salute Church towers overhead as if squirted from a can of Catholic Reddi-wip. Like Venice itself,

the church rests upon pilings. To build the foundation for the city, more than a million trees were piled together, reaching beneath the mud to the solid clay. Much of the surrounding countryside was deforested by Venice. Trees were exported and consumed locally to fuel the furnaces of Venice's booming glass industry, to build Europe's biggest merchant marine, and to prop up this city in the mud.

As the Grand Canal opens up into the lagoon, the last building on the right with the golden ball is the 17th-century **Customs House,** which now houses the Punta della Dogana Museum of Contemporary Art (see page 82). Its two bronze Atlases hold a statue of Fortune riding the ball. Arriving ships stopped here to pay their tolls.

San Marco: Up ahead on the left, the green pointed tip of the Campanile marks **St. Mark's Square,** the political and religious

center of Venice...and the final destination of this tour. You could get off at the San Marco stop and go straight to St. Mark's Square. But I'm staying on the boat for one more stop, just past St. Mark's Square (it's a quick walk back).

Survey the lagoon. Opposite St. Mark's Square, across the water, the ghostly white church with the pointy bell tower is **San Giorgio Maggiore,** with great views of Venice. Next to it is the residential island Giudecca, stretching from close to San Giorgio Maggiore past the Venice youth hostel (with a nice view, directly across) to the Hilton Hotel (good nighttime view, far right end of island).

Still on board? If you are, as we leave the San Marco stop, prepare for a drive-by view of St. Mark's Square. First comes the bold white facade of the old mint (where Venice's golden ducat, the "dollar" of the Venetian Republic, was made) and the library facade. Then the twin columns, topped by St. Theodore and St. Mark, who've welcomed visitors since the 15th century. Between the columns, catch a glimpse of two giant figures atop the **Clock Tower**—they've been whacking their clappers every hour since 1499. The domes of **St. Mark's Basilica** are soon eclipsed by the lacy facade of the **Doge's Palace.** Next you'll see the **Bridge of Sighs** (currently under scaffolding), and then the grand harborside promenade—the **Riva.**

Follow the Riva with your eye, past elegant hotels to the green area in the distance. This is the largest of Venice's few **parks,** which hosts the Biennale art show every odd year, including in 2011. Much farther in the distance is the **Lido,** the island with Venice's beach. Its sand and casinos are tempting, but its car traffic disrupts the medieval charm of Venice.

San Zaccaria: OK, you're at your last stop. Quick—muscle your way off this boat! (If you don't, you'll eventually end up at the Lido.)

At San Zaccaria, you're right in the thick of the action. A number of other *vaporetti* depart from here (see page 54). Otherwise, it's a short walk back along the Riva to St. Mark's Square. Ahoy!

Sights in Venice

San Marco District

For information on the San Marco Museum Plus Pass and the pricier Museum Pass, which cover most of the sights on the square, see page 45.

▲▲▲**St. Mark's Square (Piazza San Marco)**—This grand square is surrounded by splashy, historic buildings and sights: St. Mark's Basilica, the Doge's Palace, the Campanile bell tower, and the Correr Museum. The square is filled with music, lovers, pigeons, and tourists by day, and is your private rendezvous with the Venetian past late at night, when Europe's most magnificent dance floor is *the* romantic place to be.

With your back to the church, survey one of Europe's great urban spaces, and the only square in Venice to merit the title "Piazza." Nearly two football fields long, it's surrounded by the offices of the republic. On the right are the "old offices" (16th-century Renaissance). At left are the "new offices" (17th-century High Renaissance). Napoleon called the piazza "the most beautiful drawing room in Europe," and added to the intimacy by building the final wing, opposite the basilica, that encloses the square.

For a slow and pricey evening thrill, invest about €12–20 (including the cover charge for the music) in a glass of wine or coffee at one of the elegant cafés with the dueling orchestras (see "Cafés on St. Mark's Square," page 75). For an unmatched experience that offers the best people-watching, it's worth the small splurge.

The **Clock Tower** (Torre dell'Orologio), built during the Renaissance in 1496, marks the entry to the main shopping drag, called the Mercerie, which connects St. Mark's Square with the Rialto. From the piazza, you can see the bronze men (Moors) swing their huge clappers at the top of each hour. In the 17th century, one of them knocked an unsuspecting worker off the top

and to his death—probably the first-ever killing by a robot. Notice one of the world's first "digital" clocks on the tower facing the square (with dramatic flips every five minutes). You can go inside the Clock Tower only with a pre-booked guided tour that takes you close to the clock's innards and out to a terrace with good views over the square and city rooftops. Reserve in person at the Correr Museum, by calling 848-082-000, or online at www.museiciviciveneziani.it (€12 combo-ticket includes Correr Museum; tours in English Mon–Wed at 10:00 and 11:00, plus 13:00 in peak season; also Thu–Sun at 13:00, 14:00, and 15:00, plus 17:00 in peak season). Book a day in advance or show up at the Correr Museum prior to a scheduled tour to see if space is available.

A good **TI** is on the square (with your back to the basilica, it's in the far-left, southwest corner of the square; daily 9:00–15:30), and a €1.50 WC is 30 yards beyond St. Mark's Square (see *Albergo*

VENICE

St. Mark's Square

TO RIALTO

TO RIALTO

SAN ZULIAN

ST. MARK'S BAG CHECK

L. S. MARCO

MERCERIE

SPADARIA

PIAZZETTA D. LEONCINI

FABBRI

C. FIUBERA

❻

TRON

OLD OFFICES

CLOCK TOWER

❿

ST. MARK'S BASILICA

RAMO SELVA.

❾

❶❷

CAMPA-NILE

FRENNERIA

PIAZZA SAN MARCO

DOGE'S PALACE

POST

CORRER MUSEUM + Napoleon's Wing

❽

⓭

PIAZZETTA

WC

❶❶

S. MARCO COLUMN

SAL

SAN

MOISE

CALLE VALLARESSO

NEW OFFICES

❼

GIARDINETTI REALI

S. THEODORE COLUMN

SAN MOISÈ

WC

TO ACCADEMIA

🅥 San Marco - Giardinetti

SAN   MARCO

🅥 San Marco - Vallaresso

🆃

TO SALUTE

◀ ENTRANCES TO SIGHTS

🅥 VAPORETTO STOP

🆃 TRAGHETTO CROSSING

🅖 GONDOLA STATION

🔱 VIEW

100 YARDS

100 METERS

DCH

VENICE

Eateries
1 Ristorante alla Conchiglia & Trattoria da Giorgio ai Greci
2 Ristorante Antica Sacrestia
3 "Sandwich Row": Birreria Forst
4 Bar Verde
5 Ristorante alla Basilica
6 Rizzo
7 Todaro Gelateria

Nightlife
8 Caffè Florian
9 Gran Caffè Quadri
10 Gran Caffè Lavena
11 Gran Caffè Chioggia
12 Eden Bar
13 Caffè Aurora

Diorno sign marked on pavement, WC open daily 9:00–17:30). Another TI is on the lagoon (daily 10:00–18:00, walk toward the water by the Doge's Palace and go right, €1.50 WCs nearby).

▲▲▲**St. Mark's Basilica (Basilica di San Marco)**—Built in the 11th century to replace an earlier church, this basilica's dis-

tinctly Eastern-style architecture underlines Venice's connection with Byzantium (which protected it from the ambition of Charlemagne and his Holy Roman Empire). It's decorated with booty from returning sea captains—a kind of architectural Venetian trophy chest. The interior glows mysteriously with gold mosaics and colored marble. Since about A.D. 830, the saint's bones have been housed on this site.

Cost and Hours: Basilica entry is free, open Mon–Sat 9:45–17:00, Sun 14:00–17:00 (Sun until 16:00 Nov–March), St. Mark's Square, vaporetto stops: San Marco or San Zaccaria, tel. 041-270-8311, www.basilicasanmarco.it. The dress code is strictly enforced for everyone (no bare shoulders or bare knees). Lines can be long, and bag check is mandatory, free, and can save you time in line. No photos are allowed inside.

Three separate exhibits within the church charge admission: the **Treasury** (€3, includes free audioguide), **Golden Altarpiece** (€2), and **San Marco Museum** (€4). The San Marco Museum has the original bronze horses (copies of these overlook the square), a balcony offering a remarkable view over St. Mark's Square, and various works related to the church.

Bag Check (and Skipping the Line): Small purses and shoulder-slung bags may be allowed inside the church, but larger bags and backpacks are not. Check them for free for up to one hour at the nearby Ateneo San Basso, 30 yards to the left of the basilica, down narrow Calle San Basso (see map on next page for location; open Mon–Sat 9:30–17:30, Sun 14:00–16:30).

Those with a bag to check actually get to skip the line. Leave your bag at Ateneo San Basso and pick up your claim tag. Two people per tag are allowed to enter the basilica. Take your tag to the basilica's tourist entrance. Keep to the left of the railing where the line forms and show your tag to the gatekeeper. He'll let you in, ahead of the line. After touring the church, come back and pick up your bag. (Note: Ateneo San Basso may not let you check small bags that would be allowed inside.)

Dress Code: Modest dress (no shorts or bare shoulders) is strictly enforced, even for kids.

St. Mark's Basilica

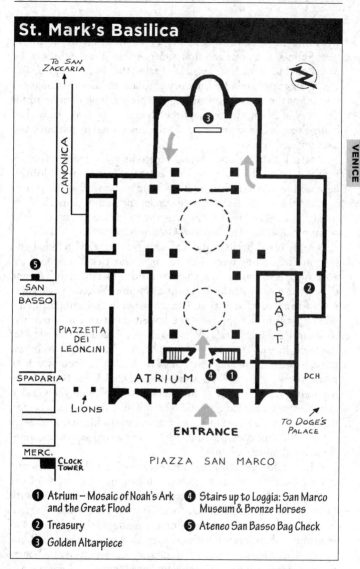

TO SAN ZACCARIA

CANONICA

3

5
SAN BASSO

2

PIAZZETTA DEI LEONCINI

B A P T.

SPADARIA

ATRIUM

4 **1**

DCH

LIONS

MERC.

CLOCK TOWER

TO DOGE'S PALACE

ENTRANCE

PIAZZA SAN MARCO

1 Atrium – Mosaic of Noah's Ark and the Great Flood
2 Treasury
3 Golden Altarpiece

4 Stairs up to Loggia: San Marco Museum & Bronze Horses
5 Ateneo San Basso Bag Check

VENICE

Theft Alert: St. Mark's Basilica is the most dangerous place in Venice for pickpocketing—inside, it's always a crowded jostle.

Tours: Free hour-long English **tours** (heavy on the mosaics' religious symbolism) are generally offered daily at 11:00; meet in the atrium. But the schedule varies, so see the schedule board in the atrium. Those traveling with an iPod or other MP3 player can download a free **Rick Steves Audio Tour** at www.ricksteves.com (or search for "Rick Steves Audio Tours" in iTunes).

VENICE

The Mosaics: St. Mark's Basilica has 4,750 square yards of Byzantine mosaics, the best and oldest of which are in the atrium (turn right as you enter and stop under the last dome—this may be roped off, but dome is still visible). Facing the church, gape up (it's OK, no pigeons) and read the story of Adam and Eve that rings the bottom of the dome. Now, facing the piazza, look domeward for the story of Noah, the ark, and the flood (two by two, the wicked being drowned, Noah sending out the dove, a happy rainbow, and a sacrifice of thanks).

Step inside the church and notice how the marble floor is richly decorated in mosaics. As in many Venetian buildings, because the best foundation pilings were made around the perimeter, the floor rolls. As you shuffle under the central dome, look up for the Ascension. Follow the one-way tourist route and consider stopping off at the Treasury and Golden Altarpiece.

Additional Sights: The Treasury (ask for the included and informative audioguide when you buy your ticket) and Golden Altarpiece give you the best chance outside of Istanbul or Ravenna to see the glories of the Byzantine Empire. Venetian crusaders looted the Christian city of Constantinople and brought home piles of lavish loot (perhaps the lowest point in Christian history until the advent of TV evangelism). Much of this plunder is stored in the Treasury (Tesoro) of San Marco. As you view these treasures, remember that most were made in about A.D. 500, while Western Europe was stuck in the Dark Ages. Beneath the high altar lies the body of St. Mark ("Marce") and the Golden Altarpiece (Pala d'Oro), made of 250 blue-backed enamels with religious scenes, all set in a gold frame and studded with 15 hefty rubies, 300 emeralds, 1,500 pearls, and assorted sapphires, amethysts, and topaz (c. 1100).

In the San Marco Museum (Museo di San Marco) upstairs you can see an up-close mosaic exhibition, a fine view of the church interior, a view of the square from the balcony with bronze horses, and (inside, in their own room) the original horses. These well-traveled horses, made during the days of Alexander the Great (fourth century B.C.), were taken to Rome by Nero, to Constantinople/Istanbul by Constantine, to Venice by crusaders, to Paris by Napoleon, back "home" to Venice when Napoleon fell, and finally indoors and out of the acidic air. The staircase up to the museum is in the atrium, near the basilica's main entrance, marked by a sign that says Loggia dei Cavalli, Museo.

▲▲▲**Doge's Palace (Palazzo Ducale)**—The seat of the Venetian government and home of its ruling duke, or doge, this was the most powerful half-acre in Europe for 400 years. The Doge's Palace was built to show off the power and wealth of the

Cafés on St. Mark's Square

Cafés line the square. Those with live music feature similar food, prices, and a three- to five-piece combo playing a selection of classical and pop hits, from Brahms to "Bésame Mucho." If you sit outside and get just a drink, expect to pay €12-20, including a €6 cover charge when the orchestra is playing. A coffee—your cheapest option—costs about €6 if you sit at an outside table, plus the €6 cover charge when the music plays, bringing it to €12 total. It's perfectly acceptable to nurse a cappuccino for an hour—you're paying for the music with the cover charge.

Caffè Florian (on the right as you face the church— see map on page 70) is the most famous Venetian café and one of the first places in Europe to serve coffee. It's been a popular spot for a discreet rendezvous in Venice since 1720. The orchestra plays a more classical repertoire than the other cafés. The outside tables are the main action, but do walk inside through the richly decorated old-time rooms where Casanova, Lord Byron, Charles Dickens, and Woody Allen have all paid too much for a drink (reasonable prices at bar in back).

Gran Caffè Quadri, opposite the Florian, has an equally illustrious history of famous clientele, including the writers Stendhal and Dumas, and composer Richard Wagner. **Gran Caffè Lavena,** near the Clock Tower, is newer and less prestigious.

Gran Caffè Chioggia, on the Piazzetta facing the Doge's Palace, charges slightly less, with one or two musicians, usually a pianist, playing cocktail jazz.

The following less-expensive options don't have live music, but you can enjoy overhearing music from nearby cafés: **Eden Bar,** next to Gran Caffè Quadri, is touristy, but that doesn't matter when you're enjoying your hot dog and Coke while sitting out on the piazza. **Caffè Aurora,** in the shadow of the Campanile, features nearly all the ambience of the orchestra cafés at half the price.

Republic. The doge lived with his family on the first floor near the halls of power. From his once-lavish (now sparse) quarters, you'll follow the one-way tour through the public rooms of the top floor, finishing with the Bridge of Sighs and the prison. The place is wallpapered with masterpieces by Veronese and Tintoretto. Don't worry much about the great art. Enjoy the building.

You'll see the restored facades from the **courtyard.** Notice a grand staircase (with nearly naked Moses and Paul Newman at the top). Even the most powerful visitors climbed this to meet the doge. This was the beginning of an architectural power trip.

In the **Senate Hall,** the 120 senators met, debated, and passed laws. Tintoretto's large *Triumph of Venice* on the ceiling (central painting, best viewed from the top) shows the city in all its glory. Lady Venice is up in heaven with the Greek gods, while barbaric lesser nations swirl up to give her gifts and tribute.

The **Armory**—a dazzling display originally assembled to intimidate potential adversaries—shows remnants of the military might that the empire employed to keep the East–West trade lines open (and the local economy booming).

The giant **Hall of the Grand Council** (175 feet by 80 feet, capacity 2,600) is where the entire nobility met to elect the senate and doge. It took a room this size to contain the grandeur of the Most Serene Republic. Ringing the room are portraits of the first 76 doges (in chronological order). The one at the far end that's blacked out is the notorious Doge Marin Falier, who opposed the will of the Grand Council in 1355. He was tried for treason, beheaded, and airbrushed from history.

On the wall over the doge's throne is Tintoretto's monsterpiece, *Paradise,* the largest oil painting in the world. Christ and Mary are surrounded by a heavenly host of 500 saints. The painting leaves you feeling that you get to heaven not by being a good Christian, but by being a good Venetian.

Cross the covered **Bridge of Sighs** over the canal to the **prisons.** Circle the cells. Notice the carvings made by prisoners—from olden days up until 1930—on some of the stone windowsills of the cells, especially in the far corner of the building.

Cross back over the Bridge of Sighs, pausing to look through the marble-trellised windows at all of the tourists.

Cost and Hours: Covered by €13 San Marco Museum Plus Pass, which also includes admission to the Correr Museum (both sights also covered by €18 Museum Pass); no individual tickets are sold to this sight. If the line is long at the Doge's Palace, buy your pass at the Correr Museum across the square; then you can go directly through the Doge's turnstile without waiting in line. Open daily April–Oct 8:30–18:30, Nov–March 9:00–18:00, last entry one hour before closing.

Location: Next to St. Mark's Basilica, just off St. Mark's

Square. Vaporetto stops: San Marco or San Zaccaria.

Tours: The audioguide costs €5. For a live guided tour, consider the Secret Itineraries Tour, which takes you into palace rooms otherwise not open to the public (€18, or €12 with San Marco Museum Plus Pass; two or three English-language tours each morning). Reserve ahead for this tour in peak season—they can fill up as much as a month in advance. Book online at www.museiciviciveneziani.it, reserve by phone (tel. 848-082-000, or from the US dial 011-39-041-4273-0892), or ask at the info desk.

▲▲**Correr Museum (Museo Civico Correr)**—This uncrowded museum gives you a good overview of Venetian history and art. In the Napoleon Wing, you'll see fine Neoclassical sculpture by Antonio Canova. Then peruse armor, banners, and paintings that re-create festive days of the Venetian republic. The upper floor lays out a good overview of Venetian art, including several paintings by the Bellini family. There are English descriptions and breathtaking views of St. Mark's Square throughout.

Cost and Hours: Covered by €13 San Marco Museum Plus Pass, which also includes the Doge's Palace—both also covered by €18 Museum Pass, daily April–Oct 9:00–19:00, Nov–March 9:00–17:00, last entry one hour before closing, enter at far end of square directly opposite basilica, tel. 041-240-5211, www.museiciviciveneziani.it.

Avoid long lines at the crowded Doge's Palace by buying either of the museum passes listed above at the Correr Museum. For €12 you can get a combo-ticket for the Correr Museum and a tour of the Clock Tower on St. Mark's Square, but your ticket won't include the Doge's Palace. For more on reserving a Clock Tower tour, see page 69.

▲**Campanile (Campanile di San Marco)**—This dramatic bell tower replaced a shorter lighthouse, once part of the original fortress that guarded the entry of the Grand Canal. The lighthouse

crumbled into a pile of bricks in 1902, a thousand years after it was built. For the next few years, you'll see construction work being done to strengthen the base of the tower. Ride the elevator 300 feet to the top of the bell tower for the best view in Venice (especially at sunset). For an ear-shattering experience, be on top when the bells ring. The golden archangel Gabriel at the top always faces into the wind.

Cost and Hours: €8, daily April–June and Oct 9:00–19:00, July–Sept 9:00–21:00, Nov–March 9:30–15:45, closed from Christmas to mid-Jan, tel. 041-522-4064. Lines are longest at midday; beat the crowds and enjoy the crisp

VENICE

A Dying City?

Venice's population (about 60,000) is half what it was just 30 years ago, and people are leaving at a rate of a thousand a year. Of those who stay, 25 percent are 65 or older.

Sad, yes, but imagine raising a family here: Apartments are small, high up, and expensive. Humidity and occasional flooding make basic maintenance a pain. Home-improvement projects require navigating miles of red tape, and you must follow regulations intended to preserve the historical ambience. Everything is expensive because it has to be shipped in from the mainland. You can easily get glass and tourist trinkets, but it's hard to find groceries or get your shoes fixed. Running basic errands involves lots of walking and stairs—imagine  crossing over arched bridges while pushing a child in a stroller and carrying a day's worth of groceries.

With over 12 million visitors a year (150,000 a day at peak times), on any given day Venetians are likely outnumbered by tourists. Despite government efforts to subsidize rents and build cheap housing, the city is losing its residents. The economy itself is thriving, thanks to tourist dollars and rich foreigners buying second homes. But the culture is dying. Even the most hopeful city planners worry that in a few decades, Venice will not be a city at all, but a museum, a cultural theme park, a decaying Disneyland for adults.

morning air at 9:00 or the cool evening breeze at 18:00.

La Fenice Opera House (Gran Teatro alla Fenice)—During Venice's glorious decline in the 18th century, this was one of seven  opera houses in the city, and one of the most famous in Europe. For 200 years, great operas and famous divas debuted here, applauded by ladies and gentlemen in their finery. Then in 1996, an arson fire completely gutted the theater. But La Fenice ("The Phoenix") has risen from the ashes, thanks to an eight-year effort to rebuild the historic landmark according to photographic archives of the interior. To see the results at their most glorious, attend an evening performance.

You can also tour the opera house during the day. All you really see is the theater itself; there's no "backstage" tour of dressing rooms, or an opera museum. The auditorium, ringed with box seats, is impressive: pastel blue with sparkling gold filigree, muses depicted on the ceiling, and a starburst chandelier. It's also a bit saccharine and brings sadness to Venetians who remember the place before the fire. Other than a minor exhibit of opera scores and Maria Callas memorabilia, there's little to see from the world of opera. The dry audioguide recounts two centuries of construction.

Cost and Hours: €7, includes 45-minute audioguide, generally open daily 10:00–19:30, but schedule varies greatly depending on rehearsal and performance schedule, concert box office open daily 9:30–18:30, call center open daily 7:30–20:00, on Campo San Fantin between St. Mark's Square and Accademia Bridge, vaporetto stop: Santa Maria del Giglio, tel. 041-2424, www.teatro lafenice.it.

Behind St. Mark's Basilica

▲**Bridge of Sighs**—Connecting two wings of the Doge's Palace high over a canal, this enclosed bridge will be surrounded by scaf-

folding for the next few years for restoration. Travelers popularized this bridge in the Romantic 19th century. Supposedly, a condemned man would be led over this bridge on his way to the prison, take one last look at the glory of Venice, and sigh. Though overhyped, when it's uncovered the bridge is undeniably tingle-worthy—especially after dark, when the crowds have dispersed and it's just you and floodlit Venice. A local legend says that lovers will be assured eternal love if they kiss on a gondola at sunset under the bridge. The bridge is around the corner from the Doge's Palace: Walk toward the waterfront, turn left along the water, and look up the first canal on your left. You can walk across the bridge (from the inside) by visiting the Doge's Palace.

Church of San Zaccaria—This historic church is home to a sometimes-waterlogged crypt, a Bellini altarpiece, a Tintoretto painting, and the final resting place of St. Zechariah, the father of John the Baptist.

Cost and Hours: Free, €1 to enter crypt, €0.50 coin to light up Bellini's altarpiece, Mon–Sat 10:00–12:00 & 16:00–18:00, Sun 16:00–18:00 only, 2 canals behind St. Mark's Basilica.

Across the Lagoon from St. Mark's Square

▲**San Giorgio Maggiore**—This is the dreamy church-topped island you can see from the waterfront by St. Mark's Square. The striking church, designed by Palladio, features art by Tintoretto, a daily Gregorian Mass, a bell tower, and good views of Venice.

Cost and Hours: Free entry to church; May–Sept Mon–Sat 9:30–12:30 & 14:30–18:00, Sun 8:30–11:00 & 14:30–18:00; Oct–April until 16:30.

Gregorian Mass is sung Mon–Sat at 8:00 and on Sun at 11:00. The bell tower costs €3 and is accessible by elevator (runs from 30 minutes after the church opens until 30 minutes before the church closes).

Getting There: To reach the island from St. Mark's Square, take the five-minute ride on vaporetto #2 (€2, 6/hour, ticket valid for one hour; leaves from San Zaccaria–M.V.E. stop located east of Bridge of Sighs by equestrian statue; catch boat in direction: Tronchetto).

Dorsoduro District

▲▲**Accademia (Gallerie dell'Accademia)**—Venice's top art museum, packed with highlights of the Venetian Renaissance, features paintings by the Bellini family, Titian, Tintoretto, Veronese, Tiepolo, Giorgione, Canaletto, and Testosterone. It's just over the wooden Accademia Bridge from the San Marco action.

The Venetian love of luxury shines through in this collection, which starts in the Middle Ages and runs to the 1700s. Look for grand canvases of colorful, spacious settings, peopled with happy locals in extravagant clothes having a great time. Medieval highlights include elaborate altarpieces and golden-haloed Madonnas. Among early masterpieces of the Renaissance are Mantegna's studly *St. George* and Giorgione's mysterious *The Tempest*. As the Renaissance reaches its heights, so do the paintings, such as Titian's magnificent *Presentation of the Virgin*, a religious scene, yes, but it's really just an excuse to display secular splendor (Titian was the most famous painter of his day—perhaps even more famous than Michelangelo). End your tour with Guardi's and Canaletto's painted "postcards" of the city—landscapes for visitors who lost their hearts to the romance of Venice.

Cost and Hours: €6.50, Mon 8:15–14:00, Tue–Sun 8:15–19:15, last entry 45 minutes before closing, no photos allowed. The dull audioguide costs €5 (€7/2 people). One-hour guided tours in

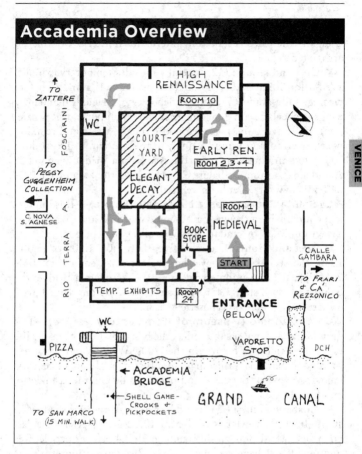

Accademia Overview

TO ZATTERE

FOSCARINI

TO PEGGY GUGGENHEIM COLLECTION

C. NOVA S. AGNESE

TERRA

RIO

WC

HIGH RENAISSANCE
ROOM 10

COURT-YARD

ELEGANT DECAY

EARLY REN.
ROOM 2,3 & 4

ROOM 1

MEDIEVAL

BOOKSTORE

START

TEMP. EXHIBITS

ROOM 24

ENTRANCE
(BELOW)

CALLE GAMBARA

TO FRARI & CA' REZZONICO

WC

PIZZA

← ACCADEMIA BRIDGE →

SHELL GAME - CROOKS & PICKPOCKETS

TO SAN MARCO (15 MIN. WALK) ↓

VAPORETTO STOP

DCH

GRAND CANAL

VENICE

English are €5 (€7/2 people, Sat–Sun at 11:00). At Accademia Bridge, vaporetto stop: Accademia. Tel. 041-522-2247, www.gallerieaccademia.org.

Avoiding Crowds: Expect long lines in the late morning, because they allow only 300 visitors in at a time; visit early or late to miss the crowds, or make a reservation at least a day in advance (€1 fee; calling 041-520-0345 is easier than reserving online at their clunky website).

There's a decent canalside pizzeria (Pizzeria Accademia Foscarini, closed Tue) at the base of the Accademia Bridge.

▲▲**Peggy Guggenheim Collection**—The popular museum of far-out art, housed in the American heiress' former retirement palazzo, offers one of Europe's best reviews of the art of the first half of the 20th century. Stroll through styles represented by artists whom Peggy knew personally—Cubism (Picasso, Braque), Surrealism (Dalí, Ernst), Futurism (Boccioni), American Abstract

Expressionism (Pollock), and a sprinkling of Klee, Calder, and Chagall. The place is staffed by international interns working on art-related degrees.

Cost and Hours: €12, generally includes temporary exhibits, Wed–Mon 10:00–18:00, closed Tue, last entry 15 minutes before closing, audioguide-€7, mini-guidebook-€6, free and mandatory baggage check for anything bigger than a small purse, pricey café, photos allowed only in garden and terrace—a fine and relaxing perch overlooking Grand Canal; near Accademia, Dorsoduro 704, a five-minute walk from the Accademia Bridge (vaporetto: Accademia) or from La Salute Church (vaporetto: Salute); tel. 041-240-5411, www.guggenheim-venice.it.

▲**La Salute Church (Santa Maria della Salute)**—This impressive church with a crown-shaped dome was built and dedicated to the Virgin Mary by grateful survivors of the 1630 plague.

Cost and Hours: Church—free, daily 9:00–12:00 & 15:00–17:30; sacristy—€2, may have shorter hours than church; tel. 041-274-3928. It's a 10-minute walk from the Accademia Bridge; the Salute vaporetto stop is at its doorstep (the hop from San Marco–Vallaresso to Salute on vaporetto #1 is €2).

▲**Ca' Rezzonico (Museum of 18th-Century Venice)**—This grand Grand Canal palazzo offers the best look in town at the life of Venice's rich and famous in the 1700s. Wander under ceilings by Tiepolo, among furnishings from that most decadent century, enjoying views of the canal and paintings by Guardi, Canaletto, and Longhi.

Cost and Hours: €7, covered by passes, April–Oct Wed–Mon 10:00–18:00, Nov–March Wed–Mon 10:00–17:00, closed Tue, last entry one hour before closing, audioguide-€4 or €6/2 people, free and mandatory baggage check, at Ca' Rezzonico vaporetto stop, tel. 041-241-0100, www.museiciviciveneziani.it.

▲**Punta della Dogana**—This new museum of contemporary art, housed in the former Customs House at the end of the Grand Canal, features cutting-edge 21st-century art in spacious rooms. This isn't Picasso and Matisse, or even Pollock and Warhol—those guys are ancient history. But if you're into the likes of Jeff Koons, Rachel Whiteread, and a host of newer artists, the museum is world-class. The displays change completely about every year, drawn from the museum's large collection. In fact, the art spreads over two locations—the triangular Customs House and Palazzo Grassi.

Cost and Hours: €15 for one locale, €20 for both, Wed–Mon 10:00–19:00, closed Tue, last entry one hour before closing, audioguide-€5 or €8/2 people, small café. The Customs House is near La Salute Church (Dogana *traghetto* or vaporetto: Salute). Palazzo Grassi is a bit upstream, on the east side of the Grand

Canal (vaporetto: San Samuele). Tel. 199-139-139, www.palazzo grassi.it.

Santa Croce District

▲▲▲Rialto Bridge—One of the world's most famous bridges, this distinctive and dramatic stone structure crosses the Grand

Canal with a single confident span. The arcades along the top of the bridge help reinforce the structure...and offer some enjoyable shopping diversions, as does the **market** east of the bridge (souvenir stalls open daily, produce market closed Sun–Mon, fish market closed Sun).

▲Ca' Pesaro International Gallery of Modern Art—This museum features 19th- and early-20th-century art in a 17th-century canalside palazzo. The collection is strongest on Italian (especially Venetian) artists, but also presents a broad array of other well-known artists. The highlights are in one large room: Klimt's beautiful/creepy *Judith II*, with eagle-talon fingers; Kandinsky's *White Zig Zags* (plus other recognizable shapes); the colorful *Nude in the Mirror* by Bonnard, which flattens the 3-D scene into a 2-D pattern of rectangles; and Chagall's surprisingly realistic portrait of his hometown rabbi, *The Rabbi of Vitebsk*. The adjoining Room VII features small-scale works by Matisse, Max Ernst, Mark Tobey, and a Calder mobile. Admission also includes an Oriental Art wing.

Cost and Hours: €5.50, covered by passes, Tue–Sun 10:00–17:00, closed Mon, last entry one hour before closing, 2-minute walk from San Stae vaporetto stop, tel. 041-524-0662.

Palazzo Mocenigo Costume Museum—The Museo di Palazzo Mocenigo offers a walk through six rooms of a fine 17th-century mansion with period furnishings, family portraits, ceilings painted (c. 1790) with family triumphs (the Mocenigos produced seven doges), Murano glass chandeliers in situ, and a paltry collection of costumes with sparse descriptions.

Cost and Hours: €6, covered by passes, Tue–Sun 10:00–16:00, closed Mon, a block in from San Stae vaporetto stop, tel. 041-721-798.

San Polo District

▲▲Frari Church (Chiesa dei Frari)—My favorite art experience in Venice is seeing art in the setting for which it was designed—as it is at the Frari Church. The Franciscan "Church of the Brothers" and the art that decorates it is warmed by the spirit of St. Francis.

Frari Church

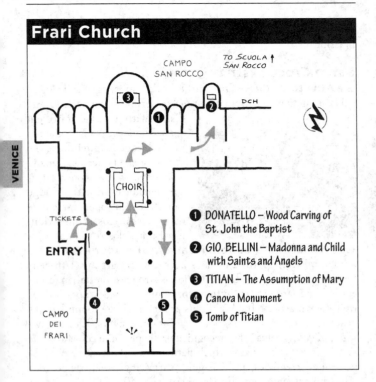

CAMPO SAN ROCCO

TO SCUOLA SAN ROCCO

DCH

CHOIR

TICKETS

ENTRY

CAMPO DEI FRARI

❶ DONATELLO – Wood Carving of St. John the Baptist

❷ GIO. BELLINI – Madonna and Child with Saints and Angels

❸ TITIAN – The Assumption of Mary

❹ Canova Monument

❺ Tomb of Titian

It features the work of three great Renaissance masters: Donatello, Giovanni Bellini, and Titian—each showing worshippers the glory of God in human terms.

In **Donatello's wood carving of St. John the Baptist** (just to the right of the high altar), the prophet of the desert—dressed in animal skins and nearly starving from his diet of bugs 'n' honey—announces the coming of the Messiah. Donatello was a Florentine working at the dawn of the Renaissance.

Bellini's *Madonna and Child and Angels* painting (in the sacristy farther to the right) came later, done by a Venetian in a more Venetian style—soft focus without Donatello's harsh realism. While Renaissance humanism demanded Madonnas and saints that were accessible and human, Bellini places them in a physical setting so beautiful that it creates its own mood of serene holiness. The genius of Bellini, perhaps the greatest Venetian painter, is obvious in the pristine clarity, rich colors (notice Mary's clothing), believable depth, and reassuring calm of this three-paneled altarpiece.

Is Venice Sinking?

Venice has been battling rising water levels since the fifth century. But today, the water is winning. Due to many factors, including global warming, Venice now floods about 100 times a year—usually from October until late winter—a phenomenon called the *acqua alta*.

Simply put, Venice is sinking and the water is rising. Venice sits atop sediments deposited at the ancient mouth of the Po River, which are still compacting and settling. Twentieth-century industry worsened things by pumping out massive amounts of groundwater from the aquifer beneath the lagoon for nearly 50 years before the government stopped it in the 1970s.

Meanwhile, as the ground sinks beneath this sea-level city, the waters around Venice are rising, especially during the winter. The notorious *acqua alta* happens when a high tide combines with strong sirocco winds and a storm. Although tides are miniscule in the Mediterranean, the narrow, shallow Adriatic Sea has about a three-foot tidal range. When a storm, which is an area of low pressure, travels over a body of water, it pulls the surface of the water up into a dome. As strong sirocco winds from Africa blow storms north up the Adriatic, they push this high water ahead of the front, causing a storm tide, or storm surge. Add to that the effects of climate change—rising sea level from melting polar ice caps, thermal expansion of the water itself as temperatures rise (remember high-school chemistry), and storms that are more frequent and more powerful—and it makes a high sea that much higher.

So what is Venice doing about the flooding? Since the 1966 flood, officials knew something had to be done, but it took about four decades to come up with a solution that some are still unhappy about. In 2003, a consortium of engineering firms began construction on the MOSE or Moses Project, which is expected to be operational by 2014. Named for the acronym of its Italian name, *Modulo Sperimentale Elettromeccanico*, it's also a nod to Moses and his (albeit temporary) mastery over the sea.

Underwater "mobile" gates are being built on the floor of the sea that will lie flat at the entrances of the three inlets that lead into Venice's lagoon. When the seawater rises above a certain level, air will be pumped into the gates, causing them to rise, and shutting out the Adriatic.

Will it work? Time...and tides...will tell.

Finally, glowing red and gold like a stained-glass window over the high altar, **Titian's *The Assumption of Mary*** sets the tone of exuberant beauty found in the otherwise sparse church. Titian the Venetian—a student of Bellini—painted steadily for 60 years... you'll see a lot of his art. As stunned apostles look up past the swirl of arms and legs, the complex composition of this painting draws you right to the radiant face of the once-dying, now-triumphant Mary as she joins God in heaven.

Feel comfortable to discreetly freeload off passing tours. For many, these three pieces of art make a visit to the Accademia Gallery unnecessary (or they may whet your appetite for more). Before leaving, check out the Neoclassical pyramid-shaped Canova monument and (opposite that) the grandiose tomb of Titian. Compare the carved marble *Assumption* behind Titian's tombstone portrait with the painted original above the high altar.

Cost and Hours: €3, Mon–Sat 9:00–18:00, Sun 13:00–18:00, last entry 15 minutes before closing, no visits during services, modest dress recommended. On Campo dei Frari, near San Tomà vaporetto and *traghetto* stops.

Tours: Audioguides are available (€2, €3/2 people). Those traveling with an iPod or other MP3 player can download a free Rick Steves audio tour at www.ricksteves.com (or search for "Rick Steves Audio Tours" in iTunes).

Concerts: The church occasionally hosts evening concerts (€15, buy ticket at church). For concert details, look for fliers, check www.basilicadeifrari.it, or call the church at 041-272-8611.

▲▲**Scuola San Rocco**—Sometimes called "Tintoretto's Sistine Chapel," this lavish meeting hall (next to the Frari Church) has some 50 large, colorful Tintoretto paintings plastered to the walls and ceilings. The best paintings are upstairs, especially the *Crucifixion* in the smaller room. View the neck-breaking splendor with one of the mirrors available at the entrance.

Cost and Hours: €7, audioguide-€1, daily 9:30–17:30, last entry 30 minutes before closing, tel. 041-523-4864, www.scuola grandesanrocco.it.

Church of San Polo—This nearby church, which pales in comparison to the two sights just listed, is only worth a visit for art-lovers. One of Venice's oldest churches (from the ninth century), San Polo features works by Tintoretto, Veronese, and Tiepolo and son.

Cost and Hours: €3, Mon–Sat 10:00–17:00, closed Sun, last entry 15 minutes before closing.

Cannaregio District

Jewish Ghetto—In medieval times, Jews were grudgingly allowed to do business in Venice, but they weren't permitted to live there until 1385 (subject to strict laws and special taxes). Anti-

Water, Water Everywhere, but...

As you explore Venice, notice the wells that grace nearly every square. Well water in the middle of the sea? Venice, surrounded by water, originally had no natural source of drinking water. For centuries, residents collected water from  the mainland with much effort and risk. Eventually, in the ninth century, they devised a way to collect rainwater by using town squares as catchment systems. The rain falls into the square, flows down through the slightly sloped pavement, drains through the limestone grates, and filters through sand into a large clay tub under the pavement. Citizens could drop their buckets down the "well" to draw up fresh rainwater. With a safe local source of drinking water, Venice's population began to grow. Several thousand of these cisterns provided lagoon communities with drinking water right up until 1886, when an aqueduct was built (paralleling the railroad tracks across the lagoon) to bring in water from nearby mountains. Since then, the clay tubs have rotted out and the wells have been capped. Now, with a high tide, the floods show first on these limestone grates, which mark the low point of each town square.

Semitic forces tried to oust them from the city, but in 1516, the doge compromised by restricting Jews to a special (undesirable) neighborhood. It was located on an easy-to-isolate island near the former foundry *(geto)*, coining the word "ghetto" for a segregated neighborhood.

The population swelled with immigrants from elsewhere in Europe, reaching 5,000 in the 1600s, the Golden Age of Venice's Jews. Restricted within their tiny neighborhood (the Ghetto Nuovo, or "New Ghetto"), they expanded upward, building six-story "skyscrapers" that still stand today. The community's five synagogues were built atop the high-rise tenements. (As space was very tight and you couldn't live above a house of worship, this was the most practical use of precious land.) Only two synagogues are still active. You can spot them (with their five windows) from the square, but to visit them you have to book a tour through the Jewish Museum.

This original Ghetto becomes most interesting after touring the **Jewish Museum** (Museo Ebraico), which consists of two parts: a museum and a synagogue. The humble two-room museum has silver menorahs, cloth covers for the Torah scrolls, various religious objects, artifacts from the old community, and scant English explanations (€3, June–Sept Sun–Fri 10:00–17:00, Oct–May Sun–Fri 10:00–16:30, closed Sat and Jewish holidays, Campo di Ghetto Nuovo, vaporetto stop: San Marcuola, tel. 041-715-359, small café and bookstore). To see the **synagogue,** you must sign up for a half-hour English tour (€8.50, tours run hourly on the half-hour June–Sept Sun–Fri 10:00–19:00, Oct–May Sun–Fri 10:00–17:30, closed Sat and Jewish holidays). Group sizes are limited (the 11:30 tour is often booked full), so show up 20 minutes early to be sure you get in.

Calatrava Bridge (a.k.a. Ponte della Costituzione)—This controversial bridge, officially called "Constitution Bridge," is

just upstream and around the bend from the train station. Only the fourth bridge to cross the Grand Canal, it carries foot traffic between the train station and Piazzale Roma. A modern structure of glass, steel, and stone, the bridge finally opened in 2008 after delays, cost overruns, and questions about its stability.

The bridge was designed by Spanish architect Santiago Calatrava, whose other projects include a museum in his hometown of Valencia, Spain; the twisting torso skyscraper in Malmö, Sweden; and the Olympic Sports complex in Athens, Greece.

The bridge draws snorts from Venetians. With an original price tag of €4 million, the cost rose to around €11 million. The modern design of the bridge is also a sore point for a city with such rich medieval and Renaissance architecture. And, to add practical insult to aesthetic injury, the heavy bridge is crushing the centuries-old foundations at either end, threatening nearby buildings.

Interestingly, Calatrava's modern structure harkens back to the past, employing the same low-arch design of many older Venetian bridges. Pedestrians walk over similar shallow stair steps, and the bridge uses local Istrian stone.

Ca' d'Oro—This "House of Gold" palace, fronting the Grand Canal, is quintessential Venetian Gothic (Gothic seasoned with Byzantine and Islamic accents—see page 61). Inside, the permanent collection includes a few big names in Renaissance painting—Ghirlandaio, Signorelli, and Mantegna; a glimpse at a lush courtyard; and a grand view of the Grand Canal.

Cost and Hours: €5, slow and dry audioguide-€4, Mon 8:15–14:00, Tue–Sun 8:15–19:15, free peek through hole in door of courtyard, vaporetto stop: Ca' d'Oro, Calle Ca' d'Oro 3932.

Castello District

▲**Scuola Dalmata di San Giorgio**—This little-visited "school" (which means "meeting place") features an exquisite wood-paneled chapel decorated with the world's best collection of paintings by Vittorio Carpaccio (1465–1526).

The Scuola, a reminder that cosmopolitan Venice was once Europe's melting pot, was one of a hundred such community centers for various ethnic, religious, and economic groups, supported by the government partly to keep an eye on foreigners. It was here that the Dalmatians (from the southern coast of present-day Croatia) worshipped in their own way, held neighborhood meetings, and preserved their culture.

Cost and Hours: €3, Mon 14:45–18:00, Tue–Sat 9:15–13:00 & 14:45–18:00, Sun 9:15–13:00, on Calle dei Furlani, tel. 041-522-8828.

Santa Elena—For a pleasant peek into a completely non-touristy, residential side of Venice, walk or catch vaporetto #1 from St. Mark's Square to the neighborhood of Santa Elena (at the fish's "tail"). This 100-year-old suburb lives as if there were no tourism. You'll find a kid-friendly park, a few lazy restaurants, and beautiful sunsets over San Marco.

La Biennale—Every odd year (including 2011), Venice hosts a world's fair of contemporary art. Participating countries send their best and most outrageous art to be displayed in buildings and pavilions scattered over the Giardini park and the Arsenale (roughly June–Nov, take vaporetto #1 or #2 to Giardini-Biennale stop, www.labiennale.org).

Venice's Lagoon

The island of Venice sits in a lagoon—a calm section of the Adriatic protected from wind and waves by the natural breakwater of the Lido. Beyond the church-topped island of San Giorgio Maggiore (directly in front of St. Mark's Square—see page 80), four interesting islands hide out in the lagoon: Cimitero, Murano, Burano, and Torcello.

San Michele (a.k.a. Cimitero) is the cemetery island—the final resting place of Venetians and a few foreign VIPs, from poet Ezra Pound to composer Igor Stravinsky. Consider getting off for a look, since boats come every 10 minutes. If you enjoy wandering through old cemeteries, you'll dig this one. Many visitors find this island—expectedly—pretty dead (daily April–Sept 7:30–18:00, Oct–March 7:30–16:30; reception is to the left as you enter, WC to the right).

Murano is famous for its glass factories. Upon arrival (at the Colonna vaporetto stop), wander up the "main street"—**Via Fondamenta Vetrai**—along the canal of the glassmakers. The canal/street is lined with factories (*fabriche)* and their furnaces

VENICE

Venice's Lagoon

(fornaci). They each offer a similar, usually free, 20-minute glassblowing demonstration of an artisan in action firing up something in a furnace, followed by an almost comically high-pressure sales pitch. (The spiel is brief, and there's absolutely no obligation to buy anything.)

Murano's **Glass Museum** displays the very best of 500 years of Venetian glassmaking. While the display is pretty old-school musty, it's well-described in English (€6.50, covered by passes, daily April–Oct 10:00–18:00, Nov–March 10:00–17:00, last entry 30 minutes before closing, tel. 041-739-586, www.museicivici veneziani.it).

Burano, known for its lace and picturesque pastel houses, is a sleepy island with a sleepy community—village Venice without the glitz. The main drag from the vaporetto stop into town is packed with tourists and lined with shops, some of which sell Burano's locally produced white wine. Wander to the far side of the island, and the mood shifts. Explore to the right of the leaning tower for a peaceful yet intensely pastel small-town lagoon world. Benches lining a little promenade at the water's edge make another pretty picnic spot.

Torcello is the birthplace of Venice, where the first mainland refugees settled, escaping the barbarian hordes. Yet today, it's the least-developed island (pop. 20) and is mostly in its natural state, marshy and shrub-covered. There's little for tourists to see except the church (a 10-minute walk from the dock), which claims to be the oldest in Venice and has impressive mosaics.

The church complex consists of four sights: the church itself (Santa Maria Assunta), the bell tower (behind the church, climb a ramped stairway for great lagoon views), a sacristy, and a small museum (facing the church, in two separate buildings) that displays Roman sculpture and medieval sculpture and manuscripts. Tickets cost €3 for any one sight, or €10 for all sights, including an audio-guide (most open daily March–Oct 10:30–17:30, Nov–Feb 10:00–17:00, museum closed Mon, last entry 30–60 minutes before closing, museum tel. 041-730-761, church/bell tower tel. 041-730-119).

Getting There: You can travel to any of the four islands by vaporetto. Since single vaporetto tickets (€6.50) expire after one hour, using a vaporetto pass for this lagoon excursion makes more sense (e.g., a €16 12-hour pass; see page 52 for more on vaporetto tickets).

Here's a way to see all of the islands, sailing from Venice to Murano (stopping at San Michele en route) to Burano to Torcello:

Venice to Murano (via San Michele, takes 40 minutes): From St. Mark's Square, catch vaporetto #41 to Murano. Boats leave every 10 minutes from the San Zaccaria–Jolanda dock, located just past the Bridge of Sighs along the Riva. They travel around the "tail" of fish-shaped Venice, making several stops (including the Cimitero stop on San Michele) before reaching Murano-Colonna.

If you're already on the north shore of Venice (the "back" of the fish), you could catch the #41 or #42 from the Fondamenta Nuove vaporetto stop. Five minutes later, it stops at San Michele (Cimitero stop), then continues on to Murano-Colonna. (Fondamenta Nuove is a 15-minute walk from Rialto and 25 minutes from St. Mark's Square.)

From Murano to Burano (30 minutes): To continue on to Burano, catch the LN vaporetto, which leaves from the Murano-Faro stop twice hourly. Our tour takes us from the Murano-Colonna stop on foot to the Murano-Faro stop (the #41 and #42 *vaporetti* stop at both Murano stops).

From Burano to Torcello (5 minutes): Line T shuttles between Burano and Torcello, on the hour and half-hour.

From Torcello to Venice (75 minutes): Return to Burano (5 minutes) and catch the LN back to Venice, either on a 70-minute trip through the lagoon to San Zaccaria near St. Mark's Square (hourly), or on a 45-minute trip to Fondamenta Nuove (leaves twice an hour; from there you can catch the #42 back to San Zaccaria—leaves every 10 minutes, takes 30 minutes).

Experiences in Venice

Gondola Rides

Gondolas cost lots more after 19:00 but are also more romantic and relaxing under the moon. A rip-off for some, this is a traditional must for romantics. Gondoliers charge about €80 for a 40-minute ride during the day; from 19:00 on, figure on €100. To add music (a singer and an accordionist), it'll cost an additional €110 before 19:00, or €130 after 19:00. You can divide the cost—and the romance—among up to six people per boat, but you'll need to save two seats for the musicians if you choose to be serenaded. Only two seats (the ones in back) are next to each other. If you want to haggle, you'll find softer prices during the day. (Note that gondoliers have a trick where one guy says "No," and another, acting secretive, comes to you a bit later and says, "OK, but don't let my friend know I'm offering you this

incredible price.") Establish the price and duration before boarding, enjoy your ride, and pay only when you're finished.

If you've hired musicians and want to hear a Venetian song *(un canto Veneziano),* try requesting *"Venezia La Luna e Tu."* Asking to hear *"O Sole Mio"* (which comes from Naples) is like asking a bartender in Cleveland to sing *"The Eyes of Texas."*

Glide through nighttime Venice with your head on someone's shoulder. Follow the moon as it sails past otherwise unseen buildings. Silhouettes gaze down from bridges while window glitter spills onto the black water. You're anonymous in the city of masks, as the rhythmic thrust of your striped-shirted gondolier turns old crows into songbirds. This is extremely relaxing (and, I think, worth the extra cost to experience at night). Because you might get a narration plus conversation with your gondolier, talk with several and choose one you like who speaks English well. Women, beware...while gondoliers can be extremely charming, local women say that anyone who falls for one of these Romeos "has slices of ham over her eyes."

For cheap gondola thrills during the day, stick to the €0.50 one-minute ferry ride on a Grand Canal *traghetto.* At night, *vaporetti* are nearly empty, and it's a great time to cruise the Grand Canal on the slow boat #1. Or hang out on a bridge along the gondola route and wave at romantics.

Festivals

Venice's most famous festival is **Carnevale,** the celebration Americans call Mardi Gras (Feb 26–March 8 in 2011, www.carnevale.venezia.it). Carnevale, which means "farewell to meat," originated centuries ago as a wild two-month–long party leading up to the austerity of Lent. In Carnevale's heyday—the 1600s and 1700s—you could do pretty much anything with anybody from any social class if you were wearing a mask. These days it's a tamer 10-day celebration, culminating in a huge dance lit with fireworks on St. Mark's Square. Sporting masks and costumes, Venetians from kids to businessmen join in the fun. Drawing the biggest crowds of the year, Carnevale has nearly been a victim of its own success, driving away many Venetians (who skip out on the craziness to go skiing in the Dolomites).

Every odd year (including 2011), the city hosts the **Venice Biennale International Art Exhibition,** a world-class contemporary art fair spread over the Arsenale and sprawling Castello Gardens. Artists representing 70 nations from around the world offer the latest in contemporary art forms: video, computer art, performance art, and digital photography, along with painting and sculpture (take vaporetto #1 or #2 to Giardini-Biennale; for details and an events calendar, see www.labiennale.org). The actual exhibition usually runs from June through November, but other events—film, dance, theater—loosely connected with the Biennale are held throughout the year (starting as early as Feb) in various venues on the island.

Other typically Venetian festival days filling the city's hotels with visitors and its canals with decked-out boats are **Feast of the Ascension Day** (June 2 in 2011), **Feast and Regatta of the Redeemer** (third Sun in July and the preceding evening—July 16–17 in 2011), and the **Historical Regatta** (old-time boats and pageantry, first Sat and Sun in Sept—Sept 3–4 in 2011). Smaller regattas include the **Murano Regatta** (early July) and the **Burano Regatta** (mid-Sept).

Venice's patron saint, **St. Mark,** is commemorated every April 25. Venetian men celebrate the day by presenting roses to the women in their lives (mothers, wives, and lovers).

Every November 21 is the **Feast of Our Lady of Good Health.** On this local "Thanksgiving," a bridge is built over the Grand Canal so that the city can pile into La Salute Church and remember how Venice survived the gruesome plague of 1630. On this day, Venetians eat smoked lamb from Dalmatia (which was the cargo of the first ship admitted when the plague lifted).

For more information on festivals, try the TI (www.turismo venezia.it) and the free *Un Ospite di Venezia* magazine (www .aguestinvenice.com).

Shopping in Venice

Shoppers like Murano glass (described earlier), Burano lace (fun lace umbrellas for little girls), Carnevale masks (fine shops and artisans all over town), art repro- ductions (posters, postcards, and books), prints of Venetian scenes, traditional stationery (pens and marbled paper products of all kinds), calendars with Venetian scenes, silk ties, scarves, and plenty of goofy knickknacks (Titian mousepads, gondolier T-shirts, and little plastic gondola condom holders).

Shops are generally open from 9:00 to 13:00 and from 15:00 to 19:30. In touristy Venice, more shops are open on Sunday than the Italian norm. If you're buying a substantial amount from nearly any shop, bargain—it's accepted and almost expected. Offer less and offer to pay cash; merchants are very conscious of the bite taken by credit-card companies. Anything not made locally is pricey to bring in and therefore generally more expensive than elsewhere in

Italy. The shops near St. Mark's Square charge the most.

Popular **Venetian glass** is available in many forms: vases, tea sets, decanters, glasses, jewelry, lamps, mod sculptures (such as solid-glass aquariums), and on and on. Shops will ship it home for you, but you're likely to pay as much or more for the shipping as you are for the item(s). Make sure the shop insures their merchandise *(assicurazione),* or you're out of luck if it breaks. If your item arrives broken and it has been insured, take a photo of the pieces, send it to the shop, and they'll replace it for free. For a cheap, packable souvenir, consider the glass-bead necklaces sold at vendors' stalls throughout Venice.

If you're serious about glass, visit the small shops on **Murano Island.** Their glassblowing demonstrations are fun; you'll usually see a vase and a "leetle 'orse" made from molten glass. You'll find greater variety on Murano, but prices are usually the same as in Venice.

Around St. Mark's Square, various companies offer glass-blowing demos for tour groups. **Galleria San Marco,** a tour-group staple just off St. Mark's Square, offers great demos every few minutes. They have agreed to let individual travelers flashing this book sneak in with tour groups to see the show (and sales pitch). And, if you buy anything, show this book and they'll take 20 percent off the listed price. The gallery faces the square behind the orchestra nearest the church; at #139, go through the shop and climb the stairs (daily 9:00–18:00, tel. 041-271-8650, manager Ferdinando).

Along Venice's many shopping streets, you'll notice fly-by-night street vendors selling knockoffs of famous-maker handbags (Louis Vuitton, Gucci). These vendors are willing to bargain. But buyer beware: If you're caught purchasing fakes, you could get hit with a fine. Legitimate manufacturers are raising a stink about these street merchants, and the government is trying to rid the city of them. Authorities frustrated in their attempts to actually arrest the merchants have made it illegal to buy counterfeit items. Their hope: The threat of a huge fine will scare potential customers away—so unlicensed merchants will be driven out of business and off the streets.

Nightlife in Venice

You must experience Venice after dark. The city is quiet at night, as tour groups stay in the cheaper hotels of Mestre on the mainland, and the masses of day-trippers return to their beach resorts and cruise ships. **Gondolas** cost more, but are worth the extra expense (see page 92). At night, *vaporetti* are nearly empty, and it's a great time to cruise the Grand Canal on the slow boat #1.

Venice has a busy schedule of events, festivals, and entertainment. Check at the TI for listings, and keep an eye out for publications such as the free *Un Ospite di Venezia* magazine (monthly, bilingual, available at top-end hotels and the TI, www.aguestin venice.com).

Baroque Concerts—Venice is a city of the powdered-wig Baroque era. For about €25 (prices vary), you can take your pick of traditional Vivaldi concerts in churches throughout town. Homegrown Vivaldi is as trendy here as Strauss is in Vienna and Mozart is in Salzburg. In fact, you'll find frilly young Vivaldis hawking concert tickets on many corners. The TI has a list of this week's Baroque concerts. Shows start at 21:00 and generally last 1.5 hours. You'll see posters in hotels all over town (hotels sell tickets at face-value). A one-stop shop for concerts is the Vivaldi Store, at the east end of Rialto Bridge (5537 Salizada del Fontego dei Tedeschi). Tickets for Baroque concerts in Venice can usually be bought the same day as the concert, so don't bother with websites that sell tickets with a surcharge.

Consider the venue carefully. The general rule of thumb: Musicians in wigs and tights offer better spectacle; musicians in black-and-white suits are better performers. **San Vitale Church** (at the north end of Accademia Bridge) and the **Interpreti Veneziani orchestra** (which often plays there) are reliably top-notch (tel. 041-277-0561, www.interpretiveneziani.com). For the latest on church concerts, check any TI or visit www.turismovenezia.it.

Other Performances—Venice's most famous theaters are **La Fenice** (grand old opera house, box office tel. 041-786-5111, see page 78), **Teatro Goldoni** (mostly Italian live theater), and **Teatro della Fondamenta Nuove** (theater, music, and dance).

Musica a Palazzo is a unique evening of opera at the Doge's Palace. You'll spend about 45 minutes in three sumptuous rooms as eight musicians (generally four instruments and four singers) perform. With these kinds of surroundings, under Tiepolo frescoes, you'll be glad you dressed up. As there are only 70 seats, you must book by phone or online in advance. Opera-lovers find this to be a wonderful evening (€50, nightly shows at 20:30, Palazzo Barbarigo-Minotto, Fondamenta Duodo o Barbarigo—on the Grand Canal next to the Santa Maria del Giglio vaporetto stop, mobile 340-971-7272, www.musicapalazzo.com).

Venezia is advertised as "the show that tells the great story of Venice" and "simply the best show in town." I found the performance to be slow-moving and a bit cheesy, and the venue to be disappointing (€40, nightly at 19:00, 80 minutes, ticket includes a 30-minute video on Venice at 18:00, Teatro San Gallo, just off St. Mark's Square on Campo San Gallo, tel. 041-241-2002, www .teatrosangallo.net).

St. Mark's Square—For tourists, St. Mark's Square is the high-light, with lantern light and live music echoing from the cafés. Just being here after dark is a thrill, as **dueling café orchestras** entertain (see sidebar on page 75). Every night, enthusiastic musicians play the same songs, creating the same irresistible magic. Hang out for free behind the tables (allowing you to move easily on to the next orchestra when the musicians take a break), or spring for a seat and enjoy a fun and gorgeously set concert. If you sit a while, it can be €12–20 well spent (for a drink and the cover charge for music). Dancing on the square is free (and encouraged). Streetlamp halos, live music, floodlit history, and a ceiling of stars make St. Mark's magic at midnight. You're not a tourist, you're a living part of a soft Venetian night...an alley cat with money. In the misty light, the moon has a golden hue. Shine with the old lanterns on the gondola piers, where the sloppy lagoon splashes at the Doge's Palace...reminiscing.

VENICE

Sleeping in Venice

For hassle-free efficiency and the sheer magic of being close to the action, I favor hotels that are handy to sightseeing activities. I've listed rooms in four neighborhoods: St. Mark's bustle, the Rialto action, the quiet Dorsoduro area behind the Accademia art museum, and near the train station (handy for train travelers, but far from the action). I also mention several apartment rentals, big fancy hotels, cheap dorms, and places on the mainland.

Hotels in Venice can be tricky to locate. While I've tried to

---

Sleep Code

(€1 = about $1.25, country code: 39)
S = Single, **D** = Double/Twin, **T** = Triple, **Q** = Quad, **b** = bathroom, **s** = shower only. Unless otherwise noted, credit cards are accepted, breakfast is included, and English is generally spoken.

To help you easily sort through these listings, I've divided the rooms into three categories based on the price for a standard double room with bath:

$$$ Higher Priced—Most rooms €180 or more.
$$ Moderately Priced—Most rooms between €130-180.
$ Lower Priced—Most rooms €130 or less.

Prices can change without notice; verify the hotel's current rates online or by email. For other updates, see www.ricksteves.com/update.

give clear directions, you'll do best by following the arrival instructions provided on your hotel's website.

Book a room as soon as you know when you'll be in town. Venice gets booked up during its festivals (see page 93), religious holidays such as Easter, and Fridays and Saturdays year-round. Also see "Holidays and Festivals" on page 981 of the appendix.

Over the past decade, Venice's supply of hotel rooms has mushroomed. This glut of hotels means that demand is soft and, therefore, so are prices. Hotels have tossed straight pricing out the window. Smart travelers will email several places and see who offers the best rates. It's important to email the hotel directly (rather than going through a booking service) and to say you are a Rick Steves reader who expects their best price. Then survey your results, and pick what you think is the best value for that day.

I've done my best to predict prices for peak season: April, May, June, September, and October. Prices will be higher during festivals, and almost all places drop prices from November through March (except during Carnevale and Christmas) and in July and August.

Many hotels in Venice list rooms on www.venere.com, especially for last-minute vacancies (two to three weeks before the date). Before you bite, check to see if rates are lower than the prices in this chapter.

Near St. Mark's Square

Located near the Bridge of Sighs, just off the Riva degli Schiavoni waterfront promenade, these places rub drainpipes with Venice's most palatial five-star hotels. To get here from the train station or Piazzale Roma bus stop, ride the vaporetto to San Zaccaria—either the slow #1 or the fast #2 (from the Tronchetto parking lot, it's #2 only). Consider using your ride to follow my tour of the Grand Canal (see page 57); to make sure you arrive via the Grand Canal, confirm that your boat goes "*via Rialto*."

The nearest laundry is **Lavanderia Gabriella,** which offers full service a few streets north of the square (€15/load wash and dry, Mon–Fri 8:00–12:30, closed Sat–Sun; with your back to the door of San Zulian Church, go over Ponte dei Ferali, take first right down Calle dei Armeni, then first left on Rio Terra de le Colonne to #985; tel. 041-522-1758, Elisabetta).

$$$ Hotel Campiello, lacy and bright, was once part of a 19th-century convent. Ideally located 50 yards off the waterfront, on a tiny square, its 16 rooms offer a tranquil, friendly refuge for travelers who appreciate comfort and professional service (Sb-€130, Db-€180, 10 percent discount with cash and this book, air-con, elevator, Wi-Fi; from the waterfront street—Riva degli Schiavoni—take Calle del Vin, between pink Hotel Danieli and Hotel Savoia e Jolanda, to #4647, Castello; tel. 041-520-5764, fax 041-520-5798, www.hcampiello.it, campiello@hcampiello.it; family-run for four generations, currently by Thomas, Monica, Nicoletta, and Marco). They also rent three modern family apartments, under rustic timbers just steps away (up to €380/night).

$$ Locanda al Leon is a basic place renting 14 decent rooms just off Campo S.S. Filippo e Giacomo (Db-€135–150, Tb-€170, Qb-€220, these prices with cash and this book, air-con, Internet access and Wi-Fi, Campo S.S. Filippo e Giacomo 4270, Castello, tel. 041-277-0393, fax 041-521-0348, www.hotelalleon.com, leon @hotelalleon.com, Giuliano and Marcella). From the San Zaccaria–Danieli vaporetto stop, take Calle dei Albanesi (two streets left of pink Hotel Danieli) to its far end.

$$ Hotel Fontana is a two-star family-run place with 15 rooms near a school, two bridges behind St. Mark's Square. Their annex across the street has much lower ceilings and slightly lower prices (Sb-€110, Db-€140–170, family rooms, 10 percent cash discount, quieter rooms on garden side, 2 rooms have terraces for €10 extra, air-con, elevator, Internet access and Wi-Fi, Campo San Provolo 4701, Castello, tel. 041-522-0579, fax 041-523-1040, www .hotelfontana.it, info@hotelfontana.it, Diego and Gabriele). From the San Zaccaria vaporetto dock, take Calle delle Rasse—to the left of pink Hotel Danieli—then turn right at the end, and continue to the first square.

$$ Hotel la Residenza is a grand old palace facing a peaceful square. It has 15 great rooms on three levels and a huge, luxurious old lounge. This is a great value for romantics—you'll feel like you're in the Doge's Palace after-hours. Hang out in the living room and you become royalty (Sb-€100, Db-€130–165, air-con, Wi-Fi, Campo Bandiera e Moro 3608, Castello, tel. 041-528-5315, fax 041-523-8859, www.venicelaresidenza.com, info@venicela residenza.com, Giovanni). From the Bridge of Sighs, walk east along Riva degli Schiavoni, cross three bridges, and take the first left up Calle del Dose to Campo Bandiera e Moro.

$$ Locanda Casa Querini rents six bright, high-ceilinged rooms on a quiet square tucked away behind St. Mark's. You can enjoy your breakfast or a sunny picnic/happy hour sitting at their tables right on the sleepy little square (Db-€150, third person-€20–25, one cheaper small double, ask for cash discount, air-con, Wi-Fi, halfway between San Zaccaria vaporetto stop and Campo Santa Maria Formosa at Campo San Giovanni in Oleo 4388, Castello, tel. 041-241-1294, fax 041-523-6188, www.locanda querini.com, casaquerini@hotmail.com, Patrizia and Silvia). From the San Zaccaria vaporetto stop, take the street to the right of the Bridge of Sighs to Campo S.S. Filippo e Giacomo, continue on Calle drio la Chiesa, take the second left, and curl around to the left into the little square, Campo San Giovanni Novo.

VENICE

Hotels near St. Mark's Square

TO RIALTO

TO RIALTO

SAN ZULIAN

⑩

MERCERIE

LARGA S. MARCO

⑨

R.T. COLONNE

FABBRI

C. FIUBERA

SPADARIA

⑧

PIAZZETTA D. LEONCINI

TRON

OLD OFFICES

CLOCK TOWER

ST. MARK'S BASILICA

CAMPA- NILE

RAMO SELVA.

PIAZZA SAN MARCO

DOGE'S PALACE

FRENZARIA

CORRER MUSEUM & NAPOLEON'S WING

PIAZZETTA

POST WC

NEW OFFICES

S. MARCO COLUMN

ℹ

SAN MOISÈ

GIARDINETTI REALI

SAL.

SAN MOISÈ

CALLE VALLARESSO

G

S. THEODORE COLUMN

WC

ℹ

SAN MOISÈ

TO ACCADEMIA

Ⓥ SAN MARCO - GIARDINETTI

Ⓥ SAN MARCO - VALLARESSO

SAN   MARCO

Ⓣ

TO SALUTE

◄ ENTRANCES TO SIGHTS

Ⓥ VAPORETTO STOP

Ⓣ TRAGHETTO CROSSING

Ⓖ GONDOLA STATION

100 YARDS

100 METERS

VENICE

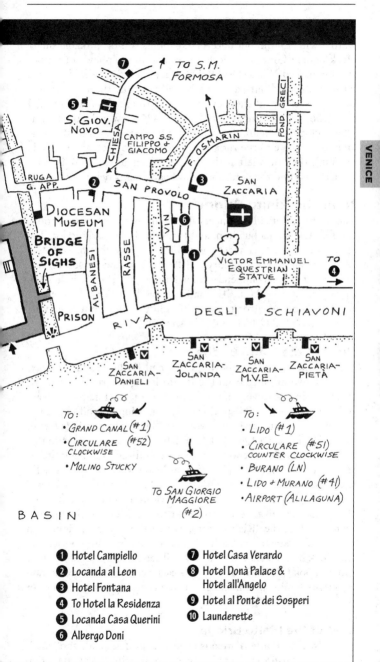

TO S.M. FORMOSA

FOND GRECI

S. GIOV. NOVO

CHIESA

CAMPO S.S. FILIPPO & GIACOMO

F. OSMARIN

RUGA G. APP.

SAN PROVOLO

SAN ZACCARIA

DIOCESAN MUSEUM

VIA

BRIDGE OF SIGHS

RASSE

ALBANESI

VICTOR EMMANUEL EQUESTRIAN STATUE

TO

PRISON

RIVA DEGLI SCHIAVONI

SAN ZACCARIA-DANIELI

SAN ZACCARIA-JOLANDA

SAN ZACCARIA-M.V.E.

SAN ZACCARIA-PIETÀ

To:
• GRAND CANAL (#1)
• CIRCULARE (#52) CLOCKWISE
• MOLINO STUCKY

To:
• LIDO (#1)
• CIRCULARE (#51) COUNTER CLOCKWISE
• BURANO (LN)
• LIDO + MURANO (#41)
• AIRPORT (ALILAGUNA)

TO SAN GIORGIO MAGGIORE (#2)

BASIN

❶ Hotel Campiello
❷ Locanda al Leon
❸ Hotel Fontana
❹ To Hotel la Residenza
❺ Locanda Casa Querini
❻ Albergo Doni

❼ Hotel Casa Verardo
❽ Hotel Donà Palace & Hotel all'Angelo
❾ Hotel al Ponte dei Sosperi
❿ Launderette

$ Albergo Doni is dark, clean, and quiet—a bit of a time warp—with 13 dim but once-classy rooms run by a likable smart aleck named Gina, her niece Tessa, and her nephew, an Italian stallion named Nikos (D-€90, Db-€115, T-€120, Tb-€155, reserve with credit card but pay in cash, ceiling fans, three Db rooms have air-con, avoid their overflow apartment, Fondamenta del Vin 4656, Castello, tel. & fax 041-522-4267, www.albergodoni.it, albergodoni@hotmail.it). From the San Zaccaria vaporetto stop, cross one bridge to the right and take the first left (marked Calle del Vin), then turn left at the little square named Ramo del Vin, jog left, and find the hotel ahead on Fondamenta del Vin.

Near the Rialto Bridge

Vaporetto #2 quickly connects the Rialto with the train station, the Piazzale Roma bus stop, and the Tronchetto parking lot. The slower vaporetto #1 connects everything but Tronchetto.

You can do your laundry at **Effe Erre,** a modern self-service *lavanderia* near recommended Hotel al Piave at Ruga Giuffa 4826 (open daily 6:30–23:00, €11/small load wash and dry; full-service for just a couple euros more, 9:00–13:00, winter hours may be shorter, mobile 349-058-3881, Massimo).

West of the Rialto Bridge

$ Pensione Guerrato, above the colorful Rialto produce market and just two minutes from the Rialto Bridge, is run by friendly, creative, and hardworking Roberto and Piero. Their 800-year-old building—with 24 spacious, air-conditioned, and charming rooms—is simple, airy, and wonderfully characteristic (D-€90, Db-€130, Tb-€150, Qb-€170, Quint/b-€185, these prices with this book and cash, check website for special discounts, Rick Steves readers can ask for €5/night discount below Web specials, Wi-Fi, Calle drio la Scimia 240a, San Polo, tel. & fax 041-528-5927, www.pensioneguerrato.it, hguerrat@tin.it, Monica and Rosanna). From the train station, take vaporetto #1 to the Mercato Rialto stop (comes before the "Rialto" stop), exit the boat to your right, and follow the waterfront. Calle drio la Scimia (not simply Scimia, the block before), is on the left—you'll see the hotel sign. My tour groups book this place for 50 nights each year. Sorry. The Guerrato also rents family apartments in the old center (great for groups of 4–8) for around €55 per person.

East of the Rialto Bridge

$$$ Hotel al Ponte Antico is exquisite, professional, and small. With nine plush rooms and a velvety royal living/breakfast room, it's perfect for a romantic anniversary. Because its wonderful terrace overlooks the Grand Canal, Rialto Bridge, and market action, its non-canal-view rooms may be a better value (Db-€290, superior Db-€380, deluxe canal-front Db-€450, air-con, Wi-Fi; 100 yards from Rialto Bridge, follow Salizzada S. Grisostomo behind post office and past Coin department store, turn left down the dark and empty Calle del Aseo to #5768, Cannaregio; tel. 041-241-1944, fax 041-241-1828, www.alponteantico.com, info@alponteantico.com).

$ **Locanda la Corte,** a three-star hotel, is perfumed with elegance. Its 19 attractive high-ceilinged wood-beamed rooms—done in earthy pastels—circle a small, quiet courtyard (Sb-€100, standard Db-€120, superior Db-€150, 10 percent discount with cash, ask for Rick Steves discount, suites and family rooms available, air-con, Wi-Fi, Castello 6317, tel. 041-241-1300, fax 041-241-5982, www.locandalacorte.it, info@locandalacorte.it, Marco, Raffaela, and Tommy the cat). Take vaporetto #52 from the train station to Fondamenta Nuove, exit the boat to your left, follow the waterfront, and turn right after the second bridge to reach S.S. Giovanni e Paolo. Facing the Rosa Salva bar, take the street to the left (Calle Bressana); the hotel is a short block away at #6317, before the bridge.

$ **Casa Pisani Canal Hotel** is a sweet little place renting five rooms (Db-€100–120, huge Db suite overlooking canal-€240, air-con, Wi-Fi, Calle de le Erbe 6105, Cannaregio, tel. 041-724-1030, www.casapisanicanal.it, info@casapisanicanal.it, Tortorelle family). It's just off Campo S.S. Giovanni e Paolo, on Calle de le Erbe.

$ **Alloggi Barbaria** rents eight quiet, spacious backpacker-type rooms on one floor around a bright and institutional-feeling common area. Beyond Campo S.S. Giovanni e Paolo, this Ikea-style place is a long walk from the action but a good value and a chance to see the real Venice (Db-€90–100, third or fourth person-€25 each, pay cash for best price, family deals, air-con, tel. 041-522-2750, fax 041-277-5540, www.alloggibarbaria.it, info@alloggibarbaria.it, Giorgio and Fausto). Take vaporetto #52 to Ospedale stop, turn left as you get off the boat, then right down Calle de le Capucine to #6573.

Southeast of the Rialto Bridge

$$ **Hotel al Piave,** with 27 fine air-conditioned rooms above a bright and classy lobby, is fresh, modern, and comfortable. You'll enjoy the neighborhood and always get a cheery welcome (Db-€150, Tb-€200; family suites-€280 for 4, €300 for 5, or €320 for 6; cash discount, Internet access and Wi-Fi, Ruga Giuffa 4838/40, Castello, tel. 041-528-5174, fax 041-523-8512, www.hotelalpiave .com, info@hotelalpiave.com, Mirella, Paolo, and Ilaria speak English). From the San Zaccaria vaporetto stop, take the street to the right of the Bridge of Sighs to Campo S.S. Filippo e Giacomo,

Hotels near the Rialto Bridge

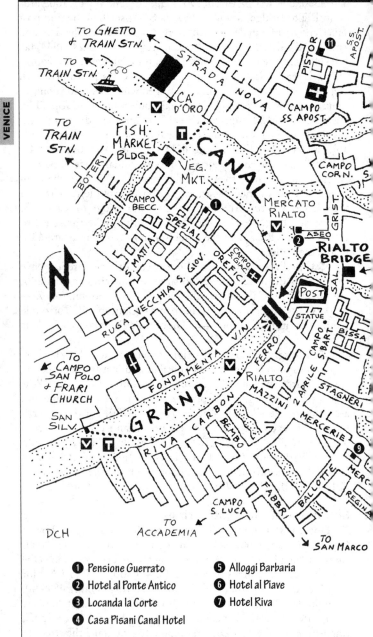

1 Pensione Guerrato

2 Hotel al Ponte Antico

3 Locanda la Corte

4 Casa Pisani Canal Hotel

5 Alloggi Barbaria

6 Hotel al Piave

7 Hotel Riva

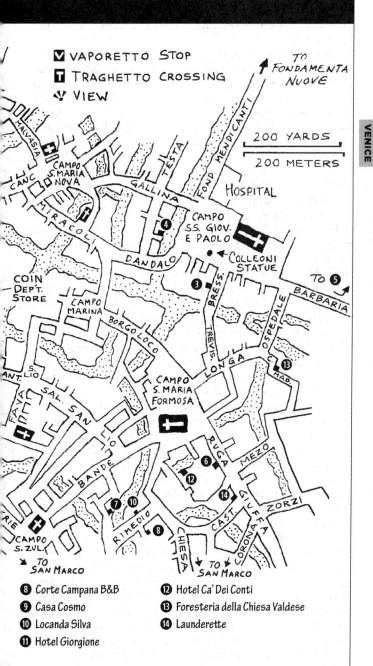

VAPORETTO STOP
TRAGHETTO CROSSING
VIEW

TO FONDAMENTA NUOVE

200 YARDS
200 METERS

MALVASIA
CAMPO S.MARIA NOVA
CANC.
MIRACOLI
TESTA
GALLINA
FOND MENDICANTI
HOSPITAL

CAMPO S.S. GIOV. E PAOLO
④
DANDALO
← COLLEONI STATUE
③
BRESS.
TO ⑤
BARBARIA

COIN DEP'T. STORE
CAMPO MARINA
BORGO LOCO
TREVIS.
LONGA
OSPEDALE
C. MAD.
⑬

S. LIO
ANT.
FAVA
SAL. SAN
CAMPO S. MARIA FORMOSA
RUGA
MEZO
⑥
⑫
⑭
GIUFFA
CAST.
ZORZI

BANDE
⑦ ⑩
RIMEDIO
⑧
CHIESA
CORONA

CAMPO S. ZUL.
TO SAN MARCO
TO SAN MARCO

⑧ Corte Campana B&B
⑨ Casa Cosmo
⑩ Locanda Silva
⑪ Hotel Giorgione
⑫ Hotel Ca' Dei Conti
⑬ Foresteria della Chiesa Valdese
⑭ Launderette

and continue on Calle drio la Chiesa. Cross the bridge, continue straight, then turn left onto Ruga Giuffa; find the hotel on your left at #4838.

VENICE

$ **Hotel Riva,** with gleaming marble hallways, big exposed beams, fine antique furnishings, and bright rooms, is romantically situated on a canal along the gondola serenade route. You could actually dunk your breakfast rolls in the canal (but don't). Ten of the 30 rooms come with air-conditioning for the same price—request one when you reserve. Or, if you prefer lots of light but no air-conditioning, you can ask Sandro to hold a corner *(angolo)* room for you (Sb-€90, D-€100, Db-€120, Tb-€170, €20 extra for view, reserve with credit card but pay with cash only, Ponte dell'Angelo, tel. 041-522-7034, fax 041-528-5551, www.hotelriva .it, info@hotelriva.it, Daniella). Facing St. Mark's Basilica, walk behind it on the left along Calle de la Canonica, take the first left (at blue *Pauly & C* mosaic in street), continue straight, go over the bridge, and angle right to the hotel at Ponte dell'Angelo.

$ **Corte Campana B&B,** run by enthusiastic and helpful Riccardo, rents three quiet and characteristic rooms just behind St. Mark's Square, plus two apartments (Db-€125, Tb or Tb apartment-€165, Qb-€190, prices are soft, cash only, 2-night minimum, €10/night less for stays of 4 nights, air-con, Internet access, Calle del Remedio 4410, Castello, tel. & fax 041-523-3603, mobile 389-272-6500, www.cortecampana.com, info@cortecampana.com). From nearby Locanda Silva—described below—go 30 yards down the canal, turn right onto Calle del Remedio, follow it to #4410, and ring the bell at the black gate.

$ **Casa Cosmo** is a humble little five-room place run by Davide and his parents. While it comes with minimal services and no public spaces, it's air-conditioned, very central, inexpensive, and quiet (Db-€110, cash discount, no breakfast, Calle di Mezo 4976, San Marco, tel. & fax 041-296-0710, www.casacosmo.com, info @casacosmo.com). From the Rialto vaporetto stop, head inland on Larga Mazzini (which becomes Merceria). Turn right onto San Salvador, then immediately left onto tiny Calle di Mezo to #4976 (it's just behind Foot Locker).

$ **Locanda Silva** is a big, basic, beautifully located, institutional-feeling place renting 23 decent old-school rooms (S-€65, Sb-€80, D-€85, weekday Db-€110, weekend Db-€130, substantially less during slow times, request 10 percent Rick Steves discount, closed Dec–Jan, Fondamenta del Remedio 4423, tel. 041-522-7643, fax 041-528-6817, www.locandasilva.it, info@locanda silva.it, Sandra and Massimo). From San Marco, head north toward Campo Santa Maria Formosa, go down Calle del Remedio, and turn left at the canal to Fondamenta del Remedio.

Near the Accademia Bridge

When you step over the Accademia Bridge, the commotion of touristy Venice is replaced by a sleepy village laced with canals. This quiet area, next to the best painting gallery in town, is a 15-minute walk from the Rialto or St. Mark's Square.

The fast vaporetto #2 connects the Accademia Bridge with the train station (15 minutes), Piazzale Roma bus stop (20 minutes), Tronchetto parking lot (25 minutes), and St. Mark's Square (5 minutes). For hotels south of the Accademia Bridge, vaporetto #51 to Zattere (or the Alilaguna speedboat from the airport to Zattere) are good options.

South of the Accademia Bridge

$$$ Hotel Belle Arti has a grand entry and a formal, stern staff. With the ambience of a modern American hotel, its 64 rooms feel out of place in musty Old World Venice (Sb-€130, Db-€240, Tb-€280, air-con, elevator; 100 yards behind Accademia art museum: facing museum, jog left, then right, down Via Dorsoduro to #912, Dorsoduro; tel. 041-522-6230, fax 041-528-0043, www.hotelbellearti.com, info@hotelbellearti.com).

$$$ Pensione Accademia fills the 17th-century Villa Maravege like a Bellini painting. Its 27 rooms are comfortable, elegant, and air-conditioned. You'll feel aristocratic gliding through its grand public spaces and lounging in its wistful, breezy gardens (Sb-€145, standard Db-€235, bigger "superior" Db-€280, Qb-€330, ask for discount when you book; facing Accademia art museum, go right, cross the bridge, go right to where the small canal hits the big one, Dorsoduro 1058; tel. 041-521-0188, fax 041-523-9152, www.pensioneaccademia.it, info@pensioneaccademia.it).

$$$ Hotel Agli Alboretti is a cozy family-run 23-room place in a quiet neighborhood a block behind the Accademia art museum. With red carpeting and wood-beamed ceilings, it feels classy (Sb-€115, Db-€200, Tb-€225, Qb-€250, air-con, elevator, 100 yards from the Accademia vaporetto stop on Rio Terra A. Foscarini at #884, Dorsoduro, tel. 041-523-0058, fax 041-521-0158, www.aglialboretti.com, info@aglialboretti.com, Anna).

$$ Pensione la Calcina, the home of English writer John Ruskin in 1876, maintains a 19th-century formality. It comes with all the three-star comforts in a professional yet intimate package. Its 32 rosy, perfumed rooms are squeaky clean, with nice wood furniture, hardwood floors, and a peaceful canalside setting facing Giudecca Island (Sb-€140, Sb with view-€150, Db-€150–310 depending on size and view, Qb-€280, air-con, Wi-Fi, rooftop terrace, floating buffet-breakfast terrace, near Zattere vaporetto stop at south end of Rio di San Vio at #780, Dorsoduro, tel. 041-520-6466, fax 041-522-7045, www.lacalcina.com, info@lacalcina.com).

VENICE

Hotels near the Accademia Bridge

TO FRARI & RIALTO

CAMPO S. MARG.

CA' REZZONICO

SAN SAM.

PALAZZO GRASSI

16 BO TT.

CA' REZZ.

CAMPO SANTO STEFANO

TO 5

CAMPO S. BARNABA

TRAGHETTO

GRAND

FRUTT.

15

CALLE

TOLETTA

ROMITE

BORGO

2

CORFU GAMB.

ACC.

ACCADEMIA BRIDGE

ACCADEMIA MUSEUM

CAMPO SAN TROVASO

PISTOR

CAMPO S. VIO

6

CAMPO NUOVA

8

BONILI

NANI

GONDOLA WORKSHOP

RINI

POMP.

3

CHIESA

FOSCARINI

CARITA VENIER

S. MARIA GESUATI

CAMPO S. AGNESE

BRAGADIN

ZATTERE

1

ALILAGUNA DOCK

PONTE LONGO

7

4

DRIO INC.

ZATTERE V

V

ZATTERE

GIUDECCA

200 YARDS
200 METERS

1 Hotel Belle Arti
2 Pensione Accademia
3 Hotel Agli Alboretti
4 Pensione la Calcina
5 To Casa Rezzonico

6 Hotel Galleria
7 Don Orione Religious
  Guest House
8 Ca' San Trovaso &
  Casa di Sara

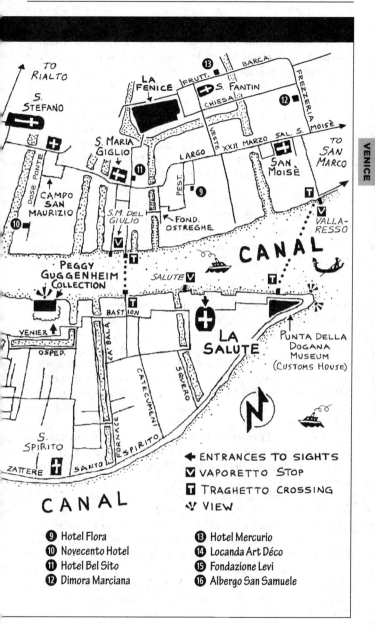

VENICE

ENTRANCES TO SIGHTS
V VAPORETTO STOP
T TRAGHETTO CROSSING
⚘ VIEW

⑨ Hotel Flora
⑩ Novecento Hotel
⑪ Hotel Bel Sito
⑫ Dimora Marciana

⑬ Hotel Mercurio
⑭ Locanda Art Déco
⑮ Fondazione Levi
⑯ Albergo San Samuele

Guests get discounted meals at their La Piscina restaurant.

$$ Casa Rezzonico is a silent getaway far from the madding crowds. Its private garden terrace has perhaps the lushest grass in Italy, and its seven spacious, very Venetian rooms have garden/ canal views (Sb-€120, Db-€160, Tb-€190, Qb-€220, ask for discount when you book, air-con, Wi-Fi, Fondamenta Gherardini 2813, Dorsoduro, tel. 041-277-0653, fax 041-277-5435, www .casarezzonico.it, info@casarezzonico.it). Take vaporetto #1 to Ca' Rezzonico, head up Calle del Traghetto, cross Campo San Barnaba to the canal, and continue on Fondamenta Gherardini to #2813.

$$ Hotel Galleria has nine tight, velvety rooms, most with views of the Grand Canal. Some rooms are quite narrow. It's run with a family feel by Luciano and Stefano (S-€85, D-€120, skinny Grand Canal view Db-€150, palatial Grand Canal view Db-€180, includes breakfast in room, fans, 30 yards from Accademia art museum, next to recommended Foscarini pizzeria, Dorsoduro 878a, tel. 041-523-2489, fax 041-520-4172, www.hotelgalleria.it, galleria@tin.it).

$$ Don Orione Religious Guest House is a big cultural center dedicated to the work of a local man who became a saint in modern times. Filling an old monastery, it feels institutional, like a modern retreat center—clean, peaceful, and strictly run, with 74 rooms. It's beautifully located, comfortable, and a fine value (Sb-€84, Db-€140, Tb-€180, profits go to mission work in the developing world, groups welcome, air-con, Dorsoduro, tel. 041-522-4077, fax 041-528-6214, www.donorione-venezia.it, info @donorione-venezia.it). From the Zattere vaporetto stop, turn right, then turn left. It's just after the church at #909a.

$ Ca' San Trovaso rents seven simple, spacious rooms split between the main hotel and a nearby annex. The location is peaceful, on a small canal (Sb-€90, Db-€115, Db with bigger canal view and air-con-€130, Tb-€145, these prices with cash, includes breakfast in your room, air-con, small roof terrace, Dorsoduro 1350/51, tel. 041-277-1146, mobile 339-445-8821, fax 041-277-7190, www .casantrovaso.com, s.trovaso@tin.it, Mark and his son Alessandro). From the Zattere vaporetto stop, exit left, and cross a bridge. Turn right at tiny Calle Trevisan, cross another bridge, cross the adjacent bridge, take an immediate right, and then the first left. Nearby, Mama Cristina's **Casa di Sara** is a brightly colored B&B with quiet rooms, a tiny roof terrace, and the same prices (mobile 345-070-8547, www.casadisara.com, info@casadisara.com).

Between the Accademia Bridge and St. Mark's Square

$$$ Hotel Flora sits buried in a sea of fancy designer boutiques and elegant hotels almost on the Grand Canal. It's formal, with uniformed staff and grand public spaces, yet the 43 rooms have a homey warmth and the garden oasis is a sanctuary for foot-weary guests (generally Db-€260, check website for special discounts or email Sr. Romanelli for 10 percent Rick Steves discount off standard prices, air-con, elevator, Calle dei Bergamaschi 2283a, San Marco, tel. 041-520-5844, fax 041-522-8217, www.hotelflora.it, info@hotelflora.it). It's at the end of Calle dei Bergamaschi, a long, skinny dead-end lane just off Calle Larga XXII Marzo.

$$$ Novecento Hotel rents nine plush rooms. Owned by Hotel Flora (described above), this boutique hotel is decorated circa-1900 throughout, with a big lounge and an elegant living room (Db-€240–260, air-con, Wi-Fi, Calle del Dose 2683, off Campo San Maurizio, San Marco, tel. 041-241-3765, fax 041-521-2145, www.novecento.biz, info@novecento.biz).

$$$ Hotel Bel Sito offers pleasing yet well-worn Old World character, 38 rooms, generous public spaces, a peaceful courtyard, and a picturesque location—facing a church on a small square between St. Mark's Square and the Accademia (Sb-€110, Db-€185, air-con, Wi-Fi, elevator; catch vaporetto #1 to Santa Maria del Giglio stop, take street inland to square, hotel is at far end to your right at Santa Maria del Giglio 2517, San Marco; tel. 041-522-3365, fax 041-520-4083, www.hotelbelsito.info, info@hotelbelsito.info, manager Rossella).

$$ Dimora Marciana, a mod place furnished in a traditional Venetian style, has seven rooms in a quiet alley just a two-minute walk from St. Mark's Square (Db-€165, Tb-€190, 2-room Qb-€230, mention Rick Steves when you book to get the best prices, cash discount, air-con, Wi-Fi, small bar, tel. 041-522-0755, www.dimoramarciana.com, info@dimoramarciana.com, Daniel). From behind the Correr Museum, turn right on Frezzeria, then take Calle Bognolo—the second street on the left—to #1604.

$$ Hotel Mercurio offers 19 peaceful, comfortable, and recently renovated rooms near La Fenice Opera House. Some rooms offer canal views (Sb-€130, Db-€170, Tb-€200, €10 less with cash, less mid-June–Aug and Nov–Feb except Christmas week, air-con, Wi-Fi, Calle del Fruttariol 1848, San Marco, tel. 041-522-0947, fax 041-582-5270, www.hotelmercurio.com, info @hotelmercurio.com, Monica, Vittorio, and Natale). From the San Marco–Vallaresso vaporetto stop, follow Calle Vallaresso to Calle Frezzaria, turn right, and follow it over a bridge as it becomes Calle del Frutariol. The hotel is on the left just before La Fenice Opera House.

$$ Locanda Art Déco is a charming little place. While the Art Deco theme is scant, a wrought-iron staircase leads from the inviting lobby to six thoughtfully decorated rooms (Db-€150–170, Tb-€200, 3-night minimum on weekends, 5 percent cash discount,

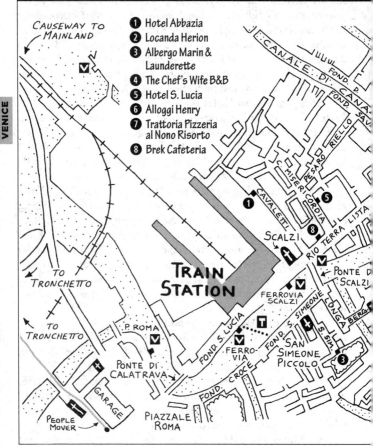

Hotels near the Train Station

- ❶ Hotel Abbazia
- ❷ Locanda Herion
- ❸ Albergo Marin & Launderette
- ❹ The Chef's Wife B&B
- ❺ Hotel S. Lucia
- ❻ Alloggi Henry
- ❼ Trattoria Pizzeria al Nono Risorto
- ❽ Brek Cafeteria

air-con, free Wi-Fi, just north of the Accademia Bridge off Campo Santo Stefano at Calle delle Botteghe 2966, San Marco, tel. 041-277-0558, fax 041-270-2891, www.locandaartdeco.com, info @locandaartdeco.com). They also rent loft apartments.

$ Fondazione Levi, run by a foundation that promotes research on Venetian music, offers 35 quiet institutional yet comfortable and spacious rooms (Sb-€70, Db-€110 or less, Tb-€120, Qb-€140, twin beds only, elevator, San Vidal 2893, San Marco, tel. 041-786-711, fax 041-786-766, www.fondazionelevi.it, foresterialevi@libero.it). It's 80 yards from the Accademia Bridge on the St. Mark's side. Leaving the bridge (opposite the Accademia vaporetto stop), take an immediate left, cross the bridge, and go down Calle Giustinian straight to the Fondazione. Buzz the *Foresteria* door to the right.

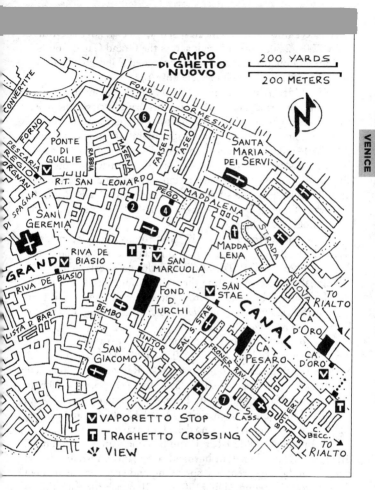

$ Albergo San Samuele's is a backpacker place: dumpy but in a great locale. It rents 12 basic rooms in a crumbling old palace near Campo Santo Stefano. Sleep here only if their price is far less than other listings (S-€60, D-€80, Db-€100, extra bed-€30, no breakfast, Salizada San Samuele 3358, San Marco, tel. 041-520-5165, fax 041-522-8045, www.albergosansamuele.it, info@albergo sansamuele.it).

Near the Train Station

I don't recommend the train station area. It's crawling with noisy, disoriented tourists with too much baggage and people whose life's calling is to scam visitors out of their money. It's so easy just to hop a vaporetto upon arrival and sleep in the Venice of your dreams. Still, for those who like to park their bags near the station, these places work well. The nearest self-service laundry is **Orange** (daily 7:30–22:30, €5/small load; across the Grand Canal from the station—follow directions to recommended Albergo Marin, on the right at Ramo delle Chioverete 665a/b).

$$$ Hotel Abbazia, in the dreary hotel zone near the train station, fills a former abbey with both history and class. The refectory makes a grand living room for guests, a garden fills the old courtyard, and the halls leading to 50 rooms are monkishly wide (Db-€180–200, larger superior rooms-€25 extra—choose Venetian or modern style, ask for Rick Steves discount when you book direct, air-con, Wi-Fi, no elevator but plenty of stairs, fun-loving staff, 2 blocks from the station on the very quiet Calle Priuli dei Cavaletti 68, tel. 041-717-333, fax 041-717-949, www.abbaziahotel .com, info@abbaziahotel.com).

$ Locanda Herion rents 17 basic rooms for a decent price (Db-€100–120, 10 percent discount with cash, air-con, tel. 041-275-9426, fax 041-275-6647, www.locandaherion.com, info @locandaherion.com). Exiting the train station, turn left to follow Rio Terra Lista de Spagna. Cross the Ponte di Guglie and turn right at the yellow *San Marcuola traghetto* sign to find Campiello Picutti o del Magazen 1697a.

$ Albergo Marin and its staff offers 17 good-value quiet rooms handy to the train station (Sb-€110, D-€90, Db-€120, Tb-€150, 5 percent cash discount, fans on request, Ramo delle Chioverete #670b, Santa Croce, tel. 041-718-022, fax 041-721-485, www.albergo marin.it, info@albergomarin.it). From the station, cross the Grand Canal and turn immediately right. Take the first left, then the first right, then right again to Ramo delle Chioverete.

$ The Chef's Wife B&B is run by American Stacy Gibboni. The "chef" is her Venetian husband, who runs a restaurant next door. Together they rent one sprawling and very cozy apartment for two to four people (Db-€100, Qb-€150, ask for Rick Steves rate, 2-night minimum, huge living room, no air-con, Wi-Fi, adjacent to Stacy's art studio, Corte del Pegoloto 1801, Cannaregio, mobile 328-365-8753, www.thechefswife.eu, stacysguesthouse @hotmail.it). It's near the San Marcuola vaporetto stop—see Stacy's website for directions.

$ Hotel S. Lucia, 150 yards from the train station, is oddly modern and sterile, with bright and spacious rooms and tight showers. Its 15 rooms are simple and clean. Guests enjoy their sunny garden area out front (S-€60, Db-€105, Tb-€145, discounts for three or more nights, 5 percent cash discount, breakfast-€5, air-con, Calle della Misericordia 358, Cannaregio, tel. 041-715-180, fax 041-710-610, www.hotelslucia.com, info@hotelslucia.com, Gianni and Alessandra). Exit the station, head left, then take the second left onto Calle della Misericordia. The hotel is 100 yards ahead on the right.

$ Alloggi Henry, a homey little family-owned hotel, rents 15 simple and flowery rooms in a quiet residential neighborhood. It's a 10-minute walk from the train station (D-€80, Db-€100, Tb-€130, prices good with cash and this book through 2011, no breakfast, air-con, Calle Ormesini 1506e, Cannaregio, tel. 041-523-6675, fax 041-715-680, www.alloggihenry.com, info@alloggi henry.com, Manola and Henry). From the station, follow Lista de Spagna, San Leonardo, and Farsetti. Turn left on Calle Ormesini, then turn right into tiny Campiello Briani. They also rent a three-room apartment that sleeps up to nine.

Big, Fancy Hotels that Discount Shamelessly

Here are several big, plush four-star places with greedy sky-high rack rates (around Db-€300) that often have great discounts (as low as Db-€120) for drop-ins, off-season travelers, or online booking through their websites. If you want sliding-glass-door, uniformed-receptionist kind of comfort and formality in the old center, these are worth considering: **$$$ Hotel Giorgione** (big, garish, shiny, near Rialto Bridge, www.hotelgiorgione.com, see map on page 104); **$$$ Hotel Casa Verardo** (elegant and quietly parked on a canal behind St. Mark's, more stately, www.casaverardo.it, see map on page 100); **$$$ Hotel Donà Palace** (sitting like Las Vegas in the touristy zone a few blocks behind St. Mark's Basilica, works with neighbors **$$$ Hotel all'Angelo** and **$$$ Hotel al Ponte dei Sosperi** to rent 100 overpriced but often discounted rooms, all on Calle Larga San Marco, www.donapalace.it, see map on page 100); and **$$$ Hotel Ca' Dei Conti** (five minutes northeast of St. Mark's Square, palatial and perfectly located but €500 rooms worth it only when deeply discounted, www.cadeiconti.com, see map on page 104).

Cheap Dormitory Accommodations

$ Foresteria della Chiesa Valdese, run by the Methodist Church, offers 60 beds in doubles and 6- to 8-bed dorms, halfway between St. Mark's Square and the Rialto Bridge. This chilly run-down yet charming old place has elegant ceiling paintings (dorm bed-€28, Db-€92, Tb-€111, Qb-€136, discount for stays of 2 nights or more; includes breakfast, sheets, towels, and lockers; room lock-out 10:00–13:30, must check in and out when office is open—8:30–20:00, reservations by phone only—no email, Fondamenta Cavagnis 5170, Castello, tel. 041-528-6797, fax 041-241-6238, www .foresteriavenezia.it, info@foresteriavenezia.it). From Campo Santa Maria Formosa, walk past Bar all'Orologio to the end of Calle Longa and cross the bridge onto Fondamenta Cavagnis.

$ Venice's youth hostel, on Giudecca Island with 260 beds and grand views across the Bay of San Marco, is a godsend for backpackers shell-shocked by Venetian prices (€25 beds with sheets and breakfast in 8- to 20-bed dorms, cheaper for hostel members, lockers, room lock-out 10:30–13:30, office open daily 7:00–24:30, catch vaporetto #2 from station to Zittele, tel. 041-523-8211, can reserve online at www.ostellovenezia.it).

On the Mainland

$ Villa Dolcetti, about 12 miles from Marco Polo Airport, is a 1635 building with nine comfortable rooms. Art-lovers Diego and Tatiana provide a buffet breakfast, free parking, and lots of sightseeing advice (Db-€70, superior Db-€80, Tb-€90–110, request discount, Internet access and Wi-Fi, tel. 041-563-1077, fax 041-563-1139, www.villadolcetti.com, info@villadolcetti.com). It's on the Venice–Padua road in the Venetian suburb of Oriago di Mira, at Via Venezia 85. Email them for driving and bus directions (buses run to/from Piazzale Roma, 2/hour, 25 minutes).

$ Villa Mocenigo Agriturismo, about 10 miles from Marco Polo Airport, is a working family-run farm in a peaceful rural location between Venice and Padua. Its 10 rooms are furnished with antiques, and regional specialties are served for dinner (Sb-€40–60, Db-€60–80, extra bed-€15–25, dinner and wine-€15–25 per person, air-con, Via Viasana 59 in Mirano-Venezia, tel. & fax 041-433-246, mobile 335-547-4728, www.villamocenigo.com, info@villamocenigo.com). Email them for directions by car or bus. Buses to Venice leave directly from the villa (3/hour, 45 minutes).

Eating in Venice

While touristy restaurants are the scourge of Venice, the following places are still popular with Venetians and respect the tourists who happen in. First trick: Walk away from triple-language menus. Second trick: Order the daily special. Third trick: For freshness, eat fish. Most seafood dishes are the catch-of-the-day. Remember that seafood can be sold by weight rather than a set price (if you see "100 g" or *"l'etto"* by a too-good-to-be-true price on the menu, that's the cost per 100 grams—about a quarter pound). The abbreviation *s.q.* is similar, meaning according to quantity (you pay for the weight of the particular piece).

Near the Rialto Bridge
North of the Bridge

These restaurants are located between Campo S.S. Apostoli and Campo Santa Maria Nova.

Trattoria da Bepi, bright and alpine-paneled, feels like a classic. Owner Loris scours the market for only the best ingredients—especially seafood—and takes good care of the hungry clientele. Ask for his seasonal specialties—the crab dishes are excellent. There's good seating inside and out (€10 pastas, €15 *secondi,* Fri–Wed 12:00–14:30 & 19:00–22:00, closed Thu, near Rialto Bridge, half a block north of Campo Santi Apostoli on Salizada Pistor, tel. 041-528-5031).

Little **Vini da Gigio** has a passion for good food, serving traditional Venetian dishes (€13 pastas, €20 *secondi,* no cover, Wed–Sun 19:00–late, last order at 22:30, closed Mon–Tue, 4 blocks from Ca' d'Oro vaporetto stop, behind the church on Campo San Felice, tel. 041-528-5140).

Trattoria Ca' d'Oro, while a little less accessible and inviting to the tourist, is a venerable favorite with a small, appealing menu and an enthusiastic following. Just to sip a wine and enjoy *cicchetti* at the bar is a treat—their *polpette* (tuna and potato meatballs) are famous, and the house wine will set you back just €0.50. It's also fine for a meal (€9 pastas, €10 *secondi,* closed Thu, reservations recommended; from the Ca' d'Oro vaporetto dock, walk 100 yards directly away from the canal, cross Strada Nuova, and you'll hit it; tel. 041-528-5324).

Osteria al Bomba is a *cicchetti* bar with a female touch, thanks to Giovanna. It's unusual (clean, no toothpicks, no cursing) and quite good, with lots of veggies. You can stand and eat at the bar—try a little €3 *crostino* with polenta and cod—or oversee the construction of the house *"antipasto misto di cicchetti"* plate (€15, enough fish and vegetables for two) and choose your wine by the glass from the posted list. A seat at the long table comes with a €2 *coperto* (daily 12:00–15:00 & 18:00–23:00, near Campo S.S. Apostoli, go a block off Strada Nuova down a small alley, then take the first right on Calle dell'Oca, tel. 041-520-5175).

East of the Rialto Bridge, near Campo San Bartolomeo

Osteria "Alla Botte," despite being located a minute from the Rialto Bridge, is packed with a casual neighborhood clientele in two simple woody rooms. For a classic Venetian taste, try the €18 all-seafood *antipasto misto* (daily 12:00–15:00 & 19:00–23:00, two short blocks off Campo San Bartolomeo in the corner behind the statue—down Calle de la Bissa, notice the "day after" photo showing a debris-covered Venice after the notorious 1989 Pink Floyd open-air concert, tel. 041-520-9775, Cristiano).

Osteria di Santa Marina, on the wonderful Campo Marina, serves pricey near-gourmet cuisine in a dressy dining room. The presentation is impressive, but you feel there's more pretense than love of food. Cheap-eating tricks are frowned on in this elegant,

Restaurants near the Rialto Bridge

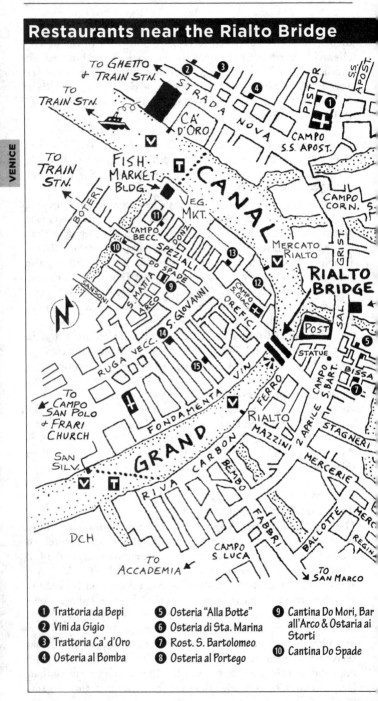

1. Trattoria da Bepi
2. Vini da Gigio
3. Trattoria Ca' d'Oro
4. Osteria al Bomba
5. Osteria "Alla Botte"
6. Osteria di Sta. Marina
7. Rost. S. Bartolomeo
8. Osteria al Portego
9. Cantina Do Mori, Bar all'Arco & Ostaria ai Storti
10. Cantina Do Spade

VENICE

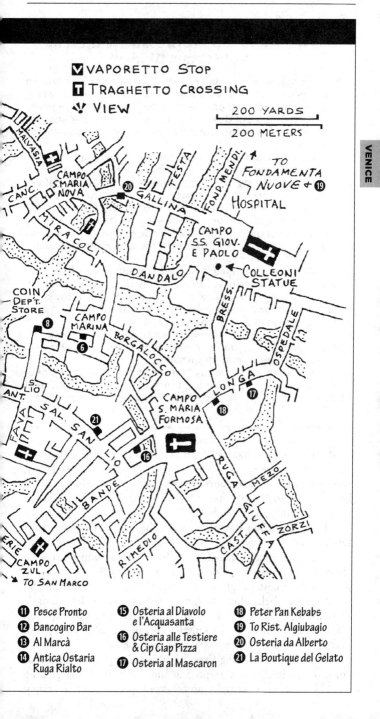

11	Pesce Pronto
12	Bancogiro Bar
13	Al Marcà
14	Antica Ostaria Ruga Rialto
15	Osteria al Diavolo e l'Acquasanta
16	Osteria alle Testiere & Cip Ciap Pizza
17	Osteria al Mascaron
18	Peter Pan Kebabs
19	To Rist. Algiubagio
20	Osteria da Alberto
21	La Boutique del Gelato

The Stand-Up Progressive Venetian Pub-Crawl Dinner

My favorite Venetian dinner is a pub crawl (giro d'ombra)—a tradition unique to Venice, where no cars means easy crawling. (Giro means stroll, and ombra—slang for a glass of wine—means shade, from the old days when a portable wine bar scooted with the shadow of the Campanile bell tower across St. Mark's Square.)

Venice's residential back streets hide plenty of character-istic bars (bacari) with countless trays of interesting toothpick munchies (cicchetti) and blackboards listing the wines that are uncorked and served by the glass. This is a great way to mingle and have fun with the Venetians. Bars don't stay open very late, and the cicchetti selection is best early, so start your evening by 18:00. Most bars are closed on Sunday. For a stress-free pub crawl, consider taking a tour with the charming Alessandro Schezzini (see page 56).

Cicchetti bars have a social stand-up zone and a cozy gaggle of tables where you can generally sit down with your cic-chetti or order from a simple menu. In some of the more popular places, the crowds happily spill out into the street. Food gener-ally costs the same price whether you stand or sit.

I've listed plenty of pubs in walking order for a quick or extended crawl. If you've crawled enough, most of these bars make a fine one-stop, sit-down dinner.

While you can order a plate, Venetians prefer going one-by-one...sipping their wine and trying this...then give me one of those...and so on. Try deep-fried mozzarella cheese, gorgon-

borderline stuffy restaurant (enticing menu with €15 pastas and €25 *secondi*, Tue–Sat 12:30–14:30 & 19:30–22:00, closed Sun, reserve for dinner, eat indoors or outdoors on pleasant little square, between Rialto Bridge and Campo Santa Maria Formosa on Campo Marina, tel. 041-528-5239).

Rosticceria San Bartolomeo is a cheap—if confusing—self-service diner, a throwback budget eatery with a likeably surly staff. Take out, grab a table, munch at the bar, or pay a bit more to eat at the restaurant upstairs (good €6–7 pasta, great fried *mozzarella al prosciutto* for €1.50, delightful fruit salad, €1 glasses of wine, prices listed on wall behind counter, no cover or service charge, daily 9:00–21:30, tel. 041-522-3569). To find it, imagine the statue on Campo San Bartolomeo walking backward 20 yards, turning left, and going under a passageway—now, follow him.

If you're pub crawling from Rosticceria San Bartolomeo, con-tinue over a bridge to Campo San Lio. Here, turn left, passing Hotel Canada on your right, and follow Calle Carminati straight

zola, calamari, artichoke hearts, and anything ugly on a toothpick. *Crostini* (small toasted bread with something on it) are popular, as are marinated seafood, olives, and prosciutto with melon. Meat and fish (*pesce;* PESH-ay) munchies can be expensive; veggies (*verdure*) are cheap, at about €3 for a meal-sized plate. In many places, there's a set price per food item (e.g., €1.50). To get a plate of assorted appetizers for €8 (or more, depending on how hungry you are), ask for *"Un piatto classico di cicchetti misti da €8"* (oon pee-AH-toh KLAH-see-koh dee cheh-KET-tee MEE-stee dah OH-toh ay-OO-roh). Bread sticks (*grissini*) are free for the asking.

Bar-hopping Venetians enjoy an *aperitivo,* a before-dinner drink. Boldly order a Bellini, a *spritz con Aperol,* or a prosecco, and draw approving looks from the natives.

Drink the house wines. A small glass of house red or white wine (*ombra rosso* or *ombra bianco*) or a small beer (*birrino*) costs about €1. The house keg wine is cheap—€1 per glass, about €4 per liter. *Vin bon,* Venetian for fine wine, may run you from €1.50 to €6 per little glass. There are usually several fine wines uncorked and available by the glass. A good last drink is *fragolino,* the local sweet wine—*bianco* or *rosso*. It often comes with a little cookie (*biscotti*) for dipping.

about 50 yards over another bridge. On the left is the pastry shop (*pasticceria*), and straight ahead is Osteria al Portego (at #6015).

Osteria al Portego is a friendly neighborhood bar—one of the best in town. Carlo serves good meals and excellent *cicchetti*—best enjoyed early, around 18:00 (from 19:00 to 21:00, tables are reserved for those ordering from the menu; the *cicchetti* are picked over by 21:00). Prices for food and wine are posted clearly on the wall. The *cicchetti* here can make a great meal, but you should also consider sitting down for a dinner from their fine menu. This place can get very busy, so reserve ahead if you want a table (€13 pastas, €2 glasses of wine, Mon–Sat 10:30–15:00 & 18:00–21:30, Sun 18:00–21:30, near Campo Marina at Calle Malvasia 6015, tel. 041-522-9038).

West of the Rialto Bridge

All of these places are informal, serving *cicchetti* and/or light meals. The first group of bars are within 200 yards of each other, a few steps behind the Rialto fish market; the rest are a short walk from this hive of eateries (see map on page 118). This area is very crowded by day, nearly empty early in the evening, and crowded with young Venetians later.

Cicchetti and Light Meals West of the Rialto

Most bars are closed 15:00–18:00 (though Cantina Do Mori and Ostaria ai Storti stay open all day), and offer glasses of house wine for under a euro, better wine for around €2, and *cicchetti* for €1–2. At each place, look for the list of snacks and wine by the glass at the bar or on the wall. If you're ready for desert, try dipping a Burano biscuit in a glass of strawberry-flavored *fragolino* or another sweet dessert wine.

Cantina Do Mori has been famous with locals (since 1462) and savvy travelers (since 1982) as a convivial place for fine wine. You'll choose from a forest of little edibles on toothpicks and *francobolli* (a spicy selection of 20 tiny mayo-soaked sandwiches nicknamed "stamps"). Go here to be abused in a fine atmosphere—the frowns are part of the shtick (Mon–Sat 8:00–20:00, closed Sun, stand-up only, arrive early before the *cicchetti* are gone, San Polo 429, tel. 041-522-5401). From the Rialto Bridge, walk 200 yards down Ruga degli Orefici, away from St. Mark's Square—then turn left on Ruga Vecchia S. Giovanni, then right at Sotoportego Do Mori.

Bar all'Arco, a bustling one-room joint across from Cantina Do Mori, is particularly enjoyable for its tiny open-face sandwiches (closed Sun, tel. 041-520-5666).

Ostaria ai Storti serves lots of veggies and a few homemade pastas (check the daily specials) at great prices. With a homey feel, it's a fun place to congregate. Check out the photo of the market in 1909, below the bar. Alessandro speaks English and enjoys helping educate travelers while serving *fragolino* (daily 9:00–22:30, 20 yards from Cantina Do Mori on Calle delle Do Spade 819, tel. 041-523-6861).

Cantina Do Spade is run by Sebastiano, who clearly lists the *cicchetti* and wines of the day (daily 11:00–15:00 & 18:00–21:00, 30 yards down Calle delle Do Spade from Ostaria ai Storti at Calle delle Do Spade 19, tel. 041-521-0583).

At **Pesce Pronto,** you can actually sample fish while watching the market action. Bruno and Umberto serve artful fish hors d'oeuvres, *sfornato con pesce* (a savory baked pastry), and many other fresh fish tidbits—all at a fair price. This fancy hole-in-the-wall is fun for a quick bite—eat standing up or take it to go. At 12:30, they serve €10–12 "express plates" of pasta and other choices (Tue–Sat 9:00–14:30 & 17:00–19:30, closed Sun–Mon, facing the fish market at Calle de le Beccarie o Panataria 319, tel. 041-822-0298).

Youthful *Cicchetti* Bars near Campo San Giacometto

A strip of five places between Campo San Giacometto and the Grand Canal, several with canal-front tables, together make a thriving youth *spritz* scene that's worth a look even if you don't eat or drink there.

The **Bancogiro Bar** is good for strong cheese and its canalside tables (€3.50/person cover, €15 cheese plate, wine by glass is listed on board, Tue–Sun 12:00–23:00, closed Mon, tel. 041-523-2061).

Al Marcà, a few steps away and off the canal, is an even livelier little nook with a happy crowd, where young locals gather to grab drinks and little snacks. The price list is clear, and I've found the crowd to be welcoming to tourists interested in connecting (Mon–Sat 9:00–15:00 & 18:00–21:00, closed Sun, on Campo Cesare Battisti).

More *Cicchetti* Bars West of the Rialto Bridge

Antica Ostaria Ruga Rialto, a.k.a. "the Ruga," is a neighborhood fixture where Giorgio and Marco serve great bar snacks and wine to a devoted clientele. Treats here are their polenta, sardine with onions, and veggies. Bar or table, no problem—they're happy to make you a €3, €6, or €10 mixed plate (daily 11:00–14:30 & 19:00–24:00, easy to find—just past the Chinese restaurant at Ruga Vecchia San Giovanni 692, tel. 041-521-1243).

Osteria al Diavolo e l'Acquasanta, three blocks west of the Rialto Bridge, serves good—if pricey—Venetian-style pasta, and makes a handy lunch stop for sightseers and gondola riders. Though they list *cicchetti* and wine by the glass on the wall, I'd come here for a light meal rather than for appetizers (Mon 12:00–14:30, Wed–Sun 12:00–21:30, closed Tue, hiding on Calle della Madonna—a quiet street just off Ruga Vecchia San Giovanni, tel. 041-277-0307).

Pizza and Pasta Farther West of the Rialto Bridge

Antica Birraria la Corte is an everyday eatery on the delightful Campo San Polo, between the Rialto Bridge and the Frari Church. Popular with locals for its pizza, calzones, and salads, it fills the far side of this cozy, family-filled square. While the interior is a sprawling beer hall, it's a joy to eat on the square, where metal tables teeter on the cobbles, the wind plays with the paper mats, and children run free (daily 12:00–14:30 & 19:00–22:30, Campo San Polo 2168; tel. 041-275-0570).

Trattoria Pizzeria al Nono Risorto is unpretentious, inexpensive, youthful, and famous for serving some of the best pizza in town. You'll sit in a gravelly garden under a leafy canopy, surrounded by an enthusiastic waitstaff and Italians enjoying huge €8 salads, pastas, and pizzas, and €12 grilled meat or fish dishes

(Thu–Tue 12:00–14:30 & 19:00–22:30, closed Wed, reservations smart on weekends; from Rialto fish market, walk 3 minutes to Campo San Cassiano—it's just over the bridge on Sotoportego de Siora Bettina; see map on page 112; tel. 041-524-1169).

Near Campo Santa Maria Formosa

Campo Santa Maria Formosa is one of my favorite community scenes. While the restaurants fronting the square aren't much, several good options for dining lie a short walk away. For locations, see the map on page 118.

Osteria alle Testiere is my top dining recommendation in Venice. Hugely respected, they are dedicated to quality, serving up creative, artfully presented market-fresh seafood (there's no meat on the menu), homemade pastas, and fine wine in what the chef calls a "Venetian Nouvelle" style. With only 22 seats, it's tight and homey, yet elegant. They have daily specials, 10 wines by the glass, and one agenda: a great dining experience. Luca, the owner-host, is gracious and passionate about his food. This is one place to let loose and trust your host. Reservations are required for their three seatings: 12:30, 19:00, and 21:30 (€19 pastas, €25 *secondi,* plan on spending €50 for dinner, closed Sun–Mon, just off Campo Santa Maria Formosa at Calle del Mondo Novo 5801, tel. 041-522-7220).

Osteria al Mascaron is where I've gone for years to watch Gigi, Momi, and their food-loving band of ruffians dish up rustic-yet-sumptuous pastas with steamy seafood to salivating foodies. The pastas, while pricey, are for two (it's OK to ask for single portions). The €16 *antipasto misto* plate—have fun pointing—and two glasses of wine make a terrific light meal, and their seafood pastas make beautiful memories (Mon–Sat 12:00–15:00 & 19:00–23:00, closed Sun, reservations smart Fri–Sat, a block past Campo Santa Maria Formosa at Calle Longa Santa Maria Formosa 5225, tel. 041-522-5995).

Fast and Cheap Eats: The Campo Santa Maria Formosa area has plenty of ways to sit and munch cheap. The veggie stand on the square is a fixture. For *döner kebabs* to go, head down Calle Longa to **Peter Pan** (€3.50). For pizza to go, it's **Cip Ciap** (next to Osteria alle Testiere at the bridge).

Near St. Mark's Square

For locations, see the map on page 70.

Dining near St. Mark's Square

The following three places are a few blocks east of St. Mark's Square and offer classy dining experiences. The first two listings are the best canalside dining values I've found in Venice. Both specialize in fish, and have a reasonable-for-the-romantic-setting menu; if you want a canalside seat for dinner, call to reserve it. To reach these from St. Mark's Square, head behind the basilica to Campo San Provolo, then follow Calle Osmarin to Fondamenta dei Greci. To get to the third, head up Chiesa from Campo San Provolo.

Ristorante alla Conchiglia seats its guests at lovely tables that line the sleepy canal (€10 pizzas, big €14 salads, €15 fixed-price meals, daily specials, daily, closed Dec and Jan, Fondamenta dei Greci, tel. 041-528-9095).

Trattoria da Giorgio ai Greci, right next door, is enthusiastically run by Giorgio and sons Davide and chatty Roberto (€17–21 fixed-price meals, daily 12:00–22:30, Ponte dei Greci 4988, tel. 041-528-9780).

Ristorante Antica Sacrestia is a classic restaurant where the owner, Pino, takes a hands-on approach to greeting guests. His staff serve a delightful antipasto spread (€18), are proud of their fish, and offer €20–45 fixed-price meals of fish, meat, or vegetarian dishes. It's also a local favorite for pizza. This is the kind of place where you are best off going with the waiters' suggestions. My readers are welcome to a free *sgroppino* (lemon vodka after-dinner drink) upon request (immediately behind San Giovanni Novo Church at Calle della Sacrestia 4442, Castello, tel. 041-523-0749).

Budget Eateries near St. Mark's Square

Picnicking isn't allowed on St. Mark's Square, but you can legally take your snacks to the nearby Giardinetti Reali, the small park along the waterfront west of the Piazzetta.

"Sandwich Row": On Calle delle Rasse, just steps away from the tourist intensity at St. Mark's Square, is a strip I call "Sandwich Row." Lined with sandwich bars, it's the closest place to St. Mark's to get a decent sandwich at an affordable price with a place to sit down (most places open daily 7:00–24:00, €1 extra to sit; from the Bridge of Sighs, head down the Riva and take the second lane on the left). I particularly like **Birreria Forst,** which serves a selection of meaty €2.70 sandwiches with tasty sauce on wheat bread, or made-to-order sandwiches for around €3.50 (daily 10:00–20:30, air-con, rustic wood tables, Calle delle Rasse 4540, tel. 041-523-0557) and **Bar Verde,** a more modern sandwich bar with fun people-watching views from its corner tables (big €4 sandwiches, splittable €8 salads, fresh pastries including Sicilian cannoli, at the end of Calle delle Rasse, facing Campo S.S. Filippo e Giacomo).

Ristorante alla Basilica, just one street behind St. Mark's Basilica, is a church-run institutional-feeling place serving a solid €13 three-course lunch daily from 11:45 to 15:00 (modern, air-con, Calle degli Albanesi 4255, tel. 041-522-0524).

Rizzo is a convenient bar/*alimentari* market located north of St. Mark's Square on the main drag of Calle dei Fabbri. Grab

€4.50 homemade lasagna and other reasonably priced snacks, such as yogurt, sautéed spinach, or fried sandwiches. It's stand-and-eat only—there's no seating (Mon–Sat 8:00–20:00, closed Sun, Calle dei Fabbri 933A, tel. 041-522-3388).

In Dorsoduro
Near the Accademia Bridge
For locations, see pages 128–129.

Ristorante/Pizzeria Accademia Foscarini, next to the Accademia Bridge and Galleria, offers decent €8–11 pizzas in a great canalside setting. Their toasted *fareiti* sandwich is a local favorite (€6.50 at the table). Though the pizzas may be forgettable, this place is both scenic and practical—on each visit to Venice, I grab a pizza lunch here while I ponder the Grand Canal bustle (May–Oct Wed–Mon 7:00–21:30, Nov–April until 20:00, closed Tue, Dorsoduro 878C, tel. 041-522-7281).

Enoteca Cantine del Vino Già Schiavi is much-loved for its €1 *cicchetti* and €3.50 sandwiches (order from list on board). It's also a good place for a €2 glass of wine and appetizers (Mon–Sat 8:00–20:30, closed Sun, 100 yards from Accademia art museum on San Trovaso canal; facing Accademia, take a right and then a forced left at the canal to the second bridge—S. Trovaso 992, tel. 041-523-0034). You're welcome to enjoy your wine and finger food hanging out at the bar, sitting on the bridge out front, or in the nearby square—which actually has grass. This is primarily a wine shop with great prices for bottles to go—and plastic glasses for picnickers.

Terrazza del Casin dei Nobili, located in Zattere (on the Venice side of the Giudecca Canal), takes full advantage of the warm, romantic evening sun. They serve finely crafted regional specialties with creativity at reasonable prices. The canalside seating is breezy and beautiful, but comes with the rumble of *vaporetti* from the nearby stop. The interior is bright and hip (good €10 pizzas, €10 pastas, €15 *secondi*, €2 cover, Fri–Wed 12:00–23:00, closed Thu, exit vaporetto at Zattere stop and turn left to Zattere 924/5, tel. 041-520-6895). The canalfront Zattere district has a fun youthful vibe, with bars that do a good job of entertaining.

Near Campo San Barnaba
A number of restaurants are near this small square, a short walk from the Accademia. As these are each within a few steps of each other and the energy and atmosphere can vary, I like to survey the options before choosing (although reservations may be necessary later in the evening).

Casin dei Nobili ("Pleasure Palace of Nobles")—related to the Terrazza del Casin dei Nobili, listed above—has a high-energy, informal, modern setting. The patio is filled with simple

Romantic Canalside Settings

Of course, if you want a meal with a canal view, it generally comes with lower quality or a higher price. But if you're aiming for a canalside memory, these places can be great. I've listed the better-value places below, along with advice for coping with the tourist traps.

Near the Rialto Bridge: Several *cicchetti* bars line the Grand Canal, with front tables just off **Campo San Giacometto,** between the market and the Rialto Bridge (described on page 122). You can get good light meals in this area, but these bars don't offer romantic dining per se.

Rialto Bridge Tourist Traps: Venetians are embarrassed by the lousy food and aggressive "service" at the string of joints dominating the best romantic, Grand Canal–fringing real estate in town. Still, if you want to linger over dinner with a view of the most famous bridge and the songs of gondoliers oaring by (and don't mind eating with other tourists), this can be enjoyable. Don't trust the waiter's recommendations for special meals. The budget ideal would be to get a simple pizza or pasta and a drink for €15, and savor the ambience without getting ripped off. But few restaurants will allow you to get

off that easy. To avoid a dispute over the bill, ask if there's a minimum charge—before you sit down (most places have one).

East of St. Mark's Square: **Ristorante alla Conchiglia** and **Trattoria da Giorgio ai Greci,** a few blocks behind St. Mark's, have the best canalside dining I've found anywhere in town (see page 125).

Overlooking the Giudecca Canal: **Terrazza del Casin dei Nobili,** located in Zattere—on the Venice side of the wide Giudecca Canal—gets the warm, romantic evening sun (page 126).

On Fondamenta Nuove with a View of the Open Lagoon: **Ristorante Algiubagio** is a good opportunity to eat well while overlooking the lagoon (page 130).

On Burano: **Ristorante Gatto Nero** sits on a tranquil canal under a tilting bell tower in the pastel townscape of Burano. If you're touring the lagoon and want to enjoy Burano without the crowds, go late and consider a dinner here (see page 91).

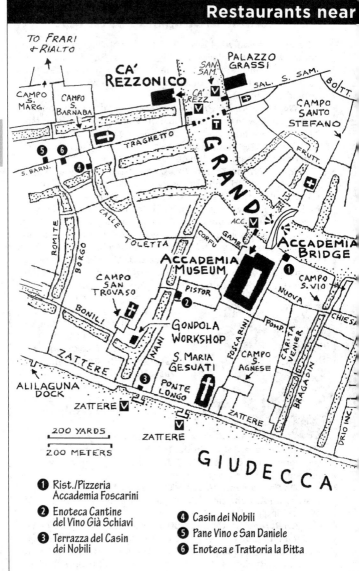

Restaurants near

1. Rist./Pizzeria Accademia Foscarini
2. Enoteca Cantine del Vino Già Schiavi
3. Terrazza del Casin dei Nobili
4. Casin dei Nobili
5. Pane Vino e San Daniele
6. Enoteca e Trattoria la Bitta

the Accademia Bridge

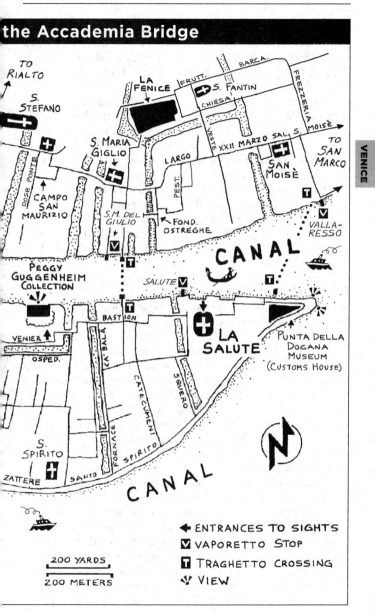

VENICE

Map labels:

TO RIALTO

S. STEFANO

LA FENICE

FRUTT.

BARCA

S. FANTIN

CHIESA

FREZZERIA

S. MARIA GIGLIO

DOSE PONTE

CAMPO SAN MAURIZIO

LARGO

VESTE

PEST.

XXII MARZO SAL. S. MOISÈ

SAN MOISÈ

TO SAN MARCO

S.M. DEL GIULIO

FOND. OSTREGHE

VALLA-RESSO

CANAL

PEGGY GUGGENHEIM COLLECTION

SALUTE

VENIER

OSPED.

BASTION

CA BALA

CATECUMENI

SQUERO

FORNACE

SPIRITO

SANTO

ZATTERE

S. SPIRITO

LA SALUTE

PUNTA DELLA DOGANA MUSEUM (CUSTOMS HOUSE)

CANAL

N

← ENTRANCES TO SIGHTS

▽ VAPORETTO STOP

⊤ TRAGHETTO CROSSING

✷ VIEW

200 YARDS

200 METERS

tables, happy tourists, and inviting €11 daily lunch specials (€12 pastas, €20 *secondi*, good pizzas, and "fantasy salads," Tue–Sun 12:00–15:00 & 19:00–23:00, closed Mon, cash only, a half-block south of Campo San Barnaba at Calle delle Casin 2765, tel. 041-241-1841, Damiano).

Pane Vino e San Daniele is a busy little place that feels real, with the TV on, an enticing blackboard listing the day's specials, and the kitchen action filling its dining room (€7 pastas, €10 salads and *secondi*, Calle Longa San Barnaba 2861, tel. 041-243-9865).

Enoteca e Trattoria la Bitta is dark and woody, with a soft-jazz bistro feel and a small, forgettable back patio. They serve beautifully presented traditional Venetian food with—proudly—no fish. Their helpful waitstaff and small menu is clearly focused on quality. Reservations are required (€10 pastas, €15 *secondi*, dinner only, Mon–Sat 18:30–23:00, closed Sun, cash only, between previous two listings at Calle Longa San Barnaba 2753, tel. 041-523-0531).

Elsewhere in Venice

On Fondamente Nuove: **Ristorante Algiubagio** is a good opportunity to eat well overlooking the lagoon. The name is a combination of the owners' four names—Alberto, Giulio, Barbara, and Giovanna—who strive to impress visitors with quality, creative Venetian cuisine made using the best ingredients. Reserve a table on the lagoon facing the island of San Michele or in their classy cantina dining room (€16 pastas, €25 *secondi*, €3 cover, Wed–Mon 12:00–15:00 & 19:00–22:30, closed Tue, to the left of the vaporetto dock as you face the water at Fondamenta Nuove 5039, Cannaregio, tel. 041-523-6084). This is a convenient place to eat if you're taking the vaporetto out to the islands in the lagoon (described on page 89; see map on page 90).

Near Campo Santa Maria Nova: **Osteria da Alberto,** with excellent daily specials, €13 seafood plates, €10 pastas, a good house wine, and a woody and characteristic interior, is one of my standbys. It's smart to reserve at night—I'd request a table in the front (Mon–Sat 12:00–15:00 & 18:00–23:00, closed Sun, midway between Campo S.S. Apostoli and Campo S.S. Giovanni e Paolo, next to Ponte de la Panada on Calle Larga Giacinto Gallina, tel. 041-523-8153, run by Graziano and Giovanni).

Near the Train Station: There are piles of eateries near the station. The **train station food circus** in the station is quite good, with peaceful garden seating out back. A block away is the efficient and economic **Brek,** a popular chain self-service cafeteria (daily 11:30–22:00, head left as you leave the station and walk about 50 yards past the bridge to Rio Terra Lista di Spagna 124).

Cheap Meals

The keys to eating affordably in Venice are pizza, bars/cafés, and picnics. *Panini* and *tramezzini* (sandwiches, described on page 32) are sold fast and cheap at bars everywhere and can stave off mid-morning hunger. There's a great "sandwich row" of cheap cafés near St. Mark's Square (see page 125). For speed, value, and ambience, you can get a filling plate of typically Venetian appetizers at nearly any bar. For budget eating, I like stand-up mini-meals at *cicchetti* **bars** best (see page 120).

Picnics

The **produce market** that sprawls for a few blocks just past the Rialto Bridge is a fun place to assemble a picnic (best Mon–Sat 8:00–13:00, closed Sun). The adjacent fish market is wonderfully slimy (closed Sun–Mon). Side lanes in this area are speckled with fine little hole-in-the-wall munchie bars, bakeries, and cheese shops. Remember that the only legal place to picnic in public in Venice is Giardinetti Reali, the waterfront park near St. Mark's Square.

Gelato

La Boutique del Gelato, as lines attest, is considered the best *gelateria* in Venice. They dish up generous €1.20 scoops (daily 10:00–22:00, closed Dec–Jan, located on map on page 119, leave Campo Santa Maria Formosa from the corner with the bell tower, cross the bridge, turn right on Salizada San Lio, and find it next to Hotel Bruno at #5727).

On St. Mark's Square, there are two venerable *gelaterie:* **Gran Caffè Lavena** (daily until 24:00, first café to left of the Clock Tower, behind the first orchestra) and **Todaro Gelateria** (on the corner of the Piazzetta, near the Grand Canal and just under St. Theodore slaying the dragon, tel. 041-528-5165).

Venice Connections

From Venice by Train to: Padua (2/hour, 30 minutes), **Vicenza** (2/hour, 1 hour), **Verona** (roughly 2/hour, 1.5 hours), **Ravenna** (hourly, 3–4 hours, transfer in Ferrara or Bologna), **Florence** (hourly, 2–3 hours, may transfer in Bologna; often crowded so make reservations), **Dolomites** (to Bolzano about hourly, 3–4 hours, transfer in

Verona; catch bus from Bolzano into mountains), **Milan** (hourly, 2.5 hours), **Cinque Terre/Monterosso** (almost hourly, 6–7 hours, with 1–3 changes), **Cinque Terre/La Spezia** (almost hourly, 5–6 hours, with 1–3 changes), **Rome** (hourly, 3.5 hours, may transfer in Bologna, overnight possible), **Naples** (almost hourly, 5.5–7 hours, with changes in Bologna or Rome), **Brindisi** (7/day, 9–14 hours, most change in Bologna; 1 direct night train, 11 hours), **Bern** (3/day, 6 hours, change in Milan or Brig), **Munich** (4–6/day, 7 hours, change in Verona; 1 direct night train, 8 hours), **Paris** (3/day, 10–16 hours with change in Milan, may also transfer in Basel or Zürich; 1 direct night train, 12.5 hours, important to reserve ahead), **Ljubljana** (3/day, 7.5 hours—take bus from Piazzale Roma to Villach in Austria, then transfer to train; 1 direct night train, 4 hours, but arrives at 2:00 in the morning), and **Vienna** (3/day, 8 hours—take bus from Piazzale Roma to Villach in Austria, then transfer to train; 1 direct night train, 11 hours).

Airports

Venice has two airports—Marco Polo and the small Treviso. For budget flights within Europe, easyJet uses Marco Polo, while Ryanair, Wizz Air, and Blue use Treviso. (For more on budget carriers, see page 975.)

Marco Polo Airport

Venice's modern airport is on the mainland, six miles north of the city. It's a sleek wood beam–and-glass terminal, with a TI (daily 9:00–21:00), ATMs, car-rental agencies, a bank, a post office, and a few shops and eateries. For flight information, call tel. 041-260-9260, visit www.veniceairport.com, or ask at your hotel for help.

There are three ways to get between the airport (which is on the mainland) and downtown Venice (on an island):
- Alilaguna water bus—medium in speed and cost
- Water taxis—fastest and most expensive
- Buses to Piazzale Roma—slowest and least expensive

Each of these options is explained in detail below. The Alilaguna water buses are the simplest way to reach most of this book's recommended hotels—except those near the train station, in which case the bus to Piazzale Roma may be the better choice.

When flying out of Venice, travelers are advised to get to the airport two hours before departure (even for flights within Europe), so allow yourself plenty of time.

Alilaguna Water Bus

These boats make the scenic (if slow) journey across the lagoon, shuttling passengers between the airport and a number of different stops on the island of Venice (€13, 60–90-minute trip depending on your destination; boats leave every 30–60 minutes). There are several lines (blue, red, orange), and it can get confusing. But if you know what stop you want, it's easy to find the line that goes there.

Here are some key stops in Venice:
• San Marco–Giardinetti—Hotels west of St. Mark's Square
• San Zaccaria—Hotels east of St. Mark's Square
• Zattere—Dorsoduro hotels
• Guglie—Hotels near Santa Lucia train station
• Rialto—Hotels near the Rialto Bridge
• Fondamenta Nuove—Hotels on the north side of the city, on the fish's "back"

From the Airport to Venice: The airport's boat dock is an eight-minute walk from the terminal. Exit the arrivals terminal and turn left, following signs along a paved, level covered sidewalk (easy for wheeled bags). You can buy tickets at the airport's TI or the "Public Transport" window (often crowded), at vending machines inside the airport terminal (cash only), or simply at the ticket booth at the dock. Any ticket-seller can tell you which line to catch to get to your destination. Boats from the airport run from roughly 7:00 to midnight.

From Venice to the Airport: Give yourself plenty of time to make your flight. Ask your hotelier what dock and what line is best. Boats start leaving Venice as early as 3:40 so that passengers can catch early flights.

For a full schedule, see the Alilaguna website (www.alilaguna .it), call 041-523-5775, ask your hotelier, scan the schedules posted at Alilaguna docks, or ask at the TI. Note that the Alilaguna water bus is not part of the ACTV vaporetto system, so it is not covered by city transit passes.

Water Taxi
Luxury taxi speedboats zip directly between the airport and your hotel, getting you within steps of your final destination in about 30 minutes. The official price is €100 for up to four people, though you'll often get a higher quote (around €110)—talk them down. A taxi can be a smart investment for small groups and those with an early departure. From the airport, arrange your ride at the airport's water-taxi desk or at the dock (next to the Alilaguna dock). From Venice, book your taxi trip through your hotel the day before you leave.

Airport Shuttle Buses
Buses take you across the bridge from the mainland to the island, dropping you at the "mouth" of the fish, on a square called Piazzale Roma. From there, you can catch a vaporetto down the

Grand Canal—convenient for hotels near the Rialto Bridge and St. Mark's Square.

Two companies compete for the airport shuttle business. The ATVO "Venezia Express" and the ACTV bus #5 both connect the airport and Piazzale Roma (€2.50–3, 20–40 minutes, 2/hour, 5:00–24:00, www.atvo.it or www.actv.it). The ATVO is slightly faster and pricier.

From the Airport to Venice: Both buses leave from just outside the arrivals terminal. Buy tickets at the TI, from ticket machines in the terminal or outside next to the buses, or sometimes directly from the driver. Check which ticket you are buying—ATVO tickets are not valid on ACTV buses and vice versa.

When you arrive at Piazzale Roma, you'll find the vaporetto dock by walking to the six-story white building, then taking a right. To go down the Grand Canal, catch either the slow vaporetto #1 or faster #2 toward St. Mark's Square (€6.50 for either boat; for more info, see "Getting Around Venice," page 52). To reach Zattere (and the Dorsoduro hotels), go the other direction on #51. If you're confused, a local commuter or the ticket-seller can help you.

If your hotel is near the train station, you can walk there from Piazzale Roma across the Calatrava Bridge.

From Venice to the Airport: Buses leave Piazzale Roma between 5:00 and 20:40, departing from the northeast corner of the lot near Hotel Santa Chiara.

Other Services

Private Shuttle Bus: Treviso Car Service offers a private minivan service between Marco Polo Airport and Piazzale Roma (€50 per minivan, seats up to 8, tel. 338-204-4390, www.trevisocarservice .com, Andrea).

Connecting to Padua: There's a cheap and easy SITA bus connection from Venice's Marco Polo Airport to Padua's bus station (buy €4.20 ticket from "Public Transport" desk inside airport near TI or pay driver €5, €1/bag in advance, €2/bag on board; 2/hour, 1 hour; as you exit the airport, catch just beyond platform 3 at the far right of the buses, www.sitabus.it).

Treviso Airport

Several budget airlines, such as Ryanair and Blue, use Treviso Airport, 12 miles northwest of Venice (www.trevisoairport.it). Regular ATVO buses take you to Piazzale Roma (€6, 2–3/hour, 1.25 hours, www.atvo.it). Buy your tickets at the ATVO desk in the airport and stamp them on the bus. The buses also stop at Mestre's train station. Treviso Car Service offers minivan service to Piazzale Roma (€55 per minivan; see "Private Shuttle Bus" listing above).

Venice Cruise-Ship Terminal

Cruise ships visiting Venice dock at the Stazione Marittima, which is roughly between the Tronchetto parking garage and Santa Lucia train station. The terminal forms the "mouth" of Venice's fish shape. The San Basilio vaporetto stop is the nearest to the cruise ships, and vaporetto #2 provides regular boat service between the terminal and St. Mark's Square. At night, it is replaced by vaporetto #N. Tickets can be bought from machines or on board (€6.50, buy immediately before you sit down to avoid a fine).

For those moving on from Venice, the new People Mover monorail (€1) links Marittima with Piazzale Roma, which has bus connections to Marco Polo Airport (see page 132) and is also near the Santa Lucia train station (see page 42).

VENICE

NEAR VENICE

• *Padua* • *Verona* • *Ravenna*

Venice is just one of many towns in the Italian region of Veneto (VEN-eh-toh), but few visitors venture off the lagoon. Several important towns and possible side trips, in addition to the lakes and the Dolomites, make zipping directly from Venice to Milan (or Florence) a route strewn with temptation.

Planning Your Time

The towns of Padua, Verona, and Ravenna are great stops. Each gives visitors a low-key slice of Italy that complements the urbanity of Venice, Florence, and Rome. If you can't make it to all three, pick the one that most interests you. Art-lovers will want to head to Padua to see Giotto's celebrated Scrovegni Chapel, or to Ravenna for its sumptuous Byzantine mosaics. History buffs should see the impressive Roman ruins in Verona. Verona is also the pick for star-crossed lovers retracing Romeo and Juliet's steps. Architecture fans could consider a quick trip to Palladio-designed Vicenza, located about halfway between Padua and Verona.

Towns near Venice

Visiting Padua and Verona couldn't be easier:

They are roughly 30–45 minutes apart on the Venice–Milan line. Spending a day town-hopping between Venice and Milan—with stops at Padua and Verona—is exciting and efficient. Trains run frequently enough to allow flexibility and little wasted time. Of the towns included in this chapter, only Ravenna (2.5 hours from Padua and 3–3.5 hours from Florence) is not on the main Venice–Milan train line.

If you're Padua-bound, remember that you need to reserve ahead to see the Scrovegni Chapel. Mondays are not ideal for a trip to Verona, when most sights are closed in the morning, or Vicenza, where the major sights are closed.

Padua

Living under Venetian rule for four centuries seemed only to sharpen Padua's independent spirit. Nicknamed "the brain of Veneto," Padua (Padova in Italian) has a prestigious university (founded in 1222) that hosted Galileo, Copernicus, Dante, and Petrarch. Padua's old town center is elegantly arcaded, filled with students, and sprinkled with surprises. And Padua's museums and churches hold their own in Italy's artistic big league.

Planning Your Time: Padua in Six Hours

Day-trippers can do a quick but enjoyable blitz of Padua—including a visit to the Scrovegni Chapel—in six hours. Trains come and go twice an hour, making for a great day trip from Venice. Once in Padua, everything is a 10-minute walk or quick tram ride apart.

Your Scrovegni Chapel reservation will dictate the order of your sightseeing (see "Reservations" on page 147). When planning your day, also consider these factors: The station has a reliable baggage check desk; the market is vibrant in the morning, dead in the evening; student life is best at the university late in the day; and the Basilica of St. Anthony is open all day, but the reliquary chapel closes from 12:40 to 14:30.

Ideally, I'd do it this way: 9:00—Market action and sightseeing in town center, 11:00—Basilica of St. Anthony, 14:00—Scrovegni Chapel tour.

Orientation to Padua

Padua's main tourist sights lie on a north–south axis through the heart of the city, from the train station to Scrovegni Chapel to the market squares (the center of town) to the Basilica of St. Anthony. It's roughly a 10-minute walk between each of these sights, or about 30 minutes from end to end. Padua's wonderful single tram line makes lacing things together quick and easy (see "Getting Around Padua," later).

Tourist Information

Padua has three TIs: at the **train station** (Mon–Sat 9:15–19:00, Sun 9:00–12:30, tel. 049-875-2077), in the **center** (across the street from Caffè Pedrocchi, Mon–Sat 9:00–13:30 & 15:00–19:00, closed Sun, tel. 049-876-7927), and at the **Basilica of St. Anthony** (April–Oct daily 9:00–13:30 & 15:00–18:00, closed Nov–March, tel. 049-875-3087). Pick up a map, a list of sights, and the seasonal *Padova Today* entertainment listing. The free I-PADova audio tour is creative and works really well. You can download it for free from their website (www.turismopadova.it), or just borrow one of their MP3 players and follow any of the five routes in town.

The **Padova Card** gives you (and one child under 14) unlimited tram travel, free parking, various discounts, and entry to all the recommended sights in Padua, except the university's Anatomy Theater and the Basilica of St. Anthony's Oratory of St. George. While the card includes the Scrovegni Chapel, you still need to make a reservation to enter. Padova Cards are also sold at all TIs, at included sights, and online at www.padovacard.it (€15/48 hours, €20/72 hours).

Arrival in Padua

By Train: The station is a user-friendly shopping mall with whatever you might need (Despar **supermarket** open daily 7:00–21:00). **WCs** and **baggage deposit** (€4, daily 6:30–18:00, bring your passport) are near track 1.

You can buy train tickets or make seat reservations in the station (at the desk or, to avoid the line, at the gray-and-yellow automatic ticket machines). Leonardi Viaggi-Turismo offers the same services for a small fee a block away (Mon–Fri 9:00–13:00 & 14:30–19:00, Sat 9:00–13:00, closed Sun, up the main drag in front of the station, Corso del Popolo 14, tel. 049-650-455).

The easiest way to get downtown is to simply hop on Padua's handy **tram** (see "Getting Around Padua," later). Leaving the station, the tram stop is 30 yards to the right at the foot of the bridge (avoid the shady characters around here at night). A **taxi** into town (a good option after dark) costs about €8.

By Long-Distance Bus: If you're arriving in Padua by bus (including buses from Venice's Marco Polo Airport), you'll end up at the main bus station at Piazzale Boschetti, several blocks north of the Scrovegni Chapel. From there, Via Gozzi leads into town.

Helpful Hints

Pronunciation: You say Padua (PAD-joo-wah), they say Padova (PAH-doh-vah).

Internet Access: Oddly, for a college town, Padua has few Internet cafés. The central TI offers free access for 15 minutes (if you fill out a form and show your passport). You can also try **Internet Point** (€2/hour, Mon–Sat 10:00–24:00, Sun 16:00–24:00, Via Altinate 145, 5-minute walk from Porta Altinate, tel. 049-659-292).

Bookstore: Feltrinelli's International Bookstore, with books in English, is near the university (daily 9:00–19:30, Via San Francesco 7, tel. 049-875-4630).

Local Guide: Charming **Cristina Pernechele** is a great teacher (€105/half-day, mobile 338-495-5453, cristina@pernechele.eu).

Best Gelato: People line up at *gelateria* **Grom**'s two locations for its fresh ingredients and honest flavors (at Via Roma 101 and on Piazza dei Signori).

Getting Around Padua

While a tangle of buses serve Padua, visitors should pretend there is only the **tram** and rely on it. There's just one line, which stresslessly and efficiently connects everything you care about (€1.10 ticket good for 75 minutes, departs every 8 minutes, www.trampadova .it). If you see tracks in the street, you know it's the tram.

Before boarding, note the tram direction on posted schedules and above the front window (Pontevigodarzere is northbound, Capolinia Sud is southbound). Stops that matter include the following: Stazione FS (train station), Eremitani (Scrovegni Chapel), Ponti Romani (old town center, market squares, university), Tito Livio (ghetto, old town center, Hotel Majestic Toscanelli), Santo (Basilica of St. Anthony and neighborhood hotels), and Prato della Valle.

You'll see **hop-on, hop-off buses** at the station and around town. While these ubiquitous tourist transporters make sense in some places, they're not worth the time or money in Padua.

Sights in Padua

▲▲▲Basilica of St. Anthony

Friar Anthony of Padua, "Christ's perfect follower and a tireless preacher of the Gospel," is buried here. Construction of this impressive Romanesque/Gothic church (with its Byzantine-style

NEAR VENICE

Padua

400 YARDS TO TRAIN STATION

TRIESTE ⓣ

VIA GARIBALDI

CARMINE

GIOTTO

CHAPEL ENTRANCE

SCROVEGNI CHAPEL

SCROV. TICKETS

PALAZZO ZUCKERMANN

EREMITANI ⓣ

V. FERMO

P. ERM.

TABARELLA

CORSO

P. INS. 28 APR.

V. VERDI

V. EM. FIL.

VIA

PONTE ROMAN

VIA S. LUCIA

② ✚

⑲ ⑪

PIAZZA DEI SIGNORI

PZZA. FRUTTA

⑮ ⓣ

PIAZZA CAVOUR

⑬

BAPTISTERY

TADI

⑧ V. MANIN

P.R. ⑫

PZZA. ERBE

②⓪

⑭ ⓘ

Post

PZZA. DUOMO

⑳

V. 8 FEB.

DUOMO ✚

SONCIN

⑨

⑩ S OLF.

VIA VESCOVADO

①

MARSALA

V. ROMA

P. TITO LIVIO

ANTENORE

TITO LIVIO ⓣ

V. STAMPA

V. LIVIO

⑲

VIA S

VIA

20 SETT.

V. S. CHIARA

V. RUDENA

VIA DEL SANTO

V. ⑯

⑥

V. ROGATI

VIA UMB.

RIV. RUZZANTE

STATUE

MARKET SQUARES w/ PALAZZO RAGIONE (BETWEEN THEM)

ⓘ

⑦

VIA ALEARDI

V. SEM.

TORRESINO

SANTO

ⓘ

③ ④

⑱

DCH

✚

PRATO DELLA VALLE ⓣ

BELLUDI

PRATO DELLA VALLE

↓ TO ⑰

N

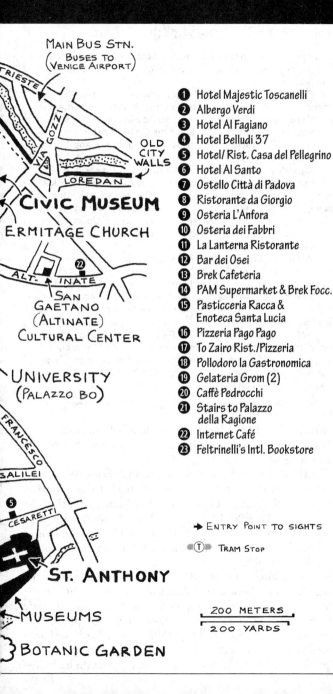

MAIN BUS STN.
(BUSES TO
VENICE AIRPORT)

TRIESTE

VIA GOZZI

OLD CITY WALLS

LOREDAN

CIVIC MUSEUM

ERMITAGE CHURCH

ALT- INATE
SAN GAETANO
(ALTINATE)
CULTURAL CENTER

UNIVERSITY
(PALAZZO BO)

FRANCESCO

GALILEI

CESARETTI

ST. ANTHONY

MUSEUMS

BOTANIC GARDEN

❶ Hotel Majestic Toscanelli
❷ Albergo Verdi
❸ Hotel Al Fagiano
❹ Hotel Belludi 37
❺ Hotel/ Rist. Casa del Pellegrino
❻ Hotel Al Santo
❼ Ostello Città di Padova
❽ Ristorante da Giorgio
❾ Osteria L'Anfora
❿ Osteria dei Fabbri
⓫ La Lanterna Ristorante
⓬ Bar dei Osei
⓭ Brek Cafeteria
⓮ PAM Supermarket & Brek Focc.
⓯ Pasticceria Racca &
   Enoteca Santa Lucia
⓰ Pizzeria Pago Pago
⓱ To Zairo Rist./Pizzeria
⓲ Pollodoro la Gastronomica
⓳ Gelateria Grom (2)
⓴ Caffè Pedrocchi
㉑ Stairs to Palazzo
   della Ragione
㉒ Internet Café
㉓ Feltrinelli's Intl. Bookstore

➜ ENTRY POINT TO SIGHTS

◖T◗ TRAM STOP

200 METERS
200 YARDS

NEAR VENICE

St. Anthony of Padua
(1195–1231)

One of Christendom's most popular saints, Anthony is known as a powerful speaker, a miracle worker, and the finder of lost articles.

Born in Lisbon to a rich, well-educated family, his life changed at age 25, when he saw the mutilated bodies of some Franciscan martyrs. Their sacrifice inspired him to join the poor Franciscans and dedicate his life to Christ. He moved to Italy and lived in a cave, studying, meditating, and barely speaking to anyone.

One day, he joined his fellow monks for a service. The appointed speaker failed to show up, so Anthony was asked to say a few off-the-cuff words to the crowd. He started slowly, but, filled with the Spirit, he became more confident and amazed the audience with his eloquence. Up in Assisi, St. Francis heard about Anthony and sent him on a whirlwind speaking tour.

Anthony had a strong voice, knew several languages, had encyclopedic knowledge of theology, and could speak spontaneously as the Spirit moved him. It's said he even stood on the shores of the Adriatic Sea in Rimini and enticed a school of fish to listen. Anthony also was known as a prolific miracle worker.

In 1230, Anthony retired to Padua, where he founded a monastery and initiated reforms for the poor. An illness cut his life short at age 36. Anthony said, "Happy is the man whose words issue from the Spirit and not from himself!"

domes) started immediately after St. Anthony's death in 1231. And for nearly 800 years, his remains and this glorious church have attracted pilgrims to Padua.

Cost and Hours: The basilica is free and open daily in summer 6:15–19:45, in winter 6:30–18:45. Note that the following sights within the basilica close around lunchtime: Chapel of the Reliquaries (daily 8:00–12:40 & 14:30–19:30, shorter hours in winter), museum (€2.50, daily 9:00–13:00 & 14:30–18:00, shorter hours and closed Mon in winter), and the Oratory of St. George (€2.50, daily 9:00–12:30 & 14:30–19:00).

Information: A modest dress code is enforced inside the basilica. A helpful information desk with Anthony-related pamphlets is in the cloisters, on the right side of the church (daily 8:30–13:00 & 14:00–18:30, shorter hours in winter, public WC nearby, Santo tram stop, tel. 049-878-9722, www.basilicadelsanto.org). If the information desk doesn't have English versions of the pamphlets—one on the saint's life and another about the basilica—

head to the Chapel of the Reliquaries and offer a donation. A TI is on the square facing the church.

Basilica Exterior

St. Anthony looks down from the red-brick facade and blesses all. He holds a book, a symbol of all the knowledge he accumulated as

a quiet monk before starting his preaching career.

Guarding the church is Donatello's life-size equestrian statue of the Venetian mercenary general, Gattamelata. Though it looks like a thousand other man-on-a-horse statues, it was a landmark in Italy's budding Renaissance—the first life-size secular equestrian statue cast out of bronze in a thousand years. The church is technically outside of Italy. When you pass the banisters that mark its property line, you're passing into Vatican territory.

Interior

Entering the basilica, grab a pew in the center of the nave. Sit and appreciate the space. Gaze past the crowds and through the incense haze to Donatello's glorious crucifix rising from the altar, and realize that this is one of the most important pilgrimage sites in Christendom.

Along with the crucifix, Donatello's bronze statues—Mary with Padua's six favorite saints—grace the high altar. Late in his career, the great Florentine sculptor spent more than a decade in Padua (1444–1455), creating the altar and Gattamelata.

St. Anthony's Tomb

Head to the left side of the nave to find the gleaming marble masterpiece that is the focus of the pilgrim visitors—the tomb of St. Anthony. Pilgrims file slowly through this side chapel around the tomb, so focused on the saint that they hardly notice the nine fine marble reliefs. These Renaissance masterpieces were carved during the 16th century, and show scenes and miracles from the life of the saint. As you enjoy each scene, notice the Renaissance mastery of realism and 3-D perspective and the intricate frames celebrating life with a burst of exuberance.

First Relief: This depicts St. Anthony receiving the Franciscan tunic. The open door illustrates the new ability to show depth with math. The cityscape above is Padua in about 1500.

Second Relief: A jealous husband has angrily stabbed his wife. Notice the musculature, the emotion, and the determination in the faces of loved ones. Above, Anthony intercedes with God to bring the woman back to life. Notice the etchings of familiar Paduan architecture at the top of the sculptures.

Third Relief: Above this panel, which shows Anthony bringing a young man back to life, is the Palazzo della Ragione, looking as it still does today.

Fourth Relief: This scene, by the famous Florentine sculptor Jacopo Sansovino, shows three generations: a dead girl, her distraught mom, and a grandmother who's seen it all. Of course, Anthony will eventually change the mood, but right now it's pretty dire. Above is a relief of this basilica.

Fifth Relief: A fisherman holds a net, sadly having retrieved a drowned boy. The mother looks at Anthony, who blesses and revives the boy. Across from here is the saint's actual tomb. Under thoughtful lighting, it reads *Corpus S. Antonii*. Letters of prayer are dropped behind the iron grill.

Sixth Relief: This shows "the miracle of the miser's heart." Anthony's helper dips his hand into a moneylender's side to demonstrate the absence of his heart. At his foot, the square tray with coins and a heart illustrates the scriptural verse "for where your treasure is, there your heart will be also."

Seventh Relief: Anthony holds the foot of a young man who confessed to kicking his mother. Taking a lesson from the saint about respecting your mother a little too literally, the man has cut off his own foot. The hysterical mother implores Anthony's help, and the saint's prayers to God enable him to reattach the foot.

Stand in the corner for a moment, observing the passionate devotion that pilgrims and Paduans alike have for Anthony. Touching his tomb or kneeling in prayer, the faithful believe Anthony is their protector—a confidant and intercessor for the poor. And they believe he works miracles. Believers leave offerings, votives, and written prayers to ask for help or to give thanks for miracles they believe Anthony has performed. By putting their hands on his tomb while saying silent prayers, pilgrims show devotion to Anthony and feel the saint's presence.

Popular Anthony is the patron saint of dozens of things: travelers, amputees, donkeys, pregnant women, infertile women, flight attendants, and pig farmers. Most pilgrims ask for his help in his role as the "finder of things"—from lost car keys to a life companion.

Eighth Relief: This scene makes the point that—unlike St. Francis, who was a rowdy youth—Anthony was holy even as a child. He tosses the glass (representing his faith), which, rather than shattering, breaks the marble floor.

Ninth Relief: An angry husband accuses his wife of cheating. The wife asks Anthony to identify her baby's father. Anthony asks the child, who speaks to assure all that the husband is his real dad and mother was not messing around. Whew!

Between scenes eight and nine, go into the next room, where you'll enter the oldest part of the church—the original chapel, where Anthony was first buried in 1231. To the left of the altar, note the fine (and impressively realistic for the 14th century) view of medieval Padua, with this church outside the wall (finished by 1300 and still looking as it does today).

Below the cityscape, in a circa-1380 fresco, Anthony on his cloud promises he'll watch over his town. Because people wanted to be buried near a saint, graves lie all around. If you could afford it, this was about the best piece of real estate a dead person could want. (The practice was ended with Napoleonic reforms in 1806.)

Chapel of the Reliquaries

Continue your circuit of the church by going behind the altar into the apse, to the Chapel of the Reliquaries. The most prized relic is in the glass case at center stage—Anthony's tongue. When Anthony's remains were exhumed 32 years after his death (1263), his body had decayed to dust, but his tongue was found miraculously unspoiled and red in color. How appropriate for the great preacher who, full of the Spirit, couldn't stop talking about God.

Work clockwise around the chapel, starting under the dome in front of the staircase at St. Anthony's holy, and holey, tunic *(tonaca)*. His rough-hewn wood coffin is on the left wall. His pillow—a comfy rock—is up the stairs (chest level in first glass case). The center display case contains (top to bottom) the Saint's lower jaw *(il mento)*, his uncorrupted tongue *(lingua)*, and, finally, his vocal chords *(apparato vocale)*, discovered intact when his remains were examined in 1981. In the last display case, a fragment of the True Cross *(la croce)* is held in a precious crucifix reliquary.

Above the relics is the *Glorification of St. Anthony*. In this Baroque fantasy, a cloud of angels and giddy *putti* tumble to the left and right in jubilation as they celebrate his presence in heaven.

Cloisters

From the right side of the nave as you face the altar, follow signs to *chiostro;* from outside, find signs on the right side of the church. The main cloister is dominated by an exceptionally bushy magnolia tree, planted in 1810, and by the graves of the most illustrious Padovans, such as Gabriel Fallopius, the scientist who gave his name to his discovery, the Fallopian tube.

Wander around the various cloisters. Picnic tables invite pilgrims and tourists to enjoy meals within the solitude of one of the cloisters (it's covered and suitable even when rainy, also has WCs). The **multimedia exhibit** on the life of St. Anthony is a bit kitschy, as pilgrimage multimedia exhibits tend to be (30 minutes, you move three times as you use headphones to listen to the story of each tableau).

At the far end, a fascinating little **museum** is filled with votives and folk art recounting miracles attributed to Anthony. The abbreviation *PGR* you'll see on many votives stands for *per grazia ricevuta*—for answered prayers.

Oratory of St. George

The small but sumptuous Oratory of St. George faces the little square in front of the basilica. The oratory ("ora" means prayer) is not actually a church, though it's certainly a fine place to pray—it's filled with vivid circa-1370 frescoes showing scenes not of Anthony, but from the life of St. Catherine. Because many lovers credit St. Anthony with finding their partners—and this is the closest place to St. Anthony where you can be married—it's popular for weddings. While you can see it all from the door, paying the entry fee lets you sit and enjoy this peaceful spot.

Near the Basilica

Prato della Valle—The square is 150 yards southwest of the basilica (down Via Luca Belludi). Once a Roman theater and later

Anthony's preaching grounds, this square claims to be the largest in Italy. It's a pleasant 400-yard-long oval-shaped piazza with fountains, walkways, dozens of statues of Padua's eminent citizens, and grass. It's also a lively **market** scene: fruit and vegetables (Mon–Fri 8:00–13:00), clothing, shoes, and household goods (Sat 8:00–19:00), and antiques (third Sun 8:00–19:00).

Botanical Garden (Orto Botanico di Padova)—Green thumbs appreciate this nearly five-acre botanical garden, which contains the university's vast collection of rare plants. Founded in 1545 to cultivate medicinal plants, it's the world's oldest academic botanical garden still in its original location. A visitors center—in a little cottage to the right of the garden's entrance—houses models of the garden's layout and computer programs that describe the history and composition of the garden in English.

Cost and Hours: Garden—€4; April–Oct daily 9:00–13:00 & 15:00–19:00; Nov–March Mon–Sat 9:00–13:00, closed Sun; entrance 150 yards south of Basilica of St. Anthony—with your back to the facade, take a hard left, Santo tram stop, tel. 049-827-2119, www.ortobotanico.unipd.it.

▲▲▲Scrovegni Chapel (Cappella degli Scrovegni)

You must make reservations in advance to see this glorious recently renovated chapel (see "Reservations," below). Wallpapered with

Giotto's beautifully preserved cycle of nearly 40 frescoes, the chapel holds scenes depicting the lives of Jesus and Mary.

Painted by Giotto and his assistants from 1303 to 1305 and considered by many to be the first piece of modern art, this work makes it clear: Europe was breaking out of the Middle Ages. A sign of the Renaissance to come, Giotto placed real people in real scenes, expressing real human emotions. These frescoes were radical for their 3-D nature, lively colors, light sources, emotion, and humanism.

The chapel was built out of guilt for white-collar crimes. Reginaldo degli Scrovegni (skroh-VEHN-yee) charged sky-high interest rates at a time when that practice was forbidden by the Church. He even caught the attention of Dante, who placed him in one of the levels of hell in his *Inferno*. When Reginaldo died, the Church denied him a Christian burial. His son Enrico tried to buy forgiveness for his father's sins by building this superb chapel. After seeing Giotto's frescoes for the Franciscan monks of St. Anthony, Enrico knew he'd found the right artist to decorate the interior (and, he hoped, to save his father's soul).

Cost and Hours: €13 combo-ticket with Civic Museum (and its worthwhile Pinacoteca and Multimedia Room). The chapel is open Mon 9:00–19:00, Tue–Sun 9:00–22:00 except off-season until 19:00. When the Civic Museum is closed—after 19:00 and on Monday—tickets are €8. The Multimedia Room, adjacent to the Civic Museum, is open daily 9:00–19:00.

Entry Times: Every 15 minutes (on the quarter-hour), the chapel opens for 15-minute visits. After 19:00, the chapel opens every 20 minutes for 20-minute visits (last entry at 21:40).

Reservations: To protect the paintings from excess humidity, only 25 people are allowed in the chapel at a time. Prepaid reservations are required. You can reserve online at www.cappella degliscrovegni.it (also sells Padova Cards—described on page 138). If you reserve by phone, you may need to be persistent and call several times (tel. 049-201-0020; booking office open Mon–Fri 9:00–19:00, Sat 9:00–13:00, closed Sun, provide your credit-card number and hotel telephone number where you can be reached if necessary the day before your visit).

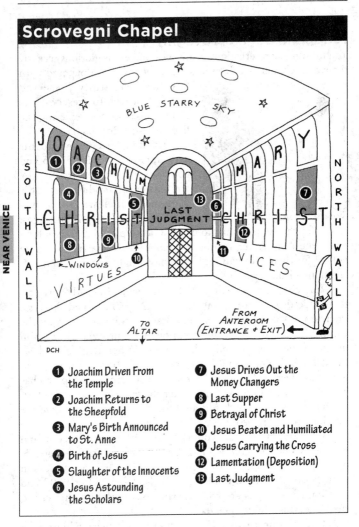

Scrovegni Chapel

1. Joachim Driven From the Temple
2. Joachim Returns to the Sheepfold
3. Mary's Birth Announced to St. Anne
4. Birth of Jesus
5. Slaughter of the Innocents
6. Jesus Astounding the Scholars
7. Jesus Drives Out the Money Changers
8. Last Supper
9. Betrayal of Christ
10. Jesus Beaten and Humiliated
11. Jesus Carrying the Cross
12. Lamentation (Deposition)
13. Last Judgment

Book your visit at least 48 hours in advance. It's sometimes possible to buy a ticket for the same day at the ticket office, but don't count on it. (A sign on the desk indicates the next available time.)

Getting There: From the train station, it's a 10–15-minute walk, or a quick tram ride to the Eremitani stop.

Getting In: You'll be instructed to pick up your tickets at the ticket office at least an hour before your visit. In practice, I've found that you can arrive later, but give yourself a minimum of 30 minutes to weather any commotion at the desk. Present your confirmation number, verify your time, and pick up your ticket.

While waiting for your reserved time, blitz the Civic Museum and Multimedia Room (described later). Read the chapel description (below) before you enter, since you'll only have a short time in the chapel itself.

Be at the chapel doors (well-signed, 100 yards to the right of the ticket office as you exit) at least five minutes before your scheduled visit. The chapel doors are automatic, and if you're even a minute late, you'll forfeit your visit and have to rebook and repay to enter.

At your appointed time, you first enter an anteroom to watch a very instructive 15-minute video (with English subtitles) and to establish humidity levels before continuing into the chapel (no photos are allowed). Although you have only a short visit inside the chapel, it is divine. You're inside a Giotto time capsule, looking back at an artist ahead of his time.

Giotto's Frescoes in the Scrovegni Chapel

Giotto painted the entire chapel in 200 working days over two years, but you'll get only 15 minutes to see it.

As you enter the long, narrow chapel, look straight to the far end—the rear wall is covered with Giotto's big *Last Judgment*. Christ in a bubble is flanked by crowds of saints and by scenes of heaven and hell. This is the final, climactic scene of the story told in the chapel's 38 panels—the three-generation history of Jesus, his mother Mary, and Mary's parents.

The story begins with Jesus' grandparents, on the long south wall (with the windows) in the upper-left corner. ❶ In the first frame, a priest scolds the man who will be Mary's father (Joachim, with the halo) and kicks him out of the temple for the sin of being childless. ❷ In the next panel to the right, Joachim returns dejectedly to his sheep farm. ❸ Meanwhile (next panel), his wife is in the bedroom, hearing the miraculous news that their prayers have been answered—she'll give birth to Mary, the mother of Jesus.

From this humble start, the story of Mary and Jesus spirals clockwise around the chapel, from top to bottom. The top row (both south and north walls) covers Mary's birth and life.

Jesus enters the picture in the middle row of the south (windowed) wall. ❹ The first frame shows his birth in a shed-like manger. In the next frame, the Magi arrive and kneel to kiss his little toes. Then the child is presented in the tiny temple. Fearing danger, the family gets on a horse and flees to Egypt. ❺ Meanwhile, back home, all the baby boys are slaughtered in an attempt to prevent the coming of the Messiah *(Slaughter of the Innocents)*.

Spinning clockwise to the opposite (north) wall, you see (in a badly damaged fresco) ❻ the child Jesus astounding the scholars with his wisdom. Next, Jesus is baptized by John the Baptist. His first miracle, at a wedding, is turning jars of water into wine. Next, he raises a mummy-like Lazarus from the dead. Riding a donkey, he enters Jerusalem triumphantly. ❼ In the temple, he drives the wicked money changers out.

Turning again to the south wall (bottom row), we see scenes from Jesus' final days. ❽ In the first frame, he and his followers gather at a table for a Last Supper. Next, Jesus kneels humbly to wash their feet. ❾ He is betrayed with a kiss and arrested. Jesus is tried. ❿ Then he is beaten and humiliated.

⓫ Finally (north wall, bottom row), he is forced to carry his own cross, crucified, and prepared for burial, while his followers mourn (⓬ *Lamentation*). Then he is resurrected and ascends to heaven, leaving his disciples to carry on.

⓭ The whole story concludes on the rear wall, where Jesus reigns at the Last Judgment. The long south wall (ground level) features the Virtues that lead to heaven, while the north wall has the (always more interesting) Vices. And all this unfolds beneath the blue, starry sky overhead on the ceiling.

Some panels deserve a closer look:

Joachim Returns to the Sheepfold (south wall, upper left, second panel): Though difficult to appreciate from ground level, this oft-reproduced scene is groundbreaking. Giotto—a former shepherd himself—uses nature as a stage, setting the scene in front of a backdrop of real-life mountains, and adding down-home details like Joachim's jumping dog, frozen in midair.

Betrayal of Christ, a.k.a. *Il Bacio*, "The Kiss" (south wall, bottom row, center panel): Amid the crowded chaos of Jesus' arrest, Giotto focuses our eyes on the central action, where Judas ensnares Jesus in his yellow robe (the color symbolizing envy), establishes meaningful eye contact, and kisses him.

Lamentation, a.k.a. *Deposition* (north wall, bottom row, middle): Jesus has been crucified, and his followers weep and wail over the lifeless body. John the Evangelist spreads his arms wide and shrieks, his cries echoed by anguished angels above. Each face is a study in grief. Giotto emphasizes these saints' human vulnerability.

Last Judgment (big west wall): Christ in the center is a glorious vision, but the action is in hell (lower right). Satan is a Minotaur-headed ogre munching on sinners. Around him, demons give sinners their just desserts in a scene right out of Dante...who was Giotto's friend and fellow Florentine. Front and center is Enrico Scrovegni in a violet robe (the color symbolizing penitence), donating the cha-

Giotto di Bondone
(c. 1267–1337)

Though details of his life are extremely sketchy, we know that as a 12-year-old shepherd boy, Giotto was discovered painting pictures of his father's sheep on rock slabs. He became the wealthiest and most famous painter of his day. His achievement is especially remarkable because painters at that time weren't considered anything more than craftsmen and weren't expected to be innovators.

After making a name for himself by painting the life of St. Francis frescoes in Assisi, the Florentine tackled the Scrovegni Chapel (c. 1303–1305). At age 35, he was at the height of his powers. His scenes were more realistic and human than anything done for a thousand years. Giotto didn't learn technique by dissecting corpses or studying the mathematics of 3-D perspective. He had innate talent. And his personality shines through in the humanity of his art.

The Scrovegni frescoes break ground by introducing nature—rocks, trees, animals—as a backdrop for religious scenes. Giotto's people, with their voluminous, deeply creased robes, are as sturdy and massive as Greek statues, throwbacks to the Byzantine icon art of the Middle Ages. But these figures exude stage presence. Their gestures are simple but expressive: A head tilted down says dejection, an arm flung out indicates grief, clasped hands are hope. Giotto created his figures not just by drawing outlines and filling them in with single colors, but as patchworks of lighter and darker shades, pioneering modern modeling techniques. Giotto's storytelling style is straightforward, and anyone with knowledge of the episodes of Jesus' life can read the chapel like a comic book.

The Scrovegni represents a turning point in European art and culture—away from scenes of heaven and toward a more down-to-earth, human-centered view.

pel to the Church in exchange for forgiveness of his father's sins.

Before the guard scoots you out, take a look at the actual altar. Though Enrico's father's tomb is lost, Enrico Scrovegni himself is in the tomb at the altar. The three statues are by Giovanni Pisano—Mary (in the center) supports baby Jesus on her hip with a perfectly natural maternal S-shape. She's flanked by no-name deacons.

Civic Museum (Musei Civici Eremitani)

This museum, next to the Scrovegni Chapel (and covered by the same combo-ticket), was once an Augustinian hermit's monastery. While you can skip the ground-floor Archaeological Museum (with Roman and Etruscan artifacts and no English descriptions), the Pinacoteca and the Multimedia Room are worth visiting.

Cost and Hours: €12 combo-ticket with Scrovegni Chapel, €10 without the chapel. The Civic Museum is open Tue–Sun 9:00–19:00, closed Mon. The Multimedia Room is open daily 9:00–19:00. Another part of the museum, Palazzo Zuckermann (Tue–Sun 9:00–19:00, closed Mon), is across the street. No photos are allowed, and there's a mandatory and free bag check. The museum is on Piazza Eremitani (Eremitani tram stop). Tel. 049-820-4551.

Pinacoteca

The museum's highlight is upstairs, in the Pinacoteca (picture gallery). The collection has 13th- to 18th-century paintings by Titian, Tintoretto, Giorgione, Tiepolo, Veronese, Bellini, Canova, Guariento, and other Veneto artists. But I'd make a beeline for the room with the Giotto crucifix. Ask for it: *"La Croce di Giotto?"*

Originally hung in the Scrovegni Chapel between the Scrovegni family's private zone and the public's worshipping zone, this crucifix is painted on wood by Giotto. If you actually sit on the floor and look up, the body really pops. The adjacent "God as Jesus" piece was the only painting in the otherwise frescoed chapel. (This is hung here due to preservation concerns. Its copy is the only non-original art in the chapel.) Studying these two masterpieces affirms Giotto's greatness.

Behind the crucifix room is a collection of 14th- and 15th-century art. While the works here are exquisite—and came well after Giotto—they're clearly not as modern.

Multimedia Room

The Multimedia Room, dedicated to taking a closer look at the Scrovegni Chapel, is adjacent to the Civic Museum (in the same building). To head straight from the museum entrance to the Multimedia Room, use the entrance to the right of the main entry, step into the courtyard, make a sharp right, and head down the stairs.

Rows of computer screens offer a virtual Scrovegni Chapel visit and provide cultural insights into daily life in the Middle Ages. There are explanations of the individual panels, Giotto's fresco technique, close-ups of the art, and a description of the restoration. They show a 12-minute video (English headphones available) that is similar—but not identical—to the one that precedes your chapel visit. For me, it's worth just taking some time to enjoy a second video that features a mesmerizing, slow montage of close-ups of the Giotto frescoes.

Between the museum and the chapel are the scant remains of Roman Padua. The remnants are from the wall of an arena and nicely fitting pipes that once channeled water so that the arena could be flooded for special spectacles.

Palazzo Zuckermann

This little-visited wing of the Civic Museum, just across a busy street, is included in the same ticket as the Pinacoteca and Multimedia Room. Its first two floors offer a commotion of applied and decorative arts—such as clothes, furniture, and ceramics—from the Venetian Republic (1600s–1700s). On the top floor, the Bottacin collection takes you to the 19th century with coins and delightful (but no-name) pre-Impressionist paintings.

More Sights in the Center

Palazzo della Ragione—This grand 13th-century palazzo, commonly called *il Salone* (great hall), once held the medieval law courts. The first floor consists of a huge hall—265 feet by 90 feet—

that was at one time adorned with frescoes by Giotto. A fire in 1312 destroyed those paintings, and the palazzo was redecorated with the 15th-century art you see today: a series of 333 frescoes depicting the signs of the zodiac, labors of the month, symbols representing characteristics of people born under each sign, and, finally, figures of saints to legitimize the power of the courts in the eyes of the Church.

The hall is topped with a hull-shaped roof, which helps to support the structure without the use of columns—quite an architectural feat in its day, considering the building's dimensions. The curious black stone in the corner opposite the big wooden horse is the "Stone of Shame," which was the seat of debtors being punished during the Middle Ages. It was introduced as a compassionate alternative to prison by St. Anthony in 1230. Instead of being executed or doing prison time, debtors sat upon this stone, surrendered their possessions, and denounced themselves publicly before being exiled from the city. The computer kiosks (choose "English") provide excellent information with entertaining videos.

Cost and Hours: €4, Tue–Sun 9:00–19:00, closed Mon. Enter through the east end of Piazza delle Erbe, and go up the long staircase. Tel. 049-820-5006, Ponti Romani tram stop. The WCs are through the glass doors at the opposite end of the hall from the wooden horse.

▲▲**Market Squares: Piazza delle Erbe, Piazza della Frutta, and Piazza dei Signori**—The stately Palazzo della Ragione (described above) provides a dramatic backdrop for Padua's almost exotic-feeling market that fills the surrounding squares—**Piazza delle Erbe** and **Piazza della Frutta**—each morning and all day

Saturday (Mon–Fri roughly 8:00–13:00, Sat 8:00–19:00, closed Sun). Second only to the produce market in Italy's gastronomic capital of Bologna, this market has been renowned for centuries as having the freshest and greatest selection of herbs, fruits, and vegetables. As you wander, appreciate the local passion for good food: Residents can tell the month by the seasonal selections. Merchants share recipe tips with shoppers. The presentation is an art in itself. And don't miss the ground floor of the Palazzo della Ragione. Wandering through this H-shaped arcade—where you'll find various butchers, *salumerie* (delicatessens), cheese shops, bakeries, and fishmongers at work—is a sensuous experience.

Students gather in the squares after the markets have closed, spilling out of colorful bars and cafés—drinks in hand. Pizza by the slice is dirt cheap. A typical snack stand selling all kinds of fresh, hot, and ready-to-eat seafood appetizers sets up in Piazza della Frutta between 17:00 and 20:30 (daily except Sun). Belly up to the bar with your drink and try whatever's being served.

Piazza dei Signori, just a block away, is a busy clothing market in the morning and the most popular gathering place in the evening for students out for a drink. The circa-1400 clock decorates the former palace of the ruling family. The aggressive lion with unfurled wings on the column was a reminder of the Venetian determination to assert its control. Today that lion can be seen as representing the Veneto region's independence from Rome: Italy's north (Veneto and Lombardy) is tired of subsidizing the south. Grumbling about this issue continues to stir talk of splitting the country.

Drinking a *Spritz* with the Student Crowd—Each early evening, before dinner, students enliven Padua by enjoying a convivial drink in their favorite places. Piazza dei Signori (described above) is the favorite square. Or you could sit in front of the university, nurse your drink, and watch the graduates get roasted with their crazy gangs of friends (see "Graduation Antics in Padua" sidebar, later). The drink of choice is a *spritz,* an aperitif generally made with Campari (liquor infused with bitter herbs), white wine, and sparkling water, and garnished with a blood-orange wedge. Most Paduan women seem to prefer a lighter *spritz* made with Aperol (orange-flavored liquor, less alcohol content).

Grab a table to be part of the scene, or get your *spritz* to take away *(da portar via)*, and join the young people out on the piazza. Either way, this is a classic opportunity to enjoy a real discussion with smart, English-speaking students who see tourists not as pests, but as interesting people from far away. For an instant conversation starter, ask about the current political situation in Italy, the right-wing party's policy on immigrants, or the cultural differences between Italy's north and south. Or ask how President Berlusconi manages to control the media so effectively.

Caffè Pedrocchi—This white-columned Neoclassical café is much more than just a café. A complex of meeting rooms and entertainment venues, it stirs the Italian soul (at least, patriotic Italian souls). Built in 1831 during the period of Austrian rule, the Caffè Pedrocchi was inaugurated for the fourth Italian Congress of Scientists, which convened during the mid–19th century to stir up nationalistic fervor as Italy struggled to become a united nation. As a symbol of patriotic hope, it was the target (no surprise) of a student uprising plot in 1848. You can still see a bullet hole (framed in silver) in the wall of the Sala Bianca, where one of the insurgents was killed. Nowadays, you get more foam than fervor.

Each room is decorated and furnished in a different color: red, white, or green—representing the colors of the Italian flag. In the Sala Verde (Green Room), people are welcome to sit and enjoy the beautiful interior without ordering anything or having to pay. This is where Italian gentlemen read their newspapers and gather with friends to chat about the old days. In the red room, the clock over the bar is flanked by marble reliefs of morning and night, signaling that it was open 24 hours a day (in the 19th century). The maps of the hemispheres with south up top reflect the anti-conventional spirit of the place. The menu offers teahouse fare, including salads, sandwiches, and the writer Stendhal's beloved *zabaglione*, a creamy custard made with *marsala* wine (daily 9:00–24:00, until 21:00 off-season; entrance is at intersection of Oberdan and VIII Febbraio, between Piazza delle Erbe and Piazza Cavour, Ponti Romani tram stop; tel. 049-878-1231).

Piano Nobile: This upper "noble floor" is more elaborate. The rooms are all in different styles, such as Greek, Etruscan, or Egyptian, with good English descriptions throughout. These rooms were intended to evoke memories of the glory of past epochs, which a united Italy had hopes of reliving.

Museum of the Risorgimento: The Piano Nobile hosts a small museum that traces Padua's role in Italian history, from the downfall of the Venetian Republic (1797) to the founding of the Republic of Italy (1948). Exhibits, a few with English descriptions, include uniforms, medals, weaponry, old artillery, Fascist propaganda posters, and a 30-minute propagandistic video (in Italian, but mostly fascinating footage without narration). The video, played on demand, is a "Luce" production (meaning a Mussolini production) and features great scenes of the town in the 1930s, including clips of Il Duce's visit and later WWII bombardments. The war and propaganda posters in the last room are haunting. An old woman pleads to those who might question the Fascist-driven war effort: "Don't betray my son." Another declares, "The Germans are truly our friends." And another asks, "And you...what are you doing?" (€4, Tue–Sun 9:30–12:30 & 15:30–18:00, closed Mon, tel. 049-820-5007). Reach Piano Nobile by a stairway to the right of the Caffè's entrance.

▲**Baptistery**—This richly frescoed little building was originally the private chapel of Padua's ruling family. Then, in 1405, Venice took over, killing Padua's ruling family, and making it a baptistery. Located next to the Duomo, the Baptistery was frescoed (c. 1370) by Giusto de' Menabuoi.

While created 70 years after Giotto, the Baptistery feels older. Because the artist was working for a private family, he needed to be politically correct and not threaten or offend the family's allies, especially the Church. While still mind-blowing, the Baptistery's art seems relatively conservative compared to Giotto's Scrovegni Chapel. Giotto, supported by the powerful Scrovegni family and the Franciscans, could get away with being more progressive and bold.

The Baptistery's complex design must have made perfect and cohesive sense to the faithful in centuries past. Almighty Christ is in majesty on top, while approachable Mary and the multitude of saints provide the devout with access to God. Find the world as was known in the 14th century (the disk below Mary's feet). It kicks off a cycle of scenes illustrating creation (clockwise from the creation of Adam). The four evangelists (Matthew, Mark, Luke, and John) with their books and symbols fill the corners. A vivid crucifixion scene faces a gorgeous annunciation. And the altar niche features a dim blue-toned literal Apocalypse from the book of Revelation.

Cost and Hours: €3, daily 10:00–18:00.

University of Padua—The main building of this prestigious university, known as Palazzo Bo, is adjacent to Caffè Pedrocchi. Founded in 1222, it's one of the first, greatest, and most progressive universities in Europe. Back when the Church controlled university curricula, a group of professors and students broke free from the University of Bologna, creating this liberal school, independent of Catholic constraints and accessible to people of alternative faiths.

A haven for free thought, the university attracted intellectuals from all over Europe, including the great astronomer Copernicus, who realized here that the universe didn't revolve around him. And Galileo—notorious for disagreeing with the Church's views on science—called his 18 years on the faculty here the best of his life.

Graduation Antics in Padua

With 60,000 students, Padua's university graduates individuals on any given day. There's a constant trickle of happy grads and their friends and families celebrating the big event.

During the school year, every 20 minutes or so, a student steps into a formal room (upstairs, above the university courtyard) to formally meet with the leading professors of his or her faculty. When they're finished, the students are given a green laurel wreath. They pose for formal group photos and family snapshots. It's a sweet scene. Then, craziness takes over.

The new graduates replace their somber clothing with raunchy outfits, as gangs of friends gather around them on Via VIII Febbraio, the street in front of the university. The roast begins. The gang rolls out a giant butcher-paper poster with a generally obscene caricature of the student and a litany of *This Is Your Life* photos and stories. The new grad, subject to various embarrassing pranks, reads the funny statements out loud. The poster is then taped to the university wall for all to see. (Find the plastic panels to the right of the main entry, facing Via VIII Febbraio. Graduation posters are allowed to stay there for 24 hours. The panels are emptied each morning, but by nighttime a new set of posters are affixed to the plastic shields.)

During the roast, the friends sing the catchy but obscene local university anthem reminding their newly esteemed friend not to get too huffy: *Dottore, dottore, dottore del buso del cul. Vaffancul, vaffancul* (loosely translated: "Doctor, doctor. You're just a doctor of the a-hole...go f-off, go f-off"). After you've heard this song (with its fanfare and oom-pah-pah catchiness) and have seen all the good-natured fun, you can't stop singing it.

The crazy show is usually staged late in the afternoon. Outdoor café tables afford great seats to enjoy the spectacle.

The gawking public is not really welcomed in the university, but you can poke into two courtyards. Enter from the front of the main building (facing city hall on Via VIII Febbraio, 30 yards from Caffè Pedrocchi at #7). You'll pop into a 16th-century courtyard, the school's historic core. It's littered with the coats of arms of important faculty and leaders of the university over the ages. Classrooms, which open onto the square, are still used. Today, students gather here, surrounded by memories of illustrious alumni, including the first woman ever to receive a university degree (in 1678).

A passageway leads from here to an adjacent second courtyard from the Fascist era (c. 1938). The relief celebrates heroic students in World War I. Off this courtyard, notice the richly decorated stairway, frescoed in the 1930s with themes celebrating art, science, and the pursuit of knowledge.

The big attraction among tourists is Europe's first great **Anatomy Theater** (from 1594), which you can visit only on a guided tour (explained below). Try to get a ticket, but keep in mind that it's not worth any heroics to see. The first two rooms of the tour are underwhelming: One features the supposed "pulpit of Galileo" (c. 1550) and portraits of 40 famous alums. The second is the Aula Magna, a ceremonial room for festivities. The historic Anatomy Theater itself is more impressive. Despite the Church's strict ban on autopsies, more than 300 students would pack this theater to watch professors dissect human cadavers (the bodies of criminals from another town). This had to be done in a "don't ask, don't tell" kind of way, because the Roman Catholic Church only started allowing the teaching of anatomy through dissection in the late 1800s.

Cost and Hours: While it's free to visit the university, you must sign up for a 30-minute tour (€5) to see the Anatomy Theater. Only 30 people may enter at a time. Tours run three times a day (March–Oct Mon, Wed, and Fri at 15:15, 16:15, and 17:15; Tue, Thu, and Sat at 9:15, 10:15, and 11:15; no tours on Sun, call for times Nov–Feb—see number below, Ponti Romani tram stop, www.unipd.it). School groups often book the entire visit, and many of the guides speak no English.

Confirm tour times and availability by calling 049-827-3047 or stopping by the ticket window (opens 15 minutes before each tour, located just inside the palace, in the hall reached from the Fascist-era courtyard described above). The bar there is fun for a cheap drink and to see photos of university life.

Sleeping in Padua

Rooms in Padua's hotels are more spacious and a better value than those in Venice. Keep in mind that when large conventions take over the town—several times a year—all hotels raise prices. I've listed two hotels in the center and a group of accommodations near the basilica. All but Albergo Verdi are easily reached from the station by the tram.

In the Center

Tito Livio is the nearest tram stop for these two hotels.

$$$ Hotel Majestic Toscanelli is a central, fancy hotel with 34 pleasant, air-conditioned rooms and a touch of charm, buried in

---

Sleep Code

(€1 = about $1.25, country code: 39)
S = Single, **D** = Double/Twin, **T** = Triple, **Q** = Quad, **b** = bathroom, **s** = shower only. Unless otherwise noted, credit cards are accepted, breakfast is included, and English is spoken.

To help you easily sort through these listings, I've divided the rooms into three categories based on the price for a standard double room with bath:

$$$ **Higher Priced**—Most rooms €130 or more.
$$ **Moderately Priced**—Most rooms between €90-130.
$ **Lower Priced**—Most rooms €90 or less.

Prices can change without notice; verify the hotel's current rates online or by email. For other updates, see www.ricksteves.com/update.

---

a characteristic ghetto with wonderful cobbled ambience. This area is popular with students at night, and it can be noisy until about 1:00 in the morning; as the hotel's windows are single-paned, request a quiet room on the back side (Sb-€95–110, Db-€150–160, 10 percent Rick Steves discount, superior rooms and suites available at extra cost, check website for special discounts, includes a wonderful breakfast, Wi-Fi, 2 blocks south of Piazza delle Erbe at Via dell'Arco 2, tel. 049-663-244, fax 049-876-0025, www.toscanelli.com, majestic@toscanelli.com). From Piazza delle Erbe, head up Via dei Fabbri and take the first left to Via dell'Arco.

$$ Albergo Verdi, a modern little place, is crammed into an old building on a forgettable street at the edge of the old town, away from the tram. While public spaces are very tight, the 14 rooms are modern and spacious (Db-€90–100, extra person-€30, air-con, elevator, a couple of blocks behind Piazza Duomo at Via Dondi dall'Orologio 7, tel. 049-836-4163, www.albergoverdipadova.it, info@albergoverdipadova.it).

Near the Basilica of St. Anthony
Santo is the nearest tram stop for the following hotels.

$$ Hotel Al Fagiano feels like an art gallery with crazy, sexy modern art everywhere. The hotel is all about the union of a man and a woman (quite romantic). They rent 30 bright and cheery air-conditioned rooms, each uniquely decorated with Rossella Fagiano's canvases (Sb-€64, Db-€100, Tb-€115, ask for Rick Steves discount, €7 per person less without breakfast, Wi-Fi, 50 yards from the Santo tram stop at Via Locatelli 45, tel. & fax 049-875-3396, www.alfagiano.com, info@alfagiano.com).

$$ Hotel Belludi 37 is a slick, borderline-pretentious place renting 15 modern rooms shoehorned into an old building. The decor is dark, woody, fresh, and stylish (S-€57, Sb-€80, D-€90, Db-€120, bigger Db-€135, ask for 10 percent Rick Steves discount, €7 less per person without breakfast, air-con, Wi-Fi, free minibar, a block from the Santo tram stop at Via Luca Belludi 37, tel. 049-665-633, fax 049-658-685, www.belludi37.it, info@belludi37.it).

$$ Hotel Casa del Pellegrino, with 150 spotless, cheap, institutional rooms and straight pricing, is home to the pilgrims who come to pay homage to St. Anthony in the basilica next door, but any visitor to Padua is welcome (S-€54, Sb-€71, D-€74, Db-€92, Tb-€109, Qb-€138, air-con, ask for a room off the street, €7 less per person without breakfast, elevator, Via Cesarotti 21, tel. 049-823-9711, fax 049-823-9780, www.casadelpellegrino.com, info@casadelpellegrino.com). For better accommodations, request one of the 24 rooms in the *dipendenza*, the hotel's modern wing (€5 extra/night).

$ Hotel Al Santo, run with charm by Valentina and Antonio, offers 15 spacious rooms with all the comforts a few steps from the basilica (Sb-€65–70, Db-€90, Tb-€120, Qb-€135, double-paned windows, air-con, quieter rooms off street, some rooms have views of basilica, Wi-Fi, Via del Santo 147, tel. 049-875-2131, fax 049-878-8076, www.alsanto.it, alsanto@alsanto.it).

Hostel: **$ Ostello Città di Padova,** near Prato della Valle, is well-run and has 80 beds in 4-, 6-, and 9-bed rooms (beds with sheets and breakfast-€19; 4-person family rooms-€80, with bath-€90; self-service laundry, bike rentals available in summer, lockers, reception open 7:00–9:30 & 16:30–23:30, rooms locked during afternoon but reception staffed if you need to leave bags, 23:30 curfew; Via Aleardi 30—take tram from station to Prato della Valle, then it's a 5-minute walk: walk along Via Cavaletto, turn right on Via Marin, turn left after Torresino church; tel. 049-875-2219, www.ostellopadova.it, ostellopadova@ctgveneto.it).

Eating in Padua

The university population means cheap, good food abounds. For picnic shopping, see "Market Squares," on page 153. My recommended restaurants are all centrally located in the historic core. You'd think there would be fine dining on the charming market squares, but on the piazzas it's a take-out-pizza-and-casual-bar scene (dominated by students after dark). La Lanterna, at the neighboring Piazza dei Signori, is the best on-square option I've found—but it's basically pizza. The dreamily atmospheric ghetto neighborhood (just two blocks off the market squares) thrives after dark with trendy bars and a lively student *spritz* scene.

Fine Dining Near the Center

Ristorante da Giorgio is a respected fixture in town for its dressy white-tablecloth dining and good international cuisine. They are passionate about their vegetarian *secondi* and proud of their bean soup, fish soup, cod, and squid. Reservations are smart at night (€12 pastas, €25 *secondi*, meals served from 12:00 and from 19:30, closed Sun, Via Daniele Manin 8, tel. 049-836-0973).

Osteria L'Anfora is a classic place serving classic dishes in a rustic, fun-loving space. Don't be put off by the woody, ruffian decor and the fact that it's a popular hangout for a pre-meal drink. They take food seriously and serve it at good prices, and the energy and commotion add to a great dining experience (€8 pastas, €12 *secondi*, €2 cover, closed Sun, Via dei Soncin 13, tel. 049-656-629, no reservations taken).

Osteria dei Fabbri, with shared rustic tables, offers a good mix of class and accessibility, quality and price. The dining room is spacious, and the dishes are traditional Venetian (€9 pastas, €13 *secondi*, Mon-Sat 12:30–14:30 & 19:30–22:30, closed Sun, Via dei Fabbri 13, tel. 049-650-336).

Cheap Eats Near the Center

La Lanterna has a forgettable interior, but a pizza here on Piazza dei Signori includes a rare-in-Padua chance to sit in a grand square under the stars, surrounded by great architecture. Its pizzas are a local favorite, and reservations are recommended (€8 pastas and pizzas, €14 *secondi*, Fri–Wed 12:00–14:30 & 18:00–24:00, closed Thu, Piazza dei Signori 39, tel. 049-660-770).

Bar dei Osei, on Piazza della Frutta, is a very simple sandwich bar with some of the best seats in town. While Paduans love their delicate *tremazzini* (white bread sandwiches with crusts cut off, €1.80), I'd choose their grilled *porchetta*—pulled pork— sandwiches. The two-foot-long mother lode awaits on the counter for you to say how big a slice you'd like. Wines are listed on the board (Mon–Sat 7:00–21:00, closed Sun, Piazza della Frutta 1, tel. 049-875-9606). With fast, cheap meal and drink in hand, grab a seat and enjoy the market scene.

Brek, tucked into a corner of Piazza Cavour at #20, is an easy self-service chain *ristorante* with healthy and affordable choices. It's big, bright, practical, and family-friendly (daily 11:30–15:00 & 18:30–22:00, tel. 049-875-3788).

Brek Foccacceria, a new branch across from Caffè Pedrocchi and next door to the PAM supermarket, sells big sandwiches that you can eat at outdoor tables (daily 8:00–22:00, Piazzetta della Garzeria 6, tel. 049-876-1651).

If the markets are closed, stock up on picnic items at the **PAM supermarket,** in a tiny *piazzetta* east of Caffè Pedrocchi (Mon–Sat

8:00–21:00, closed Wed evenings and all day Sun, Piazzetta Garzeria 3, tel. 049-657-006).

Pasticceria Racca is a pastry shop–café offering an exquisite selection of chocolates and pastries. Consider a stop here to attend to your sweet tooth, Padua-style (tiny seats, on Piazza Cavour, kitty-corner from Caffè Pedrocchi at Via Pietro Fortunato Calvi 8).

Enoteca Santa Lucia provides a modern alternative for a drink or meal. With a New York jazz-bar sense of style, they serve fine wine by the glass with generous free tapas around the bar or with seating on the square, and modern Mediterranean meals in the cellar with mod decor (€10 pastas, €20 *secondi*, closed Sun, Piazza Cavour at the corner of Via Pietro Fortunato Calvi, tel. 049-655-545).

Near the Basilica of St. Anthony

Pizzeria Pago Pago dishes up wood-fired Neapolitan pizzas (a local favorite) and daily specials depending on what's in season. Get there early for dinner or wait (€5–8.50 pizzas, Wed–Mon 12:00–14:00 & 19:00–23:00, closed Tue; 2 blocks from Basilica of St. Anthony, up Via del Santo and right onto Via Galileo Galilei to #59; tel. 049-665-558, Gaetano and Modesto).

Casa del Pellegrino Ristorante caters to St. Anthony pilgrims with simple, basic, and hearty meals, served in a cheery dining room just north of the basilica. *Baccalà* (cod) is a favorite here (€4.50 pastas, €8 *secondi*, €14 three-course fixed-price meal, daily 12:00–14:00 & 19:30–21:30, Via Cesarotti 21, tel. 049-876-0715).

Zairo is a huge *ristorante*-pizzeria with reasonable prices, delicious homemade pastas, Veneto specialties, snappy service, and a local clientele (Tue–Sun 12:00–14:30 & 19:00–24:00, closed Mon, east side of Prato della Valle at #51, tel. 049-663-803).

Pollodoro la Gastronomica, a take-out deli near the basilica, sells roast chicken, pastas, and veggies, and will make sandwiches (Wed–Mon 8:00–13:30 & 17:00–20:00, closed Tue, 100 yards from basilica at Via Belludi 34; tel. 049-663-718). You can picnic at the nearby cloisters of the basilica.

Padua Connections

From Padua by Train to: Venice (2/hour, 30 minutes), **Vicenza** (2/hour, fewer on weekends, 20 minutes), **Milan** (1–2/hour, 2.5 hours), **Verona** (2/hour, 1 hour), Ravenna (9/day, 2.5 hours).

By Bus to Venice's Airports: Cheap buses connect Padua and **Marco Polo Airport** (€5 from driver, cheaper if you buy ticket from office, €2/bag, 2/hour from 5:00 to 22:25, 1 hour, departs from Padua's bus station at Piazzale Boschetti, run by SITA, www.sitabus.it).

A **minibus service** runs from Padua to **Marco Polo Airport** (€28/person) or **Treviso Airport** (€39/person, reservations required, tel. 049-870-4425, www.airservicepadova.it).

Near Padua: Vicenza

To many architects, Vicenza (vih-CHEHN-zah) is a pilgrimage site. Entire streets look like the back of a nickel. This is the city of Andrea Palladio (1508–1580), the 16th-century Renaissance architect who gave us the Palladian style that is so influential in countless British country homes. But as grandiose as Vicenza's Palladian facades may feel, there is little marble here. The city lacked the wealth to build with much more than painted wood and plaster. If you're an architecture buff, Vicenza merits a quick stop (on any day but Monday, when major sights are closed). For my expanded coverage of Vicenza, see www.ricksteves.com/vicenza.

Tourist Information: The main TI is at Piazza Matteotti 12 (tel. 0444-320-854, www.vicenzae.org); a smaller office is at Piazza dei Signori 8. Architecture fans appreciate the TI's *Vicenza Città e le Ville del Palladio nel Veneto* booklet (in English). Two websites cover most of the sights in town: www.comune.vicenza.it and www.museicivicivicenza.it.

Arrival in Vicenza: From the train station, it's a five-minute **walk** up wide Viale Roma to the bottom of Corso Palladio. Drivers can park in one of the cheap parking lots (Parcheggio Bassano and Parcheggio Cricoli) and catch a free shuttle bus to the center.

Helpful Hints: Most of Vicenza's sights are covered by a combo-ticket, **Card Musei** (€8/3 days, sold only at the Olympic Theater), but it doesn't cover the villas outside of town. The only **baggage check** in town is at the hostel, L'Ostello Olimpico, near Piazza Matteotti (long hours, Viale Giuriolo 7/9, tel. 0444-540-222).

Sights in Vicenza

▲▲**Olympic Theater (Teatro Olimpico)**—Palladio's last work is one of his greatest. The theater is a wood-and-stucco festival of classical columns, statues, and an oh-wow stage bursting with perspective tricks (entry only with €8 Card Musei, which covers other Vicenza sights; audioguide available, Tue–Sun 9:00–17:00, closed Mon, occasionally closed when theater is in use, entrance to the left of TI, tel. 0444-222-800). When you step back outside, look up the town's main drag—named after Palladio. It's the same main street you saw in his theater.

▲**Church of Santa Corona**—A block away from the Olympic Theater, this "Church of the Holy Crown" was built in the 13th century to house a thorn from the Crown of Thorns, given to the

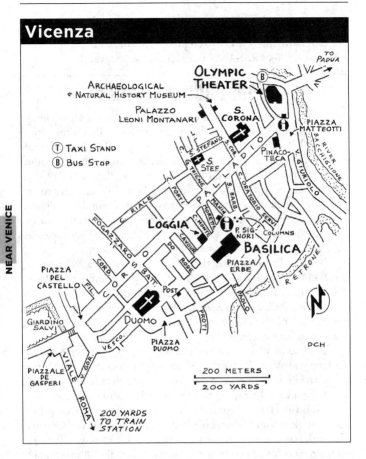

Vicenza

OLYMPIC THEATER

TO PADUA

ARCHAEOLOGICAL & NATURAL HISTORY MUSEUM

PALAZZO LEONI MONTANARI

S. CORONA

PIAZZA MATTEOTTI

RIVER BACCHIGLIONE

Ⓣ TAXI STAND
Ⓑ BUS STOP

S. STEFANO

S. STEF.

PINACO-TECA

C. G. THIENE

G. PORTI

VIA G. THIENE

LOGGIA

C. RIALE

FOGAZZARO S. O

C. CAVOUR

V. MANIN

C. MONTE

C. ROBERTI

P. SIG-NORI

Ⓘ

COLUMNS

BASILICA

PIAZZA PEL CASTELLO

CORD O.

R. S. BATT.

DO RODE

Post

PIAZZA ERBE

VIA APOLLO

RETRONE

PIAZZA DEL CASTELLO

GIARDINO SALVI

VIALE V. GOR.

VESCO.

DUOMO

PIAZZA DUOMO

PROTI

N

DCH

200 METERS
200 YARDS

PIAZZALE DE GASPERI

VIALE ROMA

200 YARDS TO TRAIN STATION

Bishop of Vicenza by the French King Louis IX. The church has two artistic highlights: the art embellishing its high altar and Giovanni Bellini's fine painting, *Baptism of Christ* (church entry free, small fee to light the Bellini, Tue–Sun 8:30–12:00 & 15:00–17:00, closed Mon).

Archaeological and Natural History Museum—Located next door to the Church of Santa Corona, this museum has a ground floor featuring Roman antiquities (mosaics, statues, and artifacts excavated from Rome's Baths of Caracalla, plus swords) and a barbarian warrior skeleton complete with sword and helmet. Prehistoric scraps are upstairs. Look for English description sheets near exhibit entryways throughout (covered by Card Musei, Tue–Sun 9:00–17:00, closed Mon).

Palazzo Leoni Montanari—Across the street from the Church of Santa Corona, this small museum is a palatial riot of Baroque, with cherub-cluttered ceilings jumbled like a preschool in heaven.

A quick stroll shows off Venetian paintings and a floor of Russian icons (small entry fee, Tue–Sun 10:00–18:00, closed Mon, Contrà Santa Corona 25, www.palazzomontanari.com).

Piazza dei Signori—Vicenza's main square has been the center of town ever since it was the site of the ancient Roman forum. The commanding **Basilica Palladiana,** with its 270-foot-tall 13th-century tower, dominates the square. It was a meeting place for local big shots. It was young Palladio's proposal—to redo Vicenza's dilapidated Gothic palace of justice in the Neo-Greek style—that established him as the city's favorite architect. The rest of Palladio's career was a one-man construction boom. When the basilica is open, it hosts frequent special exhibitions that sometimes involve a fee, but you can often pop in for a free look.

Villas on the Outskirts of Vicenza—Vicenza is surrounded by dreamy Venetian villas. Venice's commercial empire receded in the 1500s when trade began to pick up along the Atlantic seaboard and dwindle in the Mediterranean. Venice redirected its economic agenda to agribusiness, which led to the construction of lavish country villas, such as **Villa la Rotonda** (the inspiration for Thomas Jefferson's Monticello) and **Villa Valmarana ai Nani** (www.villavalmarana.com). Both houses are furnished with period pieces and come with good English descriptions (closed Mon). Pick up the free English brochure on Palladio's villas from the TI if you plan to visit.

Vicenza Connections

From Vicenza by Train to: Venice (2/hour, 1 hour), **Padua** (2/hour, fewer on weekends, 20 minutes), **Verona** (2/hour, 40 minutes), **Milan** (2/hour, 2 hours), **Ravenna** (roughly hourly, 3.5–4 hours, changes in Padua and Ferrara or Bologna).

Verona

Romeo and Juliet made Verona a household word. Alas, a visit here has nothing to do with those two star-crossed lovers. You can pay to visit the house that falsely claims to be Juliet's (with an almost-believable balcony and a courtyard swarming with tour groups), join in the tradition of rubbing the breast of Juliet's statue to help find a lover (or pick up the sweat of someone who can't), and even make a pilgrimage to what isn't "La Tomba di Giulietta."

Despite the fiction, Verona—Italy's fourth-most-visited city—has been an important crossroads for 2,000 years and is therefore packed with genuine history. R and J fans will take some solace in

the fact that two real feuding families, the Montecchi and the Cappellos, were the models for Shakespeare's Montagues and Capulets. And, if R and J had existed and were alive today, they would recognize much of their "hometown."

Verona's main attractions are its wealth of Roman ruins; the remnants of its 13th- and 14th-century political and cultural boom; its 21st-century quiet pedestrian-only ambience; and a world-class opera festival each summer (www.arena.it). After Venice's festival of tourism, Veneto's second city (in population and in artistic importance) is a cool and welcome sip of pure Italy, where dumpsters are painted by schoolchildren as class projects and public spaces are the domain of locals, not tourists. If you like Italy but don't need blockbuster sights, this town is a joy.

Orientation to Verona

The vibrant and enjoyable core of Verona is along Via Mazzini between Piazza Brà (pronounced "bra") and Piazza Erbe, Verona's market square since Roman times. Head straight for Piazza Brà—and stroll. While Via Mazzini attracts mob scenes during the *passeggiata* (evening stroll), don't neglect the parallel Corso Porta Borsari. All sights of importance are located within an easy walk through the old town, which is defined by a bend in the river. For a good day trip to Verona, visit the Roman Arena and take my self-guided walk.

Tourist Information

Verona has two TIs: at the **train station** (Mon–Sat 9:00–19:00, Sun 9:00–15:00, tel. 045-800-0861) and at **Piazza Brà** (Mon–Sat 9:00–19:00, Sun 10:00–16:00, tel. 045-806-8680, www.tourism .verona.it). At either TI, pick up the free city map for a list of sights and opening hours, and confirm the walking-tour schedule. If you're staying the night, ask about concerts or pick up the monthly entertainment guide, *Carnet Verona* (free at TI, €1 at newsstands).

Verona Card: This tourist card covers bus transportation and entrance to all the recommended Verona sights, except the manicured Giardino Giusti garden (€10/day or €15/3 days, sold at TIs and at participating sights). If you arrive at the train station, buy the card at the TI there because it'll cover your bus ride to and from the city center as well as all your sightseeing. Here's the math:

€6 (arena) + €6 (tower climb) + €6 (castle) + €5 (two churches) + €2 (two bus rides) = €25. At €10, the card saves a day-tripper blitzing the city 60 percent.

The €5 **Church Card,** sold at all churches that require admission, pays off if you visit at least three.

Arrival in Verona

By Train: Get off at the Verona Porta Nuova Station. You'll emerge into the station from one of two passages. The TI, baggage check (€4/5 hours, daily 7:00–23:00, 45 pounds max), and waiting lounge are together. The main hall includes an efficient collection of all the services you'd hope to find in a station. *Tabacchi* shops sell bus tickets. Buses and taxis are immediately outside.

Avoid the boring 15-minute walk from the station to Piazza Brà by catching a **city bus.** To get to the center, hop on any bus leaving from platform A in front of the station. To cover your trip into town, either get a Verona Card (described earlier) or buy an individual ticket before boarding from a *tabacchi* shop inside the station (€1/1 hour, €3.50 valid until midnight). Confirm the route by asking, *"Per il centro?"* (pehr eel CHEN-troh). If you have an individual ticket, validate it by stamping it in the machine in the bus. If you have a Verona Card, you'll just need to show it if a "controller" asks you for your ticket.

Buses stop on Piazza Brà, the square with the can't-miss-it Roman Arena. The TI is just a few steps beyond the bus stop (located along the medieval walls). You can catch return buses (#11, #12, or #13) to the station from here or from the bus stop just outside the city wall (on the right), where Corso Porta Nuova hits Piazza Brà.

Taxis pick up only at taxi stands (at Piazza Brà and train station) and cost about €8 for the quick ride between the train station and Piazza Brà.

By Car: The town center is closed to traffic, but if you're staying here, your hotel can get you permission to drive in—ask when you book. Otherwise your license plate could be photographed, and you could have a €100 ticket waiting for you in the mail when you get home.

Drivers will find cheap parking in well-marked lots and garages farther from the center (including two lots in front of the train station). For more central and expensive parking, consider either Garage Arena (off Via Porta Nuova just outside the walls) or Garage Italia (Corso Porta Nuova 91; both guarded, about €2.50/hour, 6:00–24:00, tel. 045-800-6312). Street parking costs €1.50 per hour (buy ticket at *tabacchi* shop to put on dashboard, spaces marked with blue lines, maximum two hours).

By Plane: Efficient shuttle buses connect Verona's airport

(Verona-Villafranca, 12 miles southwest of the city) with its train station (€4.50, buy tickets on board or at *tabacchi* shop, daily 6:30–22:30, 3/hour, 15 minutes).

From Brescia Airport, 40 miles west of Verona, a shuttle bus meets Ryanair flights and takes passengers to the Porta Nuova train station (€11, bus schedule is coordinated with Ryanair arrivals and departures).

Helpful Hints

Sightseeing Schedules: Many sights are closed on Monday morning.

Opera: From mid-June through August, Verona's opera festival brings the city to life, with 15,000 music fans filling the Roman Arena for almost nightly performances. The city is packed and festive, as restaurants have pre-scheduled seatings for dinner and hotels jack up their prices (upper-level seats about €26, book tickets either online at www.arena.it or by calling 045-800-5151; box office open Mon–Fri 9:00–12:00 & 15:15–17:45, Sat–Sun 9:00–12:00; during opera season, open daily 10:00–17:45, or until 21:00 on performance days; Via Dietro Anfiteatro 6B).

Internet Access: Try **Verona Web** (Mon–Fri 10:00–22:00, Sat–Sun 14:00–20:00, a couple of blocks off Piazza Brà toward Castelvecchio at Via Roma 17A, tel. 045-801-3394) or **Internet Etc.** (Tue–Sat 9:30–19:45, Sun–Mon 15:30–19:45, off Via Mazzini on Via Quattro Spade 3B, tel. 045-800-0222).

Travel Agency: Welcome Travel is handy if you want to buy a train ticket without going to the station (just outside the gate from Piazza Brà at Corso Porta Nuova 11, tel. 045-806-0126).

Tours in Verona

Walking Tours—The TI organizes 1.5-hour tours daily (often English-only, but sometimes in Italian too) for €10 per person. Tours meet inside the Piazza Brà TI and stroll all the way through the old town (call to find out schedule, no reservation necessary, tel. 045-806-8680, mobile 333-219-9645).

Private Guides—Two excellent and enthusiastic Verona guides enjoy giving private tours of the town and region to readers of this book (€105/2 hours and €210/5 hours per group, tours tailored to your interests—villas, wine-tasting, etc.). They are **Marina Menegoi** (tel. 045-801-2174, mobile 328-958-1108, www.veneto guide.it, mmenegoi@gmail.com) and **Valeria Biasi** (mobile 348-9034-238, www.veronatours.com, valeria@veronatours.com). Valeria also offers a Safari Verona tour suitable for families with children (€108/3 hours).

Self-Guided Walk

Welcome to Verona Town Walk

This walk covers the essential sights in the town core, starting at Piazza Brà and ending at the cathedral. Allow 1.5 hours (including the tower climb and dawdling, more with the optional detours).

❶ Piazza Brà

If you're wondering where the name came from, it means "open space" in a local dialect. A generation ago this piazza was noisy with cars. Now it's open and people-friendly—the community family room and natural festival grounds.

Grab a bench near the central fountain called "The Alps." This was a gift from Verona's sister city Munich, which is just over the mountains. You'll see the symbols of the two cities with the peaks carved out of pink marble from this region.

The ancient Arena looming over the piazza is a reminder that the city's history goes back to Roman times. A major East–West trading route once cut across Verona, which fills an easy-to-defend bend in the river. On this walk, we'll meander across what was the ancient city, from the Arena on this side to the theater across the river.

With the fall of Rome, Verona became a favored capital of barbarian kings. In the Middle Ages, noble families had to choose sides (Guelfs or Ghibellines) in the civil struggles between emperors and popes. During this time, the town bristled with San Gimignano–type towers, built by different families to symbolize their power. When the Scaligeri family rose to power here in the 14th century, they established stability on their terms and made the noble families lop off their proud towers—only they were allowed to have a tower. But inter-family feuds made it impossible for the Scaligeri to maintain a stable government, and in 1405 the town essentially gave itself to Venice, which ruled Verona until Napoleon stopped by in 1796. During the 19th century, a tug-of-war between France and Austria in this area actually divided the city for a time, with the river marking the border of each country's domains. Eventually Verona fell into Austrian hands. The huge Neoclassical city hall facing Piazza Brà (look for the flags) was built by the Austrians to serve as their 19th-century military head-quarters. The big statue is of Italy's first king, Victor Emmanuel, and celebrates Italian independence and unity, won in the 1860s.

Apart from all its history, Piazza Brà is about strolling...the *passeggiata* is a national sport in Italy. The broad, shiny sidewalk was named the "Liston" (ribbon) by 17th-century Venetians who made it big and wide (better for promenading socialites to see and be seen in all their finery).

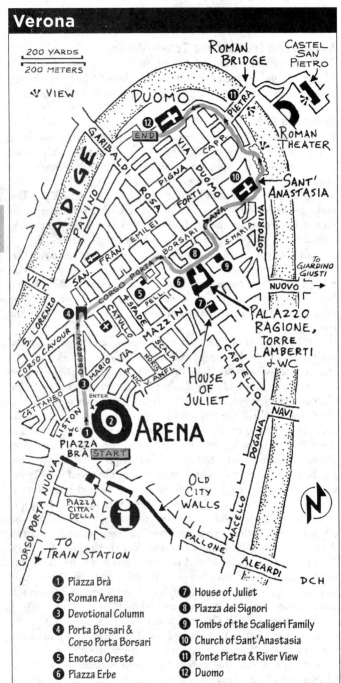

Verona

200 YARDS

200 METERS

✔ VIEW

ROMAN BRIDGE

CASTEL SAN PIETRO

DUOMO

⑪ PIETRA

ROMAN THEATER

ADIGE

⑫ END

VIA CAPP.

VIA DUOMO

PIGNA

ROSA

FORTI

⑩

SANT' ANASTASIA

GARIBALDI

PAVINO

S. ANA.

BORSARI

⑧

S. MARIA

SOTTORIVA

TO GIARDINO GIUSTI

NUOVO →

VITT

SAN. FRAN.

EMILEI

CORSO PORTA

⑨

⑥

⑦

PALAZZO RAGIONE, TORRE LAMBERTI & WC

S. LORENZO

⑤

PELL.

4 SPADE

CATULLO

MAZZINI

CORSO CAVOUR

④

OBERDAN

VIA MARIO

SCALA

NORIS

V. ANFI.

S. NC.

CAPPELLO

HOUSE OF JULIET

CATTANEO

③

ENTER

CAPPELLO

NAVI

LISTON

WC

① ② ARENA

PIAZZA BRÀ START

OLD CITY WALLS

DOGANA

MACELLO

N

CORSO PORTA NUOVA

PIAZZA CITTA-DELLA

ℹ

TO TRAIN STATION

PALLONE

ALEARDI

DCH

NEAR VENICE

❶ Piazza Brà	❼ House of Juliet
❷ Roman Arena	❽ Piazza dei Signori
❸ Devotional Column	❾ Tombs of the Scaligeri Family
❹ Porta Borsari & Corso Porta Borsari	❿ Church of Sant'Anastasia
❺ Enoteca Oreste	⓫ Ponte Pietra & River View
❻ Piazza Erbe	⓬ Duomo

❷ Roman Arena

Just as modern stadiums are usually located outside of downtown districts, Romans built this stadium outside the town walls.

With 72 aisles, this elliptical 466-by-400-foot amphitheater is the third largest in the Roman world (and it was originally 50 percent taller). Most of the stone you see is original. Dating from the first century A.D., it looks great in its pink marble. Over the centuries, crowds of up to 25,000 spectators have cheered Roman gladiator battles, medieval executions, and modern plays—including the popular opera festival (held every summer), which takes advantage of the Arena's famous acoustics. While there's little to see inside except for the impressive stonework, it is memorable to visit a Roman arena that is still a thriving venue for concerts. If you climb to the top, you'll enjoy great city views (€6, don't bother with the combo-ticket that includes the unimpressive Maffei Museum, Tue–Sun 8:30–19:30, Mon 13:30–19:30, closes at 14:00 during opera season, last entry one hour before closing, WC near entry, tel. 045-800-3204).

• *As you exit the Arena, look to your right. Where the street splits you'll see a column.*

❸ Devotional Column

In the Middle Ages, this column blessed a marketplace held here. Ten yards in front of it, a bronze plaque in the sidewalk shows the Roman city plan—a town of 20,000 placed strategically in the bend of the river, which provided protection on three sides. A wall enclosed the peninsula. The center of the grid was the forum, today's Piazza Erbe. (If you look down Via Mazzini, the busy main pedestrian drag, the bell tower in the distance marks Piazza Erbe.)

• *After viewing the bronze plaque, turn around so your back is to the Arena. Head straight down Via Oberdan and continue a couple of blocks to an ancient gate, the Porta Borsari.*

❹ Porta Borsari and Corso Porta Borsari

You're standing before the main entrance to Roman Verona; back in the day, this functioned as a toll booth (*borsari* means purse, referring to the collection of tolls here). Below the spiral fluted columns (which parents nickname "tortiglioni"—a pasta kids can relate to), you'll see the names of patrons ("this arch was brought to you by the generous support of..."). Outside the café, the stone on the curb is from a tomb—in Roman times, the roads outside the

NEAR VENICE

walls were lined with tombstones, as no one could be buried within the town itself. Step into the café. A glass panel in the floor shows the original Roman foundations and pavement stones below.

Now cross into the ancient city and walk down Corso Porta Borsari, the ancient main drag, toward what was the forum. Make it a scavenger hunt. As you walk, discover bits of the town's illustrious past—chips of Roman columns, medieval reliefs, fine old facades, fossils in marble—as well as its elegant present of fancy shops in a setting that prioritizes pedestrians over cars.

• *A block before you reach Piazza Erbe, at Vicolo San Marco in Foro, detour right, following the Pozzo dell'Amore sign. Twenty yards off Corso Porta Borsari, you'll find...*

❺ Enoteca Oreste

This funky wine and grappa bar is still run by Oreste (with his Chicagoan wife, Beverly) like a 1970s old-style *enoteca*. Browse, munch, sample. There's no formal food, but an abundance of fun and hearty bar snacks instead. This historic *enoteca* was once the private chapel of the archbishop of Verona. Traces of the past hide between the bottles—ask Beverly to tell you the story (daily 8:00–20:00, Vicolo San Marco in Foro 7, tel. 045-803-4369).

• *Return to Corso Porta Borsari and continue on until you hit a big square.*

❻ Piazza Erbe

This bustling market square is a photographer's delight. Its pastel buildings corral the fountains, pigeons, and people who have congregated here since Roman times, when this was a forum. Notice the Venetian lion hovering above the square, reminding locals of their conquerors since 1405. During medieval times, the stone canopy in the center held the scales where merchants measured the weight of goods they bought and sold, such as silk, wool, and wood. A fountain has bubbled here for 2,000 years. Its statue, originally Roman, had lost its head and arms. After a sculptor added a new head and arms, the statue became Verona's Madonna. She holds a small banner that reads, "I want justice and I bring peace."

If you were standing here in the Middle Ages, you would have been surrounded by proud noble family towers. Medieval nobles showed off with towers. Renaissance nobles showed off with finely painted facades on their palaces. If you look carefully, you can see remnants of the 16th-century days when Verona was nicknamed "the painted city."

While Piazza Brà is left for the tourists, Pizza Erbe is for the locals, who start their evening with an *aperitivo* here. It's a trendy scene, as young Veronans fill the bars to enjoy their refreshing *spritz* drinks, olives, and chips.

• *At the far end of Piazza Erbe, a market column featuring St. Zeno, the patron of Verona, looks at the crazy crowds flushing into the city's silly claim to touristic fame...the House of Juliet (100 yards down Via Cappello to #23—just follow the crowds). Side-trip there now (but watch your wallet—it's a pickpocket's haven).*

❼ House of Juliet

The tiny, admittedly romantic courtyard is a spectacle in itself, with tourists from all over the world posing on the balcony,

Nebraskans polishing Juliet's bronze breast, and amorous graffiti everywhere. Residents marvel that each year, about 1,600 Japanese tour groups break their Venice-Milan ride for an hour-long stop in Verona just to see this courtyard. Hang out and savor the scene. The information boxes (€1 for two people) offer a good history: "While no documentation has been discovered to prove the truth of the legend, no documentation has disproved it either." The "museum," which displays art inspired by the love story, plus costumes and the bed from Franco Zeffirelli's film *Romeo and Juliet,* is certainly not worth the €6 entry fee (Tue–Sun 8:30–19:30, Mon 13:30–19:30, tel. 045-803-4303).

Was there a Juliet Capulet? You just walked down Via Cappello, the street of the cap makers. Above the courtyard entry (looking out) is a coat of arms featuring a hat—representing a family that made hats and which would be named, logically, Capulet.

The world does love Juliet. Upstairs (through the embroidery store on the left as you enter the courtyard) is the home of Verona's Juliet Club (www.julietclub.com). Every day, volunteers respond to countless letters addressed simply to Juliet, Verona, Italy. You can see them at work and read a smattering of love letters (9:00–21:00). There's also a fine view of the courtyard from here.

Watch out: The house may become an even more popular destination thanks to the 2010 movie *Letters to Juliet,* about a young woman (played by Amanda Seyfried) who finds a letter to Juliet and travels through Italy to help the author find her lost love.

• *Return to Piazza Erbe. From the center, head right to Via della Costa—it's marked by a whale's rib suspended under an arch. It was likely a souvenir brought home by a traveling merchant, reminding the townspeople of a big world out there. Walk down Via della Costa, into the big square.*

❽ Piazza dei Signori

Literally the "square of the lords," this is Verona's sitting room, more quiet and harmonious than Piazza Erbe. The buildings—which span five centuries—define the square and are all linked by arches. The long portico on the left is inspired by Brunelleschi's Hospital of the Innocents (considered the first Renaissance building) in Florence.

Locals call the square Piazza Dante for the statue of the Italian poet Dante Alighieri that dominates it. Dante—always pensive, never smiling—seems to wonder why the tourists choose Juliet over him. Dante was expelled from Florence for political reasons and was granted asylum in Verona by the Scaligeri family. With the whale's rib behind you, you're facing the brick, crenellated 14th-century Scaligeri residence. Behind Dante is the yellowish 15th-century Venetian Renaissance–style Portico of the Counsel. In front of Dante to his right (follow the white *WC* signs) is the 12th-century Romanesque **Palazzo della Ragione.**

Facing the Palazzo della Ragione, a lane on the right leads into its courtyard. Enter the courtyard. The impressive staircase—which goes nowhere—is the only surviving Renaissance staircase in Verona. For a grand city view, you can climb to the top of the 13th-century **Torre dei Lamberti** (€6 for stairs or elevator, daily 8:30–19:30, ticket office just beyond the whalebone on the right). The elevator saves you 245 steps—but you'll still need to climb about 45 more to get to the first viewing platform. It's not worth continuing up the endless spiral stairs to the second viewing platform.

• *Exit the courtyard the way you entered and turn right, continuing downhill. Within a block, you'll find the...*

❾ Tombs of the Scaligeri Family

These exotic and very Gothic 14th-century tombs, with their fine, original wrought-iron protective cages, evoke the age when one family ruled Verona. The Scaligeri family was to Verona what the Medici family was to Florence. These were powerful people. They changed the law so that they could be buried within the town. They forbade the presence of any towers but their own. And, by building tombs atop pillars, they arranged to be looked up to even in death.

• *Continue 15 yards to the next corner and take a left on Vicolo Cavalletto. At the first corner, turn right and walk to the big unfinished brick facade of Verona's largest church. For a fragrant and potentially tasty diversion, pop into the recommended **Albertini** and **Gastronomia,** two classic family-run alimentari, both located on Corso Sant'Anastasia as you approach the Church of Sant'Anastasia. Either can rustle up tasty sandwiches (about €3), and Albertini sells cold beers and juices.*

❿ Church of Sant'Anastasia

This church was built from the late 13th century through the 15th century. Although the facade was never finished (as the builders ran out of steam), the interior was—and still is—brilliant. Step inside to see the delightful way this region's medieval churches were painted. Note the grimacing hunchbacks holding basins of

 holy water on their backs (near main entrance at base of columns). And don't miss Pisanello's fresco of *St. George and the Princess* (at the tip of the arch, high above chapel to right of altar). Once colorful, it has oxidized over time to its current monochrome state. For a closer look at its wonderful detail, check out the images on the computer terminal below. Ask for the English brochure, which describes the story of the church (€2.50, March–Oct Mon–Sat 9:00–18:00, Sun 13:00–18:00; Nov–Feb closes daily at 17:00).

• *Leaving the church, make two lefts, and walk along the right side of the church to Via Sottoriva. To the right, the Sottoriva arcade was once busy with colorful wine bars and* osterie, *some of which still exist (see "Eating in Verona," later). But for now, head to the left on Via Sottoriva. In a block, you'll reach a small riverfront area with stone benches that usually have a few modern-day Romeos and Juliets gazing at each other rather than the view. Belly up to the river view.*

⓫ Ponte Pietra and a River View

The white stones of the Ponte Pietra are from the original Roman bridge that stood here. After the bridge was bombed in World War II, the Veronese fished the marble chunks out of the river to rebuild it. From here, you can see the Roman Theater, built into the hillside behind the green hedge (see page 177). Way above the theater (behind the cypress trees) is the fortress, Castello San Pietro.

Continue up the river toward the bridge. You'll pass Gelateria Ponte Pietra (at #23, no sign because of city codes), where Mirko and Stefano dish out fine gelato—try the *riso* (daily 14:30–20:00, until 23:00 in summer). Walk to the high point on the bridge and find the padlocks on the left side. They are locked in place by romantic couples as proof of the permanence of their love—and they throw the key in the river. For some exercise, break away, cross the bridge, and visit the Roman Theater or head up to the Castello for an expansive city view (at the end of the bridge, go up the little road called Scalone Castello San Pietro, or climb the stairs to the left of the theater). Me? I'll just enjoy the view from here.

• From the bridge, look back 200 yards at the tall spire…that's where you're heading.

⑫ Duomo

Started in the 12th century, this church was built over a period of several hundred years. Before entering, note the fine Romanesque carvings on its facade. Also notice the elevated tomb (high above on the left)—a donor was buried this way at his request. Step inside, and pick up the leaflet that explains the church's highlights (€2.50, March–Oct Mon–Fri 10:00–17:30, Sat 10:00–16:00, Sun 13:30–17:30, shorter hours off-season, Nov–Feb closed Mon).

Directly ahead is Titian's *Assumption* (Mary calmly rides a cloud—direction up—to the shock and bewilderment of the crowd below). To the right of the Titian (through the last wooden door, left of high altar) are the ruins of an older church. These are the 10th-century foundations of the Church of St. Elena, turned intriguingly into a modern-day chapel featuring exposed fourth-century mosaic floors from the Roman church that originally stood here. Don't miss the adjacent baptistery, with its clean Romanesque lines, hanging 14th-century crucifix, and fine marble font. Try to identify the eight scenes depicted before referring to my answers. (Answers: Annunciation; first Christmas, with animals licking baby Jesus and giving him a barnyard welcome; announcement to shepherds of Jesus' birth; Epiphany, with the Three Kings giving their gifts to baby Jesus; Herod commanding to have firstborn sons killed; Slaughter of the Innocents; flight to Egypt; and finally, facing the entry door, John the Baptist baptizing Christ.) The peaceful Romanesque cloister is to the right as you leave the church, with mosaics from a fifth-century Christian church exposed below the walk.

Sights in Verona

▲▲**Evening *Passeggiata***—For me, the highlight of Verona is the *passeggiata* (stroll)—especially in the evening. Make a big circle from Piazza Brà through the old town on Via Mazzini (one of Europe's many "first pedestrian-only streets") to the colorful Piazza Erbe, and then back down Corso Porta Borsari to Piazza Brà. Consider a small town, where people know each other, all out on parade. Like peacocks, the young and nubile spread their wings. The classy shop windows are integral to the *passeggiata* as, for the ladies, shopping is a sport. Their never-finished wardrobes are considered a work in progress. This is when they gather ideas. If you're going to complement your stroll with a sit in a café or bar, the best plan is to enjoy a *spritz* drink on Piazza Erbe (the oldest and most elegant bars are on the end farthest from Juliet's balcony).

▲**Castelvecchio**—Verona's powerful Scaligeri family built this castle (1343–1356) as both a residence and a fortress. Today, it's a museum showing off Verona's glory days. The extensive collection of Verona's finest art is well-displayed throughout the huge building. The religious statues, once brightly painted, were the city's medieval forte. The paintings were the city's Renaissance forte. There's also armor, and a chance to roam the ramparts with fine views of the city and river. Info sheets with good English descriptions are available throughout, but the audioguide (€3.60, or €5/2 people) is worthwhile (€6, Tue–Sun 8:30–19:30, Mon 13:30–19:30, see map on page 180 for location).

Next to Castelvecchio, the **Fortress Bridge** (Ponte Scaligero) is free, open to the public, and fun to stroll across. Destroyed by the Germans in World War II, it was rebuilt in the 1950s. Today it's understandably a favorite for wedding-day photos.

▲**Basilica of San Zeno Maggiore**—This church is dedicated to the patron saint of Verona, whose remains are buried in the crypt under the main altar. In addition to being a fine example of Italian Romanesque, the basilica features Mantegna's *San Zeno Triptych*, with its marvelous perspective, peaceful double-columned cloisters, and a set of 48 paneled 11th-century bronze doors nicknamed "the poor man's Bible." Pretend you're an illiterate medieval peasant and do some reading. Facing the altar, on the walls of the right-side aisle, you can see frescoes painted on top of other frescoes and graffiti dating from the 1300s. These were done by people who fled into the church in times of war or flooding and scratched prayers into the walls. Druidic-looking runes are actually decorated letters typical of the Gothic period, like those in illuminated manuscripts (March–Oct Mon–Sat 8:30–18:00, Sun 13:00–18:00; Nov–Feb Tue–Sat 10:00–13:00 & 13:30–16:00, Sun 13:00–17:00, closed Mon; located on Piazza San Zeno, less than a mile northwest of Castelvecchio).

Roman Theater (Teatro Romano)—Dating from the first century A.D., this ancient theater was discovered in the 19th century and restored. Admission includes the Roman Museum, located high in the building above the theater (reach it via elevator—start at the stage and walk up the middle set of stairs, then continue straight on the path through the bushes).

The museum displays a model of the theater, a small Jesuit chapel, and Roman artifacts, including mosaic floors, busts and other statuary, clay and bronze votive figures, and architectural fragments. You'll find helpful English information sheets throughout (€4.50, Tue–Sun 8:30–19:30, Mon 13:30–19:30, last entry 45 minutes before closing, theater located across the river near Ponte Pietra, tel. 045-800-0360). From mid-June through August, the theater stages Shakespeare plays—only a little more difficult to understand in Italian than in Elizabethan English.

Giardino Giusti—If you'd enjoy a Renaissance garden with manicured box hedges and towering cypress trees, you might find this worth the walk and fee.

Cost and Hours: (€6, daily April–Sept 9:00–19:00, Oct–March 9:00–17:00; cross river at Ponte Nuovo, continue up Via Carducci, and turn left on Via Giardino Giusti, or take bus #72 from Piazza Brà and get off at Via Carducci.

Sleeping in Verona

I've listed rates you'll pay in regular season—most of April through May, and September through October. Prices soar above these (about €20–30 more per night) in late June, July, and August (during opera season), early April (during the Vinitaly wine festival—see Wines sidebar on page 183), and during big trade fairs or major holidays. Prices are lower from November to March. Hotel websites clearly explain their rates.

Near Piazza Erbe

$$$ Hotel Aurora, just off Piazza Erbe, has friendly family management, a terrace overlooking the piazza, and 19 fresh air-conditioned rooms (S-€70, Sb-€110, Db-€130, Tb-€160, Qb-€200, elevator, Wi-Fi, Piazza Erbe, tel. 045-594-717, fax 045-801-0860, www.hotelaurora.biz, info@hotelaurora.biz, Rita).

$ Casa della Giovane, run by an association that houses poor women, also rents rooms and dorm beds to female tourists. Buried deep in the old town and up several flights of stairs, the place offers 50 cheap beds in a clean, institutional, and peaceful setting (women only, €22/bed in 11-bed dorm, Sb-€35, Db-€60, Tb-€75, no breakfast, reception open 7:00–23:00, Via Pigna 7, tel. 045-596-880, fax 045-088-5449, www.casadellagiovane.com, info@casadella giovane.com).

$ L'Ospite, a 10-minute walk from Piazza Erbe, has six cozy, immaculate, fully equipped apartments and lots of stairs. The rooms, warmly managed by Federica De Rossi, sleep from two to

---

Sleep Code

(€1 = about $1.25, country code: 39)
S = Single, **D** = Double/Twin, **T** = Triple, **Q** = Quad, **b** = bathroom, **s** = shower only. Hotels accept credit cards and provide breakfast unless otherwise noted. Everyone speaks English.

To help you easily sort through these listings, I've divided the rooms into three categories, based on the price for a standard double room with bath:

$$$ Higher Priced—Most rooms €130 or more.
$$ Moderately Priced—Most rooms between €100–130.
$ Lower Priced—Most rooms €100 or less.

Prices can change without notice; verify the hotel's current rates online or by email. For other updates, see www.ricksteves.com/update.

---

four, and include air-conditioning, and—for those who stay longer—free laundry service (Db-€95, Tb/Qb-about €40–55/person, discounts for cash and longer stays, no daily cleaning; cross Ponte Navi bridge and continue straight, hotel is to the left of the San Paolo church at Via XX Settembre 3; tel. 045-803-6994, mobile 329-426-2524, www.lospite.com, info@lospite.com).

Near Piazza Brà

You'll find several options in the quiet streets just off Piazza Brà, within 200 yards of the bus stop. From the square, yellow signs point you to the hotels. The first three are big business-class places with the service and formality you'd expect. The Torcolo is more homey and friendly.

$$ Hotel Milano, just behind the Arena, is an art hotel with 52 rooms. The lobby and fancier rooms are tricked out in black and chrome (Sb-€75–100, basic Db-€120, fancy Db-€143, aircon, elevator, Wi-Fi, garage-€20/day, Vicolo Tre Marchetti 11, tel. 045-591-692, fax 045-801-1299, www.hotelmilano-vr.it, info @hotelmilano-vr.it).

$$ Hotel Giulietta e Romeo is on a quiet side street just 50 yards behind the Roman Arena. Its 40 well-designed rooms (nine with balconies) are decorated in dark colors (Sb-€95–110, Db-€120, bigger Db-€140, prices vary with season, non-smoking rooms available, air-con, elevator, Wi-Fi, free loaner bikes, laundry, garage-€19/day, Vicolo Tre Marchetti 3, tel. 045-800-3554, fax 045-801-0862, www.giuliettaeromeo.com, info@giuliettae romeo.com).

Verona Hotels & Restaurants

1 Hotel Aurora
2 Casa della Giovane
3 To L'Ospite Apartments
4 Hotels Milano & Giulietta e Romeo
5 Hotel Europa
6 Hotel/Rist. Torcolo
7 Hotel Arena
8 To Villa Francescatti
9 Osteria al Duca
10 Bottega del Vin
11 Osteria le Vecete & Pizzeria Du de Cope
12 Osteria Sottoriva
13 Enoteca Can Grande
14 Trattoria al Pompiere
15 Rist. Olivo, Trattoria de Giovanni Rana & Brek Cafeteria
16 PAM Supermarket
17 Albertini & Gastronomia
18 Internet Cafés (2)
19 Welcome Travel

$$ Hotel Europa offers sleek, modern comfort in springtime colors. Most of its 46 rooms are non-smoking, and a few rooms have little balconies overlooking the *piazzetta* below (Db-€120–180, 10 percent discount with this book, air-con, elevator, Wi-Fi, Via Roma 8, tel. 045-594-744, fax 045-800-1852, www.verona hoteleuropa.com, hoteleuropavr@tiscali.it).

$ Hotel Torcolo offers 19 comfortable, lovingly maintained non-smoking rooms with Grandma's furnishings (Sb-€65, Db-around €100, €8–14 for breakfast—optional except during opera season, air-con, fridge in room, elevator, garage-€20/day; from Piazza Brà promenade, head down the alley to the right of #16 and walk to Vicolo Listone 3; tel. 045-800-7512, fax 045-800-4058, www.hoteltorcolo.it, hoteltorcolo@virgilio.it, well-run by Silvia, Diana, and helpful Caterina).

Near Castelvecchio

$ Hotel Arena, while borderline dreary, is a good value for those on a tight budget. Located in a peaceful courtyard off a busy street just west of Castelvecchio, it offers 17 very basic, institutional, quiet rooms (S-€45, Sb-€60, D-€75, Db-€85, no air-con, Wi-Fi, 200 yards from Piazza Brà at Stradone Porta Palio #2, tel. & fax 045-803-2440, www.albergoarena.it, info@albergoarena.it, Beatrice).

Hostel

$ Villa Francescatti is a good hostel (€18 beds with breakfast, 6- or 8-bed rooms, one dorm with 35 beds, some family rooms with private bathrooms, €8 dinners, launderette, rooms closed from 9:00 to 17:00 but reception open all day, 24:00 curfew; bus #73 from train station on weekdays or #91 at night and Sun to Piazza Isolo stop, walk over the river beyond Ponte Nuovo at Salita Fontana del Ferro 15; tel. 045-590-360, fax 045-800-9127).

Eating in Verona

Osteria al Duca is a fun family-run place with a lively atmosphere and good traditional dishes. Locals line up for its affordable two-course €15 fixed-price meal. I much prefer their ground floor (*piano terra*—worth requesting). Reservations are advised (closed Sun, half-block from Scaligeri family tombs at Via Arche Scaligere 2, tel. 045-594-474, Alessandro or Daniele).

Ristorante Torcolo is a warm family restaurant, with mom (Paola) running the kitchen and father and son (Roberto and Luca) serving. It's dressy but without pretense, and the service is professional yet fun-loving. There's a happy energy, stoked by carts of boiled meat and desserts rolling temptations through the dining room. They serve all the classic dishes, with an accessible menu and an extensive wine list (€9 pastas, €18 *secondi*, €3 cover, closed Mon, just behind the Piazza Brà scene on a quiet street, Via Carlo Cattaneo 11, tel. 045-803-3730).

Bottega del Vin is pricey, venerable, and proud to have a sister establishment in New York City. Under a high ceiling and walls of wine bottles, brisk black-vested waiters match traditional dishes (polenta, duck, game) with glasses of fine wine. Choose from 100 open bottles—glasses range from €1 to €15. The waitstaff, ambience, and food have deep roots in local culture. I like their front room best (€12 pastas, €21 *secondi*, good daily specials, Wed–Mon 12:00–15:00 & 19:00–24:00, opens at 18:00 for appetizers, closed Tue; take third left off Via Mazzini as you're coming from Piazza Erbe, Via Scudo di Francia 3; tel. 045-800-4535, reservations smart for dinner).

Osteria le Vecete, consisting of just one room under open beams and walls of wine, has an enjoyable, intimate pub ambience. Slide up to the bar for wine and *tartine* (elaborate little open-faced sandwiches), or sit down and order a meal. Choose from daily specials of homemade pastas and Veronese dishes—as well as salads or a selection of *tartine*. The blackboard lists plenty of wines by the glass (€9 pastas, €18 *secondi*, daily 12:30–15:30 & 18:30–23:00, drinks and snacks served between mealtimes and until late; buried in an alley between Via Mazzini and Corso Sant'Anastasia; from Piazza Brà, go down Via Mazzini and turn left onto Via Quattro Spade, then right onto Via Pelliciai to #32A; tel. 045-594-748, Karen).

Pizzeria Du de Cope is a high-energy place that buzzes with smartly attired young waiters and locals who consider the pizza here to be the best in town (big €9 salads, €9 pizzas, Wed–Mon 12:00–14:00 & 19:00–23:00, flamboyant desserts, family-friendly, no reservations, near Osteria le Vecete at Galleria Pelliciai 10, tel. 045-595-562).

Osterie *on Via Sottoriva*: Historically, Verona's river served as the motorway. Along the river, a fine old covered arcade (the portico of Via Sottoriva) was the setting for places where business deals could be made over a glass of wine. Several of these survive as rustic, characteristic eateries serving finger food. Browse around and consider the wonderful **Osteria Sottoriva,** with simple soups and pastas, and both indoor and outdoor seating (open from 18:30, behind the Church of Sant'Anastasia in the covered arcade, Via Sottoriva 9).

Enoteca Can Grande enjoys turning people on to great, well-matched food and wine. Their cold plates, designed for wine appreciation, make a fine main dish. I'd trust Giuliano and Corrina to come up with a creative meal that fits your budget. For €35 per person plus wine, they'll blow you away with a *degustatione menu* extravaganza that just keeps on coming. It's a festival of *antipasti*

The Wines of Verona

Wine connoisseurs love the high-quality wines of this area. The hills to the east are covered with grapes to make Soave; to the north is Valpolicella country; and Bardolino comes from vineyards to the west.

Valpolicella grapes, which are used to make the fruity red Valpolicella table wine (found everywhere), are also used to make the full-bodied red Amarone and the sweet dessert wine, Recioto. To produce Amarone, grapes are partially dried (*passito*) before fermentation, then aged for a minimum of four years in oak casks, resulting in a rich, velvety, full-bodied red. Recioto, which in local dialect means "ears," uses only the grapes from the top of the cluster (so they sort of look like the ears of a face). Because these grapes get the most sun, they mature the fastest and have the highest concentration of sugar. The grapes are dried for months until all moisture has gone out before pressing, and aged for one to three years.

Bardolino, from the vineyards near Lake Garda, is a light, fruity wine, like a French Beaujolais. It's a perfect picnic wine.

Soave, which might be Italy's best-known white wine, goes well with seafood and risotto dishes. While Soave can vary widely in quality, the best are called "Soave Classico" and come from the heart of the region, near the Soave Castle. Soave is sometimes aged in oak casks, giving it a mellow, rounded flavor.

Sample these and many others at the numerous *enoteche* (wine-tasting bars) or at any restaurant around town. In early April, Verona hosts Vinitaly, the most important international convention of domestic and international wines. Vintners vie for prestigious awards for the past year's vintage. Tourists are welcome to attend at the end of the week, and are shuttled to the convention hall from Piazza Brà. Hotels book up months in advance. Check with the TI and www.vinitaly.com for details.

If you're visiting the area in the fall, consider a day trip to nearby Monteforte d'Alpone, east of Verona. The town hosts a fun, raucous wine festival in September—ask at the TI for more information on this and other regional wine festivals.

treats, followed by an imaginative pasta. Complementing the food with just the right wines can leave you with a meal you'll never forget. This is a rich and unique gourmet experience that costs no more than dinner at your basic, dressy restaurant (Wed–Mon 12:00–15:30 & 18:00–24:00, closed Tue; a block off Piazza Brà at Via Dietro Liston 19D—if the equestrian statue jogged slightly right, he'd head straight here; tel. 045-595-022).

Trattoria al Pompiere, which has a commitment to regional traditions, is a favorite of foodies and has earned its huge local following. Amid the bustle (contained by walls plastered with photos of local big shots), Stefano and his gang serve gourmet meats and cheeses as *antipasti*, ideal for a mixed plate to complement the huge selection of fine wines. There's not a bad table in this grand old-style dining room. Reservations are wise (€12 pastas, €15 *secondi*, lunch from 12:30, dinner from 19:30, closed Sun, ladies' menus without prices, Vicolo Regina d'Ungheria 5, tel. 045-803-0537).

Eating on Piazza Brà: A cancan of mainly nondescript restaurants lines the *passeggiata* action along Piazza Brà. You may be sacrificing service, value, and quality for the chance to enjoy a view of the floodlit Roman Arena and Verona on parade while you dine. Except for Brek Cafeteria, restaurants on the piazza tend to charge a cover and service fee, making even pizza here a pricey stop. **Ristorante Olivo** and the more upmarket **Trattoria de Giovanni Rana** are fixtures. For the same view at self-service prices, consider the well-run and modern **Brek Cafeteria** (€5 pastas, €6 *secondi*, cheap salad plates, daily, breakfast and sandwiches from 9:30, full menu 11:30–15:00 & 18:30–22:00, indoor/outdoor seating, facing the equestrian statue at Piazza Brà 20, tel. 045-800-4561).

Eating Cheap near Piazza Brà: **PAM supermarket** is just outside the historic gate on Piazza Brà (daily 8:00–21:00, exit Piazza Brà through the gate and take the first right). The *döner kebab* place—just behind Hotel Europa and a few steps off Via Roma—is cheap, fast, and not Italian (great €4 meals).

Eating Cheap near Piazza Erbe: You'll find two family-run *alimentari*—**Albertini** and **Gastronomia** (both Mon–Sat 8:00–20:00, Sun 9:00–13:30)—on Corso Sant'Anastasia, between the end of Vicolo Cavoletto and Church of Sant'Anastasia.

A list of "official" picnicking spots can be picked up at the TI—freelance picnicking in Verona is strongly discouraged. One good spot is along the river by Ponte Pietra.

Verona Connections

From Verona by Train to: Venice (2/hour, 1.5 hours), **Padua** (2/hour, 1 hour), **Vicenza** (2/hour, 40 minutes), **Florence** (about hourly, often with transfer in Bologna, 3 hours, note that all Rome-bound trains stop in Florence—listed as *Firenze* on train schedules), **Bologna** (hourly, 2 hours), **Milan** (2/hour, 1.5–2 hours), **Rome** (hourly, 4–5 hours, often with transfer in Bologna), **Bolzano** (2/hour, 1.5–2 hours, note that Brennero-bound trains stop in Bolzano).

Ravenna

Ravenna is on the tourist map for one reason: its 1,500-year-old churches, decorated with best-in-the-West Byzantine mosaics. The city's churches and mosaics date from the time (c. A.D. 400–600) when it was the center of Western civilization—a civilization in transition, from Roman to barbarian to Byzantine to medieval. You'll see all these layers in Ravenna.

In 402, barbarian tribes were zeroing in on the city of Rome. The Roman emperor moved his capital to Ravenna, a city well-known as a home port for the imperial navy (today's Classe). Because of its location, Ravenna kept close ties with the other Roman capital at Constantinople (called Byzantium).

Ravenna was conquered by the Goths from Hungary in 476, and the 1,000 years of the Roman Empire came to an end. But Ravenna continued on as the Goths' capital. They kept much of the Roman infrastructure and legitimized their rule by building sophisticated palaces and churches in the Roman style.

In 540, the Byzantine emperor Justinian conquered the Goths. This reunited Italy with the still-thriving Empire to the east. Justinian turned Ravenna into a pinnacle of civilization. It remained a flickering light in Europe's Dark Ages for another 200 years, until the Lombard tribe of Germany booted out the Byzantines (in 751). Ravenna melted into the backwaters of medieval Italy, staying out of historical sight for a thousand years.

In your sightseeing, you'll see art from each of these periods: Roman (Mausoleum of Galla Placidia, Neonian Baptistery), Gothic (Arian Baptistery, Basilica di Sant'Apollinare in Nuovo, Archiepiscopal Museum), Byzantine (Basilica di San Vitale, House of Stone Carpets, Church of Sant'Apollinare in Classe), and medieval (Tomb of Dante, Basilica di San Francesco).

Today, Ravenna's economy booms with a big chemical industry, the discovery of offshore gas deposits, and the construction of a new ship canal. The bustling town center is Italy's best for bicyclists. Residents go about their business, while busloads of tourists slip quietly in and out of town for the best look at the glories of Byzantium this side of Istanbul—specifically, the richest collection of mosaics from the fifth and sixth centuries anywhere.

Ravenna is a 90-minute detour from the main Venice–Florence train line and worth the effort for those interested in old mosaics. While its sights don't merit an overnight stop, many find that the peaceful charm of this untouristy and classy town makes it a pleasant surprise in their Italian wandering. The only downside of a quick visit is that Ravenna provides no official place for visitors to check their bags (although the Strada Facendo café has offered to watch bags for my readers—see "Helpful Hints," below).

Orientation to Ravenna

Central Ravenna is quiet, with a pedestrian-friendly core and more bikes than cars. Keep to the sides of the streets; bikes take the center lane (subtly indicated by white brick paving) down the brick "pedestrian" streets. Listen for the outta-my-way bells.

On a quick visit to Ravenna, follow my self-guided walk and visit the Basilica di San Vitale, its adjacent Mausoleum of Galla Placidia, and the Basilica di Sant'Apollinare Nuovo. While the main sights are easily walkable from the station, it's fun to do the city by bike. A handy bike-rental place is at the train station. If arriving by car, park near the station and pretend you arrived by train.

Tourist Information

The TI is a 15-minute walk (or a 5-minute pedal) from the train station (April–Sept Mon–Sat 8:30–19:00, Sun 10:00–18:00; Oct–March closes one hour earlier; Via Salara 8, tel. 0544-35404, www.turismo.ra.it).

City Pass: Most of Ravenna's sights are covered by a single combo-ticket. The ticket is a great deal. At the first sight, pay €10.50 (€8.50 July–Feb) and then nearly everything is covered: Basilica di San Vitale, Mausoleum of Galla Placidia, Basilica di Sant'Apollinare Nuovo, Archiepiscopal Museum and Chapel of Sant'Andrea, and the Neonian Baptistery. All of the included sights have the same hours (daily April–Sept 9:00–19:00, Oct–March 10:00–17:00 or 17:30).

Helpful Hints

Baggage Storage: Remarkably, Ravenna has no place to deposit a bag. The train station or the bike-rental place at the station may store bags in 2011, but don't count on it. Friendly Mauro at the Strada Facendo café (just to the right as you're leaving the station) has said he'd be happy to let travelers with this book drop bags there.

Laundry: A self-service launderette is a five-minute walk from the train station (€3.50 wash, €3.50 dry, daily 7:00–22:00, go left as you exit the station, then take your first left to Via Candiano 16, mobile 334-572-6354).

Bike Rental: Coop San Vitale next to the train station rents bikes (€1.10/hour, €8.50/day, Mon–Fri 7:00–19:00, closed Sat–Sun, photo ID required, tel. 0544-37031). Many hotels have loaner bikes. The TI loans 10 one-speed bikes on a first-come, first-served basis (bring your passport). Ask the TI for the free bike-trail map, which includes rides to the sea, parks, and historical sights.

Parking: Two lots are near the historic center: one accessible from the west side of Via Roma, at Via Mura di Porta Serrata (€1.50/day), and another at Largo Giustiniano just north of San Vitale (€2.80/day). Or find a lot near the station. Many lots are free overnight (20:00–8:00).

Local Guide: For a private guide, Claudia Frassineti is excellent (€95/half-day, mobile 335-613-2996, www.abacoguide.it, abacoguide@tiscalinet.it).

Self-Guided Walk

Welcome to Ravenna (A Four-Hour Tour)

A visit to Ravenna can be as short as a four-hour loop from the train station. This walk is followed by visits to the Basilica di San Vitale, Mausoleum of Galla Placidia, and Basilica di Sant'Apollinare Nuovo.

Main Drag from Station into Town: The station and surrounding neighborhood were bombed in World War II. Walk (or pedal) the main drag, Viale Farini, from the station directly into town. You'll pass the St. John the Evangelist church on the left, with a rebuilt facade. This was the palace church of the fifth-century Empress Galla Placidia. She and her children were caught at sea in a storm, prayed to St. John (the protector of sailors), and survived. As a thanks of votive offering, she had this church built at the site of their first safe step ashore. At least that's the story. It is true that in ancient times, the town harbor came right to here. Historic churches are so common in Ravenna that we'll skip this one.

The next big building is the high school, with students' motorbikes parked in front. After that, the boulevard becomes Via Diaz, an arcaded pedestrian shopping street. Remember that the lighter cobbles are for the bikes.

• *At Via degli Ariani, side-trip to the right 50 yards to find the...*

Arian Baptistery: Built during the reign of the Goths (c. 526), this small octagonal building marks the center of their Arian-style Christian faith (free, daily 8:30–19:30, off-season until 16:00, tel. 0544-543-711). Theodoric the Great, the Gothic king of Italy (r. 493–526), built the church next door, with this as his baptistery. Imagine the small baptismal pool that once stood beneath this gloriously decorated dome.

Ravenna

Self-Guided Walk

P Parking

B Bus Stop

TO VENICE VIA A-14

SAN ALBERTO

CIRC. SAN GAETANINO

P

SAN VITALE

GALLA PLACIDIA MAUSOLEUM

PORTA ADRIANO

P

ENTER

PORTA SERRATA

G. ROSSI

V.

SAN VITALE

V. ALIGHIERI   GHISELL

MARKET

SALARA

ARIAN BAPT.

CIRC. FIUME

CAVOUR

BARB.

❹

❷

❾

⓫

❶

❺

COSTA

VIA ARIANI

❷

ℹ

V. DIAZ

PIAZZA BARACCA

D'AZEGLIO

ZIRA

MOR.

CAIR.

NOV.

PIAZZA DEL POPOLO

P. GARI. MARIANI

HOUSE OF STONE CARPETS

P

RASPONI

❽

DANTE'S TOMB

NEONIAN BAPTISTERY

DUOMO

P

GASPERI

B

SAN FRANCESCO

❿

PIAZZA CADUTI

ARCHIEPISCOPAL MUSEUM + CHAPEL OF SANT'ANDREA

DCH

❶ Hotel Bisanzio	❺ Casa Masoli B&B
❷ Albergo Cappello Hotel	❻ Hotel al Giaciglio
❸ Hotel Italia	❼ To Ostello Dante
❹ M Club Delux B&B	❽ Ca' de Ven Restaurant

NEAR VENICE

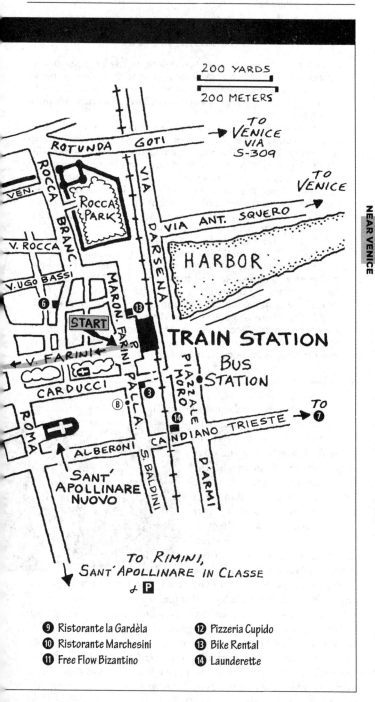

NEAR VENICE

9 Ristorante la Gardèla
10 Ristorante Marchesini
11 Free Flow Bizantino

12 Pizzeria Cupido
13 Bike Rental
14 Launderette

The Arian Heresy

Ravenna's art reflects a centuries-long battle of ideas among Europe's Christians that came to a violent head right here. As you wonder at the beauty of Ravenna's mosaics, you're also witnessing an epic clash between two different interpretations of Christianity.

Around 320 A.D., a devout Christian priest named Arius (c. 256–336) began preaching a seemingly simple idea: Jesus, being the Son of God, was therefore created by God the Father. This idea touched off a firestorm of debate and division unmatched in Christianity until the Protestant Reformation. Arius had raised questions about the very nature of the Christian God: Is God a single entity (as the head of a monotheistic religion should be); three different persons (God the Father, Jesus Christ, and the Holy Spirit); or something in between?

To keep the peace, Roman Emperor Constantine convened a Council at Nicea (in 325 A.D., near modern Istanbul). Arius was accused of doubting the divinity of Christ, by making him separate from and inferior to God the Father. The Council branded Arius a heretic and burned his books. After splitting many theological hairs, they issued the Nicene Creed, which defined God as a Trinity: There was one God, existing in three persons "of the same substance." (Don't make me try to explain it further, or this book may end up getting burned by some sect somewhere.) The three-in-one Trinity became the standard throughout the Empire,

The mosaic-covered dome shows Christ standing waist-deep in the River Jordan, being baptized by John the Baptist (in leopard-skin robe), as the dove of the Holy Spirit descends. The body builder on the left is the personified River Jordan, next to a vase from which the river springs. Notice the realism in John's stance. The 12 apostles, dynamic, with feet in motion, proceed around the dome. The

empty throne between Paul (with scroll) and Peter (with keys) is a reminder that Judgment Day will come.

The mosaic is Arian, stressing Jesus' human rather than divine nature. Jesus is naked, with his genitals only partly obscured by the water. This emphasizes his mortal body, not his divine spirit. He's a beardless youth, suggesting his recent creation by God. The descending dove spews water to purify Jesus, marking the exact moment when Arians believed Jesus' divine nature emerged.

and Arian sects were brutally suppressed.

But that did not settle the matter. Constantine's own son, a fervent Arian, sent missionaries north across the Danube to convert the barbarian Goths to Arian-style Christianity. A century later, as Rome was falling, those same Goths came knocking on Italy's doorstep. They overran Ravenna (476) and made Arian Christianity the official religion of state, though they tolerated the Nicene Christianity of their Italian subjects.

The churches the Goths built—the Arian Baptistery, Basilica di Sant'Apollinare Nuovo, and Chapel of Sant'Andrea (at the Archiepiscopal Museum)—reflected their Arian faith. Arian mosaics of Jesus emphasized his humanness rather than his divinity. (Don't confuse the Arian sect with Nazi Germany's Aryan race.)

In 540, the Byzantine Emperor Justinian drove out the Goths. To unite his empire, he demanded both political and theological conformity. Anything with the slightest whiff of Arianism was wiped out. Mosaics were stripped from the walls, statues defaced, and churches were renamed for saints famous for fighting heretics. In their place came art that reflected Byzantine tastes and Trinitarian theology. You'll see evidence of this shift at many of Ravenna's top sights.

Ravenna was Arianism's Waterloo. Sects were snuffed out, Trinitarians triumphed, and the Nicene Creed (in some form) is still said in many Christian churches today.

Besides heretical Arian elements, there's also the pagan river god, shown in (pagan) Roman fashion as a bearded old man with a vase and river plant.

To modern eyes, these subtle details mean little. But to Emperor Justinian and the Nicenes, these were red flags announcing heresy. While most Arian art was destroyed when Justinian took control, this ceiling is one of the rare survivors.

The adjacent church is closed to the public. It was the cathedral of the Goths, with a simple main structure surviving from the sixth century and a Renaissance portico.

• *Now, return to the pedestrian boulevard, turn right, and continue to...*

Piazza del Popolo: Marking the town center, this square was created by the Venetians in the 15th century. The river once flowed to about where the two columns stand. But it got mucky and full of mosquitoes. (Dante died here...of malaria.) One column was topped by a Venetian lion until 1509 when, with the support of Rome, Ravenna won its independence from Venice. Ravenna's citizens toppled that symbol of Venetian rule and did the local equivalent of tarring and feathering it. The lion was replaced by

St. Vitale (a first-century Christian martyr). The column on the left is topped by Ravenna's first bishop, St. Apollinare. This square is a fine place to join the old guys on benches, watching the community parade by.

• *At the end of Piazza del Popolo, turn left down Via Cairoli two blocks and find the...*

Basilica di San Francesco: Pop into this basilica to enjoy its simple Franciscan interior and flooded mosaic-covered crypt below the main altar. Today's water table is one yard above the Roman floor level. There's actually a pond with goldfish under the altar and over the fifth-century mosaics (spend a coin to turn on the light). The altar features a fourth-century Christian sarcophagus with Jesus in the center and the 12 apostles (daily 7:00–12:00 & 15:00–19:00, tel. 0544-33256).

• *Adjacent to the church, in a small wooded park at the end of Via Dante Alighieri, is the...*

Tomb of Dante: After he was exiled from Florence for his political beliefs, Dante lived out the rest of his life in Ravenna. The Florentines forgave Dante posthumously and wanted to bring their famous poet's bones home to rest. To protect Dante's relics from theft by the Florentines, in 1519 Ravenna hid his bones in the Monastery of San Francesco. There they lay forgotten for three centuries, until they were rediscovered and eventually placed here in 1865 (free, daily April–Sept 9:30–18:30, Oct–March 9:00–12:00 & 14:00–17:00, Via Alighieri Dante 9, tel. 0544-33662). The Dante memorial—often mistaken for a tomb—in Florence's Santa Croce Church is empty.

• *Back on Piazza del Popolo, Via IV Novembre leads a block to the colorful...*

Covered Market: The Mercato Coperto, built in 1921, is good for picnic fixings (Mon–Sat 7:00–14:00, closed Sun). Ravenna's most important sights, the Basilica di San Vitale and Mausoleum of Galla Placidia, and—in the opposite direction—the Basilica di Sant'Apollinare Nuovo, are just a few blocks away.

Sights in Ravenna

Of the following sights, all except the House of Stone Carpets and the Church of Sant'Apollinare in Classe are open the same hours (daily April–Sept 9:00–19:00, Oct–March 10:00–17:00 or 17:30), and covered by the €10.50 City Pass (€8.50 July–Feb); see page 186.

▲▲▲**Basilica di San Vitale**—Imagine: It's A.D. 540. The city of Rome has been looted, the land is crawling with barbarians, and the infrastructure of Rome's thousand-year empire is crumbling fast. Into this chaotic world comes the emperor of the East

(Justinian), bringing order and stability, briefly reassembling the empire, and making Ravenna a beacon of civilization.

Justinian's Basilica di San Vitale is a rambling complex of buildings with two stops of interest to visitors: the basilica itself with its dazzling mosaics and, across the yard, the small Mausoleum of Galla Placidia.

The basilica gift shop rents a slow-talking but thorough audioguide (on Via San Vitale, tel. 0544-541-688).

NEAR VENICE

◑ Self-Guided Tour: Step inside the church. The basilica—standing as a sanctuary of order in the midst of the fall of Rome madness—is covered with lavish mosaics: gold and glass chips the size of your fingernail. It's impressive enough to see a 1,400-year-old church. But it's rare to see one decorated in brilliant mosaics, still managing to convey the intended feeling that "This peace and stability was brought to you by your emperor and God." The art is an intricate ensemble of images that, with the help of a medieval priest, would teach volumes.

Stand before the altar. The centerpiece, high above, is God in heaven, portrayed as Christ sitting on a celestial orb. He oversees his glorious creation, symbolized by the four rivers.

Running the show on earth is Justinian (left side), sporting both a halo and a crown to indicate that he's both leader of the

Church and the state. Here, Justinian brings together the military leaders and the church leaders, all united by the straight line of eyes. The bald bishop of Ravenna—the only person who was actually here—is portrayed most realistically (with a name tag above reading *Maximanus*).

Facing the emperor (from the right side) are his wife, Theodora, and her entourage. Decked out in jewels and pearls, the former dancer who became Justinian's mistress (and then empress)

carries a chalice with which to consecrate the new church.

The border inside the apse is decorated with horns of plenty (cornucopia), promising prosperity in return for the people's obedience to the Church and State (Justinian and Theodora).

Sit in a wooden pew, front and center. Get in a medieval frame of mind and study the scene: On the floor a 16th-century inlaid marble labyrinth leads to the center, evocative of the belief that the pilgrimage of life on earth leads to salvation through Christ. The inlaid shell is the scallop shell of St. James—symbol of pilgrims.

While the decor behind you is Baroque and of no particular artistic importance, the walls and ceilings above and in front sparkle with colorful biblical scenes told with a sixth-century exuberance. (The Viennese artist Gustav Klimt sat right here around 1900 and was inspired by the glint of the light on the gold leaf.)

Okay. Now take a longitudinal, ground-up tour from your seat: The inlaid floor maze leads to the sixth-century marble altar (busy with iconography). Above that is Christ on the globe. Appreciate the symmetry. Two angels hold rays of sun (Christ is the origin of light). The scene is flanked by two cities: Bethlehem and Jerusalem (where Jesus was born and died). Above each city are potted grape vines producing wine, symbols of the blood of Christ. The circle with the monogram of Christ (I for Jesus and X for Christ) symbolizes perfection and eternity.

The ceiling above is a festive celebration of God's creation, with 80 different birds from the sixth century—most still flying around Ravenna today. (Bird-watchers—who visit with binoculars—can easily identify these by their exquisitely detailed and accurate feathers.) All creation swirls around Christ as the sacrificial lamb, supported by four angels.

Leading to the apse, arcing high above, is a triumphal arch.

Its 15 medallions depict 12 apostles, two sons of St. Vitale, and a medieval bearded Christ.

The mid-sixth century was a time of transition, and many consider Ravenna's mosaics to be both the last ancient Roman and the first medieval European works of art. The beardless Christ (as he was depicted by ancient Romans) above the altar and the standard medieval portrayal atop the arch (with a beard) were created within the same generation.

The church's octagonal design—clearly Eastern in origin—inspired at least two churches, including Hagia Sofia, the church-turned-mosque-turned-museum built 10 years later in Constantinople (today's Istanbul). Emperor Charlemagne, the greatest ruler in Europe in A.D. 800, traveled to Ravenna, and was so impressed that when he returned to his capital, Aix-la-Chapelle (present-day Aachen in Germany), he built a church that many consider to be the first great stone building in northern Europe, modeled after this one.

The pilasters surrounding you are brick, covered by sliced marble veneers. Similar marble sheets once covered all the walls. Many were scavenged by Charlemagne to provide flooring for his great church.

From the church, head across the grounds to the Mausoleum of Galla Placidia. Along the way, you'll see a bit of contemporary mosaic art—a glassy round of hay (described on the adjacent plaque). Left over from a recent international festival of mosaics, it reminds visitors that the art form survives today.

▲▲**Mausoleum of Galla Placidia**—Just across the courtyard from the Basilica di San Vitale is a tiny, humble-looking mausoleum, with the oldest—and, to many, the most precious—mosaics in Ravenna (on Via degli Ariani, tel. 0544-541-688). Ninety-five percent of the mosaics here are originals, dating from the late Roman period, when Ravenna was capital of a declining West.

The Mausoleum of Galla Placidia (plah-CHEE-dee-ah) was likely designed to be the burial place of this daughter, sister, and

mother of emperors, who died around A.D. 450. But Galla Placidia died in Rome, and wasn't buried here. The three sarcophagi, built for the imperial family but likely only used by later Christian leaders, stand empty today. The original floor was about four feet lower, explaining the stunted feel of the interior. The art's realistic portrayal of tunics and sandals gives us a peek at the fashions of fifth-century Romans.

The little light that sneaks through the thin alabaster panels brings a glow and a twinkle to the early Christian symbolism that fills the small room. Opposite the door is St. Lawrence martyred on a fiery grill. He's legendary for mocking his executors, reportedly saying something like "I'm done on this side, you can turn me over now." He was famous as an example of the strength of the feisty early Christians. Note the four Gospels clearly labeled on the bookshelf, another inspiration for these first believers as they were persecuted by the Romans.

The dome is filled with stars. Along with Mark's lion, Luke's ox, Matthew's Archangel, and John's eagle, the golden cross rises from the east, bringing life to all. Doves drink from fountains, symbolic of souls finding nourishment in the Word of God. In both transepts are deer, reminding worshippers of Psalms 42: "Like the thirsty deer longs for spring water, so my soul longs for you, my God."

Look toward the back of the mausoleum. Cover the light

from the door with your hand (or close the curtain) to see the standard Roman portrayal of Christ—beardless and as the Good Shepherd. Jesus, dressed in gold and purple like a Roman emperor, is the King of Paradise—receiving the faithful (represented by lambs). The Eastern influence (perhaps inspired by the designs on fine Persian carpets or silks) is apparent in the vault's decorative patterns.

▲▲Basilica di Sant'Apollinare Nuovo—This austere sixth-century church, with a typical early-Christian-basilica floor plan,

has two huge and wonderfully preserved side panels. One is a procession of haloed virgins, each bringing gifts to the Madonna and the Christ Child. Opposite, Christ is on his throne with four angels, awaiting a solemn procession of 26 martyrs. Ignoring the Baroque altar from a thousand years later, we can clearly see the rectangular Roman hall of justice (basilica) floor plan—which was adopted by churches and used throughout the Middle Ages (on Via di Roma, tel. 0544-541-688).

This basilica started (c. 500) as an Arian church—the palace church of King Theodoric of the Goths. Theodoric decorated it with scenes of himself and his royal palace amid Christ and the saints. Look for original, surviving Arian art in the front (on the left, Mary and baby Jesus, on the right—Jesus and four angels) and in the rear (two cityscapes: Classe and Ravenna).

When Justinian arrived, he transformed the church in the Byzantine (and Nicene) style. If you study the arcades in the cityscapes you can see where Arian figures were erased, leaving only bits of hands and fingers on the columns, and blotted-out haloes behind the curtains. The brilliant white-robed figures parading on both sides were remade in the mid-500s with a Byzantine rather than Arian message. The upper zone is original Theodoric Arian: prophets (between windows), miracles of Christ (on the left), and scenes from the last week of Jesus' life and his Resurrection (on the right).

You can have a quick lunch at the air-conditioned, efficient Sant'Apollinare Self-Serve cafeteria right on the church grounds (Mon–Fri 12:00–14:30, closed Sat–Sun). To see contemporary mosaic artists at work, follow the signs up to the second-floor mosaic laboratory in the church's courtyard.

House of Stone Carpets—Discovered in 1993, this sixth-century Byzantine domus (house) offers an extensive array of geometric, animal, and humanistic designs in colored stone floor mosaics. Excavations revealed many layers, dating back to the second century B.C. All were peeled away and preserved elsewhere. Only the sixth-century floor (12 rooms on one level) was put back and exhibited here, very close to its original location. Because this was a private home, its art could break from the conservative norms for public art of the age. The highlight is in the middle: the wonderfully realistic Dance of the Four Seasons. Don't miss the fourth-century Christ as a Shepherd, which some consider the earliest portrayal of Jesus (it's hung on a wall; the face was lost to modern excavations). A visit here is almost meaningless without the €1 audioguide (€4, daily 10:00–18:30, July–Aug may stay open until 23:00; off-season Tue–Sun 10:00–17:00, closed Mon; ask for the 10-minute English-language video—the computer-generated images help visitors envision the place in action; entrance through Church of Sant'Eufemia, on Via Barbiani just off Via Cavour near Piazza Baracca, tel. 0544-32512).

▲**Archiepiscopal Museum**—This museum, in Ravenna's Duomo, contains the sixth-century Chapel of Sant'Andrea (on Piazza Arcivescovado, tel. 0544-541-655). Built as the private prayer chapel for Theodoric's bishop (c. 500), today it anchors a fine collection of Roman, Byzantine-Christian, and pagan statues, reliefs, and mosaics.

You'll enter the chapel under a sixth-century mosaic showing Christ as a religious warrior, stepping triumphantly on a lion and snake (ancient symbols of evil) and carrying the cross as if it were a weapon. The book he holds reads in Latin, "I am the way, the truth, and the life." This is a strong pro-Trinity statement (Jesus, God, and the Holy Spirit are one) against the Arian heresy. The main chamber of the charming chapel is covered in rich mosaics, with lots of sixth-century symbolism and realistic portrait medallions.

The museum's highlight is an exquisite sixth-century Byzantine ivory throne, decorated with scenes from the life of Christ. It was carved for Bishop Maximian, Justinian's Trinitarian appointee, the man who oversaw construction of the Basilica di San Vitale, and whose bald head appears in its mosaics.

▲Neonian Baptistery—Also known as the Baptistery of the Orthodox, this octagonal space dates from about the year 400 (on Piazza Duomo, tel. 0544-219-938). Imagine pagan adults immersed in the pool under glorious ceiling mosaics as they convert to Christianity. The mosaic portrays the common baptistery theme: John the Baptist baptizing Christ, with the personification of the River Jordan looking on. The scene is ringed by empty chairs waiting to welcome you into the eternal heavenly banquet. Twelve apostles with dancing feet—their tunics and cloaks alternating between gold and white—give the room a joyful visual sense of rhythm. The acanthus flowers dividing the apostles were the botanic inspiration for the Corinthian capital, the Roman capital of choice. Decoration on the lower walls features green disks made of precious porphyry stone and a gold leafy arcade creating almond frames for the prophets.

Near Ravenna
▲▲Church of Sant'Apollinare in Classe—The final major sight for Byzantine mosaic fans in Ravenna is a church standing a couple miles outside of town in the suburb of Classe (€3, daily 8:30–19:00, Via Romea Sud, tel. 0544-473-569). It's impressive, but comes in fourth place after the Basilica di San Vitale, Mausoleum of Galla Placidia, and Basilica di Sant'Apollinare Nuovo.

The statue of Emperor Augustus, standing in front of the church, is a reminder that Classe was a strategic navy base in Roman times. In early Christian days, Classe was a big pilgrimage destination and home to a large Christian community. Today, little remains other than its church, and even that was nearly bombed-out in World War II when the Germans used its medieval tower as a lookout.

The artistic treasure here is the mosaic work in the apse, 90 percent of which is original from the sixth century. The scene is an abstract portrayal of the Transfiguration of Jesus. The cross with a tiny portrait of Christ in its center beams light. God's hand above affirms that "This is the Truth." The three lambs represent James, John, and Peter. The landscape is of pine trees, which once forested the region. And St. Apollinare, the first local bishop, is celebrated because it was he who brought Christianity to the area.

The rest of the church—its mosaics lost over time—is pretty plain. While many churches this old have settled and the bases of their columns are no longer visible, here the floor level remains unchanged and you can admire the columns' original bases.

Getting There: The church is two miles out of town. It's an easy bike ride, or catch bus #4 or #44 across the street from the train station (on the corner by the park) or from Piazza Caduti (€1, 3/hour, 15 minutes, reduced service Sun; with your back to the *tabacchi* shop, stop is on the corner; buy bus tickets from any *tabacchi* shop). To head back to town, walk down the same road; the stop is about 100 yards ahead on the right.

Overrated Sight—The nearby beach town of Rimini is a crowded mess.

Sleeping in Ravenna

Summer weekends and all of August are high season for Ravenna.

$$$ Hotel Bisanzio is a business-class splurge renting 38 rooms in the city center (Sb-€98, small Db-€114, mid-size Db-€124, large Db-€154, air-con, Wi-Fi; from Piazza del Popolo take Via IV Novembre to the market, turn left onto Via Cavour and take the first right, Via Salara 30; tel. 0544-217-111, fax 0544-32539, www.bisanziohotel.com, info@bizanziohotel.com).

$$$ Albergo Cappello Hotel fills a renovated Venetian palace with elegant chandeliers, painted open-beam ceilings, and a splendid lounge. It has seven rooms; the bigger rooms are worth

---

Sleep Code

(€1 = about $1.25, country code: 39)

S = Single, **D** = Double/Twin, **T** = Triple, **Q** = Quad, **b** = bathroom, **s** = shower only. Unless otherwise noted, credit cards are accepted, English is spoken, and prices include breakfast.

To help you easily sort through these listings, I've divided the rooms into three categories, based on the price for a standard double room with bath:

$$$ Higher Priced—Most rooms €100 or more.
$$ Moderately Priced—Most rooms between €70–100.
$ Lower Priced—Most rooms €70 or less.

Prices can change without notice; verify the hotel's current rates online or by email. For other updates, see www.ricksteves.com/update.

the expense (Db-€130, Db suite-€180, Wi-Fi, immediately across from the market at Via IV Novembre 41, tel. 0544-219-813, fax 0544-219-814, www.albergocappello.it, info@albergocappello.it).

$$ Hotel Italia, located 100 yards from the train station, feels like a posh chain hotel but is actually family-owned. Its 45 rooms provide modern comforts and lots of space (Sb-€60, Db-€90, Tb-€110, Qb-€130, free loaner bikes, free parking on first-come, first-served basis, turn left out of station, Viale Pallavicini 4, tel. 0544-212-363, fax 0544-217-004, www.hitalia.it, info@hotelitaliaravenna.com, Lucia and Mauro).

$$ M Club Delux B&B is an amazingly comfortable and stylish little place with generous public spaces, an elegant breakfast room, spacious bedrooms, and thoughtful touches. Each unique room is described on their website (straight pricing: Db-€70–120 depending on size, Qb suite-€130, facing town gate at edge of old town at Piazza Baracca 26, tel. 333-955-6466, www.m-club.it, info@m-club.it).

$$ Casa Masoli B&B's six elegantly outfitted rooms include bathrooms fit for an emperor. Grandmotherly Signora Masoli works quietly alongside daughter Anna and granddaughter Chiara (Sb-€50, Db-€70, Tb suite-€90, 4th and 5th person-€20 each, peaceful garden, big family room, Wi-Fi, library, Via G. Rossi 22, tel. 335-609-9471, mobile 339-544-8405, www.casamasoli.it, anna@casamasoli.it).

$ Hotel al Giaciglio, near the train station, has 16 back-packer-style budget rooms run by Barbara and Moanely. They offer loaner bikes in the summer (S-€35, D-€50, Db-€60, fans, Via R. Brancaleone 42, tel. & fax 0544-39403, www.albergoalgiaciglio.com, info@albergoalgiaciglio.com).

Hostel: **$ Ostello Dante,** a 15-minute walk from the station, has Internet access, laundry service, loaner bikes, and a game room (110 beds, €15/bed, 4-bed rooms, Db-€44, family rooms-€18/person with bath, €3/night extra for non-hostel members, includes breakfast and sheets, towels-€1, 11:00–14:30 lockout, 23:30 curfew or pay €1 for magnetic entrance key, Via Nicolodi 12, bus #70 or tiny bus #80 from train station, tel. & fax 0544-421-164, www.hostelravenna.com, hostelravenna@hotmail.com).

Eating in Ravenna

Ca' de Ven ("House of Wine") is the most famous restaurant in town. It fills a 16th-century warehouse with residents enjoying quality wine and traditional regional cuisine. The seating is communal and *piadina* (peeah-DEE-nah) dominates the menu. An unleavened bread that local kids are raised on, it's served plain or with pizza-type stuffing. Their dessert specialty, *torta di* *marzapane*—a decadent almond-and-cocoa brownie—is best with sweet red wine. Reserve ahead for dinner (€3–6 *piadina*, Tue–Sun 11:00–14:30 & 18:30–22:30, closed Mon, 2-minute walk from Piazza del Popolo on Via Cairoli, which turns into Via C. Ricci, Via C. Ricci 24, tel. 0544-30163).

Ristorante la Gardèla, which offers reasonable prices and cuisine specialties from Italy's mountainous Emilia-Romagna region, is a favorite. The *cappelletti*, a cheese-stuffed pasta, is served *in brodo* (soup) or *in ragu* (meat sauce). If Ravenna had a town dining room, this would be it. The fun-loving waitstaff has been here for years and the restaurant has all the nice touches without the pretense. While there are a few tables outside and upstairs, I like the jolly main floor (closed Thu, from Piazza del Popolo follow Via IV Novembre past Piazza della Costa to corner of Via Ponte Marino 3, tel. 0544-217-147).

Ristorante Marchesini offers an above-average self-serve menu that includes delicious salads and homemade pastas (€7 pastas, €10 *secondi*, Mon–Sat 12:00–14:30, closed Sun, 5-minute walk from Piazza del Popolo, on corner of Piazza Caduti at Via Mazzini 6—ride elevator to first floor, tel. 0544-212-309).

Free Flow Bizantino, inside the covered market, is a self-serve cafeteria serving lunch only (€4 pastas, €5 *secondi*, Mon–Fri 11:45–14:40, closed Sat–Sun, tel. 0544-32073). Or assemble a picnic at the market and enjoy your feast in the shady gardens of the Rocca Brancaleone fortress (open daily until 18:00; 5-minute walk from station, follow Via Maroncelli until you see the walls).

Pizzeria Cupido is good for a cheap and traditional lunch or snack. Consider their *piadina* or *crescione* (calzone-like) sandwich. These tasty sandwiches (€3–5) come stuffed with a variety of meats, cheeses, and vegetables. Try one filled with *squacquerone*, a soft regional cream cheese (Tue–Sun 11:00–15:00, closed Mon, just up Via Cavour from the market at Via Cavour 43, tel. 0544-37529).

Ravenna Connections

From Ravenna by Train to: Venice (hourly, 3–4 hours, transfer in Ferrara, Faenza, or Bologna), **Padua** (9/day, 2.5 hours), **Florence** (about hourly, 3–3.5 hours, requires transfer in Bologna).

THE DOLOMITES

Dolomiti

Italy's dramatic rocky rooftop, the Dolomites, offers some of the best mountain thrills in Europe. Bolzano is the gateway to the Dolomites, and Castelrotto is a good home base for your exploration of Alpe di Siusi, Europe's largest alpine meadow.

The sunny Dolomites are well-developed, and the region's famous valleys and towns suffer from après-ski fever. The cost for the comfort of reliably good weather is a drained-reservoir feeling. Lovers of other parts of the Alps may miss the lushness that comes with the unpredictable weather farther north. But the bold, light-gray cliffs and spires flecked with snow, above green meadows and beneath a blue sky, offer a powerful, unique, and memorable mountain experience. Dolomite, a sedimentary rock similar to limestone, gives these mountains their distinctive shape and color.

A hard-fought history has left the region bicultural, with an emphasis on the German. Locals speak German first, and some wish they were still part of Austria. In the Middle Ages, as part of the Holy Roman Empire, the region faced north. Later, it was firmly in the Austrian Habsburg realm. By losing World War I, Austria's South Tirol became Italy's Alto Adige. Mussolini did what he could to Italianize the region, including giving each town an Italian name. But even as recently as the 1990s, local secessionist groups agitated violently for more autonomy with some success (see page 204).

The government has wooed locals with economic breaks that make it one of Italy's richest areas (as local prices attest), and today all signs and literature in the province of Alto Adige/Süd Tirol are in both languages. Many include a third language, Ladin—an

The Dolomites

TO INNSBRUCK

AUSTRIA

N

BRENNER PASS

ITALY

10 MILES
10 KM

VIPITENO/ STERZING

BRUNICO/ BRUNECK

DOBBIACO/ TOBLACH

TO LIENZ & SALZBURG

REIFEN- STEIN CASTLE

FORTEZZA

S.49

S.51

BRESSANONE/ BRIXEN

TRE CIME

CASTELROTTO/ KASTELRUTH

ORTISEI PASSO SELLA

PASSO GARDENA

LAGO MISURINA

VAL GARDENA

COMPATSCH

SELLA

CORVARA

CORTINA D'AMPEZZO

BOLZANO/ BOZEN

SIUSI

SASSO- LUNGO

S.48

CANAZEI

PASSO CAMPO- LONGO

PASSO FALZARAGO

A.22

S.241

PASSO PORDOI

ALLEGHE

PIEVE DI CADORE

VIGO

MARMOLADA

S.203

S.51

S.48

CAVALESE

TO BELLUNO

TO VENICE

TO TRENTO & VERONA

DCH

ALPE DI SIUSI/ SEISER ALM
(SEE DETAIL MAP)

⌐ AUTOSTRADA
⌐ OTHER ROADS
⊢⊢ RAIL
↟ MTN. PASS

THE DOLOMITES

ancient Latin-type language still spoken in a few traditional areas. (I have listed both the Italian and German, so the confusion caused by this guidebook will match that experienced in your travels.)

In spite of all the glamorous ski resorts and busy construction cranes, the local color survives in a warm blue-aproned, ruddy-faced, felt-hat-with-feathers way. There's yogurt and yodeling for breakfast. Culturally as much as geographically, the area is reminiscent of Austria. The Austrian Tirol is named for a village that is now part of Italy.

Ich bin ein Italiener

Four in ten Italians living in the Dolomites region speak German. Many are fair-skinned and blue-eyed, eating strudel after their pasta, and feeling a closer bond with their ancestors in Austria than to their swarthy countrymen to the south. In the province of Alto Adige/Süd Tirol, along the Austrian border, German-speakers are the majority. Most have a passing knowledge of Italian, but they watch German-language TV, read newspapers in *Deutsch,*

and live in Tirolean-looking villages. (Bolzano has both Italian and German grade schools, while in more-remote Castelrotto, the children are educated only in German.)

At the end of World War I, the region was ceded by (loser) Austria to (winner) Italy. Mussolini suppressed the Germanic elements as part of his propaganda campaign to praise all things Italian. Many German-speakers hoped that Hitler would "liberate" them from Italy, but Hitler's close alliance with Mussolini prevented that from happening. Instead, in June 1939, residents were given six months to make a hard choice—move north to the Fatherland and become German citizens, or stay in their homeland *(Heimat)* under Italian rule. The vast majority (212,000, or 85 percent) made the decision to leave, but because of the outbreak of World War II, only 75,000 actually moved.

At the war's end, German-speakers were again disappointed when the Allied powers refused to grant them autonomy or repatriation (citizenship) with Austria, instead sticking with the prewar arrangement.

The region rebuilt and the two linguistic groups got along, but for the remainder of the 20th century, there was always an underlying problem: German-speakers were continually outvoted by the Italian-speaking majority in the regional government (comprising both Italian-speaking Trentino and German-speaking Alto Adige/Süd Tirol). German-speakers lobbied the national government for more control on the provincial (not regional) level, even turning to demonstrations and violence. Over the years, Rome has slowly and grudgingly granted increased local control.

Today, Alto Adige/Süd Tirol has a large measure of autonomy written into the country's 2001 constitution, though it's still officially tied to Trentino. Roads, water, electricity, communications, and schools are all under local control, including the Free University of Bozen-Bolzano, founded in 1998.

Planning Your Time

Train travelers can side-trip into the mountains from Bolzano (90 minutes north of Verona). To get a feel for the alpine culture, spend at least one night in Castelrotto. But with two nights there, you can actually get out and hike. Tenderfeet ride the bus, catch a cable car, and stroll. For serious mountain thrills, do a six-hour hike. And for a memory that won't soon fade away, spend a night in a mountain hut. Always remember to check the latest transportation timetables before you embark on an outing.

If you have a car, you can drive the three-hour loop from Bolzano or Castelrotto (Val Gardena–Sella Pass–Val di Fassa) and ride one of the lifts to the top for a ridge walk. Connecting Bolzano and Venice by the Great Dolomite Road takes two hours longer than by the autostrada, but it is far more scenic (see "More Sights in the Dolomites" at the end of this chapter).

Hiking season is mid-June through mid-October. The region is particularly crowded, booming, and blooming from mid-July through mid-September. It's packed with Italian vacationers in August. Spring is usually dead, with lifts shut down, huts closed, and the most exciting trails still under snow. Many hotels and restaurants close in April and November. Ski season (Dec–Easter) is busiest of all. For more information, visit www.visitdolomites.com.

Bolzano (Bozen)

Willkommen to the Italian Tirol! If it weren't so sunny, you could be in Innsbruck. This enjoyable old town of 100,000 is the most convenient gateway to the Dolomites, especially if you're relying on public transportation. It's just the place to take a Tirolean stroll.

Orientation to Bolzano

Tourist Information

Bolzano's TI is helpful (Mon–Fri 9:00–19:00, Sat 9:30–18:00, closed Sun, Piazza Walther 8, tel. 0471-307-000, www.bolzano -bozen.it, info@bolzano-bozen.it). Pick up the city map and the *Historic and Cultural Route* brochure (also downloadable from website). Don't bother with the Bolzano City Card (offering discounts at five Bolzano museums and the skippable Runkelstein Castle), because the only sight that merits your time is the archaeological museum, with its famous Ice Man.

The excellent-for-hikers **Alpine Information Center** (Alpenverein Südtirol) is buried deep in the old town, on an alley between Via dei Portici/Lauben Strasse and Via Vintler Strasse at

Galleria Vintler–Durch-gang 16 (Mon–Tue and Thu 10:30–12:00 & 14:00–16:00, Fri 10:30–12:00, closed Wed and Sat–Sun, tel. 0471-999-955, office@alpenverein.it).

Arrival in Bolzano

There are two train stations for Bolzano—you want just *Bolzano,* not *Bolzano Süd*. To get to the TI and downtown from the train station, veer left up the tree-lined Viale della Stazione/Bahnhofallee, and walk past the bus station (on your left) two blocks to **Piazza Walther.** You'll see the TI on the right side of the square.

Walking through Piazza Walther, you hit the medieval heart of town. The arcaded Via dei Portici leads to **Piazza Erbe/Obstplatz,** which has an open-air produce market (see "Markets," below); the Ice Man is a couple of blocks farther beyond.

Helpful Hints

Sleepy Sundays: The city is really dead on Sunday (young locals add "and during the rest of the week, too").

Markets: Piazza Erbe/Obstplatz hosts an ancient and still-thriving open-air produce market (Mon–Fri all day, Sat morning only, closed Sun). Wash your produce in the handy drinking fountain in the middle of the market. Another market (offering more variety, not just food) is held Saturday mornings on Piazza della Vittoria.

Internet Access: Multi Kulti Internet Point is a few blocks east of Piazza Walther at Via Dottore Streiter/Streitergasse 9 (€3/hour, passport required, Mon–Sat 10:00–22:00, closed Sun, tel. 0471-056-056).

Baggage Storage: While there's no baggage-storage service at the train station, there is a *deposito bagagli* at the bus station just a block away (€3/24 hours, €10 refundable deposit, out back from where the buses leave, at the entrance to the bathrooms).

Laundry: Lava e Asciuga launderette is at Via Rosmini/Rosmini Strasse 81, about two blocks west of the South Tirol Museum of Archaeology (€3 wash, €3 dry, daily 7:00–22:00, last wash 21:00, mobile 340-220-2323).

Bike Rental: The city has a well-developed bike-trail system and rental bikes are curiously cheap here. Plenty of bikes are available for rent just off Piazza Walther on Viale della Stazione/Bahnhofallee on the right side (€1/6 hours, €2/6–24 hours, €5/24 hours, €10 refundable deposit, ID required, mid-May–Oct Mon–Sat 7:30–19:50, closed Sun and Nov–mid-May, tel. 0471-997-578). The TI also has 10 bikes to rent for €5 per day (€10 refundable deposit, ID required, April–mid-Nov, ask for a map).

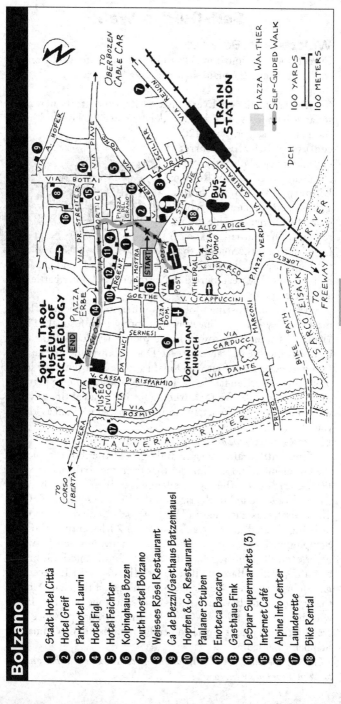

Bolzano

1. Stadt Hotel Città
2. Hotel Greif
3. Parkhotel Laurin
4. Hotel Figl
5. Hotel Feichter
6. Kolpinghaus Bozen
7. Youth Hostel Bolzano
8. Weisses Rössl Restaurant
9. Ca' de Bezzi/Gasthaus Batzenhäusl
10. Hopfen & Co. Restaurant
11. Paulaner Stuben
12. Enoteca Baccaro
13. Gasthaus Fink
14. DeSpar Supermarkets (3)
15. Internet Café
16. Alpine Info Center
17. Launderette
18. Bike Rental

THE DOLOMITES

Self-Guided Walk

Welcome to Bolzano

Everything mentioned in Bolzano is a 10-minute walk from the train station and the main square, Piazza Walther.

• Start in...

Piazza Walther: Every visit to Bolzano starts here. The square's namesake, Walther von der Vogelweide, honored by the statue in the center, was a 12th-century politically incorrect German poet who courageously stood up to the Holy Roman Emperor. Walther's spunk against a far bigger power represents the Germanic pride of this region. (The statue is made of Lasa marble—the marble that the US chose for the 86,000 crosses and Stars of David needed to mark the WWII dead buried at Normandy and other battlefields across Europe.)

When not hosting Bolzano's Christmas Market, flower market (May Day), or Speck Fest (a spring ham festival), Piazza Walther is simply the town's living room. And locals care about it. It was the site of Italy's first McDonald's, which—in the early 1990s—became the first McDonald's to be shut down by locals protesting American fast food. Today, the square is home to trendy cafés such as Café Walther, where (outside of meal times) you're welcome to nurse a "Venetian" spritz or a pricier cocktail as long as you like.

• Cross the street to the big church.

The Cathedral: The cathedral's glazed-tile roof is typical of the Germanic world, a reminder that from the sixth century until 1919, German was the region's language. Then, suddenly: *Buon giorno!* Walk around to the right to the Romanesque Lion's Gate. The church was flattened in World War II (a distinct downside of being located near a train station in 20th-century Europe). Stepping inside, you get a sense of Germany, not Venice (which never controlled this region). The mostly Gothic interior is broken by an impressive Baroque tabernacle. There's a stiff 15th-century *pietà* (obviously pre-Michelangelo) to the left of the altar. Most of the art here is by Bavarian artists. The sandstone pulpit (c. 1500), with its reliefs of the four Church fathers (whose presence gave credibility to sermons preached here) is reminiscent of Vienna's St. Stephen's Cathedral.

• Leaving the church, walk diagonally across Piazza Walther and one block into the old town, to...

Piazza del Grano/Kornplatz: The rich architecture surrounding you is a reminder that this was a wealthy merchant's town. The traditional food stand selling *Vollkornbrot* (sourdough rye bread) and pretzels is a reminder of the German heritage. In the little garden, a bronze relief on a large stone shows Bolzano's street plan in the 12th century—a one-street arcaded merchants' town huddled within a fortified wall. Continue uphill into the original medieval town, passing the "Wurstel Boutique" on your left (another reminder of this region's Germanic orientation).

Via dei Portici: This was the main street in 12th-century Bolzano. Step into the center (dodging bikes). Looking east and west, you see the width of the original town. Thirty yards to the left is the old city hall—the street's only Gothic building (with frescoed pointed arches). The other buildings are all basically the same: Each had a storm cellar, cows out back, a ground-level shop, and living quarters upstairs. Bay windows were designed for maximum light—just right for clerks keeping track of accounts and for women doing their weaving. The arcades enabled merchants to exhibit their goods even in bad weather. The only balcony on the street marks the one Baroque building on the arcade—once the mercantile center (with a fine worth-a-look courtyard), now a skippable museum.

• *Turn left on arcaded Via dei Portici and continue to the end, where you'll find a bustling market.*

Piazza Erbe/Obstplatz: This square hosts an open-air produce market, liveliest in the morning (Mon–Fri all day, Sat mornings, closed Sun). The historic market fountain gives Bolzano its only hint of the sea—a 17th-century statue of Neptune. Stroll around and see what's in season. The breads, strudel, and German hams all *schmecken gut.*

• *From the market, Museumstrasse (called Butcher Street until the 19th century, when a museum opened) leads straight to Frozen Fritz.*

Sights in Bolzano

▲▲South Tirol Museum of Archaeology (Museo Archeologico dell'Alto Adige/Südtiroler Archäologiemuseum)—This excellent museum features the actual corpse of Ötzi the Ice Man. The frozen body was discovered high in the mountains on the Italian/Austrian border by some German hikers in 1991. Initially thinking the corpse was a lost hiker, officials chopped him out of the glacier, damaging his left side. But upon discovering his pre–Bronze Age hatchet, they realized what they had found: a 5,300-year-old, nearly perfectly preserved man with clothing and gear in excellent condition for his age. With Ötzi as the centerpiece, the museum takes you on an intriguing journey through time, recounting the evolution of humanity—from the Paleolithic era to the Roman period and finally to the Middle Ages—in vivid detail. The exhibit offers informative displays and models, video demonstrations of Ötzi's extraction and his personal effects, a great audioguide, and interactive computers. You'll see Ötzi himself—still frozen—and glass cases that display his incredibly well-preserved and fascinating clothing and gear, including a finely stitched

two-color coat, his loincloth, a fancy hat, shoes, a well-crafted hatchet, and fire-making gadgets (€9, essential audioguide-€2; Tue–Sun 10:00–18:00, closed Mon except in July, Aug, and Dec; last entry 30 minutes before closing, no photos, near the river at Via Museo/Museumstrasse 43, tel. 0471-320-100, www.iceman.it, museum@iceman.it).

Dominican Church (Chiesa dei Domenicani)—Drop by this 13th-century church to see its Chapel of St. John (San Giovanni; chapel is near farthest altar from the entrance and on the right), frescoed in the 14th century by the Giotto School (free, €0.50 coin lights dim interior, Mon–Sat 9:30–17:00, Sun 12:00–18:00; also see peaceful cloisters farther to right of Piazza Domenicani, entrance at #19, cloisters closed on Sat afternoon and all day Sun, www .bolzano.net/english/dominican-church.html).

Funiva Lift to Oberbozen—There are three cable cars that can whisk you out of Bolzano, with the most popular ride being the new **Renon/Rittner** *funiva* lift to the touristy town of Oberbozen (€3.50 round-trip, departs Bolzano every 4 minutes, 12 minutes to the top, daily about 6:40–21:00, runs year-round but shorter hours off-season; from Bolzano train station walk 5 blocks to the right down Via Renon to the Sielbahn *funivia* lift; toll-free tel. 840-000-471 or tel. 0471-345-245 for cable-car info and trail conditions).

Up on top, **Oberbozen** has its own TI (Mon–Fri 9:00–12:30 & 15:00–18:00, Sat 9:00–12:30, closed Sun in summer, tel. 0471-345-245, tvritten@tin.it).

More interesting than Oberbozen itself are the nearby **"earth pyramids,"** a 20-minute walk from the cable-car station. The pyramids, which are eroding glacial debris dumped at the end of the last ice age, are Bryce Canyon–like pinnacles that rise out of the ridge (www.ritten.com).

The little narrow-gauge Ritten train runs along the ridge nearly hourly, connecting Oberbozen with other villages, including **Collalbo** (€3.50 round-trip, leaves daily every 30 minutes year-round, Collalbo TI open Mon–Fri 8:30–18:00, Sat 8:30–12:00, closed Sun, tel. 0471-356-100, www.ritten.com, info@ritten .com). From Collalbo, you can hike another 45 minutes to more pyramids.

Many are tempted to wimp out on the Dolomites and see them from a distance by hiking two hours from Oberbozen to the Pemmern chairlift (€8.50 one-way, €10.50 round-trip, www.ritt nerhorn.com), riding to Schwarzseespitze, and walking 45 more minutes to the **Rittner Horn.** You'll be atop a 7,000-foot peak with distant but often-hazy Dolomite views. It's not worth the trouble.

Sleeping in Bolzano

All of the listed hotels are in the city center.

$$$ Stadt Hotel Città, a venerable old hotel with 99 modern if basic rooms, is ideally situated on Piazza Walther. The hotel's café spills out onto the piazza, offering a prime spot for people-watching (Sb-€98, Db-€140, bigger Db with view-€180, Tb-€195, air-con in some rooms, elevator, Wi-Fi, Piazza Walther 21, tel. 0471-975-221, fax 0471-976-688, www.hotelcitta.info, info @hotelcitta.info, Francesco). This place is an especially good value if you plan to spend an afternoon in their free-for-guests Wellness Center (mid-Sept–mid-June Mon–Sat 16:30–22:00, closed some Sun; closed mid-June–mid-Sept; Turkish bath, whirlpool, Finnish

---

Sleep Code

(€1 = about $1.25, country code: 39)
S = Single, **D** = Double/Twin, **T** = Triple, **Q** = Quad, **b** = bathroom, **s** = shower only. Unless otherwise noted, credit cards are accepted, English is spoken, and breakfast is included.

To help you sort easily through these listings, I've divided the rooms into three categories based on the price for a standard double room with bath:

$$$ Higher Priced—Most rooms €100 or more.
$$ Moderately Priced—Most rooms between €60–100.
$ Lower Priced—Most rooms €60 or less.

Prices can change without notice; verify the hotel's current rates online or by email. For other updates, see www .ricksteves.com/update.

sauna, biosauna, massage by appointment)—a fine way to unwind after a day of hiking in the Dolomites.

$$$ Hotel Greif is also right on Piazza Walther. When you walk into any of their 33 rooms, which were designed by artists, you'll feel like you're in a modern-art installation (its fine website gives a room-by-room tour). It's not cozy, but it is striking, and a stay here comes with perhaps the best breakfast in Italy (comfort Sb-€148, comfort Db-€192, superior Db-€233, discounted Sat–Sun by request, ask for the 10 percent Rick Steves discount when you book online—availability limited, includes buffet breakfast, most rooms non-smoking, air-con, in-room Internet access, Piazza Walther, entrance on Via della Rena/Raing, tel. 0471-318-000, fax 0471-318-148, www.greif.it, info@greif.it). Drivers follow signs to *Parking Walther* (€17/day) and enter the hotel from the garage.

$$$ Parkhotel Laurin is an Old World luxury hotel, with 100 tastefully decorated rooms, marble bathrooms, chic dining room and terrace, swimming pool, extensive garden, attentive staff, and frescoes throughout the grand lobby depicting the legend of King Laurin (standard Sb-€111, standard Db-€142, comfort Db-€176, discounted Sat–Sun by request, includes buffet breakfast, parking-€13/day, Via Laurin 4, tel. 0471-311-000, fax 0471-311-148, www.laurin.it, info@laurin.it).

$$$ Hotel Figl, warmly run by Anton and Helga Mayr, has 23 comfy, bright, modern rooms and an attached café on a pedestrian square located a block from Piazza Walther. With rooms better than its humble public spaces and exterior, it's a fine value (Sb-€87–95, Db-€120–125, junior suite-€130–135; discount with this book for longer stays—ask when you reserve; breakfast extra, air-con, elevator, non-smoking, free Internet access and Wi-Fi, Kornplatz 9, tel. 0471-978-412, fax 0471-978-413, www.figl.net, info@figl.net, include a backup fax number if you email).

$$ Hotel Feichter is a bright, cheery lodging with a characteristic alpine feel and 30 rooms—many sharing a communal terrace—overlooking the rooftops of Bolzano. Papà Walter, Mamma Hedwig, Hannes, and Wolfi Feichter have run this homey hotel since 1969 (Sb-€60, Db-€90, Tb-€110, includes breakfast; leave Piazza Walther on Via Rena/Raing, then take left fork to Via Grappoli/Weintraubengasse, hotel is a few steps ahead on the right at #15; tel. 0471-978-768, fax 0471-974-803, www.hotel feichter.it, info@hotelfeichter.it).

$$ Kolpinghaus Bozen, modern, clean, and church-run, has 34 rooms with two twin beds (placed head to toe) and 71 new air-conditioned single rooms with all the comforts. Though institutional, it makes one feel thankful (Sb-€65, Db-€100, Tb-€150, includes breakfast, elevator, cable Internet, parking-€12/day, 4 blocks from Piazza Walther near Piazza Domenicani at A. Kolping

Strasse 3, tel. 0471-308-400, fax 0471-973-917, www.kolping.it, kolping@tin.it). The line of people in front of the building at lunchtime consists mainly of workers waiting for the cafeteria to open (€10 lunch, Mon–Fri 11:45–14:00, Sat 12:00–13:30, closed Sun).

$ Youth Hostel Bolzano, slick and new, is the most comfortable and inviting hostel that I've seen in Italy. It has 18 four-bed rooms (two bunk beds and a full bathroom each) and 10 delightful singles. The bright, clean, modern rooms make it feel like a dorm in a fancy university. With no age limit, no need for membership, easy reservations by email, great lockers, and cheap Internet access, it is the utopian hostel (bed in quad-€21, Sb-€24, €2 extra for 1-night stays, includes linens and buffet breakfast, laundry, towels-€1, kitchen, free luggage storage, checkout time 9:00, 100 yards to the right as you leave the train station, Via Renon 23, tel. 0471-300-865, fax 0471-300-858, http://bozen.jugendherberge.it, bozen@jugendherberge.it).

Eating in Bolzano

All of these recommendations are in the center of the old town. Prices are consistent (you can generally get a good plate of meat and veggies for €10). While nearly every local-style place serves a mix of Germanic Tirolean and Italian fare, I favor the Tirolean places. My recommendation: Eat German here in Bozen.

Weisses Rössl offers affordable, mostly Tirolean food with meat, fish, and fine vegetarian options. Located in a traditional woody setting, it's good for dining indoors among savvy locals (€10 plates, daily specials, Mon–Fri 11:00–15:00 & 17:30–23:30—light meals available between 16:00–17:30, Sat 11:00–15:00 only, closed Sun, 2 blocks north of Piazza Municipio at Via Bottai/Bindergasse 6, tel. 0471-973-267).

Ca' de Bezzi/Gasthaus Batzenhausl is historic. It's Bolzano's oldest inn, with a Teutonic-feeling top floor; by contrast, the patio and back room are refreshingly modern and untouristy. They make their own breads and pastas, and serve traditional Tirolean fare with a focus on fine wine—about 30 bottles are open to serve by the glass (€12 plates, daily 11:30–24:00, limited menu between mealtimes, one of the rare places open on Sun, Via Andreas Hofer Strasse 30, tel. 0471-050-950).

Hopfen and Company fills an 800-year-old house with happy eaters, drinkers, and the beer-lover's favorite aroma: hops... or *Hopfen*. A tavern since the 1600s, it's a stylish, fresh microbrewery today. This high-energy, boisterous place is packed with locals who come for its homemade beer, delicious Tirolean/Italian food, and reasonable prices. You'll enjoy the friendly English-speaking waitstaff (€10–15 main courses, great €8 salads, heavy traditional

Tirolean Cuisine

During your visit to the Dolomites, take a break from Italian-style pizzas and pastas to sample some of the region's traditional cuisine...with a distinctly Austrian flavor. To reduce confusion, I've generally listed Italian names here, though local menus are in both Italian and German (and usually also English).

Wurst and sauerkraut are the Tirolean clichés. More adventurous eaters seek out *speck,* a raw (prosciutto-style) ham smoked for five months then thinly sliced and served as an antipasto or in sandwiches. *Canederli*—large dumplings with bits of *speck,* liver, spinach, or cheese—are often served in broth, or with butter and cheese. (Never cut a dumpling with a knife—it'll destroy the chef.)

The stars of Tirolean cuisine are the hearty meat dishes—which, unlike traditional Italian main courses, are nearly always served with side dishes of doughy dumplings or vegetables and potatoes. Try *stinco di maiale* (roasted pork shank, usually garnished with potatoes) and *crauti rossi* (a sweetish sauerkraut made from red cabbage). *Carrè affumicato* is pork shank that is first smoked, then boiled. *Selvaggine,* or wild game, comes in the form of *capriolo* (fawn), *cervo* (venison), or *camoscio* (chamois/antelope). Game is eaten smoked and thinly sliced in *antipasti;* in meat sauce *(ragù)* with fresh pasta or as ravioli stuffing; or in entrées, as tender chunks grilled or roasted in a rich sauce *(spezzatino).*

For dessert, strudel is everywhere, filled with the harvest from this region's renowned apple orchards. Cakes and pies are loaded with other locally grown fruits, raisins, and nuts. *Kaiserschmarrn* is an interesting alternative: a tall, eggy crêpe prepared with raisins and topped with powdered sugar and red currant jam.

Bier (birra) is king in the Alto Adige (the best-known brand, Forst, is brewed in nearby Merano), but the wines of the area are well-matched to the local fare. *Magdalaner* is a light, dry red made from Schiava grapes. *Lagrein scuro* is a full-bodied red, dry and fruity, similar to a cabernet sauvignon or merlot. *Gewürztraminer* is a dry white wine with a spicy fruit flavor. For something stronger, try grappa made from Williams pears (and served with a wedge of fresh pear), or *grappa Nocino*—a darker, sweeter brew similar to Jägermeister. *Guten Appetit und Prost!*

THE DOLOMITES

beer dumplings, daily 9:30–24:00, Piazza Erbe/Obstplatz 17, tel. 0471-300-788).

Paulaner Stuben is a restaurant-pizzeria-*Bierstube* serving good food and a favorite Bavarian beer with good outside seating and a take-me-to-Germany *Stube*, or cellar, downstairs (€5–10 pizzas, pastas, and salads, €9–18 dinner plates, daily 11:30–24:00, Via dei Portici 51 and Via Argentieri 16, tel. 0471-980-407).

Enoteca Baccaro, a nondescript hole-in-the-wall wine bar, is an intriguing spot for a glass of wine (€1–4) and bar snacks amid locals. Wines available by the glass are listed on the blackboard (Mon–Fri 9:00–13:00 & 15:30–20:30, Sat 9:00–15:30, closed Sun, located a half-block east of Hopfen and Company on a hidden alley off Via Argentieri/Silbergasse 17, look for *vino* or *wein* sign next to fountain on south side of street, tel. 0471-971-421).

Gasthaus Fink, a busy diner, serves typical Tirolean and Italian dishes with indoor and on-the-street seating on a quiet pedestrian lane, just off Piazza Walther (€8 pastas, €12 *secondi,* Fri–Tue 8:00–22:00, Wed 8:00–15:00 only, closed Wed evening and all day Thu, Via della Mostra 9, tel. 0471-975-047).

Picnic: Assemble the ingredients at the **Piazza Erbe/Obstplatz** market and dine in the park along the Talvera River (the green area with benches past the museum). There are three **DeSpar supermarkets:** One is on Piazza Erbe, one is on Via Bottai, and the other is on Via della Rena/Raing near Piazza Walther (all are open Mon–Fri 8:30–19:15, Sat 8:30–18:00, closed Sun; to find the Villa della Rena/Raing location from Piazza Walther, face the TI, take street to the left for 2 blocks, supermarket is at bottom of stairs on your left).

Bolzano Connections

From Bolzano by Train to: Milan (about hourly, 3.5–4 hours, change in Verona), **Verona** (about hourly, 1.75–2.15 hours), **Trento** (about 2/hour, 45 minutes), **Venice** (about hourly, 3.25–3.5 hours, change in Verona), **Florence** (every 1–2 hours, 4–5.25 hours, change in Verona and/or Bologna), **Innsbruck** (every 1–2 hours, 2–2.5 hours, some change in Brennero), **Munich** (called "Monaco" in Italy, 5/day direct, 3.75 hours).

By Bus to: Castelrotto (at least 2/hour, fewer on weekends, 50 minutes, generally leaves Bolzano at :10 and :40, pick up free schedule at bus station, last departure 19:10, toll-free tel. 800-846-047 or toll tel. 840-000-471, www.sii.bz.it). The bus leaves from Bolzano's bus station (1 block west of train station), stops at the train station, and then winds high into the mountains, dropping you in the center of Castelrotto.

Buy a *carta di valore* ticket (€3.50 one-way €5 round-trip) from

The Dramatic Dolomites

Located in northeastern Italy, the Dolomites have been called the most beautiful mountains on earth, and certainly they are among the most dramatic. They differ from the rest of the Alps because of their dominant rock type, dolomite, which forms sheer vertical walls of white, gray, and pink that rise abruptly from green valleys and meadows. There is one national park (Dolomiti Bellunesi National Park) in this region, and many regional parks, such as Alpe di Siusi. Rail lines, roads, and a huge system of lifts make this group of mountains very accessible.

Once dubbed the "Pale Mountains" or the "Venetian Alps," this mountain range was named after French mineralogist Dolomieu, who in the late 1700s first described the rock type responsible for the region's light-colored bluffs and peaks. These sedimentary rocks (similar to limestone) were formed in warm tropical seas during the Triassic Period (about 250 million years ago). The marine sediments, along with the fossilized remains of coral reefs and other animals, were buried, hardened, and later scooped upward along with the rest of the Alps by the tectonic-plate action of Africa slowly smashing into Europe. Today, marine fossils are found atop the region's highest peaks, including the skyscraping, nearly 11,000-feet-high Marmolada (east of Bolzano).

During World War I, the front line between the Italian and Austro-Hungarian forces ran through these mountains, and many paths were cut into the range for military use. Today mountaineers follow a network of metal rungs, cables, and ladders called the *Via Ferrata*. One famous wartime trail is the "Road of Tunnels," which passes through 52 tunnels. Along with being a paradise for hikers and climbers, the Dolomites are a popular skiing destination. The 1956 Olympics in Cortina di Ampezzo put the region on the map. A popular winter activity for intrepid skiers is the "Sella Ronda"—circling the Sella massif using a system of lifts and 28 miles of ski runs.

Whether you experience the Dolomites with your hand on a walking stick, a ski pole, or an *aperitivo* while mountain-gazing from a café, it's easy to enjoy this spectacular region.

the driver. If you're heading directly to **Alpe di Siusi,** take the same bus, get off just past the Seiseralm Bergbahn station, and ascend on the cable car. For more on Alpe di Siusi, see page 224.

Castelrotto (Kastelruth)

The ideal home base for exploring Alpe di Siusi, Castelrotto (town population: 2,000; district population: 6,000; altitude: 3,475 feet) has more village character than any other town I know in the region. With its traffic-free center, a thousand years of history, an oversized and hyperactive bell tower, and traditionally clad locals, it seems lost in another world. Against a backdrop of mountains, Castelrotto conveys the powerful message that simple pleasures are enough. Stay two nights!

Orientation to Castelrotto

Tourist Information

The helpful TI is on the main square, Piazza Kraus 2 (daily mid-May–Oct 8:30–12:00 & 14:30–18:00, shorter hours and closed Sun off-season, tel. 0471-706-333, www.seiseralm.it, info@kastelruth .com). If you plan to do any hiking, pick up the TI's list of suggested hikes, including estimated walking times and trail numbers. The TI sells transport passes such as the combi-card (described next).

Helpful Hints

Combo-Tickets: For a longer stay, consider the **Combi-Card** (€34/any 3 days out of a 7-day validity period, €43/unlimited usage for 7 days, expires 1 week after time stamp). It covers the Alpe di Siusi Express bus, Seiseralm Bergbahn cable car, Compatsch–Saltria shuttle bus (Almbus #11), other shuttle buses, regional orange SAD buses, such as the one to Bolzano from Castelrotto, and all trains in the Sudtirol/Alto Adige region. For €70 the **Seiser Alm Card Gold** gets you all of the above-listed transport options plus free rides on all Alpe di Siusi lifts.

Annual Events: The Oswald-von-Wolkenstein Riding Tournament, held on the first weekend of June, features equestrian

Castelrotto

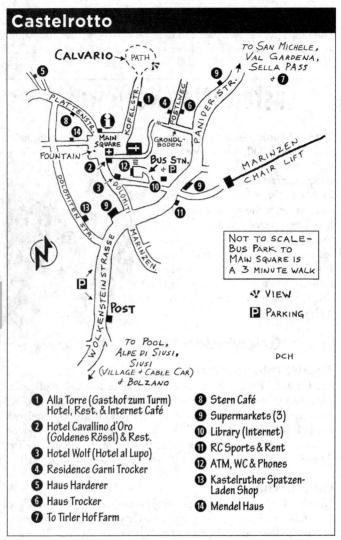

CALVARIO — PATH

TO SAN MICHELE,
VAL GARDENA,
SELLA PASS
& 7

PLATTENSTR.

KOFELSTR.

POSTLWEG

PANIDER STR.

MAIN SQUARE

FOUNTAIN

GRONDL-
BODEN

BUS STN.
& P

MARINZEN
CHAIR LIFT

DOLOMITEN STR.

DOLOMITI

MARINZEN

WOLKENSTEINSTRASSE

N

P

Post

TO POOL,
ALPE DI SIUSI,
SIUSI
(VILLAGE & CABLE CAR)
& BOLZANO

NOT TO SCALE—
BUS PARK TO
MAIN SQUARE IS
A 3 MINUTE WALK

VIEW

P PARKING

DCH

1 Alla Torre (Gasthof zum Turm) Hotel, Rest. & Internet Café

2 Hotel Cavallino d'Oro (Goldenes Rössl) & Rest.

3 Hotel Wolf (Hotel al Lupo)

4 Residence Garni Trocker

5 Haus Harderer

6 Haus Trocker

7 To Tirler Hof Farm

8 Stern Café

9 Supermarkets (3)

10 Library (Internet)

11 RC Sports & Rent

12 ATM, WC & Phones

13 Kastelruther Spatzen-Laden Shop

14 Mendel Haus

medieval-style tournament games, followed by a feast. The town also holds religious processions with locals dressed in traditional costumes, usually on Corpus Christi (June 23 in 2011); the feast day of the village protectors, saints Peter and Paul (June 26); and on the local Thanksgiving (first weekend in Oct).

Internet Access: You can get online at the recommended **Alla Torre** hotel, which has an Internet café (Thu–Tue 8:00–23:00, closed Wed , closed April and Nov, behind TI at Kofelgasse

8, tel. 0471-706-349). Or visit the public **library** (Mon 14:00–18:00, Tue 9:00–12:00, Thu 15:00–19:00, Fri 9:00–12:00, bring your passport, tel. 0471-708-023).

Recreation: A heated outdoor swimming pool with alpine views and nearby tennis courts is near town (€5, open mid-May–mid-Sept 9:00–21:00, tel. 0471-705-090, ask your hotel for details). You can rent a horse at **Ober-Lanzinerhof Tezfen** (tel. 339-868-6868, www.suedtirol.info, Karin speaks some English).

For more excitement, tandem paragliding flights—you and the pilot—depart from Alpe di Siusi and land either where you started or in Castelrotto (tel. 335-603-6400, www.tandem-pilot.com, Marco, Ruben, and Kurt). You can rent skis and snowboards at **RC Sports and Rent** (Via Panider/Paniderstrasse 10, tel. 0471-711-079, Robert—mobile 339-293-9725, Christian—mobile 328-303-8045).

Arrival in Castelrotto

The **bus station** *(Bushof)* is a few steps below the town's main square. The bus parking lot has a shelter with timetables. An ATM, WC, and phones are located in a building to the right. Take the stairs to get to the main square and TI.

Drivers can park in one of the two underground parking lots—one is in front of the bus station (first hour free). Each of the recommended hotels also has free parking: For Alla Torre and Hotel al Lupo, email for directions. For Hotel Cavallino d'Oro, drive through the traffic-free town center, drop off your luggage in front of the hotel, and then park in their garage. The recommended private homes will advise you of your options (see "Sleeping in Castelrotto," later).

Self-Guided Walk

Welcome to Castelrotto

Castelrotto has little to distract you other than the surrounding mountains and hikes. This quick walk will trace the town's history, from the ruling Krauses to yodelers who rule. Note that shops in Castelrotto close for siesta from 12:00–15:00—a good time for a long lunch, a hike in the hills...or a siesta of your own.

• Start in the...

Main Square: Piazza Kraus is named for the family who ruled the town 1550–1800. Their palace, now the City Hall and TI, overlooks the square and sports the Kraus family coat of arms.

Castelrotto uses its square well. The farmers market takes place here Friday mornings in the summer (June–Oct), and a clothing market fills the square most Thursday mornings. While touristy, Castelrotto is not a full-blown resort; if you're on the square weekdays at 14:45, you'll see local moms gather their preschoolers, chat, then stop by the playground on Plattenstrasse. Before and after Sunday Mass, the square is crowded with villagers and farmers (who fill the church) dressed in traditional clothing. The main Mass (at 20:00 on Sat—19:30 in winter—or 10:00 on Sun) is in German. Another Mass takes place in Italian throughout tourist season (at 11:00) for visitors.

• *A landmark in the square is the...*

Bell Tower: At 250 feet, the freestanding bell tower dominates the town. It was once attached to a church, which burned in 1753. While the bell tower was quickly rebuilt, the present-day church was constructed a century later next to the gutted church (which was then torn down to make space for the square). The wire between the church and tower connects the noisy bells. The sacristan can easily ring them using an electric switch.

When you feel the pride that the locals have in their tower—which symbolizes their town—you'll better understand why Italy is called "the land of a thousand bell towers." The bells of Castelrotto—a big part of the town experience—ring on the hour throughout the day and night. While sleepy tourists wonder why they clang through the wee hours, locals—who grew up with the chimes—find them comforting. The bells mark the hours, summon people to Mass, announce festivals, and warn when storms threaten. In the days when people used to believe that thunder was the devil approaching, the bells called everyone to pray. (Townspeople thought the bells' sound cleared the clouds.) Bells ring big at 7:00, noon, and 19:00. The biggest of the eight bells (7,500 pounds) peals only on special days. On Fridays, the bells ring at 15:00, commemorating Christ's sacrifice at the supposed hour of his death. The colorful poles in front of the church (yellow and white for the Vatican, red and white for Tirol) fly flags on festival days.

• *Also on the square is the...*

Church: Before entering, notice the plaque on the exterior. This commemorative inscription honors the tiny community's WWI dead—*Dorf* means from the village itself, and *Fraktion* is from an outlying district. Stepping into the church, you're surrounded by harmonious art from about 1850. The church is dedicated to Sts. Peter and Paul, and the paintings that flank the high altar show how each was martyred (crucifixion and beheading). The pews (and smart matching confessionals) are carved of walnut wood.

• *Back outside, belly up to the...*

Fountain: Opposite the bell tower, Castelrotto's fountain

THE DOLOMITES

dates from 1884. St. Florian, the protector against fires, keeps an eye on it today as he did when villagers (and their horses) first came here for a drink of water.

· *With your back to the bell tower, look a half-block down the lane to see the finely frescoed...*

Mendel Haus: This house has a traditional facade and a wood-carvers' shop. Its frescoes (from 1886) include many symbolic figures, as well as an emblem of a carpenter above the door—a relic from the days when images, rather than address numbers, identified the house. Notice St. Florian again; this time, he's pouring water on a small painting of this very house engulfed in flames. Inside Mendel Haus are fine carvings, a reminder that this region—especially nearby Val Gardena—is famous for its woodwork. You'll also see many witches, folk figures that date back to

when this area was the Salem of this corner of Europe. Women who didn't fit society's mold—including midwives, healers, redheads, and so on—were burned as witches.

· *Walk around behind Mendel Haus, turn left, and climb the stairs to Dolomitenstrasse. In 20 yards, on the left at the end of the street, is a shop dedicated to Castelrotto's hometown heroes...*

Kastelruther Spatzen-Laden: The ABBA of yodeling, the folk-singing group Kastelruther Spatzen is a gang of local boys who put Castelrotto on the map. They have a huge following here and throughout the German-speaking world. At the big Castelrotto festival on the second weekend in October, they put on hometown concerts—filling Castelrotto with fans from as far away as the Alsace, Switzerland, and the Netherlands. They also have an open-air concert in June and usually perform a Christmas concert.

Inside this shop—where you'll undoubtedly hear their inimitable music—is a yodelers' Carnaby Street. Downstairs is a folksy little museum slathered with gifts, awards, and gold records. The group has won 10 Echo Awards..."more than Robbie Williams." Watch the continuously playing video (€2 museum downstairs, refunded if you spend €5 in the shop, Mon–Fri 9:00–12:00 & 14:00–18:00, Sat 9:00–12:00, closed Sun, Via Dolomitenstrasse 21, tel. 0471-707-439, www.spatzenladen.it, info@spatzenladen.it).

Sights in Castelrotto

Calvario Stroll—For a scenic stroll, take a short walk around the town's hill, originally the site of the ancient Roman fortress and later the fortified home of the medieval lord. One lane circles the hill while another spirals to the top past seven little chapels, each depicting a scene from Christ's Passion and culminating in the Crucifixion. Facing the TI, take the road under the arch to the right, and then follow signs to *Kofel* (to go around the hill) or *Kalvarienberg* (to get directly to the top). This 15-minute stroll is great after dark—romantically lit and under the stars. (The lead singer of Kastelruther Spatzen enjoyed his first kiss right here.)

Marinzen Lift—The little Marinzen chairlift zips you up the mountain to the Marinzenhütte café, which has an animal park for kids (open when the cable car runs). You can come back on the lift, or it's a one-hour hike down (€6 one-way, €8 round-trip, runs daily late May–mid-Oct 9:00–17:00, July–Aug Wed until 22:00, closed off-season and rainy mornings, tel. 0471-707-160, www.seiseralm.it). From the town square, head downhill toward Wolkensteinstrasse, turn left and go another 50 yards down the road toward San Michele, and find the chairlift a few steps off the road on the right, behind the Gol supermarket.

Sleeping in Castelrotto

(€1 = about $1.25, country code: 39)

$$$ Alla Torre (in German, **Gasthof zum Turm**) is comfortable, clean, and alpine-traditional, with great beds and modern bathrooms (small Db-€78–120, big Db-€88–136, Tb-€121–187, price depends on season—highest in Aug, includes breakfast, €4 extra for one-night stays, closed April and Nov, elevator, behind TI at Kofelgasse 8, tel. 0471-706-349, fax 0471-707-268, www.zumturm .com, info@zumturm.com, Gabi and Günther).

$$$ Hotel Cavallino d'Oro (in German, **Goldenes Rössl**), on the main square, has plenty of Tirolean character and plush, welcoming public rooms. Run by friendly and helpful Stefan and Susanne, the entire place is dappled with artistic woodsy touches and historic photos. If you love antiques by candlelight, this 650-year-old hotel is the best in town (Sb-€45–65, Db-€88–115, Db suite-€120–190 depending on season, 2 percent discount with cash, discount for 4-night stay, includes breakfast, elevator, Internet access and Wi-Fi, laundry, free parking, Piazza Kraus 1, tel. 0471-706-337, fax 0471-707-172, www.cavallino.it, cavallino @cavallino.it). Stefan converted his wine cellar into a Roman steam bath and Finnish sauna (free for guests, great after a hike, can book an hour for exclusive use)—complete with heated tile seats, massage rooms, a solarium for tanning, and tropical plants.

$$ Hotel Wolf (in Italian, **al Lupo**) is pure Tirolean, with all the comforts in 23 neat-as-a-pin rooms, most with balconies (Sb-€35–55, Db-€60–100, prices vary with season and view, includes buffet breakfast, non-smoking rooms, elevator, Wi-Fi, coin-op laundry, closed April–mid-May and Nov–mid-Dec, free parking, a block below main square at Wolkensteinstrasse 5, tel. 0471-706-332, fax 0471-707-030, www.hotelwolf.it, info@hotelwolf.it, Arno).

$$ Residence Garni Trocker is run by the Moser family, who rent 13 great rooms in a place that's bomb-shelter solid yet warm-wood cozy. Their compound is beautifully laid out with a café-bar, garden, and top-notch plumbing (Sb-€34–48, Db-€60–86 depending on season, includes breakfast, Fostlweg 3, tel. 0471-705-200, fax 0471-707-427, www.residencetrocker.com, garni@residencetrocker.com, Stefan). Nonsmokers should request a room far from the smoking rooms. Sunday is the family's day of rest; if you're coming on a Sunday, be sure to let them know in advance what time you'll arrive.

$ Haus Harderer, below Hotel Kastelruth (take the middle lane where it forks), rents a single plush, woody apartment for up to four (Db-€55, Tb-€65, no breakfast, cash only, 3-night minimum stay in summer, lots of stairs, view balcony, Plattenstrasse 20, tel. 0471-706-702, run by Oswald, Heinz, and Ida).

$ Haus Trocker, on the edge of town, is a modern home where Frau Trocker rents two delightful rooms that share one WC. Frau Trocker doesn't speak English, but her son Roland does (D-€50; from the bus station, walk away from the church spire, past Hotel Kastel Seiseralm to Fostlweg 6, look for yellow *Zimmer* sign at top of steps; tel. 0471-707-087).

$ Tirler Hof, the storybook Jaider family farm, has 40 cows, four Old World–comfy guest rooms, and a great mountain view. The ground-floor double has a private bath. The top-floor rooms share a bathroom and a great balcony. Take a stroll before breakfast (D/Db-€56, discount for stays longer than one night, includes breakfast, cash only, open year-round, definitely most practical for drivers; it's the first farm outside of town on the right on road to San Michele, Via Panider/Paniderstrasse 44; tel. 0471-706-017, info@tirlerhof.it).

Eating in Castelrotto

Note that the first two options are also listed earlier under "Sleeping in Castelrotto."

Cavallino d'Oro Restaurant offers a variety of beautifully presented, homemade Tirolean cuisine—including wild game, *canederli* dumplings, and strudel—in a dressy but relaxed and woodsy ambience. The waiters, Marco and Monica, are very helpful; quiz them before you order (€25 meals, daily 12:00–14:00 & 18:00–21:00, tel. 0471-706-337). Lunch is by reservation only, unless you're staying at the hotel.

Alla Torre Restaurant, homier and with the best terrace

in town, is another fine option for traditional and international dishes. Try their *risotto ai funghi* (Thu–Tue 12:00–14:00 & 18:00–20:45, closed Wed, closed April and Nov, tel. 0471-706-349).

Dessert: For strudel, locals like the no-nonsense **Stern** café, with its terrace seating (Tue–Sun 7:30–19:00, closed Mon; on Plattenstrasse—facing TI, go left through arch; tel. 0471-706-382).

Picnics: You can put together a picnic at **EuroSpar** (Mon–Sat 8:00–19:00, closed Sun, on Wolkensteinstrasse, tel. 0471-706-222), **M-Preis** (Mon–Sat 8:00–19:00, closed Sun, Via Paniderstrasse 21, tel. 0471-710-014), or **Co-op/Konsum-Market** (sells locally produced food, Mon–Sat 7:30–12:30 & 15:00–19:00, closed Sun and off-season Sat afternoons, Via Paniderstrasse 24, tel. 0471-706-330).

Castelrotto Connections

From Castelrotto by Bus to: Bolzano (€3.50 one-way, €5 round-trip, buy *carta di valore* from driver, 2/hour, departures generally on the half-hour, fewer on weekends, 50 minutes, runs 6:15–19:00; in Bolzano, the bus stops at the more central Bahnhofplatz, or train station—get off here to avoid the 200-yard walk from the bus station, where the bus terminates), **Canazei** (late June–mid-Sept only, 3–4/day, 2–2.25 hours), and **Ortisei/St. Ulrich** and **St. Cristina** (8/day, 30 minutes to Ortisei, then another 10 minutes to St. Cristina). Get bus schedules at the TI, call toll-free tel. 800-846-047, toll tel. 840-000-471, or check www.sii.bz.it or www.silbernagl.it. For **Alpe di Siusi** connections, see the next page.

To Munich: On Saturdays only, a bus departs Alpe di Siusi at 6:00 and Castelrotto at 6:25, and heads for Munich's main train station (arrives 11:00, €37) and airport (arrives 12:00, €45). You can be picked up at your hotel for an extra €5. For information and booking, contact the Castelrotto TI.

Alpe di Siusi (Seiser Alm)

Europe's largest high-alpine meadow, Alpe di Siusi separates two of the most famous Dolomite ski-resort valleys. Eight miles wide, 20 miles long, and soaring up to 6,500 feet high, Alpe di Siusi is dotted by farm huts and wildflowers (mid-June–July), surrounded by dramatic—if distant—Dolomite peaks and cliffs, and much appreciated by hordes of walkers.

Compatsch, the modern little tourist town at the entrance of the meadow, has a TI, food, a little strip mall, and services (described on page 228).

The Sasso Lungo mountains (Langkofel in German, Long Stone in English) at the head of the meadow provide a storybook Dolomite backdrop, while the spooky Schlern peak stands boldly staring into the haze of the peninsula. The Schlern, looking like a devilish *Winged Victory,* gave ancient peoples enough willies to spawn legends of supernatural forces. The Schlern witch, today's tourist-brochure mascot, was the cause of many a broom-riding medieval townswoman's fiery death.

Alpe di Siusi is my recommended one-stop look at the Dolomites because of Castelrotto's charm as a home base, its quintessential Dolomite mountain views, its easy accessibility for those with and without cars, and its variety of walks, hikes, and mountain-bike routes. While most hikers will enjoy the easy meadow strolls, the nearby Schlern tempts and rewards those with more energy and an adventurous spirit.

The meadow is famous for its wildflowers—a fragrant festival (best in June) blooming with flowers that grow only 5,900–7,800 feet above sea level. The cows munching away in this vast meadow produce 2.5 million gallons of milk annually, much of which is sent to Bolzano to make cheese. After tourism, dairy is the leading industry here. While cows winter in Castelrotto, they summer in Alpe di Siusi. The meadow is also dotted with small, idyllic hotels and chalet restaurants. It's extremely family-friendly, with playgrounds at each stop and plenty of animals to pet. Being here on a sunny summer day comes with the ambience of a day at the beach.

THE DOLOMITES

Orientation to Alpe di Siusi

Getting to Alpe di Siusi

By Car: A nature preserve, Alpe di Siusi is closed to cars during the day (9:00–17:00), unless you're staying in one of the area hotels. (Show your reservation confirmation as proof.) Parking at Compatsch (€13.50/day) requires that you arrive before the road closes at 9:00 in the morning, though you can drive back down at any time. Park officials encourage visitors to use the free parking lot located at the Seiseralm Bergbahn cable-car station in Siusi/Seis (see below); park your car and take the cable car *(cabinovia)* up to Compatsch.

By Cable Car from Siusi/Seis up to Alpe di Siusi: A cable car (Seiseralm Bergbahn) runs hikers and skiers from the village of

Alpe di Siusi

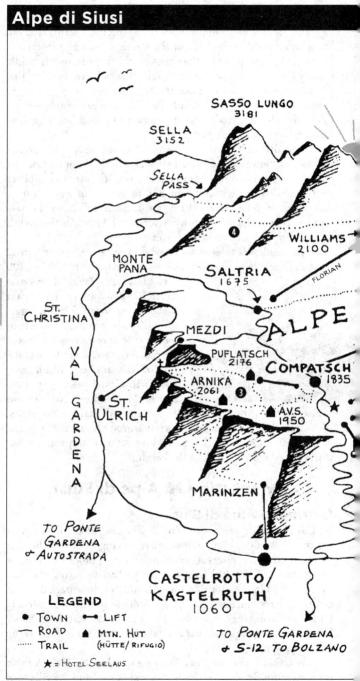

THE DOLOMITES

SASSO LUNGO
3181

SELLA
3152

SELLA PASS

④

WILLIAMS
2100

FLORIAN

MONTE PANA

SALTRIA
1675

ALPE

St. CHRISTINA

MEZDI

PUFLATSCH
2176

COMPATSCH
1835

VAL GARDENA

ARNIKA
2061

③

St. ULRICH

A.V.S.
1950

★

MARINZEN

TO PONTE GARDENA & AUTOSTRADA

CASTELROTTO/ KASTELRUTH
1060

TO PONTE GARDENA & S-12 TO BOLZANO

LEGEND
● TOWN   ●—● LIFT
— ROAD   ▲ MTN. HUT
····· TRAIL   (HÜTTE/RIFUGIO)
★ = HOTEL SEELAUS

NOTE: THIS 3-D VIEW LOOKS
SOUTHEAST & IS NOT TO SCALE.
ELEVATIONS IN METERS

MARMOLADA
3342

PLATTKOFEL

ZALLINGER
2054

TIERSER ALPL
2441

MOLIGNON
2060

DI SIUSI

PANORAMA
2014

SPITZBÜHL
1979

SCHLERN-
HAUS
2450

MT.
PEZ
2563

SCHLERN

SALTNER
SCHWAIGE
"TSCHAPIT"
1830

SEISER ALM
BERGBAHN

SIUSI/SEIS
1002

TO
BOLZANO
& AUTOSTRADA

1 Panorama to Zallingerhütte Hike
2 Summit Hike of Schlern
3 "Trail of the Witches"
4 Loop around Sasso Lungo

DCH

THE DOLOMITES

Siusi/Seis to Compatsch, the gateway to the meadow (late May–mid-Sept daily 8:00–19:00, off-season 8:00–18:00, 15-minute ride to the top, €9 one-way, €13.50 round-trip, www.seiseralmbahn.it). From Compatsch, you can take a shuttle bus farther into Alpe di Siusi to Saltria (€1 one-way, €2 round-trip).

By Bus from Castelrotto: Buses shuttle hikers between Castelrotto's bus station *(Bushof)* and the Seiseralm Bergbahn cable car near the village of Siusi/Seis (2–4/hour in season, daily 8:00–19:30, fewer midday, €3 one-way, does not include cable-car ticket). Bus #3 links Castelrotto, Siusi, and the Seiseralm Bergbahn cable-car station about twice hourly.

Regional buses (such as the orange SAD bus to and from Bolzano) stop at Siusi/Seis and just past the Seiseralm Bergbahn (frequent in summer, 4/day in each direction off-season, €2 one-way).

The Alpe di Siusi Express is a shuttle bus that runs from Castelrotto all the way to Compatsch—denying you the fun experience of approaching the high meadow by cable car (6/day, 20 minutes, €9 one-way, €13 round-trip, see www.silbernagl.it for schedules).

Getting Around Alpe di Siusi

Shuttle Buses: As the meadow is essentially car-free, the park's buses shuttle visitors to and from key points along the tiny road all the way from Compatsch—at the entry to the meadow—to the end of the line at Saltria—at the foot of the postcard-dramatic Sasso peaks (every 20 minutes 9:00–18:30, 15 minutes, €1, buy from driver). At the end of the day, buses can be jam-packed.

Cable Cars and Chair Lifts: The entire meadow is served by various lifts (marked on maps). These are worth the roughly €5–8 per ride to get you into the higher and more scenic hiking areas (or back to the shuttle buses quickly). Keep in mind that lifts and shuttle buses stop running fairly early (typically at about 17:00)—which can be a major disappointment if you're running out of steam and time, and are still high up after a long day's hike.

Compatsch

This tourist village (6,048 feet) at the entrance to the meadow is served by the Seiseralm Bergbahn cable car from the town of Siusi/Seis. You can drive to Compatsch if you are staying at a hotel in Alpe di Siusi (or if you arrive very early or leave very late, outside of park opening hours). Parking costs €13.50 per day.

Compatsch has a **TI** (Mon–Fri 8:15–12:30, Sat 8:15–12:00, closed Sun, WCs at cable-car station, tel. 0471-727-904, www.seiseralm.it/en). You'll also find a grocery store (open mid-June–

mid-Oct), ATM, hotels, restaurants, and shops.

You can rent mountain bikes at **Sporthaus Trocker** (€8/1 hour, €25/day, mid-May–mid-Oct only, 50 yards and across the street from TI in strip mall under the Plaza Hotel, tel. 0471-727-824, www.sporthaustrocker.it). There's a world of tiny paved and gravel lanes to pedal on. Pick up their suggested routes and consider those I've described later. Rentable baby buggies are popular for those hiking with toddlers.

Trocker rents horses and provides guides (about €28/1 hour, €38/2 hours, €54/3 hours, open July–Sept, near cable-car station, follow gravel road between Pensione Animone and Station to end, tel. 0471-727-807, no English spoken).

Horse-drawn carriage rides are available to the left of the TI (May–Oct 9:00–16:00). Prices vary widely; check the sign near the road for details.

Sleeping near the Park Entrance: **$$$ Hotel Seelaus,** a 10-minute walk downhill from Compatsch, is a cozy, friendly family-run place with a Germanic feel and down comforters (Sb-€60–130, Db-€110–260, prices vary with season and type of room; includes buffet breakfast and hearty dinner, free and easy parking, and use of Wellness Center with sauna, hydro-massage, and mini-pool; Via Compatsch 8, tel. 0471-727-954, fax 0471-727-835, www.hotelseelaus.it, info@hotelseelaus.it, Roberto). There are many more chalets and huts with rooms for rent in Alpe di Siusi (which generally cost as much as a normal hotel; ask TI for details).

Hiking in Alpe di Siusi

Easy meadow walks abound in Alpe di Siusi, giving novice hikers classic Dolomite views from baby-stroller trails. Experienced hikers should consider the tougher and more exciting treks. Before attempting a hike, call or stop by the local TI to confirm your understanding of the time and skills required. As always, when hiking in the mountains, assume weather can change quickly, and pack accordingly. Many lifts operate only mid-June through mid-October—check with the TI for specifics on open lifts. Meadow walks, for flower-lovers and strollers, are pretty—or may be pretty boring. Chairlifts are springboards for more dramatic and demanding hikes. Trails are very well-marked, and the brightly painted numbers are keyed into local maps. For simple hikes, you can basically string together three or four hut names. For anything more serious, invest in a good map, about €5 at the TI. The Kompass Bolzano map #54 covers everything in this chapter (scale 1:50,000). The Wanderkarte map of Alpe di Siusi (produced by Tabacco) offers more detail and focuses on just Alpe di Siusi (scale 1:25,000).

Walks and Hikes from Compatsch

Panorama to Zallingerhütte: The "Easy" Route—This is a basic four-hour mostly level walk that is moderately strenuous. It promises fine vistas from both ends of the meadow, fun stops along the way, and lifts up and down on each end. Start by riding the €5 lift to Panorama (6,600 feet), then hike 1.25 hours to Molignonhütte (6,725 feet). Continue hiking two hours (fairly level, follow trails #2 and then #7) to Zallingerhütte (6,725 feet). From here it's a 10-minute walk to Williamshütte (6,888 feet), where you catch the €8 Florian lift back to Saltria and the shuttle-bus stop (for Compatsch). Both Molignonhütte and Zallingerhütte have great restaurants for a drink or meal. For shorter or cheaper versions, you can ride the lift up and stroll back down.

Panorama to Plattkofelhütte: The High Route—For a more thrilling two-hour extension of the previous hike, climb from Molignonhütte (6,725 feet) up to Plattkofelhütte (7,544 feet), follow the high trail #4 along the ridge for an hour, with commanding views both left and right, and then hike steeply back down to Williamshütte (6,888 feet).

Summit Hike of Schlern (Sciliar)—For a challenging 12-mile (six-hour) hike—with a possible overnight in a traditional mountain refuge (generally open mid-June–mid-Oct)—consider hiking to the summit of Schlern and spending a night in Rifugio Bolzano/Schlernhaus. This route is popular with serious hikers as the best hike in the region.

Start at the Spitzbühl chairlift (€4.50 one-way, €6.50 round-trip, 5,659 feet, free parking lot, first bus stop in park, www.seiseralm.it), which drops you at Spitzbühl (6,348 feet). Trail #5 takes you through a high meadow, down to the Saltner dairy farm (6,004 feet—you want the Saltner dairy farm at Tschapit, not the one near Zallingerhütte), across a stream, and steeply up the Schlern mountain. About three hours into your hike, you'll meet trail #1 and walk across the rocky tabletop plateau of Schlern to the mountain hotel **Rifugio Bolzano/Schlernhaus** (7,544 feet, 60 beds, S-€24, D-€48, dorm beds-€20, breakfast-€7, open early June–Sept, cold water only, summer only tel. 0471-612-024 or mobile 335-606-1905, can reserve by email before hut opens in June, www.schlernhaus.it, info@schlernhaus.it). From this dramatic setting, you can enjoy a meal and get a great view of the Rosengarten range. Hike 20 more minutes up the nearby peak (Mount Pez, 8,399 feet) where you'll find a lofty meadow, cows in the summer, and the region's ultimate 360-degree alpine panorama. From Rifugio Bolzano/Schlernhaus, you can hike back the way you came or walk farther along the Schlern (7 miles, 2 hours; past **Rifugio Alpe di Tires/Tierser Alpl,** 8,005 feet, €31 beds, €21 bunks, half-board available for €48/€38, open June–mid-Oct, showers-€3, tel. 0471-727-958 or 0471-707-460, mobile 333-654-6865, www.tierseralpl.com, info@tierseralpl.com) and descend back into Alpe di Siusi, to the road where the bus or cable car will return you to your starting point or hotel.

The "Trail of the Witches"—Take a lift from Compatsch to Puflatsch (€5 one-way, €7 round-trip) for the two-hour loop north to Arnikahütte (with a café) and back (elevation gain about 660 feet). An engraved map on the platform near the top of the lift gives the names of the surrounding mountains. Walking among the legendary stone seats of witches, you'll enjoy fine views of the valley all the way down to Castelrotto.

Loop Around Sasso Lungo—Another dramatic but easy hike is the eight-hour walk around the Sasso Lungo (Langkofel) mountains, called the Federico Augusto/Friederich August trail. Ride the bus to Saltria (end of the line), take the chairlift to Williamshütte, walk past the **Zallingerhütte** (overnight possible, €41/person in dorm room, Db-€62, includes breakfast and dinner, open late-May–mid-Oct, tel. 0471-727-947), and circle the Sasso Lungo group (get details and advice from the TI). On the opposite side, at Sella Pass, you ride a lift up Sasso Lungo to the Leo Demetz hut (8,790 feet), cross the saddle between Sasso Lungo and Sasso Piatto, and zigzag back into Alpe di Siusi with breathtaking views of rock climbers.

Biking in Alpe di Siusi

Mountain bikes are easy to rent, welcome on the lifts, and permitted on Alpe di Siusi lanes. The Compatsch TI has a good information flier that lists the best routes (I've listed three here). Get local advice to confirm difficulty levels and your plan before starting any ride.

Mountain-Bike Rides from Compatsch

Easy High Alp Ride (2.5 Hours, Medium)—This ride stays in Alpe di Siusi and gives you the best basic look at this high meadow, with little altitude gain and easy lanes throughout.

Start from Compatsch (6,048 feet), bike or ride the lift to Panorama (6,600 feet), and take road #7, which runs generally level to Goldknopf/Punta d'Oro and then Mahlknechthütte/Molignonhütte (6,725 feet). Then follow road #8 down to Saltria (5,575 feet), and back to Compatsch (6,048 feet).

Alpe di Siusi Meadow and Val Gardena (4 Hours, Medium to Difficult)—This route covers the great views of the Alpe di

Siusi meadow, gets you into Val Gardena (a classic Süd Tirol valley) to see two resort towns, and then a lift gets you easily back to your starting point.

Start at Compatsch (6,048 feet), and take the road to Saltria (5,575 feet); from the bus stop, ride the unpaved road down to Monte Pana (5,366 feet). From here, an asphalt road zigzags steeply to St. Cristina (4,592 feet on valley floor far below), then heads down the valley to St. Ulrich/Ortisei (4,264 feet), where you take the cable car to Mezdi (6,560 feet), back in the Alpe di Siusi high meadow. Complete your loop by rolling back down on a good road to Compatsch (6,048 feet).

Dramatic High Ridge Ride (4 Hours, Difficult)—This ride takes you into the dramatic rocks so characteristic of the Dolomites, with grand views and only the sound of your hardworking body and the rocks under your tires. If you get an early start, you can leave the bike at the Tierser Alpl/Alpe di Tires hut (8,006 feet) and hike to Schlernhausern/Rifugio Bolzano near the summit of the mighty Schlern—Monte Pez (2 hours, 8,400 feet).

Start at Compatsch (6,048 feet), ride the paved road downhill for 3.5 miles to Saltria (5,575 feet), then take road #8 for a huge uphill slog to the Tierser Alpl hut (8,006 feet; or you can ride the lift to Williamshütte to avoid half the altitude gain). From the Tierser Alpl hut, return the way you came until just below Hotel Floralpina/Seiser Alm Haus, where you'll take the left fork and follow road #7 to Mahlknechthütte/Molignonhütte (6,725 feet) and on through Goldknopt/Punta d'Oro (6,560 feet), and back down to Compatsch (6,048 feet).

More Sights in the Dolomites

▲▲Great Dolomite Road—This is the definitive Dolomite drive: Belluno–Cortina–Pordoi Pass–Val di Fassa–Bolzano. Connecting Venice with Bolzano this way (the Belluno–Venice autostrada is slick) takes three hours longer than the direct Bolzano–Verona–Venice autostrada. No public transit does this trip. In spring and early summer, passes labeled "closed" are often bare, dry, and, as far as local drivers are concerned, wide-open. Call 0471-200-198 for road conditions (in Italian or German only).

▲▲Abbreviated Dolomite Loop Drive—See the biggies in half the miles (allow four hours, Bolzano–Castelrotto–Val Gardena–Sella Pass–Val di Fassa–Bolzano). Val Gardena (Grodner Tal) is famous for its skiing and hiking resorts, traditional Ladin culture, and wood-carvers (the wood-carving company ANRI is from the Val Gardena town of St. Cristina). It's a bit overrated, but even if its culture has been suffocated by the big bucks of hedonistic European fun-seekers, it remains a good jumping-off point for trips into the mountains. Within an hour, you'll reach Sella Pass (7,349 feet). After a series of tight hairpin turns a half-mile or so over the pass, you'll see some benches and cars. Pull over and watch the rock climbers.

The town of Canazei, at the head of the valley and the end of the bus line, has the most ambience and altitude (4,642 feet). From there, a lift (€5 one-way, €8 round-trip) and a gondola (€6 one-way, €8.50 round-trip; or both lifts for €9.50 one-way, €14 round-trip; late June–late Sept daily 8:30–12:30 & 14:00–17:30, both closed Oct–Easter) take you to Col dei Rossi Belvedere, where you can hike the Bindelweg trail past Rifugio Belvedere along an easy but breathtaking ridge to Rifugio Viel del Pan (Canazei TI for lift info: tel. 0462-609-600, www.fassa.com, infocanazei@fassa.com). This three-hour round-trip hike has views of the highest mountain in the Dolomites—the Marmolada—and the Dolo-mighty Sella range.

▲▲**Reifenstein Castle**—For one of Europe's most intimate looks at medieval castle life, let the friendly lady of Reifenstein (Frau Steiner) show you around her wonderfully preserved castle. She leads tours in German and Italian, squeezing in whatever English she can (€6, open May–Oct; tours Sun–Fri at 10:30, 14:00, and 15:00; mid-July–mid-Sept also at 16:00, always closed Sat, best to call ahead to reserve tour, minimum of 4 people needed for tour to run, picnic spot at drawbridge, tel. 339-264-3752, or TI tel. 0472-765-325, www.sterzing.com).

To drive to the castle, follow the A-22 autostrada toward Brenner Pass, exit at Vipiteno (Sterzing), and follow signs toward *Bolzano,* taking three rights. The castle is just west of the freeway; park at the base of the castle's rock. Of the two castles here, Reifenstein is the one to the west. While this is easy by car, it's probably not worth the trouble by train (6/day from Bolzano, one-hour train ride followed by a one-hour hike).

▲**Glurns**—Drivers connecting the Dolomites and Lake Como by the high road via Meran and Bormio can spend the night in the amazing little town of Glurns (45 minutes west of touristy Meran, between Schluderns and Taufers). Glurns still lives within its square wall on the Adige River, with a church bell tower that has a thing about ringing, and real farms rather than boutiques. The town's short archways seem to cause the locals, whose families go back eons, to take on a Quasimodo-like posture. There are several small hotels in the town, but I'd stay in a private home (such as **Family Hofer,** 4 rooms, €26/person with breakfast, less for 3 nights, cash only, 100 yards from town square, near church, just outside wall on river, Via Adige 1, tel. 0473-831-597, fax 0473-835-864, www.hofer.bz.it, privatzimmer.hofer@rolmail.net).

THE LAKES

Commune with nature where Italy is welded to the Alps, in the lovely Italian lakes district. In this land of lakes, the million-euro question is: Which one? For the best mix of accessibility, scenery, and offbeat-ness, Varenna on Lake Como is my top choice, followed by Stresa on Lake Maggiore. You'll get a complete dose of Italian-lakes wonder and aristocratic-old-days romance. Bustling Milan, just an hour away from either lake, doesn't even exist. Now it's your turn to be *chiuso per restauro* (closed for restoration). If relaxation's not on your agenda, the lakes shouldn't be either. If you must choose between Lake Como and Lake Maggiore, the former is a better place to linger, while the latter makes a good day trip from Milan.

Lake Como

Planning Your Time

Lake Como (Lago di Como) is Milan's quick getaway, and the sleepy mid-lake village of Varenna is the gateway to the lake and the handiest base of operations. With good connections to Milan, Malpensa Airport, and mid-lake destinations, Varenna is my favorite home base for the lakes. Even though there are no essential activities, plan for at least two nights so that you'll have an uninterrupted day to see how slow you can get your pulse.

Lake Como—lined with elegant 19th-century villas, crowned by snowcapped mountains, and busy with ferries, hydrofoils, and slow passenger-only boats—is a good place to take a break from

The Lakes

the intensity and obligatory-turnstile culture of central Italy. It seems like half the travelers you'll meet have tossed their itineraries into the lake and are actually relaxing.

Today, the hazy, lazy lake's only serious industry is tourism. Thousands of lakeside residents travel daily to nearby Lugano, in Switzerland, to find work. The lake's isolation and flat economy have left it pretty much the way the 19th-century Romantic poets described it.

Getting Around Lake Como

By Boat: Lake Como is well-served by boats and hydrofoils. The lake service is divided into three parts: south–north from Como to Colico; mid-lake between Varenna, Bellagio, Menaggio, and Cadenabbia (Villa Carlotta); and the southeastern arm to Lecco. Unless you're going through Como, you'll probably limit your cruising to the mid-lake service (boat info: toll-free tel. 800-551-801 or tel. 031-579-211, www.navigazionelaghi.it). Boats go about every 40–60 minutes between Varenna, Menaggio, and Bellagio (€3.60 per hop, 15–20 minutes, daily approximately 7:00–22:30, confirm return trip when you disembark). Overnight stopovers

Boat Schedule Literacy Tips

Feriali	Monday–Saturday
Festivi	Sundays and holidays
Partenze da...	Departing from
Traghetto or *Autotraghetto*	Car Ferry (walk-on passengers, too)
Aliscafo or *Servizio rapido*	Hydrofoil
Battello ship	Slow passenger-only boat going all the way to Como
Battello navetta	Shuttle ship serving mid-lake only

aren't allowed, so buy individual tickets for each ride if you aren't planning to return the same day. The one-day €11 mid-lake pass costs the same as three rides and can be used to make unlimited trips between seven different villages bordering the lake, using either the *autotraghetti* (car ferry) or the passenger-only *battello* (but note that many travelers take only two rides in a day—a round-trip between Varenna and Bellagio).

The free schedule (available at TIs, hotels, and boat docks) lists boat times. Rates are displayed on posters at ticket windows. Confusingly, the schedule requires you to scan four different time-tables to know all the departures:

• car and passenger ferry (mid-lake "ferry-boat," or *auto-traghetto* on the schedule)

• hydrofoil (*servizio rapido,* costs a third more, enclosed, stuffy, speedy, less scenic)

• all-lake slow boat *(battello ship)*

• mid-lake shuttle ferry *(battello navetta)*

I find the schedule impossible to decipher and simply ask at each dock when the next boat is leaving and which dock it's leaving from (Bellagio has several docks). Be sure to note whether you are traveling on a weekday (*feriali,* Mon–Sat) or a Sunday *(festivi).* Review your possible connections (ask your hotelier for help) before you set out so you can pace your day smartly. It's a shame to miss a boat and lose out on a hike or an eagerly anticipated meal because of confusing timetables.

THE LAKES

By Car: With the parking problems, traffic jams, and expensive car ferries, this is no place to drive if you don't have to. While you can drive around the lake, the road is narrow, congested, and lined with privacy-seeking walls, hedges, and tall fences. Parking in Bellagio is more difficult than in Varenna. If you have a car in Varenna, leave it there and use the boat.

While you can rent cars in Bellagio, for most travelers, it's best to take the train to Milan and pick up a car there, either at the central train station or at an airport.

Varenna

This town of 800 people offers the best of all lake worlds. Easily accessible by train, on the less-driven side of the lake, Varenna

has a romantic promenade, a tiny harbor, narrow lanes, and its own villa. It's just the right place to savor a lakeside cappuccino or *aperitivo*. There's wonderfully little to do here, and it's very quiet at night, unless you're here during one of the hundred or so annual American-wedding parties. The *passerella* (lakeside walk, unlit but safe after dark) is adorned with caryatid lovers pressing silently against each other in the shadows. Varenna is a popular destination with my readers and European vacationers—book well in advance for visits in summer (May–Oct). Between November and mid-March, Varenna practically shuts down; hotels close for the winter, and restaurants and shops reduce their hours.

THE LAKES

Orientation to Varenna

Tourist Information

Don't count on any tourist information. You may find a small office with sporadic hours at the train station, on the main square, or at the boat dock. Pro Loco Varenna, on the main square, may be open weekends during high season only (April–Sept Sat–Sun 10:00–12:30 & 15:30–18:30, just past the tobacco shop, tel. 0341-830-367, www.varennaitaly.com, prolocovarenna@tin.it). Your hotel may have the latest edition of the *Varenna Tourist Info* booklet, with updated info on sights around Varenna and a list of restaurants, bars, and services in town.

Arrival in Varenna

By Train: From any destination covered in this book, you'll get to Lake Como via Milan. The quickest, easiest, and cheapest Milan connection to any point mid-lake (Varenna, Bellagio, or Menaggio) is via the train to Varenna. On arrival, set up and limit your activities to the scenic mid-lake area (Varenna and Bellagio).

Here are the specifics: Leaving from Milan's central station, catch a train heading for Sondrio or Tirano—sometimes the departure board also says "Lecco/Tirano." (Tirano is often confused with Torino...wrong city.) And, if you're heading for Varenna, be sure you don't accidentally catch a train to Verona. All Sondrio trains stop in Varenna, as noted in the fine print on the *Partenze* (departures) schedule posted at Milan's train station. Trains leave Milan about every two hours (€5, likely schedule: 6:20, 8:20, 10:20, 12:20, 14:20, 16:20, 17:20, 19:20, 20:20, and 21:25; confirm these times, 1 hour). Get a second-class ticket, since first-class train cars are rare on the Sondrio–Tirano route. Stamp the ticket in the yellow box at the front of the tracks or risk a €50 fine. Sit on the left for maximum lake view beauty. Get off at Varenna–Esino. Even though train schedules simply list Varenna, Varenna–Esino is what you'll see at the train station—same place.

Long trains serve Varenna's tiny station and stop for only about a minute. Know what time you're supposed to arrive in Varenna, so you can be ready to disembark with luggage in hand. Otherwise you'll be carried on to the next town and have to backtrack. You may have to open the train door yourself, and because trains can be longer than the station, your car may actually stop before or after the platform (causing you to mistakenly think that you're not there yet). Look out the window. If part of the train's at the station, you'll need to get out and walk to the platform. Tips: Board mid-train to land next to a platform. Leave from the door by which you entered, since you know it's working. If necessary, pull hard on the red handle to open the door.

By Bus/Train from Malpensa Airport (Milan): You can take the airport bus from Malpensa Airport to Milan's train station (see page 313), then catch a Varenna-bound train (see above).

By Boat via Como: For a less convenient but more scenic trip, you can also get to Varenna from Milan via the town of Como (or vice versa). Trains take you from Milan to Como (hourly, 30- to 90-minute ride). It's a 10-minute walk to the dock, where you catch a boat for the one-hour hydrofoil or two-hour *battello* (slow boat—great for enjoying the scenery) ride up the lake to Varenna (slow boat: 3/day, €8, last departure about 15:00; hydrofoil: 5/day except 1/day Sun, €12, last departure about 19:00).

By Taxi: A taxi costs roughly €130–165 between Varenna and downtown Milan or Milan's airports. For a reputable taxi service,

Central Lake Como

2 MILES
3 KM

N

TO TIRANO &
ST. MORITZ
(SWITZ)

BELLANO

MONTE GRONA

VARENNA-
ESINO STN.

MENAGGIO

CASTLE
VEZIO

12 MILES TO
LUGANO, SWITZ.
(SCENIC BUS)

VARENNA

SOURCE OF
RIVER

PUNTA
SPARTI-
VENTO

FIUME-
LATTE
(TINY
RIVER)

CADENABBIA

PESCALLO

VILLA CARLOTTA
TREMEZZO

BELLAGIO

LENNO

LAGO
DI
LECCO

OSPEDA-
LETTO

CAMPO

MANDELLO

VILLA
BALBIANELLO

TO
MILAN
1 HOUR

TO
COMO

ISOLA
COMACINA

••• MID-LAKE BOATS
▪▪▪ SELF-GUIDED
    FERRY TOUR
· · · OTHER BOATS
+ + RAIL
- - - TRAIL

DCH

CENTRAL
LAKE
COMO

LAKE
COMO

VARENNA

LECCO

COMO

BELLAGIO

THE LAKES

see "Helpful Hints," page 242.

By Car: In Varenna, look for the color-coded lines to decipher the parking options: white is free anytime; yellow is for residents only; and blue means you pay (look for signs, €1/hour, payment times vary—often 8:00–12:00 & 14:00–19:00, otherwise free). Buy tickets from the newsstand on the main square, the *tabacchi* shop just south of the square, or Bar Cambusa near the ferry dock (scratch off the date and time you'll be parked and leave the ticket on your dashboard; overnight until 8:00 is OK).

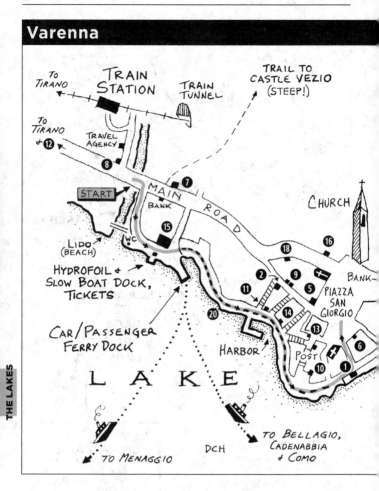

Parking is free Monday–Friday at the train station, but you'll have to pay on Saturdays and Sundays during the high season (8:00–19:00, feed coins into meter at center of the lot and put the printed ticket on the dashboard). In general, parking in Varenna is complicated—it's best to confirm with your hotelier that you are safely parked.

Getting Around Varenna

Varenna is small, and everything is within a 15-minute walk (except for Hotel Eremo Gaudio). From the dock, walk up to the main road to avoid carting your luggage across the cobblestones.

If you'd prefer a taxi, you'll find them waiting at the train station and dock. From either arrival point, a taxi should charge €9 for a ride to your hotel (see "Taxi," page 242).

- ❶ Hotel du Lac
- ❷ Albergo Milano & Ristorante la Vista
- ❸ Villa Cipressi & Rist. la Contrada
- ❹ To Eremo Gaudio
- ❺ Albergo/Rist. del Sole
- ❻ Villa Elena
- ❼ Hotel/Rist. Montecodeno
- ❽ Albergo Beretta
- ❾ Rist. il Cavatappi & Osteria Quatro Pass
- ❿ Nilus Bar, Bar il Molo & La Frulleria
- ⓫ Gelateria la Giazzera
- ⓬ To Rist. il Caminetto & Cooking Course
- ⓭ Rist. Isola Nuova
- ⓮ Vecchia Varenna
- ⓯ Hotel/Rist. Olivedo
- ⓰ Grocery Stores (2)
- ⓱ Ornithology & Natural Science Museum; Internet Café
- ⓲ Laundry
- ⓳ Villa Monastero
- ⓴ Christ of the Lake

TRAIN TUNNEL

TO MILAN

TRAIL TO ❹ & FIUMELATTE

TO LECCO

MAIN RD.

GARDENS

C O M O

→ SELF-GUIDED WALK
---- PASSERELLA (LAKESIDE PROMENADE)
ⅢⅢ STEPPED STREETS

NOT TO SCALE:
(TRAIN STN. TO CHURCH
IS A 10 MIN. WALK)

THE LAKES

Helpful Hints

Money: A bank (with a cash machine) is near Varenna's main square; another is located inland from the boat dock (see town map).

Internet Access: Try **Barilott,** which also sells Milan train tickets, fresh *panini,* and wines by the glass (Internet access €6/hour, Mon–Sat 7:00–20:00, closed Sun, Via IV Novembre 6, tel. 0341-815-045, Claudia and Fabrizio).

Post Office: It's just off the main square (Mon–Fri 8:30–14:00, Sat 8:30–12:30, closed Sun).

Laundry: Lavanderia Pensa Barbara can wash and dry your laundry within 24 hours (€3.50/kilo, no self-service, no underwear but socks are OK, Mon–Fri 9:00–12:30 & 15:00–19:30, Sat 9:00–12:30, closed Sun, Via Venini 31, tel. 0341-830-478).

Taxi: Reliable **Marco Barili** (or his wife Nelli) will meet you at the train station if you know your exact arrival time in Varenna. He can also get you to Milan and its airports and, unlike other drivers, he doesn't add surcharges for baggage or early/late departures (€130 to central Milan or Linate Airport, €140 to Malpensa Airport for up to 4 people, €210 for 5–8 passengers in a minibus, tel. 0341-815-061, taxi.varenna@tiscali.it).

Travel Agency: For bus and boat tours, consider Varenna's travel agency, **I Viaggi del Tivano,** next to Albergo Beretta, a block below the train station. They book planes, trains, and automobiles, and can offer half-day and daylong tours of the region and into Switzerland from April through October; book tours by noon the day before (office open Mon–Fri 8:30–12:30 & 15:00–19:00, Sat 9:00–12:00, closed Sun, can book rental cars here but pick up elsewhere, Via Esino 3, tel. 0341-814-009, www.tivanotours.com, info@tivanotours.com, helpful Cristina and Eleonora).

Self-Guided Walk

Welcome to Varenna

Since you came here to relax, this short walk gives you just the town basics.

Bridge Just Below Train Station: This main bridge spans the tiny Esino River. The river divides two communities: Perledo (which sprawls up the hill—notice the church spire high above) and the old fishing town of Varenna (huddled around its harbor). The train station is called Varenna–Esino, named for a third community situated eight miles higher in the hills. Follow the river down to the lakeside promenade by the ferry dock. The town's public beach (or *lido*) is just over the cute pedestrian bridge (free beach, lounge chairs for rent). The inn facing the ferry dock, Hotel Olivedo, has greeted ferry travelers since the 19th century, and is named for the olive groves you can see growing halfway up the hill. Natives claim this is the farthest north that olives grow in Europe.

• *Across from Hotel Olivedo is Varenna's...*

Ferry Landing: Since the coming of the train in 1892, Varenna has been *the* convenient access point from "mid-lake" (the communities of Bellagio, Menaggio, and Varenna) to Milan. From this viewpoint, you can almost see how Lake Como is shaped like a man. The head is the north end (to the right, up by the Swiss Alps). Varenna is the man's left hip (to the east). Menaggio, across the lake, is the right hip (to the west). And Bellagio (hiding behind the smaller wooded hill to your left) is where the legs come together—you can see the point (Punta Spartivento—literally, "point that divides the wind"). In a more colorful description, a traditional poem says, "Lake Como is a man, with Colico the head, Lecco and Como the feet, and Bellagio the testicles." (In the regional dialect, this rhymes—ask a native to say it for you.)

The farthest ridges high above the right hip mark the border of Switzerland. The region's longtime poverty shaped the local character (much like the Great Depression shaped the outlook of a generation of Americans). Many still remember that this side of the lake was the poorest, because those on the other side (Menaggio) controlled the lucrative cigarette-smuggling business over the Swiss border. Today, the entire region is thriving—thanks to tourism.

• *Walk past the ferry dock to Varenna's elevated shoreline walk, called the...*

Passerella: A generation ago, Varenna built this elegant lakeside promenade, which connects the ferry dock with the old town center. Strolling this lane, you'll come to the tiny two-dinghy concrete breakwater of a villa. Lake Como is lined with swanky  19th-century villas; their front doors face the lake to welcome visitors arriving by boat. At this point, the modern *passerella* cuts between this villa's water gate and its private harbor. Around the next corner, a plaque marks *Il Signore del Lago,* which means the Christ of the Lake. The divers' association placed this crucifix (floodlit after dark) about 10 feet underwater, declaring, "We are committing ourselves to love, because this is the only certainty." (Their commitment to replacing a burnt-out lightbulb, however, is not so certain.) From here, enjoy a good Varenna town view. These buildings are stringently protected by preservation laws; you can't even change the color of your villa's paint.

Just over the hump (which allows boats into a covered moorage), look up at another typical old villa—with a private *passerella*, a lovely veil of wisteria, and a prime lakeview terrace. Many of these villas are owned by the region's "impoverished nobility." They were bred and raised not to work and, therefore, are now unable to pay for the upkeep of their sprawling houses. Lately, these villas are being bought by the region's nouveau riche.

• *At the community harbor, walk to the end of the pier for a town overview, then continue under the old-time arcades to the fishermen's multi-hued homes, which face the harbor.*

Varenna Harborfront: There are no streets in the old town... just characteristic stepped lanes called *contrade*. Varenna was originally a fishing community. Even today, old-timers enjoy Lake Como's counterpart to the Norwegian lutefisk: *missoltino,* air-dried and salted lake "sardines." They're served with the region's polenta (different from Venice's because buckwheat is mixed in with the corn).

Imagine the harbor 200 years ago—busy with coopers expertly fitting chestnut and oak staves into barrels, stoneworkers carving the black marble that was quarried just above town, and fishing boats dragged onto the sloping beach. The little stone harbor dates from about 1600. Today, the fishing boats are just for recreation, and residents gather here with their kids to relax by the lake.

At the south end of the harbor (across from La Frulleria), belly up to the banister of the terrace for another colorful town view. Another traditional ditty goes, "If you love Lake Como, you know Bellagio is the pearl...but Varenna is the diamond."

• *Continue straight, leaving the harbor. A lane leads around past Hotel du Lac (its fine lakeside terrace welcomes non-guests for a drink) to the tiny pebbly town beach. From here, climb uphill to the town square, called...*

Piazza San Giorgio: Four churches face Varenna's town square. The main church dates from the 13th century. Romantic Varenna is an understandably popular spot for weddings—rice often litters the church's front yard. Stepping inside, you'll find a few humble but centuries-old bits of carving and frescoes. The black floor and chapels are made from the local marble. Outside, past the WWI monument, is the TI and the Ornithology and Natural Science Museum, with its small collection of stuffed birds and other wildlife (both open Sat–Sun only).

The Royal Victoria Hotel, also on the main square, recalls the 1839 visit of Queen Victoria, who registered herself as the Countess of Clare in an attempt to remain anonymous. The trees are planted to make a V for Varenna. The street plan survives from Roman times, when gutters flowed down to the lake. The little church on the lake side of the square is the baptistery. Dating from the ninth century, it's one of the oldest churches on the lake, but is rarely open for visits.

As you wander the lanes of Varenna, you'll notice plastic water bottles left out by the door. Residents believe that these keep cats from peeing on their doorstep. Something about seeing their reflection causes the cats to get self-conscious...

Your walk is over. From this square, you can head south to the gardens (described below, under "Sights in Varenna"), north to go to the train station or ferry dock, or hike up to reach the castle.

Sights in Varenna

Castle—A steep and stony trail leads to Varenna's ruined hilltop castle, Castello di Vezio, located in a peaceful, traffic-free one-chapel town. Start at the stairs to the left of Hotel Montecodeno, and figure on a 20-minute walk one-way. The castle is barren, but livened up by occasional art exhibits and a falconry-training center (€4, daily June–Aug 9:00–17:00, March–May and Sept–Nov until 18:00, closed in winter and when rainy; falconry shows Sat–Sun around 16:00, Mon–Fri likely once daily—call in morning for times; sleepy café at entrance, mobile 333-448-5975, www.castellodivezio.it, Nicola).

Gardens—Two manicured lakeside gardens—the terraces of Villa Cipressi and the adjacent, more open grounds of the Villa Monastero—are open to the public. The former noble residence of the Villa Monastero, filled with overly ornate furnishings from the late 1800s, is also open to the public as a museum (gardens-€3; Villa Monastero museum-€6, price includes garden; daily April–Oct 9:00–19:00, closed Nov–March, villa closed for lunch 13:00–14:00, bar in garden).

Swimming—There are three spots to swim in Varenna: the little free beach behind the Royal Victoria Hotel off Piazza San Giorgio, the central lakefront area by Nilus Bar, and the *lido*. The *lido* is by far the best equipped for swimmers. Just west of the boat dock, it's essentially a wide concrete slab with sand and a swimming area off an old boat ramp. It has showers, bathrooms, a bar, and lounge chairs for rent.

Speedboat Tours—**Taxiboat** organizes "villa-viewing trips" around the lake, gives personalized tours on the water, and provides a water-taxi service. Their 40-minute "Varenna seen from the water" tour (€10/person, €50 minimum, up to 10 people) is fun, and chartering the boat for 1.25 hours gets you a mid-lake tour (mobile 349-229-0953, www.taxiboatlecco.com, info@taxiboatlecco.com, Luca). A similar company works out of Bellagio.

Near Varenna

▲▲Self-Guided Ferry Tour: Lake Como—The best simple day out is to simply take the *battello navetta* (mid-lake ferry) on its entire 50-minute Varenna–Bellagio–Cadenabbia–Villa Carlotta–Tremezzo–Lenno route. On the return trip, stop at any sights that interest you (Lenno to see Villa del Balbianello, Villa Carlotta, and/or Bellagio). This commentary describes what you'll see along the way.

Leaving Varenna: Looking back at Varenna from the lake, you'll see the castle above, new Varenna on the left (bigger buildings and modern ferry dock), and old Varenna on the right (tighter buildings). You'll also see a big development high on the hillside—an ugly example of cronyism (without the mayor involved, this would never have happened). Under the castle is a grove of olives (reputedly the most northern ones grown in Italy). As the lake is protected from the north wind, exotic flowers grow well in the lake's many fine gardens. From Varenna's castle to the right are the town cemetery, a lift up to the recommended Eremo Gaudio hotel (a former hermitage), and a spurt of water gushing out of the mountain just above lake level. This is the tiny Fiumelatte, Italy's shortest river.

Mid-Lake: The Swiss Alps rise to the north. Across the lake is Menaggio, and just over the ridge from that is Lugano and the Swiss Riviera. The winds alternate between north and south. In pre-industrial times, traders harnessed the wind to sail up and down the lake. Notice the V-shaped fjord-like terrain. Lake Como is glacier cut. And at more than 1,200 feet deep, it's Europe's deepest lake. You'll cruise past the Punta Spartiventa, the point that literally splits the wind, and where the two "legs" of the lake join (Lecco is on the left and Como on the right).

Approaching Bellagio: Survey the park to the left on the tip—it's a pleasant walk from town. Bellagio has 10 times the number of hotel rooms as Varenna, as you can see upon approach. The town, with its strip of three-star hotels, is bookended by Villa Serbelloni (5 stars) on the left, dominating the lakefront, and the sprawling Grand Hotel Bretagne (4 stars) on the right. In the 19th century, the Russians hung out in the Serbelloni and the English chose the Bretagne. These days, the Serbelloni is the second-most luxurious hotel on the lake after Villa Este, while Bretagne is mired in a long renovation project.

Approaching Cadenabbia: From Bellagio you cross the lake to Cadenabbia. Above Cadenabbia, the Church of St. Martin seems stranded halfway up the mountain. This side of the lake has nearly all of the area's traffic, thanks to a big road that ended up separating many fine lakefront gardens from their villas. Farther north is the village of Dongo, where Mussolini and his girlfriend were captured in the last months of World War II as they tried to escape into Switzerland. They were shot here on the lake, and their bodies were hung ingloriously in Milan for public viewing.

Villa Carlotta: Because of lake taxes and high maintenance costs, owners of once-elite villas have been forced to either turn them into hotels, or else open their doors to the paying public. This is an example of the latter. One of the finest villas on the lake, Villa Carlotta is most visited for its Canova statue and lush garden (see listing on page 260).

Tremezzo: Notice the Grand Hotel Tremezzo, with its striking Liberty-style facade and floating pool. Above the town is a villa built in the 19th-century Romantic age as a medieval castle. After the Tremezzo stop (just before the Tremezzo church), you'll see a fine public park with a fountain. When the road split this land off from its villa, its owners gave it to the community. Here along the lake you'll see a string of fine old villas with elegant landings and gated boat houses. Built in the days before motors, they are now too small for most modern lake boats. Tullio Abbate is famous in this area for building top-end and speedy lake boats.

Lenno: This is your last stop. About 400 yards farther along the shore is a tiny dock for shuttle boats headed for Villa del Balbianello (of *Star Wars: Episode II* and *Casino Royale* fame, see page 260).

Sailing Home: From here you return to Bellagio or Varenna, stopping along the way as you like.

Hiking—The town of Fiumelatte, about a half-mile south of Varenna, was named for its milky river. It's the shortest river in Italy (at 800 feet) and runs—like most of the area tourist industry—only from April through September. The *La Sorgente del Fiumelatte* brochure, available at Varenna's TI, lays out a walk from Varenna to the Fiumelatte to the castle and back. It's a 30-minute hike to the source *(sorgente)* of the milky river (at Varenna's monastery, take the high road, drop into the tranquil and evocative cemetery, and climb steps to the wooded trail leading to the peaceful and refreshing cave from which the river sprouts).

For a longer hike with lake views, ask the TI about the Wayfarers' Path (hike one-way up the lake, about 1.5 hours, not quite as steep as Fiumelatte hike). You can return by train from Bellano (€4, Bellano not included on mid-lake pass, check schedule before you go), or take the ferry to Menaggio and catch a connecting boat back to Varenna.

▲**Cooking Course**—Chef Moreno of the recommended Ristorante il Caminetto picks you up in Varenna, zips you up the mountain to his restaurant (experience Italian driving!), and then teaches you some basics of Italian cooking. Learn how to handcraft fresh pasta or prep regional specialties. Classes last about three hours, plus add time to *mangiare* (€35 includes trip, lesson, and a lunch complete with wine, cookies, and coffee; Mon, Tue, Thu, and Fri; 10:00 pick-up from Varenna landing, return by 16:00, reservations mandatory, tel. 0341-815-225, www.ilcaminettoonline.com, info@ilcaminettoonline.com). People love the experience and find Moreno a charming teacher and host.

Sleeping in Varenna

Reservations are tight in August, snug May through October, and wide open most of the rest of the year. Many places close in winter. High-season prices are listed here; prices get soft off-season (Nov–April).

$$$ Hotel du Lac, filling a refined and modernized 19th-century villa, is the finest hotel in town. From its exclusive private perch on the point, it offers a quiet lakefront breakfast terrace, generous public spaces, a friendly, professional staff, and 16 delightful rooms, all with lake views (standard Db-€187, bigger Db-€240, prices straight May through mid-Oct, €20 less in April, closed off-season, air-con, Wi-Fi, parking-€15, Via del Prestino 11, tel. 0341-830-238, fax 0341-831-081, www.albergodulac.com, albergodulac@tin.it).

$$$ Albergo Milano, located right in the old town, is graciously run by Egidio and his Swiss wife, Bettina. Fusing the best of Italy with the best of Switzerland, this well-run, romantic hotel has eight comfortable rooms with extravagant views, balconies, or big terraces (Sb-€125, Db-€160, €10 extra for view terrace, €5/day cash discount, no elevator, closed Dec–Feb; from the station, take main road to town and turn right at steep alley where sidewalk and guardrail break; Via XX Settembre 35; tel. 0341-830-298, fax 0341-830-061, www.varenna.net, hotelmilano@varenna.net). This place whispers *luna di miele*—honeymoon (see website for 3-night honeymoon deal). Nearby are three comfortable apartments that work well for families (Db-€130–160, proportionately more for third or fourth person, breakfast served at main hotel). Their Ristorante la Vista is worth considering for dinner.

$$ Villa Cipressi is a sprawling centuries-old lakeside mansion with 33 warmly outfitted, modern rooms, and public spaces that are often busy with wedding parties. Rooms without views face the street and can be noisy. The villa sits in a huge, quiet terraced garden that non-guests pay to see (Sb-€125, non-view Db-€140, view Db-€170–180, extra cot-€40, extra bed-€60, prices promised with this book, elevator, Wi-Fi, Jacuzzi, garden access, free mountain bike use for guests, Via IV Novembre 22, tel. 0341-830-113, fax 0341-830-401, www.hotelvillacipressi.it, info@hotelvillacipressi.it, Davide).

$$ Eremo Gaudio stands out with a commanding lake view high above Varenna. Once an orphanage, it became a hermitage run by the Catholic Church, and then—since 2000—a modern hotel accessed by a private funicular. Perfect for monks with champagne

Sleep Code

(€1 = about $1.25, country code: 39)

S = Single, **D** = Double/Twin, **T** = Triple, **Q** = Quad, **b** = bathroom, **s** = shower only. Unless otherwise noted, you can assume the price includes breakfast, credit cards are accepted, and English is spoken.

To help you sort easily through these listings, I've divided the rooms into three categories based on the price for a standard double room with bath:

$$$ **Higher Priced**—Most rooms €150 or more.

$$ **Moderately Priced**—Most rooms between €100–150.

$ **Lower Priced**—Most rooms €100 or less.

Prices can change without notice; verify the hotel's current rates online or by email. For other updates, see www.ricksteves.com/update.

tastes, it's peaceful, with awe-inspiring view balconies and a breakfast terrace. Thirteen bright, plain-but-comfy rooms climb up the main building, and 15 less-dramatic but equally comfortable rooms huddle below at the foot of the funicular (upper rooms: Sb-€100, Db-€120, Db with balcony-€135; lower rooms: Db-€100–125; 7 percent discount with cash and 3-night stay, closed Nov–Feb, all rooms have lake views, air-con, taxi from station recommended, quarter-mile south of Varenna's main square at Via Roma 15, tel. 0341-815-301, fax 0341-815-314, www.eremogaudio.it, eremogaudio@yahoo .it). Suppers are served on the upper terrace, weather permitting.

$$ Albergo del Sole is a no-frills hotel over a basic restaurant right on the town square. Run by a straight-faced family, the hotel has seven comfy rooms and no hint of a lake view (Sb-€70–85; Db-€120, €105 off-season; fans, hardwood floors, shiny bathrooms, Wi-Fi, no elevator, Piazza San Giorgio 17, tel. & fax 0341-815-218, www.albergodelsole.lc.it, albergo.sole@virgilio.it).

$ Villa Elena, a grandmotherly, low-energy place on the main square, offers a tranquil rest and the best budget beds in town. English-speaking Signora Seta ("Silk") Vitali, who lives downstairs, rents her three characteristic antique-filled rooms at the same price—room #1 has a shabby bathroom and view terrace (first come, first served); room #3 also has a private bathroom, but room #2 does not. With only twin beds, it's not for romantics, but it is a great value (D-€45 with or without bath, cash only, no breakfast, it's the vine-covered facade at Piazza San Giorgio 7 near Via San Giovanni, tel. 0341-830-575, www.villaelenavarenna.it, info@villaelenavarenna.it).

$ Hotel Montecodeno, with 11 decent rooms and no views, is a functional concrete box just off the main road between the train station and lake (Sb-€70, Db-€90, extra bed-€10, air-con, attached restaurant serves fresh fish and a €23 "Rick Steves" fixed-price meal; if you stay 3 nights and pay cash, you get one meal included per guest or a 15 percent cash discount—take your pick; Via della Croce 2, tel. 0341-830-123, fax 0341-815-227, www.hotel montecodeno.com, ferrcas@tin.it, Marina Castelli). Their nearby apartments sleep up to six for €35–40 per person.

$ Albergo Beretta, on the main road a block below the station, has 10 pleasant rooms, several with balconies (and street noise). Second-floor rooms are quietest. This place, above a coffee shop that doubles as the reception, feels homey, lacks any lakeside glamour, and sometimes smells smoky (D-€60, Db-€70, extra bed-€12, breakfast-€6 but free with this book, no elevator, Via per Esino 1, tel. & fax 0341-830-132, www.hotelberetta.it, hotel beretta@iol.it, Signora Tosca doesn't speak English, but Giulia and Ariana do).

Eating in Varenna

Dining with a Lake View

Ristorante la Vista, at Albergo Milano, feels like a private hotel restaurant, but also welcomes non-guests. On a balmy evening, their six-table terrace overlooking the town and the lake is hard to beat. Egidio (or Egi—pronounced "edgy") and his staff give traditional cuisine a creative twist, and his selection is great for foodies with discerning tastes. I'd go with his €35 three-course fixed-price dinner (Mon and Wed–Sat 19:00–22:00, closed Sun and Tue, reservations required, Via XX Settembre 35, tel. 0341-830-298).

Ristorante la Contrada, with its terrace-side location, takes advantage of Villa Cipressi's elegant garden, trickling fountain, and lake view. Indoor seating glows with a warm and romantic air, and the garden is a delight on warm summer evenings. Fresh daily specialties and professional service make this a worthwhile splurge. However, weddings and groups can crowd the place and distract from the service (€30 meals plus wine, daily 12:30–14:00 & 19:15–21:45, may close for weddings, Via IV Novembre 18, tel. 0341-830-113).

Dining Without a Lake View

Ristorante il Cavatappi, a tiny place on a quiet lane just off the town square, serves old-time specialties, such as *missoltino* (the air-dried lake fish that natives like more than tourists do) as an antipasto. Helpful owner-chef Mario is happy to be considered a lunatic gourmet. With just five tables, he can connect personally with diners.

Talk with him, make a plan, then let him loose. Plan on spending €25 plus wine (Thu–Tue 12:30–14:30 & 19:30–21:45, closed Wed, reservations recommended for dinner, tel. 0341-815-349).

Osteria Quatro Pass is a welcoming bistro known for its homemade pasta and fish. It offers 10 candlelit tables under picturesque vaults, plus sidewalk seating (Thu–Tue 12:30–14:00 & 19:00–22:00, closed Wed, Via XX Settembre 20, tel. 0341-815-091, Lollo).

Eating Simple on the Harbor

The harborfront is lined with several simple eateries, all with great lakefront seating.

Nilus Bar, with a young waitstaff, serves dinner crêpes, pizzas, big mixed salads, hot sandwiches, soup of the day, and cocktails with a smile. Pricing includes cover and service (March–Nov Wed–Mon 12:00–22:30, hours can vary and bar open longer, closed Tue and Dec–Feb, cash only, tel. 0341-815-228, Fulvia and Giovanni).

Bar il Molo, next door, is good for a pizza or pasta on the harbor (€9 pizzas and pastas, salads, toasted sandwiches, daily 11:00–24:00, tel. 0341-830-070). They also have a room full of gifty edibles.

La Frulleria is a sweet stop for drinks and desserts. It's a youthful place serving cold, sugary, and fruity treats from a fun menu. If you're eating dinner elsewhere without a lake view, consider skipping dessert and coming here for your finale (May–Oct Tue–Sun 12:00–24:00, closed Mon and Nov–April, 2 doors down from Nilus Bar, Samantha). To sit at a lakeside table, you need to order from the menu (€4–6 menu items).

At **Gelateria la Giazzera,** you can get a cup or cone to go, or grab a little pillow on the bulkhead. Eros is the only guy in town who makes his gelato fresh every day. Try their *nocciola* (hazelnut), then make your choice (daily 13:00–21:00, open later June–Aug).

Eating Simple Without a Lake View

Ristorante del Sole, facing the town square, serves edible meals and Naples-style pizzas (€5–9). Making few concessions to the tourist crowds, this family-friendly restaurant caters to residents, providing a fun atmosphere and a cozy, walled-in garden in back, or tables on the square (daily 12:00–15:00 & 19:00–22:00, pizza until 24:00, Piazza San Giorgio 21, tel. 0341-815-218).

Ristorante il Caminetto is a homey backwoods mountain trattoria in Gittana, a tiny town high above Varenna. Getting there entails a free curvy 10-minute drive. They pick you up in Piazza San Giorgio at 19:30, deliver you to their restaurant, and then dish up classic fare at small-town prices. Specialties such as grilled meats and risotto with porcini mushrooms and berries are made with pride by husband and wife Moreno and Rossella. This is a good place to set a price and trust your host to bring whatever's best (€15–19 *dégustation* menu, Thu–Tue 12:30–14:30 & 19:30–21:30, closed Wed, reservations mandatory to confirm pickup from Varenna at 19:30, Viale Progresso 6, tel. 0341-815-225 or 0341-815-127, mobile 347-331-2238).

Other Eateries

Ristorante Montecodeno, a cozy little place on the big road in the new part of town, serves a plate of eight different lake fish including *missoltino*. **Ristorante Isola Nuova** is a new restaurant with a fresh atmosphere, buried in the old town with no sea view. The venerable **Vecchia Varenna** is the only classy restaurant actually on the harbor (old place with new management). And at **Hotel Olivedo,** a grand old hotel facing the ferry dock, you can eat in a classic dining hall.

Picnics: Varenna's two little grocery stores have all you need for a classy balcony or breakwater picnic dinner. The *salumeria* on the square is best for meats, cheese, and bread (Tue–Sun 7:30–12:30 & 15:30–19:30, Mon 7:30–12:30 only), while the store just north of the main square by the pharmacy stocks fresh fruits and veggies (daily 7:30–12:30, Tue–Sat also 16:00–19:30).

Varenna Connections

If leaving Varenna by train, you can't purchase tickets at the station. Instead, you'll have to buy them from the Barilott *tabacchi* shop just off the main square, or the travel agency, I Viaggi del Tivano, next door to the recommended Albergo Beretta hotel. Stamp your ticket in the yellow machine at the station before boarding. If both places are closed, win the sympathy of the conductor and buy your ticket on board for an additional fee. (Seek him out. If he finds you, you'll likely be charged a stiff penalty.)

Varenna to Milan by Train: Trains leave Varenna for Milano Centrale (around €5, likely schedule for daily and direct trains: 5:36, 6:23, 6:39, 7:37, 8:37, 10:37, 12:37, 14:37, 16:37, 18:37, and 20:37; 1 hour; if you take a train at a time not listed here, it's likely a local milk-run train taking twice as long).

Varenna to Stresa by Train: Trains run about every two hours (2.75–4 hours, transfer in Milan).

Varenna to St. Moritz in Switzerland by Train: From Varenna, you have easy access to the Bernina Express scenic train to St. Moritz. Note that this is only realistic from April through October. First, take the train to Tirano, and then transfer to the Bernina Express train to St. Moritz (3/day, allow 4–5 hours with transfer; for details see www.rhb.ch—click "E" for English). For information on this route, stop by the I Viaggi del Tivano travel agency (see listing on page 242), or ask your hotelier if they have the handy tourist information book produced by the travel agency.

Bellagio

The self-proclaimed "Pearl of the Lake" is a classy combination of tidiness and Old World elegance. If you don't mind that "tramp in

a palace" feeling, it's a fine place to shop for ties and umbrellas while surrounding yourself with the more adventurous posh travelers. The heavy curtains between the arcades keep the visitors and their poodles from sweating. Thriving yet still cute, Bellagio is a much more substantial town than Varenna (which has one-tenth the number of hotel beds and almost no shops).

Orientation to Bellagio

Tourist Information: The TI is right downtown, at the passenger boat dock (April–Oct Mon–Sat 9:00–12:30 & 13:00–18:00, Sun 10:00–14:00; Nov–March shorter hours and closed Sun and Tue; tel. 031-950-204, www.bellagiolakecomo.com, iat@promobellagio .it). They often offer guided tours of the town a couple of times a week (€8, 2 hours).

Arrival in Bellagio: Bellagio is best reached via ferry from Varenna (€3.60) or via ferry, hydrofoil, or slow boat from Como (see "Arrival in Varenna," page 238).

Parking is difficult, but you can try near the lakeside or the parking lot at the ferry dock (white lines are always free, blue lines €1/hour, yellow lines are for residents only, pay with coins in gray machines and stick ticket in car window).

The Docks: Bellagio has two docks a few minutes' walk apart. The northern docks are for the passenger-only slow boat (*battello* or *battello navetta*) and the hydrofoil *(servizio rapido)*. The southern dock is for all "ferry-boats" *(traghetto):* both the car ferry (cars and foot passengers) and the passenger-only ferry. To make sure you're waiting at the correct dock, ask a resident. Remember that if you want to know all your departure options beyond Varenna, Cadenabbia, and Menaggio, you need to study four different timetables (see "Getting Around Lake Como," page 235). Confirm your intentions at the kiosk near either dock.

Helpful Hints

Internet Access: Bellagio Point has a slick Internet café, complete with great sandwiches, wine-tasting options, and free Wi-Fi if you buy a drink (€2/15 minutes, daily 10:00–22:00, Salita Plinio 8, tel. 032-950-437, www.bellagiopoint.com). Julio also rents apartments (listed later, under "Sleeping in Bellagio").

Post Office: It's on the south end of Lungo Lago Mazzini (Mon–Fri 8:30–14:00, Sat 8:30–12:30, closed Sun).

Laundry: La Lavandera is bright and new (daily 9:00–21:00; €7.50 wash/dry, Salita Carlo Grandi 21—this street is also marked as Via Specula, tel. 339-410-6852).

Sights in Bellagio

Villa Serbelloni Park—If you need a destination, you can visit this park, which overlooks the town, with a guide (€8.50, April–Oct, tours Tue–Sun at 11:00 and 15:30, no tours Mon and when rainy, 1.5 hours, first two-thirds of walk is uphill, show up at the little tour office in the medieval tower on Piazza della Chiesa 15 minutes before tour time to buy tickets, confirm time at office, tel. 031-951-555). The villa itself, owned by the Rockefeller Foundation, is not open to the public.

Strolling—Explore the steep-stepped lanes rising from the harborfront. While Johnnie Walker and jewelry sell best at lake level, the natives shop up the hill. Piazza della Chiesa, near the top of town, has a worth-a-look church (with its art described in an English-language handout).

The administrative capital of the mid-lake region, Bellagio is located where the two southern legs of the lake split off. For an easy break in a park with a great view, wander right on out to the crotch. Meander past the rich and famous Hotel Villa Serbelloni, and walk five minutes to Punta Spartivento ("point that divides the wind"). You'll find a Renoir atmosphere complete with an inviting bar-restaurant, a tiny harbor, and a chance to sit on a park bench and gaze north past Menaggio, Varenna, and the end of the lake to the Swiss Alps.

For another stroll, head south from the car-ferry dock down the tree-shaded promenade. Ten minutes later, you'll pass the town's concrete swimming area (closed indefinitely). The grassy,

Bellagio

P PARKING

TO PUNTO
SPARTIVENTO
14

NOT TO SCALE
PASSENGER DOCK
TO CHURCH IS A
5 MINUTE WALK
UPHILL.

TO
VARENNA

VIA EUGENIO

VIA ROMA

SALITA MARAFFIO

4

CHURCH

SLOW BOAT
& HYDROFOIL
DOCK,
TICKETS

7   1

SALITA

3

SALITA

PIAZZA
MAZZINI

VIA CENTRALE

MONASTERO

PLINIO

PIAZZA
CHIESA

17

TO
VILLA
SERBELLONI
PARK

SALITA

9   6   15   5

BOAT
TICKETS

PIAZZA
MAZZINI

SALITA

VIA MELLA

VIA GARIBALDI

VIA RONCATI

12

SALITA

CAVOUR

18   GRANDI   16

13

TO CADENABBIA &
MENAGGIO

CERNAIA

SPECULA

8

2

SERBELLONI

L A K E
C O M O

LUNGO MANZONI

BELLUSIO

GARIBALDI

11

CAR/PASSENGER
FERRY DOCK

BOAT
TICKETS

P

10

DCH

SAL. CAPP.

SAL. GENAZZINI

POST +
BUS STOP
TO COMO

TO
PESCALLO

TO
VILLA MELZI
10 MIN. WALK

TO COMO

THE LAKES

1 Hotel Florence
2 Hotel/Rist./Snack Bar
   Metropole
3 Hotel Centrale
4 Albergo Europa
5 Bellagio B&B Apartments
6 Il Borgo Apartments
7 The Florence Ristorante
8 Trattoria San Giacomo
9 Rist. Terrazza Barchetta

10 Enoteca Cava Turacciolo
11 Aperitivo Et Al
12 Gelateria del Borgo
13 Gilardoni Alimentari
14 To La Punta Ristorante
15 Bellagio Point Internet Café
16 Launderette
17 Villa Serbelloni Park Tickets
18 Water-Taxi Tours

pebbly public San Giovanni beach (no showers) is another 20 minutes farther south from there.

Villa Melzi Gardens—A 10-minute walk south from the ferry dock is this picture-perfect lakeside expanse of exotic plants, flowers, trees, and Neoclassical sculpture, assembled by the vice president of Napoleon's Italian Republic in the early 19th century (€6, March–Oct daily 9:30–18:30, www.giardinidivillamelzi.it).

Hikes and Walks—The TI has free brochures on three well-crafted walking tours that explore the city and environs, varying from one to three hours. Sites include villas, gardens, churches, an old-fashioned dairy shop, medieval towers, and a nautical instruments museum. The TI also sells a hiking map for €3 that shows four different hikes ranging in difficulty and duration.

Water-Taxi Tour—With a small stand at the boat docks, Jennine and Luca offer tours and private service in their luxurious and powerful boat. Their basic 2.5-hour tour, guided by Luca, includes a fun hour on mid-lake, with a float-by of Richard Branson's villa, as well as a stop at Villa del Balbianello (see listing on page 260), where you'll take an English tour (generally at 14:00, €45 with a 10 percent discount for readers of this book, price includes entry and tour of villa—worth €11, check blackboard for day's offerings or call, mobile 338-524-4914).

Sleeping in Bellagio

(€1 = about $1.25, country code: 39)

This is a "boom or bust" lake resort, with high-season prices (those listed here) straight through from May–September, plus a brief shoulder season (with discounted prices) in April and October–November. Off-season (Dec–March), nearly everything is closed down.

$$$ Hotel Florence has a prime lakefront setting in the center of town. The 150-year-old family-run place features 30 rooms, hardwood floors, bold earth tones, and a rich touch of Old World elegance (Sb-€120, Db-€140–200, Db suite-€230–260, prices depend on view and balcony, closed Nov–March, handheld showers, fans on request, Wi-Fi, tel. 031-950-342, fax 031-951-722, www.hotelflorencebellagio.it, info@hotelflorencebellagio.it, run by Austrian Ketzlar family).

$$ Hotel Metropole, dominating Bellagio's waterfront between the ferry docks, is a grand old place with plush public spaces. Its modern rooms have all the comforts but also have an institutional feel. Many of its 42 rooms have lake views (Db-€130–150, €20–40 more with terrace, air-con, Wi-Fi, stunning roof terrace, tel. 031-950-409, fax 031-951-534, www.albergometropole.it, info@albergometropole.it).

$$ Hotel Centrale, managed with pride and care by Giacomo Borelli, warmly welcomes its guests into a true-blue family operation: Signore Borelli's wife and two sons help out, his mama painted the art, and grandpa crafted much of the Art Deco–era furniture. This place has generous public spaces and many thoughtful touches—and its 17 comfortable rooms are a great value, even without lake views (Db-€90–110, larger Db-€110–130, €10/night discount with this book, air-con, elevator, free Wi-Fi, Salita Plinio 7, tel. 031-951-940, fax 031-952-682, www.hc-bellagio.com, info @bellagio.com).

$ Albergo Europa, run with low energy, is in a concrete annex behind a restaurant, away from the waterfront. Its 10 rooms have no charm but are comfortable (Db-€60–90, breakfast-€8, no elevator, free parking, Via Roma 21, tel. & fax 031-950-471, www .hoteleuropabellagio.it, albeuropa@tiscali.it, family Marchesi).

$ Bellagio B&B Apartments, with five units for rent, are located behind the *gelateria* at the top of town. Julio also runs the Bellagio Point Internet café, which serves as the reception (Db-€60, more for 3 or 4 people, two-night minimum, no breakfast, Wi-Fi, reception located at Salita Plinio 8, apartments located at Salita Cavour n. 37, tel. 031-951-680, fax 031-953-0025, www .bellagiobedandbreakfast.com, info@bellagiobedandbreakfast .com).

$ Il Borgo Apartments rents six modern *Better Homes and Gardens*–quality apartments with kitchenettes in the old center at great prices. Easygoing Flavio is available for check-in daily 9:00–12:00, or by appointment (Db-€80, 2 bigger apartments for up to 6 people-€100, cash discount, no breakfast, 2-night minimum required, air-con, Salita Plinio 4, tel. & fax 031-952-497, mobile 338-193-5559, fax 031-951-585, www.borgoresidence.it, info@borgo residence.it).

Eating in Bellagio

On the Lakefront

The following places offer wonderful lakeside tables and, considering the setting, reasonable prices.

Hotel Metropole Ristorante, while a mediocre food value, has a full menu and is a relaxing delight for a meal with good service (€14 pastas, €16 *secondi,* daily April–Oct 12:00–14:30 & 19:00–21:30, closed Nov–March, tel. 031-950-409).

Hotel Metropole Snack Bar, next to the hotel's restaurant, is quite good, with simple pastas (€9), fine salads, and sandwiches (no cover charge, daily 12:00–21:30, good service, great locale).

The Florence is nicely situated under a trellis of flowers across from the Florence Hotel and away from the ferry fumes. This is a lovely perch for a drink or meal (€16 pastas, €20 *secondi*, no cover charges, more simple lunch menu of salads and such, bar open all day).

In the Old Town Without Lake Views

Trattoria San Giacomo is a high-energy place that's respected for its traditional cuisine, such as *riso e filetto di pesce* (rice and perch fillet in butter and sage). It has daily, seasonal specials and an inviting €20–25 fixed-price meal based on regional specialties. Choose between fun seating on a steep, cobbled lane or tight seating inside (Mon and Wed–Thu 12:00–14:30 & 19:00–21:30, Fri–Sun open later midday and evenings, closed Tue, Salita Serbelloni 45, tel. 031-950-329, run by Aurelio).

Ristorante Terrazza Barchetta, set on a bamboo-covered terrace with no lake view and bedecked with summery colors, puts a creative twist on regional specialties. The €48 tasting menu pairs three glasses of wine with a fish dish, a meat dish, and dessert (available in high season only). Don't confuse it with the street-level bar-trattoria—head up the stairs to the second floor. Reservations are recommended (€15 pastas, €20 *secondi*, Wed–Mon 12:00–15:00 & 19:00–22:30, closed Tue, Salita Mella 13, tel. 031-951-389).

Other Options

Wine Tasting: Step into the vaulted stone cellar rooms of the funky **Enoteca Cava Turacciolo** to taste three regional wines with a sampling of cheeses, meats, and breads (€18/person with this book, Thu–Tue 10:30–24:00, closed Wed, Salita Genazzini, tel. 031-950-975, Norberto and Rosy). **Aperitivo Et Al,** slick and jazzy, is a trendier wine bar, offering mixed *salumi* and *formaggi* plates (€12), big fresh salads (€11), and light lunches, along with a great selection of wines by the glass (€14 three-glass tasting totaling a half bottle of wine per person, add antipasto plate for €25, Wed–Mon 11:30–1:00 in the morning, closed Tue, free Wi-Fi, Salita Serbelloni 34, tel. 031-951-523, run by Aussie expat Sarah).

Gelato: Residents agree that you won't find the best *gelateria* in town among the sundaes served on the waterfront. Instead, climb to the top of town to **Gelateria del Borgo** (daily April–Oct 10:00–22:30, closed Nov–March, Via Garibaldi 46, tel. 031-950-755, Stefania and Gianfranco).

Picnics: You'll find benches at the park, along the waterfront in town, and lining the promenade south of town. Pick up your picnic supplies at **Gilardoni Alimentari.** They have roast chicken, ribs, and focaccia, and are happy to make fresh sandwiches to your order (Tue–Sat 7:30–13:00 & 15:30–19:30, Sun–Mon 7:30–13:00 only, shorter hours off-season, on corner of Via Garibaldi and Via Carlo Bellosio, tel. 031-951-815).

Punto Spartivento: This dramatic park, a 10-minute walk north of town (see "Strolling," page 254), is a great place for either a picnic or a meal at **La Punta Ristorante** (€9 pastas, €13 fish, €22 meat courses; daily April–Oct 12:00–14:30 & 19:00–22:00, bar open through the afternoon for snacks only, closed Nov–March, tel. 031-951-888).

Menaggio

Menaggio has more urban bulk than its neighbors. Since many visitors find Lake Como too dirty for swimming, consider spending  ing time in Menaggio's fine public pool (look for the "Lido"). This is the starting point for a few hikes. Only a few decades ago, these trails were used by cigarette smugglers, sneaking through at night from Switzerland back into Italy with their tax-free booty. The TI has information about mountain biking, and catching the bus to trailheads on nearby Mount Grona (TI open daily 9:00–12:30 & 14:30–18:00, closed Sun and Wed Nov–March, tel. 0344-32-924, www.menaggio .com, infomenaggio@tiscali.it).

THE LAKES

Getting to Menaggio: Buses run between Milan's Malpensa Airport and Como (€13, 1 hour, buy tickets at Airport 2000 ticket desk in arrivals hall), where you change to public bus #C10 to get to Menaggio (€3, about hourly, 1–1.25 hours).

Sleeping in Menaggio

(€1 = about $1.25, country code: 39)
$ La Marianna B&B has eight rooms and a fine restaurant in Cadenabbia, about a mile south of Menaggio on a busy road (Db with view–€90, optional €30 dinner, lakeside terrace at restaurant, air-con, free Wi-Fi, tel. 0344-43095, www.la-marianna.com, inn @la-marianna.com, Ty and Paola). The hourly Como–Menaggio bus #C10 stops here, and the ferry dock for mid-lake towns via Bellagio is 300 yards away.

$ La Primula Youth Hostel has a great location on the lake, a two-minute walk from the ferry dock (€17/person in dorm room, €18/person in family room with bathroom, €3 extra/night for non-members, €5 pizzas, Internet access and Wi-Fi, sailing school, kayak and mountain bike rentals, rock-climbing nearby, tel. &

fax 0344-32356, www.lakecomohostel.com, info@lakecomohostel
.com). The bus from Como (55 minutes) stops right by the hostel.

Menaggio Connections

From Menaggio to Milan: It's a 20-minute ferry to Varenna (boats hourly), where trains connect to Milan (every 1–2 hours, 1 hour, see "Varenna Connections," page 252). More fast trains depart from Como than Varenna. From Menaggio, take hourly local bus #C10 (€3, 1–2/hour, 1 hour) to Como, where you can catch the train (hourly, 30–60 minutes).

From Menaggio to Switzerland: Public bus #C12 departs about every hour or two from Piazza Garibaldi for Lugano (Sunday buses depart from Via Mazzini, €10 round-trip, 1 hour, buy tickets at newspaper shop in Piazza Garibaldi). In summer the yellow Palm Express bus runs once daily to **Lugano** (1 hour) and **St. Moritz** (3 hours). Off-season (mid-Oct–mid-June) the bus runs only on weekends and by advance reservation (www.postbus.ch).

More Sights on Lake Como

Villa Carlotta—If you plan to tour one of Lake Como's famed villas, this is the best for gardens and flowers (its forte). I see the lakes as a break from Italy's art, but if you're in need of a place that charges admission, Villa Carlotta offers an elegant Neoclassical interior, a famous Antonio Canova statue, and a garden that is its highlight and best in spring (€8.50, daily April–mid-Oct 9:00–18:00, until 16:00 last 2 weeks of March and mid-Oct–mid-Nov, closed mid-Nov–mid-March, tel. 034-440-405, www.villacarlotta.it). Nearby Tremezzo and Cadenabbia are pleasant lakeside resorts an easy walk away. Boats serve both places (5-minute walk from either dock to the villa) and are reached by *traghetto* (ferry, dock in Cadenabbia) or the *battello* (slow boat), dock in Tremezzo).

Villa del Balbianello—On a romantic promontory overlooking Lake Como and facing Bellagio is the dreamiest villa on the lake. Built for a cardinal at the end of the 18th century on the remains of an old Franciscan church, the villa was the cardinal's palace of delights, where he could study and brainstorm with his friends. Today it reflects the exotic vision of its last owner, explorer Guido Monzino, who died in 1988, leaving the villa, his rich art collection, and mementos of his expeditions to the state. The upper floor serves as a museum of his expeditions, with memorabilia from his North Pole and Mount Everest adventures. The real masterpiece here is the terraced garden and elegant loggia, where the land fits the architecture and landscaping in a lovely way. This is a favorite choice for movie directors when they need a far-out villa to feature; scenes from *Casino Royale* and *Star Wars: Episode II* were filmed here (€8-garden only, €11-garden with villa tour, Thu–Sun and Tue 10:00–18:00, closed Mon and Wed; access by walking six-tenths of a mile from Lenno through park, weekends only, or catching the €6 ferry shuttle from Lido di Lenno; tel. 034-456-110).

Isola Comacina—This remote little island (just south of Bellagio) offers peace, ancient church foundations, goats, sheep, nice swimming, and a lovely view of Lake Como. It takes 30–45 minutes to walk around the island, but longer to savor it. Bring a picnic or try the snack bar at the dock. Look for trips to Isola Comacina on the Colico–Como *battello* schedule (listed in Lago di Como boat timetable, free at ticket booths at ferry docks, see page 235). The *isola* is accessible from Varenna (1 hour), Menaggio (50 minutes), or Bellagio (35 minutes). Check return times carefully (Como–Colico direction) and don't miss your boat. Usually only one trip a day each way works out for a visit. Allow about six hours, including travel time.

Como—On the southwest tip of the lake, Como has a good, traffic-free old town, an interesting Gothic/Renaissance cathedral, and a pleasant lakefront with a promenade (TI June–Sept Mon–Sat 9:00–13:00 & 14:30–18:00, Sun 9:30–13:00, tel. 031-330-0128, www.lakecomo.it, lakecomo@tin.it). It's an easy 10-minute walk from the boat dock to the train station (trains to Milan depart at least hourly, 30–60 minutes). Boats leave Como about hourly for mid-lake (ferries-€8–10, 2 hours, departures 7:35–16:45; hydrofoils-€11–13, 1 hour, departures 8:45–19:10; tel. 031-579-211, www.navigazionelaghi.it).

Sleeping in Como: For a cheap overnight, try the **$ Villa Olmo Hostel** (€16, includes breakfast and sheets, €3/night extra for non-members, dinners-€6.50–10.50, free Wi-Fi and pay Internet access, laundry service available, baggage storage, free parking, bike rental, reception open 7:00–10:00 & 16:00–24:00, lockout 10:00–16:00, 24:00 curfew, closed Dec–Feb, 20-minute walk from train station or dock, Via Bellinzona 2, tel. & fax 031-573-800, www.aighostels.com, ostellocomo@tin.it).

All-Day Lugano Side-Trip—From Varenna or Bellagio you can nip into Switzerland to see the elegant lake resort of Lugano and the town of Como, as well as cruise a good part of Lake Como. Here's a good day plan: 9:00—ferry to Mennagio, 10:00—bus to Lugano (45 minutes), 11:30—explore Lugano, train to Como (2/hour), 16:00—fast boat from Como to Varenna (departures also at about 17:00, 18:00, and 19:00). For information on Lugano, see www.ricksteves.com/lugano.

Lake Maggiore

Lake Maggiore is ringed by mountains, snowcapped in spring and fall, and lined with resort towns such as Stresa. While crassly touristic, the town of Stresa is a handy base from which to explore the exotic garden islands of Lake Maggiore. And many consider it a pleasant last stop before flying home from nearby Malpensa Airport.

A visit to this region is worth the trouble for two islands, each with exotic gardens and Borromeo family villas. The Borromeo family—through many generations since 1630—lovingly turned their islands into magical retreats, with elaborate villas and fragrant gardens. Isola Bella has the palace and terraced garden; Isola Madre has a villa and sprawling English-style (more casual) garden. A third island, Isola Pescatori (a.k.a. Superiore), is simply small, serene, and residential. The Borromeos, who made their money from trade and banking, enjoyed the arts—from paintings (hung in lavish abundance throughout the palace and villa) to plays (performed in an open-air theater on Isola Bella) and marionette shows (you'll see the puppets that performed here).

Tourists flock to the lakes in May and June, when flowers are in bloom, and in September. Concerts held in scenic settings draw music-lovers, particularly during the Musical Weeks in August (get details from Stresa TI). For fewer crowds, visit in April, July, August (when Italians prefer the Mediterranean beaches), or October. In winter, the snow-covered mountains (with resorts a 1.5-hour drive away) attract skiers.

Planning Your Time

This region is best visited on a sunny day, when the mountains are clear, the lake is calm, and the heat of the sun brings out the scent of the blossoms. The two top islands for sightseeing are Isola Bella and Isola Madre. Isola Pescatori has no sights, but is a peaceful place for lunch.

Day Trip from Milan: Catch an early train from Milan to Stresa (take a one-hour fast train). Upon arrival in Stresa, walk 10 minutes downhill to the boat dock, and catch a boat to Isola Madre. Then work your way back to Isola Pescatori for a lazy lunch, and on to Isola Bella for the afternoon, before returning to the town of Stresa and back to Milan.

Overnight: Small, touristy Stresa makes a fine first or last stop in Italy—its connections with Milan's airport, which is located about halfway between Stresa and Milan, don't involve a transfer in big Milan (see "Stresa Connections," page 272).

Getting Around Lake Maggiore

Boats link the islands and Stresa, running about twice hourly. Allow roughly 10 minutes between stops. Since short round-trip hops add up fast (€6.80 each for Isola Bella and Isola Pescatori, €8.80 for Isola Madre), it's best to simply buy the **all-day pass:** €9.80 for two islands (Bella and Pescatori); or €14.70 for all the islands plus Pallanza (a town on the opposite shore) and Villa Taranto. A **combo-ticket** combining the villas on Isola Bella and Isola Madre with the all-day boat pass may be available for about €28 (credit cards accepted).

Boats run daily April through September. The map on page 265 shows the route: Stresa, Carciano/Lido, Isola Bella, Isola Pescatori, Baveno (lakeside town), Isola Madre, Pallanza, and Villa Taranto. This route is part of a longer one. To follow the boat schedule (free, available at boat docks, TI, and maybe your hotel), look at the Arona–Locarno timetable for trips from Stresa to the islands, and the Locarno–Arona timetable for the return trip to Stresa.

Buy boat tickets directly from the dock ticket booth to the left of the TI. Don't be fooled by the private taxi-boat drivers and their little sales booth on the sidewalk in front of the public boat launch. They'll try to talk you into paying way too much (public boat info: tel. 800-551-801 or 0322-233-200, www.navigazionelaghi.it, info maggiore@navigazionelaghi.it).

THE LAKES

Stresa

Stresa—which means "thin stretch"—was named for the original strip of fishermen's huts that lined the shore. Today, grand old hotels run along that same shore. The old town—basically a traffic-free touristy shopping mall—is just a few blocks deep, stretching inland from the main boat dock. A fine waterfront promenade leads past the venerable old hotels to the Lido (with the Carciano boat dock and a mountain cable car). Stresa's stately 19th-century lakeside hotels date back to the days when this town was on the "Grand Tour" circuit. In any Romantic-age resort like Stresa, hotels had names designed to appeal to Victorian aristocrats...like Palace (rather than Palazzo), Astoria, Bristol, and Victoria.

Nineteen-year-old Ernest Hemingway first came here in 1918. Wounded in Slovenia as an ambulance driver for the Italian Red Cross, he was taken to the Grand Hotel des Iles Borromees. This was the first hotel on the shore (from 1862), and it served—like its regal neighbors—as an infirmary during World War I. Hemingway returned to the same hotel in 1948, stayed in the same room (#205, now called the "Hemingway suite"—you can stay there for a couple of thousand dollars a night), and signed the guest book as "an old client." Another "old client" was Winston Churchill, who honeymooned here.

Orientation to Stresa

Tourist Information: The helpful TI, located to the right of the ticket window at the boat dock, has free maps and boat schedules (daily March–Oct 10:00–12:30 & 15:00–18:30; Nov–Feb Mon–Fri 10:00–12:30 & 15:00–18:30, Sat 10:00–12:30, closed Sun; Piazza Marconi 16, tel. 0323–30150, www.distrettolaghi.it, info@stresa turismo.it).

Arrival in Stresa: At the train station, ask for a free city map at the newsstand (to the far right of the tracks as you exit the train). To get downtown, exit right from the station and take your first left (on Viale Duchessa di Genova). This takes you straight down to the lake (the boat dock is about four blocks to your right; ask for boat schedule at ticket window). The TI is next door on the same dock. Taxis charge a fixed rate of €8 for even the shortest ride in town.

Internet Access: The **Newdata Internet Point** is a block off Piazza Cadorna in the old center (daily 9:30–12:30 & 15:00–22:00, until 19:30 in winter, Via de Vit 15A, tel. 0323-30323, new datastresa@virgilio.it).

Sights in Stresa

Islands and Gardens

▲▲**Isola Bella**—This island, nearest Stresa, has the formal garden and the fanciest Baroque palace. Looking like a stepped pyramid from the water, the island was named by Charles Borromeo (sponsor of Milan's Duomo) for his wife, Isabella. The island itself is touristy, with a gauntlet of souvenir stands and a corral of restaurants. A few back streets provide evidence that people actually live here. While the Borromeo family now lives in Milan, they spend a few weeks on Isola Bella each summer (when their blue-and-red family flag flies from the top of the garden).

Your visit is a one-way tour, starting with the palace and finishing with the garden. (There's no way to see the garden without the palace.) From the dock, head left to the huge palace, passing

Stresa & the Borromeo Islands

1/2 MILE
1 KM

LAKE MAGGIORE

PALLANZA

TO VILLA TARANTO

ISOLA MADRE

TO/FROM BAVENO

ISOLA PESCATORI (SUPERIORE)

BORROMEO PALACE

ISOLA BELLA

GARDENS

TO SANTA CATERINA DEL SASSO

TO SWITZ.

CARCIANO/ LIDO

CABLE CAR

CORSO UMBERTO I

VIA DUCH.

PIAZZA MARCONI

BOAT DOCK

TO ALPINA & MONTE MOTTARONE 1491 m.

TRAIN STATION

CORSO ITALIA

PIAZZA CADORNA

DCH

STRESA CENTER
(SEE DETAIL MAP)

TO MILAN

the public WCs. In the lavishly decorated Baroque palace, stairs lead to stucco crests of Italy's top families (balls signify the Medici, bees mean the Barberini, and a unicorn symbolizes the Borromeo's motto: Humility). The next room shows a portrait of the first Borromeo. It's followed by a richly stuccoed grand hall, with an 80-foot-high dome and featuring an 18th-century model of the villa, including a grand entry that never materialized. Next, the room with the musical instruments was the site of the 1935 Stresa Conference, in which Mussolini met with British and French diplomats in a united attempt to scare Germany out of starting World War II. This "Stresa Front" soon fizzled when Mussolini attacked Ethiopia and joined forces with Hitler. A photocopy of the treaty with Mussolini's signature is on the wall next to the exit. Napoleon's bedroom comes with an engraving that depicts his 1797 visit. (Napoleon is on a bench with his wife and sister enjoying festivities in his honor.) The last rooms display souvenirs and gifts that the Borromeo family picked up over the generations.

Downstairs, many of the famous Borromeo marionettes are on display. (A larger collection is on Isola Madre.) The 18th-century grotto, decorated from ceiling to floor with shell motifs and black-and-white stones, still serves its original function of providing a cool refuge from Italy's heat. The dreamy marble statues are by Gaetano Monti, a student of Canova. Climbing out of the basement, look up at the unique cantilevered stairs; they're from a 16th-century fortress that predates this building.

The ornate hall of 16th-century Flemish tapestries leads to the finale of this island visit: the garden, complete with Chinese white peacocks to give it all an exotic splash. Baroque—which is exactly what you see here—is all about controlling nature. The terraced gardens are crowned by the Borromeo family unicorn. Circle around the garden to the left to visit the bookshop; or head to the right to go straight to the exit. Gardeners continue on to the second exit to pass through Elisa's Greenhouse, named for Napoleon's sister and home to tropical plants.

Cost and Hours: Palace and garden-€12, €17.50 combo-ticket includes Isola Madre, daily mid-March–mid-Oct 9:00–18:00, last entry 30 minutes before closing, closed mid-Oct–mid-March, tel. 0323-30556, www.borromeoturismo.it. A fine €3 audioguide describes the palace, which also has posted English descriptions. A WC is at the garden entrance. Note that there are two docks on this island (one for each direction). Departure times are indicated by clocks at each dock. Picnicking is not allowed in the garden, but you can picnic at the point of the island (free and open to the public); take the mosaic sidewalk to the left of the palace entrance.

▲**Isola Pescatori**—This sleepy island—home to 35 families—is the smallest and most residential of the three. It has a couple of good seafood restaurants, picnic benches, views, and, blissfully, nothing to do—under arbors of wisteria. A

delight for photographers and painters, the island is never really crowded, except at lunchtime.

▲▲**Isola Madre**—Don't come here unless you intend to tour the sight, because that's all there is: an interesting furnished villa and a lovely garden filled with exotic birds and plants. Visiting is a

one-way affair, starting with a long stroll through the garden and finishing with the villa. The sightseeing route is clearly signed, taking you through the gardens and villa, and ending at the chapel.

Eight gardeners (with the help of water continually pumped from the lake) keep this English-style garden paradise lush and a joy, even for those bored by flowers and foliage. You'll see trees from around the world, and an exotic bird menagerie with silver pheasants and Chinese peacocks. In front of the villa, a once-magnificent Himalayan cypress tree paints your world a streaky green. It was knocked down by a tornado in 2006, and earnest rescue efforts are underway to save the 150-year-old tree. It's still green, but with several amputated limbs and the trunk in traction, its survival is uncertain.

The 16th-century villa is the first of the Borromeo palaces. A century older than the other, it's dark, somber, and from the Renaissance. The clever angled hinges keep the doors from flapping in the lake breeze. The family's huge collection of dolls, marionettes, and exquisite 17th-century marionette theater sets—painted by a famous La Scala opera set designer—fills several rooms. A corner room is painted to take you into an 18th-century Venetian Rococo sitting room under a floral greenhouse. You'll see some of the garden's best flowers immediately after leaving the villa.

Cost and Hours: €10, €17.50 combo-ticket includes Isola Bella, mid-March–mid-Oct daily 9:00–18:00, last entry 30 minutes before closing, closed mid-Oct–mid-March, no photos in villa, WC next to chapel, tel. 0323-30556, www.borromeoturismo .it. The €3 audioguide is devoted almost entirely to the garden—a good investment to properly appreciate the plantings.

While eating is best on Isola Pescatori, Isola Madre has one eatery: **La Piratera Ristorante Bar** (€23 fixed-price tourist meal, daily 8:00–18:00, sit-down meals 12:00–15:00 and simple sandwiches to go anytime, picnic at rocky beach a minute's walk from restaurant, tel. 0323-31171).

▲**Villa Taranto Botanical Gardens**—Garden-lovers will enjoy this large landscaped park, located on the mainland a 10-minute boat ride beyond Isola Madre (across the lake from Stresa). The gardens are a Scotsman's labor of love. Starting in the 1930s, Neil McEacharn created this garden of delights—bringing in thousands of plants from all over the world—and here he stays, in the small mausoleum. The park's highlight is the terraced garden with a series of cascading pools. Villa Taranto is directly across the street from the boat dock.

Cost and Hours: €9, daily April–Sept 8:30–18:30, Oct until 17:00, closed Nov–March, tel. 0323-404-555, www.villataranto.it.

Mountain Cable Car—From Stresa's Lido, a cable car takes you up—in two stages and a 20-minute ride—to the top of Mount Mottarone (about 5,000 feet). From here, you get great views of neighboring peaks and, by taking a short hike, a bird's-eye view of the small, neighboring Lake Orta (€17.50 round-trip, €10.50 one-way, includes Alpine Gardens entry, daily 9:30–17:40 in summer, 8:30–17:00 in winter, closed Nov, 2–3/hour, tel. 0323-30295, www.stresa-mottarone.it).

To visit the **Alpine Gardens,** get off at the midway Alpina stop, where a 10-minute walk leads to the gardens (turn left as you leave; included in round-trip cable-car ticket, April–Oct daily 9:30–18:00, closed Nov–March). The gardens come with great lake views and picnic spots, but can't compare to what you'll see on the islands.

If you plan to **hike** down, pick up the Trekking Map from the TI and allow 3.5 hours from the top of Mount Mottarone, or 1.5 hours from the Alpine Gardens.

You can rent a **bike** at the base of the cable-car lift (full-suspension mountain bike or road bike-€5/hour, €22/half-day, €27/day, €45/weekend, includes helmet, tel. 338-839-5692, Giorgio) and bring it on the cable car with you (€11 extra). It's a treacherous ride, enjoyable only for serious bikers. While the ride is nice on top, you'll fight traffic on congested, rough, and windy roads for the rest of the trip.

Day Trips from Stresa

▲**Scenic Boat and Rail Trip to Locarno and Centovalli**—This enjoyable all-day excursion from Stresa involves three segments. Confirm all times, particularly the departure of the last boat from Locarno, before you embark on the trip. Take the train from Stresa to Domodossola, then catch the "Centovalli" train for a 1.5-hour ride that links together remote mountain villages on your way to

Locarno, in the Italian-speaking Swiss canton of Ticino (bring your passport). Spend an hour or so exploring this town, on the far end of Lake Maggiore. Then take the boat past loads of small lakeside hamlets back to Italy. As a relaxing finale, you'll cruise into your home port of Stresa. The trip can also be done in reverse (with the boat trip first). A special €30 "Lago Maggiore Express" ticket covers both the train and boat (you must reserve in advance; fax 0322-249-530 or email infomaggiore@navigazionelaghi.it—indicate the date you'll travel, number of passengers, and a return fax number or email address; call 800-551-801 or 0322-233-200, www.lagomaggioreexpress.com).

▲**Lake Orta**—Just on the other side of Mount Mottarone is the small lake of Orta. The lake's main town, Orta San Giulio, has a beautiful lakeside piazza ringed by picturesque buildings. The

piazza faces the lake with a view of Isola San Giulio. Taxi boats (€2.50 round-trip) make the five-minute trip throughout the day. The island is worth a look for the Church of San Giulio and the circular "path of silence" that takes about 10 minutes. In peak season, Orta is anything but silent, but off-season or early or late in the day, this place is full of peace and magic (**TI** open Wed–Sun 9:00–13:00 & 14:00–18:00, closed Mon–Tue, located on Via Panoramica next to the parking lot downhill from the train station, tel. 0322-905-163).

The train ride from Stresa to Orta–Miasino (a short walk from the lakeside piazza) takes 1.5–2 hours and requires a change or two (9/day). Public buses from Stresa's Piazza Marconi to Orta depart from near the TI (around €8 round-trip, 3/day mid-June–mid-Sept departing at 10:00, 14:00, and 17:00; return trip from Orta to Stresa departing at 11:00, 15:00, and 18:00; confirm schedule at TI).

Sleeping in Stresa

(€1 = about $1.25, country code: 39)
Because Stresa town is just a resort, I'd day-trip from Milan. But here are good options if you'd like to stay.

$$ **Hotel Milan Speranza** is an impersonal four-star corporate-style hotel that caters mostly to tour groups, with 175 predictably comfortable rooms across from the boat dock (Db-€100–150 depending on season and view, €20–30 extra for lake views, air-con, elevator, tel. 0323-31178, fax 0323-32729,

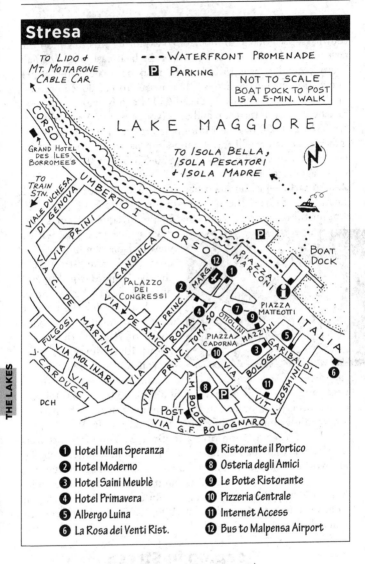

Stresa

- - - WATERFRONT PROMENADE
- P Parking

NOT TO SCALE
BOAT DOCK TO POST
IS A 5-MIN. WALK

TO LIDO &
MT. MOTTARONE
CABLE CAR

LAKE MAGGIORE

GRAND HOTEL
DES ILES
BORROMEES

TO ISOLA BELLA,
ISOLA PESCATORI
& ISOLA MADRE

TO
TRAIN
STN.

N

CORSO
VIALE DUCHESA
DI GENOVA
VIA PRINI
UMBERTO I
CORSO

BOAT
DOCK

VIA C. DE
VIA CANONICA
PIAZZA MARCONI

PALAZZO
DEI
CONGRESSI

ITALIA

PIAZZA
MATTEOTTI

VIA DE AMICIS
VIA PRINC.
VIA ROMA
TOMASO
OTTOLINI
MAZZINI
PIAZZA
CADORNA

FULGOSI
MARTINI
PRINC. TOMASO
GARIBALDI
ROSMINI

VIA MOLINARI
VIA
CARDUCCI

A.M. BOLOG.
P.L.
BOLOG.
VIT.

DCH
Post

VIA G.F. BOLOGNARO

- ① Hotel Milan Speranza
- ② Hotel Moderno
- ③ Hotel Saini Meublè
- ④ Hotel Primavera
- ⑤ Albergo Luina
- ⑥ La Rosa dei Venti Rist.
- ⑦ Ristorante il Portico
- ⑧ Osteria degli Amici
- ⑨ Le Botte Ristorante
- ⑩ Pizzeria Centrale
- ⑪ Internet Access
- ⑫ Bus to Malpensa Airport

THE LAKES

www.milansperanza.it, info@milansperanza.it).

$$ Hotel Moderno offers 54 peaceful and well-maintained pastel rooms on a pedestrian street a block from the main square (Db-€140, discount for Rick Steves readers depending on availability, closed Nov–mid-March, air-con, elevator, Internet access, Via Cavour 33; from the main square, with your back to the lake, find the church—hotel is behind the church on pedestrian street parallel to main road; tel. 0323-933-773, fax 0323-933-775, www.hms.it, moderno@hms.it).

   $$ Hotel Saini Meublè is a cozy place with rustic stonework and warm hardwood floors, located in a pedestrian zone a couple of blocks from the boat dock in the old center. Its 14 rooms are big, modern, and quiet (Sb-€82, Db-€102, lower prices off-season, these rates promised to my readers through 2011, elevator, Internet access, from Piazza Matteotti head up Via Mazzini and turn left on Via Garibaldi, Via Garibaldi 10, tel. 0323-934-519, fax 0323-31169, www.hotelsaini.it, info@hotelsaini.it). Gianni (Johnny) greets you at reception.

   $ Hotel Primavera, next door to Hotel Moderno, rents 34 cheaper, decent air-conditioned rooms, most with little terraces that overlook the action in the streets below (Db-€75–100, Via Cavour 39, tel. 0323-31286, fax 0323-33458, www.stresa.it, hotel primavera@stresa.it).

   $ Albergo Luina is a clean and homey family-run cheap sleep, with seven basic rooms above a restaurant (Sb-€35–52, Db-€50–80, some with little balconies for no extra charge, these prices for Rick Steves readers, mention this book when you reserve, breakfast-€4; Via Garibaldi 21, 2 blocks off Piazza Matteotti—with back to lake, go left up small street; tel. & fax 0323-30285, luinastresa@yahoo.it). Papa Marco cooks in the restaurant while Mamma Renata tends to the guests.

Eating in Stresa

La Rosa dei Venti, on the main drag, caters to locals with great €7 pizzas and lakefront dining. They proudly offer homemade pastas and creative risottos for €7 (big €7 salads, €13 *secondi*, Wed–Mon 12:00–15:00 & 19:00–24:00, closed Tue, everything made to order, 2 blocks south of the boat dock at Corso Italia 50, tel. 0323-31431).

   Ristorante il Portico is a cheerful, energetic place featuring several €16–26 multicourse tasting samplers and daily market specials on sidewalk tables or in their airy, fresh dining room. It's smart to reserve (piping-hot €6 pizzas, €7 pastas, €9 *secondi*, daily 12:00–16:00 & 19:00–24:00, Via Ottolini 9, tel. 0323-934-510).

   Osteria degli Amici serves up tasty €9 risottos and pastas, with fast and friendly service under a canopy of grape and kiwi leaves (€7 wood-fired pizzas, daily 12:00–14:30 & 19:00–22:30, closed Wed Sept–June, deep in the old town past Piazza Cadorna at Via Bolongaro 33, tel. 0323-30453).

   Le Botte offers a variety of Piedmont's regional specialties in a pub-grub casual atmosphere (€9 pastas, €13 *secondi*, daily 12:00–15:00 & 19:00–22:30 in summer, closed Thu Oct–March and all of Dec–Feb, Via Mazzini 6/8, tel. 0323-30462).

   The main square, **Piazza Cadorna,** is a carnival of residents selling things to tourists. Still, at night it has a certain charm. It

THE LAKES

seems anyone who claims to be a musician can get a gig singing for eaters. The **Pizzeria Centrale** (on a platform in the center) is a good place to enjoy the ambience. Their pizzas are decent, but don't order any serious food here.

Stresa Connections

From Stresa by Train to: Milan (about hourly, 1-hour fast train, 70- to 90-minute slow train), **Varenna** (roughly every two hours, 2.75–4 hours, transfer in Milan), **Venice** (7/day, 4–4.5 hours, transfer in Milan), **Domodossola** (near the Swiss border, almost hourly, 30 minutes).

To Malpensa Airport: For a **train-bus combination,** take the train toward Milan (departs hourly) and get off at Gallarate (about 40 minutes, first train departs at 5:23, connects with first bus departure for Malpensa), where frequent, cheap shuttle buses run to Malpensa's Terminal 1 (€1.50, pay driver, about 1–2/hour, 25 minutes). From Gallarate, the bus departs from the train station and runs 5:55–20:15; from Malpensa's Terminal 1, the bus runs 5:34–19:50, tel. 0331-258-411, www.sea-aeroportimilano.it/en).

Alibus Airport buses run between Stresa and Malpensa (€9, April–Oct, 50 minutes; leaves airport from bus stop 22 outside Terminal 1 at 7:30, 10:30, 12:30, 14:30, 17:30, and 20:30; leaves Stresa from in front of the church next to Hotel Milan Speranza—near the ferry dock and TI—at 6:30, 9:30, 11:30, 13:30, 16:30, and 19:30; confirm schedule, must reserve by 11:00 the previous day or by 11:00 Sat if booking for Sun or Mon bus—call 0323-552-172, book online at www.safduemila.com, or email alibus@safduemila .com).

Taxis to the airport cost €90 (1–5 people, €100 if traveling between 22:00–7:00) and take about an hour; your hotel can arrange the taxi for you, but will charge you extra for booking it. It's easy to arrange a taxi on your own at the train station's taxi stand. Salvo Taxi is reliable (mobile 335-707-8894).

THE LAKES

MILAN

Milano

For every church in Rome, there's a bank in Milan. Italy's second city and the capital of Lombardy, Milan is a hardworking, fashion-conscious, time-is-money city of 1.3 million. It's a melting pot of people and history. Milan's industriousness may come from the Teutonic blood of its original inhabitants, the Lombards, or from the region's Austrian heritage. Milan is Italy's fashion, industrial, banking, TV, publishing, and convention capital. The economic success of post-war Italy can be blamed on this city of publicists and pasta power lunches.

As if to make up for its rough, noisy big-city-ness, its people are works of art. Milan is an international fashion capital with a refined taste. Window displays are gorgeous, cigarettes are chic, and even the cheese comes gift-wrapped. Yet, thankfully, Milan is no more expensive for tourists than other Italian cities.

Three hundred years before Christ, the Romans called this place Mediolanum, or "the central place." By the fourth century A.D., it was the capital of the western half of the Roman Empire. Emperor Constantine issued the Edict of Milan from here, legalizing Christianity. After some barbarian darkness, medieval Milan rose to regional prominence under the Visconti and Sforza families. By the time of the Renaissance, it was nicknamed "the New Athens," and was enough of a cultural center for Leonardo da Vinci to call home. Then came 400 years of foreign domination (Spain, Austria, France, more Austria). Milan was a center of the 1848 revolution against Austria, and helped lead Italy to unification in 1870.

Mussolini left a heavy fascist touch on the architecture here (such as the central train station). His excesses also led to

Greater Milan

the WWII bombing of Milan. But the city rose again. The 1959 Pirelli Tower (the skinny skyscraper in front of the station) was a trendsetter in its day. Today, Milan is people-friendly, with a great transit system and inviting pedestrian zones. And the city is busy with construction projects in an effort to beef up both its infrastructure and cultural offerings as it prepares to host the 2015 World's Fair.

Many tourists come to Italy for the past. But Milan is today's Italy, and no Italian trip is complete without visiting it. While it's not big on the tourist circuit, the city has plenty to see. And fortunately, seeing Milan—so manageable and well-organized—is not difficult.

For pleasant excursions from the city, consider visiting Lake Como or Lake Maggiore—both are about an hour from Milan by train (see The Lakes chapter).

Planning Your Time

OK, it's a big city, so you probably won't linger. Compared to Rome and Florence, Milan's art is mediocre, but the city does have unique and noteworthy sights: the Duomo and Galleria Vittorio Emanuele, Pinacoteca Ambrosiana, La Scala Opera House, Brera Art Gallery, Michelangelo's last *Pietà* in the Sforza Castle, and Leonardo's *Last Supper*. It's best to reserve several months in advance to see *The Last Supper* (see page 297); if you haven't booked ahead, your best option is to take a bus-and-walking tour (see "Tours in Milan," later).

With two nights and a full day, you can gain an appreciation for the town and see the major sights. On a short visit, I'd focus on  the center. Tour the Duomo, hit what art you like, browse through the elegant shopping area and the Galleria Vittorio Emanuele, and try to see an opera. Technology buffs like the Leonardo da Vinci National Science and Technology Museum, while history and art buffs dig the city's early Christian churches, Brera Gallery, Pinacoteca Ambrosiana, and the Museum of Art and Science. People-watchers and pigeon-feeders could spend their entire visit never losing sight of the Duomo. And if you dig burial grounds, rattle through Milan's evocative Monumental Cemetery. To maximize your time in Milan, use the Metro and note which places stay open through the siesta.

Since Milan is a cold Italian plunge, and most flights to the US leave Milan early in the morning, you could save it for the end of your trip and start your journey softly by going directly by train from Milan to Lake Como (one-hour ride to Varenna), Lake Maggiore (about an hour to Stresa), or the Cinque Terre (4 hours to Vernazza). Then spend a night or two in Milan at the end of your trip before flying home.

Monday is a terrible sightseeing day, since many museums are closed (including Leonardo's *Last Supper*). August is rudely hot and muggy. Locals who *can* vacate, do, leaving the city pretty quiet. Those visiting in August find the nightlife sleepy; many shops, restaurants, and some hotels closed; and hotel rooms on the discounted push list.

Rome vs. Milan: A Classic Squabble

In Italy, the North and South bicker about each other, hurling barbs, quips, and generalizations. All the classic North/South traits can be applied to Milan (the business capital) and Rome (the government capital). Although the differences have become less pronounced lately, the sniping continues.

The Milanesi say the Romans are lazy. Roman government jobs come with short hours—cut even shorter by too many coffee breaks, three-hour lunches, chats with colleagues, and phone calls to friends and relatives. Milanesi contend that Roma *ladrona* (Rome, the big thief) is a parasite that lives off the taxes of people up North. There's still a strong Milan-based movement seriously promoting secession from the South.

Romans, meanwhile, dismiss the Milanesi as uptight workaholics with nothing else to live for—gray like their foggy city. Romans do admit that in Milan, job opportunities are better and based on merit. And the Milanesi grudgingly concede the Romans have a gift for enjoying life.

While Rome is more of a family city, Milan is the place for

A Three-Hour Tour: If you're just changing trains in Milan (as, sooner or later, you will), consider this blitz tour: Check your bag at the station, pick up a city map at the station TI, ride the subway to the Duomo (for specifics, see "Arrival in Milan," later), peruse the square, explore the cathedral's rooftop and interior, have a scenic coffee in the Galleria Vittorio Emanuele, spin on the floor mosaic of the bull for good luck, see a museum or two (most are within a 10-minute walk of the main square), and return by subway to the station. Art fans could make time for *The Last Supper* (if they've made reservations), the Michelangelo *Pietà* in the Sforza Castle (no reservations necessary), the Brera Art Gallery, or the Pinacoteca Ambrosiana (with its Leonardo exhibit).

Orientation to Milan

My coverage focuses on the old center. Most sights and hotels are within a 10-minute walk of the cathedral (Duomo), which is a straight eight-minute Metro ride from the train station.

high-powered singles on the career fast track. Milanese yuppies mix with each other...not the city's longtime residents. Milan is seen as wary of foreigners and inward-looking, and Rome as fun-loving, tolerant, and friendly. In Milan, bureaucracy (like social services) works logically and efficiently, while in Rome, accomplishing even small chores can be exasperating. Everything in Rome—from finding a babysitter to buying a car—is done through friends. Meanwhile, people in Milan are more private.

Milanesi find Romans vulgar. The Roman dialect is considered one of the coarsest in the country. Much as they try, Milanesi  just can't say "Damn your dead relatives" quite as effectively as the Romans. Still, Milanesi enjoy Roman comedians and love to imitate the accent.

The Milanesi feel that Rome is dirty and Roman traffic nerve-wracking. But despite the craziness, Rome maintains a genuine village feel. People share family news with their neighborhood grocer. Milan lacks people-friendly piazzas, and entertainment comes at a high price. But in Rome, *la dolce vita* is as close as the nearest square, and a full moon is enjoyed by all.

Tourist Information

Milan has two TIs: on Piazza del Duomo and at the train station. The main TI on **Piazza del Duomo** is in a former subterranean day hotel for railworkers (left of the entrance to the Galleria, down the staircase next to the pharmacy, Mon–Sat 8:45–13:00 & 14:00–18:00, Sun 9:00–13:00 & 14:00–17:00, tel. 02-7740-4343, www.visitamilano.it, iat.info@provincia.milano.it). You can book Autostradale and Zani Viaggi city tours (see "Tours in Milan," later) at the desks farthest from the entrance.

The TI at the **central train station** is in front of track 13 (Mon–Sat 9:00–18:00, Sun 9:00–13:00 & 14:00–17:00, tel. 02-7740-4318).

At either TI, confirm your sightseeing plans and pick up a free map. Also ask for the two free booklets listing Milan's sights (including hours, prices, and directions), events, concerts, films in English, expatriate groups, and cultural insights. *Hello Milano* is a monthly newspaper in English (www.hellomilano.it); *Milano Mese* is less helpful (scant event descriptions in English, events listed by category rather than date).

I've listed enough sights to keep you very busy for two days, but there's much more to see in Milan. Its many thousand-year-old churches make it clear that Milan was an important beacon in the Dark Ages. The TI, local guidebooks, and newspapers can point you in the right direction if you have more time.

Arrival in Milan

By Train: The huge sternly decorated, fascist-built (in 1931) central train station is a sight in itself. Newly cleaned, the halls feel more monumental than ever. Notice how the art makes you feel that a powerful state is a good thing. In the front lobby, heroic people celebrate "modern" transportation (circa-1930 ships, trains, and cars) opposite reliefs depicting old-fashioned sailboats and horse carts.

The station has three levels of **shops and services.** On the ground level to the left (with your back to the tracks), you'll find taxis, travel agencies, shuttle buses to the airports, and a baggage check (marked *deposito,* €4/5 hours, €10/12 hours, 5-day maximum, daily 6:00–24:00, passport required, 45-pound bag limit). A supermarket is outside on the right (daily 8:00–22:00). ATMs are in front of the station, outside and to the right. Also in front of the station are the Metro and car-rental offices (clearly marked). The 24-hour pharmacy has a big green neon cross.

From the track level, down the moving walkways, you'll find Trenitalia **ticket** booths (daily 5:45–22:45) and user-friendly ticket sales machines (gray for local train services only, gray-and-green for all trains, credit cards and cash accepted).

The **365 Travel Agency** has two offices at the station (one across from the baggage check *deposito* desk and another outside, facing the airport shuttle buses on Piazza Luigi di Savoia). They sell train tickets, supplements, and night-train berth reservations (daily 8:00–19:30, tel. 02-669-0039 and 02-669-0351). The 6 percent commission can be a reasonable price to pay to skip the Trenitalia ticket lines.

Taking the Metro to the Duomo and Back: For a quick visit, it's a straight shot on the underground from the station to the Duomo (buy €1 ticket at the kiosk or from machines, validate in the orange machine). Follow signs for yellow line 3 (direction: San Donato); after an eight-minute ride (four stops), you'll be facing the cathedral. To return, ride the same yellow line 3 back the other way (direction: Maciachini).

By Car: Driving is bad enough in Milan to make the €20/day fee for a downtown garage a blessing. If you're driving, do Milan (and Lake Como) before or after you rent your car, not while you've got it. If you have a car, use the well-marked suburban *parcheggi* (parking lots), which offer affordable (€6/day) and safe parking at city-edge subway stations, with extremely easy access to the center by Metro.

By Plane: Frequent shuttle trains and buses connect the airports and train station. See "Milan Connections" at the end of this chapter.

Helpful Hints

Theft Alert: Be on guard. Milan's thieves target tourists, especially at the station, getting in and out of the subway, and around the Duomo. They can be dressed as tourists, businessmen, or beggars, or they can be gangs of too-young-to-arrest children. Watch out for ragged people carrying newspaper and cardboard—they'll thrust this item at you as a distraction while they pick your pocket. If you're ripped off and plan to file an insurance claim, fill out a report with the police (Police Station, "Questura," Via Fatebenefratelli 11, Metro: Turati, open daily 24 hours, tel. 02-62261). For police emergencies, call 113. For lost or stolen credit cards, see page 14.

US Consulate: It's at Via Principe Amedeo 2/10 (Metro: Turati, tel. 02-290-351 for recorded info and phone tree, http://milan.usconsulate.gov).

Medical Help: Dial 118 for medical emergencies. There are two medical clinics with emergency care facilities: the International Health Center in Galleria Strasburgo 3 (Mon–Thu 9:00–19:00, Fri 9:00–18:00, closed Sat–Sun, between Via Durini and Corso Europa, third floor, Metro: San Babila, tel. 02-7634-0720) and the American International Medical Center at Via Mercalli 11 (Mon–Fri 9:00–17:30, closed Sat–Sun, Metro: Missori or Crocetta, call for appointment, tel. 02-5831-9808, mobile 335-570-1055). A 24-hour pharmacy is in the central train station; look for the neon-green cross.

Street Markets: Milan has two very popular flea markets. **Fiera di Sinigallia** spills into a lot at Porta Genova every Saturday (8:30–17:00, later in summer, Metro: Porta Genova). If you continue along Viale d'Annunzio to Viale Papiniano, you'll run into the **Papiniano** market (Tue morning and Sat all day). Small street markets are held every morning except Sunday in various neighborhoods; *Hello Milano* has a complete listing (free at TI).

Internet Access: A **Mondadori Mediacenter** shop is near the Duomo on Piazza del Duomo at the corner of Via Marconi (daily 9:00–22:00, see map on page 305). Purchase an Internet card (*tessera*, €3/hour) on the ground floor, then go up two flights of stairs to the second floor to register, using your passport.

Bookstores: The handiest major bookstore is **Libreria Feltrinelli**, under the Galleria Vittorio Emanuele. Books in English—fiction and guidebooks—are at opposite ends of the store (Mon–Sat 10:00–23:00, Sun 10:00–20:00; enter at Ricordi Mediastore next to McDonald's in center of Galleria and go downstairs, or through Autogrill restaurant on Piazza del Duomo, store is in basement level; also sells maps; tel. 02-8699-6903). The **American Bookstore** is at Via Camperio 16, near the Sforza Castle (Mon 13:30–19:00, Tue–Sat 10:30–19:00, closed Sun, tel. 02-878-920).

Travel Agencies: You can buy train tickets and reserve an overnight berth *(cuccetta)* at the **365 Travel Agency**'s train station locations (6 percent commission but faster than ticket windows; listed earlier, under "Arrival in Milan") or at a downtown travel agency such as **American Express,** near the Duomo (Mon–Fri 9:00–17:30, closed Sat–Sun, Italian train tickets only, Via Larga 4, two blocks southeast of the Duomo, tel. 02-721-041).

Getting Around Milan

By Public Transit: Use Milan's great subway system. The clean, spacious, fast, and easy three-line Metro zips you nearly anywhere you may want to go, and trams and city buses fill in the gaps. The handiest Metro line for a quick visit is the yellow line 3, which connects the train station to the Duomo. The other lines are red (1) and green (2). "ATM" is the acronym for the Milan public transit system.

A **ticket,** valid for 1.25 hours, can be used for one subway, tram, or bus ride, including a transfer either within the same or another system, but not a round-trip on the same system (€1, sold at newsstands, *tabacchi* shops, shops with *ATM* sticker in window, and at machines in subway stations).

Validate tickets in the yellow or orange machines at the turnstiles, and keep them until you exit the Metro system. If you're caught riding on an unvalidated ticket, the fine is €33.

Other ticket options include: a *carnet* (€9.20 for 10 rides; one magnetic ticket that can be validated 10 times); a **24-hour pass** (€3, worthwhile if you take four rides); and a **48-hour pass** (€5.50). Passes use the same validation machines as standard tickets.

For transit information, visit the ATM Point (at Duomo stop, near Arengario exit, to right of Duomo as you face it, Mon–Sat 7:45–19:15, closed Sun, tel. 800-808-181, www.atm-mi.it).

I've keyed sightseeing to the subway system. Though most sights are within a few blocks of each other, Milan is an exhausting city for walking. With the Metro, you'll rarely wait more than five minutes for a train. The well-marked trams can also be useful, especially to get to *The Last Supper* (tram #16) and the Monumental

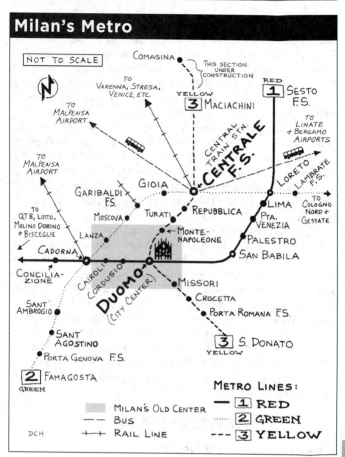

Milan's Metro

NOT TO SCALE

COMASINA

THIS SECTION UNDER CONSTRUCTION

TO VARENNA, STRESA, VENICE, ETC.

YELLOW [3] MACIACHINI

RED [1] SESTO F.S.

TO MALPENSA AIRPORT

TO MALPENSA AIRPORT

CENTRAL TRAIN STN. CENTRALE F.S.

TO LINATE & BERGAMO AIRPORTS

LORETO TO LAMBRATE F.S.

TO COLOGNO NORD & GESSATE

GIOIA

GARIBALDI F.S.

REPUBBLICA

LIMA PTA. VENEZIA

TO QT8, LOTTO, MOLINO DORINO & BISCEGLIE

MOSCOVA

TURATI

PALESTRO

LANZA

MONTE-NAPOLEONE

CADORNA

SAN BABILA

CONCILIA-ZIONE

CAIROLI CORDUSIO

DUOMO (CITY CENTER)

MISSORI

CROCETTA

SANT' AMBROGIO

PORTA ROMANA F.S.

SANT' AGOSTINO

[3] S. DONATO
YELLOW

PORTA GENOVA F.S.

[2] FAMAGOSTA
GREEN

METRO LINES:

[ ] MILAN'S OLD CENTER
— — BUS
+++ RAIL LINE

DCH

━━ [1] RED
······ [2] GREEN
--- [3] YELLOW

Cemetery (#12 or #14).

By Taxi: Small groups go cheap and fast by taxi (drop charge-€3.10, €0.70/kilometer; drop charge doubles on Sun, holidays, and from 21:00 to 6:00 in the morning). It can be easier to walk to a taxi stand than to flag down a cab. Handy stands are at Piazza del Duomo and in front of Sforza Castle.

Tours in Milan

Bus Tours—The three-hour **Autostradale** bus-and-walking tour is a good value, has a live guide describing the city's monuments in English, and guarantees you'll see Leonardo's *Last Supper*—useful if you haven't booked ahead for this important sight. The jam-packed itinerary also includes visits to the Duomo, Galleria Vittorio Emanuele, Sforza Castle, and La Scala Opera House (€60, departs Tue–Sun at 9:30). Tours leave from Piazza del Duomo, next to the taxi stand at the far end of the square from the church. There are four ways to reserve this tour: Book in advance online at www.autostradale.it; ask your hotelier to book it for you; call the TI at 02-7740-4343; or drop into the TI at Piazza del Duomo before the morning departure to see if tickets are available. To confirm details, call 02-3391-0794.

Zani Viaggi does a similar tour that includes *The Last Supper*. Guides lead two-language tours (which always includes English), departing Tuesday through Sunday at 9:30 and 14:30 from their office at Foro Bonaparte 76, near the Sforza Castle (€60, 3 hours, no Mon tours, office open Mon–Fri 9:00–19:00, Sat 9:00–17:00, closed Sun, tel. 02-867-131, www.zaniviaggi.it, excursions@zani viaggi.it).

CitySightseeing Milano has hop-on, hop-off buses that do a circuit of the major sights accompanied by a recorded commentary; you can get off at a stop, tour the sight, and hop back on the bus to resume your tour (€20/24 hours, buy ticket on board, buses depart daily every 1.25 hours from 9:30–17:30, tel. 02-867-131). While you can hop on anywhere, it's easy at the Duomo and La Scala.

Local Guide—Lorenza Scorti is a hardworking young woman who knows her city's history and how to teach it. She can be booked well in advance (necessary in May and Sept) or on short notice (€120/3-hour tour, €240/day, same price for individuals or groups, evenings OK, tel. 02-4801-7042, mobile 347-735-1346, lorenza.scorti@libero.it).

Sights in Milan

The Cathedral and Nearby

▲▲Duomo (Cathedral)—The city's centerpiece is the fourth-largest church in Europe—after the Vatican's, London's, and Seville's. Back when Europe was fragmented into countless tiny kingdoms and dukedoms, the dukes of Milan wanted to impress their counterparts in Ger-

many and France. Their goal was to earn Milan recognition and respect from both the Vatican and the kings and princes of northern Europe by building a massive, richly ornamented cathedral. Even after Renaissance-style domes were in vogue else-

—re in Italy, conservative Milan's cathedral stayed on Gothic

t. The dukes—thinking northerners would relate better to

MILAN

Central Milan

M METRO STATION

TO CENTRAL TRAIN STN.

GIARDINI PUBBLICI

MUSEUM OF ANCIENT ART & SFORZA CASTLE

BRERA GALLERY

TURATI
MARCHI
TURATI
M TURATI
MANIN

LANZA
M

PONTACCIO
FATEBENE FRAT.

MUSEUM OF ARTS & SCIENCE
F. CHIARI
F. OSCURI

SELLA
CARMINE
P. VET.
BRERA
NUOVO
GIARDINI
FATE BENE FRAT.

MANZONI

BAGATTI VALSECCHI MUSEUM

RISORGI-MENTO MUSEUM

GADIO

GESÙ
ANDREA
SENATO

CAIROLI **M** LARGO CAIROLI
FORO BUON.
CUSANI
ORSO
ROVELLO
DANTE
P. VET.
VERDI
MONTE PIETA
POLDI PEZZOLI MUSEUM
SANT'
VIA MONTENAPOLEONE

LA SCALA
OPERA MUSEUM

LEO.

SAN ANDREA

SAN BABILA
M

PIAZZA CORDUSIO

VIA MERAVIGLI **M**

To Last Supper

VIA OREFICI

GALLERIA

MATTEOTTI

CORSO VIT. EM.

DUOMO

PINACOTECA AMBROSIANA

DUOMO

VIA SPERONARI

DUOMO MUSEUM (CLOSED UNTIL 2015)

VIA TORINO
VIA MAZZINI
VIA LARGA

SAN SATIRO

DC H

MISSORI **M**

¼ MILE
400 METERS

❶ Tram #16 to Last Supper, Leo's Horse & Meazza Stadium
❷ Trams #12, #14 to Mon. Cemetery
❸ Zani Viaggi Tours
❹ Via Montenapoleone (High-Fashion Shops)
❺ Museum of Ancient Art Entrance
❻ Stairs to Duomo Roof
❼ Elevators to Duomo Roof (2)
❽ American Bookstore
❾ Obikà Mozzarella Bar
❿ Bar Brera

MILAN

Gothic—loaded it with pointed arches and spires. For good measure, the cathedral was built not from ordinary stone, but from marble, top to bottom. Pink Candoglia marble was rafted in from a quarry about 60 miles away, across Lake Maggiore and down a canal to a port at the cathedral.

Cost and Hours: Free, daily 7:00–18:45, Metro: Duomo, tel. 02-7202-2656, www.duomomilano.it. The new Duomo Point info

Milan at a Glance

▲▲Duomo Milan's showpiece cathedral, with an amazing roof you can walk on, amid a forest of spires. **Hours:** Church—daily 7:00-18:45, rooftop stairs—daily 9:00-17:20, until 16:20 in winter; rooftop elevator—daily April-Oct 9:00-22:00, closes earlier off-season. See page 282.

▲▲Galleria Vittorio Emanuele Glass-domed arcade on the main square, perfect for window-shopping and people-watching. **Hours:** Always open. See page 289.

▲▲La Scala Opera House and Museum The world's most prestigious opera house. **Hours:** Museum daily 9:00-12:30 & 13:30-17:30. See page 290.

▲▲Pinacoteca Ambrosiana Oldest museum in Milan, with works by Raphael, Leonardo, Botticelli, Titian, and Caravaggio, and a special exhibit of Leonardo sketches (until 2015). **Hours:** Tue-Sun 9:00-19:00, closed Mon. See page 292.

▲Piazza del Duomo Milan's main square, full of energy, history, and pickpockets. **Hours:** Always open. See page 288.

▲Brera Art Gallery World-class collection of Italian paintings (13th-20th centuries), including Raphael, Caravaggio, Gentile da Fabriano, Piero della Francesca, Mantegna, and the Bellini brothers. **Hours:** Tue-Sun 8:30-19:00, closed Mon. See page 293.

▲Risorgimento Museum History of Italian unification. **Hours:** Tue-Sun 9:00-13:00 & 14:00-17:30, closed Mon. See page 294.

▲Sforza Castle Milan's castle containing a museum whose highlight is an unfinished Michelangelo *Pietà*. **Hours:** Tue-Sun 9:00-17:30, closed Mon. See page 295.

▲Via Dante Human traffic buzzes to lilting accordions on one of Europe's longest pedestrian-only boulevards. **Hours:** Always open. See page 297.

MILAN

center behind the cathedral on the right-hand side rents audioguides and sells tickets for the Duomo's south elevator (Mon–Fri 9:00–18:00, Sat 9:00–17:30, Sun 13:00–18:00, tel. 02-7202-3375, staff are helpful and most speak English).

Audioguide: €4 for 1.5-hour audioguide, €2 if rented in last hour before closing (available from Duomo Point or kiosk located de to right of entrance, kiosk open Mon–Fri 9:30–17:30, Sat

▲The Last Supper Leonardo da Vinci's masterpiece, viewable only with a reservation—book several months in advance. **Hours:** Tue-Sun 8:15–18:45 (last visit), closed Mon. See page 297.

▲Leonardo da Vinci National Science and Technology Museum Leonardo's designs illustrated in wooden models, plus a vast collection of historical, scientific, and technological bric-a-brac and machines. **Hours:** Wed-Fri 9:30–17:00, Sat-Sun 9:30–18:30, closed Mon-Tue. See page 299.

▲Monumental Cemetery Evocative outdoor art gallery with tombs showcasing expressive art styles from 1870–1930. **Hours:** Tue-Sun 8:00–18:00, closed Mon. See page 301.

Church of Santa Maria presso San Satiro Pilgrim church with impressive 3-D paintings. **Hours:** Mon-Fri 7:30–11:30 & 15:30–18:30, Sat 15:30–19:00, Sun 10:00–12:00 & 15:30–19:00. See page 291.

Poldi Pezzoli Museum Italian paintings (15th–18th centuries), weaponry, and decorative arts. **Hours:** Tue-Sun 10:00–18:00, closed Mon. See page 295.

Bagatti Valsecchi Museum 19th-century Italian Renaissance furnishings. **Hours:** Tue-Sun 13:00–17:45, closed Mon. See page 295.

Branca Tower Great 365-degree views over the city. **Hours:** Erratic—call or confirm at TI before heading there, closed Mon and in bad weather. See page 296.

Museum of Art and Science Leonardo da Vinci's art and inventions, with hands-on exhibits on authenticating and dating various forms of art. **Hours:** Mon-Fri 10:00–18:00, closed Sat-Sun. See page 296.

Leonardo's Horse Gargantuan equestrian monument built according to Leonardo's designs. **Hours:** Tue-Sun 9:00–17:30, closed Mon. See page 300.

MILAN

9:30–17:00, closed Sun, ID required).

Dress Code: Modest dress is required. Don't wear shorts or anything sleeveless. Even kids with exposed shoulders or knees are likely to be turned away at the door.

❷ **Self-Guided Tour:** At 525 by 300 feet, the place is immense, with more than 2,000 statues inside and 52 hundred-foot-tall, sequoia-size pillars representing the weeks of the year and the liturgical calendar. If you do two laps, you've done your daily walk. It was built to hold 40,000 worshippers, the entire population of Milan when construction began.

Built 1386–1810, with the final touches added in 1965, this construction project originated the Italian phrase for "never-ending": "like building a cathedral." It started out Gothic (best seen in the apse behind the altar) and was finished in the early 1800s under Napoleon (particularly the noteworthy west facade, which is wonderful late in the day, with the sun low in the sky). While the church is a good example of the Flamboyant, or "flamelike," overripe final stage of Gothic, architectural harmony is not its forte.

Exterior: Walk around the entire church exterior and notice the statues, made between the 14th and 20th centuries by sculptors from all over Europe. There are hundreds of these statues—each different and quite creative. Look at the statues on the tips of the many spires...they seem so relaxed, like they're just hanging out, waiting for their big day. Functioning as drain spouts, the 96 fanciful gargoyle monsters are especially imaginative.

As you stand outside at the back, behind the altar, imagine the glory of this first wall. These were the earliest stones, laid in 1390. The sun-in-rose window was the proud symbol of the city's leading Visconti family; it's flanked by the angel telling Mary she's going to bear the Messiah. And behind you is a shrine to the leading religion of the 21st century: soccer. The Football Team store is filled with colorful vestments and relics of local soccer saints (go upstairs, daily 10:00–19:00).

Return to the front and enjoy the statues enlivening the facade. The lower ones—full of energy and movement—are early Baroque, from about 1600. Of the five doors, the center one is biggest. Made in 1907 in the Liberty style, it features the Joy and Sorrow of the Virgin Mary. Sad scenes are on the left, joyful ones on the right, and on top is the coronation of Mary in heaven by Jesus with all the saints and angels looking on.

Interior: Enter the church. Stand at the back of the fourth-longest nave in Christendom. The apse at the far end was started in 1386. The wall behind you wasn't finished until 1520. Even though the Renaissance had begun, builders stuck with the Gothic style. The two single stone-marble pillars behind you are the most precious ones in the church.

Notice two tiny lights: The little red one above the altar marks where a nail from the cross of Jesus is kept. This relic was brought to Milan by St. Helen (Emperor Constantine's mother) in the fourth century, when Milan was the capital of the Western Roman Empire. It's on display for three days a year (in mid-Sept). Now look high to the right and find a tiny pinhole of white light. This is designed to shine a 10-inch sunbeam at noon onto the bronze line that runs across the floor, indicating where we are on the zodiac (but local guides claim they've never seen it work).

Stained-Glass Windows: Wander deeper into the church up the right aisle. Check out the windows—15th-century mosaics of brilliant and expensive colored glass (stained, not painted). Bought by wealthy families seeking the Church's favor, they face the south and get the most light. The altars below generally honor the patron who made that window possible. Pick out familiar scenes in the windows. The purpose was to teach the illiterate masses the way to salvation through stories of the Old Testament and the life of Jesus. On the opposite wall (left side), many of the windows date from the time of Napoleon and are either made of dimmer, cheaper painted glass or are replacements for ones bombed out in World War II.

One window is clearly more modern, dating from the 1980s and celebrating the three top local cardinals, two of whom became saints (St. Ambrose, St. Charles Borromeo, and Cardinal Ferrari).

Altar: Belly up to the bar facing the high altar. While the church is Gothic, the area around the altar was made Baroque— the style of the Vatican in the 1570s (a Roman Catholic statement to counter the Protestant churches of the north, which were mostly Gothic). Napoleon crowned himself King of Italy under this dome in 1805. Now look to the rear up at the ceiling and see the fancy "carving" (between the ribs)—nope, that's painted. It looks expensive, but paint is more affordable than carved stone.

Statue: Find the bald statue lit by the open door, by the wall in the south transept. This is a grotesque 16th-century statue of St. Bartolomeo, an apostle and first-century martyr skinned alive by the Romans. Walk behind the poor guy wearing his skin like a robe to see his face, hands, and feet. Carved by a student of Leonardo da Vinci, this is a study in human anatomy learned by dissection, forbidden by the Church at the time.

Floor: Walk toward the altar and around the corner 30 steps to a gate blocking entry to the apse. Look down at the fine 16th-century inlaid-marble floor. The pieces around the altar are original. You can tell that the black marble (quarried from Lake Como) is harder because it looks and feels less worn than the other colors (the white is from Lake Maggiore, pink from Verona).

The apse is lit by three huge windows, all 19th-century painted copies. The originals, destroyed in Napoleonic times, were made of precious stained glass.

Treasury: Steps lead under the altar to the treasury and to the tombs of St. Charles Borromeo (1538–1584) and his family. Charles was bishop of Milan, and the second most important hometown saint after St. Ambrose. Silver reliefs around the ceiling show scenes from Charles' life. The treasury, or *tesoro*, features empty reliquaries and carved ivories (€1).

Paleo-Christian Baptistery: In the rear of the church (buy €4 ticket at bookshop kiosk, same hours as the Duomo), you can climb down into the church that stood here long before the present one. Milan was an important center of early Christianity. In Roman times, Mediolanum's street level was 10 feet below today's level. You'll see the scant remains of an eight-sided baptistery (where saints Augustine and Ambrose were baptized) and a little church. Back then, since you couldn't enter the church until you were baptized (which didn't happen until age 18), churches had a little "holy zone" just outside for the unbaptized. This included a baptistery like this one.

Cathedral Rooftop: This is the most memorable part of a Duomo visit. You'll wander through a fancy forest of spires with great views of the city, the square, and—on clear days—the crisp and jagged Italian Alps. And, 330 feet above everything, La Madonnina overlooks it all. This 15-foot-tall gilded Virgin Mary is a symbol of the city.

Climb the stairs for €5 (daily 9:00–17:20, until 16:20 in winter), or ride the elevator for €8 (daily April–Oct 9:00–22:00, closes earlier off-season). The entrances to both the stairs and elevator are outside the church. Enter the stairs from the north side (across from La Rinascente department store). Access the elevator by the north or south transept.

▲▲**Duomo Museum (Museo del Duomo)**—This fine museum, currently closed for extensive renovation, offers an excellent opportunity to understand Milan's cathedral and see its original art close up. It's likely to reopen in 2015.

▲**Piazza del Duomo**—Milan's main square is a classic European scene and a popular local gathering point. Professionals scurry, fashion-conscious kids loiter, young thieves peruse. Teens hang

out near the Galleria entrance in the afternoons, waving at the balcony above in hopes of being filmed by MTV cameras located in an upper-floor studio.

Standing in the square (midway between the statue and the Galleria), you're surrounded by history. The statue is Victor Emmanuel II, first king of Italy. He's looking at the grand Galleria named for him. The words above the triumphal arch entrance read: "To Victor Emmanuel

II, from the people of Milan."

Behind the statue (opposite the cathedral) is the center of medieval Milan: Piazza Mercanti. Dating from 1220, the medieval City Hall (look for its red-brick arches) marked the center of town back when the entire city stood within its immense fortified walls. The merchant's square is a strangely peaceful place today, with a fine smattering of old-time Milano architecture that escaped the bombs of World War II.

Opposite the Galleria are twin fascist buildings. Mussolini made grandiose speeches from their balconies. Study the buildings' relief panels telling—with fascist drama—the history of Milan. Between these buildings and the cathedral (set back a bit) is the historic ducal palace, Palazzo Reale. This building, now a venue for temporary art exhibits, was redone in the Neoclassical style by Maria Theresa in the late 1700s, when Milan was ruled by the Austrian Habsburgs. For a fine view of the Duomo and the piazza, climb the steps to the balcony of the skinny fascist-style building closest to the cathedral (can be closed for frequent *manifestazioni*—demonstrations—or any other perceived security threat). Behind the Duomo is a vibrant pedestrian shopping zone along Corso Vittorio Emanuele.

▲▲**Galleria Vittorio Emanuele**—A symbol of Milan is its great four-story glass-domed arcade on the cathedral square. Built dur-

ing the heady days of Italian unification (c. 1870), it was the first building in town to have electric lighting. Here you can turn an expensive cup of coffee into a good value by enjoying Europe's best people-watching (or get the same view for peanuts from the strategically placed McDonald's).

The venerable **Bar Zucca** (at the entry), with a friendly staff and an Art Deco interior typical of the 1920s, is the former haunt of famous opera composer Giuseppe Verdi and conductor Arturo Toscanini, who used to stop by after their performances at La Scala. It's a fine place to enjoy a drink and people-watch (€3 for an espresso is a great deal if you relax and enjoy the view, or €1 at the bar just to enjoy the sumptuous interior). Once called the Campari café, this is considered the birthplace of the famous Campari bitter. Now a bitter aperitif, Zucca, is their signature drink (€3.40 standing or €8.70 seated, Tue–Sun 7:30–20:00, closed Mon and Aug, tel. 02-8646-4435).

Wander around the gallery. Its art celebrates the establishment of Italy as an independent country. Around the central dome, patriotic mosaics symbolize the four major continents. The mosaic floor is also patriotic. The white cross in the center represents the king. The she-wolf with Romulus and Remus (on the south side—facing Rome) honors the city that, since 1870, has been the national capital. On the west side (facing Torino, the provisional capital of Italy from 1861–1865), you'll find that city's symbol: a *torino* (little bull). For good luck, locals step on his irresistible little testicles. Two local girls explained to me that it works better if you spin. Find the poor little bull and observe for a few minutes...it's a cute scene. With so much spinning, the mosaic is replaced every few years.

Piazza della Scala—This smart little traffic-free square, out the back between the Galleria and the opera house, is dominated by a statue of Leonardo da Vinci. The statue (from 1870) is a reminder that Leonardo spent many years in Milan working for the Sforza family (who dominated Milan as the Medici family dominated Florence). Under the great Renaissance genius stand four of his greatest "Leonardeschi." (He apprenticed a sizable group of followers.) The reliefs show his various contributions as painter, architect, and engineer. Leonardo, wearing his hydro-engineer hat, re-engineered Milan's canal system, complete with locks. (Until the 1920s, Milan was one of Italy's major ports, with canals connecting the city to the Po River and Lake Maggiore.)

▲▲**La Scala Opera House and Museum**—The statue of Leonardo behind the Galleria is looking at a plain but famous Neoclassical building, arguably the world's most prestigious opera house: Milan's Teatrale alla Scala. La Scala opened in 1778 with an opera by Antonio Salieri (of *Amadeus* fame).

At Milan's famous opera house and its adjacent museum, opera buffs can see the museum's extensive collection and get a glimpse of the theater.

Museum: Well-described in English, the collection features things that mean absolutely nothing to the hip-hop crowd: Verdi's top hat, Rossini's eyeglasses, Toscanini's baton, Fettuccini's pesto, original scores, diorama stage sets, costumes, busts, portraits, and death masks of great composers and musicians. The museum allows you to peek into the actual theater. The stage is as big as the seating area on the ground floor. (You can see the towering stage box from Piazza della Scala across the street.) A recent five-year renovation corrected acoustical problems caused by WWII bombing and subsequent reconstruction. The royal box is just below your vantage point, in the center rear. Notice the massive chandelier made of Bohemian crystal (€5, daily 9:00–12:30 & 13:30–17:30, last entry 30 minutes before closing, Piazza della Scala, tel. 02-887-974-73, www.teatroallascala.org).

MILAN

Opera: The show goes on at the world-famous La Scala Opera House. Schedules vary, but the opera season is nearly year-round (show time 20:00), and ballet and classical concerts are held from October through June. No performances are held in August (for information, call Scala Infotel Service, daily 9:00–18:00, tel. 02-7200-3744; for automated booking, call 02-860-775 and press 2 for English; or book online at www.teatroallascala.org). On the opening night of an opera, a dress code is enforced for men (suit and tie).

Tickets generally go on sale one month before a performance. Seats sell out quickly. On performance days, 140 sky-high gallery tickets are sold at a discount only at the box office (located down the left side of the theater toward the back on Via Filodrammatici, and marked with *Biglietteria Serale* sign). If you want a same-day discounted (but still not cheap) ticket, show up at 13:00 to get your name on the list. Return at 17:30 for the roll call. You must be present when your name is called in order to receive a voucher, which you'll then show at the ticket window to purchase a discounted ticket. One hour before show time, the box office sells any remaining tickets at a 25 percent discount. You can also buy tickets—but not the discounted ones—at a handy ticket office in the Duomo Metro station (daily 12:00–18:00, entrance is to right of the Duomo as you face it, underground, follow signs to *ATM Point*), as well as on the Internet (Web sales end one hour before show time).

Via Speronari—A block off Piazza del Duomo, this is one of Milan's oldest streets, and the most charming drag in the old center. Via Speronari—named for the spurs once made and sold here—is worth a wander. Street names around here recall their medieval crafts: *speronari*—spurs, *spadari*—swords, *armorari*—armor. The weaponry made on these streets was high fashion among Europe's warrior class...like having an Armani dagger. While right in the city center, the neighborhood feels vital because it's also a residential street. Banks of doorbells indicate that families live above the shops. Start at the corner of Via Mazzini and Via Speronari, one block southwest of the Duomo. A shop on your right—*L'Ortolan Pusae Vecc de Milan*—brags in the old Milanese language that this is the oldest fruit-and-veggie store in the city. The neighboring Princi bakery is understandably popular. Its brioches are rarely more than a few minutes old. The *tavola calda*—hot table—across the street sells fresh, hearty take-out to hungry businesspeople.

Where Via Speronari hits Via Torino, go 20 yards to the left to find the...

Church of Santa Maria presso San Satiro (Church of St. Mary at St. Satiro)—Hiding behind its Baroque facade, this church was the scene of a temper tantrum in 1242, when a losing gambler vented his anger by hitting the baby Jesus in the Madonna-and-Child altarpiece. Blood "miraculously" spurted out, and the beautiful little church has been on the pilgrimage trail ever since. While I've never seen any blood, I'd swear I've seen a 3-D background behind the basically flat altar (a *trompe l'oeil* illusion—only about a foot deep). This church—squeezed between the earlier church of San Satiro and a street—had no room for a real apse, so, with the help of math, the Renaissance architect Donato Bramante made what looks like an apse.

In the north transept, you'll find that original ninth-century church of San Satiro (brother of St. Ambrogio, patron saint of Milan). This tiny church—with surviving bits of Byzantine fresco—predated the rest. From this chapel, look back at the main altar to see Bramante's 3-D work collapsed. On the opposite side (near entry)—with dimensions mirroring this old chapel—an eight-sided baptistery by Bramante from the 1480s shows the mathematically based values of the Renaissance. If you have a prayer in need of an extra boost, pop a coin into the box and "light" an electric candle.

Cost and Hours: Free entry, Mon–Fri 7:30–11:30 & 15:30–18:30, Sat 15:30–19:00, Sun 10:00–12:00 & 15:30–19:00, Via Torino at Via Speronari, tel. 02-874-683.

▲▲**Pinacoteca Ambrosiana (with Leonardo exhibit)**—This oldest museum in Milan was inaugurated in 1618 to house Cardinal Federico Borromeo's painting collection. And until 2015, the museum is both more expensive and more important, thanks to a long-running special exhibit displaying 22 pages from Leonardo's notebook. Think of your visit in two parts: the permanent collection of paintings (including the Leonardo Hall), and the last room, which has the notebook pages. While it's exciting to see the pages, the permanent material is still the highlight. Pick up the English-language map locating major works, and rent the €1 audioguide, which explains highlights of both the permanent and special exhibits.

Pinacoteca Ambrosiana began as a teaching academy, which explains its many replicas of famous works of art. Highlights include original paintings by Botticelli, Caravaggio, and Titian. As Cardinal Borromeo was a friend of Jan Brueghel, you'll find an entire room (#7) filled with delightful works by Brueghel and other Flemish masters. Study the wonderful detail in Brueghel's *Allegory of Fire* and *Allegory of Water*. The Flemish paintings are extremely detailed—many painted on copper to heighten the effect—and offer an insight into the psyche of the age. If the cardinal were asked why he enjoyed paintings that celebrated the secular life, he'd likely say, "Secular themes are God's book of nature."

Filling an entire wall, Raphael's charcoal-on-canvas cartoon served as an outline for the famous *School of Athens* fresco at the Vatican Museum. (A cartoon—*cartone* in Italian—is a large sketch that functions as a model for the making of a fresco.) While the

Vatican's much-adored fresco is attributed entirely to Raphael, it was painted mostly by his students. But this *cartone* was wholly sketched by the hand of Raphael. To make the fresco, his assistants riddled this cartoon with pinpricks along the outlines of the characters, stuck it to the wall of the pope's study, and then applied a colored powder. When they removed the *cartone,* the characters' shapes were marked on the wall, and completing the fresco was a lot like filling in a coloring book. If you've seen the original fresco at the Vatican, you'll notice that the figure of Michelangelo (as a brooding stonecutter lounging on the steps in the foreground) is missing from the cartoon. Raphael added him to the fresco as a tribute after seeing his awe-inspiring work on the ceiling of the Sistine Chapel.

Leonardo Exhibit: As Leonardo da Vinci spent many of his most productive years working in Milan, the city has an affinity for the Renaissance genius. The Leonardo Hall, with more of the gallery's permanent collection, features da Vinci's *Portrait of a Musician*, a copy of *The Last Supper*, and several fine Leonardo-type paintings by Luini and other disciples. During his Milan years, Leonardo created *The Last Supper* and painted several other famous canvases. Of these other paintings, only the *Portrait of a Musician*—as delicate, mysterious, and thought-provoking as the *Mona Lisa*—remains in Milan. The large fresco filling the far wall—with Christ receiving the crown of thorns—is by Luini. I find the painting of *The Last Supper* most interesting. When the cardinal realized that Leonardo's marvelous frescoed original was fading, he commissioned a careful copy to be created here for posterity. Today, this copy gives a rare chance to appreciate the original colorful richness of the now-faded masterpiece.

The Leonardo Hall leads into the somber library called Federiciana Hall, where you'll find the special Leonardo exhibit. The gallery, which owns da Vinci's *Codex Atlanticus,* is showing 22 of its 1,100 pages in themed exhibits changing quarterly until 2015. Soft period music accompanies your time with the 22 glass cases, each displaying a well-lit page from the notebook (the audioguide, which explains each page of the current exhibit, is essential to fully enjoy your visit). Don't enter the special exhibit until you are done with the permanent collection, as it's a one-way system and re-entry isn't allowed.

Cost and Hours: €15, Tue–Sun 9:00–19:00, closed Mon, near Piazza del Duomo at Piazza Pio XI 2, tel. 02-8069-2221, www .ambrosiana.eu.

In the Brera Neighborhood

▲**Brera Art Gallery**—Milan's top collection of Italian paintings (13th–20th centuries) is world-class, but it can't top Rome's or Florence's. Established in 1809 to house Napoleon's looted art, it fills the first floor above a prestigious art college.

Enter the grand courtyard of a former monastery, where you'll be greeted by the nude *Napoleon with Tinkerbell* (by Antonio Canova). Climb the stairway (following signs to *Pinacoteca*, past all the art students), buy your ticket, and pick up an English map of the museum's masterpieces.

The gallery's highlights include works by Gentile da Fabriano, hinting at the realism of the coming Renaissance (check out the lifelike flowers and realistic, bright gold paint—he used real gold powder, Room IV). Andrea Mantegna's *The Dead Christ* is a textbook example of feet-first foreshortening (Room VI). Room XVIII hosts a permanent glass-enclosed restoration lab, allowing you to see various restoration works in progress.

In Room XXI, notice how Crivelli employs Renaissance technique (he was a contemporary of Leonardo), yet clings to the mystique of the Gothic Age (that's why I like him so much). Find eight Crivellis. Also, don't miss Raphael's *Wedding of the Madonna,* Piero della Francesca's *Madonna and Child with Four Angels* (Room XXIV), and the gritty-yet-intimate realism of Caravaggio's *Supper at Emmaus* (Room XXIX). Room XXXV features several of Canaletto's picture-postcards of Venetian cityscapes. This is Impressionism—not a single line in the works, just strategically placed daubs of paint that render palazzos and canals bathed in Venetian light with photographic precision. To spice things up, look for Francesco Hayez's hot and heavy *The Kiss (Il Bacio)* in Room XXXVII.

Cost and Hours: €5, more during special exhibits, Tue–Sun 8:30–19:00, closed Mon, last entry 45 minutes before closing, free lockers just before the ticket counter, no photos, Via Brera 28, Metro: Lanza or Montenapoleone, tel. 02-722-631, www.brera .beniculturali.it. Since there are no English descriptions, consider the audioguide (€3.50, €5.50/2 people, ID required), or pick up the fine *Guide to the Galleries* (€8.20) in the bookshop. Java junkies will seek out the great, cheap cappuccino machine: Go through Napoleon's courtyard and straight through the art school to the end of the long hall; the machine's on your left. It's fun to explore the art school on the ground floor, mill about among the many young students, and wonder if there's a 21st-century Leonardo in your midst.

▲**Risorgimento Museum**—With a quick 30-minute swing through this quiet one-floor museum thoughtfully described in English, you'll learn the interesting story of Italy's rocky road to unity: from Napoleon (1796) to the victory in Rome (1870). It's just around the block from the Brera Art Gallery at Via Borgonuovo 23.

Cost and Hours: €2, Tue–Sun 9:00–13:00 & 14:00–17:30,

closed Mon, Metro: Montenapoleone, tel. 02-8846-4176, www
.museodelrisorgimento.mi.it.

Near Montenapoleone

Poldi Pezzoli Museum—This classy house of art features top
Italian paintings of the 15th through 18th centuries, old weaponry,
and lots of interesting decorative arts, such as a roomful of old
sundials and compasses.

Cost and Hours: €8, Tue–Sun 10:00–18:00, last entry 1 hour
before closing, closed Mon, ask for English brochure and map at
ticket desk, free English audioguides, Via Manzoni 12, Metro:
Montenapoleone, tel. 02-796-334, www.museopoldipezzoli.it.

Bagatti Valsecchi Museum—This unique 19th-century collection of Italian Renaissance furnishings was assembled by two
aristocratic brothers who spent a wad turning their home into a
Renaissance mansion. Museum guards pack flashlights for closer
examination of fine wood carvings.

Cost and Hours: €8, half-price on Wed, open Tue–Sun 13:00–
17:45, closed Mon, free English audioguides and good English
descriptions throughout, Via Gesù 5, Metro: Montenapoleone, tel.
02-7600-6132, www.museobagattivalsecchi.org.

Sforza Castle and Nearby

▲**Sforza Castle (Castello Sforzesco)**—The castle of Milan tells
the story of the city in brick. Built in the late 1300s as a military
fortress, it guarded the gate to the city wall and defended Milan
from enemies "within and without." It was beefed up by the Sforza
duke in 1450 in anticipation of a Venetian attack. Later, it was the
Renaissance palace of the Sforza family and was even home to
their in-house genius, Leonardo. During the many years of foreign
rule (16th–19th centuries), it was a barracks for occupying Spanish,
French, and Austrian soldiers. Today, it houses several museums.

The **gate** stands above the ditch once filled with water. A relief
celebrates Umberto I, the second king of Italy. Above that, a statue
of St. Ambrosius, the patron of Milan (and a local bishop in the
fourth century), oversees the action. Notice the chart, just outside
the gate, showing how the city was encircled first by a crude medieval wall, and then by a state-of-the-art 16th-century wall—of
which this castle was a key element. It's apparent from the enor-
mity of these walls that Milan was a strategic prize. Today, the
walls are gone, giving the city two circular boulevards.

This immense much-bombed-and-rebuilt brick fortress—
exhausting at first sight—can only be described as heavy. But
its courtyard has a great lawn for picnics and siestas. Its main
museum, the **Museum of Ancient Art,** is fascinating, unlike
the other museums in the castle. Enter the museum just past the

ticket counter. It fills the old Sforza family palace with interesting medieval armor, furniture, early Lombard art, an Egyptian collection, and—for your finale—Michelangelo's unfinished *Pietà Rondanini* in Room XV.

This is a rare opportunity to enjoy a Michelangelo with no crowds. Michelangelo died while still working on this piece—his fourth *Pietà*. A *pietà*, by definition, is a representation of a dead Christ with a sorrowful Virgin Mary. This unfinished statue is surrounded by a fortress-like concrete wall to limit its viewing to a few tourists at a time, and is unique in that it shows the genius of Michelangelo midway through a major rework—Christ's head is cut out of Mary's right shoulder, and an earlier arm is still just hanging there. But there's a certain power to this rawness. Walk around the back to see the strain in Mary's back (and Michelangelo's rough chisel work) as she struggles to support her son. The sculpture's elongated form hints at the Mannerist style that would follow. Notice the ancient Roman altar underneath the *Pietà*. This sculpture was owned by the Rondanini family until just after World War II.

At the far end of the castle's grounds is the monumental Arco della Pace, a **triumphal arch.** They built the arch facing Paris to welcome Napoleon's rule, because locals believed he would bring with him the ideals of the French Revolution. When they learned he was just another megalomaniac, they turned the horses around, their tails facing France.

Cost and Hours: €3, free entry 16:30–17:00 and Fri 14:00–17:00, open Tue–Sun 9:00–17:30, closed Mon, WCs and limited free lockers are downstairs from the ticket counter—get key and give ID at ticket desk, English info fliers throughout, Metro: Cairoli, tel. 02-8846-3700, www.milanocastello.it.

Branca Tower—This tower, a five-minute walk from the Sforza Castle through Milan's equivalent of Central Park, offers a commanding city view. For €4, an elevator takes you as high as the Mary that crowns the cathedral (hours are erratic, call or confirm at TI before heading out, closed Mon and in bad weather, tel. 02-331-4120).

Museum of Art and Science (Museo d'Arte e Scienza)—This hands-on museum offers an interesting look at Leonardo's works during the 20 years he spent in Milan. It includes his paintings and sketches, and inventions such as a clever drum machine and war machines in miniature. Another part of the museum describes how to tell the difference between genuine art and copies or fakes, with 10 demonstration stations. Oddly, a third collection features

African and Buddhist art.

Cost and Hours: €8, Mon–Fri 10:00–18:00, closed Sat–Sun, English descriptions throughout, Via Q. Sella 4; tel. 02-720-2488, www.museoartescienza.com.

▲**Via Dante**—This grand pedestrian boulevard and popular shopping street leads from the Sforza Castle toward the town center and the Duomo. Since Via Dante was carved out of a medieval tangle of streets to celebrate Italian unification (c. 1870), all the facades lining it are relatively new. Over the vigorous complaints of merchants, the street became traffic-free in 1995. Today, they'd have it no other way. Enjoy strolling this beautiful people zone, where you'll hear the whir of bikes and the lilting melodies of accordion players instead of traffic noise. Photo exhibits are frequently displayed up and down the street. In front of the Sforza Castle, a commanding statue of Giuseppe Garibaldi, one of the heroes of the unification movement, looks down one of Europe's longest pedestrian zones. From here you can walk to the Duomo and beyond (about 1.5 miles) down streets that are all nearly traffic-free. Stroll and appreciate Italian design both in people and in windows (ignore the Foot Locker).

The Last Supper and Nearby

▲**Leonardo da Vinci's *The Last Supper (Cenacolo)***—Housed in the Church of Santa Maria delle Grazie, this is one of the ultimate masterpieces of the Renaissance. Milan's leading family, the Sforza, hired da Vinci to decorate the dining hall of the Dominican monastery that adjoins the church. This gift was essentially a bribe to the monks so that the Sforzas could locate their family tomb in the church. Ultimately, the French drove the Sforzas out of Milan, they were never buried here, and the Dominicans got a great fresco for nothing. Note that this is a rare sight, and entry must be booked months in advance (explained later).

MILAN

Because of Leonardo's experimental fresco technique, deterioration began within six years of its completion. The church was bombed in World War II, but—miraculously, it seems—the wall holding *The Last Supper* remained standing. A 21-year restoration project (completed in 1999) peeled away 500 years of touch-ups, leaving Leonardo's masterpiece faint but vibrant.

In a big, vacant whitewashed room, you'll see faded pastels and not a crisp edge. The feet under the table look like negatives. But the composition is dreamy—Leonardo captures the psychological drama as the Lord says, "One of you will betray me," and the apostles huddle in stressed-out groups of three, wondering, "Lord, is it I?" Some are scandalized. Others want more information. Simon (on the far right) gestures as if to ask a question that has no answer. In this agitated atmosphere, only Judas (fourth from left and the only one with his face in shadow)—clutching his 30 pieces of silver and looking pretty guilty—is not shocked.

The circle meant life and harmony to Leonardo. Deep into a study of how life emanates in circles—like ripples on a pool hit by a pebble—Leonardo positioned the 13 characters in a semicircle. Jesus is in the center, from whence the spiritual force of God emanates, or ripples out.

The room depicted in the painting seems like an architectural extension of the church. The disciples form an apse, with Jesus as the altar—in keeping with the Eucharist. Jesus anticipates his sacrifice—his face sad, all-knowing, and accepting. His feet even foreshadowed his death by crucifixion. Had the door, which was cut out in 1652, not been added, you'd see how Leonardo placed Jesus' feet atop each other, ready for the nail.

The room was a refectory or dining room for the Dominican friars. Traditionally, they'd gather here to eat with a Last Supper scene on one wall facing a Crucifixion scene on the opposite wall.

The perspective is mathematically correct. In fact, restorers found a tiny nail hole in Jesus' left eye, which anchored the strings Leonardo used to establish these lines. The table is cheated out to show the meal. Notice the exquisite lighting. The walls are lined with tapestries (as they would have been), and the one on the right is brighter in order to fit the actual lighting in the refectory (which has windows on the left). With the extremely natural effect of the light and the drama of the faces, Leonardo created an effective masterpiece.

Reservations: Reservations are mandatory. Even though the hype surrounding the blockbuster novel and movie *The Da Vinci Code* has died down, spots are still booked more than a month in advance—so plan ahead. To minimize the humidity problem—even though the damage has already been done—only 900 visitors a day are allowed in. That's 25 tourists popping in every 15 minutes for exactly 15 minutes. Prior to your appointment time, you wait in several rooms to dehumidify, while doors close behind you and open up slowly in front of you. The posted information about Leonardo is mainly in Italian.

If you book by **phone,** you'll have a greater selection of days and time slots to choose from, since the website doesn't reflect cancellations (tel. 02-9280-0360, or from the US dial 011-39-02-9280-0360, office open Mon–Fri 8:00–18:30, closed Sat–Sun; the number is often busy—once you get through, dial 2 for an English-speaking operator; the process takes about two minutes and you'll hang up with an appointed entry time and a number; pay with credit card upon booking).

If you book **online** using the official website, you'll see a calendar that shows available time slots for the current month. If the days are blank, it means that all the slots for those days have been filled. If you can't find a spot when you need it, try calling instead, because cancellations show up on the website as booked slots (www.cenacolovinciano.net).

Cost and Hours: €8, includes €1.50 reservation fee (9:30 and 15:30 visits require €3.25 extra for provided guided English tour). Open Tue–Sun 8:15–18:45 (last visit), closed Mon. Show up 20 minutes before your scheduled time. When an attendant calls your time, get up and move into the next room. Consider the fine €2.50 audioguide. Its spiel fills every second of the time you're in the room—so try to start listening to it just before you enter (ideally in the waiting room while studying the reproduction of *The Last Supper*). No photos are allowed.

Last-Minute Tickets: While "reservations are required," if spots are available (more likely on weekdays and first thing in the morning) you can sometimes book one at the desk (even if *Sold Out* sign is posted). If fewer than 25 people show up for a particular time slot, you can get lucky. But those who show up without a reservation generally kill lots of time waiting around. Note that the Autostradale and Zani Viaggi bus tours (see "Tours in Milan," earlier) include entry to *The Last Supper.*

Getting There: Take the Metro to Cadorna or Conciliazione (plus a 5-minute walk), or hop on tram #16 (catch it just off Piazza del Duomo on corner of Via Mazzini and Via Dogana), which drops you off in front of the Church of Santa Maria delle Grazie. The Science Museum (next listing) is two blocks away.

▲Leonardo da Vinci National Science and Technology Museum (Museo Nazionale della Scienza e Tecnica "Leonardo da Vinci")—The spirit of Leonardo lives here. Most tourists visit for the hall of Leonardo designs illustrated in wooden models, but Leonardo's mind is just as easy to appreciate by paging through a coffee-table edition of his notebooks in any bookstore.

The rest of this immense collection of industrial cleverness is fascinating, with planes, trains, and automobiles, ships, radios, old musical instruments, computers, batteries, telephones, chunks of the first transatlantic cable, interactive science workshops, and on and on. Many exhibits include English descriptions. Some of the best exhibits (such as the Marconi radios) branch off the Leonardo hall. Ask for an English museum map from the ticket desk—you'll need it. Allow at least 1.5 hours here.

Cost and Hours: €8, Wed–Fri 9:30–17:00, Sat–Sun 9:30–18:30, closed Mon–Tue, Via San Vittore 21; bus #50 or #58 from the Sforza Castle; tram #16—catch it just off Piazza del Duomo, direction: San Siro; or Metro: Sant'Ambrogio; tel. 02-485-551.

Away from the Center

Leonardo's Horse—The largest equestrian monument in the world is a modern reconstruction of a model created in 1482 by Leonardo da Vinci for the Sforza family. The model was destroyed in 1499 by invading French forces, who used it for target practice. In 1999, American Renaissance-art collector Charles Dent decided to build the 15-ton, 24-foot-long statue from Leonardo's design. He presented it to the Italians in appreciation for their role in the Renaissance and in homage to Leonardo's genius. The exhibit, described in English, includes statue casts and photos of the construction.

Cost and Hours: Free, Tue–Sun 9:00–17:30, closed Mon, located on outskirts near Meazza soccer stadium and San Siro racetrack; from corner of Via Mazzini and Via Dogana, take tram #16, direction: San Siro, to Stratico Palatino stop—ask conductor when to get off, then head right on Via Palatino, and left on Piazzale dello Sport to #9; or you can walk a half-mile from Metro: Lotto.

Soccer—The Milanesi claim that their soccer (football, or *calcio*, in Italian) teams are the best in Europe. For a dose of Europe's soccer mania (which many believe provides a necessary testosterone vent to keep Europe out of a third big war), catch a match while you're here. A.C. Milan and Inter Milan are the ferociously competitive home teams (tickets-€10–350).

A.C. Milan tickets are sold at Intesa Sanpaolo banks (one's at Via Verdi 8, Mon–Fri 8:45–13:45 & 14:45–15:45, closed Sat–Sun), online at www.acmilan.com, or at the Milan Point Shop (Tue–Sat 10:00–19:00, closed Sun–Mon, Piazza XXVI Maggio next to Via San Gottardo). Inter Milan tickets are sold at Banca Popolare di Milano banks (one's at Piazza Meda 4, Metro: San Babila; Mon–Fri 8:45–13:45 & 14:45–15:45, closed Sat–Sun) or online at www.inter.it.

Games are held in the 85,000-seat Meazza stadium most Sunday afternoons from September to June (Metro: Lotto, or tram #16—catch it just off Piazza del Duomo, on corner of Via Mazzini and Via Dogana, direction: San Siro; take it to last stop, where you'll find the stadium). You'll need to have your passport when you buy your ticket and bring it with you to the stadium for security reasons. For more on the Italian passion for soccer, see page 776.

▲**Monumental Cemetery (Il Cimitero Monumentale)**—Europe's most artistic and dreamy cemetery experience, this grand

place was built just after unification to provide a suitable final resting spot for the city's "famous and well-deserving men." Any cemetery is evocative, but this one—with its super-emotional portrayals of the deceased and their heavenly escorts (in art styles c. 1870–1930)—is in a class by itself. It's a vast garden art gallery of proud busts and grim reapers, heartbroken angels and weeping widows, too-young soldiers and countless old smiles, frozen on yellowed black-and-white photos.

Cost and Hours: Free, Tue–Sun 8:00–18:00, closed Mon, pick up map at the entrance gate, a long walk from Metro: Garibaldi FS, or catch tram #12 or #14 from the corner of Via Orefici and Via Cantu' near the Duomo.

Shopping in Milan

For world-class window-shopping, visit the "**Quadrilateral**," an elegant high-fashion shopping area around Via Montenapoleone. This was the original Beverly Hills of Milan. In the 1920s, the top fashion shops moved in, and today it remains *the* place for designer labels. Most places close Sunday and for much of August. On Mondays, stores open only after 16:00. In this land where fur is still prized, the people-watching is as entertaining as the window-shopping. Notice also the exclusive penthouse apartments with roof gardens high above the scene. Via Montenapoleone and the pedestrianized Via della Spiga are the best streets.

Whether you're gawking or shopping, here's the best route: From La Scala, walk up Via Manzoni to the Metro stop at Montenapoleone, browse down Via Montenapoleone, cut left on Via Santo Spirito (lined with grand aristocratic palazzos—peek into the courtyard at #7), turn right to window-shop down Via della Spiga, turn right on Via Sant'Andrea and then left, back onto Montenapoleone, which leads you through a final gauntlet of temptations to Piazza San Babila. Then (for less-expensive shopping thrills), walk back to the Duomo down the pedestrian-only

Corso Vittorio Emanuele. From the Duomo, go down Via Dante to the Sforza Castle.

La Rinascente, next to the Duomo, is a Nordstrom-type department store with something for everyone and an especially good toy selection. Each floor has a fine collection of designer names sold out of independent shops, all functioning within the walls of this vast and venerable store. Simply riding the escalator up and up gives a fun overview of Italian design and marketing. The seventh floor is a top-end food circus, with terrace views of the Duomo and a public WC. Its name, meaning "the place reborn," fits its history. In an earlier life, it was a fine Liberty-style building until it burned down in 1918. It was rebuilt, only to be bombed in World War II and rebuilt once again (Mon–Thu 9:30–21:00, Fri–Sat 9:30–22:00, Sun 10:00–21:00, has a VAT refund office and recommended restaurants, faces north side of the Duomo on Piazza del Duomo).

Nightlife in Milan

For evening action, check out the artsy Brera area in the old center, with several swanky sidewalk cafés to choose from and lots of bars that stay open late. Home to Brera's Art University, this district has a sophisticated, lively people-watching scene. Another great neighborhood for nightlife, especially for a younger scene, is Navigli, Milan's formerly bohemian, now gentrified "Little Venice" (Metro: Porta Genova).

There are always concerts and live music playing in the city at various clubs and concert halls. Specifics change quickly, so it's best to rely on the entertainment information in periodicals from the TI.

Sleeping in Milan

All recommended hotels are within a few minutes' walk of Milan's subway system. With Milan's fine Metro, you can get anywhere in town in a flash. Anytime in March, April, September, and October, the city can be completely jammed by conventions, and hotel prices jump way up. I've listed high-season prices, but not convention-gouging prices. (For the convention schedule, see www.fieramilano.it.) Summer is usually wide-open and prices are discounted, though many hotels close in August for vacation. Hotels cater more to business travelers than to tourists, so Fridays and Saturdays are generally cheaper and available.

Lately I've noticed a trend in which small family-style hotels in the center are being neglected, and the big, modern business-class hotels around the train station are proliferating. I've tried to collect central places, where travelers feel appreciated and the staff

---

Sleep Code

(€1 = about $1.25, country code: 39)
S = Single, **D** = Double/Twin, **T** = Triple, **Q** = Quad, **b** = bathroom,
s = shower only. Unless otherwise noted, credit cards are
accepted, English is spoken, and breakfast is included.

To help you sort easily through these listings, I've divided
the rooms into three categories based on the price for a
standard double room with bath:

$$$ Higher Priced—Most rooms €150 or more.
$$ Moderately Priced—Most rooms between €110–150.
$ Lower Priced—Most rooms €110 or less.

Prices can change without notice; verify the hotel's current
rates online or by email. For other updates, see www.ricksteves
.com/update.

---

feels like part of the family. If the following places are booked up,
go online—there are lots of hotels near the train station.

Near the Duomo

The Duomo area is thick with people-watching, reasonably priced
eateries, and the major sightseeing attractions. From the central
train station to the Duomo, it's just four stops on a direct Metro
line (yellow line 3, direction: San Donato) to Metro: Duomo.

$$$ Hotel Grand Duca di York is oddly stuck in the middle
of banks and big-city starkness three blocks southwest of Piazza
del Duomo. It's got lavish public spaces and 33 modern, bright
rooms that are thoughtfully designed and decorated (Sb-€98–128,
Db-€148–188, €30 more for balconies, air-con, elevator, free Wi-Fi,
free minibar, closed Aug, near Metro stops: Cordusio or Duomo,
Via Moneta 1, tel. 02-874-863, fax 02-869-0344, www.ducadiyork
.com, info@ducadiyork.com).

$$$ Hotel Spadari boasts an Art Deco interior designed by
the Milanese artist Giò Pomodoro ("Joe Tomato" in English). The
40 rooms have billowing drapes, big paintings, and designer doors.
It's next door to the recommended Peck deli, and two blocks from
the Duomo (standard Db-€198–248, deluxe Db-€268–328, no need
for the pricier suites, Via Spadari 11, tel. 02-7200-2371, fax 02-861-
184, www.spadarihotel.com, reservation@spadarihotel.com).

$ Hotel Vecchia Milano is a humble but clean well-run place
buried deep in the old town on a narrow lane. The Rossi family
rents 27 comfortable rooms at a great price for the location (Sb-
€65, Db-€80–85, air-con, free Wi-Fi with this book, next to recommended Hostaria Borromei at Via Borromei 4, tel. 02-875-042,

fax 02-8645-4292, www.hotelvecchiamilan.com, hotelvecchia milano@tiscalinet.it).

Between La Scala and the Sforza Castle

$$$ Hotel Star, comfortable and modern, rents 30 sparkling, fresh, and spacious rooms (Sb-€160, Db-€210, prices drop about €40 outside convention times, interior rooms are quieter, air-con, fridge, Wi-Fi, closed Aug, Via dei Bossi 5, tel. 02-801-501, fax 02-861-787, www.hotelstar.it, info@hotelstar.it).

$$$ Antica Locanda dei Mercanti is a work in progress, with a major renovation under way. It's in a great location and rents 15 rooms (Db-€175–250, more during conventions, air-con, free Internet access and Wi-Fi, Via San Tomaso 6, Metro: Duomo or Cordusio; tel. 02-805-4080, fax 02-805-4090, www.locanda.it, locanda@locanda.it, Eri).

$$ London Hotel, a simple 30-room hotel with overstuffed little living rooms, an inviting breakfast room, and all the amenities, is tucked away on a quiet side street just off vibrant Via Dante. It's warmly run by the friendly Gambino family: mom and pop Elda and Franco don't speak English, but daughters Tanya and Licia do (S-€70, Sb-€90, D-€120, Db-€150, Tb-€180, prices much higher during conventions, skip their €8 breakfast and grab something on Via Dante, cheaper in July and Aug, book direct for these rates and get an additional 10 percent off with cash, air-con, elevator, near Metro: Cairoli at Via Rovello 3, tel. 02-7202-0166, fax 02-805-7037, www.hotellondonmilano.com, info@hotel londonmilano.com).

Near the Train Station

The train station neighborhood is more practical than characteristic. Its hotels are utilitarian business-class hotels with prices that bounce all over depending upon the convention schedule. You'll find more shady characters than shady trees in the parks, and lots of massage parlors. But you can't beat the convenience (near station, Metro to the center, shuttles to airports), and if you hit it outside of convention times, the prices are hard to beat. Here are two decent options:

$$ Hotel Florida is a comfortable, well-maintained business-class hotel with 55 rooms on a quiet street one block from the station. Prices plummet if you book direct and are not visiting during a convention (normally Db-€240 but often more like Sb-€70–100 and Db-€90–130, Wi-Fi, Via Lepetit 33, tel. 02-670-5921, fax 02-669-2867, www.hotelfloridamilan.com, reception@hotelfloridamilan.com). With the tracks to your back, leave the station's upper hall to the left, cross the taxi stand, and then cross the road. The hotel is on Via Lepetit, around the

Hotels & Restaurants in Milan

1. Hotel Grand Duca di York
2. Hotel Spadari & Peck Gourmet Deli
3. To Hotel Vecchia Milano & Hostaria Borromei
4. Hotel Star
5. Antica Locanda dei Mercanti
6. London Hotel
7. To Train Station Area Hotels
8. Trattoria Milanese
9. Ristorante Bruno
10. Peck Italian Bar
11. Elevator to La Rinascente Dept. Store Eateries
12. Latteria Cucina Vegetariana
13. Pastarito Pizzarito
14. Ciao Cafeteria
15. Ristorante Rita
16. McDonald's & Bar Zucca
17. Odeon Gelateria
18. Gelateria Grom
19. Princi Bakeries (2)
20. Luini Panzerotti
21. Supermarket
22. To Da Rita e Antonio
23. Le Briciole Ristorante
24. Antica Osteria Milanese
25. Via Dante Eateries
26. Internet Café

corner from Ristorante Giglio Rosso.

$$ Hotel Garda has 55 tidy, spotless rooms two and a half blocks from the station (Sb-€50–100, Db-€80–180, use website for special offers, good breakfast included but cheaper without, air-con, elevator, Via N. Torriani 21, tel. 02-6698-2626, fax 02-6698-2576, www.hotelgardamilan.com, info@hotelgardamilan.com). Exit the train station and head straight across the square, veering left onto Via N. Torriani. It's ahead on your right.

Hostels

For beds costing about €20–25, consider Milan's hostels. Most are away from the center, but the first one I've listed is closer to town.

$ Ostello la Cordata, a good choice, has 83 beds in both private rooms and in shared dorm rooms (€21–25 for beds in 6-, 8-, and 16-bed dorms; hotel-type rooms on the third floor—Sb-€40–50, Db-€70–80, Tb-€90–105; reserve ahead, 14:30–24:00 check-in, no curfew, elevator, free Internet access and Wi-Fi, self-serve laundry, Via Burigozzo 11, Metro: Missori—on the yellow line 3, tel. 02-5831-4675, fax 02-5830-3598, www.ostellolacordata .com, ostello@lacordata.it).

$ AIG Piero Rotta is larger and offers cheap, basic accommodation with a simple breakfast (€20 beds in 4-to 6-bed dorms, hostel membership required, non-members pay €3/night more, near Metro: QT8—on the red line, at Viale Salmoiraghi 1, tel. 02-3926-7095, fax 02-3300-0191, www.ostellomilano.it, milano @ostellionline.org).

Eating in Milan

This is a fast-food city, but fast food in a fashion capital isn't a burger and fries. Milan's bars, delis, *rosticcerie,* and self-service cafeterias cater to people with plenty of taste and more money than time. You'll find delightful eateries all over town (note that they take Aug off).

I find the price difference between basic and classy restaurants to be negligible (for example, pastas-€7–12, *secondi*-€12–20, cover-€1–3), so it's worth springing for the places that give the best experience. To eat mediocre food on a famous street with great people-watching, choose an eatery on the pedestrian-only Via Mercanti or Via Dante. To eat with students in trendy little trattorias, explore the Brera neighborhood. To eat well near the Duomo, consider the recommended places below.

Locals like to precede a lunch or dinner with an *aperitivo* (while Campari made its debut in Milan, a simple glass of *vino bianco* or prosecco, the Italian champagne, is just as popular). Bars fill their counters with inviting baskets of munchies, which

---

Milanese Specialties

Milan's signature dishes (often served together as a *piatto unico*, or "single dish") are *risotto alla milanese* and *ossobuco*. The risotto is flavored with saffron, which gives it its intense yellow color. It's said that a 16th-century Belgian glassworker first stumbled on the use of saffron as a spice. Initially, he used saffron to tint the glass mixture for completing the stained-glass windows of the Duomo in 1574. His master joked that he'd end up adding the precious spice to his food as well. On the day of his master's daughter's wedding, the glassworker persuaded the chef to add saffron to the rice cooked for the reception. After the guests got over their initial surprise, the dish was a great success, and has been a staple on Milan's menus ever since. The subtle flavor of the saffron pairs nicely with the *ossobuco* (meaning "marrow," or literally "hole in the bone," of the veal shank). The prized marrow is extracted with special little forks and considered the best part of the meal.

---

are served free with these drinks, at about 17:00. A cheap drink (if you're either likable or discreet) can become a light meal. For example, check out the wonderful buffet spread at the recommended Bar Brera.

Breakfast is a bad value in hotels and fun on Via Dante or in bars. It's OK to quasi-picnic. Bring in a banana (or whatever) and order a toasted ham-and-cheese sandwich (called and pronounced *tost*) or brioche with your cappuccino.

Near the Duomo

Dining with Class

Trattoria Milanese, sophisticated and family-run, is a splurge. It has an enthusiastic and local clientele—the restaurant didn't even bother to get a phone until 1988. Expect a Milanese ambience and quality traditional cuisine (closed Sat–Sun and mid-July–Aug, air-con, Via Santa Marta 11, 5-minute walk from the Duomo, near Pinacoteca Ambrosiana, tel. 02-8645-1991).

Ristorante Bruno serves Tuscan cuisine with a passion for fresh fish. This place impresses with its dressy waiters, hearty food, inexpensive desserts, and a fine self-serve antipasto buffet (a plate full of Tuscan specialties for €9). You can eat inside or on the sidewalk under fascist columns (Sun–Fri 12:00–15:00 & 19:00–23:00, closed Sat and Aug, moderate prices, air-con, Via M. Gonzaga 6, reservations wise, tel. 02-804-364). Giuseppe (from Volterra) and Graziella take good care of their eaters.

Hostaria Borromei is where Milanese yuppies go for power lunches to impress clients with market-fresh traditional Italian dishes. Dine under an awning of vines in an elegant mellow-yellow interior courtyard or in their cantina-chic dining rooms. Reservations are recommended (€15 pastas, €20 *secondi*, €3 cover and service charge, Mon–Fri 12:30–14:45 & 19:30–22:45, Sat 19:30–22:45, closed Sun, Via Borromei 4, tel. 02-8645-3760).

Peck Italian Bar is a hit with the sophisticated office crowd, which mobs the place at lunch for its fast, excellent meals. It's owned by the same people who run the recommended high-end Peck deli (listed later), so be prepared to spend—this place's classi-ness alone makes it worth the money. Any time you find yourself among such a quality-conscious group of Milanesi, you know you're getting good food (€12 pastas, €17 *secondi,* Mon–Fri 7:30–20:30, Sat 9:00–20:30, closed Sun, Via Cantù 3, tel. 02-869-3017).

Dining at the Top of a Top-End Department Store with a Duomo View

The seventh floor of the La Rinascente department store, along-side the Duomo, has a Milanese-style food court, including a sunny outdoor terrace. You'll dine accompanied by views of the cathedral's rooftop (though anyone can pop up for a look at the cathedral). All three of the terrace-seating establishments are open 10:00–24:00, include cover charge with service, and can be accessed after store hours from elevators on Via S. Radegonda. (During open hours, you can go through the department store to take escalators to the top, but it's faster to take the elevators.)

Obikà is a swanky mozzarella bar offering this heavenly cheese in all its various forms—cow's milk, buffalo, and smoked—in sal-ads or on splittable €10–19 antipasto sampler plates, accompanied by *salumi,* tapanades, and vegetables.

At the opposite end of the terrace, **Ristorante Maio** has pricey full-meal service (€13 pastas and pizzas, €22 *secondi*). In between is **Il Bar,** living-room cozy with cushy divans and low coffee tables, and serving light meals (salads, pasta), coffee, desserts, and cocktails.

Eating Simply

Latteria Cucina Vegetariana is a bright hole-in-the-wall that serves a good vegetarian Italian lunch. This busy joint is over-run with tables where neighborhood workers enjoy soup, salads, pastas, and imaginative veggie entrées at affordable prices. Try the €13 *piatto misto al forno* for a delicious assortment of soufflés, quiches, and roasted and sautéed veggies (€8–13 meals, Mon–Fri 12:00–16:00, Sat 13:00–16:00, closed Sun, just off Via Torino at Via dell'Unione 6, 2 blocks southwest of the Duomo, tel. 02-874-401). Giorgio is a hit with camera-toting eaters.

Pastarito Pizzarito is a pasta-and-pizza chain with a wonderful formula. In a bright atmosphere under literal walls of pasta, you can choose from 10 big fresh pastas and lots of sauces to create a huge dish (€5–11), or try a *bis* (two different sauces) for €11. Splitting is welcome. Find plenty of seating on the ground floor or upstairs. Pizzas run €4–9, large salads are €7, and the wine is reasonably priced (daily 12:00–15:00 & 19:30–23:00, air-con, 4 blocks from the Duomo, a block behind opera house at Via Verdi 6, tel. 02-862-210).

Ciao, a self-service cafeteria, offers a low-stress, affordable meal above a fast-food arcade on Piazza del Duomo (daily 11:30–23:00, inexpensive pasta and good salad bar, easy public WC). It's to the right of the Galleria entrance—enter through the ground floor Autogrill and go up to the second floor.

Ristorante Rita, a block behind Ciao, is a smart budget option (€4–5 pastas and *secondi*) without the Italian fast-food feel. While the downstairs has a take-out place, there's a sleek, modern restaurant upstairs with good food and cafeteria prices (Mon–Sat 12:00–15:00, closed Sun, on Via Marconi between Piazza del Duomo and Piazza Diaz, tel. 02-8699-7387).

Fast-food cheapskates enjoy the best people-watching in Milan inside the Galleria at **McDonald's** (long hours daily, salad/pasta plate and tall orange juice for around €5).

Gelato: Floodlit Mary gazes down on the **Odeon Gelateria** from the top of the Duomo for good reason (next to a McDonald's on Piazza del Duomo, on far side of square opposite Duomo facade, open nightly until 24:00). While Odeon is convenient, **Gelateria Grom** (two blocks toward La Scala on Via Santa Margherita) is the connoisseurs' choice.

Picnics Milan-style

For a fun adventure, assemble an elegant dinner picnic by hitting the colorful deli, cheese, and produce shops on Via Speronari. The **Princi bakery** is mobbed with locals vying for focaccia, olive breadsticks, and luscious pastries. Notice the stacked-wood-oven action in the back. For most pastry items (like the brioche), pay the cashier first; for items sold by weight (such as pizza and cake), get it weighed before you pay. Consider a piping-hot pasta lunch (12:00–15:00 only) for €6 per plate (Mon–Sat 7:00–20:00, closed Sun, on Via Speronari, off Via Torino, a block southwest of Piazza del Duomo; a larger Princi bakery, more like a café, is near the Sforza Castle and is listed later).

Peck Gourmet Deli is an aristocratic deli with a fancy café/lunchroom/pastry and gelato shop upstairs, a gourmet grocery and *rosticceria* on the main level, and an expensive *enoteca* wine cellar in the basement. Even if all you can afford is the aroma, peek in. Check out the classic circa-1930 salami slicers and the gourmet assembly line in the kitchen in the back (Mon 15:30–19:30, Tue–Sat 9:15–19:30, closed Sun, Via Spadari 9, tel. 02-802-3161).

The *rosticceria* serves fancy food to go for a superb picnic dinner in your hotel. It's delectable, beautiful, sold by weight (order by the *etto*—100-gram unit, 250 grams equals about a half-pound), and pricey. Try the risotto.

Luini Panzerotti serves up piping-hot mini-calzones *(panzerotti)* stuffed with mozzarella, tomatoes, ham, or whatever you like for €3–5 (Mon 10:00–15:00, Tue–Sat 10:00–20:00, closed Sun and Aug, Via S. Radegonda 16, tel. 02-8646-1917). From the back of the Duomo, head north and look for the lines of hungry locals out front. Order from the small menus posted behind the cash registers. Traditionally, Milanesi munch their hot little meals on nearby Piazza San Fedele. Don't overlook the *dolce* half of their menu—Panzerotti is popular for its sweets all day long.

Billa Superfresco Supermarket is within a few blocks of the Duomo (Mon–Sat 8:00–21:00, Sun 9:00–20:00, small deli on ground level, big supermarket in basement, on Via Torino at intersection with San Maurilio).

Near the Sforza Castle

Da Rita e Antonio is a favorite neighborhood restaurant, serving up well-prepared, reasonably priced Milanese specialties such as *costoletta* (breaded veal chop) and *ossobuco* (veal shank and risotto), as well as delicious €9 Neapolitan-style pizzas. It's a high-energy, dressy place, complete with bow ties and vests (€10 pastas, €20 *secondi*, Tue–Fri and Sun 12:00–14:30 & 19:00–23:00, Sat 19:00–23:00, closed Mon, Via G. Puccini 2a, tel. 02-875-579). Facing the Sforza Castle from Via Dante, it's about 100 yards to your left, built into the far side of the pink-and-white theater.

Le Briciole, run by the Campenella family, is small and folksy, drawing a local crowd for its quality Ligurian cuisine (pesto, seafood) and friendly-family feel (€11 homemade pastas, Mon–Sat 12:15–14:30 & 19:15–22:30, closed Sun; Via Camperio 17, a block in front of castle, on small street at end of Via Dante, tel. 02-804-114; Anamaria and Sara).

Antica Osteria Milanese is a hardworking family place with a smart local following and spacious, stylish seating. They serve good-quality typical Milanese favorites (€8 pastas, €12 *secondi*, €2 cover, closed Sun, Via Camperio 12, tel. 02-861-367).

Fancy Via Dante Bars and Cafés: Thriving and central, Via Dante is lined with hardworking eateries where you can join locals for a lively lunch. Or, for about the price of your forgettable hotel breakfast, you can start your day watching the parade of Milanesi heading to work.

Princi bakery, near the castle, works the same as the one on Via Speronari (listed earlier), only it's more of a restaurant, with seating both inside and on the street. While the bakery and café are open all day, they serve hot cafeteria-style lunches only between 12:00 and 15:00 (Mon–Sat 7:00–20:00, closed Sun, Via Ponte Vetero 10, tel. 02-7201-6067).

In the Brera Neighborhood

The Brera neighborhood surrounding the Church of St. Carmine is laced with narrow, inviting pedestrian streets. Make an evening of your visit by having an *aperitivo* (pre-dinner drink) with snacks at recommended Bar Brera or any bar—most serve munchies with pre-dinner drinks 17:00–21:00. Afterwards, stroll along restaurant row (Via Fiori Chiari) to survey the sidewalk cafés. To locate these eateries, see the map on page 283.

Obikà is a trendy mozzarella bar with a sleek, minimalist sushi-bar feel. It features fresh cow, buffalo, and smoked mozzarella; big organic gourmet salads; and top-quality *salumi*. Show up at happy hour (daily 18:30–21:00) to enjoy a generous buffet and select from a long list of €10 drinks (€9 pastas, daily 12:00–15:30 & 18:30–24:00, on corner of Via Mercato and Via Fiori Chiari, at Via Mercato 28, tel. 02-8645-0568).

Bar Brera, across the street from the Brera Art Gallery, serves salads, sandwiches, and pastas to throngs of art students. During happy hour (daily 17:00–21:00), have a seat, order a drink, and then help yourself to the buffet (17:00–19:00), which has a generous variety of *antipasti,* from marinated veggies to prosciutto (buffet is free if you buy drinks; bar open daily 7:00–2:00 in the morning, great streetside seating, Via Brera 23, tel. 02-877-091).

Milan Connections

From Milan by Train to: Venice (at least hourly, most departures at :05 or :35 past the hour, most are direct on high-speed ES trains, 2.5 hours), **Florence** (hourly, 1.75 hours), **Genoa** (about hourly, 2 hours, also look for trains to La Spezia or Livorno that stop at Genoa), **Rome** (hourly, 3.5–8 hours, overnight possible), **Brindisi** (4 direct/day, 2 are night trains, 9–12 hours, more with changes), **Cinque Terre/La Spezia** (about hourly, 3 hours direct or with change in Genoa; trains from La Spezia to the villages go nearly hourly), **Cinque Terre/Monterosso al Mare** (about hourly, 3–4 hours direct or with change in Genoa), **Varenna** on Lake Como (small line direct to Lecco/Sondrio/Tirano leaves at 6:20, 8:20, 10:20, 12:20, 14:20, 16:20, 17:20, 19:20, 20:20, and 21:25; 1 hour; confirm these times—if you take a train at a time not listed here, it's likely a local milk-run train that will take twice as long), **Stresa** on Lake Maggiore (about hourly, 1-hour fast train, 70- to 90-minute slow train; also look for trains to Domodossola and some international destinations that stop at Stresa), **Como** (at least hourly, 30–60 minutes, boats go from Como to Varenna until 19:10), **Naples** (direct trains hourly, 5 hours, more with change in Rome, overnight possible).

International Destinations: Amsterdam (1 direct/day, hourly with several changes, 15 hours), **Barcelona** (13–20 hours, several with 1–5 changes), **Bern** (3 direct/day, more with change in Brig, 3–3.5 hours), **Frankfurt** (1 direct overnight, more with changes in Basel or Zurich, 9–10 hours), **London** (3/day, 12–18 hours with changes), **Munich** (7/day, 8–12 hours with changes), **Nice** (2 direct/day, 5 with changes, night train possible, 5–6.5 hours), **Paris** (4 direct/day, 7–8 hours), **Lyon** (8/day, 6–8.5 hours with changes), **Vienna** (1 direct/day, more with 1–3 changes, 11–14 hours). With dozens of budget airlines serving Europe's hub cities, flying to your international destination is often the most efficient and economical option (see "Cheap Flights," on page 975).

Airports

To get flight information for Malpensa or Linate airports or the current phone number of your airline, call 02-74851 and wait for English options, or try 02-7485-2200 (www.sea-aeroportimilano.it).

Malpensa Airport

Most international flights land at the manageable Malpensa Airport, 28 miles northwest of Milan. Customs guards fan you through, and even the customs dog seems friendly. You'll most likely land at Terminal 1 (international flights), rather than Terminal 2 (charter flights); buses connect the two. Both have ATMs (at Terminal 1, between exit 4 and 5 at Banca Nazionale del Lavoro), banks, and exchange offices. Terminal 1 has a pharmacy, eateries, and a hotel reservation service disguised as a TI (daily 7:00–20:00; when you exit the baggage-carousel area, go right to reach services and exit; tel. 02-5858-0080). The *tabacchi* shop sells phone cards—handy for confirming your hotel reservation.

You have three easy ways to get to downtown Milan: by train, shuttle bus, or taxi.

By Train: The Malpensa Express zips between Malpensa Airport and Milan's Cadorna station, which is both a Metro stop and a small train station, closer to the Duomo than the central train station (€11, credit cards accepted, 2/hour, 40 minutes; usually departs airport at :23 and :53 past the hour from 5:53–23:23, generally departs Cadorna at :27 and :57 past the hour from 5:57–23:27, not covered by railpasses, www.malpensaexpress.it). At the airport, as you pop out through customs, you'll see a *Treno per Malpensa* kiosk selling tickets and a big electric board on the wall indicating how many minutes until the next departure. Follow signs (*Treni* and *Malpensa Express*) down the stairs to the tracks.

Train Connections from Milan

If you're leaving Milan to go to the airport, take the Metro to the Cadorna stop, surface, and buy a ticket at the Malpensa Express office in the station. Purchase your ticket before you board, or you'll pay €2.50 extra to buy it on the train. Trains depart Cadorna from track 1. Note that there are some earlier and later departures to and from Cadorna by bus—ask when you buy your ticket. If your departure is by bus, the stop is outside the station; head left as you exit to find the stop 50 yards to the left on Via Paleocapa.

By Bus: Two bus companies offer virtually identical, competing services between Malpensa Airport and Milan's central train station. They each charge about €8 for the one-hour trip (buy ticket from driver) and depart from the same places: in front of the airport (outside exit 5, at stops 2 and 3) and from Piazza Luigi di Savoia (on the east side of Milan's train station—with your back to the tracks exit to the left). You'll generally find a bus leaving about every 15 minutes, every day, nearly all day (from downtown roughly 4:30–23:00 and from the airport roughly 5:30–00:15 in the morning; Malpensa Shuttle tel. 02-5858-3185, www.malpensashuttle .it; Autostradale tel. 02-3391-0794, www.autostradale.it). They're almost comically competitive, with one offering three rides for the price of two. Play around a bit and you may save some money.

By Taxi: Taxis into Milan cost a fixed rate of €85; avoid hustlers in airport halls (catch taxis outside exit 6). Considering how far the city is from the airport and how good the train and bus services are, Milan is the last place I'd take a taxi to the airport. To get from Milan to the airport, I taxi to the Cadorna station and then catch the Malpensa Express train.

Getting Between Malpensa and Linate: The Malpensa Shuttle company runs a bus between the airports about hourly (€13, from Malpensa to Linate runs 7:50–00:25 in the morning, 1.25 hours, catch bus outside Malpensa's exit 3, stop 20, buy tickets from Airport 2000 offices; from Linate to Malpensa buses depart 4:30–21:30, bus stops at Malpensa's Terminal 1—you must request stop if you need Terminal 2; tel. 02-5858-3185, www.malpensa shuttle.it).

Linate Airport

Most European flights land at Linate, five miles east of Milan. The airport has a bank (just past customs; ATM, decent rates) and a hotel-finding service disguised as a TI (daily 7:30–23:30, tel. 02-7020-0443).

You can get to downtown Milan by bus or taxi (or to Malpensa Airport by bus; see above).

By Bus: Two different buses—Starfly and ATM—take you from Linate Airport to downtown. The Starfly bus zips you to the central train station (€4.50, buy ticket from driver, 3/hour, 30 minutes, bus runs from airport 6:05–23:45, from station 5:40–23:30, leaves from east side of train station at Piazza Luigi di Savoia, tel. 02-717-106, www.autostradale.com.). The cheaper ATM city bus gets you to the San Babila Metro stop (specifically to Corso Europa, just around the corner from Piazza San Babila and its Metro station; from here it's one stop to the Duomo on red line 1, direction: Molino Dorino or Bisceglie, or a 7-minute walk). The bus costs €1, departs every 10 minutes, and takes 20 minutes (departures leave city center 5:35–00:35, from airport 6:00–01:05, www.atm-mi.it). Either bus company works fine: Wait for the one that's handier to your hotel, or hop on the first one that shows up. From where it drops you off, take the Metro or a taxi to your hotel. Both buses leave the airport from outside the arrivals hall.

By Taxi: Taxis from Linate to the Duomo cost about €18.

Bergamo (Orio Al Serio) Airport

Some budget airlines, such as Ryanair and Wizzair, use Bergamo Airport as their Milan hub (about 30 miles from Milan, tel. 035-326-323, www.sacbo.it). An express bus, Orioshuttle, connects the airport to Milan's central train station (€7, daily 4:00–23:15, 2/hour, 1 hour, buy tickets from driver or online at http://ticketon line.orioshuttle.com, tel. 035-330-706).

THE CINQUE TERRE

The Cinque Terre (CHINK-weh TAY-reh), a remote chunk of the Italian Riviera, is the traffic-free, lowbrow, underappreciated alternative to the French Riviera. There's not a museum in sight. Just sun, sea, sand (pebbles), wine, and pure, unadulterated Italy. Enjoy the villages, swimming, hiking, and evening romance of one of God's great gifts to tourism. For a home base, choose among five *(cinque)* villages, each of which fills a ravine with a lazy hive of human activity—callused locals, sunburned travelers, and no Vespas. While the Cinque Terre is now discovered (and can be quite crowded midday, when tourist boats drop by), I've never seen happier, more relaxed tourists.

The chunk of coast was first described in medieval times as "the five lands." In the feudal era, this land was watched over by castles. Tiny communities grew up in their protective shadows, ready to run inside at the first hint of a Turkish Saracen pirate raid. Marauding pirates from North Africa were a persistent problem until about 1400. Many locals were kidnapped and ransomed or sold into slavery, and those who remained built fires on flat-roofed watchtowers to relay warnings—alerting the entire coast to imminent attacks. The last major raid was in 1545.

As the threat of pirates faded, the villages prospered, catching fish and growing grapes. Churches were enlarged with a growing population. But until the advent of tourism in this generation, the towns remained isolated. Even today, traditions survive, and each of the five villages comes with a distinct dialect and its own proud heritage.

Sadly, a few ugly, noisy Americans give tourism a bad name here. Even hip, young residents are put off by loud, drunken

The Cinque Terre

tourists. They say—and I agree—that the Cinque Terre is an exceptional place. It deserves a special dignity. Party in Viareggio or Portofino, but be mellow in the Cinque Terre. Talk softly. Help keep it clean. In spite of the tourist crowds, it's still a real community, and we are its guests.

In this chapter, I cover the five towns in order from east to west, from Riomaggiore to Monterosso. Since I still get the names of the towns mixed up, I think of them by number: #1 Riomaggiore (a workaday town), #2 Manarola (picturesque), #3 Corniglia (on a hilltop), #4 Vernazza (the region's cover girl, the most touristy and dramatic), and #5 Monterosso al Mare (the closest thing to a beach resort of the five towns).

Arrival in the Cinque Terre

Big, fast trains from elsewhere in Italy speed past the Cinque Terre (though some stop in Monterosso and Riomaggiore). Unless you're coming from a nearby town, you'll have to change trains at least once to reach Manarola, Corniglia, or Vernazza.

Generally, if you're coming from the north, you'll change

trains in Sestri Levante or Genoa (specifically, Genoa's Piazza Principe station). If you're coming from the south or east, you'll most likely have to switch trains in La Spezia (change at La Spezia  Centrale station). No matter where you're coming from, it's best to check in the station before you leave to see your full schedule and route options (use the computerized kiosks or ask at a ticket window). Don't forget to validate your ticket by stamping it— ka-CHUNK!—in the yellow machines located on train platforms and elsewhere in the station. Conductors here are notorious for levying stiff fines on forgetful tourists. For more information on riding the train between Cinque Terre towns, see "Getting Around the Cinque Terre," later in this chapter.

If the Cinque Terre is your first, last, or only stop on this trip, consider flying into Pisa or Genoa, rather than Milan. These airports are less confusing than Milan's, and closer to the Cinque Terre.

If you're driving in the Cinque Terre (but given the narrow roads and lack of parking, I wouldn't), see "Cinque Terre Connections" at the end of this chapter for directions.

Planning Your Time

The ideal stay is two or three full days; my recommended minimum stay is two nights and a completely uninterrupted day. The Cinque Terre is served by the local train from Genoa and La Spezia. Speed demons arrive in the morning, check their bags in La Spezia, take the five-hour hike through all five towns, laze away the afternoon on the beach or rock of their choice, and zoom away on the overnight train to somewhere back in the real world. But be warned: The Cinque Terre has a strange way of messing up your momentum. (The evidence is the number of Americans who have fallen in love with the region and/or one of its residents...and are still here.) Frankly, staying fewer than two nights is a mistake that you'll likely regret.

The towns are just a few minutes apart by hourly train or boat. There's no checklist of sights or experiences—just a hike, the towns themselves, and your fondest vacation desires. Study this chapter in advance and piece together your best day, mixing hiking, swimming, trains, and a boat ride. For the best light and coolest temperatures, start your hike early.

Market days perk up the towns from 8:00 to 13:00 on Tuesday

in Vernazza, Wednesday in Levanto, Thursday in Monterosso and Sestri Levante, and Friday in La Spezia. (Levanto, Sestri Levante, and La Spezia are covered in the next chapter.)

The winter is really dead—most hotels and some restaurants close in December and January. The long Easter weekend (April 22–25 in 2011) and July and August are peak of peak, the toughest time to find rooms. In spring, the towns can feel inundated with Italian school groups day-tripping on spring excursions (they can't afford to sleep in this expensive region). For more information on the region, see www.cinqueterre.it.

The Cinque Terre National Park

The creation of the Cinque Terre National Marine Park in 1999 has brought lots of money (all visitors pay a fee to hike the trails), new restrictions on land and sea to protect wildlife, and lots of concrete bolstering walkways, trails, beaches, breakwaters, and docks. Each village has a park-sponsored information center, and two towns have tiny, nearly worthless folk museums. The park is run by its president, Franco Bonanini, a powerful man—nicknamed "The Pharaoh" for his grandiose visions—who used to be Riomaggiore's mayor. For the latest on the park, see www.parconazionale 5terre.it.

Cinque Terre Cards

Visitors hiking between the towns need to pay a park entrance fee. This fee keeps the trails safe and open, and pays for viewpoints, picnic spots, WCs, and more. The popular coastal trail generates enough revenue to subsidize the development of trails and outdoor activities higher in the hills.

You have three options for covering the park fee: the Cinque Terre Card (the best deal), the Cinque Terre Treno Card, or the Cinque Terre Treno e Batello Card. All are valid until midnight on the expiration date. Write your name on your card or risk a big fine (see www.parconazionale5terre.it).

The **Cinque Terre Card,** good for one day of hiking, costs €5 (includes map; €8/2 days, €10/3 days, €20/7 days). It covers all trails, shuttle buses, and park museums, but not trains or boats, and a three-hour bike rental. Buy it at trailheads, at national park offices, and at most train stations (no validation required).

The **Cinque Terre Treno Card** covers what the Cinque Terre Card does, plus the use of the local trains (from Levanto to La Spezia, including all Cinque Terre towns). It's sold at TIs inside train stations—but not at trailheads—and comes with a map, information brochure, and train schedule (€9/1 day, €15/2 days, €20/3 days, €37/week, validate card at train station by punching it in the yellow machine). This card is not a good value, because you'd have to hike and take three train trips every day just to break even.

The **Cinque Terre Treno e Batello Card,** valid for one day, covers the same things as the Cinque Terre Treno Card, plus boats between Monterosso and Riomaggiore (€19.50). It's a poor value unless you plan to hike and take several boat or train rides all in one day—determine the individual cost for each leg of your trip before buying this pass.

Getting Around the Cinque Terre

Within the Cinque Terre, you'll get around the villages more cheaply by train, but more scenically by boat. And any way you do it, a visit here comes with lots of stairs and climbing.

By Train

Along the coast here, trains go in only two directions: "per [to] Genova" (the Italian spelling of Genoa) or "per La Spezia."

Assuming you're on vacation, accept the unpredictability of Cinque Terre trains (they're often late...unless you are, too—in which case they're on time). Relax while you wait—buy a cup of coffee at a station bar. When the train comes (know which direction to look for: La Spezia or Genova), casually walk over and hop on. This is especially easy in Monterosso, with its fine café-with-a-view on track #1 (direction: Milano/Genova).

Use the handy TV monitors in the station to make sure you're headed for the right platform. Most of the northbound trains that stop at all Cinque Terre towns and are headed toward Genova will list Sestri Levante as the *destinazione*.

By train, the five towns are just a few minutes apart. Know your stop. After the train leaves the town before your destination, go to the door and get ready to slip out before the mob packs in. Words to the wise for novice tourists, who often miss their stop: The stations are small and the trains are long, so (especially in Vernazza) you might have to get off deep in a tunnel. Also, the doors don't open automatically—you may have to flip open the handle of the door yourself. If a door isn't working, go quickly to the next car to leave. (When leaving a town by train, if you find the platform jammed with people, walk down the platform into the tunnel where things quiet down.)

It's cheap to buy individual train tickets to travel between the towns. Since a one-town hop costs the same as a five-town hop (about €1.40), and every ticket is good for six hours with stopovers, save money and explore the region in one direction on one ticket. Or buy a round-trip ticket from one end to the other of the region (e.g., round-trip from Monterosso to Riomaggiore and back)—it functions as a six-hour pass. Stamp the ticket at the station machine before you board. Riding without a validated ticket can be expensive ("minimum €25 fine" means they charge what they want—usually €50) if you meet a conductor. If you have a Eurailpass, don't spend one of your valuable flexi-days on the cheap Cinque Terre.

In general, I'd skip the train from Riomaggiore to Manarola (the trains are unreliable, and the 15-minute Via dell'Amore stroll is a delight—see page 325 for more on this path).

Cinque Terre Train Schedule: Since the train is the Cinque Terre's lifeline, many shops and restaurants post the current schedule, and most hotels offer copies of it. Carry a schedule with you—it'll come in handy (one comes with the Cinque Terre Card). Note that fast trains leaving La Spezia zip right through the Cinque Terre; some stop only in Monterosso (town #5) and Riomaggiore (town #1). But any train that stops in Manarola, Corniglia, and Vernazza (towns #2, #3, and #4) will stop in all five towns (including the trains on the schedule below).

All of the times listed below were accurate as of this printing; most are daily and a few run Monday through Saturday, while others (not listed here) operate only on Sundays. Confirm times locally.

Trains leave La Spezia Centrale for all or most of the Cinque Terre villages at 7:12, 8:12, 10:07, 11:10, 12:00, 13:17, 13:27, 14:06, 15:10, 15:27, 16:01, 17:05, 17:13, 17:27, 18:06, 19:10, 19:29, 20:18, 21:23, 23:10, and 00:50.

Going back to La Spezia, trains leave Monterosso at 6:20, 7:12, 8:15, 9:29, 10:20, 11:00, 11:58 12:19, 13:26, 14:09, 14:20, 15:24, 16:07, 16:17, 17:30, 18:08, 18:20, 19:24, 20:20, 20:32, 20:43, 21:32, 22:24, 23:11, and 23:44 (same trains depart Vernazza about four minutes later).

Convenient TV monitors posted at several places in each station clearly show exactly what times the next trains are leaving in each direction (and if they're late, how late they are expected to be). I trust these monitors much more than my ability to read any printed schedule.

By Boat

From Easter through October, a daily boat service connects Monterosso, Vernazza, Manarola, Riomaggiore, and Portovenere. Boats provide a scenic way to get from town to town and survey what you just hiked. And boats offer the only efficient way to visit

Events in the Cinque Terre in 2011

For more festival information, check www.cinqueterre.it and www.turismoinliguria.it. The food festivals in particular are subject to change.

April 24–25	All towns: Easter Sunday and Monday
April 25	All towns: Liberation Day (stay away from the Cinque Terre this day, as locals literally shut down the trails)
May 1	All towns: Labor Day (another local holiday that packs the place)
May 14–15	Monterosso: Lemon Feast
June 2	All towns: Ascension Day
June 23	Monterosso: Feast of Corpus Domini (procession on carpet of flowers at 18:00)
June 18–19	Monterosso: Anchovies Festival
June 24	Riomaggiore and Monterosso: Festival in honor of St. John the Baptist (procession and fireworks; big fire on Monterosso's old town beach the day before)
June 29	Corniglia: Festival of St. Peter and St. Paul
July 20	Vernazza: Festival with fireworks for patron saint, St. Margaret
Aug 10	Manarola: Festival for patron saint, St. Lawrence
Aug 14	Monterosso: Fireworks on eve of Assumption of Mary (*Ferragosto*)
Aug 15	All towns: Assumption of Mary (*Ferragosto*)
Sept 17–18	Monterosso: Anchovies and Olive Oil Festival

the nearby resort of Portovenere (see next chapter; the alternative is a tedious train-bus connection via La Spezia). In peaceful weather, the boats can be more reliable than the trains, but if seas are rough,

they don't run at all. Because the boats nose in and tourists have to gingerly disembark onto little more than a plank, even a small chop can cancel some or all of the stops.

I see the tour boats as a syringe, injecting each town with a boost of euros. The towns are addicted, and they shoot up hourly through the summer. (Between 10:00–15:00—especially on weekends—masses of gawkers unload from boats, tour buses, and cruise ships, inundating the villages and changing the tenor of the region.)

Boats depart Monterosso about hourly (10:30–17:00), stopping at the Cinque Terre towns (except at Corniglia) and ending up an hour later in Portovenere. (Portovenere–Monterosso boats run 9:00–17:00.) The ticket price depends on the length of the boat ride (short hops-€5–6, longer hops-€8–10, five-town all-day pass-€15). Round-trip tickets are slightly cheaper than two one-way trips. You can buy tickets at little stands at each town's harbor (tel. 0187-732-987 and 0187-818-440). Another all-day boat pass for €23 extends to Portovenere and includes a 40-minute scenic ride around three small islands (2/day). Boats are not covered by the Cinque Terre Card, but are included in the Cinque Terre Treno e Batello Card. Boat schedules are posted at docks, harbor bars, Cinque Terre park offices, and hotels (www.navigazionegolfodeipoeti.it).

By Shuttle Bus

Shuttle buses connect each Cinque Terre town with its distant parking lot and various points in the hills (for example, from Corniglia's beach and train station to its hilltop town center). Note that these shuttle buses do not connect the towns with each other. Most rides cost €1.50 (and are covered by the Cinque Terre Card)—pick up bus schedules from a Cinque Terre park office or note the times posted on bus doors and at bus stops. Some (but not all) departures from Vernazza, Manarola, and Riomaggiore go beyond the parking lots and high into the hills. Pay for a round-trip ride and just cruise both ways to soak in the scenery (round-trip 30–45 minutes).

Hiking the Cinque Terre

All five towns are connected by good trails, marked with red-and-white paint, white arrows, and some signs. You'll experience the area's best by hiking all the way from one end to the other. While you can detour to dramatic hilltop sanctuaries, I'd keep it simple

by following trail #2—the low route between the villages. The entire seven-mile hike can be done in about four hours, but allow five for dawdling. Germans (with their task-oriented *Alpenstock* walking sticks) are notorious for marching too fast through the region. Take it slow...smell the cactus flowers and herbs, notice the lizards, listen to birds singing in the olive groves, and enjoy vistas on all sides.

Trails can be closed in bad weather or because of landslides. Remember that hikers need to pay a fee to enter the trails (see "Cinque Terre Cards," earlier in this chapter). If you're hiking the entire five-town route, consider that the trail between Riomaggiore (#1) and Manarola (#2) is easiest. The hike between Manarola and Corniglia (#3) has minor hills. The trail from Corniglia to Vernazza (#4) is challenging, while the path from Vernazza to Monterosso (#5) is the most challenging. For that hike, you might want to start in Monterosso in order to tackle the toughest section while you're fresh—and to enjoy the region's most dramatic scenery as you approach Vernazza.

Other than the wide, easy Riomaggiore–Manarola segment, the trail is generally narrow, rocky, and comes with lots of steps. Be warned that I get many emails from readers who say the trail was tougher than they expected. The rocks and metal grates can be slippery in the rain. Some readers wish they had brought their walking sticks or trekking poles, since there aren't any for sale here. While the trail is a bit of a challenge, it's perfectly doable for any fit hiker...and worth the sweat.

Maps aren't necessary for the basic coastal hikes described here. But for the expanded version of this hike (12 hours, from Portovenere to Levanto) and more serious hikes in the high country, pick up a good hiking map (about €5, sold everywhere). To leave the park cleaner than when you found it, bring a plastic bag *(sacchetto di plastica)* and pick up a little trail trash along the way. It would be great if American visitors—who get so much joy out of this region—were known for this good deed.

Riomaggiore–Manarola (20 minutes): Facing the front of the train station in Riomaggiore (#1), go up the stairs to the

right, following signs for *Via dell'Amore.* The photo-worthy promenade—wide enough for baby strollers—winds along the coast to Manarola (#2). It's primarily flat, and it's even wheelchair accessible since there are elevators at each end (elevators at Riomaggiore included in pass, elevator at Manarola for disabled use only). While there's no beach along the trail, stairs lead down to sunbathing rocks. A long tunnel and mega-nets protect hikers from mean-spirited rocks. The classy park-run Bar & Vini A Pie de Ma wine bar—located at the Riomaggiore trailhead—offers light meals, awesome town views, and clever boat storage under the train tracks (for more info, see page 336). There's also the scenic, peaceful cliffside Bar Via dell'Amore, serving homemade hot meals, closer to the Manarola end of the trail (daily in summer 9:00–24:00, until 20:00 off-season, light meals any time, full meals 12:00–15:00 & 19:30–21:30). The official park picnic area steeply rises above Bar Via dell'Amore on several terraces, with shaded picnic tables and a WC.

Manarola–Corniglia (45 minutes): The walk from Manarola (#2) to Corniglia (#3) is a little longer and more rugged and steep than the Via dell'Amore. It's also less romantic. To avoid the last stretch (switchback stairs leading up to the hill-capping town of Corniglia), end your hike at Corniglia's train station and catch the shuttle bus to the town center (2/hour, €1.50, free with Cinque Terre Card, usually timed to meet the trains).

Corniglia–Vernazza (90 minutes): The hike from Corniglia (#3) to Vernazza (#4)—the wildest and greenest section of the coast—is very rewarding but very hilly (going the other direction from Vernazza to Corniglia is steeper). From the Corniglia station and beach, zigzag up to the town (via the steep stairs, the longer road, or the shuttle bus). Ten minutes past Corniglia, toward Vernazza, you'll see Guvano beach far beneath you (once the region's nude beach). The scenic trail leads past a bar and picnic tables, through lots of fragrant and flowery vegetation, into Vernazza. If you need a break before reaching Vernazza, stop by Franco's Ristorante and Bar La Torre; it has a small menu but big views (between meal times only drinks are served; see listing on page 365).

Vernazza–Monterosso (90 minutes): The trail from Vernazza (#4) to Monterosso (#5) is a scenic up-and-down-a-lot trek. Trails are narrow and rough with a lot of steps (some readers report "very dangerous"), but easy to follow. Locals frown on camping at the picnic tables located midway. The views just out of Vernazza, looking back at the town, are spectacular.

Longer Hikes: Above the trails that run between the towns, higher-elevation hikes crisscross the region. Shuttle buses make the going easier, connecting coastal villages and trailheads in the hills. Ask locally about the more difficult six-mile inland hike to Volastra. This tiny village, perched between Manarola and Corniglia, hosts lots of Germans and Italians in the summertime. Just below its town center, in the hamlet of Groppo, is the Cinque Terre Cooperative Winery (see page 341). For the whole trip on the high road between Manarola and Corniglia, allow two hours one-way. In return, you'll get sweeping views and a closer look at the vineyards. Shuttle buses run from Manarola to Volastra (€2.50 or free with Cinque Terre Card, pick up schedule from park office,

Via dell'Amore

The Cinque Terre towns were extremely isolated until the last century. Villagers rarely married anyone from outside their town. After the blasting of the second train line in the 1920s, a trail was made between the first two towns: Riomaggiore and Manarola. A gunpowder warehouse was built along the way, safely away from the townspeople. (That building is today's Bar dell'Amore.)

Happy with the trail, the villagers asked that it be improved as a permanent connection between neighbors. But persistent landslides kept the trail closed more often than it was open. After World War II, the trail was reopened, and became established as a lovers' meeting point for boys and girls from the two towns. (After one extended closure in 1949, the trail was reopened for a Christmas marriage.) A journalist, who noticed all the amorous graffiti along the path, coined the trail's now-established name, Via dell'Amore: "Pathway of Love."

This new lane changed the social dynamics between the two villages, and made life much more fun and interesting for courting couples. Today, many tourists are put off by the cluttered graffiti that lines the trail. But it's all part of the history of the Cinque Terre's little lovers' lane.

You'll see padlocks locked to wires, cables, and fences. Closing a padlock with your lover at a lovey-dovey spot—often a bridge—is a common ritual in Italy (it was re-popularized by a teen novel a few years ago). In case you're so inclined, the hardware store next to Bar Centrale in Riomaggiore sells these locks.

The big news a few years ago was the completion of major construction work—including the addition of tunnels—to make the trail safer and keep it open permanently. Notice how the brick-lined arcades match the train tunnel below. Rock climbers from the north ("Dolomite spiders") were imported to help with the treacherous construction work. As you hike, look up and notice the massive steel netting bolted to the cliffside. Look down at the boulders that fell before the nets were added, and be thankful for those Dolomite spiders.

8/day, more departures in summer, 15 minutes); consider taking the bus up and hiking down.

Swimming, Kayaking, and Biking

Every town in the Cinque Terre has a beach or a rocky place to swim. Monterosso has the biggest and sandiest, with beach umbrellas and beach-use fees (but it's free where there are no umbrellas). Vernazza's is tiny—better for sunning than swimming. Manarola and Riomaggiore have the worst beaches (no sand), but Manarola offers the best deep-water swimming.

Wear your walking shoes and pack your swim gear. Several of the beaches have showers (no shampoo, please). Underwater sight-seeing is full of fish—goggles are sold in local shops. Sea urchins can be a problem if you walk on the rocks, and sometimes jellyfish wash up on the pebbles. If you have swim shoes, this is the place to wear them.

You can rent kayaks in Riomaggiore, Vernazza, and Monterosso. (For details, see individual town listings in this chapter.) Some readers say kayaking can be dangerous—the kayaks tip easily, training is not provided, and lifejackets are not required.

Mountain biking is also possible (park info booths in each town have details on rentals and maps of trails high above the coast). A free three-hour bike rental is included with the Cinque Terre Card (note that these bikes can be used only on specific bike trails, not the standard hiking trails).

Sleeping in the Cinque Terre

If you think too many people have my book, avoid Vernazza. You get fewer crowds and better value for your money in other towns. Monterosso is a good choice for sun-worshipping softies, those who prefer the ease of a real hotel, and the younger crowd (more nightlife). Hermits, anarchists, wine-lovers, and mountain goats like Corniglia. Sophisticated Italians and Germans choose Manarola. Riomaggiore is bigger than Vernazza and less resorty than Monterosso.

While the Cinque Terre is too rugged for the mobs that ravage the Spanish and French coasts, it's popular with Italians, Germans, and in-the-know Americans. Hotels charge more and are packed on holidays (including Easter), in July and August, and on Fridays and Saturdays all summer. August weekends are worst. But €65–70 doubles are available May–June and September–October—you'll end up paying at least €10–20 extra for July and August. The prices I've listed are the maximum for July–August. For a terrace or view, you might pay an extra €20 or more. Apartments for four can be economical for families—figure on €100–120.

In general, you'll pay the most for the comforts of a hotel in Monterosso, and the cheapest rooms are in Corniglia. Prices in Riomaggiore and Manarola are comparable (a double averages around €75). Rooms in Vernazza are smaller, and for a recently remodeled room, expect to pay €15–25 more.

Book ahead if you'll be visiting in June, July, August, on a weekend, or around a holiday (for specific dates, see "Events in the Cinque Terre in 2011," earlier in this chapter, and the list of Italian holidays in the appendix). At other times, you can land a double

room on any day by just arriving in town (ideally by noon) and asking around at bars and restaurants, or simply by approaching locals on the street. Many travelers enjoy the opportunity to shop around a bit and get the best price by bargaining. Private rooms—called *affitta camere*—are no longer an intimate stay with a family. They are generally comfortable apartments (often with small kitchens) where you get the key and come and go as you like, rarely seeing your landlord. Many landowners rent the buildings by the year to local managers, who then attempt to make a profit by filling them night after night with tourists.

For the best value, visit two private rooms and snare the best. Going direct cuts out a middleman and softens prices. Staying more than one night gives you bargaining leverage. Plan on paying cash. Private rooms are generally bigger and more comfortable than those offered by the pensions and offer the same privacy as a hotel room.

If you want the security of a reservation, make it at a hotel long in advance (smaller places generally don't take reservations very far ahead). Query by email, not fax. If you do reserve, honor your reservation (or, if you must cancel, do it as early as possible). Since people renting rooms usually don't take deposits, they lose money if you don't show up. Cutthroat room hawkers at the train stations might try to lure you away from a room that you've already reserved with offers of cheaper rates. Don't do it. You owe it to your hosts to stick with your original reservation.

Some hoteliers and individuals renting rooms in the Cinque Terre take advantage of the demand by artificially bumping up prices. This problem seems most prevalent in Vernazza and Riomaggiore. Shop around before you commit. Due to the global economic slump, travelers will have more negotiating power this year.

Eating in the Cinque Terre

Hanging out at a seaview restaurant while sampling local specialties could become one of your favorite memories.

Tegame alla Vernazza is the most typical main course in Vernazza: anchovies, potatoes, tomatoes, white wine, oil, and herbs. Anchovies (*acciughe*; ah-CHOO-gay) are ideally served the day they're caught. If you've always hated anchovies (the harsh, cured-in-salt American kind), try them fresh here. *Pansotti* are ravioli with ricotta and a mixture of greens, often served with a walnut sauce...delightful and filling.

While antipasto means cheese and salami in Tuscany, here you'll get *antipasti frutti di mare*, a plate of mixed "fruits of the sea" and a fine way to start a meal. Many restaurants are particularly proud of their *antipasti frutti di mare*. Splitting one of these and a pasta dish can be plenty.

This region is the birthplace of pesto. Basil, which loves the temperate Ligurian climate, is ground with cheese (half parmigiano cow cheese and half pecorino sheep cheese), garlic, olive oil, and pine nuts, and then poured over pasta. Try it on spaghetti, *trenette*, or *trofie* (made of flour with a bit of potato, designed specifically for pesto to cling to). Many also like pesto lasagna, always made with white sauce, never red. If you become addicted, small jars of pesto are sold in the local grocery stores and gift shops. If it's refrigerated, it's fresh; this is what you want if you're eating it today. For taking home, get the jar-on-a-shelf pesto.

Focaccia, the tasty pillowy bread, also originates here in Liguria. Locals say the best focaccia is made between the Cinque Terre and Genoa. It's simply flatbread with olive oil and salt. The baker roughs up the dough with finger holes, then bakes it. Focaccia comes plain or with onions, sage, or olive bits, and is a local favorite for a snack on the beach. Bakeries sell it in rounds or slices by the weight (a portion is about 100 grams, or *un etto*).

Farinata, a humble fried bread snack, is made from chickpea meal, water, oil, and pepper, and baked on a copper tray in a wood-burning stove. *Farinata* is sold at pizza and focaccia places.

The *vino delle Cinque Terre*, while not one of Italy's top wines, flows cheap and easy throughout the region. It's white—great with seafood. For a sweet dessert wine, the *sciacchetrà* wine is worth the splurge (€4 per small glass, often served with a cookie). You could order the fun dessert, *torta della nonna* (grandmother's cake), and dunk chunks of it into your glass. Aged *sciacchetrà* is dry and costly (up to €12/glass). While 10 kilos of grapes yield seven liters of local wine, *sciacchetrà* is made from near-raisins, and 10 kilos of grapes make only 1.5 liters of *sciacchetrà*. The word means "push and pull"—push in lots of grapes, pull out the best wine. If your room is up a lot of steps, be warned: *Sciacchetrà* is 18 percent alcohol, while regular wine is only 11 percent.

In the cool, calm evening, sit on Vernazza's breakwater with a glass of wine and watch the phosphorescence in the waves.

Nightlife in the Cinque Terre

While the Cinque Terre is certainly not noted for bumping beach-town nightlife like nearby Viareggio, you'll find some sort of travel-tale-telling hub in Monterosso, Vernazza, and Riomaggiore (Manarola and Corniglia are sleepy). Monterosso has a lively scene, especially in the summertime—but no discoteca yet. In Vernazza the nightlife centers in the bars on the waterfront piazza, which is the small-town-style place to "see and be seen." Bar Centrale in Riomaggiore is, well, the central place for cocktails and meeting fellow travelers (see "Nightlife" in each village for more details). Wherever your night adventures take you, have fun, but please remember that residents live upstairs.

Helpful Hints for the Cinque Terre

Tourist and Park Information: Each town (except Corniglia) has a well-staffed TI and park office (listed throughout this chapter).

Money: Banks and ATMs are plentiful throughout the region.

Baggage Storage: You can store bags at La Spezia's train station (see page 409) and the National Park kiosk at Riomaggiore's train station (but not overnight).

Services: Every train station has a handy public WC. Otherwise, pop into a bar or restaurant.

Taxi: Cinqueterre Taxi covers all five towns (mobile 328-583-4969, www.cinqueterretaxi.com, info@cinqueterretaxi.com).

Local Guides: Andrea Bordigoni (€110/half-day, €175/day, mobile 347-972-3317, bordigo@inwind.it) and **Paola Tommarchi** (€120/half-day, €175/day, mobile 334-109-7887, paolatomma @alice.it) both offer good tours.

Booking Agency: Miriana and Filippo at **Cinque Terre Riviera** book rooms in the Cinque Terre towns, Portovenere, and La Spezia for a 10 percent markup over the list price (can also arrange transportation, cooking classes, and weddings; Via Picedi 18 in La Spezia; tel. 0187-520-702, Miriana—mobile 340-794-7358, Filippo—mobile 393-939-1901, www .cinqueterreriviera.com, info@cinqueterreriviera.com, English spoken).

Cheap Tricks: Consider arriving without a reservation and bargaining with locals for a private room; staying more than one night and paying cash should get you a double for around €65 (this is possible anytime, but safest on weekdays Sept–May). Many rooms come with kitchenettes, and bakeries and food shops make meals to go. Picnic tables along the trail come with a first-class view. Even hobos can afford the major delights of the Cinque Terre: hiking, nursing a drink at the harbor, strolling with the locals through town, and enjoying the beach.

Riomaggiore (Town #1)

The most substantial non-resort town of the group, Riomaggiore is a disappointment from the train station. But once you leave that neighborhood, you'll discover a fascinating tangle of pastel homes leaning on each other like drunken sailors. Just walk through the tunnel next to the train tracks (or ride the elevator through the hillside to the top of town). You'll find the rooms are priced right.

Orientation to Riomaggiore

Tourist Information

The TI is in the train station at the ticket desk (daily 6:30–20:00, tel. 0187-920-633). If the TI in the station is crowded, buy your hiking pass at the Cinque Terre park shop/ information office next door by the mural (daily 8:00–19:30, tel. 0187-760-515, net pointriomaggiore@parconazionale5terre .it). For a less-formal information source, try Ivo and Alberto, who run Bar Centrale (described later in this section).

Arrival in Riomaggiore

The bus shuttles locals and tourists up and down Riomaggiore's steep main street and continues to the parking lot outside of town (€1.50 one-way, €2.50 round-trip, free with Cinque Terre Card, 2/hour, main stop at the fork of Via Colombo and Via Malborghetto, or flag it down as it passes). If you park at the lot (€3/hour or €22/day), use cash—some readers have been overcharged on their credit cards. About seven buses a day head into the hills, where you'll find the region's top high-country activities (for details, see "Sights in Riomaggiore," later).

Helpful Hints

Internet Access: The **park shop** and information office has eight Internet terminals upstairs and Wi-Fi (€5/hour, daily May–Sept 8:00–22:00, Oct–April until 19:30). **Hotel Zorzara** has

Riomaggiore

VIA DELL'AMORE TO MANAROLA

MURALS

SAN GIOVANNI CHURCH

ELEVATOR

ELEVATOR TO HIGH ROAD

TRAIN STATION

VIA GASPERI

VIA SIGNORINI

CINQUE TERRE INFO

PED. TUNNEL

VIA

V. MALB.

VIA COLOMBO

VIA SANT.

LIGURIAN SEA

NOT TO SCALE

N

HARBOR & BOAT DOCK

TO 20

BOAT TICKETS

"BEACH" SWIMMING & SHOWERS

STAIRS

DCH

1. Locanda del Sole
2. Locanda Ca' dei Duxi
3. Mar Mar/Il Grifone Rooms
4. La Dolce Vita Rooms
5. Locanda dalla Compagnia
6. Edi's Rooms & Launderette
7. Villa Argentina
8. Ristorante la Lampara
9. La Lanterna Restaurant
10. Ristorante Ripa del Sole
11. Te La Do Io La Merenda Snack Bar
12. Enoteca & Ristorante Dau Cila
13. Bar & Vini A Pie de Ma
14. Co-op Groceries (2)
15. Bar Centrale & Gelateria
16. Bar dell'Amore
17. Internet Access (Hotel Zorzara)
18. Boat Dock
19. To Madonna di Montenero Trail
20. To Torre Guardiola Pathway & WWII Bunkers
21. Park Office Kiosk (Bag Storage)

THE CINQUE TERRE

two terminals in town and charges about the same (daily 11:00–21:30, under the archway just past the first Co-op grocery store).

Baggage Storage: The attendant at the train station park office will open the kiosk next door to store your bags (€0.50/hour per piece, €6 surcharge if left longer than 6 hours, daily 8:00–19:45, no overnight storage, passport required).

Laundry: A self-service launderette is on the main street (€3.50 wash, €3.50 dry, daily 8:30–20:00, run by Edi's Rooms next door, Via Colombo 111).

Bike Rental: Ask at the TI about where to go to pick up a bike (first 3 hours free with Cinque Terre Card, then €1.50/hour, passport or €50 deposit required).

Self-Guided Walk

Welcome to Riomaggiore

Here's an easy loop trip that maximizes views and minimizes uphill walking.

• *Start at the train station. (If you arrive by boat, cross beneath the tracks and take a left, then hike through the tunnel along the tracks to reach the station.) You'll come to some...*

Colorful Murals: These murals, with subjects modeled after real-life Riomaggiorians, glorify the nameless workers who constructed the nearly 300 million cubic feet of dry stone walls (without cement). These walls run throughout the Cinque Terre, giving the region its characteristic *muri a secco* terracing for vineyards and olive groves. These murals, done by Argentinean artist Silvio Benedetto, are well-explained in English but may be covered for restoration on your visit.

• *Head to the railway tunnel entrance, and ride the elevator to the top of town (€0.50 or €1 family ticket, free with Cinque Terre Card, daily 8:00–19:45). You're at the...*

Top o' the Town: Here you're treated to spectacular sea views. To continue the view-fest, go right and follow the walkway (ignore the steps marked *Marina Seacoast* that lead to the harbor). It's a five-minute level stroll to the church. You'll pass under the city hall (flying two flags) with murals celebrating the heroic grape pickers and fishermen of the region (also by Silvio Benedetto).

• *Before reaching the church, pause to enjoy the...*

Town View: The major river of this region once ran through this valley, as implied by the name Riomaggiore (local dialect for "river" and "major"). As in the other Cinque Terre towns, the river ravine is now paved over, and the romantic arched bridges that once connected the two sides have been replaced by a practical modern road.

Notice the lack of ugly aerial antennae. In the 1980s, every residence got cable. Now, the TV tower on the hilltop behind the church steeple brings the modern world into each home. While the church was rebuilt in 1870, it was first built in 1340. It's dedicated to St. John the Baptist, the patron saint of Genoa, a maritime republic that dominated the region. The elevator next to the church may be completed by the time you get here. It's to help seniors get around the steep town, and also to link to the elevator near the Via dell'Amore trailhead.

• *Continue past the church down to Riomaggiore's main street, named...*

Via Colombo: Walk about 30 feet after the WC, go down the stairs, and pop into the tiny Cinque Terre Antiche museum (€0.50, free with Cinque Terre Card, daily 9:30–13:00 & 14:00–18:00). Sit down for a few minutes to watch a circa-1950 video of the Cinque Terre.

Continuing down Via Colombo, you'll pass a bakery, a couple of grocery shops, and the self-service laundry. There's homemade gelato next to the Bar Centrale. When Via Colombo dead-ends, to the left you'll find the stairs down to the Marina neighborhood, with the harbor, the boat dock, a 200-yard trail to the beach *(spiaggia)*, and an inviting little art gallery. To the right of the stairs is the tunnel, running alongside the tracks, which takes you directly back to the station and the trail to the other towns. From here, you can take a train, hop a boat, or hike to your next destination.

Sights in Riomaggiore

Beach—Riomaggiore's rugged and tiny "beach" is rocky, but it's clean and peaceful. Take a two-minute walk from the harbor: Face the harbor, then follow the path to your left. Passing the rugged boat landing, stay on the path to the beach.

Kayaks and Water Sports—The town has a diving center (scuba, snorkeling, kayaks, and small motorboats; office down the stairs and under the tracks on Via San Giacomo, daily May–Sept 9:00–18:00, tel. 0187-920-011, www.5terrediving.it).

Hikes—Consider the cliff-hanging Torre Guardiola trail that leads from the beach up to old WWII bunkers and a hilltop botanical pathway of native flora and fauna with English information (free with Cinque Terre Card, daily 10:00–18:30, steep 20-minute climb, take the stairs between the boat dock and the beach). Another trail rises scenically to the 14th-century Madonna di Montenero sanctuary, high above the town (45 minutes, take the main road inland until you see signs, or ride the green shuttle bus 12 minutes from the town center to the sanctuary trail, then walk uphill five minutes, details at park office next to the train station, park center at the sanctuary offers bike rental).

THE CINQUE TERRE

Nightlife in Riomaggiore

Bar Centrale, run by sociable Ivo, Alberto, and the gang, offers "nightlife" any time of day—making it a good stop for Italian breakfast and music. Ivo, who lived in San Francisco and speaks good English, fills his bar with San Franciscan rock and a fun-loving vibe. During the day, this is a shaded place to relax with other travelers. At night, it offers the younger set the liveliest action (and best *mojitos*) in town. They also serve €5 fast-food pastas and microwaved pizzas (daily 7:30–24:00 or later, closed Mon in winter, in the town center at Via Colombo 144, tel. 0187-920-208). There's a good *gelateria* next door.

Enoteca & Ristorante Dau Cila, a cool little hideaway down at the miniscule harbor with a mellow jazz-and-Brazilian-lounge ambience, is a counterpoint to wild Bar Centrale (snacks and meals, fine wine by the glass; see "Eating in Riomaggiore," page 336).

Bar & Vini A Pie de Ma, at the beginning of Via dell'Amore, has piles of charm, often music, and stays open until midnight in the summer.

The marvelous **Via dell'Amore** trail, lit only with subtle ground lighting so that you can see the stars, welcomes romantics after dark. The trail is free after 19:30 (for its history, see the "Via dell'Amore" sidebar, page 325).

Sleeping in Riomaggiore

Riomaggiore has arranged its private-room rental system better than its neighbors. Several agencies—with regular office hours, English-speaking staff, and email addresses—line up within a few yards of each other on the main drag. Each manages a corral of local rooms for rent. These offices can close unexpectedly, so it's smart to settle up the day before you leave in case they're closed when you need to depart. Expect lots of stairs. If you don't mind the hike, the street above town has safe overnight parking (free 20:00–8:00).

Room-Finding Services

$$$ Locanda del Sole has seven modern, basic, and overpriced rooms with a shared and peaceful terrace. Located at the utilitarian top end of town, it's a five-minute walk downhill to the center. Easy parking makes it especially appealing to drivers (Db-€130, free parking with this book, Via Santuario 114, tel. & fax 0187-920-773, mobile 340-983-0090, www.locandadelsole.net, info @locandadelsole.net, Enrico).

$$$ Locanda Ca' dei Duxi rents 10 good rooms from an efficient little office on the main drag (Db-€100–130 depending on

Sleep Code

(€1 = about $1.25, country code: 39)
S = Single, **D** = Double/Twin, **T** = Triple, **Q** = Quad, **b** = bathroom, **s** = shower only. Unless otherwise noted, credit cards are accepted, English is spoken, and breakfast is included (except in Vernazza).

To help you sort easily through these listings, I've divided the rooms into three categories based on the price for a standard double room with bath:

$$$ Higher Priced—Most rooms €100 or more.
$$ Moderately Priced—Most rooms between €50-100.
$ Lower Priced—Most rooms €50 or less.

Prices can change without notice; verify the hotel's current rates online or by email. For other updates, see www.ricksteves.com/update.

view and season, extra person-€20, air-con; parking-€10/day, book when you reserve; open year-round, Via Colombo 36, tel. & fax 0187-920-036, mobile 329-825-7836, www.duxi.it, info@duxi.it, Samuele).

$$ Mar Mar/Il Grifone Rooms offers 12 rooms and 15 apartments, with American expats Amy and Maddy smoothing communications (Db-€60–90 depending on view, Db suite with top view-€120, cash only, reception open 9:00–17:00 in season, Via Colombo 181, tel. & fax 0187-920-932, www.5terre-marmar.com, info@5terre-marmar.com). Try calling if you don't get a return email. They also run a mini-hostel in a fine communal apartment with a cool living room, terrace, and kitchen in a good, quiet location. Take care of this little treasure so it survives (9 beds in 3 rooms, €22/bed).

$$ La Dolce Vita offers three rooms on the main drag and two apartments around town (Db-€60–80, open daily 9:30–19:30; if they're closed, they're full; Via Colombo 120, tel. & fax 0187-760-044, mobile 349-326-6803, agonatal@interfree.it, helpful Giacomo and Simone).

$$ Locanda dalla Compagnia rents five modern rooms at the top of town, just 300 yards below the parking lot and the little church. All rooms—nice but rather dim—are on the same ground floor, sharing an inviting lounge. Franca runs it with Giovanna's help (Db-€70, cash only, air-con, mini-fridge, no view, Via del Santuario 232, tel. 0187-760-050, fax 0187-920-586, lacomp @libero.it).

THE CINQUE TERRE

$$ Edi's Rooms rents 20 rooms and apartments. You pay extra for views (Db-€70–120 depending on room, apartment Qb-€100–160, reserve with credit card, office open daily 8:30–20:00 in summer, winter 10:30–12:30 & 14:30–19:00, some rooms involve climbing a lot of steps—ask before viewing or reserving, Via Colombo 111, tel. 0187-760-842, tel. & fax 0187-920-325, www.lancoracinqueterre.com, edi-vesigna@iol.it).

For Drivers: **$$$ Villa Argentina** has 16 plain rooms, many with views overlooking the town. It makes up for its sterility with friendly staff, easy access to the elevator to San Giovanni Church, and a sunny, communal terrace (Db-€130 with view, fans, parking-€15/day, Via de Gasperi 170, tel. 0187-920-213, fax 0187-760-531, www.villargentina.com, villaargentina@libero.it).

Eating in Riomaggiore

Ristorante la Lampara serves a *frutti di mare* pizza, *trenette al pesto,* and the aromatic *spaghetti al cartoccio*—€11 oven-cooked spaghetti with seafood in foil (daily 7:00–24:00, closed Tue in winter, just above tracks off Via Colombo at Via Malborghetto 10, tel. 0187-920-120).

La Lanterna, dressier than the Lampara, is wedged into a niche in the Marina, overlooking the harbor under the tracks (daily 12:00–22:00, Via San Giacomo 10, tel. 0187-920-589).

Ristorante Ripa del Sole is the local pick for an elegant night out, with the same prices and better quality than the Lampara and Lanterna. The €13 antipasto "Cinque Terre" gives you five tastes of anchovy specialties (Tue–Sun 12:00–14:00 & 18:30–21:30, closed Mon, closed Jan–Feb, 10-minute hike above town, Via de Gasperi 282, tel. 0187-920-143).

Te La Do Io La Merenda ("I'll Give You a Snack") is good for a snack, pizza, or takeout. Their counter is piled with an assortment of munchies, and they have pastas, roasted chicken, and focaccia sandwiches to go (daily 9:00–21:00, Via Colombo 161, tel. 0187-920-148).

Enoteca & Ristorante Dau Cila is the *nuovo chic* of the Cinque Terre, decked out like a black-and-white movie set in a centuries-old boat shed. Try their antipasto specialty of several seafood appetizers, and listen to jazz with the waves lapping at the harbor below (€12 pastas, €18 *secondi,* March–Oct daily until 24:00, Via San Giacomo 65, tel. 0187-760-032, Luca).

Bar & Vini A Pie de Ma, at the trailhead on the Manarola end of town, is a nice place for a scenic light bite or quiet drink at night. Enjoying a meal at a table on its dramatically situated terrace provides an indelible Cinque Terre memory (daily 10:00–20:00, until 24:00 in summer, tel. 0187-921-037).

Picnics: Groceries and delis on Via Colombo sell food to go, including pizza slices, for a picnic at the harbor or beach. The two **Co-op groceries,** one at the top and one at the bottom of the main street, are the least expensive and will make sandwiches to go (daily 7:30–13:00 & 17:00–19:30, Via Colombo 55 and 205).

Manarola (Town #2)

Like Riomaggiore, Manarola is attached to its station by a 200-yard-long tunnel. During WWII air raids, these tunnels provided refuge and a safe place for rattled villagers to sleep. The town itself fills a ravine, bookended by its wild little harbor to the west and a diminutive church square inland to the east. A delightful and gentle stroll, from the church down to the harborside park, provides the region's easiest little vineyard walk (described in my "Self-Guided Walk," next page).

Orientation to Manarola

Arrival in Manarola

The TI next to the train station is open daily 7:00–20:00. A shuttle bus runs between the low end of Manarola's main street (at the *tabacchi* shop and newsstand) and the parking lot (€1.50 one-way, €2.50 round-trip, free with Cinque Terre Card, 2/hour, just flag it down). Shuttle buses also run about hourly from Manarola to Volastra, near the Cinque Terre Cooperative Winery (see "Sights in Manarola," later).

To get to the dock and the boats that connect Manarola with the other Cinque Terre towns, find the steps to the left of the harbor view—they lead down to the ticket kiosk. Continue around the left side of the cliff (as you're facing the water) to catch the boats.

Note that the Cassa di Risparmio della Spezia ATM at the bottom of the main street (near the entrance to the train-station tunnel) is notorious for running out of euros, especially in summer. It's been known to charge users' accounts without spitting out the *soldi* (cash)—avoid using it.

THE CINQUE TERRE

Self-Guided Walk

Welcome to Manarola

From the harbor, this 30-minute circular walk shows you the town and surrounding vineyards, and ends at a fantastic viewpoint, perfect for a picnic.

• *Start down at the waterfront.*

The Harbor: Manarola is tiny and picturesque, a tumble of buildings bunny-hopping down its ravine to the fun-loving waterfront. Notice how the I-beam crane launches the boats. Facing the harbor, look to the right, at the hillside Punta Bonfiglio cemetery and park (where this walk ends).

The town's swimming hole is just below. Manarola has no sand, but offers the best deep-water swimming in the area. The first "beach" has a shower, ladder, and wonderful rocks. The second has tougher access and no shower, but feels more remote and pristine (follow the paved path toward Corniglia, just around the point). For many, the tricky access makes this beach dangerous.

• *Hiking inland up the town's main drag, you'll come to the train tracks covered by Manarola's new square, called...*

Piazza Capellini: Built in 2004, this square is an all-around great idea, giving the town a safe, fun zone for kids. Locals living near the tracks also enjoy a little less noise. Check out the mosaic that displays the varieties of local fish in colorful enamel.

• *Fifty yards uphill, you'll find the...*

Sciacchetrà Museum: Run by the national park, it's hardly a museum. But pop in to its inviting room to see a tiny exhibit on the local wine industry (€0.50, free with Cinque Terre Card, daily 9:30–13:00 & 13:30–18:00, 15-minute video in English by request, 100 yards uphill from train tracks, across from the post office).

• *Hiking farther uphill, you can still hear...*

Manarola's Stream: As in Riomaggiore, Monterosso, and Vernazza, Manarola's stream was covered over by a modern sewage system after World War II. Before that time, romantic bridges arched over its ravine. A modern waterwheel recalls the origin of the town's name—local dialect for "big wheel" (one of many possible derivations). Mills like this once powered the local olive oil industry.

• *Keep climbing until you come to the square at the...*

Top of Manarola: The square is faced by a church, an oratory—now a religious and community meeting place—and a bell tower, which served as a watch tower when pirates raided the town

Manarola

NOT TO SCALE
)))) STAIRS   ⚘ VIEW

TO CORNIGLIA

SWIMMING

PUNTA BONFIGLIO

CEMETERY   PIAZZA

SWIMMING & SHOWER

BOAT DOCK

SAN LORENZO CHURCH

TO PARKING, & CINQUE TERRE CO-OP WINERY &

BELL TOWER   CHAPEL

MAIN ST.

PEDESTRIAN TUNNEL

TRAIN STATION

LIGURIAN SEA

VIA DELL' AMORE TRAIL

TO RIOMAGGIORE

❶ La Torretta Rooms
❷ Marina Piccola Rooms & Restaurant
❸ Albergo Ca' d'Andrean
❹ Carugiu B&B & Casa Capellini
❺ Michela Rooms
❻ Ariadmare Rooms
❼ Ostello 5-Terre
❽ To Hotel il Saraceno
❾ Trattoria Il Porticciolo
❿ Trattoria Dal Billy
⓫ Shuttle Bus to Parking Lot & Volastra
⓬ Manarola Vineyard Walk

(the cupola was added once the attacks ceased). Behind the church is Manarola's well-run youth hostel—originally the church's schoolhouse. To the right of the oratory, a lane leads to Manarola's sizable tourist-free zone.

While you're here, check out the church. According to the white marble plaque in its facade, the Parish Church of St. Lawrence dates from "MCCCXXXVIII" (1338). Step inside to see two paintings from the unnamed "Master of the Cinque Terre," the only painter of any note from the region (left wall and above main altar). While the style is Gothic, the work dates from the late 15th century, long after Florence had entered the Renaissance.

• Walk 20 yards below the church and find a wooden railing. It marks the start of a delightful stroll around the high side of town, and back to the seafront. This is the beginning of the...

Manarola Vineyard Walk: Don't miss this experience. Simply follow the wooden railing, enjoying lemon groves and wild red valerian (used for insomnia since the days of the Romans). Along the path, which is primarily flat, you'll get a close-up look at the region's famous dry-stone walls and finely crafted vineyards (with dried-heather thatches to protect the grapes from the southwest winds). Smell the rosemary. Study the structure of the town, and pick out the scant remains of an old fort. Notice the S-shape of the main road—once a riverbed—that flows through town. The town's roofs are traditionally made of locally quarried slate, rather than tile, and are held down by rocks during windstorms. As the harbor comes into view, you'll see the breakwater, added just a decade ago.

Out of sight above you on the right are simple wooden religious scenes, the work of local resident Mario Andreoli. Before his father died, Mario promised him he'd replace the old cross on the family's vineyard. Mario has been adding figures ever since. After recovering from a rare illness, he redoubled his efforts. On religious holidays, everything's lit up: the Nativity, the Last Supper, the Crucifixion, the Resurrection, and more. Some of the scenes are left up year-round.

• *This trail ends at a T-intersection, where it hits the main coastal trail. Turn left. (A right takes you to the trail to Corniglia.) Before descending back into town, take a right, detouring into...*

The Cemetery: Ever since Napoleon—who was king of Italy in the early 1800s—decreed that cemeteries were health risks, Cinque Terre's burial spots have been located outside of town. The result: The dearly departed generally get first-class sea views. Each cemetery—with its evocative yellowed photos and finely carved Carrara marble memorial reliefs—is worth a visit. (The basic structure for all of them is the same, but Manarola's is most easily accessible.)

In cemeteries like these, there's a hierarchy of four places to park your mortal remains: a graveyard, a spacious death condo (*loculo*), a mini bone-niche (*ossario*), or the communal ossuary. Because of the tight space, a time limit is assigned to the first three options (although many older tombs are grandfathered in). Bones go into the ossuary in the middle of the chapel floor after about a generation. Traditionally, locals make weekly visits to loved ones here, often bringing flowers. The rolling stepladder makes access to top-floor *loculi* easy.

• *The Manarola cemetery is on Punta Bonfiglio. Walk just below it, farther out through a park (playground, drinking water, WC, and picnic benches). Your Manarola finale: the bench at the tip of the point, offering one of the most commanding views of the entire region. The easiest way back to town is to take the stairs at the end of the point.*

Sights in Manarola

Wine Tasting—Hike or ride the green shuttle bus to the Cinque Terre Cooperative Winery (La Cantina Sociale) in the village of Groppo for a tour and wine tasting. Depending on the weather, a guide will take you around the vineyards as well as the winery, where they produce a dry white and the prized *sciacchetrà* sweet wine (€5–11, English may be spotty, Mon–Sat 7:00–19:00, Sun 9:00–12:30 & 14:30–19:00, tel. 0187-920-076).

Getting There: To hike, follow the road past the Manarola parking lot, look for trail markers, stay straight when trail #2 splits to the right, and then go uphill once the trail hits the street. It takes about 30 minutes. By bus, catch the shuttle at the lower end of the main street or flag it down. Ask the driver to drop you off at La Cantina or it might not stop (€1.50 one-way, €2.50 round-trip, free with Cinque Terre Card, 8/day, more in summer, 10 minutes).

Sleeping in Manarola

(€1 = about $1.25, country code: 39)
Manarola has plenty of private rooms. Ask in bars and restaurants. There's a modern three-star place halfway up the main drag, a sea-view hotel on the harbor, a big modern hostel, and a cluster of options around the church at the peaceful top of the town (a 5-minute hike from the train tracks).

$$$ La Torretta is a trendy, upscale 13-room place that caters to a demanding clientele. It's a peaceful refuge with all the comforts for those happy to pay, including a communal hot tub with a view. Enjoy a complimentary snack and glass of prosecco on arrival and free wine tastings during your stay (smaller Db-€135, regular Db-€180, Db suite-€250, 8 percent discount with cash, book several months in advance as it is justifiably popular, Wi-Fi, on Piazza della Chiesa beside the bell tower at Vico Volto 20, tel. 0187-920-327, fax 0187-760-024, www.torrettas.com, torretta @cdh.it, Gabriele).

$$$ Marina Piccola offers 13 bright, slick rooms on the water—so they figure a warm welcome is unnecessary (Db-€115, buffet breakfast, air-con, Via Birolli 120, tel. 0187-920-103, fax 0187-920-966, www.hotelmarinapiccola.com, info@hotelmarina piccola.com).

$$$ Albergo Ca' d'Andrean, run by Simone, is quiet, comfortable, and modern—except for its antiquated reservation system. While the welcome is formal at best, it has 10 big, sunny air-conditioned rooms and a cool garden oasis complete with lemon trees (Sb-€72, Db-€100, breakfast-€6, cash only, send personal or traveler's check to reserve from US—or call if you're reserving from the road, closed Nov–Christmas, up the hill at Via A. Discovolo 101, tel. 0187-920-040, fax 0187-920-452, www.cadandrean.it, cadandrean@libero.it).

$$ Carugiu B&B rents two no-view rooms at the top of town (Db–€65, Db suite–€80, €5/day less with 3-night stay, Via Ettore Cozzani 42, tel. 0187-920-359, English-speaking daughter-in-law Cristina's mobile 349-346-9208, www.carugiu.com, info@carugiu.com).

$$ Casa Capellini rents four rooms: One has a view balcony, another a 360-degree terrace—book long in advance (Sb–€40, Db–€70; €90 for the *alta camera* on the top, with a kitchen, private terrace, and knockout view; two doors down the hill from the church—with your back to the church, it's at 2 o'clock; Via Ettore Cozzani 12, tel. 0187-920-823 or 0187-736-765, www.casa capellini-5terre.it, casa.capellini@tin.it, Gianni and Franca don't speak English).

$$ Michela Rooms has two spacious, modern rooms—one is an apartment (Db–€75) and the other is a simple double (Db–€65). You trek up the hill for the good prices, not for good views (no breakfast, air-con, located near recommended Trattoria Dal Billy at Via Rollando 221, she'll meet you at the station, mobile 320-184-0930, www.michelarooms5terre.com).

$$ Ariadmare Rooms rents four modern, sunny rooms and an apartment 20 yards beyond Trattoria Dal Billy at the very top of town. Three rooms have spacious terraces with knockout views (Db–€80, 2 adults and 1 child–€80, Db apartment–€90, these prices promised through 2011, no breakfast, Wi-Fi, up stairs on the left at Via Aldo Rollandi 137, tel. 0187-920-367, mobile 349-058-455, http://ariadimare.info, ask at Billy's if no one's home). Maurizio speaks a little English, while Mamma Franca communicates with lots of Italian and toothy smiles.

$ Ostello 5-Terre, Manarola's modern and pleasant hostel, occupies the former parochial school above the church square and offers 48 beds in four- to six-bed rooms. Nicola and Riccardo run a calm and peaceful place—it's not a party hostel—and quiet is greatly appreciated. They rent dorm rooms as doubles. Reserve well in advance. Full means full—they don't accommodate the desperate on the floor (Easter–mid-Oct: dorm beds–€23, Db–€65, Qb–€100; off-season: dorm beds–€20, Db–€55, Qb–€88; closed Nov–Feb; not co-ed except for couples and families; no membership necessary; optional €5 breakfast and €5–6 pasta; in summer, office closed 13:00–17:00, rooms closed 10:00–17:00, 1:00 curfew; off-season, office and rooms closed until 16:00, strict midnight curfew; open to all ages, laundry, safes, phone cards, Internet access, book exchange, elevator, great roof terrace and sunset views, Via B. Riccobaldi 21, tel. 0187-920-215, fax 0187-920-218, www.hostel5terre.com, info@hostel5terre.com). Book online with your credit-card number; note that you'll be charged for one night if you cancel with fewer than three days' notice.

For Drivers: $$$ Hotel il Saraceno, with seven spacious, modern rooms, is a deal for drivers. Located above Manarola in the tiny town of Volastra (chock full of vacationing Germans and Italians in summer), it's serene, clean, and right by the shuttle bus to Manarola (Db-€100, buffet breakfast, Wi-Fi, free parking, Via Volastra 8, tel. 0187-760-081, fax 0187-760-791, www.thesaraceno.com, hotel@thesaraceno.com, friendly Antonella).

Eating in Manarola

Many hardworking places line the main drag. I like the Scorza family's friendly **Trattoria Il Porticciolo** (€7 pastas, tasty seafood-based dishes, free glass of *sciacchetrà* dessert wine with this book, Thu–Tue 10:30–22:30, closed Wed, reservations smart for dinner, just below the train tracks at Via R. Birolli 92, tel. 0187-920-083, Davide).

For harborside dining, **Marina Piccola** is the winner. While less friendly and a little more expensive, the setting is memorable (€10 pastas, Wed–Mon 11:30–16:30 & 18:30–22:00, closed Tue, tel. 0187-920-923).

Trattoria Dal Billy is a hidden gem, high on the hill but well worth the climb, with impressive views over the valley. It's run by two friends, Edoardo and Dario; the original "Billy"—a retired sea captain—still helps out and will regale you with fisherman's tales as you survey the photo gallery of impressive catches. Among your choices are black pasta with seafood and squid ink, green pasta with artichokes, mixed seafood starters, and homemade desserts. Dinner reservations are a must (€11 pastas, €14 *secondi,* generally daily 8:00–10:00, 12:00–15:00 & 19:00–23:30, sometimes closed Thu, Via Aldo Rollandi 122, tel. 0187-920-628). Exit the church square at the top of Manarola right at the back by the dry-stone wall, follow the steps, and continue ahead.

Corniglia (Town #3)

This is the quiet town—the only one of the five not on the water—with a mellow main square. According to a (likely fanciful) local legend, the town was originally settled by a Roman farmer who named it for his mother, Cornelia (how Corniglia is pronounced). The town and its ancient residents produced a wine so famous that—some say—vases found at Pompeii touted its virtues. Regardless of the veracity of the legends, wine remains Corniglia's

THE CINQUE TERRE

lifeblood today. Follow the pungent smell of ripe grapes into an alley cellar and get a local to let you dip a straw into a keg. Remote and less visited than the other Cinque Terre towns, Corniglia has fewer tourists, cooler temperatures, a few restaurants, a windy overlook on its promontory, and plenty of private rooms for rent (ask at any bar or shop, no cheaper than other towns).

Orientation to Corniglia

Arrival in Corniglia

From the station, a footpath zigzags up nearly 400 steps to the town. Or take the green shuttle bus, generally timed to meet arriving trains (€1.50 one-way, €2.50 round-trip, free with Cinque Terre Card, 2/hour). Before leaving for the bus, confirm departure times at the TI in the train station or consult the schedule posted at the stop (daily 6:30–19:30). If you're driving, be aware that only residents can park on the main road between the recommended Villa Cecio and the point where the steep switchback staircase meets the road. Beyond that area, parking is €1.50 per hour.

Self-Guided Walk

Welcome to Corniglia

We'll explore this tiny town—population 240—and end at a scenic viewpoint.

• *Begin near the bus stop, located at a...*

Town Square: The gateway to this community is "Ciappà" square, with an ATM, phone booth, old wine press, and bus stop. The Cinque Terre's designation as a national park has sparked a revitalization of the town. Corniglia's young generation might now stay put, rather than migrate into big cities the way locals did in the past.

• *Stroll the spine of Corniglia, Via Fieschi. In the fall, the smell of grapes (on their way to becoming wine) wafts from busy cellars. Along this main street, you'll see...*

Corniglia's Enticing Shops: The enjoyable wine bar and restaurant, Enoteca Il Pirun—named for a type of oddly shaped old-fashioned wine pitcher—is located in a cool cantina at Via Fieschi 115 (daily, tel. 0187-812-315). Mario and Marilena don't speak

Corniglia

100 YARDS
100 METERS

TO GUVANO BEACH & VERNAZZA

VIEW

LOC. CANALE

VIA SERRA

LOC. CHIOSO

ALLA STAZIONE

HUNDREDS OF STEPS

FIESCHI

VIA ALLA MARINA

VIA

HARBOR

LARGO TARAGIO, ORATORY

SANTA MARIA BELVEDERE

'CIAPPA' SQUARE & BUS STOP

VIA LARDARINA

TO MANAROLA

LIGURIAN SEA

TRAIN STATION

SWIMMING

DCH

① Pan e Vin Bar (Ricci Rooms Check-In)

② Villa Cecio Rooms

③ Corniglia Hostel

④ La Lanterna Restaurant

⑤ Osteria Mananan

⑥ Enoteca Il Pirun

⑦ Gelateria

⑧ Butiega Shop

much English, but they try. Sample some local wines—generally free for small tastes. For a fun experience and a souvenir to boot, order a €3 glass of wine, which is served in a *pirun* and comes with a bib to keep. The *pirun* aerates the wine to give the alcohol more kick. Mario's recently opened small restaurant upstairs offers local cuisine (see "Eating in Corniglia," later).

Across from Enoteca Il Pirun, Alberto and Cristina's *gelateria* dishes up the best homemade gelato in town. Before ordering, get a free taste of Alberto's *miele di Corniglia,* made from local honey.

In the Butiega shop at Via Fieschi 142, Vincenzo and Lorenzo sell organic local specialties (daily 8:00–19:30). For picnickers, they offer €2.50 made-to-order ham-and-cheese sandwiches and a fun €3.50 *antipasto misto* to go. (There are good places to picnic farther along on this walk.)

• *Following Via Fieschi, you'll end up at the...*

Main Square: On Largo Taragio, tables from two bars and a trattoria spill around a WWI memorial and the town's old well. It once piped in natural spring water from the hillside to locals living without plumbing. What looks like a church is the Oratory of Santa Caterina. (An oratory is a kind of a spiritual clubhouse for a service group doing social work in the name of the Catholic

Church. For more information, see "Oratory of the Dead" on page 369.) Behind the oratory, you'll find a clearing that local children have made into a soccer field. The stone benches and viewpoint make this a peaceful place for a picnic (less crowded than the end-of-town viewpoint, described below).

• *Opposite the oratory, notice how steps lead steeply down on Via alla Marina to Corniglia's non-beach. It's a five-minute paved climb to sunning rocks, a shower, and a small deck (with a treacherous entry into the water). From the square, continue up Via Fieschi to the...*

End-of-Town Viewpoint: The Santa Maria Belvedere, named for a church that once stood here, marks the scenic end of Corniglia. This is a super picnic spot. From here, look high to the west, where the village and sanctuary of San Bernardino straddle a ridge (a good starting point for a hike; accessible by shuttle bus from Monterosso or a long uphill hike from Vernazza). Below is the tortuous harbor, where locals hoist their boats onto the cruel rocks.

Sights in Corniglia

Beaches—This hilltop town has rocky sea access below its train station (toward Manarola). Once a beach, it's all been washed away and offers no services. Look for signs that say *al mare* or *Marina*.

Guvano beach is in the opposite direction (toward Vernazza). Guvano (GOO-vah-noh) was created by an 1893 landslide that cost the village a third of its farmland. The big news is that after decades as a nude beach, Guvano has been sold to the national park, which plans to improve access (and keep sunbathers clothed). Look for upgrades to what has been a dark, uneven walk through a long tunnel to reach the beach, and avoid the steep, overgrown, unofficial trail.

Sleeping in Corniglia

(€1 = about $1.25, country code: 39)
Perched high above the sea on a hilltop, Corniglia has plenty of private rooms (generally Db-€65). To get to the town from the station, catch the shuttle bus or make the 15-minute uphill hike. The town is riddled with humble places that charge too much and have meager business skills and a limited ability to converse with tourists—so it's almost never full.

$$ Cristiana Ricci is an exception to the rule. She communicates well and is reliable, renting four small, clean, and peaceful rooms—two with kitchens and one with a terrace and sweeping view—just inland from the bus stop (Db-€60-70, Qb-€90, €10/day less when you stay 2 or more nights, free Internet access, check in at the Pan e Vin bar at Via Fieschi 123, mobile 338-937-6547, cri_affittacamere@virgilio.it, Stefano). Her mom rents a big, modern apartment (€90 for 2–4 people).

$$ Villa Cecio feels like an abandoned hotel. They offer eight well-worn rooms on the outskirts of town, with saggy beds and little character or warmth (Db-€65 promised in 2011, no breakfast, cash preferred, great views, on main road 200 yards toward Vernazza at Via Serra 58, tel. 0187-812-043, fax 0187-812-138, mobile 334-350-6637, www.cecio5terre.com, info@cecio5terre .com, Giacinto). They also rent eight similar rooms in an annex on the square where the bus stops.

$ Corniglia Hostel, brand-new in 2009, was formerly the town's schoolhouse. It's in a pastel-yellow building up some steps from the main square where the bus stops. The playground in front is often busy with happy kids. Despite its institutional atmosphere, the hostel's prices, central location, and bright and clean rooms ensure its popularity (€24/bed in two 8-bed dorms, €27 with minimal breakfast; four Db-€55, €60 with breakfast; air-con, self-serve laundry, lockers, no public spaces except lobby, office open 7:00–13:00 & 15:00–24:00, rooms closed 13:00–15:00, 1:30 curfew, Via alla Stazione 3, tel. 0187-812-559, fax 0187-763-984, www.ostellocorniglia.com but reserve at www.hostelworld.com, ostellocorniglia@gmail.com, helpful Daniele).

Eating in Corniglia

Corniglia has few restaurants. **Cecio,** above the town, has terrace seating with a view of the sea. The trattoria **La Lantera,** on the main square, is the most atmospheric. (Neither comes with particularly charming service.)

Restaurant **Osteria Mananan**—between the Ciappà bus stop and the main square on Via Fieschi—serves the best food in town in its small stony and elegant interior (Fri–Wed 12:15–14:30 & 19:45–21:15, closed Thu, no outdoor seating, tel. 0187-821-166). **Enoteca Il Pirun,** on Via Fieschi, has a small restaurant above the wine bar, where Mario serves typical local dishes (€28 fixed-price meal includes homemade wine, daily 12:00–16:00 & 19:30–23:30, tel. 0187-812-315).

THE CINQUE TERRE

Vernazza (Town #4)

With the closest thing to a natural harbor—overseen by a ruined castle and a stout stone church—Vernazza is the jewel of the Cinque Terre. Only the occasional noisy slurping up of the train by the mountain reminds you of the modern world.

The action is at the harbor, where you'll find outdoor restaurants, a bar hanging on the edge of the castle, a breakwater with a promenade, and a tailgate-party street market every Tuesday

morning. In the summer, the beach becomes a soccer field, where teams fielded by local bars and restaurants provide late-night entertainment. In the dark, locals fish off the promontory, using glowing bobbers that shine in the waves.

Proud of their Vernazzan heritage, the town's 500 residents like to brag: "Vernazza is locally owned. Portofino has sold out." Fearing the change it would bring, keep-Vernazza-small proponents stopped the construction of a major road into the town and region. Families are tight and go back centuries; several generations stay together. In the winter, the population shrinks, as many people return to their more comfortable big-city apartments to spend the money they reaped during the tourist season.

Leisure time is devoted to taking part in the *passeggiata*—strolling lazily together up and down the main street. Sit on a bench and study the passersby doing their *vasche* (laps). Explore the characteristic alleys, called *carugi*. Learn—and live—the phrase *"la vita pigra di Vernazza"* (the lazy life of Vernazza).

Orientation to Vernazza

Tourist Information

The TI and park information booths are both at the train station. The park office is more of a souvenir shop, while the combination TI/train-ticket desk sells Cinque Terre Cards (park office—daily April–Oct 9:30–20:00, Nov–March until 19:30, tel. 0187-812-524, TI/train-ticket desk—daily 7:00–19:30, tel. 0187-812-533 but often busy). Some of the staff at the TI/train desk will ring the owner of the room you have reserved so that he or she can meet you, but they cannot make reservations. Public WCs are nearby in the station.

Arrival in Vernazza

By Train: Vernazza's train station is only about three cars long, but the trains are much longer, so most of the cars come to a stop in a long, dark tunnel. Get out anyway, and walk through the tunnel to the station.

By Car: There's a non-resident parking lot, but be aware that parking is tough—the lot fills up quickly from May through September (€2/hour, €12/24 hours, cash only, about 500 yards above town, pay first at the parking stand before getting your spot). A hardworking shuttle service, generally with friendly English-speaking Beppe or Simone behind the wheel, connects the lot to the top of town (€1.50, free with Cinque Terre Card, 3–4/hour, runs 7:00–19:00). Yellow lines mark parking spots for residents. The highest lot (a side-trip uphill) is for overnight stays.

Helpful Hints

Internet Access: The **Blue Marlin Bar,** run by Massimo and Carmen, has the lowest prices and longest hours (€0.10/minute, open earlier but Internet available Fri–Wed 9:30–22:30, closed Thu, see listing on page 362). The slick six-terminal **Internet Point,** run by Alberto and Isabella, is in the village center (€0.15/minute, €0.10/minute after 30 minutes, daily June–Oct 9:30–23:00, until 20:00 Nov–May, Wi-Fi, will burn your digital photos to a CD or DVD for €6, sells international phone cards, 10 percent discount for Rick Steves readers in their **Cantina Del Molo Enoteca** across the street, tel. 0187-812-949).

Laundry: Lavanderia il Carugetto is completely self-serve (coin-op, wash-€6, dry-€5, daily 8:00–22:00, on a narrow lane a block off the main drag opposite the Internet Point, operated by the fish shop).

Massage: Stephanie, an American expat, gives a good, strong therapeutic massage in a neat little studio at the top of town (€50/hour, mobile 338-9429-494, stephsette@gmail.com).

Best Views: A steep 10-minute hike in either direction from Vernazza gives you a classic village photo op (for the best light, head toward Corniglia in the morning, and toward Monterosso in the evening). Franco's **Bar La Torre,** with a panoramic terrace, is uphill from his restaurant on the trail toward Corniglia (listed in "Eating in Vernazza," later).

THE CINQUE TERRE

Vernazza

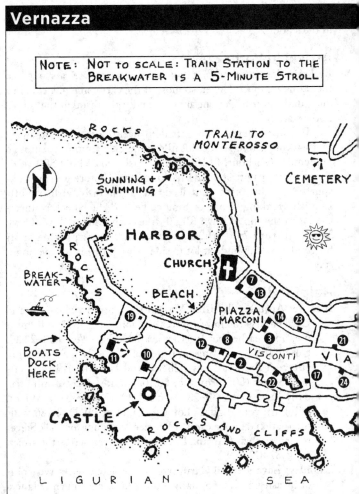

NOTE: NOT TO SCALE: TRAIN STATION TO THE BREAKWATER IS A 5-MINUTE STROLL

ROCKS

TRAIL TO MONTEROSSO

CEMETERY

SUNNING & SWIMMING

HARBOR

CHURCH

BREAK-WATER →

BEACH

PIAZZA MARCONI

BOATS DOCK HERE

CASTLE

ROCKS AND CLIFFS

LIGURIAN   SEA

Self-Guided Walks

Welcome to Vernazza

This tour includes Vernazza's characteristic town squares, and ends on its scenic breakwater.

• *From the train station, walk uphill until you hit the parking lot, with a bank, a post office, and a barrier that keeps out all but service vehicles. Vernazza's shuttle buses run from here to the parking lot and into the hills. Walk to the tidy, modern square called...*

Fontana Vecchia: Named after a long-gone fountain, this is where older locals remember the river filled with townswomen

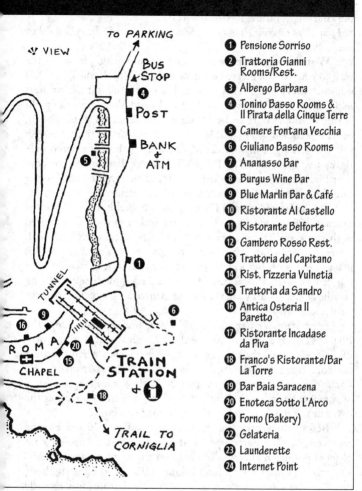

TO PARKING

↘ VIEW

BUS STOP ■ ❹

■ POST

■ BANK & ATM

❺

❶

TUNNEL

❾

❶❻

R O M A ✚ CHAPEL

❷❶ ❷❹ ❶❺

TRAIN STATION ✚ ⓘ

❻

❶❽

TRAIL TO CORNIGLIA

❶ Pensione Sorriso
❷ Trattoria Gianni Rooms/Rest.
❸ Albergo Barbara
❹ Tonino Basso Rooms & Il Pirata della Cinque Terre
❺ Camere Fontana Vecchia
❻ Giuliano Basso Rooms
❼ Ananasso Bar
❽ Burgus Wine Bar
❾ Blue Marlin Bar & Café
❿ Ristorante Al Castello
⓫ Ristorante Belforte
⓬ Gambero Rosso Rest.
⓭ Trattoria del Capitano
⓮ Rist. Pizzeria Vulnetia
⓯ Trattoria da Sandro
⓰ Antica Osteria Il Baretto
⓱ Ristorante Incadase da Piva
⓲ Franco's Ristorante/Bar La Torre
⓳ Bar Baia Saracena
⓴ Enoteca Sotto L'Arco
㉑ Forno (Bakery)
㉒ Gelateria
㉓ Launderette
㉔ Internet Point

doing their washing. Now they enjoy checking on the baby ducks. The trail leads up to the cemetery. Imagine the entire village sadly trudging up here during funerals. (The cemetery is peaceful and evocative at sunset, when the fading light touches each crypt.)

• *Glad to be here in happier times, begin your saunter downhill to the harbor. Just before the* Pensione Sorriso *sign, on your right (big brown wood doors), you'll see the...*

Ambulance Barn: A group of volunteers is always on call for a dash to the hospital, 40 minutes away in La Spezia. Opposite the barn is a big empty lot. Like many landowners, the owner of Pensione Sorriso had plans to expand, but since the 1980s, the government said no. While some landowners are frustrated, the old character of these towns survives.

• *A few steps farther along (past the town clinic and library), you'll see a...*

World Wars Monument: Look for a marble plaque in the wall to your left, dedicated to those killed in the World Wars. Not a family in Vernazza was spared. Listed on the left are soldiers *morti in combattimento,* who died in World War I; on the right is the World War II section. Some were deported to *Germania;* others—labeled *Part* (stands for *partigiani,* or partisans)—were killed while fighting against Mussolini. Cynics considered partisans less than heroes. After 1943, Hitler called up Italian boys over 15. Rather than die on the front for Hitler, they escaped to the hills. They became "resistance fighters" in order to remain free.

The path to Corniglia leaves from here (behind and above the plaque). Behind you is a small square and playground, decorated with three millstones, once used to grind local olives into oil. There's a good chance you'll see an expat mom here at the village playground with her kids. I've met many American women who fell in love with a local guy, stayed, and are now happily raising families here. (But I've never met an American guy who moved in with a local girl.)

From here, Vernazza's tiny river goes underground. Until the 1950s, Vernazza's river ran openly through the center of town. Old-timers recall the days before the breakwater, when the river cascaded down and the surf crashed along Vernazza's main drag. Back then, the town was nicknamed "Little Venice" for the series of romantic bridges that arched over the stream, connecting the two sides of the town before the main road was built.

Before the tracks (on the left), the wall has 10 spaces, one reserved for each party's political ads during elections—a kind of local pollution control. The map on the right, under the railway tracks, shows the region's hiking trails. Trail #2 is the basic favorite. The second set of tracks (nearer the harbor) was recently renovated to lessen the disruptive noise, but locals say it made no difference.

• *Follow the road downhill to...*

Vernazza's "Business Center": Here, you'll pass many locals doing their *vasche* (laps). At Enoteca Sotto l'Arco, Gerry and Paola sell wine—they can uncork it and throw in plastic glasses—and delightful jars of local pesto, which goes great on bread (Wed–Mon 9:00–21:00, Tue 12:30–21:00, Via Roma 70). Next, you'll pass the Blue Marlin Bar (Vernazza's top nightspot) and the tiny Chapel of Santa Marta (the small stone chapel with iron grillwork over the window), where Mass is celebrated only on special Sundays. Farther down, you'll walk by a grocery, *gelateria,* bakery, pharmacy, another grocery, and another *gelateria*. There are plenty of fun and cheap food-to-go options here.

• *On the left, in front of the second* gelateria, *an arch (with a peaceful little sitting perch atop it) leads to what was a beach, where the town's stream used to hit the sea back in the 1970s. Continue down to the...*

Harbor Square and Breakwater: Vernazza, with the only natural harbor of the Cinque Terre, was established as the sole place boats could pick up the fine local wine. The two-foot-high square stone at the foot of the stairs by the recommended Burgus Wine Bar is marked *Sasso del Sego* (stone of tallow). Workers crushed animal flesh and fat in its basin to make tallow, which drained out of the tiny hole below. The tallow was then used to waterproof boats or wine barrels. For more town history, step into the Burgus to see fascinating old photos of Vernazza on the wall.

On the far side (behind the recommended Ristorante Pizzeria Vulnetia), peek into the tiny street with its commotion of arches. Vernazza's most characteristic side streets, called *carugi*, lead up from here. The trail (above the church, toward Monterosso) leads to the classic view of Vernazza (see "Best Views," under "Helpful Hints" earlier in this section).

Located in front of the harborside church, the tiny piazza—decorated with a river-rock mosaic—is a popular hangout spot. It's where Vernazza's old ladies soak up the last bit of sun, and kids enjoy a patch of level ball field.

Vernazza's harborfront church is unusual for its strange entryway, which faces east (altar side). With relative peace and prosperity in the 16th century, the townspeople doubled the church in size, causing it to overtake a little piazza that once faced the west facade. From the square, use the "new" entry and climb the steps, keeping an eye out for the level necessary to keep the church high and dry. Inside, the lighter pillars in the back mark the 16th-century extension. Three historic portable crosses hanging on the walls are carried through town during Easter processions. They are replicas of crosses that Vernazza ships once carried on crusades to the Holy Land.

• *Finish your town tour seated out on the breakwater (and consider starting the following tour).*

The Burned-Out Sightseer's Visual Tour of Vernazza

• *Sit at the end of the harbor breakwater (perhaps with a glass of local white wine or something more interesting from a nearby bar—borrow the glass, they don't mind), face the town, and see...*

The Harbor: In a moderate storm, you'd be soaked, as waves routinely crash over the *molo* (breakwater, built in 1972). Waves can even wash away tourists squinting excitedly into their cameras.

(I've seen it happen.) In 2007, an American woman was swept away and killed by a rogue wave. Enjoy the new waterfront piazza—carefully.

The train line (to your left) was constructed in 1874 to tie together a newly united Italy, and linked Turin and Genoa with Rome. A second line (hidden in a tunnel at this point) was built in the 1920s. The yellow building alongside the tracks was Vernazza's first train station. You can see the four bricked-up alcoves where people once waited for trains.

Vernazza's fishing fleet is down to just a couple of fishing boats (with the net spools). Vernazzans are still more likely to own a boat than a car. Boats are on buoys, except in winter or when the red storm flag indicates bad seas (in which case they're allowed to be pulled up onto the square—which is usually reserved for restaurant tables). In the 1970s, tiny Vernazza had one of Italy's top water polo teams, and the harbor was their "pool." Later, when the league required a real pool, Vernazza dropped out.

The Castle: On the far right, the castle, which is now a grassy park with great views (and nothing but stones), still guards the

town (€1.50 donation supports the local Red Cross, daily 10:00–19:00; from harbor, take stairs by Trattoria Gianni and follow *Ristorante Al Castello* signs, tower is a few steps beyond). It was the town's lookout back in pirate days. The highest umbrellas mark the recommended Ristorante Al Castello. The squat tower on the water is great for a glass of wine or a meal. From the breakwater, you could follow the rope to the Ristorante Belforte, and pop inside, past the submarine-strength door. A photo of a major storm showing the entire tower under a wave (not uncommon in the winter) hangs near the bar.

The Town: Vernazza has two halves. *Sciuiu* (Vernazzan dialect for "flowery") is the sunny side on the left, and *luvegu* (dank) is the shady side on the right. Houses below the castle were connected by an interior arcade—ideal for fleeing attacks. The "Ligurian pastel" colors are regulated by a commissioner of good taste in the regional government. The square before you is locally famous for some of

THE CINQUE TERRE

the area's finest restaurants. The big red central house—on the site where Genoan warships were built in the 12th century—used to be a guardhouse.

In the Middle Ages, there was no beach or square. The water went right up to the buildings, where boats would tie up, Venetian-style. Imagine what Vernazza looked like in those days, when it was the biggest and richest of the Cinque Terre towns. There was no pastel plaster, just fine stonework (traces of which survive above the Trattoria del Capitano). Apart from the added plaster, the general shape and size of the town has changed little in five centuries. Survey the windows and notice inhabitants quietly gazing back.

Above the Town: The small, round tower above the red guardhouse—another part of the city fortifications—reminds us of Vernazza's importance in the Middle Ages, when it was a key ally of Genoa (whose archenemies were the other maritime republics, especially Pisa). Franco's Ristorante and Bar La Torre, just behind the tower, welcomes hikers who are finishing, starting, or simply contemplating the Corniglia–Vernazza hike, with great town views. Vineyards fill the mountainside beyond the town. Notice the many terraces. Someone—probably after too much of that local wine—calculated that the roughly 3,000 miles of dry-stone walls built to terrace the region's vineyards have the same amount of stonework as the Great Wall of China.

Wine production is down nowadays, as the younger residents choose less physical work. But locals still maintain their tiny plots and proudly serve their family wines. The patchwork of local vineyards is atomized and complex because of inheritance traditions. Historically, families divided their land between their children. Parents wanted each child to get some good land. Because some lots were "kissed by the sun" while others were shady, the lots were split into increasingly tiny and eventually unviable pieces.

A single steel train line winds up the gully behind the tower. It is for the vintner's *trenino*, the tiny service train. Play "Where's *trenino?*" and see if you can find two trains. The vineyards once stretched as high as you can see, but since fewer people sweat in the fields these days, the most distant terraces have gone wild again.

The Church, School, and City Hall: Vernazza's Ligurian Gothic church, built with black stones quarried from Punta Mesco (the distant point behind you), dates from 1318. Note the gray stone that marks the church's 16th-century expansion. The gray-and-red house above the spire is the local elementary school (about 25 children attend). High-schoolers go to the "big city": La Spezia. The red building to the right of the schoolhouse, a former monastery, is the City Hall. Vernazza and Corniglia function as one community. Through most of the 1990s, the local government was Communist. In 1999, they elected a coalition of many parties working to rise above ideologies and simply make Vernazza a better place. Finally, on the top of the hill, with the best view of all, is the town cemetery.

Sights in Vernazza

Tuesday-Morning Market—Vernazza's meager business community is augmented Tuesday mornings (8:00–13:00) when a gang of cars and trucks pull into town for a tailgate market.

Beach—The harbor's sandy cove has sunning rocks and showers by the breakwater. There's also a ladder on the breakwater for deep-water access.

Boat Rental—Nord Est rents canoes and small motorboats from their stand on the harbor. With a rental boat, you can reach a tiny *acqua pendente* (waterfall) cove between Vernazza and Monterosso; locals call it their *laguna blu* (motorboats-€60/2 hours, €80/4 hours; plus gas, usually about €15; includes snorkeling gear; May–Oct only, mobile 338-700-0436, manuelamoggia@tiscali.it).

Shuttle Bus Joyride—For a cheap and scenic joyride, with a chance to chat about the region with friendly Beppe or Simone, ride the shuttle bus for the entire route for the cost of a round-trip ticket. Some buses also head to two sanctuaries in the hills above town (4/day—usually at 7:00, 9:45, 12:00, and 15:00; schedule posted at park office, train station, and bus stop in front of post office; €2.50 one-way, free with Cinque Terre Card, churches at sanctuaries usually closed). The high-country 40-minute loop—buses are marked *Drignana*—gives you lots of scenery without having to hike (don't take buses marked *No panoramic,* as these won't take scenic routes).

Nightlife in Vernazza

Vernazza's younger generation of restaurant workers lets loose after-hours. They work hard through the tourist season, travel in the winter, speak English, and enjoy connecting with international visitors. After the restaurants close down, the town is quiet except for a couple of nightspots. For more information on the Blue Marlin, Ananasso, Il Pirata, and Ristorante Incandase, see their listings under "Eating in Vernazza," later.

Blue Marlin Bar dominates the late-night scene with a mix of locals and tourists, home-cooked food until 22:00, good drinks, and piano jam sessions. If you're young and hip, this is *the* place to hang out.

Ananasso Bar offers early-evening happy-hour fun and cocktails (called *"aperitivi"*) that both locals and visitors enjoy. Its harborfront tables get the last sunshine of the day.

THE CINQUE TERRE

Burgus Wine Bar, chic and cool with a jazz ambience, is a popular early-evening and after-dinner harborside hangout. Sip local wine or a cocktail, and sample Lorenza's artful complimentary snack foods, available 18:00–20:30. Let her explain the historic town photos and museum cases of artifacts (Tue–Sun 6:45–24:00, closed Mon, also handy for early breakfast, Piazza Marconi 4, tel. 0187-812-556).

Il Pirata delle Cinque Terre, at the top of the town, features the entertaining Canoli brothers, who fill a happy crowd of tourists with wonderful Sicilian pastries and drinks each evening. Many come for dinner and end up staying because of these two wild and crazy guys and the camaraderie they create among their diners.

Ristorante Incadase da Piva (tucked up the lane behind the pharmacy) is the haunt of Piva, Vernazza's troubadour. Piva often gets out his guitar and sings traditional local songs as well as his own compositions. If you're looking for a local Hemingway, check here.

Franco's **Bar La Torre,** clinging to the terraces above Ristorante La Torre, has more evening life than nightlife—it closes around 22:00. Wine bottles are reasonably priced around €12, and the soaring view is intoxicating.

Really Late: There's a little cave on the beach just under the church that lends itself to fun in the wee hours, when everything else is closed.

Sleeping in Vernazza

(€1 = about $1.25, country code: 39)
Vernazza, the spindly and salty essence of the Cinque Terre, is my top choice for a home base. Off-season (Oct–March), you can generally arrive without a reservation and find a place, but at other times, it's smart to book ahead (especially for June–Aug, any weekend, and holidays such as Easter).

People recommended here are listed for their communication skills (they speak English, have email, are reliable with bookings) and because they rent several rooms. Consequently, my recommendations charge more than comparable rooms you'll find if you shop around. Comparison-shopping will likely save you €10–20 per double per night—and often get you a better place and view to boot. The real Vernazza gems are stray single rooms with owners who have no interest in booking in advance or messing with email. Arrive by early afternoon and drop by any shop or bar and ask; most locals know someone who rents rooms.

Anywhere you stay here requires some climbing, but keep in mind that more climbing means better views. Most do not include breakfast. Cash is preferred or required almost everywhere. Night noise can be a problem if you're near the station. Rooms on the harbor come with church bells (but only between 7:00 and 22:00).

Pensions

These pensions are located on the Vernazza map, earlier in this chapter.

$$$ Pensione Sorriso is the oldest pension in town (and where I stayed on my first visit in 1975). Above the train station, it's run by Aldo and Francesca—the local Sonny and Cher—who welcome guests to their 19 rooms. While the main building has the charm, it comes with train noise and saggy beds; the annex, up the street, is in a quieter apartment that feels forgotten (Sb-€70, D-€85, Db-€110 without air-con, Db-€125 with air-con, Tb-€130, includes breakfast, peaceful garden, Via Gavino 4, tel. 0187-812-224, fax 0187-821-198, www.pensionesorriso.com, info@pensione sorriso.com).

$$$ Trattoria Gianni rents 27 small rooms and three apartments just under the castle. The rooms are in three buildings—one funky, two modern—up a hundred tight, winding spiral stairs. The funky ones, which may or may not have private baths, are artfully decorated à la shipwreck, with tiny balco-  nies and grand sea views *(con vista sul mare)*. The comfy new *(nuovo)* rooms lack views. Both have modern bathrooms and access to a super-scenic cliff-hanging guests' gar- den. Steely Marisa requires check-in before 16:00 or a phone call to explain when you're coming. Emanuele (Gianni's son, who now runs the restaurant), Simona, and the staff speak a little English (S-€45, D-€80, Db-€120, Tb-€140, 10 percent discount with cash and this book in 2011—request when you reserve, cancellations required a week in advance or you'll be charged one night's deposit, break-fast-€5, closed Jan–Feb, Piazza Marconi 5, tel. & fax 0187-812-228, tel. 0187-821-003, on Wed call mobile 393-9008-155 instead, www.giannifranzi.it, info@giannifranzi.it). Pick up your keys at Trattoria Gianni's restaurant/reception on the harbor square. If they're booked up, Simona may show you a room in a friend's place (no Rick Steves discount).

$$ Albergo Barbara rents nine simple but clean and modern rooms overlooking the harbor square—most with small windows and small views. It's run by English-speaking Giuseppe and his no-nonsense Swiss wife, Patricia (D-€55, Db-€65–70, big Db with nice harbor view-€110, 2-night stay preferred, free Wi-Fi, closed Dec–Feb, Piazza Marconi 30, tel. & fax 0187-812-398, mobile

338-793-3261, reserve online with credit card but pay cash, www .albergobarbara.it, info@albergobarbara.it).

Private Rooms (Affitta Camere)

Vernazza is honeycombed with private rooms year-round, offering the best values in town. Owners may be reluctant to reserve rooms far in advance. It's easiest to call a day or two ahead or simply show up in the morning and look around. Doubles cost €55–90, depending on the view, season, and plumbing—you get what you pay for. Most places accept only cash. Some have killer views, come with lots of stairs, and cost the same as a small, dark place on a back lane over the train tracks. Little English is spoken at many of these places. If you call to let them know your arrival time (or call when you arrive, using your mobile phone or the pay phone just below the station), they'll meet you at the train station.

Well-Managed and Well-Appointed Rooms in the Inland Part of Town

$$$ **Tonino Basso** rents four super clean, modern rooms—at a steep price. Each room has its own computer for free Internet access. He's in the only building in Vernazza with an elevator. You get tranquility and air-conditioning, but no views (Sb-€65, Db-€120, Tb-€150, Qb-€180, prices go down Nov–March, call Tonino's mobile number upon arrival and he'll meet you, tel. 0187-821-264, mobile 335-269-436, fax 0187-812-807, toninobasso @libero.it). If you can't locate Tonino, ask his friends at Enoteca Sotto L'Arco at Via Roma 70.

$$ **Camere Fontana Vecchia** is a delightful place, with four bright, spacious, quiet rooms and an apartment near the post office (no view). As the only place in Vernazza with almost no stairs to climb and the sound of a babbling brook outside your window, it's perhaps the best value in town (D-€70, Db-€80, T-€95, Tb-€110, super-trendy 2-person apartment-€100, fans and heat, open all year, Via Gavino 15, tel. 0187-821-130, mobile 333-454-9371, fax 0187-812-261, m.annamaria@libero.it, youthful and efficient Anna speaks English). If no one answers, ask at Enoteca Sotto L'Arco on the main drag.

$$ **Giuliano Basso** rents four pleasant rooms, crafted with care, just above town in the terraced wilds (sea views from terraces). Straddling a ravine among orange trees, it's an artfully decorated Robinson Crusoe–chic wonderland, proudly built out of stone by Giuliano himself (Db-€80, Db suite with air-con-€100, Db suite with private rooftop balcony-€100, extra bed-€25, fridge access, free Internet access; above train station, take the ramp just before Pensione Sorriso, more train noise than others, mobile 333-341-4792,

THE CINQUE TERRE

or have Enoteca Sotto L'Arco contact him or his American partner Michele, www.cdh.it/giuliano, giuliano@cdh.it).

Other Reliable Places Scattered Through Town and the Harborside

These places are not identified on this book's map; ask for directions when you reserve.

$$$ La Malà is Vernazza's jetsetter pad. Four pristine white rooms boast four-star-hotel-type extras, a common terrace looking out over the rocky shore, and air-conditioning (Db-€150, Db suite-€210, includes breakfast at a designated bar, tel. 334-287-5718, fax 0187-812-218, www.lamala.it, info@lamala.it, Giamba and Armanda). It's a climb—way, way up to the top of town. They also rent the simpler "Armanda's Room" nearby (no view, Db-€70) and an apartment (€150/2 people, extra bed-€20, ring bell at Piazza Marconi 15).

$$ Monica Lercari rents several classy rooms with modern comforts, perched at the top of town (Db-€80, sea-view D-€100, grand sea-view terrace D-€120, "honeymoon suite" Db-€180 also covers your choice of bike or rowboat rental; includes breakfast, air-con, next to recommended Ristorante Al Castello, tel. 0187-812-296, alcastellovernazza@yahoo.it).

$$ Antonio and Ingrid Fenelli Camere rent three very central, comfy, and fairly priced rooms that are an excellent value. You'll meet friendly Antonio—a hulking man in a huge white T-shirt and bathing suit who's a fixture on the village streets—and his charming petite English-speaking wife Ingrid (small Db-€55, Db-€70, Tb-€80, two-person apartment with terrace-€95, air-con, 10 steps above pharmacy at Via Carattino 2, tel. 0187-812-183). They have no email, but getting a room by phone or in person is worth the trouble.

$$ Memo Rooms has three clean and spacious rooms that offer good value. They overlook the main street, in what feels like a miniature hotel. Enrica will meet you if you call upon arrival (Db-€70, Via Roma 15, tel. 0187-812-360, mobile 338-285-2385).

$$ Martina Callo's four air-conditioned rooms overlook the square; they're up plenty of steps near the silent-at-night church tower (room #1: Tb-€100 or Qb-€115 with harbor view; room #2: huge Qb family room with no view-€110; room #3: Db with grand view terrace-€75; room #4: roomy Db with no view-€60; ring bell at Piazza Marconi 26, tel. & fax 0187-812-365, mobile 329-435-5344, www.roomartina.com, roomartina@roomartina.com).

$$ Nicolina rents five recently renovated units with double-paned windows. Two rooms are in the center over the pharmacy, up a few steep steps, one has only sleeper sofas (Db-€80); another two are in a different building with great views (Db-€100,

Tb-€120, Qb-€150); and the last unit is a two-bedroom quadruple with even better views (€200). Inquire at Pizzeria Vulnetia on the harbor square (Piazza Marconi 29, tel. & fax 0187-821-193, www .camerenicolina.it, camerenicolina.info@cdh.it).

$$ Rosa Vitali rents two four-person apartments across from the pharmacy overlooking the main street. One has a terrace and fridge (top floor); the other has windows and a full kitchen (Db-€85, Tb-€110, Qb-€130, reception at Via Visconti 10 between the grotto and Piazza Marconi, tel. 0187-821-181, mobile 340-267-5009, www.rosacamere.it, rosa.vitali@libero.it).

$$ Francamaria and her kind husband Andrea rent eight sharp, comfortable, and creatively renovated but expensive rooms— all described in detail on her website (small no-view Db-€75, big and modern no-view Db-€90, larger view Db-up to €115, Qb-€125–160, family apartments, prices depend on view and size, few steps, reception at Piazza Marconi 30, don't confuse with Albergo Barbara at same address, tel. & fax 0187-812-002, mobile 328-711-9728, www .francamaria.com, francamaria@francamaria.com).

More Private Rooms in Vernazza

$$ Maria Capellini rents a couple of simple, clean rooms, including one on the ground floor right on the harbor (Db with kitchen-€85, Tb-€110, cash only, fans, mobile 338-436-3411, www.mariacapellini.com, mariacapellini@hotmail.it, Maria and Giacomo).

$$ Il Pirata delle Cinque Terre has a few big, basic rooms with the sounds of the river below. Managed by Noelia and Leyla, wives of the drink-slinging Canoli brothers (see listing under "Eating in Vernazza"), it's a two-minute walk from the bar and a five-minute walk to the sea (Db-€90, Tb-€130, Qb-€160; includes breakfast with this book at the Il Pirata bar—which also functions as the reception; 2-night minimum, cash only, guaranteed hot water, convenient to parking; from the Il Pirata, hike up 100 yards to the yellow building that was the old mill; tel. 0187-812-047, mobile 338-596-2503, www.ilpiratarooms.com, ilpiratarooms @libero.it).

$$ Ivo's Camere rents two simple no-terrace rooms high above the main street (Db-€70, Via Roma 6, includes breakfast at a nearby bar, reception at Pizzeria Fratelli Basso, Via Roma 1, tel. 0187-821-042, mobile 333-477-5521, www.ivocamere.com, post @ivocamere.com).

$$ Daria Bianchi rents 12 clean, spacious, and comfortable rooms near the station. Four rooms are above the Blue Marlin looking down on the main street, and eight are near the City Hall (Db-€70, Qb-€100–120, fans, reception next to Blue Marlin Bar, tel. 0187-812-151, mobile 338-581-4688, www.vernazzarooms.com).

$$ Emanuela Colombo has two rooms—one spacious and basic on the main square, the other *molto* chic and located in a quiet side street (Db-€90, Tb-€110, check in at Enoteca Sotto L'Arco, tel. 339-834-2486, www.vacanzemanuela.it, manuela @libero.it).

More Options: **$$ Affitta Camere Alberto Basso** (a clean, modern room with a noisy harbor/piazza view, Db-€75, check in at Internet Point, albertobasso@hotmail.com), **$$ Capitano Rooms** (3 recently remodeled rooms above the main drag, Db-€90, ask for Paolo or Barbara at the recommended Trattoria del Capitano restaurant, tel. 0187-812-201), **$$$ Eva's Rooms** (3 rooms, Db-€60–80, overlooking main street with some train noise, ring at Via Roma 56, tel. 0187-821-134, www.evasrooms .it, massimoeva@libero.it), **$$$ Manuela Moggia** (Db-€80, Tb-€95, Qb with kitchen-€125, top of the town at Via Gavino 22, tel. 0187-812-397, mobile 333-413-6374, www.manuela-vernazza. com, manuelamoggia@tiscali.it), **$$$ Villa Antonia** (2 nice rooms sharing 1 bathroom, D-€70, on the main drag, mobile 320-372-4570 or 333-971-5602), and **$$$ Elisabetta Rooms** (3 rooms that need updating but have fantastic views, Db-€65, fans, Via Carattino 62, mobile 347-451-1834, www.elisabettacarro.it, carroelisabetta @hotmail.com).

Eating in Vernazza

Breakfast

Locals take breakfast about as seriously as flossing. A cappuccino and a pastry or a piece of focaccia from a bar or bakery does it. Most of my recommended accommodations don't come with breakfast (when they do, I've noted so in my listings). Instead, you have several fun options. The first two, on the harborfront square, have the best ambience.

Ananasso Bar feels Old World, with youthful energy and a great location. They offer toasted *panini,* pastries, and designer cappuccino. You can eat a bit cheaper at the bar (you're welcome to picnic on the nearby bench or seawall rocks with a Mediterranean view) or enjoy the best-situated tables in town (Fri–Wed 8:00–late, closed Thu).

Burgus Wine Bar, described earlier in "Nightlife in Vernazza," serves a continental breakfast by the harbor for early birds (€4, from 6:45).

Blue Marlin Bar (mid-town, just below the train station) serves a good array of clearly priced à la carte items including eggs and bacon, adding up to the priciest breakfast in town (likely to total €10). It's run by Massimo and Carmen (Fri–Wed 7:00–24:00, closed Thu, tel. 0187-821-149). If you're awaiting a train any time of day, the Blue Marlin's outdoor seats beat the platform.

Il Pirata delle Cinque Terre is located at the top of the town, where the dynamic Sicilian duo Gianluca and Massimo (twins, a.k.a. the Canoli brothers) enthusiastically offer a great assortment of handcrafted authentic Sicilian pastries. Their fun and playful service makes up for the lack of a view. Gianluca is a pastry artist, hand-painting fanciful sculptured marzipan. Their sweet pastry breakfasts are a hit, with a stunning array of hot-out-of-the-oven treats like *panzerotto* (made of ricotta, cinnamon, and vanilla, €2.50) and hot meat-and-cheese bruschetta (€3). Other favorites include their *granite* (slushees made from fresh fruit), but, proudly, they serve no bacon and eggs (since "this is Italy"). While the atmosphere of the place seems like suburban Milan, it has a curious charisma among its customers—bringing Vernazza a welcome bit of Sicily (daily 6:30–24:00, also simple lunches and tasty dinners, Via Gavino 36, tel. 0187-812-047).

Lunch and Dinner

If you enjoy Italian cuisine and seafood, Vernazza's restaurants are worth the splurge. All take pride in their cooking. Wander around at about 20:00 and compare the ambience, but don't wait too late to eat—many kitchens close at 22:00. To get an outdoor table on summer weekends, reserve ahead. Expect to spend €10 for pastas, €12–16 for *secondi*, and €2–3 for a cover charge. Harborside restaurants and bars are easygoing. You're welcome to grab a cup of coffee or glass of wine and disappear somewhere on the breakwater, returning your glass when you're done. If you dine in Vernazza but are staying in another town, be sure to check train schedules before dining, as trains run less frequently in the evening. While kitchens are generally closed 15:00–19:00, snacks and drinks are served all day.

Above the Harbor, by the Castle

Ristorante Al Castello is run by gracious and English-speaking Monica, her husband Massimo, kind Mario, and the rest of her family (you won't see mamma—she's busy personally cooking each home-style *secondo*). Hike high above town to just below the castle for commanding views. Their *lasagne al pesto* and scampi crêpes are time-honored family specialties. For simple fare and a special evening, reserve one of the dozen romantic cliff-side sea-view tables for two (Thu–Tue 12:00–15:00 for lunch, 19:00–22:00 for dinner, closed Wed and Nov–April, tel. 0187-812-296).

Ristorante Belforte's experimental and creative cuisine includes a hearty *zuppa Michela* (€21 for a boatload of seafood), fishy *spaghetti Bruno* (€13), and *trofie al pesto* (hand-rolled noodles with pesto). Their classic *antipasto del nostro chef* (€36 for six plates) is designed to be plenty for two people. From the breakwater, follow either the stairs or the rope that leads up and around to the restaurant. You'll find a tangle of tables embedded in four levels of the lower part of the old castle. For the ultimate seaside perch, call and reserve one of four tables on the *terrazza con vista* (terrace with view). Most of Belforte's seating is outdoors—if the weather's bad, the interior can get crowded (€13 pastas, €23 *secondi*, Wed–Mon 12:00–22:00, limited menu 15:00–19:00, closed Tue and Nov–March, tel. 0187-812-222, Michela).

Harborside
Gambero Rosso ("red prawn," the same name as Italy's top restaurant guide) is considered Vernazza's most venerable restaurant. It feels classy and costs more than the others. Try Chef Claudio's namesake risotto (€15 pastas, €20 *secondi*, €3 cover, Tue–Sun 12:00–15:00 & 19:00–22:00, closed Mon and Dec–Feb, Piazza Marconi 7, tel. 0187-812-265).

Trattoria del Capitano might serve the best food for the money, including *spaghetti con frutti di mare* (pasta entangled with various types of seafood) and *grigliata mista*—a mix of seasonal Mediterranean fish (€10 pastas, €16 *secondi*, €2 cover, Wed–Mon 12:00–15:00 & 19:00–22:00, closed Tue except in Aug, closed Nov–Dec, tel. 0187-812-201, while Paolo speaks English, grandpa Giacomo doesn't need to).

Trattoria Gianni is an old standby for locals and tourists who appreciate the best prices on the harbor. You'll enjoy well-prepared seafood and receive steady, reliable, and friendly service from Emanuele and Alessandro (€10 pastas, €13 *secondi*, €3 cover, check their *menù cucina tipica Vernazza*, Thu–Tue 12:00–15:00 & 19:00–22:00, closed Wed except July–Aug, tel. 0187-812-228).

Ristorante Pizzeria Vulnetia is simpler, serving regional specialties such as prize-winning *tegame alla Vernazza*—anchovies, tomatoes, and potatoes baked in the oven (€8 pizzas, €10 pastas, €15 *secondi*, €2 cover, Tue–Sun 12:00–15:30 & 18:30–22:00, closed Thu, Piazza Marconi 29, tel. 0187-821-193).

Inland, on or near the Main Street
Several of Vernazza's inland eateries manage to compete without the harbor ambience, but with slightly cheaper prices.

Trattoria da Sandro, on the main drag, mixes Genovese and Ligurian cuisine with friendly service. It can be a peaceful alternative to the harborside scene, plus they dish up award-winning stuffed mussels (Wed–Mon 12:00–15:00 & 18:30–22:00, closed Tue, Via Roma 62, tel. 0187-812-223, Gabriella and Alessandro).

Antica Osteria Il Baretto is another solid bet for homey, reasonably priced traditional cuisine, run by Simone and Jenny. As it's

THE CINQUE TERRE

off the harbor and a little less glitzy than the others, it's favored by locals who prefer less noisy English while they eat (Tue–Sat 8:00–16:00 & 18:00–24:00, closed Mon, indoor and outdoor seating, Via Roma 31).

Ristorante Incadase da Piva is a rare bit of old Vernazza. For 25 years, charismatic Piva has been known for his *tegame alla Vernazza*, his *risotto con frutti di mare* (seafood risotto), and his love of music. The town troubadour, he often serenades his guests when the cooking's done (€13 pastas, €16 *secondi*, Fri–Wed 10:30–15:00 & 18:00–22:30, closed Thu, tucked away 20 yards off the main drag, up a lane behind the pharmacy).

Other Eating Options

Il Pirata delle Cinque Terre, popular for breakfast, is also a favorite for lunch and dinner (€9 pastas, salads, Sicilian specialties), and its homemade desserts and drinks. The Canoli twins entertain while they serve, as diners enjoy delicious meals while laughing out loud in this simple café/pastry shop (at the top of town; for complete description, see listing under "Breakfast," earlier).

Franco's Ristorante La Torre, sitting humbly above Vernazza on the trail to Corniglia, offers family-run warmth, a spectacular view, perfect peace, and especially romantic dinners at sunset. Hours can be sporadic, so confirm that he's open before hiking up (Wed–Mon 12:00–21:30, sometimes also open Tue, kitchen closed 15:00–19:30 but drinks served all day, cash only, tel. 0187-821-082, mobile 338-404-1181).

Bar Baia Saracena ("Saracen Bay") serves decent pizza and microwaved pastas out on the breakwater. Eat here for the economy and the view (€5–7 salads, €9 pizza, closed Wed July–Aug, closed Fri Sept–June, tel. 0187-812-113, Luca).

Pizzerias, Sandwiches, and Groceries: Vernazza's main street creatively fills tourists' needs. Two pizzerias stay busy, and while they mostly do take-out, each will let you sit and eat for the same cheap price. One has tables on the street, and the other **(Ercole)** hides a tiny terrace and a few tables out back (it's the only pizzeria in town with a wood-fired oven). **Rosticceria Ar Tian** sells pasta and cooked dishes by weight for a cheap meal to go (at bottom of Via Roma across from Gelateria Stalin). **Forno Bakery** has good focaccia and veggie tarts, and several bars sell sandwiches and pizza by the slice. **Grocery stores** also make inexpensive sandwiches to order (generally Mon–Tue and Thu–Sat 8:00–13:00 & 17:00–19:30, Wed 8:00–13:00, closed Sun). Tiny jars of pesto spread give elegance to picnics.

Gelato: The town's three *gelaterias* are good. What looks like Gelateria Amore Mio (near the grotto, mid-town), is actually Gelateria Stalin—founded in 1968 by a pastry chef with that unfortunate name. His niece Sonia, who speaks "ice cream," and nephew Francesco now run the place, and are generous with free tastes. They have a neat little licking zone with tiny benches hidden above the crowds; look for it on the little bridge a few steps past their door (daily 8:00–24:00, closes at 19:00 off-season, 24 flavors, sit there or take it to go).

Monterosso al Mare (Town #5)

This is a resort with a few cars and lots of hotels, rentable beach umbrellas, crowds, and a thriving late-night scene. Monterosso al Mare—the only Cinque Terre town built on flat land—has two parts: A new town (called Fegina) with a parking lot, train station, and TI; and an old town (Centro Storico), which cradles Old World charm in its small, crooked lanes. In the old town, you'll find hole-in-the-wall shops, pastel townscapes, and a new generation of creative small-businesspeople eager to keep their visitors happy.

A pedestrian tunnel connects the old with the new—but take a small detour around the point for a nicer walk. It offers a close-up view of two sights: a 16th-century lookout tower, built after the last serious pirate raid in 1545; and a Nazi "pillbox," a small, low concrete bunker where gunners hid. (During World War II, nearby La Spezia was an important Axis naval base, and Monterosso was bombed while the Germans were here.)

Strolling the waterfront promenade, you can pick out each of the Cinque Terre towns decorating the coast. After dark, they sparkle. Monterosso is the most enjoyable of the five for young travelers wanting to connect with other young travelers and looking for a little evening action. Even so, Monterosso is not a full-blown Portofino-style resort—and locals appreciate quiet, sensitive guests.

Orientation to Monterosso

Tourist Information

The TI Proloco is next to the train station (April–Oct daily 9:00–19:00, closed Nov–March, exit station and go left a few doors, tel. 0187-817-506, www.prolocomonterosso.it, info@proloco monterosso.it, Annamaria). The Cinque Terre has park offices

THE CINQUE TERRE

on Piazza Garibaldi in the old town and in the train station in the new town (daily 8:00–20:00, tel. 0187-817-059, www.parco nazionale5terre.it, parcoragazze@hotmail.com). If you arrive late on a summer day, head to the Internet café for tourist information (see below).

Arrival in Monterosso

By Train: Train travelers arrive in the new town, from which it's a scenic, flat 10-minute stroll to all the old-town action (leave station to the left; but for hotels in the new town, turn right out of station).

Shuttle buses run along the waterfront between the old town (Piazza Garibaldi, just beyond the tunnel), the train station, and the parking lot at the end of Via Fegina (*Campo Sportivo* stop). While the buses can be convenient, saving you a 10-minute schlep with your bags, they only go once an hour, and are likely not worth the trouble (€1.50, free with Cinque Terre Card).

The other alternative is to take a **taxi** (certain vehicles have permission to drive in the old city center). They usually wait outside the train station, but you may have to call (€7 from station to the old town, mobile 335-616-5842 or 335-628-0933).

By Car: Monterosso is 30 minutes off the freeway (exit: Levanto-Carrodano). Note that about three miles above Monterosso, a fork directs you to Centro Storico (old part of town—Via Roma parking lot with a few spots) or Fegina (the new town and beachfront parking, most likely where you want to go). You have to choose which area, because you can't drive directly from the new town to the old center, which is closed to cars without special permits.

Parking is easy (except July–Aug and summer weekends) in the huge beachfront guarded lot in the new town (€12/24 hours). If you're heading to the old town, the lot is on Via Roma, a 10-minute downhill walk to the main square (€1.50/hour, €15/24 hours in the parking structure). Near the lot you can parallel park along the road, but you pay €1.50 per hour and there's no daily limit. For the cheapest Monterosso rates, park at blue lines (5 minutes further uphill from Via Roma parking structure) for €8 per day. See "Cinque Terre Connections" at the end of this chapter for directions from Milan and tips on driving in the Cinque Terre.

Helpful Hints

Medical Help: The town's bike-riding, leather bag–toting, English-speaking doctor is Dr. Vitone, who charges €50–80 for a simple visit (less for poor students, mobile 338-853-0949).

Internet Access: The Net, a few steps off the main drag (Via

Roma), has 10 high-speed computers (€1.50/10 minutes) and Wi-Fi. Enzo happily provides information on the Cinque Terre, has a line on local accommodations, and can burn your photos onto a CD for €6 (daily 9:30–23:00, off-season closes for lunch and dinner breaks, Via Vittorio Emanuele 55, tel. 0187-817-288, mobile 335-778-5085, www.monterosso net.com).

Laundry: Lavarapido, in the new part of town, will return your laundry to your hotel for you (€12/13 pounds, daily 8:30–22:00, Via Molinelli 17, mobile 339-484-0940, Lucia).

Massage: Giorgio Moggia, the local physiotherapist, gives good massages at your hotel or in his studio (€60/hour, tel. 339-314-6127, giomogg@tin.it).

Self-Guided Walk

Welcome to Monterosso

• *Hike out from the dock in the old town and climb a few rough steps to the very top of the...*

Breakwater: If you're visiting by boat, you'll start here anyway. From this point, you can survey the old town and the new town (stretching to the left, with train station and parking lot). The little fort above is a private home. The harbor now hosts more paddleboats than fishing boats. Sand erosion is a major problem. The partial breakwater is designed to save the beach from washing away. While old-timers remember a vast beach, their grandchildren truck in sand each spring to give tourists something to lie on. (The Nazis liked the Cinque Terre, too—find two of their bomb-hardened bunkers, near left and far right.)

The fancy €300-a-night four-star Hotel Porto Roca (on the far right) marks the trail to Vernazza. High above, you see the costly road built in the 1980s to connect Cinque Terre towns with the freeway over the hills. The two capes (Punta di Montenero and Punta Mesco) define the Cinque Terre region—you can just about make out the towns from here. The closer cape, Punta Mesco, marks an important sea-life sanctuary, home to a rare sea grass that provides an ideal home for fish eggs. Buoys keep fishing boats away. The cape was once a quarry, providing employment to locals who chipped out the stones used to cobble the streets of Genoa. On the far end of the new town, marking the best free beach around, you can just see the statue named *Il Gigante*. It's 45 feet tall and once held a trident. While it looks as if it was hewn from the rocky cliff, it's actually made of reinforced concrete and dates from the beginning of the 20th century, when it supported a dancing terrace for a *fin de siècle* villa. A violent storm left the giant holding nothing but memories of Monterosso's glamorous age.

• *From the breakwater, walk to the old-town square (just past the train tracks and beyond the beach). Find the statue of a dandy holding what looks like a box cutter in...*

Piazza Garibaldi: The statue honors Giuseppe Garibaldi, the dashing firebrand revolutionary who, in 1870, helped unite the people of Italy into a modern nation. Facing Garibaldi, with your back to the sea, you'll see (from right to left) the City Hall (with the now-required European Union flag aside the Italian one), a big home and recreation center for poor and homeless elderly, and a park information center (in a building bombed in 1945 by the Allies, who were attempting to take out the train line). You'll also see the A Ca' du Sciensa pub (with historic town photos inside and upstairs, you're welcome to pop in for a look—see "Nightlife in Monterosso," later in this section). There's a little "anchovy visitors center" behind the City Hall, in case you've got a hankering for a salty little snack.

Just under the bell tower (with back to the sea, it's on your left), a set of covered arcades facing the sea is where the old-timers hang out (they see all and know all). The crenellated bell tower marks the church.

• *Go to church (the entrance is on the inland side).*

Church of St. John the Baptist: This black-and-white church, with marble from Carrara, is typical of this region's Romanesque style. Note the lacy stone rose window above the entrance. The church dates from 1307—the proud inscription on the middle column inside reads "MilleCCCVII." Outside the church, on the side facing the main street, find the high-water mark from a November 1966 flood (the same month as the flood that devastated Florence).

• *Leaving the church, turn left immediately and go to church again.*

Oratory of the Dead: During the Counter-Reformation, the Catholic Church offset the rising influence of the Lutherans by creating brotherhoods of good works. These religious Rotary clubs were called "confraternities." Monterosso had two, nicknamed White and Black. This building is the oratory of the Black group, whose mission—as the macabre decor indicates—was to arrange for funerals and take care of widows, orphans, the shipwrecked, and the souls of those who ignore the request for a €1 donation. It dates from the 16th century, and membership has passed from father to son for generations. Notice the fine 17th-century carved choir stalls just inside the door. Look up on the ceiling to find the symbol of the confraternity: a skull, crossbones, and an hourglass... death awaits us all.

• *Return to the beach and find the brick steps that lead up to the hill-capping convent (starting between the train tracks and the pedestrian tunnel).*

The Switchbacks of the Friars: Follow the yellow brick road

THE CINQUE TERRE

Monterosso al Mare

NOTE: NOT TO SCALE –
TRAIN STATION TO
PIAZZA GARIBALDI
IS A 5-MINUTE STROLL

TO LEVANTO & AUTOSTRADA
EXIT: CARRODANO OR BRUGNATO

VIA MESCO

VIA IV

VIA PADRE SEM

VIA IV NOV.

NEW TOWN
(FEGINA)

MOLINELLI

TRAIN
STATION

TO
TRAIL TO
LEVANTO

VIA E. MONTALE

BEACH

VIA

P

FREE BEACH

FREE
BEACH

L I G U R I A N

↙ FREE BEACH
IL GIGANTE STATUE

1. Hotel Villa Steno
2. Albergo Pasquale
3. La Poesia Rooms
4. Locanda il Maestrale
5. Albergo Marina
6. Hotel la Colonnina
7. Il Giardino Incantato & Rist. L'Alta Marea

8. L'Antica Terrazza
9. Manuel's Guesthouse
10. Buranco Agriturismo
11. Hotel Souvenir
12. Albergo al Carugio
13. Il Timone Rooms

14. A Cà du Gigante
15. Hotel Baia
16. Hotel Punta Mesco
17. Pensione Agavi
18. Ristorante Belvedere
19. Ciak Restaurant

(OK, it's orange...but I couldn't help singing as I skipped skyward). Go constantly uphill until you reach a convent church, then a cemetery, in a ruined castle at the summit. The lane *(Salita dei Cappuccini)* is nicknamed *Zii di Frati* ("switchbacks of the friars"). Midway up the switchbacks, you'll see a statue of St. Francis and a wolf enjoying a grand view.

• *From here, backtrack 20 yards and continue uphill. When you reach a gate marked* Convento e Chiesa Cappuccini, *you have arrived.*

Church of the Capuchin Friars: The former convent (until recently a hotel) now accommodates friars. Before stepping inside, notice the church's striped Romanesque facade. It's all fake. Tap

20 Via Venti Restaurant
21 Miky Restaurant
22 La Cantina Di Miky
23 Ristorante Tortuga
24 Il Frantoio Focacceria

25 Pizzeria la Smorfia & The Net
26 Focacceria de Ely
27 Il Casello Bar
28 A Ca' du Sciensa Pub

29 Enoteca Eliseo
30 Fast Bar
31 Lavarapido Laundry
32 "Anchovy Visitors Center"

it—no marble, just cheap 18th-century stucco. Sit in the rear pew. The high altarpiece painting of St. Francis can be rolled up on special days to reveal a statue of Mary, which stands behind it. Look at the statue of St. Anthony to the right and smile (you're on convent camera). Wave at the security camera—they're nervous about the precious painting to your left.

This fine painting of the Crucifixion is attributed to Antony Van Dyck, the Flemish master who lived and worked for years in nearby Genoa (though art historians suspect that, at best, it was painted by someone in the artist's workshop). When Jesus died, the earth went dark. Notice the eclipsed sun in the painting, just to the right of the cross. Do the electric candles work? Pick one up, pray for peace, and plug it in. (Leave €0.50, or unplug it and put it back.)

• *Leave and turn left to hike uphill to the cemetery that fills the remains of the castle, capping the hill. Look out from the gate and enjoy the view.*

Cemetery and Ruined Castle: In the Dark Ages, the village huddled within this castle. Slowly it expanded. Notice the town view from here—no sea. You're looking at the oldest part of Monterosso, huddled behind the hill, out of view of 13th-century pirates. Explore the cemetery, but remember that cemeteries are sacred and treasured places (as is clear by the abundance of fresh flowers). Ponder the black-and-white photos of grandparents past. *Q.R.P.* is *Qui Riposa in Pace* (a.k.a. R.I.P.). Rich families had their own little tomb buildings. See if you can find the Odoardo family tomb—look to the wall on the left (apparently, February 30 happened in Monterosso). Climb to the very summit—the castle's keep, or place of last refuge. Priests are buried in a line of graves closest to the sea, but facing inland—the town's holy sanctuary high on the hillside (above the road, hiding behind trees). Each Cinque Terre town has a lofty sanctuary, dedicated to Mary and dear to the village hearts.

• *From here, your tour is over—any trail leads you back into town.*

Sights in Monterosso

Beaches—Monterosso's beaches, immediately in front of the train station, are easily the Cinque Terre's best and most crowded. This town is a sandy resort with rentable beach extras: Figure €20 to rent two chairs and an umbrella for the day. Light lunches are served by beach cafés to sunbathers at their lounge chairs. It's often worth the euros to enjoy a private beach. Beaches are free (and marked on the Monterosso al Mare map) only where you see no umbrellas. Don't use your white hotel towels; most hotels will give you beach towels—sometimes for a fee. The local hidden beach, which is free and generally less crowded, is tucked away under Il Casello restaurant at the east end of town, near the trailhead to Vernazza. The beach is gravelly, and for some, best enjoyed with water shoes. The bocce ball court (next to Il Casello) is busy with the old boys enjoying their favorite pastime.

Kayaks—Samba rents kayaks on the beach (€7/hour for 1-person kayak, €12/hour for 2-person kayak, to the right of train station as you exit, mobile 339-681-2265, Domenico). The paddle to Vernazza is a favorite.

Shuttle Buses for High-Country Hikes—Monterosso's bus service (described earlier in "Arrival in Monterosso") continues beyond the town limits, but check the schedules—only one or two departures a day head into the high country. Some buses go to the Sanctuary of Soviore, where you can hike back down to Monterosso (1.5 hours, moderately steep). Rides cost €1.50 (free with Cinque Terre Card, pick up schedule from park office). Or you can hike to Levanto (no Cinque Terre card necessary, not as stunning as the rest of the coastal trail, 2.5 hours, straight uphill and then easy decline, follow signs at west end of the new town). For hiking details, ask at either park info booth (at the train station or Piazza Garibaldi).

Wine Tasting—Buranco Agriturismo offers visits to their vineyard and cantina daily at 12:00. You'll taste two of their wines plus a grappa and a *limoncino*—along with home-cooked food (€25/person with snacks, €40/person for full lunch, reservations required at least three days in advance, English may be limited, follow Via Buranco uphill to path, 10 minutes above town, tel. 0187-817-677, www.burancocinqueterre.it). They also rent apartments; see "Sleeping in Monterosso," on the next page.

Boat Rides—From the old-town harbor, boats run nearly hourly (10:30–17:00) to Vernazza, Manarola, Riomaggiore, and Portovenere. Schedules are posted in Cinque Terre park offices (for details, see "Getting Around the Cinque Terre: By Boat," on page 320).

Angelo's Boat Tours—Local fisherman Angelo and his American wife Paula are now fishers of tourists who'd love to take you out for a scenic cruise. You'll swim, explore the coast, snorkel in a private cove below a waterfall, and lunch on freshly caught fish. Paula enjoys cooking for guests (4–10 people: €500/4-hour cruise, €600/5 hours; 1–3 people: €85/hour for the boat plus €35/person for the meal—no meal charge for kids 13 and under; €85/person for 2-hour sunset tapas cruise, mobile 333-318-2967, angelosboat tours@yahoo.com).

Nightlife in Monterosso

A Ca' du Sciensa has nothing to do with science—it's the last name of the town moneybags who owned this old mansion. The antique dumbwaiter is still in use—a remnant from the days when servants toiled downstairs while the big shots wined and dined up top. This classy yet laid-back pub offers breezy square seating, bar action on the ground level, an intimate lounge upstairs, and discreet balconies overlooking the square to share with your best travel buddy. It's a good place for light meals such as salads (until 24:00) and plenty of drinks. Luca encourages you to wander around the place and enjoy the old Cinque Terre photo collection (daily 10:00–2:00 in the morning, serves late-night sandwiches and microwaved pasta, closed Nov–March, Piazza Garibaldi 17, tel. 0187-818-233).

Enoteca Eliseo, the first wine bar in town, comes with operatic ambience. Eliseo and his wife, Mary, love music and wine. You can select a fine bottle from their shop shelf, and for €7 extra, enjoy it and the village action from their cozy tables. Wines sold by the glass *(bicchiere)* are posted (Wed–Mon 9:00–24:00, closed Tue, Piazza Matteotti 3, a few blocks inland behind church, tel. 0187-817-308).

Fast Bar, the best bar in town for young travelers and night owls, is located on Via Roma in the old town. Customers mix travel tales with big, cold beers, and the crowd (and the rock 'n' roll) gets noisier as the night rolls on. Come here to watch Italian or American sporting events on their TV any time of day (sandwiches and snacks usually served until midnight, open nightly until 2:00, closed Thu Nov–March).

La Cantina Da Miky, in the new town just beyond the train station, is a trendy downstairs bar-restaurant with an extensive cocktail and grappa menu. Run by Manuel, son of well-known local restaurateur Miky, it sometimes hosts live music. Take advantage of its outdoor seating by the beach. This could be just the place to meet your future well-heeled Ligurian *amore* (daily until well after 24:00, Via Fegina 90, tel. 0187-802-525).

Sleeping in Monterosso

(€1 = about $1.25, country code: 39)

Monterosso, the most beach–resort-y of the five Cinque Terre towns, offers maximum comfort and ease. The TI Proloco just outside the train station can give you a list of €70–80 double rooms. Rooms in Monterosso are a better value for your money than similar rooms in crowded Vernazza, and the proprietors seem more genuine and welcoming. To locate the hotels, see the Monterosso al Mare map.

In the Old Town

$$$ Hotel Villa Steno is lovingly managed and features great view balconies, private gardens off some rooms, air-conditioning, and the friendly help of English-speaking Matteo and his wife Carla. Of their 16 rooms, 12 have view balconies (Sb-€100, Db-€165, Tb-€190, Qb-€220, includes hearty buffet breakfast, €10 per night discount with cash and this book in 2011, Internet access and Wi-Fi in lobby, laundry, Via Roma 109, tel. 0187-817-028 or 0187-818-336, fax 0187-817-354, www.villasteno.com, steno@pasini.com). It's a 10-minute hike (or €7 taxi ride) from the train station to the top of the old town. Readers get a free Cinque Terre info packet and a glass of the local sweet wine, *sciacchetrà*, when they check in—ask for it. The Steno has a tiny parking lot for guests (€5/day, reserve in advance).

$$$ Albergo Pasquale is a modern, comfortable place, run by the same family as the Hotel Villa Steno (above). It's conveniently located just a few steps from the beach, boat dock, tunnel entrance to the new town, and train tracks. While there is some traffic and train noise, it's located right on the harbor and has an elevator, offering easier access than most (same prices and welcome drink as Villa Steno; air-con, all rooms with sea view, Via Fegina 8, tel. 0187-817-550 or 0187-817-477, fax 0187-817-056, www.hotel pasquale.com, pasquale@pasini.com, Felicita and Marco).

$$$ La Poesia has four warmly colored rooms that share a peaceful garden terrace, where you'll enjoy a complimentary *aperitivo* upon arrival. A shuttle to/from the train station is also included (Db-€150, suite not worth €40 extra, air-con, Via Genova 4, tel. 0187-817-283, www.lapoesia-cinqueterre.com, info@lapoesia -cinqueterre.com, mamma Nicoletta speaks little English, daughter Veronica speaks more).

$$$ Locanda il Maestrale rents six small, stylish rooms in a sophisticated and peaceful little inn. While renovated with all the modern comforts, it retains centuries-old character under frescoed ceilings. Its peaceful sun terrace overlooking the old town and Via Roma action is a delight (small Db-€110, Db-€140, suite-€170, less off-season, 10 percent discount with cash and this book, air-con, Wi-Fi, Via Roma 37, tel. 0187-817-013, mobile 338-4530-531, fax 0187-817-084, www.locandamaestrale.net, maestrale@monterosso net.com, Stefania).

$$$ Albergo Marina, creatively run by enthusiastic husband-and-wife team Marina and Eraldo, has 23 thoughtfully appointed rooms and a garden with lemon trees. With a free, delicious buffet featuring local specialties from 14:00 to 19:00 daily, they offer a great value (standard Db-€115, big Db-€128, 10 percent discount with cash and this book in 2011, elevator, air-con; free use of bikes, kayak, and snorkel equipment; two-person wine-barrel hot tub costs extra; Via Buranco 40, tel. 0187-817-613, fax 0187-817-242, www.hotelmarina5terre.com, marina@hotel marina5terre.com).

$$$ Hotel la Colonnina, a comfy, modern place with 21 big and pretty rooms, is buried in the town's fragrant and sleepy back streets with no sea views (Db-€142, Tb-€200, Qb-€225, €15 more for bigger rooms with viewless terrace, cash or traveler's checks only, air-con, Internet access and Wi-Fi, fridges, elevator, inviting rooftop terrace with sun beds, garden, Via Zuecca 6, tel. 0187-817-439, fax 0187-817-788, www.lacolonninacinqueterre.it, info@lacolonninacinqueterre.it, Christina). The hotel is in the old town behind the statue of Garibaldi (take street to left of A Ca' du Sciensa one block up).

$$$ **Il Giardino Incantato** ("The Enchanted Garden") is a charming four-room B&B in a tastefully renovated 16th-century Ligurian home in the heart of the old town. Breakfast is served in a hidden garden (choose from an extensive list the night before), and the garden is illuminated with candles in the evening (Db-€170, Db suite-€200, air-con, free minibar and tea and coffee service, Via Mazzini 18, tel. 0187-818-315, mobile 333-264-9252, www.ilgiardinoincantato.net, giardino_incantato@libero.it, kind and eager to please Fausto and Mariapia).

$$$ **L'Antica Terrazza** rents four classy rooms right in town. With a pretty terrace overlooking the pedestrian street and minimal stairs, Raffaella offers a good deal (Db-€110, 5 percent discount with cash, air-con, Wi-Fi and Internet access, Vicolo San Martino 1, tel. 0187-817-499, mobile 347-132-6213, anticaterrazza @libera.it).

$$$ **Manuel's Guesthouse,** perched among terraces, is a garden getaway ruled by disheveled artist Manuel and run by his nephew Lorenzo. They have seven big, bright rooms and a grand view. Their killer terrace is hard to leave—especially after a few drinks (Db-€120, Db suite with view-€140, prices good with this book, cash only, air-con, Wi-Fi and Internet access, in old town, up about 100 steps behind church at top of town, Via San Martino 39, mobile 333-439-0809 or 329-547-3775, www.manuelsguest house.com, info@manuelsguesthouse.com).

$$$ **Buranco Agriturismo,** a 10-minute walk from the old town, has wonderful gardens and views over the vine-covered valley. Its primary business is wine and olive-oil production (their wine is judged among the 100 best in Italy), but they offer three apartments for a great value. It's a rare opportunity to stay in a farmhouse but still be able to get to town on foot (2–6 people-€60/ person including breakfast, €30/child under 12, dinner on request, air-con, free shuttle from station, bottle of their wine included, open year-round, tel. 0187-817-677, mobile 349-434-8046, fax 0187-802-084, www.burancocinqueterre.it, info@buranco.it, informally run by Loredana, Mary, and Giulietta).

$$ **Hotel Souvenir** is Monterosso's cash-only backpacker's hotel. Family-run, it has two buildings, each utilitarian but comfortable (one more stark than the other). Both share a lounge and pleasant leafy courtyard. The first is for students (S-€30, Sb-€35, D-€55, Db-€70, T-€105, breakfast-€5); the other is nicer and pricier (Sb-€45, Db-€80, Tb-€120, includes breakfast; guests receive 20 percent discount at La Pineta beach-chair rental near the train station). Walk three blocks inland from the main old-town square to Via Gioberti 24 (tel. 0187-817-822, tel. & fax 0187-817-595, hotel_souvenir@yahoo.com, helpful Beppe).

$$ Albergo al Carugio is a simple, practical nine-room place in a big apartment-style building at the top of the old town. It's quiet, comfy, yet forgettable, with no discernable management, and run in a crooked-painting-on-the-wall way (Db-€90 July–Aug, otherwise €65–80, air-con, Via Roma 100, tel. 0187-817-453, alcarugio@virgilio.it).

$$ Il Timone Rooms, a little B&B by the post office, has three tidy, modern rooms. Francesco also rents a few rooms near the cemetery, but they aren't worth the hike (Db-€90, breakfast at a bar, air-con, Via Roma 75, tel. 349-870-8666, www.iltimonedi monterosso.it).

In the New Town
$$$ A Cà du Gigante, despite its name, is a tiny yet stylish refuge with nine rooms. About 100 yards from the beach (and surrounded by blocky apartments on a modern street), the interior is done with taste and modern comfort in mind (Db-€160, Db sea-view suite-€180, includes parking, air-con, 10 percent discount with 3-night stay and this book in 2011, occasional last-minute deals, Via IV Novembre 11, tel. 0187-817-401, fax 0187-817-375, www.ilgigante cinqueterre.it, gigante@ilgigantecinqueterre.it, Claudia).

$$$ Hotel Baia (by-yah), overlooking the beach near the station, has clean high-ceilinged dimly lit rooms, dark hallways, and impersonal staff. Of the hotel's 28 rooms, half have views. The best little two-chair view balconies are on top floors (Db-€180, non-view Db in back-€150, elevator only for baggage and guests with disabilities, minimum 2-night stay May–Sept, Via Fegina 88, tel. 0187-817-512, fax 0187-818-322, www.baiahotel.it, info@baiahotel.it).

$$$ Hotel Punta Mesco is a tidy and well-run little haven renting 17 quiet, modern rooms without views, but 10 have small terraces. For the price, it's perhaps the best comfort in town (Db-€126, Tb-€170, 5 percent discount with cash, air-con, Wi-Fi, free bike loan, free parking, Via Molinelli 35, tel. & fax 0187-817-495, www.hotelpuntamesco.it, info@hotelpuntamesco.it, Diego).

$$$ Pensione Agavi has 10 bright, airy, quiet, and overpriced rooms, about half overlooking the beach near the big rock. This is not a place to party—it feels like an old hospital with narrow hallways (D-€80, Db-€110, Tb-€140, no breakfast, cash only, refrigerators, turn left out of station to Fegina 30, tel. 0187-817-171, mobile 333-697-4071, fax 0187-818-264, hotel.agavi@libero.it).

Eating in Monterosso

Ristorante Belvedere is *the* place for a good-value meal indoors or outdoors on the harborfront. Their *amfora belvedere*—mixed seafood stew—is huge, and can easily be shared by up to four

(€45). Share with your group and add pasta for a fine meal. Mussel fans will enjoy the *tagliolini della casa* (€8). It's energetically run by Federico and Roberto (€9 pastas, €12 *secondi*, €2 cover, Wed–Mon 12:00–14:30 & 19:00–22:00, usually closed Tue, on the harbor in the old town, tel. 0187-817-033).

L'Alta Marea offers special fish ravioli, the catch of the day, and huge crocks of fresh, steamed mussels. Young chef Marco cooks with charisma, while his wife, Anna, takes good care of the guests. This place is quieter, buried in the old town two blocks off the beach, and has covered tables out front for people-watching. This is a good opportunity to try rabbit (€9 pastas, €12–15 *secondi*, €2 cover, 10 percent discount with cash and this book in 2011, Thu–Tue 12:00–15:00 & 18:00–22:00, closed Wed, Via Roma 54, tel. 0187-817-170).

Ciak—a cut above its neighbors in elegance and also a little higher in price—is known for their huge sizzling terra-cotta crocks for two, crammed with the day's catch and either accompanied by risotto or spaghetti, or swimming in a soup *(zuppa)*. Another popular choice is the seafood *antipasto Lampara*. Stroll a couple of paces past the outdoor tables up Via Roma to see what Ciak's got on the stove (Thu–Tue 12:00–15:00 & 19:00–22:30, closed Wed, tel. 0187-817-014).

Via Venti is a fun little trattoria, buried in an alley deep in the heart of the old town, where Papa Ettore creates imaginative seafood dishes using the day's catch and freshly made pasta. Ilaria and her partner Michele serve up delicate and savory gnocchi (tiny potato dumplings) with crab sauce, tender ravioli stuffed with fresh fish in a swordfish sauce, and pear-and-cheese pasta. There's nothing pretentious here...just good cooking, service, and prices (€11 pastas, €16 *secondi*, Fri–Wed 12:00–15:30 & 18:30–22:00, closed Thu, tel. 0187-818-347). From the bottom of Via Roma, with your back to the sea and the church to your left, head to the right down Via XX Settembre and follow it to the end, to #32.

Miky is packed with well-dressed locals who know their seafood and want to eat it in a classy environment, but don't want to spend a fortune. For elegantly presented, top-quality food, this is my Cinque Terre favorite. It's clearly a proud family operation: Miky (dad), Simonetta (mom), and charming Sara (daughter) all work hard. All their pasta is "pizza pasta"—cooked normally but finished in a bowl that's encased in a thin pizza crust. They cook the concoction in a wood-fire oven to keep in the aroma. Miky's has a fine wine list with many available by the glass if you ask. If I was ever to require a dessert, it would be their mixed sampler plate, *dolce mista*—€10 and plenty for two (€15 pastas, €22 *secondi*, €8 sweets, Wed–Mon 12:00–15:00 & 19:00–23:00, closed Tue, reservations wise in summer, diners tend to dress up a bit; in the new town 100 yards north of train station at Via Fegina 104; tel. 0187-817-608).

La Cantina Di Miky, a few doors down toward the station, serves Ligurian specialties, following in Miky's family tradition of quality (it's run by son Manuel). It's more trendy and informal than Miky's, and you can sit downstairs or on the outdoor terrace (€15 anchovy tasting plate, €12 pastas, €15 *secondi,* creative desserts, daily 11:00–24:00 or later, Via Fegina 90, tel. 0187-802-525). This place doubles as a cocktail bar in the evenings—see "Nightlife in Monterosso," earlier in this section.

Ristorante Tortuga is the top option in Monterosso for sea-view elegance, with gorgeous outdoor seating on a bluff and an elegant white tablecloth–and-candles interior. If you're out and about, drop by to consider which table you'd like to reserve for later (€15 pastas, €20 *secondi,* closed Mon, just outside the tunnel that connects the old and new town, daily 12:00–14:30 & 18:00–22:00, tel. 0187-800-065, mobile 333-240-7956, Silvia and Giamba).

Light Meals, Take-Out Food, and Breakfast

Lots of shops and bakeries sell pizza and focaccia for an easy picnic at the beach or on the trail. At **Il Frantoio,** Simone makes tasty pizza to go or to munch perched on a stool (Fri–Wed 9:00–14:00 & 16:00–19:30, closed Thu, just off Via Roma at Via Gioberti 1, tel. 0187-818-333). **Pizzeria la Smorfia** also cooks up good pizza to eat in or take out (Tue–Sun 11:30–15:00 & 18:00–23:00, closed Mon, 73 Via Vittorio Emanuele, tel. 0187-818-395). **Focacceria de Ely** makes airy focaccia and thick-crust pizzas for casual seating or take-out (daily 10:30–20:00, until 24:00 in summer, Emigliano).

Il Casello is the only place for a fun meal on a terrace over-looking the old town beach. With outdoor tables on a rocky outcrop, it's a good bet for a salad or a sandwich, or a well-prepared pasta or *secondi.* For an economic meal with romance, reserve the balcony upstairs (daily June–Aug, meals from 11:30 and 22:30, closed Nov–March, tel. 333-492-7629, Bacco).

Cinque Terre Connections

By Train

The five towns of the Cinque Terre are on a pokey milk-run train line (described in "Getting Around the Cinque Terre," on page 319). Erratically timed but roughly hourly trains connect each town with the others, plus La Spezia, Genoa, and Riviera towns to the north. While a few of these local trains go to more distant points (Milan or Pisa), it's much faster to change in La Spezia, Monterosso, or Sestri Levante to a bigger train (local train info tel. 0187-817-458).

From La Spezia Centrale by Train to: Rome (7/day, 4 hours, more with changes, €45), **Pisa** (about hourly, 1–1.5 hours, €5), **Florence** (5/day direct, otherwise nearly hourly, 2.5 hours, €10), **Milan** (about hourly, 3 hours direct or with change in Genoa, €22), **Venice** (about hourly, 5–6 hours, 1–3 changes, €50).

From Monterosso by Train to: Venice (about hourly, 6–7 hours, 1–3 changes, €52), **Milan** (8/day direct, otherwise hourly, 3–4 hours, more with change in Genoa, €22), **Genoa** (hourly, 1.2–2 hours, €8), **Turin** (8/day, 3–4 hours, €20), **Pisa** (hourly, 35–60 minutes, €6-10), **Sestri Levante** (hourly, 20–40 minutes, most trains to Genoa stop here, €3), **La Spezia** (hourly, 20–30 minutes), **Levanto** (nearly hourly, 4 minutes), **Santa Margherita Ligure** (at least hourly, 45 minutes, €2), **Rome** (hourly, 4.5 hours, change in La Spezia, €50). For destinations in **France,** change trains in Genoa.

By Car

Because these towns are close together and have frequent transportation connections, bringing a car to the Cinque Terre is not the best idea. If your plans require it, however, here are some basic tips: stay in a hotel that includes parking, use public transportation or hike between towns, and for day-trip parking, go to Monterosso (€12–15/day), Riomaggiore (€22/day), or Manarola (€15/day). Don't drive to Vernazza, as finding a spot is tough. Parking anywhere on the Cinque Terre is truly a mess in July and August.

Milan to the Cinque Terre (130 miles): Drivers speed south on autostrada A-7 from Milan, skirt Genoa, and drive a little bit of Italy's curviest and narrowest freeways, passing the Cinque Terre toward the port of La Spezia (A-12). Another option is to take the slightly more straight A-1 via the city of Parma, followed by the A-15 to La Spezia. This route takes the same amount of time (about 2.5 hours), even though it covers more miles.

Coming from either direction, and for either Monterosso or Vernazza, exit autostrada A-12 at *uscita Carrodano*, northwest of La Spezia. Don't take Cinque Terre exits before Carrodano to reach these towns.

Monterosso is 30 minutes from the autostrada. Remember that the highway divides as you approach Monterosso—you must choose between the road to Centro Storico (the old town) or the one to Fegina (the new town and beachfront parking). **Vernazza** is 45 minutes from the autostrada. The drive down to Vernazza is scenic, narrow, and scary, and you'll probably lose time looking for parking.

To drive to **Riomaggiore, Corniglia,** or **Manarola,** leave the freeway at La Spezia.

Within the Cinque Terre: On busy weekends, holidays, and in July and August, both Vernazza and Monterosso fill up, and police at the top of town will deny entry to anyone without a hotel reservation. It's smart to have a confirmation in hand. If you don't, insist (politely) that they allow you to enter—but only if you actually have a room reserved (the police might call your hotel to check your story).

Parking Tips: Each Cinque Terre town has a parking lot and a once-an-hour shuttle bus to get you into town (except Corniglia), though all parking areas are no more than a 10-minute walk uphill from the center.

White signs post valid hours for pay parking, which usually don't charge 24:00–8:00. Anyone can park where there are blue lines. Parking is cash only in all towns (except Riomaggiore, where some readers have been overcharged on their credit cards—best to pay in cash).

If you plan to find parking in any of the Cinque Terre towns, try to arrive between 10:00–11:00, when overnight visitors are usually departing. Or you can park your car in La Spezia or Levanto (see next chapter), then take the train into the town of your choice. In these bigger towns, confirm that your parking spot is OK, and leave nothing inside to steal.

A few hotels offer parking for free or a daily charge. In **Monterosso,** consider Hotel Villa Steno, A Cà du Gigante, or Hotel Punta Mesco. For **Riomaggiore,** try Locanda del Sole, Locanda Ca' dei Duxi, or Villa Argentina. In Volastra (a shuttle ride above **Manarola**), try Hotel il Saraceno. Rooms listed in this book for Corniglia and Vernazza do not offer parking.

RIVIERA TOWNS NEAR THE CINQUE TERRE

Levanto • Sestri Levante • Santa Margherita Ligure • Portofino • La Spezia • Carrara • Portovenere

The Cinque Terre is tops, but several towns to the north have a breezy beauty and more beaches. Towns to the south offer a mix of marble, trains, and yachts.

Levanto, the northern gateway to the Cinque Terre, has a long beach and a scenic, strenuous trail to Monterosso al Mare. Sestri Levante, on a narrow peninsula flanked by two beaches, is for sun-seekers. Santa Margherita Ligure is more of a real town, with actual sights, beaches, and easy connections with Portofino by trail, bus, or boat. All three towns are a straight shot to the Cinque Terre by train.

South of the Cinque Terre, you'll likely pass through (don't stay unless you're desperate) the workaday town of La Spezia, the southern gateway to the Cinque Terre. Carrara is a quickie for marble-lovers who are driving between Pisa and La Spezia. The picturesque village of Portovenere, near La Spezia, has scenic boat connections with Cinque Terre towns.

Public transportation is the best way to get around this region. All of the places in this chapter are well connected by train and/or boat.

North of the Cinque Terre

Levanto

Graced with a long, sandy beach, Levanto is packed in summer. The rest of the year, it's just a small, sleepy town, with less colorful charm and fewer tourists than the Cinque Terre. With quick connections to Monterosso (4 minutes by train), Levanto makes a decent home base if you can't snare a room in the Cinque Terre.

Levanto has a new section (with a regular grid street plan) and a twisty old town (bisected by a modern street), plus a few pedestrian streets and a castle (not tourable). From Levanto, you can take a no-wimps-allowed hike to Monterosso (2.5 hours) or hop a boat to the Cinque Terre towns and beyond.

Orientation to Levanto

Tourist Information

The TI is on Piazza Mazzini (Mon–Sat 9:00–13:00 & 15:00–18:00, Sun 9:00–13:00, tel. 0187-808-125, www.comune.levanto.sp.it, info@comune.levanto.sp.it).

Arrival in Levanto

By Train: It's a 10-minute walk from the Levanto train station to the TI in town (head down stairs in front of station, turn right, cross bridge, then follow Corso Roma to Piazza Mazzini).

By Car: Drivers can use the cheap short-term parking in the lots in front of and on either side of the train station (€6/8 hours, €9/24 hours, note that you have to pay at the machines each day—so long-term parking is difficult). Another option is the lot across the river from the hospital on the way into town (first left after the hospital, cross bridge and immediately turn left), or north of the church on Via del Mercato (can be free during high season, except Wed before 14:00). For long-term parking, try the lots at Piazza Mazzini or either side of the TI (€15/day). Parking is always in flux, so confirm rates and availability with your hotelier or the TI.

Helpful Hints

Markets: Levanto's modern covered *mercato*, which sells produce and fish, is on Via del Mercato, between the TI and train station (Mon–Sat 8:00–13:00, closed Sun). On Wednesday morning, an **open-air market** with clothes, shoes, and housewares fills the street in front of the *mercato*.

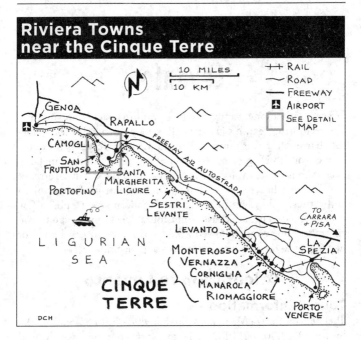

Riviera Towns near the Cinque Terre

Internet Access: Try **Viaggi Beraldi** at Via Garibaldi 102 (€2/30 minutes, Mon–Sat 9:00–13:00 & 15:30–19:30, closed Sun, tel. 0187-800-818).

Baggage Storage: None is available at the station. The nearest baggage storage is in Riomaggiore (see page 331) or Santa Margherita Ligure (page 395).

Laundry: A self-service launderette is at Piazza Staglieno 38 (wash-€5 including soap, dry-€5, open 24 hours daily, mobile 335-653-5964).

Bike Rental: Cicli Raso North Shore rents bikes (€8–20/day depending on type of bike, daily 9:30–12:30 & 15:30–19:30, closed Sun Nov–April, Via Garibaldi 63, tel. 0187-802-511, www.cicliaraso-levanto.com).

Sights in Levanto

Beach—The beach is just two blocks away from the TI. As you face the harbor, the boat dock is to your far left, and the diving center is to your far right (rental boats available at either place in summer). You can also rent a kayak or canoe on the beach, just below the east end of the Piazza Mazzini parking lot.

During the summer, three parts of the beach are free: both sides of the boat dock, and behind the TI. The rest of the beach is broken up into private sections that charge admission. You can always stroll along the beach, even through the private sections—just don't sit down. Off-season, roughly October through May, the entire beach is free, and you can lay your towel anywhere you like.

Old Town and Trailhead—The old town, several blocks from the TI and beach, clusters around Piazza del Popolo. Until a few decades ago, the town's open-air market was held at the 13th-century loggia (covered set of archways) in the square. Explore the back streets.

To reach the trailhead to Monterosso: From Piazza del Popolo, head uphill to the striped church, Chiesa di Sant'Andrea (with your back to the loggia, go straight ahead—across the square and up Via Don Emanuele Toso to the church). From the church courtyard, follow the sign to the *castello* (a private residence), go under the stone arch, and continue uphill. Or, if you're coming from the seaside promenade (Via Gaetano Semenza), head under the arches and up the stairs, and follow the signs to the *castello*. Either route leads you to a sign that points you toward Punta Mesco, the rugged tip of the peninsula. From here, you can hike up to Monterosso (2.5 hours).

Hike or Bike to Bonassola—Cross the river bridge located by the TI to wander along this new waterfront path, good for walking or cycling. You'll encounter shaded tunnels and two sunny beaches on the way to the small but modern town of Bonassola with its sandy beach (25 minutes by foot, 10 minutes by bike, public beaches located a minute's walk down from trail).

Sleeping in Levanto

In this popular beach town, many hotels want you to take half-pension (lunch or dinner) in summer, especially in July and August. Prices listed here are the maximum for high season (July–Aug); smaller rooms or those without views may have a lower maximum. Expect to pay €10–30 less per night for April–June and September–October, and even less for the rest of the year. The longer your stay, the greater your bargaining power. The high number of four-person rooms in Levanto makes it particularly welcoming to families who want to explore the Cinque Terre. Many hotels rent out large apartments with kitchenettes (without a half-pension requirement), and parking is free or very reasonable.

$$$ Albergo Primavera is family-run, with 17 vibrantly colored rooms—10 with balconies but no views—just a half-block from the beach. Owner Carlo is a good cook. Try dining here once during your visit (€25 fixed-price meal); let him know a couple of hours in advance if you'd like dinner (Db-€120, request a quiet room off the street, includes hearty breakfast buffet, air-con, Wi-Fi and Internet access; parking-€8/day June–Sept, free

Levanto

1. Albergo Primavera
2. Villa Margherita
3. A Durmì Guesthouse
4. Rist. la Loggia Rooms/Rist.
5. Villa Clelia B&B
6. La Rosa dei Venti Rooms
7. Garden Hotel
8. To Erba Persa Agriturismo
9. Ostello Ospitalia del Mare
10. Osteria Tumelin
11. Da Rino Trattoria
12. Taverna Garibaldi & Bike Rental
13. La Picea Pizzeria
14. Focacceria il Falcone
15. Crai Supermarkets (2)
16. Il Pinguino Gelateria
17. Il Porticciolo Gelateria
18. Internet Café
19. Launderette
20. Canoe & Kayak Rental

RIVIERA TOWNS

Sleep Code

(€1 = about $1.25, country code: 39)
S = Single, **D** = Double/Twin, **T** = Triple, **Q** = Quad, **b** = bathroom, **s** = shower only. Unless otherwise noted, credit cards are accepted, English is spoken, and breakfast is included.

To help you sort easily through these listings, I've divided the rooms into three categories based on the price for a standard double room with bath:

$$$ Higher Priced—Most rooms €110 or more.
$$ Moderately Priced—Most rooms between €50-110.
$ Lower Priced—Most rooms €50 or less.

Prices can change without notice; verify the hotel's current rates online or by email. For other updates, see www .ricksteves.com/update.

off-season; Via Cairoli 5, tel. 0187-808-023, fax 0187-801-588, www.primaverahotel.com, info@primaverahotel.com). Friendly Carlo and Daniela speak a little English, and daughters Gloria and Giuditta do their homework in the dining room.

$$$ Villa Margherita is 300 yards out of town, but the shady gardens, 11 characteristic colorfully tiled rooms (some with little view terraces), and tranquility are worth the walk (Db-€155, Tb-€170, 5 percent discount with cash and this book, elevator one flight up from street level, Internet access and Wi-Fi, free parking, 10-minute walk to town with stairs, 5-minute walk to train station, free shuttle service from station if you tell them when you'll arrive, Via Trento e Trieste 31, tel. & fax 0187-807-212, mobile 328-842-6934, www.villamargherita.net, info@villamargherita.net). They also have centrally located apartments for 2–6 people (some are noisy, request quiet lodging, 3-night minimum stay, www.levanto.net).

$$ A Durmi is a happy little *affitta camere* (guesthouse) owned by Graziella, Gianni, and their two daughters, Elisa and Chiara. Their sunny patios, green leafy gardens, six immaculate modern new rooms, and five sunlit apartments make a welcoming place to stay (Db-€80, extra bed-€20; apartments-€100, no minimum stay required; breakfast-€6, air-con, Internet access, bar, parking-€5/ day, Via D. Viviani 12, tel. 0187-800-823, mobile 349-105-6016, www.adurmi.it, info@adurmi.it).

$$ Ristorante la Loggia has four pleasant, cozy, summery rooms perched above the old loggia on Piazza del Popolo (Db-€70, cash only, request balcony, quieter rooms in back, two basic side-by-side apartments great for families of 4–8, air-con, free parking, Piazza del Popolo 7, tel. & fax 0187-808-107, mobile

335-641-7701, www.tigulliovino.it).

$$ Villa Clelia B&B has six peaceful, dark, air-conditioned rooms (named for the winds—*scirocco, maestrale,* and so on) with mini-fridges and terraces in a garden courtyard just 50 yards from the sea (Db-€70–90, minimal in-room breakfast, free parking, with loggia on your left it's straight ahead at Piazza da Passano 1, tel. 0187-808-195, mobile 328-797-6403, www.villaclelia.it, info @villaclelia.it). They also have seven central apartments that economically sleep up to five (€700/week, 3-night minimum stay). B&B rooms are cleaned daily; you're on your own at the apartments.

$$ La Rosa dei Venti is an *affitta camere* just a couple of blocks from the beach. Enthusiastic Rosanna and her son Marco rent five super-clean rooms with dark hardwood floors, comfy rugs, and a hodgepodge of seashore decor (Db-€100, Tb €135, includes homemade breakfast and free parking, behind Enoteca Tumelin across from Piazza del Popolo, Via della Compera, tel. 0187-808-165, mobile 333-701-3213, www.larosadeiventilevanto.com, larosa deiventi1983@libero.it).

$$ Garden Hotel offers 17 simple, bright, and modern rooms, all with balconies (but most lack views due to the elevated street), a block from the beach on busy Corso Italia (Db-€108, new fifth-floor rooms with views and terraces go for Db-€135, 5 percent discount with cash and this book, lower floors closed mid-Nov–mid-March, air-con, elevator for some floors, free Internet access and Wi-Fi, free parking but not on-site—can unload bags and then park near the station, Corso Italia 6, tel. 0187-808-173, fax 0187-803-652, www.nuovogarden.com, info@nuovogarden.com, Davide and Damiano).

$$ Erba Persa Agriturismo, a rustic farmhouse run by sunny Grazia Lizza and her gardener husband Claudio, hosts cats, dogs, pet rabbits, and donkeys among their plots of organic fruits and vegetables. It's a 10-minute walk from the train station and about a 20-minute walk from town (D-€50 or Db with balcony and view-€70, Tb-€80, free Internet access, free parking, free mosquitoes, Via N. S. della Guardia 21, mobile 339-400-8587, fax 0187-801-376, www.erbapersa.it, erbapersa@alice.it).

Hostel: **$ Ostello Ospitalia del Mare** has 70 beds, airy rooms, an elevator, Internet access, and a terrace in a well-renovated medieval palazzo a few steps from the old town (beds-€19–27 in 4-, 6-, and 8-bed rooms with private bath, Db-€70, includes breakfast, towels, and sheets, self-service laundry-€8, microwave, fridge, non-members welcome, co-ed unless you strenuously object, no curfew, no lockout, office open daily April–Oct 8:00–12:30 & 16:00–19:30—later weekend nights, may be closed Nov–March, Via San Nicolò 1, tel. 0187-802-562, fax 0187-803-696, www .ospitaliadelmare.it, info@ospitalitadelmare.it).

Eating in Levanto

Osteria Tumelin, a local favorite, is more expensive than other options, but has great ambience and fresh seafood (daily 12:00–14:30 & 19:00–22:00, closed Thu Oct–May, reservations recommended in summer, Via d. Grillo 32, across street from loggia, tel. 0187-808-379).

Da Rino, a small trattoria on a quiet pedestrian street, dishes up reasonably priced fresh seafood and homemade Ligurian specialties prepared with care. Consider the grilled *totani* (squid), *pansotti con salsa di noci* (cheese ravioli with walnut sauce), and *trofie al pesto* (local pasta with pesto sauce). Dine indoors, or at one of the few outdoor tables (€8 pastas, €13 *secondi,* cash only, daily mid-March–Oct 19:00–22:00, closed on Tue Nov–mid-March, Via Garibaldi 10, mobile 328-3890-350).

Ristorante la Loggia (also recommended under "Sleeping in Levanto"), next to the old loggia, makes fine gnocchi with scampi and saffron sauce, *gattafini* (Levanto-style fritters filled with herbs and cheese), and daily fish specials served in a homey wood-paneled dining room or on a little terrace overlooking the square (€10 pastas, €15 *secondi,* Thu–Tue 12:30–14:00 & 19:00–22:00, closed Wed, closed Nov–Feb, Piazza del Popolo 7, tel. 0187-808-107).

Taverna Garibaldi is a good-value, cozy place on the most characteristic street in Levanto, serving focaccia with various toppings, made-to-order *farinata* (savory chickpea crêpe), pizzas, and salads (€8 light meals, daily in summer 19:30–22:00, closed Tue Sept–June, Via Garibaldi 57, tel. 0187-808-098).

La Picea serves up wood-fired pizzas to go, or dine at one of the few small tables (Tue–Sun 16:30–21:45, closed Mon, just off the corner near Via Varego at Via della Concia 18, tel. 0187-802-063).

A Picnic or Bite on the Go: Focaccerie, rosticcerie, and delis with take-out pasta abound on Via Dante Alighieri. **Focacceria il Falcone** has a great selection of focaccia with different toppings (daily 9:30–22:00, until 20:00 Oct–May, Via Cairoli 19, tel. 0187-807-370). For more picnic options, try the *mercato* (mornings except Sun; see "Helpful Hints," page 383). There are two **Crai supermarkets:** One is just off Via Jacopo da Levanto at Via del Municipio 5 (Mon–Sat 8:00–13:00 & 17:00–20:00, Sun 8:00–13:00 & 17:30–20:00); the other is nearby on Piazza Staglieno (for a shaded setting, lay out your spread on a bench in the grassy park at this piazza). Another excellent picnic spot is Piazza Cristoforo Colombo, located just east of the swimming pool, with benches and sea views.

And for Dessert: Compare **Il Pinguino Gelateria** at Piazza Staglieno 2 (daily until late) with **Il Porticciolo Gelateria,** at the end of Via Cairoli at Piazzetta Marina (daily in summer, closed Mon Sept–June, mobile 393-228-1570).

Levanto Connections

From Levanto: To get to the Cinque Terre, take the **train** (nearly hourly, 4 minutes to Monterosso) or the **boat,** which stops at every Cinque Terre town—except Corniglia—before heading to Portovenere (2/day Easter–Oct, none Nov–Easter; €5 one-way to Monterosso, €10 round-trip, or €18 for half-day pass to Portovenere and scenic ride—departing Levanto at about 10:10 and 14:30, with 1-hour stop before return to Levanto; as much as €25 for all-day pass on a weekend to Portovenere; 1 return boat each day from Portovenere departs at about 17:00; pick up boat schedule and price sheet from TI or boat dock, or call 0187-732-987, or 0187-732-200 on weekends).

Sestri Levante

This peninsular town is squeezed as skinny as a hot dog between its two beaches. The pedestrian-friendly Corso Colombo, which runs down the middle of the peninsula, is lined with shops that sell take-away pizza, pastries, and beach paraphernalia.

Hans Christian Andersen enjoyed his visit here in the mid-1800s, writing, "What a fabulous evening I spent in Sestri Levante!" One of the bays—Baia delle Favole—is named in his honor (*favole* means "fairy tale"). The small mermaid curled on the edge of the fountain behind the TI is another nod to the beloved Danish storyteller.

During the last week of May, the town holds a street festival, culminating in a ceremony for locals who write the best fairy tales (four prizes for four age groups, from pre-kindergarten to adult). The "Oscar" awards are little mermaids.

Orientation to Sestri Levante

Tourist Information
From the train station, it's a five-minute walk to the TI, where you can pick up a map (May–Sept Mon–Sat 9:30–12:30 & 14:30–19:00, Sun 9:30–12:30 & 15:00–18:00, Oct–April closes at 17:30 and on Sun; go straight out of station on Via Roma, turn left at fountain in park, TI in next square—Piazza Sant'Antonio 10; tel. 0185-457-011, iat.sestrilevante@provincia.genova.it).

Helpful Hints
Market Day: It's on Saturday at Piazza Aldo Moro (8:00–13:00).
Internet Access: Spazio Libero has two computers (closed Sat-Sun, Via Roma 11; from station, take road straight ahead and

it's on the right).

Baggage Storage: None is available at the station. The nearest baggage storage is in Santa Margherita Ligure (see page 395).

Sights in Sestri Levante

Stroll the Town—From the TI, take Corso Colombo (to the left of Bermuda Bar, eventually turns into Via XXV Aprile), which runs up the peninsula. Follow this street—lively with shops and eateries—for about five minutes. Just before you get to the large white church at the end, turn off for either beach (free Silenzio beach is on your left). Or take the street on the left of the church to head uphill. You'll pass the evocative arches of a ruined chapel (bombed during World War II, and left as a memorial). Continue a few minutes farther to the Hotel Castelli and consider a drink at their view café (so-so view, reasonably priced drinks, daily 10:00–24:00, café entrance is at end of parking lot). The rocky, forested bluff at the end of the town's peninsula is actually the huge private backyard of this fancy hotel.

Beaches—These are named after the bays *(baie)* that they border. The bigger beach, Baia delle Favole, is divided up much of the year (May–Sept) into sections that you must pay to enter. The fees, which can soar up to €30 per day in August (no hourly rate), generally include chairs, umbrellas, and fewer crowds. There are several small free sections: at the ends and in the middle (look for *libere* signs, and ask *"Gratis?"* to make sure that it's free). For less-expensive sections of beach (where you can rent less than the works), ask for *spiaggia libera attrezzata* (spee-AH-jah LEE-behr-ah ah-treh-ZAHT-tah). The usual beach-town activities are clustered along this *baia:* boat rentals, sailing lessons, and bocce courts—ask if you can get in on a game.

The town's other beach, Baia del Silenzio, is narrow, virtually all free, and packed, providing a good chance to see Italian families at play. There isn't much more to do here than unroll a beach towel and join in. At the far end of Baia del Silenzio is Citto Beach bar, which offers front-row seats of bay views (daily June–Aug 10:00–24:00, May and Sept–Oct until 20:00, closed Nov–April, Gilberto).

Sleeping in Sestri Levante

(€1 = about $1.25, country code: 39)

Prices listed here are the maximum during the high season (July–Aug). Prices will be €10–20 less April–June and September–October, and soft the rest of the year. Some hotels are closed off-season, so call ahead.

$$$ Hotel Due Mari, located in an old Genoese palazzo, has three stars, 65 fine rooms, and a rooftop terrace with a super view of both beaches. Ideally, reserve well in advance. The extra services and grand communal spaces are the draw (Db-€140–190 depending on view and type of room, half-pension in aristocratic restaurant required July–Aug-€35/person, closed mid-Oct–Dec, air-con, Wi-Fi, elevator, garden, outdoor and heated indoor sea-water swimming pools, wet sauna, small gym, parking-€12/day, take Corso Colombo to the end, hotel is behind church in Piazza Matteotti—take either alleyway flanking church, Vico del Coro 18, tel. 0185-42695, fax 0185-42698, www.duemarihotel.it, info @duemarihotel.it).

$$$ Hotel Helvetia, overlooking Baia del Silenzio, is another three-star bet, with 21 bright rooms, a large sun terrace, and a peaceful garden atmosphere—but an apathetic management (view-less Db-€170, Db with view/balcony-€200, closed Nov–March, air-con, elevator, swimming pool, off-site parking-€5–15/day with free shuttle, from Corso Colombo turn left on Via Palestro and angle left at the small square to Via Cappuccini 43, tel. 0185-41175, fax 0185-457-216, www.hotelhelvetia.it, helvetia@hotelhelvetia.it).

$$$ Hotel Genova, run by the Bertoni family, is a shipshape hotel with 27 shiny-clean, modern, and cheery rooms, sunny lounge, rooftop sundeck, free loaner bikes, and a good location just two blocks from Baia delle Favole (Sb-€75, Db-€125, superior Db-€140, Tb-€169, ask for quieter room in back, air-con, elevator, Internet access and Wi-Fi, parking-€5/day; from the train station, walk straight ahead, turn right at the T-intersection and find the cream building with flags ahead on the right, Viale Mazzini 126; tel. 0185-41057, fax 0185-455-739, www.hotelristorantegenova.com, info@hotelristorantegenova.com).

$$$ Hotel Celeste, a dream for beach-lovers, rests along the waterfront. Its 41 rooms are modern and plainly outfitted—you pay for the sea breeze (Db-€140, with view and balcony €15–25 more, optional half-pension, air-con, elevator, Internet access, deals on beach chairs, attached beachside bar, a free *aperitivo* for Rick Steves guests, Lungomare G. Descalzo, 14, tel. 0185-485-005, fax 0185-411-166 www.hotelceleste.com, info@hotelceleste .com, Franco).

$$ Albergo Marina's friendly Magda and her brother Santo rent 22 bright, peaceful, and clean rooms done in sea-foam green. Though the hotel is located on a busy boulevard, all rooms are at the back facing a quiet courtyard and parking lots...and priced right (Db-€60–70, half-pension optional, air-con, elevator, self-service laundry, pool table; exit the train station and angle left down Via Eraldo, at Piazza Repubblica take an easy left onto Via Fasce and find the hotel ahead on the right, Via Fasce 100; tel. & fax 0185-

487-332, www.marinahotel.it, marinahotel@marinahotel.it).

$$ Villa Jolanda is a homey, kid-friendly basic *pensione* with 17 simple rooms, five with little balconies but no views, new bathrooms, and a garden courtyard/sun terrace—perfect for families on a budget...and the owner's cats (Db-€75–90, Qb-€100–120, 3-night minimum stay if you want to reserve in advance, €6.50 breakfast isn't worth it but owner Mario's €23 home-cooked dinners are, free parking, located near Baia del Silenzio—take alley just to the right of the church on Piazza Matteotti, Via Pozzetto 15, tel. & fax 0185-41354, www.villaiolanda.com, info@villaiolanda.com).

Eating in Sestri Levante

Everything I've listed is on classic Via XXV Aprile, which also abounds with *focaccerie,* take-out pizza by the slice, and little grocery shops. Assemble a picnic or try one of the places below.

At **L'Osteria Mattana,** where everyone shares long tables in two dining rooms (the second one is in the back, past the wood oven and brazier), you can mix with locals while enjoying traditional cuisine, listed on the chalkboard menus (Tue–Fri 19:30–23:00, Sat–Sun 12:30–14:30 & 19:30–22:30, closed Mon except in Aug, follow Corso Colombo from TI as it turns into Via XXV Aprile, restaurant on right at #36, tel. 0185-457-633, Marco).

Polpo Mario is classier but affordable, with a fun people-watching location on the main drag (€35 fixed-price tasting menu, Tue–Sun 12:15–14:30 & 19:30–22:30, closed Mon, Via XXV Aprile 163, tel. 0185-480-203).

Ristorante Mainolla offers pizzas, big salads, focaccia sandwiches, and reasonably priced pastas near Baia del Silenzio (daily in summer 12:00–16:00 & 19:00–22:00, closed Tue off-season, Via XXV Aprile 187, mobile 338-157-0877).

Gelato: Locals flock to **Ice Cream's Angels** at the intersection of Via XXV Aprile and Via della Chiusa. Riccardo and Elena artfully load up your cone with intermingling flavors, and top it with a dollop of Nutella chocolate-hazelnut cream (open daily until late in summer, closed Tue off-season, mobile 348-402-1604). **Bacciolo** enjoys a similar popularity among residents (closed Thu, Via XXV Aprile 51, on the right just before the church).

Supermarket: You can stock up on picnic supplies at two locations of **Per Di supermarket** on Piazza della Repubblica, at #1 and #28 (Mon–Sat 8:00–20:00, Sun 8:30–13:00 & 15:30–20:00).

Deli: For a take-out meal, head to **Rosticceria Bertolone** for roasted anything—beef, pork, chicken, or vegetables. Assemble an entire meal from their deli and ask them to heat it for you (Mon–Sat 7:30–13:00 & 16:00–19:30, closed Wed afternoon and all day Sunday, Via Fasce 12, tel. 0185-487-098).

Sestri Levante Connections

Sestri Levante is just 20–40 minutes away from Monterosso by **train** (hourly connections with Monterosso, nearly hourly with other Cinque Terre towns).

    Boats depart to the Cinque Terre, Santa Margherita Ligure, Portofino, and San Fruttuoso from the dock *(molo)* on the peninsula (boats run Easter–Oct, see "Santa Margherita Ligure Connections," page 403, for details; to get to the dock: facing the church in Piazza Matteotti, take the road on the right with the sea on your right, about halfway down Via P. Queirolo; tel. 0185-284-670, www.traghettiportofino.it).

Santa Margherita Ligure

If you need the movie stars' Riviera, park your yacht at Portofino. Or you can settle down in the nearby and more personable Santa

Margherita Ligure (15 minutes by bus from Portofino and 1 hour by train from the Cinque Terre). While Portofino's velour allure is tarnished by snobby residents and a nonstop traffic jam in peak season, Santa Margherita tumbles easily downhill from its train station. The town has a fun resort character and a breezy harborfront.

    On a quick day trip from Milan or the Cinque Terre, walk the beach promenade and see the small old town of Santa Margherita Ligure before catching the bus (or boat) to Portofino to see what all the fuss is about. With more time, Santa Margherita makes a fine overnight stop.

Orientation to
Santa Margherita Ligure

Tourist Information

Pick up a map at the harborside TI (daily April–Sept 9:30–12:30 & 14:30–19:00, Oct–March closes at 17:30 and all day Sun, tel. 0185-287-485, www.turismoinliguria.it, iat.santamargheritaligure @provincia.genova.it).

Arrival by Train

To get from the station to the city center, take the stairs marked *Mare* (sea) down to the harbor. The harborfront promenade is as wide as the skimpy beach. (The real beaches, which are pebbly, are a 10-minute walk further on, past the port.)

To reach the pedestrian-friendly old town and the TI, take a right at Piazza Veneto (with the roundabout, flags, and park) onto Largo Antonio Giusti. For the TI, angle left on Via XXV Aprile. For the old town (a block off Piazza Veneto), head toward the TI, but turn left on Via Torino, which opens almost immediately onto Piazza Caprera, a square with a church and morning fruit vendors in the midst of pedestrian streets.

Helpful Hints

Internet Access: Plant Shop may still be open when you visit (daily 9:00–13:00 & 14:30–20:00, Via Roma 15, tel. 0185-286-615). If it has closed, ask your hotelier or the TI for suggestions.

Post Office: It's just under the train station (Mon–Fri 8:00–18:30, Sat 8:00–12:30, closed Sun, Via Roma 36).

Baggage Storage: Day-trippers arriving by train can stash their bags at the station's café-bar (€2.50/day per piece, daily 5:00–19:30).

Bike Rental: GM Rent is at Via XXV Aprile 11 (€10/5 hours, €20/24 hours, also rents scooters and Smart Cars, daily 10:00–13:00 & 16:30–20:00, mobile 329-406-6274, www.gmrent.it, Francesco).

Taxi: A taxi ride from the train station to anywhere in town costs a minimum of €13 (they justify the high price by the short tourist season). Taxis wait outside the station (mobile 338-860-2349, Alessandro).

Parking: The recommended **Hotel Mediterraneo, Hotel Tigullio,** and **Villa Anita** offer free parking to their guests, and a few hotels have limited spots for a fee. When you reserve your room, mention that you'll have a car. Otherwise, try a private lot (about €10–15/half-day, €15–20/24 hours) such as **Autorimessa Europa,** next to the post office (Via Roma 38, tel. 0185-287-818). The TI has a list of parking spots (generally free where there are white lines) and paid parking lots.

Local Guide: Roberta De Beni knows the Ligurian Coast, its history, and its art very well (€100/half-day, €165/day, mobile 349-530-4778, www.xeniaguide.it, diodebe@inwind.it).

Santa Margherita Ligure

NOT TO SCALE - TRAIN STATION TO BOAT DOCK IS A 10 MIN. WALK

TRAIN STATION

TRIESTE

VIA ZARA

CORSO E. RAINUSSO

COSTA GEMELLI

VIA ROMA

P POST

PAGANA

TO RAPALLO & FREEWAY

T.I. KIOSK

VIA XXV APRILE

CORSO MATTEOTTI

PALESTRO

PIAZZA CAMERA

LARGO GIUSTI

PIAZZA VENETO

FREE BEACH

Bus KIOSK

PIAZZA DELLA LIBERTÀ

PEZZA. MAZZ

CAVOUR

CAIROLI

SOLIMANO

VITT

DOGALI

SANTA MARGHERITA

GIUNCHETO

VIRGIN MARTYR STATUE

BOAT DOCK

CASTLE

VIA BELVEDERE

VIA P. CENT

VILLA DURAZZO PARK

SAN GIACOMO

S. GIACOMO

SANT' ERASMO

G. MARCONI

S. FRANCESCO

TRE NOV.

CORSO G. MARCONI

FISH MARKET

VIA FAVALE

LIGURIAN SEA

P PARKING

DCH

TO MARINA, PORTOFINO & ⑧

❶ La Locanda di Colombo	❿ To Dal Baffo
❷ Hotel Jolanda	⓫ Da Pezzi Ristorante
❸ Hotel Tigullio	⓬ Il Portico Gelateria
❹ Hotel Mediterraneo	⓭ Gelateria Centrale
❺ Hotel Laurin	⓮ Seghezzo Grocery
❻ Hotel Fasce	⓯ D'Oro Centry Supermarket
❼ Hotel Nuova Riviera	⓰ Bike Rental
❽ To Villa Anita, Rist. A' Lampara & Via Tomaso Bottaro Eateries	⓱ Internet Café
❾ Rist. il Nostromo	⓲ Portofino Bus Stop

Self-Guided Walk

Welcome to Santa Margherita Ligure

Explore Santa Margherita Ligure on the following stroll.

• *Begin at Piazza della Libertà. Walk out to the tip of the boat dock and turn around to survey the...*

Town View: From here you can take in all of Santa Margherita Ligure, from the villas dotting the hills and the castle built in the 16th century (closed except for special exhibitions) to the exclusive hotels. Sharing the dock with you is a statue of "Santa Margherita Virgin Martyr."

• *Wander along the harborfront (down Corso Marconi) past the castle and to the...*

Marina: What's left of the town's fishing fleet ties up here. The fishing industry survives, drag-netting octopus, shrimp, and miscellaneous "blue fish"—plus mountains of anchovies attracted to midnight lamps. The fish market (inside the rust-colored building with arches and columns) wiggles weekdays at about, oh, maybe 16:00–20:00 or so. Residents complain that it's easier to buy their locally caught fresh fish in Milan than here.

• *Behind the fish market stands the...*

Oratory of Sant'Erasmo: This small church is named for St. Erasmus (a.k.a. "St. Elmo"), the protector of sailors. Notice the fine and typically local black-and-white pebble mosaic *(riseu)* in front of the church (with maritime themes). The church is actually an "oratory," where a brotherhood of faithful men who did anonymous good deeds congregated and worshipped. It's decorated with ships and paintings of storms that—thanks to St. Erasmus—the local seafarers survived. The huge crosses are carried through town on special religious holidays (the church is supposedly open only during Mass, but often open at other times, too).

• *Next, double back to climb the loooong stairway (Via Tre Novembre) overlooking the bay to reach the...*

Church of San Giacomo: Even though this is a secondary church in a secondary town, it's impressively lavish (daily 7:30–19:00, avoid visiting during Mass, usually 8:00–9:00). The region's aristocrats amassed wealth from trade in the 11th to 15th centuries. When Constantinople fell to the Turks, free trade in the Mediterranean stopped and Genovese traders became bankers—making even more money. A popular saying of the day was, "Silver is born in America, lives in Spain, and dies in Genoa." Bankers here served Spain's 17th-century royalty and aristocracy, and the accrued wealth paid for a Golden Age of art. Wander the church, noticing the inlaid-marble floors and chapels.

• *Step out of the church and enjoy the sea view. Then turn left and step into...*

Rise of a Resort: The History of Santa Margherita Ligure

This town, like the entire region (from the border of France to La Spezia), was once ruled by the Republic of Genoa. In the 16th century, when Arab pirates from North Africa plagued the entire coastal area, Genoa built castles in the towns and lookout towers in the neighboring hills.

At the time, Santa Margherita was actually two bickering towns—each with its own bay. In 1800, Napoleon came along, took over the Republic of Genoa, and turned the rival towns into one city—naming it Porto Napoleone. When Napoleon fell in 1815, the town stayed united and took the name of the patron saint of its leading church, Santa Margherita.

In 1850, residents set to work creating a Riviera resort. They imported palm trees from North Africa and paved a fine beach promenade. Santa Margherita and the area around it was studded with fancy villas built by the aristocracy of Genoa (which was controlled by just 35 families). English, Russian, and German aristocrats also discovered the town in the 19th century. Mass tourism only hit in the last generation. Even with the increased crowds, the town decided to stay chic and kept huge developments out. Its neighbor, Rapallo, chose the extreme opposite—giving Italian its word for uncontrolled growth ruining a once-cute town: *rapallizzazione*.

Durazzo Park (Parco Comunale Villa Durazzo): This park was an abandoned shambles until 1973, when the city took it over (free, daily May–Sept 9:00–19:00, maybe until 20:00 July–Aug; Oct–April 9:00–17:00). Today it's a delight, with a breezy café enjoyed mostly by locals (closed Tue May–Aug, closed entirely Oct–March). The garden has two distinct parts: the carefully coiffed Italian garden (designed to complement the villa's architecture) and the calculatedly wild "English garden" below. The Italian garden is famous for its collection of palm trees—each one is different.

• *In the building next to the café, you'll see...*

Villa Durazzo: Typical of the region, this palazzo has some period furniture, several grand pianos, chandeliers, and paintings strewn with cupids on the walls and ceilings. For most people, it's not worth the entry fee (€5.50, more for special exhibits; daily 9:00–13:00 & 14:00–18:00; Oct–April until 17:00; last entry one hour before closing, WC opposite entry on left, tel. 0185-293-135, www.villadurazzo.it, villa.durazzo@comunesml.it). Classical music concerts are held here in July and August (ask at TI or villa ticket desk, or call for the schedule).

• *Your self-guided walk is over. Enjoy the park.*

Sights in Santa Margherita Ligure

Church of Santa Margherita (Basilica di Nostra Signora Della Rosa)—The town's main church is textbook Italian Baroque. Its 18th-century facade hides a 17th-century interior. The chapels to the right of the high altar contain religious "floats" used in local festival parades. The wooden groups in the niches higher up used to be part of the processions, too. The altar is typical of 17th-century Ligurian altars—shaped like a boat, with lots of shelf space for candles, flowers, and relics. Remember, Baroque is like theater. After Vatican II in the 1960s, priests began to face their flocks, turning their back on the old altars rather than the people. For this reason, all over the Catholic world, modern tables serving as post–Vatican II altars stand in front of earlier altars that are no longer the center of attention during the Mass (daily 7:30–12:00 & 15:00–18:30, tel. 0185-286-555).

Via Palestro—This promenade (a.k.a. *caruggio*—"the big street" in local dialect) is *the* strolling street for window-shopping, people-watching, and studying the characteristic Art Nouveau house painting from about 1900. Before 1900, people distinguished their buildings with pastel paint and distinctive door and window frames. Then they decided to get fancy and paint entire exteriors with false balconies, weapons, saints, beautiful women, and 3-D Gothic concentrate.

As you wander from the Church of Santa Margherita inland, pop into the fanciest grocer-deli in town—**Seghezzo** (immediately to the right of the church on Via Cavour, see "Eating in Santa Margherita Ligure"). Locals know that this venerable institution has whatever odd ingredient the toughest recipe calls for.

Farther up Via Palestro, you might drop into the traditional old **Panificio** bakery (closed Wed) for a slice of fresh focaccia. Saying *"Vorrei un etto di focaccia"* will get you a Ligurian olive–oily 100-gram €1.50 hunk of every kid's favorite beach munchie. Locals claim the best focaccia in Italy is made along this coast.

Markets—On weekday afternoons, fishing boats unload their catch, which is then sold to waiting customers at **Mercato del Pesce** (roughly Mon–Fri 17:00–20:00, opens an hour earlier for wholesalers, Oct–April may open at 15:30). Find it in the rust-colored building with arches and columns on Corso Marconi, on the harbor, just past the castle. The open-air market, a commotion of clothes and produce, is held every Friday morning along Corso Matteotti, inland from Piazza Mazzini (8:00–13:00). Piazza Caprera (facing the main church) daily hosts a few farmers selling their produce from stalls.

Beaches—The handiest free Santa Margherita beaches are just below the train station toward the boat dock. But the best beaches are on the south side of town. Among these, I like "Gio and Rino beach" (just before Covo di Nord Est)—not too expensive, with fun, creative management and a young crowd. Also nice is the beach on the south side of Hotel Miramare, which offers a more relaxing sun-worshipping experience. Both beaches have free entry and rentable chairs and umbrellas. They're a 20-minute walk from downtown, or take the bus from either the train station or Piazza Veneto (€1 each way, buy tickets from kiosk, newsstands, *tabacchi* shops, or the green ATP ticket office next to the TI).

Paraggi beach, which is halfway to Portofino (with an easy bus connection, see "Portofino," later in this chapter), is better than any Santa Margherita beach, but it's *very* expensive. One Paraggi beach operator, Bosetti, offers a reasonable rate (€25/day, no hourly rates, includes umbrella, lounge chair, and towel), while rates at other beaches may soar up to €50 per day in July and August. In high season, the Paraggi beach may be all booked up by big shots from Portofino, which has no beach—only rocks. A skinny patch of sand smack-dab in the middle of Paraggi beach is free.

Sleeping in Santa Margherita Ligure

In the Center
(€1 = about $1.25, country code: 39)

To locate these hotels, see the map on page 396. Hotel Tigullio, Hotel Jolanda, and La Locanda di Colombo are closest to the station. Prices listed here are the maximum price for the high season of July–August. Expect April–June and September–October to be €10–15 cheaper, and the rest of the year to be cheaper still.

$$$ La Locanda di Colombo has six stylish and contemporary rooms and two small, relaxing patios (Db-€150, tell them "Rick sent me" to get a 5 percent discount on stays of 1–3 days, 10 percent discount on longer stays; air-con, disabled access, Via XXV Aprile 12, tel. 0185-293-129, fax 0185-291-937, www.lalocanda dicolombo.it, sml@lalocandadicolombo.it). Welcoming hosts Massimiliano and Raffaella also run a restaurant with a 10 percent discount for readers of this book.

$$$ Hotel Jolanda, just around the corner from La Locanda di Colombo, is a solid, professionally run hotel with 50 rooms, a revolving door, a good breakfast buffet, and a friendly staff. With the lavish public spaces and regal colors, you'll feel like nobility here (Db-€150, superior Db-€170, 10 percent discount with this book if you mention it when you reserve, air-con, elevator, free one-hour use of small weight room, wet and dry saunas, Jacuzzi for a charge, at Via Luisito Costa 6, tel. 0185-287-512, fax 0185-284-763, www.hoteljolanda.it, info@hoteljolanda.it). They have 10 free loaner bikes on request.

$$$ Hotel Tigullio, run by Giuseppe of Hotel Jolanda, has equally fine rooms with creamy hues and lower prices. You don't get all the luxury extras, but the breezy sun terrace on top—with a bar in summertime—makes for a relaxing retreat (Db-€135, bigger Db with terrace-€145, 10 percent discount with this book if you mention it when you reserve, air-con, elevator but lots of stairs down to reception, free parking but request it when you reserve, Via Rainusso 6, tel. 0185-287-455, fax 0185-281-860, www .hoteltigullio.eu, info@hoteltigullio.eu).

$$$ Hotel Mediterraneo, run by the Melegatti family, offers 30 spacious rooms (a few with balconies or sun terraces) in a family-friendly, comfy 18th-century palazzo a five-minute walk from Piazza Veneto. They have a park-like sun garden with lounge chairs and lots of semi-private space. Pia Pauli makes great Ligurian specialties for dinner (Sb-€100, Db-€150, Tb-€160, great breakfast, five-course dinner-€30/person, free laundry service with 3-day stay or longer, free parking, free loaner bikes, closed Jan–March, take street immediately to the right of Church of Santa Margherita and find hotel straight ahead at Via della Vittoria 18A, tel. 0185-286-881, fax 0185-286-882, www.sml-mediterraneo.it, info@sml-mediterraneo.it).

$$$ Hotel Laurin offers slick, modern air-conditioned American-style lodgings fixated on harborfront views. All of its 43 rooms face the sea, most have terraces, and there's a small pool on the sundeck, as well as a gym and wet sauna. As it's a Best Western, it feels corporate (Sb-€157, Db-€222, 10 percent discount if you book directly with the hotel, mention this book when you reserve and show book on arrival, double-paned windows, elevator, 15-yard walk past the castle, or €15 taxi ride from station, Corso Marconi 3, tel. 0185-289-971, fax 0185-285-709, www.laurinhotel .it, info@laurinhotel.it).

$$$ Hotel Fasce, a 16-room hotel surrounded by flowers and greenery, is run enthusiastically by intense Englishwoman Jane Fasce, her husband Aristide, and son Alessandro. Jane gets mixed reviews from my readers—some find her helpful, while others find her rules too strict...my advice is to toe the line (Sb-€100, Db-€120, Tb-€140, Qb-€160, see website for deals, no-nonsense 21-day cancellation policy, two rooms have private bathroom located across the hall, no elevator, free loaner bikes, rooftop garden, laundry service-€18, parking-€20/day, free round-trip train tickets to

Cinque Terre with 3-night stay if you book room direct or through their website, 10-minute walk or €15 cab ride from station at Via Bozzo 3, tel. 0185-286-435, fax 0185-283-580, www.hotelfasce.it, hotelfasce@hotelfasce.it).

$$$ Hotel Nuova Riviera is a stately old villa surrounded by a peaceful garden. The Sabini family rents nine non-smoking rooms (Db-€115, Tb-€138, Qb-€165, these prices good in 2011 if you book direct and mention this book when you reserve, additional 5 percent discount with cash, special weeklong offers, fans, some balconies, no elevator, 15-minute walk from station or easy cab ride; if you're driving, follow signs to hospital, then watch for hotel signs on Piazza Mazzini; if you're walking, enter Piazza Mazzini and see signs from there; Via Belvedere 10, tel. & fax 0185-287-403, www.nuovariviera.com, info@nuovariviera.com). They also run a nearby annex with six spotless renovated rooms and one apartment with a tiny kitchen corner (Db-€95, Tb-€110, Qb-€125, cash only, breakfast at Hotel Nuova Riviera is optional and extra, tel. 0185-287-403, www.sabinirentals.com, sabinirentals@gmail.com).

$$$ Villa Anita is a homey family *pensione* run by Daniela and her son Sandro. They rent 12 simple, tidy rooms (nearly all have terraces) overlooking a peaceful residential neighborhood just a five-minute walk from the seaside boulevard. While they require half-pension in July and August, Daniela is a good cook and offers a varying menu of Ligurian specialties (Db-€120, half-pension-€85/person, air-con, free Wi-Fi, free parking, €15 taxi from station, Via Tigullio 10, tel. 0185-286-543, fax 0185-283-005, www.hotelvillaanita.com, info@hotelvillaanita.com).

Eating in Santa Margherita Ligure

For information on some of the regional specialties, see page 328.

Ristorante "A' Lampara" is the locals' favorite for *casalinga* (home-style) Genovese cuisine, prepared by the endearing Barbieri family: Mamma Maria Luisa oversees the dining room, son Mario cooks, and daughter Natalina serves. Try their specialties, such as *ravioli di pesce* (homemade fish ravioli with red mullet sauce) or *pansotti con salsa di noci*—cheese ravioli with walnut sauce (Fri–Wed 12:30–14:00 & 19:30–22:00, closed Thu, veggie options; follow Corso Marconi 4 blocks past the fish market, turn right onto Via Maragliano and find #33 a block and a half ahead on left; tel. 0185-288-926).

Ristorante il Nostromo, more central, specializes in artfully presented contemporary cuisine, based on the freshest catch of the day and seasonal ingredients. Enjoy the sidewalk seating in summertime and candlelit ambience as Anna, Delia, and Gianluca share their warm hospitality (daily 12:30–14:30 & 19:30–22:30, Oct–June closed Mon, a block off Piazza Veneto, take Via Gramsci and turn inland on Via dell'Arco to #6, tel. 0185-165-0000).

Dal Baffo is a bustling mom-and-pop eatery popular with locals for its traditional Ligurian specialties, including homemade pasta, wood-fired pizzas (folks queue up to watch the *pizzaioli* make their €7 pies to go), fresh fish, and grilled steaks at reasonable prices (Wed–Mon 12:00–15:00 & 19:00–23:30, closed Tue; from Piazza Caprera, head inland—both pedestrian streets eventually turn into busy Corso Matteotti; Corso Matteotti 56, tel. 0185-288-987).

Da Pezzi, with a cheap cafeteria-style atmosphere, is packed with locals at midday and at night. They're munching *farinata* (crêpe made from chickpeas, available Oct–May) standing at the bar, or enjoying pesto and fresh fish in the dining room. Consider the deli counter for picnic ingredients (Sun–Fri 12:00–14:00 & 18:15–21:00, closed Sat, Via Cavour 21, tel. 0185-285-303).

Waterfront Dining: All along Via Tomaso Bottaro, you'll find restaurants, pizzerias, and bars serving food with a harbor view. **Da Gennaro Pizzeria,** in Piazza della Libertà by the boat dock, makes popular Neapolitan-style pizzas. **Bar Giuli,** the only place actually on the harbor, serves forgettable salads and sandwiches for a reasonable price (about 150 yards south of the fish market).

Gelato: The best *gelateria* I found in town—with chocolate-truffle *tartufato*—is **Il Portico** (daily 8:30 until late, closed Mon off-season, under the castle, closest to the water at Piazza della Libertà 48). **Gelateria Centrale,** just off Piazza Veneto near the cinema, serves up their specialty—*pinguino* (penguin), a cone with your choice of gelato dipped in chocolate (daily 7:00–late, closed Wed Sept–May).

Groceries: **Seghezzo** is classiest and great for a meal to go—ask them to *riscaldare* (heat up) their white *lasagne al pesto* or grilled veggies (daily June–Aug 7:30–13:00 & 15:30–20:00, closed Wed Sept–May, right of the church on Via Cavour). The **D'Oro Centry** supermarket, just off Piazza Mazzini, has better prices (Mon–Sat 8:00–13:30 & 15:30–19:30, Sun 8:00–13:00, during summer Sat open all day long, across from Hotel Fiorina at Piazza Mazzini 38, tel. 0185-286-470).

Santa Margherita Ligure Connections

From Santa Margherita Ligure by Train to: Sestri Levante (2/hour, 30 minutes, €2), **Monterosso** (at least hourly, 45 minutes, €2), **La Spezia** (hourly, 1–1.5 hours, €5), **Pisa** (2/hour, 2.5 hours, transfer in La Spezia, €14), **Milan** (8/day, 2–2.5 hours, more with transfer in Genoa, €18), **Ventimiglia**/French border (4/day, 4 hours; or hourly with change in Genoa), **Venice** (8/day, 6–7 hours with 1–3 changes, €41–50). For **Florence,** transfer in Pisa (8/day, 3.5–4 hours, €20–26). See "Getting Around the Cinque Terre," page 319, for details.

By Boat to the Cinque Terre: For the latest, pick up a schedule of departures and excursion options from the TI, ask at your hotel, call 0185-284-670, or check online at www.traghetti portofino.it.

The routes mentioned below run at least twice weekly from May through September or October, increasing in frequency in July and August.

The "Linea 3" boat does an all-day trip that includes two stopovers: one hour in Vernazza and three hours in Portovenere, plus a scenic trip around an island (May–mid-Oct depart Sun at 9:00, plus Tue and Thu late July–mid-Sept, €21 one-way, €32 round-trip).

The half-day "Linea 4" boat sails to the Cinque Terre with a one-hour stopover in Vernazza (May–Oct depart Mon and Fri at 13:30, €17 one-way, €24.50 round-trip).

The "Super Cinque Terre, Linea 5" boat offers day-trip cruises from Santa Margherita Ligure to the Cinque Terre, departing at 8:45 and stopping in three Cinque Terre towns: three hours in Monterosso, and an hour each in Vernazza and Riomaggiore (May–Sept Wed and Sat only, €21 one-way, €32 round-trip).

Portofino

Santa Margherita Ligure, with its aristocratic architecture, hints at old money, whereas nearby Portofino, with its sleek shops, reeks of new money. Fortunately, a few pizzerias, *focaccerie*, bars, and grocery shops are mixed in with Portofino's jewelry shops, art galleries, and haute couture boutiques, making the town affordable. The *piccolo* harbor, classic Italian architecture, and wooded peninsula can even turn glitzy Portofino into an appealing package. It makes a fun day trip from Santa Margherita Ligure.

Ever since the Romans founded Portofino for its safe harbor, it has had a strategic value (appreciated by everyone from Napoleon to the Nazis). In the 1950s, *National Geographic* did a beautiful exposé

Portofino Area

--- BUS
···· BOAT
···· TRAIL

TO GENOA
CAMOGLI
PORT
STATION
(TUNNEL)

1 MILE
1 KM

SEE DETAIL MAP

TO RAPALLO, CINQUE TERRE + PISA

TRAIN STATION
BUS STOP Ⓑ

SANTA MARGHERITA LIGURE

MONTE PORTOFINO

CHURCH

TO RAPALLO

BOAT DOCK

SAN FRUTTUOSO

TRAIL

GIO + RINO BEACHES

PARAGGI

CHRIST OF THE ABYSS

PORTOFINO

CASTELLO BROWN

LIGURIAN SEA

LIGHT-HOUSE

DCH

on the idyllic port, and locals claim that's when the Hollywood elite took note. Liz Taylor and Richard Burton came here annually (as did Liz Taylor and Eddie Fisher). During one famous party, Rex Harrison dropped his Oscar into the bay (it was recovered). Ava Gardner came down from her villa each evening for a drink—sporting her famous fur coat. Greta Garbo loved to swim naked in the harbor, not knowing that half the town was watching. Truman Capote also called Portofino home. But VIPs were also here a century earlier. In one of his books, Friedrich Nietzsche wrote about philosophizing with mythical prophet Zarathustra on the path between Portofino and Santa Margherita.

My favorite Portofino plan: Visit for the evening. Leave Santa Margherita on the bus at about 16:30 and hike the last 20 minutes from Paraggi beach. Explore Portofino. Splurge for a drink on the harborfront, or get a take-out fruity sundae (*paciugo*; pah-CHOO-goh) and sit by the water. Then return by bus to Santa Margherita for dinner (confirm late departures). Portofino does offer fancy harborside dining, but the quality doesn't match the high prices.

Getting to Portofino

Portofino makes an easy day trip from Santa Margherita by bus, boat, bike, or foot.

RIVIERA TOWNS

By Bus: Catch bus #82 or #882 from Santa Margherita's train station or at bus stops along the harbor (€1, 2–3/hour, 15 minutes, goes to Paraggi or Portofino). Buy tickets at the bar next to the station, at Piazza Veneto's green bus kiosk (which it shares with the TI; daily 7:15–19:45), from the green machine on the side of the kiosk, or at any newsstand, *tabacchi,* or shop that displays a *Biglietti Bus* sign. You can usually buy tickets on the bus for double the cost. If you're at the Piazza Veneto kiosk, grab a bus schedule, which will come in handy if you travel in the evening (last bus around 23:00).

In Portofino, get tickets at the newsstand or from the machine next to the bus stop (go uphill and you'll come to Piazza Martiri della Libertà, machine and bus stop on right side, directions in English).

By Boat: The boat makes the trip with more class and without the traffic jams (€5.50 one-way, €8.50 round-trip, €0.50 more on Sun and holidays; daily May–Sept nearly hourly departures 10:15–16:15, Oct–April at 10:15 and 14:15 only; dock is a 2-minute walk from Piazza Veneto off Piazza Martiri della Libertà, call to confirm or pick up schedule from TI or your hotel, tel. 0185-284-670, mobile 336-253-336, check at www.traghettiportofino.it). These boats also run to the Cinque Terre (see page 320).

The boats run between Rapallo and the San Fruttuoso Abbey, stopping in between at Santa Margherita Ligure and Portofino. (Another boat line runs from Recco, Camogli, and Punta Chiappa to the abbey.)

By Bike: The 25-minute bike ride from Santa Margherita to Portofino is a popular option. Many of my recommended hotels provide free loaner bikes (though they may not be in the best condition); you can also rent your own wheels (see "Helpful Hints" in the Santa Margherita Ligure section). Biking along the narrow road isn't too dangerous, as traffic is slow in summer, and there are no steep hills to struggle up.

On Foot: To hike the entire distance from Santa Margherita Ligure to Portofino, you have two options: You can follow the sidewalk along (and sometimes hanging over) the sea (1 hour, 2.5 miles)—although traffic can be noisy. Or, if you're hardy and ambitious, you can take a quieter two-hour hike by leaving Santa Margherita at Via Maragliano, then follow the Ligurian-symbol trail markers (look for red-and-white stripes—they're not always obvious, sometimes numbered according to the path you're on, usually painted on rocks or walls, especially at junctions). This hike takes you high into the hills. Keep left after Cappelletta delle Gave. Several blocks past a castle, you'll drop down into the Paraggi beach, where you'll take the Portofino trail the rest of the way.

Bus and Hike Option: For a shorter hike (20 minutes) into Portofino, ride bus #82 or #882 only as far as the ritzy Paraggi beach. At the far end of the beach, cross the street and follow the paved trail marked *Pedonali per Portofino* high above the road. Twenty minutes later, you'll enter Portofino at a yellow-and-gray-striped church labeled *Divo Martino*—which I figure means "the divine Martin" and has something to do with Dean Martin giving us all "Volare" (which I couldn't get out of my head for the rest of the day).

Orientation to Portofino

Tourist Information

Portofino's snooty TI—downhill from the bus stop, on your right under the portico—reluctantly gives out information. Pick up a free town map and a rudimentary hiking map (daily Easter–Sept 10:00–13:00 & 14:00–19:00; Oct–Easter Tue–Sun 10:30–13:30 & 14:30–17:30, closed Mon; Via Roma 35, tel. 0185-269-024, iat.porto fino@provincia.genova.it).

Sights in Portofino

Museo del Parco—For an artsy break, stroll around a park littered with 148 contemporary sculptures by top artists (€5, May–Oct Wed–Mon 10:00–13:00 & 15:00–19:00, closed Tue, closed Nov–April and in bad weather, mobile 337-333-737).

Hikes—One option is the paved stone path that winds up and down to the lighthouse *(faro)* at a scenic point with a bar (bar open May–Sept, hedges block views until the end, 25-minute walk). Consider popping into **Castello Brown,** a medieval castle, on the way. It features lush gardens and a black-and-white portrait gallery of stars and famous personages who once frequented Portofino, including Clark Gable, Sophia Loren, Kim Novak, Grace Kelly, John Wayne, Ernest Hemingway, Humphrey Bogart, and Lauren Bacall. Original decorations and photos are explained in English (€4, daily in summer 10:00–19:00, only Sat–Sun in winter, tel. 0185-267-101).

Or you could stroll the pedestrian promenade from Portofino to Paraggi beach, and, if you're lucky, see a wild boar en route (20 minutes, path starts to the right of yellow-and-gray-striped Divo Martino church—look for clock tower, parallels main road, ends at ritzy Paraggi beach, where it's easy to catch bus back to Santa Margherita Ligure).

Or you can hike out to San Fruttuoso Abbey (see below, 2.5 hours, steep at beginning and end, trail starts on the inland-most point of town in Santa Margherita past Piazza della Libertà; from

Portofino, pick up the trailhead at the top of town, past the *cara-binieri* station).

Near Portofino

San Fruttuoso Abbey—This 11th-century abbey, accessible only by foot or boat (from Portofino or Santa Margherita), isn't the main attraction (€5, more for special exhibits; May–Sept daily 10:00–16:45; Oct–April daily 10:00–15:45 except closed Mon in winter; tel. 0185-772-703). The more intriguing draw is 60 feet underwater offshore from the abbey: the statue *Christ of the Abyss (Cristo degli Abissi)*. A rowboat will take you from the dock below the Portofino boat dock to the statue, where you can look down through a lens to just barely see the arms of Jesus—outstretched, reaching upward. Some people bring goggles and dive in for a better view. As the statue might be removed for restoration, and the rowboats

don't run in rough seas, call the abbey to confirm before making the trip (about €4 for the 20-minute round-trip, these rowboats run only during boat arrival hours from Portofino—generally daily May–Sept 9:00–17:00). From Easter through September, boats continue north from San Fruttuoso Abbey to Punta Chiappa and Camogli (€5 one-way, can return to Santa Margherita by train or buy round-trip boat tickets, call 0185-772-091 or inquire at Portofino or Santa Margherita TI for information).

South of the Cinque Terre

La Spezia

While just a quick train ride away from the fanciful Cinque Terre (20–30 minutes), the working town of La Spezia feels like reality Italy. Primarily a jumping-off point for travelers, the town is slim on sights, and has no beaches.

The pedestrian zone on Via del Prione to the gardens along the harbor makes a pleasant stroll. The nearly deserted **Museo Amedeo Lia** displays Italian paintings from the 13th to 18th centuries, including minor works by Venetian masters Titian, Tintoretto, and Canaletto (€6.50, Tue–Sun 10:00–18:00, closed Mon, last entry 30 minutes before closing, English descriptions on laminated sheets in most rooms, audioguide-€3, WCs down the hall from ticket desk, no photos allowed, 10-minute walk

from station at Via del Prione 234, tel. 0187-731-100, http://mal
.spezianet.it).

Stay in the Cinque Terre if you can, but if you're in a bind I've
listed several La Spezia accommodations later in this section. To
grab a meal while you wait for a train, see "Eating in La Spezia."

Orientation to La Spezia

Tourist Information

The TI is in a separate building in front of the north end of the
train station (daily April–Sept 9:00–19:00, Oct–March closes at
16:00, tel. 0187-770-900). The Cinque Terre National Park office
is located inside the train station (daily 7:00–20:00, www.parco
nazionale5terre.it).

A second TI is near the waterfront (with same phone and summer hours as TI at station, open until 17:00 in winter, Viale Italia 5,
www.turismoprovincia.laspezia.it, iat_spezia@provincia.sp.it).

Arrival in La Spezia

By Train: Get off at the La Spezia Centrale stop. You can check
your bags in the train station (see "Helpful Hints," below). Most of
the recommended hotels are an easy walk from here.

By Car: The parking lot being built underneath the train
station won't be finished by your visit. You'll find free parking at
Piazza d'Armi; from there it's a 20-minute walk to the train station, or take the €1 shuttle service to Piazza Brin, a five-minute
walk from the station (3/hour). To reach Piazza d'Armi from
the highway, follow the La Spezia autostrada as it becomes Viale
Carducci and ends at Viale Italia, then turn left and follow the
road as it bends right, following signs for parking.

A guarded parking garage is on Via Crispi, just after the
Galleria (tunnel) Spallanzani on the right. Look for the *AciPark* sign
(€20/day for 1–3 days, €16/day for longer stays, Mon–Fri 7:00–20:15,
Sat 7:00–13:30, closed Sun, reserve in advance only if you'll be arriving when they're closed, tel. 0187-510-545, acipark@libero.it).

Helpful Hints

Market Days: A colorful covered market sets up in Piazza Cavour
(Mon–Sat 8:00–13:00). On Fridays, a huge all-day open-air
market sprawls along Viale Garibaldi, about six blocks from
the station.

Baggage Storage: A left-luggage service is at the train station
along track 1 (facing the tracks on platform 1, go left; it's next
to the WC). It's secure, though it isn't always staffed—ring
the bell to the left of the doorway to call the attendant. Since
you may have to wait, allow plenty of time to pick up your

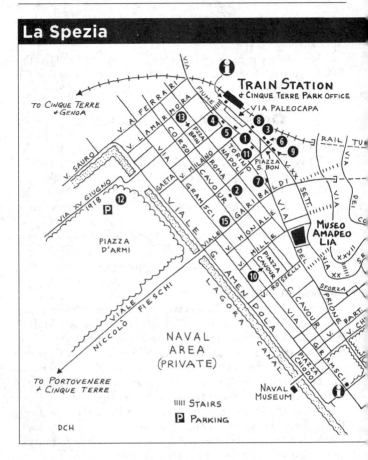

La Spezia

TO CINQUE TERRE & GENOA

TRAIN STATION & CINQUE TERRE PARK OFFICE
VIA PALEOCAPA
VIA FIUME
VIA A. FERRARI
V. LA MARMORA
V. SAURO
V. CORSO
PIAZZA BRIN
VIA MILANO
V. GAETANI
V. GRAMSCI
VIA CAVOUR
VIA TORINO
VIA NAPOLI
VIA ROMA
PIAZZA S. BON
VIA GARIBALDI
VIA SETT.
VIA MONALE
VIALE G. AMENDOLA
VIALE NICCOLÒ FIESCHI
VIA LAGORA CANAL
VIA DELLA
MUSEO AMADEO LIA
PIAZZA CAVOUR
PIAZZA ROSSELLI
C. CAVOUR
VIA SFORZA
VIA DEL PRIONE
V. CHIODO
PIAZZA CHIODO
NAVAL MUSEUM
RAIL
VIA XV GIUGNO 1918
PIAZZA D'ARMI
NAVAL AREA (PRIVATE)
TO PORTOVENERE & CINQUE TERRE

||||| STAIRS
P PARKING

DCH

baggage before departing (€3/12 hours, daily 8:00–22:00, they'll photocopy your passport).

Laundry: A handy self-service launderette is just below the train station. Head down toward town and immediately at the first piazza take a sharp right on Via Fiume, it's on your left at #95 (€7 wash and dry, Mon–Sat 8:00–22:00, Sun 9:00–22:00, mobile 346-492-2893).

Supermarket: DiMeglio is at the bottom of the train-station staircase, near the recommended launderette (Mon–Sat 8:00–20:00, closed Sun, tel. 0187-704-059).

Booking Agency: Cinque Terre Riviera books rooms and apartments in La Spezia, the Cinque Terre, and Portovenere for a 10 percent markup (check website for day trips and cooking lessons, Via Picedi 18, tel. 0187-520-702, www.cinqueterre riviera.com, info@cinqueterreriviera.com).

Getting to the Cinque Terre: Trains leave at least twice hourly for the Cinque Terre, though not all trains stop at all towns. The Cinque Terre Treno Card (covers train ride to Cinque Terre as well as hiking fee—see page 318) is sold at the train-station ticket window and at the national park office in the station (see "Tourist Information," at the beginning of this section). For more details, see "Getting Around the Cinque Terre" on page 319.

Sleeping in La Spezia

(€1 = about $1.25, country code: 39)
Remember, sleep in La Spezia only as a last resort. These hotels and rooms are within a five-minute walk of La Spezia's station—except the last two listings, which are for drivers only.

Hotels

$$$ Hotel Firenze e Continentale is grand and Old World, but newly restored with a mountain-view breakfast room to boot. Its 67 rooms have all the usual comforts. Maria Gabriella will throw in a Cinque Terre food specialty for my readers (Sb-€85, Db-€125, large superior Db-€150, these special prices when you book direct with this book, cheaper during slow times, non-smoking rooms, double-paned windows, air-con, elevator, outdoor parking-€8/day, indoor parking-€18/day, Via Paleocapa 7, tel. 0187-713-200, fax 0187-714-930, www.hotelfirenzecontinentale.it).

$$ Hotel Astoria, with 56 decent rooms, has a combination lobby and breakfast room as large as a school cafeteria. It's a fine backup if the hotels nearer the train station are full (Db without air-con-€80; Db-€130 for the 10 summery, modern rooms with air-con and double-paned windows; elevator, free parking garage, take Via Milano left of Albergo Parma, go 3 blocks and turn left to reach Via Roma 139, tel. 0187-714-655, fax 0187-714-425, www.albergoastoria.com, info@albergoastoria.com).

$$ Hotel Venezia, across the street from Hotel Firenze e Continentale, is run with low energy and the lobby can smell smoky, but its 19 rooms are pleasantly modern and recently remodeled (Sb-€55, Db-€90, air-con, elevator, free parking out front but must request when you reserve, Via Paleocapa 10, tel. & fax 0187-733-465, www.hotelvenezialaspezia.it, hotelvenezia@telematica italia.it).

$$ Albergo Parma, with 36 rooms, is a little worn around the edges but inexpensive (D-€50, Db-€60, breakfast-€4, no fans, double-paned windows, just below train station and down the stairs at Via Fiume 143, tel. 0187-743-010, fax 0187-743-240, albergo parma@libero.it, some English spoken, Aurelio).

Private Rooms

Affitta camere, meaning rented rooms with no official reception, abound near the station. Expect good deals, modest English skills, and no breakfast (buy yourself a coffee and pastry at a nearby bar).

$$ La Stazione del Golfo dei Poeti rents four cute, clean, and contemporary rooms on the busy Via Fiume (Db-€80, cash only, air-con, Via Fiume 52, mobile 345-352-6567, www.lastazione delgolfodeipoeti.it, info@lastazionedelgolfodeipoeti.it, welcoming Mariapia).

$$ Casa da Nè/Tre Frè has 11 chic rooms with comfy linens, located so close to the station that some rooms look out at the tracks. Luckily the windows are double-paned (Db-€80, air-con, Wi-Fi, clarify that you want to stay in the building at Via Paleocapa 4 or else you're farther from the station, mobile 347-351-3239, www.trefre.it, info@trefre.it, Giovanna).

$$ **L'Arca di Noè** is homey, with three bright and artsy rooms that share one bathroom for one of the best deals on the Cinque Terre. A group could take the entire massive apartment (D-€55, Q-€80, air-con, communal kitchen, a five-minute walk from station at Via Fiume 39, mobile 320-485-2434, Brunella and Alessandra).

Near La Spezia
$$ **Il Gelsomino,** for drivers only, is a homey B&B in the hills above La Spezia overlooking the Gulf of Poets. It has three tranquil rooms: one with a bay-view terrace, one with hillside views, and a third that lacks views or a terrace. Don't confuse it with another B&B called Il Gelsomino d'Oro (Db-€70, Tb/Qb-€100, reconfirm a day in advance with your arrival time, large breakfast, Via dei Viseggi 9, tel. & fax 0187-704-201, www.ilgelsomino.biz, ilgelsomino@inwind.it, gracious Carla and Walter Massi).

$ **Santa Maria del Mare Monastery,** a last resort for drivers, rents 15 comfortable rooms to spiritual travelers high above La Spezia in a scenic but institutional setting (donation only, recommended offerings dorm bed-€30, Db-€80, includes breakfast, additional €10/person for a meal, Via Montalbano 135B, tel. 0187-711-382, fax 0187-708-490, mobile 347-848-3993, www.santamaria delmare.it, madre@santamariadelmare.191.it).

Eating in La Spezia

Ristorante Roma da Marcellin, a one-minute walk from the station, has a cool, leafy terrace that's ideal for relaxing while you await your train. Grandpa Ottorino cooks up the freshest catch and a homemade filled pasta called *cappelletti* (daily 12:15–15:00 & 19:30–23:00; as you exit the station, turn left, across from Hotel Firenze e Continentale at Via Paleocapa 18; tel. 0187-715-921).

Il Pomodoro Pizzeria, just a few doors farther down on the corner of Via Zampino, offers more reasonable prices and a good selection of pizzas. Practice your Italian with the chalkboard display of pastas of the day (Mon–Sat 12:00–14:00 & 19:00–23:00, closed Sun, Piazza S. Bon 5, tel. 0187-739-911).

La Spezia Connections

From La Spezia by Train to: Monterosso (2/hour, 25 minutes, €2), **Carrara** (2/hour, 25 minutes, €3), **Viareggio** (2/hour, 30–60 minutes, €4), **Pisa** (hourly, 1–1.5 hours, €5–9), **Florence** (3/day direct, otherwise nearly hourly, 2.5 hours, change in Pisa, €9), **Rome** (every 2 hours, 4–5 hours, €35–45), **Milan** (about hourly, 3 hours direct or with change in Genoa, €22–29), **Venice** (12/day, 5 hours, 1–3 changes, €50–55).

By Bus to Portovenere: City buses generally depart from Viale Garibaldi (2/hour, 30 minutes, €1.45 each way, buy tickets at *tabacchi* shops or newsstands, bus stop 11P—just past Corso Cavour; but note that Friday buses depart from Corso Cavour). From the La Spezia train station, exit left and head downhill, following the street to the first square (Piazza S. Bon). Continue down Via Fiume to Piazza Garibaldi, then turn right at the fountain in the square onto Viale Garibaldi; the bus stop for Portovenere-bound buses is after the first stoplight on the right side of the street.

Carrara

Perhaps the world's most famous marble quarries are just east of La Spezia in Carrara. Michelangelo himself traveled to these val-

leys to pick out the marble that he would work into his masterpieces. The towns of the region are dominated by marble. The quarries higher up are vast digs that dwarf their hardworking trucks and machinery. The Marble Museum traces the story of marble-cutting here from pre-Roman times until today (€4.50, May–Sept Mon–Sat 9:30–13:00 & 14:30–18:00, Oct–April until 17:00, closed Sun, Viale XX Settembre 85, tel. 0585-845-746, http://urano.isti.cnr.it:8880/museo/home.php).

For a guided visit, **Sara Paolini** is excellent (€80/half-day tour, mobile 373-711-6695, sarapaolini@hotmail.com). She is accustomed to meeting drivers at the Carrara freeway exit, or she can pick you up at the train station.

Portovenere

While the gritty port of La Spezia offers little in the way of redeeming touristic value, the nearby resort of Portovenere is enchanting. This Cinque Terre–esque village clings to a rocky promontory that juts into the sea and protects the harbor from the crashing waves. On the harbor, next to colorful bobbing boats, a row of restaurants—perfect for al fresco dining—feature local specialties such as *trenette* pasta with pesto and *spaghetti con frutti di mare*.

RIVIERA TOWNS

Local boats take you on a 40-minute excursion around three nearby islands or over to Lerici, the town across the bay. Lord Byron swam to Lerici (not recom-mended). Hardy hikers enjoy the five-hour (or more) hike to Riomaggiore, the nearest Cinque Terre town.

Getting There: Portovenere—not to be confused with Portofino—is an easy day trip from the Cinque Terre by **boat** (Easter–Oct, 4–6/day 9:00–15:00, 1 hour, €12 one-way, €23 day pass includes hopping on and off and either Lerici or a jaunt around three small islands near Portovenere, www.navigazionegolfodei poeti.it). You can also cruise between Portovenere and Santa Margherita Ligure, with stops in Vernazza and Sestri Levante, using another boat line (www.traghettiporto fino.it). Pick up a schedule of departures and excursion options from the TI, or ask at your hotel. Or you can take the **bus** from La Spezia (2/hour, 30 minutes, €1.45, in La Spezia buy tickets at *tabacchi* shops or newsstands; in Portovenere get tickets at TI; for directions to the bus stop in La Spezia, see page 414). **Parking** is a nightmare here from May through September, but Albergo Il Genio offers free parking. In peak season, buses shuttle drivers from the parking lot just outside Portovenere to the harborside square. Otherwise, test your luck with the spots on the seaside (€1.50/hour).

Tourist Information: The TI is easy to find in the main square (June–Sept Thu–Tue 10:00–12:00 & 16:00–19:00, closed Wed; Oct–May Thu–Tue 10:00–12:00 & 15:00–18:00, closed Wed; Piazza Bastreri 7, tel. 0187-790-691).

Sleeping in Portovenere: If you forgot your yacht, try **$$$ Albergo Il Genio,** in the building where the main street hits the piazza (Db-€130, some rooms with views, no elevator, Internet access, free parking but request when you reserve, Piazza Bastreri 8, tel. & fax 0187-790-611, www.hotelgenioportovenere.com, info@hotelgenioportovenere.com). If your *vita* is feeling *dolce*, consider **$$$ Grand Hotel Portovenere,** which has striking sea views (from €117 for a viewless Db off-season to €227 for a view suite in summer, optional half-pension-€30–39/person, Internet access, tel. 0187-792-610, fax 0187-790-661, Via Garibaldi 5, www.portovenerehotel.it, ghp@village.it).

FLORENCE

Firenze

Florence, the home of the Renaissance and birthplace of our modern world, has the best Renaissance art in Europe.

Get your bearings with a Renaissance walk. Florentine art goes beyond paintings and statues—there's food, fashion, and handicrafts. You can lick Italy's best gelato while enjoying some of Europe's best people-watching.

Planning Your Time

If you're in Italy for three weeks, Florence deserves at least a well-organized day: see the Accademia, tour the Uffizi Gallery, visit the underrated Bargello (best statues), and do the Renaissance ramble (explained on page 437; to avoid heat and crowds, do this walk in the morning or late afternoon). Art-lovers will want to chisel out another day of their itinerary for the many other Florentine cultural treasures. Shoppers and ice-cream–lovers may need to do the same.

Plan your sightseeing carefully: Opening hours can be erratic, and crowds can cause long lines. Before heading into Florence, carefully check all the opening and closing times of your must-see museums at the TI, by phone, or online. This is especially true if you'll be in town for only a day or two during the crowded summer months.

The Uffizi Gallery and Accademia (starring Michelangelo's *David*) nearly always have long ticket-buying lines, especially in peak season (April–Oct) and on holiday weekends. Crowds thin out weekdays in the off-season. Whatever time of year you visit, you can easily avoid the wait by making reservations (see page 430). Note that both of these major sights are closed on Monday.

The Museum of San Marco closes at 13:50 on weekdays and at 16:50 on weekends. Other museums close early only on certain days (e.g., the first Sunday of the month, second and fourth Monday, etc.). In general, Sundays and Mondays are bad, with many museums either closed or with shorter hours.

Connoisseurs of smaller towns should consider taking the bus to Siena for a day or evening trip (75 minutes one-way, confirm when last bus returns). Siena is magic after dark. For more information, see the Siena chapter.

Orientation to Florence

The best of Florence lies on the north bank of the Arno River. The main historical sights cluster around the red-brick dome of the cathedral (Duomo). Everything is within a 20-minute walk of the train station, cathedral, or Ponte Vecchio (Old Bridge). The less-impressive but more characteristic Oltrarno area (south bank) is just over the bridge. Though small, Florence is intense. Prepare for scorching summer heat, kamikaze motor scooters, slick pickpockets, few WCs, steep prices, and long lines.

Tourist Information

There are three TIs in Florence: across from the train station, near Santa Croce Church, and on Via Cavour.

The TI across the square from the train station is most crowded—expect long lines (Mon–Sat 8:30–19:00, Sun 8:30–14:00; with your back to tracks, exit the station—it's 100 yards away, across the square in wall near corner of church at Piazza Stazione 4; tel. 055-212-245, www.firenzeturismo.it). In the train station, avoid the Hotel Reservations "Tourist Information" window (marked *Informazioni Turistiche Alberghiere*) near the McDonald's; it's not a real TI but a hotel-reservation business instead.

The TI near Santa Croce Church is pleasant, helpful, and uncrowded (Mon–Sat 9:00–19:00, Sun 9:00–14:00, shorter hours off-season, Borgo Santa Croce 29 red, tel. 055-234-0444, turismo2 @comune.fi.it).

Another winner is the TI three blocks north of the Duomo (Mon–Sat 8:30–18:30, Sun 8:30–13:30, Via Cavour 1 red, tel. 055-290-832, international bookstore across street).

At any TI, pick up these free, handy resources:
- a city map (ask for the "APT" map, which has bus routes of interest to tourists on the back)
- a current museum-hours listing (extremely important, since no guidebook—including this one—has ever been able to accurately predict the hours of Florence's sights for the coming year). Also check www.comune.fi.it (select "Museums,"

FLORENCE

then "Museums' Opening Hours").

- information on entertainment, including the TI's monthly *Florence and Tuscany News* (good for events and entertainment listings)
- the ad-driven monthly *Florence Concierge Information* magazine (which lists museums, plus concerts, markets, sporting events, church services, shopping ideas, some bus and train connections, and an entire similar section on Siena)
- *The Florentine* newspaper (published every other Thu in English, for expats and tourists, with great articles giving cultural insights; download latest issue at www.theflorentine .net).

These English freebies are available at TIs and hotels all over town.

Arrival in Florence

By Train: Florence's main train station is called **Santa Maria Novella** (*Firenze S.M.N.* on schedules and signs). Built in Mussolini's "Rationalism" style back between the wars, in some ways the station seems to have changed little—notice the 1930s-era lettering and architecture.

Florence also has two suburban train stations: **Firenze Rifredi** and **Firenze Campo di Marte.** Note that some trains don't stop at the main station—before boarding, confirm that you're heading for S.M.N., or you may overshoot the city. (If this happens, don't panic; the other stations are a short taxi ride from the center.)

Minimize time in the main station—doing business here is generally intense, crowded, and overpriced. It's also rife with pickpockets. The banks of user-friendly automated ticket machines are handy. They take euros and credit cards, display schedules, issue tickets, and even make reservations for railpass-holders. Still, it can be quicker to get tickets and train info from travel agencies in town.

With your back to the tracks, look left to see a 24-hour pharmacy (*Farmacia*, near McDonald's), the fake "Tourist Information" office (funded by hotels), city buses, bus ticket booth, the taxi stand (fast-moving line, except on holidays), and the entrance to the Galleria S.M. Novella underground mall/passage that leads from the station under the square to the Church of Santa Maria Novella. (Warning: Pickpockets—often dressed as tourists—frequent this tunnel, especially the surface point near the church.) Baggage check is near track 16 (€4/5 hours, then €0.60/hour for 6–12 hours and €0.20/hour for 13-plus, daily 6:00–23:50, passport required, maximum 40 pounds, no explosives—sorry).

To get to the TI, walk away from the tracks and exit the train station to the left (going straight out of the station leads you to

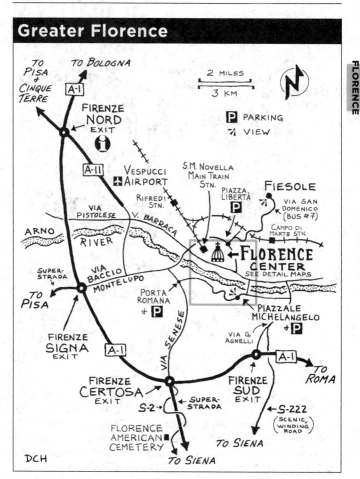

Greater Florence

Map labels:

TO PISA & CINQUE TERRE

TO BOLOGNA

A-1

2 MILES / 3 KM

P PARKING

⚲ VIEW

FIRENZE NORD EXIT

ⓘ

A-11

VESPUCCI ✈ AIRPORT

S.M. NOVELLA MAIN TRAIN STN.

RIFREDI STN.

V. BARRACA

PIAZZA LIBERTÀ **P**

FIESOLE

VIA SAN DOMENICO (BUS #7)

VIA PISTOLESE

CAMPO DI MARTE STN.

ARNO RIVER

SUPER-STRADA

VIA BACCIO MONTELUPO

TO PISA

PORTA ROMANA ✝ **P**

FLORENCE CENTER — SEE DETAIL MAPS

PIAZZALE MICHELANGELO ✝ **P**

VIA SENESE

VIA G. AGNELLI

FIRENZE SIGNA EXIT

A-1

FIRENZE CERTOSA EXIT

S-2 →

SUPER-STRADA

FIRENZE SUD EXIT

A-1

TO ROMA

S-222 (SCENIC WINDING ROAD)

FLORENCE AMERICAN CEMETERY

TO SIENA

TO SIENA

DCH

---

an uninviting wasteland of construction). The real TI is across the square by the stone church, 100 yards in front of the station (see "Tourist Information"). Pick up picnic supplies at the Conad supermarket, located along the west side of the station on Via Luigi Alamanni (Mon–Sat 8:00–20:00, closed Sun).

Most recommended hotels are within a 10- or 15-minute walk of the station. The Duomo, though not visible from here, is located to the left (east) down busy Via dei Panzani, a 10-minute walk away.

By Bus: The bus station is next to the train station, with the TI across the square. For more information on buses, see page 428.

By Car: The autostrada has several exits for Florence. Get off at the Nord, Sud, or Certosa exits and follow signs toward—but

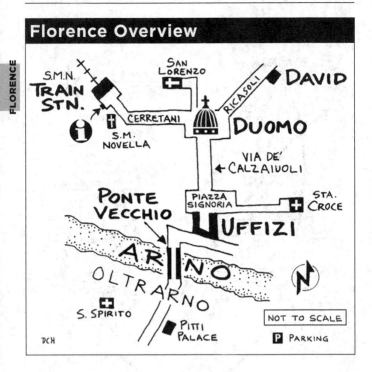

Florence Overview

not into—the *Centro*.

Don't even attempt driving into the city center. Florence has a traffic-reduction system that's complicated and confusing even to locals. Every car passing into the *Zona Traffico Limitato (ZTL)* is photographed; those who haven't jumped through bureaucratic hoops to get a permit can expect to receive a €100 ticket in the mail. If you get lost and cross the line several times...you get several fines. The no-go zone (defined basically by the old medieval wall, now a boulevard circling the historic center of town—watch for *Zona Traffico Limitato* signs) is roughly the area between the river, main train station, Piazza della Libertà, Piazza Donatello, and Piazza Beccaria.

Fortunately, the city center is ringed with big, efficient parking lots (signposted with the standard big *P*), each with taxi and bus service into the center. Check www.firenzeparcheggi.it for details on all their parking lots, availability, and prices. From the freeway, follow the signs to *Centro,* then *Stadio,* then *P*. I usually head for "Parcheggio del Parterre," just beyond Piazza della Libertà (€1.50/hour, €18/day, €65/week, open 24 hours daily, tel. 055-500-1994, 600 spots, automated, pay with cash or credit card, never fills up completely). To get into town, find the taxi stand at the elevator exit, or ride one of the *elettrico* minibuses that connect all of the major parking lots with the city center (see www.ataf.net for routes).

You can also park for free along any suburban curb near a bus stop that feels safe, and take the bus into the city center from there. Check for signs that indicate parking restrictions—for example, a circle with a slash through it and "*dispari giovedi,* 0,00–06,00" means don't park on Thursdays between midnight and six in the morning.

Free parking is easy up at Piazzale Michelangelo (see page 454), but don't park where the buses drop off passengers; park on the side of the piazza farthest from the view. To get from Piazzale Michelangelo to the center of town, take bus #12 or #13.

If you're picking up a rental car upon departure, don't struggle with driving into the center. Taxi with your luggage to the car-rental office, and head out from there.

By Plane: Amerigo Vespucci Airport, also called Peretola Airport, is about five miles northwest of Florence (open 5:10–24:00, no overnighting allowed, TI, cash machines, car-rental agencies, airport info tel. 055-306-1630, flight info tel. 055-306-1700—domestic only, www.aeroporto.firenze.it). Shuttle buses (far right of airport as you exit arrivals hall) connect the airport with Florence's SITA bus station, 100 yards west of the train station on Via Santa Caterina da Siena (2/hour, 30 minutes, daily 6:00–23:30, €5, first bus leaves for airport from Florence at 5:30). Allow about €20 and 30 minutes for a taxi.

By Cruise Ship: For detailed instructions for arriving at Florence's port, Livorno, see page 484.

Helpful Hints

Theft Alert: Florence has particularly hardworking thief gangs who hang out where you do: near the train station, the station's underpass (especially where the tunnel surfaces), and major sights. American tourists—especially older ones—are considered easy targets. Some thieves even dress like tourists to fool you. Also be on guard at two squares frequented by drug pushers (Santa Maria Novella and Santo Spirito). Bus #7 (to the nearby town of Fiesole, with great Florence views) is a favorite with tourists and, therefore, with thieves.

Medical Help: There's no shortage of English-speaking medical help in Florence. To reach a doctor who speaks English, call **Medical Service Firenze** at 055-475-411; the phone is answered 24/7. Rates are reasonable. For a doctor to come to your hotel within an hour of your call, you'd pay €100–200 (higher rates apply on Sun, holidays, or late visits). You pay only €50 if you go to the clinic when the doctor's in (Mon–Fri 11:00–12:00 & 17:00–18:00, Sat 11:00–12:00, closed Sun, no

Daily Reminder

Sunday: The Duomo's dome, Museum of Precious Stones, and Mercato Centrale are closed. At the Church of Santa Maria Novella, the Museum and Cloisters are closed, but the church itself is open (11:00–17:00). These sights close early: Duomo Museum (at 13:40) and the Baptistery's interior (at 14:00). A few sights are open only in the afternoon: Duomo (13:30–16:45), Santa Croce Church (13:00–17:30), Church of San Lorenzo (13:30–17:00), Brancacci Chapel and Church of Santa Maria Novella (both 13:00–17:00), and Santo Spirito Church (15:00–17:30). The Museum of San Marco and the Bargello are closed on the first, third, and fifth Sundays of the month. Palazzo Davanzati and the Medici Chapels close on the second and fourth Sundays. Need a calendar? Look in the appendix.

It's not possible to reserve tickets by phone on Sunday for the major sights (Accademia and Uffizi Gallery) because the telephone-reservation office for both is closed; try other options instead (see page 430 for details).

Monday: The biggies are closed, including the Accademia *(David)* and the Uffizi Gallery, as well as the Orsanmichele Church, and the Pitti Palace's Palatine Gallery, Royal Apartments, and Modern Art Gallery.

The Museum of San Marco and the Bargello close on the second and fourth Mondays. At the Pitti Palace, the Argenti Museum and the Boboli and Bardini Gardens close on the first and last Mondays. Palazzo Davanzati is closed on the first, third, and fifth Mondays. The San Lorenzo Market is closed Monday in winter.

Target these sights on Mondays: Duomo and its dome, Duomo Museum, Campanile, Baptistery, Medici-Riccardi Palace, Brancacci Chapel, Mercato Nuovo, Mercato Centrale, Casa Buonarroti, Galileo Science Museum, Palazzo Vecchio, and churches (including Santa Croce and Santa Maria Novella). Or take a walking tour.

appointment necessary, Via L. Magnifico 59, near Piazza della Libertà). A second clinic is available at Via Porta Rossa 1 (Mon–Sat 13:00–15:00, closed Sun).

Dr. Stephen Kerr is an English doctor specializing in helping sick tourists (clinic open for drop-ins Mon–Fri 15:00–17:00, other times by appointment, €50 per visit, Piazza Mercato Nuovo 1, between Piazza della Repubblica and Ponte Vecchio, tel. 055-288-055, mobile 335-836-1682, www.dr-kerr.com). The TI has a list of other English-speaking doctors.

There are 24-hour **pharmacies** at the train station and on Borgo San Lorenzo (near the Baptistery).

Tuesday: All sights are open, except Casa Buonarroti and the Brancacci Chapel. The Galileo Science Museum closes early (13:00).

Wednesday: All sights are open, except the Medici-Riccardi Palace and Santo Spirito Church.

Thursday: All sights are open. These sights close early: Duomo (15:30 in May and Oct, 16:30 in winter, 17:00 in summer) and Palazzo Vecchio (14:00).

Friday: All sights are open except the Museum and Cloisters at the Church of Santa Maria Novella (church open 11:00-17:30).

Saturday: All sights are open, but the Duomo's dome closes earlier than usual, at 17:40.

Early-Closing Warning: Some of Florence's sights close surprisingly early every day (or most days). Palazzo Davanzati closes daily at 13:50, the Museum of San Marco closes at 13:50 on weekdays (open later Sat and some Sun), and the Medici Chapels close at 13:50 in winter. The Museum of Precious Stones and Casa Buonarroti close at 14:00, as does the Mercato Centrale (except in winter, when it stays open until 17:00 on Sat).

Late-Hours Relief: The Accademia, Uffizi Gallery, and Palatine Gallery in the Pitti Palace are open until 18:50 daily except Monday.

Many sights are open until 19:00 on a particular day or more: San Lorenzo Market (daily, but closed Mon in winter), Medici-Riccardi Palace (Thu-Tue), the Duomo's dome (Mon-Fri), the Baptistery (Mon-Sat, except first Sat of month until 14:00), Palazzo Vecchio (Fri-Wed), and the Leonardo Museum (daily but closes at 18:00 in winter).

These sights are open until 19:30: Campanile (daily), Duomo Museum (Mon-Sat), San Miniato Church (daily but closes at 18:00 in winter), and the Boboli and Bardini Gardens at the Pitti Palace (daily, June-Aug only). The Mercato Nuovo is open daily until 20:00.

Reservations: To avoid standing in long lines, book ahead to visit the Accademia and Uffizi Gallery (see page 430 for details); you'll pay about a €4 booking fee, but it's worth it for the efficiency and peace of mind of having an assured entry time. One sight, the Brancacci Chapel, requires reservations, though these are free and easy to make; just call at least a day in advance (see page 453).

Price Hike Alert: Some of Florence's museums have found a clever way to squeeze more money out of visitors. They host a special exhibit that few tourists really care to see, and require you to pay extra for your ticket, even if all you want to see is the permanent collection.

Churches: Many churches now operate like museums, charging an admission fee to see their art treasures. Modest dress for men, women, and even children is required in some churches, and recommended for all of them—no bare shoulders, short shorts, or short skirts. Be respectful of worshippers and the paintings; don't use a flash. Churches usually close from 12:00 or 12:30 to 15:00 or 16:00.

Freebies: Many of Florence's sights and activities are free. There is no charge for entry to the Duomo, Orsanmichele Church, Santo Spirito Church, and San Miniato Church. It's free to visit the leather school at Santa Croce Church and the perfumery near the Church of Santa Maria Novella, and fun to browse at the three markets (Centrale for produce, Nuovo and San Lorenzo for goods).

Free public spaces include the Uffizi and Palazzo Vecchio courtyards; the art-filled loggia on Piazza della Signoria; and Piazzale Michelangelo, with glorious views over Florence. A walk across the picturesque Ponte Vecchio costs nothing at all—unless you succumb to temptation at one of the many shops along the way. A stroll anywhere in Florence with a gelato in hand is an inexpensive treat.

Addresses: Street addresses list businesses in red and residences in black (color-coded on the actual street number and indicated by a letter following the number in printed addresses: "r" = red; no indication or "n" = black, for *nero*). *Pensioni* are usually black but can be either. The red and black numbers each appear in roughly consecutive order on streets but bear no apparent connection with each other. I'm lazy and don't concern myself with the distinction (if one number's wrong, I look for the other) and can easily find my way around.

Internet Access: In bustling, tourist-filled Florence, you'll see small Internet cafés on virtually every street (remember to bring your passport). **V.I.P. Internet** has cheap rates, numerous terminals, and long hours (€1.50/hour, daily 9:00–24:00, near recommended hotel Katti House at Via Faenza 49 red, tel. 055-264-5552). **Internet Train,** the dominant chain, is pricier, with bright and cheery rooms, speedy computers, and decent hours (€4.30/hour, cheaper for students, reusable card good for any other Internet Train location, open daily roughly 9:00–20:00, www.internettrain.it). Find branches near Piazza della Repubblica (Via Porta Rossa 38 red), behind the Duomo (Via dell'Oriolo 40), on Piazza Santa Croce (Via de Benci 36 red), near *David* and recommended hotels (Via Guelfa 54 red), and near Ponte Vecchio (Borgo San Jacopo 30 red). Internet Train also offers Wi-Fi, phone

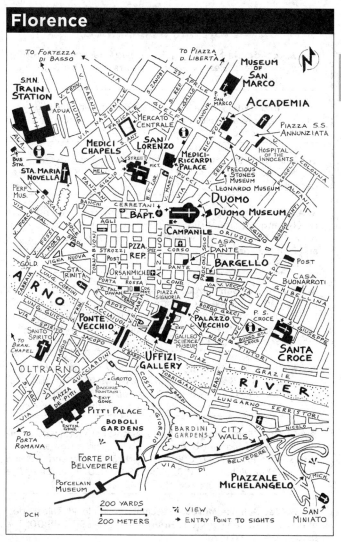

Florence

TO FORTEZZA DI BASSO
TO PIAZZA D. LIBERTA
MUSEUM OF SAN MARCO
SMN. TRAIN STATION
ACCADEMIA
MERCATO CENTRALE
PIAZZA S.S. ANNUNZIATA
MEDICI CHAPELS
SAN LORENZO
MEDICI-RICCARDI PALACE
HOSPITAL OF THE INNOCENTS
STA. MARIA NOVELLA
BUS STN.
PERF. MUS.
PRECIOUS STONES MUSEUM
LEONARDO MUSEUM
DUOMO
BAPT.
DUOMO MUSEUM
CAMPANILE
CASA DI DANTE
PZZA. REP.
POST
BARGELLO
POST
CASA BUONARROTI
ORSANMICH.
PIAZZA SIGNORIA
ARNO
PONTE VECCHIO
PALAZZO VECCHIO
GALILEO SCIENCE MUSEUM
SANTA CROCE
UFFIZI GALLERY
RIVER
OLTRARNO
GROTTO
BACCHUS FOUNTAIN
PITTI PALACE
BOBOLI GARDENS
BARDINI GARDENS
CITY WALLS
TO PORTA ROMANA
FORTE DI BELVEDERE
PORCELAIN MUSEUM
PIAZZALE MICHELANGELO
SAN MINIATO
200 YARDS
200 METERS
VIEW
ENTRY POINT TO SIGHTS
DCH

cards, CD-burning, and other related services.

Bookstores: Local guidebooks (sold at kiosks) are cheap and give you a map and a decent commentary on the sights. For brand-name guidebooks in English, try **Feltrinelli International** (Mon–Sat 9:00–19:30, closed Sun, a few blocks north of the Duomo and across the street from TI and Medici-Riccardi Palace at Via Cavour 12 red, tel. 055-219-524); **Edison Bookstore** (also has CDs, plus novels on the Renaissance and much more on its four floors; Mon–Sat 9:00–24:00, Sun

Florence at a Glance

▲▲▲**Accademia** Michelangelo's *David* and powerful (unfinished) *Prisoners*. Reserve ahead. **Hours:** Tue–Sun 8:15–18:50, closed Mon. See page 433.

▲▲▲**Uffizi Gallery** Greatest collection of Italian paintings anywhere. Reserve at least one month in advance. **Hours:** Tue–Sun 8:15–18:50, closed Mon. See page 446.

▲▲▲**Duomo Museum** Underrated cathedral museum with sculptures. **Hours:** Mon–Sat 9:00–19:30, Sun 9:00–13:40. See page 442.

▲▲▲**Bargello** Underappreciated sculpture museum (Michelangelo, Donatello, Medici treasures). **Hours:** Tue–Sat April-Oct 8:15–16:50, Nov–March 8:15–13:50; also open first, third, and fifth Mon of each month and second and fourth Sun of each month. See page 443.

▲▲**Museum of San Marco** Best collection anywhere of artwork by the early Renaissance master Fra Angelico. **Hours:** Tue–Fri 8:15–13:50, Sat 8:15–16:50; also open 8:15–16:50 on second and fourth Sun and 8:15–13:50 on first, third, and fifth Mon of each month. See page 435.

▲▲**Medici Chapels** Tombs of Florence's great ruling family, designed and carved by Michelangelo. **Hours:** Tue–Sat April-Oct 8:15–16:50, Nov–March 8:15–13:50; also open first, third, and fifth Sun and second and fourth Mon of each month. See page 438.

▲▲**Duomo (Santa Maria del Fiore)** Gothic cathedral with colorful facade and the first dome built since ancient Roman times. **Hours:** Mon–Fri 10:00–17:00, Thu until 15:30 in May and Oct and until 16:30 in winter, Sat 10:00–16:45, Sun 13:30–16:45. See page 440.

▲▲**Galileo Science Museum** Fascinating old clocks, telescopes, maps, and Galileo's fingers. **Hours:** Wed–Mon 9:30–18:00, Tue 9:30–13:00. See page 448.

▲▲**Santa Croce Church** Precious art, tombs of famous Florentines, and Brunelleschi's Pazzi Chapel in 14th-century church. **Hours:** Mon–Sat 9:30–17:30, Sun 13:00–17:30. See page 449.

▲▲**Church of Santa Maria Novella** Thirteenth-century Dominican church with Masaccio's famous 3-D painting. **Hours:** Mon–Thu 9:00–17:30, Fri 11:00–17:30, Sat 9:00–17:00, Sun 13:00–17:00. See page 451.

FLORENCE

▲▲**Pitti Palace** Several museums in lavish palace plus sprawling Boboli and Bardini Gardens. **Hours:** Palatine Gallery, Royal Apartments, and Modern Art Gallery: Tue–Sun 8:15–18:50, closed Mon; Argenti Museum, Costume Gallery, Porcelain Museum, and Boboli and Bardini Gardens: Daily 8:15–18:30, until 19:30 June–Aug, closed first and last Mon of the month, shorter hours in winter. See page 451.

▲▲**Brancacci Chapel** Works of Masaccio, early Renaissance master who reinvented perspective. **Hours:** Mon and Wed–Sat 10:00–17:00, Sun 13:00–17:00, closed Tue. Reservations required. See page 453.

▲▲**San Miniato Church** Sumptuous Renaissance chapel and sacristy showing scenes of St. Benedict. **Hours:** Daily April–Oct 8:00–19:30, Nov–March 8:00–13:00 & 14:30–18:00. See page 454.

▲**Medici-Riccardi Palace** Lorenzo the Magnificent's home, with fine art, frescoed ceilings, and Gozzoli's lovely Chapel of the Magi. **Hours:** Thu–Tue 9:00–19:00, closed Wed. See page 439.

▲**Climbing the Duomo's Dome** Grand view into the cathedral, close-up of dome architecture, and, after 463 steps, a glorious Florence vista. **Hours:** Mon–Fri 8:30–19:00, Sat 8:30–17:40, closed Sun. Long and slow lines, go early, no reservations accepted. See page 441.

▲**Campanile** Views similar to Duomo's, 50 fewer steps, and fewer lines. **Hours:** Daily 8:30–19:30. See page 441.

▲**Baptistery** Bronze doors fit to be the gates of paradise. **Hours:** Doors always viewable; interior open Mon–Sat 12:15–19:00 except first Sat of month 8:30–14:00, Sun 8:30–14:00. See page 442.

▲**Palazzo Vecchio** Fortified palace, once the home of the Medici family, wallpapered with history and Renaissance themes. **Hours:** Fri–Wed 9:00–19:00, Thu 9:00–14:00. See page 448.

▲**Ponte Vecchio** Famous bridge lined with gold and silver shops. **Hours:** Bridge always open (shops closed at night). See page 449.

▲**Casa Buonarroti** Early, lesser-known works by Michelangelo. **Hours:** Wed–Mon 9:30–14:00, closed Tue. See page 450.

▲**Piazzale Michelangelo** Hilltop square with stunning view of Duomo and Florence. **Hours:** Always open. See page 454.

FLORENCE

10:00–24:00, facing Piazza della Repubblica, tel. 055-213-110); **Paperback Exchange** (cheaper, all books in English, bring in your used book for a discount on a new one, Mon–Fri 9:00–19:30, Sat 10:30–19:30, closed Sun, just south of the Duomo on Via delle Oche 4 red, tel. 055-293-460); or **BM Bookshop** (with perhaps the city's largest collection of English books and guidebooks—including mine; Mon–Sat 9:30–19:30, closed Sun, near Ponte alla Carraia at Borgognissanti 4 red, tel. 055-294-575).

Maps: While the city is awash in free tourist maps, which work fine for most visits, if you want to invest in a durable, detailed, and smartly designed map, consider Rough Guide's *Map of Florence & Siena* (€9).

Services: WCs are scarce. Use them when you can, in cafés or museums you patronize.

Laundry: The **Wash & Dry Lavarapido** chain offers long hours and efficient, self-service launderettes at several locations (about €7 for wash and dry, daily 8:00–22:00, tel. 055-580-480 or toll-free 800-231-172). These are close to recommended hotels: Via dei Servi 105 red (and a rival launderette at Via Guelfa 55, off Via San Zanobi; both near *David*), Via del Sole 29 red and Via della Scala 52 red (between train station and river), Via Ghibellina 143 red (Palazzo Vecchio), Via Faenza 26 (near station), and Via dei Serragli 87 red (across the river in Oltrarno neighborhood).

Travel Agency: Get train tickets, reservations, and supplements at travel agencies rather than at the congested train station. The cost is either the same or the charge is minimal. Ask your hotel for the nearest travel agency.

Water: Carry a water bottle to refill at Florence's twist-the-handle public fountains.

Chill Out: Schedule several cool breaks into your sightseeing where you can sit, pause, and refresh yourself with a sandwich, gelato, or coffee.

Getting Around Florence

I organize my sightseeing geographically and do it all on foot. I think of Florence as a Renaissance treadmill—it requires a lot of walking.

Buses: The city's full-size buses don't cover the old center well, especially now that the whole area around the Duomo has been declared off-limits to motorized traffic. Of the many bus lines, I found these of most value for seeing outlying sights: Lines #12 and #13 go from the train station to Porta Romana, up to San Miniato Church and Piazzale Michelangelo, and on to Santa Croce. Most other lines leave from Piazza San Marco (near the

Accademia and Museum of San Marco), including bus #7, which goes to Fiesole, a small town with big views of Florence. To get from the train station to Piazza San Marco, either walk or take bus #1, #6, #14, or #23.

Fun little *elettrico* **minibuses** wind through the tangled old center of town and up and down the river—just €1.20 gets you a 90-minute joyride. These buses, which run every 10 minutes, are popular with sore-footed sightseers and eccentric local seniors. *Elettrico* #C2 twists through the congested old center from the train station to Piazza Beccaria. *Elettrico* #C3 goes up and down the Arno River from Ognissanti to Santa Croce Church and beyond; #C1 winds around Piazza Repubblica, then heads north up to Piazza Libertà. *Elettrico* #D goes from the train station to Ponte Vecchio, cruising through Oltrarno, and finishing at Ponte San Niccolò. The minibuses connect many major parking lots with the historical center (tickets sold at machines at lots). Routes are shown on the free TI map (see the handy inset) and the "La Rete dei Bussini Potenziata" leaflet, free at the ATAF bus office, located just east of the train station, on Piazza della Stazione.

Buy bus tickets at *tabacchi* (tobacco) shops, newsstands, or the ATAF bus office (€1.20/90 minutes, €4.50/4 tickets, €5/24 hours, €12/3 days, 1-day and 3-day passes aren't always available in *tabacchi*, validate in machine on the bus, tel. 800-424-500, www.ataf .net). You can buy tickets on board, but you'll pay more (€2) and you'll need exact change. Follow general bus etiquette: Board at front or rear doors, exit out the center.

Hop-on, hop-off bus tours stop at the major sights (see "Hop-on, Hop-off Bus Tours" in the following section).

Taxi: The minimum cost for a taxi ride is €5, or €6 after 22:00 and on Sundays (rides in the center of town should be charged as tariff #1). A taxi ride from the train station to Ponte Vecchio costs about €9. Taxi fares and supplements (e.g., €2 extra if you call a cab rather than hail one) are clearly explained on signs in each taxi.

Tours in Florence

Tour companies big and small offer plenty of tours that go out to smaller towns in the Tuscan countryside (the most popular day trips: Siena, San Gimignano, Pisa, and into Chianti country for wine-tasting). They also do city tours, but for most people, the city is really best on foot (and the book you're holding provides as much information as you'll get with a generic bus tour).

For extra insight with a personal touch, consider the tour companies and individual Florentine guides listed here. They are hardworking, creative, and offer a worthwhile array of organized sightseeing activities. Study their websites for details. If you're

Make Reservations to Avoid Lines

Florence has an optional reservation system for its state-run sights, which include the Accademia, Uffizi Gallery, Bargello, Medici Chapels, and Pitti Palace. I highly recommend getting reservations for the Accademia (Michelangelo's *David*) and the Uffizi (Renaissance paintings), but not the others.

The Brancacci Chapel is the only sight in Florence that requires reservations. These are free and simple to make. Call at least a day in advance and sign up for the film, too. Sometimes same-day reservations are available (tel. 055-276-8224 or 055-276-8558, English spoken, call center open daily 9:00–17:00). For more information, see page 453.

The Uffizi and Accademia

Your best strategy is to get reservations for these two top sights as soon as you know when you'll be in town. Although you can generally get an entry time for the Accademia within a few days, the Uffizi can be booked more than a month in advance.

There are several ways to make a reservation: Have your hotelier arrange it, call the reservation number directly, book online, take a tour, or go in person in advance to the museums or the Orsanmichele Church ticket window. Here are details on the options:

- When you make your **hotel** reservation, ask if they can book your museum reservations for you (some hoteliers will do this for free; others charge a €3–5 fee). This is your easiest option.
- Reserve by **phone** before you leave the States (from the US, dial 011-39-055-294-883, or within Italy call 055-294-883; €4/ticket reservation fee; booking office open Mon–Fri 8:30–18:30, Sat 8:30–12:30, closed Sun). The reservation line is often busy, and even if you get through, you may be dis-

taking a city tour, remember that individuals save money with a scheduled public tour (such as those offered daily by Artviva Tours of Florence, listed next). If you're traveling as a family or small group, however, you're likely to save money by booking a private guide (since rates are based on roughly €55/hour for any size of group).

Artviva Walking Tours—This company offers a variety of tours (up to 12/day year-round) featuring downtown Florence, museum highlights, and Tuscany day trips. Their guides are native English-

connected while on hold. Be persistent and try again. When you do get through, an English-speaking operator walks you through the process, and a few minutes later you say *grazie,* with an appointment and a six-digit confirmation number. Bring the confirmation(s) with you and pay cash at the sight(s). The advantage to phoning versus booking online is that you pay nothing upfront when you phone.

- Using a credit card, you can reserve your visit **online.** Pricey middleman sites—such as www.uffizi.com and www.tickitaly .com—are reliable, but their booking fees are exorbitant, running about €10 per ticket. Or you could take your chances with the city's troublesome official site (www.firenzemusei .it) in the hopes that its glitches have been fixed. It's the cheapest place to make reservations online (€4/ticket reservation fee), but even when it's working, the site often reverts to Italian-only (*"Annulia Operazione"* means "cancel"), you can't book a time before noon, and some readers report not receiving vouchers they've paid for.

- Take a **tour** that includes your museum admission. Artviva Walking Tours offers tours of the Uffizi (€39/person, 2 hours), Accademia (€35/person, 1 hour), and both museums (€94/person, 6 hours; see listing on page 430, or visit www .italy.artviva.com).

- To **reserve in Florence,** here are your choices: call the reservation number (see above); ask your hotelier for help; or head to the booking window at Orsanmichele Church (€4 reservation fee, daily 10:00–17:00, along Via Calzaiuoli—see location on map on page 436). For another Uffizi option, go to its ticket office and pay cash (Tue–Sun 8:15–18:50, use the *Main Entrance*—door #2, enter to the left of the line).

Off-Season: If you're in Florence off-season (Oct–March), you can probably get into the Uffizi or Accademia without a reservation in the late afternoon (after 16:00). At worst, you can make a reservation for later that day or the next day. But why hassle with it when you can make a reservation in advance? After seeing hundreds of bored, sweaty tourists waiting in lines without reservations, it's hard not to be amazed at their cluelessness.

speakers. The three-hour "Original Florence" walk hits the main sights but gets offbeat to weave a picture of Florentine life in medieval and Renaissance times. Tours go rain or shine with as few as four participants (€25, daily at 9:15). Museum tours include the Uffizi (€39, includes admission, 2 hours), Accademia (called "Original *David*" tour, €35, includes admission, 1 hour), and "Original Florence in One Day" (€94, includes admission to Uffizi and Accademia, 6 hours). Their "Florence Orientation" talk starts in their office and is followed by a wine-tasting in an atmospheric bar (€10, daily at 17:00). They also offer talks by artists, writers, and wine and culinary experts (usually €20/person, late April–Oct Mon–Fri at 17:50, one hour, reserve at least one day ahead, dress is "elegant casual"—do your best).

Reservations are necessary for all tours and talks. For specifics and schedules, pick up their extensive brochure in your hotel lobby or their office (Mon–Sat 8:00–18:00, Sun 8:30–13:30 but off-season closed Sun and for lunch, near Piazza della Repubblica at Via dei Sassetti 1, second floor, above Odeon Cinema, tel. 055-264-5033 during day or mobile 329-613-2730 18:00–20:00, www.italy.artviva.com, staff@artviva.com).

Florentia—Top-notch private walking tours—geared for thoughtful, well-heeled travelers with longer-than-average attention spans—are led by Florentine scholars. The tours range from introductory city walks and museum visits to in-depth thematic walks, such as the Oltrarno neighborhood, "Unusual Florence," and side-trips into Tuscany (tours-€175/half-day, €350/day, reserve in advance, tel. 338-890-8625, www.florentia.org, info@florentia.org).

Context Florence—This scholarly group of graduate students and professors leads "walking seminars," such as a three-hour study of Michelangelo's work and influence (€85/person, includes Accademia admission) and a two-hour evening orientation stroll (€35/person). I enjoyed the fascinating three-hour fresco workshop (€75/person, you take home a fresco you make yourself). See their website for other innovative offerings: Medici walk, lecture series, food walks, kids' tours, and programs in Venice, Rome, Naples, London, and Paris (tel. 069-762-5204, US tel. 888-467-1986, www.contexttravel.com, info@contexttravel.com).

Local Guides—Good guides include **Paola Barubiani** and her art historian partners at Walks Inside Florence (€55/hour for up to 4 people, €50/person for small-group 3-hour tour, €165/group of 2–6 people for private 3-hour tour, special rates for family tours, ask about Rick Steves discount, mobile 335-526-6496, www.walksinsideflorence.com, paola@walksinsideflorence.it). **Alessandra Marchetti,** a Florentine who has lived in the US, gives private walking tours of Florence and driving tours of Tuscany (€60–75/hour, mobile 347-386-9839, aleoberm@tin.it). **Paola Migliorini** and her partners at Tuscany Tours offer museum tours, city walking tours, private cooking classes, wine tours, and Tuscan excursions by van—you can tailor tours as you like (€55/hour without car, €65/hour in an 8-seat van, tel. 055-472-448, mobile 347-657-2611, www.florencetour.com, info@florencetour.com).

Hop-on, Hop-off Bus Tours—Around town, you'll see big double-decker sightseeing buses double-parking near major sights. Tourists on the top deck can listen to brief recorded descriptions of the sights, snap photos, and enjoy an effortless drive-by look at the major landmarks. Tickets cost €22, are valid for two days, and include two bus lines. Line A takes one hour with a trip up to Piazzale Michelangelo; Line B takes two hours with a side-trip to Fiesole (first bus at 9:30, last bus at 18:00, pay as you board, www .firenze.city-sightseeing.it). As the name implies, you can hop off when you want and catch the next bus (usually every 30 minutes, depending on the season). Hop-on stops include the train station and Pitti Palace. As most sights are buried in the old center where big buses can't go, Florence doesn't really lend itself to this kind of tour bus. Look at the route map before committing.

Sights in Florence

North of the Arno River
North of the Duomo (Cathedral)

▲▲▲**Accademia (Galleria dell'Accademia)**—When you look into the eyes of Michelangelo's magnificent sculpture of *David*, you're looking into the eyes of Renaissance Man.

In 1501, Michelangelo Buonarroti, a 26-year-old Florentine, was commissioned to carve a large-scale work. The figure comes from a Bible story. The Israelites are surrounded by barbarian war-

riors led by a brutish giant named Goliath. When the giant challenges the Israelites to send out someone to fight him, a young shepherd boy steps forward. Armed only with a sling, David defeats the giant. This 17-foot-tall symbol of divine victory over evil represents a new century and a whole new Renaissance outlook.

Originally, *David* was meant to stand on the roofline of the Duomo, but was placed more prominently at the entrance of Palazzo Vecchio (where a copy stands today). In the 19th century, *David* was moved indoors for his own protection, and stands under a wonderful Renaissance-style dome designed just for him.

Nearby are some of the master's other works, including his powerful (unfinished) *Prisoners, St. Matthew,* and a *Pietà* (possibly by one of his disciples). Michelangelo, who would work tirelessly through the night, believed that the sculptor was a tool of God, responsible only for chipping away at the stone until the intended sculpture emerged. Beyond the magic marble are some mildly interesting pre-Renaissance and Renaissance paintings, including a couple of lighter-than-air Botticellis, the plaster model of Giambologna's *Rape of the Sabines,* and a musical instrument collection with an early piano.

FLORENCE

Heart of Florence

MUSEUM OF SAN MARCO

P. SAN MARCO

ACCADEMIA

P. S. S. ANNUNZ.

200 YARDS
200 METERS

MEDICI CHAPELS

SAN LORENZO

MEDICI-RICCARDI PALACE

PRECIOUS STONES MUSEUM

HOSPITAL OF THE INNOCENTS

STREET

MKT.

TO TRAIN STN.

B. S. LOR.

V. MARTELLI

PUCCI

VIA

SERVI

V. ALF

LEONARDO MUSEUM

PANZ.

CERRETANI

DUOMO

DUOMO MUSEUM

AGLI

BAPT.

CAMPANILE

ORIUOLO

STROZZI

PZZA. REP.

SPEZ.

S. MARIA RICCI

CORSO

CASA DI DANTE

CASA BUONA-RROTI

ORSAN-MICHELE

TAVO. DANTE

BARGELLO

PORTA ROSSA

COND.

VIA

V. G. VECCHIA

GHIB.

V. PAL. DAVAN.

COV. MKT.

PIAZZA SIGNORIA

ANG.

TERME

MARIA

BORGO GRECI

P. S. CROCE

B. S. APOST.

L. ACCIAIUOLI

PALAZZO VECCHIO

BENCI

BORGO STA. CROCE

SANTA CROCE

EXIT

GALILEO SCIENCE MUSEUM

V. D. NERI

TINTORI

S. JAC.

GUICC.

UFFIZI GALLERY

LUNG. DIAZ

PONTE VECCHIO

DCH

ARNO

↗ VIEW
→ ENTRY POINT TO SIGHTS

TO PITTI PALACE

OLTRARNO

Cost and Hours: €6.50, plus €4 fee for recommended reservation (see page 430 for details), Tue–Sun 8:15–18:50, closed Mon, last entry 45 minutes before closing (Via Ricasoli 60, tel. 055-238-8609 or 055-294-883, www.polomuseale.firenze.it).

Nearby: Piazza S.S. Annunziata, behind the Accademia, displays lovely Renaissance harmony. Facing the square are two fine buildings: the 15th-century Santissima Annunziata church (worth a peek) and Filippo Brunelleschi's Hospital of the Innocents (Spedale degli Innocenti, not worth going inside), with terra-cotta medallions by Luca della Robbia. Built in the 1420s, the hospital is considered the first Renaissance building. I love sleeping on this square (at the recommended Hotel Loggiato dei Serviti) and picnicking here during the day (with the riffraff, who remind me of the persistent gap—today as in Medici times—between

those who appreciate fine art and those just looking for some cheap wine).

▲▲**Museum of San Marco (Museo di San Marco)**—Located one block north of the Accademia, this 15th-century monastery houses the greatest collection anywhere of frescoes and paintings by the early Renaissance master Fra Angelico. The ground floor features the monk's paintings, along with some works by Fra

Bartolomeo. Upstairs are 43 cells decorated by Fra Angelico and his assistants. While the monk-painter was trained in the medieval religious style, he also learned and adopted Renaissance techniques and sensibilities, producing works that blended Christian symbols and Renaissance realism. Don't miss the cell of Savonarola, the

charismatic monk who rode in from the Christian right, threw out the Medicis, turned Florence into a theocracy, sponsored "bonfires of the vanities" (burning books, paintings, and so on), and was finally burned himself when Florence decided to change channels.

Cost and Hours: €4, Tue–Fri 8:15–13:50, Sat 8:15–16:50; also open 8:15–16:50 on second and fourth Sun and 8:15–13:50 on first, third, and fifth Mon of each month; last entry 30 minutes before closing, reservations possible but unnecessary, on Piazza San Marco, tel. 055-238-8608, www.polomuseale.firenze.it.

FLORENCE

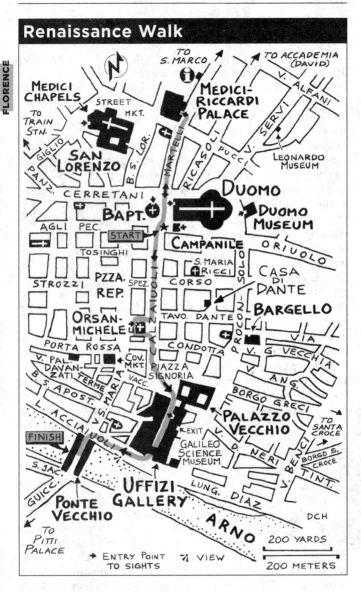

Renaissance Walk

Museum of Precious Stones (Museo dell'Opificio delle Pietre Dure)—This unusual gem of a museum features room after room of exquisite mosaics of inlaid marble and stones. Upstairs, you'll see remnants of the Medici workshop from 1588, including 500 different precious stones and the tools used to cut and inlay them. The helpful loaner booklet available next to the ticket window describes it all in English.

A Renaissance Walk Through Florence

During the Dark Ages, it was especially obvious to the people of Italy—sitting on the rubble of Rome—that there had to be a brighter age before them. The long-awaited rebirth, or Renaissance, began in Florence for good reason. Wealthy because of its cloth industry, trade, and banking; powered by a fierce city-state pride (locals would pee into the Arno with gusto, knowing rival city-state Pisa was downstream); and fertile with more than its share of artistic genius (imagine guys like Michelangelo and Leonardo attending the same high school)—Florence was a natural home for this cultural explosion.

Take a two-hour walk through the core of Renaissance Florence by starting at the Accademia (home of Michelangelo's *David*) and cutting through the heart of the city to Ponte Vecchio on the Arno River (see map on opposite page).

At the Accademia, you'll see *David,* the ultimate Renaissance Man. Then walk to the cathedral (Duomo) to marvel at the dome that kicked off the architectural Renaissance. Step inside the Baptistery to view a ceiling covered with preachy 2-D medieval mosaic art. Then, to learn what happened when art met math, check out the realistic 3-D reliefs on the doors. The painter, Giotto, also designed the bell tower—an early example of a Renaissance genius who could excel in many areas. Continue toward the river on Florence's great pedestrian mall, Via de' Calzaiuoli—part of the original grid plan given to the city by the ancient Romans. Stop by any gelato shop for some cool refreshment. Down a few blocks, compare medieval and Renaissance statues on the exterior of the Orsanmichele Church. Via de' Calzaiuoli connects the cathedral with the central square (Piazza della Signoria), the city palace (Palazzo Vecchio), and the Uffizi Gallery, which contains the greatest collection of Italian Renaissance paintings in captivity. Finally, walk through the Uffizi courtyard—a statuary think tank of Renaissance greats—to the Arno River and Ponte Vecchio.

Cost and Hours: €4, Mon–Sat 8:15–14:00, closed Sun, around corner from Accademia at Via degli Alfani 78, tel. 055-265-1357.

Church of San Lorenzo—This red-brick dome—which looks like the Duomo's little sister—is the Medici church and the burial place of the family's founder, Giovanni di Bicci de' Medici (1360–1429). The facade is big, ugly, and unfinished, because Pope Leo X (also a Medici) pulled the plug on the project due to dwindling funds—after Michelangelo had labored on it for four years (1516–1520). Inside, though, is the spirit of Florence in the 1420s, with gray-and-white columns and arches in perfect Renaissance symmetry and simplicity. The Brunelleschi-designed church is lit

by an even, diffused light. The Medici coat of arms (with the round pills of these "medics") decorates the ceiling, and everywhere are images of St. Lawrence, the Medici patron saint who was martyred on a grill.

Highlights of the church include two finely sculpted Donatello pulpits (in the nave). In the Martelli Chapel (left wall of the left transept), Filippo Lippi's *Annunciation* features a smiling angel greeting Mary in a sharply 3-D courtyard. Light shines through the vase in the foreground, like the Holy Spirit entering Mary's womb. The Old Sacristy (far left corner), designed by Brunelleschi, was the burial chapel for the Medicis. Bronze doors by Donatello flank the sacristy's small altar. Overhead, the dome above the altar shows the exact arrangement of the heavens on July 4, 1442, leaving scholars to hypothesize about why that particular date was used. Back in the nave, the round inlaid marble in the floor before the main altar marks where Cosimo the Elder—Lorenzo the Magnificent's grandfather—is buried. Assistants in the church provide information on request, and the information brochure is free and in English.

Cost and Hours: €3.50, Feb–Oct Mon–Sat 10:00–17:00, Sun 13:30–17:00, closed Nov–Jan, www.basilicasanlorenzo.it.

Nearby: Outside the church, along the left side, is a cloister with peek-a-boo Duomo views and two sights: The San Lorenzo Museum (of fancy reliquaries) is included in your church admission, but is hardly worth the walk, except to see Donatello's grave. Next door is the Laurentian Library (*Biblioteca Laurenziana,* not included in church entry), starring Michelangelo's impressive staircase entrance. The library is worthwhile if it's open (€3, only opens during special exhibits, generally 9:30–13:00). A street market bustles outside the church (listed after the Medici Chapels, below).

Around the back end of the church is the entrance to the Medici Chapels and the New Sacristy, designed by Michelangelo for a later generation of dead Medicis.

▲▲**Medici Chapels (Cappelle Medicee)**—The burial site of the ruling Medici family in the Church of San Lorenzo includes the dusky Crypt; the big, domed Chapel of Princes; and the magnificent all-Michelangelo New Sacristy, featuring the master's architecture, tombs, and statues. The Medicis made their money in textiles and banking and patronized a dream team of Renaissance

artists that put Florence on the cultural map. Michelangelo, who spent his teen years living with the Medicis, was commissioned for the family's final tribute.

Cost and Hours: €6, Tue–Sat April–Oct 8:15–16:50, Nov–March 8:15–13:50; also open first, third, and fifth Sun and second and fourth Mon of each month; last entry 30 minutes before closing, confirm latest hours at TI or chapel, tel. 055-238-8602, www.polomuseale.firenze.it. Don't waste money on a reservation to visit this sight.

▲**San Lorenzo Market**—Florence's vast open-air market sprawls around the Church of San Lorenzo. Most of the leather stalls are run by Iranians selling South American leather that was tailored in Italy. Prices are soft (daily 9:00–19:00, closed Mon in winter, between the Duomo and train station).

▲**Mercato Centrale (Central Market)**—Florence's giant iron-and-glass-covered central market, a wonderland of picturesque produce, is fun to explore. While the nearby San Lorenzo Market—with its garment stalls in the streets—feels like a step up from a haphazard flea market, the Mercato Centrale retains a Florentine elegance. Wander around. You'll see parts of the cow you'd never dream of eating (no, that's not a turkey neck), enjoy generous free samples, watch pasta-making, and have your pick of plenty of fun eateries sloshing out cheap and tasty pasta to locals (Mon–Sat 7:00–14:00, in winter open Sat until 17:00, closed Sun). For eating ideas in and around the market, see "Eating in Florence," later.

▲**Medici-Riccardi Palace (Palazzo Medici-Riccardi)**—Lorenzo the Magnificent's home is worth a look for its art. The tiny Chapel of the Magi contains colorful Renaissance gems like the *Procession of the Magi* frescoes by Benozzo Gozzoli. The former

library has a Baroque ceiling fresco by Luca Giordano, a prolific artist from Naples known as "Fast Luke" *(Luca fa presto)* for his ambidextrous painting abilities. While the Medicis originally occupied this 1444 house, in the 1700s it became home to the Riccardi family, who added the Baroque flourishes.

Cost and Hours: €5, €7 with mandatory special exhibits,

Thu–Tue 9:00–19:00, closed Wed, last entry 30 minutes before closing; kitty-corner from Church of San Lorenzo, one long block north of Duomo, ticket entrance is north of the main gated entrance, Via Cavour 3, tel. 055-276-0340.

Leonardo Museum—This small entrepreneurial venture is fun for anyone who wants to crank the shaft and spin the ball bearings of Leonardo's genius inventions. While there are no actual historic artifacts, it shows about 30 of Leonardo's inventions and experiments made into models. You'll see a full-size armored tank, walk into a chamber of mirrors, operate a rotating crane, and watch experiments in flying.  Each is described in English. What makes this exhibit special is that you're encouraged to touch and play with the models—it's great for kids.

Cost and Hours: €6, daily 10:00–19:00, closes at 18:00 in winter, Via dei Servi 66 red, tel. 055-282-966, www.mostredi leonardo.com.

Duomo and Nearby

▲▲**Duomo (Cattedrale di Santa Maria del Fiore)**—Florence's Gothic cathedral has the third-longest nave in Christendom. The

church's noisy Neo-Gothic facade from the 1870s is covered with pink, green, and white Tuscan marble. In the interior, you'll see a huge *Last Judgment* by Giorgio Vasari and Federico Zuccari (inside the dome). Much of the church's great art is stored in the Duomo Museum behind the church.

The cathedral's claim to artistic fame is Brunelleschi's magnificent dome—the first Renaissance dome and the model for domes to follow. Think of the confidence of the age: The Duomo was built with a big hole in its roof awaiting a dome. This was before the technology to span it with a dome was available. No *problema*. They knew that someone soon could handle the challenge...and the local architect Filippo Brunelleschi did. First, he built the grand white skeletal ribs, which you can see, then filled them in with interlocking bricks in a herringbone pattern. The dome grew upward like an igloo, supporting itself as it proceeded from the base. At the top, Brunelleschi arched the ribs in and fixed them in place with the lantern. His dome, built in only 14 years, was the largest since Rome's Pantheon.

Massive crowds line up to see the huge church. The church is a major sight, but not worth a long wait. Either go late (the crowds subside by late afternoon), or take the Terraces tour mentioned below.

Cost and Hours: Free entry, Mon–Fri 10:00–17:00, Thu until 15:30 in May and Oct and until 16:30 in winter, Sat 10:00–16:45, Sun 13:30–16:45, modest dress code enforced, tel. 055-230-2885, www.operaduomo.firenze.it.

Crowd-Beating Tip: Taking the "**Terraces of the Cathedral and Dome**" tour allows you to skip the long lines to enter the cathedral and to climb the dome. After a short guided tour of the interior, you'll climb up onto the exterior terrace, where great views reward the stair hike (see "Climbing the Duomo's Dome," next). When the tour is finished on the terrace, you can continue on your own up to the top of the dome (€15, 45 minutes; offered Mon–Fri at 10:30, 12:00, and 15:00; at 10:30 and 12:00 on Sat, no tours on Sun, buy tickets at nearby Duomo Museum and they'll tell you where to meet your guide). If you're planning to climb the dome anyway (€8), the tour is a fine value.

▲**Climbing the Duomo's Dome**—For a grand view into the cathedral from the base of the dome, a peek at some of the tools used in the dome's construction, a chance to see Brunelleschi's "dome-within-a-dome" construction, a glorious Florence view from the top, and the equivalent of 463 plunges on a Renaissance StairMaster, climb the dome. Michelangelo, setting out to construct the dome of St. Peter's in Rome, drew inspiration from the dome of Florence. He said, "I'll make its sister...bigger, but not more beautiful." To avoid the long, dreadfully slow-moving line, arrive by 8:30 or drop by very late. Those taking the "Terraces" tour of the Duomo (see above) can skip the line.

Cost and Hours: €8, Mon–Fri 8:30–19:00, Sat 8:30–17:40, closed Sun, last entry 40 minutes before closing, enter from outside church on north side, tel. 055-230-2885.

▲**Campanile (Giotto's Tower)**—The 270-foot bell tower has 50 fewer steps than the Duomo's dome (but that's still 414 steps—no elevator); offers a faster, less-crowded climb; and has a view of the

Duomo to boot, but the cage-like top makes taking good photographs difficult.

Cost and Hours: €6, daily 8:30–19:30, last entry 40 minutes before closing.

▲Baptistery—Michelangelo said its bronze doors were fit to be the gates of paradise. Check out the gleaming copies of Lorenzo Ghiberti's bronze doors facing the Duomo. Making a breakthrough in perspective, Ghiberti used mathematical laws to create the illusion of receding distance on a basically flat surface.

The doors on the north side of the building were designed by Ghiberti when he was young; he'd won the honor and opportunity by beating Brunelleschi in a competition (the rivals' original entries are in the Bargello).

Inside, sit and savor the medieval mosaic ceiling, where it's

always Judgment Day and Jesus is giving the ultimate thumbs-up and thumbs-down. The rest of the ceiling mosaics tell the history of the world, from Adam and Eve (over the north/entrance doors, top row) to Noah and the Flood (over south doors, top row), to the life of Christ (second row) to the beheading of John the Baptist (bottom row), all bathed in the golden glow of pre-Renaissance heaven.

Cost and Hours: €4, interior open Mon–Sat 12:15–19:00 except first Sat of month 8:30–14:00, Sun 8:30–14:00, last entry 30 minutes before closing, audioguide-€2, photos allowed inside, tel. 055-230-2885; bronze doors are on the outside, so always "open"; original panels are in the Duomo Museum.

▲▲▲Duomo Museum (Museo dell' Opera del Duomo)—The underrated cathedral museum, behind the church (at Via del Proconsolo 9), is great if you like sculpture. On the ground floor, look for a late Michelangelo *Pietà,* the eight restored panels of Ghiberti's north doors for the Baptistery, and statues from the original Baptistery facade. Upstairs, you'll find Brunelleschi's models for his dome, as well as Donatello's

anorexic *Mary Magdalene* and playful choir loft. The museum features most of Ghiberti's original "Gates of Paradise" panels; the panels on the Baptistery's doors today are copies.

Cost and Hours: €6, Mon–Sat 9:00–19:30, Sun 9:00–13:40, last entry 40 minutes before closing, one of the few museums in Florence always open on Mon, Via del Proconsolo 9, tel. 055-230-2885. At this museum, you can purchase €15 tickets for the "Terraces of the Cathedral and Dome" tour mentioned earlier (page 441), which allows you to bypass the long cathedral-entry and dome-climbing lines.

Nearby: If you find this church art intriguing, head to the left around the back of the Duomo to find Via dello Studio (near the south transept), then walk a block toward the river to #23a. You can look through the open doorway of the Opera del Duomo art studio and see workers sculpting new statues, restoring old ones, or making exact copies. They're carrying on an artistic tradition that dates back to the days of Brunelleschi.

Between the Duomo and Piazza della Signoria

▲▲▲**Bargello (Museo Nazionale)**—This underappreciated sculpture museum is in a former police station–turned-prison that looks like a mini–Palazzo Vecchio. It has Donatello's painfully beautiful *David* (the very influential first male nude to be sculpted in a thousand years), works by Michelangelo, and rooms of Medici treasures explained only in Italian (politely suggest  to the staff that English descriptions would be wonderful). Moody Donatello, who embraced realism with his lifelike statues, set the personal and artistic style for many Renaissance artists to follow. The best works are in the ground-floor room at the foot of the outdoor staircase and in the room directly above.

Cost and Hours: €4, but mandatory special exhibitions often increase the price to €7, Tue–Sat April–Oct 8:15–16:50, Nov–March 8:15–13:50; also open first, third, and fifth Mon and the second and fourth Sun of each month; last entry 40 minutes before closing, reservations possible but unnecessary, Via del Proconsolo 4, reservation tel. 055-238-8606, www.polomuseale.firenze.it.

Casa di Dante (Dante's House)—Dante Alighieri (1265–1321), the poet who gave us *The Divine Comedy*, is the Shakespeare of Italy, the father of the modern Italian language, and the face on the country's €2 coin. However, most Americans know little of

him, and this museum is not the ideal place to start. Even though it has English information, this small museum (in a building near where he likely lived) assumes visitors have prior knowledge of the poet. Dante-lovers can trace his interesting life and works through pictures, models, and artifacts. And because the exhibits are as much about medieval Florence as they are about the man, novices can learn a little about Dante and the city he lived in.

Cost and Hours: €4, summer daily 10:00–18:00; winter Tue–Sun 10:00–17:00, closed Mon; last entry 30 minutes before closing, near the Bargello at Via Santa Margherita 1, tel. 055-219-416, www.museocasadidante.it.

▲**Orsanmichele Church**—In the ninth century, this loggia (covered courtyard) was a market used for selling grain (stored upstairs). Later, it was enclosed to make a church.

Outside are dynamic statue-filled niches, some with accompanying symbols from the guilds that sponsored the art. Donatello's *St. Mark* and *St. George* (on the northeast and northwest corners) step out boldly in the new Renaissance style.

The interior has a glorious Gothic tabernacle (1359) housing the painted wooden panel that depicts *Madonna delle Grazie* (1346). The iron bars spanning the vaults were the Italian Gothic answer to the French Gothic external buttresses. Look for the rectangular holes in the piers—these were once wheat chutes that connected to the upper floors.

Cost and Hours: Free entry, Tue–Sun 10:00–17:00, closed Mon, niche sculptures always viewable from the outside.

Concerts and Ticket Office: You can give the *Madonna della Grazie* a special thanks if you're in town when an evening concert is held inside the Orsanmichele (tickets sold on day of concert from door facing Via de' Calzaiuoli; also books Uffizi and Accademia tickets, ticket window open daily 10:00–17:00).

A block away, you'll find the...

▲**Mercato Nuovo (a.k.a. the Straw Market)**—This market loggia is how Orsanmichele looked before it became a church. Originally a silk and straw market, Mercato Nuovo still functions as a rustic yet touristy market (at the intersection of Via Calimala and Via Porta Rossa). Prices are soft, but the San Lorenzo Market (listed earlier) is much better for haggling. Notice the circled X in the center, marking the spot where people hit after being hoisted up to the top and dropped as punishment for bankruptcy. You'll also find *Porcellino* (a statue of a wild boar nicknamed "little pig"), which people rub and give coins to in order to ensure their return to Florence. This new copy, while only a few years old, already has a polished snout. At the back corner, a wagon sells tripe (cow innards) sandwiches—a local favorite (daily 9:00–20:00).

▲**Piazza della Repubblica and Nearby**—This large square sits on the site of Florence's original Roman Forum. The lone column—

nicknamed "the belly button of Florence"—once marked the intersection of the two main Roman roads. All that survives of Roman Florence is its grid street plan and this column. Look at any map of Florence today (there's one by the benches—where the old boys hang out to talk sports and politics), and you'll see the ghost of Rome in its streets: a grid-plan city center surrounded by what was the Roman wall. Roman Florence was a garrison town, a rectangular fort with this square marking the intersection of the two main roads (Via Corso and Via Roma).

Today's piazza, framed by a triumphal arch, is a nationalistic statement celebrating the unification of Italy. Florence, the capital of the country (1865–1870) until Rome was "liberated" (from the Vatican), lacked a square worthy of this grand new country. So the neighborhood here—once the Jewish quarter—was razed to open up an imposing, modern forum surrounded by stately circa-1890 buildings.

Venerable cafés and stores line the square. The La Rinascente department store, facing Piazza della Repubblica, is one of the city's mainstays (WC on fourth floor, continue up the stairs from there to the bar with a view terrace).

▲**Palazzo Davanzati**—This five-story late-medieval tower house offers a rare look at a noble dwelling built in the 14th century. Currently only the ground and first floors are open to visitors, though the remaining floors can be visited by appointment. Like

other buildings of the age, the exterior is festooned with 14th-century horse-tethering rings made out of iron, torch holders, and poles upon which to hang laundry and fly flags. Inside, though the furnishings are pretty sparse, you'll see richly painted walls, a long chute that functioned as a well, plenty of fireplaces, a lace display, and even a modern toilet.

Cost and Hours: €2, Tue–Sat 8:15–13:50; also open second and fourth Mon and first, third, and fifth Sun; Via Porta Rossa 13, tel. 055-238-8610.

On and near Piazza della Signoria

Piazza della Signoria, the main civic center of Florence, is dominated by Palazzo Vecchio, the Uffizi Gallery, and the marble greatness of old Florence littering the cobbles. This square still vibrates with the echoes of Florence's past—executions, riots, and great celebrations. Today, it's a tourist's world with pigeons, postcards, horse buggies, and tired hubbies. If it would make your tired companion happy, stop in at the recommended but expensive **Rivoire** café to enjoy its fine desserts, pudding-thick hot chocolate, and the best view seats in town.

▲▲▲**Uffizi Gallery**—This greatest collection of Italian paintings anywhere features works by Giotto, Leonardo, Raphael,

Caravaggio, Rubens, Titian, and Michelangelo, and a roomful of Botticellis, including his *Birth of Venus*.

The museum is nowhere near as big as it is great. Few tourists spend more than two hours inside. The paintings are displayed on one comfortable U-shaped floor in chronological order from the 13th through 17th centuries. The left wing, starring the Florentine Middle Ages to the Renaissance, is the best. The connecting corridor contains sculpture, and the right wing focuses on the High Renaissance and Baroque.

Essential stops are (in this order): Gothic altarpieces (narrative, pre-Realism, no real concern for believable depth) including Giotto's altarpiece, which progressed beyond "totem-pole angels"; Paolo Uccello's *Battle of San Romano,* an early study in perspective with a few obvious flubs (recently restored but likely back on display in 2011); and Fra Filippo Lippi's cuddly Madonnas. The Botticelli room is filled with masterpieces and classical fleshiness (the famous *Birth of Venus* and the *Allegory of Spring*), plus two minor works by Leonardo da Vinci. The octagonal classical sculpture room (which may be under renovation when you visit, and after that, viewable through glass) has a copy of Praxiteles' *Venus de' Medici,* considered the epitome of beauty in Elizabethan Europe. Next comes the view of Ponte Vecchio through the window, dreamy at sunset. Rounding it off are Michelangelo's only

FLORENCE

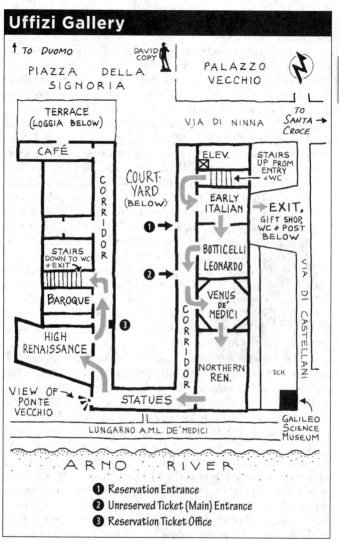

Uffizi Gallery

↑ TO DUOMO

DAVID COPY

PIAZZA DELLA SIGNORIA

PALAZZO VECCHIO

TO SANTA CROCE →

TERRACE (LOGGIA BELOW)

VIA DI NINNA

CAFÉ

CORRIDOR

COURT-YARD (BELOW)

ELEV.

STAIRS UP FROM ENTRY & WC

EARLY ITALIAN

EXIT, GIFT SHOP, WC & POST BELOW

❶ →

STAIRS DOWN TO WC & EXIT

BOTTICELLI LEONARDO

❷ →

BAROQUE

VENUS DE' MEDICI

❸

CORRIDOR

HIGH RENAISSANCE

NORTHERN REN.

DCH

VIA DI CASTELLANI

VIEW OF PONTE VECCHIO →

STATUES

LUNGARNO A.M.L. DE' MEDICI

GALILEO SCIENCE MUSEUM

ARNO RIVER

❶ Reservation Entrance
❷ Unreserved Ticket (Main) Entrance
❸ Reservation Ticket Office

surviving easel painting, the round *Holy Family;* Raphael's noble *Madonna of the Goldfinch;* and Titian's voluptuous *Venus of Urbino.* Enjoy Duomo views from the café terrace.

Cost, Hours, Reservations: €6.50 but mandatory special exhibits generally bump the price to €10, extra €4 for recommended reservation, cash required to pick up reserved tickets, Tue–Sun 8:15–18:50, closed Mon, last entry 45 minutes before closing, museum info tel. 055-238-8651, www.polomuseale.firenze .it. To avoid the long ticket lines, get reservations at least a month ahead in high season. For details on making reservations, check the sidebar on page 430.

In the Uffizi's Courtyard: Enjoy the courtyard (free), full of artists and souvenir stalls. (Swing by after dinner when it's completely empty.) The surrounding statues honor earthshaking Florentines: artists (Michelangelo), philosophers (Niccolò Machiavelli), scientists (Galileo), writers (Dante), explorers (Amerigo Vespucci), and the great patron of so much Renaissance thinking, Lorenzo "the Magnificent" de' Medici.

▲**Palazzo Vecchio**—With its distinctive castle turret, this fortified palace—the Town Hall, officially called the Palazzo della Signoria—is a Florentine landmark. But

if you're visiting only one palace interior in town, the Pitti Palace is better. The interior of Palazzo Vecchio is best for fans of coffered and gilded ceilings, of Florentine history, or of the artist Giorgio Vasari, who wallpapered the place with mediocre magnificence.

The museum's most famous statues are Michelangelo's *Victory* and Donatello's bronze statue of *Judith and Holerfernes.*

Cost and Hours: €6, €8 combo-ticket with Brancacci Chapel, skippable audioguide, tours are free and in English but require reservation, Fri–Wed 9:00–19:00, Thu 9:00–14:00, ticket office closes one hour earlier, tel. 055-276-8224.

Nearby: Even if you don't go to the museum, do step into the **free courtyard** behind the fake *David* just to feel the essence of the Medicis. Until 1873, Michelangelo's *David* stood at the entrance, where the copy is today. While the huge statues in the square are important only as the whipping boys of art critics and as rest stops for pigeons, the nearby **loggia** has several important statues. Look for Benvenuto Cellini's bronze statue of Perseus holding the head of Medusa. The plaque on the pavement in front of the fountain marks the spot where the monk Savonarola was burned in MCDXCVIII, or 1498.

▲▲**Galileo Science Museum (Museo Galilei e Istituto di Storia della Scienza)**—When we think of the Florentine Renaissance, we think of visual arts: painting, mosaics, architecture, and sculpture. But when the visual arts declined in the 1600s (abused and co-opted by political powers), music and science flourished in Florence. The first opera was written here. And Florence hosted many scientific breakthroughs, as you'll see in this fascinating collection of Renaissance and later clocks, telescopes, maps, and ingenious gadgets. Trace the technical innovations as modern science emerges from 1000 to 1900. One of the most talked-about bottles in Florence is the one here that contains Galileo's finger. Exhibits include various tools for gauging the world, from a compass and thermometer to Galileo's telescopes. Other displays delve into clocks, pumps, medicine, and chemistry. Some English information is available,

and the docents are helpful. It's friendly, comfortably cool, never crowded, and just a block east of the Uffizi on the Arno River.

Cost and Hours: €8, €20 family ticket, Wed–Mon 9:30–18:00, Tue 9:30–13:00, Piazza dei Giudici 1, tel. 055-265-311, recorded info tel. 055-293-493, www.museogalileo.it.

▲**Ponte Vecchio**—Florence's most famous bridge is lined with shops that have traditionally sold gold and silver. A statue of Benvenuto Cellini, the master goldsmith of the Renaissance,

stands in the center, ignored by the flood of tacky tourism. This is a very romantic spot late at night (when lovers gather, and a top-notch street musician performs).

Notice the "prince's passageway" above the bridge, called the **Vasari Corridor.**
In less-secure times, the city leaders had a fortified passageway connecting Palazzo Vecchio and the Uffizi with the mighty Pitti Palace, to which they could flee in times of attack. This passageway is sometimes open to the public, but a visit is almost impossible to arrange, and if you do manage it, it's usually a disappointment (you could check at the Uffizi to see if it's open or try a private tour company such as Artviva Walking Tours; see page 430).

East of Piazza della Signoria

▲▲**Santa Croce Church**—This 14th-century Franciscan church, decorated with centuries of precious art, holds the tombs of great Florentines.

The loud 19th-century Victorian Gothic facade faces a huge square ringed with tempting shops and littered with tired tourists. Escape into the church and admire its sheer height and spaciousness. Start at the back of the nave (farthest from the altar). On the left wall (as you face the altar) is the **tomb of Galileo Galilei** (1564–1642), the Pisan who lived his last years under house arrest

near Florence. Having defied the Church by saying that the earth revolved around the sun, his heretical remains were only allowed in the church long after his death. Directly opposite (on the right wall) is the **tomb of Michelangelo Buonarroti** (1475–1564).

The first chapel to the right of the main altar features the famous fresco by Giotto of the *Death of St. Francis*. With simple but eloquent gestures, Francis' brothers bid him a sad farewell. One folds his hands and stares longingly at Francis' serene face. Another bends to kiss Francis' hand, while others raise their arms in grief. It's one of the first expressions of human emotion in modern painting. It's also one of the first to create a real three-dimensional grouping of figures.

At the end of the right transept, a left turn at the first door leads into the sacristy, where you'll find a rumpled bit of **St. Francis' tunic** (*Parte della Tonaca*, scrunched up in a small gold frame). In the hallway near the bookstore, notice the photos of the devastating flood of 1966. Beyond that is the leather school, the first shop of what is now a popular leather district. Wander through the former dorms for monks, watch the leatherworking in action, and browse the finished products—for sale, of course.

Exit between the Rossini and Machiavelli tombs into the cloister (open-air courtyard). On the left, enter Brunelleschi's Pazzi Chapel, which captures the Renaissance in miniature.

Cost, Hours, Location: €5 includes the church, Pazzi Chapel, and museum; Mon–Sat 9:30–17:30, Sun 13:00–17:30, last entry 30 minutes before closing, modest dress code enforced, 10-minute walk east of Palazzo Vecchio along Borgo de' Greci, tel. 055-246-6105. The leather school is free and sells tickets to the church. If the church has a long line, come here to avoid the line (daily 10:00–18:00, has own entry behind church plus an entry within the church, www.leatherschool.com).

▲**Casa Buonarroti (Michelangelo's House)**—Fans enjoy a house standing on property once owned by Michelangelo. The house was built after Michelangelo's death by the artist's grand-nephew, who turned it into a little museum honoring his famous relative. You'll see some of Michelangelo's early, less-than-monumental statues and a few sketches. Be warned: Michelangelo's descendants attributed everything they could to their famous relative, but very little here (beyond two marble relief panels and a couple of sketches) is actually by Michelangelo.

Cost, Hours, Location: €6.50, Wed–Mon 9:30–14:00, closed Tue, English descriptions, Via Ghibellina 70, tel. 055-241-752.

Near the Train Station

▲▲Church of Santa Maria Novella—This 13th-century Dominican church is rich in art. Along with crucifixes by Giotto

and Brunelleschi, there's every textbook's example of the early Renaissance mastery of perspective: *The Holy Trinity* by Masaccio. The exquisite chapels trace art in Florence from medieval times to early Baroque. The outside of the church features a dash of Romanesque (horizontal stripes), Gothic (pointed arches), Renaissance (geometric shapes), and Baroque (scrolls). Step in and look down the 330-foot nave for a 14th-century optical illusion.

Cost and Hours: €3.50, Mon–Thu 9:00–17:30, Fri 11:00–17:30, Sat 9:00–17:00, Sun 13:00–17:00, last entry 30 minutes before closing, tel. 055-219-257.

Nearby: A palatial **perfumery** (Farmacia di Santa Maria Novella) is a block from Piazza Santa Maria Novella, 100 yards down Via della Scala at #16 (free but shopping encouraged, inconsistent hours but likely daily 9:30–19:30, see map on page 458, tel. 055-216-276, www.smnovella.com). Thick with the lingering aroma of centuries of spritzes, it started as the herb garden of the Santa Maria Novella monks. Well-known even today for its top-quality products, it is extremely Florentine. Pick up the history sheet at the desk, and wander deep into the shop. From the back room, you can peek at one of Santa Maria Novella's cloisters with its dreamy frescoes and imagine a time before Vespas and tourists.

You can get a closer look inside the **Museum and Cloisters,** adjacent to the church, but they're definitely lesser sights (€2.70, entry to the left of the church's facade; Mon–Thu and Sat 9:00–17:00, closed Fri and Sun).

South of the Arno River

To locate these sights, see the map on page 468.

▲▲Pitti Palace—The imposing Pitti Palace, several blocks southwest of Ponte Vecchio, is not only home to the second-best collection of paintings in town, the **Palatine Gallery,** but also happens to be the most sumptuous palace you can tour in Florence. The building itself is mammoth, holding several different museums and anchoring two gardens. Stick primarily to the gallery, forget about everything else, and the palace becomes a little less exhausting.

You'll walk through one palatial room after another, walls sagging with masterpieces by 16th- and 17th-century masters, including Rubens, Titian, and Rembrandt. Its Raphael collection is the second-biggest anywhere—the Vatican beats it by one. Each room has some descriptions in English, though the paintings themselves have limited English labels.

The collection is all on one floor. To see the highlights, walk straight down the spine through a dozen or so rooms. Before you exit, consider a visit to the Royal Apartments. These 14 rooms (of which only a few are open at any one time) are where the Pitti's rulers lived in the 18th and 19th centuries. Each room features a different color and time period. Here, you get a real feel for the splendor of the dukes' world.

The Rest of the Pitti Palace: If you've got the energy and interest, it'd be a Pitti to miss the palace's other offerings.

The **Modern Art Gallery,** on the second floor, features Romantic, Neoclassical, and Impressionist works by 19th- and 20th-century Tuscan painters.

The **Argenti Museum** (on the ground and mezzanine floors) is the Medici treasure chest, with jeweled crucifixes, exotic porcelain, and gilded ostrich eggs, made to entertain fans of the applied arts.

The **Boboli and Bardini Gardens,** located behind the palace, offer a pleasant and shady refuge from the city heat. Enter the Boboli Gardens from the Pitti Palace courtyard. The less-visited Bardini Gardens are behind the Boboli, rising in terraces toward Piazzale Michelangelo.

Cost and Hours: The main reason to visit is to see the Palatine Gallery, but you can't buy a ticket for the gallery alone; to see it you'll need to buy ticket #1, which includes the Palatine Gallery, Royal Apartments, and Modern Art Gallery (€8.50 but often €12 with mandatory special exhibits, Tue–Sun 8:15–18:50, closed Mon, tel. 055-238-8614, www.polomuseale.firenze.it). Ticket #2 covers the Boboli and Bardini Gardens, Argenti Museum (the Duke's treasures), Costume Gallery, and Porcelain Museum (€6, more with special exhibits, daily 8:15–18:30, until 19:30 June–Aug, same phone and website as above). An €11.50 combo-ticket covers the whole palace complex (valid 3 days). If there's a long line, you can bypass it by buying a reservation for immediate entry at the ticket window (€3 reservation fee).

▲▲**Brancacci Chapel**—For the best look at works by Masaccio (the early Renaissance master who reinvented perspective), see his restored frescoes here.

Instead of medieval religious symbols, Masaccio's paintings feature simple, strong human figures with facial expressions that reflect their emotions. The accompanying works of Masolino and Filippino Lippi provide illuminating contrasts.

Reservations are free and required (see below). Your ticket includes a 40-minute film in English on the church, the frescoes, and Renaissance Florence (reserve a viewing time when you book your entry). The film starts promptly at the top of the hour. Computer animation brings the paintings to life—making them appear to move and giving them 3-D depth—while narration describes the events depicted in the panels. Yes, it's a long time commitment, and the film takes liberties with the art. But it's visually interesting and your best way to see the frescoes close up. The film works great either before or after you visit the frescoes.

Cost and Hours: €4, free reservations required—it's very easy...just call at least a day in advance, €8 combo-ticket with Palazzo Vecchio, both tickets include worthwhile 40-minute film in English—reserve film when you book entry, limit of 30 visitors every 15 minutes, Mon and Wed–Sat 10:00–17:00, Sun 13:00–17:00, closed Tue, ticket office closes at 16:30; in Church of Santa Maria del Carmine—cross Ponte Vecchio and turn right on Borgo San Jacopo, walk 10 minutes, then turn left into Piazza del Carmine; tel. 055-276-8224 or 055-276-8558.

Reservations: Call the chapel at least a day ahead for free, mandatory reservations; tickets are sometimes available for the same day (tel. 055-276-8224 or 055-276-8558, English spoken, call center open daily 9:00–17:00). If the line is busy, keep trying—it's best to call around 14:00–15:00 or just before the ticket office closes at 16:30. Reservation times begin every 15 minutes, with a maximum of 30 visitors per time slot (you have 15 minutes inside the chapel). When you call to reserve, you can also book a time to see the film.

Santo Spirito Church—This church has a classic Brunelleschi interior and a painted, carved wooden crucifix attributed to 17-year-old Michelangelo. The sculptor donated this early work to the monastery in appreciation for allowing him to dissect and learn

about bodies. The Michelangelo *Crocifisso* is displayed in the sacristy, through a door midway down the left side of the nave (if it's closed, ask someone to let you in). Copies of Michelangelo's *Pietà* and *Risen Christ* flank the nave. Beer-drinking, guitar-playing rowdies decorate the church steps.

Cost and Hours: Free entry, Mon–Tue and Thu–Sat 9:30–12:30 & 16:00–17:30, Sun 15:00–17:30 only, closed Wed, Piazza Santo Spirito, tel. 055-211-716.

▲**Piazzale Michelangelo**—Overlooking the city from across the river (look for the huge statue of *David*), this square has a superb view of Florence and the stunning dome of the Duomo (see photo on page 416).

It's worth the 30-minute hike, drive (free parking), or bus ride (either #12 or #13 from the train station— takes a long time). It makes sense to take a taxi or ride the bus up, and then enjoy the easy downhill walk back into town. An inviting café with great views is just below the overlook. The best photos are taken from the street immediately below the overlook (go around to the right and down a few steps). Off the west side of the piazza is a somewhat hidden terrace, an excellent place to retreat from the mobs. After dark, the square is packed with school kids licking ice cream and each other. About 200 yards beyond all the tour groups and teenagers is the stark, beautiful, crowd-free Romanesque San Miniato Church (next listing).

The hike down is quick and enjoyable. Take the steps between the two bars on the San Miniato Church side of the parking lot (Via San Salvatore al Monte), and in a couple of minutes you walk through the old wall (Porta San Miniato) and emerge in the delightful little Oltrarno neighborhood of San Niccolò.

▲▲**San Miniato Church**—According to legend, the martyred St. Minias—this church's namesake—was beheaded on the banks of the Arno in A.D. 250. He picked up his head and walked here (this was before the #12 bus), where he died and was buried in what became the first Christian cemetery in Florence. In the 11th century, this church was built to house Minias' remains. Imagine this fine

church all alone—without any nearby buildings or fancy stairs—a peaceful refuge where white-robed Benedictine monks could pray and work (their motto: *ora et labora*). The church's green-and-white marble facade (12th century) is classic Florentine Romanesque. The church has wonderful 3-D paintings, a plush ceiling of glazed terra-cotta panels by Luca della Robbia, and a sumptuous Renaissance chapel (located front and center). The highlight for me is the brilliantly preserved art in the sacristy (behind altar in the room on right) showing scenes from the life of St. Benedict (circa 1350, by a follower of Giotto). Drop a euro into the box to light the room for five minutes.

Cost and Hours: Free entry, daily April–Oct 8:00–19:30, Nov–March 8:00–13:00 & 14:30–18:00, Gregorian chants April–Sept daily at the 17:30 Mass—17:00 in winter, 200 yards above Piazzale Michelangelo, bus #12 or #13 from train station, tel. 055-234-2731.

Shopping in Florence

Florence is a great shopping town—known for its sense of style since the Medici days. Many people spend entire days shopping. Smaller stores are generally open 9:00–13:00 and 15:30–19:30, usually closed on Sunday, often closed on Monday, and sometimes closed for a couple of weeks around August 15. Many stores have promotional stalls in the market squares.

Busy street scenes and markets abound, especially near San Lorenzo, near Santa Croce, on Ponte Vecchio, and at Mercato Nuovo (the covered market square 3 blocks north of Ponte Vecchio, described on page 444). Prices are soft in the markets—go ahead and bargain. Leather, gold, silver, art prints, and tacky plaster mini-*David*s are most popular.

For shopping ideas, ads, and a list of markets, see *The Florentine* newspaper or *Florence Concierge Information* magazine (free from TI and many hotels). For a list of bookstores, see page

425. For information on VAT refunds and customs regulations, see page 16.

For ritzy Italian fashions, browse along Via de' Tornabuoni, Via della Vigna Nuova, Via del Parione, and Via Strozzi. The main **Ferragamo** store fills a classy 800-year-old building with a fine selection of shoes and bags (daily 10:00–19:30, Via de' Tornabuoni 2).

Typical chain department stores are **Coin,** the Italian equivalent of Macy's (Mon–Sat 10:00–19:30, Sun 10:30–19:30, on Via de' Calzaiuoli, near Orsanmichele Church); the similar, upscale **La Rinascente** (Mon–Sat 9:00–21:00, Sun 10:30–20:00, on Piazza della Repubblica); and **Oviesse,** the local JCPenney, a discount clothing chain (Mon–Sat 9:00–19:30, Sun 9:00–13:00 & 15:00–17:30, near train station at intersection of Via Panzani and Via del Giglio).

Sleeping in Florence

Nearly all of my recommended accommodations are located in the center of Florence, within minutes of the great sights.

The accommodations scene varies wildly with the season. Spring and fall are very tight and expensive, while mid-July through August is wide open and discounted. November through February is also generally empty. I've listed prices for peak season: April, May, June, September, and October.

In Florence, you can snare a stark, clean, and comfortable double with breakfast and a private bath for about €100 (less in smaller towns). You get elegance in peak season for €160.

Florence is notorious for its mosquitoes. If your hotel lacks air-conditioning, request a fan and don't open your windows, especially at night. Many hotels furnish a small plug-in bulb *(zanzariere)*—usually set in the ashtray—that helps keep the blood-suckers at bay. If not, you can purchase one cheaply at any pharmacy *(farmacia)*.

Museum-goers take note: When you book your room, ask if your hotelier will reserve entry times for you to visit the popular Uffizi Gallery and the Accademia (Michelangelo's *David*). This service is fast, easy, and offered free or for a small fee by most hotels—the only requirement is advance notice. Ask them to book your visits for any time the day after your arrival. If you'd rather make the reservations yourself, see page 430 for details.

North of the Arno River
Between the Duomo and the Train Station

$$ Hotel Accademia, which comes with marble stairs, parquet floors, and attractive public areas, has 21 pleasant rooms and a floor plan that defies logic (Db-€150, Tb-€180, 5 percent cash

---

Sleep Code

(€1 = about $1.25, country code: 39)
S = Single, **D** = Double/Twin, **T** = Triple, **Q** = Quad, **b** = bathroom,
s = shower only.

You can assume a hotel takes credit cards unless you see "cash only" in the listing. Unless otherwise noted, hotel staff speak basic English and breakfast is included.

To help you easily sort through these listings, I've divided the rooms into three categories based on the price for a standard double room with bath during high season:

$$$ **Higher Priced**—Most rooms €160 or more.
$$ **Moderately Priced**—Most rooms between €100–160.
$ **Lower Priced**—Most rooms €100 or less.

Prices can change without notice; verify the hotel's current rates online or by email. For other updates, see www.ricksteves.com/update.

---

discount with this book, air-con, Internet access and Wi-Fi, Via Faenza 7, tel. 055-293-451, fax 055-219-771, www.hotelaccademia firenze.com, info@hotelaccademiafirenze.com, Tea, Francesca, and Paolo).

$$ Hotel Centrale, with 20 spacious rooms, is indeed central (Db-€150, superior Db-€176, Tb-€182, 5 percent discount with this book, ask for Rick Steves rate when you reserve, air-con, elevator, Internet access and Wi-Fi, Via dei Conti 3, tel. 055-215-761, fax 055-215-216, www.hotelcentralefirenze.it, info@hotelcentrale firenze.it, Margherita and Roberto).

$ Katti House and the nearby **Soggiorno Annamaria** are run by house-proud mama-and-daughter team Maria and Katti, who keep their 15 rooms spotless, inviting, and well-maintained. While both offer equal comfort, Soggiorno Annamaria has a more historic setting, with frescoed ceilings, unique tiles, timbered beams, and quieter rooms (Db-€70–100, air-con, Internet access and Wi-Fi, Via Faenza 21, tel. & fax 055-213-410, www.kattihouse .com, info@kattihouse.com).

$ Hotel Lorena, just across from the Medici Chapels, has 19 rooms (six of which share a bathroom) and a tiny, cramped lobby. Though it's a bit like a youth hostel, it's cheap and conveniently located. Roberto speaks little English, but seems eager to please (Sb-€40, D-€55, Db-€65, Tb-€90, air-con, Wi-Fi, curfew from 2:00 in the morning to 7:00, Via Faenza 1, tel. 055-282-785, fax 055-288-300, www.hotellorena.com, info@hotellorena.com).

FLORENCE

Florence Hotels

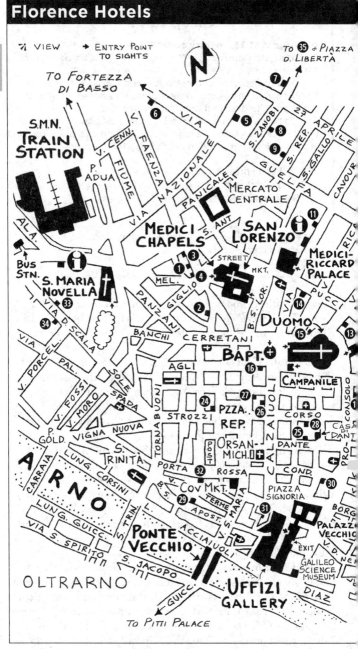

⇗ VIEW   ➔ ENTRY POINT TO SIGHTS

TO 35 & PIAZZA D. LIBERTÀ

TO FORTEZZA DI BASSO

S.M.N. TRAIN STATION

MERCATO CENTRALE

MEDICI CHAPELS

SAN LORENZO

MEDICI-RICCARD PALACE

BUS STN.

S. MARIA NOVELLA

STREET MKT.

DUOMO

BANCHI   CERRETANI

Bapt.

CAMPANILE

AGLI

PZZA. REP.

ORSAN-MICH.

DANTE

STROZZI

CORSO

CASA DI DANT

P. GOLD.   VIGNA NUOVA

S. TRINITA

PORTA ROSSA

PIAZZA SIGNORIA

A R N O

LUNG. CORSINI

COV. MKT.

TERME

APOST.

PALAZZ VECCHIO

PONTE VECCHIO

ACCIAIUOLI

EXIT

GALILEO SCIENCE MUSEUM

OLTRARNO

UFFIZI GALLERY

DIAZ

TO PITTI PALACE

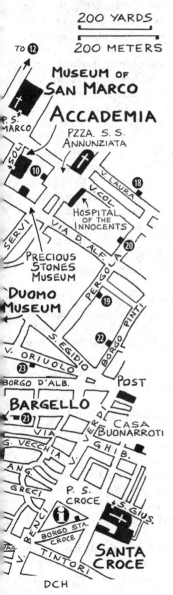

200 YARDS
200 METERS

TO ⑫

MUSEUM OF SAN MARCO

ACCADEMIA

P. S. MARCO

PZZA. S. S. ANNUNZIATA

V. LAURA

V. COL.

HOSPITAL OF THE INNOCENTS

PRECIOUS STONES MUSEUM

DUOMO MUSEUM

SERVI

VIA D. ALF.

PERGOLA

BORGO PINTI

S. EGIDIO

V. ORIUOLO

BORGO D'ALB.

POST

BARGELLO

VIA

G. VECCHIA

GHIB.

CASA BUONARROTI

ANG.

GRECI

P. S. CROCE

BENCI

BORGO STA. CROCE

SANTA CROCE

S. GIUS.

TINTORI

DCH

① Hotel Accademia
② Hotel Centrale
③ Katti House & Soggiorno Annamaria
④ Hotel Lorena
⑤ Galileo Hotel
⑥ Hotel Il Bargellino
⑦ Hotel Enza
⑧ Casa Rabatti
⑨ Soggiorno Magliani
⑩ Hotel Loggiato dei Serviti
⑪ Hotel Dei Macchiaioli & Hotel Europa
⑫ To Athenaeum Personal Hotel
⑬ Palazzo Niccolini al Duomo
⑭ Residenza dei Pucci
⑮ Hotel Duomo
⑯ Soggiorno Battistero
⑰ La Residenza del Proconsolo B&B
⑱ Hotel Morandi alla Crocetta
⑲ Panella's Residence
⑳ Residenza il Villino
㉑ B&B Il Bargello
㉒ Hotel Cardinal of Florence & Oblate Sisters of the Assumption
㉓ Hotel Dalí
㉔ Hotel Pendini
㉕ B&B Dei Mori
㉖ Hotel Axial & Hotel Maxim
㉗ Residenzia Giotto B&B
㉘ Albergo Firenze
㉙ Hotel Torre Guelfa & Hotel Alessandra
㉚ In Piazza della Signoria B&B
㉛ Relais Ufizzi
㉜ Hotel Davanzati
㉝ Hotel Alba Palace
㉞ Bellevue House
㉟ To Villa Camerata & Hostel 7 Santi

North of the Duomo
North of the Mercato Centrale

After dark, this neighborhood can feel a little sketchy, but I've never heard of anyone running into harm here. It's a short walk from the train station and an easy stroll to all the sightseeing action. Plenty of good budget restaurants and markets are nearby.

$$ Galileo Hotel, a classy business hotel of 31 rooms, is run with familial warmth (Db-€130, Tb-€150, ask for 10 percent Rick Steves discount when you book direct, quadruple-pane windows effectively shut out street noise, Wi-Fi, Via Nazionale 22a, tel. 055-496-645, fax 055-496-447, www.galileohotel.it, info@galileo hotel.it, Rhuna).

$ Hotel Il Bargellino, run by Bostonian Carmel and her Italian husband Pino, is a bit farther out and consequently feels like it's in a residential neighborhood. They rent 10 summery rooms decorated with funky antique furniture and Pino's modern paintings. Guests enjoy relaxing with Carmel and Leopoldo the parrot on the big, breezy momentum-slowing terrace adorned with lemon shrubs (S-€45, D-€80, Db-€90, extra bed-€25, no breakfast, Wi-Fi, north of the train station at Via Guelfa 87, tel. & fax 055-238-2658, www.ilbargellino.com, carmel@ilbargellino.com).

$ Hotel Enza rents 19 relaxing rooms (Sb-€55, Db-€80, prices promised through 2011 with this book, extra bed-€20, optional breakfast by request only-€5, air-con, Internet access and Wi-Fi, Via San Zanobi 45 black, tel. 055-490-990, fax 055-473-672, www .hotelenza.it, info@hotelenza.it, Diana).

$ Casa Rabatti is the ultimate if you always wanted to have a Florentine mama. Its four simple, clean rooms are run with warmth by Marcella. This is a great place to practice your Italian, since Marcella loves to chat and speaks minimal English. Seeing nearly two decades of my family Christmas cards on the walls, I'm reminded of how long she has been keeping budget travelers happy (D-€50, Db-€60, €25 extra per bed in shared quad or quint, prices good with this book, cash only but secure reservation with credit card, no breakfast, fans available, 5 blocks from station at Via San Zanobi 48 black, tel. 055-212-393, casarabatti@inwind.it).

If Marcella's booked, she'll put you up in her daughter's place nearby, at Via Nazionale 20 (five big, airy family-friendly rooms; €25/person, fans, no breakfast, closer to the station). While daughter Patrizia works, her mom runs the place. Getting bumped to Patrizia's gives you slightly more comfort and slightly less personality...certainly not a net negative.

$ Soggiorno Magliani is central and humble, with six no-frills rooms (sharing two baths) that feel and smell like a great-grandmother's home. It's run by the friendly duo Vincenza and her English-speaking daughter Cristina, and the price is right (S-€36, D-€46, T-€63, cash only but secure reservation with credit card, no breakfast, near Via Guelfa at Via Santa Reparata 1, tel. 055-287-378, hotel-magliani@libero.it).

Between the Duomo and the Accademia

$$$ Hotel Loggiato dei Serviti, at the most prestigious address in Florence on the most Renaissance square in town, gives you Old World romance with hair dryers. Stone stairways lead you under open-beam ceilings through this 16th-century monastery's monumental public rooms—it's so artful, you'll be snapping photos everywhere. The 33 cells—with air-conditioning, TVs, mini-bars, and telephones—would be unrecognizable to their original inhabitants. The hotel staff is both professional and warm (Sb-€120, Db-€160–170, superior Db-€180, family suites from €263, ask for Rick Steves rate when you book, elevator, Piazza S.S. Annunziata 3, tel. 055-289-592, fax 055-289-595, www.loggiatodeiservitihotel .it, info@loggiatodeiservitihotel.it, Fabio, Chiara, and Simonetta). When full, they rent five spacious and sophisticated rooms in a 17th-century annex a block away. While it lacks the monastic mystique, the annex rooms are bigger, gorgeous, and cost the same.

$$$ Hotel Dei Macchiaioli, which opened in 2010, is managed by the same friendly team as the recommended Hotel Accademia. With 15 rooms, the hotel is located in a restored *palazzo* owned for generations by a noble Florentine family. You'll eat breakfast under original frescoed ceilings while enjoying modern comforts (Sb-€100, Db-€180, Tb-€220, 10 percent Rick Steves discount if you book direct, air-con, Wi-Fi, Via Cavour 21, tel. 055-213-154, www.hoteldeimacchiaioli.com, info@hoteldei macchiaioli.com, helpful Tea).

$$ Hotel Europa, run by cheery Miriam, Roberto, and daughter Priscilla since 1970, has a welcoming atmosphere. The breakfast room is spacious, and some of the 20 rooms have views of the Duomo (Sb-€89, Db-€140, Tb-€165, 10 percent cash discount, elevator, Wi-Fi, Via Cavour 14, tel. 055-239-6715, fax 055-268-984, www.webhoteleuropa.com, firenze@webhoteleuropa.com)

$$ Athenaeum Personal Hotel is a classy, ultra-modern place with 60 rooms located a block from the Accademia and a 10-minute walk from the Duomo. It has a comfy lounge, modern art on the walls, and a spacious courtyard with a miniature waterfall where you can dine al fresco (Sb-€128, Db-€150, Tb-€180, check website for seasonal price variations, elevator, Wi-Fi, Via Cavour 88, tel. 055-589-456, fax 055-561-408, www.hotelathenaeumflorence.com, info@hotelathenaeum.com).

Near the Duomo

All of these places are within a block of Florence's biggest church and main landmark.

$$$ **Palazzo Niccolini al Duomo,** one of five elite Historic Residence Hotels in Florence, is run by Sra. Niccolini da Camugliano. The lounge is palatial (free chamomile tea served in the evenings), and the 12 rooms are big and splendid, with original 16th-century frescoes. If you have the money and want a Florentine palace to call home, this is a very good bet, located just one block from the Duomo (Db-€150 and up, fancier and pricier suites with DVD players, ask for 10 percent Rick Steves discount when you book, check online to choose a room and consider last-minute deals, Via dei Servi 2, tel. 055-282-412, fax 055-290-979, www.niccolinidomepalace.com, info@niccolinidomepalace.com).

$$ **Residenza dei Pucci** rents 12 tastefully decorated rooms (each one different) spread over three floors. The decor is a mix of soothing earth tones and aristocratic furniture (Sb-€135, Db-€150, Tb-€170, Qb-€238, 10 percent discount with cash and this book, air-con, no elevator, reception open 9:00–20:00—let them know if you'll arrive late, Via dei Pucci 9, tel. 055-281-886, fax 055-264-314, www.residenzadeipucci.com, residenzadeipucci@residenzadeipucci.com, Mirella).

$$ **Hotel Duomo,** big and venerable, rents 24 rooms four floors up. The Duomo looms like a monster outside the hotel's windows. The rooms, while pretty forgettable, are comfortable enough, and the location can't be beat (Db-€100–170, 10 percent cash discount with this book, Internet access, Piazza del Duomo 1, tel. 055-219-922, www.hotelduomofirenze.it, info@hotelduomofirenze.it, Alberto).

$$ **Soggiorno Battistero** rents seven simple, airy rooms, most with great views, literally overlooking the Baptistery and the Duomo square. Choose a view or a quieter room in the back when you book by email. It's a pristine, fresh, and minimalist little place run by Italian Luca and his American wife Kelly, who makes the hotel particularly welcoming (Sb-€78, Db-€103, Tb-€140, Qb-€150, prices good with this book, 5 percent cash discount, breakfast served in room, air-con, Wi-Fi, Piazza San Giovanni 1, third floor—no elevator, tel. 055-295-143, fax 055-268-189, www.soggiornobattistero.it, info@soggiornobattistero.it).

$$ **La Residenza del Proconsolo B&B,** run by helpful Mariano, has five pleasantly appointed rooms a minute from the Duomo (three rooms have Duomo views). The place lacks public spaces, but the rooms are quite large—perfect for eating breakfast, which is served in your room (Sb-€90, Db-€140, Tb-€160, Wi-Fi, Via del Proconsolo 18n, tel. 055-264-5657, mobile 335-657-4840, www.proconsolo.com, info@proconsolo.com).

East of the Duomo

$$ Hotel Morandi alla Crocetta, a former convent, envelops you in a 16th-century cocoon. Located on a quiet street with 12 rooms, period furnishings, parquet floors, and wood-beamed ceilings, it takes you back a few centuries (Sb-€70–100, Db-€100–140, breakfast included if you book direct, air-con, a block off Piazza S.S. Annunziata at Via Laura 50, tel. 055-234-4747, fax 055-248-0954, www.hotelmorandi.it, welcome@hotelmorandi.it, well-run by Maurizio, Rolando, and Frank).

$$ Panella's Residence, once a convent and today part of owner Graziella's extensive home, is a classy B&B, with six chic and romantic rooms, antique furnishings, and historic architectural touches (Db-€140, superior Db-€165, these prices are with cash, discounts for 3 or more nights, air-con, Wi-Fi, Via della Pergola 42, tel. 055-234-7202, fax 055-247-9669, www.panellaresidence .com, panella_residence@yahoo.it).

$$ Residenza il Villino, popular and friendly, aspires to offer a Florentine home. It has 10 rooms and a picturesque, peaceful little courtyard (small Db-€110, Db-€130, family suite that sleeps up to six—price upon request, 5 percent discount with cash and this book, ask for special Rick Steves rates in low season, air-con, Internet access and Wi-Fi, just north of Via degli Alfani at Via della Pergola 53, tel. 055-200-1116, fax 055-200-1101, www.il villino.it, info@ilvillino.it, Sergio, Elisabetta, and son Lorenzo).

$ B&B Il Bargello is a home away from home, run by friendly and helpful Canadian expat Gabriella. Hike up three long flights to reach Gabriella's six smart, relaxing rooms. She offers a cozy communal living room, kitchen access, book exchange, and an inviting rooftop terrace with close-up views of Florence's towers (Db-€100, ask for Rick Steves rate when you book direct and pay cash, air-con, Internet access and Wi-Fi, 20 yards off Via Proconsolo at Via de' Pandolfini 33 black, tel. 055-215-330, mobile 339-175-3110, www .firenze-bedandbreakfast.it, info@firenze-bedandbreakfast.it).

$ Hotel Cardinal of Florence is a third-floor walk-up with 17 new, tidy, and sun-splashed rooms overlooking either a silent courtyard (many with views of Brunelleschi's dome) or quiet street. Relax and enjoy Florence's rooftops from the sun terrace (Sb-€60, Db-€95, these prices for Rick Steves readers, additional €5 cash discount, €15/day limited parking—request when you reserve, Borgo Pinti 5, tel. 055-234-0780, fax 055-234-3389, www.hotel cardinaloflorence.com, info@hotelcardinaloflorence.com, Mauro and Ida).

$ Hotel Dalí has 10 decent, basic rooms with new baths in a nice location for a great price. Samanta and Marco run this guesthouse with a charming passion; they offer no Wi-Fi "because it burns your brains" (S-€40, D-€65, Db-€80, extra bed-€25, no breakfast, fans but no air-con, request quiet room when you book, free parking, 2 blocks behind the Duomo at Via dell'Oriuolo 17, tel. & fax 055-234-0706, hoteldali@tin.it).

$ Oblate Sisters of the Assumption run an institutional 30-room hotel in a Renaissance building with a dreamy garden, great public spaces, appropriately simple rooms, and a quiet, prayerful ambience (S-€40, Db-€80, Tb-€120, Qb-€160, cash only, single beds only, optional breakfast-€5, air-con, elevator, €10/day limited parking—request when you book, Borgo Pinti 15, tel. 055-248-0582, fax 055-234-6291, sroblateborgopinti@virgilio.it, sisters are likely to speak French but not English, Sister Theresa is very helpful).

Between the Duomo and Piazza della Signoria

These are the most central of my accommodations recommendations (and therefore a little overpriced). They're worth the extra cost for many, but given Florence's walkable core, nearly every hotel can be considered central.

$$ Hotel Pendini, with three tarnished stars, fills the top floor of a grand building constructed to celebrate Italian unification in the late 19th century. It overlooks Piazza della Repubblica, and as you walk into the lobby, you feel as if you are walking back in time. Its 40 rooms are well-worn and pretty stodgy, though a few have been redecorated recently. The place is memorable—and a good value (Db-€89–155, Internet access and Wi-Fi, Via Strozzi 2, tel. 055-211-170, www.hotelpendini.it, info@hotelpendini.it).

$$ B&B Dei Mori, a peaceful haven, has five newly remodeled rooms ideally located on a quiet pedestrian street near the Casa di Dante. Accommodating hostess Suzanne offers lots of tips on dining and sightseeing in Florence (D-€100, Db-€120, 10 percent discount for my readers—ask when you book, air-con-€5 extra, reception open 8:00–19:00, Via Dante Alighieri 12, tel. 055-211-438, www.deimori.com, deimori@bnb.it).

$$ Hotel Axial (run by the same folks who own Hotel Maxim—see next listing) offers 14 soundproofed, tidy, and plain rooms on Florence's main pedestrian drag (Sb-€89–109, Db-€139, 5 percent discount if you book on their website, another 5 percent off for cash, check for website promotions, air-con, elevator, Wi-Fi, Via de' Calzaiuoli 11, tel. 055-218-984, fax 055-211-733, www.hotel axial.it, info@hotelaxial.it).

$$ Hotel Maxim, right on Via de' Calzaiuoli, is a big and institutional-feeling place warmly run by a family team: father Paolo, son Nicola, and daughter Chiara. Its halls are narrow, but the 26 basic rooms are comfortable and well-maintained (Sb-€75, Db-€110, Tb-€138, Qb-€155, 10 percent discount with cash and this book, air-con, elevator, Internet access and Wi-Fi, Via de'

Calzaiuoli 11, tel. 055-217-474, fax 055-283-729, www.hotelmaxim firenze.it, reservation@hotelmaximfirenze.it).

$$ Residenzia Giotto B&B offers you the chance to stay on Florence's upscale shopping drag, Via Roma. Occupying the top floor of a 19th-century building, this place has six bright rooms and a terrace with knockout views of the Duomo's tower (Sb-€90, Db-€140, extra bed-€25, 10 percent discount for stays of more than 3 nights, elevator, Via Roma 6, tel. 055-214-593, fax 055-264-8568, www.residenzagiotto.it, info@residenzagiotto.it, Giorgio speaks good English). Let them know your arrival time in advance.

$$ Albergo Firenze, a big, efficient place, offers 58 basic rooms in a central locale two blocks behind the Duomo. It's institutional and often busy with big groups (Sb-€84, Db-€114, Tb-€147 but these are the hotel's wishful-thinking prices—ask for a discount, air-con, elevator, noisy, at Piazza Donati 4 across from Via del Corso 8, tel. 055-214-203, fax 055-212-370, www.albergo firenze.net, info@albergofirenze.net, Enrico).

Near Piazza della Signoria and Ponte Vecchio

$$$ Hotel Torre Guelfa is topped by a fun medieval tower with a panoramic rooftop terrace and a huge living room. Its 24 pricey rooms vary wildly in size. Room 15, with a private terrace (€245), is worth reserving several months in advance (standard Db-€170–190, Db junior suite-€235, family deals, 5 percent discount with cash, air-con, elevator, a couple blocks northwest of Ponte Vecchio, Borgo S.S. Apostoli 8, tel. 055-239-6338, fax 055-239-8577, www.hoteltorreguelfa.com, info@hoteltorreguelfa.com, Sabina, Giancarlo, and Sandro).

$$$ In Piazza della Signoria B&B, overlooking Piazza della Signoria, is peaceful, refined, and homey at the same time. Fit for a honeymoon, the 10 rooms come with all the special touches and little extras you'd expect in a top-end American B&B—such as being served fresh-squeezed orange juice for breakfast (viewless Db-€220, view Db-€250, Tb-€280, ask for 10 percent discount when you book direct with this book, family apartments, lavish bathrooms, air-con, tiny elevator, Internet access and Wi-Fi, Via dei Magazzini 2, tel. 055-239-9546, mobile 348-321-0565, fax 055-267-6616, www.inpiazzadellasignoria.com, info@inpiazzadella signoria.com, Sonia and Alessandro).

$$$ Relais Uffizi is a peaceful little gem, with 15 classy rooms tucked away down a tiny alleyway off Piazza della Signoria. The lounge has a huge window overlooking the action in the square below (Sb-€140, Db-€180, Tb-€220, buffet breakfast, elevator, Wi-Fi, Chiasso de Baroncelli/Chiasso del Buco 16, tel. 055-267-6239, fax 055-265-7909, www.relaisuffizi.it, info@relaisuffizi.it, charming Alessandro).

$$$ Hotel Davanzati, bright and shiny with artistic touches, has 19 cheerful rooms with all the comforts. The place is a family affair, thoughtfully run by friendly Tommaso and father Fabrizio, who offer drinks and snacks each evening at their candlelit happy hour (Sb-€122, Db-€189, Tb-€259, these rates good with this book though prices soft off-season, 10 percent cash discount; PlayStation 2, DVD player, and laptop with free Wi-Fi in every room; air-con, next to Piazza Davanzati at Via Porta Rossa 5, tel. 055-286-666, fax 055-265-8252, www.hoteldavanzati.it, info@hoteldavanzati.it).

$$ Hotel Alessandra is 16th-century, tranquil, and sprawling, with 27 big, tasteful rooms (S-€67, Sb-€110, D-€110, Db-€150, Tb-€195, Qb-€215, 5 percent cash discount, air-con, Internet access and Wi-Fi, Borgo S.S. Apostoli 17, tel. 055-283-438, fax 055-210-619, www.hotelalessandra.com, info@hotelalessandra.com, Anna and son Andrea).

Near the Train Station

As with any big Italian city, the area around the train station is a magnet for hardworking pickpockets on the alert for lost, vulnerable tourists with bulging money belts hanging out of their khakis.

$$ Hotel Alba Palace is a three-star hotel with a welcoming reception, cushy red leather sofas, and a piano in the lounge. Breakfast is served in a glass-roofed patio area, and the rooms have been tastefully redone in traditional Florentine style (Sb-€90, Db-€150, Tb-€170, check website for price fluctuations, elevator, Wi-Fi, Via della Scala 22/38 red, tel. 055-282-610, fax 055-288-358, www.hotelalbafirenze.it, info@hotelalbafirenze.it).

$ Bellevue House is a third-floor (no elevator) oasis of tranquility, with six spacious rooms flanking a long mellow-yellow lobby. It's a peaceful time warp thoughtfully run by Rosanna and Antonio di Grazia (Db-€70–90, family deals, 5 percent cash discount, optional €3 breakfast in street-level bar, Via della Scala 21, tel. 055-260-8932, mobile 333-612-5973, fax 055-265-5315, www.bellevuehouse.it, info@bellevuehouse.it).

Hostels Away from the Center

These two hostels, northeast of the downtown, are a bus ride from the action. A far more central hostel is in Oltrarno (see end of next section).

$ Villa Camerata, classy for an IYHF hostel, is in a pretty villa three miles northeast of the train station, on the outskirts of Florence (€20/bed with breakfast, 4- to 6-bed rooms, must have hostel membership card or pay additional €3/night, self-serve laundry; take bus #17 from the train station to Salviatino stop; Via Righi 2, tel. 055-601-451, fax 055-610-300, www.aighostels.com, firenze@aighostels.com).

FLORENCE

$ Hostel 7 Santi calls itself a "travelers' haven." It fills a former convent, but you'll feel like you're in an old school. Still, it offers some of the best cheap beds in town; is friendly to older travelers; and comes with the services you'd expect in a big, modern hostel, including free Wi-Fi and a self-serve laundry. It's in a more residential neighborhood near the Campo di Marte stadium, about a 10-minute bus ride from the center (200 beds in 60 rooms, mostly 4- or 6-bed dorms with a floor of doubles and triples, €20/dorm bed, Sb-€40, Ds-€60, Db-€70; includes breakfast, sheets, and towels; no curfew; from the station, take bus #17 direction: Campo di Marte to bus stop Chiesa dei Sette Santi; Viale dei Mille 11, tel. 055-504-8452, www.7santi.com, info@7santi.com).

South of the Arno River, in the Oltrarno

Across the river in the Oltrarno area, between the Pitti Palace and Ponte Vecchio, you'll still find small, traditional crafts shops, neighborly piazzas, and family eateries. The following places are an easy walk from Ponte Vecchio. Only the first one is a real hotel—the rest are a ragtag gang of budget alternatives.

$$$ Hotel Silla is a classic three-star hotel with 35 cheery, spacious, pastel, and modern rooms. It faces the river and overlooks a park opposite the Santa Croce Church (Db-€180, Tb-€220, ask for Rick Steves rate when you book, air-con, elevator, Wi-Fi, Via dei Renai 5, tel. 055-234-2888, fax 055-234-1437, www.hotelsilla.it, hotelsilla@hotelsilla.it, Laura, Chiara, Massimo, and Stefano).

$ Istituto Gould is a Protestant Church–run place with 40 clean and spartan rooms that have twin beds and modern facilities (Sb-€45, Db-€56–68, Tb-€75, Qb-€92, breakfast-€5 extra, quieter rooms in back, no air-con but rooms have fans, Via dei Serragli 49, tel. 055-212-576, fax 055-280-274, www.istitutogould.it, foresteriafirenze@diaconiavaldese.org). You must arrive when the office is open (Mon–Fri 8:45–13:00 & 15:00–19:30, Sat 9:00–13:30 & 14:30–18:00, no check-in Sun or holidays).

$ Soggiorno Alessandra has five bright, comfy, and smallish rooms. Because of its double-paned windows, you'll hardly notice the traffic noise (D-€58–73, Db-€78, Tb-€98, Qb-€128, 5 percent discount with 2-night stay, air-con-€8, just past the Carraia Bridge at Via Borgo San Frediano 6, tel. 055-290-424, fax 055-218-464, www.soggiornoalessandra.it, info@soggiornoalessandra.it, Alessandra).

$ Casa Santo Nome di Gesù is a grand 29-room convent whose sisters—Franciscan Missionaries of Mary—are thankful to rent rooms to tourists. Staying in this 15th-century palace, you'll be immersed in the tranquil atmosphere created by a huge, peaceful garden, generous and prayerful public spaces, and smiling nuns (D-€70, Db-€85, elevator, no air-con but rooms have fans, twin

FLORENCE

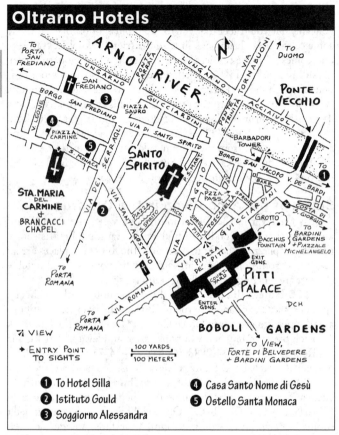

Oltrarno Hotels

(Map labels:)

TO PORTA SAN FREDIANO

ARNO RIVER

PONTE CARRARA

LUNGARNO

VIA TORNABUONI

↑ TO DUOMO

SAN FREDIANO

❸

BORGO SAN FREDIANO

VI. LEONE

❹

PIAZZA SAURO

GUICCIARDINI

PONTE TRINITA

PONTE ACCIAIUOLI

PONTE VECCHIO

PIAZZA CARMINE

❺

S. MONACA

VIA DI SANTO SPIRITO

BARBADORI TOWER

SANTO SPIRITO

BORGO SAN JACOPO V. DE' BARDI

TO ❶

STA. MARIA DEL CARMINE & BRANCACCI CHAPEL

VIA DE SERRAGLI

❷

VIA SANT'AGOSTINO

PIAZZA S. SPIRITO

PZA. PASS.

SPRONE

BARB.

GUICCIARDINI

COSTA DI S. GIORGIO

VIA MICH.

TOSCANELLA

SPRUCE DE' PITTI

GROTTO

TO BARDINI GARDENS + PIAZZALE MICHELANGELO

TO PORTA ROMANA

VIA ROMANA

VIA DE' PITTI

PIAZZA DE' PITTI

BACCHUS FOUNTAIN

EXIT GDNS.

PITTI PALACE

COURT YARD

TO PORTA ROMANA

VIA ROMANA

ENTER GDNS.

DCH

🔭 VIEW

→ ENTRY POINT TO SIGHTS

BOBOLI GARDENS

TO VIEW, FORTE DI BELVEDERE + BARDINI GARDENS

100 YARDS / 100 METERS

❶ To Hotel Silla
❷ Istituto Gould
❸ Soggiorno Alessandra
❹ Casa Santo Nome di Gesù
❺ Ostello Santa Monaca

beds only, memorable convent-like breakfast room, strict 23:29
curfew, Piazza del Carmine 21, tel. 055-213-856, fax 055-281-835,
www.fmmfirenze.it, info@fmmfirenze.it).

Hostel: **$ Ostello Santa Monaca**, a long block south of the
Brancacci Chapel, is well-run and attracts a young backpacking
crowd (€15–24/bed with sheets, 2- to 20-bed dorms, 10:00–14:00
lock-out, 2:00 in the morning curfew, free Internet access and
Wi-Fi, self-serve laundry, kitchen, Via Santa Monaca 6—see map
on this page, tel. 055-268-338, fax 055-280-185, www.ostellodi
firenze.it, info@ostello.it).

Eating in Florence

To save money and time for sights, keep lunches fast and simple,
eating in one of the countless pizzerias and self-service cafeterias
(or picnicking your way though the Mercato Centrale).

For good sit-down meals, consider the following listings. Remember, restaurateurs like to serve what's fresh. If you're into flavor, go for the seasonal best bets—featured in the *piatti del giorno* ("special of the day") sections of menus.

For dessert, it's gelato (see the sidebar on page 478).

North of the Arno River
Near the Train Station

Trattoria al Trebbio serves traditional food with simple Florentine elegance in its candlelit interior. Tables spill out onto a romantic little square—an oasis of Roman Trastevere-like charm (€8 pastas, €13 *secondi*, daily 12:00–15:00 & 19:15–23:00, reserve for outdoor seating, half a block off Piazza Santa Maria Novella at Via delle Belle Donne 47, tel. 055-287-089, Antonio).

Trattoria "da Giorgio" is a family-style diner serving up piping-hot, delicious home cooking to happy locals and tourists alike. Their three-course fixed-price meal is a great value for €12, including water and a drink. Choose from among the daily specials or the regular menu (Mon–Sat 12:00–14:30 & 18:00–22:00, closed Sun, Via Palazzuolo 100 red, tel. 055-284-302, Silvano).

Osteria Belle Donne makes you feel like you're eating dinner in a crowded terrarium piled high with decorative knickknacks. Old-fashioned Tuscan food is served on tight tables, with a few spilling onto a tiny deck outside. They take no reservations and tend to steamroll tourists; arrive early or wait (€10 pastas, €12 *secondi*, daily 12:00–15:00 & 19:00–23:00, Via delle Belle Donne 16 red, tel. 055-238-2609, run by sprightly Giacinto).

Trattoria Marione serves sincerely home-cooked-style meals to a mixed group of tourists and Florentines in a happy, crowded, food-loving, and steamy ambience (€8 pastas, €10 *secondi*, daily 12:00–17:30 & 19:00–23:00, Via della Spada 27 red, tel. 055-214-756, Fabio).

Trattoria Sostanza-Troia, characteristic and well-established, is famous for its beef. Hearty steaks and pastas are splittable. Whirling ceiling fans and walls strewn with old photos evoke earlier times, while the artichoke pies remind locals of Grandma's cooking. Crowded, shared tables with paper tablecloths give this place a bistro feel. They offer two dinner seatings, at 19:30 and 21:00, which require reservations (dinners for about €30 plus wine, cash only, lunch Mon–Sat 12:30–14:00, closed Sun, closed Sat in off-season, Via del Porcellana 25 red, tel. 055-212-691).

Trattoria 13 Gobbi ("13 Hunchbacks") is a trendy favorite, glowing with candles around a tiny garden. Romantic in front and kid-friendly in back, it serves beautifully presented Tuscan food on big, fancy plates to a mostly tourist crowd (€8.50 pastas, €15 *secondi*, daily 12:00–15:00 & 19:30–23:00, Via del Porcellana 9 red, tel. 055-284-015, Enrico).

FLORENCE

Florence Restaurants

TO PIAZZA D. LIBERTA

TO FORTEZZA DI BASSO

S.M.N. TRAIN STATION

P. ADUA

V. CENN.

V. FIUME

V. FAENZA

VIA NAZIONALE

VIA PANICALE

S. ANT.

S. ZANOBI

27 APRILE

S. REP.

S. GALLO

GUELFA

CAVOUR

MERCATO CENTRALE

MEDICI CHAPELS

STREET MKT.

SAN LORENZO

B.S. LOR.

RICA

MEDICI-RICCARDI PALACE

PUCCI

VIA

DUOMO

BUS STN.

ALA.

S. MARIA NOVELLA

VIA D. SCALA

PORC. SCALA

V. PAL.

V. FOSS.

V. MORO

SPADA

SOLE

PANZANI

MEL.

GIGLIO

BANCHI

CERRETANI

BAPT.

CAMPANILE

SOLO

AGLI

TOSINGHI

TORNABUONI

STROZZI

PZZA. REP.

POST

ORSAN-MICH.

PORTA ROSSA

CALZAIUOLI

CORSO

CASA DI DANTE

DANTE

PROCON.

V.

P. GOLD.

VIGNA NUOVA

S. TRINITA

ARNO

CARRAIA

LUNG. CORSINI

LUNG. GUICC.

VIA S. SPIRITO

TRIN.

B.S.

COV. MKT.

V. TERME

APOST.

S. MARIA

PIAZZA SIGNORIA

COND.

PALAZZO VECCHIO

BORGO

PONTE VECCHIO

S. JACOPO

ACCIAIUOLI

VINEGI.

V. DE' NER.

EXIT

GALILEO SCIENCE MUSEUM

V. SAP.

OLTRARNO

GUICC.

DIAZ

UFFIZI GALLERY

TO PITTI PALACE

1. Trattoria al Trebbio
2. Trattoria "da Giorgio"
3. Osteria Belle Donne
4. Trattoria Marione
5. Trattoria Sostanza-Troia
6. Trattoria 13 Gobbi
7. Trattoria Zà-Zà & Trattoria Mario's
8. Trattoria la Burrasca
9. Osteria la Congrega
10. Trattoria Lo Stracotto
11. Osteria Vineria i'Brincello
12. Trattoria Nerone Pizzeria
13. Mercato Centrale & Nerbone in the Market
14. Casa del Vino
15. Il Pirata
16. Pasticceria Robiglio
17. La Mescita Fiaschetteria
18. Il Centro Supermercati
19. Self-Service Rist. Leonardo
20. The Oil Shoppe
21. Rivoire Café
22. Frescobaldi Rist. & Wine Bar
23. Ristorante Paoli & Cantinetta dei Verrazzano
24. Trattoria Nella
25. Osteria Vini e Vecchi Sapori
26. I Fratellini
27. L'Antico Trippaio
28. 'Ino Bottega di Alimentari e Vini
29. Trattoria Icche C'è C'è
30. Ristorante del Fagioli
31. Boccadama Enoteca Rist.
32. Trattoria Anita
33. Gelateria Grom
34. Gelateria Carrozze
35. Gelateria Carabè
36. Festival del Gelato
37. Perchè No! Gelateria
38. Vivoli's Gelateria
39. Gelateria de' Neri
40. La Congrega Lounge Bar

Near the Mercato Centrale

The following market-neighborhood eateries are distinct but within a hundred yards of each other. Scout around and choose your favorite.

Dining near the Mercato Centrale

Trattoria Zà-Zà is a fun, characteristic, high-energy place facing the Mercato Centrale. It's a family-friendly festival of standard Tuscan dishes such as *ribollita* and *bistecca alla fiorentina*, plus a variety of big, splittable salads. Florentines lament the invasion of tourists, but everyone's happy, and the food is still great. Arrive early or make a reservation, especially for the wonderful outdoor piazza seating. Understand your itemized bill (as they are reportedly math-challenged), and don't mistake their outside seating with the neighboring restaurant's (daily 11:00–23:00, Piazza del Mercato Centrale 26 red, tel. 055-215-411).

Trattoria la Burrasca is Flintstone-chic. Friendly duo Elio and Simone offer a limited menu with daily specials of rib-stickin' Tuscan home cooking. It's small—10 tables—and often filled with my readers. If Archie Bunker were Italian, he'd eat at this trattoria for special nights out (€7 pastas, €10 *secondi,* no cover or service charge, Tue–Sun 12:00–15:30 & 19:00–23:00, closed Mon, Via Panicale 6, north corner of Mercato Centrale, tel. 055-215-827).

Osteria la Congrega brags that it's "a Tuscan wine bar designed to help you lose track of time." In a fresh, imaginative, two-level setting, chef-owner Mahyar (mai-AR) takes pride in his fun, easy menu, which features modern Tuscan cuisine, top-notch meat, and seasonal produce. He offers quality vegetarian dishes, creative salads, and an inexpensive but excellent house wine. There are just 10 tables, and reservations are required for dinner (€8 pastas, €12 nightly specials, Mon–Sat 12:00–15:00 & 19:00–23:00, closed Sun, a block from Mercato Centrale, Via Panicale 43 red, tel. 055-264-5027). Mahyar offers fine wines by the glass (see list on blackboard) and occasional live jazz. Between meals, he's busy teaching cooking classes here (www.osterialacongrega.it).

Trattoria Lo Stracotto is a stylish new truffle-colored eatery just steps away from the Medici Chapels. It's run with enthusiasm and flair by two cousins, who serve up tasty traditional dishes such as *bistecca alla fiorentina* and *ribollita* (based on grandfather's recipe), and good chocolate soufflé. Enjoy the candlelit ambience and soft music as you sit either in the dining room or out on the terrace (€7 pastas, €10 *secondi,* daily 11:00–23:00, Piazza Madonna degli Aldobrandi 16/17, tel. 055-230-2062, Francesco and Tomasso).

Osteria Vineria i'Brincello—a bright, happy no-frills diner with lots of spirit and friendly service—is great for a simple lunch. Notice the list of Tuscan daily specials on the blackboard hanging from the ceiling (€7 pastas, daily 12:00–15:00 & 19:00–23:00, corner of Via Nazionale and Via Chiara at Via Nazionale 110 red, tel. 055-282-645, Shahid cooks while Claudia serves).

Trattoria Nerone Pizzeria serves up cheap, hearty Tuscan dishes and decent pizzas. The lively, flamboyantly outfitted space (once the garden courtyard of a convent) feels like a good but kitschy American Italian chain restaurant (€7 pizzas, €7 pastas, €10 *secondi,* daily 12:00–15:00 & 18:30–23:00, just north of Via Nazionale at Via Faenza 95 red, tel. 055-291-217, Tulio).

Eating Cheaply in or near the Mercato Centrale

Notice that all of these eateries, except the last one, are open only for lunch.

Mercato Centrale (Central Market) is great for an ad-lib lunch. It offers colorful piles of picnic produce, people-watching, and rustic sandwiches (Mon–Sat 7:00–14:00, Sat in winter until 17:00, closed Sun, a block north of San Lorenzo street market). Meat, fish, and cheese are sold on the ground level, with fruit and veggies mostly upstairs. The thriving ground-level eateries within the market (such as Nerbone, described next) serve some of the cheapest hot meals in town. The fancy deli, Perini, is famous for its quality products and generous free samples. Buy a picnic of fresh mozzarella cheese, olives, fruit, and crunchy bread to munch on the steps of the nearby Church of San Lorenzo, overlooking the bustling street market.

Nerbone in the Market is a venerable café and the best place for a sit-down meal within Mercato Centrale. Join the shoppers and workers who crowd up to the bar to grab their €5 plates—tripe is very big here—and then find an informal table to eat at nearby. Of the several cheap market diners, this feels the most authentic (lunch only, cash only, inside Mercato Centrale on the side closest to the Church of San Lorenzo, mobile 339-648-0251).

Trattoria Mario's, around the corner from Trattoria Zà-Zà (listed earlier), has been serving hearty lunches to market-goers since 1953 (Fabio and Romeo are the latest generation). Their simple formula: bustling service, old-fashioned good value, a lunch-only fixed-price meal, and shared tables. It's *cucina casalinga*—home cooking *con brio.* This place is extremely popular, and their best dishes often sell out first, so go early. If there's a line, put your name on the list (€5 pastas, €8 *secondi,* cash only, Mon–Sat 12:00–15:30, closed Sun and Aug, no reservations, Via Rosina 2, tel. 055-218-550).

Casa del Vino, Florence's oldest operating wine shop, offers glasses of wine from among 25 open bottles. Owner Gianni, whose family has owned the Casa for more than 70 years, is a class act. Gianni's *carta dei panini* lists many delightful €3.50 sandwiches (the crostini are notable). Some opened bottles behind the counter are marked with prices for wine by the glass; otherwise, see the list tacked to the bar. During busy times, it's a mob scene. You'll eat standing outside, with workers on a quick lunch break (Mon–Sat 9:30–17:00, closed Sat in summer and Sun year-round, hidden behind stalls of San Lorenzo Market at Via dell'Ariento 16 red, tel. 055-215-609).

Il Pirata, a deli and rotisserie, puts out a €7.50 all-you-can-eat buffet each evening (18:00–22:00, includes water). They offer budget travelers an array of homemade Italian dishes and roasted meats for takeout or to dine in at the counter. Pick up a plastic plate, fill it, get it microwaved if you like, grab a stool, and chow down (closed Sun, 2 blocks from the Accademia at Via de' Ginori 56 red, tel. 055-218-625). You don't want to linger here (and the owner is a bit of a smart aleck)—but at least you'll fill your stomach.

Budget Lunches Between the Duomo and the Accademia

Pasticceria Robiglio, a smart little café, opens up its stately dining area and sets out a few tables on the sidewalk for lunch on workdays. They have a small menu of daily pasta and *secondi* specials, and seem determined to do things like they did in the elegant pre-tourism days (generous €8 plates, a great €7.50 *niçoise*-like "fantasy salad," pretty pastries, good wines by the glass, smiling service, daily 12:00–15:00, longer hours as a café, a block toward the Duomo off Piazza S.S. Annunziata at Via dei Servi 112 red, tel. 055-212-784). Before you leave, be tempted by their pastries—famous among Florentines.

La Mescita Fiaschetteria is a characteristic hole-in-the-wall just around the corner from *David*—but a world away from all the tourism. It's where locals and students enjoy daily pasta specials and hearty sandwiches with good €1 house wine. You can trust Mirco—just point to what looks good (such as their €5 pasta plate), and you'll soon be eating well and inexpensively. The place can either be mobbed by students or in a peaceful time warp, depending on when you stop by (Mon–Sat 12:00–16:00, closed Sun, Via degli Alfani 70 red, mobile 347-795-1604).

Picnic on the Ultimate Renaissance Square: Il Centro Supermercati, a handy supermarket across from the Accademia *(David)*, happily makes sandwiches to your specs (Mon–Sat 8:00–20:00, Sun 10:00–19:00, Via Ricasoli 109). Choose your fresh bread and tasty meat and cheese (assembled and sold by the weight); embellish with some veggies, milk, yogurt, or juice; and hike around the block to Piazza S.S. Annunziata, the first Renaissance square in Florence. There's a fountain for washing fruit on the square. Grab a stony seat anywhere you like, and savor one of my favorite cheap

> ## Döner Kebab—Cheap, Fast, and Not a Hint of Pasta
>
> Because of the influx of Middle Eastern immigrants into Italy, "ethnic cuisine" has become more prevalent in recent years. Today, shops selling döner kebab (roasted meat wrapped in thin bread) are sprouting everywhere.
>
> Döner kebab shops offer cheap, filling, healthy alternatives to your average slice of pizza or ham-and-cheese *panino*. The kebab itself consists of chicken or veal and turkey, which has been cut into thick slabs, piled high onto a skewer, and slow-roasted on a vertical spit. Once it's cooked, the rich, savory meat is sliced ultra-thin with a razor and stuffed into your choice of pita bread *(panino)* or a wrap *(piadina)*, along with tomatoes, onions, lettuce, tangy yogurt sauce, and (optional) hot chili sauce. A vegetarian alternative is falafel (a fried garbanzo-bean patty) served with the same works. Either dish costs about €3-4, and shops are generally open from 11:00 in the morning until midnight.

Florence eating experiences. (Or, drop by either of the two places listed earlier for a sandwich and juice to go.)

Fast and Cheap near the Duomo

Self-Service Ristorante Leonardo is inexpensive, air-conditioned, quick, and handy. Eating here, you'll get the sense that they're passionate about the quality of their food. Stefano and Luciano (like Pavarotti) run the place with enthusiasm, and put out free pitchers of tap water. It's just a block from the Duomo, southwest of the Baptistery (tasty €4 pastas, €5 main courses, Sun–Fri 11:45–14:45 & 18:45–21:45, closed Sat, upstairs at Via Pecori 11, tel. 055-284-446).

The Oil Shoppe cobbles together huge gourmet hot and cold sub sandwiches *all'Italiana* from creative ingredients (€3.50). You can get a sandwich plus fries and water (€5), or build your own salad and pair it with a homemade soup of the day for a fast, cheap, and hearty lunch. Eat at the skinny counter or take your food to go (generally Mon–Fri 10:30–18:00 or until the bread runs out, closed Sat–Sun, 2 long blocks east of the Duomo at Via S. Egidio 22 red, cheery Alberto runs the show).

Near Piazza della Signoria and Ponte Vecchio

Dining

Piazza della Signoria, the scenic square facing Palazzo Vecchio, is ringed by beautifully situated yet touristy eateries serving overpriced, bad-value, and probably microwaved food. If you're determined to eat on the square, have pizza at Ristorante il

Cavallino or bar food from the Irish pub next door. The Piazza della Signoria's saving grace is **Rivoire** café, famous for its fancy desserts and thick hot chocolate. While obscenely expensive, it has the best view tables on the square (Tue–Sun 7:30–24:00, closed Mon, tel. 055-214-412).

Frescobaldi Ristorante and Wine Bar, the showcase of Italy's aristocratic wine family, is a good choice for a formal dinner in Florence. Candlelight reflects on glasses, and high-vaulted ceilings complement the sophisticated dishes and fine wines. They offer the same menu in three different dining areas: cozy interior, woody wine bar, and breezy terrace. If coming for dinner, make a reservation, dress up, and hit an ATM (€12 appetizers and pastas, €20 *secondi,* lunch salads, Tue–Sat 12:00–14:30 & 19:00–22:30, Mon 19:00–22:30, closed Sun and Aug, air-con, half a block north of Palazzo Vecchio at Via dei Magazzini 2–4 red, tel. 055-284-724). Don't let them railroad you into ordering things you don't want.

Ristorante Paoli dishes up wonderful traditional cuisine to loads of cheerful eaters being served by jolly little old men under a richly frescoed Gothic vault. Because of its fame and central location, it's filled mostly with tourists, but for a sophisticated, traditional Tuscan splurge meal, this is a fine choice. Salads are dramatically cut and mixed from a trolley right at your table. The walls are sweaty with memories that go back to 1824, and the service is flamboyant and fun-loving (but don't get taken—confirm prices). Woodrow Wilson slurped spaghetti here—his bust looks down on you as you eat (€11 pastas, €15 *secondi,* €25 tourist fixed-price meal, daily 12:00–15:00 & 19:00–23:00, reserve for dinner, between Piazza della Signoria and the Duomo at Via dei Tavolini 12 red, tel. 055-216-215).

Trattoria Nella serves good typical Tuscan cuisine at affordable prices. Twin brothers Federico and Lorenzo carry on their father Sergio's tradition of keeping their clientele well-fed and happy. Their ravioli with walnuts is a hit with regulars (daily specials, €9 pastas, €14 *secondi,* daily 12:00–15:00 & 19:00–22:00, reserve for dinner, 3 blocks northwest of Ponte Vecchio, Via delle Terme 19 red, tel. 055-218-925).

Cheap and Simple near Piazza della Signoria

Cantinetta dei Verrazzano, a long-established bakery-café–wine bar, serves delightful sandwich plates in an old-time setting. Their *specialità Verrazzano* is a fine plate of four little crostini (like mini-bruschetta) proudly featuring different breads, cheeses, and meats from the Chianti region (€7.50). The *tagliere di focacce,* a sampler plate of mini-focaccia sandwiches, is also fun (price depends on quantity). Add a glass of Chianti to either of these dishes to make a fine light meal. Office workers pop in for a quick lunch, and it's traditional to share tables (Mon–Sat 8:00–21:00, closed Sun, just off Via de' Calzaiuoli on a side street across from Orsanmichele Church at Via dei Tavolini 18, tel. 055-268-590). They also have benches and tiny tables for eating at "take-out" prices. Simply step to the back and point to the hot *focacce* sandwich (€3) you'd like, order a drink at the bar, and take away your food or sit with locals and watch the action while you munch.

Osteria Vini e Vecchi Sapori, half a block north of Palazzo Vecchio, is a colorful 16-seat hole-in-the-wall serving Tuscan food, including plates of mixed crostini (€1 each—step right up and choose at the bar) and €10 daily specials. Be sure to try their raspberry *(lampone)* tiramisu. In the evening, it becomes a little restaurant with a fun, accessible menu of delicious €8 pastas and €10 *secondi* (Tue–Sat 12:30–15:00 & 19:30–22:00, Sun 12:30–15:00, closed Mon, reserve for dinner; facing the bronze equestrian statue in Piazza della Signoria, go behind its tail into the corner and to your left; Via dei Magazzini 3 red, tel. 055-293-045, run by Mario while wife Rosanna cooks and son Thomas serves).

I Fratellini is an informal little eatery where the "little brothers" have served peasants 29 different kinds of sandwiches and cheap glasses of Chianti wine (see list on wall) since 1875. Join the local crowd to order, then sit on a nearby curb or windowsill to munch, placing your glass on the wall rack before you leave (€4 for sandwich and wine, daily 9:00–20:00 or until the bread runs out, closed Sun in winter, 20 yards in front of Orsanmichele Church on Via dei Cimatori, tel. 055-239-6096). Be adventurous with the menu (easy-order by number). Consider *finocchiona* (a special Tuscan salami), *lardo di Colonnata* (lard aged in Carrara marble), and *cinghiale piccante* (spicy wild boar) sandwiches. Order the most expensive wine they're selling by the glass (Brunello for €4; bottles are labeled).

L'Antico Trippaio, an antique tripe stand, is a fixture in the town center (daily 9:00–20:00, on Via Dante Alighieri, mobile 339-742-5692). Cheap and authentic as can be, this is where Florentines come daily for €3.50 sandwiches *(panini)* featuring specialties like *trippa alla fiorentina* (tripe), *lampredotto* (cow's stomach), and a list of more appetizing sandwiches. Roberto offers a free plastic glass of his Chianti with each sandwich for travelers with this book. The best people-watching place to munch your sandwich is three blocks away, on Piazza della Signoria.

'Ino Bottega di Alimentari e Vini is a mod little shop filled with gifty edibles. Serena and Alessandro serve sandwiches and wine—you'll get your €5-7 sandwich on a napkin with an included glass of their wine of the day as you perch on a tiny stool. They can also make a fine *piatto misto* of cheeses and meats; just say how much you'd like to spend (daily 11:00–17:00, immediately behind

Gelato

Gelato is an edible art form. Italy's best ice cream is in Florence—one souvenir that can't break and won't clutter your luggage. But beware of scams at touristy joints on busy streets that turn a simple request for a cone into a €10 "tourist special" rip-off. To avoid this, survey the size options and be very clear in your order (for example, "a €3 cone").

A key to gelato appreciation is sampling liberally and choosing flavors that go well together. Ask, as Italians do, for *"Un assaggio, per favore?"* (A taste, please?; oon ah-SAH-joh pehr fah-VOH-ray) and *"Che si sposano bene?"* (What marries well?; kay see spoh-ZAH-noh BEN-ay).

Artiginale, nostra produzione, and *produzione propia* mean gelato is made on the premises; also, gelato displayed in covered metal tins (rather than white plastic) is more likely to be homemade. Gelato aficionados avoid colors that don't appear in nature—for fewer chemicals and real flavor, go for mellow hues (bright colors attract children). These places are open daily for long hours.

Near the Duomo: The recent favorite in town, **Grom** uses organic ingredients and seasonal fresh fruit, along with biodegradable spoons and tubs. Their traditional approach and quality give locals déjà vu, reminding them of the good old days and the ice cream of their childhood. Mario, who really cares, sees "gelato as cuisine," and adjusts the menu monthly to fit what's in season (daily 10:30–24:00, Via delle Oche 24 red). Their *liquirizia* (licorice) flavor is worth a sample.

Uffizi Gallery on Ponte Vecchio side, Via dei Georgofili 3 red, tel. 055-219-208).

East of Piazza della Signoria

Trattoria Icche C'è C'è (EE-kay chay chay; dialect for "whatever there is, there is") is a small family-style restaurant where fun-loving Gino and his wife Mara serve quality local food, including a €13 three-course fixed-price meal (€6 pastas, €10 *secondi,* Tue–Sun 12:30–14:30 & 19:30–22:30, closed Mon and two weeks in Aug, midway between Bargello and river at Via Magalotti 11 red, tel. 055-216-589).

Ristorante del Fagioli is an enthusiastically run eatery where you feel the heritage. The dad, Gigi, commands the kitchen, while family members Antonio, Maurizio, and Simone keep the throngs

Near Ponte Vecchio: Gelateria Carrozze is a longtime favorite (daily 11:00–20:00, until 1:00 in the morning in summer, on riverfront 30 yards from Ponte Vecchio toward the Uffizi at Piazza del Pesce 3).

Near the Accademia: A Sicilian choice on a tourist thoroughfare, **Gelateria Carabè** is particularly famous for its luscious *granite*—Italian ices made with fresh fruit. Antonio, whose family has made ice cream the Sicilian way for more than 100 years, can tell you why that's important (daily 11:00–20:00; from the Accademia, it's a block toward the Duomo at Via Ricasoli 60 red).

Near Orsanmichele Church: For gelato served in a brash, neon environment, it's **Festival del Gelato** or **Perchè No!,** both located just off the busy main pedestrian drag (Via de' Calzaiuoli). They serve a stunning array of brightly colored kid-pleasing flavors (Festival del Gelato is at Via del Corso 75; Perchè No! is at Via dei Tavolini 19).

Near the Church of Santa Croce: The venerable favorite, **Vivoli's** still serves great gelato—but it's more expensive and stingy in its servings. Before ordering, try a free sample of their rice flavor—*riso* (closed Mon, Aug, and Jan; opposite the Church of Santa Croce, go down Via Torta a block and turn right on Via Stinche). Locals flock to **Gelateria de' Neri** (Via de' Neri 26 red), also owned by Vivoli's.

Across the River: If you want an excuse to check out the little village-like neighborhood across the river from Santa Croce, enjoy a gelato at the tiny **Il Gelato di Filo** (named for Filippo and Lorenzo) at Via San Miniato 5 red, a few steps toward the river from Porta San Miniato. Gelato chef Edmir is proud of his fruity sorbet as well.

of loyal customers returning. The cuisine: home-style bread soups, hearty steaks, and Florentine classics. Don't worry—while *fagioli* means "beans," that's the family name, not the extent of the menu (€9 pastas, €9 *secondi*, closed Sat–Sun, reserve for dinner, cash only, between Santa Croce Church and the Alle Grazie bridge at Corso dei Tintori 47, tel. 055-244-285).

Boccadama Enoteca Ristorante is a stylish shabby-chic wine bistro serving creative Tuscan fare based on seasonal produce. Eat in the intimate candlelit dining room or at a few tables lining tranquil Piazza Santa Croce. Reservations are smart (€9 *primi*, €14 *secondi*, daily 11:00–16:00 & 18:30–24:00, on south side of Piazza Santa Croce at 25–26 red, tel. 055-243-640).

Trattoria Anita, midway between the Uffizi and Santa Croce, offers a good lunch special: three hearty Tuscan courses—pasta, *secondo,* and *contorno* (side dish)—for €8 (Mon–Sat 12:00–14:30 & 19:00–22:15, closed Sun, on the corner of Via Vinegia and Via del Parlagio at #2 red, tel. 055-218-698, Gianni and Maurizio).

South of the River, in the Oltrarno
Dining with a Ponte Vecchio View

Golden View Open Bar is a lively, trendy bistro, good for a romantic meal or just a salad, pizza, or pasta with fine wine and a fine view of Ponte Vecchio and the Arno River. Reservations for window tables are essential (reasonable prices, €10 pizzas and big salads, daily 11:30–24:00, impressive wine bar, 50 yards upstream from Ponte Vecchio at Via dei Bardi 58, tel. 055-214-502, run by Antonio, Marco, and Tomaso). They have four seating areas (with the same menu and prices) for whatever mood you're in: a riverside pizza place, a classier restaurant, a jazzy lounge, and a wine bar (they also serve a buffet of appetizers free with your drink from 19:00 to 22:00). Mixing their fine wine, river views, and live jazz makes for a wonderful evening (jazz nightly at 21:00 except Tue and Thu off-season).

In the Heart of the Oltrarno

Of the many good and colorful restaurants in the Oltrarno, these are my favorites. Reservations are smart in the evening.

Dining in the Oltrarno

Ristorante Enoteca le Barrique, with eight tables, offers a delightful, quiet, intimate break from traditional Italian cuisine. The Japanese chef fuses Tuscan and Asian with a fun, inviting menu. The list is short, as everything is fresh and seasonal. While the candlelit interior is calm and sweet, the garden out back is a welcome option on a hot summer night (€10 homemade pastas, €14 *secondi,* €2 cover, Tue–Sun 21:00–late, closed Mon, two blocks beyond Piazza del Carmine at Via del Leone 40, tel. 055-224-192, mobile 338-963-2334, Allessandro). If Le Barrique doesn't work for you, **Ristorante Pandemonio,** a block farther down the street, is also good (closed Sun, Via del Leone 50, tel. 055-224-002).

Trattoria 4 Leoni creates the quintessential Oltrarno dinner scene. The Tuscan-style food is made with an innovative twist and an appreciation for vegetables. You'll enjoy the fun energy and characteristic seating, both inside and on the colorful square, Canto ai Quattro Pagoni (informally known as Piazza della Passera). While the wines by the glass are pricey, the house wine is very good (€10 pastas, €15 *secondi,* daily 12:00–24:00; from Ponte Vecchio walk four blocks up Via de' Guicciardini, turn right on Via dello Sprone, then slightly left to Via de' Vellutini 1; tel. 055-218-562).

Oltrarno Restaurants

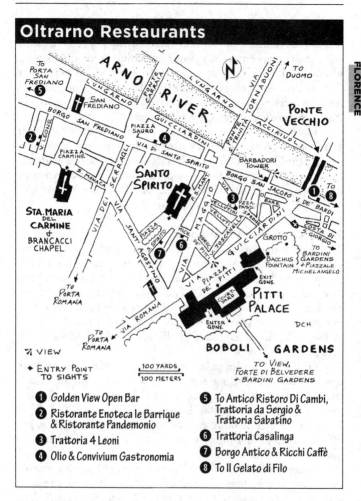

1. Golden View Open Bar
2. Ristorante Enoteca le Barrique & Ristorante Pandemonio
3. Trattoria 4 Leoni
4. Olio & Convivium Gastronomia
5. To Antico Ristoro Di Cambi, Trattoria da Sergio & Trattoria Sabatino
6. Trattoria Casalinga
7. Borgo Antico & Ricchi Caffè
8. To Il Gelato di Filo

Olio & Convivium Gastronomia started as an elegant deli whose refined oil-tasting room morphed into a romantic, aristocratic restaurant. Their three intimate rooms are surrounded by fine *prosciutti*, cheeses, and wine shelves. It's an intimidating place and a little pretentious, but one that foodies will appreciate for its quiet atmosphere. Use it for a special evening. Their list of €13–20 *gastronomia* plates offers an array of taste treats and fine wines by the glass (€14 pastas, €18 *secondi*, stylish €18 lunches, €3 cover, Tue–Sat 12:00–14:30 & 19:00–22:30, Mon lunch only, closed Sun, strong air-con, Via di Santo Spirito 4, tel. 055-265-8198, Monica).

Antico Ristoro Di Cambi is a meat-lover's dream—thick with Tuscan traditions, rustic touches, and T-bone steaks. The bustling scene has a memorable beer-hall energy. As you walk in, you'll pass

FLORENCE

a glass case filled with red chunks of Chianina beef that's priced by weight (and splittable by two or even more). This is a good chance to enjoy the famous *bistecca alla fiorentina*, sitting inside the convivial woody interior or outside on a square (€8 pastas, €12 *secondi*, closed Sun, reserve on weekends and to sit outside, Via Sant'Onofrio 1 red, one block south of Ponte Amerigo Vespucci, tel. 055-217-134, run by Stefano and Fabio, the Cambi cousins).

Trattoria da Sergio, a tiny eatery about a block before Porta San Frediano, has charm and a strong following—reservations are a must. The food is on the gourmet side of home-cooking—mama's favorites with a modern twist—and therefore a bit more expensive (€10 pastas, €15 *secondi*, daily 19:30–23:00, Borgo San Frediano 145 red, tel. 055-223-449, Sergio and Marco).

Eating Cheaply in the Oltrarno

Trattoria Sabatino, farthest away and least touristy of my Oltrarno listings, is a spacious, brightly lit mess hall—disturbingly cheap—with family character and a simple menu. It's a super place to watch locals munch. You'll find it just outside the Porta San Frediano, one of Florence's medieval gates, a 15-minute walk from Ponte Vecchio (€4 pastas, €5 *secondi*, Mon–Fri 12:00–15:00 & 19:15–22:00, closed Sat–Sun, Via Pisana 2 red, tel. 055-225-955, little English spoken).

Trattoria Casalinga, an inexpensive standby, comes with aproned women bustling around the kitchen. Florentines and tourists alike pack the place and leave full and happy, with euros to spare for gelato (€6 pastas, €7 *secondi*, Mon–Sat 12:00–14:30 & 19:00–21:45, after 20:00 reserve or wait, closed Sun and Aug, just off Piazza Santo Spirito, near the church at Via de' Michelozzi 9 red, tel. 055-218-624, Andrea).

Borgo Antico is the hit of Piazza Santo Spirito, with enticing pizzas, big deluxe plates of pasta, a delightful setting, and a trendy and boisterous young crowd (€9 pizza and pasta, €16 *secondi*, daily 12:00–24:00, best to reserve for a seat on the square, Piazza Santo Spirito 6 red, tel. 055-210-437, Andrea).

Ricchi Caffè, next to Borgo Antico, has fine gelato, homemade desserts, shaded outdoor tables, and pasta dishes at lunch (daily 7:00–24:00, tel. 055-215-864). After noting the plain facade of the Brunelleschi church facing the square, step inside the café and pick your favorite picture of the many ways it might be finished.

Florence Connections

Florence is Tuscany's transportation hub, with fine train, bus, and plane connections to virtually anywhere in Italy. The city has several train stations, a bus station (next to the main train station), and an airport (plus Pisa's airport nearby). Livorno, on the coast west of Florence, is a major cruise-ship port for passengers visiting Florence, Pisa, and other nearby destinations.

Trains

From Florence by Train to: Pisa (2–3/hour, 1.25 hours, €6.50), **Lucca** (2/hour, 1.5 hours, €5), **Siena** (direct trains hourly, 1.5 hours, €6.20; bus is better because Siena's train station is far from the center), **Livorno**—port of call for many cruise ships (hourly, 1.5 hours, some change in Pisa, Lucca connection possible), **La Spezia** (for the Cinque Terre, 5/day direct, 1.75 hours, nearly hourly with change in Pisa, €9.20), **Milan** (hourly, 1.75 hours), **Venice** (hourly, 2–3 hours), **Assisi** (8/day direct, 2–3 hours, €11), **Orvieto** (hourly, 2 hours, some with change in Campo di Marte or Rifredi station), **Rome** (at least hourly, 2 hours, many stop at Orvieto en route, most connections require seat reservations, €44), **Naples** (hourly, 3–5 hours, some change in Rome), **Brindisi** (8/day, 8 hours with change in Bologna or Rome, €90), **Frankfurt** (1/day, 12 hours, 1–3 changes), **Paris** (3/day, 10–15 hours, 1–2 changes, important to reserve overnight train ahead), **Vienna** (1 direct overnight train, or 5/day with 1–3 changes, 10–16 hours).

Buses

The SITA bus station (100 yards west of the Florence train station on Via Santa Caterina da Siena) is traveler-friendly—a big old-school lot with numbered stalls and all the services you'd expect. Schedules for regional trips are posted everywhere, and TV monitors show imminent departures. Bus service drops dramatically on Sunday.

By Bus to: San Gimignano (hourly, 1.25–2 hours, change in Poggibonsi, less frequent on Sat–Sun, €6.25), **Siena** (2/hour, 1.25-hour *corse rapide* buses are fastest—even faster than the train, €7), **Volterra** (4/day, 2/day Sun, 2 hours, change in Colle Val d'Elsa, €7.60), Florence's **Amerigo Vespucci Airport** (2/hour, 30 minutes, €5). Buy tickets in the station if possible, as you'll pay 30 percent more if you buy tickets on the bus (except for the airport bus). Bus info: www.sitabus.it or tel. 800-373-760 (Mon–Fri 8:30–18:30, Sat 8:30–12:30, closed Sun); some schedules are listed in the *Florence Concierge Information* magazine.

Taxis

For small groups with more money than time, zipping to nearby towns by taxi can be a good value (e.g., €120 from your Florence hotel to your Siena hotel).

A more comfortable alternative is to hire a private car service. Florence-based **Transfer Chauffeur Service** has a fleet of modern vehicles with drivers who can whisk you between cities, to and from the cruise-ship port, and through the Tuscan countryside for around the same price as a cab (€130 for Florence to Siena, tel. 055-614-2182, mobile 338-862-3129, www.transfercs.com, marco .masala@transfercs.com, Marco).

Airports

For information on Florence's **Amerigo Vespucci Airport,** see page 421. For information on Pisa's **Galileo Galilei Airport,** see page 508.

Livorno Cruise-Ship Port

Florence's port is Livorno (sometimes called "Leghorn" in English), a coastal town located about 60 miles west of Florence.

Of the excursion options, **Florence** is the most time-consuming to reach (roughly two hours each way by public transit). **Pisa** is closer (about an hour for transit each way), and—since Pisa is well-connected with **Lucca**—it's possible to combine those two cities into one long day. (If doing this, save Pisa until after lunch to avoid the cruise crowds in the morning, and be aware that most shops and restaurants in Lucca are closed Sun–Mon.) No matter where you go, allow ample time to get back to your ship, as trains can be delayed.

Tourist Information: The TI kiosk is in Piazza del Municipio (daily June–Oct 8:00–18:00, Nov–May 9:00–17:00, arranges taxi-sharing and guides, tel. 0586-204-611). Public **WCs** are in the city hall, across the street from the TI.

Livorno Arrival and Connections

Cruise ships dock at the harbor on the western edge of the city, generally either at **Molo 75** (in the **Porto Mediceo**) or the adjacent **Molo Capitaniera.** The port is a mile away from the city center, which clusters around two nearby squares: **Piazza Grande** (ATMs, bus stop to Livorno Centrale train station) and **Piazza del Municipio** (TI, public WCs). These piazzas are several blocks apart, connected by Via Cogorano.

When you disembark at the port, you can join a cruise-line shore excursion, or hire your own taxi (explained later).

If you're going to Florence, Pisa, or Lucca on your own, it's a three-step process: first you'll head into downtown Livorno (15-minute walk along Via Grande to Piazza Grande), then take bus #1 to Livorno Centrale train station (€1, buy ticket at *tabacchi* and buy return ticket to save time, 8/hour, 10 minutes), and finally you'll catch the train to your destination.

Alternatively, from the port, cruise-line **shuttle buses** take you directly to the TI kiosk in Piazza del Municipio (about €5 round-trip). It's illegal for the **shuttle buses** to go all the way to the train station; on the rare occasion that your cruise offers this service for free, take it. Unfortunately, only a few **taxi** drivers at the port are wiling to take you directly to the train station (about €10–20).

Public Transportation Between Livorno and Florence, Pisa, and Lucca

Most connections are best by train. Roughly estimate 30 minutes to get between Livorno's port and its train station: 15-minute walk to the town center, then another 10 minutes by bus to the station.

To Florence: The train takes you to Florence's central Santa Maria Novella train station, Firenze S.M.N. (hourly, usually departs at :11 after the hour, 80 minutes, €7).

To Pisa: Trains runs to Pisa Centrale train station (2–3/hour, 20 minutes, €2, the few €8 Eurostar trains aren't much quicker).

To Lucca: Lucca works best in conjunction with Pisa, since they're on the same train line (hourly, 1 hour, transfer at Pisa Centrale, €4, check schedules as some routes take 1.5 hours).

Taxi Excursions

You can get a cab on your own at the port or in town. Since the cost is per cab rather than per person, you can minimize costs by gathering a small group of cruise-ship pals to go with you. Alternatively, the TI can arrange taxi-sharing. For a day trip, the cabbie drops you off for a designated amount of time in one or two cities. Ballpark round-trip fares: **Pisa**-€120, **Pisa and Lucca**-€220, **Florence**-€320 (some cabs fit 8 people, bringing the cost down to about €40 per person). The fare can vary, depending on the number of people and the season (taxis both at the port and in the city offer the same rates). Confirm a set fare beforehand, even though by law the driver must have the meter on (the price will usually be less than the meter).

Near Florence: Fiesole

Perched on a hill overlooking the Arno valley, Fiesole gives weary travelers a break in the action and—during the heat of summer—a breezy location from which to admire the city below. It's a small town with a main square, a few restaurants and shops, a few minor sights, and a great view. The ancient Etruscans knew a good spot when they saw one, and chose to settle here, establishing Fiesole about 400 years before the Romans founded Florence. Wealthy Renaissance families in pre-air-conditioning days also chose

Fiesole (fee-AY-zoh-lay) as a preferred vacation spot, building villas in the surrounding hillsides. Later, 19th-century Romantics spent part of the Grand Tour admiring the vistas, much like the hordes of tourists do today. Most come here for the view—the actual sights pale in comparison to those in Florence. Shutterbugs visit in the morning for the best light.

Getting to Fiesole: From Florence's Piazza San Marco, take bus #7—enjoying a peek at gardens, vineyards, orchards, and villas—to the last stop, Piazza Mino (4/hour, fewer after 20:00, 30 minutes, €1.20 or €2 if bought on bus; departs Florence from Piazza San Marco; wear your money belt—thieves frequent this bus). Taxis from Florence cost about €20 (ride to highest point you want to visit—La Reggia Ristorante for view terrace or Church of San Francesco—then explore downhill).

Tourist Information: The TI is immediately to the right of the Roman Archaeological Park (see next page), at Via Portigiani 3 (daily 9:30–18:30, closes at 16:00 on weekends in winter, tel. 055-598-720, info.turismo@comune.fiesole.fi.it).

Market Day: A modest selection of food and household items fills Via Portigiani, just off Piazza Mino, on Saturday mornings until 13:00.

Sights in Fiesole

Fiesole's main sights are either free or covered under one €10 combo-ticket, available at the Roman Theater (described below).

▲▲**Terrace with a View**—Catch the sunset (and your breath) from the view terrace just below La Reggia Ristorante. It's a steep seven-minute hike from the Fiesole bus stop: Face the bell tower and take Via San Francesco, on the left. (For similar views and a peek at residential Fiesole, climb up the opposite side of the square, along the road hugging the ridgeline.)

Church of San Francesco—For even more hill-climbing, continue up from the view terrace to this charming little church. The small scale and several colorful altar paintings make this church more enjoyable than Fiesole's Duomo (free, Mon–Sat 8:00–12:00 & 15:00–19:00, Sun 7:00–11:00 & 15:00–19:00, Via San Francesco 13, tel. 055-59175).

Ethnographic Missionary Museum—This eclectic little collection, hidden beneath the church of San Francesco, includes an Egyptian mummy, ancient coins, Chinese Buddhas, and the *in* *situ* ruins of a third-century Etruscan wall (donation suggested, Tue–Sun 7:00–12:00 & 15:00–19:00, closed Mon, unmarked door inside church leads to cloisters and museum).

Duomo—While this church has a drab 19th-century exterior, the interior is worth a look, if only for the blue-and-white glazed Giovanni della Robbia statue of St. Romulus over the entry door (free, daily 10:00–17:00, across Piazza Mino from the bus stop).

Roman Theater and Archaeological Park—Occasionally used today for plays, this well-preserved theater held up to 2,000 people. The site's other ruins are, well, ruined, and lacking in explanation. But the valley view and peaceful setting are lovely (€10 combo-ticket also covers Civic and Bandini museums, daily 10:00–18:00; from the bus stop cross Piazza Mino, heading toward the back of the Duomo). Warning: They have a greedy habit of forcing visitors to pay extra for special exhibits (often totaling around €12)—more than this sight is worth.

Civic Museum—Located within the Archaeological Park, the museum imparts insight into Fiesole's Etruscan and Roman roots with well-displayed artifacts and with a few English description sheets in the corners (covered by €10 combo-ticket, daily 10:00–18:00).

Bandini Museum—This petite museum displays the wooden panels of lesser-known Gothic and Renaissance painters as well as the glazed terra-cotta figures of Andrea della Robbia (covered by €10 combo-ticket, daily 10:00–18:00, behind Duomo at Via Dupre 1).

Sleeping in Fiesole

(€1 = about $1.25, country code: 39)

$ **Villa le Scalette** has six clean, tidy rooms a short distance from the bus stop on Piazza Mino (Db-€85–100, family deals, air-con, Wi-Fi, elevator, Via Cannelle 1, tel. 055-597-8484, fax 055-597-9970, www.villascalette.it, info@villascalette.it, Marco). From the square, take Via Portigiani to Via Cannelle, a stepped alleyway.

$ **Hotel Villa Bonelli** in Fiesole has three stars, 20 dim, outdated rooms, an abandoned ambience, and a good price (Sb-€70, Db-€90, Tb-€100, air-con, free Wi-Fi, 250 yards from bus stop up Via Gramsci, go right on Via Poeti to #1, tel. 055-59-513, fax 055-598-942, www.hotelvillabonelli.com, info@hotelvillabonelli.com).

Eating in Fiesole

These two restaurants are on Piazza Mino, where the bus from Florence stops.

Ristorante Perseus, a local favorite, serves authentic Tuscan dishes at a fair price in a rambling interior. They also have seating at a few sidewalk tables or on a shady garden terrace in fair weather (daily 12:30–14:30 & 19:30–23:30, tel. 055-59-143, Leonardo).

Ristorante Aurora is an upscale alternative with a view terrace overlooking the city of Florence (daily 12:00–14:30 & 19:00–22:30, tel. 055-59-363).

Picnics: Fiesole is made-to-order for a scenic and breezy picnic. Grab a pastry at Fiesole's best *pasticceria,* **Alcedo** (head up the main drag from the bus stop to Via Gramsci 27). Round out your goodies at the **Co-op** supermarket on Via Gramsci before walking up to the panoramic terrace. Or, for more convenience and less view, picnic at the shaded park on the way to the view terrace (walk up Via San Francesco about halfway to the terrace, and climb the stairs to the right).

PISA AND LUCCA

Florence is within easy striking distance of a number of great cities—as their fortifications attest. Along with Siena (which merits solo coverage in another chapter), Pisa and Lucca show that Florence wasn't the only power and cultural star of the late Middle Ages and Renaissance.

Pisa's famous Field of Miracles (Leaning Tower, Duomo, and Baptistery) is touristy but worth a visit. Lucca, contained within its fine Renaissance wall, has a charm that causes many connoisseurs of Italy to claim it as a favorite stop.

The two towns are 30 minutes from each other by hourly bus. Each is a 90-minute train ride from Florence and well-served by excellent highways. Using public transportation, you could day-trip from Florence to both cities within the same day. But with more time, spend at least a half-day in Pisa and an overnight in Lucca. For example, take the train to Pisa, do your sightseeing, catch the bus to Lucca late in the afternoon, enjoy the evening scene, and stay the night. Sightsee  Lucca the next day, then move on to your next destination by train.

Pisa

In A.D. 1200, Pisa's power peaked. For nearly three centuries (1000–1300), Pisa rivaled Venice and Genoa as a sea-trading power, exchanging European goods for luxury items in Muslim lands. As a port near the mouth of the Arno River (six miles from the coast), the city enjoyed easy access to the Mediterranean, plus the protection of sitting a bit upstream. The Romans had made it a navy base, and by medieval times it was a major player.

Pisa's 150-foot galleys cruised the Mediterranean, gaining control of the islands of Corsica, Sardinia, and Sicily, and trading with other Europeans, Muslims, and Byzantine Christians as far south as North Africa and as far east as Syria. European Crusaders hired Pisan boats to carry them and their supplies as they headed off to conquer the Muslim-held Holy Land. The Pisan "Republic" prided itself on its independence from both popes and emperors. The city used its sea-trading wealth to build the grand monuments of the Field of Miracles, including the now-famous Leaning Tower.

But the Pisan fleet was routed in battle by Genoa (1284, at Meloria, off Livorno), their overseas outposts were taken away, the port silted up, and Pisa was left high and dry, with only its Field of Miracles and its university keeping it on the map.

Pisa's three important sights—the Duomo, Baptistery, and the Tower—float regally on the best lawn in Italy. The style throughout is Pisa's very own "Pisan Romanesque." Even as the church was being built, Piazza del Duomo was nicknamed the "Campo dei Miracoli," or Field of Miracles, for the grandness of the undertaking.

The Tower has reopened after a decade of restoration and topple-prevention. To ascend, you'll have to make a reservation when you buy your €15 ticket (for details, see page 500).

Planning Your Time

For most visitors, Pisa is a touristy quickie—seeing the Tower, visiting the square, and wandering through the church are 90 percent of their Pisan thrill. But it's a shame to skip the rest of the city. Considering Pisa's historic importance and the wonderful ambience created by its rich architectural heritage and the vibrant student population, the city deserves a half-day visit. For many, the lack of tourists outside the Field of Miracles is both a surprise and a relief.

By car, it's best to leave the freeway at *Pisa Nord* and use the big parking lot (described in "Arrival in Pisa—By Car," later). From there, a regular city bus shuttles you to the Field of Miracles. By

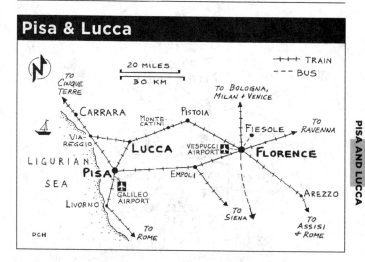

Pisa & Lucca

20 MILES
30 KM

+++ TRAIN
--- BUS

TO CINQUE TERRE

TO BOLOGNA, MILAN + VENICE

CARRARA

MONTE-CATINI

PISTOIA

FIESOLE

TO RAVENNA

VIA-REGGIO

LUCCA

VESPUCCI AIRPORT

FLORENCE

LIGURIAN

PISA

EMPOLI

SEA

GALILEO AIRPORT

AREZZO

LIVORNO

TO SIENA

TO ASSISI + ROME

TO ROME

DCH

train, it's a snap (and train travelers may need to change trains in Pisa anyway). From Pisa Centrale train station, head to the Tower, either by following my walk through the town center, or hopping on the bus to go directly there (a 15-minute ride each way).

If you want to climb the Tower, go straight to the ticket office to snag an appointment—usually for a couple of hours later. For an extra €2, you can book a time online (at least 15 days in advance) at www.opapisa.it. If you'll be seeing both the town and the Field of Miracles, plan on a six-hour stop. If just blitzing the Field of Miracles, three hours is the minimum. Spending the night lets you savor a great Italian city scene.

If you're day-tripping to Pisa from Lucca, or doing a Lucca/Pisa day trip from Florence, note that a handy bus runs hourly between the Field of Miracles and Lucca, saving time and hassle (30 minutes, €3; more details on page 508).

Orientation to Pisa

The city of Pisa is framed on the north by the Field of Miracles (Leaning Tower) and on the south by Pisa Centrale train station. The Arno River flows east to west, bisecting the city. Walking

from Pisa Centrale train station directly to the Tower takes about 30 minutes (but allow up to an hour if you take my self-guided walk). The two main streets for tourists and shoppers are

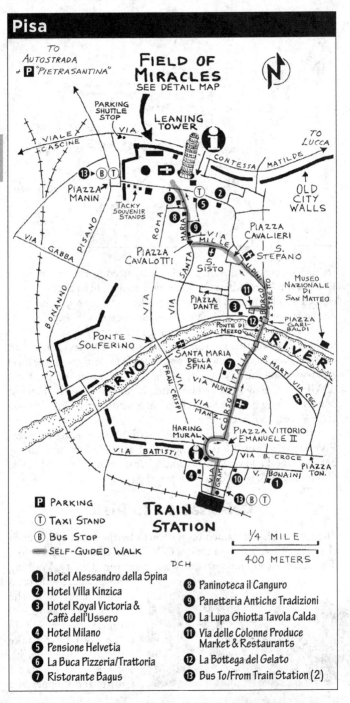

Pisa

Pisa

TO AUTOSTRADA & P "PIETRASANTINA"

FIELD OF MIRACLES
SEE DETAIL MAP

N

PARKING SHUTTLE STOP

VIA

LEANING TOWER

VIALE CASCINE

TO LUCCA

CONTESSA MATILDE

OLD CITY WALLS

PIAZZA MANIN

TACKY SOUVENIR STANDS

ROMA

VIA GABBA

VIA BONANNO PISANO

PISANO

SANTA MARIA

PIAZZA CAVALLOTTI

PIAZZA CALLOTTI

S. SISTO

VIA MILLE

PIAZZA CAVALIERI

S. STEFANO

ULDINI

BORGO STRETTO

MUSEO NAZIONALE DI SAN MATTEO

PIAZZA DANTE

VIA

PONTE SOLFERINO

ARNO

SANTA MARIA DELLA SPINA

FRAU CRISPI

PONTE DI MEZZO

PIAZZA GARI-BALDI

RIVER

VIA NUNZ

CORSO ITALIA

S. MART

VIA CECI

VIA MANZ

HARING MURAL

PIAZZA VITTORIO EMANUELE II

VIA BATTISTI

VIA B. CROCE

PIAZZA TON.

V. BONAINI

VIA GRAMF

TRAIN STATION

DCH

P PARKING
T TAXI STAND
B BUS STOP
— SELF-GUIDED WALK

¼ MILE
400 METERS

1 Hotel Alessandro della Spina
2 Hotel Villa Kinzica
3 Hotel Royal Victoria & Caffè dell'Ussero
4 Hotel Milano
5 Pensione Helvetia
6 La Buca Pizzeria/Trattoria
7 Ristorante Bagus

8 Paninoteca il Canguro
9 Panetteria Antiche Tradizioni
10 La Lupa Ghiotta Tavola Calda
11 Via delle Colonne Produce Market & Restaurants
12 La Bottega del Gelato
13 Bus To/From Train Station (2)

Via Santa Maria (running south from the Tower) and Corso Italia/Borgo Stretto (running north from the station).

Tourist Information

One TI is about 200 yards from Pisa Centrale train station—exit and walk straight up the left side of the street to the big circular Piazza Vittorio Emanuele II. The TI is on the left, around the corner from #16 (Mon–Sat 9:00–19:00, Sun 9:00–16:00, tel. 050-42291, www.pisaturismo.it). Another, less-enthusiastic TI is east of the Tower, in the Duomo Museum (daily April–Sept 9:30–19:30, Oct–March 10:00–17:00). There's also a TI at the airport (daily 11:00–23:00).

PISA AND LUCCA

Arrival in Pisa

By Train: Most trains (and visitors) arrive at Pisa Centrale station, about a mile south of the Tower and Field of Miracles. A few trains also stop at the smaller Pisa S. Rossore station, which is just four blocks from the Tower (not all trains stop here, but if yours does, hop off).

Pisa Centrale train station has a baggage-check desk—look for *deposito bagagli* (€3/bag for 12 hours, daily 6:00–21:00, they photocopy your passport to check ID). As you get off the train, it's to the right at the far end of platform 1, behind the nonfunctional lockers (installed just days before 9/11, and never used).

To get from this station to the Field of Miracles, you can **walk** (get free map from TI, 30 minutes direct, 60 minutes if you follow my self-guided walk), take a **taxi** (€7–10, tel. 050-541-600, taxi stand at station), or go by **bus.** Take bus LAM Rossa (4–6/hour, after 20:00 3/hour, 15 minutes), which stops across the street from the train station, in front of the NH Cavalieri Hoteles. Buy a €1 bus ticket from the *tabacchi*/magazine kiosk in the train station's main hall or at any *tabacchi* shop (€1.50 if you buy it on board, smart to have exact change, good for 1 hour, round-trip permitted). Before getting on the bus, confirm that it is indeed going to "Campo dei Miracoli" (ask driver, a local, or TI) or risk taking a long tour of Pisa's suburbs. The correct buses let you off at Piazza Manin, in front of the gate to the Field of Miracles; drivers make sure tourists don't miss the stop.

To return to the train station from the Tower, catch the bus in front of the BNL bank, across the street from where you got off (again, confirm the destination—"Stazione Centrale"). You'll also find a taxi stand 30 yards from the Tower (at Bar Duomo).

To get from **Pisa S. Rossore train station** to the Field of Miracles, it's just a four-block walk: Follow Viale delle Cascine east, continuing as it turns into Via Contessa Matilde, and follow signs to *La Torre*—or just head toward the dome of the Baptistery. From this station, the nearest TI is the one at the Duomo Museum.

By Car: Driving in the city center will likely net you a steep fine (cameras catch you and the city sends you a ticket by mail). Instead, use the big Pietrasantina parking lot, designed for tour buses (which pay €110 to park) and tourists with cars (who park for free). To reach the parking lot, exit the autostrada at *Pisa Nord* and follow signs to *Pisa* (on the left). Pass the second traffic light and turn left toward the city center. Go straight, following the *Bus Parking* signs, until you see the gas station. The parking lot is on the left. Here you'll find a cafeteria, WC, lots of big buses, and a bus stop for the Line C shuttle that goes back and forth between the lot and the Largo Cocco Griffi bus stop, just behind the walls of the Field of Miracles (€1, buy round-trip ticket on board, daily 8:30–19:20, 6/hour). Or, if you have more time and want to follow my self-guided walk through Pisa to the Field of Miracles, take bus LAM Rossa to Pisa Centrale train station (€1 if you buy ticket at parking-lot cafeteria, or €1.50 if purchased on board, 4–6/hour, after 20:00 3/hour, en route also stops near the Tower).

By Plane: For details on Pisa's Galileo Galilei Airport, see page 508.

Helpful Hints

Markets: An open-air **produce market** attracts picnickers to Piazza della Vettovaglie, one block north of the Arno River near Ponte di Mezzo, and nearby Piazza Sant'Uomobuono (Mon–Sat 7:00–18:00, main section closes at 13:00, closed Sun). A **street market**—with more practical goods than food—bustles on Wednesday and Saturday mornings between Via del Brennero and Via Paparrelle (8:00–13:00, just outside of wall, about 6 blocks east of the Tower).

Festivals: The first half of June has many events, culminating in a celebration for Pisa's patron saint (June 16–17).

Local Guide: Dottore Vincenzo Riolo is a great guide for Pisa and the surrounding area (€130/3 hours, mobile 338-211-2939, www.pisatour.it, info@pisatour.it).

Tours: To get beyond the tourist mobs and understand the cultural powerhouse that was Pisa, consider the "Walking in Pisa" tour. Local guides lead a two- to three-hour walking tour in English (and Italian) that covers the city rather than the famous Tower sights. (€12, ask at hotel or check website for times, tel. 050-830-253, mobile 328-144-6855 after hours, www.pisatour.it, Vincenzo).

Self-Guided Walk

Welcome to Pisa: From Pisa Centrale Train Station to the Tower

A leisurely one-hour stroll from the station to the Tower is a great way to get acquainted with the more subtle virtues of this Renaissance city. Because almost none of the hordes who descend daily on the Tower bothers with the rest of the town, you'll find most of Pisa to be delightfully untouristy—a student-filled classy Old World town with an Arno-scape much like its upstream rival, Florence. Pisa is pretty small, with just 100,000 people. But its 45,000 students keep it lively, especially at night.

• *From Pisa Centrale train station, walk north up Viale Gramsci to the circular square called...*

Piazza Vittorio Emanuele II

As Pisa was considered strategic in World War II, both the train station and its main bridge were targeted. For that reason, 40 per-

cent of this district was destroyed. Looking at the makeshift walls that surround the square, you may think it's still a bombed-out zone. The piazza is being rebuilt to include an underground parking lot, but the project was delayed after workers accidentally damaged an ancient structure while digging. The entire wall of a building just to the left of the piazza was painted by American artist Keith Haring in 1989 to create *Tuttomondo (Whole Wide World)*. Haring (who died of AIDS in 1990) brought New York City graffiti into the mainstream. This painting is a celebration of diversity, chaos, and the liveliness of our world, vibrating with energy. On the piazza, you'll also find a TI.

• *Walk up Corso Italia to the river.*

Corso Italia

Cutting through the center of town, this is Pisa's main drag. As it leaves Piazza Vittorio Emanuele II, look to the right to see the circa-1960 wall map of Pisa with a steam train (on the wall of the bar on the corner). You'll also see plenty of youthful fashions, as kids are out making the scene here. Be on guard for pickpockets—too young to arrest, they can only be kicked out of town. Pushed out of their former happy hunting grounds, the Field of Miracles, they now work the crowds here, often dressed as tourists.

• *Follow the pedestrianized Corso Italia straight north to the Arno River and Ponte di Mezzo. Stop in the center of the bridge.*

Ponte di Mezzo

This modern bridge, constructed on the same site where the Romans built one, marks the center of Pisa. In the Middle Ages, this bridge (like Florence's Ponte Vecchio) was lined with shops. It's been destroyed several times by floods and in 1943 by British and American bombers. Enjoy the view from the center of the bridge, with its long lines of elegant mansions recalling days of trading glory—the cityscape feels a bit like Venice's Grand Canal. Pisa sits on shifting delta sand, making construction tricky. The entire town leans. With innovative arches above ground and below, architects didn't stop the leaning—but they have made buildings that wobble without falling down.

• *Cross the bridge to...*

Piazza Garibaldi

This square is named for the charismatic leader of the Risorgimento, the unification movement that led to Italian independence in 1870. Knowing Pisa was strongly nationalist, Garibaldi came here when wounded to be nursed back to health. Many Pisans died in the national struggle. **La Bottega del Gelato,** Pisa's favorite gelato place, is on Piazza Garibaldi (daily 11:30–24:00). You can side-trip about 100 yards downstream to **Caffè dell'Ussero** (famous for its fine 14th-century red terra-cotta original facade, at #28, Sun–Fri 7:00–21:00, closed Sat) and browse its time-warp interior, lined with portraits and documents from the struggle for Italian independence.

• *Continue north up the elegantly arcaded...*

Borgo Stretto

Welcome to Pisa's main shopping street. On the right, the Church of St. Michael, with its fine Pisan Romanesque facade, still sports some 16th-century graffiti. I'll bet you can see some modern graffiti across the street. Students have been pushing their causes here—or simply defacing things—for five centuries.

From here, look farther up the street and notice how it undulates like a flowing river. In the sixth century B.C., Pisa was born when two parallel rivers were connected by canals. This street echoes the flow of one of those canals. An 11th-century landslide rerouted the second river, destroying ancient Pisa, and the entire city regenerated.

• *After a few steps, detour left onto Via delle Colonne, and walk one block down to...*

Piazza delle Vettovaglie

Pisa's historic market square, Piazza delle Vettovaglie, is lively day and night. Its Renaissance loggia has hosted the fish and vegetable market for generations. The stalls are set up in this piazza during the morning (Mon–Sat 7:00–13:00, closed Sun), and stay open later in the neighboring piazza to the west (Piazza Sant'Uomobuono, Mon–Sat 7:00–18:00, closed Sun). You could cobble together a picnic from the sandwich shops and fruit-and-veggie stalls ringing these squares.

• *Continue north on Borgo Stretto another 100 yards, passing an ugly bomb site on the right, with its horrible 1960s reconstruction. Take the second left on nondescript Via Ulisse Dini (it's not obvious—turn left immediately at the arcade's end, just before the pharmacy). This leads to Pisa's historic core, Piazza dei Cavalieri.*

Piazza dei Cavalieri

With its old clock and colorfully decorated palace, this piazza was once the seat of the independent Republic of Pisa's government. In around 1500, Florence decapitated Pisa and made this square the training place for the knights of its navy. The statue of Cosimo I de' Medici shows the Florentine who ruled Pisa in the 16th cen-

tury. With a foot on a dolphin, he reminded all who passed that the Florentine navy controlled the sea—at least a little of it. The frescoes on the exterior of the square's buildings, though damaged by salty sea air and years of neglect, reflect Pisa's fading glory under the Medicis.

With Napoleon, this complex of grand buildings became part of the University of Pisa. The university is one of Europe's oldest, with roots in a law school that dates back as far as the 11th century. In the mid-16th century, the city was a hotbed of controversy, as spacey professors like Galileo Galilei studied the solar system—with results that challenged the Church's powerful doctrine. More recently, the blind tenor Andrea Bocelli attended law school in Pisa before embarking on his well-known musical career.

From here, take Via Corsica (to the left of the clock). The humble **Church of San Sisto,** ahead on the left (side entrance on Via Corsica), is worth a quick look. With simple bricks, assorted reused columns, heavy walls, and few windows, this was the typical Romanesque style before the more lavish Pisan Romanesque of the Field of Miracles structures.

Follow Via Corsica as it turns into Via dei Mille (and grab a quick bite at the recommended **Panetteria Antiche Tradizioni**), and then turn right on Via Santa Maria, which leads north, through increasingly touristy claptrap, directly to the Field of Miracles and the Tower.

Sights in Pisa

▲▲▲Leaning Tower—A 15-foot lean from the vertical makes the Tower one of Europe's most recognizable images. You can see it for free; it's always viewable. And, after years of stabilization efforts, it's open again if you want to climb it for a fee.

Rising up alongside the cathedral, the Tower is nearly 200 feet tall and 55 feet wide, weighing 14,000 tons and currently leaning at a five-degree angle (15 feet off the vertical axis). It started to lean almost immediately after construction began. There are eight stories—a simple base, six stories of columns (forming arcades), and a belfry on top. The inner structural core is a hollow cylinder built of limestone bricks, faced with white marble barged here from San Giuliano, northeast of the city. The thin columns of the open-air arcades make the heavy Tower seem light and graceful.

The Tower was built over two centuries by at least three different architects. You can see how each successive architect tried to correct the leaning problem—once halfway up (after the fourth story), once at the belfry on the top.

The first stones were laid in 1173, probably under the direction of the architect Bonanno Pisano (who also designed the Duomo's bronze back door). Five years later, just as they'd finished the base and the first arcade, someone said, "Is it just me, or does that look crooked?" The heavy Tower—resting on a very shallow 13-foot foundation—was obviously sinking on the south side into the marshy, multilayered, unstable soil. (Actually, all the Campo's buildings tilt somewhat.) They carried on anyway, until they'd finished four stories (the base, plus three arcade floors). Then, construction suddenly halted—no one knows why—and for a century the Tower sat half-finished and visibly leaning.

Around 1272, the next architect continued, trying to correct the problem by angling the next three stories backward, in the opposite direction of the lean. The project then again sat mysteriously idle for nearly another century. Finally, Tommaso Pisano put the belfry on the top (c. 1350–1372), also kinking it backward.

After the Tower's completion, several attempts were made to stop its slow-motion fall. The architect-artist-writer Giorgio Vasari reinforced the base (1550), and it actually worked. But in

Pisa's Field of Miracles

▢ GRASS ON FIELD OF MIRACLES
← ENTRANCE
Ⓣ TAXI STAND
Ⓑ BUS STOP
Ⓟ PARKING

TO AUTOSTRADA
Ⓟ "PIETRASANTINA"

V. CASCINE
PARKING SHUTTLE STOP
VIA CONTESSA

VIA CARLO

LARGO C. GRIFFI
Ⓟ

VIA NICO

JEWISH CEMETERY

CAMEO

Ⓑ ④

PIAZZA MANIN
③ Ⓑ Ⓣ

VIA PISANO

BAPTISTERY
PORTA LEONE
TACKY SOUVENIR STANDS
① ❶

CAMPOSANTO CEMETERY

MATILDE

WC

① ❶

CITY WALLS

DUOMO

① ❶

LEANING Tower

VIA MAFFI

MUSEUM OF THE SINOPIAS

VIA ROMA

LA BUCA

V. S. MARIA

Ⓣ

Duomo MUSEUM

BAR DUOMO

200 YARDS
200 METERS

V. A. TASSI

TO REST OF THE TOWN & TRAIN STATION

DCH

❶ Ticket Offices (2 Locations)
❷ Tower Bag Check
❸ Bus to Train Station
❹ Bus to Lucca

PISA AND LUCCA

1838, well-intentioned engineers pumped out groundwater, destabilizing the Tower and causing it to increase its lean at a rate of a millimeter per year.

It got so bad that in 1990 the Tower was closed for repairs, and $30 million was spent trying to stabilize it. Engineers dried the soil with steam pipes, anchored the Tower to the ground with steel cables, and buried 600 tons of lead on the north side as a counterweight (not visible)—all with little success. The breakthrough came when they drilled 15-foot holes in the ground on the north side and sucked out 60 tons of soil, allowing the Tower to sink on the north side and straighten out its lean by about six inches.

In addition to gravity, erosion threatens the Tower. Since its construction, 135 of the Tower's 180 marble columns have had to be replaced. Stone decay, deposits of lime and calcium phosphate,

Field of Miracles Tickets

Pisa has a combo-ticket scheme designed to get you into its neglected secondary sights: the Baptistery, Camposanto Cemetery, Duomo Museum, and Museum of the Sinopias (fresco pattern museum).

For €5, you get your choice of one of the following: the Baptistery, Camposanto Cemetery, Museum of the Sinopias, or Duomo Museum; for two of these sights or one plus the Duomo, the cost is €6; for three of the above you pay €8; and for the works, you'll pay €10 (credit cards accepted). By comparison, the Duomo alone is a bargain (€2).

You can buy any of these tickets either behind the Leaning Tower or at the Museum of the Sinopias (near Baptistery, almost suffocated by souvenir stands). Both ticket offices have big yellow triangle-shaped signs.

No matter what ticket you get, you'll have to pay an additional €15 if you want to climb the Tower. Tickets for the Tower are sold at the ticket offices or online at least 15 days in advance at www.opapisa.it (€2 fee).

accumulations of dirt and moss, cracking from the stress of the lean—all of these are factors in its decline.

Thanks to the Tower's lean, there are special trouble spots. The lower south side (which is protected from cleansing rain and wind) is black from dirty airborne particles, while the stone on the upper areas, though clean, has more decay (from eroding rain and wind).

The Tower, now stabilized, is getting cleaned. Cracks are filled, and accumulations removed, using atomized water sprays and poultices of various solvents.

All the work to shore up, straighten, and clean the Tower has probably turned the clock back a few centuries. In fact, art historians figure it leans today as much as it did for Galileo.

Cost and Hours: €15, kids under 8 not allowed, daily March 9:00–17:00, April–mid-June and Sept 8:30–20:30, mid-June–Aug 8:00–23:30, Oct 9:00–19:30, Nov–Feb 10:00–16:30, ticket office opens 30 minutes early, last entry 30 minutes before closing.

Reservations: Reservations are required to climb the Tower. You can reserve in person or, for an extra €2, book a time at www.opapisa.it.

Online bookings are accepted no more than 45 days—and no

fewer than 15 days—in advance. You must pick up your ticket(s) at least 30 minutes before your time slot. Show up 10 minutes before your appointment at the meeting point outside the ticket office.

To reserve in person, go to the ticket office behind the Tower, on the left in the yellow building, or to the Museum of the Sinopias ticket office hidden behind the souvenir stalls. You choose a 30-minute time slot for your visit. If you visit in summer, it will likely be a couple of hours before you're able to go up (see the rest of the monuments and grab lunch while waiting). The wait is usually much shorter at the beginning or end of the day.

Climbing the Tower: Every 30 minutes, 40 people can clamber up the 294 tilting stairs to the top. Note that children under age eight are not allowed to go up. Children ages 8–12 must be accompanied by—and hold hands at all times with—an adult. Teenagers between 12 and 18 are allowed with an adult.

You can't take any bags up the Tower, but day bag–size lockers are available at the ticket office—show your Tower ticket to check your bag. You may check your bag 10 minutes before your reservation time and must pick it up immediately after your Tower visit.

You wind your way up the outside of the Tower along a spiraling ramp. For your 30-minute time slot, figure about 10 minutes to climb and 10 to descend, leaving about 10 minutes for vertigo at the top. Even though it's technically a "guided" visit, that only means you're accompanied by a museum guard who makes sure you don't stay up past your scheduled appointment time.

Caution: There are skinny railings, the steps are slanted, and rain makes the marble slippery. Anyone with balance issues of any sort should think twice before ascending.

▲▲Duomo (Cathedral)—The gargantuan Pisan Romanesque cathedral, with its carved pulpit by Giovanni Pisano, is artistically more important than its more famous bell tower.

Begun in 1063, the Duomo is the centerpiece of the Field of Miracles' complex of religious buildings. The architect Buschetto created the style of Pisan Romanesque that set the tone for the Baptistery and Tower.

The **bronze back doors** (Porta San Ranieri) at the Tower end were designed by Bonnano Pisano (c. 1186). The doors have 24 different panels that show Christ's story using the same simple, skinny figures found in Byzantine icons. (The doors are actually copies; the originals are

housed—but not always on display—in the Duomo Museum.) Cast using the lost-wax technique, these doors were an inspiration for Lorenzo Ghiberti's bronze doors in Florence.

The 320-foot nave was the longest in Christendom when it was built. The striped marble and arches-on-columns give it an exotic, almost mosque-like feel. Dim light filters in from the small upper windows of the galleries, where the women worshipped. The gilded coffered ceiling has shields of Florence's Medicis, including the round symbols (pills). This powerful family—who began as doctors, later became cloth merchants, and finally bankers—took over Pisa after its glory days.

In the apse (behind the altar) is a **mosaic** (c. 1300, partly done by Cimabue) showing Christ as the Ruler of All (Pantocrator) between Mary and John the Evangelist. Looking up into the **dome,** the heavens open, and rings of saints and angels spiral up to a hazy God. Beneath the dome is an inlaid-marble Cosmati-style mosaic floor.

The 15-foot-tall octagonal **pulpit** by Giovanni Pisano (c. 1250–1319) is the last, biggest, and most complex of the four pulpits by the Pisano father-and-son team. Christ's life unfolds in a series of panels crammed with figures. Giovanni left no stone uncarved in his pursuit of beauty. Originally, this and the other pulpits were frosted with paint, gilding, and colored pastes.

The bronze **incense burner** that hangs from the ceiling (near the pulpit) is a replica of the one that supposedly caught teenage Galileo's attention when a gust of wind set the lamp swinging. He timed the swings, and realized that the burner swung back and forth in the same amount of time regardless of how wide the arc. (This pendulum motion was a constant that allowed Galileo to measure this ever-changing universe.) Legend says the Pisa-born Galileo also threw objects off the Tower to time their falls, fascinated by gravity.

Pause at the **tomb of Holy Roman Emperor Henry VII,** the German king (c. 1275–1313) who invaded Italy and was welcomed by Pisans as a leader of unity and peace. Unfortunately, Henry took ill and died young, leaving Ghibelline Pisa at the mercy of its Guelph rivals, such as rising Florence. Pisa never recovered.

In a glass-lined casket on the altar, Pisa's patron saint—**St. Ranieri**—lies mummified, encased in silver at his head and feet, with his hair shirt covering his body. The son of a rich sea-trader, Ranieri (1117–1161) was a hard-partying touring musician who was later inspired to give away his money, join a monastery, and give spirited sermons from the Duomo pulpit.

Cost, Hours, Information: €2; Mon–Sat March 10:00–18:00, April–Sept 10:00–20:00, Oct 10:00–19:00, Nov–Feb 10:00–17:00; Sun 13:00–17:30 all year; last entry 30 minutes before closing. Shorts are OK as long as they're not too short, and shoulders should be covered (although it's not really enforced). Big backpacks are not allowed, nor is storage provided. If you have a day bag, carry it.

▲▲▲**Field of Miracles (Campo dei Miracoli)**—Scattered across a golf course–green lawn are five grand buildings: the cathedral (or Duomo), its bell tower (the Leaning Tower), the

Baptistery, the hospital (today's Museum of the Sinopias), and the Camposanto Cemetery (see map on page 499). The buildings are constructed from similar materials—bright white marble—and have comparable decoration. Each has a simple ground floor and rows of delicate columns and arches that form open-air arcades, giving the Campo a pleasant visual unity.

The style is dubbed Pisan Romanesque. Where traditional Romanesque has a heavy fortress-like feel—thick walls, barrel arches, few windows—Pisan Romanesque is light and elegant. At ground level, most of the structures have simple half-columns and arches. On the upper levels, you'll see a little of everything—tight rows of thin columns; pointed Gothic gables and prickly spires; Byzantine mosaics and horseshoe arches; and geometric designs (such as diamonds) and striped colored marbles inspired by mosques in Muslim lands.

Architecturally, the Campo is unique and exotic. Theologically, the Campo's buildings mark the main events of every Pisan's life: christened in the Baptistery, married in the Duomo, honored in ceremonies at the Tower, healed in the hospital, and buried in the Camposanto Cemetery.

Lining this field of artistic pearls is a gauntlet of Europe's tackiest souvenir stands, as well as dozens of amateur mimes "propping up" the Leaning Tower while tourists take photos.

▲Baptistery—Located in front of the Duomo, the round Baptistery is the biggest in Italy. It's interesting for its pulpit and interior ambience, and especially great for its acoustics.

The building is 180 feet tall—John the Baptist on top looks eye-to-eye with the tourists atop the nearly 200-foot Leaning Tower. Notice that the Baptistery leans nearly six feet to the north (the Tower leans 15 feet to the south). The building (begun 1153) is modeled on the circular domed Church of the Holy Sepulchre in Jerusalem, seen by Pisan Crusaders who occupied Jerusalem in 1099.

Inside, it's simple, spacious, and baptized with light. Tall arches encircle just a few pieces of religious furniture. In the center sits the **octagonal font** (1246, topped with a statue of the first baptist, John), which contains plenty of space for baptizing adults by immersion (the medieval custom), plus four wells for dunking babies.

Nicola Pisano's **pulpit** is arguably the world's first Renaissance sculpture. It's the first authenticated (signed) work by the "Giotto of sculpture," working in what came to be called the Renaissance style. The pulpit is a free-standing sculpture that has classical columns, realistic people and animals, and 3-D effects in the carved panels.

The speaker's platform stands on columns that rest on the backs of animals, representing Christianity's triumph over paganism. The relief panels, with scenes from the life of Christ, are more readable than the Duomo pulpit. Read left to right, starting from the back: Nativity, Adoration of the Magi, Presentation in the Temple, Crucifixion, Last Judgment.

Make a sound in here and it echoes for a good 10 seconds. A priest standing at the baptismal font (or a security guard today) can sing three tones within the 10 seconds—"Ave Maria"—and make a chord, singing haunting harmonies with himself. This medieval form of digital delay is due to the 250-foot-wide dome. Recent computer analysis suggests that the 15th-century architects who built the dome intended this building to function not just as a Baptistery, but also as a musical instrument. A security guard sings every half-hour, starting when the doors open in the morning. Climb 75 steps to the interior gallery (midway up) for an impressive view back down on the baptismal font.

Cost and Hours: €5, for combo-ticket see "Field of Miracles

Tickets" sidebar, daily March 9:00–17:30, April–Sept 8:00–19:30, Oct 8:30–19:00, Nov–Feb 10:00–17:00, last entry 30 minutes before closing.

Camposanto Cemetery—This site, bordering the Field of Miracles on the north, has been a cemetery since ancient times. Lined with faint frescoes, the ancient cemetery is famous for its "Holy Land" dirt, said to reduce a body into a skeleton within a day. Highlights are the building's cloistered open-air courtyard (with intricately carved arches); some ancient Roman and Greek sarcophagi; and the 1,000-square-foot 14th-century fresco, *The Triumph of Death*. The fresco captures Pisa's mood in the wake of the bubonic plague (1348), which killed one in three Pisans. Grim stuff, but appropriate for the Camposanto's permanent residents.

Cost and Hours: €5, for combo-ticket see "Field of Miracles Tickets" sidebar, same hours as Baptistery.

Museum of the Sinopias (Museo delle Sinopie)—Across from the Baptistery, housed in a 13th-century hospital (with its entrance nearly obscured by souvenir stands), this museum displays some of the original sketches (made on walls) that were used to make the frescoes in the Camposanto Cemetery.

This museum comes with two free short introductory videos that you can watch even without a ticket. Good students might want to start here first for this orientation to the square: a 10-minute 3-D computer tour of the complex, and a 15-minute story of the Tower, its tilt, and its fix.

"Sinopias" are sketches in red paint made directly on the wall, designed to guide the making of the final colored fresco. The master always did the sinopia himself; if he liked the results, his assistants made a "cartoon" by tracing the sinopia onto large sheets of paper *(cartone)*. Then the sinopia was plastered over and the assistants redrew the outlines, using the cartoon as a guide. While the plaster was still wet, the master and his team quickly filled in the color and details, producing the final frescoes (now on display at the Camposanto). These sinopias—never meant to be seen—were uncovered by the bombing and restoration of the Camposanto and brought here.

Cost and Hours: €5, for combo-ticket see "Field of Miracles Tickets" sidebar, same hours as Baptistery.

Duomo Museum (Museo dell'Opera del Duomo)—This museum behind the Leaning Tower is big on Pisan art, displaying treasures of the cathedral, paintings, silverware, and sculptures (from the 12th to 14th centuries, particularly by the Pisano dynasty), as well as ancient Egyptian, Etruscan, and Roman artifacts. It houses many of the original statues and much of the artwork that once adorned the Campo's buildings (where copies stand today), notably the statues by Nicola and Giovanni Pisano. You can stand face-to-face with the Pisanos' very human busts that once ringed the outside of the Baptistery. You'll see a mythical sculpted hippogriff (a medieval jackalope) and other oddities brought back from the Holy Land by Pisan Crusaders. The museum also has several large-scale wooden models of the Duomo, Baptistery, and Tower.

Cost and Hours: €5, for combo-ticket see "Field of Miracles Tickets" sidebar, same hours as Baptistery, Piazza Arcivescovado 18.

Museo Nazionale di San Matteo—On the river and in a former convent, this art museum displays 12th- to 15th-century sculptures, illuminated manuscripts, and paintings on wood by Martini, Masaccio, and others. This fine collection—especially its painted wood crucifixes—gives you a chance to see Pisan innovation in 11th- to 13th-century art, before Florence took the lead.

Cost and Hours: €4, Tue–Sat 8:30–19:00, Sun 8:30–13:00, closed Mon, near Piazza San Paolo at Lungarno Mediceo, a 5-minute walk upriver from the main bridge, tel. 050-541-865.

Sleeping in Pisa

To locate these hotels, see the map on page 492.

$$$ Hotel Alessandro della Spina, in a nondescript neighborhood near Pisa Centrale train station, has 16 elegant and colorful rooms, each named after a flower (Sb-€120, Db-€140, discounts off-season and for drop-ins, air-con, parking-€10/day; head straight out of train station, turn right on Viale F. Bonaini, and take the third right on Via Alessandro della Spina to find the hotel on your left at #5; tel. 050-502-777, fax 050-20583, www.hotel dellaspina.it, info@hoteldellaspina.it).

$$ Hotel Villa Kinzica has 30 tired but decent rooms with high ceilings, indifferent management, and a prime location just steps away from the Field of Miracles—ask for a room with a view of the Tower (Sb-€80, Db-€110, Tb-€126, Qb-€137, air-con, elevator, attached restaurant, Piazza Arcivescovado 2, tel. 050-560-419, fax 050-551-204, www.hotelvillakinzica.it, info@hotelvilla kinzica.it).

$$ Hotel Royal Victoria, a classy place on the Arno River, is conveniently located dead-center between the Tower and Pisa Centrale train station (D-€80, standard Db-€100, better Db-€130, suite-€190, family room-€200, check website for special deals, lush communal terrace, Lungarno Pacinotti 12, tel. 050-940-111, fax 050-940-180, www.royalvictoria.it, mail@royalvictoria.it, Piegaja family).

$ Hotel Milano, near Pisa Centrale train station, offers 10 spacious, recently remodeled rooms; ask for a room off the street

---

Sleep Code

(€1 = about $1.25, country code: 39)

S = Single, **D** = Double/Twin, **T** = Triple, **Q** = Quad, **b** = bathroom, **s** = shower only. Unless otherwise noted, credit cards are accepted, breakfast is included, and English is generally spoken.

To help you sort easily through these listings, I've divided the rooms into three categories based on the price for a standard double room with bath:

$$$ Higher Priced—Most rooms €120 or more.
  $$ Moderately Priced—Most rooms between €80-120.
    $ Lower Priced—Most rooms €80 or less.

Prices can change without notice; verify the hotel's current rates online or by email. For other updates, see www.ricksteves.com/update.

---

when you book (D-€55, Db-€78, breakfast extra, air-con, Via Mascagni 14, tel. 050-23-162, fax 050-44-237, www.hotelmilano.pisa.it, info@hotelmilano.pisa.it).

$ Pensione Helvetia is a no-frills homey, clean, and quiet inn just 100 yards from the Tower. Its 29 economical rooms are spread over four floors (no elevator); the lower your room number, the lower your altitude. They prefer reservations by phone or fax, but are trying to move into the Internet Age. Let them know your arrival time, since they don't ask for deposits to secure reservations (S-€37, Sb-€52, D-€48, Db-€65, vending-machine breakfast, ceiling fans, Via Don G. Boschi 31, tel. 050-553-084, www.pensione helvetiapisa.com, info@pensionehelvetiapisa.com, Michele).

Eating in Pisa

La Buca, a pizzeria-trattoria just a block from the Tower, is adequate and convenient for a quick lunch or dinner (Sat–Thu 12:00–15:00 & 18:00–22:30, closed Fri, at Via Santa Maria 171 and Via A. G. Tassi 6b, tel. 050-560-660).

Ristorante Bagus boasts trendy twists on Tuscan fare—their specialty is an extra-rare burger made with the famous Chianina beef. For a change from the basic Italian trattoria or tourist traps, this place promises an upscale lunch or dinner (€25 fixed-price meal, Mon–Fri 12:30–14:30 & 19:30–22:00, Sat 19:30–22:00 only, closed Sun, heading south on Corso Italia turn right on Via Nunziata and take your first right, Piazza dei Facchini 13, tel. 050-26196).

At **Paninoteca il Canguro,** friendly Fabio makes warm, hearty sandwiches to order. Try the popular primavera sandwich (Mon–Sat 10:00–24:00, closed Sun, Via Santa Maria 151, tel. 050-561-942).

Panetteria Antiche Tradizioni—not too be confused with another *panetteria* across the street—is a sandwich/bread shop with complete fixings for a picnic on the lawn at the Field of Miracles or a sit-down lunch ordered from their menu (limited pastas, soups, and salads). Build your own sandwich with homemade bread or focaccia, then choose fruit from the counter, fresh pastries from the window, and cold drinks or wine to round out your meal (daily 8:00–20:00, Via Santa Maria 66, mobile 347-675-2940).

Drop by cheery **La Lupa Ghiotta Tavola Calda** for a cheap, fast, and tasty meal a few steps from Pisa Centrale train station. It's got everything you'd want from a *ristorante* at half the price and with faster service (build your own salad—five ingredients for €4.50; Mon and Wed–Sat 12:15–15:00 & 19:15–23:30, Tue 12:15–15:00 only, closed Sun, Viale F. Bonaini 113, tel. 050-21018).

The street that houses the daily market, **Via delle Colonne** (a block north of the Arno, west of Borgo Stretto), has a few atmospheric mid-priced restaurants and several fun greasy take-out options.

Pisa Connections

Pisa is well-connected by trains, buses (particularly with Lucca), and highways, with a busy airport nearby.

From Pisa Centrale Station by Train to: Florence (2–3/hour, 1.25 hours, €6.50), **Rome** (hourly, many change in Florence, 3–4 hours, €45), **La Spezia,** gateway to Cinque Terre (about hourly, 1–1.5 hours, €12), **Siena** (2/hour, 1.75 hours, change at Empoli, €7), **Lucca** (1–2/hour, 30 minutes, bus is better, €3). Even the fastest trains stop in Pisa, so you might change trains here whether you plan to stop or not.

By Bus to Lucca: A handy bus connects the Field of Miracles with Lucca's Piazzale Verdi in 30 minutes with hourly departures (in Pisa, wait at the Vai Bus signpost, immediately outside the wall behind the Baptistery; buy €3 ticket on bus, toll-free tel. 800-602-947). This makes a half-day side-trip to Pisa from Lucca particularly easy.

By Car: The drive between Pisa and Florence is that rare case where the non-autostrada highway (free, more direct, and at least as fast) is a better deal than the autostrada.

By Plane: Pisa's **Galileo Galilei Airport** handles more and more international and domestic flights (TI open daily 11:00–23:00, cash machine, car-rental agencies, baggage storage from 8:00–20:00 only, €7/bag; self-service cafeteria, tel. 050-849-300, www.pisa-airport.com).

To get into **Pisa,** you can take bus LAM Rossa (4–6/hour, after 20:00 3/hour, 15 minutes, €1, departs from in front of the arrivals hall); a train (departs from the far left of the arrivals hall as you face the exits); or a taxi (€10–12).

You can connect to **Florence** easily by train (2/hour, 1.5 hours, €5.50, most transfer at Pisa Centrale) or by Terravision bus (about hourly, 1.25 hours, €10 one-way, ticket kiosk is at the right end of the arrivals hall as you're facing the exits, catch bus outside and to the far right of the bus parking lot, www.terravision.eu).

Lucca

Surrounded by well-preserved ramparts, layered with history, alternately quaint and urbane, Lucca charms its visitors. The city

is a paradox. Though it hasn't been involved in a war since 1430, it is Italy's most impressive fortress city, encircled by a perfectly intact wall. Most cities tear down their wall to make way for modern traffic. But Lucca's wall effectively keeps out both traffic and, it seems, the stress of the modern world. Locals are very protective of their wall, which they enjoy like a community roof garden.

Lucca, known for being Europe's leading producer of toilet paper and Kleenex (with a monopoly on the special machinery that makes it), is nothing to sneeze at. However, the town has no single monumental sight to attract tourists—it's simply a uniquely human and undamaged never-bombed city. Romanesque churches seem to be around every corner, as do fun-loving and shady piazzas filled with soccer-playing children. Still, it's hard to focus on anything in particular within the walls.

Locals say Lucca is like a cake with a cherry filling in the middle...every slice is equally good. Despite Lucca's charm, few tourists seem to put it on their maps, and it remains a city for the Lucchesi (loo-KAY-zee).

Orientation to Lucca

Tourist Information

The main TI is just inside the Porta Santa Maria gate, on Piazza Santa Maria (daily May–Oct 9:00–20:00, Nov–April 9:00–12:30

& 15:00–18:30, pricey Internet access, WCs, no-fee room booking, Piazza Santa Maria 35, tel. 0583-919-931, www.luccatourist.it, info@luccaturismo.it).

Another TI, on Piazzale Verdi, offers information, a no-fee room-booking service, and baggage check (daily 9:00–18:30, futuristic WC, bike rental, 80-minute city-walk audioguide-€9, additional audioguide-€3 more; bag storage-€1.50/hour per bag, they need to photocopy your passport; tel. 0583-583-150).

A third TI, at Piazza Curtatone, has the handiest baggage check near the train station (daily 9:00–17:30, bag storage-€1.50/day per bag; exit the station, cross the square, and it's just ahead on the right; tel. 0583-583-150).

Arrival in Lucca

To reach the city center from the **train** station, walk toward the walls and head left, to the entry at Porta San Pietro. Taxis are sparse, but try calling 0583-333-434 (ignore any recorded message—just wait for a live operator); a ride from the station to Piazza Anfiteatro costs about €6. There is no baggage check at the train station, but there is one at the TI in nearby Piazza Curtatone (see "Tourist Information," above).

Drivers: The key for drivers—don't try to drive within the walls. The old town is ringed by lots. Parking is always free in Piazzale Don Franco, a five-minute walk north of the city walls. Otherwise, try lots at Porta Santa Maria and Porta Sant'Anna, a.k.a. Vittorio Emanuele (€1/hour), or consider parking outside the gates near the train station or on the boulevard surrounding the city (meter rates vary; about €1/hour). Lucca's TIs have maps showing the location of free parking lots just outside the walls. Overnight parking (20:00–8:00) is free in the lots at Porta Santa Maria and Porta Sant'Anna/Vittorio Emanuele and €1.50/night at Ex-Caserma Mazzini, just inside Porta Elisa.

Helpful Hints

Combo-Tickets: A €6 combo-ticket includes visits to the Ilaria del Carretto tomb in San Martino Cathedral (€2), Cathedral Museum (€4), and San Giovanni Church (€2.50). A €5 combo-ticket combines the Guinigi Tower (€3.50) and the Clock Tower (€3.50). Yet another combo-ticket covers Palazzo Mansi and Villa Guinigi for €6.50 and is valid for three days (€4 each if purchased separately).

Shops and Museums Alert: Shops close most of Sunday and Monday mornings. Many museums are closed on Monday as well.

Markets: Lucca's atmospheric markets are worth visiting. Every third Sunday and the preceding Saturday of the month, one of the largest **antiques markets** in Italy unfurls in the blocks from Piazza Antelminelli to Piazza San Giovanni (8:00–19:00). The last weekend of the month, local artisans sell **arts and crafts** around town, mainly near the cathedral (also 8:00–19:00). At the **general market,** held Wednesdays and Saturdays, you'll find produce and household goods (8:30–13:00, from Porta Elisa to Porta San Jacopo on Via dei Bacchettoni).

Concerts: San Giovanni Church hosts one-hour concerts featuring a pianist and singers performing highlights from hometown composer Giacomo Puccini (€17 at the door, some hotels offer tickets for the same price or cheaper, April–Oct nightly at 19:00, Nov–March check schedule and location at www .puccinielasualucca.com).

Festival: On September 13 and 14, the city celebrates Volto Santo ("Holy Face"), with a procession of the treasured local crucifix and a fair in Piazza Antelminelli.

Internet Access: You can get online at the main **TI** (see "Tourist Information," earlier) or at **Betty Blue,** a wine bar handy to the recommended launderette (€4.50/hour, two terminals and cables to plug in your laptop, Thu–Tue 11:00–24:00, closed Wed, Via del Gonfalone 16, tel. 0583-492-166).

Laundry: Lavanderia Self-Service Niagara is just off Piazza Santa Maria at Via Rosi 26 (€9 wash and dry, daily 7:00–23:00).

Bike Rental: Several places with identical prices cluster around Piazza Santa Maria (€2.50/hour, €12.50/day, tandem bikes available, free helmets, daily about 9:00–19:30 or sunset). These easygoing shops rent good bikes: **Antonio Poli** (Piazza Santa Maria 42, tel. 0583-493-787, enthusiastic Cristiana) and **Cicli Bizzarri** (Piazza Santa Maria 32, tel. 0583-496-682, Australian Dely). At the west end of town, the **TI** on Piazzale Verdi rents bikes. At the south end, you'll find **Promo Turist** at Porta San Pietro (same rates and hours as the competition, Via Francesco Carrara, mobile 348-380-0126, Marco). A one-hour rental gives you two leisurely loops around the ramparts.

Magazine: For insights into American and British expat life and listings of concerts, markets, festivals, and other special events, pick up a copy of *The Grapevine* (€2), available at newsstands.

Cooking Class: Gianluca invites you to the hills above Lucca to learn to make Tuscan fare. You prepare and then eat a three-course meal. Depending on how many others attend, the price ranges from €50 (a steal) to a whopping €125 per person. This is great for groups of four or more (€14 cab ride from town, 3-hour lesson plus time to dine, includes wine, reserve at least 2 days in advance, Via di San Viticchio 414, mobile 347-678-7447, www.italiancuisine.it, info@italiancuisine.it).

Lucca

RAMPARTS

••• PATHWAY ATOP RAMPARTS

--- OTHER PATHS

P PARKING

1 La Romea B&B
2 La Locanda Sant'Agostino
3 La Bohème B&B
4 Hotel la Luna
5 Alla Dimora Lucense
6 Hotel Universo
7 Hotel Diana
8 La Magnolia B&B
9 Le Violette B&B
10 Ostello San Frediano
11 To Hotel San Marco
12 Hotel Rex
13 To Sogni d'Oro Guest House

- ⑭ Ristorante Canuleia
- ⑮ Vineria I Santi & Osteria Baralla
- ⑯ Osteria Via San Giorgio
- ⑰ Vecchia Trattoria Buralli
- ⑱ Trattoria da Leo
- ⑲ Bella 'Mbriana Pizzeria
- ⑳ Il Cuore Enogastronomia
- ㉑ Pizzeria da Felice
- ㉒ Betty Blue (Internet Access)
- ㉓ Launderette
- ㉔ Bike Rentals (3)
- ㉕ Bus to Pisa's Leaning Tower

Local Guide: **Gabriele Calabrese** knows and shares his hometown well (€120/3 hours, by foot or bike, mobile 347-788-0667, www.turislucca.com, turislucca@turislucca.com).

Sights in Lucca

▲▲**Bike the Ramparts**—Lucca's most remarkable feature, its Renaissance wall, is also its most enjoyable attraction—especially when circled on a rental bike. Stretching for 2.5 miles, this is an ideal place to come for an overview of the city by foot or bike.

Lucca has had a protective wall for 2,000 years. You can read three walls into today's map: the first rectangular Roman wall, the later medieval wall (nearly the size of today's), and the 16th-century Renaissance wall that survives today.

With the advent of cannons, thin medieval walls were suddenly vulnerable. A new design—the same one that stands today—was state-of-the-art when it was built (1550–1650). Much of the old medieval wall (look for the old stones) was incorporated into the Renaissance wall (with uniform bricks). The new wall was squat: a 100-foot-wide mound of dirt faced with bricks, engineered to absorb a cannonball pummeling. The townspeople cleared a wide no-man's-land around the town, exposing any attackers from a distance. Eleven heart-shaped bastions (inviting picnic areas today) were designed to minimize exposure to cannonballs and to maximize defense capabilities. The ramparts were armed with 130 cannons.

The town invested a third of its income for more than a century to construct the wall, and—since it kept away the Florentines and nasty Pisans—it was considered a fine investment. In fact, nobody ever bothered to try to attack the wall. Locals say that the only time it actually defended the city was during an 1812 flood of the Serchio River, when the gates were sandbagged and its ramparts kept out the high water.

Today, the ramparts seem made-to-order for a leisurely bike ride (20-minute pedal, wonderfully smooth). You can rent bikes cheaply and easily from one of several bike-rental places in town (listed earlier, under "Helpful Hints").

Piazza Anfiteatro—Just off the main shopping street, the architectural ghost of a Roman amphitheater can be felt in the delightful Piazza Anfiteatro. With the fall of Rome, the theater (which seated 10,000) was gradually cannibalized for its stones and

The History of Lucca

Lucca began as a Roman settlement. In fact, the grid layout of the streets (and the shadow of an amphitheater) survives from Roman times. Trace the rectangular Roman wall—indicated by today's streets—on the map. As in typical Roman towns, two main roads quartered the fortified town, crossing at what was the forum (main market and religious/political center)—today's Piazza San Michele.

Christianity came here early; it's said that the first bishop of Lucca was a disciple of St. Peter. While churches were built here as early as the fourth century, the majority of Lucca's elegant Romanesque churches date from about the 12th century.

Feisty Lucca, though never a real power, enjoyed a long period of independence (maintained by clever diplomacy). Aside from 30 years of being ruled from Pisa in the 14th century, Lucca was basically an independent city-state until Napoleon came to town.

In the Middle Ages, wealthy Lucca's economy was built on the silk industry, dominated by the Guinigi (gwee-NEE-gee) family. Without silk, Lucca would have been just another sleepy Italian town. In 1500, the town had 3,000 silk looms employing 25,000 workers. Banking was also big. Many pilgrims stopped here on their way to the Holy Land, deposited their money for safety…and never returned to pick it up.

In its heyday, Lucca packed 160 towers—one on nearly every corner—and 70 churches within its walls. Each tower was the home of a wealthy merchant family. Towers were many stories tall, with single rooms stacked atop each other: ground-floor shop, upstairs living room, and top-floor fire-safe kitchen, all connected by exterior wooden staircases. The rooftop was generally a vegetable garden with trees providing shade. Later, the wealthy city folk moved into the countryside, trading away life in their city palazzos to establish farm estates complete with fancy villas. (You can visit some of these villas today—the TI has a brochure—but they're convenient only for drivers and are generally not worth the cost of admission.)

In 1799, Napoleon stormed into Italy and took a liking to Lucca. He liked it so much that he gave it to his sister as a gift. It was later passed on to Napoleon's widow, Marie Louise. With a feminine sensitivity, Marie Louise was partially responsible for turning the city's imposing (but no longer particularly useful) fortified wall into a fine city park that is much enjoyed today.

inhabited by a mishmash of huts. The huts were cleared away at the end of the 19th century to better appreciate the town's illustrious past. Today, the square is a circle of touristy shops and mediocre restaurants that becomes a lively bar-and-café scene after dark. Today's street level is nine feet above the original arena floor. The only bits of surviving Roman stonework are a

few arches on the northern exterior (at Via Fillungo 42 and on Via Anfiteatro).

Via Fillungo—This main pedestrian drag stretches southwest from Piazza Anfiteatro. The street to stroll, Via Fillungo takes you from the amphitheater almost all the way to the cathedral. Along the way, you'll get a taste of Lucca's rich past, including several elegant century-old storefronts. Many of the original storefront paintings, reliefs, and mosaics survive—even if today's shopkeeper sells something entirely different.

At #97 is a classic old **jewelry store** with a rare storefront that has kept its T-shaped arrangement (when closed, you see a wooden T, and during open hours it unfolds with a fine old-time display). This design dates from a time when the merchant sold his goods in front, did his work in the back, and lived upstairs.

Di Simo Caffè, at #58, has long been the hangout of Lucca's artistic and intellectual elite. Composer and hometown boy Giacomo Puccini tapped his foot while sipping coffee here. Pop in to check out the 1880s ambience (handy €10 buffet lunch served daily 12:30–14:30, café open 9:00–24:00).

A surviving five-story **tower house** is at #67. There was a time when nearly every corner sported its own tower (see "The History of Lucca" sidebar). The stubby stones that still stick out once supported wooden staircases (there were no interior connections between floors). So many towers cast shadows over this part of town that the street just before it is called Via Buia (Dark Street). Look away from the tower down Via San Andrea for a peek at the town's tallest tower, Guinigi, in the distance—with its characteristic oak trees sprouting from the top.

At #45 and #43, you'll see two more good examples of tower houses. Across the street, the **Clock Tower** (Torre delle Ore) has a hand-wound Swiss clock that has clanged four times an hour since 1754 (€3.50 to climb up and see the mechanism flip into action on the quarter-hour—if it's actually working, €5 combo-ticket includes Guinigi Tower, daily April–Oct 9:30–18:30, Nov–March 9:30–16:30, corner of Via Fillungo and Via del'Arancio).

The intersection of Via Fillungo and Via Roma/Via Santa

Croce marks the center of town (where the two original Roman roads crossed). As you go right down Via Roma, you'll pass the fine Edison Bookstore on your left before reaching Piazza San Michele.

Piazza San Michele—This square has been the center of town since Roman times, when it was the forum. It's dominated by the Church of San Michele. Towering above the church's fancy Pisan Romanesque facade, the archangel Michael stands ready to flap his wings—which he actually did on special occasions.

The square is surrounded by an architectural hodgepodge. The loggia, which dates from 1495, is the first Renaissance building in town. There's a late-19th-century interior in Buccellato Taddeucci, a 130-year-old pastry shop (#34). The left section of the BNL bank (#5; in front of the church) sports an Art Nouveau facade that celebrates both Amerigo Vespucci and Cristoforo Colombo.

You'll notice that no statues of big shots decorate Lucca squares. That's because unlike Venice, Florence, and Milan—which were dominated by a few powerful dynasties—Lucca was traditionally run by an oligarchy of a hundred leading families. But after Italian unification, when leaders were fond of saying, "We have created Italy...now we need to create Italians," stirring statues of national heroes popped up everywhere—even in Lucca. The statue on Piazza San Michele is of a two-bit local guy, dredged up centuries after his death because he favored strong central government.

Look back at the church facade, which also has an element of patriotism—designed to give roots and legitimacy to Italian statehood. Perched above many of the columns are the faces of heroes in the Italian independence and unification movement: Victor Emmanuel II (above the short red column on the right), the Count of Cavour (next to Victor, above the column with black zigzags), and Giuseppe Mazzini.

▲San Martino Cathedral—This cathedral, begun in the 11th century, is an entertaining mix of architectural and artistic styles. Its elaborate Pisan Romanesque **facade**—featuring Christian teaching scenes, animals, and candy-cane-striped columns—dominates the piazza. The facade's central figure is St. Martin, a Roman military officer from Hungary who, by offering his cloak to a beggar, more fully understood the beauty of Christian compassion. (The impressive original, a fine example of Romanesque sculpture, hides from pollution just inside, to the right of the main entrance.) Each of the columns on the facade is unique. Notice how the facade is asymmetrical: The 11th-century bell tower was already in place when the rest of the cathedral was built, so the builders cheated on the right side to make it fit the space. Over the right portal (as if leaning against the older tower), the architect Guideo from Como holds a document declaring that he finished the facade in 1204. On the right (at eye level on the pilaster), a labyrinth is set into the wall.

The maze relates the struggle and challenge our souls face in finding salvation. (French pilgrims on their way to Rome could relate to this, as it's the same pattern they knew from the floor of the church at Chartres.) The Latin plaque just left of the main door is where moneychangers and spice traders met to seal deals (on the doorstep of the church—to underscore the reliability of their promises). Notice the date: *An Dni MCXI* (A.D. 1111).

The **interior** features Gothic arches, Renaissance paintings, and stained glass from the 19th century. On the left side of the nave, a small, elaborate birdcage-like temple contains the wooden crucifix—beloved by locals—called Volto Santo. It's said to have been sculpted by Nicodemus in Jerusalem and set afloat in an unmanned boat that landed on the coast of Tuscany, from where wild oxen miraculously carried it to Lucca in 782. The sculpture (which is actually 12th-century Byzantine-style) has quite a jewelry collection, which you can see in the Cathedral Museum (described next).

On the right side of the nave, the sacristy houses the enchantingly beautiful **memorial tomb of Ilaria del Carretto** by Jacopo della Quercia (1407). Pick up a handy English description to the right of the door as you enter the sacristy. This young bride of silk baron Paolo Guinigi is decked out in the latest, most expensive fashions, with the requisite little dog curled up at her feet in eternal sleep. She's so realistic that the statue was nicknamed "Sleeping Beauty." Her nose is partially worn off because of a long-standing tradition of lonely young ladies rubbing it for luck in finding a boyfriend.

Cost and Hours: Cathedral—free, Ilaria tomb—€2, €6 combo-ticket includes Cathedral Museum and San Giovanni Church; Mon–Fri 9:30–17:45, Sat 9:30–18:45; Sun open sporadically between Masses: 9:30–10:45 & 12:00–17:45; Piazza San Martino.

Cathedral Museum (Museo della Cattedrale)—This beautifully presented museum houses original paintings, sculptures, and vestments from the cathedral and other Lucca churches. The first room displays jewelry made to dress up the Volto Santo crucifix, including gigantic gilded silver shoes. Upstairs, notice the fine red brocaded silk—a reminder that this precious fabric is what brought riches and power to the city. The exhibits in this museum have very brief descriptions and are meaningful only with the slow-talking €1 audioguide—if you're not in the mood to listen, skip the place altogether.

Cost and Hours: €4, €6 combo-ticket includes Ilaria tomb and San Giovanni Church; April–Oct daily 10:00–18:00; Nov–March Mon–Fri 10:00–14:00, Sat–Sun 10:00–17:00; to the left of the cathedral as you're facing it, Piazza Antelminelli, tel. 0583-490-530, www.museocattedralelucca.it.

San Giovanni Church—This first cathedral of Lucca is interesting only for its archaeological finds. The entire floor of the 12th-century church has been excavated in recent decades, revealing layers of Roman houses, ancient hot tubs that date back to the time of Christ, early churches, and theological graffiti. Eager students can request an English translation of the floor plans from the ticket office to learn what's what. As you climb under the church's present-day floor and wander the lanes of Roman Lucca, remember that the entire city sits on similar ruins.

Cost and Hours: €2.50, €6 combo-ticket includes Ilaria tomb and Cathedral Museum, audioguide-€1; mid-March–Oct daily 10:00–18:00; Nov–mid-March Sat–Sun 10:00–17:00, closed Mon–Fri; see concert info on page 511; kitty-corner from cathedral at Piazza San Giovanni.

Church of San Frediano—This impressive church was built in 1112 by the pope to counter Lucca's bishop and his spiffy cathedral. Lucca was the first Mediterranean stop on the pilgrim route from northern Europe, and the pope wanted to remind pilgrims that the action, the glory, and the papacy awaited them in Rome. Therefore, he had the church made "Roman-esque." The pure marble facade frames an early Christian Roman-style mosaic of Christ with his 12 apostles. Step inside and you're struck by the sight of 40 powerful (if recycled) ancient Roman columns. The message: Lucca may be impressive, but the finale of your pilgrimage—in Rome—is worth the hike.

Inside, there's a notable piece of art in each corner: At rear left is the 12th-century baptistery, with some interesting Church propaganda showing the story of Moses (the evil Egyptians are played by Holy Roman Empire troops). At rear right is St. Zita's actual body, put there in 1278. At front left is a particularly elegant Virgin Mary, depicted at the moment she gets the news that she'll bring the Messiah into the world (carved and painted by Lucchesi artist Matteo Civitali, c. 1460). And at front right is a painting on wood of the *Assumption of the Virgin* (c. 1510), with Doubting Thomas receiving Mary's red belt as she ascends so he'll doubt no more. The pinball-machine composition serves as a virtual catalog of the fine silk material produced in Lucca—a major industry in the 16th century.

Cost and Hours: Free, Mon–Sat 8:30–12:00 & 15:00–17:30, Sun 9:00–11:30 & 15:00–17:30, Piazza San Frediano, tel. 0583-493-627.

Palazzo Mansi—Minor paintings by Tintoretto, Pontormo, Veronese, and others vie for attention, but the palace itself—a sumptuously furnished and decorated 17th-century confection—steals the show. This is your chance to appreciate the wealth of Lucca's silk merchants.

Cost and Hours: €4, €6.50 combo-ticket includes Villa Guinigi, Tue–Sat 8:30–19:30, Sun 8:30–13:30, closed Mon, no photos, request English booklet at ticket desk, Via Galli Tassi 43, tel. 0583-55-570. All visitors must be accompanied by a museum employee, so there may be a bit of a wait during high season.

Guinigi Tower (Torre Guinigi)—Many Tuscan towns have towers, but none is quite like the Guinigi family's. Up 227 steps is a small garden with fragrant trees surrounded by fantastic views.

Cost and Hours: €3.50, €5 combo-ticket includes Clock Tower, likely open daily April–Sept 9:00–19:30, Oct 10:00–18:00, Nov–March 9:30–16:30, Via Sant'Andrea 41.

Puccini's House—Opera enthusiasts (but nobody else) will want to visit the home where Giacomo Puccini (1858–1924) grew up, but—tragedy—it's closed. A pitched battle is going on between Puccini's grandniece—who actually owns the house and wants to renovate the museum—and the city of Lucca, which wants to preserve the house unchanged. Until one or the other relents, the museum's curtains will remain closed.

Palazzo Pfanner—Garden enthusiasts (and anyone needing a break from churches) will enjoy this 18th-century palace built for a rich Swiss expat who came to Lucca to open a brewery. His sudsy legacy includes Baroque furniture, elaborate frescoes, a centuries-old kitchen, and a lavish garden.

Cost and Hours: Garden or residence-€4 apiece, or €5.50 for both, April–Oct daily 10:00–18:00, closed Nov–March, Via degli Asili 33, tel. 0583-954-029, www.palazzopfanner.it.

Villa Guinigi—Built by Paolo Guinigi in 1418, the family villa is now a stark, abandoned-feeling museum displaying a hodgepodge of Etruscan artifacts, religious sculptures, paintings, inlaid wood-work, and ceramics. Monumental paintings by the multi-talented Giorgio Vasari are the best reason to visit.

Cost and Hours: €4, €6.50 combo-ticket includes Palazzo

Mansi, Tue–Sat 8:30–19:30, Sun 8:30–13:30, closed Mon, may have to wait in high season for a museum employee to accompany you, Via della Quarquonia, tel. 0583-496-033.

Sleeping in Lucca

(€1 = about $1.25, country code: 39)

Fancy Little Boutique B&Bs Within the Walls

$$$ La Romea B&B, in an air-conditioned restored 14th-century palazzo near Guinigi Tower, feels like a royal splurge. Its four posh rooms and one suite are lavishly decorated in handsome colors, and surround a big plush lounge with stately Venetian-style floors (Db-€100–135 depending on season, big suite-€160, extra bed-€20–25, 3 percent cheaper with cash, Wi-Fi; from the train station, take Via Fillungo, turn right on Via Sant'Andrea, then take the second right to Vicolo delle Ventaglie 2; tel. 0583-464-175, www.laromea.com, info@laromea.com, Giulio and wife Gaia).

$$$ La Locanda Sant'Agostino, run by gracious Sarah, has three romantic, bright, and spacious rooms. The vine-draped terrace and quaint views invite you to relax (Db-€160, extra bed-€25, 5 percent discount with cash and this book, air-con, Internet access and Wi-Fi, from Via Fillungo take Via San Giorgio to Piazza Sant'Agostino 3, best to reserve by email, tel. & fax 0583-467-884, www.locandasantagostino.it, info@locandasantagostino.it). Sarah's husband, Irio, runs an antique shop/art gallery—as reflected in the tasteful furnishings.

$$$ La Bohème B&B has a cozy yet elegant ambience, offering six large charming chandeliered rooms, each painted with a different rich color scheme (Db-€120, less off-season, 10 percent discount with cash and this book, air-con, free Wi-Fi, Via del Moro 2, tel. & fax 0583-462-404, www.boheme.it, info@boheme.it, Sara).

Sleeping More Forgettably Within the Walls

$$ Hotel la Luna, run by the Barbieri family, has 29 classy, spotless rooms in the heart of the city. Updated rooms are split between two adjacent buildings right off the main shopping street (Sb-€83, Db-€113, suite-€175, these prices for Rick Steves readers, air-con, elevator in one of the two buildings, pay Internet access, parking-€15/day, Via Fillungo at Corte Compagni 12, tel. 0583-493-634, fax 0583-490-021, www.hotellaluna.com, info@hotellaluna.com, Sara).

$$ Alla Dimora Lucense's seven new rooms are bright, modern, clean, and peaceful, with all the comforts. Enjoy their relaxing, sunny interior courtyard (Db-€115, suite for 2–4 people-€150–200, optional breakfast-€5, air-con, half a block from Via Fillungo at Via Fontana 17, tel. 0583-495-722, fax 0583-441-210, www.dimora lucense.it, info@dimoralucense.it).

$$ Hotel Universo, renting 56 rooms right on Piazza Napoleone and facing the theater and Palazzo Ducale, is a 19th-century town fixture. While it clearly was once elegant, now it's old and tired, with a big Old World lounge and soft prices ("comfort" Db-€100, "superior" Db with updated bath-€130, Wi-Fi, Piazza del Giglio 1, tel. 0583-493-678, www.universolucca.com, info @universolucca.com).

$$ La Magnolia B&B offers five basic rooms and one apartment with an intimate atmosphere and relaxing garden. It's buried in a ramshackle old palace in a central location (Sb-€65, Db-€85, Qb-€90, includes breakfast at nearby bar, 5 percent discount with cash and this book, a block behind amphitheater at Via Mordini 63, tel. 0583-467-111, www.lamagnolia.com, info@lamagnolia .com, Andrea and Laura).

$ Hotel Diana is a dreary little family-run hotel, with nine rooms in the main building and another six slightly nicer sound-proofed and air-conditioned rooms in the annex just around the corner (D-€50, Db-€67, annex Db-€85, south of the cathedral at Via del Molinetto 11, tel. 0583-492-202, fax 0583-467-795, www .albergodiana.com, info@albergodiana.com).

$ At Le Violette B&B, friendly Anna (who's still learning English; her granddaughter Sara speaks English) will settle you into one of her six homey rooms near the train station inside Porta San Pietro (D-€60, Db-€75, extra bed-€15, communal kitchen, €5 to use washer and dryer, Via della Polveriera 6, tel. 0583-493-594, mobile 349-823-4645, fax 0583-429-305, www.leviolette.it, le violette@virgilio.it).

$ Ostello San Frediano, in a central, sprawling ex-convent with a peaceful garden, is a cut above the average hostel. Older travelers and families feel comfortable here. Its 29 rooms are bright and modern, and some have fun lofts (140 beds, Db-€58, Tb-€78, Qb-€100, €20 beds in 6- to 8-person dorms, includes sheets, €3 extra/night for non-members, cash only, breakfast extra, no curfew, lockers, Internet access, cheap restaurant, free parking, Via della Cavallerizza 12, tel. 0583-469-957, fax 0583-461-007, www .ostellolucca.it, info@ostellolucca.it).

Outside the Walls

$$$ Hotel San Marco, a seven-minute walk outside the Porta Santa Maria, is a postmodern place decorated à la Stanley Kubrick. Its 42 recently remodeled rooms are sleek, with all the comforts (Sb-€87, Db-€126, extra bed-€10, includes nice breakfast spread, air-con, Wi-Fi, elevator, pool, bikes-€5/half-day, free parking, taxi from station–€6, Via San Marco 368, tel. 0583-495-010, fax 0583-490-513, www.hotelsanmarcolucca.com, info@hotelsanmarco lucca.com).

$$ Hotel Rex rents 25 rooms in a practical modern building on the train station square. While in the modern world, you're just 200 yards away from the old town and get more space for a better price (Db–€90–100, air-con, Wi-Fi, free bike rental, a few steps from the train station at Piazza Ricasoli 19, tel. 0583-955-443, www.hotelrexlucca.com, info@hotelrexlucca.com).

$ Sogni d'Oro Guest House ("Sleep like Gold"), run by Davide, is a handy budget option for drivers, with five basic rooms and a cheery communal kitchen (grocery store next door). It's a 10-minute walk from the train station and a five-minute walk from the city walls (D-€45, Db-€55, Q-€60, 10 percent discount with cash; free ride to and from station with advance notice—then call when your train arrives in Lucca; from the station, head straight out to Viale Regina Margherita and turn right, follow the main boulevard as it turns into Viale Giuseppe Giusti, at the curve turn right onto Via Antonio Cantore to #169; tel. 0583-467-768, mobile 329-582-5062, fax 0583-957-612, www.bbsognidoro.com, info @bbsognidoro.com).

Eating in Lucca

Ristorante Canuleia makes everything fresh in their small kitchen. While the portions aren't huge, the food is tasty. You can eat in their dressy little dining room or outside on the garden courtyard (€9 pastas, €15 *secondi*, Mon–Sat 12:30–14:00 & 19:30–21:30, closed Sun, Via Canuleia 14, tel. 0583-467-470, reserve for dinner).

Vineria I Santi is pricey but good if you appreciate quality food and fine wine, and just want to lie back and be pampered. Leonardo serves food with a sexy jazz ambience that would work well in a bordello. Relax in the peaceful indoors among wine bottles, or on a quiet square outside (€11 pastas, €18 *secondi*, Thu–Tue 12:30–14:30 & 19:30–22:00, closed Wed, Via Anfiteatro 29, tel. 0583-496-124).

Osteria Via San Giorgio, owned by Daniela and her brother Piero, is a cheery family eatery that satisfies both fish-lovers and meat-lovers. Sample the splittable *antipasto fantasia*—five small courses such as *ceviche* (seafood salad), scallops au gratin, squid sautéed with potatoes, or whatever else was caught that day in Viareggio. Dinner-size salads are bright and fresh, pasta is home-made, and Daniela's desserts tempt (daily 12:00–16:00 & 19:00–23:00, Via San Giorgio 26, tel. 0583-953-233).

Vecchia Trattoria Buralli, on quiet Piazza Sant'Agostino,

Specialties in Lucca

Lucca has some tasty specialties worth seeking out. *Ceci* (CHEH-chee), also called *cecina* (cheh-CHEE-nah), makes an ideal cheap snack any time of day. This garbanzo-bean crêpe is sold in pizza shops and is best accompanied by a nip of red wine.

Farro, a grain (spelt) dating back to ancient Roman cuisine, shows up in restaurants in soups or as a creamy rice-like dish *(risotto di farro).*

Tordelli, the Lucchesi version of *tortelli,* is homemade ravioli. It's traditionally stuffed with meat and served with more meat sauce, but chefs creatively pair cheeses and vegetables, too.

Meat, not fish, is the star at most restaurants, especially steak, which is listed on menus as *filetto di manzo* (filet), *tagliata di manzo* (thin slices of grilled tenderloin), or the king of steaks, *bistecca alla fiorentina.* Order *al sangue* (rare), *medio* (medium rare), *cotto* (medium), or *ben cotto* (well). Anything more than *al sangue* is considered a travesty for steak connoisseurs.

Note that steaks (as well as fish) are often sold by weight, noted on menus as *s.q.* (according to quantity ordered) or *l'etto* (cost per 100 grams—250 grams is about an 8-ounce steak).

For something sweet, bakeries sell *buccellato*, bread dotted with raisins, lightly flavored with anise, and often shaped like a wreath. It's only sold in large sizes, but luckily it stays good for a few days (and it also pairs well with *vin santo*—fortified Tuscan dessert wine). An old proverb says, "Coming to Lucca without eating the *buccellato* is like not having come at all." *Buon appetito!*

is a good bet for traditional cooking and juicy steaks, with fine indoor and piazza seating (€7 pastas, €10 *secondi,* €12–30 fixed-price meals, Thu–Tue 12:00–14:45 & 19:00–22:30, closed Wed, Piazza Sant'Agostino 10, tel. 0583-950-611).

Osteria Baralla, on the street that circles Piazza Anfiteatro, is popular with locals for its quality mid-priced meals. They have a breezy, spacious dining room under medieval vaults, and a few quiet tables on the pedestrian street (Mon–Sat 12:30–14:15 & 19:30–22:15, closed Sun, reservations smart for dinner, Via Anfiteatro 7/9, tel. 0583-440-240).

Trattoria da Leo, a brother of Vecchia Trattoria Buralli, packs in chatty locals for typical, cheap home-cooking in a hash-slingin' Mel's Diner atmosphere. This place is a high-energy winner...you know it's going to be good as soon as you step in. Arrive early or reserve in advance (€6 pastas, €10 *secondi,* Mon–Sat 12:00–14:30

& 19:30–22:30, sometimes open Sun, cash only, leave Piazza San Salvatore on Via Asili and take the first left to Via Tegrimi 1, tel. 0583-492-236).

Bella 'Mbriana Pizzeria focuses on doing one thing very well: turning out piping-hot wood-fired pizzas to happy locals in a welcoming wood-paneled dining room. Order and pay at the counter, take a number, and they'll call you when your pizza's ready. Consider take-out to munch atop the nearby walls. Prices range from €5 for your basic *Napolitano* to €8 for their specialty, with buffalo mozzarella and other gourmet ingredients (Wed–Mon 12:30–14:30 & 18:30–23:00, closed Tue, to the right as you face the Church of San Frediano, Via della Cavalerizza 29, tel. 0583-495-565).

Il Cuore Enogastronomia includes a delicatessen and restaurant. For a fancy picnic, drop in the deli for ready-to-eat lasagna, saucy meatballs, grilled and roasted vegetables, vegetable soufflés, Tuscan bean soup, fruit salads, and more, sold by weight and dished up in disposable trays to go. Ask them to heat your order *(riscaldare),* then picnic on nearby Piazza Napoleone. For curious traveling foodies on a budget who want to eat right there, they can assemble a €10 "degustation plate"—point to direct the construction from among the array of tasty treats under the glass (Tue–Sun 9:30–19:30, closed Mon, Via del Battistero 2, tel. 0583-493-196, Marianna).

Il Cuore Ristorante, located across the way, is a trendy find for wine-tasting or a meal on a piazza. Try the €8 *aperitivo* (available 18:00–20:00), which includes a glass of wine and a plate of cheese, *salumi,* and snacks, or feast on fresh pastas and other high-quality dishes from their lunch and dinner menus (Wed–Sun 12:00–22:00 with limited menu 15:00–19:30, Tue 12:00–15:00, closed Mon, Via del Battistero, tel. 0583-493-196).

Pizzeria da Felice is a little mom-and-pop hole-in-the-wall serving *cecina* (chickpea crêpes) and slices of freshly baked pizza to throngs of snackers. Grab a *cecina* and a short glass of wine for €2.50 (Mon–Sat 10:00–20:30, closed Sun and 3 weeks in Aug, Via Buia 12, tel. 0583-494-986).

Lucca Connections

From Lucca by Train to: Florence (2/hour, 1.5 hours, €5), **Pisa** (roughly 1–2/hour Mon–Sat, 30 minutes, bus is better, €3), **Milan** (2/hour except Sun, 4–5 hours, transfer in Florence, €60), **Rome** (1/hour except Sun, 3–4 hours, change in Florence, €50).

From Lucca by Bus to Pisa: Direct buses from Lucca's Piazzale Verdi drop you right at the Leaning Tower, making Pisa an easy day trip (hourly, 30 minutes, €3). Even with a car, I'd opt for this much faster and cheaper option.

SIENA

Siena was medieval Florence's archrival. And while Florence ultimately won the battle for political and economic superiority, Siena still competes for the tourists. Sure, Florence has the heavyweight sights. But Siena seems to be every Italy connoisseur's favorite pet town. In my office, whenever Siena is mentioned, someone moans, "Siena? I looove Siena!"

Once upon a time (about 1260–1348), Siena was a major banking and trade center, and a military power in a class with Florence, Venice, and Genoa. With a population of 60,000, it was even bigger than Paris. Situated on the north–south road to Rome (the Via Francigena), Siena traded with all of Europe. Then, in 1348, the Black Death (bubonic plague) that swept through Europe hit Siena and cut the population by more than a third. Siena never recovered. In the 1550s, Florence, with the help of Philip II's Spanish army, conquered the flailing city-state, forever rendering Siena a non-threatening backwater. Siena's loss became our sightseeing gain, as its political and economic irrelevance pickled the city in a purely medieval brine. Today, Siena's population is still 60,000, compared with Florence's 420,000.

Siena's thriving historic center, with red-brick lanes cascading every which way, offers Italy's best medieval city experience. Most people do Siena, just 35 miles south of Florence, as a day trip, but it's best experienced at twilight. While Florence has the blockbuster museums, Siena has an easy-to-enjoy soul: Courtyards sport flower-decked wells, alleys dead-end at rooftop views, and the sky is a rich blue dome.

For those who dream of a Fiat-free Italy, Siena is a haven. Pedestrians rule in the old center of Siena. Sit at a café on the main square. Wander narrow streets lined with colorful flags and iron rings to tether horses. Take time to savor the first European city to eliminate automobile traffic from its main square (1966) and then, just to be silly, wonder what would happen if they did it in your hometown.

Planning Your Time

On a quick trip, consider spending two nights in Siena (or three nights with a whole-day side trip into Florence). Whatever you do, enjoy a sleepy medieval evening in Siena. The next morning, you can see the city's major sights in half a day.

Orientation to Siena

Siena lounges atop a hill, stretching its three legs out from Il Campo. This main square, the historic meeting point of Siena's

neighborhoods, is pedestrian-only. And most of those pedestrians are students from the local university.

Just about everything mentioned in this chapter is within a 15-minute walk of the square. Navigate by three major landmarks (Il Campo, Duomo, and Church of San Domenico), following the excellent system of street-corner signs. The typical visitor sticks to the Il Campo–San Domenico axis. Make a point to stray from the current of this main artery.

Siena itself is one big sight. Its individual sights come in two little clusters: the square (Civic Museum and City Tower) and the cathedral (Baptistery and Duomo Museum with its surprise viewpoint). Check these sights off, and then you're free to wander.

Tourist Information

The TI on Il Campo can be an exasperating place, but you can pick up some good handouts and buy a €0.50 map (daily 9:00–19:00, on Il Campo at #56, tel. 0577-280-551, www.terresiena.it, incoming @terresiena.it). The helpful booklet *Siena* from their *Terre di Siena* series lists current hours and prices for sights in Siena and outlying towns. The TI organizes walking tours of the old town and San Gimignano (€20, daily April–Sept).

There's also a little TI, which is primarily for hotel promotion, across the street from the Church of San Domenico, and a TI at the train station (daily 9:30–13:30, tel. 0577-270-600).

Greater Siena

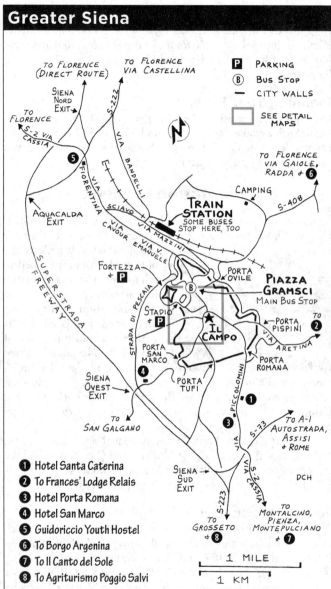

P PARKING
B BUS STOP
— CITY WALLS
☐ SEE DETAIL MAPS

TO FLORENCE (DIRECT ROUTE)
TO FLORENCE VIA CASTELLINA
SIENA NORD EXIT
TO FLORENCE
S-2 VIA CASSIA
S-222
VIA BANDELLI
VIA FIORENTINA
AQUACALDA EXIT
SCIAVO
VIA CAVOUR
VIA MAZZINI
VIA V. EMANUELE
TRAIN STATION
SOME BUSES STOP HERE, TOO
CAMPING
S-408
TO FLORENCE VIA GAIOLE, RADDA & ⑥
SUPERSTRADA FREEWAY
FORTEZZA **P**
STRADA DI PESCAIA
STADIO **P**
B
IL CAMPO
PORTA OVILE
PIAZZA GRAMSCI
MAIN BUS STOP
PORTA PISPINI
TO ②
VIA ARETINA
PORTA ROMANA
PORTA SAN MARCO
SIENA OVEST EXIT
④
PORTA TUFI
VIA PICCOLOMINI
①
③
TO SAN GALGANO
TO A-1 AUTOSTRADA, ASSISI & ROME
S-73
VIA S-2 CASSIA
SIENA SUD EXIT
S-223
DCH
TO GROSSETO ⑧
TO MONTALCINO, PIENZA, MONTEPULCIANO ⑦

① Hotel Santa Caterina
② To Frances' Lodge Relais
③ Hotel Porta Romana
④ Hotel San Marco
⑤ Guidoriccio Youth Hostel
⑥ To Borgo Argenina
⑦ To Il Canto del Sole
⑧ To Agriturismo Poggio Salvi

1 MILE
1 KM

SIENA

Arrival in Siena

By Train: The small train station, located on the edge of town, has a bar, a TI (daily 9:30–13:30), a bus office (Mon–Sat 6:15–20:15, Sun 7:30–12:30 & 14:30–18:30), and a newsstand (which sells bus tickets—buy one now if you're taking the city bus into town), but no baggage check or lockers (check bags at Piazza Gramsci—see "By Intercity Bus," below). A shopping mall is right in front of the station.

To get from the station to the city center by **city bus,** exit the station, go left 15 yards, and head across the road to the shopping mall, a brick-and-glass building labeled *Galleria Porta Siena*. Enter the right-hand glass door and use the elevator to go down one floor. If you didn't buy bus tickets in the train station, you can get tickets (€1) from the blue machine (touch the screen for English and select "urban" for type of ticket). Most orange or red-and-silver buses go to the city center (6/hour, fewer on Sun and after 22:00). Double-check the destination with the driver by asking *"Centro?"* Punch your ticket in the machine onboard to validate it. Ride to the last stop, Piazza Gramsci (or nearby Piazza del Sale).

If you're leaving Siena and you need to get to the train station, catch an orange or red-and-silver city bus from Piazza Gramsci. Confirm with the driver that the bus is going to the *stazione* (stat-zee-OH-nay); remember to purchase your ticket in advance from a *tabacchi* shop, then validate it on board.

The **taxi stand** is to your far right as you exit the train station, but as the city is chronically short on cabs, getting one here can take forever (about €9 to Il Campo, taxi tel. 0577-49222).

By Intercity Bus: Some buses arrive in Siena at Piazza Gramsci (a few blocks from the city center), though most arrive at the train station. (Some go first to the train station, then continue to Piazza Gramsci.) The main bus companies are Sena and the confusingly named Tra-In (pronounced TRAH-in). Day-trippers can store baggage underneath Piazza Gramsci in Sottopassaggio la Lizza (€5.50/day, open daily 7:00–19:00, carry-on-sized luggage no more than 33 pounds, no overnight storage). For more on buses, see the very end of this chapter.

By Car: Drivers coming from the autostrada take the *Siena Ovest* exit and follow signs for *Centro,* then *Stadio* (stadium). The soccer-ball signs take you to the stadium lot (Parcheggio Stadio, €1.60/hour, pay when you leave) near the huge bare-brick Church of San Domenico. The Fortezza lot nearby charges the same amount. For the Il Campo parking lot, take exit *Siena Sud,* follow *Direzione Roma,* then turn immediately left and follow the sign for *Il Campo* (special €25/day rate, ask at your hotel).

On parking spots, blue stripes mean "pay and display"; white stripes mean free parking. You can park for free in the lot west of

SIENA

Siena at a Glance

▲▲▲Il Campo Best square in Italy. **Hours:** Always open. See page 534.

▲▲▲Duomo Art-packed cathedral with mosaic floors and statues by Michelangelo and Bernini. **Hours:** March–Sept Mon–Sat 10:30–19:30, June–Aug until 20:00, Sun 13:30–17:30; Oct–Feb Mon–Sat 10:30–18:00, Sun 13:30–17:30. See page 538.

▲▲Duomo Museum Displays cathedral art (including Duccio's *Maestà*) and offers sweeping Tuscan view. **Hours:** Daily March–Sept 9:30–20:00, Oct–Feb 10:00–17:00. See page 541.

▲Civic Museum City museum in City Hall with Sienese frescoes of Good and Bad Government. **Hours:** Daily March–Oct 10:00–19:00, Nov–Feb 10:00–17:15. May be open later in summer. See page 535.

▲City Tower 330-foot tower climb. **Hours:** Daily March–Oct 10:00–19:00, Nov–Feb 10:00–16:00. See page 537.

▲Pinacoteca Fine Sienese paintings. **Hours:** Sun–Mon 9:00–13:00, Tue–Sat 10:00–18:00. See page 538.

▲Baptistery Cave-like building has baptismal font decorated by Ghiberti and Donatello. **Hours:** Daily 9:30–19:00. See page 542.

▲Santa Maria della Scala Museum with vibrant ceiling and wall frescoes depicting day-to-day life in a medieval hospital, much of the original *Fountain of Joy,* and an Etruscan artifact exhibit. **Hours:** Daily 10:30–18:30. See page 542.

Church of San Domenico Huge brick church with St. Catherine's head and thumb. **Hours:** Daily March–Oct 7:00–18:30, Nov–Feb 9:00–18:30. See page 543.

Sanctuary of St. Catherine Home of St. Catherine. **Hours:** Daily 9:30–19:00. See page 544.

the Fortezza; in white-striped spots behind the Hotel Villa Liberty (behind the Fortezza); and overnight in most city lots from 20:00 to 8:00. Watch for signs showing a street cleaner and a day of the week—that's when the street is closed to cars for cleaning.

Driving within Siena's city center is restricted to local cars, and policed by automatic cameras. If you drive or park anywhere marked *Zona Traffico Limitato (ZTL)*, you'll likely have a hefty ticket waiting for you in the mail back home.

Technically, hotel customers are allowed to drop off bags at their hotel before finding a place to park overnight, but getting permission to do so isn't worth the trouble.

Helpful Hints

Combo-Tickets: A deranged person cobbled together a pile of illogically paired combo-tickets for the sights in Siena—nothing covers everything, and the meager savings are just not worth the brainpower it takes to figure out the system. Only three of these combo-tickets are really worth considering: The best is the **"My Name is Duccio"** (DOO-choh) ticket, which covers the Duomo, Duomo Museum, Crypt, and Baptistery (€10, buy ticket at museum to skip line at Duomo). The **Civic Museum** offers two different combo-tickets (€12 combined with City Tower, €11 combined with Santa Maria della Scala—but no ticket combines all three).

Wednesday-Morning Market: The weekly market (clothes, knickknacks, and food) sprawls between the Fortezza and Piazza Gramsci along Viale Cesare Maccari and the adjacent Viale XXV Aprile.

Internet Access: In this university town, there are lots of places to get plugged in. **Cheap Phone Center** is hidden in a small shopping mall at Via Angiolieri Cecco 16 (€2/hour to use terminals, €1/hour to access Wi-Fi with your laptop, Mon–Sat 10:00–22:00, Sun 11:00–23:00; coming from Il Campo, go uphill past recommended Albergo Tre Donzelle, turn left, and after 20 yards, look for the *Buffet Restaurant* sign on your left). **Internet Point** is located upstairs at Via di Città 80, with the entrance around the corner on Via delle Campane (€3/hour, daily 9:00–21:00).

Post Office: It's on Piazza Matteotti (Mon–Fri 8:15–19:00, Sat 8:15–13:30, closed Sun).

Books: Libreria Senese sells books (including my guidebooks), newspapers, and magazines in English, with an emphasis on Italian-related topics (daily 9:00–20:00, Via di Città 62, tel. 0577-280-845). The **Feltrinelli** bookstore at Banchi di Sopra 52 also sells books and magazines in English (Mon–Sat 9:00–19:30, closed Sun, tel. 0577-271-104).

Laundry: Two modern self-service launderettes are **Express Wash** (near Logge del Papa at Via di Pantaneto 38) and **Onda Blu** (50 yards from Il Campo at Via del Casato di Sotto 17). Both are open daily 8:00–22:00 with last loads at 21:00.

Travel Agency: Palio Viaggi, on Piazza Gramsci, sells train tickets (downstairs under the arch) and plane tickets (upstairs), but no bus tickets (Mon–Fri 9:00–12:45 & 15:00–18:30, Sat 9:00–12:30, closed Sun, opposite the columns of NH Excelsior Hotel at La Lizza 12, tel. 0577-280-828, info@palio viaggi.it).

Wine Classes: The Tuscan Wine School gives two-hour classes in English on Italian wines and includes samples of five vintages (a one-hour "crash course" may also be available). Rebecca and her fellow sommeliers keep things entertaining. They also have an outlet store that sells wine from local producers at cost (€40/person, daily, 2-hour classes at 11:00 and 16:00, later class specializes in Tuscan wines, Via Stalloreggi 26, 30 yards from recommended Hotel Duomo, tel. 0577-221-704, mobile 333-722-9716, www.tuscanwineschool.com, info@tuscanwines chool.com).

Tours in Siena

Local Guides—Roberto Bechi, a hardworking Sienese guide, specializes in off-the-beaten-path tours of the surrounding countryside by minibus (up to eight passengers, convenient pickup at hotel). Married to an American (Patti) and having run restaurants in Siena and the US, Roberto communicates well with Americans. His passions are Sienese culture, Tuscan history, and local cuisine. It's ideal to book well in advance, but you might be able to schedule a tour if you call the day before (seven different tours, full-day tours are €90/person—mention this book for a free gift, off-season 4-hour tours are €60/person, entry fees are extra; assistant Anna can schedule city tours as well as other guides if Roberto is booked; Anna's mobile 320-147-6590, Roberto's mobile 328-425-5648, www.toursbyroberto .com, toursbyroberto@gmail.com).

Federica Olla is a smart young guide with a knack for creative teaching (€55/hour, mobile 338-133-9525, info@ollaeventi.com).

Bus Tour—Wine & Tours runs half-day guided bus tours from Siena into Chianti, Montalcino, Montepulciano, and San Gimignano country—including winery visits and tastings—and the Tuscan countryside (€38, 10 percent discount with this book, daily 14:00–19:00, four different 5-hour tours, leave from Piazza Gramsci, office at Via Il Casato di Sotto 12, tel. 0577-46091, www .enocuriosi.com, info@wineandtours.it).

SIENA

Siena

100 YARDS
100 METERS

➤ VIEW
🅿 PARKING
➡ ENTRY POINT TO SIGHTS

TO TRAIN STATION

VIALE FRANCHI
LA LIZZA
ENOTECA ITALIANA
V. MACCARI
25 APR.
FORTEZZA
STADIO
🅿

V. GARI.
STUPA SECCA
VIA MONTAN INI
VIA TOZZI
VIA STUFA SECCA

PIAZZA DEL SALE

PIAZZA GRAMSCI   BUSES TO FLORENCE, ROME, ETC.

PIAZZA MATTEOTTI

POST

PIAZZA SALIMBENI

V. DEI MILLE
VIA CURTATONE
PARADISO
McD

ⓘ
WC
VIA SAPIENZA
CAMPOREGIO
S. PITTORI
S. ANT.
S. CAT.
TERME
BANCHI DI SOPRA
ROSSI
CECCO

PIAZZA TOLOMEI

SAN DOMENICO

SANCT. S. CAT.
GALLUZZA
P. IND.
TERMINI
LOGGIA
BANCHI DI SOTTO

CIVIC MUSEUM, CITY HALL & TOWER

ESTERNA FONT.
COSTONE
BAPT.
FONT.
CUCETO
WC
IL CAMPO
ⓘ
PANTANETO

DUOMO
FRANC.
VIA PELL.
DUOMO MUSEUM
VIA DI CITTÀ
SALICOTTO
PORRIONE

PIAZZA DUOMO

CASTORO
CAPITANO
CAS. DI SOTTO
DUPRE

SANTA MARIA DELLA SCALA

WC

PIAZZA D. MERCATO

STALLOREGGI
S. PIETRO

PINACOTECA
(PAINTING GALLERY)

❶ Sottopassaggio la Lizza (Underground Bus Depot, Bag Storage & Bus Tickets)
❷ Libreria Senese Bookstore
❸ Feltrinelli Bookstore
❹ Palio Viaggi Travel Agency
❺ Wine & Tours
❻ Tuscan Wine School

Sights in Siena

▲▲▲Il Campo: Siena's Main Square

Il Campo is the heart—geographically and metaphorically—of Siena. The square fans out from the City Hall (Palazzo Pubblico)

to create an amphitheater, where the citizens are the stars.

Originally, this area was just a field *(campo)* located outside the former city walls. You can still see some of the old blocks made of volcanic tuff incorporated into today's red-brick Caffè Fonte Gaia (along the right side of the square as you face City Hall).

As the city expanded, Il Campo eventually became the historic junction of Siena's various competing districts, or *contrade,* and the old marketplace. The brick surface is divided into nine sections, representing the council of nine merchants and city bigwigs who ruled medieval Siena. The square and its buildings are the color of the soil upon which they stand...a color known to Crayola-users and other artists as "Burnt Sienna."

The City Hall and its 330-foot tower dominate the square. In medieval Siena, this secular building was the center of the city, and the whole focus of Il Campo still flows down to it. The **City Tower** (Torre del Mangia), Italy's

tallest secular tower, was named after a hedonistic watchman who consumed his earnings like a glutton consumes food—his chewed-up statue is in the courtyard, to the left as you enter. (For details on climbing the tower, see "City Tower," page 537.)

The chapel located at the base of the tower was built in 1348 as thanks to God for ending the Black Death (after it killed more than a third of the population). It should also be used to thank God that the tower—just plunked onto the building with no extra foundation—still stands. These days, the chapel is used solely to bless the Palio contestants, and the tower's bell only rings for the race.

The *Fountain of Joy (Fonte Gaia),* by Jacopo della Quercia, marks the square's high point. Find the snake-handler woman, the two naked guys about to be tossed in, and the pigeons politely waiting their turn to tightrope gingerly down slippery spouts to

slurp a drink from wolves' snouts. The relief panel on the left (as you face the fountain) shows God creating Adam by helping him to his feet. It's said that this reclining Adam influenced Michelangelo when he painted his Sistine Chapel ceiling. This fountain is a copy—you can see most of the original fountain in an interesting exhibit at Siena's Santa Maria della Scala (described later).

To say that Siena and Florence have always been competitive is an understatement. In medieval times, a statue of Venus stood on Il Campo. After the plague hit Siena, the monks blamed the pagan statue. The people cut it to pieces and buried it along the walls of Florence.

Picture Il Campo during the famous Palio horse races (every year on July 2 and Aug 16). Ten snorting horses and their nervous riders (selected from 17 *contrade,* or neighborhoods) line up near the Antica Siena shop (right side of square) to await the starting signal. Then they race like crazy three times around the perimeter (the gray pavement), which is covered with

dirt. Mattresses pad the sharpest turns. Spectators waving the banners of their neighborhoods cram (for free) into the center of the square or, if they have the money, watch from temporary bleachers or the balconies above. Every possible vantage point and perch is packed with people straining to see the action. The winner crosses the line, and 1/17th of Siena goes berserk for the next 365 days. For more on the Palio, see the sidebar on page 536.

▲**Civic Museum (Museo Civico)**—At the base of the tower is Siena's City Hall, the spot where secular government got its start in early Renaissance Europe. There you'll find city government still at work, along with a sampling of local art.

In the following order, you'll see: the Sala Risorgimento, with dramatic scenes of Victor Emmanuel II's unification of Italy (surrounded by statues that don't seem to care); the chapel, with impressive inlaid-wood chairs in the choir; and the Sala del Mappamondo, with Siena's first fresco, Simone Martini's *Maestà* (*Enthroned Virgin*—a groundbreaking depiction of a down-to-earth Madonna), facing the faded *Guidoriccio da Fogliano* (a

Siena's Palio

In the Palio, the feisty spirit of Siena's 17 *contrade* (neighbor-hoods) lives on. Each *contrada* has a parish church, well, or fountain, and sometimes even a historical museum. Each is represented by a mascot (porcupine, unicorn, wolf, etc.) and unique colors worn proudly by residents.

Contrada pride is evident year-round in Siena's parades and colorful banners, lamps, and wall plaques. (If you hear the thunder of distant drumming, run to it for some medieval action, often featuring flag-throwers.) You are welcome to participate in these lively neighborhood festivals. Buy a scarf in *contrada* colors, grab a glass of Chianti, munch on some *panforte,* and join in the merriment.

Contrada passion is most visible twice a year—on July 2 and August 16—when the city erupts during its world-famous horse race, the Palio di Siena. Ten of the 17 neighborhoods compete (chosen by rotation and lot), hurling themselves with medieval abandon into several days of trial races and traditional revelry. Jockeys—usually from out of town—are considered hired guns, no better than paid mercenaries. Bets are placed on which *contrada* will win...and lose. Despite the shady behind-the-scenes dealing, on the big day the horses are taken into their *contrada*'s church to be blessed. ("Go and return victorious," says the priest.) It's considered a sign of luck if a horse leaves droppings in the church.

On the evening of the race, Il Campo is stuffed to the brim with locals and tourists. Dirt is brought in and packed down to create the track's surface, while mattresses pad the walls of surrounding buildings. The most treacherous spots are the sharp

mercenary providing a more concrete form of protection).

Next is the Sala della Pace—where the city's fat cats met. Looking down on the oligarchy during their meetings were two fascinating frescoes showing the *Effects of Good and Bad Government*, by Ambrogio Lorenzetti. Notice the whistle-while-you-work happiness of the utopian community ruled by the utopian government (in the better-preserved fresco) against the fate of a community ruled by politicians with more typical values (in a terrible state of disrepair). The message: Without justice, there can be no prosperity.

Take a moment to savor one of those to-sigh-for rural panoramas out the window of the Sala della Pace. The view is essentially the same as the one from the top of the big stairs you'll pass as you exit—enjoy it from here.

corners, where many a rider bites the dust. One lap around the course is about a third of a mile (350 meters); three laps make a full circuit. In this literally no-holds-barred race—which lasts just over a minute—a horse can win even without its rider (jockeys perch precariously without saddles on the sweaty horses' backs, and often fall off).

The winning neighborhood is the scene of grand celebrations afterward. Winners receive a *palio* (banner), typically painted by a local artist and always featuring the Virgin Mary. But the true prize is proving that your *contrada* is *numero uno,* and mocking your losing rival.

All over town, sketches and posters depict the Palio. This is not some folkloristic event—it's a real medieval moment. If you're packed onto the square with 60,000 people, all hungry for victory, you won't see much, but you'll feel it. Bleacher and balcony seats are expensive, but it's free to join the masses in the square. Be sure to go with an empty bladder as there are no WCs, and be prepared to surrender any sense of personal space.

While the actual Palio packs the city, you could side-trip in from Florence to see the horse-race trials—called *prove* (prohvay)—on any of the three days before the main event (usually at 9:00 and about 19:30, free seats in bleachers). For more information, visit www.ilpalio.org.

Cost and Hours: 7.50, €12 combo-ticket includes City Tower, €11 combo-ticket includes Santa Maria della Scala, daily March–Oct 10:00–19:00—may be open later in summer, Nov–Feb 10:00–17:15, last entry 45 minutes before closing, tel. 0577-292-615.

▲**City Tower (Torre del Mangia)**—Siena gathers around its City Hall more than its church. Medieval Siena was a proud republic,

and this tall tower is the exclamation point of its "declaration of independence." Its 300 steps get pretty skinny at the top, but the reward is one of Italy's best views.

Cost and Hours: €7, €12 combo-ticket includes Civic Museum, daily March–Oct 10:00–19:00, Nov–Feb 10:00–16:00, last entry 45 minutes before closing, closed in rain, limited to 30 tourists at a time so be prepared for long lines—avoid midday crowds, often sold out, free and mandatory bag check.

Near Il Campo

▲**Pinacoteca**—If you're into medieval art, you'll likely find this quiet, uncrowded colorful museum delightful. The museum walks you through Siena's art chronologically, from the 12th through the 16th century, when a revolution in realism was percolating in Tuscany. For the casual sightseer, the Sienese art in the Civic and Duomo museums is adequate. But art fans enjoy this opportunity to trace the evolution of Siena's delicate and elegant works, from stiff, gold-backed icon-like Madonnas to curvy, graceful Madonnas to Italian Renaissance. Concentrate on pieces by Duccio (artist of the *Maestà* in the Duomo Museum), Simone Martini (who did the *Maestà* in the Civic Museum), the brothers Ambrogio and Pietro Lorenzetti (Ambrogio created the *Effects of Good and Bad Government* in the Civic Museum), Pinturicchio (who did the frescoes in the Piccolomini Library in the Duomo), and Domenico Beccafumi (who inlaid pavement in the Duomo).

Cost and Hours: €4, Sun–Mon 9:00–13:00, Tue–Sat 10:00–18:00, last entry 30 minutes before closing, free and mandatory bag check, tel. 0577-281-161 or 0577-286-143. To reach the museum from Il Campo, walk out Via di Città and go left on Via San Pietro.

Siena's Cathedral Area

▲▲▲**Duomo**—If the Campo is the heart of Siena, the Duomo (or cathedral) is its soul. The white-and-dark-green-striped church, sitting on an artificial platform atop Siena's highest point, is visible for miles around. The current structure dates back to 1215, with the major decoration done during Siena's heyday from 1250 to 1350. This ornate but surprisingly secular shrine to the Virgin Mary is stacked with colorful art inside and out, from the inlaid-marble floors to the stained-glass windows. The interior is a Renaissance riot of striped columns, intricate marble inlays, Michelangelo statues, and Bernini sculptures. In the Piccolomini Library, a series of captivating frescoes by the Umbrian painter Pinturicchio tells the story of Aeneas Piccolomini, Siena's consummate Renaissance Man, who became Pope Pius II.

Cost and Hours: €3 includes cathedral and Piccolomini Library; €10 "My Name is Duccio" combo-ticket also includes the Duomo Museum (sold 100 yards away at the museum, allows you to skip cathedral line), Crypt, and Baptistery. There's a €5 audioguide for the church and the library (€7/2 people); an €8 combo-audioguide also covers the Duomo Museum (€12/2 people, ID required for deposit). The Duomo and library are both open March–Sept Mon–Sat 10:30–19:30, June–Aug until 20:00, Sun 13:30–17:30; Oct–Feb Mon–Sat 10:30–18:00, Sun 13:30–17:30; last entry 30 minutes before closing. Modest dress is required to enter, but paper ponchos are provided if needed.

❷ **Self-Guided Tour:** In the **nave,** the heads of 172 popes—who reigned from Peter to the 12th century—peer down from above, looking over the fine inlaid art on the floor. With a forest of striped columns, a coffered dome, a large stained-glass window at the far end (it's a copy—the original is viewable up close in the nearby Duomo Museum), and an art gallery's worth of early Renaissance art, this is one busy interior. If you look closely at the popes, you'll see the same four faces repeated over and over.

For almost two centuries (1373–1547), 40 artists paved the marble floor with scenes from the Old Testament, allegories, and intricate patterns. The earliest designs are simple black-and-white with engraved details, but the later ones use inlay technique with many colored marbles. The series starts near the entrance with historical allegories; the larger, more elaborate scenes surrounding the altar are mostly stories from the Old Testament. Many of the floor panels are roped off to prevent further wear and tear.

Grab a seat under the dome. It sits on a 12-sided base, but its "coffered" ceiling is actually a painted illusion. Get oriented to the array of sights by thinking of the church floor as a big 12-hour clock. You're the middle, and the altar is high noon: You'll find the *Slaughter of the Innocents* roped off on the floor at 10 o'clock, Pisano's pulpit between two pillars at 11 o'clock, a copy of Duccio's round stained-glass window at high noon, Bernini's chapel at 3 o'clock, the Piccolomini Altar with the Michelangelo statue (next to doorway leading to a shop, snacks, and WC) at 7 o'clock, the Piccolomini Library at 8 o'clock, and a Donatello statue at 9 o'clock.

Nicola Pisano's octagonal Carrara marble **pulpit** (1268) rests on the backs of lions, symbols of Christianity triumphant. Like the lions, the Church eats its catch (devouring paganism) and nurses its cubs. The seven relief panels tell the life of Christ in rich detail. (Buy light from the coin-op machine.) This is a copy of the original window, which was moved to the Duomo Museum a couple of years ago. The famous rose window was created in 1288 and dedicated to the Virgin Mary.

Look for the *Slaughter of the Innocents* inlaid pavement panel. Herod (left), sitting enthroned amid Renaissance arches, orders the massacre of all babies to prevent the coming of the promised Messiah. It's a chaotic scene of angry soldiers, grieving mothers, and dead babies, reminding locals that a republic ruled by a tyrant will experience misery.

Donatello's rugged *St. John the Baptist* in his famous rags stands in a chapel to the right of the library. To understand why Giovanni Lorenzo Bernini is considered the greatest Baroque sculptor, step into the sumptuous **Bernini Chapel.** This last work in the cathedral (1659) is enough to make even a Lutheran light a candle. Move up to the altar and look back at the two Bernini statues: Mary Magdalene in a state of spiritual ecstasy, and St. Jerome playing the crucifix like a violinist lost in beautiful music.

Over the altar is the *Madonna del Voto,* a Madonna and Child painted by Duccio and adorned with a real crown of gold and jewels. Tilting her head, she looks out sympathetically. This is the Mary to whom the Palio is dedicated, dear to the hearts of the Sienese. The faithful's prayers to Mary are accompanied by offerings, found outside the chapel, hanging on the wall to the left as you exit.

The **Piccolomini Altar** (left wall, marble altarpiece decorated with statues) was designed for the tomb of the Sienese-born Pope Pius III. It's most interesting for Michelangelo's statue of St. Paul (lower right, who is clearly more interesting than the bland, bored popes above him). Paul has the look of Michelangelo's *Moses,* the broken-nosed self-portrait of the sculptor himself, and the relaxed hand of his *David.* It was the chance to sculpt *David* in Florence that convinced Michelangelo to abandon the Siena project.

The brilliantly frescoed **Piccolomini Library** captures the exuberant, optimistic spirit of the 1400s, when humanism and the Renaissance were born. The never-restored frescoes look nearly as vivid now as the day they were finished 550 years ago. (With the bright window light, candles were not necessary in this room—and didn't sully the art with soot.) The painter Pinturicchio (c. 1454–1513) was hired to celebrate the life of one of Siena's hometown boys—a man many call "the first humanist," Aeneas Piccolomini (1405–1464), who became Pope Pius II. Start from the window and work clockwise, following 10 scenes framed with arches, as if Pinturicchio were opening a window onto the spacious 3-D world we inhabit. The library also contains intricately decorated, illuminated music scores, and a statue (a Roman copy of a Greek original) of the Three Graces.

Exit the Duomo, and make a U-turn to the left, walking alongside the church to Piazza Jacopo della Quercia to view the unfinished cathedral. The nave of the Duomo was supposed to be where the piazza is today. Worshippers would have entered the church from the far end of the piazza through the unfinished wall. (Look way up at the highest part of the wall. That's the viewpoint accessible from inside the Duomo Museum.)

After rival republic Florence began its grand cathedral (1296), proud Siena planned to build one even bigger, the biggest church in all Christendom. Construction began in the 1330s on an extension off the right side of the existing Duomo (today's cathedral would have been used as a transept). Some of the nave's green-and-white-striped columns were built, and are now filled in with a brick wall. The wall connecting the Duomo with the museum of the cathedral was as far as Siena got before a plague hit, killing the city's ability to finish the project. Round white stones in the pavement mark where a row of pillars would have been. Look through the unfinished entrance facade, note blue sky where the stained-glass windows would have been, and ponder the struggles, triumphs, and failures of the human spirit.

▲▲**Duomo Museum (Museo dell'Opera e Panorama)**— Located at the back of the Duomo on the right, Siena's most enjoyable museum was built to house the cathedral's art. The ground floor is filled with the cathedral's original Gothic sculptures by Giovanni Pisano (who spent 10 years in the late 1200s carving and orchestrating the decoration of the cathedral) and a fine Donatello *Madonna and Child*. A slender, tender Mary gazes down at her chubby-cheeked baby, and her sad eyes say that she knows the eventual fate of her son.

Until a couple of years ago, this original window was located above and behind the Duomo's altar. Now the church has a copy, and art-lovers can enjoy a close-up look at this masterpiece. The rose window—20 feet across, made in 1288—is dedicated (like the church and the city itself) to the Virgin Mary, and combines elements from rigid Byzantine icons with a budding sense of 3-D realism.

Upstairs to the left awaits a private audience with Duccio's *Maestà* (*Enthroned Virgin*, 1311). Grab a seat and study one of the great pieces of medieval art. The flip side of the *Maestà* (displayed on the opposite wall) features 26 smaller panels—the medieval equivalent of pages—showing colorful scenes from the Passion of Christ.

Climb onto the Panorama del Facciatone for a surprise view of Siena. At the landing just before the top floor, turn right and walk past the rooms, going through the small doorway to the stairwell. Climb down the steps and then up about 60 claustrophobic spiral stairs to the first viewpoint. You can continue up another similar spiral staircase to reach the very top. Look back over toward the Duomo and consider this: If grandiose plans for the church had been completed, you'd be looking straight down the nave.

Cost and Hours: €6; €10 "My Name is Duccio" combo-ticket also includes the Duomo, Crypt, and Baptistery; €3 for worthwhile 40-minute audioguide; €8 combo-audioguide includes Duomo and the library—rentable only at the Duomo, €12/2 people, ID required for deposit; daily March–Sept 9:30–20:00, Oct–Feb 10:00–17:00, tel. 0577-283-048, www.operaduomo.siena.it.

▲**Baptistery**—Siena is so hilly that there wasn't enough flat ground on which to build a big church. What to do? Build a big church anyway and prop up the overhanging edge with the Baptistery. This dark and quietly tucked-away cave of art is worth a look for its cool tranquility bronze panels and angels by Ghiberti, Donatello, and others that adorn the pedestal of the baptismal font (€3; €10 "My Name is Duccio" combo-ticket also includes Duomo, Duomo Museum, and Crypt; daily 9:30–19:00, last entry 30 minutes before closing).

The nearby cathedral "crypt" entrance (halfway up the stairs between the Baptistery and the Duomo Museum) is important archaeologically—several frescoed rooms have been discovered here within the last 10 years. It may be of little interest to the average tourist, but fresco fans will enjoy it.

Cost and Hours: €6, also covered by €10 "My Name is Duccio" combo-ticket, daily 9:30–19:30.

▲**Santa Maria della Scala**—This museum (opposite the Duomo entrance) was used as a hospital until the 1980s. Its labyrinthine 12th-century cellars—carved out of volcanic tuff and finished with brick—go down several floors, and during medieval times were used to store supplies for the hospital upstairs. Today, the hospital and its cellars are filled with museum exhibits, including these main attractions: the fancily frescoed Pellegrinaio Hall (ground floor), most of the original *Fountain of Joy,* St. Catherine's Oratory chapel (first basement), and the Etruscan collection in the Archaeological Museum (second basement). Just inside the complex is the Church of the Santissima Annunziata (which you can see for free by entering from the square, through the left-side wooden door opposite the Duomo entrance).

Cost and Hours: €6, €11 combo-ticket includes Civic Museum, daily 10:30–18:30, last entry 30 minutes before closing, bookstore, café, tel. 0577-534-511, www.santamariadellascala.com.

Pellegrinaio Hall: Sumptuously frescoed, this hall shows medieval Siena's innovative health care and social welfare system in action (c. 1442, wonderfully described in English). Starting in the 11th century, the hospital nursed the sick and cared for abandoned children, as is vividly portrayed in these frescoes. The good works paid off, as bequests and donations poured in, creating the wealth that's evident throughout this building.

Fountain of Joy **Exhibit:** Downstairs you'll find an engaging exhibit on Jacopo della Quercia's early 15th-century *Fountain of Joy (Fonte Gaia)*—and the disassembled pieces of the original fountain itself. In the 19th century, after serious deterioration, the ornate fountain was dismantled and plaster casts were made. (From these casts, they formed the replica that graces Il Campo today.) Here you'll see the eroded original panels paired with their restored casts, along with the original statues that once stood on the edges of the fountain.

On the same floor, pop into **St. Catherine's Oratory,** the small chapel where she prayed and received visions. A holy nail thought to be from Jesus' cross is on the altar.

Archaeological Museum: Descend into the cavernous second basement under groin vaults to be alone with piles of ancient Etruscan stuff excavated from tombs dating centuries before Christ (displayed in a labyrinthine exhibit). Remember, the Etruscans dominated this part of Italy before the Roman Empire swept through—some historians think even Rome originated as an Etruscan town.

Siena's San Domenico Area

Church of San Domenico—This huge brick church is worth a quick look. The spacious, plain interior (except for the colorful flags of the city's 17 *contrade,* or neighborhoods) fits the austere philosophy of the Dominicans and invites meditation on the thoughts and deeds of St. Catherine. Walk up the steps in the rear to see paintings from the life of St. Catherine, patron saint of Siena. Halfway up the church on the right, find a metal bust of

St. Catherine, a small case housing her thumb (sometimes loaned out to other churches), and a reliquary on the lowest shelf containing the chain she used to scourge herself. In the chapel (15 feet to the left) surrounded with candles, you'll see Catherine's actual head atop the altar. Through the door just beyond are the sacristy and the bookstore.

Cost and Hours: Free, daily March–Oct 7:00–18:30, Nov–Feb 9:00–18:30, gift shop tel. 0577-286-848, www.basilicacateriniana.com. A WC (€0.50) is at the far end of the parking lot, to the right as you face the church entrance.

Sanctuary of St. Catherine—Step into Catherine's cool and peaceful home. Siena remembers its favorite hometown gal, a simple, unschooled, but mystically devout soul who, in the mid-1300s, helped convince the pope to return from France to Rome. Because of her intervention, Catherine is honored today as Europe's patron saint. Pilgrims have visited her home since 1464, and architects and artists have greatly embellished what was probably once a humble home (her family worked as wool-dyers). Enter through the courtyard, and walk down the stairs at the far end. The church on your right contains the wooden crucifix upon which Catherine was meditating when she received the stigmata. The chapel on your left was originally the kitchen. Go down the stairs to the left of the kitchen to reach the saint's room. Catherine's bare cell is behind wrought-iron doors. Much of the art throughout the sanctuary depicts scenes from her life.

Cost and Hours: Free, daily 9:30–19:00, a few downhill blocks toward the center from San Domenico—follow signs to *Santuario di Santa Caterina*—at Costa di Sant'Antonio 6, tel. 0577-288-175.

Shopping and Nightlife in Siena

Shopping

The main drag, Via Banchi di Sopra, is a cancan of fancy shops. The big local department store is **Upim** (Mon–Sat 8:30–20:00, Sun 10:00–20:00, Piazza Matteotti).

For easy-to-pack souvenirs, get some of the colorful scarves/flags that depict the symbols of Siena's 17 different neighborhoods (such as the wolf, the turtle, and the snail). They're good for gifts or to decorate your home (sold in varying sizes at souvenir stands).

Sweets: All over town, **Prodotti Tipici** shops sell Sienese

St. Catherine of Siena
(1347–1380)

The youngest of 25 children born to a Sienese cloth-dyer, Catherine began experiencing heavenly visions as a child.

At 16 she became a Dominican nun, locking herself away for three years in a room in her family's house. She lived the life of an ascetic, which culminated in a vision wherein she married Christ. Catherine emerged from solitude to join her Dominican sisters, sharing her experiences, caring for the sick, and gathering both disciples and enemies. At age 23, she lapsed into a spiritual coma, waking with the heavenly command to spread her message to the world. She wrote essays and letters to kings, dukes, bishops, and popes, imploring them to find peace for a war-ravaged Italy. While visiting Pisa during Lent of 1375, she had a vision in which she received the stigmata, the wounds of Christ.

Still in her twenties, Catherine was invited to Avignon, France, where the pope had taken up residence. With her charm, sincerity, and reputation for holiness, she helped convince Pope Gregory XI to return the papacy to the city of Rome. Catherine also went to Rome, where she died young. She was canonized in the next generation (by a Sienese pope), and her relics were distributed to churches around Italy.

specialties. Siena's claim to caloric fame is its *panforte*, a rich, chewy concoction of nuts, honey, and candied fruits that impresses even fruitcake-haters. There are a few varieties: *Margherita*, dusted in powdered sugar, is more fruity, while *panpepato* has a spicy, peppery crust. Locals prefer a chewy white macaroon-and-almond cookie called *ricciarelli*.

Nightlife

Join the evening *passeggiata* (peak strolling time is 19:00) along Via Banchi di Sopra with gelato in hand.

The **Enoteca Italiana** is a good wine bar in a cellar in the Fortezza. To get there, enter the Fortezza via the bridge, cross the running track, and—after passing a tree—go left down a ramp (sample glasses in three different price ranges: €3, €4, and €6.50; Mon–Sat 12:00–24:00, closed Sun; bottles available from all over Italy, snacks served when the bar's pricey restaurant is between mealtimes; outside terrace, tel. 0577-228-832).

Sleeping in Siena

Finding a room in Siena is tough during Easter (April 24 in 2011) or the Palio (July 2 and Aug 16). Many hotels won't take reservations until the end of May for the Palio, and even then they might require a four-night stay. If you're traveling any other time of year, you should still call ahead, as all the guidebooks list Siena's few budget places. While day-tripping tour groups turn the town into a Gothic amusement park in midsummer, Siena is basically yours in the evenings and off-season.

Most of the listed hotels lie between Il Campo and the Church of San Domenico. Part of Siena's charm is its lively, festive character—this means that all hotels can be plagued with noise, even (and sometimes especially) the hotels in the pedestrian-only zone. If tranquility is important for your sanity, ask for a room that's off the street, or consider staying at one of the recommended places outside the center.

Simple Places near Il Campo

Most of these listings are forgettable but inexpensive, and just a horse wreck away from one of Italy's most wonderful civic spaces.

$$ Palazzo Masi is a modern B&B run by husband-and-wife team Alizzardo and Daniela. Just steps away from Il Campo, it has six pleasant, quiet rooms—some furnished with antiques—and shared common areas on the second and third floors of a renovated

---

Sleep Code

(€1 = about $1.25, country code: 39)

S = Single, **D** = Double/Twin, **T** = Triple, **Q** = Quad, **b** = bathroom, **s** = shower only. Breakfast is not included unless noted. If your hotel doesn't provide breakfast, eat at a bar on Il Campo or near your hotel. Credit cards are generally accepted, but I note in the listings if they aren't. (If not, there are ATMs all over town.) Hotel staff generally speak English unless noted otherwise.

To help you easily sort through these listings, I've divided the rooms into three categories based on the price for a standard double room with bath:

$$$ Higher Priced—Most rooms €130 or more.
 $$ Moderately Priced—Most rooms between €90-130.
   $ Lower Priced—Most rooms €90 or less.

Prices can change without notice; verify the hotel's current rates online or by email. For other updates, see www.ricksteves.com/update.

Siena Hotels

1. Palazzo Masi & Launderette
2. To Palazzo Bruchi B&B
3. Piccolo Hotel Etruria
4. Albergo Tre Donzelle
5. Locanda Garibaldi
6. Hotel Cannon d'Oro
7. To Hotel Duomo & Pensione Palazzo Ravizza
8. To Hotel Villa Elda & Hotel Villa Liberty
9. Hotel Chiusarelli
10. Alma Domus
11. Albergo Bernini
12. Internet Cafés (2)
13. Launderette

medieval 14th-century townhouse (D-€80, Db-€120, these rates promised to readers through 2011 if you book direct, discounts for 4 or more nights, cash only, free Wi-Fi, take the road to the far right of City Hall as you're facing it and head down Casato di Sotto about 50 yards to #29, mobile 349-600-9155, www.palazzo masi.com, info@palazzomasi.it).

$$ Palazzo Bruchi B&B offers six tranquil rooms in a 17th-century palazzo overlooking the Tuscan countryside. There's one fancy, spacious room *(luxe)* that features Old World heavy walnut furnishings and period paintings. The other six rooms are smaller and simpler, with bright, cheery decor and views of the quiet interior courtyard. Camilla takes good care of her guests (Sb-€90, Db-€100, *luxe* Db/Tb-€150, Tb-€120–175, Qb-€200, 4 percent cash discount, includes breakfast, free Internet access and Wi-Fi; take Via Banchi di Sotto until it turns into Via Pantaneto, located on left, just before the Church of San Giorgio at #105; tel. & fax 0577-287-342, www.palazzobruchi.it, masignani@hotmail.com).

$$ Piccolo Hotel Etruria has 20 decent air-conditioned rooms but not much soul. The hotel is overpriced for what it is, though well-located and sleepable (S-€50, Sb-€55, Db-€110, Tb-€138, Qb-€170, optional breakfast-€6, curfew at 1:00 in the morning, next to recommended Albergo Tre Donzelle at Via Donzelle 1–3, tel. 0577-288-088, fax 0577-288-461, www.hoteletruria.com, info @hoteletruria.com, Fattorini family).

$ Albergo Tre Donzelle is a fine budget value with 20 plain, institutional, well-worn rooms. Although the showers have seen better days, these may be the cheapest rooms in the center. Don't hang out here...think of Il Campo, a block away, as your terrace (S-€38, D-€49, Db-€60, T-€70, Tb-€85, no rooms available for Palio; with your back to the tower, head away from Il Campo toward 2 o'clock to Via Donzelle 5; tel. 0577-280-358, www .tredonzelle.com, info@tredonzelle.com).

$ Locanda Garibaldi is a modest, characteristically Sienese place. Gentle Marcello rents seven pleasant rooms up a funky, artsy staircase (Db-€75, Tb-€95, only takes reservations a month in advance, half a block downhill from Il Campo at Via Giovanni Dupre 18, tel. 0577-284-204, Marcello and Sonia speak a little English).

$ Hotel Cannon d'Oro, a few blocks up Via Banchi di Sopra, has 30 airy and comfortable rooms, but is a bit noisy and group-friendly (Sb-€71, Db-€90, Tb-€115, Qb-€136, these discounted prices good with this book through 2011, family deals, includes breakfast, a couple blocks from the bus hub at Via Montanini 28, tel. 0577-44-321, fax 0577-280-868, www.cannondoro.com, info @cannondoro.com, Maurizio).

Sleeping Fancy, Southwest of Il Campo

These two classy and well-run places are a 10-minute walk from Il Campo.

$$$ Hotel Duomo has 20 spacious rooms and a bizarre floor plan (Sb-€105, Db-€130, Db suite-€180, Tb-€180, Qb-€230, includes breakfast, air-con, elevator, Internet access, picnic-friendly roof terrace, discounted parking; follow Via di Città, which becomes Via Stalloreggi, to #38; tel. 0577-289-088, fax 0577-43-043, www.hotelduomo.it, booking@hotelduomo.it, Svetlana and Vasilika). If arriving by train, take a taxi (€8) or bus #3 to the Porta Tufi stop, just a few minutes' walk from the hotel; if driving, go to Porta San Marco, turn right, and follow signs to the hotel—drop your bags, then park in the nearby Il Campo lot.

$$$ Pensione Palazzo Ravizza is elegant and friendly, with an aristocratic feel, a peaceful garden, and a Steinway in the upper lounge. It was a noble's luxurious residence, where John F. Kennedy once stayed (Sb-€150, small loft Db-€130, standard Db-€170, superior Db-€200, Tb-€240, family suites-€300, see website for room differences, rooms in back overlook countryside, includes breakfast, air-con, elevator, cable Internet in rooms, Wi-Fi in public spaces, free parking, Via Piano dei Mantellini 34, tel. 0577-280-462, fax 0577-221-597, www.palazzoravizza.com, bureau @palazzoravizza.it, Ariol).

Near San Domenico Church

These hotels are within a 10-minute walk northwest of Il Campo. Albergo Bernini and Alma Domus, which offer views of the old town and cathedral, are about the best values in town.

$$$ Hotel Villa Elda rents 11 bright and light rooms in a newly renovated villa. Classy, stately, and overpriced, it's in a fine neighborhood just a few minutes' walk past the Church of San Domenico (Db-€89–170, more with view, extra person-€20, includes breakfast, air-con, garden and view terrace, Viale Ventiquattro Maggio 10, tel. 0577-247-927, www.villaeldasiena.it, info@villaeldasiena.it).

$$$ Hotel Chiusarelli, with 48 recently renovated rooms in a beautiful Neoclassical villa, has a handy location but is on a very busy street, making it a last resort. Expect traffic noise at night—ask for a quieter room in the back (can be guaranteed with reservation). The bells of San Domenico are your 7:00 wake-up call (Sb-€98, Db-€138, Tb-€175, ask for Rick Steves discount when you book, air-con, Wi-Fi, rental bikes-€4/half-day, across from San Domenico at Viale Curtatone 15, tel. 0577-280-562, fax 0577-271-177, www.chiusarelli.com, info@chiusarelli.com).

$$ Hotel Villa Liberty, a bit farther out, is a former private mansion that was renovated in 2010. It has 18 big, bright, comfortable rooms and lots of street noise (Sb-€70, Db-€100–130, Tb-€130–160, junior suite-€160–180, air-con, elevator, free Wi-Fi, bar, courtyard, free and easy street parking, facing fortress at Viale V. Veneto 11, tel. 0577-44-966, fax 0577-44-770, www.villaliberty .it, info@villaliberty.it).

$ Alma Domus is a church-run hotel offering 43 clean, quiet little rooms for a steal. Bright lamps, quaint balconies, fine views, grand public rooms, top security, and a pleasant atmosphere make this a great value—but they offer only a limited number of doubles. The 10:00 checkout time is strict, but they will store your luggage in their secure courtyard (Sb-€45, Db-€75, Tb-€95, Qb-€110, breakfast included, ask for view room—*con vista,* central air-con, elevator, Internet access; from San Domenico, walk downhill toward the view with the church on your right, turn left down Via Camporegio, make a U-turn at the little chapel down the brick steps to Via Camporegio 37; tel. 0577-44-177, fax 0577-47-601, www.hotelalmadomus.it, info@hotelalmadomus.it).

$ Albergo Bernini makes you part of a Sienese family in a modest, clean home with nine traditional rooms (ask for a quiet room away from the restaurant). Giovanni, wife Daniela, and their three daughters welcome you to their spectacular view terrace for breakfast and picnic lunches and dinners (Sb-€78, D-€65, Db-€85, less in winter, optional breakfast-€7.50, cash only, non-smoking, free Wi-Fi, on the main Il Campo–San Domenico drag at Via della Sapienza 15, tel. & fax 0577-289-047, www.albergobernini .com, hbernin@tin.it).

Farther from the Center

City buses will get you to any of the following places. See locations on the map on page 528.

$$$ Hotel Santa Caterina is a three-star 18th-century place that is professionally run with real attention to quality. Most of the hotel's 22 comfortable rooms were recently renovated, and there's a delightful garden outside (Sb-€115, small Db-€115, Db-€155, Tb-€195, prices promised with this book through 2011—ask for special Rick Steves rate when you reserve, includes buffet breakfast, air-con, fridge in room, elevator, garden side is quieter, but street side—with multipaned windows—isn't bad, parking-€15/ day—request when you reserve, 100 yards outside Porta Romana city gate at Via E.S. Piccolomini 7, tel. 0577-221-105, fax 0577-271-087, www.hscsiena.it, info@hscsiena.it, Lorenza and Andrea). To get to and from downtown Siena, catch shuttle bus #A. To connect with the bus and train stations, take bus #2 (which becomes #17 at Piazza del Sale).

$$$ Frances' Lodge Relais is a small farmhouse B&B less than a mile out of Siena. Franca and Franco rent six modern rooms and one apartment suite in a rustic-yet-elegant old place with an inviting breakfast room, peaceful garden, eight acres of olive trees and vineyards, and great views of Siena and its countryside—even from the swimming pool (small Db-€170, Db-€190, Db suite-€200, Tb-€210–220, Tb suite-€250, Qb suite-€300, these prices promised to Rick Steves readers through 2011, includes great breakfast, air-con-€10, Internet access, free parking, Strada di Valdipugna 2, tel. & fax 0577-42379, mobile 337-671-608, www .franceslodge.it). It's an easy five-minute bus ride from the center (shuttle bus #B) plus a five-minute walk, or €10 by taxi. Consider having an al fresco picnic dinner there, complete with view.

$$ Hotel Porta Romana is at the edge of town off a busy road. Fourteen rooms face the open countryside, and breakfast is served in the garden (Sb-€90, Db-€110, Qb-€130, extra person-€20, 10 percent Rick Steves discount if you book direct, cash preferred, Internet access, free parking, 50 yards from convenient connection to town center via shuttle bus #A—desk has tickets, Via E.S. Piccolomini 35, tel. 0577-42299, fax 0577-232-905, www .hotelportaromana.com, info@hotelportaromana.com, Marco and Evelia).

$$ Hotel San Marco, in a new and characterless building just outside Porta San Marco, has 28 pleasing modern rooms with all the comforts. While it's easiest to drive here, city bus #54 stops 100 yards from the hotel every 15 minutes (Db-€120, discounts for 3 or more nights, air-con, Wi-Fi, free parking, Via Massetana 70, tel. 0577-271-556, fax 0577-271-826, www.sanmarcosiena.it, info @sanmarcosiena.it).

$ Guidoriccio Youth Hostel, which has 100 cheap beds and an institutional ambience, welcomes anyone (€20/bed in doubles, triples, and dorms with sheets; co-ed rooms, includes breakfast, Internet access, self-service laundry-€6, lock-out 10:00–14:00; take bus #10 or #77 from train station or bus #10 or #15 from Piazza Gramsci—about 20 minutes to Via Fiorentina 89 in Stellino neighborhood; tel. 0577-52212, fax 0577-50277, www.ostellosiena .it, info@ostellosiena.it).

Outside of Siena

The following accommodations are set in the lush, peaceful countryside surrounding Siena, and are best for those traveling by car (see locations on the map on page 528).

$$$ Borgo Argenina is a well-maintained, pricey splurge of a B&B. Run by helpful Elena Nappa, it's 20 minutes north of Siena by car in the Chianti region (Db-€170, beautiful gardens, tel. 0577-747-117, www.borgoargenina.it, info@borgoargenina.it).

$$ Il Canto del Sole is a lovingly restored 18th-century farmhouse turned family-friendly B&B located about six miles outside of the Porta Romana city gate. Run by Laura, Luciano, and their son Marco, it features six bright and airy rooms and two apartments with original antique furnishings, a saltwater swimming pool, a game room, and bike rentals (Db-€90–110, Tb-€130, extra bed-€15, apartment-€180–220, air-con in swimming pool–facing rooms and apartment only, Wi-Fi, Val di Villa Canina 1292, 53014 Loc. Cuna, tel. 0577-375-127, fax 0577-373-378, www.ilcantodel sole.com, info@ilcantodelsole.com). An optional five-course dinner is available by request for €20 (wine is extra).

$ **Agriturismo Poggio Salvi** has three pleasant, spacious apartments—rentable only by the week in high season—set in a grassy field near the tiny burg of Poggio Salvi, 15 minutes southwest of Siena. Dwellings are separate, with modern conveniences (rentals from Sat–Sat, €625/2 people and €970/4 people during high season, Internet access, Loc. Poggio Salvi 249, 53010 San Rocco a Pilli, tel. & fax 0577-349-443, mobile 333-290-7890, www .poggiosalvi.net, info@poggiosalvi.net).

Eating in Siena

Sienese restaurants are reasonable by Florentine and Venetian standards. You can enjoy ordering high on the menu here without going broke.

Dining in the Old Town

Antica Osteria Da Divo is *the* place for a dressy and atmospheric €45 meal. The kitchen is creative, the ambience is candlelit, and the food is fresh and top-notch. While the cuisine is flamboyant and almost over-the-top, they serve up my favorite splurge dinner in town. Chef Pino is fanatic about fresh ingredients, enjoys giving traditional dishes his creative spin, and is understandably proud of his desserts (Wed–Mon 12:00–14:30 & 19:00–22:30, closed Tue, reservations smart; facing Baptistery door, take the far right street and walk one long curving block to Via Franciosa 29; tel. 0577-284-381). Those dining here with this book can finish with a complimentary biscotti and *vin santo* or coffee (upon request).

Hostaria Il Carroccio seats guests in an artsy sea-foam-green dining room and serves elegantly presented traditional "slow food" recipes with innovative flair at affordable prices. Musician Sting's wife Trudie Styler (they have a home in Tuscany) pops in now and again with buddies such as Bruce Springsteen to sample the home-made desserts (€7 pastas, €15 *secondi*, €30 tasting *menu*—minimum two people, cash only, reservations wise, Thu–Tue 12:30–15:00 & 19:30–22:00, closed Wed, Via Casato di Sotto 32, tel. 0577-41-165, sweet Renata and Mauro).

Siena Restaurants

100 YARDS
100 METERS

VIEW

P PARKING

→ ENTRY POINT TO SIGHTS

TO TRAIN STATION

BUSES TO FLORENCE, ROME, ETC.

SIENA

1 Antica Osteria Da Divo
2 Hostaria Il Carroccio
3 Osteria Boccon del Prete
4 Trattoria La Torre, Key Largo Bar, Ciao Cafeteria & Spizzico Pizza
5 To Taverna San Giuseppe
6 To Osteria Nonna Gina
7 Trattoria Papei
8 Ristorante Guidoriccio
9 Osteria la Chiacchera
10 Osteria Trombicche

11 La Taverna Di Cecco
12 Locanda Garibaldi
13 Pizzeria La Speranza & Bar Paninoteca San Paolo
14 Bar il Palio
15 Il Bandierino
16 Osteria Liberamente
17 Costarella Gelateria
18 Antica Pizzicheria al Palazzo della Chigiana
19 Consorzio Agrario Siena Grocery
20 Enoteca Italiana

Osteria Boccon del Prete puts an artistic spin on Tuscan favorites using the freshest seasonal ingredients. Their sultry dining room is intimate and tiny, making reservations a must (Mon–Sat 12:30–15:00 & 19:30–22:00, closed Sun, Via S. Pietro 17, tel. 0577-280-388).

Eating Traditional and Rustic in the Old Town

Trattoria La Torre is a thriving *casalinga* (home-cooking) eatery, popular for its homemade pasta, plates of which entice eaters as they enter. The sound of its busy open kitchen adds to the conviviality. Ten tables are packed under one medieval brick arch. Ask for a written menu, or study the one in the window before entering; otherwise, the owner likes to just recite his long string of dishes (Fri–Wed 12:00–15:00 & 19:00–22:00, closed Thu, just steps below Il Campo at Via Salicotto 7, tel. 0577-287-548, Alberto Boccini).

Taverna San Giuseppe, a local favorite, offers modern Tuscan cuisine in a chic grotto atmosphere. Check the posters tacked around the entry for daily specials. Reserve or arrive early to get a table (€8 pastas, €18 *secondi,* Mon–Sat 12:00–14:30 & 19:00–22:00, closed Sun, reservations wise, air-con, 7-minute climb up street to the right of City Hall at Via Giovanni Dupre 132, tel. 0577-42-286, Matteo).

Osteria Nonna Gina wins praise from locals for its good-quality, rustic cuisine and reasonable prices. The front room is more charming than the cellar (€8 pastas, €9 *secondi,* Tue–Sun 12:30–14:30 & 19:30–22:30, closed Mon, 10-minute walk from Il Campo—two blocks beyond Hotel Duomo—at Piano dei Mantellini 2, tel. 0577-287-247).

Trattoria Papei is a Sienese favorite, featuring a bright, bustling family atmosphere and friendly servers dishing out generous portions of rib-stickin' Tuscan specialties and grilled meats (daily 12:00–15:00 & 19:00–22:30, closed Mon off-season, Piazza del Mercato 6, tel. 0577-280-894; Signora Giuliana rules the kitchen, while Amadeo speaks English).

Ristorante Guidoriccio, just a few steps below Il Campo, feels warm and welcoming. You'll get smiling service from Ercole and Elisabetta (€8 pastas, €13 *secondi,* Mon–Sat 12:30–14:30 & 19:00–22:30, closed Sun, air-con, Via Giovanni Dupre 2, tel. 0577-44-350).

Osteria la Chiacchera is a youthful hole-in-the-brick-wall that plays hip music and serves "peasant food" at peasant prices on simple tables and paper placemats. It's an eat-it-and-beat-it, pasta-slinging place, with rickety outside tables clinging to the steep, stepped lane (€5.50 pastas, €7 *secondi,* Wed–Mon 12:00–15:30 &

19:00–24:00, closed Tue, great cakes, skip the *trippa*—tripe, down the street to the left of Albergo Bernini at Costa di S Antonio 4, tel. 0577-280-631, Anna).

Osteria Trombicche is cheap and small, with tight indoor seating and two tiny outdoor tables from which to watch the street scene. They serve fast, hearty food to a young crowd (€5 *ribollita*—bean-and-vegetable soup, €6–12 vegetarian sampler plates, hand-cut prosciutto, Mon–Sat 11:00–22:00, closed Sun, Via delle Terme 66, tel. 0577-288-089).

La Taverna Di Cecco is a clean, comfortable little eatery where earnest Luca serves tasty dishes made from fresh ingredients for a fair price. Try the yummy salads and traditional Sienese specialties (€8 pastas, €12 *secondi*, daily 12:00–16:00 & 19:00–24:00, Via Cecco Angiolieri 19, tel. 0577-288-518).

Locanda Garibaldi, just around the corner from Il Campo, gives you a chance to imagine Siena before the tourist hordes discovered it. Join Marcello, kindly wife Sonia, and their son Simone for an unpretentious Sienese meal in a rustic setting, while the TV murmurs quietly in the corner. The pasta is handmade, the house wine is cheap, and the almond pie *(torta di mandorle)* is sweet and crunchy (€6 pastas, €9 *secondi*, €20 fixed-price meal with house wine, Sun–Fri 12:00–14:00 & 19:00–21:00, closed Sat, Via Giovanni Dupre 18, tel. 0577-284-204).

Eating on Il Campo

If you choose to eat (or drink) on perhaps the finest town square in Italy, you'll pay a premium, meet waiters who don't need to hustle, and get mediocre food. And yet I recommend it. The clamshell-shaped square is lined with venerable cafés, bars, restaurants, and pizzerias. **Caffè Fonte Gaia,** long the classic place to see and be seen, is now a bit tired. **Pizzeria La Speranza** serves good but pricey pizzas with full-frontal views. **Bar il Palio** is best for drinks (straight prices, no cover, decent waiters, great perch). For value, everyone agrees: it's **Il Bandierino,** with the square's best food but worst view. Their *pici* (pee-chee), a fat Sienese spaghetti, is good (€9 salads, €11 pizzas, €11 pastas; no cover but a 20 percent service fee, daily 11:00–23:00, tel. 0577-282-217). For a trendy vibe popular with young people, pick the dynamic little **Osteria Liberamente** (fine wine by the glass, cocktails with good tapas, breakfasts, noisy music inside but great outdoor tables, rotating art exhibit, tastings on Wed, open daily 12:00–late, tel. 0577-274-733, Pino).

If your hotel doesn't serve breakfast or if you'd like something more memorable, consider breakfast on Il Campo—there are plenty of options. A cappuccino and a *cornetto* (croissant) run about €5–6.

Drinks or Snacks from Balconies Overlooking Il Campo

Three places have skinny balconies with benches overlooking the main square for their customers. Sipping a coffee or nibbling a pastry here while marveling at the Il Campo scene is one of my favorite things to do in Europe. And it's very cheap. Survey these three places from Il Campo (from the base of the tower, imagine a 12-hour clock—they are at 10 o'clock, high noon, and 3 o'clock, respectively).

The little **Costarella Gelateria,** on the corner of Via di Città and Costa dei Barbieri, has good ice cream, drinks, and light snacks such as cute little €1.50 sandwiches (Fri–Wed 8:00–late, closes at 22:30 and all day Thu in off-season, Via di Città 33).

Bar Paninoteca San Paolo has a youthful pub ambience and a row of stools overlooking the square. It serves big salads and 50 kinds of sandwiches, hot and cold (€3.50 each, €0.50 extra if you sit outside, order and pay at the counter, food served daily 12:00–2:00, on Vicolo di S. Paolo at the stairs leading down to the top of Il Campo—look for "great hot sandwiches" written on a brown canopy).

Key Largo Bar has two benches in the corner offering a great secret perch. Buy your drink or snack at the bar (no extra charge to sit), climb upstairs, and slide the ancient bar to open the door. Suddenly you're imagining Palio ponies zipping wildly around the corner (daily 7:00–23:00 or until 24:00 in summer, on the corner of Via Rinaldini).

Eating Cheaply in the Center

Antica Pizzicheria al Palazzo della Chigiana may be the official name, but I bet locals just call it Antonio's. For most of his life, frenzied Antonio has carved salami and cheese for the neighborhood. Most of the day, a hungry line spills onto the street as locals wait for their sandwiches—meat and cheese sold by weight—with a good bottle of Chianti (Italian law dictates that he must sell you a bottle of wine and lend you the glasses). Antonio and his boys offer a big cheese-and-meat plate (about €18 gets you 30 minutes of eating) and pull out a tiny tabletop in the corner so you can munch or sip while standing and watch the ham-hock-y scene. He's also got a small table outside (daily 8:00–20:00, Via di Città 95, tel. 0577-289-164). Even if you don't get a sandwich, pop in to inhale the commotion or peruse Antonio's gifty traditional edibles.

Ciao Cafeteria, at the bottom of Il Campo, offers good-value self-service lunches, but no ambience or views (daily 12:00–15:00). The crowded **Spizzico,** a pizza counter in the front half of Ciao, serves huge, inexpensive quarter-pizzas; on sunny days, people take the pizza—trays and all—out on Il Campo for a picnic (daily

11:00–21:00, to left of City Tower as you face it).

Budget eaters look for *pizza al taglio* shops, scattered throughout Siena, selling pizza by the slice. Of all the grocery shops, the biggest is **Consorzio Agrario Siena.** Ask them to make you up a *panino* (Mon–Sat 8:00–19:30, sometimes open Sun, a block off Piazza Matteotti, toward Il Campo at Via Pianigiani 5).

Siena Connections

Siena has sparse train connections but is a great hub for buses to the hill towns, though frequency drops on Sundays and holidays. For most, Florence is the gateway to Siena. Even if you are a railpass-user, connect these two cities by bus—it's faster than the train, and Siena's bus station is more convenient and central than its train station.

SIENA

By Train

Siena's train station is at the edge of town. For details on getting between the town center and the station, see page 529.

From Siena by Train to: Florence (direct trains hourly, 1.5–2 hours, €6.20; bus is better), **Pisa** (2/hour, 1.75 hours, change at Empoli, €7), **Assisi** (8/day, 4–5 hours, most involve 2 changes, bus is faster), **Rome** (1–2/hour, 3.25–3.75 hours, transfer in Florence or Chiusi, €13–21 depending on type of train), **Orvieto** (12/day, 2–2.5 hours, change in Chiusi). For more information, visit www .trenitalia.com.

By Bus

The main bus companies are Sena (www.sena.it) and Tra-In (skip Tra-In's notoriously unreliable website—it's better to get schedule info in person). On schedules, the fastest buses are marked *rapida.* I'd stick with these. Some buses depart Siena from Piazza Gramsci; others leave from the train station (confirm when you buy your ticket). Note that if a schedule lists your departure point as either Via Tozzi or Piazza la Lizza, you actually catch the bus at Piazza Gramsci (Via Tozzi is the street that runs alongside Piazza Gramsci, and Piazza la Lizza is the name of the bus-hub square). Confusing? *Assolutamente!*

Tickets and Information: You can get tickets for Tra-In buses and Sena buses at the train station's bus-ticket kiosk (cash only, Mon–Sat 6:15–20:15, Sun 7:30–12:30 & 14:30–18:30). You can also buy tickets at **Sottopassaggio la Lizza,** located under Piazza Gramsci—look for stairwells to the underground passageway in front of NH Excelsior Hotel (credit cards accepted; Tra-In bus office: Mon–Sat 7:00–19:30, Sun 7:30–19:30, tel. 0577-204-246, www.trainspa.it; Sena bus office: Mon–Sat 7:15–19:45, closed

Sun, tel. 0577-208-282, www.sena.it; on Sundays, when the Sena bus-ticket office is closed, buy tickets next door at Tra-In office). If necessary, you can buy tickets from the driver, but it costs €5 extra.

Services: Sottopassaggio la Lizza also has luggage storage (€5.50/day, carry-on-sized luggage no more than 33 pounds, open daily 7:00–19:00, no overnight storage), posted bus schedules, TV monitors listing all imminent departures for several bus companies, and WCs (€0.50).

By Bus to: Florence (2/hour, 1.25-hour *corse rapide* buses are faster than the train, avoid the 2-hour *diretta* buses unless you have time to enjoy the beautiful scenery en route, €7, by Tra-In bus, tickets available at *tabacchi* shops if bus-ticket office is closed, Florence-bound buses depart from in front of NH Excelsior Hotel on Piazza Gramsci), **San Gimignano** (8/day, 1.25 hours, €5.50, by Tra-In bus, tickets sometimes available at *tabacchi* shops), **Assisi** (daily at 16:40, 2 hours, €12, by Sena bus, bus departs from the train station; terminates 3 miles below Assisi at Santa Maria degli Angeli, where a city bus finishes the ride), **Rome** (8/day, 3 hours, €21, by Sena bus, arrives at Rome's Tiburtina station on Metro line B with easy connections to the central Termini train station), **Milan** (3/day, 4 hours, €31, by Sena bus, departs from Siena's train station, arrives at Milan's Cadorna Station with Metro access and direct trains to Malpensa Airport), **Pisa's Galileo Galilei Airport** (2/day, 1.75 hours, €14, by Tra-In bus, via Poggibonsi); to reach the town center of **Pisa,** the train is better (see earlier).

SIENA

ASSISI

Assisi is famous for its hometown boy, St. Francis, who made very good. While Francis the saint is interesting, Francesco Bernardone the man is even more so, and mementos of his days in Assisi are everywhere—where he was baptized, a shirt he wore, a hill he prayed on, and a church where a vision changed his life.

About the year 1200, this simple friar from Assisi countered the decadence of Church government and society in general with a powerful message of non-materialism and a "slow down and smell God's roses" lifestyle. Like Jesus, Francis taught by example, living without worldly goods and aiming to love all creation. A huge monastic order grew out of his teachings, which were gradually embraced (some would say co-opted) by the Church. Christianity's most popular saint and purest example of simplicity is now glorified in beautiful churches, along with his female counterpart, St. Clare. In 1939, Italy made Francis one of its patron saints.

Francis' message of love, simplicity, and sensitivity to the environment has a broad and timeless appeal. But every pilgrimage site inevitably gets commercialized, and Francis' legacy is now Assisi's basic industry. In summer, this Umbrian town bursts with flash-in-the-pan Francis fans and Franciscan knickknacks. Those able to see past the glow-in-the-dark rosaries and bobblehead friars can actually have a "travel on purpose" experience.

Planning Your Time

Assisi is worth a day and a night. Its old town has a half-day of sightseeing and another half-day of wonder. The essential sight is the Basilica of St. Francis. For a good visit, take my self-guided "Welcome to Assisi" walk, ending at the Basilica of St. Francis.

Schedule time to wander the back streets and linger on the main square, Piazza del Comune.

Most visitors are day-trippers. While the town's a zoo by day, it's a delight at night. Assisi after dark is closer to a place Francis could call home.

Orientation to Assisi

Crowned by a ruined castle, Assisi spills downhill to its famous Basilica of St. Francis. The town is beautifully preserved and rich in history. A 5.5-magnitude earthquake in 1997 did more damage to the tourist industry than to the town's buildings. Fortunately, tourists—whether art-lovers, pilgrims, or both—have returned, drawn by Assisi's special allure.

The city sprawls across a ridge that rises from a flat plain. The Basilica of St. Francis sits at the low end of town; Piazza Matteotti (with bus station and parking lot) is at the high end; and the main square, Piazza del Comune, lies in between. Via San Francesco runs from Piazza del Comune to the basilica. Capping the hill above the town is a ruined castle called the Rocca Maggiore, and rising above that is Mount Subasio. The town is small, and slopes uphill from west to east. Walking uphill from the basilica to Piazza Matteotti takes 30 minutes, while the downhill journey takes about 15 minutes. Some Francis sights lie outside the city walls, both in the valley beneath the ridge and in the hills above.

Tourist Information
The TI is in the center of town on Piazza del Comune (Mon–Sat 8:00–14:00 & 15:00–18:00, Sun 10:00–13:00 & 14:00–17:00 except Sept–May Sun 9:00–13:00, tel. 075-813-8680).

The **Assisi Card** is free to hotel guests staying in town; otherwise it costs €2 from the TI, or from *tabacchi* and other stores around town. The card doesn't give discounted admission to any sites, but it does get you reduced parking fees at the Piazza Matteotti garage, and a 10 percent discount in numerous restaurants, bars, and shops around town (www.assisicard.com).

If you're interested in Assisi's Roman roots, ask at the TI if the excavations of the recently discovered **Domus Romane** (Roman houses) are open yet to the public. If so, they may be worth a look for their original frescoes and mosaic floors (under Piazza del Comune).

Arrival in Assisi
By Train and Bus: City buses connect Assisi's train station with the old town of Assisi on the hilltop (2/hour, 15 minutes, €1), stopping at Piazzale Giovanni Paolo II (near Basilica of St. Francis),

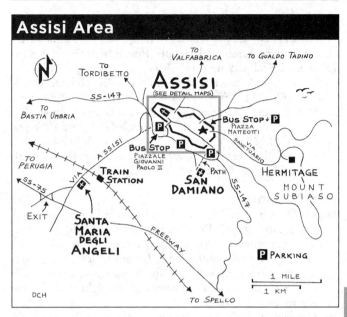

Assisi Area

then Largo Properzio (near Basilica of St. Clare), and finally Piazza Matteotti (top of old town). Buses usually leave from the train station at :15 and :45 past the hour (buy tickets at the train station's newsstand). You can check bags at the newsstand (€3/12 hours, daily 6:00–19:00), but not in the old town.

Going from the old town to the train station, buses usually run from Piazza Matteotti at :10 and :40 past the hour (stopping outside Porta Nuova at Largo Properzio a couple minutes later, and in Piazzale Giovanni Paolo II a few minutes after that).

At Piazzale Giovanni Paolo II (the big parking lot #A for cars and buses below the Basilica of St. Francis), there are two bus stops *(fermata bus):* one sign reads *per f.s. S.M. Angeli, Linea C* (to the train station; this is also where the bus headed for Piazza Matteotti stops—check the front of the bus for its destination), and the other is for Linea B, a short line that runs through the center of the old town to Piazza del Comune. Hop on a bus marked *Piazza Matteotti* if you're exhausted after your basilica visit and need a sweat-free five-minute return to the top of the old town (near many of my recommended hotels).

Taxis from the train station to the old town cost about €15. Extra charges for luggage, night service, and additional people (four is customary) are legitimate. When departing the old town, you'll find taxi stands at Piazzale Giovanni Paolo II, the Basilica of St. Francis, the Basilica of St. Clare, and Piazza del Comune (or have your hotel call for you, tel. 075-813-100). Expect to pay a minimum of €10 for any ride.

By Car: Drivers just coming in for the day should follow the signs to several handy parking lots. Piazza Matteotti's wonderful underground parking garage is at the top of the town (which comes with bits of ancient Rome in the walls; €1/hour, €16/24 hours, or €10/24 hours with Assisi Card, daily 7:00–21:00, until 23:00 in summer). Another big lot, Parking Giovanni Paolo II, is 200 yards below the Basilica of St. Francis (€1/hour for the first two hours, €1.50/hour thereafter). The Parking Mojano lot, while below the wall, comes with an escalator that transports you nearly to the Basilica of St. Clare (€1.50/hour, €12/day).

Helpful Hints

Combo-Ticket: One €8 ticket covers three minor sights: Rocca Maggiore (castle), Pinacoteca (paintings), and the newly restored Roman Forum (*biglietto cumulativo*, valid for 1 day, may include audioguide). It's available at these three sights, but not from the TI. The Assisi Card, which is sold at the TI, doesn't grant discounts on any sights (see "Tourist Information," earlier).

Best Shopping: Tacky knickknacks line the streets leading to the Basilica of St. Francis. For better shops (with local handicrafts), head to Via San Rufino and Corso Mazzini (both just off Piazza del Comune, shops described later in the "Welcome to Assisi" self-guided walk). A Saturday-morning market fills Piazza Matteotti (which has a good parking garage).

Festivals: Assisi annually hosts several interesting festivals commemorating St. Francis and life in the Middle Ages. **Festa di Calendimaggio** is a springtime medieval festival featuring costume parades, concerts, and competitions among Assisi's rival neighborhoods (www.calendimaggiodiassisi.it). Rustic medieval "taverns" pop up around the center offering *porchetta* (roasted pig) and *vino* (starts the first Thu–Sun in May). The **Settimana Francescana** commemorates the beginning of the end of Francis' life, when he made his way for the last time to the Porziuncola Chapel (Sept 28). This week-long celebration culminates in the **Festa di San Francesco,** which marks his death with religious processions, special services, and an arts, crafts, and folklore fair (Oct 3–4). The TI has an *Info Assisi* booklet with details on upcoming festivals and celebrations.

Internet Access: Facing the Cathedral of San Rufino, the recommended **Caffè Duomo** offers free Internet access to anyone ordering even just a drink (otherwise €2.50/hour, daily 7:30–23:00, snacks, Piazza San Rufino 5, tel. 075-815-5209).

Laundry: Belleblu' Lavanderia has a few self-service machines (€5/wash, €4/dry, Mon–Fri 9:00–18:00, Sat 9:00–13:00, closed

St. Francis of Assisi
(1181/82-1226)

In 1202, young Francesco Bernardone donned armor and rode out to battle the Perugians (residents of Umbria's capital city). The battle went badly, and 20-year-old Francis was captured

and imprisoned for a year. He returned a changed man. He avoided friends and his father's lucrative business, and spent more and more time outside the city walls fasting, praying, and searching for something.

In 1206, a vision changed his life, culminating in a dramatic confrontation. He stripped naked before the town leaders, threw his clothes at his father—turning his back on the comfortable material life—and declared his loyalty to God alone.

Idealistic young men flocked to Francis, and they wandered Italy like troubadours, spreading the joy of the Gospel to rich and poor. Francis became a cult figure, attracting huge crowds. They'd never seen anything like it—sermons preached outdoors, in the local language (not Church Latin), making God accessible to all. Francis' new order of monks was also extremely non-materialist, extolling poverty and simplicity. Despite their radicalism, the order eventually gained the pope's own approval and spread through the world. Francis, who died in Assisi at the age of 45, left a legacy of humanism, equality, and love of nature that would eventually flower in the Renaissance.

In Francis' Sandal-Steps
1. Baptized in Assisi's **Cathedral of San Rufino** (then called St. George's).
2. Raised in the family home just off Piazza del Comune (now the **Chiesa Nuova**).
3. Heard call to "rebuild church" in **San Damiano.** (The crucifix of the church is now in the **Basilica of St. Clare.**)
4. Settled and established his order of monks at the **Porziuncola Chapel** (today's St. Mary of the Angels Basilica).
5. Met Clare. (Her tomb and possessions are at the **Basilica of St. Clare.**)
6. Received the pope's blessing for his order (1223 document in the **Basilica of St. Francis' relic chapel**).
7. Had many visions and was associated with miracles during his life (depicted in **Giotto's frescoes** in the Basilica of St. Francis' upper level).
8. Died at the **Porziuncola,** his body later interred beneath the **Basilica of St. Francis.**

Sun, Via Borgo Aretino 6a, tel. 075-816-084).

Travel Agencies: You can purchase train and most bus tickets (except for Siena) at **Agenzia Viaggi Stoppini,** between Piazza del Comune and the Basilica of St. Clare (Mon–Fri 9:00–12:30 & 15:30–18:30, Sat 9:00–12:00, closed Sun, Corso Mazzini 31, tel. 075-812-597). Fabrizio, who runs the agency, is patient with tourists' needs and charges exactly what you'd pay at the train station for tickets.

Bus tickets for Siena and many other destinations are sold at **Agenzia Viaggi Mavitur** (Mon–Fri 8:30–13:00 & 15:00–18:30, Sat 8:30–13:00, closed Sun, Via Frate Elia 1b, below the Basilica of St. Francis, tel. 075-812-377). This agency sells tickets only for buses and planes, not trains. Some tickets can be bought on the bus, though it'll cost you an extra couple of euros (see "Assisi Connections," at the end of this chapter).

Local Guide: Giuseppe Karabotis is a good, licensed guide (€110/2 hours, mobile 328-867-0567, iokarabot@tele2.it); if he's busy, he can recommend other guides.

Getting Around Assisi

Cute electrical minibuses, labeled *Linea A* and *Linea B,* connect the top of the town with the bottom. While it's only a 15-minute stroll down the hill, the climb back up can have you looking for a lift. Before boarding, confirm the destination (below the Basilica of St. Francis at the Porta San Francisco, Piazza del Comune, or Piazza Matteotti). You can buy a bus ticket (good on any city bus) at a newsstand or kiosk for €1, or get a ticket from the driver for €1.50.

Self-Guided Walk

▲▲Welcome to Assisi

There's much more to Assisi than St. Francis and what the blitz tour groups see. This walk covers the town from Piazza Matteotti at the top, down to the Basilica of St. Francis at the bottom. To get to Piazza Matteotti, ride the bus from the train station (or from Piazzale Giovanni Paolo II) to the last stop; drive there (underground parking with Roman ruins); or hike five minutes uphill from Piazza del Comune.

• *Start 50 yards beyond Piazza Matteotti (away from city center—see map).*

❶ The Roman Amphitheater

A lane named Via Anfiteatro Romano leads to a cozy circular neighborhood built around a Roman amphitheater—a reminder that Assisi was once an important Roman town. Circle the amphitheater counterclockwise. Imagine how colorful the town laundry

Welcome to Assisi Walk

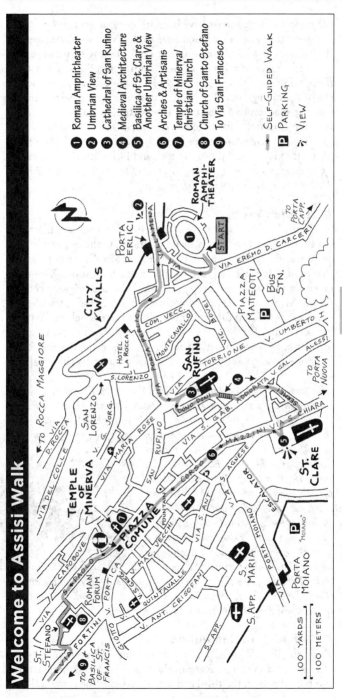

1. Roman Amphitheater
2. Umbrian View
3. Cathedral of San Rufino
4. Medieval Architecture
5. Basilica of St. Clare & Another Umbrian View
6. Arches & Artisans
7. Temple of Minerva/ Christian Church
8. Church of Santo Stefano
9. To Via San Francesco

- Self-Guided Walk
- P Parking
- ⚲ View

ASSISI

basin (on the right) must have been in previous generations, when the women of Assisi gathered here to do their wash. Adjacent to the laundry is a small rectangular pool filled with water; above it are the coats of arms of Assisi's leading families. A few steps farther, hike up the stairs to the top of the hill for an aerial view of the oval amphitheater. The Roman stones have long been absorbed into the medieval architecture. It was Roman tradition to locate the amphitheater outside of town...which this used to be. While the amphitheater dates from the first century A.D., the buildings filling it today were built in the 13th and 14th centuries.

• *Continue on, enjoying the grand view of the fortress in the distance. The lane leads down to a city gate and an...*

❷ Umbrian View

Step outside of Assisi at the Porta Perlici for a commanding view. Umbria, called the "green heart of Italy," is the country's geographical center and only landlocked region. Enjoy the various shades of green: silver green on the valley floor (olives), emerald green (grapevines), and deep green on the hillsides (evergreen oak trees). Also notice Rocca Maggiore ("big fortress"), which provided townsfolk a refuge in times of attack, and, behind you atop the nearer hill, Rocca Minore ("little fortress"), which provides the town's young lovers a little privacy. The quarry (under the Rocca Maggiore) was a handy source for Assisi's characteristic pink limestone.

• *Go back through the gate and follow Via Porta Perlici downhill—it's immediately on your right—into town (toward Hotel La Rocca). Enjoy the higgledy-piggledy architecture (this neighborhood has some of the most photogenic back lanes in town).*

You'll pass a wall containing an aqueduct (on the left) that goes back to Roman times. It still brings water from a mountain spring into the city (push the brass tap for a taste). After about 200 yards, turn left through a medieval town gate (with Hotel La Rocca on your right). Just after the hotel, you'll pass a second gate dating from Roman times. Follow Via Porta Perlici downhill until you hit a fine square facing a big church. (Caffè Duomo, facing Piazza San Rufino, is a nice place for a drink or snack; it also has free Internet access for customers.)

❸ Cathedral of San Rufino

Trick question: Who's Assisi's patron saint? While Francis is one of Italy's patron saints, Rufino (the town's first bishop, martyred and buried here in the third century) is Assisi's. The cathedral (seat

of the local bishop) is 11th-century Romanesque with a Neoclassical interior. Although it has what is considered to be one of the best and purest Romanesque facades in all of Umbria, the big triangular top of it (just a decorative wall) was added in Gothic times. Study the lions at the base of the facade: One is eating a Christian martyr, reminding worshippers of the courage of early Christians.

Enter the church (Mon–Fri 7:00–12:30 & 14:30–19:00, Sat–Sun 7:00–19:00, tel. 075-812-283). While the front of the church is an unremarkable mix of 17th- and 18th-century Baroque and Neoclassical, the rear (near where you enter) has several points of interest. Notice first the two fine statues: St. Francis and St. Clare (by Giovanni Dupré, 1888). To your right is an old baptismal font (in the corner with the black iron grate). In about 1182, a baby boy was baptized in this font. His parents were upwardly mobile Francophiles who called him Francesco ("Frenchy"). In 1194, a nobleman baptized his daughter Clare here. Eighteen years later, their paths crossed in this same church, when Clare attended a class and became mesmerized by the teacher—Francis. Traditionally, the children of Assisi are still baptized here.

The striking glass panels in the floor reveal foundations preserved from the ninth-century church that once stood here. You're walking on history. After the 1997 earthquake, structural inspectors checked the church from ceiling to floor. When they looked under the paving stones, they discovered graves (until Napoleon decreed otherwise, it was common practice to bury people in churches). Underneath that level, they found Roman foundations and some animal bones (suggesting the possibility of animal sacrifice). There might have been a Roman temple here; churches were often built upon temple ruins. As you're standing at the back of the church facing the altar, look left to the Roman cistern (inside the great stone archway). If you take the three steps down, an automatic light should go on. Marvel at the fine stonework and Roman engineering. In the Middle Ages, this was the town's emergency water source when under attack.

Underneath the church, incorporated into the Roman ruins, are the foundations of an earlier Church of San Rufino, now the crypt and Diocesan museum. When open, you can go below to see the saint's sarcophagus and the small museum featuring the cathedral's art from centuries past (€3, mid-March–mid-Oct Thu–Tue 10:00–13:00 & 15:00–18:00, in winter closes at 17:30, closed Wed except in Aug, tel. 075-812-712, www.assisimuseodiocesano.com).

• *Leaving the church, take a sharp left (on Via Dono Doni), following the sign for Santa Chiara. After 20 yards, take a right and go down the stairway to see some...*

❹ Medieval Architecture

At the bottom of the stairs, notice the pink limestone pavement, part of the surviving medieval town. The arches built over doorways indicate that the buildings date from the 12th through the 14th centuries, when Assisi was booming. Italian cities such as Assisi—thriving on the north–south trade between northern Europe and Rome—were in the process of inventing free-market capitalism, dabbling in democratic self-rule, and creating the modern urban lifestyle. The vaults you see that turn lanes into tunnels are reminders of medieval urban expansion (mostly 15th century). While the population grew, people wanted to live within its protective walls. Medieval Assisi had several times the population density of today's Assisi.

Notice the blooming balconies; Assisi holds a flower competition each June.

• *Continue steeply downhill. When you arrive at a street, turn left, going slightly uphill for a block, then take the low road at the Y, and head down Via Sermei. Continue ahead, following the* S. Chiara *sign downhill to the big church.*

❺ Basilica of St. Clare (Basilica di Santa Chiara)

Dedicated to the founder of the Order of the Poor Clares, this Umbrian Gothic church is simple, in keeping with the nuns' dedication to a life of contemplation (daily 6:30–12:00 & 14:00–19:00, until 18:00 in winter). In Clare's lifetime, the order was located in the humble Church of San Damiano, in the valley below, but after Clare's death, they needed a bigger and more glorious building. The church was built in 1265, and the huge buttresses were added in the next century. The interior's fine frescoes were whitewashed in Baroque times.

The Chapel of the Crucifix of San Damiano, on the right, has the wooden crucifix that changed Francis' life. In 1206, an emaciated, soul-searching, stark-raving Francis knelt before this crucifix (then located in the Church of San Damiano) and asked for guidance. The crucifix spoke: "Go and rebuild my Church, which you can see has fallen into ruin." Francis followed the call.

Stairs lead from the nave down to the tomb of St. Clare. Her tomb is at the far end (the image is wax; her bones lie underneath). As you circulate with the crowd of pilgrims, notice the paintings on the walls depicting spiritual lessons from Clare's life and death (see sidebar). At the opposite end of the crypt (back between the stairs, in a large glassed-in area) are important relics: the saint's

---

St. Clare
(1194-1253)

The 18-year-old rich girl of Assisi fell in love with 30-year-old Francis' message, and made secret arrangements to meet him. The night of Palm Sunday, 1212, she slipped out of her father's mansion in town and escaped to the valley below. A procession of friars with torches met her and took her to (what is today) the St. Mary of the Angels Basilica. There, Francis cut her hair, clothed her in a simple brown tunic, and welcomed her into a life of voluntary poverty. Clare's father begged, ordered, and physically threatened her to return, but she would not budge.

Clare was joined by other women who banded together as the Poor Clares. She spent the next 40 years of her life within the confines of the convent of San Damiano: barefoot, vegetarian, and largely silent. Her regimen of prayer, meditation, and simple manual labor—especially knitting—impressed commoners and popes, leading to her canonization almost immediately after her death. St. Clare is often depicted carrying a monstrance (a little temple holding the Eucharist wafer).

---

robes, hair (in a silver box), and an enormous tunic she made—along with relics of St. Francis (including a blood-stained stocking he wore after receiving the stigmata). The attached cloistered community of the Poor Clares has flourished for 700 years.

• *Leave the church and belly up to the viewpoint at the edge of the square for...*

Another Umbrian View

On the left is the convent of St. Clare (global headquarters of all the Poor Clares). Below you lies the olive grove of the Poor Clares, which has been there since the 13th century. In the distance is a grand Umbrian view. Assisi overlooks the richest and biggest valley in otherwise hilly and mountainous Umbria. The municipality of Assisi has a population of 25,000, but only 3,500 people live in the old town. The lower town grew up with the coming of the railway in the 19th century. In the haze, the blue-domed church is St. Mary of the Angels (Santa Maria degli Angeli, described later), the cradle of the Franciscan order. A popular pilgrimage site today, it marks the place where St. Francis lived and worked.

Spanish-speaking Franciscans settled in California. Three of their missions grew into major cities: Los Angeles (named after this church), San Francisco (named after St. Francis), and Santa Clara (named after St. Clare).

• *From the church square, step out into Via Santa Chiara. You can see gates in both directions.*

❻ Arches and Artisans

The gate over the road behind the church dates from 1265. (Beyond it, you can just see the crenellations of the 1316 Porta Nuova, which marks the final expansion of Assisi.) Toward the city center (on Via Santa Chiara, the high road), an arch marks the site of the Roman wall. These three gates represent the town's three walls, illustrating how much the city has grown since ancient times.

Walk uphill along Via Santa Chiara (which becomes Corso Mazzini) to the city's main square. The street is lined with interesting shops selling traditional embroidery, religious souvenirs, and gifty local edibles. About 20 yards before the arch, at #1b, a plaque over the door explains that the old printing press (a national monument now, just inside the door) was used to make fake documents for Jews escaping the Nazis in 1943 and 1944.

The shops on Corso Mazzini, on the stretch between the gate and the main square, show off many local crafts. As you browse, watch for the following shops: Galleria d'Arte Pena (on the left, #20) sells the medieval fantasy townscapes of Paolo Grimaldi, a local painter who runs this shop with his brother. A helpful travel agency is across the street (Agenzia Viaggi Stoppini; see "Helpful Hints," earlier). Next, the shop L'Ulivo Sculture (on the left at #14d) sells olive-wood carvings, as does Poiesis, across the street at #23. It's said that St. Francis made the first nativity scene to help humanize and, therefore, teach the Christmas message. That's why you'll see so many crèches in Assisi. (Even today, nearby villages are enthusiastic about their "living" manger scenes, and Italians everywhere enjoy setting up elaborate crèches in churches for Christmas.) Adjacent to #14 is a bakery, Bar Sensi, selling the traditional raisin-and-apple strudel called *rocciata* (€3.50 each). Farther along on the left (at #9) is Il Duomo, selling religious art, manger scenes, and crucifixion figurines. Across the street, on the right, is a respected embroidery shop. And on the square (at #34, opposite the flags), La Bottega dei Sapori is worth a visit for edible and drinkable souvenirs.

You've walked up what was, in ancient times, the main drag into town. Ahead of you, the six fluted Corinthian columns of the Temple of Minerva marked the forum (today's Piazza del Comune). Sit at the fountain on the piazza for a few minutes of people-watching—don't you love Italy? Within a few hundred yards of this square, on either side, were the medieval walls. Imagine the commotion of 5,000 people confined within these walls. No wonder St. Francis needed an escape for some peace and quiet.

• *Now, head over to the temple on the square.*

❼ Temple of Minerva/Christian Church

Assisi has always been a spiritual center. The Romans went to great lengths to make this first-century B.C. Temple of Minerva a centerpiece of their city. Notice the columns that cut into the stairway. It was a tight fit here on the hilltop. In ancient times, the stairs went down—about twice as far as they do now—to the main drag, which has gradually been filled in over time. The Church of Santa Maria sopra ("over") Minerva was added in the ninth century. The bell tower is from the 13th century. Pop inside the temple/church (Mon–Sat 7:15–19:30, Sun 8:00–19:30, closes at sunset and midday in winter).

Today's interior is 17th-century Baroque. Flanking the altar are the original Roman temple floor stones. You can even see the drains for the bloody sacrifices that took place here. Behind the statues of Peter and Paul, the original Roman embankment peeks through.

Across the square at #11, step into the 16th-century frescoed vaults from the old market. Notice the Italian flair for design. Even this smelly market was once finely decorated. The art style was "grotesque"—literally, a painting in a grotto. This was painted sometime after 1492. How do art historians know? Because it features turkeys—first seen in Europe after Columbus returned with his bag of exotic souvenirs. The turkeys painted here may have been that bird's European debut.

• *From the main square, hike past the temple up the high road, Via San Paolo. After 200 yards, a sign directs you down a lane to the...*

❽ Church of Santo Stefano

Surrounded by cypress, fig, and walnut trees, Santo Stefano—which used to be outside the town walls in the days of St. Francis—is a delightful bit of offbeat Assisi. Legend has it that Santo Stefano's bells miraculously rang on October 3, 1226, the day St. Francis died. Step inside. This is the typical rural Italian Romanesque church—no architect, just built by simple stonemasons who put together the most basic design (daily 8:30–21:30, Sept–May until 18:30).

• *The lane zigzags down to Via San Francesco. Turn right and walk under the arch toward the Basilica of St. Francis.*

❾ Via San Francesco

This was the main drag that led from the town to the basilica holding the body of St. Francis. Francis was a big deal even in his own day. He died in 1226 and was made a saint in 1228—the same year that the basilica's foundations were laid—and his body was moved here by 1230. Assisi was a big-time pilgrimage center, and this street was its booming main drag. The arch marks the end of what was Assisi in St. Francis' day. Notice the fine medieval balcony just below the arch. A few yards farther down (on the left), cool yourself at the fountain. The hospice next door was built in 1237 to house pilgrims. Notice the three surviving faces of its fresco: Jesus, Francis, and Clare.

• *Continuing on, you'll eventually reach Assisi's main sight, the Basilica of St. Francis.*

Self-Guided Tour

▲▲▲Basilica of St. Francis

The Basilica di San Francesco is one of the artistic and religious highlights of Europe. In 1226, St. Francis was buried (with the

outcasts he had stood by) outside of his town on the "Hill of the Damned"—now called the "Hill of Paradise." The basilica is frescoed from top to bottom by the leading artists of the day: Cimabue, Giotto, Simone Martini, and Pietro Lorenzetti. A 13th-century historian wrote, "No more exquisite monument to the Lord has been built."

From a distance, you see the huge arcades "supporting" the basilica. These were 15th-century quarters for the monks. The arcades that line the square and lead to the church housed medieval pilgrims.

Cost and Hours: Free entry; lower basilica daily 6:00–18:45, until 17:45 in winter; relic chapel in lower basilica supposedly open 9:00–18:00 but often closed; upper basilica daily 8:30–18:45, until 18:00 in winter. Modest dress is required to enter the church—no sleeveless tops or shorts for men, women, or children.

The church courtyard at the entrance of the lower basilica has an info office (Mon–Sat 9:15–12:00 & 14:15–17:30, closed Sun, tel. 075-819-001). Audioguides (boring and old-school) are available at the kiosk located outside the entrance of the lower basilica (€4–5 donation requested, daily 9:00–17:00, 40 minutes). You can also take an English tour, offered daily except Sunday (€10 donation requested, call or email to reserve, tel. 075-819-0084, www.sanfrancescoassisi.org, assisisanfrancesco@libero.it). The church bookshop, behind the upper and lower basilica, sells the excellent guidebook *The Basilica of Saint Francis—A Spiritual Pilgrimage* (€3, by Goulet, McInally, and Wood; I used it as a source for my self-guided tour). To worship in the basilica, consider joining the Franciscan brothers in the lower basilica in the morning at 7:00 or

Assisi

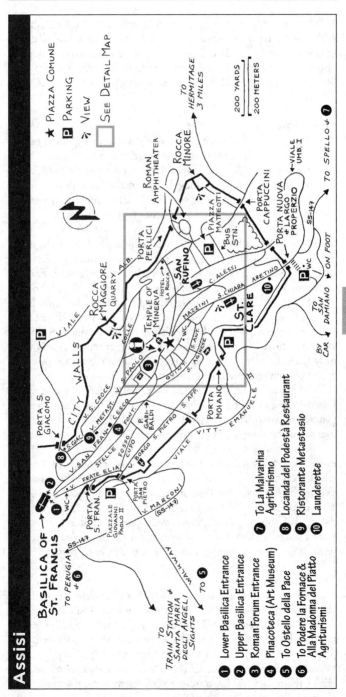

Assisi

① Lower Basilica Entrance
② Upper Basilica Entrance
③ Roman Forum Entrance
④ Pinacoteca (Art Museum)
⑤ To Ostello della Pace
⑥ To Podere la Fornace & Alla Madonna del Piatto Agriturismi
⑦ To La Malvarina Agriturismo
⑧ Locanda del Podestà Restaurant
⑨ Ristorante Metastasio
⑩ Launderette

★ PIAZZA COMUNE
🅿 PARKING
⚲ VIEW
☐ SEE DETAIL MAP

200 YARDS
200 METERS

11:00, or experience a sung Mass Sundays at 10:30. English and additional sung Mass services don't follow a set schedule. Call the basilica to find out when English-speaking pilgrimage groups or choirs have reserved Masses and attend with them (tel. 075-819-001). You can also call to ask about upcoming concerts (tel. 075-819-0032).

Overview

The Basilica of St. Francis, a theological work of genius, can be difficult for the 21st-century tourist/pilgrim to appreciate.

Since the basilica is the reason that most people visit Assisi, and the message of St. Francis has even the least-devout blessing the town Vespas, I've designed this self-guided tour with an emphasis on the place's theology (rather than art history).

A disclaimer before we start: Just as Francis used many Bible legends to help teach the Christian message, legends from the life of Francis were used in later ages to teach the same message. Are they true? In general, probably not. Are they in keeping with Francis' message? Yes. Do I share legends here as if they are historic? Sure.

The church has three parts: the upper basilica, the lower basilica, and the saint's tomb (below the lower basilica). In the 1997 earthquake, the lower basilica—with walls nearly nine feet thick—was unscathed. The upper basilica, with bigger windows and walls only three feet thick, was damaged. Following a restoration, the entire church reopened to visitors in late 1999.

To get oriented, stand at the lower entrance in the courtyard. Opposite the entry to the lower basilica is the information center. (There are two different pay WCs within a half block—up the road in a squat building, and halfway down the big piazza on the left.)

Enter through the grand doorway of the lower basilica. Just inside, decorating the top of the first arch, look up and see St. Francis, who greets you with a Latin inscription. Sounding a bit like John Wayne, he says the equivalent of "Slow down and be joyful, pilgrim. You've reached the Hill of Paradise. And, if you're observant and thoughtful, this church will knock your spiritual socks off."

• *Start with the tomb. Enter the nave and turn left; midway down the nave, follow signs to your right and go downstairs to the tomb.*

The Tomb

The saint's remains are above the altar in the stone box with the iron ties. In medieval times, pilgrims came to Assisi because St. Francis was buried here. Holy relics were the "ruby slippers" of medieval Europe. Relics gave you power—they answered your prayers and won your wars—and ultimately helped you get back to your eternal Kansas. Assisi made no bones about promoting the saint's relics, but hid his tomb for obvious reasons of security. His

The Franciscan Message

Francis' message caused a stir. Not only did he follow Christ's teachings, he adopted his lifestyle, living as a poor, wandering preacher. He traded a life of power and riches for one of obedience, poverty, and chastity. He was never ordained as a priest, but his influence on Christianity was monumental.

The Franciscan existence (Brother Sun, Sister Moon, and so on) is a space where God, man, and the natural world frolic harmoniously. Francis treated every creature—animal, peasant, pope—with equal respect. He and his "brothers" (*fratelli,* or friars) slept in fields, begged for food, and exuded the joy of non-materialism. Franciscan friars were known as the "Jugglers of God," modeling themselves on French troubadours (*jongleurs,* or jugglers) who roved the countryside singing, telling stories, and cracking jokes.

In an Italy torn by conflict between towns and families, Francis promoted peace and the restoration of order. (He set an example by reconstructing the crumbled San Damiano chapel.) While the Church was waging bloody Crusades, Francis pushed ecumenism and understanding. Even today the leaders of the world's great religions meet here for summits.

This richly decorated basilica seems to contradict the teachings of the poor monk it honors, but it was built as an act of religious and civic pride to remember the hometown saint. It was also designed—and still functions—as a pilgrimage center and a splendid classroom. Though monks in robes may not give off an "easy-to-approach" vibe, the Franciscans of today are still God's jugglers (and most of them speak English).

Here is Francis' message, in his own words:

The Canticle of the Sun

Good Lord, all your creations bring praise to you!
Praise for Brother Sun, who brings the day. His radiance
reminds us of you!
Praise for Sister Moon and the stars, precious and beautiful.
Praise for Brother Wind, and for clouds and storms and
rain that sustain us.
Praise for Sister Water. She is useful and humble, precious and pure.
Praise for Brother Fire who cheers us at night.
Praise for our sister, Mother Earth, who feeds us and
rules us.
Praise for all those who forgive because you have forgiven them.
Praise for our sister, Bodily Death, from whose embrace
none can escape.
Praise and bless the Lord, and give thanks, and, with
humility, serve him.

ASSISI

body was buried secretly while the basilica was under construction, and over the next 600 years, the exact location was forgotten. When the tomb was to be opened to the public in 1818, it took a month and a half to find his actual remains.

Francis' four closest friends and first followers are memorialized in the corners of the room. Opposite the altar, up four steps in between the entrance and exit, notice the small copper box behind the metal grill. This contains the remains of Francis' rich Roman patron, Jacopa dei Settesoli. She traveled to see him on his deathbed, but was turned away because she was female. Francis waived the rule and welcomed "Brother Jacopa" to his side.

The candles you see are the only real candles in the church (others are electric). Pilgrims pay a coin, pick up a candle, and place it at the tomb. Franciscans will light it later.

• *Climb back to the lower nave.*

Nave of Lower Basilica

Appropriately Franciscan—subdued and Romanesque—this nave was frescoed with parallel scenes from the lives of Christ (right) and Francis (left), connected by a ceiling of stars. Unfortunately, after the church was built and decorated, side chapels needed to be erected to provide mausoleums for the rich families that patronized the work of the order. Huge arches were cut out of some scenes, but others survive. In the fresco directly above the entry to the tomb, Christ is being taken down from the cross (just the bottom half of his body can be seen, to the left), and it looks like the story is over. Defeat. But in the opposite fresco (above the tomb's exit), we see Francis preaching to the birds, reminding the faithful that the message of the Gospel survives.

These stories directed the attention of the medieval pilgrim to the altar, where he could meet God through the sacraments. The church was thought of as a community of believers sailing toward God. The prayers coming out of the nave (*navis,* or ship) fill the triangular sections of the ceiling—called *vele,* or sails—with spiritual wind. With a priest for a navigator and the altar for a helm, faith propels the ship.

Stand behind the altar (toes to the bottom step, facing the entrance) and look up. The three scenes in front of you represent the creed of the Franciscans: Directly above the tomb of St. Francis, you'll see to the right, **Obedience** (Francis appears twice, wearing a rope harness and kneeling in front of Lady Obedience); to the left, **Chastity** (in a tower of purity held up by two angels); and straight ahead, **Poverty.** Here Jesus blesses the marriage as Francis slips a ring on Lady Poverty. In the foreground, two "self-sufficient" yet pint-size merchants (the new rich of a thriving northern Italy) are throwing sticks and stones at the bride. But Poverty, in her patched

Basilica of St. Francis—Lower Level

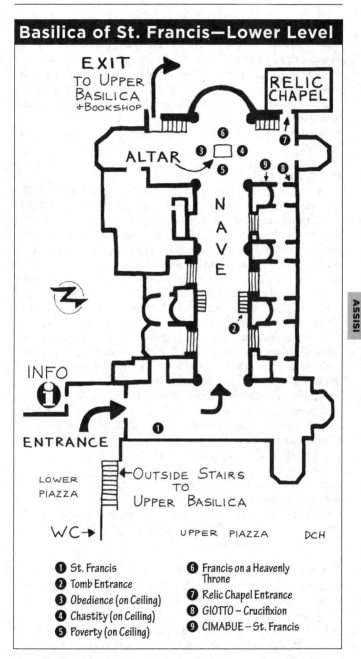

EXIT
TO UPPER
BASILICA
& BOOKSHOP

RELIC CHAPEL

ALTAR

6

3   4

5

7

9   8

NAVE

2

INFO

ENTRANCE

2

LOWER PIAZZA

← OUTSIDE STAIRS TO UPPER BASILICA

WC →

UPPER PIAZZA   DCH

1 St. Francis
2 Tomb Entrance
3 Obedience (on Ceiling)
4 Chastity (on Ceiling)
5 Poverty (on Ceiling)

6 Francis on a Heavenly Throne
7 Relic Chapel Entrance
8 GIOTTO – Crucifixion
9 CIMABUE – St. Francis

ASSISI

wedding dress, is fertile and strong, and even those brambles blossom into a rosebush crown. The three knots of the rope that tie the Franciscan robe symbolize obedience, chastity, and poverty.

Putting your heels to the altar and bending back like a drum major, look up for a peek at the reward for a life of obedience, chastity, and poverty: **Francis on a heavenly throne** in a rich, golden robe. He traded a life of earthly simplicity for glory in heaven.

• *Now, turn to the right and march to the corner, where steps lead down into the...*

Relic Chapel

This chapel is filled with fascinating relics (which a €0.50 flier explains in detailed English). Step in and circle the room clockwise. You'll see the silver chalice and plate that Francis used for the bread and wine of the Eucharist (in small, dark windowed case set into wall, marked *Calice e Patena*). Francis believed that his personal possessions should be simple, but the items used for worship should be made of the finest materials. In the corner display case is a small section of the itchy haircloth *(cilizio)*—not sheep's wool, but cloth made from scratchy horse or goat hair—worn by Francis as penitence. In the next corner are the tunic and slippers that Francis donned during his last days. Next, find a prayer (in a fancy silver stand) that St. Francis wrote for Brother Leo, signed with his tau cross. The last letter in the Hebrew alphabet, tav ("tau" in Greek) is symbolic of faithfulness to the end. Francis signed his name with this simple capital-T-shaped character. Next is a papal document (1223) legitimizing the Franciscan order and assuring his followers that they were not risking a (deadly) heresy charge. Finally, see the tunic that was lovingly patched and stitched by followers of the five-foot, four-inch-tall St. Francis.

Before leaving the chapel, notice the modern paintings done in the last year or so by local artists. Over the entrance, Francis is shown being born in a stable like Jesus (by Capitini). Scenes from the life of Clare and Padre Pio (a Capuchin priest, huge in Italy, who was sainted in 2002) were painted by Stefanelli and Antonio.

• *Return up the stairs to the...*

Transept of Lower Basilica

This church brought together the greatest Sienese (Lorenzetti and Simone Martini) and Florentine (Cimabue and Giotto) artists of the day. Look around at the painted scenes. In 1300, this was radical art—believable homespun scenes, landscapes, trees, real people. Study **Giotto's painting of the Crucifixion,** with the eight sparrow-like angels. For the first time, holy people are expressing emotion: One angel turns her head sadly at the sight of Jesus, and another scratches her hands down her cheeks, drawing blood.

ASSISI

Mary (lower left), previously in control, has fainted in despair. The Franciscans, with their goal of bringing God to the people, found a natural partner in Europe's first modern (and therefore natural-ist) painter, Giotto.

To grasp Giotto's Renaissance leap, compare his work with the painting to the right, by Cimabue. It's Gothic, without the 3-D architecture, natural backdrop, and slice-of-life real-ity of Giotto's work. **Cimabue's St. Francis** (far right) shows the saint with the stigmata—Christ's marks of the Crucifixion. Contemporaries described Francis as being short, with a graceful build, dark hair, and sparse beard. (This is considered the most accurate portrait of Francis—done according to the descrip-tion of one who knew him.) The sunroof haircut (tonsure) was standard for monks of the day. According to legend, the brown robe and rope belt were inventions of necessity. When Francis stripped naked and ran away from Assisi, he grabbed the first clothes he could, a rough wool peasant's tunic and a piece of rope, which became the uniform of the Franciscan order. To the left, at eye level under the sparrow-like angels, are paintings of saints and their exquisite halos (by Simone Martini or his school).

Francis' friend, "Sister Bodily Death," was really not all that terrible. In fact, Francis would like to introduce you to her now (above and to the right of the door leading into the relic chapel). Go ahead, block the light from the door with this book and meet her. Before his death, Francis added a line to *The Canticle of the Sun:* "Praise for our sister, Bodily Death, from whose embrace none can escape."

• *Now cross the transept to the other side of the altar (enjoying some of the oldest surviving bits of the inlaid local-limestone flooring—c. 13th century) and find the staircase going up. Immediately above the stairs is Pietro Lorenzetti's* Francis Receiving the Stigmata. *(Francis is considered the first person ever to earn the marks of the cross through his great faith and love of the Church.) Make your way to the...*

Courtyard

The courtyard overlooks the 16th-century cloister, the heart of this monastic complex. The courtyard functioned as a cistern to collect rainwater, supplying enough for 200 monks (today, there are about 40). The Franciscan order emphasizes teaching. This place functioned as a kind of theological center of higher learning designed to rotate monks in for a six-month stint, then send them back home more prepared and inspired to preach effectively. That explains the complex narrative of the frescoes wallpapering the walls and halls here. The treasury *(Museo del Tesoro)* to the left of the bookstore is free (donation requested) and features ornately

Basilica of St. Francis—Upper Level

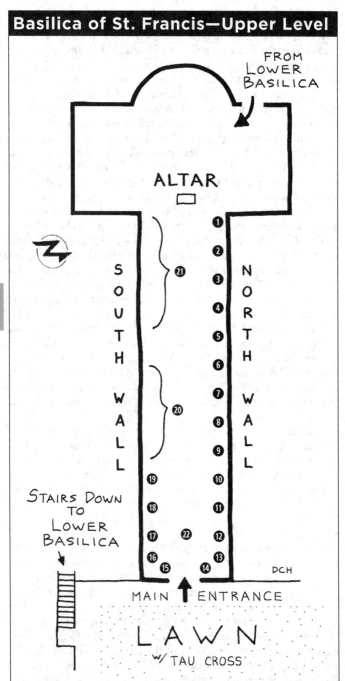

FROM LOWER BASILICA

ALTAR

SOUTH WALL

NORTH WALL

㉑

⑳

① ② ③ ④ ⑤ ⑥ ⑦ ⑧ ⑨ ⑩ ⑪ ⑫ ⑬ ⑭

⑮ ⑯ ⑰ ⑱ ⑲

㉒

STAIRS DOWN TO LOWER BASILICA

DCH

MAIN ENTRANCE

LAWN
w/ TAU CROSS

ASSISI

Basilica Key

① A Common Man Spreads his Cape before Francis

② Francis Offers his Cape to a Needy Stranger

③ Francis is Visited by the Lord in a Dream

④ Francis Prays to the Crucifix

⑤ Francis Relinquishes his Possessions

⑥ The Pope has a Dream

⑦ The Pope Confirms the Franciscan Order

⑧ A Vision of the Flaming Chariot

⑨ A Vision of Thrones

⑩ Exorcism of Demons in Arezzo

⑪ St. Francis Before the Sultan

⑫ Ecstasy of St. Francis

⑬ The Crèche at Greccio

⑭ Miracle of the Spring

⑮ Sermon to the Birds

⑯ The Knight of Celano Invites Francis to his Deathbed

⑰ Preaching for Pope Honorius III

⑱ The Apparition at Arles

⑲ Francis Receives the Stigmata

⑳ Francis' Death, Funeral, and Canonization

㉑ Three "Post Mortem Miracles" Associated with St. Francis

㉒ Tan Patches on Ceiling (1997 Earthquake Damage)

decorated chalices, reliquaries, vestments, and altarpieces.

• *From the courtyard, climb the stairs (next to the bookshop) to the...*

Upper Basilica

Built later than its counterpart below, the brighter upper basilica is considered the first Gothic church in Italy (started in 1228).

Local guides say it has the oldest stained glass in Italy (behind the apse), but the basilica's draw for art-lovers is that it was practically wallpapered by Giotto and his assistants in about 1297–1300. Or perhaps it was subcontracted to other artists—scholars debate it (for more on Giotto, see page 151). The gallery of frescoes shows 28 scenes from the life of St. Francis. The events are a mix of documented history and folk legend.

• *Get oriented by facing the basilica's main altar. Working clockwise, start on the right-hand (north) wall. Note that the subtitles in the black strip below the frescoes describe each scene in clear Latin—and affirm my interpretation.*

❶ **A common man spreads his cape before Francis** in front of the Temple of Minerva on Piazza del Comune. Before his conversion, young Francis was the model of Assisian manhood—handsome, intelligent, and well-dressed, befitting the son of a wealthy cloth dealer. Above all, he was liked by everyone, a natural charmer who led his fellow teens in nights of wine, women, and song. Medieval pilgrims understood a deeper meaning in this scene: The "eye" of God (symbolized by the rose window in the Temple of Minerva) looks over 20-year-old Francis, a dandy "imprisoned" in his own selfishness (the Temple—with barred windows—was once a prison).

❷ **Francis offers his cape to a needy stranger** (next panel). Francis was always generous of spirit. He became more so after being captured in battle and held for a year as a prisoner of war, then suffering from illness. Charity was a Franciscan forte.

❸ **Francis is visited by the Lord in a dream.** Still unsure of his calling, Francis rode off to the Crusades. One night, he dreams of a palace filled with armor marked with crosses. Christ tells him to leave the army—to become what you might consider the first "conscientious objector"—and go home to wait for a non-military assignment in a new kind of knighthood. He returned to Assisi and, though reviled as a coward, would end up fighting for spiritual wealth, not earthly power and riches.

❹ **Francis prays to the crucifix** in the Church of San Damiano. After months of living in a cave, fasting, and meditating, Francis kneels in the run-down church and prays. The crucifix speaks, telling him: "Go and rebuild my Church, which you can see has fallen into ruin." Francis hurried home and sold his father's cloth to pay for God's work. His furious father dragged him before the bishop.

❺ **Francis relinquishes his possessions.** In front of the bishop and the whole town, Francis strips naked and gives his dad his clothes, credit cards, and time-share on Capri. Francis raises his hand and says, "Until now, I called you father. From now on, my only father is my Father in Heaven." He then ran off into the hills, naked and singing. In this version, Francis is covered by the bishop, symbolizing his transition from a man of the world to a man of the Church. Notice the disbelief and concern on the bishop's advisors' faces; subtle expressions like these wouldn't have made it into other medieval frescoes of the day.

❻ **The pope has a dream.** Francis headed to Rome, seeking the pope's blessing on his fledgling movement. Initially rebuffing Francis, the pope then dreams of a simple, barefooted man propping up his teetering Church, and then...

❼ **The pope confirms the Franciscan order,** handing Francis and his gang the document now displayed in the relic chapel.

Francis' life was surrounded by visions and miracles, shown in three panels in a row: (❽) **A vision of the flaming chariot,** (❾) **A vision of thrones,** and (❿) **Exorcism of demons in Arezzo.**

• *Next see...*

❶ St. Francis before the sultan. Francis' wandering ministry took him to Egypt during the Crusades (1219). He walked unarmed into the Muslim army camp. They captured him, but the sultan was impressed with Francis' manner and let him go, reportedly whispering, "I'd convert to your faith, but they'd kill us both." Here the sultan gestures from his throne.

❷ Ecstasy of St. Francis. This oft-painted scene shows the mystic communing with Christ.

❸ The Crèche at Greccio. A creative teacher, Francis invents the tradition of manger scenes in 1223.

• *Around the corner, see the...*

❹ Miracle of the spring. Shown here getting water out of a rock to quench a stranger's thirst, Francis felt closest to God when in the hills around Assisi, seeing the Creator in the creation.

❺ Sermon to the birds. In his best-known miracle, Francis is surrounded by birds as they listen to him teach. Francis embraces all levels of creation. One interpretation of this scene is that the birds, which are of different species, represent the diverse flock of humanity and nature, all created and beloved by God and worthy of each other's love.

• *Continue to the south wall for the rest of the panels.*

Despite the hierarchical society of his day, Francis was welcomed by all classes, shown in these three panels: (**❻**) **The knight of Celano invites Francis to his deathbed;** (**❼**) **Preaching for Pope Honorius III,** who listens carefully; and (**❽**) **The apparition at Arles,** which illustrates how Francis could be in two places at once (something only Jesus and saints can pull off). The proponents of Francis, who believed he was destined for sainthood, show him performing the necessary miracles.

❾ Francis receives the stigmata. It's September 17, 1224,

and Francis is fasting and praying on nearby Mount Alverna when a six-winged angel (called a seraph) appears with holy laser-like powers to burn in the marks. For the strength of his faith, Francis is given the marks of his master, the "battle scars of love"...the stigmata. These five wounds Christ suffered during crucifixion (nails in palms and feet, lance in side) marked Francis' body for the rest of his life.

The next panels (**❿**) deal with **Francis' death, funeral, and canonization.** The last panels (**㉑**) show **miracles** associated with the saint after his death, proving that he's in heaven and bolstering his eligibility for sainthood.

Before you leave the front entrance, look up at the ceiling and the walls near the rose window to see (㉒) **large tan patches.** In 1997, when a 5.5-magnitude quake hit Assisi, it shattered the upper basilica's frescoes into 300,000 fragments that had to be meticulously picked up and pieced back together. Shortly after the quake, two monks and two art scholars were standing here when an aftershock shook the ceiling frescoes down, killing them.

Outside, on the lawn, are the Latin *pax* (peace) and the Franciscan tau cross. For a drink or snack, the Bar San Francisco (facing the upper basilica) is handy. For *pax,* take the high lane back to town, up to the castle, or into the countryside.

Sights in Assisi

▲**Roman Forum (Foro Romano)**—For a look at Assisi's Roman roots, tour the Roman Forum, which is actually under Piazza del Comune. The floor plan is clearly explained in English, as are the surviving odd bits and obscure pieces. During your visit, you'll walk on an ancient Roman road.

Cost and Hours: €4, included in €8 combo-ticket that also covers next two sights, daily 10:00–13:00 & 14:30–19:00, closes at 17:00 in winter; from Piazza del Comune, go one-half block down Via San Francesco—it's on your right; tel. 075-815-5077.

Pinacoteca—This small museum attractively displays its 13th- to 17th-century art (mainly frescoes), with general English information in nearly every room. There's a damaged Giotto Madonna and a rare secular fresco (to the right of the Giotto art), but it's mainly a peaceful walk through a pastel world—best for art-lovers.

Cost and Hours: €3, included in €8 combo-ticket, daily 10:00–18:00, June–Aug until 19:00, Nov–Feb closes at 17:00, Via San Francesco, no building number—look for banner above entryway, on main drag between Piazza del Comune and Basilica of St. Francis, tel. 075-815-5077.

▲**Rocca Maggiore**—The "big castle" offers a good look at a 14th-century fortification and a fine view of Assisi and the Umbrian countryside. If you're pinching your euros, the view is just as good from outside the castle. There's talk of restoring some rooms in their original medieval style, possibly in time for your visit.

Cost and Hours: €5, included in €8 combo-ticket, daily from 10:00 until an hour before sunset—about 19:15 in summer, tel. 075-815-5077.

Commune with Nature—For a picnic with the same birdsong and views that inspired St. Francis, leave the tourists behind and hike to the Rocca Minore (small private castle, not tourable) above Piazza Matteotti.

In Santa Maria degli Angeli

This modern part of Assisi sits in the flat valley below the hill town (see "Assisi Area" map, earlier). It has two sights: the basilica that marks the spot where Francis lived, worked, and died; and the church where the crucifix spoke to him.

▲▲St. Mary of the Angels Basilica (Basilica Patriarcale di Santa Maria degli Angeli in Porziuncola)—This huge basilica,

towering above the buildings below Assisi, was built in the 16th century around the tiny but historic Porziuncola Chapel (now directly under the dome). The last part of the church's Italian name ("in Porziuncola") means literally "over the Porziuncola Chapel." After Francis' conversion, some local monks gave him this *porzi-uncola,* or "small portion"—a little land with a fixer-upper chapel.

Francis lived here after he founded the Franciscan Order in 1208, and this was where he consecrated St. Clare as a Bride of Christ. What would humble Francis think of the huge church—Christianity's 10th largest—that was built over his tiny chapel?

Behind the chapel on the right, find the Cappella del Transito, which marks the site of Francis' death on October 3, 1226. Francis died as he'd lived—simply, in a small hut located here. On his last night on earth, he invited some friars to join him in a Last Supper–style breaking of bread. Then he undressed, lay down on the bare ground, and began to recite Psalm 141, "Lord, I cry unto thee." He spoke the last line, "Let the wicked fall into their own traps, while I escape"...and he passed on.

Follow *Roseto* signs to the rose garden. Francis, fighting a temptation that he never named, once threw himself onto the roses. As the story goes, the thorns immediately dropped off. Thornless roses have grown here ever since.

When you reach the statue of Francis petting a sheep, look to the right, through the window at the rose garden. The Rose Chapel (Cappella delle Rose) is built over the place where Francis lived.

In the autumn, a room in the next hallway displays a giant animated nativity scene (a reminder to pilgrims that Francis first established the tradition of manger scenes as a teaching aid). The bookshop has some works in English, while the Porziuncola Museum features a few monastic cells of interest to pilgrims, a model of Assisi during Francis' lifetime, and religious art and objects from the basilica (€2.50, museum open May–mid-Sept Tue–Sun 9:30–12:30 & 15:30–19:00, mid-Sept–April Tue–Sun 9:30–12:30 & 15:00–18:00, closed Mon, tel. 075-805-1419, www .porziuncola.org).

Cost and Hours: The basilica is free to enter and open Mon–Sat 6:15–12:50 & 14:30–19:30; it opens 30 minutes later on Sun (tel. 075-805-11). A little TI kiosk is across the street from the souvenir stands (generally daily 10:00–12:30 & 16:00–18:30, tel. 075-804-4554). As you face the church, the best WC is on your right.

Getting There: To get to St. Mary of the Angels Basilica from Assisi's train station, it's a five-minute walk (exit station left, take first left at McDonald's—you'll see the dome in the distance). When you leave the basilica, you can catch a bus that goes to the station and on to Assisi's old town (leaving church, stop is on your right). The orange city buses run twice hourly (buses to the old town depart the basilica at :10 and :40 after the hour; tickets cost €1 if you buy at *tabacchi* or the newsstand near the TI, €1.50 if you buy from driver; 20-minute ride up to old town). It's efficient to visit this basilica either on your way to the old town of Assisi or when you leave.

Museo Pericle Fazzini—This new museum, housed in the arcaded building opposite St. Mary of the Angels Basilica, features works by the contemporary Italian sculptor Pericle Fazzini. The collection includes bronzes of St. Francis and the original sketch of "The Resurrection"—Fazzini's famous bronze of Jesus rising from a nuclear-bomb crater, commissioned by the pope for the audience hall of the Vatican.

Cost and Hours: €5, Tue–Sun 10:00–13:00 & 16:00–19:00, closed Mon, tel. 075-804-4586, www.museo.periclefazzini.it.

Church of San Damiano—Located in the valley beneath the Basilica of St. Clare, this church and convent was where Francis received his call and where Clare spent her days as Mother Superior of the Poor Clares. Today, there's not much to see, but it's a relatively peaceful escape from touristy Assisi. Drivers can zip right there, while walkers descend pleasantly from Assisi for 15 minutes through an olive grove.

In 1206, Francis was inside the church when he heard the

wooden crucifix order him to rebuild the church. (The crucifix in San Damiano is a copy; the original is now displayed in the Basilica of St. Clare.) Francis initially interpreted these miraculous words as a call to rebuild crumbling San Damiano. He sold his father's cloth for money to fix the church. (The church we see today, however, was rebuilt later by others.) Eventually, Francis realized the call was to revitalize the Christian Church at large.

As he approached the end of his life, Francis came to San Damiano to visit his old friend Clare. She set him up in a simple reed hut in the olive grove where, in September 1225, he was inspired to write his poem *The Canticle of the Sun* (see page 575).

Cost and Hours: Daily, 10:00–12:00 & 14:00–18:00, closes at 16:30 in winter, tel. 075-812-273, www.assisiofm.org; start walking from Porta Nuova parking lot at south end of town and follow the signs.

Outside of Assisi

Hermitage (Eremo delle Carceri)—If you want to follow further in St. Francis' footsteps, take a trip up the rugged slopes of nearby Mount Subasio to the humble hermitage Francis and his followers retreated to for solitude. The highlight is a look at the tiny, dank cave where Francis would retire for private prayer.

Cost and Hours: Free, daily 6:30–19:00, until 17:30 off-season, tel. 075-812-301, www.eremocarceri.it. Guided visits may be available.

Getting There: There is no public transportation right to the top; either drive, take a taxi, or hike. Starting from Assisi's Porta Cappuccini gate, it's a stiff three-mile, 1.5-hour hike with an elevation gain of 800 feet. The Linea A bus from Piazza del Comune will cut your hike by 30 minutes; get off at the Camping Fortemaggiore stop. Wear sturdy shoes and bring water. A souvenir kiosk at the entrance sells drinks and sandwiches.

Sleeping in Assisi

Assisi accommodates large numbers of pilgrims on religious holidays (see list on page 981). Finding a room at any other time should be easy. Few hotels are air-conditioned. Locals suggest that you keep your windows closed in the middle of the day so that your room will be as cool as possible in the evening.

Hotels and Rooms

$$$ Hotel Umbra, a quiet villa in the middle of town, has 24 spacious rooms with great views and fine accommodations (Sb-€75, standard Db-€110, superior Db-€123, Tb-€155, 10 percent cash discount for 2 or more nights with this book, air-con, elevator,

---

Sleep Code

(€1 = about $1.25, country code: 39)
S = Single, **D** = Double/Twin, **T** = Triple, **Q** = Quad, **b** = bathroom, **s** = shower only. Unless otherwise noted, credit cards are accepted, English is spoken, and breakfast is included.

To help you sort easily through these listings, I've divided the rooms into three categories based on the price for a standard double room with bath:

  $$$ Higher Priced—Most rooms €100 or more.
   $$ Moderately Priced—Most rooms between €55–100.
    $ Lower Priced—Most rooms €55 or less.

Prices can change without notice; verify the hotel's current rates online or by email. For other updates, see www .ricksteves.com/update.

ASSISI

peaceful garden and view sun terrace, most rooms have views, good restaurant, dinner only, closed Dec–Feb, just off Piazza del Comune under the arch at Via degli Archi 6, tel. 075-812-240, fax 075-813-653, www.hotelumbra.it, info@hotelumbra.it, family Laudenzi).

$$ Hotel Ideale, on a ridge overlooking the valley, offers 14 airy, modern rooms (all with views, 10 with balconies), a tranquil garden setting, and free parking (Sb-€50, Db-€90, prices good with this book through 2011, 10 percent discount for stays of 3 or more nights, may be cheaper off-season, air-con, confirm your arrival time especially if it's after 17:00, Piazza Matteotti 1, tel. 075-813-570, fax 075-813-020, www.hotelideale.it, info@hotelideale .it, friendly sisters Lara and Ilaria). The hotel is close to the bus stop (and parking lot) at Piazza Matteotti at the top end of town.

$$ Hotel Belvedere, a great value, is a modern building with 16 big, spacious rooms—nine come with sweeping views (Sb-€45, Db-€65, breakfast-€5, elevator, large communal view terrace, 2 blocks past Basilica of St. Clare at Via Borgo Aretino 13, tel. 075-812-460, fax 075-816-812, www.assisihotelbelvedere.it, info @assisihotelbelvedere.it, run by Enrico and Mary from New Jersey).

$$ La Pallotta offers seven clean, bright rooms and a communal view room on the top floor (Sb-€45, Db-€75, free Internet access, Wi-Fi, free use of washer and clothesline, free hot drinks and cake at teatime, free use of an Assisi audioguide; a block off Piazza del Comune at Via San Rufino 6—go up a short flight of stairs outside building, above the arch, to reach entrance; tel. & fax 075-812-307, www.pallottaassisi.it, pallotta@pallottaassisi.it, helpful Stefano, Serena, and family). They also have a good restaurant

Assisi Hotels & Restaurants

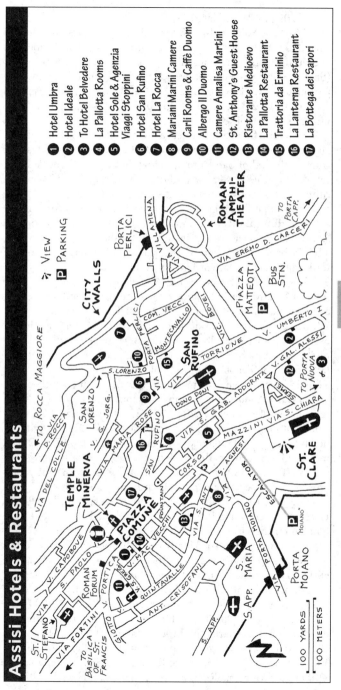

1. Hotel Umbra
2. Hotel Ideale
3. To Hotel Belvedere
4. La Pallotta Rooms
5. Hotel Sole & Agenzia Viaggi Stoppini
6. Hotel San Rufino
7. Hotel La Rocca
8. Mariani Marini Camere
9. Carli Rooms & Caffè Duomo
10. Albergo Il Duomo
11. Camere Annalisa Martini
12. St. Anthony's Guest House
13. Ristorante Medioevo
14. La Pallotta Restaurant
15. Trattoria da Erminio
16. La Lanterna Restaurant
17. La Bottega dei Sapori

ASSISI

(see "Eating in Assisi," later).

$$ Hotel Sole, renting 38 rooms in a 15th-century building, is tired and forgettable. Service comes with a shrug, but the location is central. Half of its rooms are in a newer annex across the street (Sb-€45, Db-€65, Tb-€85, breakfast-€5, ask for a discount, easy parking, 100 yards before Basilica of St. Clare at Corso Mazzini 35, tel. 075-812-373, fax 075-813-706, www.assisihotelsole.com, info@assisihotelsole.com).

$$ Hotel San Rufino offers a great locale, solid stone quality, and 11 comfortable rooms (Sb-€46, Db-€56, Tb-€75, breakfast-€4; from Cathedral of San Rufino, follow sign to Via Porta Perlici 7; tel. & fax 075-812-803, www.hotelsanrufino.it, info@hotelsanrufino.it). Their nine-room annex, Albergo Il Duomo (listed later), saves you about €6 a night for a double with no loss in comfort.

$$ Hotel La Rocca, on the peaceful top end of town, has 32 solid and modern rooms in a medieval shell (Sb-€43, Db-€56, Tb-€75, breakfast-€4, parking-€6, sunny rooftop terrace, 3-minute walk from Piazza Matteotti at Via Porta Perlici 27, tel. & fax 075-812-284, www.hotelarocca.it, info@hotelarocca.it).

$ Mariani Marini Camere, in a utilitarian building rebuilt after the earthquake, rents 10 basic, perfectly sleepable rooms. While there's a tiny sun deck and a little reception area, it's an extremely basic place (Db-€45 for two or more nights, €50 for one-night stay, extra bed-€10, cash only, Via A. Cristofani 5, tel. and fax 075-812-508, mobile 348-733-2610, www.cameremarianimarini.com, info@cameremarianimarini.com, Antonio and Fabrizio).

$ Carli Rooms has six shiny, spacious, new rooms in a solid, minimalist place above a shop (Sb-€37, Db-€48, Qb-€60, show this book to get these prices, family lofts, Wi-Fi, free parking nearby, facing the Duomo at Via Porta Perlici 1, tel. 075-812-490, mobile 339-531-1366, carliarte@live.it, Carli).

$ Albergo Il Duomo is tidy and *tranquillo,* with nine rooms on a stair-stepped lane one block up from San Rufino. Check in at Hotel San Rufino (Sb-€40, Db-€50, breakfast-€4, Vicolo San Lorenzo 2, tel. & fax 075-812-742, www.hotelsanrufino.it, info@hotelsanrufino.it).

$ Camere Annalisa Martini is a cheery home in the town's medieval core that swims in vines, roses, and cats. Annalisa enthusiastically accommodates her guests with a picnic garden, a washing machine (€7/small load, includes line drying), a communal refrigerator, and six homey rooms (S-€27, Sb-€30, D-€38, Db-€42, Tb-€58, Qb-€68, cash only but credit card required for deposit, 3 rooms share 2 bathrooms, no breakfast; 1 block from Piazza del Comune—go downhill toward basilica, turn left on Via San Gregorio to #6; tel. & fax 075-813-536, cameremartini@libero.it, Mamma Rosignoli—"roh-sin-YOH-lee"—doesn't speak English, but Annalisa does).

   $ *Hostel:* Francis probably would have bunked with the peasants in Assisi's **Ostello della Pace** (€17 beds in 4- to 8-bed rooms, €19/person in private 2- to 4-person rooms with bath, dinner-€10.50, laundry service-€3.50, lockout 9:30–16:00, midnight curfew; get off bus at Piazzale Giovanni Paolo II, then walk 15 minutes downhill to Via di Valecchie 177—see map on page 573; tel. & fax 075-816-767, www.assisihostel.com, assisi.hostel@tiscali net.it).

Sweet Dreams in a Convent

Assisi is filled with convents, most of which rent rooms to pilgrims and travelers. While you don't need to be a pilgrim or even a Christian to be welcome, it's just common sense to stay in a convent *only* if you're approaching Assisi with a contemplative mindset. Convents feel institutional, house many groups, and are not particularly cheap—but they come with all the facilities you might need to enjoy a spirit-filled visit to Assisi.

   $$ St. Anthony's Guest House is where the Franciscan Sisters of the Atonement (including several Americans and Canadians) offer a very warm and tranquil welcome. Their oasis of peace is just above the Basilica of St. Clare. With only 35 beds in 20 rooms at a reasonable price, they book up literally months in advance (Sb-€40–45, Db-€60–65, Tb-€80–85, 2-night minimum, cash only for short stays, no problem if couples want to share a bed, 23:00 curfew, closed mid-Nov–Feb, library, views, picnic garden, parking-€3 donation/day, just below Piazza Matteotti at Via Galeazzo Alessi 10, tel. 075-812-542, fax 075-813-723, atoneassisi@tiscali.it).

Agriturismi near Assisi

If you're looking for some rest and relaxation on your journey, retire to the country at a farmhouse (see map on page 573).

   $$ Podere la Fornace is a renovated farmhouse in the tiny village of Tordibetto, just a few miles outside Assisi. The five apartments have 1–3 bedrooms, full kitchens, and a living room that can sleep an extra person. Local wine, olive oil, and pasta are available on-site (Db-€65–110, apartment-€80–195, price depends on size and season, 2-night minimum, games for children, swimming pool, bikes, cooking lessons, Via Ombrosa 3, tel. 075-801-9537, mobile 338-990-2903, fax 075-801-9630, www.lafornace .com, info@lafornace.com).

   $$ Alla Madonna del Piatto is a six-room *agriturismo* located about five miles outside of Assisi, with impressive views of the countryside. The Dutch-Italian owners have taken a centuries-old farm into the modern age, making organic olive oil on the premises and offering cooking classes that include visits to the market.

Ruurd and Letizia offer useful tips on sightseeing, the culture, dining, and wineries in the area (Db-€80–115, 2-night minimum, non-smoking, closed Dec–mid-March, at Via Petrata 37 in the parish of Pieve San Nicolò, tel. 075-819-9050, mobile 328-702-5297, www.incampagna.com, letizia.mattiacci@gmail.com).

$$ La Malvarina *agriturismo* invites visitors to its farm, where the owners keep horses, raise their own poultry, harvest truffles, tend sheep for cheesemaking, and produce their own extra-virgin organic olive oil, honey, and marmalade. The 13 rooms and three apartments are homey and comfortable. Guests can take cooking lessons with Mamma Maria, enjoy walking tours of the countryside, join guided visits to nearby Umbrian hill towns, or just relax by the swimming pool and enjoy the views of the countryside (Db-€95, Tb-€110, Qb-€140, apartments-€100—or €660/week, cooking lessons-€25/person up to 4 people, €100/lesson more than 4 people, optional 5-course dinner with wine-€30, Via Pieve di Sant'Apollinare 32, tel. & fax 075-806-4280, www.malvarina.it, info@malvarina.it; Claudio, Filippo, and Piera).

Eating in Assisi

I've listed decent, central, good-value restaurants. Assisi's food is heavy and rustic. Locals brag about their sausage and love to grate truffles on pasta. To bump up any meal, consider a glass or bottle of the favorite homegrown red wine, Sagrantino de Montefalco. Umbria's answer to Brunello (although many here would say it's Brunello that has to measure up to Sagrantino), it stirs dancing girls and flames.

Fine Dining

Ristorante Medioevo is my vote for your best splurge. With heavy but spacious cellar vaults, this restaurant is an elegant, accessible playground of gastronomy. William Ventura will guide you to the best of Umbrian cuisine. He features traditional cuisine with a modern twist, dictated by what's in season. While his first passion is cooking, his second is music—mellow jazz and bossa nova give a twinkle to the medieval atmosphere. Dishes are well-presented, knives are sharpened at your table, beef and game dishes are the specialties, and the wonderful Sagrantino wine is served by the glass (€10 pastas, €14 *secondi*, Tue–Sun 12:30–15:00 & 19:30–22:45, closed Mon; from the fountain on Piazza del Comune, hike downhill two blocks to Via Arco dei Priori 4; tel. 075-813-068).

La Pallotta, a local favorite run by a friendly and hardworking family, offers delicious, well-presented regional specialties, such as *piccione* (squab, a.k.a. pigeon) and *coniglio* (rabbit). Margarita is in charge of the kitchen. Reservations are smart (€8 pastas, €10 *secondi*, interesting €25 fixed-price sampler of local specialties, Wed–Mon 12:15–14:30 & 19:00–21:30, closed Tue, vegetarian options, a few steps off Piazza del Comune across from temple/church at Vicolo della Volta Pinta 2, tel. 075-812-649).

Casual Eateries

Trattoria da Erminio is charming, with peaceful tables on a tiny square, or indoor seating under a big medieval brick vault. Run by Federico and his family for three generations, it specializes in local meat cooked on an open-fire grill. They have good Umbrian wines—before you order, ask Federico for a taste of the Petranera wine (€12 grilled meats, €13–22 tourist fixed-price meal featuring local recipes based on seasonal produce—changes weekly, Fri–Wed 12:00–14:30 & 19:00–21:00, closed Thu; from Piazza San Rufino, go a block up Via Porta Perlici and turn right to Via Montacavallo 19; tel. 075-812-506).

At **Locanda del Podestà,** chef Selvio cooks up tasty grilled Umbrian sausages, *gnocchi alla locanda,* and all manner of truffles, while Romina graciously serves happy diners who know a good value. Try the tasty *scottaditto* ("scorch your fingers") lamb chops (€7 pastas, €12 *secondi*, Thu–Tue 12:00–14:30 & 19:00–21:30, closed Wed and Jan, 5-minute walk uphill along Via Cardinale Merry del Val from basilica, San Giacomo 6c—see map on page 573, tel. 075-816-553).

Ristorante Metastasio, just up the street from Podestà, has Assisi's best view terrace for dining (€9 pastas, €12 *secondi*, closed Wed, Via Metastasio 9, tel. 075-816-525).

Caffè Duomo, which faces the Cathedral of San Rufino, has a cozy interior with a jazzy ambience and great outdoor seating. It's run by enthusiastic young stallions, has a good selection of beers, and offers free Internet access to anyone ordering even just a drink. They also sell sandwiches and ice cream (daily 7:30–23:00, Piazza San Rufino 5, tel. 075-815-5209, Francesco and Ada speak English). Across the street, you can get pizza by the slice.

La Lanterna, up a small alleyway at the top of Via San Rufino, is a sleek, newly renovated eatery where you can dine by candlelight. Their €18 fixed-price meal (served all day), consisting of a starter, *secondo,* and side dish, is a good deal. It's run by a Neapolitan family who also make tasty pizzas in their wood-fired oven. Show this book for a free after-dinner *limoncello* from Luigi (daily 12:00–15:30 & 18:00–23:00, Via San Rufino 39, tel. 075-816-399, chef Massimiliano speaks English).

Picnic on the Main Square

There are many little grocery stores *(alimentari)* nearby.

Try **La Bottega dei Sapori** for a picnic of Umbrian treats: good prosciutto sandwiches and specialty items, including truffle paste and olive oil. Friendly Fabrizio, who is a slow-food enthusiast, may give you a taste. He also stocks the best Umbrian wines at good-to-go prices—nice if you have an appointment with your terrace for sunset (daily 9:00–20:00, closed Jan–Feb, Piazza del Comune 34, tel. 075-812-294).

Assisi Connections

From Assisi by Train to: Rome (13/day, 2–3.5 hours, 5 direct, most others change in Foligno), **Florence** (6/day direct, 2–3 hours), **Orvieto** (roughly hourly, 2–2.5 hours, with transfer in Terantola), **Siena** (8/day, 4–4.5 hours, most involve 2 transfers; bus is faster), **Cortona** (every 2 hours, 70 minutes to Camucia-Cortona station). The train-station ticket office is often closed until 13:30; on those mornings only, a ticket machine is available. You can get train information and tickets from Agenzia Viaggi Stoppini in the middle of town (see "Helpful Hints" on page 562). Train station tel. 075-804-0272 (generally unresponsive; you're better off asking at Agenzia Viaggi Stoppini or checking online at www.trenitalia .com).

By Bus: Several different bus companies offer service to **Rome** (2/day, 3 hours, €16, pay driver, departs from Piazzale Giovanni Paolo II below the basilica, arrives at Rome's Tiburtina station—the train makes much more sense), **Siena** (2/day at about 10:45 and 17:00, Nov–April no morning departure, 2 hours, €12). You can't buy Siena tickets from the driver; you must buy them at Assisi's Agenzia Viaggi Mavitur at Via Frate Elia 1b (see "Helpful Hints" on page 562). The 17:00 bus to Siena leaves from Porta San Pietro; the 10:45 bus departs from St. Mary of the Angels Basilica (stopping immediately at the side of the church).

Don't take the bus to **Florence**; the train is better. To see either **Gubbio** or **Todi** as a side-trip from Assisi, you'll need a car—bus schedules don't accommodate day-trippers. Day trips to **Spello, Perugia,** and **Lake Trasimeno** also aren't doable by bus, but you can do them by train.

By Plane: Perugia/San Egidio Airport, about 10 miles from Assisi, has daily connections to London Stansted airport (on Ryanair) and to Milan. No public transport runs between Assisi and the airport; a taxi costs about €25 (tel. 075-592-141, www .sangallo.it/perugiaairport).

HILL TOWNS
OF CENTRAL ITALY

San Gimignano • Volterra • Montalcino • Pienza •
Montepulciano • Cortona • Orvieto • Civita di Bagnoregio

The sun-soaked hill towns of central Italy offer what to many is the quintessential Italian experience: sun-dried tomatoes, homemade pasta, wispy cypress-lined driveways following desolate ridges to fortified 16th-century farmhouses, atmospheric *enoteche* serving Tuscany's famously tasty wines, and dusty old-timers warming the same bench day after day while soccer balls buzz around them like innocuous flies.

The hill towns of central Italy—in Tuscany, Le Marche, and Umbria—retain their medieval charm, and are best enjoyed by adapting to the pace of the countryside. So, slow...down...and savor the delights that these villages offer. Spend the night if you can, as many hill towns are mobbed by day-trippers.

Planning Your Time

How in Dante's name does a traveler choose from Italy's hundreds of hill towns? I've listed some of my favorites in this chapter. The one(s) you visit will depend on your interests, time, and mode of transportation.

Multi-towered San Gimignano is a classic, but because it's such an easy hill town to visit (1.25-hour bus ride from Florence), peak-season crowds can overwhelm the town's charms. For rustic vitality not completely trampled by tourist crowds, out-of-the-way Volterra is the clear winner. Wine aficionados head for Montalcino and Montepulciano—each a happy gauntlet of wine shops and art galleries (Montepulciano being my favorite). Fans of architecture and urban design appreciate Pienza's well-planned streets and squares. Art-lovers and those enamored by Frances Mayes' memoir *(Under the Tuscan Sun)* make the pilgrimage to Cortona. Urbino,

Hill Towns of Central Italy

CINQUE TERRE
• LA SPEZIA
• CARRARA
LUCCA
PISA
ARNO
AMERICAN CEM.
CHIANTI
SAN GIMIGNANO
VOLTERRA •
SAN GALGANO •
TUSCANY
MONTE-PULCIANO
MONTALCINO •
ELBA
PIENZA
LAKE BOLSENA
CIVITA DI BAGNOREGIO
TARQUINIA •
TYRRHENIAN SEA
50 MILES
50 KM

VENICE ↑
RAVENNA
ADRIATIC SEA
RIMINI
• FIESOLE
FLORENCE
• SAN MARINO
• POPPI
ANCONA
• AREZZO
LE MARCHE
• URBINO
• SIENA
GUBBIO •
CORTONA •
LAKE TRASIMENO
• PERUGIA
• ASSISI
• SPELLO
DERUTA •
BEVAGNA •
UMBRIA
CHIUSI
TODI •
• MONTEFALCO
ORVIETO
BOMARZO
LAZIO
CERVETERI •
TIBER RIVER
ROME
OSTIA
DCH

HILL TOWNS

well off the tourist track and quite remote, is known for its huge Ducal Palace. The grand, classic town of Orvieto is famous for its wine, ceramics, and colorful cathedral. But my longtime favorite is the tiny, obscure hill town of Civita di Bagnoregio (pictured on previous page). Assisi and Siena, while hill towns, are in a category by themselves. Bigger and with more major artistic and historic sights, they each get their own chapter.

For a relaxing break from big-city Italy, settle down in an *agriturismo*—a farmhouse that rents out rooms to travelers (usually for a minimum of a week in high season). These rural B&Bs—almost by definition in the middle of nowhere—provide a good home base from which to find the magic of Italy's hill towns. I've listed several

Hill Towns: Public Transportation

TO GENOA
TO MILAN
TO VENICE
CINQUE TERRE
FERRARA
LA SPEZIA
LUCCA
BOLOGNA
FLORENCE
CARRARA
EMPOLI
FIESOLE
RAVENNA
PISA
A   B
POGG.
CORTONA
RIMINI
LIVORNO
SALINE
CAM.
TERONTOLA
GUBBIO
PESARO
CECINA
SIENA
PERUGIA URBINO
FALCONARA
C   D   E
ASSISI
CHIUSI
SPELLO
CIVITA
TODI
FOLIGNO
SPOLETO
VITERBO
ORVIETO
ANCONA
TARQUINIA
CIVITAVECCHIA
ORTE
TO BARI & BRINDISI
CERVETERI
ROME
TO NAPLES
DCH

A - VOLTERRA
B - SAN GIMIGNANO
C - MONTALCINO
D - PIENZA
E - MONTEPULCIANO

NOT TO SCALE

--- BUS
— RAIL
✈ AIRPORT

HILL TOWNS

good options throughout this chapter (for more information, see "Agritourism" on page 25).

Getting Around the Hill Towns

Bigger destinations (such as Cortona and Orvieto) are doable by public transportation, but most hill towns are easier and more efficient to visit by car.

By Bus or Train

Traveling by public transportation is cheap and connects you with the locals. While trains link some of the towns, hill towns—being on hills—don't quite fit the railroad plan. Stations are likely to be in the valley a couple of miles from the town center, usually connected efficiently by a local bus.

Buses are often the only public-transportation choice to get between small hill towns. If you're pinched for time, it makes sense to narrow your focus to one or two hill towns, or rent a car to see more. For more on traveling by bus in Italy, see page 970.

Driving in Tuscany: Distance & Time

To Cinque Terre (La Spezia)

To Milan

To Venice

EMILIA-ROMAGNA

Lucca 50m•1h Florence

50m•1h

20m•.5h

Pisa

70m•1.25h

190m•3.5h 160m•3.5h

45m•1h

45m•2h (via S-222)

70m•1.5h

75m•1.5h

15m•.5h

60m•1.25h

Livorno

55m•1.5h

40m•.75h

San Gimignano

Volterra 20m•.5h

30m•.75h

Cortona 40m•1h

To Assisi

45m•1h

30m•.75h

Siena 50m•1h

40m•1h

20m•.75h

30m•.75h 35m•1h

10m•.25h Montepulciano

Chiusi

San Galgano Monastery 55m•1.5h 15m•.5h Pienza

15m•.5h

Montalcino

UMBRIA

210m•4h

60m•1.5h Orvieto 105m•2h

75m•1.5h

15m•.5h

Bagnoregio (Civita)

To Rome LAZIO To Rome

m = miles
h = hours
Note: Your times may vary based on traffic, construction, and road conditions.

TUSCANY

HILL TOWNS

By Car

Exploring small-town Tuscany, Le Marche, and Umbria by car can be a great experience. But since a car is an expensive, worthless headache in Florence and Siena, wait to pick up your car until the last big city you visit (or pick it up at the nearest airport to avoid big-city traffic). Then use the car for lacing together the hill towns and exploring the countryside. For more on car rentals and driving in Italy, see page 970.

A big, detailed regional road map (buy one at a newsstand or gas station) and a semiskilled navigator are essential. Freeways (such as the toll autostrada and the non-toll *superstrada*) provide the fastest way to connect two points, but the smaller roads, including the super-scenic S-222 through the heart of the Chianti region (connecting Florence and Siena), are more rewarding. For more joyrides—from Siena to Montalcino, and from Montalcino to Montepulciano—see "Crete Senese Drives" on page 652.

Parking throughout this region can be challenging. Some

towns don't allow visitors to park in the city center, so you'll need to leave your car outside the walls and walk into town. Don't drive or park in any area with signs reading *Zona Traffico Limitato (ZTL)*—often above a red circle. Parking lots, indicated by big blue *P* signs, are usually free and plentiful outside city walls. In some towns, you can park on the street; nearby kiosks sell "pay and display" tickets. I'd advise, when possible, parking in guarded lots, which are worth the expense to reduce the threat of theft (no guarantees, though).

San Gimignano

The epitome of a Tuscan hill town, with 14 medieval towers still standing (out of an original 72), San Gimignano (sahn jee-

meen-YAH-noh) is a perfectly preserved tourist trap. There are no important interiors to sightsee, and the town is packed with crass commercialism. The locals seem corrupted by the easy money of tourism, and most of the rustic is faux. The fact that this small town supports two torture museums is a comment on the caliber of the masses who choose to visit. But San Gimignano is so easy to reach and visually so beautiful that it remains a good stop. I find the place enchanting at night.

In the 13th century—back in the days of Romeo and Juliet—feuding noble families ran the towns. They'd periodically battle things out from the protection of their respective family towers. Pointy skylines, like San Gimignano's, were the norm in medieval Tuscany.

San Gimignano's cuisine is mostly what you might find in Siena—typical Tuscan home cooking. *Cinghiale* (cheeng-GAH-lay, wild boar) is served in almost every way: stews, soups, cutlets, and, my favorite, salami. Most shops will give you a sample before you commit to buying. The city is well known for having some of the best saffron in Italy; look for it on menus at finer restaurants (it's fairly expensive). Although Tuscany is normally a red-wine region, the most famous Tuscan white wine comes from here: the inexpensive, light, and fruity Vernaccia di San Gimignano. Look for the green "DOCG" label around the neck for the best quality (see "Italian Wines" sidebar, page 30).

HILL TOWNS

San Gimignano

TO CERTALDO & S-429

SANT' AGOSTINO

VIA GHIACCIAIA
VIA GARIBALDI
VIA BAGNAIA

PORTA SAN JACOPO

PORTA SAN MATTEO

VIA FOLGORE DI SAN GIM.

PORTA DELLE FONTI

VIA SETT.
VIA X
VIA XX
VERG.
VIA D'ACCETO
VIA SAN MATTEO
VIA CADASSI
VIA DELLE FONTI
VIA D. ROMITE

Duomo

PIAZZA DEL DUOMO

WELL

CASTELLO

Rocca

PRUN.

WC.

STER

DI BONDA

QUERCECCHIO

San Gimignano 1300

INNOCENTI

VIA DI

PIAZZA DELLA CISTERNA

PORTA QUER-CECCHIO

VIALE DEI FOSSI

VIA SAN GIOVANNI

CIVIC MUSEUM, TOWER & ℹ️

Post

PORTA SAN GIOVANNI

START

300 YARDS
300 METERS

BUS STOP ⓑ -DEPART-

BUS STOP -ARRIVAL-

SELF-GUIDED WALK

ⓑ BUS STOP

DCH

P

TO ➍

STEPPED STREETS

P PARKING

VIEW

ONE-WAY STREETS

TO VOLTERRA

TO POGGIBONSI & SIENA

HILL TOWNS

➊ Hotel l'Antico Pozzo
➋ Hotel la Cisterna
➌ Palazzo al Torrione
➍ To Ponte a Nappo Rooms & Co-op Supermarket
➎ Le Vecchie Mura Camere & Ristorante

➏ Locanda il Pino
➐ Trattoria Chiribiri
➑ Dulcis in Fundo Ristorante
➒ Locanda di Sant'Agostino
➓ Gelateria Pluripremiata "di Piazza"

Orientation to San Gimignano

While the basic ▲▲▲ sight here is the town of San Gimignano itself, there are a few worthwhile stops. From the town gate, head straight up the traffic-free town's cobbled main drag to Piazza della Cisterna (with its 13th-century well). The town sights cluster around the adjoining Piazza del Duomo.

Tourist Information: The helpful TI is in the old center on Piazza del Duomo (daily March–Oct 9:00–13:00 & 15:00–19:00, Nov–Feb 9:00–13:00 & 14:00–18:00, free maps, sells bus tickets, books rooms, tel. 0577-940-008, www.sangimignano.com).

The town offers a two-hour **guided walk** in English and Italian several days a week (April–Oct Sat–Sun at 11:00, €20; includes admission to Civic Museum and Tower; pay and meet at TI). Two-hour guided walks into the surrounding countryside are also available on request.

Arrival in San Gimignano: The bus stops at the main town gate, Porta San Giovanni. There's no baggage storage anywhere in town, so you're better off leaving your bags in Siena or Florence. You can't drive within the walled town. There are three pay lots a short walk outside the walls; the handiest is Parcheggio Montemaggio, just outside Porta San Giovanni. The one below the roundabout and Co-op supermarket is least expensive (€1/hour, €6/day, Giubileo 1).

Helpful Hints: Thursday is **market** day on Piazza del Duomo (8:00–13:00), but for local merchants, every day is a sales frenzy. A public **WC** is just off Piazza della Cisterna (€0.50), and another is around the corner from Porta San Giovanni. A little electric **shuttle bus** does its laps all day from Porta San Giovanni to Piazza della Cisterna to Porta San Matteo (€0.50, 2/hour, buy ticket from TI, *tabacchi* shop, or from coin-operated machine on bus).

Self-Guided Walk

Welcome to San Gimignano

This quick walking tour will take you across town from the bus stop at Porta San Giovanni through the town's main squares to the Duomo, and on to the Sant'Agostino Church.

• *Start, as most tourists do, at the Porta San Giovanni gate at the bottom end of town.*

Porta San Giovanni: San Gimignano lies about 25 miles from both Siena and Florence, a good stop for pilgrims en route to those cities, and on a naturally fortified hilltop that encouraged settlement. The town's walls were built in the 13th century, with gates like this that helped regulate who came and went. Today, modern posts keep out all but service and emergency vehicles. The small square just outside the gate features a memorial to the town's WWII dead. Follow the pilgrims' route (and flood of modern tourists) through the gate and up the main drag.

About 100 yards up, on the right, is a pilgrims' shelter (12th-century, Pisan Romanesque). The Maltese cross indicates that this was built by the Knights of Malta. It was one of 11 such shelters in town. Today, only the wall of this shelter remains.

• *Carry on, up to the town's central Piazza della Cisterna. Sit on the steps of the well.*

Piazza della Cisterna: The piazza is named for the cistern that is served by the old well standing in the center of this square.

A clever system of pipes drained rainwater from the nearby rooftops into the underground cistern. This square has been the center of the town since the ninth century. Turn in a slow circle and observe the commotion of rustic-yet-proud facades crowding in a tight huddle around the well. Imagine this square in pilgrimage times, lined by inns and taverns for the town's guests. Now finger the grooves in the lip of the well and imagine generations of maids and children fetching water. Each Thursday, the square fills with a market—as it has for more than a thousand years.

• *Notice San Gimignano's famous towers.*

The Towers: Of the original 72 towers, only 14 survive. Before effective city walls were developed, rich people fortified their own

homes with these towers: They provided a handy refuge when ruffians and rival city-states were sacking the town. These towers became a standard part of medieval skylines. Even after town walls were built, the towers continued to rise—now to fortify noble families feuding within a town (Montague and Capulet–style).

In the 14th century, San Gimignano's good times turned very bad. In the year 1300, about 13,000 people lived within the walls. Then in 1348, a six-month plague decimated the population, leaving the once-mighty town with barely 4,000 survivors. Once fiercely independent, now crushed and demoralized, San Gimignano came under Florence's control and was forced to tear down its towers. (The Banca Toscana building occupies the remains of one such toppled tower.) And, to add injury to injury, Florence redirected the vital trade route away from San Gimignano. The town never recovered, and poverty left it in a 14th-century architectural time warp. That well-preserved cityscape, ironically, is responsible for the town's prosperity today.

• *From the well, walk 30 yards uphill to the adjoining square with the cathedral.*

Piazza del Duomo: The square faces the former cathedral. The twin towers to the right are 10th-century, among the first in

town. The stubby tower opposite the church is typical of a merchant's tower: main door on ground floor, warehouse upstairs, holes to hold beams that once supported wooden balconies and exterior staircases, heavy stone on the first floor, cheaper and lighter brick for upper stories.

• *On the piazza are the Civic Museum and Tower, worth checking out (see "Sights in San Gimignano," later). You'll also see the...*

Duomo (or Collegiata): Walk inside San Gimignano's Romanesque cathedral. Sienese Gothic art (14th century) lines the nave with parallel themes, Old Testament on the left and New Testament on the right. (For example: the suffering of Job opposite the suffering of Jesus, Creation facing the Annunciation, and the birth of Adam facing the Nativity.) This is a classic use of art to teach. Study the fine Creation series (top left). Many scenes are portrayed with a local 14th-century "slice of life" setting, to help lay townspeople relate to Jesus—in the same way that many white Christians are more comfortable thinking of Jesus as Caucasian (€3.50, €5.50 combo-ticket includes mediocre Religious Art Museum, daily April–Oct 10:00–18:40, Nov–March 10:00–16:40).

From the church, hike uphill (passing the church on your left) following signs to *Rocca e Parco di Montestaffoli*. Keep walking until you enter a peaceful hilltop park and olive grove within the shell of a 14th-century fortress. On the far side, a few steps take you to the top of a little tower (free) for the best views of San Gimignano's skyline; the far end of town and the Sant'Agostino Church (where this walk ends); and a commanding 360-degree view of the Tuscan countryside. San Gimignano is surrounded by olives, grapes, cypress trees, and—in the Middle Ages—lots of wild dangers. Back then, farmers lived inside the walls and were thankful for the protection.

• *Return to the bottom of Piazza del Duomo, turn left, and continue your walk across town, cutting under the double arch (from the town's first wall). In around 1200, this defined the end of town. The Church of San Bartolo stood just outside the wall. The Maltese cross indicates that it likely served as a hostel for pilgrims. Continuing on down Via San Matteo, you pass a fascinating array of stone facades from the 13th and 14th centuries—now a happy cancan of wine shops and galleries. Eventually you reach...*

Sant'Agostino Church: This tranquil church, at the opposite end of town (built by the Augustinians who arrived in 1260), has fewer crowds and more soul. Behind the altar, a lovely fresco cycle by Benozzo Gozzoli (who painted the exquisite Chapel of the Magi in the Medici-Riccardi Palace in Florence) tells of the life of St. Augustine, a North African monk who preached simplicity. The kind English-speaking friars (from Britain and the US) are happy to tell you about their church and way of life, and also have Mass in English on Sundays at 11:00. Pace the tranquil cloister before heading back into the tourist mobs (free, €0.50 lights the frescoes; April–Oct daily 7:00–12:00 & 15:00–19:00; Nov–March Tue–Sun 7:00–12:00 & 15:00–18:00, Mon 16:00–18:00). Their fine little shop, with books on the church and its art, is worth a look.

Sights in San Gimignano

Civic Museum and Tower (Museo Civico and Torre Grossa)—This small, fun museum, consisting of just three unfurnished rooms and a tower, is inside City Hall (Palazzo Comunale). The main room, called Sala di Consiglio (a.k.a. Danti Hall), is covered in festive frescoes, including the *Maestà* by Lippo Memmi. This virtual copy of Simone Martini's *Maestà* in Siena proves that Memmi doesn't have quite the same talent as his famous brother-in-law. Upstairs, the Pinacoteca displays a classy little painting collection, with a 1422 altarpiece by Taddeo di Bartolo honoring St. Gimignano. You can see the saint, with the town—bristling with towers—in his hands, surrounded by events from his life.

As you exit, be sure to stop by the Mayor's Room (Camera del Podesta). Frescoed in 1310 by Memmo di Filippuccio, it offers an intimate and candid peek into the 14th century. The theme: profane love. As you enter, look to the left corner where a young man is ready to experience the world. He hits his parents up for a bag of money and is free. Almost immediately he's entrapped by two prostitutes, who lead him into a tent where he loses his money (above the window), is turned out, and is beaten. Above the door from left to right you see a parade of better choices: marriage, the cradle of love, the bride led to the groom's house, and newlyweds bathing together and retiring happily to their bed.

The highlight for most visitors is a chance to climb the **Tower** (Torre Grossa). The city's tallest tower, 200 feet and 218 steps up, rewards those who climb it with a commanding view. You leave via a delightful stony loggia and courtyard out back.

Cost and Hours: €5, includes museum and tower, audioguide may be available for €2, daily March–Oct 9:30–19:00, Nov–Feb 10:00–17:30, Piazza del Duomo.

San Gimignano 1300—This new attraction is a trip back in time. Located inside the Palazzo Ficarelli in the town center, it features a scale model of San Gimignano at the turn of the 14th century. You can see the 72 original "tower houses," peek into cross-sections of buildings, and view scenes of medieval life within the city walls

Cost and Hours: €5, daily 8:00–20:00, June–Sept until 23:00, Via Berignano 23, tel. 0577-941-078, www.sangimignano1300.com.

Sleeping in San Gimignano

Although the town is a zoo during the daytime, locals outnumber tourists when evening comes, and San Gimignano becomes peaceful and enjoyable. Drivers can unload near their hotels, then park outside the walls in recommended lots. Hotel websites provide instructions.

$$$ Hotel l'Antico Pozzo is an elegantly restored 15th-century townhouse with 18 tranquil, comfortable rooms, a peaceful interior courtyard terrace, and an elite air (Db-€140 and higher depending on the room, air-con, elevator, Wi-Fi, near Porta San Matteo at Via San Matteo 87, tel. 0577-942-014, fax 0577-942-117, www.anticopozzo.com, info@anticopozzo.com, Emanuele).

$$$ Hotel la Cisterna, right on Piazza della Cisterna, offers 49 predictable rooms, some with panoramic view terraces (Sb-€78, Db-€100, Db with view-€120, Db with view terrace-€145, 10 percent discount with this book, buffet breakfast, air-con, elevator, Wi-Fi, good restaurant with great view, closed Jan–Feb, Piazza della Cisterna 23, tel. 0577-940-328, fax 0577-942-080, www.hotelcisterna.it, info@hotelcisterna.it, Alessio).

$$$ Ponte a Nappo, run by enterprising Carla Rossi (who doesn't speak English) and her son Francesco (who does), has seven comfortable rooms and two apartments in a kid-friendly farmhouse. Located a long half-mile below town, this place has killer views (Db-€110, 2-to-6-person apartment-€130–220, air-con extra, free Wi-Fi, parking, pool, free loaner bikes, 15-minute

HILL TOWNS

Sleep Code

(€1 = about $1.25, country code: 39)
S = Single, **D** = Double/Twin, **T** = Triple, **Q** = Quad, **b** = bathroom,
s = shower only. Unless otherwise noted, credit cards are accepted and breakfast is included (but usually optional). English is generally spoken, but I've noted exceptions.

To help you sort easily through these listings, I've divided the rooms into three categories based on the price for a standard double room with bath:

$$$ Higher Priced—Most rooms €100 or more.

$$ Moderately Priced—Most rooms between €70–100.

$ Lower Priced—Most rooms €70 or less.

Prices can change without notice; verify the hotel's current rates online or by email. For other updates, see www.ricksteves.com/update.

walk or 5-minute drive from Porta San Giovanni, tel. 0577-955-041, mobile 349-882-1565, fax 0577-941-268, www.accommodation-sangimignano.it, info@rossicarla.it). A picnic dinner—lounging on their comfy garden furniture as the sun sets—is good Tuscan living. About 100 yards below the monument square at Porta San Giovanni, find Via Vecchia (not left or right, but down a tiny road) and follow it down a dirt road for five minutes by car. They also rent a dozen or so rooms and apartments in town (each described on their website).

$$ Palazzo al Torrione, just inside Porta San Giovanni, is quiet and handy, and generally better than most hotels, though they don't have a full-time reception. Their 10 modern rooms are spacious and tastefully appointed (Db-€80, terrace Db-€100, Tb-€98, terrace Tb-€113, Qb-€120–130, 10 percent discount with this book, breakfast-€5, communal kitchen, parking-€6/day, inside and left of gate at Via Berignano 76; operated from *tabacchi* shop 2 blocks away, on the main drag at Via San Giovanni 59; tel. 0577-940-480, mobile 338-938-1656, fax 0577-955-605, www.palazzoaltorrione.com, palazzoaltorrione@palazzoaltorrione.com, Vanna and Francesco).

$ Le Vecchie Mura Camere offers three good rooms above their restaurant in the old town (Db-€60, no breakfast, air-con, Via Piandornella 15, tel. 0577-940-270, www.vecchiemura.it, info@vecchiemura.it, Bagnai family).

$ Locanda il Pino is tiny (five rooms), but has a big living room. It's dank but super-clean, quiet, and run by English-speaking Elena and her family above their elegant restaurant just inside Porta San Matteo (Db-€55, no breakfast, easy parking just outside the gate, Via Cellolese 4, tel. 0577-940-415, locanda @ristoranteilpino.it). While far from the bus stop, this is a good value for those with a car.

Eating in San Gimignano

Trattoria Chiribiri, just inside Porta San Giovanni, serves home-made pastas and desserts at remarkably fair prices. It's petite with tight seating and, though hot in the summer, is a fine value (€6 pastas, €8.50 *secondi,* daily 11:00–23:00, Piazza della Madonna 1, tel. 0577-941-948, Beatrice and Maurizio).

Dulcis in Fundo Ristorante, small and family-run, proudly serves local cuisine with a modern twist, gourmet presentation, and slow-food values in a jazz ambience (€12 pastas, €15 *secondi,* meals served Thu–Tue 12:30–14:30 and 19:30–22:00, closed Wed, Vicolo degli Innocenti 21, tel. 0577-941-919).

Le Vecchie Mura Ristorante is my choice for good service, great prices, tasty home cooking, and the ultimate view. It's romantic indoors or out. They have a dressy, modern interior where you can dine with a view of the busy stainless-steel kitchen under rustic vaults, but I'd come for the incredible cliffside garden terrace. Cliffside tables are worth reserving in advance by calling or dropping by: Ask for "front view" (€8 pastas, €12 *secondi,* Wed–Mon dinner only from 18:00, last order at 22:00, closed Tue, Via Piandornella 15, tel. 0577-940-270, Bagnai family).

Locanda di Sant'Agostino spills out onto the peaceful square, facing Sant'Agostino Church. It's cheap and cheery, serving lunch and dinner daily—a great place for salads, pizza, or a rustic dish of pasta. Dripping with wheat stalks and atmosphere on the inside, there's shady on-the-square seating outside (€8 pastas, €12 *secondi,* daily 11:00–22:00, closed Tue off-season, also closed Jan–Feb, Piazza Sant'Agostino 15, tel. 0577-943-141, Genziana and sons).

Picnics: The big, modern **Co-op supermarket** sells all you need for a nice spread (Mon–Sat 8:30–20:00, closed Sun, at parking lot below Porta San Giovanni). Or browse the little shops guarded by wild boar heads within the town walls; they sell boar meat *(cinghiale).* Pick up 100 grams (about a quarter pound) of boar, cheese, bread, and wine and enjoy a picnic in the garden at the Rocca or the park outside Porta San Giovanni.

Gelato: To cap the evening and sweeten your late-night city stroll, stop by **Gelateria Pluripremiata "di Piazza"** on Piazza della Cisterna (at #4). Gelato-maker Sergio was a member of the Italian team that won the official Gelato World Cup (daily 8:00–24:00, tel. 0577-942-244, Dondoli family).

San Gimignano Connections

Bus tickets are sold at the bar just inside the town gate or at the TI.

From San Gimignano by Bus to: Florence (hourly, less on Sat–Sun, 1.25–2 hours, change in Poggibonsi, €6.25), **Siena** (8 direct/day, 1.25 hours, €5.50), **Volterra** (4/day Mon–Sat; on Sun only 1/day—usually crowded—with no return to San Gimignano; 2 hours, change in Colle Val d'Elsa).

By Car: San Gimignano is an easy 45-minute drive from Florence (take the A1 exit marked *Firenze Certosa,* then a right past tollbooth following *Siena per 4 corsie* sign; exit the freeway at Poggibonsi). From San Gimignano, it's a scenic and windy half-hour drive to Volterra.

Volterra

Encircled by impressive walls and topped with a grand fortress, Volterra sits high above the rich farmland. More than 2,000 years ago, Volterra was one of the most important Etruscan cities, a city much larger than the one we see today. Greek-trained Etruscan artists worked here, leaving a significant stash of art, particularly funerary urns. Eventually Volterra was absorbed into the Roman Empire, and for centuries it was an independent city-state. Volterra fought bitterly against the Florentines, but like many Tuscan towns, it lost in the end and was given a fortress atop the city to "protect" its citizens. For more information on the Etruscans, see page 616.

Unlike other famous towns in Tuscany, Volterra feels not cutesy or touristy...but real, vibrant, and almost oblivious to the allure of the tourist dollar. A refreshing break from its more commercial neighbors, it's my favorite small town in Tuscany.

Orientation to Volterra

Compact and walkable, the city stretches out from the pleasant Piazza dei Priori to the old city gates.

Tourist Information: The helpful TI is on the main square, at Piazza dei Priori 19 (daily 10:00–13:00 & 14:00–18:00, tel. 0588-87257, www.volterratur.it). The TI's excellent €5 audioguide narrates 20 stops (2-for-1 discount on audioguides with this book).

Arrival in Volterra: Buses stop at Piazza Martiri della Libertà in the town center. Drivers will find the town ringed with easy numbered parking lots (#3 and #5 are free; #3 is most likely to have a place, but comes with a steeper hike into town). The most central lots are the pay lots at Porta Fiorentina and underground at Piazza Martiri della Libertà (€1.50/hour, €11/24 hours).

Helpful Hints

Market Day: Market day is Saturday morning near the Roman Theater (8:00–13:00, in Piazza dei Priori in winter).

Festivals: Volterra's Medieval Festival takes place the third and fourth Sundays of August (Aug 21 and 28 in 2011). Fall is a popular time for food festivals—check with the TI for dates and events planned.

Internet Access: Web & Wine has a few terminals and fine wine by the glass (€3/hour, no minimum, summer daily 9:30–1:00 in the morning, off-season closed Thu, Via Porta all'Arco 11–15, tel. 0588-81531, www.webandwine.com, Lallo speaks English). **Enjoy Café Internet Point** has a couple of terminals in their basement (€3/hour, daily 6:30–1:00 in the morning, Piazza dei Martiri 3, tel. 0588-80530).

Local Guide: American **Annie Adair** married into the local community; she organizes American weddings in Tuscany, is an excellent private guide, and can organize wine and food tours (€125/half-day, €250/day, tel. 0588-87774, mobile 347-143-5004, www.tuscantour.com, info@tuscantour.com).

Sights in Volterra

▲▲Guided Volterra Walk—Annie Adair and her colleagues offer a great one-hour English-only introductory walking tour of Volterra for €5. The walk touches on Volterra's Etruscan, Roman, and medieval history, as well as the contemporary cultural scene (April–Sept daily, rain or shine, at 18:00; depart from Piazza Martiri della Libertà, at the bus terminal above the underground parking lot; no need to reserve—just show up, they need a minimum of 4 people—or €20—to make the tour go, www.volterrawalkingtour.com or www.tuscantour.com, info@volterrawalkingtour.com). There's no better way to spend €5 and one hour in this city.

▲▲Self-Guided Historic Town Walk—You can easily lace the town's top sights and my descriptions together to make your own handy little town walk. Here's the spine of the walk (all described

HILL TOWNS

Volterra

TO PISA & 8
TO 4
PORTA S. FRAN.
VIALE FRANCESCO
ETRUSCAN WALLS
PORTA DIANA
PORTA FIORENTINA
FERRUCCI
ROMAN THEATER
VIA S. LINO
PORTA SAN FELICE
V. FRAN.
L. TRENTO E TRIESTE
MANDORLO
PINACOTECA
PALAZZO DEI PRIORI
V. RICC.
ROMA
V. SARTI
PAL. VITI
PRIG.
14
MATTEOTTI
GRAM.
SETT
VIA FONTE
SACRED ART MUS.
BAPT.
DUOMO
11
10
i
2
15
V. SOTTO
PORTA ALL'ARCO
19
18
PIAZZA MARTIRI
5
V. CASTELLO
P. X SETT
PORTA ALL'ARCO ETRUSCAN ARCH
19
9
BUS STN.
12
ARCHAEOLOGICAL PARK
VIA
VIALE DEI PONTI
100 YARDS
100 METERS
VIALE GARIBALDI
TO 1
V. BATTISTI
DCH

in this order below): Start with the Etruscan Arch, browse up what I call "Artisan Lane," follow my tour of Via Matteotti, side-trip to the main square and Duomo, detour (if you like) to the Pinacoteca and Roman Theater, head over to the Etruscan Museum and Alabaster Workshop, and finish with a drink under all the bras with Bruno and Lucio at La Vena di Vino. The town's other sights are easily grafted onto this route.

▲**"Porta all'Arco" Etruscan Arch**—Volterra's most famous sight is its Etruscan arch, built of massive volcanic tuff stones in the fourth century B.C. (for more information on tuff, see the sidebar on page 675). Volterra's original wall was four miles around—twice the size of the wall that encircles it today. With 25,000 people, Volterra was a key Etruscan trade center—one of 12 leading towns that made up the Etruscan *Dodecapolis* (a league of Etruscan cities). The three seriously eroded heads, dating from the first century B.C., show what happens when you leave something outside for

7i VIEW

P PARKING

★ PIAZZA DEI PRIORI

||||| STAIRS

❶ To Park Hotel Le Fonti
❷ Albergo Etruria
❸ Hotel La Locanda
❹ To Albergo Villa Nencini
❺ Albergo Nazionale
❻ Seminario Vescovile Sant'Andrea
❼ To Volterra Youth Hostel & Trattoria da Bado
❽ To Podere Marcampo
❾ Rist. Enoteca del Duca
❿ Trattoria Don Beta
⓫ La Vecchia Lira
⓬ Rist. Il Sacco Fiorentino
⓭ La Vena di Vino Wine Bar
⓮ Ombra della Sera & Pizzeria Tavernetta
⓯ Despar Market
⓰ Alab'Arte Alabaster Showroom
⓱ Alab'Arte Alabaster Workshop
⓲ "Artisan Lane"
⓳ Internet Cafés (2)

HILL TOWNS

2,000 years. The newer stones are part of the 13th-century city wall, which incorporated parts of the much older Etruscan wall.

A plaque just outside remembers June 30, 1944. That night, Nazi forces were planning to blow up the arch to slow the Allied advance. To save their treasured landmark, Volterrans ripped up the stones that pave Via Porta all'Arco and plugged the gate,

managing to convince the Nazi commander that there was no need to blow up the arch. Today, all the stones are back in their places, and, like silent heroes, they welcome you through the oldest standing Etruscan gate into Volterra. Locals claim this as the only surviving round arch of the Etruscan age, and believe this is where Romans got the idea for using a keystone in their arches.

"Artisan Lane"—Via Porta all'Arco (which leads to and from the Etruscan arch) is lined with interesting shops featuring the work of artisans and producers. Because of its alabaster heritage, Volterra attracted artisans and artists, who brought with them a rich variety of crafts (shops generally open Mon–Sat 10:00–13:00 & 16:00–19:00, closed Sun; the TI produces a free booklet called *Handicraft in Volterra*).

From the Etruscan Arch, browse your way up the hill, checking out these shops (listed from bottom to top): La Mia Fattoria, a co-op of producers of cheese, salami, and oil, letting you buy direct at farm prices (#52); alabaster shops (#57 and #45); book bindery and papery (#26); jewelry (#25); etchings and silk screening (#23); leather (#16); Web & Wine (Internet access; #11–15); and bronze work (#6).

▲**Via Matteotti**—The town's main drag, named after the popular Socialist leader killed by the Fascists in 1924, provides a good cultural scavenger hunt. The street starts 30 yards from Palazzo dei Priori (City Hall and cathedral, described later).

At #1 is a typical Italian bank security door. (Step in and say, "Beam me up, Scotty.") Look up and all around. Find the medieval griffin torch holder—symbol of Volterra—and imagine it holding a lit torch. The pharmacy sports the symbol of its medieval guild. As you head down Via Matteotti, notice how the doors show centuries of refitting work.

At #2, look up and imagine heavy beams cantilevered out, supporting extra wooden rooms and balconies crowding out over the street. Throughout Tuscany, today's stark and stony old building fronts once supported a tangle of wooden extensions. Doors that once led to these extra rooms are now partially bricked up to make windows. Contemplate urban density in the 14th century, before the plague thinned out the population. Be careful: There's a wild boar (a local delicacy) at #10.

At #12, notice how the typical palace, once the home of a single rich family, is now occupied by many middle-class families (judging from the line of doorbells). After the social revolution in the 18th century and the rise of the middle class, former palaces were condominium-ized. Even so, like in *Dr. Zhivago*, the original family still lives here. Apartment #1 is the home of Count Guidi.

At #16, pop in to an alabaster showroom. Alabaster, mined nearby, has long been a big industry here. Volterra alabaster—softer and more porous than marble—was sliced thin to serve as windows for Italy's medieval churches.

At #19, the recommended La Vecchia Lira is a lively cafeteria. The Bar L'Incontro across the street is a favorite for homemade gelato and pastries.

Vampire Volterra

Sitting on its stony main square at midnight, watching bats dart about as if they own the place, I realize there really is something supernatural about Volterra. The cliffs of Volterra inspired Dante's "cliffs of hell." In the winter, the town's vibrancy is smothered under a deadening cloak of clouds. The name Volterra means "land that floats"—referring to the clouds that often seem to cut it off from the rest of the world below.

The people of Volterra live in a cloud of mystery, too. Their favorite cookie, crunchy with almonds, is called Ossi di Morta ("bones of the dead"). The town's first disco was named Catacombs. And in the 1970s, when Volterra was the set of a wildly popular TV horror series called *Ritratto di Donna Velata (Portrait of a Veiled Woman),* all of Italy tuned in to Volterra every week for a good scare.

Lately the town is attracting international attention for its connection to the bestselling *Twilight* series of vampire romance novels and movies. Part of the second movie, *New Moon* (2009), is set in Volterra. Even though most of it was actually filmed in Montepulciano, the TI plays a video clip of *New Moon* continuously and is proud of Volterra's Hollywood connection.

As a result, the town is seeing lots of "Twihards," who come not for the Etruscan Museum, but to run across the sun-drenched square at noon and retrace the footsteps of Edward and Bella down dark alleyways. The movie has definitely stirred up vampire tourism—it's in their blood.

Across the way, up Vicolo delle Prigioni, is a fun bakery *(panificio)*. They're happy to sell small quantities if you want to try the local *cantuccini* (almond biscotti) or munch a cannoli.

At #51, a bit of Etruscan wall is artfully used to display more alabaster art. And #56B is the alabaster art gallery of Paolo Sabatini.

Locals gather early each evening at Osteria dei Poeti (at #57) for the best cocktails in town—served with free munchies. The cinema is across the street. Movies in Italy are rarely in *versione originale*. Italians are used to getting their movies dubbed into Italian.

At #66, the end of the street is marked by another Tuscan tower. This noble house has a ground floor with no interior access to the safe upper floors. Rope ladders were used to get upstairs. The tiny door was wide enough to let in your skinny friends...but definitely not anyone wearing armor and carrying big weapons.

Across the street stands the ancient Church of St. Michael. After long years of barbarian chaos, the Lombards moved in from the north and asserted law and order in places like Volterra. That generally included building a Christian church on the old Roman forum to symbolically claim and tame the center of town. The church standing here today is Romanesque, dating from the 12th century. Find the crude little guys under its eaves—they've been making faces at the passing crowds for 800 years.

Palazzo dei Priori—Volterra's City Hall (c. 1209) claims to be the oldest of any Tuscan city-state. It clearly inspired the more famous Palazzo Vecchio in Florence. Town halls like this were emblematic of an era when city-states were powerful. They were architectural exclamation points declaring that, around here, no pope or emperor called the shots. Towns such as Volterra were truly city-states—proudly independent and relatively democratic. They had their own armies, taxes, and even weights and measures. Notice the horizontal "cane" cut into the City Hall wall. For a thousand years, this square hosted a market, and the "cane" was the local yardstick. When not in use for meetings or weddings, the city council chambers—lavishly painted and lit with fun dragon lamps as they have been for centuries of town meetings—are open to visitors.

Cost and Hours: €1, April–Oct daily 10:30–17:30, Nov–March Sat–Sun only 10:00–17:00.

Duomo—A common arrangement in the Middle Ages was for the church to face the baptistery (you couldn't enter the church until you were baptized)...and for the hospital to face the cemetery. All of these overlooked the same square. That's how it is in Pisa. And that's how it is here.

This 12th-century church is not as elaborate as its cousin in Pisa, but the simple facade and central nave flanked by monolithic stone columns are beautiful examples of the Pisan Romanesque style. The chapel to the left of the entry has painted terra-cotta statue groups. The interior was decorated mostly in the late 16th century, during Florentine rule under the Medici family. You'll see a lot of the Medici coat of arms (with the six pills, representing the family's first trade—as doctors, or *medici*). The 12th-century marble pulpit is beautifully carved. All of the apostles are together except Judas, who's under the table with the evil dragon (his name is the only one not carved onto the relief).

Just before the pulpit (in the Rosary Chapel, on the left), check out the *Annunciation* by Fra Bartolomeo (who was a student of Fra Angelico and painted this in 1497). Bartolomeo delicately gives worshippers a way to see Mary "conceived by the Holy Spirit." Note the vibrant colors, exaggerated perspective, and Mary's *contrapposto* pose—all attributes of the Renaissance.

To the right of the main altar is a dreamy painted-and-gilded-wood *Deposition* (Jesus being taken down from the cross), restored to its original form. Painted in 1228, a generation before Giotto, it shows emotion and motion way ahead of its time.

The glowing windows in the transept and behind the altar are sheets of alabaster. These, along with the recorded Gregorian chants, add to the church's wonderful ambience.

Cost and Hours: Free, daily 8:00–12:30 & 15:00–17:00.

Sacred Art Museum—This humble four-room museum collects sacred art from deconsecrated churches and small, unguarded churches from nearby villages.

Cost and Hours: €9 combo-ticket includes Etruscan Museum and Pinacoteca, daily 9:00–13:00 & 15:00–18:00, morning only in winter, well-explained in English, next to the Duomo at Via Roma 1, tel. 0588-86290.

Pinacoteca—This museum fills a 14th-century palace with fine paintings that feel more Florentine than Sienese—a reminder of whose domain this town was in. Its highlights are Luca Signorelli's beautifully lit *Annunciation,* an example of classic High Renaissance (from the town cathedral), and (to the right) *Deposition from the Cross,* the groundbreaking Mannerist work by Rosso Fiorentino (note the elongated bodies and harsh emotional lighting and colors). Notice also Ghirlandaio's *Christ in Glory.* The two devout-looking kneeling women are actually pagan, pre-Christian Etruscan demigoddesses, Attinea and Greciniana, but the church identified them as obscure saints to make the painting acceptable.

Cost and Hours: €9 combo-ticket includes Etruscan and Sacred Art museums, daily 9:00–19:00, Nov–mid-March until 13:45, Via dei Sarti 1, tel. 0588-87580.

Palazzo Viti—Go behind the rustic, heavy stone walls of the city and see how the nobility lived (in this case, rich from 19th-century alabaster wealth). One of the finest private residential buildings in Italy, with 12 rooms open to the public, Palazzo Viti feels remarkably lived in because it is. You'll also find Senora Viti herself selling admission tickets. It's no wonder this time warp is so popular with Italian movie directors. While exquisite, it's pricey. But remember, you're helping keep a noble family in leotards.

Cost and Hours: €5, pick up the loaner English description, April–Oct daily 10:00–13:00 & 14:30–18:30, closed Nov–March, Via dei Sarti 41, tel. 0588-84047, www.palazzoviti.it.

Roman Theater—Built in about 10 B.C., this well-preserved theater is considered to have some of the best acoustics of its kind. Because of the fine aerial view you get from the city wall promenade, you may find it unnecessary to pay admission to enter. Belly up to the 13th-century wall and look down. The wall that you're standing on divided the theater from the town center...so, naturally, the theater became the town dump. Over time, the theater

Under the Etruscan Sun
(c. 900 b.c.–a.d. 1)

About 550 B.C.—just before the Golden Age of Greece—the Etruscan people of central Italy had their own Golden Age. Though their origins are mysterious, their mix of Greek-style art with Roman-style customs helped lay a civilized foundation for the rise of Rome. As you travel through Italy—particularly in Tuscany (from "Etruscan"), Umbria, and North Latium—you'll find traces of the long-lost Etruscans.

The Etruscans first appeared in the ninth century B.C., when a number of cities sprouted up in sparsely populated Tuscany and Umbria, including today's hill towns of Cortona, Chiusi, and Volterra. Perhaps they were immigrants from Western Turkey, but more likely they were just the local farmers who moved to the city, became traders and craftsmen, and welcomed new ideas from Greece.

More technologically advanced than their neighbors, they mined metal, exporting it around the Mediterranean, both as crude ingots and as some of the finest-crafted jewelry in the known world. The Etruscans drained and irrigated large tracts of land, creating the fertile farmland of central Italy's breadbasket. With their disciplined army, warships, merchant vessels, and (from the Greek perspective) pirate galleys, they ruled central Italy and the major ports along the Tyrrhenian Sea. For nearly two centuries (c. 700–500 B.C.), much of Italy lived a golden age of peace and prosperity under the Etruscan sun.

Judging from the many luxury items that have survived, the Etruscans enjoyed the good life. Frescoes show men and women looking remarkably like how the Greeks and Romans described them: healthy, vibrant, and well-dressed, playing flutes, dancing with birds, or playing party games. Etruscan artists celebrated individual people, showing their wrinkles, crooked noses, silly smiles, and funny haircuts.

Thousands upon thousands of surviving ceramic plates, cups, and vases attest to the importance of food. Hosting a banquet was a symbol that you'd arrived. Men and women ate together, propped on their elbows on dining couches, surrounded by colorful frescoes and terra-cotta tiles. According to contemporary accounts, the Etruscans (and even their slaves) were Europe's best-dressed people. They ate off dinnerware either imported from Greece or made in the Greek style—red and black ceramics, decorated with warriors, nymphs, sphinxes, and gods. The banqueters were entertained with music and dancing and served by elegant and well-treated slaves.

Scholars today have deciphered the Etruscans' Greek-style alphabet and some individual words, but they've yet to fully master the grammar or crack the code. Virtually no long-enough Etruscan documents survive.

Much of what we know of the Etruscans comes from their tombs, often clustered in a necropolis. The tomb was your home

The Etruscan Empire

in the hereafter, fully furnished for the afterlife, complete with all your belongings. The lid of the sarcophagus might have a statue of the deceased at a banquet—lying across a dining couch, spooning with his wife, smiles on their faces, living the good life for all eternity.

Seven decades of wars with Greeks (545–474 B.C.) disrupted the trade routes and drained the Etruscan League, just as a new Mediterranean power was emerging: Rome. In 509 B.C., the Romans overthrew their Etruscan king, and Rome expanded, capturing Etruscan cities one by one (the last in 264 B.C.). Etruscan resisters were killed, the survivors intermarried with Romans, their kids grew up speaking Latin, and the culture became Romanized. By Julius Caesar's time, the only remnants of Etruscan culture were Etruscan priests, who became Rome's professional soothsayers. The shape a flock of birds made, the bend in a lightning flash, or a scar on a goat's liver could tell a priest how a client's business might fare next year. Interestingly, the Etruscan prophets had foreseen their own demise, having predicted that Etruscan civilization would last 10 centuries.

But Etruscan culture lived on in Roman religion (pantheon of gods, household gods, and divination rituals), art (realism), lifestyle (the banquet), and in a taste for Greek styles—the mix that became our "Western civilization."

Etruscan Sights in Italy

Here are some of the more important and more accessible Etruscan sights (all are mentioned in this book):

Rome: Traces of original Etruscan engineering projects (e.g., Circus Maximus), Vatican Museum artifacts, and Villa Giulia Museum, with the famous "husband and wife sarcophagus."

Orvieto: Archaeological Museum (coins, dinnerware, and a sarcophagus), necropolis, and underground tunnels and caves.

Volterra: Etruscan gate (Porta dell'Arco, from fourth century B.C.) and Etruscan Museum (funerary urns).

Chiusi: Museum, tombs, and tunnels.

Cortona: Museum and dome-shaped tombs.

HILL TOWNS

was forgotten—covered in the garbage of Volterra. Luckily, it was rediscovered in the 1950s.

The stage wall was standard Roman design—with three levels from which actors would appear: one for mortals, one for heroes, and the top one for gods. Parts of two levels still stand. Gods leaped out onto the third level for the last time in the fourth century A.D., when the town decided to abandon the theater and to use its stones to build fancy baths instead. You can see the remains of the baths behind the theater, including the round sauna with brick supports to raise the heated floor.

Cost and Hours: €3, but you can view the theater free from Via Lungo le Mure, April–Oct daily 10:30–17:30, Nov–March Sat–Sun only 10:00–16:00.

View from Promenade: From the vantage point on the city wall promenade, you can trace Volterra's vast Etruscan wall. Find the church in the distance, on the left, and notice the stones just below. They are from the Etruscan wall that followed the ridge into the valley and defined Volterra five centuries before Christ.

▲▲**Etruscan Museum (Museo Etrusco Guarnacci)**—Filled top to bottom with rare Etruscan artifacts, this museum—even with few English explanations and its dusty, almost neglectful, old-school style—makes it easy to appreciate how advanced this pre-Roman culture was.

The collection starts with pre-Etruscan Villanovian artifacts (c. 1500 B.C.), but its highlight is a seemingly endless collection of Etruscan funerary urns (designed to contain the ashes of cremated loved ones).

Each urn is tenderly carved with a unique scene, offering a peek into the still-mysterious Etruscan society. While contempo-

raries of the Greeks, the Etruscans were more libertine. Their religion was less demanding, and their women were a respected part of both the social and public spheres. Women and men alike are depicted lounging on Etruscan urns. While they seem to be just hanging out, the lounging dead were actually offering the gods a banquet—in order to gain their favor in the transition to the next life. The outcome of the banquet had eternal consequences.

On urns dating from the seventh to the first century B.C., the dearly departed are often depicted holding scrolls, blank wax tablets (symbolizing blank new lives in the next world), and libation cups—offering wine to the gods. Realistic scenes show the fabled horseback-and-carriage ride to the underworld, where the dead are greeted by Caron, with his hammer and pointy ears. While the finer urns are carved of alabaster, most are made of volcanic tuff. Most lids are mismatched—casualties of reckless 18th- and 19th-century archaeology. Look at the faces, and imagine the lives they lived and the loved ones they left behind.

On the top floor is a re-created grave site, with several urns and artifacts that would have been buried with the deceased. Some of these were funeral dowry (called *corredo*) that the dead would pack along. You'll see artifacts such as mirrors, coins, hardware for vases, votive statues, pots, pans, and jewelry.

Fans of Alberto Giacometti will be amazed at how the tall, skinny figure called *The Shadow of Night (L'Ombra della Sera)* looks just like the modern Swiss sculptor's work—but is 2,500 years older.

Cost and Hours: €9 combo-ticket includes—like it or not—the Pinacoteca and Sacred Art Museum, daily 9:00–19:00, Nov–March until 13:45, ask at the ticket window for mildly interesting English pamphlet, €3 audioguide fleshes out your visit well, Via Don Minzoni 15, tel. 0588-86347, www.comune.volterra.pi.it /english.

After your visit, duck across the street to the alabaster showroom and the wine bar (both described next).

▲**Alabaster Workshop**—Alab'Arte offers a fun peek into the art of alabaster. Their showroom is across from the Etruscan Museum.

A block downhill, in front of Porta Marcoli, is their powdery workshop, where you can watch Roberto Chiti and Giorgio Finazzo at work. They are delighted to share their art with visitors. Lighting shows off the translucent quality of the stone and the expertise of these artists For more artisans in action, visit the "Artisan Lane" described earlier, or ask the TI for their list of the town's many workshops open to the public.

Cost and Hours: Showroom—daily 10:30–13:00 & 15:30–19:00, Via Don Minzoni 18; workshop—Mon–Sat 9:30–13:00 & 15:00–19:00, closed Sun, Via Orti Sant'Agostino 28; tel. 0588-87968, www.alabarte.com.

▲**La Vena di Vino (Wine-Tasting with Bruno and Lucio)**—La Vena di Vino, also just across from the Etruscan Museum, is a fun *enoteca* where two guys have devoted themselves to the wonders of wine and share it with a fun-loving passion. Each day Bruno and Lucio open six or eight bottles, serve your choice by the glass, pair it with characteristic munchies, and offer fine music (guitars available for patrons) and an unusual decor (the place is strewn with bras). Hang out here with the local characters. This is your chance to try the Super Tuscan—a creative mix of international grapes grown in Tuscany. According to Bruno, "While the Brunello (€7/glass) is just right for wild boar, the Super Tuscan (€6) is just right for meditation." Food is served all day, including some hot dishes or a plate of meats and cheeses (Wed–Mon 11:00–1:00 in the morning, closed Tue, 3- and 5-glass wine-tastings, Via Don Minzoni 30, tel. 0588-81491, www.lavenadivino.com). While Volterra is  famously quiet late at night, this place is full of action. There's a vintage dentist chair attached to the karaoke machine downstairs.

Medici Fortress and Archaeological Park—The Parco Archeologico marks what was the acropolis of Volterra from 1500 B.C. until A.D. 1472, when Florence conquered the pesky city and burned its political and historic center, turning it into a grassy commons (park closes at 20:00 in summer, 17:00 in winter) and building the adjacent Medici Fortezza. The old fortress—a symbol of Florentine dominance—now keeps people in rather than out. It's a maximum-security prison housing only about 60 special prisoners. (Note that when you're driving from San Gimignano to Volterra, you pass another big, modern prison—almost surreal in the midst of all the Tuscan wonder.) Authorities prefer to keep organized-crime figures locked up far away from their family ties in Sicily.

Sleeping in Volterra

(€1 = about $1.25, country code: 39)

$$$ Park Hotel Le Fonti, a 10-minute walk downhill from Porta al Arco, is a spacious, family-run hotel in an imposing building with 67 rooms, many with views. In addition to the swimming pool, guests can use a small spa with sauna, hot tub, and an intriguing "emotional shower" (Db-€89–165 but prices vary wildly depending on season, elevator, on-site restaurant, wine bar, free parking, Via di Fontecorrenti 5, tel. 0588-85219, fax 0588-92728, www.parkhotellefonti.com, info@parkhotellefonti.com, Pedro, Paola, and Ghebo Bessi).

$$ Albergo Etruria, on Volterra's main drag, rents 21 fresh, modern, and spacious rooms within an ancient stone structure. They have a welcoming TV lounge and a peaceful garden out back. Request a quiet room off the street (Sb-€75, Db-€95, Tb-€115, 10 percent discount with cash and this book, fans, Wi-Fi, Via

Matteotti 32, tel. 0588-87377, fax 0588-92784, www.albergoetruria .it, info@albergoetruria.it, Lisa and Giuseppina are fine hosts).

$$ Hotel La Locanda is well-located and rents 18 decent rooms (Db-€93–125, air-con, Wi-Fi, Via Guarnacci 24/28, tel. 0588-81547, www.hotel-lalocanda.com, staff@hotel-lalocanda .com, Jenny, Stefania, and Irina).

$$ Albergo Villa Nencini, just outside of town, is big, modern, and professional, with 36 fine rooms. A few rooms have terraces and many have views. There's also a large pool and free parking (Sb-€67, Db-€88, Tb-€115, 10 percent discount with cash and this book, Borgo Santo Stefano 55, a 15-minute uphill walk to main square, tel. 0588-86386, fax 0588-80601, www.villanencini .it, info@villanencini.it, Nencini family).

$$ Albergo Nazionale, with 38 big rooms, is simple, a little musty, short on smiles, popular with school groups, and steps from the bus stop (Sb-€65–70, Db-€80–90, Tb-€105, less off-season, Via dei Marchesi 11, tel. 0588-86284, fax 0588-84097, www.hotel nazionale-volterra.it, info@hotelnazionale-volterra.it).

$ Seminario Vescovile Sant'Andrea has been training priests for more than 500 years. Today, the remaining eight priests still train students, but when classes are over, their 16 rooms— separated by vast and holy halls in an echoing old mansion—are rented very cheaply. Look for the 15th-century Ascension ceramic by Andrea della Robbia, tucked away in a corner upstairs (S-€15, Sb-€20, D-€28, Db-€36, T-€42, Tb-€54, breakfast-€3, elevator, closes at 24:00, groups welcome, free parking, easy 7-minute walk from Etruscan Museum, Viale Vittorio Veneto 2, tel. 0588-86028, semvescovile@diocesivolterra.it, Alberto or Angela).

$ Volterra Youth Hostel fills a wing of the restored Convent of San Girolamo with 85 beds. It's spacious and has lots of services, but it's a 15-minute hike out of town, in a boring area, and no cheaper than the more memorable seminary option closer to town (bed in 6-bed dorm-€17, Db-€60, breakfast-€3, lockers, tel. 0588-86613, www.ostellovolterra.it, info@ostellovolterra.it).

Near Volterra

$$ Podere Marcampo is a new *agriturismo* about four miles outside Volterra on the road to Pisa. Run by Genuino (owner of the recommended Ristorante Enoteca del Duca) and his wife, this peaceful spot has three well-appointed rooms and three apartments, plus a swimming pool with panoramic views. Genuino produces his award-winning merlot on-site and offers €15 wine-tastings with cheese and homemade salami. Cooking classes are also available (Db-€90, apartment-€125–160, includes breakfast, air-con, Wi-Fi, free parking, tel. 0588-85393, mobile 348-514-9782, www.agriturismo -marcampo.com, info@agriturismo-marcampo.com).

HILL TOWNS

Eating in Volterra

Menus feature a Volterran take on regional dishes. *Zuppa alla Volterrana* is a fresh vegetable-and-bread soup, similar to *ribollita* (except that it isn't made from leftovers). *Torta di ceci,* also known as *cecina,* is a savory pancake–like dish made with garbanzo beans. Those with more adventurous palates dive into *trippa* (tripe; comes in a bowl like stew), the traditional breakfast of the alabaster carvers.

Ristorante Enoteca del Duca, with a locally respected chef named Genuino, serves well-presented and creative Tuscan cuisine. You can dine under a medieval arch with walls lined with wine bottles, in a stark dining room (with an Etruscan statuette at each table), or on a nice little patio out back. It's a good place for truffles, and has a fine wine list (which includes Genuino's own merlot) and friendly staff. The spacious seating, dressy clientele, and calm atmosphere make this a good choice for a romantic meal (€42 food-sampler fixed-price meal, €10 pastas, €17 *secondi,* Wed–Mon 12:30–15:00 & 19:30–22:00, closed Tue, near City Hall at Via di Castello 2, tel. 0588-81510).

Trattoria da Bado, a 10-minute hike out of town, is every local's favorite for its *tipica cucina Volterrana.* Giacomo and family offer a rustic atmosphere and serve food with no pretense—"the way you wish your mamma cooks" (meals Thu–Tue from 12:30 and 19:30, closed Wed, Borgo San Lazzero 9, tel. 0588-86477, reserve before you go as it's often full).

Don Beta is a family-run trattoria on the main drag, popular with trendy Volterrans for its stylish home cooking. Mirko supervises the lively young team as they whisk out steaming plates of seafood pasta and homemade desserts (€10 pastas, €15 *secondi*, reservations smart, Via Matteotti 39, tel. 0588-86730, Paolo, Azzura, and Mamica).

La Vecchia Lira, bright and cheery, is a classy self-serve eatery that's a hit with locals as a quick and cheap lunch spot by day, and a fancier restaurant at night (Fri–Wed 12:00–14:30 & 19:00–22:30, closed Thu, Via Matteotti 19, tel. 0588-86180, Lamberto and Massimo).

Ristorante il Sacco Fiorentino is a local favorite for traditional cuisine and seasonal seafood specials (€8 pastas, €15 *secondi,* Thu–Tue 12:00–14:30 & 19:00–21:30, closed Wed, Piazza XX Settembre 18, tel. 0588-88537).

La Vena di Vino is an *enoteca* serving up simple and traditional dishes and the best of Tuscan wine in a fun atmosphere (Wed–Mon 11:00–1:00 in the morning, closed Tue, Via Don Minzoni 30, tel. 0588-81491, www.lavenadivino.com). For more details, read the description on page 619.

Pizzerias: **Ombra della Sera** dishes out what local kids consider the best pizza in town. At €6 and big enough to split, they make for a cheap date (Tue–Sun 12:00–15:00 & 19:00–22:00, closed Mon, Via Guarnacci 16, tel. 0588-85274).

Pizzeria Tavernetta, next door, is more romantic, with delightful indoor and on-the-street seating. Marco, who looks like Billy Joel, serves splittable €7 pizzas (Thu–Tue, closed Wed, Via Guarnacci 14, tel. 0588-87630).

Picnics: You can assemble a picnic at the few *alimentari* around town (try Despar Market at Via Gramsci 12, Wed 7:30–13:00, Thu–Tue 7:30–13:00 & 17:00–20:00) and eat in the breezy Archaeological Park.

Volterra Connections

The nearest train station is in **Saline di Volterra,** a 15-minute bus ride away (7/day, 4/day Sun). In Volterra, buses come and go from Piazza Martiri della Libertà (buy tickets at any *tabacchi* shop).

From Volterra by Bus to: Florence (4/day, 2/day Sun, 2 hours, change in Colle Val d'Elsa), **Siena** (4/day, 1/day Sun, 2 hours, change in Colle Val d'Elsa), **San Gimignano** (4/day, 2/day Sun, 2 hours, change in Colle Val d'Elsa), **Pisa** (9/day, 2 hours, change in Pontedera). For Siena, Florence, and San Gimignano, C.P.T. bus tickets get you only as far as Colle Val d'Elsa (4/day, 50 minutes, €2.50); you must then buy another ticket (from another bus company) at the newsstand near the bus stop.

Montalcino

On a hill overlooking vineyards and valleys, Montalcino—famous for its delicious and pricey Brunello di Montalcino red wines—is a must for wine-lovers. Everyone touring this area seems to be relaxed and in an easy groove...as if enjoying a little wine buzz.

In the Middle Ages, Montalcino (mohn-tahl-CHEE-noh) was considered Siena's biggest ally. Originally allied with Florence, the town switched sides after the Sienese beat up Florence in the Battle of Montaperti in 1260. The Sienese persuaded the Montalcini to join their side by forcing them to sleep one night in the bloody Florentine-strewn battlefield.

Montalcino prospered under Siena, but like its ally, it waned after the Medici family took control of the region. The village became a humble place. Then, in the late 19th century, the Biondi Santi family created a fine, dark red wine, calling it "the brunette" (Brunello). Today's affluence is due to the town's much-sought-after wine.

Non-wine-lovers may find Montalcino a bit too focused on *vino*, but one sip of Brunello makes even wine skeptics believe that Bacchus was onto something. Note that Rosso di Montalcino (a younger version of Brunello) is also very good, at half the price. Those with a sweet tooth will enjoy crunching the Ossi di Morta ("bones of the dead") cookies popular in Tuscany.

Orientation to Montalcino

Sitting atop a hill amidst a sea of vineyards, Montalcino is surrounded by walls and dominated by the Fortezza (a.k.a. "La Rocca"). From here, roads lead down into the two main squares: Piazza Garibaldi and Piazza del Popolo.

Tourist Information: The TI, just off Piazza Garibaldi in the City Hall, can find you a room (Db-€50–80) for no fee. They have information on taxi service to nearby towns, abbeys, and monasteries (daily 10:00–13:00 & 14:00–17:30, tel. & fax 0577-849-331, www.prolocomontalcino.it).

Arrival in Montalcino: The bus station is on Piazza Cavour, about 300 yards from the town center. Drivers coming in for a short visit should drive right through the old gate under the fortress (follow signs to *Fortezza;* it looks almost forbidden) and grab a spot in the pay lot at the fortress (€1.50/hour, free 20:00–8:00). Otherwise, park for free a short walk away.

Helpful Hints: Market day is Friday (7:00–13:00) on Viale della Libertà. Day-trippers be warned: Montalcino has **no baggage storage.**

Sights in Montalcino

Fortezza—This 14th-century fort, built under the rule of Siena, is now little more than an empty shell. People visit for its *enoteca* (wine bar—see page 628). You can climb the ramparts to enjoy a panoramic view of the Asso and Orcia valleys, or enjoy a picnic in the park surrounding the fort.

Montalcino

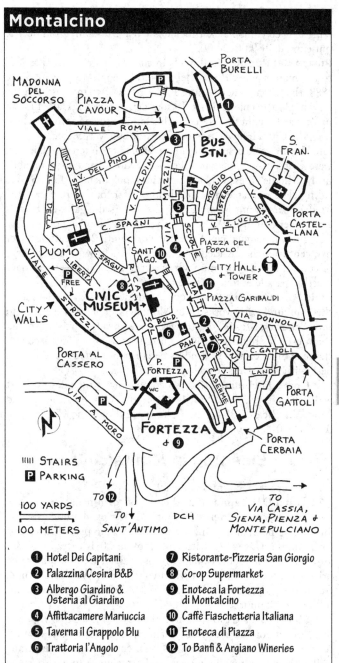

IIIII STAIRS
P PARKING

100 YARDS
100 METERS

1 Hotel Dei Capitani
2 Palazzina Cesira B&B
3 Albergo Giardino & Osteria al Giardino
4 Affittacamere Mariuccia
5 Taverna il Grappolo Blu
6 Trattoria l'Angolo
7 Ristorante-Pizzeria San Giorgio
8 Co-op Supermarket
9 Enoteca la Fortezza di Montalcino
10 Caffè Fiaschetteria Italiana
11 Enoteca di Piazza
12 To Banfi & Argiano Wineries

Cost and Hours: €4 for rampart walk—buy ticket in the wine bar, €6 combo-ticket includes Civic Museum—sold only at museum, daily 9:00–20:00.

Piazza del Popolo—All roads in tiny Montalcino seem to lead to the main square, Piazza del Popolo ("People's Square"). Since 1888, the recommended Caffè Fiaschetteria Italiana has been the elegant place to enjoy a drink. Its founder, inspired by Caffè Florian in Venice, brought fine coffee to this humble town of woodcutters.

The City Hall was the fortified seat of government. It's decorated by the coats of arms of judges who, in the interest of fairness, were from outside of town. Like Siena, Montalcino was a republic in the Middle Ages. When Florentines took Siena in 1555, Siena's ruling class retreated here and held out for four more years. The Medici coat of arms (with the six pills) superseding all the others is a reminder that in 1559 Florence finally took Montalcino.

The one-handed clock was the norm until 200 years ago. For five centuries the arcaded loggia hosted the town market. And, of course, it's fun to simply observe the *passeggiata*—these days mostly a parade of tourists here for the wine.

Civic Museum (Museo Civico)—Gothic sacred art is the star of this museum, with works from Montalcino's heyday, the 13th to 16th centuries. Most of the art was created by local artists. Among the museum's highlights are a glazed terra-cotta altarpiece and statue of St. Sebastian by Andrea della Robbia. The ground floor is best, with an impressive collection of crucifixes.

Cost and Hours: €4.50, €6 combo-ticket includes rampart walk at Fortezza, Tue–Sun 10:00–13:00 & 14:00–17:50, closed Mon, Via Ricasoli 31, to the right of Sant'Agostino Church, tel. 0577-846-014.

Sleeping in Montalcino

(€1 = about $1.25, country code: 39)

$$$ Hotel Dei Capitani, at the end of town near the bus station, is well-run and rents 29 rooms. It has plush public spaces, an inviting pool, and a cliffside terrace offering plenty of reasons for lounging (Db-€120 with this book in 2011, extra bed-€30, air-con, half the rooms come with vast Tuscan views for the same price—request a view room when you reserve, Wi-Fi in lounge, free parking, Via Lapini 6, tel. 0577-847-227, www.deicapitani.it, info@deicapitani.it).

$$ Palazzina Cesira, right in the heart of the old town, rents five spacious and tastefully decorated rooms in a fine 13th-century residence with a palatial lounge. You'll enjoy a refined and tranquil ambience, a nice breakfast, and the chance to get to know Lucilla and her American husband Roberto (Db-€95, suites-€115,

HILL TOWNS

cash only, 2-night minimum except 3-night minimum on holiday weekends, Wi-Fi, Via Soccorso Saloni 2, tel. & fax 0577-846-055, www.montalcinoitaly.com, p.cesira@tin.it).

$ Albergo Giardino, old and basic, has nine big simple rooms, no public spaces, and a fine locale (Db-€55–60, 10 percent discount with this book, no breakfast, Piazza Cavour 4, tel. & fax 0577-848-257, mobile 338-684-3163, albergoilgiardino@virgilio.it, Roberto and his dad, Mario).

$ Affittacamere Mariuccia has three basic, Ikea-chic rooms on the main drag over a heaven-scented bakery (Db-€50, no breakfast, check-in across the street at Enoteca Pierangioli before 20:00 or let them know arrival time, Piazza del Popolo 16, rooms at #28, tel. 0577-849-113, mobile 348-392-4780, www.affittacamere mariuccia.it, enotecapierangioli@hotmail.com, Alessandro speaks English).

Near Montalcino

$$ La Crociona, an *agriturismo* farm and working vineyard, rents seven fully equipped apartments. Fiorella Vannoni and Roberto and Barbara Nannetti offer cooking classes and tastes of the Brunello wine grown and bottled on the premises (Db-€95, or €65 in Oct–mid-May; Qb-€130, or €95 in Oct–mid-May; lower weekly rates, metered gas heating, laundry-€8/load, pool, La Croce 15, tel. 0577-847-133, fax 0577-846-994, www.lacrociona .com, crociona@tin.it). The farm is two miles south of Montalcino on the road to the Sant'Antimo Monastery (look for big yellow *Piombaia La Crociona* sign on left, then follow directions to Tenuta Crocedimezzo e Crociona). A good restaurant is next door.

Eating in Montalcino

Taverna il Grappolo Blu is unpretentious, friendly, and serious about its wine, serving local specialties and vegetarian options to an enthusiastic crowd (€8.50 pastas, €12.50 *secondi,* daily 12:00–15:00 & 19:00–22:00, reservations smart, near the main square, a few steps off Via Mazzini at Scale di Via Moglio 1, tel. 0577-847-150).

Trattoria l'Angolo, a family-run hole-in-the-wall, has nine small tables and homemade desserts (€7 pastas, €8 meat dishes, Wed–Mon 12:00–14:30 & 19:00–21:30, closed Tue, Via Ricasoli 9, tel. 0577-848-017). The other **l'Angolo,** at the Fortezza end of Via Ricasoli, is mainly a food store with just a couple of tables for munching on plates of cheese and salami (closed Tue).

Osteria al Giardino is small and dressy, serving near-gourmet creative Tuscan cuisine at the bus-station end of town. Owner and chef Giovanni Luca makes everything fresh, from the bread to the desserts, always has a veggie option, and offers a tasting *menu* (€10 pastas, €14 *secondi,* Mon–Sat 12:30–14:30 & 19:30–21:45, closed Sun, Piazza Cavour 1, tel. 0577-849-076). Giovanni's wife, Paola, runs the dining room.

Ristorante-Pizzeria San Giorgio is a homely trattoria-pizzeria with kitschy decor and great prices, run by the same family as Trattoria l'Angolo (pizza €4.50–7 served evenings only, daily 12:00–15:00 & 19:00–22:30, near recommended hotel Palazzina Cesira at Via S. Saloni 10–14, tel. 0577-848-507, Mara).

Gather ingredients for a picnic at the **Co-op supermarket** on Via Sant'Agostino (just off Via Ricasoli in front of Sant'Agostino Church, closed Sun), then enjoy your feast up at the Madonna del Soccorso Church, with vast territorial views.

Wine-Tasting and Wineries

Enoteca la Fortezza di Montalcino offers a chance to taste top-end wines by the glass, each with an English explanation. While wine snobs turn up their noses, the medieval setting inside Montalcino's fort is a hit for most visitors. Spoil yourself with Brunello in the cozy *enoteca* or at an outdoor table (€12 for 3 tastings; €5–9 sampler plates of cheeses, *salumi,* honeys, and olive oil; daily 9:00–20:00, closes at 18:00 in off-season, inside the Fortezza, tel. 0577-849-211, www.enotecalafortezza.com).

Caffè Fiaschetteria Italiana was founded by Ferruccio Biondi Santi, who created the famous Brunello wine. The wine library in the back of the café boasts many local wine choices. A meeting place since 1888, this grand café also serves light lunches and espresso to tourists and locals alike (€6–15 for a glass of Brunello and plate of snacks; same prices inside, outside, or in back room; Fri–Wed 7:30–23:00, closed Thu, Piazza del Popolo 6, tel. 0577-849-043). And if it's coffee you need, this place—with its classic 1961 espresso machine—is considered the best in town.

Enoteca di Piazza is one of a chain of wine shops with a system of mechanical wine dispensers. You get a card that keeps track of the samples you take, and you'll pay from €1 to €9 for each 50-mililiter taste of 100 different wines kept fresh in the fancy machines. The only nibbles are saltine-type crackers. They hope you'll buy a bottle of the samples you like, and are happy to educate you in English. (Rule of thumb: a bottle costs about 10 times the cost of the sample. If you buy a bottle, the sample of that wine is free.) While the place feels a little formulaic and sterile, it can be fun—and the wine is great (daily 9:00–20:00, near Piazza del Popolo at Via Matteotti 43, tel. 0577-848-104, www.enotecadipiazza.com).

Wineries: While there are plenty of *enoteche,* there are no real wineries inside the city. The nearby countryside, however, is littered with them, and some offer tastings. While some require an appointment, many also are happy to serve a glass to potential buyers and show them around. **Banfi** is run by the Italian-American Mariani brothers. Huge and the most touristy, it produces well-respected wines (daily 10:00–18:00, tours daily at 16:00, reserve in advance, 10-minute drive south of Montalcino in Sant'Angelo Scalo, tel. 0577-877-500, www.castellobanfi.com, reservations @banfi.it). **Argiano** claims to be the oldest working winery in the region, dating back to 1580. Not far from Banfi at Sant'Angelo in Colle, their one-hour tour in English includes the vineyards, the exterior of a historic villa, and ancient moldy cellars full of wine casks. They also rent on-site apartments—handy for those who have oversampled (€20 tour includes six wine samples, reserve in advance, tel. 0577-844-037, www.argiano.net, argiano@argiano .net, coming by car the last two miles are along a rough-but-drivable track through vineyards). The Montalcino TI can give you a list of more than 150 regional wineries. Or check with the vintners' consortium (tel. 0577-848-246, www.consorziobrunello dimontalcino.it, info@consorziobrunellodimontalcino.it).

Montalcino Connections

The nearest train station is a 30-minute bus ride (running nearly hourly) away in Buonconvento. Montalcino's bus station is on Piazza Cavour, within the town walls. Bus tickets are sold at the bar on Piazza Cavour or at *tabacchi* shops, but not on board. Check schedules at the TI, at the bus station, or at www.sienamobilita.it.

From Montalcino by Bus to: Siena (6/day, 1.5 hours, €3.50), **Pienza** (5/day, none on Sun, change to line #114 in Torrenieri, 1 hour plus changing time), **Sant'Antimo** (3/day, none on Sun, 15 minutes, €1.50, buy tickets on board). Anyone going to Florence changes in Siena—the most convenient route is by bus to Buonconvento, then take the train.

Pienza

Set on a crest, surrounded by green, rolling hills, the small town of Pienza packs a lot of Renaissance punch. In the 1400s, locally born Pope Pius II of the Piccolomini family decided to remodel his birthplace in the style that was all the rage: Renaissance. Propelled by papal clout, the town of Corsignano was transformed—in only five years' time—into a jewel of Renaissance architecture. It was renamed Pienza, after Pope Pius. The plan was to remodel the entire town, but work ended in 1464 when both the pope and his architect, Bernardo Rossellino, died. Their vision—what you see today—was completed a century later. The architectural focal point

is the square, Piazza Pio II, surrounded by the Duomo and the
pope's family residence, Palazzo
Piccolomini. While Piazza Pio II
is Pienza's pride and joy, the entire
town—a mix of old stonework,
potted plants, and grand views—
is fun to explore, especially with
a camera or sketchpad in hand.

You can walk each lane in the tiny town in a few minutes.

Cute as the town is, it also feels a bit greedy and is entirely
given over to snaring the tourist dollar. Because of that, I'd recommend popping in to enjoy the setting, and perhaps touring the
palace, but not lingering for an overnight.

Nearly every shop sells the town's specialty: Pecorino cheese.
This pungent sheep's cheese is available fresh *(fresco)* or aged *(secco)*,
and sometimes contains other ingredients, such as truffles or peppers. Look on menus for warm Pecorino *(al forno* or *alla griglia)*,
often topped with honey or pears and served with bread. Along
with a glass of local wine, this just might lead you to a new understanding of *la dolce vita.*

Orientation to Pienza

Tourist Information: The TI is 10 yards up the street from
Piazza Pio II, inside the Diocesan Museum (daily 10:00–13:00 &
15:00–18:00, shorter hours Nov–March, tel. 0578-749-905). Ignore
the kiosk just outside the gate, labeled *Informaturista,* which is a
private travel agency.

Arrival in Pienza: Free street parking is available—if you can
find it. Otherwise you can park at the large lot near Largo Roma
outside of the old town (€1.50/hour, often completely full in the
morning).

Helpful Hints: Market day is Friday morning. A public **WC,**
marked *gabinetto,* is on the right just outside the town gate on
Piazza Dante Alighieri.

Sights in Pienza

▲**Piazza Pio II**—One of Italy's classic piazzas, this square is
famous for its elegance and artistic unity. The square and the surrounding buildings were all designed by Rossellino to form an
"outdoor room." Spinning around clockwise, you'll see the City
Hall (13th-century bell tower with a Renaissance facade and a fine
loggia), the Bishop's Palace (now an art museum), the Duomo, and
the Piccolomini family palace. Just to the left of the church, a lane

leads to the best viewpoint in town.

Duomo—Its classic, symmetrical Renaissance facade—dated 1462 with the Piccolomini family coat of arms immodestly front and center—dominates Piazza Pio II. The interior is charming, with several Gothic altarpieces and painted arches. Windows feature the crest of Pius II, with five half-moons advertising the number of crusades that his family funded. The interior art is Sienese Gothic on the cusp of the Renaissance. As the local clay and

tufa stone were not ideal building material for the foundation, the church is slouching. See the cracks in the apse walls, and get seasick behind the main altar.

Cost and Hours: Free, generally open daily 7:00–13:00 & 14:30–19:00.

▲▲Palazzo Piccolomini—The home of Pius II (see page 540 in the Siena chapter) and the Piccolomini family (until 1962) can be visited with a guided tour. While the 30-minute tour (in English and Italian) visits only six rooms and the loggia, it offers a fascinating slice of 15th-century aristocratic life and is the sightseeing highlight of the town. In fact, it's the most impressive small-town palace experience I've found in Tuscany. You can check out the well-preserved painted courtyard for free. In Renaissance times, most buildings were covered with elaborate paintings like these.

Cost and Hours: €7, Tue–Sun 10:00–13:00 & 14:00–18:30, closed Mon, tel. 0578-748-392, www.palazzopiccolominipienza.it.

Diocesan Museum (Museo Diocesano)—This collection of religious paintings from local churches fills the cardinal's Renaissance palace. The art is provincial Sienese, displayed in chronological order from the 12th through 17th centuries, conveniently all on one floor.

Cost and Hours: €4; mid-March–Dec Wed–Mon 10:00–13:00 & 15:00–18:00, closed Tue; Jan–mid-March Sat–Sun only 10:00–13:00 & 15:00–18:00; Corso il Rossellino 30.

View Terrace—As you face the church, the upper lane leading left brings you to the panoramic promenade. Views from the terrace include the Tuscan countryside and Monte Amiata, the largest mountain in southern Tuscany, in the distance.

Pienza Connections

Bus tickets are sold at the *edicola/libreria* just outside Pienza's town gate and at some *tabacchi* (or pay a little extra and buy tickets from the driver). Montepulciano is the nearest transportation hub to other points.

From Pienza by Bus to: Siena (5/day, none on Sun, 1.5 hours), **Montepulciano** (8/day, 30 minutes).

Montepulciano

Curving its way along a ridge, Montepulciano (mohn-teh-pull-cheeAH-noh) delights visitors with *vino* and views. Alternately under Sienese and Florentine rule, the city still retains its medieval *contrade* districts, each with a mascot and flag. The neighborhoods compete the last Sunday of August in the Bravio delle Botti, where teams of men push large wine casks uphill from Piazza Marzocco to Piazza Grande,

all hoping to win a banner and bragging rights. The entire last week of August is a festival: Each *contrada* arranges musical entertainment and prepares food at outdoor eateries that offer generous tastings of the local *vino*.

The city is a collage of architectural styles, but the elegant San Biagio Church, at the base of the hill, is its most impressive Renaissance building. Most visitors ignore the architecture and focus more on the city's other creative accomplishment, Vino Nobile di Montepulciano, a tasty red wine.

Orientation to Montepulciano

The commercial action in Montepulciano centers in the lower town, mostly along Via di Gracciano nel Corso (nicknamed Corso). Strolling here, you'll find cheap eateries, gift shops, and tourist traps. The back streets are worth exploring. The main square at the top of town is Piazza Grande. Standing proudly above all the touristy sales energy, it has a more noble, Florentine feel.

Tourist Information: The TI is near the bus station, in Piazza Don Minzoni. It books hotels and rooms for no fee, sells train tickets, has an Internet terminal (€3.50/hour), and can book one of the town's two taxis (Mon–Sat 9:30–12:30 & 15:00–18:00, Sun 9:30–12:30, daily until 19:00 in summer except until 20:00 in Aug, tel. 0578-757-341, www.prolocomontepulciano.it).

Note that there's a more central office that looks like a TI, but is actually a privately run "Strada del Vino" (Wine Road) agency. They don't have city info, but provide wine-road maps and organize **wine tours** in the city, and minibus winery tours farther afield. They also offer other tours (olive oil, cheese, and slow food), cooking classes, and more, depending on season and demand (Mon–Sat 10:00–13:00 & 15:00–18:00, closed Sun, closed Sat off-season, Piazza Grande 7, tel. 0578-717-484, www.strada vinonobile.it).

Arrival in Montepulciano: Most visits begin at the fortified Porta al Prato gate, near the bus station. From the gate, it's a 15-minute walk uphill along the Corso, the bustling main drag (note the Etruscan reliefs on the foundation of Palazzo Bucelli—see photo on previous page), to the main square, Piazza Grande. If you arrive at the bus station, an orange shuttle bus can take you to Piazza Grande (2/hour); it's a good strategy to take the bus up and walk back down.

Drivers arriving by car should park outside the walls (don't try to tackle the tiny roads inside the city), either at the bus station or the numerous lots on the edge of town. For a free spot near the top of the hill, follow signs for lots #7 and #8. If you're sleeping in town, your hotelier will give you a permit to park within the walls.

Helpful Hints: Market day is Thursday. There's no official **baggage storage** in town, but the TI might let you leave bags with them if they have space. Public **WCs** are located at the TI, to the right of Palazzo Comunale, and at the Sant'Agostino Church. A self-service **laundry** is at Via del Paolino 2 (€4 wash, €4 dry, daily 8:00–22:00, tel. 0578-717-544). For a **taxi,** call 335-617-7126.

Sights in Montepulciano

Piazza Grande—This pleasant, lively piazza is surrounded by a grab bag of architectural sights. If the medieval Palazzo Comunale

 reminds you of Palazzo Vecchio in Florence, it's because Florence dominated this town in the 15th and 16th centuries. The crenellations along the roof were never intended to hide soldiers—they're meant just to symbolize power. A cistern system fed by rainwater draining from surrounding palaces supplied the courtyard's fine well. Check out its 19th-century pulleys, the grills to keep animals from contaminating the water supply, and the Medici coat of arms (with lions symbolizing political power of Florence).

Montepulciano

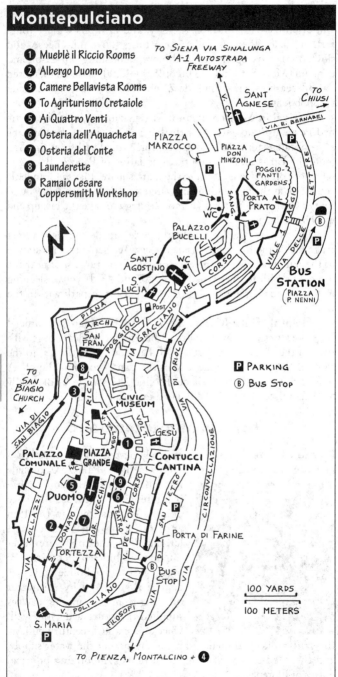

1. Mueblè il Riccio Rooms
2. Albergo Duomo
3. Camere Bellavista Rooms
4. To Agriturismo Cretaiole
5. Ai Quattro Venti
6. Osteria dell'Aquacheta
7. Osteria del Conte
8. Launderette
9. Ramaio Cesare Coppersmith Workshop

TO SIENA VIA SINALUNGA & A-1 AUTOSTRADA FREEWAY

TO CHIUSI

SANT' AGNESE

V. CAL

VIA E. BERNABEI

PIAZZA MARZOCCO

PIAZZA DON MINZONI

POGGIO-FANTI GARDENS

PORTA AL PRATO

WC

PALAZZO BUCELLI

SANT' AGOSTINO

WC

S. LUCIA

NEL CORSO

SANG

VIALE I MAGGIO

VIA DELLE LETTERE

BUS STATION (PIAZZA P. NENNI)

Post

PIANA

ARCHI

SAN FRAN.

POGGIOLO

VIA GRACCIANO

VIA DI ORIOLO

TO SAN BIAGIO CHURCH

VIA DI SAN BIAGIO

P PARKING

B BUS STOP

VIA RICCI

VIA TALOSA

CIVIC MUSEUM

VOLT.

GESÙ

PALAZZO COMUNALE

WC

PIAZZA GRANDE

CONTUCCI CANTINA

DUOMO

FIOR. VECCHIA

V. DELL'ORIO CORSO

TEATRO

VIA DI SAN PIETRO

CIRCONVALLAZIONE

P

PORTA DI FARINE

DONATO

FORTEZZA

V. DEL

B BUS STOP

VIA COLLAZZI

100 YARDS

100 METERS

S. MARIA

P

V. POLIZIANO

FILOSOFI

VIA DI

TO PIENZA, MONTALCINO & 4

Climbing the **tower** rewards you with a windy but commanding view from the terrace below the clock. Go into the Palazzo Comunale, head up the stairs to your left, and pay on the second floor (€2, daily 10:00–18:00, closed in winter). The Palazzo de' Nobili-Tarugi is a Renaissance arcaded confection; meanwhile, the unfinished Duomo looks glumly on, wishing the city hadn't run out of money for its facade. The Contucci Palace (left of the church) is lucky enough to have a 16th-century Renaissance facade. The Contucci family still lives in their palace, producing and selling their own wine. The town is fortunate to be graced with so many bold and noble palazzos—Florentine nobility favored Montepulciano as a breezy and relaxed place for a secondary residence.

Duomo—This church's unfinished facade—rough stonework left waiting for the final marble veneer—is not that unusual. Many churches were built just to the point where they had a functional interior, and then, for various practical reasons, the facades were left unfinished. But step inside and you'll be rewarded with some fine art. A beautiful Andrea della Robbia glazed-terra-cotta *Altar of the Lilies* is behind the baptismal font (on the left as you enter). The high altar features a luminous early-Renaissance Assumption triptych by the Sienese artist Taddeo di Bartolo. Showing Mary in her dreamy eternal sleep as she ascends to be crowned by Jesus, it illustrates how Siena clung to the Gothic aesthetic—elaborate gold leaf and lacy pointed arches—to show heavenly grandeur at the expense of realism.

Cost and Hours: Free, daily 9:00–13:00 & 15:00–18:00.

▲▲Contucci Cantina—Montepulciano's most popular attraction isn't made of stone...it's the famous wine, Vino Nobile. This  robust red can be tasted in any of the cantinas lining Via Ricci and Via di Gracciano nel Corso, but the cantina in the basement of the Contucci Palace is both historic and fun. While the palace has a formal wine-tasting showroom facing the square, head down the lane on the right to the actual cellars, where you'll meet lively Adamo, who has been making wine since 1953 and welcomes tourists into his cellar. While at the palace, you may meet Andrea Contucci, whose family has lived here since the 11th century. He loves to share his family's products with the public. Adamo and Signor Contucci usually have a dozen bottles open (free drop-in tasting, daily 8:30–12:30 & 14:30–18:30, Piazza Grande 7, tel. 0578-757-006, www.contucci.it).

After sipping a little wine with Adamo, explore the palace basement, with its 13th-century vaults. Originally part of the town's wall, these chambers have been filled since the 1500s with huge barrels of wine. Dozens of barrels of Croatian, Italian, and French oak (1,000–2,500 liters each) cradle the wine through a two-year in-the-barrel aging process, while the wine picks up the personality of the wood. After about 35 years, an exhausted barrel has nothing left to offer its wine, so it's retired. Adamo explains that the French oak gives the wine "pure elegance," the Croatian is more masculine, and the Italian oak is a marriage of the two. Each barrel is labeled with the size in liters, the year the wine was barreled, and the percentage of alcohol (determined by how much sun shone in that year). "Nobile"-grade wine needs a minimum of 13 percent alcohol.

Civic Museum (Museo Civico)—The highlight of this small, eclectic, and forgettable museum is its colorful Andrea della Robbia ceramic altarpieces and Etruscan artifacts.

Cost and Hours: €4.20, Tue–Sun 10:00–13:00 & 15:00–18:00, closed Mon, no English, Via Ricci 10, tel. 0578-717-300.

Ramaio Cesare—Cesare the coppersmith is an institution in Montepulciano, carrying on his grandfather's trade by hammering into existence an immense selection of copper objects in his cavern-like workshop. Though his English is limited, he's happy to show you photos of his work—including the copper top of the Duomo in Siena (Via dell'Opio nel Corso 64, tel. 0578-758-753, www.rameria.com).

San Biagio Church—Just outside of town, down a picturesque driveway lined with cypresses, this church—designed by Antonio da Sangallo and built of locally quarried travertine—is Renaissance perfection. The proportions of the Greek cross floor plan give the building a pleasing rhythmic quality. Bramante, who designed St. Peter's at the Vatican in 1516, was inspired by this dome. Walk around the building to study the freestanding towers. The lone tower was supposed to have a twin, but it was never built. The soaring interior, with a high dome and lantern, creates a fine Renaissance space.

Cost and Hours: Free, normally open daily 8:30–18:30. Consider a picnic or snooze on the grass in back. The street called Via di San Biagio, leading from the church up into town, makes for an enjoyable, if challenging, walk.

Sleeping in Montepulciano

(€1 = about $1.25, country code: 39)

$$$ Mueblè il Riccio ("Hedgehog") is medieval-elegant, with six modern and spotless rooms, an awesome roof terrace, and friendly owners (Sb-€80, Db-€100, Tb-€116, breakfast-€8, air-con, Internet access and Wi-Fi, limited free parking—request when you reserve, a block below the main square at Via Talosa 21, tel. & fax 0578-757-713, www.ilriccio.net, info@ilriccio.net, Gió and Ivana speak English). Gió and his son Iacopo give country tours (€30/hour) in one of their classic Italian cars; for tour details, see their website. Ivana makes wonderful breakfast tarts.

$$ Albergo Duomo, renting 13 rooms, is big, fairly modern, and newly decorated, with a comfortable lounge downstairs and a decent breakfast (small Db-€70, standard Db-€90, Tb-€115, family deals, Wi-Fi in lounge, free parking nearby, Via di San Donato 14, tel. 0578-757-473, www.albergoduomo.it, albergoduomo @libero.it, Elisa and Saverio).

$ Camere Bellavista has 10 basic rooms, some with better views than others. Room 6 has a view terrace worth reserving (Db-€70, terrace Db-€80, optional breakfast at a bar in the piazza-€3, cash only, no elevator, Via Ricci 25, no reception—call before arriving or ring bell, mobile 347-823-2314, fax 0578-716-341, bellavista@bccmp.com, Gabriella, little English spoken).

Between Montepulciano and Montalcino: A Green Acres *Agriturismo* Holiday

$$ Agriturismo Cretaiole, in pristine farmland on the Montalcino–Pienza road, is warmly run by Isabella and her

husband, Carlo. This family-friendly farm, deeply rooted in the culture, welcomes visitors for weeklong stays (generally Sat–Sat) in six comfortable apartments. Eager to share their local traditions, they create a community of about 14–20 travelers who are looking for a rich cultural education. Isabella offers pasta-making classes, guided walks and hikes, visits to local wineries, and the chance to help with truffle-hunting and/or grape and olive harvesting. Carlo is a professional olive-oil taster (a class is included as part of your weekly stay). Carlo's father, Luciano, is in charge of the grappa and tending the vegetable garden (take your pick of the free veggies). While there's no swimming pool—for philosophical reasons—many thoughtful touches and extras, such as Wi-Fi, mountain bikes, and loaner mobile phones, are provided (Db-€750/week, small Db apartment-€890/week, large Db apartment-€1,190/week, same apartment for four-€1,390/week, prices soft mid-Nov–mid-March, non-included activities are fairly priced, tel. & fax 0578-748-083, Isabella's mobile 338-740-9245, www.cretaiole.it, info@cretaiole.it). It's on the Montalcino–Pienza road (S-146), about 11 miles out of Montalcino, and about three miles out of Pienza. While they prefer weeklong stays, when things are slow they may accept guests for as few as three nights (for this you must book less than a month in advance, Db-€110, 3-night minimum).

Eating in Montepulciano

Ai Quattro Venti is fresh, flavorful, fun, and right on Piazza Grande, offering good indoor and outdoor seating (€8.50 pastas, Fri–Wed 12:30–14:30 & 19:30–22:30, closed Thu, next to City Hall on Piazza Grande, tel. 0578-717-231, Chiara).

Osteria dell'Aquacheta is a carnivore's dream come true, famous among locals for its excellent beef steaks. Its long, narrow room is jammed with shared tables and tight seating, with an open fire in back and a big hunk of red beef lying on the counter like a corpse on a gurney. Giulio, with a pen tucked into his ponytail, whacks off slabs with a cleaver, confirms the weight and price with the diner, and tosses them on the grill—seven minutes per side. Steaks are sold by the weight (€3/100 grams, or *etto,* one kilo is about the smallest they serve, two can split it for €30). They also serve hearty €6 pastas and salads and a fine house wine (Wed–Mon 12:30–15:00 & 19:30–22:30, closed Tue, Via del Teatro 22, tel. 0578-758-443). In the tradition of old trattorias, they serve one glass, which you use alternately for wine and water.

Osteria del Conte, an attractive but humble family-run bistro, offers a €30 *menù del Conte*—a four-course dinner of local specialties including wine—as well as à la carte options and cooking like mom's (€7 pastas, €12 *secondi*, indoor and outdoor seating, Thu–Tue 12:30–14:30 & 19:30–21:30, closed Wed, Via S. Donato 19, tel. 0578-756-062).

Montepulciano Connections

All buses leave from Piazza Pietro Nenni. Check www.siena mobilita.it for schedules.

From Montepulciano by Bus to: Florence (3/day with a change in Bettole), **Siena** (8/day, 1.25 hours, none on Sun), **Pienza** (8/day, 30 minutes). There are hourly bus connections to **Chiusi,** a town on the main Florence–Rome rail line; Chiusi is a much better bet than the distant Montepulciano station (5 miles away), which is served only by milk-run trains. Buses connect Montepulciano's bus station and its train station (8/day, none on Sun).

To Montalcino: This connection is problematic by public transportation—consider asking at the TI for a taxi. Although expensive (about €50), a taxi could make sense for two or more people. Otherwise you can take a bus to Buonconvento, then change to get to Montalcino (2 hours). **Drivers** find route S-146 to Montalcino particularly scenic (see "Crete Senese Drives" on page 652).

Cortona

Cortona blankets a 1,700-foot hill surrounded by dramatic Tuscan and Umbrian views. Frances Mayes' books, such as *Under the Tuscan Sun*, placed this town in the touristic limelight, just as Peter

Mayle's books popularized the Luberon region in France. But long before Mayes ever published a book, Cortona was popular with Romantics and considered one of the classic Tuscan hill towns. Unlike San Gimignano, Cortona maintains a rustic and gritty personality—even with its long history of foreigners who, enamored with its Tuscan charm, made this their adopted home.

The city began as one of the largest Etruscan settlements, the remains of which can be seen at the base of the city walls, as well as in the nearby tombs. It grew to its present size in the 13th to 16th centuries, when it was a colorful and crowded city, eventually allied with Florence. The farmland that fills almost every view from the city was marshy and uninhabitable until about 200 years ago, when it was drained and turned into some of Tuscany's most fertile land.

Art-lovers know Cortona as the home of Renaissance painter Luca Signorelli, Baroque master Pietro da Cortona (Berretini), and the 20th-century Futurist artist Gino Severini. The city's museums and churches reveal many of the works of these native sons.

Orientation to Cortona

Most of the main sights, shops, and restaurants cluster around the level streets on the Piazza Garibaldi–Piazza del Duomo axis, but Cortona will have you huffing and puffing up some steep hills.

Tourist Information: The helpful TI is on the main drag

Cortona

TO ETRUSCAN TOMBS + AREZZO

TUSCAN SUN

PIAZZA DEL DUOMO

DIOCESAN MUSEUM

PORTA SANTA MARIA

DUOMO

PORTA COLONIA

THEATER & PIAZZA SIGNORELLI

VIA DARDANO

VIA CASALI

ETRUSCAN MUSEUM IN CASALI PALACE

ETRUSC. GATE

VIA ROMA

VIA MERCATO

P. SIG.

POST

VIA BERRETTINI

S. FRAN.

V. S. NICC.

CITY HALL

VIA GUELFA

PZA. REPUB.

VIA MAFFEI

S. FRAN.

P. SIG.

V. S.

PORTA SANT' AGOSTINO

SANTO SPIRITO

VIALE C. BATTISTI

VIA NAZIONALE

BUS STOP PIAZZA GARIBALDI

START

SAN DOMENICO

VIA SEVE

DCH

Numbered locations: 13, 12, 11, 9, 15, 10, 16, 3, 14, 1, B, 6, 7, 2

at Via Nazionale 42 (April–Oct daily 9:00–13:00 & 15:00–19:00, shorter hours and closed Sun off-season, sells train and bus tickets, tel. 0575-630-352, www.apt.arezzo.it).

Arrival in Cortona: Train travelers arrive at Camucia-Cortona train station, a long, strenuous walk from the town on roads with no sidewalks. Fortunately, buses are generally timed with the arrival of the train and zip you right up to town in 10 minutes (2/hour, €1.10, buy tickets at newsstand 200 yards from station). Buses stop at Piazza Garibaldi. From here, it's a level five-minute walk down bustling shop-lined Via Nazionale (stop by the TI) to Piazza della Repubblica, the heart of the town, dominated by City Hall (Palazzo del Comune). From this square, a two-minute stroll leads you past the interesting Etruscan Museum and theater to Piazza del Duomo, where you'll find the recommended Diocesan Museum. Steep streets, many of them stepped, go from Piazza della Repubblica up to the San Niccolò and Santa Margherita churches and the Medici Fortress (a 30-minute climb

PORTA MONTANINA

P BAR → TO MEDICI FORTRESS

VIA S. CROCE

SAN NICCOLÒ

V. CANTUCCE

PORTA BERADA

SANTA MARGHERITA

100 YARDS

100 METERS

CITY WALLS

PUBLIC GARDENS

TO CAMUCIA & TERONTOLA (NEAREST TRAIN STATIONS)

1. Hotel San Luca & Parking
2. Hotel Villa Marsili
3. Rugapiana Vacanze B&B
4. Casa Betania
5. Istituto Santa Margherita
6. San Marco Hostel
7. Casa Kita
8. To Casa San Martino, La Villetta di San Martino B&B & Castello di Montegualandro
9. Trattoria la Grotta
10. Ristorante La Loggetta
11. Ristorante La Bucaccia
12. Fufluns Tavern Pizzeria
13. Osteria del Teatro
14. Enoteca la Saletta
15. Despar Market Molesini
16. Foto Lamentini (Internet Access)

—— SELF-GUIDED WALK

P PARKING

→ ENTRY POINT TO SIGHTS

⇗ VIEW

|||| STAIRS

Ⓑ BUS STOP

HILL TOWNS

from Piazza della Repubblica).

Drivers will find several free lots right outside the walls. Viale Cesare Battisti may be your best bet. A free lot just after the big Santo Spirito Church has an escalator leading to Piazza Garibaldi. Piazza Garibaldi itself has a handful of pay spots (marked by blue lines, pay & display, cheap, free 20:00–8:00). The small town is actually very long, and it can be smart to drive to the top for sightseeing up there (parking at Santa Margherita Basilica).

Helpful Hints: Market day is Saturday on Piazza Signorelli (from early morning until 14:00). The town has **no baggage storage,** so try asking nicely at a hotel or museum to store your bag there. The best public **WC** is located in Piazza del Duomo, under Santa Margherita's statue. There are several **Internet** terminals at Foto Lamentini (€3/hour, daily April–Oct 10:00–20:00, Oct–March 10:30–13:00 & 14:00–19:00, Via Nazionale 33, tel. 0575-62588).

Local Guide: Giovanni Adreani exudes energy and a love

of his city and Tuscan high culture. He is great at bringing the fine points of the city to life and can take visitors around in his car for no extra price. As this region is speckled with underappreciated charms, having Giovanni for a day as your driver/guide promises to be a fascinating experience (€110/half-day, €200/day, tel. 0575-630-665, mobile 347-176-2830, www.adreanigiovanni .com, adreanigiovanni@alice.it).

Cooking Classes: Husband-and-wife team Romano and Agostina hold morning hands-on cooking and cheesemaking classes in the kitchen of their Ristorante La Bucaccia (described later, under "Eating in Cortona"). In the three-hour class, you'll prepare two *antipasti,* two types of pasta, an entrée, and a dessert, which you then get to eat (€70/person, price includes wine, 5 percent discount with this book, classes start at 9:30, book in advance, personalized classes available, Via Ghibellina 17, tel. 0575-606-039, www.labucaccia.it).

Self-Guided Walk

Welcome to Cortona

This introductory walking tour will take you from Piazza Garibaldi up the main strip to the town center, its piazzas, and the Duomo.

• *Start at the bus stop in...*

Piazza Garibaldi: Many visits start and finish in this square, thanks to its bus stop. While the piazza, bulging out from the town fortifications like a big turret, looks like part of an old rampart, it's really a souvenir of those early French and English Romantics— the ones who first created the notion of a dreamy, idyllic Tuscany. During the Napoleonic Age, the French built this balcony (and the scenic little park behind the adjacent San Domenico Church) simply to enjoy a commanding view of the Tuscan countryside.

With Umbria about a mile away, Cortona marks the end of Tuscany. This is a major cultural divide, as Cortona was the last town in Charlemagne's empire and the last under Medici rule. Umbria, just to the south, was papal territory for centuries. These deep-seated cultural disparities were a great challenge for the visionaries who unified the fractured region to create the modern nation of Italy during the 1860s. A statue in the center of this square honors one of the heroes of the struggle for Italian unification—the brilliant revolutionary general Giuseppe Garibaldi.

Enjoy the commanding view from here. Assisi is just over the ridge on the left. Lake Trasimeno peeks from behind the hill, looking quite normal today. But, according to legend, it was blood-red after Hannibal defeated the Romans here in 217 B.C., and 15,000 died in the battle. The only sizable town you can see, on the right, is Montepulciano. Cortona is still defined by its Etruscan walls—

remnants of these walls, with stones laid 2,500 years ago, stretch from here in both directions.

Frances Mayes put Cortona on the map for many Americans with her book (and later movie) *Under the Tuscan Sun.* The book

describes her real-life experience buying, fixing up, and living in a run-down villa in Cortona with her husband, Ed. The movie romanticized the story, turning Frances into a single, recently divorced writer who restores the villa and her peace of mind. Frances' villa isn't "under the Tuscan sun" very often; it's named "Bramasole"—literally, "craving sun." On the wrong side of the hill, it's in the shade after 15:00. She and her husband still live there part of each year and are respected members of their adopted community (outside the walls, behind the hill on the left).

• *From this square, head into town along...*

Via Nazionale: The only level road in town, locals have nicknamed Via Nazionale the *ruga piana* (flat wrinkle). This is the main commercial street in this town of 2,500, and it's been that way for a long time. Every shop seems to have a medieval cellar or an Etruscan well. Notice the crumbling sandstone door frames. The entire town is constructed out of this grainy, eroding rock.

• *Via Nazionale leads to...*

Piazza della Repubblica: The City Hall faces Cortona's main square. Note how the City Hall is a clever hodgepodge of twin medieval towers, with a bell tower added to connect them, and a grand staircase to lend some gravitas. Notice also the fine wood balconies on the left. In the Middle Ages, wooden extensions such as balconies were common features on the region's stone buildings. These balconies (not original, but rebuilt in the 19th century) would have fit right into the medieval cityscape. These days, you usually see only the holes that once supported the long-gone wooden beams.

This spot has been the town center since Etruscan times. Four centuries before Christ, an important street led from here up to the hill-capping temple. Later, the square became the Roman forum. Opposite the City Hall is the handy, recommended Despar Market Molesini, good for cheap sandwiches. Above that is the loggia—once a fish market, now a recommended restaurant.

• *The second half of the square, to the right of the City Hall, is...*

Piazza Signorelli: Dominated by Casali Palace, this square was the headquarters of the Florentine captains who used to control the city. Peek into the palace entrance for a look at the coats of arms. Every six months, Florence would send a new captain to

Cortona, who would help establish his rule by inserting his family coat of arms into the palace's wall. These date from the 15th to the 17th century, and were once painted with bright colors. Cortona's fine Etruscan Museum (described below, under "Sights in Cortona") is in the Casali Palace courtyard, which is lined with many more of these family coats of arms. The inviting Caffè del Teatro fills the loggia of the theater that is named for the town's most famous artist, Luca Signorelli.

• *Head down the street just to the right of the museum to...*

Piazza del Duomo: Here you'll find the Diocesan Museum (listed under "Sights in Cortona"), cathedral, and a statue of Santa Margherita. If the cathedral seems a little underwhelming and tucked away, that's because it is. Cortona loves its hometown saint, Margherita, and put the energy it would normally invest in its cathedral into the Santa Margherita Basilica, at the top of the hill. Margherita was a 13th-century rich girl who took good care of the poor and was an early follower of St. Francis and St. Clare. Many locals believe that Margherita protected Cortona from WWII bombs.

The Piazza del Duomo terrace comes with a commanding view of the Tuscan countryside. Find the town cemetery in the distance. If you were standing here before the time of Napoleon, you'd be surrounded by tombstones. But Cortona's graveyards—like other urban graveyards throughout Napoleon's realm—were cleaned out in the early 1800s to reclaim land and improve hygiene.

• *Next, enter the...*

Duomo: The Cortona cathedral is not—strictly speaking—a cathedral, because it no longer has a bishop. The white-and-gray Florentine Renaissance–style interior is mucked up with lots of Baroque chapels filling once-spacious side niches. In the rear (on the right) is an altar cluttered with relics. Technically, any Catholic altar, in order to be consecrated, needs a relic embedded in it. Go ahead—gently lift up the tablecloth. The priest here doesn't mind. You'll see a little marble patch that holds a bit of a saint (daily 7:30–13:00 & 15:00–18:30, shorter hours in winter, closed during Mass).

• *From here, you can visit the nearby Diocesan Museum or head back toward Piazza della Repubblica to visit the Etruscan Museum in Piazza Signorelli (both listed next), or to get a bite to eat (see "Eating in Cortona," later).*

Sights in Cortona

▲**Etruscan Museum (Museo dell'Accademia Etrusca)**— Located in the 13th-century Casali Palace, this fine gallery (established in 1727) is one of the first dedicated to artifacts from the

Etruscan civilization. You'll see an exhibit on the Roman settlement and take a virtual tour of the Etruscan "Il Sodo" tombs. The Cortona Tablet (*Tabula Cortonensis,* second century B.C.), a 200-word contract inscribed in bronze, contains dozens of Etruscan words archaeologists had never seen before its discovery in 1992. Along with lots of gold and jewelry, you'll find a seventh-century B.C. grater (for some *very* aged Parmesan cheese) and a magnificent fourth-century B.C. bronze oil lamp with 16 spouts, set in a small four-pillared temple. The library of the Etruscan Academy, founded in 1727 to promote an understanding of the city through the study of archaeology, is upstairs. This eclectic museum also has an Egyptian section, fine Roman mosaics, and a room dedicated to modern abstract works by Severini, all lovingly described in English.

Cost and Hours: €8, €10 combo-ticket includes Diocesan Museum; April–Oct daily 10:00–19:00; Nov–March Tue–Sun 10:00–17:00, closed Mon; Casali Palace on Piazza Signorelli, tel. 0575-637-235, www.cortonamaec.org.

▲**Diocesan Museum (Museo Diocesano)**—This collection of art from the town's many churches has works by Fra Angelico and Pietro Lorenzetti, and masterpieces by hometown hero and Renaissance master Luca Signorelli.

Don't miss Fra Angelico's sumptuous *Annunciation.* In this scene, Mary says "Yes," consenting to bear God's son. Notice how the house sits on a pillow of flowers...the new Eden. The old Eden, featuring the expulsion of Adam and Eve from Paradise, is in the upper left. The painting comes with comic strip–like narration of scenes from Mary's life: The angel's words are top and bottom, while Mary's answer is upside down (logically, since it's directed to God, who would be reading while looking down from heaven).

The crucifix (by Pietro Lorenzetti, c. 1325, just to the right of the Fra Angelico) is impressive in its severity. Notice the gripping realism—even the tendons in Jesus' arms are pulled tight. Another highlight is Luca Signorelli's *Mourning of the Dead Christ (Compianto sul Cristo Morto).* Signorelli was a generation ahead of Michelangelo and, with his passion for painting ideas, was an inspiration for the young artist. Everything in his painting has a meaning: The skull of Adam sits under the sacrifice of Jesus; the hammer represents the Passion (the Crucifixion leading to the Resurrection); the lake is blood; and so on. I don't understand all of the medieval symbolism, but it is intense.

Cost and Hours: €5, €10 combo-ticket includes Etruscan Museum, helpful audioguide-€3; April–Oct daily 10:00–19:00; Nov–March Tue–Sun 10:00–17:00, closed Mon; Piazza del Duomo 1, tel. 0575-62-830. For more on Signorelli, see page 665.

Church of St. Francis—Established by St. Francis' best friend, Brother Elias, this church dates from the 13th century. The wooden beams of the ceiling are original. While the place was redecorated in the Baroque age, some of the original frescoes that once wall-papered the church peek through the whitewash in a chapel on the left. Francis fans visit for its precious Franciscan relics. To the left of the altar, you'll find one of Francis' tunics, his pillow (inside a fancy cover), and his gospel book. Behind the altar is Elias' very simple tomb. It reads "Frate Elia da Cortona." Notice how the entire high altar seems designed to frame its precious relic—a piece of the cross Elias brought back from his visit to the patriarch in Constantinople. You're welcome to climb the altar for a close-up look (daily 9:00–18:30).

San Niccolò Church—Signorelli enthusiasts will want to make the pilgrimage up to this tiny church, a steep 10-minute walk beyond the Church of St. Francis. Ring the bell on the left side of the church and the caretaker might give you a short tour in Italian. The highlight of this humble church is an altarpiece painted on both sides by Signorelli. The caretaker activates a tricky arm mechanism that moves the picture away from the wall to reveal the painting behind it.

Cost and Hours: €1 donation, daily in summer 9:00–12:00 & 15:00–19:00, off-season until 17:00. Even if you can't get in, it's still worth the walk just to explore the picturesque neighborhood.

Santa Margherita Basilica—From San Niccolò Church, another steep path leads uphill 10 minutes to this basilica, which houses the remains of Margherita, the town's favorite saint. Santa Margherita, an unwed mother from Montepulciano, found her calling with the Franciscans in Cortona, tending to the sick and poor. The well-preserved and remarkably emotional 13th-century crucifix on the right is the cross that, according to legend, talked to Margherita.

Cost and Hours: Free, daily 9:00–12:00 & 15:00–19:00, tel. 0575-603-116.

Nearby: Still need more altitude? Head uphill five more minutes to the Medici Fortezza (€3, usually open daily April–Sept 9:00–12:00 & 15:00–18:00, July–Aug until 19:00, closed Oct–March). The views are stunning, stretching all the way to distant Lago Trasimeno.

Etruscan Tombs near Cortona—Guided tours to nearby "Il Sodo" tombs (called *melone* for their melon-like shape) are complicated to arrange. But the excavation site and bits of the ruins are easy to visit and can be seen from outside the fence in the morning. It's just a couple miles out of Cortona on the Arezzo road (R-71), at the edge of Camucia at the foot of the Cortona hill; ask anyone for "Il Sodo."

Sleeping in Cortona

(€1 = about $1.25, country code: 39)

$$$ **Hotel San Luca,** perched on the side of a cliff, has 57 modern, impersonal business-class rooms, half with stunning views of Lago Trasimeno. While tired and a bit run-down, it's friendly and conveniently located right at the bus stop (Sb-€85, Db-€120, Tb-€150, request a view room when you reserve, popular with Americans and groups, Piazza Garibaldi 1, tel. 0575-630-460, fax 0575-630-105, www.sanlucacortona.com, info@sanlucacortona .com). If driving, you might find a spot at the small public parking lot at the hotel (cheap and easy meters).

$$$ **Hotel Villa Marsili** is a comfortable splurge just below town. It was originally a 15th-century church, then an elegant 18th-century home. Today its 25 rooms and public areas have been recently redecorated and restored. Guests enjoy a complimentary aperitif every evening on the panoramic terrace (Db-€130–250, Db suite-€230–350, Jacuzzi in some rooms, air-con, Wi-Fi and Internet access, Viale Cesare Battisti 13, tel. 0575-605-252, fax 0575-605-618, www.villamarsili.net, info@villamarsili.net, Stefano).

$$ **Rugapiana Vacanze B&B** rents four doubles and four apartments, each described separately on their website. Located on Cortona's main drag, it's beautifully furnished with all the thoughtful touches (apartment-€100–115 or Db-€95 with breakfast at a nearby bar, 10 percent discount with this book, family suites, Wi-Fi, Via Nazionale 63, tel. & fax 0575-630-712, mobile 340-808-6879, www.rugapianavacanze.com, info@rugapianavacanze .com, Massimo).

$ **Casa Betania,** a big, wistful convent with an inviting view terrace, rents 27 fine rooms (mostly twin beds) for the best price in town. While it's primarily for "thoughtful travelers," anyone looking for a peaceful place to call home will feel welcome in this pilgrims' resort (S-€32, D-€44, Db-€48, Tb-€66, extra bed-€20, breakfast-€4, parking, about a third of a mile out of town, a few minutes' walk below Piazza Garibaldi at Via Gino Severini 50, tel. & fax 0575-630-423, www.casaperferiebetania.com, info@casa perferiebetania.com).

$ **Istituto Santa Margherita,** run by the Serve di Maria Riparatrici sisters, rents 22 cheap and simple rooms in a smaller and more institutional-feeling convent across the street (Sb-€42, Db-€58, Tb-€75, Qb-€86, breakfast-€5, elevator, free parking, Viale Cesare Battisti 15, tel. 0575-178-7203 or 0575-630-336, fax 0575-630-549, comunitacortona@smr.it).

$ **San Marco Hostel,** at the top of town, is housed in a remodeled 13th-century palace (bed in dorm-€16, in 2-bed and

4-bed rooms-€20, includes breakfast, dinner-€10.50, lockout 10:00–13:00, Via Maffei 57, tel. & fax 0575-601-392, www.cortona hostel.com, ostellocortona@libero.it).

$ Casa Kita, renting four fine rooms, is a homely place at the edge of town with breathtaking views from its terrace (Db-€60, 100 yards below Piazza Garibaldi at Vicolo degli Orti 7, tel. 389-557-9893, www.casakita.com, info@casakita.com, Lorenzini family).

Near Cortona

$$$ Casa San Martino, a 30-minute drive east of Cortona near the isolated village of Lisciano Niccone, is a 250-year-old coun-tryside farmhouse run as a B&B by American Italophile Lois Martin. While Lois reserves the summer (June–Aug) for people staying at least one week, she'll take guests staying a minimum of three nights the rest of the year (Db-€140, 10 percent discount for my readers—mention this book when you reserve, pool, Casa San Martino 19, Lisciano Niccone, tel. 075-844-288, fax 075-844-422, www.tuscanyvacation.com, csm@tuscanyvacation.com).

$$$ Castello di Montegualandro, a well-preserved castle on a hill opposite Cortona, overlooks the lake and countryside. The Marti family rents four charming medieval apartments, formerly peasants' quarters, inside the peaceful castle walls. Each one is unique and named for its former use; for example, the Fornaci's sunken living room used to be a kiln (apartments range from €400–450 for 3-night minimum stay, €700–800/week, cash only; for a 5-night stay, mention this book for a 7 percent discount; 10 percent discount for longer stays; 10 minutes southeast of Cortona in Tuoro sul Trasimeno, tel. & fax 075-823-0267, www.monte gualandro.com, info@montegualandro.com, Claudio and Franca).

$$ La Villetta di San Martino B&B is a tidy place run by Lois' neighbors, Ernestine and Gisbert Schwanke (Db-€80, 2-night minimum, cash only, common kitchen and sitting room, San Martino 36, tel. & fax 075-844-309, www.tuscanyvacation .com, erni@netemedia.net).

Eating in Cortona

Trattoria la Grotta, just off Piazza della Repubblica, is a tradi-tional place serving daily specials to an enthusiastic clientele under grotto-like vaults (€7 pastas, €8 meat dishes, good wine by the glass, Wed–Mon 12:00–14:30 & 19:00–22:00, closed Tue, Piazza Baldelli 3, tel. 0575-630-271).

Ristorante La Loggetta serves up big portions of well-presented Tuscan cuisine on the loggia overlooking Piazza della Repubblica. While they have fine indoor seating, I'd eat here for the chance to gaze at the square over a meal (€8 pastas, €7–15 meat dishes, Thu–Tue 12:30–15:00 & 19:30–23:00, closed Wed, Piazza Pescheria 3, tel. 0575-630-575).

Ristorante La Bucaccia is a family-run eatery set in a rustic medieval wine cellar. It's dressy and romantic. They take great pride in their Chianina beef entrées and homemade pastas. With an evangelical pride in their food, Romano hosts and his wife Agostina cooks (€9 pastas, €14 entrées, daily 12:00–15:30 & 19:00–24:00, show this book for a 5 percent discount and a small free antipasto, Via Ghibellina 17, tel. 0575-606-039).

Fufluns Tavern Pizzeria (that's the Etruscan name for Dionysus) is easy-going, friendly, and remarkably unpretentious for its location in the town center. It's popular with locals for its good, inexpensive Tuscan cooking and friendly staff (cheap, lots of €6 pizza and pasta plus big salads, good house wine, Wed–Mon 12:15–14:30 & 19:15–22:30, closed Tue, a block below Piazza della Repubblica at Via Ghibellina 3, tel. 0575-604-140).

Osteria del Teatro tries very hard to create a romantic Old World atmosphere, and does it well. Chef Emiliano serves nicely presented and tasty international and local cuisine (taking creative liberties with traditions). There's good outdoor seating, too (Thu–Tue 12:30–14:30 & 19:30–21:30, closed Wed, 2 blocks uphill from the main square at Via Maffei 2, tel. 0575-630-556).

Enoteca la Saletta, dark and classy, is good for fine wine and a light meal. You can sit inside surrounded by wine bottles or outside to people-watch on the town's main drag (daily 7:30–24:00, meals served 12:00–24:00, Via Nazionale 26, tel. 0575-603-366).

For a Picnic: On the main square, the chic little **Despar Market Molesini** makes tasty sandwiches (see list on counter and order by number) and sells whatever you might want for a picnic (Mon–Sat 7:00–13:30 & 16:00–19:30, closed Sun, Piazza della Repubblica 23). Munch your picnic across the square on the steps of the City Hall, or just past Piazza Garibaldi in the public gardens behind San Domenico Church.

Cortona Connections

Cortona has good train connections with the rest of Italy through its Camucia-Cortona station. To get to the train station at the foot of the hill, take a taxi or hop the bus (€1.10, 2/hour between Piazza Garibaldi and station, buy tickets at newsstand, TI, or *tabacchi* shop, or buy from driver at double the price). Note that some only take you as far as the newsstand *(edicola)* 200 yards in front of the station.

From Cortona by Train to: Rome (9/day, 2.5 hours), **Florence** (hourly, 1.5 hours), **Assisi** (every 2 hours, 70 minutes), **Montepulciano** (10/day, 1–1.25 hours, change in Chiusi—because few buses serve Montepulciano's town center from its distant train station, it's better to go by train to Chiusi, then by hourly bus to Montepulciano), **Chiusi** (hourly, 30 minutes). Most trains stop at the Camucia-Cortona train station, but some trains to/from Rome and Florence stop at Terontola, 10 miles away (bus to/from Cortona runs hourly during the week, 4/day on Sun, €2, tel. 800-115-605 or call the TI to confirm times).

More Sights in Tuscany

▲San Galgano Monastery

Of southern Tuscany's several evocative monasteries, San Galgano is the best. Set in a forested area called the Montagnolo (medium-size mountains), the isolated abbey and chapel are postcard-perfect.

St. Galgano was a 12th-century saint who renounced his past as a knight to become a hermit. Lacking a cross to display, he created his own by miraculously burying his sword up to its hilt in a stone, à la King Arthur, but in reverse. After his death, a large Cistercian monastery complex grew. Today, all you'll see is the roofless ruined abbey and, on a nearby hill, the Chapel of San Galgano with its fascinating dome and sword in the stone.

Getting There: Although a bus reportedly comes here from Siena, this sight is realistically accessible only for drivers. It's just outside of Monticiano (not Montalcino), about an hour south of Siena. A warning to the queasy: These roads are curvy.

The Abbey: This picturesque Cistercian abbey was once a powerful institution in Tuscany. Known for their skill as builders, the Cistercians oversaw the construction of Siena's cathedral. But after losing most of its population in the plague of 1348, the abbey never really recovered and was eventually deconsecrated.

The Cistercian order was centered in France, and the architecture of the abbey shows a heavy French influence. Notice the large, high windows and the pointy, delicate arches. This is pure French Gothic, a style that never fully caught on in Italy (compare it with the chunky, elaborately decorated cathedral in Siena, built about the same time).

As you enter the church, notice the small section of the cloister wall to the left. This used to surround the garden, and was the only place where the monks were allowed to talk, for one hour each day. From inside the church, the empty windows frame the view of the chapel up on the hill.

The Chapel: A path from the abbey leads up the hill to the Chapel of San Galgano. The unique beehive-like interior houses St. Galgano's sword and stone, recently confirmed to date back to the 12th century. Don't try and pull the sword from the stone—the small chapel to the left displays the severed arms of the last guy who tried. The chapel also contains some deteriorated frescoes and more interesting *sinopie* (fresco sketches). The adjacent gift shop sells a little bit of everything, from wine to postcards to herbs, some of it monk-made.

Cost and Hours: Free, summer daily 9:00–20:00, shoulder season until 18:30, erratic hours Nov–Dec, closed Jan–Feb, tel. 0577-756-738, www.sangalgano.org; concerts sometimes held here in summer—ticket info tel. 0555-978-308. For a quick snack, a small, touristy bar at the end of the driveway is your only option.

Nearby: Other, more accessible Tuscan monasteries worth visiting include Sant'Antimo (6 miles south of Montalcino) and Monte Oliveto Maggiore (15 miles south of Siena, mentioned in "Crete Senese Drives," later).

▲Chiusi

This small hill town (rated ▲▲ for Etruscan fans) was once one of the most important Etruscan cities. Today, it's a key train junction

and a pleasant, workaday Italian village with an enjoyable historic center and few tourists.

The region's trains (to Florence, Siena, Orvieto, and Assisi) go through or change at this hub, making Chiusi an easy day trip. Buses link the train station with the town center two miles away (depart every 40 minutes, tickets at *tabacchi* shop). Easy and free parking lots are a five-minute walk from the center. If you want to rent a car, there's a Hertz office near the train station (Via M. Buonarroti 21, tel. 057-822-3000).

The **TI** is on the main square (May–Sept Tue–Sun 10:00–13:00 & 15:00–17:00, closed Mon; Oct–April Tue–Sun 9:30–12:30, closed Mon; tel. 0578-227-667).

The **Archaeological Museum,** just off the main square, thoughtfully presents a high-quality collection with plenty of explanations in English. The collection of funerary urns, some in painted terra-cotta and some in *pietra fetida* ("stinky stone"), are remarkably intact (€4, July–Sept daily 9:00–20:00, Via Porsenna 93, tel. 0578-20177, www.archeotoscana.beniculturali.it). The museum also arranges tours to visit tombs outside of town. One of the tombs is multichambered, with several sarcophagi. Another, the **Tomba della Scimmia** (Tomb of the Monkey), has some well-preserved frescoes. Visiting the tombs requires a guide, a car, and an advance reservation (€2, Tue, Thu, and Sat only, March–Oct at 11:00 and 16:00, Nov–Feb at 11:00 and 14:30, 25 visitors per tour).

Troglodyte alert! The **Cathedral Museum** on the main square has a dark, underground labyrinth of Etruscan tunnels. The mandatory guided tour of the tunnels ends in a large Roman cistern from which you can climb the church bell tower for an expansive view of the countryside (museum-€2, labyrinth-€3, combo-ticket-€4, daily June–Oct 9:30–12:30 & 16:00–19:00, Nov–May 9:30–12:30 only, 30-minute tunnel tours run every 40 minutes during museum hours, Piazza Duomo 1, tel. 0578-226-490).

Craving more underground fun? The **Museo Civico** provides hourly tours of the Etruscan water system, which includes an underground lake (€3; May–Oct Tue–Sun at 10:15, 11:30, 12:45, 15:15, 16:30, and 17:45; closed Mon, fewer tours off-season, call to confirm times, Via II Ciminia 1, tel. 0578-227-667, mobile 334-626-6851).

▲Florence American Cemetery and Memorial

The compelling sight of endless rows of white marble crosses and Stars of David recalls the heroism of the young Americans who fought so valiantly to free Italy (and ultimately Europe) from the grip of fascism. This particular cemetery is the final resting place of more than 4,000 Americans who died in the liberation of Italy during World War II. Climb the hill, past the perfectly manicured lawn lined with grave markers, to

the memorial, where maps and a history of the Italian campaign detail the Allied advance.

Cost and Hours: Free, daily 9:00–17:00; 7.5 miles south of Florence, off Via Cassia, which parallels the *superstrada* between Florence and Siena, 2 miles south of Florence Certosa exit on A-1 autostrada; tel. 055-202-0020, www.abmc.gov. Buses from Florence stop just outside the cemetery.

▲▲Crete Senese Drives

South of Siena, the hilly area known as the "Sienese Crests" is full of colorful fields and curvy, scenic roads. You'll see an endless parade of classic Tuscan scenes, rolling hills topped with medieval towns, olive groves, rustic stone farmhouses, and a skyline punctuated with cypress trees. You won't find many wineries here, since the clay soil is better for wheat and sunflowers, but you will find the same pristine, panoramic Tuscan countryside that you see on calendars and postcards.

During the spring, the fields are painted in yellow and green with fava beans and broom, dotted by red poppies on the fringes. Sunflowers decorate the area during June and July, and expanses of windblown grass fill the landscape almost all year.

Most roads to the southeast of Siena will give you a taste of this area, but one of the most scenic stretches is the Lauretan road (Siena–Asciano–San Giovanni d'Asso, #438 on road maps; you can also take S-2—Via Cassia—toward Rome and turn off at *Asciano* sign, either way allows you to easily continue to Montalcino). You'll come across plenty of turnouts for panoramic photo opportunities on this road, as well as a few roadside picnic areas.

For a break from the winding road, about 15 miles from Siena, you'll find the quaint and non-touristy village of **Asciano.** With a medieval town center and several interesting churches and museums, this town offers a rare look at everyday Tuscan living—and a great place for lunch (TI open Tue–Fri 10:30–13:00 & 15:00–18:00, Sat–Sun 10:30–13:00, closed Mon, at Corso Matteotti 18, tel. 0577-719-510). If you're in town on Saturday, gather a picnic at the outdoor market (Via Amendola, 8:00–13:00).

Five miles south of Asciano, the **Abbey of Monte Oliveto Maggiore** houses a famous fresco cycle of the life of St. Benedict, painted by Renaissance masters Il Sodoma and Luca Signorelli (free, daily 9:15–12:00 & 15:15–18:00, Nov–March until 17:00, Gregorian chanting Sun at 11:00 and Mon–Sat at 18:15, call to confirm, tel. 0577-707-611, www.monteolivetomaggiore.it). Once you reach the town of **San Giovanni d'Asso,** it's only another 12 miles southwest to Montalcino.

Another scenic drive is the lovely stretch between Montalcino and Montepulciano (S-146 on road maps). This route alternates between the grassy hills of the Crete Senese and sunbathed vineyards of the Orcia River valley. Stop by Pienza en route.

Sleeping in the Crete Senese: **$$ Agriturismo il Molinello** rents five apartments, two built over a medieval mill. Hardworking Alessandro and Elisa share their organic produce and offer weekly wine-tastings for a minimum of four people. From May through October, they offer free guided tours of Siena on Tuesday afternoons. With children, friendly dogs, toys, and a swimming pool, this is ideal for families (Qb-€70–100, apartment for up to 8-€150–180, optional organic breakfast-€9.50, one-week stay required in summer, discounts and no minimum stay off-season, free Internet access, mountain-bike rentals, biking maps and guided bike tours, near Asciano, 30 minutes southeast of Siena, tel. 0577-704-791, mobile 335-692-5720, fax 0577-705-605, www.molinello.com, info@molinello.com).

HILL TOWNS

Urbino

If you're driving through central Italy, Urbino is worth a stop for its sprawling, fascinating Ducal Palace. Although Urbino is the hometown of the artist Raphael and architect Donato Bramante, it's better known for the Duke of Montefeltro, a mercenary general who built the palace and turned Urbino into an important Renaissance center. For my expanded coverage of Urbino, see www.ricksteves.com/urbino.

A classic hill town, Urbino has a medieval wall with four gates, and two main roads that crisscross at the town's main square, Piazza della Repubblica. The tiny **TI** is just across from the Ducal Palace (Tue–Fri 9:00–13:00 & 15:00–18:00, Mon and Sat 9:00–13:00 only, closed Sun, Piazza Duca Federico 35, tel. 0722-2613, www.urbinoculturaturismo.it).

The **Ducal Palace** (Palazzo Ducale), which has more than 300 rooms, was built in the mid-1400s. While the rooms are fairly bare, the palace holds a few very special paintings, as well as exquisite inlaid-wood decorations. It's a monument to how one man—the Duke of Montefeltro—brought the Renaissance to his small town (€4, but sometimes €8 for special exhibits; Mon 8:30–14:00, last entry at 12:30; Tue–Sun 8:30–19:15, last entry at 18:00; tel. 072-232-2625).

The highlights of the palace include great paintings such as Raphael's *Portrait of a Gentlewoman* (a.k.a. *La Muta*); the Renaissance **courtyard** patterned after the trendsetting Medici-Riccardi Palace in Florence; the richly paneled and inlaid-wood walls of the duke's **study;** and the vast **cellars** that include a giant stable with a clever horse-pie disposal system.

Stop by the **Oratory of St. John** to see its remarkable frescoed interior that tells the story of the life of St. John the Baptist (€2.50, Mon–Sat 10:00–12:30 & 15:00–17:30, Sun 10:00–12:30, 5-minute walk from main square—follow signs, Piazza Baricci 31; if no one's there, find attendant at the Oratory of San Giuseppe a few steps away; mobile 347-671-1181).

Finally, for the ultimate Urbino view, climb up to the grassy park surrounding the **fortress** (interior closed, but grounds open to the public). The Franciscan church spire, on the left, marks the main square.

Getting There: Urbino is easier for drivers, but public transportation is an option. Buses link Urbino with Pesaro, on the Ravenna-Pescara train line (buses run hourly, 1-hour trip). From Venice, Florence, or Rome, trains leave for Pesaro almost hourly (taking 3–5 hours). In Urbino, buses come and go from the Piazza Mercatale parking lot below the town, where an elevator lifts you up to the base of the Ducal Palace (or take a 5-minute steep walk up Via Mazzini to Piazza della Repubblica).

Sleeping in Urbino: The hotel scene is limited to a few comfortable, expensive places, including **Albergo San Domenico** (www.viphotels.it), **Hotel Raffaello** (www.albergoraffaello.com), and **Albergo Italia** (www.albergo-italia-urbino.it). The TI has a line on lots of families renting rooms.

Eating in Urbino: Try **Taverna degli Artisti** (Via Bramante 52) and **Il Coppiere** (Via Santa Margherita 1), or **Ristorante/Pizzeria Tre Piante** (Via Voltaccia della Vecchia 1).

Orvieto

Just off the freeway and the main train line, Umbria's grand hill town entices those heading to and from Rome. While no secret, it's well worth a visit.  The town sits majestically a thousand feet above the valley floor on a big chunk of tuff *(tufa)*, an easy-to-dig volcanic rock. While a regional power in the Middle Ages, it was also one of the dozen major Etruscan cities centuries before Christ. Some historians believe Orvieto may have been a kind of Etruscan Mecca (locals are looking for archaeological proof—the town and surrounding countryside are dotted with Etruscan ruins).

Orvieto, which has three popular claims to fame (cathedral, Classico wine, and ceramics), is loaded with tourists by day and quiet by night. Drinking a shot of the local white wine in a ceramic cup as you gaze up at the cathedral lets you experience Orvieto's three C's all at once. (Is the cathedral best in the afternoon, when the facade basks in golden light, or early in the morning, when it rises above the hilltop mist? You decide.) And a visit to Orvieto comes with a wonderful bonus: an easy bus connection with my favorite hill town, Civita di Bagnoregio (covered later in this chapter).

Orientation to Orvieto

Orvieto has two distinct parts: the old-town hilltop and the new town below. Whether coming by train or car, you first arrive in the forgettable, modern lower part of town. From there you can drive or take the funicular up to the medieval upper town, an atmospheric labyrinth of streets and squares where all the sight-seeing action is.

Tourist Information

A seasonal TI is at the top of the funicular, to your right as you exit into Piazza Cahen, the start of the upper town (daily May–mid-Aug 10:00–18:00, March–April and mid-Aug–Sept 10:00–13:00 & 15:00–18:00, closed Oct–Feb). The main TI is on the cathedral square at Piazza del Duomo 24 (Mon–Fri 8:15–13:50 & 16:00–19:00, Sat–Sun 10:00–13:00 & 15:00–18:00, tel. 076-334-1772, www.comune.orvieto.tr.it). Pick up the free city map and their green city guide, and ask about train and bus schedules. The ticket office (next to the main TI) sells combo-tickets, and books reservations for the underground tours (tel. 0763-340-688).

Combo-Ticket: The €18 **Carta Unica** combo-ticket covers Orvieto's top sights (virtually every sight recommended here, including Underground Orvieto Tours) and includes either five hours of parking (at *parcheggio* Campo della Fiera) or one round-trip on the bus and/or funicular (www.cartaunica.it). To cover your funicular ride into the upper town, you can buy the combo-ticket at the bar at the train station upon arrival (if they haven't run out), or at a seasonal ticket office in the train station parking lot (tel. 0763-302-378). It's also available at the ticket office on Piazza del Duomo, as well as at most of the sights it covers.

Arrival in Orvieto

By Train: From the train station at the foot of the hill town, a funicular carries you to the top. Buy your ticket at the entrance to the *funiculare;* look for the *biglietteria* sign (€1, €0.80 with same-day train ticket, good for 70 minutes, includes minibus from Piazza Cahen to Piazza del Duomo, Mon–Sat 7:20–20:30, Sun 8:00–20:30, every 10 minutes). Or buy a Carta Unica combo-ticket (described earlier) to cover your funicular ride. If you arrive outside the funicular's operating hours, you can take a bus or taxi to the upper town. Note that there's no baggage storage at the train station (the nearest place for day-trippers to store bags is the recommended Hotel Picchio, €4/bag, see page 672).

As you exit the funicular at the top, you're in Piazza Cahen, located at the east end of the upper town. To your left is a ruined fortress with a garden, WC, and a commanding view. To your right is the seasonal TI (closed Oct–Feb) and, down a steep road, St. Patrick's Well. Farther to the right is a park with Etruscan ruins and another sweeping view. Just in front of you is the orange shuttle bus, waiting to take you to Piazza del Duomo. The bus fills up fast, but the views from the ruined fortress are worth pausing for—if you miss the bus, you can wait for the next one, or just walk to the cathedral (head uphill on Corso Cavour; after about 10 minutes take a left onto Via del Duomo). The bus drops you in Piazza del Duomo just steps from the main TI and within easy walking distance of most of my recommended sights. If you forgot to check at the station for the train schedule to your next destination, no problem—the train schedule is posted at the top of the funicular and is also available at the TI.

By Car: You can park for free at the base of the hill at the huge lot behind the train station (5 minutes off the autostrada, follow the *P funiculare* signs); in Piazza Cahen (north half, with white lines); or inside the Ex-Caserma (just as you arrive at the top of Orvieto, turn right and follow signs). Otherwise go to the small pay lot to the right of Orvieto's cathedral (€1.50 for first hour, €1/hour thereafter) or the blue-lined half of Piazza Cahen (€1/hour). Generally, white lines indicate free parking, and blue lines require that you must buy a "pay and display" slip from a nearby machine. While you can drive up Via Postierla and Via Roma to get to central parking lots, Corso Cavour and other streets in the old center are closed to traffic and monitored by cameras (look for red lights).

If arriving from the southwest, Campo della Fiera is your most convenient parking lot (€0.80/hour). From its top level, it's still a steep climb up; you can avoid it by taking an escalator (7:00–24:00) or an elevator (7:00–21:00) to the upper town (both free).

By Taxi: Taxis line up in front of the station and charge about €12 for a ride to the cathedral (a ridiculous price considering the fun and ease of the €1 funicular/shuttle-bus ride to the cathedral square, tel. 360-433-057).

Helpful Hints

Market Days: On Thursday and Saturday mornings, Piazza del Popolo becomes a busy farmers market.

Internet Access: Caffè Montanucci has four terminals (€2.50/30 minutes, Corso Cavour 21, daily 7:00–24:00), **Copisteria ESPA** has three (€3/30 minutes, Via Felice Cavallotti 9, Mon–Fri 9:00–13:00 & 16:00–19:40, Sat 9:00–13:00, closed Sun), and the **library** on Piazza Febei offers free Internet access during its limited hours (Mon–Fri 8:30–13:30; Sept–June also Mon, Wed, and Fri 15:30–18:30; closed Sat–Sun).

Driver: For a private car hire, consider Giuliotaxi, enthusiastically run by charming and English-speaking Giulio and his sister Maria Serena. They charge about €50 for a ride to Bagnoregio, and provide a good way to explore the region (mobile 360-433-057, www.umbria-transfer.com).

Local Guide: Manuela Del Turco is good (€100/2.5-hour tour, mobile 333-221-9879, manueladel@virgilio.it).

HILL TOWNS

Orvieto

1. Hotel Maitani
2. Hotel Duomo
3. Grand Hotel Italia
4. Hotel Corso
5. Hotel Posta
6. Villa Mercede
7. Istituto S.S. Salvatore
8. Valentina's Rooms
9. La Magnolia B&B
10. Casa Sèlita B&B
11. Hotel Picchio
12. Picchio II B&B
13. La Palomba Restaurant
14. Antico Bucchero
15. L'Antica Trattoria dell'Orso
16. Trattoria la Grotta & Sidis Supermarket

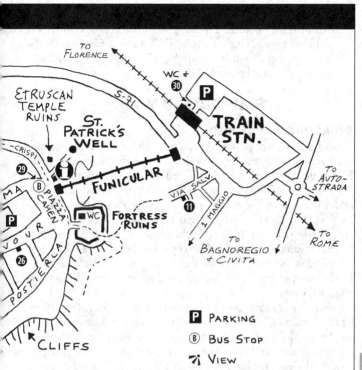

TO
FLORENCE

WC &
30

P

ETRUSCAN
TEMPLE
RUINS

S-71

ST.
PATRICK'S
WELL

TRAIN
STN.

CRISPI

29

PIAZZA
CAHEN

B

FUNICULAR

VIA SALV

11

TO
AUTO-
STRADA

O

MA

P

JOUR

WC

FORTRESS
RUINS

V. MAGGIO

TO
ROME

26

POSTIERLA

TO
BAGNOREGIO
& CIVITA

CLIFFS

P PARKING

Ⓑ BUS STOP

⊼ VIEW

➡ SELF-GUIDED WALK

--- VIEW WALKS

DCH

HILL TOWNS

⑰ Trattoria del Moro Aronne
⑱ Pizzeria Re Artù
⑲ L'Oste del Re
⑳ Enoteca Tozzi &
   Pasqualetti Gelateria
㉑ Il Vincaffè Bar
㉒ Well of the Cave
㉓ MoDo Art Galleries &
   Nat'l Arch. Museum

㉔ Archaeological Museum
㉕ Copisteria ESPA
   (Internet)
㉖ Tabacchi (Bus Tickets)
㉗ Access to View Walks (4)
㉘ Piazza Marconi
㉙ Bagnoregio Bus Stop
㉚ Combo-Ticket Kiosk

After Dark: In the evening, there's little going on other than strolling and eating. The big *passeggiata* scene is down Via del Duomo and Corso Cavour. **Il Vincaffè** is *the* place for the classy young crowd late at night, with lots of good wines by the glass (Via Filippeschi 39).

Self-Guided Walk

Welcome to Orvieto

A quickie L-shaped walk takes you through Orvieto's historic center. Each evening, this route is the scene of the local *passeggiata*. Facing the cathedral, head left. Stroll under the clock tower (first put here in 1347 for the workers building the cathedral), which marks the start of Via del Duomo, lined with shops selling ceramics. Via dei Magoni (first left) has several artisan shops and the crazy little Il Mago di Oz ("Wizard of Oz") shop, a wondrous toyland created by eccentric Giuseppe Rosella (Via dei Magoni 4, tel. 076-334-2063; he runs another store nearby at Via Pedota 9). Have Giuseppe push a few buttons, and you're far from Kansas (no photos allowed).

Via del Duomo continues to Orvieto's main intersection, where it meets Corso Cavour and a tall, stark tower—the Torre del Moro. The tower marks the center of town, serves as a handy orientation tool, and is decorated by the coats of arms of past governors. The elevator leaves you with 173 steps still to go to earn a commanding view (€3, daily March–Oct 10:00–19:00, May–Aug until 20:00, shorter hours off-season).

This crossroads divides the town into four quarters (notice the *Quartiere* signs on the corners). Residents of these four districts compete in a lively equestrian competition on Piazza del Popolo during the annual Corpus Christi celebration. Historically, the four streets led from here to the market and the fine palazzo on Piazza del Popolo, the well, the Duomo, and City Hall.

Before heading left down Corso Cavour, side-trip a block farther ahead, behind the tower, for a look at the striking Palazzo del Popolo. Built of local *tufa*, this is a textbook example of a fortified medieval public palace: a fortress designed to house the city leadership and military, with a market at its base, fancy meeting rooms upstairs, and aristocratic living quarters on the top level.

Return to the tower and head down Corso Cavour (turning right) past classic storefronts to Piazza della Repubblica and City Hall. The original vision—though it never came to fruition—was for City Hall to have five arches flanking the main central arch (marked by the flags today). The Church of Sant'Andrea (left of City Hall) sits atop an Etruscan temple that was likely the birthplace of Orvieto centuries before Christ. Inside is an interesting architectural progression: Romanesque (with scant frescoes surviving), Gothic, and a Renaissance barrel vault in the apse (behind the altar)—all lit by fine alabaster windows.

From City Hall, you can continue to the far end of town to the Church of San Giovenale—where, if you have the MoDo ticket (see page 666), you can see the statues of apostles that once stood in the Duomo (warning: these statues may be moved back inside the Duomo in 2011). From here you can take a left and walk the cliffside ramparts (see "View Walks," later).

Sights in Orvieto

▲▲Duomo

The cathedral has Italy's liveliest facade (from 1330, by Lorenzo Maitani and others). This colorful, prickly Gothic facade, divided

by four pillars, has been compared to a medieval altarpiece. Grab a gelato (buy it to the left of the church) and study this gleaming mass of mosaics, stained glass, and sculpture.

At the base of the cathedral, the four broad marble pillars carved with biblical scenes tell the story of the world from left to right in four acts: Genesis, Old Testament, New Testament, and Revelation. The relief on the far left shows the Creation (see God performing surgery as he extracts Adam's rib, and the snake tempting Eve). Next is the Tree of Jesse (Jesus' family tree—with Mary, then Jesus on top) flanked by Old Testament stories, then the New Testament (look for the unique manger scene and other famous scenes from the life of Christ). On the far right is the Last Judgment (Christ judging on top, with a commotion of sarcophagi popping open and all hell breaking loose at the bottom).

Each pillar is topped by a bronze symbol of one of the Evangelists: angel (Matthew), lion (Mark), eagle (John), and ox (Luke). The bronze doors are modern, by the Sicilian sculptor Emilio Greco. (A gallery devoted to Greco's work is to the immediate right of the church; see page 666.) In the mosaic below the rose window, Mary is transported to heaven. In the uppermost mosaic, Mary is crowned.

Step inside. The nave feels spacious and less cluttered than most Italian churches. Until 1877 it was much busier, with statues of the apostles at each column and fancy chapels. Then the people decided they wanted to "un-Baroque" their church. More recently, however, there's been talk of returning the apostles to their original locations—perhaps in time for your visit.

HILL TOWNS

Orvieto's Duomo

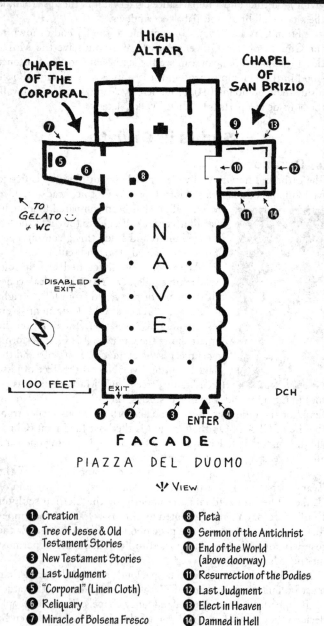

HIGH ALTAR

CHAPEL OF THE CORPORAL

CHAPEL OF SAN BRIZIO

TO GELATO ☺ & WC

NAVE

DISABLED EXIT

100 FEET

EXIT

ENTER

DCH

FACADE

PIAZZA DEL DUOMO

↯ VIEW

HILL TOWNS

① Creation
② Tree of Jesse & Old Testament Stories
③ New Testament Stories
④ Last Judgment
⑤ "Corporal" (Linen Cloth)
⑥ Reliquary
⑦ Miracle of Bolsena Fresco
⑧ Pietà
⑨ Sermon of the Antichrist
⑩ End of the World (above doorway)
⑪ Resurrection of the Bodies
⑫ Last Judgment
⑬ Elect in Heaven
⑭ Damned in Hell

The interior is warmly lit by alabaster windows, highlighting the black-and-white striped stonework. Why such a big and impressive church in such a little town? Well, first of all, it's not as big as it looks. The architect created an illusion—the nave is wider at the back and narrower at the altar so that from the back, it looks like it's a longer distance to the front. Still, it's a big and rich church. That's because of a famous blood-stained cloth, kept in a silver-gilt reliquary in the Chapel of the Corporal.

Visit the church in three parts: Chapel of the Corporal (north transept, left of altar, in front), high altar (center front), and Chapel of San Brizio (left front, paid entry).

Cost and Hours: The Duomo is open daily April–Sept 7:30–19:30, March and Oct until 18:30, Nov–Feb until 17:30. Admission is €2, or €3 if you want to see the Chapel of San Brizio, which has shorter hours than the Duomo. The Chapel of San Brizio is open Mon–Sat 9:00–19:00, Sun 13:30–18:30 (closes one hour earlier in winter). A €5 combo-ticket includes the Duomo, the chapel, and the Museo dell'Opera del Duomo—the "MoDo" (available at the chapel; MoDo alone costs €4). Admission is also covered by the €18 Carta Unica combo-ticket.

Chapel of the Corporal: In 1263, or so the story goes, a skeptical priest named Peter of Prague passed through Bolsena (a few miles from Orvieto) while on a pilgrimage to Rome. He had doubts that the bread used in Communion could really be transformed into the body of Christ. But during Mass, as he held the host aloft and blessed it, the bread began to bleed, running down his arms and dripping onto a linen cloth (a "corporal") on the altar. The bloody cloth (in the turquoise frame above the main altar) was brought to Orvieto, where Pope Urban IV happened to be visiting. The amazed pope proclaimed a new holiday, Corpus Christi (Body of Christ), and the Orvieto cathedral was built (begun in 1290) to display the miraculous relic. Find the fine gilded enamel **reliquary** (which no longer holds the blood-stained relic) in a glass case on the left. Until the 1970s, this silver-and-blue enamel reliquary (c. 1358)—considered one of the finest medieval jewels in Italy—held the linen relic as if in a frame. Notice how it evokes the facade of this cathedral. For centuries, the precious linen was paraded through the streets of Orvieto in this ornate reliquary.

The room was frescoed in the 14th century with scenes attesting to Christ's presence in the communion wafer (for example, the panel above the glass case to the left illustrates how the wafer bleeds if you cook it). You can see the **Miracle of Bolsena** depicted in the fresco on the chapel's right wall (light it with a €0.50 coin in the box).

The new cathedral put Orvieto (then known as "Urbs Vetus") on the map, and with lots of pilgrims came lots of wealth. Two future popes used the town as a refuge when their enemies forced them to flee Rome.

Now leave the Chapel of the Corporal and walk to the middle front of the church, where you'll see a patch in the marble floor, a fine marble statue, and the highly decorated high altar.

The High Altar: The brilliant stained glass from the 14th century is original and painstakingly restored. The fine organ has more than 5,000 pipes. The marble *pietà* (statue of Mary holding Jesus' just-crucified body) was carved in 1579 by local artist Ippolito Scalza. Clearly inspired by Michelangelo's *Pietà*, this exceptional piece with four figures was sculpted from one piece of marble. Notice the texture Scalza gave this wonderful work. Look at the alabaster rose window. Also note from here how the architect's trick, making the church look bigger from the rear, works in reverse from here. If you look to the back, the church feels stubbier than it actually is.

As the Roman church countered the Reformation, it made reforms of its own. For instance, altars were moved back to let people get closer to the religious action. The confused patching on the marble floor is evidence that, prior to the Counter-Reformation, the altar stood here.

Chapel of San Brizio: This chapel, to the right of the altar, is Orvieto's one must-see artistic sight. It features Luca Signorelli's brilliantly lit frescoes of the Apocalypse (painted 1499–1504). Step into the chapel and you're surrounded by vivid scenes crammed with figures. The frescoes depict events at the end of the world, but they also reflect the turbulent political and religious atmosphere of late 15th-century Italy.

The chapel is decorated in one big and cohesive story. Follow the plot (counterclockwise): Antichrist, end of world (above the arch facing the nave), Resurrection, hell, Judgment Day (Fra Angelico's Jesus above the window), and finally heaven. Now the story: In the **Sermon of the Antichrist** (left wall), a crowd gathers around a man preaching from a pedestal. It's the Antichrist, who comes posing as Jesus to mislead the faithful. This befuddled Antichrist forgets his lines mid-speech, but the Devil is on hand to whisper what to say next. His words sow wickedness through the world, including executions (upper right). The worried woman in red and white (foreground, left of pedestal) gets money from a man for something she's not proud of (perhaps receiving funds from a Jewish moneylender—notice the Stars of David on his purse).

HILL TOWNS

Most likely, the Antichrist himself is a veiled reference to Savonarola (1452–1498), the charismatic Florentine monk who defied the pope, drove the Medici family from power, and riled the populace with apocalyptic sermons. Many Italians—including the painter Signorelli—viewed Savonarola as a tyrant and heretic, the Antichrist who was ushering in the Last Days.

In the upper left, notice the hardworking angel. He looks as if he's at batting practice, hitting followers of the Antichrist back to earth as they try to get through the pearly gates. In the bottom left corner of the scene is a self-portrait of the artist, **Luca Signorelli** (c. 1450–1523), well-dressed in black with long golden hair. Signorelli, from nearby Cortona, was at the peak of his powers, and this chapel was his masterpiece. He looks out proudly as if to say, "I did all this in just five years, on time and on budget," confirming his reputation as a speedy, businesslike painter. Next to him is the artist Fra Angelico, who started the chapel decoration five decades earlier, but completed only a small part of it.

Around the arch, opposite the windows, are signs of the **end of the world:** eclipse, tsunami, falling stars, earthquakes, violence in the streets, and a laser-wielding gray angel.

On the right wall (opposite the Antichrist) is the **Resurrection of the Bodies.** Trumpeting angels blow a wake-up call, and the dead climb dreamily out of the earth to be clothed with new bodies. On the same wall (below the action, at eye level) is a gripping *pietà*. Also by Signorelli, this *pietà* gives an insight into the genius and personality of the artist. Look at the emotion in the faces of the two Marys and consider that Signorelli's son had just died. The Deposition scene (behind Jesus' leg) seems inspired by ancient Greek scenes of a pre-Christian hero's death. In the confident spirit of the Renaissance, the artist incorporates a pagan scene to support a Christian story. This 3-D realism in a 2-D sketch shows the work of a talented master.

The altar wall (with the windows) features the **Last Judgment.** To the left of the altar (and continuing on the left wall) are the **Elect in Heaven.** They spend eternity posing like bodybuilders while listening to celestial Muzak. To the right (and continuing on the right wall) are the **Damned in Hell,** in the scariest mosh pit ever. Devils torment sinners in graphic detail, while winged demons control the airspace overhead. In the center, one lusty demon turns to tell the frightened woman on his back exactly what he's got planned for their date. (According to legend, this was Signorelli's lover, who betrayed him...and ended up here. You'll see this couple all over town.) Signorelli's ability to tell a story through human actions and gestures, rather than symbols, inspired his younger contemporary, Michelangelo, who meticulously studied the elder artist's nudes.

HILL TOWNS

In this chapel, Christian theology sits physically and figuratively upon a foundation of classical logic. Below everything are Greek and Latin philosophers, plus Dante, struggling to reconcile Classic truth with Church doctrine. You can see the intellectual challenge on their faces as they ponder this puzzle. They're immersed in fanciful Grotesque decor. Dating from 1499, this is one of the first uses of the frilly, nubile, and even sexy "wallpaper pattern" so popular in the Renaissance. (It was inspired by the decorations found in Nero's Golden House in Rome, which had been discovered just a few years earlier.)

During the Renaissance, nakedness symbolized purity. When attitudes changed during the Counter-Reformation, the male figures in Signorelli's frescoes were given penis-covering sashes. During a 1982 restoration, most—but not all—of the sashes were removed. A little of that prudishness survives to this day, as those in heaven were left with their sashes modestly in place.

After leaving the cathedral, if you want to visit a **viewpoint park,** exit left and pass the small parking lot and WC.

Near the Duomo: MoDo and Other Museums

▲▲MoDo City Museum (Museo dell'Opera del Duomo)— This museum is a confusing ensemble of several different sights, scattered around town: the cathedral art collections split between two small galleries behind the cathedral; the Emilio Greco collection (next to the cathedral, in Palazzo Soliano); and, at the far end of town, the Church of San Giovenale, which has statues of the 12 apostles that were added to the Duomo in the Baroque Age (c. 1700) and removed in the late 1800s.

Cost and Hours: €4 MoDo ticket covers all MoDo sights (or get the €5 combo-ticket that includes the Duomo and Chapel of San Brizio), open daily 9:30–19:00, shorter hours off-season.

Cathedral Art Collections: Behind the Duomo in Palazzi Papali, a complex of medieval palaces shows off the city's best art. The highlight is just inside the door: the *Sala della Maestà*—a bronze Mary and child with exquisite angels, under a canopy that once filled the niche in the center of the cathedral's facade. This is proto-Renaissance, dating from around 1300.

Other highlights include fine inlaid woodwork from the original choir; a room full of sinopias (wall charts for frescoes with a roughed-up surface so the wet plaster would stick); a *Madonna with Child* from 1322 by Sienese great Simone Martini, who worked in Orvieto; and paintings from the late 1500s that decorated the side chapels with a harsher Counter-Reformation message.

Museo Emilio Greco: Emilio Greco (1913–1995) was a Sicilian artist who designed the modern doors of Orvieto's cathedral. His sketches and about 30 of his bronze statues are on display here, showing his absorption with gently twisting and turning nudes. Greco's sketchy outlines of women are simply beautiful. The artful installation of his work in this palazzo, with walkways and even a spiral staircase up to the ceiling, allows you to view his sculptures from different angles.

National Archaeological Museum of Orvieto—This small four-room collection, immediately behind the cathedral in the ground floor of Palazzi Papali (under MoDo), beautifully shows off a trove of well-preserved Etruscan bronze, terra-cotta, and ceramics—some with painted colors surviving from 500 B.C. The reconstructed Golini tombs (named after the man who discovered them in 1836) show scenes from an Etruscan afterlife banquet.

Cost and Hours: €3, daily 8:30–19:30. The overpriced audioguide gives a virtual visit to the excavation sites (€5, 30 minutes). For background on the Etruscans, see page 616.

Archaeological Museum (Museo Claudio Faina e Museo Civico)—A former palace, across from the entrance to the cathedral, holds an Etruscan collection. The highlights of the first floor are the Roman coins; push the brass buttons and they rotate so you can see both sides. The best of the Etruscan vases and bronzes are on the top floor.

Cost and Hours: €4.50; April–Sept daily 9:30–18:00; Oct–March Tue–Sun 10:00–17:00, closed Mon; English descriptions throughout, tel. 076-334-1511.

Underground Orvieto

If you're short on time and have to choose one means of going underground in Orvieto, I'd recommend Well of the Cave or St. Patrick's Well over Underground Orvieto Tours.

▲**St. Patrick's Well (Pozzo di San Patrizio)**—Modern engineers are impressed by this deep well—175 feet deep and 45 feet

wide—designed in the 16th century with a double-helix pattern. The two spiral stairways allow an efficient one-way traffic flow: intriguing now, but critical then. Imagine if donkeys and people, balancing jugs of water, had to go up and down the same stairway. At the bottom is a bridge that people could walk on to scoop up water.

The well was built because a pope got nervous. After Rome was sacked in 1527 by renegade troops of the Holy Roman Empire, the pope fled to Orvieto. He feared that even this little town (with no water source on top) would be besieged. He commissioned a well, which was started in 1527 and finished 10 years later. It was a huge project. (As it turns out, the town was never besieged, but supporters believe that the well was worth the cost and labor because of its deterrence value—attackers would think twice about besieging a town with a water source.) Even today, when a local is faced with a difficult task, people say, "It's like digging St. Patrick's Well." It's a total of 496 steps up and down—lots of exercise and not much to see other than some amazing 16th-century engineering.

Cost and Hours: €4.50; interesting €1 audioguide, ID required; daily April–Sept 9:00–20:00, shorter hours in winter, the well is to your right as you exit the funicular. Bring a sweater if you plan to descend to the chilly depths.

Well of the Cave (Pozzo della Cava)—While renovating its trattoria, an Orvieto family discovered a vast underground network of Etruscan-era caves, wells, and tunnels. The excavation started in 1984 and continues to this day. It's well-explained in English and makes for a fun subterranean wander.

Cost and Hours: €3, Tue–Sun 9:00–20:00, closed Mon, Via della Cava 28, tel. 076-334-2373.

Underground Orvieto Tours (Parco delle Grotte)—Guides weave a good archaeological history into an hour-long look at about 100 yards of Etruscan and medieval caves. You'll see the remains of an old olive press, an impressive 130-foot-deep Etruscan well shaft, and what's left of a primitive cement quarry.

Cost and Hours: €5.50; 1-hour English tours depart from ticket office next to main TI at 11:15, 12:30, 16:15, and 17:15, with more scheduled according to demand; book tour at ticket office, confirm times at TI or by calling 076-334-0688, www.orvietounderground.it.

Etruscan Necropolis—Below town, at the base of the cliff, is a remarkable "city of the dead" that dates back to about five centuries before Christ. The tombs, which are laid out in a kind of street grid, are empty, and there's precious little to see here other than the basic stony construction. But it is both eerie and fascinating to wander the streets of an Etruscan cemetery.

Cost and Hours: €3, daily April–Sept 8:30–19:00, Oct–March 8:30–17:00.

View Walks

▲Hike Around the City on the Rupe—Orvieto's Rupe is a peaceful paved path that completely circles the town at the base

of the cliff upon which it sits. With the help of the TI brochure on "la Rupe," you'll see there are three access points from the town for the three-mile walk. Once on the trail, it's fairly level and easy to follow. On one side you have the cliff, with the town high above. On the other side you have Umbrian views stretching into the distance. I'd leave the town at Piazza Marconi and walk left (counterclockwise) three-quarters of the way around the town (with a fine view down onto the Etruscan Necropolis mid-way) and ride the escalator and elevator back up to the town from the big new Campo della Fiera parking lot. If you're ever confused about the path, follow the *la Rupe* and *Giro dell'Umbria* signs.

▲**Shorter Romantic Rampart Stroll**—Thanks to its dramatic hilltop setting, several fine little walks wind around the edges of Orvieto. My favorite after dark, when it's lamplit and romantic, is along the ramparts of the far west end of town. Start at the Church of San Giovenale. With your back to the church, go a block to the right to the end of town. Then head left along the ramparts, with cypress-dotted Umbria to your right, and follow Vicolo Volsinia to the Church of San Giovanni Evangelista.

Near Orvieto

Wine-Tasting—Orvieto Classico white wine is justly famous. For a short tour of a winery with Etruscan cellars, visit **Tenuta Le Velette,** where English-speaking Corrado and Cecilia (cheh-CHEEL-yah) Bottai will welcome you—if you've called ahead to set up an appointment (€8–18 for tour and tasting, price varies depending on wines, Mon–Fri 8:30–12:00 & 14:00–17:00, Sat 8:30–12:00, closed Sun, also have accommodations—see listing on page 673, tel. 076-329-090, mobile 348-300-2002, www.levelette.it). From their sign (5-minute drive past Orvieto at top of switchbacks just before Canale, on road to Bagnoregio), cruise down a long tree-lined drive, then park at the striped gate (must call ahead; no drop-ins).

Custodi is another respected family-run winery that produces Orvieto Classico, grappa, and olive oil on their 140-acre estate. Stop by for a tour of their cantina, an explanation of the winemaking process, and a tasting of four of their wines. Reserve ahead for an assortment of *salumi* and local cheeses or lunch to go with your wine-tasting (€7/person, €11–15/person with *antipasti* or lunch, daily 8:30–12:30 & 16:00–18:30, Viale Venere S.N.C. Loc. Canale;

on the road from Orvieto to Civita, a half-mile after Le Velette, it's the first building before Canale; tel. 076-329-053, mobile 338-316-0405, www.cantinacustodi.com, info@cantinacustodi.com). Helpful Chiara and Laura Custodi speak English.

Sleeping in Orvieto

(€1 = about $1.25, country code: 39)
Most of my recommended hotels are in the old town. The exceptions: Casa Sèlita B&B and Picchio II B&B are near the Campo della Fiera elevator, and Hotel Picchio is in a more modern neighborhood near the station.

$$$ **Hotel Maitani** is an overpriced time warp with antiquated outlets and rotary phones. Still, its grand public spaces and 39 rooms—each elegant and individual—offer a memorable splurge in a venerable centuries-old building half a block from the Duomo (Sb-€79, Db-€130, Db suite-€152 and €175, claim your 8 percent Rick Steves discount if you book direct, I'd skip their €10 breakfast, calls from the room are very expensive, air-con, elevator, 20 yards from the bus stop behind the TI at Via Lorenzo Maitani 5, tel. & fax 076-334-2011, www.hotelmaitani.com, direzione @hotelmaitani.com, Giuseppi and Norma).

$$$ **Hotel Duomo** is centrally located and modern, with splashy art and 17 sleek rooms. Double-paned windows keep the sound of the church bells well-muffled (Sb-€80, Db-€120, Db suite-€140, Tb-€150, extra bed-€10, 10 percent cash discount with this book, buffet breakfast, air-con, elevator, free Internet access, pay Wi-Fi, sunny terrace, a block from Duomo behind *gelateria* at Vicolo di Maurizio 7, tel. 076-334-1887, fax 076-339-4973, www .orvietohotelduomo.com, hotelduomo@tiscalinet.it, Gianni and Maura Massaccesi don't speak English, daughter Elisa does). The Massaccesi family also owns a three-room B&B 50 yards from the hotel (Sb-€70, Db-€90, Tb-€110, breakfast at the main hotel).

$$$ **Grand Hotel Italia,** new and top-end, rents 46 modern and spacious rooms farther into the old town (Db-€140, extra bed-€20, air-con, Via di Piazza del Popolo 13, tel. 0763-342-065, www .grandhotelitalia.it, hotelita@libero.it).

$$ **Hotel Corso** is friendly, with 18 comfy, contemporary rooms—some with balconies and views. Everyone can enjoy their sunlit little terrace (Sb-€70, Db-€95, Tb-€115, 10 percent discount with this book, buffet breakfast-€6.50, ask for quieter room off street, air-con, elevator, pay Wi-Fi, free parking nearby, on main street up from funicular toward Duomo at Corso Cavour 343, tel. 076-334-2020, fax 076-334-0648, www.hotelcorso.net, info@hotel corso.net, Carla).

$ Hotel Posta is a dumpy, long-ago-elegant palazzo renting 20 quirky rooms with vintage furniture—among the cheapest in town (S-€31, Sb-€37, D-€44, Db-€56, breakfast-€6, cash only, Via Luca Signorelli 18, tel. & fax 076-334-1909, www.orvietohotels.it, hotelposta@orvietohotels.it, little English spoken).

$ Villa Mercede, a wonderful value, is a religious institution offering 23 cheap, simple twin-bedded rooms, each with a big modern bathroom and many with glorious Umbrian views (Sb-€50, Db-€70, Tb-€90, free parking, Wi-Fi, a half-block from Duomo at Via Soliana 2, tel. 076-334-1766, fax 076-334-0119, www.argoweb.it/casareligiosa_villamercede, villamercede @orvienet.it).

$ Istituto S.S. Salvatore rents 15 spotless twin rooms and four singles in their convent, which comes with a peaceful terrace and an evening curfew (Sb-€38, Db-€58 April–Sept, Db-€48 Oct–March, cash only, no breakfast, elevator, parking, just off Piazza del Popolo at Via del Popolo 1, tel. & fax 076-334-2910, istitutosuoresansalvatore@tiscali.it, no English spoken).

$ Valentina's Rooms include six clean, airy, well-appointed rooms and two apartments, all with big beds and antique furniture. Her place is located in the heart of Orvieto, behind the palace on Piazza del Popolo (Db-€54 for two or more nights, Db-€60 for one-night stops, Tb-€75, studio with kitchen-€80; bright, spacious family apartment for up to 5 people-€150 for two or more nights, €170 for one night; these special discounted cash-only prices with this book, breakfast-€3, air-con-€5, Wi-Fi, Via Vivaria 7, tel. 076-334-1607, mobile 393-970-5868, www.bandbvalentina.com, valentina.z@tiscalinet.it). Valentina also rents three rooms across the square that share a kitchen (Db-€50, no air-con).

$ La Magnolia B&B has lots of fancy terra-cotta tiles, a couple of rooms with frescoed ceilings, terraces, and other welcoming touches. Its seven unique rooms, some like mini-apartments with kitchens, are cheerfully decorated and *tranquillo* despite being on the town's main drag (Db-€65, plush Db apartment-€70–75, extra person-€15, family deals, book direct and stay at least two nights to get a 10 percent Rick Steves discount, cash only, no elevator, use of washer-€3, Via Duomo 29, tel. 076-334-2808, mobile 338-902-7400, www.bblamagnolia.it, info@bblamagnolia.it, Serena).

$ Casa Sèlita B&B, a peaceful country house, offers easy access to Orvieto for drivers and train trippers. It's nestled in an orchard just below the town cliffs (under the big Campo della Fiera parking lot, with its handy escalator up into town). Its several rooms with terraces are airy and fresh, with dark hardwood floors, fluffy down comforters, and modern baths. Enjoy the views from the relaxing garden. Sèlita, her husband Ennio, and daughter

Elena are gracious hosts (Sb-€50, Db-€70, Tb-€85, €5 more off-season for heat, these prices promised to my readers through 2011 if you book direct, cash only, fans, free Internet access and Wi-Fi, free parking, Strada di Porta Romana 8, tel. 076-334-4218, www.casaselita.com, info@casaselita.com).

$ Hotel Picchio is a hardworking little family-run place with 27 overpriced rooms stuck back in the modern world, in a forgettable zone 300 yards from the train station at the base of the hill. A trail leads from here up to the old town (Sb-€45, Db-€62, superior Db-€85, Tb-€80–95, higher rates are for newer and brighter rooms in annex across street, 10 percent discount with this book when you book direct, air-con-€6, Wi-Fi, free outdoor parking, Via G. Salvatori 17, tel. & fax 076-330-1144, hotelpicchio@tin.it, Alessandra and Giovanna, who speaks English). Alessandra and Giovanna also run **Picchio II B&B,** a classier place on the opposite side of town (works well for drivers but otherwise inconvenient, Db-€70–80, air-con, Wi-Fi, double-paned windows keep out most traffic noise, free parking, small garden, near the base of the Campo della Fiera elevator at Via Adige 3).

Near Orvieto

$$$ Agriturismo Fattoria di Vibio produces olive oil and honey, sells organic products, and offers classes and spa services. In August, its 14 rooms rent at peak prices (and for one week during the month they require a minimum seven-night stay, with arrivals and departures on Saturdays). The rest of the year, no minimum stay is required, although rates drop dramatically for longer visits (Db-€250–320, includes breakfast and dinner). Its three cottages sleep 4–7 people and rent only by the week (€980–1,680/week depending on amenities, see complicated rate table on website, located 20 miles northeast of Orvieto, tel. 075-874-9607, fax 075-878-0014, www.fattoriadivibio.com, info@fattoriadivibio.com).

$$$ Agriturismo La Rocca Orvieto, run by Emiliano and Sabrina, is a fancy spa-type place, located 15 minutes north of Orvieto by car. They produce their own olive oil and wine and have nine rooms and 10 apartments—all with air-conditioning and Wi-Fi (Db-€98–140, 10 percent discount with this book—mention when you reserve, pool, panoramic view restaurant, Wellness Center with Jacuzzi and steam room, gym, mountain bikes, bocce court, hiking paths, tel. 076-334-4210 or 076-339-3437, fax 076-339-5155, mobile 348-640-0845, www.laroccaorvieto.com, info@laroccaorvieto.com).

At **$$$ Agriturismo Locanda Rosati,** you'll be greeted by gracious hosts Cristina and Giampiero Rosati, who rent 10 tastefully decorated rooms in a pleasant, homey atmosphere (Db-€110–140, Tb-€140–160, full traditional dinners for €35 on request with this book, air-con, swimming pool, 5 miles from Orvieto on the road to Viterbo, tel. 076-321-7314, www.locandarosati.it, info @locandarosati.it).

$$ Tenuta Le Velette is a sprawling, family-run farmhouse. Cecilia and Corrado Bottai rent six fully furnished apartments and villas housing 2–14 people in perfect Umbrian rural peace and tranquility (Db apartment-€90–110, see website for details on various villas, 3-night minimum, 20 percent discount for weekly stay, cash only, pool, bocce court, 5 minutes from Orvieto—drive toward Bagnoregio-Canale and follow *Tenuta le Velette* signs, fax 076-329-114, mobile 348-300-2002, www.levelette.it, cecilia levelette@libero.it). They also offer wine-tastings (see listing on page 669).

$$ Borgo Fontanile is a vacation home with a swimming pool, terrace, and kids' play area. Its five new apartments with rustic wood beams and terra-cotta tile floors sleep 2–4 people (€50–60/night per person, discounts for longer stays, €400–800/ apartment per week, air-con, Vocabolo Fornace 159, Loc. Baschi, tel. & fax 074-495-7342, www.borgofontanile.com, info@borgo fontanile.com).

$ Agriturismo Pomonte Umbria, seven miles east of Orvieto, offers home-cooked meals, lovely vistas, and seven comfortable rooms in a recently built guest house (Db-€58, includes breakfast, €92-half-pension, €115-full pension, Loc. Canino di Orvieto 1, Corbara, tel. 076-330-4041, fax 076-330-4080, www.pomonte.it, info@pomonte.it).

Eating in Orvieto

La Palomba features game and truffle specialties in a wood-paneled dining room. Gianpiero, Enrica, and the Cinti family take care of their regulars and visiting travelers alike, offering both a fine value and a classy conviviality. Seating is comfortable and not too crowded. Truffles are ground right at your table—try the *ombricelli al tartufo* (homemade pasta with truffles). As firm believers in the slow-food movement, they use ingredients that are mostly organic and locally produced (€8 pastas, €12 *secondi,* Thu–Tue 12:30–14:15 & 19:30–22:00, closed Wed, reservations smart, just off Piazza della Repubblica at Via Cipriano Manente 16, tel. 076-334-3395).

Antico Bucchero, a bit mod under a big white vault, makes a nice splurge with its candlelit ambience and delicious food (€8 pastas, €12 *secondi,* Thu–Tue 12:00–15:00 & 19:00–23:00, closed Wed, indoor/outdoor seating, a half-block south of Corso Cavour, between Torre del Moro and Piazza della Repubblica at Via de Cartari 4, tel. 076-334-1725, Piero and Silvana).

L'Antica Trattoria dell'Orso offers well-prepared Umbrian cuisine paired with fine wines in a homey and peaceful atmosphere. Ciro and chef Gabriele enjoy getting to know their diners, and will steer you toward the freshest seasonal plates of their famous pastas and passionately prepared vegetables. Or just trust Gabriele, and go for their €30 complete tasting meal—including wine (Wed–Sun 12:00–14:00 & 19:30–22:00, closed Mon–Tue, just off Piazza della Repubblica at Via della Misericordia 18/20, tel. 076-334-1642).

Trattoria la Grotta, pricey and chic, prides itself on serving only the freshest food and finest wine. The decor is Signorelli mod and the ambience is quiet, with courteous service. Owner-chef Franco has been at it for 50 years, and promises diners a free coffee, grappa, *limoncello,* or *vin santo* with this book (Wed–Mon opens at 12:00 for lunch and at 19:00 for dinner, closed Tue, Via Luca Signorelli 5, tel. 076-334-1348).

Trattoria del Moro Aronne is a long-established family bistro run by Cristian and his mother Rolanda, who lovingly prepare homemade pasta and market-fresh meats and produce for their typical Umbrian specialties. Be sure to sample the *nidi*—folds of fresh pasta enveloping warm, gooey Pecorino cheese sweetened with honey. The crème brûlée is a winner for dessert. Three small and separate dining areas make the interior feel intimate. This place is known locally as a good value (Wed–Mon 12:00–15:00 & 19:00–22:00, closed Tue, Via S. Leonardo 7, tel. 076-334-2763).

Pizzeria Re Artù is a local favorite open only in the evenings. It's popular with families and students for casual dinners of wood-fired €7 pizzas, big salads, homemade pasta, or grilled meat. In a quiet courtyard guarded by a medieval tower, it's centrally located a block southwest of Piazza della Repubblica (Thu–Tue 18:30–22:30, closed Wed, Via Loggia dei Mercanti 14, tel. 076-339-3438).

At **L'Oste del Re,** a simple trattoria on Corso Cavour, the Re Artù team serves lunch, with a focus on local cheeses and meats (Thu–Tue 11:00–15:30, closed Wed, Corso Cavour 58, tel. 0763-343-846).

Enoteca Tozzi, to the left of the Duomo, serves up rustic *panini*—try the roast suckling pig *(porchetta)* if it's available (daily 9:00–19:00, open sporadically in winter, Piazza del Duomo 13, tel. 076-334-4393).

Sidis supermarket, tucked away two minutes from the Duomo, has what you need to put together a functional picnic or stock your hotel room pantry (daily 8:00–13:00 & 16:30–19:30, next to recommended Trattoria la Grotta at Via Luca Signorelli 23).

Gelato: For dessert, try the deservedly popular *gelateria* **Pasqualetti** (daily 11:30–21:00, open later June–Aug, closed in winter, next to left transept of church, Piazza del Duomo 14; another branch is at Corso Cavour 56, open daily 11:00–23:00).

Italy Is Made of Tuff Stuff

Tuff (or *tufa* in Italian) is a light-colored volcanic rock that is common in Italy. A part of Tuscany is even called the "Tuff Area." The seven hills of Rome are made of tuff, and quarried blocks of this stone can be seen in the Colosseum, Pantheon, and Castel Sant'Angelo. Just outside of Rome, the catacombs were carved from tuff. Sorrento rises above the sea

on a tuff outcrop. Orvieto, Civita di Bagnoregio (pictured), and many other hill towns perch on bluffs of tuff.

Italy's early inhabitants, including the Etruscans and Romans, carved caves, tunnels, burial niches, and even roads out of tuff. Blocks of this rock were quarried to make houses and walls. Tuff is soft and easy to carve when it's first exposed

to air, but hardens later, which makes it a good building stone.

Italy's tuff-producing volcanoes resulted from a lot of tectonic-plate bumping and grinding. This violent geologic history is reflected in Italy's volcanoes, like Vesuvius and Etna, and earthquakes such as the 2009 quake in the L'Aquila area northeast of Rome.

Tuff is actually just a big hardened pile of old volcanic ash. When volcanoes hold magma that contains a lot of water, they erupt explosively (think heat + water = steam = POW!). The exploded rock material gets blasted out as hot volcanic ash, which settles on the surrounding landscape, piles up, and over time welds together into the rock called tuff.

So when you're visiting an area in Italy of ancient caves or catacombs built out of this material, you'll know that at least once (and maybe more) upon a time, it was a site of a lot of volcanic activity.

HILL TOWNS

Orvieto Connections

From Orvieto by Train to: Rome (hourly, 70 minutes), **Florence** (hourly, 2 hours, use Firenze S.M.N. train station—see page 418), **Siena** (12/day, 2.5 hours, change in Chiusi, all Florence-bound trains stop in Chiusi), **Assisi** (roughly hourly, 2.5 hours, 1 or 2 transfers). The train station's Buffet della Stazione is surprisingly good if you need a quick *focaccia* sandwich or pizza picnic for the train ride.

By Bus to Bagnoregio (30-minute walk from Civita di Bagnoregio, described next): It's a one-hour trip (€2 one-way or

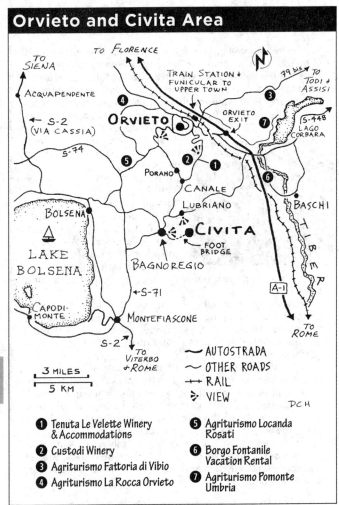

Orvieto and Civita Area

TO FLORENCE

TO SIENA

TRAIN STATION & FUNICULAR TO UPPER TOWN

ACQUAPENDENTE

79 bis TO TODI & ASSISI

③

← S-2 (VIA CASSIA)

④ **ORVIETO**

ORVIETO EXIT ⑦

S-448 LAGO CORBARA

S-74

⑤

② ①

PORANO

⑥

CANALE

LUBRIANO

CIVITA

BASCHI

BOLSENA

FOOT BRIDGE

LAKE BOLSENA

BAGNOREGIO

TIBER

CAPODI-MONTE

← S-71

A-1

MONTEFIASCONE

S-2 → TO VITERBO & ROME

TO ROME

3 MILES / 5 KM

⌒ AUTOSTRADA
⌒ OTHER ROADS
+—+ RAIL
⤢ VIEW

DCH

HILL TOWNS

① Tenuta Le Velette Winery & Accommodations
② Custodi Winery
③ Agriturismo Fattoria di Vibio
④ Agriturismo La Rocca Orvieto

⑤ Agriturismo Locanda Rosati
⑥ Borgo Fontanile Vacation Rental
⑦ Agriturismo Pomonte Umbria

€4 round-trip if bought in advance from bar or *tabacchi*, €7 one-way or €14 round-trip if purchased from driver). Here are likely departure times (but confirm) from Orvieto's Piazza Cahen on the blue Cotral bus, daily except Sunday: 6:15, 12:45, 15:45, 17:40, and 18:20 (buses stop at Orvieto's train station 5 minutes later). During the school year (roughly Sept–June), there are additional departures at 7:20, 7:50, and 13:55. Confirm the schedule and buy your round-trip ticket at the train-station bar or at the *tabacchi* shop on Corso Cavour, a block up from the funicular (remember, if you wait to buy your ticket from the driver, you'll pay much more).

The schedule is also posted across the street from the bus parking lot (look for sign saying *A.Co.Tral Capolinea*). To find the bus stop, face the funicular. The bus stop is at the far left end of Piazza Cahen. Remember to confirm departure and return times with the driver—the bus you want says *Bagnoregio* in the window. The last bus back from Bagnoregio usually leaves at 17:45. If you catch the bus down below at Orvieto's train station, wait to the left of the funicular station (as you're facing it). For schedule and tickets, visit the *tabacchi*/bar in the train station, see www.cotralspa.it, or call 0761-760-049 (may be Italian-only).

Tip for Drivers: If you're thinking of driving to Rome, consider stashing your car here instead. You can easily park the car, safe and free, behind the Orvieto train station (even for a week or more), and zip effortlessly into Rome by train (70 minutes).

Civita di Bagnoregio

Perched on a pinnacle in a grand canyon, the traffic-free village of Civita di Bagnoregio is Italy's ultimate hill town. In the last decade, the real Civita (chee-VEE-tah) has died—the last of its lifelong residents have moved away. But relatives and newcomers are moving in and revitalizing the village, and it remains an amazing place to visit. (It's even become popular as a movie backdrop—most recently for a 2008 made-for-TV version of *Pinocchio*.) Civita is connected to the world and the town of Bagnoregio by a long pedestrian bridge—and a website (www.civitadibagnoregio.it, run by B&B owner Franco).

Civita's history goes back to Etruscan and ancient Roman times. In the early Middle Ages, Bagnoregio was a suburb of Civita, which had a population of about 4,000. Later, Bagnoregio surpassed Civita in size—especially following a 1695 earthquake, after which many residents fled Civita to live in Bagnoregio, fearing their houses would be shaken off the edge into the valley below. You'll notice Bagnoregio is dominated by Renaissance-style buildings while, architecturally, Civita remains stuck in the Middle Ages.

While Bagnoregio lacks the pinnacle-town romance of Civita, it's actually a healthy, vibrant community (unlike Civita, the suburb now nicknamed "the dead city"). In Bagnoregio, get a haircut, sip a coffee on the square, and walk down to the old laundry (ask, *"Dov'è la lavanderia vecchia?"*). Off-season, when Civita and Bagnoregio are deadly quiet—and cold—I'd side-trip in quickly from Orvieto rather than spend the night.

HILL TOWNS

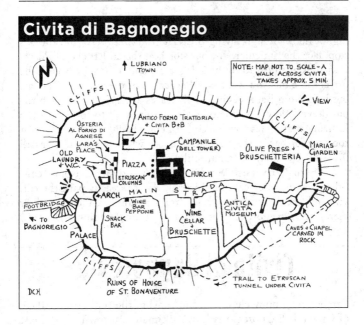

Civita di Bagnoregio

NOTE: MAP NOT TO SCALE—A WALK ACROSS CIVITA TAKES APPROX. 5 MIN.

LUBRIANO TOWN

CLIFFS

← VIEW

CLIFFS

OSTERIA AL FORNO DI AGNESE

ANTICO FORNO TRATTORIA + CIVITA B+B

LARA'S PLACE

OLD LAUNDRY + W.C.

PIAZZA

ETRUSCAN COLUMNS

CAMPANILE (BELL TOWER)

OLIVE PRESS + BRUSCHETTERIA

MARIA'S GARDEN

ARCH

MAIN   STRADA

CHURCH

FOOTBRIDGE

→ TO BAGNOREGIO

PALACE

WINE BAR PEPPONE

SNACK BAR

WINE CELLAR + BRUSCHETTE

ANTICA CIVITA MUSEUM

CAVES + CHAPEL CARVED IN ROCK

CLIFFS

RUINS OF HOUSE OF ST. BONAVENTURE

TRAIL TO ETRUSCAN TUNNEL UNDER CIVITA

DCH

Orientation to Civita

Arrival in Bagnoregio, near Civita

If you're taking the **bus** from Orvieto, you'll get off at the bus stop in Bagnoregio. Look at the posted bus schedule and write down the return times to Orvieto, or check with the driver.

From Bagnoregio to Civita: Civita sits at the opposite end of Bagnoregio, about a mile away. From Bagnoregio, you can walk (allow around 30 minutes) or take a little **shuttle bus**—yellow, orange, or white—to the base of the bridge to Civita (hourly, 10-minute ride, €1 round-trip, pay driver, first bus runs Mon–Sat at about 7:30, Sun at 8:50, last at 18:45, no buses 13:00–15:30, fewer buses June–Aug, catch bus across from gas station). From the base of the bridge, you have to walk the rest of the way (a 10-minute hike up a pedestrian bridge). If you want to return to Bagnoregio by bus, check the schedule posted near the bridge (at edge of parking lot, where bus let you off) before heading up to Civita, or ask at the recommended Trattoria Antico Forno.

To **walk** from the Bagnoregio bus stop to the base of Civita's bridge (at least 20 minutes, fairly level), take the road going uphill, Via Garibaldi (overlooking the big parking lot). Once on the road, take the first right and an immediate left onto the main drag, Via Roma. Follow this straight out to the belvedere for a superb viewpoint. From the viewpoint, backtrack a few steps (staircase at end of viewpoint is a dead end) and take the stairs down to the road leading to the bridge.

Drivers coming from Orvieto or elsewhere can avoid a long walk by driving through Bagnoregio and parking under the bridge at the base of Civita (for more tips, see "Bagnoregio Connections" on page 684).

Helpful Hints

Market Day: A lively market fills the Bagnoregio bus-station parking lot each Monday.

Baggage Storage: While there's no official baggage-check service in Bagnoregio, I've arranged with Mauro Laurenti, who runs the **Bar/Enoteca/Caffè Gianfu** and **Cinema Alberto Sordi,** to let you leave your bags there (€1/bag, Fri–Wed 6:00–13:00 & 13:30–23:00, closed Thu). As you get off the bus, go back 50 yards or so in the direction that the Orvieto bus just came from, and go right around corner.

Food near Bagnoregio Bus Stop: About 100 yards from the bus stop, within a few steps of the Porta Albana (old gate to the town), you'll find both a small grocery store and a great little bakery (**L'Arte del Pane**—with fresh pizza by the slice, Via Matteotti 5).

Bus Tickets: To save money on bus fare to Orvieto, buy a ticket before boarding from the newsstand near the Bagnoregio bus stop, across from the gas station (€2 one-way or €4 round-trip; otherwise €7 one-way or €14 round-trip if purchased from driver).

HILL TOWNS

Self-Guided Walk

Welcome to Civita

Civita was once connected to Bagnoregio, before the saddle between the separate towns eroded away. Photographs around town show the old donkey path, the original bridge. It was bombed in World War II and replaced in 1966 with the new footbridge that you're climbing today. The town's hearty old folks hang on to the bridge's handrail when fierce winter weather rolls through.

• *Entering the town, you'll pass through a cut in the rock and a 12th-century Romanesque...*

Arch: This was the main Etruscan road leading to the Tiber Valley and Rome. The stone passageway was cut by the Etruscans 2,500 years ago.

• *Inside the town gate, to the left, is an unmarked WC, behind the*

Bottega souvenir store. It faces the town's old laundry, which dates from just after World War II, when water was finally piped into the town. Until recently, this was a lively village gossip center. Nearby, inside the entry arch and on the right, are the remains of a...

Renaissance Palace: The wooden door and windows (above the door) lead only to thin air. They were part of the facade of one of five palaces that once graced Civita. Much of the palace fell into the valley, riding a chunk of the ever-eroding rock pinnacle. Today, the door leads to a remaining section of the palace—complete with Civita's first hot tub, as it was once owned by the "Marchesa," a countess who married into Italy's biggest industrialist family. Check out the canyon viewpoint a few steps to the left of the palace. Lean over the banister and listen to the sounds of the birds and the bees. Just beyond that is the site of the long-gone home of Civita's one famous son, St. Bonaventure, known as the "second founder of the Franciscans" (look for the small plaque on the wall to your right).

• *Now wander to the main square and Civita's church.*

Piazza: Here in the town square is Wine Bar Peppone (if it's chilly, go inside for the inviting fire), two restaurants, and wild donkey races on the first Sunday of June and the second Sunday of September. At Christmastime, a living nativity scene is enacted in this square, and if you're here at the end of July or beginning of August, you might catch a play here. The pillars that stand like giants' bar

stools are ancient Etruscan. The church with its *campanile* (bell tower) marks the spot where an Etruscan temple, and then a Roman temple, once stood.

• *Go into the church.*

Church: A cathedral until 1699, the church houses records of about 60 bishops that date back to the seventh century. Inside you'll see frescoes and statues from "the school of Donatello." The central altar is built upon the relics of the Roman martyr St. Victoria, who once was the patron saint of the town. St. Marlonbrando served as a bishop here in the ninth century; an altar dedicated to him is on the right.

The fine crucifix, carved out of pear wood in the 15th century, is from the school of Donatello. It's remarkably expressive and greatly venerated by locals. Jesus' gaze is almost haunting. Some say his appearance changes based on what angle you view him from: looking alive from the front, in agony from the left, and dead from the right. Regardless, his eyes follow you from side to side. On Good Friday, this crucifix goes out and is the focus of the midnight procession.

On the left side of the nave above an altar is an intimate fresco of the Madonna of the Earthquake, given this name because—in the shake of 1695—the whitewash fell off and revealed this tender fresco of Mary and her child. (During the Baroque era, a white-and-bright interior was in vogue, and churches such as these—which were covered with precious and historic frescoes—were simply whitewashed over.) On the same wall—toward the front—find a faded portrait of Santa Apollonia, the patron saint of your teeth; notice the scary-looking pincers. Say hello to Annarita, the church attendant (daily 9:30–13:00 & 15:00–18:00). Drop a coin into the offering box.

• *Just around the corner from the church, on the main street, are several...*

Eateries: At Rossana and Antonio's cool **Bruschette con Prodotti Locali,** pull up a chair and let them or their daughters, Arianna and Antonella, serve you *panini* (sandwiches), bruschetta (garlic toast with optional tomato topping), *salumi,* grilled sausages, wine, and a local cake called *ciambella.* After eating, wander down to see their cellar with its traditional winemaking gear and provisions for rolling huge kegs up the stairs. Tap on the kegs in the bottom level to see which are full (daily 11:00–17:00, in summer until 20:00, tel. 0761-793-270).

The rock below Civita is honeycombed with ancient cellars like this (for keeping wine at the same temperature all year) and cisterns (for collecting rainwater, since there was no well in town). Many date from Etruscan times.

Farther down on the left, you'll find **Antico Frantoio Bruschetteria,** a rustic, super-atmospheric place for a bite to eat. Vittoria's sons Sandro and Felice, and her grandsons Maurizio and Fabrizio, toast delicious bruschetta (roughly 10:00–20:00 in summer, off-season open weekends only 10:00–19:00, tel. 076-194-8429, mobile 328-689-9375).

Peruse the menu, choose your topping (chopped tomato is super), and get a glass of wine for a fun, affordable snack.

While waiting for your bruschetta, take a look around to see Vittoria's mill *(mulino),* an interesting collection of old olive presses. The huge **olive press** in the entry is about 1,500 years old. Until the 1960s, blindfolded donkeys trudged in the circle here, crushing olives and creating paste that filled the circular filters and was put into a second press. Notice the 2,500-year-old sarcophagus niche. The hole in the floor (with the glass top) was a garbage hole. In ancient times, residents would toss their jewels down when under attack; excavations uncovered a windfall of treasures (if you're not eating here, a €1 donation is requested).

• *Across the street and down a tiny lane, find...*

Antica Civita: This is the closest thing the town has to a museum. The new collection is the brainchild of Felice, Vittoria's husband, who has hung farm tools, olive presses, and local artifacts in a series of old caves. Felice wants to give visitors a feeling for life in Civita when it had its traditional economy. He promised me he'd be adding old black-and-white photos and English explanations to his humble exhibits (€1).

• *On the left 20 yards farther down is...*

Maria's Garden (Maria's Giardino): Maria is too frail to live in Civita these days, but you can peek into her garden and enjoy her view. She and her husband, Peppone (who passed away in 2009), used to carry goods on a donkey back and forth 40 times a day on the path between the old town and Bagnoregio. She's now the last native Civita resident still living. As you view the canyon in which Civita is stranded, imagine the work the two rivers did—in the same style as the Colorado River—to carve all this. Listen to the roosters and voices from distant farms.

• *At the end of town, the main drag winds downhill. On your right are small...*

Etruscan Caves: The first two caves were used as stables until a few years ago. The third cave is an unusual chapel, cut deep into the rock, with a barred door; this is the **Chapel of the Incarcerated** (Cappella del Carcere). In Etruscan times, the chapel—with a painted tile depicting the Madonna and child—may have originally been a tomb, and in medieval times, it was used as a jail. When Civita's few residents have a religious procession, they come here in honor of the Madonna of the Incarcerated.

• *After the chapel, the paving-stone path peters out into a dirt trail leading down and around to the right to an...*

Etruscan Tunnel: This tunnel dates from the Etruscan era. Tall enough for a woman with a jug on her head to pass through, it may have served as a shortcut to the river below. It was widened in the 1930s so that farmers could get between their scattered fields more easily. Think of the scared villagers who huddled here for refuge during WWII bombing raids.

• *Backtrack to return to the...*

Piazza: Evenings on Civita's town square are a bite of Italy.

The same people sat on the same church steps under the same moon, night after night, year after year. I love my cool, late evenings in Civita. If you visit in the morning, have cappuccino and rolls at the small café/wine bar on the town square.

Whenever you visit, stop halfway up the donkey path and listen to the sounds of rural Italy. Reach out and touch one of the Monopoly houses. If you know how to turn the volume up on the crickets, do so.

Sleeping in Civita or Bagnoregio

(€1 = about $1.25, country code: 39)
In Civita and Bagnoregio, there are 15 B&B rooms up for grabs and one newly remodeled hotel. Outside the town there are plenty of *agriturismi;* otherwise, there's always Orvieto.

$$ Romantica Pucci B&B in Bagnoregio is a haven for city-weary travelers. Its eight spacious rooms are indeed romantic, with canopied beds and flowing veils. Both homey and elegant, it's like sleeping at Katharine Hepburn's place. Pucci and Lamberto take special care of their guests (Db-€80, air-con, free time-limited Internet access, free parking, her "Trust Pucci" €20 special family-style dinner is popular with guests—non-guests are also welcome for dinner, Piazza Cavour 1, tel. 076-179-2121, www.hotel romanticapucci.it, hotelromanticapucci@libero.it). It's just above the parking lot you see when you arrive in Bagnoregio—look for a sign marking its private parking place. From the Orvieto bus stop, take Via Garibaldi uphill above the parking lot, at the *tabacchi* bear right onto Via Roma, then look for the hotel sign straight ahead.

$$ Laura's Place has four rooms decorated medieval-rustic-mod, filling the old mayor's house and overlooking Civita's piazza. The local-products shop just across the square functions as the reception (Db-€80–100 depending on demand, breakfast at nearby café, mobile 347-627-5628, raffaele_rocchi@libero.it, Laura).

$ Hotel Divino Amore, in Bagnoregio, has 23 bright, modern rooms (Db-€70, Tb-€80, Via Fidanza 25–27, tel. & fax 076-178-0882, mobile 328-071-7244, www.hoteldivinoamore.com, info @hoteldivinoamore.com). From the bus stop, follow Via Garibaldi uphill above the parking lot, where it becomes Via Fidanza, and continue straight along for about 200 yards; #25 is on the left.

$ Civita B&B, run by Franco Sala (who also owns Trattoria Antico Forno and the only dog in Civita—17-year-old Birillo), has three fine little rooms, each overlooking Civita's main square (D-€65, Db-€70, T-€90, continental breakfast, Wi-Fi, Piazza del Duomo Vecchio, tel. 076-176-0016, mobile 347-611-5426, www .civitadibagnoregio.it, fsala@pelagus.it).

Eating in Civita

Osteria Al Forno di Agnese is a delightful spot where Manuela and her friends serve visitors simple yet delicious meals on a covered patio just off Civita's main square (€8 pastas, €8 *secondi*, €1.50 cover, Wed–Mon opens at 12:30 for lunch and at 19:30 for dinner, closed Tue, tel. 340-1259-721).

Trattoria Antico Forno cooks up rustic dishes, homemade pasta, and salads at affordable prices (€7 pastas, €8 *secondi*, daily for lunch 12:30–15:30 and sporadically for dinner 19:30–22:00, on main square, also rents rooms—see Civita B&B listing on previous page, tel. 076-176-0016, Franco and his assistants Gina and Nina).

Hostaria del Ponte is *the* place for serious cooking. It offers light, creative, and traditional cuisine with a great view terrace at the parking lot at the base of the bridge to Civita. Big space heaters make it comfortable to enjoy the wonderful view as you dine from their rooftop terrace, even in spring and fall (€7 pastas, €10 *secondi*, reservations often essential, Tue–Sun 12:30–14:30 & 19:30–21:30, closed Mon; Nov–April also closed Sun eve, tel. 076-179-3565, Lorena).

Bagnoregio Connections

From Bagnoregio to Orvieto: Public buses (6/day, 1 hour, €2 one-way or €4 round-trip if purchased in advance, €7 one-way or €14 round-trip from driver) connect Bagnoregio to the rest of the world via Orvieto. Departures from Bagnoregio—daily except Sunday and some holidays—are likely to be (but confirm): 5:30, 9:55, 10:10, 13:00, 14:25, and 17:25. During the school year (roughly Sept–June), buses also run at 6:35, 6:50, and 13:35 (for info on coming from Orvieto, see "Orvieto Connections," page 675). Remember to save money by buying your ticket in Bagnoregio before boarding the bus—purchase one from the newsstand near the bus stop, across from the gas station.

Driving from Orvieto to Bagnoregio: Orvieto overlooks the autostrada (and has its own exit). The shortest way to Civita from the freeway exit is to turn left (below Orvieto) and then simply follow the signs to *Lubriano* and *Bagnoregio*.

A more winding and scenic route takes 20 minutes longer: From the freeway, pass under hill-capping Orvieto (on your right, signs to *Lago di Bolsena*, on Viale I Maggio), then take the first left (direction: Bagnoregio), winding up past great Orvieto views through Canale, and through farms and fields of giant shredded wheat to Bagnoregio.

Either way, just before Bagnoregio, follow the signs left to

Lubriano and pull into the first little square by the church on your right for a breathtaking view of Civita. You'll find an even better view farther inside the town, from the tiny square at the next church (San Giovanni Battista). Then return to the Bagnoregio road.

Drive through the town of Bagnoregio (following yellow *Civita* signs) to the lot at the base of the steep pedestrian bridge. Park for free in spaces with no blue lines (plenty under the bridge). The €1 fee for parking in the blue-lined spaces is loosely enforced. While you're supposed to pay at the restaurant or shop opposite (same family), if no one's there, just park and don't worry. The bridge at this parking lot leads up to the traffic-free 2,500-year-old canyon-swamped pinnacle town of Civita di Bagnoregio.

More Hill Towns

If you haven't gotten your fill of hill towns, here are more to check out.

▲Gubbio

This handsome town climbs Monte Ingino in northeast Umbria. Tuesday is market day, when Piazza 40 Martiri (named for 40

local martyrs shot by Nazis) bustles. Nearby are the ruins of the Roman amphitheater, and a park close by that's perfect for a picnic. Head up Via della Repubblica to the main square with the imposing Palazzo dei Consoli. Farther up, Via San Gerolamo leads to the funky lift that will carry you up the hill, in two-person "baskets," for a stunning view from the top, where the Basilica of San Ubaldo is worth a look. The **TI** is at Via della Repubblica 15 (April–Sept 8:30–13:45 & 15:30–18:30, Oct–March closes at 18:00 daily; tel. 075-922-0693, www.gubbio -altochiascio.umbria2000.it). Buses from Gubbio run directly to Rome and Perugia (where you can transfer to Florence).

▲Bevagna

This sleeper of a town south of Assisi has Roman ruins, interesting churches, and more. Locals offer their guiding services for free (usually Italian-speaking only) and are excited to show visitors their town. Get a map at the **TI** at Piazza Silvestri 1 (daily 9:30–13:00 & 15:00–19:00, tel. 074-236-1667) and wander. Highlights are the Roman mosaics, remains of the arena, a paper-making workshop, the Romanesque Church of San Silvestro, and a gem of a 19th-century theater. Bevagna has all the elements of a hill town except one: a hill. You can see the main sights easily in a couple of hours. For an overnight stay, consider the fancy **$$ Hotel Palazzo Brunamonti** (Sb-€55, Db-€80–100, Tb-€110, air-con, Corso Giacomo Matteotti 79, tel. 074-236-1932, fax 074-236-1948, www.brunamonti.com, hotel@brunamonti.com). Buses connect Bevagna with Foligno (except on Sun).

▲Spello

Umbrian hill town aficionados always include Spello on their list. Just six miles south of Assisi, this town is much less touristy than its neighbor to the north. Spello will give your legs a workout. Via Consolare goes up, up, up to the top of town. Views from the terrace of the **Il Trombone** restaurant (closed Tue, tel. 074-230-1006) will have you singing a tune. The **TI** is on Piazza Giacomo Matteotti 3 (daily 9:30–12:30 & 15:30–18:30, afternoons 15:00–17:00 in winter, tel. 074-230-1009, www.prospello.it). Spello is on the Perugia–Assisi–Foligno train line.

ROME

Roma

Rome is magnificent and brutal at the same time. It's a showcase of Western civilization, with astonishingly ancient sights and a modern vibrancy. But if you're careless, you'll be run down or pickpocketed. And with the wrong attitude, you'll be frustrated by the kind of chaos that only an Italian can understand. On my last visit, a cabbie struggling with the traffic said, *"Roma chaos."* I responded, *"Bella chaos."* He agreed.

While Paris is an urban garden, Rome is a magnificent tangled forest. If your hotel provides a comfortable refuge; if you pace yourself; if you accept—and even partake in—the siesta plan; if you're well-organized for sightseeing; and if you protect yourself and your valuables with extra caution and discretion, you'll love it. (And Rome is much easier to live with if you avoid the midsummer heat.)

For me, Rome is in a three-way tie with Paris and London as Europe's greatest city. Two thousand years ago, the word "Rome" meant civilization itself. Everything was either civilized (part of the Roman Empire, Latin- or Greek-speaking) or barbarian. Today, Rome is Italy's political capital, the capital of Catholicism, and the center of the ancient world, littered with evocative remains. As you peel through its fascinating and jumbled layers, you'll find Rome's buildings, cats, laundry, traffic, and 2.6 million people endlessly entertaining. And then, of course, there are its stupendous sights.

Visit St. Peter's, the greatest church on earth, and scale Michelangelo's 448-foot-tall dome, the world's tallest. Learn something about eternity by touring the huge Vatican Museum. You'll find the story of creation—bright as the day it was painted—in the restored Sistine Chapel. Do the "Caesar Shuffle" through ancient

Rome's Forum and Colosseum. Savor Europe's most sumptuous building, the Borghese Gallery, and take an early-evening "Dolce Vita Stroll" down Via del Corso with Rome's beautiful people. Enjoy an after-dark walk from Campo de' Fiori to the Spanish Steps, lacing together Rome's Baroque and bubbly nightspots. Dine well at least once.

Planning Your Time

Rome is wonderful, but it's huge and exhausting. On a first-time visit, many travelers find that Rome is best done quickly—Italy is more charming elsewhere. But whether you're here for a day or a week, you won't be able to see all of Rome's attractions, so don't try—you'll keep coming back to Rome. After several dozen visits, I still have a healthy list of excuses to return.

Rome in a Day: Some people actually try to "do" Rome in a day. Crazy as that sounds, if all you have is a day, it's one of the most exciting days Europe has to offer. Start at 8:30 at the Colosseum. Then explore the Forum, hike over Capitol Hill, and cap your "Caesar Shuffle" with a visit to the Pantheon. After a quick lunch, taxi to the Vatican Museum (the lines usually die down mid-afternoon). See the Vatican Museum and take a short-cut from the Sistine Chapel directly into St. Peter's Basilica (open until 19:00 April–Sept). Taxi back to Campo de' Fiori to find dinner. Finish your day lacing together all the famous floodlit spots (follow my self-guided "Night Walk Across Rome"). Note: If you only want a day in Rome, consider side-tripping in from Orvieto or Florence, or maybe before the night train to Venice.

Rome in Two to Three Days: On the first day, do the "Caesar Shuffle" from the Colosseum to the Forum, then over Capitol Hill to the Pantheon. After a siesta, join the locals strolling from Piazza del Popolo to the Spanish Steps (follow my self-guided "Dolce Vita Stroll"). On the second day, see Vatican City (St. Peter's, climb the dome, tour the Vatican Museum). Have dinner on the atmospheric Campo de' Fiori, then walk to the Trevi Fountain and Spanish Steps (following my "Night Walk Across Rome"). With a third day, add the Borghese Gallery (reservations required) and the National Museum of Rome.

Orientation to Rome

Sprawling Rome actually feels manageable once you get to know it. The old core, with most of the tourist sights, sits in a diamond formed by Termini train station (in the east), the Vatican (west), Villa Borghese Gardens (north), and the Colosseum (south). The Tiber River runs through the diamond from north to south. In the center of the diamond sits Piazza Venezia, a busy square and traffic

Rome's Neighborhoods

hub. It takes about an hour to walk from Termini train station to the Vatican.

Think of Rome as a series of neighborhoods, huddling around major landmarks.

Ancient Rome: In ancient times, this was home for the grandest buildings of a city of a million people. Today, the best of the classical sights stand in a line from the Colosseum to the Forum to the Pantheon.

Pantheon Neighborhood: The Pantheon anchors the neighborhood I like to call the heart of Rome. It stretches eastward from the Tiber River through Campo de' Fiori and Piazza Navona, past the Pantheon to the Trevi Fountain.

North Rome: With the Spanish Steps, Villa Borghese Gardens, and trendy shopping streets (Via Veneto and the "shopping triangle"), this is a more modern, classy area.

Vatican City: Located west of the Tiber, it's a compact world of its own, with two great, huge sights: St. Peter's Basilica and the Vatican Museum.

Trastevere: This seedy, colorful wrong-side-of-the-river neighborhood is village Rome. It's the city at its crustiest—and perhaps most "Roman."

Termini: Though light on sightseeing highlights, the train-station neighborhood has many recommended hotels and public-transportation connections.

Pilgrim's Rome: Several prominent churches dot the area south of Termini train station.

South Rome: South of the city center, you'll find the gritty/colorful Testaccio neighborhood, the 1930s suburb of E.U.R., and the Appian Way, home of the catacombs.

Within each of these neighborhoods, you'll find elements from the many layers of Rome's 2,000-year history: the marble ruins of ancient times; tangled streets of the medieval world; early Christian churches; grand Renaissance buildings and statues; Baroque fountains and church facades; 19th-century apartments; and 20th-century boulevards choked with traffic.

Since no one is allowed to build taller than St. Peter's dome, and virtually no buildings have been constructed in the city center since Mussolini got distracted in 1938, Rome has no modern skyline. The Tiber River is basically ignored—after the last floods (1870), the banks were built up very high, and Rome turned its back on its naughty river.

Tourist Information

Rome has two tourist information offices and numerous kiosks (generally open daily 9:30–19:00). The TI offices are at the airport (terminal 3) and Termini train station (open until 20:30, way down track 24, look for signs). Little kiosks are near the Forum (on Piazza del Tempio della Pace), in Trastevere (on Piazza Sonnino), on Via Nazionale (at Palazzo delle Esposizioni), near Castel Sant'Angelo (at Piazza Pia), at the Church of Santa Maria Maggiore (on Via dell'Olmata), near Piazza Navona (at Piazza delle Cinque Lune), and near the Trevi Fountain (at Via del Corso and Via Minghetti). The TI's website is http://en.turismoroma.it.

At any TI, ask for a city map, a listing of sights and hours (in the free *Museums of Rome* booklet), and the free *Evento* booklet, with English-language pages listing the month's cultural events. The TIs don't offer room-booking services. If a commercial info-center offers to book you a room, just say no—you'll save money by booking direct.

If all you need is a **map,** skip the TI and pick up a freebie map at your hotel. The best map I found is published by Rough Guide (€8 in bookstores).

Rome's single best source of up-to-date tourist information is its **call center,** with English-speakers on staff. Dial 06-0608 (answered daily 9:00–21:00, press 2 for English). You can call to buy museum tickets, sightseeing passes (see page 696), and theater

Greater Rome

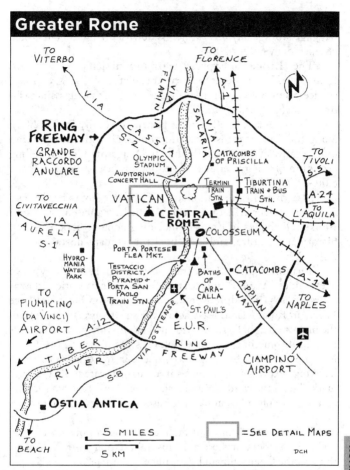

TO VITERBO

TO FLORENCE

N

RING FREEWAY →
GRANDE RACCORDO ANULARE

VIA CASSIA S-2

VIA FLAMINIA

VIA SALARIA

A-1

TO TIVOLI S-5

OLYMPIC STADIUM

CATACOMBS OF PRISCILLA

AUDITORIUM CONCERT HALL

TERMINI TRAIN STN.

TIBURTINA TRAIN & BUS STN.

A-24

TO L'AQUILA

TO CIVITAVECCHIA

VIA AURELIA S-1

VATICAN

CENTRAL ROME

COLOSSEUM

HYDRO-MANIA WATER PARK

PORTA PORTESE FLEA MKT.

CATACOMBS

APPIAN WAY

A-1

TO NAPLES

TESTACCIO DISTRICT, PYRAMID + PORTA SAN PAOLO TRAIN STN.

BATHS OF CARA-CALLA

TO FIUMICINO (DA VINCI) AIRPORT

A-12

OSTIENSE

ST. PAUL'S

E.U.R.

VIA RING FREEWAY

CIAMPINO AIRPORT

TIBER RIVER

S-8

OSTIA ANTICA

TO BEACH

5 MILES
5 KM

☐ = SEE DETAIL MAPS

DCH

ROME

tickets using your credit card. There's usually only a €1.50 fee.

Several English-oriented **websites** provide insight into events and daily life in the city: www.inromenow.com (light tourist info on lots of topics), www.wantedinrome.com (events and accommodation rentals), and http://rome.angloinfo.com (on living in and moving to Rome).

Arrival in Rome

By Train at Termini Station: Termini, Rome's main train station, is a buffet of tourist services. While information desks are jammed with travelers, very handy red info kiosks at the head of the tracks can answer your simple questions.

Along track 24, about 100 yards down, you'll find the **TI** (daily 8:00–20:30), a **post office** (Mon-Fri 8:30–14:00, Sat 8:30–13:00, closed Sun), a **hotel booking** office, and **car rental** desks. The **baggage storage** (*deposito bagagli*) is downstairs (€4/5 hours, then cheaper, daily 6:00–24:00).

The **"Leonardo Express" train** to Fiumicino Airport runs from track 25; access is at the very far end of track 24. A good self-service **cafeteria,** Ciao, is near the head of track 24, upstairs, with fine views (daily 11:00–22:30).

Near track 1, you'll find a **pharmacy** (daily 7:30–22:00); along the same track is a **waiting room** and **train information** office (daily 6:00–24:00). The handy **Drugstore Conad,** selling everything from groceries to electronics, is just downstairs (daily 6:00–24:00).

Elsewhere in the station are **ATMs,** late-hours banks, and 24-hour thievery. In the station's main entrance lobby, **Borri Books** sells books in English, including popular fiction, Italian history and culture, and kids' books, plus maps upstairs (daily 7:00–23:00).

Termini is also a local transportation hub. The city's two Metro lines (A and B) intersect at Termini Metro station (downstairs). Buses (including Rome's hop-on, hop-off bus tours—see "Tours in Rome," later) leave across the square directly in front of the main station hall. The Metro and bus areas are under construction until sometime in 2011—look for signs directing you to the Metro platform or bus stop. Taxis queue in front; avoid con men hawking "express taxi" services in unmarked cars (only use ones marked with the word *taxi* and a phone number). To avoid the long taxi line, simply hike out past the buses to the main street and hail one.

From Termini, most of my recommended hotels are easily accessible by foot (for those near this train station) or by Metro (for those in the Colosseum and Vatican neighborhoods).

The station has some sleazy sharks with official-looking business cards; avoid anybody selling anything unless they're in a legitimate shop at the station.

By Train or Bus at Tiburtina Station: Tiburtina, Rome's second-largest train station, is located in the city's northeast corner. In general, slower trains (from Milan, Bolzano, Bologna, Udine, and Reggio di Calabria) and some night trains (from Munich, Milan, Venice, Innsbruck, and Udine) use Tiburtina, as does the night bus to Fiumicino Airport. Direct night trains from Paris and Vienna use Termini Station instead. However, as Tiburtina is being redeveloped for high-speed rail, it's likely that additional major trains will soon begin using the station.

Tiburtina is better known as a hub for bus service to destinations all across Italy. Buses depart from the piazza in front of the station. Ticket offices are located in the piazza and around the

ROME

corner on Circonvallazione Nomentana.

Within the train station are a **currency-exchange office** and a 24-hour **grocery.** Tiburtina Station is on Metro line B, with easy connections to Termini (a straight shot, four stops away) and the entire Metro system. Or take bus #492 from Tiburtina to various city-center stops (such as Piazza Barberini, Piazza Venezia, and Piazza Cavour) and the Vatican neighborhood.

By Car: The Grande Raccordo Anulare circles greater Rome. This ring road has spokes that lead you into the center. Entering from the north, leave the autostrada at the Settebagni exit. Following the ancient Via Salaria (and the black-and-white *Centro* signs), work your way doggedly into the Roman thick of things. This will take you along the Villa Borghese Gardens and dump you right on Via Veneto in downtown Rome. Avoid rush hour and drive defensively: Roman cars stay in their lanes like rocks in an avalanche.

Parking in Rome is dangerous. Park near a police station or get advice at your hotel. The Villa Borghese underground garage is handy (Metro: Spagna). Garages charge about €24 per day.

Consider this: Your car is a worthless headache in Rome. Avoid a pile of stress and save money by parking at the huge, easy, and relatively safe lot behind the train station in the hill town of Orvieto (follow *P* signs from autostrada) and catching the train to Rome (hourly, 60–90 minutes).

If you absolutely must drive and park a car in Rome, try to avoid commuter traffic by arriving Friday evening, or anytime during the weekend, and by leaving town during the weekend. Park your car at Tiburtina station (€1/hour, www.atac.roma.it) and take a 10-minute ride on the Metro line B into the center.

By Plane: For information on Rome's airports and connections into the city, see page 822.

Helpful Hints

Sightseeing Tips: Avid sightseers can save money by buying the Roma Pass (see "Tips on Sightseeing in Rome" sidebar), available at TIs and participating sights—buy one before visiting the Colosseum or Forum, and you can skip the long lines there. If you want to see the Borghese Gallery, remember to reserve ahead (see page 752). To bypass the long Vatican Museum line, reserve an entry time online (see page 760 for details).

Internet Access: If your hotel doesn't offer free or cheap Internet access, your hotelier can point you to the nearest Internet café. Remember to bring your passport, which you may be asked to show before going online.

Bookstores: These stores (all open daily except Anglo American

Daily Reminder

Sunday: These sights are closed—the Vatican Museum (except for the last Sunday of the month, when it's free and even more crowded), Villa Farnesina, Santa Susanna Church, and the Catacombs of San Sebastiano. In the morning, the Porta Portese flea market hops, and the old center is delightfully quiet.

Monday: Many sights are closed, including the National Museum of Rome, Borghese Gallery, Capitoline Museums, Catacombs of Priscilla, Museum of the Bath (at the Baths of Diocletian), Museum of the Imperial Forums (includes Trajan's Market and Trajan's Forum), Castel Sant'Angelo, Ara Pacis, Montemartini Museum, E.U.R.'s Museum of Roman Civilization, Etruscan Museum, Museum of the Liberation of Rome, some Appian Way sights (Tomb of Cecilia Metella, Circus and Villa of Maxentius, and the San Sebastiano Gate and Museum of the Walls), and Ostia Antica. Many of the ancient sights (e.g., Colosseum and Forum) and the Vatican Museum, among others, are open. Churches are open as usual. The Baths of Caracalla closes early in the afternoon.

Tuesday: All sights are open in Rome. This isn't a good day to side-trip to Naples because its Archaeological Museum is closed.

Wednesday: All sights are open, except for the Catacombs of San Callisto. St. Peter's Basilica may be closed in the morning for a papal audience.

Thursday: All sights are open (though the Cappuccin Crypt occasionally closes).

Friday: All sights are open in Rome.

Saturday: Most sights are open in Rome, except for the Synagogue, Jewish Museum, and Santa Susanna Church.

and Open Door) sell travel guidebooks, including mine. The first two are chains, while the others have a more personal touch. **Borri Books** is at Termini train station, and **Feltrinelli International** has two branches (at Largo Argentina, and just off Piazza della Repubblica at Via Vittorio Emanuele Orlando 84, tel. 06-482-7878). **Anglo American Bookshop** has great art and history sections (closed Sun and Mon morning, a few blocks south of Spanish Steps at Via della Vite 102, tel. 06-679-5222). **Libreria Fanucci** is centrally located (a block toward the Pantheon from Piazza Navona at Piazza Madama 8, tel. 06-686-1141). In Trastevere, Irishman Dermot at the **Almost Corner Bookshop** stocks an Italian-interest section (Via del Moro 45, tel. 06-583-6942), and the **Open Door**

Bookshop carries the only used books in English in town (closed Sun, Via della Lungaretta 23, tel. 06-589-6478).

Laundry: Your hotelier can direct you to the nearest launderette. The **ondablu** chain usually comes with Internet access; one of their more central locations is near Termini train station (€2/hour, about €8 to wash and dry a 15-pound load, usually open daily 8:00–22:00, Via Principe Amedeo 70b, tel. 06-474-4647).

Travel Agencies: You can get train tickets and railpass-related reservations and supplements at travel agencies (at little or no additional cost), avoiding a trip to a train station. Your hotelier will know of a convenient agency nearby. The **American Express** office near the Spanish Steps sells train tickets and makes reservations for no extra fee (Mon–Fri 9:00–17:30, Sat 9:00–12:30, closed Sun, Piazza di Spagna 38, tel. 06-67641).

Dealing with (and Avoiding) Problems

Theft Alert: While violent crime is rare in the city center, petty theft is rampant. With sweet-talking con artists meeting you at the station, well-dressed pickpockets on buses, and thieving gangs of children at the ancient sites, Rome is a gauntlet of rip-offs. While it's not as bad as it was a few years ago, and pickpockets don't want to hurt you—they usually just want your money—green or sloppy tourists will be scammed. Thieves strike when you're distracted. Don't trust kind strangers. Keep nothing important in your pockets. Be most on guard while boarding and leaving buses and subways. Thieves crowd the door, then stop and turn while others crowd and push from behind. You'll find less crowding and commotion—and less risk—waiting for the end cars of a subway rather than the middle cars. The sneakiest thieves pretend to be well-dressed businessmen (generally with something in their hands), or tourists wearing fanny packs and toting cameras and even Rick Steves guidebooks.

Scams abound: Don't give your wallet to self-proclaimed "police" who stop you on the street, warn you about counterfeit (or drug) money, and ask to see your cash. If a bank machine eats your ATM card, see if there's a thin plastic insert with a tongue hanging out that thieves use to extract it.

If you know what to look out for, fast-fingered moms with babies and gangs of children picking the pockets and handbags of naive tourists are not a threat, but an interesting, albeit sad, spectacle. Pickpockets troll through the tourist crowds around the Colosseum, Forum, Piazza della Repubblica, and train and Metro stations. Watch them target tourists who are

Tips on Sightseeing in Rome

These tips will help you use your time and money efficiently, making the Eternal City seem less eternal and more entertaining. For general advice on sightseeing, see page 17.

Roma Pass: Rome offers several sightseeing passes to help you save money. For most visitors, the Roma Pass (www.romapass.it) is the clear winner. The Roma Pass costs €25 and is valid for three days, covering public transportation and free or discounted entry to Roman sights. You get free admission to your first two sights (where you also get to skip the ticket line), and then a discount on the rest within the three-day window. Sights covered (or discounted) by the pass include the following: Colosseum/Palatine Hill/Roman Forum, Borghese Gallery (though you still must make a reservation and pay the €2-3 booking fee), Capitoline Museums, Castel Sant'Angelo, Montemartini Museum, Ara Pacis, Museum of Roman Civilization, Etruscan Museum, Baths of Caracalla, Trajan's Market, and some of the Appian Way sights. The pass also covers all four branches of the National Museum of Rome, considered as a single "sight": Palazzo Massimo (clearly the most important of the lot), Museum of the Bath at the Baths of Diocletian (Roman inscriptions), Crypta Balbi (medieval art), and Palazzo Altemps (sculpture collection).

If you'll be visiting any two of the major sights in a three-day period, get the pass. It's sold at participating sights, TIs, and even the Colosseum *tabacchi* shop. Try to buy it at a less-crowded TI or sight. Don't bother to order it online because you have to physically pick up the pass in Rome, negating any time-saving advantage.

Validate your Roma Pass by writing your name and validation date on the card. Then insert it directly into the turnstile at your first two (free) sights. At other sights, show it at the ticket office to get your reduced *(ridotto)* price—about 30 percent off.

To get the most out of your pass, visit the two most expensive sights first—for example, the Colosseum (€12) and the National Museum (€10). Definitely use it to bypass the long ticket line at the Colosseum. For sights that normally sell a combined ticket (such as the Colosseum/Palatine Hill/Roman Forum or the four National Museum branches), visiting the combined sight counts as a single entry.

The Roma Pass comes with a three-day transit pass. Write your name and birth date on the transit pass, validate it on your first bus or Metro ride by passing it over a sensor at a turnstile or validation machine (look for a yellow circle), and you can take unlimited rides within Rome's city limits until midnight of the third day.

ROME

The TI's other passes—Roma and Pui Pass ("Rome and More") and the Archeologia Card—are generally not worth the trouble for most tourists.

Combo-Ticket for Colosseum, Forum, and Palatine Hill: A €12 combo-ticket covers these three adjacent sights (no individual tickets are sold per sight). The combo-ticket allows one entry per sight, and is valid for two days. Note that these sights are also covered by the Roma Pass. To avoid ticket-buying lines at the Colosseum and Forum, purchase your combo-ticket or Roma Pass at the lesser-visited Palatine Hill. If you're deciding between the combo-ticket or Roma Pass, the pass is the better deal, unless you're planning on seeing only the sights covered by the combo-ticket.

Museum Reservations: The marvelous Borghese Gallery requires reservations well in advance (for specifics, see page 752). You can reserve online to avoid long lines at the Vatican Museum (see page 760).

Opening Hours: Rome's sights have notoriously variable hours from season to season. Get a current listing of opening times from one of Rome's TIs—ask for the free booklet *Museums of Rome*. Or check online at www.060608.it (click on "Culture and Leisure"; although the pages are in English, search by using the Italian names of sights). On holidays, expect shorter hours or closures.

Churches: Many churches, which have divine art and free entry, open early (around 7:00–7:30), close for lunch (roughly 12:00–15:00), and close late (about 19:00). Kamikaze tourists maximize their sightseeing hours by visiting churches before 9:00 or late in the day, and during the siesta, seeing major sights that stay open all day (St. Peter's, Colosseum, Forum, Capitoline Museums, and National Museum of Rome). Many churches have "modest dress" requirements, which means no bare shoulders, miniskirts, or shorts—for men, women, or children. However, this dress code is only strictly enforced at St. Peter's Basilica and St. Paul's Outside the Walls. Elsewhere, you'll see many tourists in shorts (but not skimpy shorts) touring churches.

Picnic Discreetly: Public drinking and eating is no longer allowed at major sights, though the ban is proving difficult to enforce. To avoid the risk of being fined, choose an empty piazza for your picnic, or keep a low profile.

Miscellaneous Tips: I carry a plastic water bottle and refill it at Rome's many public drinking spouts. Because public restrooms are scarce, use toilets at museums, restaurants, and bars.

overloaded with bags or distracted with a video camera. The kids look like beggars and hold up newspapers or cardboard signs to confuse their victims. They scram like stray cats if you're on to them.

Reporting Losses: To report lost or stolen passports and documents, or to make an insurance claim, you must file a police report (at Termini train station, with *polizia* at track 11 or with carabinieri at track 20; offices are also at Piazza Venezia). To replace a passport, file the police report, then call your embassy to make an appointment (US embassy: tel. 06-46741, Via Vittorio Veneto 121, www.usembassy.it). To report lost or stolen credit cards, see page 14.

Emergency Numbers: Police—tel. 113. Ambulance—tel. 118.

Pedestrian Safety: Your main safety concern in Rome is crossing streets safely, using extreme caution. Scooters don't need to stop at red lights, and even cars exercise what drivers call the "logical option" of not stopping if they see no oncoming traffic. As noisy gasoline-powered scooters are replaced by electric ones, they'll be quieter (hooray) but more dangerous for pedestrians. Follow locals like a shadow when you cross a street (or spend a good part of your visit stranded on curbs). When you do cross alone, don't be a deer in the headlights. Find a gap in the traffic and walk with confidence while making eye contact with approaching drivers—they won't hit you if they can tell where you intend to go.

Staying/Getting Healthy: The siesta is a key to survival in summertime Rome. Lie down and contemplate the extraordinary power of gravity in the Eternal City. I drink lots of cold, refreshing water from Rome's many drinking fountains (the Forum has three).

There's a pharmacy (marked by a green cross) in every neighborhood. Several pharmacies stay open late in Termini train station (daily 7:30–22:00) and at Piazza dei Cinquecento 51 (open 24 hours daily, next to Termini train station on the corner of Via Cavour, tel. 06-488-0019).

Embassies can recommend English-speaking doctors. Consider MEDline, a 24-hour home-medical service; doctors speak English and make calls at hotels for €150–180 (tel. 06-808-0995). Anyone is entitled to free emergency treatment at public hospitals. The hospital closest to Termini train station is Policlinico Umberto 1 (entrance for emergency treatment on Via Lancisi, translators available, Metro: Policlinico). The American Hospital, a private hospital on the edge of town, is accustomed to helping Yankees (Via Emilio Longoni 69, tel. 06-22-551).

Getting Around Rome

Sightsee on foot, by city bus, by Metro, or by taxi. I've grouped

your sightseeing into walkable neighborhoods. Make it a point to visit sights in a logical order. Needless backtracking wastes precious time.

The public-transportation system, which is cheap and efficient, consists primarily of buses, a few trams, and the two underground subway (Metro) lines. Consider it part of your Roman experience.

Buying Tickets

All public transportation uses the same ticket (€1, valid for one Metro ride—including transfers underground—plus unlimited city buses and *elettrico* buses during a 75-minute period). Passes good on buses and the Metro are sold in increments of one day (€4, good until midnight), three days (€11), and one week (€16, about the cost of two taxi rides).

You can purchase tickets and passes at some newsstands, tobacco shops (*tabacchi*, marked by a black-and-white *T* sign), and major Metro stations and bus stops, but not onboard. It's smart to stock up on tickets early, or to buy a pass or a Roma Pass (which includes a three-day transit pass—see page 696). That way, you don't have to run around searching for an open *tabacchi* when you spot your bus approaching. Metro stations rarely have human ticket-sellers, and the machines are often either broken or require exact change (it helps to insert your smallest coin first).

Validate your ticket by sticking it in the Metro turnstile (magnetic strip–side up, arrow-side first) or in the machine when you board the bus (magnetic strip–side down, arrow-side first)—watch others and imitate. To get through a Metro turnstile with a transit pass or Roma Pass, use it just like a ticket (on buses, however, you only need to validate your pass if that's your first time using it).

If the validation machine won't work, you can ride with your ticket unstamped, but you must write the date, time, and bus number on it, or risk getting fined. For more information, visit www.atac.roma.it (which has a useful route planner in English), or call 800-431-784 or 06-57-003.

Rome's Metro

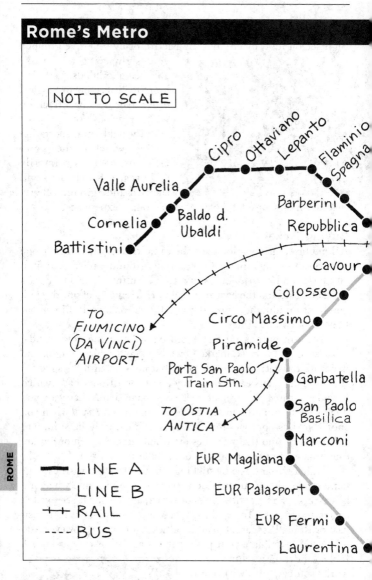

NOT TO SCALE

Cipro
Ottaviano
Lepanto
Flaminio
Spagna
Valle Aurelia
Barberini
Cornelia
Baldo d. Ubaldi
Repubblica
Battistini

TO FIUMICINO (DA VINCI) AIRPORT

Cavour
Colosseo
Circo Massimo
Piramide

Porta San Paolo Train Stn.

TO OSTIA ANTICA

Garbatella
San Paolo Basilica
Marconi
EUR Magliana
EUR Palasport
EUR Fermi
Laurentina

━━━ LINE A
━━━ LINE B
+++ RAIL
---- BUS

By Metro

The Roman subway system (Metropolitana, or "Metro") is simple, with two clean, cheap, fast lines—A and B—that intersect at Termini train station. The Metro runs from 5:30 to 23:30 (Fri–Sat until 1:30 in the morning). The subway's first and last compartments are generally the least crowded (and the least likely to harbor pickpockets).

You'll notice lots of big holes in the city as a new line is built.

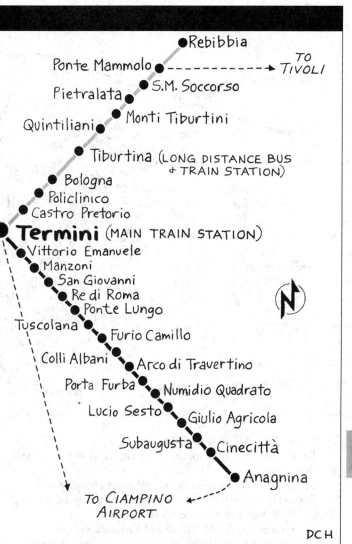

Rebibbia

Ponte Mammolo — — — — — → TO TIVOLI

S.M. Soccorso

Pietralata

Monti Tiburtini

Quintiliani

Tiburtina (LONG DISTANCE BUS & TRAIN STATION)

Bologna

Policlinico

Castro Pretorio

Termini (MAIN TRAIN STATION)

Vittorio Emanuele

Manzoni

San Giovanni

Re di Roma

Ponte Lungo

Tuscolana

Furio Camillo

Colli Albani

Arco di Travertino

Porta Furba

Numidio Quadrato

Lucio Sesto

Giulio Agricola

Subaugusta

Cinecittà

Anagnina

TO CIAMPINO AIRPORT

DCH

Line C, from the Colosseum to Largo Argentina, will likely be done in 2020.

While much of Rome is not served by its skimpy subway, the following stops are helpful:

Termini (intersection of lines A and B): Termini train station, shuttle train to airport, National Museum of Rome, and recommended hotels

Repubblica (line A): Baths of Diocletian/Octagonal Hall,

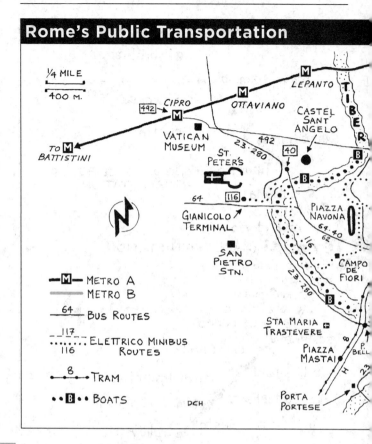

Rome's Public Transportation

¼ MILE
400 M.

CIPRO
LEPANTO
OTTAVIANO
CASTEL SANT ANGELO
TIBER
492
TO BATTISTINI
VATICAN MUSEUM
ST. PETER'S
23·280
492
40
64
116
GIANICOLO TERMINAL
PIAZZA NAVONA
64·40
62
SAN PIETRO STN.
116
23·280
CAMPO DE' FIORI

M — METRO A
—— METRO B
64 — BUS ROUTES
117 / 116 — ELETTRICO MINIBUS ROUTES
8 — TRAM
B — BOATS

STA. MARIA TRASTEVERE
PIAZZA MASTAI
P. BELL
PORTA PORTESE

DCH

Via Nazionale, and recommended hotels

Barberini (line A): Cappuccin Crypt, Trevi Fountain, and Villa Borghese

Spagna (line A): Spanish Steps, and classy shopping area

Flaminio (line A): Piazza del Popolo, start of recommended "Dolce Vita Stroll" down Via del Corso

Ottaviano (line A): St. Peter's and Vatican City

Cipro (line A): Vatican Museum and recommended hotels

Tiburtina (line B): Tiburtina train and bus station

Colosseo (line B): Colosseum, Roman Forum, bike rental, and recommended hotels

Piramide (line B): Protestant Cemetery and trains to Ostia Antica

E.U.R. (line B): Mussolini's futuristic suburb

By Bus

The Metro is handy, but it won't get you everywhere—take the

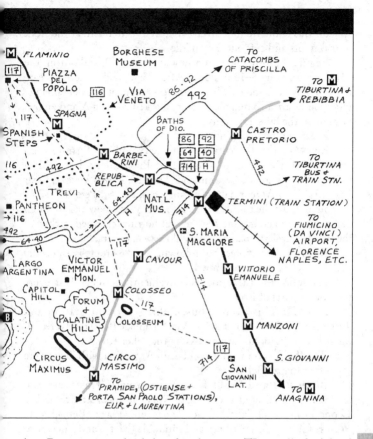

ROME

bus. Bus routes are clearly listed at the stops. TIs usually don't have bus maps, but with some knowledge of major stops, you won't necessarily need one (though if you do want a route map, buy it from *tabacchi* shops; bus info: www.atac.roma.it with good route planner in English, or tel. 06-57003, usually not in English).

Buses (especially the touristy #40 and #64) are havens for thieves and pickpockets. Assume any commotion is a thief-created distraction. If one bus is packed, there's likely a second one on its tail with far fewer crowds and thieves. Once you know the bus system, you'll find it's easier than searching for a cab.

Tickets have a barcode and must be stamped on the bus in the yellow box with the digital readout (be sure to retrieve your ticket). Validate your ticket as you board (magnetic strip–side down, arrow-side first), or you are cheating. While relatively safe, riding without a stamped ticket on the bus is stressful. Inspectors fine even innocent-looking tourists €50. Remember that there's no need to validate a transit pass or Roma Pass on the bus, unless your pass is new and hasn't yet been stamped elsewhere in the transit system. Bus etiquette (not always followed) is to board at the front or rear doors and exit out the middle.

Regular bus lines start running at about 5:30, and during the day they run every 5–10 minutes. After 23:30, and sometimes earlier (such as on Sundays), buses are less frequent but dependable. Night buses are also reliable, and are marked with an *N* and an owl symbol on the bus-stop signs.

These are the major bus routes:

Bus #64: This bus cuts across the city, linking Termini train station with the Vatican, stopping at Piazza della Repubblica (sights), Via Nazionale (recommended hotels), Piazza Venezia (near Forum), Largo Argentina (near Pantheon), and St. Peter's Basilica (get off just past the tunnel). Ride it for a city overview and to watch pickpockets in action. The #64 can get horribly crowded, awkward for female travelers uncomfortably close to male strangers.

Bus #40: This express bus following the #64 route is especially helpful—fewer stops and crowds.

The following three routes conveniently connect Trastevere with other parts of Rome:

Bus #H: This express bus, linking Termini Station and Trastevere, makes a few stops on Via Nazionale (for Trastevere, get off at Piazza Belli, just after crossing the Tiber River).

Bus #8: This tram connects Largo Argentina with Trastevere (get off at Piazza Belli).

Buses #23 and #280: Link Vatican with Trastevere and Testaccio, stopping at the Vatican Museum (nearest stop is Via Leone IV), Castel Sant'Angelo, Trastevere (Piazza Belli), Porta Portese (Sunday flea market), and Piramide (Metro and gateway to Testaccio).

Here are other useful routes:

Bus #62: Largo Argentina to St. Peter's Square.

Bus #81: San Giovanni in Laterano, Largo Argentina, and Piazza Risorgimento (Vatican).

Buses #85 and #87: Piazza Venezia, Colosseum, San Clemente, and San Giovanni in Laterano.

Bus #492: Travels east–west across the city, connecting Tiburtina (train and bus stations), Piazza Barberini, Piazza Venezia, Piazza Cavour (Castel Sant'Angelo), and Piazza Risorgimento (Vatican).

Bus #714: Termini train station, Santa Maria Maggiore, San Giovanni in Laterano, Terme di Caracalla (Baths of Caracalla), and on to E.U.R.

Elettrico Minibuses: Two cute *elettrico* minibuses wind through the narrow streets of old and interesting neighborhoods, and are great for transport or simple joyriding:

Elettrico **#116:** Through the medieval core of Rome: Ponte Vittorio Emanuele II (near Castel Sant'Angelo) to Campo de' Fiori, Pantheon, Piazza Barberini, and the southern edge of the scenic Villa Borghese Gardens.

Elettrico **#117:** San Giovanni in Laterano, Colosseo, Via dei Serpenti, Trevi Fountain, Piazza di Spagna, and Piazza del Popolo.

By Taxi

I use taxis in Rome more often than in other cities. They're reasonable and useful for efficient sightseeing in this big, hot metropolis. Taxis start at €2.80, then charge about €1.30 per kilometer (surcharges: €1 on Sun, €3 for nighttime hours of 22:00–7:00, one regular suitcase or bag rides free, tip by rounding up to the nearest euro). Sample fares: Termini train station to Vatican-€10; Termini train station to Colosseum-€6; Colosseum to Trastevere-€7 (or look up your route at www.worldtaximeter.com). Three or four companions with more money than time should taxi almost everywhere.

It's tough to wave down a taxi in Rome, especially at night. Find the nearest taxi stand by asking a passerby or a clerk in a shop, *"Dov'è una fermata dei taxi?"* (doh-VEH OO-nah fehr-MAH-tah DEHee TAHK-see). Some taxi stands are listed on my maps. To save time and energy, have your hotel or restaurant call a taxi for you; the meter starts when the call is received (generally adding a euro or two to the bill). To call a cab on your own, dial 06-4994 or 06-6645. It's routine for Romans to ask the waiter in a restaurant to call a taxi when they ask for the bill. The waiter will tell you how many minutes you have to enjoy your coffee.

Beware of corrupt taxis. A common cabbie scam is to take your €20 note, drop it, and pick up a €5 note (similar color), claiming that's what you gave him. To avoid this scam, pay in small bills; if you only have a large bill, show it to the cabbie as you state its face value.

If hailing a cab on the street, be sure the meter is restarted when you get in (should be around €2.80, or around €5 if you or your hotelier phoned for the taxi). Many meters show both the fare and the time elapsed during the ride—and some tourists pay €10 for an eight-and-a-half-minute trip (more than the fair meter rate).

When you arrive at the train station or airport, beware of hustlers conning naive visitors into unmarked rip-off "express taxis." Only use official taxis, with a *taxi* sign and phone number marked on the door. By law, they must display a multilingual official price chart. If you have any problems with a taxi, point to the chart and ask the cabbie to explain it to you. Making a show of writing down the taxi number (to file a complaint) can motivate a driver to quickly settle the matter.

If you take a Rome city cab from the airport to anywhere in central Rome within the old city walls, the cost should be €45 (covering up to four people and their bags); however, every year some readers report being ripped off. The catch is that cabbies not based in Rome can charge €60. At the airport, look specifically for a Rome city cab, with the "SPQR" shield on the door. By law, they can charge only €45 for the ride.

Tired travelers arriving at the airport will likely find it less stressful to take the airport shuttle van to their hotel, or catch the train to Termini train station and take the Metro or a cheaper taxi from there (see page 822 for details on getting from the airport to downtown Rome via taxi, shuttle, or train).

By Bike

Biking in the big city of Rome can speed up sightseeing or simply be an enjoyable way to explore. Though Roman traffic can be stressful, Roman drivers are respectful of cyclists. The best rides are on small streets in the city center. A bike path along the banks of the Tiber River makes a good 20-minute ride (easily accessed from the ramps at Porta Portese and Ponte Regina Margherita near Piazza del Popolo). Get a bike with a well-padded seat—the little stones that pave Roman streets are unforgiving.

Top Bike Rental and Tours is professionally run by Roman bike enthusiasts who want to show off their city. Your rental comes with a handy map that suggests a route and indicates less-trafficked streets. Ciro and Marta also offer four-hour-long English-only guided tours around the city and the Ancient Appian Way; check their website for days and times (rental: €8/half-day, €13/day, 10 percent discount with this book, best to reserve in advance via email; bike tours: start at €29, reservations required; daily 9:30–19:00, leave ID for deposit, from Santa Maria Maggiore TI kiosk take Via dell'Olmata and turn left one block down, Via dei Quattro Cantoni 40, tel. 06-488-2893, www.topbikerental.com, info@topbikerental.com).

Cool Rent, near the Colosseo Metro stop, is cheaper but less helpful (€3/hour, €10/day, 3-person bike cart-€10/hour, daily 9:30–20:00, driver's license or other ID for deposit, 10 yards to the right as you exit the Metro). A second outlet is just off Via del Corso (on Largo di Lombardi, near corner of Via del Corso and Via della Croce).

By Car with Driver

You can hire your own private car with driver through Autoservizi Monti Concezio, run by gentle, capable, and English-speaking

Ezio (car-€35/hour, minibus-€40/hour, 3-hour minimum for city sightseeing, long rides outside Rome are more expensive, mobile 335-636-5907 or 349-674-5643, www.montitours.com, concezio monti@gmail.com).

Tours in Rome

Walking Tours

Finding the best guided tours in Rome is challenging. Local guides are good but pricey. Tour companies are cheaper, but quality and organization are unreliable. To help, I've produced a series of free audio tours that illuminate the major sights and neighborhoods, covered the way my readers appreciate.

You have several main tour options: Download my audio tours to your iPod or other MP3 player (easy, perfectly reliable, and free—see next page for details); hire a private Italian guide (around €150–180 for a half-day tour—those listed here are excellent and worth every euro, if you can afford it); organize a group of 4–6 people from your hotel to split the cost of hiring a private guide (this ends up costing about the same as joining a tour from one of the companies listed here); or go on a scheduled walking tour with one of the companies listed below (about €25, generally expat guides).

Local Guides—Consider hiring your own personal tour guide. I've worked with each of these licensed independent local guides. They speak excellent English, and enjoy tailoring tours to your interests. Their prices (roughly €50/hour, €180/half-day) flex with the day, season, and demand. Arrange your date and price by email.

Francesca Caruso loves to teach and share her appreciation of her city, and has contributed generously to this chapter (francesca inroma@gmail.com). Popular with my readers, Francesca understandably books up quickly; if she's busy, she'll recommend one of her colleagues. **Carla Zaia** is an engaging expert on all things Roman (mobile 349-759-0723, carlaromeguide@gmail.com). **Cristina Giannicchi** has an archaeology background (mobile 338-111-4573, www.crisacross.com, crisgiannicchi@gmail.com). **Sara Magister** is a Roman with a doctorate in art history, who wrote a book on Renaissance Rome (tel. 06-583-6783, mobile 339-379-3813, a.magister@iol.it). **Giovanna Terzulli** is a personable, knowledgeable art historian (terzulli@tiscali.it).

Walking-Tour Companies—Rome has many highly competitive tour companies, each offering a series of themed walks through various slices of Rome. Three-hour guided walks generally cost €25–30 per person. Guides are usually native English-speakers, often American expats. Tours are limited to small groups, geared to American tourists, and given in English only. I've listed some here,

ROME

but without a lot of details on their offerings. Before your trip, spend some time on these companies' websites to get to know your options, as each company has a particular teaching and guiding personality. Some are highbrow, and others are less scholarly. It's sometimes required, and always smart, to book a spot in advance (easy online). I must add that we get a lot of negative feedback on some of these tour companies. Readers report that their advertising can be misleading, and that scheduling mishaps are not uncommon.

Context Rome's walking tours are more intellectual than most, designed for travelers with longer-than-average attention spans. They are more expensive than others, and are led by "docents" rather than guides (tel. 06-9762-5204, US tel. 800-691-6036, www.contextrome.com). **Enjoy Rome** offers five different walks and a website filled with helpful information (Via Marghera 8a, tel. 06-445-1843, www.enjoyrome.com, info@enjoyrome.com). **Rome Walks** has put together several particularly creative itineraries (mobile 347-795-5175, www.romewalks.com, info@romewalks .com, Annie). **Roman Odyssey** gives readers of this book a 10 percent discount on their walks and private tours (tel. 06-580-9902, mobile 328-912-3720, www.romanodyssey.com, Rahul). **Through Eternity** offers travelers with this book a 10 percent discount on most tours and a 20 percent discount on its Underground Rome and Secret Rome tours; book through their website for the best discount (tel. 06-700-9336, mobile 347-336-5298, www.through eternity.com, info@througheternity.com, Rob).

Free Rick Steves Audio Tours—With an iPod (or other MP3 player) or a smartphone, you can tour the Colosseum, Roman Forum, Pantheon, St. Peter's Basilica, Sistine Chapel, Trastevere, Jewish Ghetto, Ostia Antica, and Pompeii (download them from www.ricksteves.com, or search for "Rick Steves Audio Tours" in iTunes). If you don't mind me in your ear, these audio tours are hard to beat: Nobody will stand you up, the quality is reliable (if not live), you can take the tour exactly when you like, and they're free.

Hop-on, Hop-off Bus Tours

Several different agencies, including the ATAC public bus company, run hop-on, hop-off tours around Rome. These tours are constantly evolving and offer varying combinations of sights. You can grab one (and pay as you board) at any stop; Termini train station and Piazza Venezia are handy hubs. Although the city is perfectly walkable and traffic jams can make the bus dreadfully slow, these open-top bus tours remain popular.

Trambus #110 seems to be the best. It's operated by the ATAC city-bus lines, and offers an orientation tour on big red double-decker buses with an open-air upper deck. In less than two hours, you'll have 80 sights pointed out to you (with a next-to-worthless recorded narration). While you can hop on and off, the service can be erratic (mobbed midday, not ideal in bad weather) and it can be very slow in heavy traffic. It's best to think of this as a two-hour quickie orientation with scant information and lots of images. The 11 stops include Via Veneto, Via Tritone, Ara Pacis, Piazza Cavour, St. Peter's Square, Corso Vittorio Emanuele (for Piazza Navona), Piazza Venezia, Colosseum, and Via Nazionale. Bus #110 departs every 20 minutes (runs daily 8:30–20:30, tel. 06-684-0901, www .trambusopen.com). Buy the €20 ticket as you board.

Archeobus is an open-top bus, also operated by ATAC, that runs twice hourly from Termini train station out to the Appian Way (with stops at the Colosseum, Baths of Caracalla, San Callisto, San Sebastiano, and the Tomb of Cecilia Metella). This is a handy way to see the sights down this ancient Roman road, but it can be frustrating for various reasons—sparse narration, sporadic service, and not ideal for hopping on and off (€15, €30 combo-ticket with Trambus 110, ticket valid 24 hours, 1.5-hour loop, daily 8:30–16:30, from Termini train station and Piazza Venezia, tel. 06-684-0901, www.trambusopen.com). A similar bus laces together all the Christian sights.

Self-Guided Walks

Here are three walks that give you a moving picture of Rome, an ancient yet modern city. You'll walk through history ("Roman Forum Walk"), take a refreshing early-evening stroll ("Dolce Vita Stroll"), and enjoy the thriving night scene ("Night Walk Across Rome").

Roman Forum Walk

The Forum was the political, religious, and commercial center of the city. Rome's most important temples and halls of justice were here.

This was the place for religious processions, political demonstrations, elections, important speeches, and parades by conquering generals. As Rome's empire expanded, these few acres of land became the center of the civilized world.

Cost: €12 combo-ticket also includes Colosseum and Palatine Hill; ticket valid two consecutive days—one entry per sight; also covered by Roma Pass. If the line at the Forum is long, buy a combo-ticket or Roma Pass nearby at the less-crowded

Roman Forum Walk

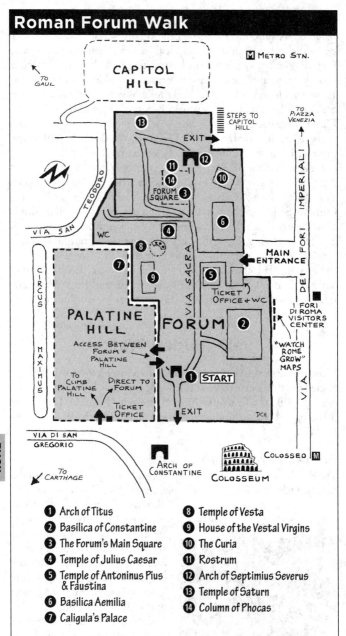

1 Arch of Titus
2 Basilica of Constantine
3 The Forum's Main Square
4 Temple of Julius Caesar
5 Temple of Antoninus Pius & Faustina
6 Basilica Aemilia
7 Caligula's Palace
8 Temple of Vesta
9 House of the Vestal Virgins
10 The Curia
11 Rostrum
12 Arch of Septimius Severus
13 Temple of Saturn
14 Column of Phocas

Palatine Hill entrance on Via di San Gregorio. The Roma Pass is also sold at the *tabacchi* shop at the Colosseum Metro stop.

Hours: The Roman Forum, Colosseum, and Palatine Hill are all open daily 8:30 until one hour before sunset: April–Sept until 19:15, Oct until 18:30, off-season closes as early as 16:30; last entry one hour before closing.

Getting There: The closest Metro stop is Colosseo. The Forum has two entrances. The main entrance is on Via dei Fori Imperiali ("Road of the Imperial Forums"). From the Colosseum Metro stop, walk away from the Colosseum on Via dei Fori Imperiali to find the low-profile Forum ticket office, located where Via Cavour spills into Via dei Fori Imperiali.

The other entrance is at the Palatine Hill ticket office on Via di San Gregorio—after buying your ticket, take the path to the right (not up the hill), and wind around to enter the Forum at the Arch of Titus.

Information: A free visitors center (called I Fori di Roma), located across Via dei Fori Imperiali from the Forum's main entrance, has a TI, bookshop, small café, WCs, and a film (daily 9:30–18:30). A bookstore is at the Forum entrance. Vendors at the Forum sell small *Rome: Past and Present* books with plastic overlays that restore the ruins (includes DVD, smaller book marked €15, prices soft, so offer €10). Info office tel. 06-3996-7700.

Tours: An unexciting yet informative **audioguide** helps decipher the rubble (€4, €6 version includes Palatine Hill, must leave ID), but you'll have to return it to one of the Forum entrances instead of being able to exit directly to Capitol Hill or the Colosseum. Official **guided tours** in English run Monday through Friday at around 13:00 (€4, 45 minutes, confirm time at ticket office). You can also download my free self-guided Roman Forum **audio tour** from www.ricksteves.com (or search for "Rick Steves Audio Tours" in iTunes).

• *Start at the Arch of Titus (Arco di Tito). It's the white triumphal arch that rises above the rubble on the east end of the Forum (closest to the Colosseum). Stand at the viewpoint alongside the arch and gaze over the valley known as the Forum.*

❶ **Arch of Titus (Arco di Tito):** This arch commemorated the Roman victory over the province of Judaea (Israel) in A.D. 70. The Romans had a reputation as benevolent conquerors who tolerated the local customs and rulers. All they required was allegiance to the empire, shown by worshipping the emperor as a god. No problem for most conquered people, who already had half a dozen gods on their prayer lists anyway. But Israelites believed in only one god, and it wasn't the emperor. Israel revolted. After a short but bitter war, the Romans defeated the rebels, took Jerusalem, destroyed their temple (leaving only the foundation wall—today's

Rome: Republic and Empire
(500 B.C.–A.D. 500)

Ancient Rome spanned about a thousand years, from 500 B.C. to A.D. 500. During that time, Rome expanded from a small tribe of barbarians to a vast empire, then dwindled slowly to city size again. For the first 500 years, when Rome's armies made her ruler of the Italian peninsula and beyond, Rome was a republic governed by elected senators. Over the next 500 years, a time of world conquest and eventual decline, Rome was an empire ruled by a military-backed dictator.

Julius Caesar bridged the gap between republic and empire. This ambitious general and politician, popular with the people because of his military victories and charisma, suspended the Roman constitution and assumed dictatorial powers in about 50 B.C. A few years later, he was assassinated by a conspiracy of senators. His adopted son, Augustus, succeeded him, and soon "Caesar" was not just a name but a title.

Emperor Augustus ushered in the Pax Romana, or Roman peace (A.D. 1–200), a time when Rome reached her peak and controlled an empire that stretched even beyond Eurail—from England to Egypt, Turkey to Morocco.

revered "Wailing Wall"), and brought home 50,000 Jewish slaves... who were forced to build this arch (and the Colosseum).

• *Walk down Via Sacra into the Forum. After about 50 yards, turn right and follow a path uphill to the three huge arches of the...*

❷ **Basilica of Constantine (a.k.a. Basilica Maxentius):** Yes, these are big arches. But they represent only one-third of the original Basilica of Constantine, a mammoth hall of justice. The arches were matched by a similar set along the Via Sacra side (only a few squat brick piers remain). Between them ran the central hall, which was spanned by a roof 130 feet high—about 55 feet higher than the side arches you see. (The stub of brick you see sticking up began an arch that once spanned the central hall.) The hall itself was as long as a football field, lavishly furnished with colorful inlaid marble, a gilded bronze ceiling, and statues, and filled with strolling Romans. At the far (west) end was an enormous marble statue of Emperor Constantine on a throne. (Pieces of this statue, including a hand the size of a man, are on display in Rome's Capitoline Museums.)

The basilica was begun by the emperor Maxentius, but after he was trounced in battle (see page 734), the victor Constantine completed the massive building. No doubt about it, the Romans built monuments on a more epic scale than any previous Europeans, wowing their "barbarian" neighbors.

• *Now stroll deeper into the Forum, downhill along Via Sacra, through the trees. Many of the large basalt stones under your feet were walked on by Caesar Augustus 2,000 years ago. Pass by the only original bronze door still swinging on its ancient hinges (the green door at the Tempio di Romolo, on the right) and continue between ruined buildings until Via Sacra opens up to a flat, grassy area.*

❸ **The Forum's Main Square:** The original Forum, or main square, was this flat patch about the size of a football field, stretching to the foot of Capitol Hill. Surrounding it were temples, law courts, government buildings, and triumphal arches.

Rome was born right here. According to legend, twin brothers Romulus (Rome) and Remus were orphaned in infancy and raised by a she-wolf on top of Palatine Hill. Growing up, they found it hard to get dates. So they and their cohorts attacked the nearby Sabine tribe and kidnapped their women. After they made peace, this marshy valley became the meeting place and then the trading center for the scattered tribes on the surrounding hillsides.

The square was the busiest and most crowded—and often the seediest—section of town. Besides the senators, politicians, and currency exchangers, there were even sleazier types—souvenir hawkers, pickpockets, fortune-tellers, gamblers, slave marketers, drunks, hookers, lawyers, and tour guides.

The Forum is now rubble, but imagine it in its prime: blinding white marble buildings with 40-foot-high columns and shining bronze roofs; rows of statues painted in realistic colors; processional chariots rattling down Via Sacra. Mentally replace tourists in T-shirts with tribunes in togas. Imagine the buildings towering and the people buzzing around you while an orator gives a rabble-rousing speech from the Rostrum. If things still look like just a pile of rocks, at least tell yourself, "But Julius Caesar once leaned against these rocks."

• *At the near (east) end of the main square (the Colosseum is to the east) are the foundations of a temple now capped with a peaked wood-and-metal roof.*

❹ **The Temple of Julius Caesar (Tempio del Divo Giulio, or "Ara di Cesare"):** Julius Caesar's body was burned on this spot (under the metal roof) after his assassination. Peek behind the wall into the small apse area, where a mound of dirt usually has fresh flowers—given to remember the man who, more than any other, personified the greatness of Rome.

Caesar (100–44 B.C.) changed Rome—and the Forum—dramatically. He cleared out many of the wooden market stalls and began to ring the square with even grander buildings. Caesar's house was located behind the temple, near that clump of trees. He walked right by here on the day he was assassinated ("Beware the Ides of March!" warned a street-corner Etruscan preacher).

ROME

Though he was popular with the masses, not everyone liked Caesar's urban design or his politics. When he assumed dictatorial powers, he was ambushed and stabbed to death by a conspiracy of senators, including his adopted son, Brutus *("Et tu, Brute?")*.

The funeral was held here, facing the main square. The citizens gathered, and speeches were made. Mark Antony stood up to say (in Shakespeare's words), "Friends, Romans, countrymen, lend me your ears. I come to bury Caesar, not to praise him." When Caesar's body was burned, the citizens who still loved him threw anything at hand on the fire, requiring the fire department to come put it out. Later, Emperor Augustus dedicated this temple in his name, making Caesar the first Roman to become a god.

• *Behind and to the left of the Temple of Julius Caesar are the 10 tall columns of the...*

❺ Temple of Antoninus Pius and Faustina: The Senate built this temple to honor Emperor Antoninus Pius (A.D. 138–161) and his deified wife, Faustina. The 50-foot-tall Corinthian (leafy) columns must have been awe-inspiring to out-of-towners who grew up in thatched huts. Although the temple has been inhabited by a church, you can still see the basic layout—a staircase led to a shaded porch (the columns), which admitted you to the main building (now a church), where the statue of the god sat. Originally, these columns supported a triangular pediment decorated with sculptures.

Picture these columns, with gilded capitals, supporting brightly painted statues in the pediment, and the whole building capped with a gleaming bronze roof. The stately gray rubble of today's Forum is a faded black-and-white photograph of a 3-D Technicolor era.

The building is a microcosm of many of the changes that occurred after Rome fell. In medieval times, the temple was pillaged. Note the diagonal cuts high on the marble columns—a failed attempt by scavengers to cut through the pillars to pull them down for their precious stone. (They used vinegar and rope to cut the marble...but because vinegar also eats through rope, they abandoned the attempt.) In 1550, a church was housed inside the ancient temple. The door shows the street level at the time of Michelangelo. The long staircase was underground until excavated in the 1800s.

• *There's a ramp next to the Temple of A. and F. Walk halfway up it and look to the left to view the...*

❻ Basilica Aemilia: A basilica was a covered public forum, often serving as a Roman hall of justice. In a society that was as legal-minded as America is today, you needed a lot of lawyers—and a big place to put them. Citizens came here to work out matters such as inheritances and building permits, or to sue somebody.

Notice the layout. It was a long, rectangular building. The stubby columns all in a row form one long, central hall flanked by two side aisles. Medieval Christians required a larger meeting hall for their worship services than Roman temples provided, so they used the spacious Roman basilica as the model for their churches. Cathedrals from France to Spain to England, from Romanesque to Gothic to Renaissance, all have the same basic floor plan as a Roman basilica.

• *Return again to the Temple of Julius Caesar. To the right of the temple are the three tall Corinthian columns of the Temple of Castor and Pollux. Beyond that is Palatine Hill—the corner of which may have been...*

❼ Caligula's Palace (a.k.a. the Palace of Tiberius): Emperor Caligula (ruled A.D. 37–41) had a huge palace on Palatine Hill overlooking the Forum. It actually sprawled down the hill into the Forum (some supporting arches remain in the hillside).

Caligula was not a nice person. He tortured enemies, stole senators' wives, and parked his chariot in handicap spaces. But Rome's luxury-loving emperors only added to the glory of the Forum, with each one trying to make his mark on history.

• *To the left of the Temple of Castor and Pollux, find the remains of a small white circular temple.*

❽ The Temple of Vesta: This is perhaps Rome's most sacred spot. Rome considered itself one big family, and this temple represented a circular hut, like the kind that Rome's first families lived in. Inside, a fire burned, just as in a Roman home. And back in the days before lighters and butane, you never wanted your fire to go out. As long as the sacred flame burned, Rome would stand. The flame was tended by priestesses known as Vestal Virgins.

• *Around the back of the Temple of Vesta, you'll find two rectangular brick pools. These stood in the courtyard of the...*

❾ House of the Vestal Virgins: The Vestal Virgins lived in a two-story building surrounding a long central courtyard with these two pools at one end. Rows of statues depicting leading Vestal Virgins flanked the courtyard. This place was the model—both architecturally and sexually—for medieval convents and monasteries.

Chosen from noble families before they reached the age of 10, the six Vestal Virgins served a 30-year term. Honored and revered by the Romans, the Vestals even had their own box opposite the emperor in the Colosseum.

As the name implies, a Vestal took a vow of chastity. If she served her term faithfully—abstaining for 30 years—she was given a huge dowry, and allowed to marry. But if they found any Virgin who wasn't, she was strapped to a funeral car, paraded through the streets of the Forum, taken to a crypt, given a loaf of bread and a lamp...and buried alive. Many women suffered the latter fate.

• *Return to the Temple of Julius Caesar and head to the Forum's west end (opposite from the Colosseum). As you pass alongside the big open space of the Forum's main square, consider how the piazza is still a standard part of any Italian town. It has reflected and accommodated the gregarious and outgoing nature of the Italian people since Roman times.*

Stop at the big, well-preserved brick building (on right) with the triangular roof and look in.

❿ The Curia (Senate House): The Curia was the most important political building in the Forum. While the present building dates from A.D. 283, this was the site of Rome's official center of government since the birth of the republic. (Note that ongoing archaeological work may restrict access to the Curia, as well as the Arch of Septimius Severus—described later—and the exit to Capitol Hill.) Three hundred senators, elected by the citizens of Rome, met here to debate and create the laws of the land. Their wooden seats once circled the building in three tiers; the Senate president's podium sat at the far end. The marble floor is from ancient times. Listen to the echoes in this vast room—the acoustics are great.

Rome prided itself on being a republic. Early in the city's history, its people threw out the king and established rule by elected representatives. Each Roman citizen was free to speak his mind and have a say in public policy. Even when emperors became the supreme authority, the Senate was a power to be reckoned with. The Curia building is well-preserved, having been used as a church since early Christian times. In the 1930s, it was restored and opened to the public as a historic site. (Note: Although Julius Caesar was assassinated in "the Senate," it wasn't here—the Senate was temporarily meeting across town.)

A statue and two reliefs inside the Curia help build our mental image of the Forum. The statue, made of porphyry marble in about A.D. 100 (with its head, arms, and feet now missing), was a tribute to an emperor, probably Hadrian or Trajan. The two relief panels may have decorated the Rostrum. Those on the left show people (with big stone tablets) standing in line to burn their debt records following a government amnesty. The other shows the distribution of grain (Rome's welfare system), some buildings in the background, and the latest fashion in togas.

• *Go back down the Senate steps and find the 10-foot-high wall just to the left of the big arch, marked...*

⓫ Rostrum (Rostra): Nowhere was Roman freedom more apparent than at this "Speaker's Corner." The Rostrum was a raised platform, 10 feet high and 80 feet long, decorated with statues, columns, and the prows of ships (rostra).

On a stage like this, Rome's orators, great and small, tried to

Rome Falls

Remember that Rome lasted 1,000 years—500 years of growth, 200 years of peak power, and 300 years of gradual decay. The fall had many causes, among them the barbar-

ians who pecked away at Rome's borders. Christians blamed the fall on moral decay. Pagans blamed it on Christians. Socialists blamed it on a shallow economy based on the spoils of war. (Republicans blamed it on Democrats.) Whatever the reasons, the far-flung empire could no longer keep its grip on conquered lands, and it pulled back. Barbarian tribes from Germany and Asia attacked the Italian peninsula and even looted Rome itself in A.D. 410, leveling many of the buildings in the Forum. In 476, when the last emperor checked out and switched off the lights, Europe plunged into centuries of igno-rance, poverty, and weak government—the Dark Ages.

But Rome lived on in the Catholic Church. Christianity was the state religion of Rome's last generations. Emperors became popes (both called themselves "Pontifex Maximus"), senators became bishops, orators became priests, and basili-cas became churches. The glory of Rome remains eternal.

draw a crowd and sway public opinion. Mark Antony rose to offer Caesar the laurel-leaf crown of kingship, which Caesar publicly (and hypocritically) refused while privately becoming a dictator. Men such as Cicero railed against the corruption and decadence that came with the city's newfound wealth. In later years, daring citizens even spoke out against the emperors, reminding them that Rome was once free. Picture the backdrop these speakers would have had—a mountain of marble buildings piling up on Capitol Hill.

In front of the Rostrum are trees bearing fruits that were sacred to the ancient Romans: olives (provided food, light, and preservatives), figs (tasty), and wine grapes (made a popular export product).

• *The big arch to the right of the Rostrum is the...*

❷ **Arch of Septimius Severus:** In imperial times, the Rostrum's voices of democracy would have been dwarfed by images of the empire, such as the huge six-story-high Arch of Septimius Severus (A.D. 203). The reliefs commemorate the African-born emperor's battles in Mesopotamia. Near ground level, see soldiers marching captured barbarians back to Rome for the victory parade.

Despite Severus' efficient rule, Rome's empire was crumbling under the weight of its own corruption, disease, decaying infrastructure, and the constant attacks by foreign "barbarians."

· *Pass underneath the Arch of Septimius Severus and turn left. On the slope of Capitol Hill are the eight remaining columns of the...*

⓭ Temple of Saturn: These columns framed the entrance to the Forum's oldest temple (497 B.C.). Inside was a humble, very old wooden statue of the god Saturn. But the statue's pedestal held the gold bars, coins, and jewels of Rome's state treasury, the booty collected by conquering generals.

· *Standing here, at one of the Forum's first buildings, look east at the lone, tall...*

⓮ Column of Phocas: This is the Forum's last monument (A.D. 608), a gift from the powerful Byzantine Empire to a fallen empire—Rome. Given to commemorate the pagan Pantheon's becoming a Christian church, it's like a symbolic last nail in ancient Rome's coffin. After Rome's 1,000-year reign, the city was looted by Vandals, the population of a million-plus shrank to about 10,000, and the once-grand city center—the Forum—was abandoned, slowly covered up by centuries of silt and dirt. In the 1700s, an English historian named Edward Gibbon overlooked this spot from Capitol Hill. Hearing Christian monks singing at these pagan ruins, he looked

out at the few columns poking up from the ground, pondered the "Decline and Fall of the Roman Empire," and thought, "Hmm, that's a catchy title...."

· *There are several ways to exit the Forum:*

1. Exiting past the Arch of Titus lands you at the Colosseum.

2. Exiting near the Arch of Septimius Severus leads you to the stairs up to Capitol Hill.

3. The Forum's main entrance spills you back out onto Via dei Fori Imperiali.

4. From the Arch of Titus, you can climb Palatine Hill to the top—see page 736.

Dolce Vita Stroll

This is the city's chic stroll, from Piazza del Popolo (Metro: Flaminio) down a wonderfully traffic-free section of Via del Corso, and up Via Condotti to the Spanish Steps each evening around 18:00. Saturdays and Sundays are best; leave earlier than 18:00 if you plan to visit the Ara Pacis, which closes at 19:00 (and is closed Mon).

Dolce Vita Stroll

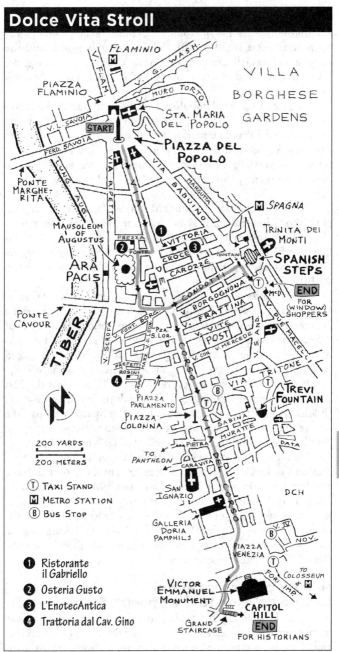

200 YARDS
200 METERS

- Ⓣ TAXI STAND
- Ⓜ METRO STATION
- Ⓑ BUS STOP

❶ Ristorante il Gabriello
❷ Osteria Gusto
❸ L'EnotecAntica
❹ Trattoria dal Cav. Gino

Shoppers, people-watchers, and flirts on the prowl fill this neighborhood of some of Rome's most fashionable stores (some open after siesta 16:30–19:30). While both the crowds and the shops along Via del Corso have gone downhill recently, elegance survives in the grid of streets between this street and the Spanish Steps.

To get to **Piazza del Popolo,** where the stroll starts, take Metro line A to Flaminio and walk south to the square. Delightfully car-free, Piazza del Popolo is marked by an obelisk that was brought to Rome by Augustus after he conquered Egypt. (It used to stand in the Circus Maximus.) In medieval times, this area was just inside Rome's main entry (for more background on the square, see page 756).

The Baroque church of **Santa Maria del Popolo** is worth popping into (Mon–Sat until 19:00, Sun until 19:30, next to gate in old wall on north side of square). Inside, look for Raphael's Chigi Chapel (KEE-gee, second chapel on left) and two paintings by Caravaggio (the side paintings in the Cerasi Chapel, left of altar; see listing on page 757).

From Piazza del Popolo, shop your way down **Via del Corso.** Historians side-trip right down Via Pontefici past the fascist architecture to see the massive rotting round-brick **Mausoleum of Augustus,** topped with overgrown cypress trees. Beyond it, next to the river, is Augustus' **Ara Pacis** (Altar of Peace), now enclosed within a protective glass-walled museum (described on page 759).

From the mausoleum, return to Via del Corso and the 21st century, continuing straight until **Via Condotti.** Window-shoppers should take a left to join the parade to the **Spanish Steps.** The streets that parallel Via Condotti to the south (Borgognona and Frattini) are more elegant, and filled with high-end boutiques.

Historians: Ignore Via Condotti and forget the Spanish Steps. Stay on Via del Corso, which has been straight since Roman times, a half-mile down to the Victor Emmanuel Monument. Climb Michelangelo's stairway to his glorious (especially when flood-lit) square atop Capitol Hill. Stand on the balcony (just past the mayor's palace on the right), which overlooks the Forum. As the horizon reddens and cats prowl the unclaimed rubble of ancient Rome, it's one of the finest views in the city.

Night Walk Across Rome: Campo de' Fiori to the Spanish Steps

Rome can be grueling. But taking an after-dark walk is a fine way to mix romance into all the history, enjoy the cool of the evening, and enliven everything with some of Europe's best people-watching. My favorite nighttime stroll laces together Rome's floodlit nightspots and fine urban spaces with real-life theater vignettes.

Sitting so close to a Bernini fountain that traffic noises evaporate; jostling with local teenagers to see all the gelato flavors; observing lovers straddling more than the bench; jaywalking past *polizia* in flak-proof vests; and marveling at the ramshackle elegance that softens this brutal city for those who were born here and can imagine living nowhere else—these are the flavors of Rome best tasted after dark.

Start this mile-long walk at the great, colorful **Campo de' Fiori,** my favorite outdoor dining room after dark (see page 809 of "Eating in Rome"). The center of the square is marked with a statue of Giordano Bruno, an intellectual heretic who was burned on this spot in 1600. Bruno overlooks this "Field of Flowers," the site of a busy produce market in the morning and a favorite of strollers after sundown. This neighborhood is still known for its free spirit and occasional demonstrations. When the statue of Bruno was erected in 1889, local riots overcame Vatican protests against honoring a heretic. Bruno faces his nemesis, the Vatican Chancellory (the big white building just outside the far-right corner of the square), while his pedestal reads, "And the flames rose up." Check out the reliefs on the pedestal for scenes from Bruno's trial and execution.

At the east end of the square (behind Bruno), the ramshackle apartments are built right into the old outer wall of ancient Rome's mammoth Theater of Pompey. This entertainment complex covered several city blocks, stretching from here to Largo Argentina. Julius Caesar was assassinated in the Theater of Pompey, where the Senate was renting space.

The square is lined with and surrounded by fun eateries. Bruno faces the **Forno** (in the left corner of the square, closed Sun), a popular place for hot and tasty take-out *pizza bianco*. Step in, at least to observe the frenzy as pizza is sold hot out of the oven. You can order *un etto* (100 grams, an average serving) by pointing, then take your snack to the counter to pay. The many bars lining the square are fine for drinks and people-watching. Late at night on weekends, the place is packed with beer-drinking kids, turning what was once a charming medieval square into one vast Roman street party.

If Bruno did a hop, step, and jump forward, then turned right on Via dei Baullari and marched 200 yards, he'd cross the busy Corso Vittorio Emanuele; then, continuing another 150 yards on Via Cuccagna, he'd find **Piazza Navona.** Rome's most interesting night scene features street music, artists, fire-eaters, local Casanovas, ice cream, fountains by Bernini, and outdoor cafés that are worthy of a splurge if you've got time to sit and enjoy Italy's human river.

This oblong square retains the shape of the original racetrack that was built around A.D. 80 by the emperor Domitian. (To see

Night Walk Across Rome

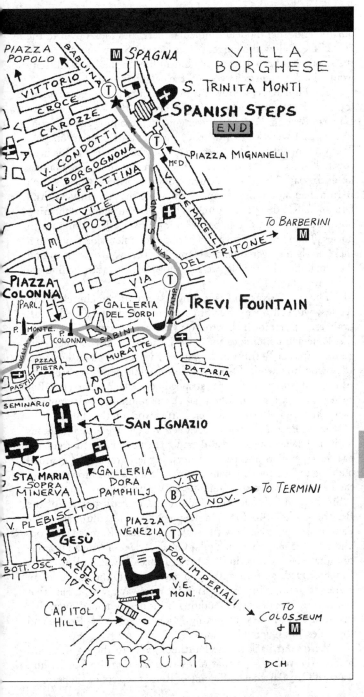

PIAZZA POPOLO

VITTORIO
CROCE
CAROZZE
BABUINA
V. CONDOTTI
V. BORGOGNONA
V. FRATTINA
V. VITE
POST

M SPAGNA
S. TRINITÀ MONTI
SPANISH STEPS
END
PIAZZA MIGNANELLI
McD

VILLA BORGHESE

S. AND.
DUE MACELLI
To BARBERINI M
DEL TRITONE

PIAZZA COLONNA
PARL.
P. MONTE. P. COLONNA
GUGLIA
PZZA PIETRA
PASTINI
SEMINARIO

GALLERIA DEL SORDI
VIA
STAMP.
SABINI
MURATTE
CORSO
DATARIA

TREVI FOUNTAIN

SAN IGNAZIO

STA. MARIA SOPRA MINERVA
V. PLEBISCITO
GESÙ
BOTT. OSC.

GALLERIA DORA PAMPHILJ
B
V. IV
NOV.
To TERMINI

PIAZZA VENEZIA

ARACOELI
CAPITOL HILL
V.E. MON.
FORI IMPERIALI
To COLOSSEUM & M

FORUM

DCH

ROME

the ruins of the original entrance, exit the square at the far—or north—end, then take an immediate left, and look down to the left 25 feet below the current street level.) Since ancient times, the square has been a center of Roman life. In the 1800s, the city would flood the square to cool off the neighborhood.

The **Four Rivers Fountain** in the center is the most famous fountain by the man who remade Rome in Baroque style, Gian Lorenzo Bernini. Four burly river gods (representing the four continents that were known in 1650) support an Egyptian obelisk. The water of the world gushes everywhere. The Nile has his head covered, since the headwaters were unknown then. The Ganges holds an oar. The Danube turns to admire the obelisk, which Bernini had moved here from a stadium on the Appian Way. And Uruguay's Río de la Plata tumbles backward in shock, wondering how he ever made the top four. Bernini enlivens the fountain with horses plunging through the rocks and exotic flora and fauna from these newly discovered lands. Homesick Texans may want to find the armadillo. (It's the big, weird armor-plated creature behind the Plata river statue.)

The Plata river god is gazing upward at the church of St. Agnes, worked on by Bernini's former student–turned-rival, Francesco Borromini. Borromini's concave facade helps reveal the dome and epitomizes the curved symmetry of Baroque. Tour guides say that Bernini designed his river god to look horrified at Borromini's work. Or maybe he's shielding his eyes from St. Agnes' nakedness, as she was stripped before being martyred. But either explanation is unlikely, since the fountain was completed two years before Borromini even started work on the church.

Leave Piazza Navona directly across from Tre Scalini (famous for its rich chocolate ice cream), and go east down Corsia Agonale, past rose peddlers and palm readers. Jog left around the guarded building (where Italy's senate meets), and follow the brown sign to the Pantheon, which is straight down Via del Salvatore.

Sit for a while under the floodlit and moonlit portico of the **Pantheon.** The 40-foot single-piece granite columns of the Pantheon's entrance show the scale the ancient Romans built on. The columns support a triangular Greek-style roof with an inscription that says "M. Agrippa" built it. In fact, it was built *(fecit)* by Emperor Hadrian (A.D. 120), who gave credit to the builder of an earlier structure. This impressive entranceway gives no clue that the greatest wonder of the building is inside—a domed room that inspired later domes, including Michelangelo's St. Peter's and Brunelleschi's Duomo (in Florence).

With your back to the Pantheon, veer to the right, uphill toward the yellow sign that reads *Casa del Caffè* on Via Orfani. **Tazza d'Oro Casa del Caffè,** one of Rome's top coffee shops, dates back to the days when this area was licensed to roast coffee beans. Locals come here for its fine *granita di caffè con panna* (coffee slush with cream).

Continue up Via Orfani to **Piazza Capranica**—home to the big, plain Florentine Renaissance–style Palazzo Capranica (directly opposite as you enter the square). Big shots, like the Capranica family, built towers on their palaces—not for any military use, but just to show off. Leave the piazza to the right of the palace, heading down Via in Aquiro.

The street leads to a sixth-century B.C. **Egyptian obelisk** taken as a trophy by Augustus after his victory in Egypt over Mark Antony and Cleopatra. The obelisk was set up as a sundial. Walk the zodiac markings to the well-guarded front door. This is Italy's **Parliament building,** where the lower house meets, and you may see politicians, political demonstrations, and TV cameras.

To your right is Piazza Colonna, where we're heading next—unless you like gelato...

A two-block detour to the left (past Albergo Nazionale) brings you to Rome's most famous *gelateria.* **Giolitti's** is cheap for take-out or elegant and splurge-worthy for a sit among classy locals (open daily until past midnight, Via Uffici del Vicario 40); get your gelato in a cone *(cono)* or cup *(coppetta).*

Piazza Colonna features a huge second-century column. Its reliefs depict the victories of Emperor Marcus Aurelius over the barbarians. When Marcus died in A.D. 180, the barbarians began to get the upper hand, beginning Rome's long three-century fall. The big, important-looking palace houses the headquarters for the deputies (or cabinet) of the prime minister.

Noisy **Via del Corso** is Rome's main north–south boulevard. It's named for the Berber horse races—without riders—that took place here during Carnevale. This wild tradition continued until the late 1800s, when a series of fatal accidents (including, reportedly, one in front of Queen Margherita) led to its cancellation. Historically the street was filled with meat shops. When it became one of Rome's first gas-lit streets in 1854, these butcher shops were banned and replaced by classier boutiques, jewelers, and antiques dealers. Nowadays most of Via del Corso is closed to traffic for a few hours every evening and becomes a wonderful parade of Romans out for a stroll (see my "Dolce Vita Stroll," earlier).

Cross Via del Corso to enter a big palatial building with columns, which houses the Galleria del Sordi shopping mall. Inside, take the fork to the right and exit out the back. (If you're here after 22:00, when the mall is closed, circle around the right side of the Galleria on Via dei Sabini.) Once out the back, head up Via de Crociferi, to the roar of the water, lights, and people of the Trevi Fountain.

Rome at a Glance

▲▲▲**Colosseum** Huge stadium where gladiators fought. **Hours:** Daily 8:30 until one hour before sunset: April–Sept until 19:15, Oct until 18:30, off-season closes as early as 16:30. See page 729.

▲▲▲**Roman Forum** Ancient Rome's main square, with ruins and grand arches. **Hours:** Same hours as Colosseum. See page 736.

▲▲▲**Pantheon** The defining domed temple. **Hours:** Mon–Sat 8:30–19:30, Sun 9:00–18:00, holidays 9:00–13:00, closed for Mass Sat at 17:00 and Sun at 10:30. See page 744.

▲▲▲**National Museum of Rome** Greatest collection of Roman sculpture anywhere. **Hours:** Tue–Sun 9:00–19:45, closed Mon. See page 747.

▲▲▲**Borghese Gallery** Bernini sculptures and paintings by Caravaggio, Raphael, and Titian. Reservations mandatory. **Hours:** Tue–Sun 9:00–19:00, closed Mon. See page 752.

▲▲▲**Vatican Museum** Four miles of the finest art of Western civilization, culminating in Michelangelo's glorious Sistine Chapel. **Hours:** Mon–Sat 9:00–18:00, last entry at 16:00, they start ushering you out at 17:30. Closed religious holidays and Sun, except last Sun of the month (when it's open 9:00–14:00, last entry at 12:30). May be open some Fri nights April–Oct 19:00–23:00 (last entry at 21:30) by reservation only. Hours are notoriously subject to constant change. See page 760.

▲▲▲**St. Peter's Basilica** Most impressive church on earth, with Michelangelo's *Pietà* and dome. **Hours:** Church—daily April–Sept 7:00–19:00, Oct–March 7:00–18:00, often closed Wed mornings; dome—daily April–Sept 8:00–18:00, Oct–March 8:00–17:00. See page 768.

▲▲**Palatine Hill** Ruins of emperors' palaces, Circus Maximus view, and museum. **Hours:** Same as Colosseum. See page 736.

▲▲**Capitoline Museums** Ancient statues, mosaics, and view of Forum. **Hours:** Tue–Sun 9:00–20:00, closed Mon. See page 741.

▲▲**Ara Pacis** Shrine marking the beginning of Rome's Golden Age. **Hours:** Tue–Sun 9:00–19:00, closed Mon. See page 759.

▲▲**Catacombs** Underground tombs, mainly Christian, outside the city. **Hours:** Generally open 9:00–12:00 & 14:00–17:00. See pages 758 and 788.

ROME

▲**Arch of Constantine** Honors the emperor who legalized Christianity. **Hours:** Always viewable. See page 733.

▲**St. Peter-in-Chains** Church with Michelangelo's *Moses*. **Hours:** Daily 8:00–12:30 & 15:00–19:00, until 18:00 in winter. See page 734.

▲**Trajan's Column** Tall column with narrative relief, on Piazza Venezia. **Hours:** Always viewable. See page 737.

▲**Museum of the Imperial Forums** Includes entry to Trajan's Market. **Hours:** Tue-Sun 9:00–19:00, closed Mon. See page 738.

▲**Capitol Hill Square** Hilltop piazza designed by Michelangelo, with a museum, grand stairway, and Forum overlooks. **Hours:** Always open. See page 739.

▲**Trevi Fountain** Baroque hot spot into which tourists throw coins to ensure a return trip to Rome. **Hours:** Always flowing. See page 747.

▲**Baths of Diocletian** Once ancient Rome's immense public baths, now a Michelangelo church. **Hours:** Mon-Sat 7:00–18:30, Sun 7:00–19:30. See page 748.

▲**Santa Maria della Vittoria** Church with Bernini's swooning *St. Teresa in Ecstasy*. **Hours:** Mon-Sat 8:30–12:00 & 15:30–18:00, Sun 15:30–18:00. See page 749.

▲**Rome from the Sky** Elevator to the top of the Victor Emmanuel Monument for a 360-degree city view. **Hours:** Mon-Thu 9:30–18:30, Fri-Sun 9:30–19:30. See page 744.

▲**Cappuccin Crypt** Decorated with the bones of 4,000 Franciscan friars. **Hours:** Daily 9:00–12:00 & 15:00–18:00, may be closed Thu. See page 756.

▲**Castel Sant'Angelo** Hadrian's Tomb turned castle, prison, papal refuge, now museum. **Hours:** Tue-Sun 9:00–19:30, closed Mon. See page 772.

▲**Galleria Doria Pamphilj** Aristocrat's ornate palace shows off paintings by Caravaggio, Titian, and Raphael. **Hours:** Daily 10:00–17:00. See page 746.

The **Trevi Fountain** shows how Rome took full advantage of the abundance of water brought into the city by its great aqueducts. This watery Baroque avalanche by Nicola Salvi was completed in 1762. Salvi used the palace behind the fountain as a theatrical backdrop for the figure of "Ocean," who represents water in every form. The statue surfs through his wet kingdom—with water gushing from 24 spouts and tumbling over 30 different kinds of plants—while Triton blows his conch shell.

The magic of the square is enhanced by the fact that no streets directly approach it. You can hear the excitement as you approach, and then—*bam!*—you're there. The scene is always lively, with lucky Romeos clutching dates while unlucky ones clutch beers. Romantics toss a coin over their shoulder, thinking it will give them a wish and assure their return to Rome. That may sound silly, but every year I go through this tourist ritual...and it actually seems to work.

Take some time to people-watch (whisper a few breathy *bellos* or *bellas*) before leaving. There's a peaceful zone at water level on the far right.

Facing the Trevi Fountain, go forward, walking along the right side of the fountain on Via della Stamperia. Cross the busy Via del Tritone. Continue 100 yards and veer right at Via delle Fratte, a street that changes its name to Via Propaganda before ending at **Piazza di Spagna,** with the very popular Spanish Steps. The piazza is named for the Spanish Embassy to the Vatican, which has been here for 300 years. It's been the hangout of many Romantics over the years (Keats, Wagner, Openshaw, Goethe, and others). In the 1700s, British aristocrats on the "Grand Tour" of Europe came here to ponder Rome's decay. The British poet John Keats pondered his mortality, then died of tuberculosis at age 25 in the pink building on the right side of the steps. Fellow Romantic Lord Byron lived across the square at #66.

The Sinking Boat Fountain at the foot of the steps, built by Bernini or his father, Pietro, is powered by an aqueduct. Actually, all of Rome's fountains are aqueduct-powered; their spurts are determined by the water pressure provided by the various aqueducts. This one, for instance, is much weaker than Trevi's gush.

The piazza is a thriving night scene. It's clear that the main sight here is not the famous steps, but the people who sit on them. Window-shop along Via Condotti, which stretches away from the steps. This is where Gucci and other big names cater to the trendsetting jet set. Facing the Spanish Steps, you can walk right, about a block, to tour one of the world's biggest and most lavish McDonald's (salad bar, WC).

Our walk is finished. If you'd like to reach the top of the

steps sweat-free, there's a free elevator just outside the Spagna Metro stop (elevator closes at 21:00; Metro stop is to the left of the Spanish Steps). Afterward, you can zip home on the Metro (usually open until 22:00) or grab a taxi at either the north or south side of the piazza.

Sights in Rome

I've clustered Rome's sights into walkable neighborhoods, some quite close together (see the "Rome's Neighborhoods" map on page 689). For example, the Colosseum and the Forum are a few minutes' walk from Capitol Hill; a 10-minute walk beyond that is the Pantheon. I like to group these sights into one great day, starting at the Colosseum and ending at the Pantheon.

Ancient Rome

The core of the ancient city, where the grandest monuments were built, is between the Colosseum and Capitol Hill. To the north, this ancient area flows into the Renaissance at Capitol Hill, then into the modern era at Piazza Venezia.

The Colosseum and Nearby

▲▲▲**Colosseum (Colosseo)**—This 2,000-year-old building is the classic example of Roman engineering. The Romans pioneered

the use of concrete and the rounded arch, which enabled them to build on this tremendous scale. While the essential structure of the Colosseum is Roman, the four-story facade is decorated with mostly Greek columns—Doric-like Tuscan columns on the ground level, Ionic on the second story, Corinthian on the next level, and at the top, half-columns with a mix of all three. Built when the Roman Empire was at its peak in A.D. 80, the Colosseum represents Rome at its grandest. The Flavian Amphitheater (the Colosseum's real name) was an arena for gladiator contests and public spectacles. When killing became a spectator sport, the Romans wanted to share the fun with as many people as possible, so they stuck two semicircular theaters together to create a freestanding amphitheater. The outside (where slender cypress trees stand today) was decorated with a 100-foot-tall bronze statue of Nero that gleamed in the sunlight. In a later age, the colossal structure was nicknamed a "coloss-eum," the wonder of its age. It could accommodate 50,000 roaring fans

Rome

(100,000 thumbs). This was where ancient Romans—whose taste for violence was the equal of modern America's—enjoyed their *Dirty Harry* and *Terminator*. Gladiators, criminals, and wild animals fought to the death in every conceivable scenario. The bit of reconstructed Colosseum floor gives you an accurate sense of the original floor and the subterranean warren where animals were held, then lifted up in elevators. Released at floor level, the animals would pop out from behind blinds into the arena—the gladiator didn't know where, when, or by what he'd be attacked.

Cost and Hours: €12 combo-ticket also includes Roman Forum and Palatine Hill; ticket valid two consecutive days—one entry per sight; also covered by the Roma Pass. Open daily 8:30 until one hour before sunset: April–Sept until 19:15, Oct until 18:30, off-season closes as early as 16:30; last entry one hour before closing; tel. 06-3996-7700.

Getting There: Metro: Colosseo. Bus #60 is handy for hotels near Via Firenze and Via Nazionale. Bus #87 links Largo Argentina with the Colosseum.

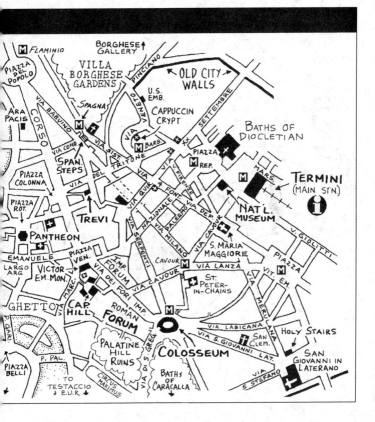

Sightseeing Strategy: It makes sense to see the Colosseum, Forum, and Palatine Hill in succession on a single visit. If you're getting a Roma Pass (you could buy it at the *tabacchi* shop in the Colosseo Metro station), this order works best: See the blockbuster Colosseum first, when you're freshest, then the Forum, then the Palatine if you have energy left over. But if you're getting a combo-ticket, this is the most efficient order: Buy your combo-ticket at the (less-crowded) Palatine entrance and sightsee the Palatine,

ending at the Forum's Arch of Titus. From there, do the Forum. Then exit the Forum at the east end (Colosseum), and finish with the Colosseum.

Avoiding Lines: The lines in front of the Colosseum are for buying tickets and for security checks, not for actually entering the sight. Everyone has to wait in

Colosseum

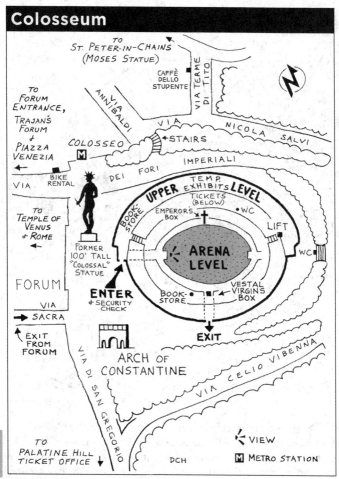

the security line to go through the metal detectors first, but once you're through that—if you have your ticket or pass already—stay to the left and muscle your way past the ticket-buying crowd to go directly to the turnstile, which never has a line. Enter by inserting your ticket in the turnstile or flashing your pass. You'll likely save lots of time if you get your ticket or pass in advance using one of these alternatives:

1. If you're planning on getting a €25 Roma Pass, buy it at a less-crowded place to bypass the ticket-buying line at the Colosseum. You can purchase the pass at the *tabacchi* shop in the Colosseo Metro station, or at the entrance to Palatine Hill on Via di San Gregorio (facing the Forum, with Colosseum at your back, go left down the street). Avoid buying it at the Forum,

which also tends to have lines.

2. If you're buying a combo-ticket, get it at the less-crowded Palatine Hill entrance. Or buy and print it online in advance at www.ticketclic.it (€1.50 booking fee, good for two consecutive days, not changeable). Note that the "free tickets" you'll see listed are valid only for EU citizens with ID.

3. Pay to join an official guided tour (€4 plus €12 combo-ticket, see "Tours," below). Once past the security check, tell one of the guards that you want to purchase a guided tour and he will usher you toward the ticket booth marked *Visite Guidate* (you'll also pay for your ticket here).

Private walking-tour guides (or their American assistants) linger outside the Colosseum, offering tours that include the admission fee and allow you to skip the line. This will cost you a few extra euros (€22 for two-hour tours of the Colosseum, Palatine Hill, and Forum, including the €12 ticket), but can save time; however, see the warning below.

Warnings: It can be hard to judge the length of the ticket line because it's tucked into the Colosseum arcade. Unscrupulous private guides tell tourists that there's a long line, when there really might be no line at all. If you do sign up with a private guide, confirm that your tour will start right away, and look at your ticket to make sure that it includes admission to Palatine Hill and Forum (some guides, claiming to cover all three sights, will purchase a group Colosseum-only ticket, then say "ciao" after the Colosseum tour).

Also beware of the **greedy gladiators.** For a fee, the incredibly crude modern-day gladiators snuff out their cigarettes and pose for photos. They take easy-to-swindle tourists for too much money. Watch out if you tangle with these guys (they're accustomed to getting as much as €100 from naive tourists). If you go for it, €4–5 for one photo usually keeps them appeased.

And finally, look out for **pickpockets.** The Colosseum's exterior is traditionally a happy hunting ground for pickpockets and con artists.

Tours: A dry but fact-filled **audioguide** is available just past the turnstiles (€4.50 for 2 hours of use). A handheld **videoguide** senses where you are in the site and plays related video clips (€5.50, pick up after turnstiles). Guided **tours** in English (which let you skip the ticket line) depart nearly hourly between 10:00 and 17:00, and last 45 minutes to one hour (€4 plus your €12 ticket, purchase inside the Colosseum near the ticket booth marked *Visite Guidate*). My self-guided Colosseum **audio tour** is free to download to an iPod or other MP3 player (at www.ricksteves.com or search for "Rick Steves Audio Tours" in iTunes).

▲**Arch of Constantine**—If you are a Christian, were raised a Christian, or simply belong to a so-called "Christian nation,"

ponder this arch. It marks one
of the great turning points in
history—the military coup
that made Christianity mainstream. In A.D. 312, Emperor
Constantine defeated his
rival Maxentius in the crucial
Battle of the Milvian Bridge.
The night before, he had seen
a vision of a cross in the sky.

Constantine—whose mother and sister were Christians—became
sole emperor and legalized Christianity. With this one battle, a
once-obscure Jewish sect with a handful of followers was now the
state religion of the entire Western world. In A.D. 300, you could
be killed for being a Christian; a century later, you could be killed
for not being one. Church enrollment boomed.

The restored arch is like an ancient museum. It's decorated
entirely with recycled carvings originally made for other buildings. By covering it with exquisite carvings of high Roman art—
works that glorified previous emperors—Constantine put himself
in their league. Hadrian is featured in the round reliefs, with
Marcus Aurelius in the square reliefs higher up. The big statues
on top are of Trajan and Augustus. Originally, Augustus drove a
chariot similar to the one topping the modern Victor Emmanuel II
monument. Fourth-century Rome may have been in decline, but
Constantine clung to its glorious past.

▲**St. Peter-in-Chains Church (San Pietro in Vincoli)**—Built
in the fifth century to house the chains that held St. Peter, this
church is most famous for its Michelangelo statue. Check out the
much-venerated chains under the high altar, then focus on mighty
Moses. (Note that this isn't the famous St. Peter's Basilica, which is
at Vatican City.)

Pope Julius II commissioned Michelangelo to build a massive tomb, with 48 huge statues, crowned by a grand statue of this
egomaniacal pope. The pope had planned to have his tomb placed
in the center of St. Peter's Basilica. When Julius died, the work
had barely been started, and no one had the money or necessary
commitment to Julius to finish the project.

In 1542, some of the remnants of the tomb project were brought
to St. Peter-in-Chains and pieced together by Michelangelo's
assistants. Some of the best statues ended up elsewhere, like the
Prisoners in Florence, and the *Slaves* in the Louvre. *Moses* and
the Louvre's *Slaves* are the only statues Michelangelo personally
completed for the project. Flanking *Moses* are the Old Testament
sister-wives of Jacob, Leah (to our left) and Rachel, both begun by
Michelangelo but probably finished by pupils.

ROME

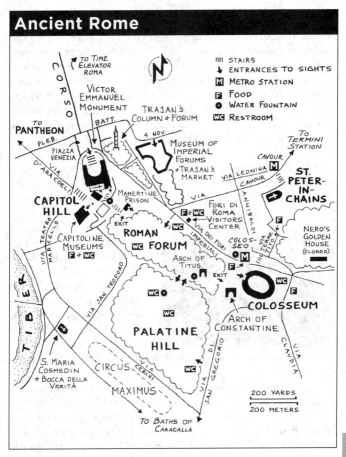

Ancient Rome

LEGEND:
- ‖‖‖ STAIRS
- ↓ ENTRANCES TO SIGHTS
- Ⓜ METRO STATION
- Ⓕ FOOD
- ◉ WATER FOUNTAIN
- WC RESTROOM

(Map labels include:) CORSO, TO TIME ELEVATOR ROMA, VICTOR EMMANUEL MONUMENT, TRAJAN'S COLUMN + FORUM, TO PANTHEON, PLEB., BATT., 4 NOV., MUSEUM OF IMPERIAL FORUMS + TRAJAN'S MARKET, PIAZZA VENEZIA, VIA D'ARA COELI, CAPITOL HILL, MAMERTINE PRISON, VIA LEONINA, CAVOUR, ST. PETER-IN-CHAINS, TO TERMINI STATION, CAPITOLINE MUSEUMS, EXIT, ROMAN FORUM, FORI DI ROMA VISITORS CENTER, VIA DEI FORI IMPERIALI, VIA ANNIBALDI, COLOSSEO, VIA TERME TITO, NERO'S GOLDEN HOUSE (CLOSED), VIA TEATRO MARCELLO, TIBER, VIA SAN TEODORO, ARCH OF TITUS, EXIT, COLOSSEUM, ARCH OF CONSTANTINE, VIA CLAUDIA, S. MARIA COSMEDIN + BOCCA DELLA VERITÀ, PALATINE HILL, CIRCUS MAXIMUS, VIA DI CERCHI, VIA DI SAN GREGORIO, TO BATHS OF CARACALLA

200 YARDS / 200 METERS

This powerful statue of Moses—mature Michelangelo—is worth studying. The artist worked on it in fits and starts for 30 years. Moses has received the Ten Commandments. As he holds the stone tablets, his eyes show a man determined to stop his tribe from worshipping the golden calf and idols...a man determined to win salvation for the people of Israel. Why the horns? Centuries ago, the Hebrew word for "rays" was mistranslated as "horns."

Cost and Hours: Free, April–Sept 8:00–12:30 & 15:30–19:00, Oct–March 8:00–12:30 & 15:00–18:00, modest dress required; the church is a 15-minute uphill, zigzag walk from the Colosseum, or a shorter, simpler walk from the Cavour Metro stop—from that station, go downhill on Via Cavour a half-block, then climb the pedestrian staircase called Via di San Francesco di Paola, which leads right to the church.

Nero's Golden House (Domus Aurea)—The sparse underground remains of Emperor Nero's "Golden House" are a faint shadow of their ancient grandeur. In its heyday, the gold leaf–encrusted residence was huge, with its original entrance all the way over at the Arch of Titus in the Forum. Nero's massive estate once sprawled across the valley (where the Colosseum now stands) and up the hill—the part that's been open on-and-off to the public. While it's exciting to think that Nero's house survives, it's in a sad state of ruin, and has been closed to the public indefinitely.

The Roman Forum and Nearby

▲▲▲**Roman Forum (Foro Romano)**—This is ancient Rome's birthplace and civic center, and the common ground between Rome's famous seven hills.

As just about anything important that happened in ancient Rome happened here, it's arguably the most important piece of real estate in Western civilization. While only a few fragments of that glorious past remain, history-seekers find plenty to ignite their imaginations amid the half-broken columns and arches.

Cost and Hours: €12 combo-ticket includes Colosseum and Palatine Hill—see page 731, audioguide available; open daily 8:30 until one hour before sunset: April–Sept until 19:15, Oct until 18:30, off-season closes as early as 16:30; last entry one hour before closing, Metro: Colosseo, tel. 06-3996-7700. See my self-guided walk on page 709.

▲▲**Palatine Hill (Monte Palatino)**—The hill overlooking the Forum is jam-packed with history—"the huts of Romulus," the huge Imperial Palace, a view of the Circus Maximus—but there's only the barest skeleton of rubble left to tell the story.

We get our word "palace" from this hill, where the emperors chose to live. The Palatine Hill was once so filled with palaces that later emperors had to build out. (Looking up at it from the Forum, you see the substructure that supported these long-gone palaces.)

The Palatine museum contains statues and frescoes that help

you imagine the luxury of the imperial Palatine. From the pleasant garden, you'll get an overview of the Forum. On the far side, look down into an emperor's private stadium and then beyond at the dusty Circus Maximus, once a chariot course. Imagine the cheers, jeers, and furious betting.

While many tourists consider the Palatine Hill just extra credit after the Forum, it offers an insight into the greatness of Rome that's well worth the effort. (And, if you're visiting the Colosseum or Forum, you've got a ticket whether you like it or not.)

Cost and Hours: €12 combo-ticket also includes Roman Forum and Colosseum—see page 730; open same hours as Roman Forum and Colosseum, Metro: Colosseo. Audioguides cost €4 (€6 version includes Roman Forum, must leave ID). Guided tours in English are offered once daily at 11:30 (€4, 45 minutes, not always available off-season); ask for information at the ticket booth. The entrance is on Via di San Gregorio (facing the Forum with the Colosseum at your back, it's down the street to your left). You can also enter the Palatine from within the Roman Forum—just climb the hill from the Arch of Titus.

▲**Mamertine Prison**—This 2,500-year-old cistern-like prison, which once held the bodies of Saints Peter and Paul, is worth a look—unless it's still closed for renovation when you visit. When you step into the room, ignore the modern floor and look up at the hole in the ceiling, through which prisoners were lowered. Then take the stairs down to the level of the actual prison floor. Downstairs, you'll see the column to which Peter was chained. It's said that a miraculous fountain sprang up in this room so that Peter could convert and baptize his jailers, who were also subsequently martyred. The upside-down cross commemorates Peter's upside-down crucifixion (donation requested, daily 9:00–19:00 if renovation completed, at the foot of Capitol Hill, near Forum's Arch of Septimius Severus).

Imagine humans, amid fat rats and rotting corpses, awaiting slow deaths. On the walls near the entry are lists of notable prisoners (Christian and non-Christian) and the ways they were executed: *strangolati, decapitato, morto per fame* (died of hunger). The sign by the Christian names reads, "Here suffered, victorious for the triumph of Christ, these martyr saints."

▲**Trajan's Column, Market, and Imperial Forums**—This grand column is the best example of "continuous narration" that we have from antiquity. More than 2,500 figures scroll around the 140-foot-high column, telling of Trajan's victorious Dacian campaign (circa A.D. 103, in present-day Romania), from the assembling of the army at the bottom to the victory sacrifice at the top. The ashes of Trajan and his wife were once held in the base, and the sun once glinted off a polished bronze statue of Trajan at the top. (Today, St. Peter is on top.) Study the propaganda that winds up the column like a scroll, trumpeting Trajan's wonderful military exploits. Viewing balconies once stood on either side, but it seems likely that Trajan fans came away only with a feeling that the greatness of their emperor and empire was beyond comprehension (for a rolled-out version of the column's story, visit the E.U.R.'s Museum of Roman Civilization). This column marked "Trajan's Forum," which was built to handle the shopping needs of a wealthy city of more than a million people. Commercial, political, religious, and social activities all mixed in the forum.

Nestled into the cutaway curve of Quirinal Hill is the semi-circular brick complex of **Trajan's Market.** It was likely part shopping mall, part warehouse, and part administration building. Or, as some archaeologists have recently suggested, it may have contained mostly government offices.

Paying the admission fee gets you inside Trajan's Market, Trajan's Forum, and the **Museum of the Imperial Forums.** The museum takes you through discoveries from the forums of emperors Julius Caesar, Augustus, Nerva, and Trajan, with fragments of statues and a slideshow that reconstructs how the forum looked in each emperor's time.

Trajan's Column is just a few steps off Piazza Venezia (a hub for major bus routes #40, #64, and #87), on Via dei Fori Imperiali, across the street from the Victor Emmanuel Monument. Trajan's Market can be entered only through the Museum of the Imperial Forums at Via IV Novembre 94. Trajan's Forum stretches southeast of the column toward the Colosseo Metro stop and the Colosseum itself.

Cost and Hours: €6.50, includes entry to the market ruins, Tue–Sun 9:00–19:00, closed Mon, last entry 30 minutes before closing, Via IV Novembre 94, up the staircase from Trajan's Column; tel. 06-0608, ww.mercatiditraiano.it.

Bocca della Verità—The legendary "Mouth of Truth" at the Church of Santa Maria in Cosmedin draws a playful crowd. Stick your hand in the mouth of the gaping stone face in the porch wall. As the legend goes (and was popularized by the 1953 film *Roman Holiday*, starring Gregory Peck and Audrey Hepburn), if you're a liar, your hand will be gobbled up. The mouth is only accessible when the church gate is open.

Cost and Hours: €0.50, daily 9:30–17:50, closes earlier off-season, Piazza Bocca della Verità, near the north end of Circus Maximus.

Capitol Hill and Nearby

Of Rome's famous seven hills, this is the smallest, tallest, and most famous—home of the ancient Temple of Jupiter and the center of city government for 2,500 years. There are several ways to

get to the top of Capitol Hill. (While I call it "Capitol Hill" for simplicity, it's correctly called "Capitoline Hill.") If you're coming from the north (from Piazza Venezia), take Michelangelo's impressive stairway to the right of the big, white Victor Emmanuel Monument. Coming from the southeast (the Forum), take the steep staircase near the Arch of Septimius Severus. From near Trajan's Forum along Via dei Fori Imperiali, take the winding road. All three converge at the top, in the square called Campidoglio (kahm-pee-DOHL-yoh).

Shortcut: A clever little "back door" gives you access from the top of Capitol Hill directly to the top of the Victor Emmanuel Monument and the Santa Maria in Aracoeli church, saving lots of uphill stair-climbing. To find the back door, locate the She-Wolf statue (to the left of the mayoral palace). Climb the wide set of stairs near the statue (the highest set of stairs you see). To reach the church, turn left at the column in the middle of the staircase, following signs to *Aracoeli*. To reach the Victor Emmanuel Monument, continue up to the top of the steps, pass through the iron gate, and enter the small unmarked door at #13 on the right. You'll soon emerge on a café terrace midway up the monument with vast views. The Rome from the Sky elevator to the top is just around the corner (see page 744).

▲**Capitol Hill Square (Campidoglio)**—This square atop the hill, once the religious and political center of ancient Rome, is still the home of the city's government. In the 1530s, the pope called on Michelangelo to re-establish this square as a grand center. Michelangelo placed the ancient equestrian statue of Marcus Aurelius as the square's focal point. Effective. (The original statue is now in the adjacent museum.) The twin buildings on either side are the Capitoline Museums. Behind the replica of the statue is the mayoral palace (Palazzo Senatorio).

Michelangelo intended that people approach the square from his grand stairway off Piazza Venezia. From the top of the stairway, you see the new Renaissance face of Rome, with its back to the Forum. Michelangelo gave the buildings the "giant order"—huge pilasters make the existing two-story buildings feel one-storied and more harmonious with the new square. Notice how the statues atop these buildings welcome you and then draw you in.

The terraces just downhill (past either side of the mayor's palace) offer grand views of the Forum. To the left of the mayor's palace is a copy of the famous She-Wolf statue on a column.

ROME

Capitol Hill & Piazza Venezia

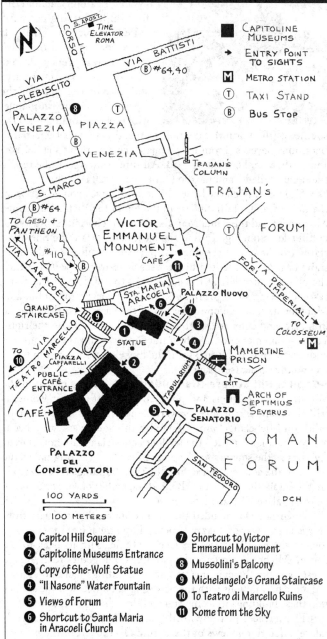

1. Capitol Hill Square
2. Capitoline Museums Entrance
3. Copy of She-Wolf Statue
4. "Il Nasone" Water Fountain
5. Views of Forum
6. Shortcut to Santa Maria in Aracoeli Church
7. Shortcut to Victor Emmanuel Monument
8. Mussolini's Balcony
9. Michelangelo's Grand Staircase
10. To Teatro di Marcello Ruins
11. Rome from the Sky

Farther down is *il nasone* ("the big nose"), a refreshing water fountain. Block the spout with your fingers, and water spurts up for drinking. Romans joke that a cheap Roman boy takes his date out for a drink at *il nasone*. Near the She-Wolf statue is the staircase leading to a shortcut to the Victor Emmanuel Monument (for details, see "Shortcut," page 739).

▲▲**Capitoline Museums (Musei Capitolini)**—This museum encompasses two buildings (Palazzo dei Conservatori and Palazzo Nuovo), connected by an underground passage that leads to the vacant Tabularium and panoramic views of the Roman Forum.

Cost and Hours: €8–11 depending on cost of temporary exhibit, €8.50–13 combo-ticket with Montemartini Museum, Tue–Sun 9:00–20:00, closed Mon, last entry one hour before closing, tel. 06-8205-9127, www.museicapitolini.org.

Overview: The museum's layout—with two different buildings connected by an underground passage—can be confusing. To identify the museum's two buildings, face the equestrian statue (with your back to the grand stairway). You'll enter at the Palazzo dei Conservatori (on your right), cross underneath the square (beneath the Palazzo Senatorio, or mayoral palace, not open to public), and exit from the Palazzo Nuovo (on your left).

At the Palazzo dei Conservatori entrance, buy your ticket and consider renting the good €5 audioguide (€6.20/2 people).

The **Palazzo dei Conservatori** claims to be one of the world's oldest museums, founded in 1471 when a pope gave ancient statues to the citizens of Rome. In the courtyard, enjoy the massive chunks of Constantine: his head, hand, and foot. When intact, this giant held the place of honor in the Basilica of Constantine in the Forum. The museum is worthwhile, with lavish rooms and several great statues. You'll see the 13th-century *Capitoline She-Wolf* (the little statues of Romulus and Remus were added in the Renaissance). Don't miss the *Boy Extracting a Thorn* and the enchanting *Commodus as Hercules*. Behind Commodus is a statue of his dad, Marcus Aurelius, on a horse. The greatest surviving equestrian statue of antiquity, this was the original centerpiece of the square (where a copy stands today). Christians in the Dark Ages thought that the statue's hand was raised in blessing, which probably led to their misidentifying him as Constantine, the first Christian emperor. While most pagan statues were destroyed by Christians, "Constantine" was spared.

The second-floor café, Caffè Capitolino, has a splendid patio

ROME

offering city views. It's lovely at sunset (public entrance for non-museum-goers off Piazza Caffarelli and through door #4).

Go downstairs to the **Tabularium.** Built in the first century B.C., these sturdy vacant rooms once held the archives of ancient Rome. The word Tabularium comes from "tablet," on which Romans wrote their laws. You won't see any tablets, but you will see a superb head-on view of the Forum from the windows.

Leave the Tabularium and enter the **Palazzo Nuovo,** which houses mostly portrait busts of forgotten emperors. But it also has two must-see statues: the *Dying Gaul* and the *Capitoline Venus* (both on the first floor up).

Santa Maria in Aracoeli—This church is built on the site where Emperor Augustus (supposedly) had a premonition of the com-

ing of Mary and Christ standing on an "altar in the sky" *(ara coeli).* The church is Rome in a nutshell, where you can time-travel across 2,000 years by standing in one spot.

Cost and Hours: Daily 9:00–12:30 & 15:00–18:30. It's atop Capitol Hill, squeezed between the Victor Emmanuel Monument and the square called Campidoglio. While dedicated pilgrims climb up the long, steep staircase from street level (the right side of Victor Emmanuel Monument, as you face it), savvy sightseers prefer to enter through the "back door" atop Capitol Hill (see "Shortcut," page 739).

Piazza Venezia

This vast square, dominated by the big, white Victor Emmanuel Monument, is a major transportation hub and the focal point of modern Rome. (The square will be dug up for years—Metro line C is under construction, and when anything of archaeological importance is uncovered, progress is interrupted.) Stand with your back to the monument and look down Via del Corso, the city's axis, surrounded by Rome's classiest shopping district. In the 1930s, Benito Mussolini whipped up Italy's nationalistic fervor from a balcony above the square (with your back to Victor Emmanuel Monument, it's the less-grand balcony on the left). Fascist masses filled the square screaming, "Four more years!"—or something like that. Mussolini created boulevard Via dei Fori Imperiali (to your right) to open up views of the Colosseum in the distance to impress his visiting friend Adolf Hitler. Mussolini lied to his people, mixing fear and patriotism to push his country to the right and embroil the Italians in expensive and regrettable wars. In 1945, they shot and hung Mussolini from a meat hook in Milan.

Circling around the right side of the Victor Emmanuel Monument, look down into the ditch on your left to see the ruins of an ancient apartment building from the first century A.D.; part of it was transformed into a tiny church (faded frescoes and bell tower). Rome was built in layers—almost everywhere you go, there's an earlier version beneath your feet. (The hop-on, hop-off Trambus 110 stops just across the busy intersection from here.)

Continuing on, you reach two staircases leading up Capitol Hill. One is Michelangelo's grand staircase up to the Campidoglio. The longer of the two leads to the Santa Maria in Aracoeli church, a good example of the earliest style of Christian churches (described earlier). The contrast between this climb-on-your-knees ramp to God's house and Michelangelo's elegant stairs illustrates the changes Renaissance humanism brought civilization.

From the bottom of Michelangelo's stairs, look right several blocks down the street to see a condominium actually built upon the surviving ancient pillars and arches of Teatro di Marcello.

Victor Emmanuel Monument—This oversize monument to Italy's first king, built to celebrate the 50th anniversary of the

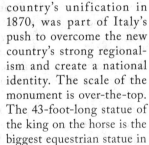

country's unification in 1870, was part of Italy's push to overcome the new country's strong regionalism and create a national identity. The scale of the monument is over-the-top. The 43-foot-long statue of the king on the horse is the biggest equestrian statue in the world. The king's moustache is over five feet wide, and a person could fit into the horse's hoof. Open to the public, the structure offers a grand view of the Eternal City (free, 242 punishing steps to the highest viewpoint accessible on foot—unless you take the shortcut from Capitol Hill described on page 739).

Locals love to hate the "Altar of the Nation." Romans think of the 200-foot-high, 500-foot-wide monument not as an altar of the fatherland, but as "the wedding cake," "the typewriter," or "the dentures." (For short, they call it "the Vittoriano.") It wouldn't be so bad if it weren't sitting on a priceless acre of ancient Rome and if they had chosen better marble (the in-your-face white picks up the pollution horribly, requiring frequent cleaning). Soldiers guard Italy's Tomb of the Unknown Soldier as the eternal flame flickers.

The Victor Emmanuel Monument also houses a little-visited **Museum of the Risorgimento**, which explains the movement and war that led to the unification of Italy in 1870 (free, daily 9:30–18:30, tel. 06-679-3598, café).

▲**Rome from the Sky**—This elevator, located near the top of the Victor Emmanuel Monument next to the outdoor café, zips

you to the rooftop for the grandest 360-degree view of the center of Rome (even better than from the top of St. Peter's dome). Helpful panoramic diagrams describe the skyline, with powerful binoculars available for zooming in on particular sights. Go in late afternoon, when it's beginning to cool off and Rome glows.

Cost and Hours: €7, Mon–Thu 9:30–18:30, Fri–Sun 9:30–19:30, ticket office closes 45 minutes earlier, tel. 06-6920-2049, follow signs inside the Victor Emmanuel Monument to *ascensori panoramici* or take the shortcut from Capitol Hill.

Pantheon Neighborhood

The area around the Pantheon is the heart of Rome. This neighborhood stretches eastward from the Tiber River through Campo de' Fiori and Piazza Navona, past the Pantheon to the Trevi Fountain. Besides being home to ancient sights and historic churches, it's also the place that gives Rome its urban-village feel. Wander narrow streets, sample the many shops and eateries, and gather with the locals in squares marked by a bubbling fountain. Exploring is especially good in the evening, when the restaurants bustle and streets are jammed with foot traffic. For more on nocturnal sightseeing, see my "Night Walk Across Rome," on page 720.

Getting There: To reach the Pantheon neighborhood, you can walk (it's a 20-minute walk from Capitol Hill), take a taxi, or catch a bus. Buses #64 and #40 carry tourists and pickpockets frequently between Termini train station and Vatican City, stopping at a chaotic square called Largo Argentina, located a few blocks south of the Pantheon. (Take either Via dei Cestari or Via di Torre Argentina north to the Pantheon.) The *elettrico* minibus #116 runs between Campo de' Fiori and Piazza Barberini via the Pantheon. The most dramatic approach is on foot coming from Piazza Navona along Via Giustiniani, which spills directly into Piazza della Rotunda, offering the classic Pantheon view.

▲▲▲**Pantheon**—For the greatest look at the splendor of Rome, antiquity's best-preserved interior is a must. Because the Pantheon became a church dedicated to the martyrs just after the fall of

Pantheon Neighborhood

TO PIAZZA
DEL POPOLO

TO
SPANISH
STEPS

TO M
BARB.

PONTE
UMBERTO

TIBER

LUNGOTEVERE MARZIO

VIA
TRITONE

PIAZZA
COLONNA

TREVI

SAN LUIGI
(CARAVAGGIO)

PARL.

UFF. VICARIO

SABINA
MURATTE

ANCIENT
STADIUM
ENTRANCE

CORONARI

COPPELLE

P.
MONT.

PATAR.

TRE
SCALINI

AQUIRO

PIAZZA DI
PIETRA

PIAZZA
NAVONA

SALV.

GIUST.

PIAZZA
ROTUNDA

SEMINARIO

SAN
IGNAZIO

PIAZZA
PASQUINO

S.EUST.

CITY
MUSEUM

CORSO VITTORIO

PANTHEON

STA. MARIA
SOPRA
MINERVA

GALLERIA
DORIA
PAMPHILJ.

IV NOV.

CAMPO
DE'
FIORI

EMAN.

VIA PLEBISCITO

GESU

PIAZZA
VENEZIA

FORI IMP.

VICTOR
EM. MON.

V. GIUBBO

VIA BOTT. OSC.

LARGO
ARGENTINA RUINS
(+ CAT HOSPICE)

CAPITOL
HILL
+ CAP.
MUSEUMS

TO
COLOSSEUM
+ M

PALAZZO
FARNESE

LUNGOTEVERE

PONTE
SISTO

TO
TRASTEVERE

FORUM

→ ENTRY POINT
TO SIGHTS

T TAXI STAND

M METRO STATION

B BUS STOP

DCH

200 YARDS

200 METERS

Rome, the barbarians left it alone, and the locals didn't use it as a quarry. The portico is called "Rome's umbrella"—a fun local gathering in a rainstorm. Walk past its one-piece granite columns (biggest in Italy, shipped from Egypt) and through the original bronze doors. Sit inside under the glorious skylight and enjoy classical architecture at its best.

The dome, 142 feet high and wide, was Europe's biggest until the Renaissance. Michelangelo's dome at St. Peter's, while much higher, is about three feet narrower. The brilliance of this dome's construction astounded architects through the ages. During the Renaissance, Brunelleschi was given permission to cut into the dome (see the little square hole above and to the right of the entrance) to analyze the material. The concrete dome gets thinner and lighter with height—the highest part is volcanic pumice.

This wonderfully harmonious architecture greatly inspired Raphael and other artists of the Renaissance. Raphael, along with

Italy's first two kings, chose to be buried here.

The Pantheon is the only ancient building in Rome continuously used since its construction. When you leave, notice that the building is sunken below current street level, showing how the rest of the city has risen on 20 centuries of rubble.

Cost and Hours: Free, Mon–Sat 8:30–19:30, Sun 9:00–18:00, holidays 9:00–13:00, closed for Mass Sat at 17:00 and Sun at 10:30, tel. 06-6830-0230. You can download my free Pantheon audio tour at www.ricksteves.com (or search for "Rick Steves Audio Tours" in iTunes).

Nearby: The nearest WCs are at bars and downstairs in the McDonald's on the Pantheon's square. Several reasonable eateries are a block or two north up Via del Pantheon. Some of Rome's best gelato and coffee are nearby. For recommendations, see page 815.

▲▲**Churches near the Pantheon**—The **Church of San Luigi dei Francesi** has a magnificent chapel painted by Caravaggio (free, daily 10:00–12:30 & 16:00–19:00). The only Gothic church in Rome is **Santa Maria sopra Minerva,** with a little-known Michelangelo statue, *Christ Bearing the Cross* (free, Mon–Fri 7:00–19:00, Sat–Sun 8:00–13:00 & 15:30–19:00, on a little square behind Pantheon, to the east). The **Church of San Ignazio,** several blocks east of the Pantheon, is a riot of Baroque illusions with a false dome (free, daily 7:30–12:30 & 15:00–19:15). A few blocks away, across Corso Vittorio Emanuele, is the rich and Baroque **Gesù Church,** headquarters of the Jesuits in Rome (free, daily 7:00–12:30 & 16:00–19:45).

▲**Galleria Doria Pamphilj**—This underappreciated gallery, tucked away in the heart of the old city, fills a palace on Piazza del Collegio Romano. It offers a rare chance to wander through a noble family's lavish rooms with the prince who calls this downtown mansion home. Well, almost. Through an audioguide, the prince lovingly narrates his family's story, including how the Doria Pamphilj (pahm-FEEL-yee) family's cozy relationship with the pope inspired the word "nepotism." Highlights include paintings by Caravaggio, Titian, and Raphael, and portraits of Pope Innocent X by Diego Velázquez (on canvas) and Gian Lorenzo Bernini (in marble). The fancy rooms of the palace are interesting, with a mini-Versailles-like hall of mirrors and paintings lining the walls to the ceiling in the style typical of 18th-century galleries.

Cost and Hours: €9.50, includes worthwhile audioguide, daily 10:00–17:00, last entry 45 minutes before closing, café, from Piazza Venezia walk 2 blocks up Via del Corso to #305, tel. 06-679-7323, www.dopart.it/roma.

Time Elevator Roma—This cheesy, overpriced show is really just for kids. The 45-minute multiscreen show jolts you through the centuries. Equipped with headphones, you get nauseous in a com-

ROME

fortable, air-conditioned theater as the history of Rome unfolds before you—from the founding of the city, through its rise and fall, to its Renaissance rebound, and up to the present.

Cost and Hours: €12, children 5–12-€9, daily 10:30–19:30, shows at the bottom of each hour, last showing at 19:30, no kids under 39 inches, just off Via del Corso, a 3-minute walk from Piazza Venezia, across from Galleria Doria Pamphilj at Via dei S.S. Apostoli 20, tel. 06-9774-6243, www.timeelevator.it.

Piazza di Pietra (Piazza of Stone)—The square was actually a quarry set up to chew away at the abandoned Roman building. You can still see the holes that hungry medieval scavengers chipped into the columns to steal the metal pins that held the slabs together (two blocks toward Via del Corso from Pantheon).

▲Trevi Fountain—The bubbly Baroque fountain, worth ▲▲ by night, is a minor sight to art scholars...but a major nighttime gathering spot for teens on the make and tourists tossing coins. The coins tourists deposit daily are collected to feed Rome's poor. (For more information, see page 728.)

Near Termini Train Station

These sights are within a 10-minute walk of the train station. By Metro, use the Termini stop for the National Museum and the Repubblica stop for the rest.

▲▲▲National Museum of Rome (Museo Nazionale Romano Palazzo Massimo alle Terme)—The National Museum's main branch, at Palazzo Massimo, houses the greatest collection of ancient Roman art anywhere. It's a historic yearbook of Roman marble statues with some rare Greek originals. On the ground floor alone, you can look eye-to-eye with Julius and Augustus Caesar, Alexander the Great, and Socrates.

On the first floor, along with statues and busts showing such emperors as Trajan and Hadrian, you'll see the best-preserved Roman copy of the Greek *Discus Thrower*. Statues of athletes like this commonly stood in the baths, where Romans cultivated healthy bodies, minds, and social skills, hoping to lead well-rounded lives. Other statues on this floor originally stood in the pleasure gardens of the Roman rich—surrounded by greenery, with the splashing sound of fountains, the statues all painted in bright, lifelike colors. Though executed by Romans, the themes are mostly Greek, with godlike humans and human-looking gods.

The second floor features a collection of frescoes and mosaics

ROME

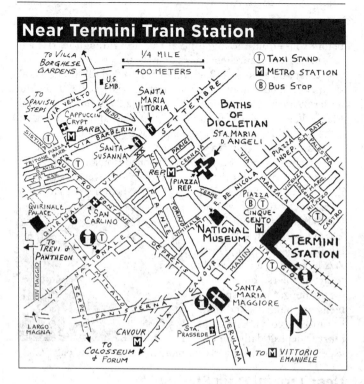

Near Termini Train Station

that once decorated the walls and floors of Roman villas. They're remarkably realistic and unstuffy, featuring everyday people, animals, flowery patterns, and geometrical designs. The Villa Farnese frescoes—in black, red, yellow, and blue—are mostly architectural designs, with fake columns, friezes, and garlands. The Villa di Livia frescoes immerse you in a leafy green garden full of birds and fruit trees.

Finally, descend into the basement to see fine gold jewelry, dice, an abacus, and vault doors leading into the best coin collection in Europe, with fancy magnifying glasses maneuvering you through cases of coins from ancient Rome to modern times.

Cost and Hours: €10 combo-ticket covers nearby Museum of the Bath and other forgettable branches, audioguide-€4, Tue–Sun 9:00–19:45, closed Mon, last entry 45 minutes before closing, Metro: Termini, tel. 06-3996-7700). The museum is about 100 yards from the train station—as you leave the station, it's the sandstone-brick building on your left. Enter at the far end, at Largo di Villa Peretti.

▲**Baths of Diocletian (Terme di Diocleziano)**—Around A.D. 300, Emperor Diocletian built the largest baths in Rome. This sprawling meeting place—with baths and schmoozing spaces to accommodate 3,000 bathers at a time—was a big deal in ancient times. While much of it is still closed, three sections are open: The Church of Santa Maria degli Angeli was once the great central hall of the baths (free, Mon–Sat 7:00–18:30, Sun 7:00–19:30, closed to sightseers during Mass, faces Piazza della Repubblica). The Octagonal Hall, once a gymnasium, is now a gallery of Roman bronze and marble statues (free, open sporadically Sun 9:00–13:00 only, faces Piazza della Repubblica). The skippable Museum of the Bath, despite its name, has nothing on the baths (€10 combo-ticket covers National Museum of Rome and more, Tue–Sun 9:00–19:45, closed Mon, last entry 45 minutes before closing, audioguide-€4, Viale Enrico de Nicola 79, entrance faces Termini train station, tel. 06-3996-7700).

Santa Maria degli Angeli: From noisy Piazza della Repubblica, step through the curved brick wall of the ancient baths and into the vast and cool church built upon the remains of a vast and steamy Roman bath complex. The church we see today was (at least partly) designed by Michelangelo (1561), who used the baths' main hall as the nave. Later, when Piazza della Repubblica became an important Roman intersection, another architect renovated the church. To allow people to enter from the grand new piazza, he spun it 90 degrees, turning Michelangelo's nave into a long transept. The eight red granite columns are original, from ancient Rome—stand next to one and feel its five-foot girth. (Only the eight in the transept proper are original. The others are made of plastered-over brick.) In Roman times, this hall was covered with mosaics, marble, and gold, and lined with statues.

Octagonal Hall: Open only on occasional Sunday mornings, this octagonal building, capped by a dome with a hole in the top, may have served as a cool room *(frigidarium),* with small pools of cold water for plunging into. Or, because of its many doors, it may simply have been a large intersection, connecting other parts of the baths. Originally, the floor was 25 feet lower—as you can see through the glass-covered hole in the floor. The graceful iron grid overhead supported the canopy of a 1928 planetarium.

▲Santa Maria della Vittoria—This church houses Bernini's statue, the swooning *St. Teresa in Ecstasy.*

The statue is to the left of the altar. Teresa has just been stabbed with God's arrow of fire. Now, the angel pulls it out and watches her reaction. Teresa swoons, her eyes roll up, her hand goes limp, she parts her

lips...and moans. The smiling, cherubic angel understands just how she feels. Teresa, a 16th-century Spanish nun, later talked of the "sweetness" of "this intense pain," describing her oneness with God in ecstatic, even erotic, terms.

Bernini, the master of multimedia, pulls out all the stops to make this mystical vision real. Actual sunlight pours through the alabaster windows, bronze sunbeams shine on a marble angel holding a golden arrow. Teresa leans back on a cloud and her robe ripples from within, charged with her spiritual arousal. Bernini has created a little stage-setting of heaven. And watching from the "theater boxes" on either side are members of the family that commissioned the work.

Cost and Hours: Free, pay €0.50 for light, Mon–Sat 8:30–12:00 & 15:30–18:00, Sun 15:30–18:00, about 5 blocks northwest of Termini train station on Largo Susanna, Metro: Repubblica.

Santa Susanna Church—The home of the American Catholic Church in Rome, Santa Susanna holds Mass in English daily at 18:00 and on Sunday at 9:00 and 10:30. They arrange papal audiences (see page 763), and their excellent website contains tips for travelers and a list of convents that rent out rooms.

Cost and Hours: Free, Mon–Fri 9:00–12:00 & 16:00–18:00, closed Sat–Sun, Via XX Settembre 15, near recommended Via Firenze hotels, Metro: Repubblica, tel. 06-4201-4554, www.santa susanna.org.

Pilgrim's Rome

East of the Colosseum (and south of Termini train station) are several venerable churches that Catholic pilgrims make a point of visiting. Near one of the churches is a small WWII museum.

Church of San Giovanni in Laterano—Built by Constantine, the first Christian emperor, this was Rome's most important church through medieval times. A building alongside the church houses the Holy Stairs (Scala Santa) said to have been walked up by Jesus, which today are ascended by pilgrims on their knees.

Cost and Hours: Free, audioguide-€5; church—daily 7:00–18:30; Holy Stairs—daily April–Sept 6:15–12:00 & 15:30–18:30, Oct–March 6:15–12:00 & 15:00–18:00; Piazza San Giovanni in Laterano, Metro: San Giovanni, or bus #85 or #87; tel. 06-6988-6409.

Museum of the Liberation of Rome (Museo Storico della Liberazione di Roma)—This small memorial museum, near the Church of San Giovanni in Laterano, is housed in the prison wing of the former Nazi police headquarters of occupied Rome. Other than a single printed sheet to help, there's little in English. Still, for those interested in resistance movements and the Nazi occupation, it's a stirring visit. You'll see a few artifacts, many photos of heroes, and a couple of cells preserved as they were

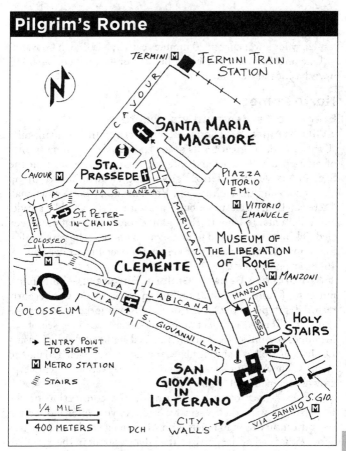

Pilgrim's Rome

TERMINI Ⓜ TERMINI TRAIN STATION

SANTA MARIA MAGGIORE

CAVOUR Ⓜ STA. PRASSEDE

PIAZZA VITTORIO EM.

Ⓜ VITTORIO EMANUELE

VIA G. LANZA

ST. PETER-IN-CHAINS

COLOSSEO

SAN CLEMENTE

MUSEUM OF THE LIBERATION OF ROME

Ⓜ MANZONI

Ⓜ COLOSSEUM

VIA LABICANA

S. GIOVANNI LAT.

HOLY STAIRS

SAN GIOVANNI IN LATERANO

S. GIO.
Ⓜ

CITY WALLS

VIA SANNIO

DCH

→ ENTRY POINT TO SIGHTS
Ⓜ METRO STATION
≋ STAIRS

¼ MILE
400 METERS

found on June 4, 1944, when the city was liberated.

Cost and Hours: Free, Tue–Sun 9:30–12:30, Tue and Thu–Fri also 15:30–19:00, closed Mon and Aug, just behind the Holy Stairs at Via Tasso 145, tel. 06-700-3866.

Church of Santa Maria Maggiore—Some of Rome's best-surviving mosaics line the nave of this church built as Rome was falling. The nearby Church of Santa Prassede has still more early mosaics.

Cost and Hours: Free, daily 8:30–18:00, Piazza Santa Maria Maggiore, Metro: Termini or Vittorio Emanuele, tel. 06-6988-6802.

▲**Church of San Clemente**—Besides visiting the church itself, with frescoes by Masolino, you can also descend into the ruins of an earlier church. Descend yet one more level and enter the eerie remains of a pagan temple to Mithras.

Cost and Hours: Upper church—free, lower church—€5, both open Mon–Sat 9:00–12:30 & 15:00–18:00, Sun 12:00–18:00, last entry for lower church 20 minutes earlier; Via di San Giovanni in Laterano, Metro: Colosseo, or bus #85 or #87; tel. 06-774-0021, www.basilicasanclemente.com.

North Rome

Borghese Gardens and Via Veneto

▲**Villa Borghese Gardens**—Rome's scruffy three-square-mile "Central Park" is great for its shade and people-watching (plenty of modern-day Romeos and Juliets). The best entrance is at the head of Via Veneto (Metro: Barberini, then 10-minute walk up Via Veneto and through the old Roman wall at Porta Pinciana). There you'll find a cluster of buildings with a café, a kiddie arcade, and bike rental (€4/hour). Rent a bike (or, for romantics, a ped-aled rickshaw—*riscio*) and follow signs to discover the park's cafés, fountains, statues, lake, great viewpoint over Piazza del Popolo, and prime picnic spots.

▲▲▲**Borghese Gallery (Galleria Borghese)**—This plush museum, filling a cardinal's mansion in the park, was recently restored and offers one of Europe's most sumptuous art experiences. You'll enjoy a collection of world-class Baroque sculpture, including Bernini's *David* and his excited statue of Apollo chasing Daphne, as well as paintings by Caravaggio, Raphael, Titian, and Rubens. The museum's slick, mandatory reservation system keeps crowds to a manageable size.

The essence of the collection is the connection of the Renaissance with the classical world. As you enter, notice the second-century Roman reliefs with Michelangelo-designed panels above either end of the portico. The villa was built in the early 17th century by the great art collector Cardinal Scipione Borghese, who wanted to prove that the glories of ancient Rome were matched by the Renaissance.

In the main entry hall, opposite the door, notice the thrilling first-century Greek sculpture of a horse falling. The Renaissance-era rider was added by Pietro Bernini, father of the famous Gian Lorenzo Bernini.

Each room seems to feature a Baroque masterpiece. The best of all is in Room III: Bernini's *Apollo and Daphne*. It's the perfect Baroque subject—capturing a thrilling, action-filled moment. In the mythological story, Apollo races after Daphne. Just as he's about to catch her, she calls to her father to save her. Magically, her fingers begin to sprout leaves, her toes become roots, her skin turns to bark, and she transforms into a tree. Frustrated Apollo will end up with a handful of leaves. Walk slowly around the statue. It's more air than stone.

ROME

North Rome

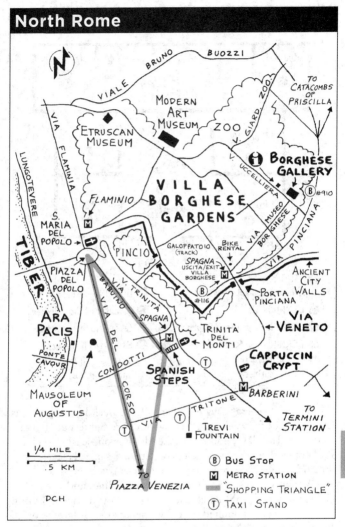

Cost, Hours, Reservations: €8.50, €12.50 during special exhibits, both prices include basic €2 reservation fee, credit cards accepted, Tue–Sun 9:00–19:00, ticket office closes one hour earlier, closed Mon. Reservations are mandatory and easy to get in English online (www.ticketeria.it, €1 extra booking fee, user-friendly website) or by calling 06-32810 (if you get an Italian recording, wait for the English translation to get the most up-to-date information, or press 2 for their standard information in English; office hours Mon–Fri 9:00–18:00, Sat 9:00–13:00, office closed Sat in Aug and Sun year-round, www.galleriaborghese.it). Reserve a

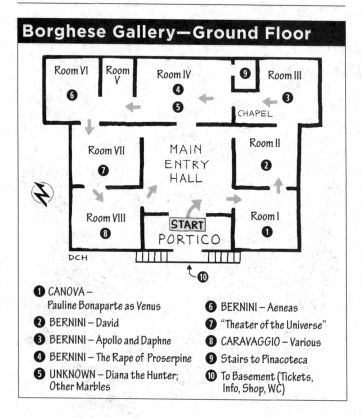

Borghese Gallery—Ground Floor

Room VI
Room V
Room IV
❾
Room III

❻
❹
❸

❺
CHAPEL

Room VII
MAIN ENTRY HALL
Room II

❼
❷

Room VIII
Room I

❽
START
PORTICO
❶

DCH

❿

❶ CANOVA – Pauline Bonaparte as Venus

❷ BERNINI – David

❸ BERNINI – Apollo and Daphne

❹ BERNINI – The Rape of Proserpine

❺ UNKNOWN – Diana the Hunter; Other Marbles

❻ BERNINI – Aeneas

❼ "Theater of the Universe"

❽ CARAVAGGIO – Various

❾ Stairs to Pinacoteca

❿ To Basement (Tickets, Info, Shop, WC)

minimum of several days in advance for a weekday visit, at least a week ahead for weekends. Reservations are tightest at 11:00 and 15:00, on Tuesdays, and on weekends. For off-season weekdays (but not weekends), your chances of getting a same-day reservation are fairly high, if you're flexible about the entry time.

When you reserve, request a day and time, and you'll get a claim number. You'll be advised to pick up your ticket 30 minutes before your appointed time. The ticket office is located on the lower level. If you're paying with a credit card, you can skip the ticket pickup line and head directly to the computer kiosks, enter your reservation number, swipe your credit card, and *pronto*—your tickets are ready.

If you're planning to use a Roma Pass for entry, you still need to make a reservation and pay the €2 fee. Call the reservations number (tel. 06-32810) to make your appointment.

If you don't have a reservation, you can try arriving near the top of the hour, when they sell unclaimed tickets to those standing by. Generally, out of 360 reservations, a few will fail to show (but more than a few may be waiting to grab them). You're most likely to land a stand-by ticket at 13:00 or 17:00.

Museum Strategy: Visits are strictly limited to two hours. Budget most of your time for the more interesting ground floor, but set aside 30 minutes for the paintings of the Pinacoteca upstairs (highlights are marked by the audioguide icons). Avoid the crowds by seeing the Pinacoteca first. The fine bookshop and cafeteria are best visited outside your two-hour entry window.

Tours: €6 guided English tours are offered at 9:10 and 11:10 (may also be offered at 13:10 and 15:10). You can't book a tour when you make your museum reservation—sign up as soon as you arrive. Or consider the excellent 1.5-hour audioguide tour for €5.

Getting There: The museum is set idyllically but inconveniently in the vast Villa Borghese Gardens. To avoid missing your appointment, allow yourself plenty of time to find the place. A taxi drops you 100 yards from the museum. Your destination is the Galleria Borghese (gah-leh-REE-ah bor-GAY-zay). Be sure *not* to tell the cabbie "Villa Borghese"—which is the park, not the museum.

The best public-transportation service is bus #910, which goes from Termini train station to the Via Pinciana stop (a few steps from the villa). Coming from Campo de' Fiori or Via del Corso (at Via Minghetti), bus #116 drops you off at the southern edge of the park. From Largo Argentina, bus #63 takes you to the American Embassy on Via Veneto; walk uphill on Via Veneto to the southern edge of the park.

By Metro, you have two options. From the Spagna Metro stop (or the Spanish Steps), it's a 15-minute walk: From inside the Metro station, follow signs to *Via Veneto* (not *Villa Borghese*). You'll continue along an underground labyrinth of escalators and moving sidewalks. Once you hit the supermarket, take a right up the stairs of the exit marked *uscita Villa Borghese*. At the top, turn left and head straight—you'll see signs to the gallery.

From the Barberini Metro stop, walk up Via Veneto, enter the park, and turn right, following signs.

Etruscan Museum (Villa Giulia Museo Nazionale Etrusco)— The fascinating Etruscan civilization thrived in this part of Italy around 600 B.C., when Rome was an Etruscan town. The Villa Giulia (a fine Renaissance palace) hosts a museum that tells the story. Aficionados of all things Etruscan come here for the famous "husband and wife sarcophagus"—a dead couple seeming to enjoy an everlasting banquet from atop their tomb (sixth century B.C. from Cerveteri); the *Apollo from Veii* statue (of textbook fame); and an impressive room filled with gold sheets of Etruscan printing and temple statuary from the Sanctuary of Pyrgi.

Cost and Hours: €4, Tue–Sun 8:30–19:30, closed Mon, last entry one hour before closing, scant English information, 20-minute walk from Borghese Gallery, Piazzale di Villa Giulia 9, tel.

06-322-6571. For more on the Etruscans, see the sidebar on page 616.

Via Veneto—In the 1960s, movie stars from around the world paraded down curvy Via Veneto, one of Rome's glitziest nightspots. Today it's still lined with the city's poshest hotels and the American Embassy, but any hint of local color has faded to bland.

▲Cappuccin Crypt—If you want to see artistically arranged bones, this is the place. The crypt is below the church of Santa Maria della Immacolata Concezione on Via Veneto, just up from Piazza Barberini.

The bones of more than 4,000 friars who died between 1528 and 1870 are in the basement, all lined up in a series of six crypts for the delight—or disgust—of the always-wide-eyed visitor. The dirt in the crypt was brought from Jerusalem 400 years ago, and the monastic message on the wall explains that this is more than just a macabre exercise: "We were what you are...you will become what we are now."

Cost and Hours: €1 donation, daily 9:00–12:00 & 15:00–18:00, sometimes closed Thu, modest dress required, no photos, turn off mobile phones, Metro: Barberini, tel. 06-487-1185. As you leave, pick up a few of Rome's most interesting postcards (proceeds support Capuchin mission work) and head back outside, where it's not just the bright light that provides contrast with the crypt. Within a few steps are the American Embassy, Hard Rock Cafe, and fancy Via Veneto cafés, filled with the poor and envious keeping an eye out for the rich and famous.

Piazza del Popolo—This vast oval square marks the traditional north entrance to Rome (its oval shape dates from the early 19th century). Today the square, known for its symmetrical design and its art-filled churches, is the starting point for the city's evening *passeggiata* (see my "Dolce Vita Stroll," on page 718).

From the Flaminio Metro stop, pass through the third-century A.D. Aurelian Wall via the Porta del Popolo, and look south. The 10-story obelisk in the center of the square once graced the temple of Ramses II

ROME

in Egypt and the Roman Circus Maximus racetrack. The obelisk was brought here in 1589 as one of the square's beautification projects. At the south side of the square, twin domed churches mark the spot where three main boulevards exit the square and form a trident. The central boulevard (running between the churches) is Via del Corso, which since ancient times has been the main north–south drag through town, running to Capitol Hill (the governing center) and the Forum. Along the north side of the square (flanking the Porta del Popolo) are two more buildings, which give the square a pleasant symmetry: the Carabinieri station and the church of Santa Maria del Popolo.

From the square, the *Tridente* of roads takes people south to the city center (along Via del Corso), to the Spanish Steps (Via Babuino), and to the Tiber River (Via Ripetta). Two large fountains grace the sides of the square—Neptune to the west and Roma to the east (marking the base of Pincio Hill). Though the name Piazza del Popolo means "Square of the People" (and it is a popular hangout), the word was probably derived from the Latin *populus,* after the poplar trees along the square's northeast side.

Santa Maria del Popolo—One of Rome's most overlooked churches, this features two chapels with top-notch art and a facade

built of travertine scavenged from the Colosseum. The church is brought to you by the Rovere family, which produced two popes, and you'll see their symbol—the oak tree and acorns—throughout.

Go inside. The Chigi Chapel (second on the left) was designed by Raphael and inspired (as Raphael was) by the Pantheon.

Notice the Pantheon-like dome, pilasters, and capitals. Above in the oculus, God looks in, aided by angels who power the eight known planets. Raphael built the chapel for his wealthy banker friend Agostino Chigi, buried in the pyramid-shaped tomb in the wall to the right of the altar. Later, Chigi's great-grandson hired Bernini to make two of the four statues, and Bernini delivered a theatrical episode. In one corner, Daniel straddles a lion and raises his praying hands to God for help. Kitty-corner across the chapel, an angel grabs Habbakuk's hair and tells him to go take some food to poor Daniel.

In the Cerasi Chapel (left of altar), Caravaggio's *The Conversion on the Way to Damascus* shows Paul sprawled on his back beside his horse while his servant looks on. The startled future saint is blinded by the harsh light as Jesus' voice asks him, "Why do you persecute me?" In the style of the Counter-Reformation, Paul receives his

new faith with open arms.

In the same chapel, Caravaggio's *Crucifixion of St. Peter* is shown as a banal chore; the workers toil like faceless animals. The light and dark are in high contrast. Caravaggio liked to say, "Where light falls, I will paint it."

Cost and Hours: Free, Mon–Sat 7:00–12:00 & 16:00–19:00, Sun 8:00–13:30 & 16:30–19:30; on north side of Piazza del Popolo—as you face gate in old wall from the square, church entrance is to your right.

▲▲**Catacombs of Priscilla (Catacombe di Priscilla)**— While most tourists and nearly all tour groups go out to the ancient Appian Way to see the famous catacombs of San Sebastiano and San Callisto, the Catacombs of Priscilla (on the other side of town) are less commercialized and crowded, and just feel more intimate, as catacombs should.

You enter from a convent and explore the result of 250 years of tunneling that occurred from the second to the fifth centuries, most likely to hold tombs for early Christians. As poorer Christians couldn't generally afford a nice plot in a cemetery, they would dig graves at a generous person's home...and dig and dig. You'll see a few thousand of the 40,000 niches carved here, along with some beautiful frescoes, including what is considered the first depiction of Mary nursing the baby Jesus.

Cost and Hours: €8, Tue–Sun 8:30–12:00 & 14:30–17:00, closed Mon, last entry 30 minutes before closing, closed one random month a year—check website or call first, tel. 06-8620-6272, www.catacombepriscilla.com. Visits are by 30-minute guided tour only (English-language tours go whenever a small group gathers—generally every 20 minutes or so).

Getting There: The catacombs are northeast of Termini Station (at Via Salaria 430), far from the center but well-served by buses (20–30 minutes). From Termini, take bus #92 or #86 from Piazza Cinquecento; from Piazza Venezia and along Via del Corso take bus #63. Tell the driver "kah-tah-KOHM-bay" and he'll let you off near Piazza Crati, which is close to the catacombs.

For more information, see "Catacombs" on page 788.

From the Spanish Steps to Ara Pacis

▲**Spanish Steps**—The wide, curving staircase, culminating with an obelisk between two Baroque church towers, makes for one of Rome's iconic sights. Beyond that, it's a people-gathering place. By day, the area hosts shoppers looking for high-end fashions; on

ROME

warm evenings, it attracts young people in love with the city. For more, see my "Night Walk Across Rome" on page 720.

"Shopping Triangle"—The triangular-shaped area between the Spanish Steps, Piazza Venezia, and Piazza del Popolo (along Via del Corso) contains Rome's highest concentration of upscale boutiques and fashion stores (see triangle at bottom of map on page 753).

▲▲▲Ara Pacis (Altar of Peace)—On January 30, 9 B.C., soon-to-be-emperor Augustus led a procession of priests up the steps

and into this newly built "Altar of Peace." They sacrificed an animal on the altar and poured an offering of wine, thanking the gods for helping Augustus pacify barbarians abroad and rivals at home. This marked the dawn of the Pax Romana (c. A.D. 1–200), a Golden Age of good living, stability, dominance, and peace (pax). The Ara Pacis (AH-rah PAH-chees) hosted annual sacrifices by the emperor until the area was flooded by the Tiber River. Buried under silt, it was abandoned and forgotten until the 16th century, when various parts were discovered and excavated. Mussolini gathered the altar's scattered parts and reconstructed them here in 1938. In 2006, the Altar of Peace reopened to the public in a striking modern building. As the first new building allowed to be built in the old center since 1938, it's been controversial, but its quiet, air-conditioned interior may signal the dawn of another new age in Rome.

The Altar of Peace was originally located east of here, along today's Via del Corso. The model shows where it stood in relation to the Mausoleum of Augustus (now next door) and the Pantheon. Approach the Ara Pacis and look through the doorway to see the raised altar. This simple structure has just the basics of a Roman temple: an altar for sacrifices surrounded by cubicle-like walls that enclose a consecrated space.

The reliefs on the north and south sides probably depict the parade of dignitaries who consecrated the altar, while reliefs on the west side (near the altar's back door) celebrate the two things Augustus brought to Rome: peace (goddess Roma as a conquering Amazon, right side) and prosperity (fertility goddess). Imagine the altar as it once was, standing in an open field, painted in bright colors—a mingling of myth, man, and nature.

Cost and Hours: €9, tightwads can look in through huge windows for free; Tue–Sun 9:00–19:00, closed Mon, last entry one hour before closing; €3.50 audioguide also available as free podcast at www.arapacis.it, good WC downstairs. The Ara Pacis is a long block west of Via del Corso on Via di Ara Pacis, on the east bank of the Tiber near Ponte Cavour, Metro: Spagna; a 10-minute walk down Via dei Condotti. Tel. 06-0608.

Vatican City

Vatican City, a tiny independent country, contains the Vatican Museum (with Michelangelo's Sistine Chapel) and St. Peter's Basilica (with Michelangelo's exquisite *Pietà*). A helpful **TI** is just to the left of St. Peter's Basilica as you're facing it (Mon–Sat 8:30–19:00, closed Sun, tel. 06-6988-1662, Vatican switchboard tel. 06-6982, www.vatican.va). The entrances to St. Peter's and to the Vatican Museum are a 15-minute walk apart (follow the outside of the Vatican wall, which links the two sights). The nearest Metro stops still involve a 10-minute walk to either sight: For St. Peter's, the closest stop is Ottaviano; for the Vatican Museum, it's Cipro.

▲▲▲Vatican Museum (Musei Vaticani)

The four miles of displays in this immense museum—from ancient statues to Christian frescoes to modern paintings—culminate in the Raphael Rooms and Michelangelo's glorious Sistine Chapel. (If you have binoculars, bring them.) This is one of Europe's top three or four houses of art. It can be exhausting, so plan your visit carefully, focusing on a few themes. Allow two hours for a quick visit, three or four hours for enough time to enjoy it.

Cost and Hours: €15 plus optional €4 reservation fee, Mon–Sat 9:00–18:00, last entry at 16:00 (though the official closing time is 18:00, the staff starts ushering you out at 17:30), closed on religious holidays and Sun except last Sun of the month (when it's free, more crowded, and open 9:00–14:00, last entry at 12:30). Hours are subject to constant change and frequent holidays; check http://mv.vatican.va for current times. Lines are extremely long in the morning—go in the afternoon, or skip the ticket-buying line altogether by reserving an entry time on their website for €19 (€15 ticket plus €4 booking fee, pay with credit card). Guided tours and audioguides are available.

The museum is closed on many holidays (mainly religious ones) including, for 2011: Jan 1 (New Year's), Jan 6 (Epiphany), Feb 11 (Vatican City established), March 19 (St. Joseph), April 24 and 25 (Easter Sunday and Monday), May 1 (Labor Day), June 29 (Saints Peter and Paul), Aug 15 plus either Aug 14 or 16—it varies

Vatican Museum Overview

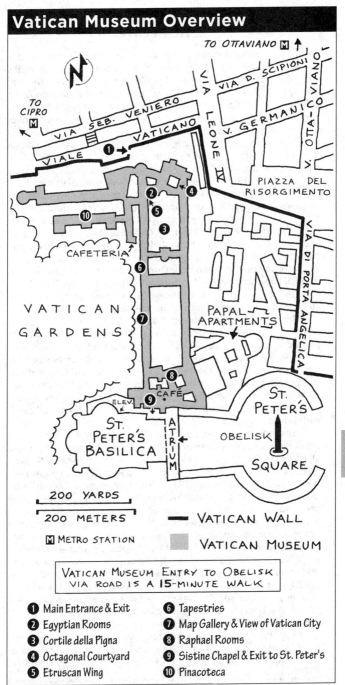

TO OTTAVIANO M ↑

TO CIPRO M

N

VIA SEB. VENIERO

VIALE VATICANO

VIA LEONE IV

VIA D. SCIPIONI

V. GERMANICO

VIA OTTA-VIANO

V. OTTAVIANO

PIAZZA DEL RISORGIMENTO

VIA DI PORTA ANGELICA

❶

❷
❹
❺

❿

❸

CAFETERIA

❻

VATICAN GARDENS

❼

PAPAL APARTMENTS

❽

CAFÉ

ELEV.

❾

ST. PETER'S BASILICA

ATRIUM

ST. PETER'S

OBELISK

SQUARE

200 YARDS

200 METERS

M METRO STATION

━━ VATICAN WALL

VATICAN MUSEUM

VATICAN MUSEUM ENTRY TO OBELISK
VIA ROAD IS A 15-MINUTE WALK

❶ Main Entrance & Exit
❷ Egyptian Rooms
❸ Cortile della Pigna
❹ Octagonal Courtyard
❺ Etruscan Wing
❻ Tapestries
❼ Map Gallery & View of Vatican City
❽ Raphael Rooms
❾ Sistine Chapel & Exit to St. Peter's
❿ Pinacoteca

ROME

Vatican City

This tiny independent country of little more than 100 acres, contained entirely within Rome, has its own postal system, dress code (dress modestly—even if you're just wandering through the square), armed guards, helipad, mini-train station, and radio station (KPOP). Politically powerful, the Vatican is the religious capital of 1.1 billion Roman Catholics. If you're not a Catholic, become one for your visit.

The pope is both the religious and secular leader of Vatican City. For centuries, locals referred to him as "King Pope." Italy and the Vatican didn't always have good relations. In fact, after unification (in 1870), when Rome's modern grid plan was built around the miniscule Vatican, it seemed as if the new buildings were designed to be just high enough so no one could see the dome of St. Peter's from street level. Modern Italy was created in 1870, but the Holy See didn't recognize it as a country until 1929, when the pope and Mussolini signed the Lateran Pact, giving sovereignty to the Vatican and a few nearby churches.

Like every European country, Vatican City has its own versions of the euro coin (with a portrait of the pope). You're unlikely to find one in your pocket, though, as they are snatched up by collectors before falling into actual circulation.

Small as it is, Vatican City has two huge sights: St. Peter's Basilica (with Michelangelo's *Pietà*) and the Vatican Museum (with the Sistine Chapel). The Vatican post office, with offices on St. Peter's Square (next to TI) and in the Vatican Museum, is famous for its stamps (Mon-Sat 8:30-18:30, closed Sun). Vatican stamps are good throughout Rome, but to use the Vatican's mail service, you need to mail your cards from the Vatican; write your postcards ahead of time. (Note that the Vatican won't mail cards with Italian stamps.)

Seeing the Pope: Your best chances for a sighting are on Sunday and Wednesday. The pope usually gives a blessing at noon on Sunday from his apartment on St. Peter's Square (except in July and August, when he speaks at his summer residence at Castel Gandolfo, 25 miles from Rome, reachable by train from Rome's Termini Station). St. Peter's is easiest (just show up) and, for most, enough of a "visit." Those interested in a more formal appearance (though not more intimate) can get a ticket for the Wednesday general audience (at 10:30) when the pope, arriving in his bulletproof Popemobile, greets and blesses the crowds at St. Peter's from a balcony or canopied platform on the square (except in winter, when he speaks at 10:30 in the 7,000-seat Paolo VI Auditorium, next to St. Peter's Basilica). If you only want to see St. Peter's—but not the pope—avoid these times (the basilica closes during papal audiences and crowds are substantial).

For the Wednesday audience, while anyone can observe from a distance, you need a (free) ticket to actually get close to the papal action (and get a seat). To find out the pope's schedule,

ROME

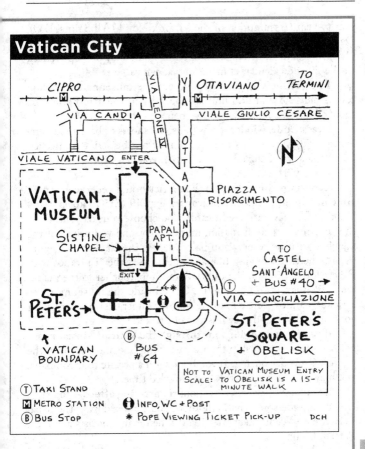

Vatican City

CIPRO Ⓜ

VIA LEONE IV

VIA OTTAVIANO Ⓜ OTTAVIANO TO TERMINI

VIA CANDIA VIALE GIULIO CESARE

Ⓝ

VIALE VATICANO ENTER

VATICAN → MUSEUM

PIAZZA RISORGIMENTO

SISTINE CHAPEL

PAPAL APT.

EXIT

TO CASTEL SANT' ANGELO + BUS #40 →

Ⓣ

VIA CONCILIAZIONE

ST. PETER'S →

ℹ *

ST. PETER'S SQUARE + OBELISK

VATICAN BOUNDARY

Ⓑ BUS #64

NOT TO SCALE: VATICAN MUSEUM ENTRY TO OBELISK IS A 15-MINUTE WALK

Ⓣ TAXI STAND
Ⓜ METRO STATION
Ⓑ BUS STOP

ℹ INFO, WC + POST
* POPE VIEWING TICKET PICK-UP

DCH

call 06-6982-3114.

Santa Susanna Church lets you order tickets online (free, with no booking charge). Pick up your reserved tickets, or check for last-minute availability, at the church the Tuesday before the audience between 17:00 and 18:30, and consider staying for the 18:00 English Mass (Via XX Settembre 15, near recommended Via Firenze hotels, Metro: Repubblica, tel. 06-4201-4554—charming Rosanna speaks English, get all the details at www.santasusanna .org).

Probably less convenient—because of the long line—is getting a ticket at St. Peter's Square from the Vatican guard at their station at the bronze doors (open Tue 12:00–19:30; last-minute tickets may be available Wed morning—just join the line). It's under the "elbow" of Bernini's colonnade, on the right side of the square as you face the basilica.

While many visitors come hoping for a more intimate audience, private audiences ended with the death of Pope John Paul II. Pope Benedict doesn't do them.

year to year (Assumption of the Virgin), Nov 1 (All Saints' Day), Dec 8 (Immaculate Conception), and Dec 25 and 26 (Christmas). Other holidays and changes in opening hours may pop up—check the hours and calendar at http://mv.vatican.va.

The Sistine Chapel closes before the museum. Individual rooms may close at odd hours, especially in the afternoon. The rooms described here are usually open.

Dress Code: Modest dress (no short shorts or bare shoulders) is required. While this dress code may not be strictly enforced here, it is at St. Peter's Basilica (which you can visit after leaving the Sistine Chapel).

Avoiding Lines: You can buy a ticket and **reserve an entry time online** at http://mv.vatican.va for €19 (€15 ticket plus €4 booking fee, pay with credit card). You choose your day and time, they email you a confirmation immediately, and you print out the voucher with its reservation bar code. At the Vatican Museum, bypass the ticket-buying line and queue up at the "Entrance with Reservations" line (to the right). Show your voucher to the guard, who will scan it and let you in. Once inside the museum, go to a ticket window (either in the lobby or upstairs), present your voucher and ID, and they'll issue your ticket.

If you book a **guided tour through the Vatican Museum** (see below), you can also skip the ticket-buying line and approach the guard with your voucher. If you book with a private tour company, you may still have a short wait at crowded times.

If you don't have a reservation, **try arriving after 14:00,** when crowds subside somewhat. Another good time is during the papal audience on Wednesday after 10:30, when many tourists are at St. Peter's Basilica.

Make sure you get in the right line. Generally, individuals without tickets line up against the Vatican City wall (to the left of the entrance as you face it), and individuals with reservations enter on the right.

Tours: The Vatican offers English tours that are easy to book online (€31, includes admission, http://mv.vatican.va). As with individual ticket reservations, present your confirmation voucher to a guard to the right of the entrance, then, once inside, go to the Guided Tours desk (in the lobby, up a few stairs).

Both private tour companies and private guides offer guided English tours of the museum, usually allowing you to skip the long ticket-buying line. For a listing of several companies, see page 707.

Audioguide Tours: If you rent an **audioguide** (€7 plus ID, available at the top of the ramp/escalator), you lose the option of taking the shortcut from the Sistine Chapel to St. Peter's (since audioguides must be returned to the museum entrance/exit). You can download a free **audio tour** of the Sistine Chapel portion of this tour at www .ricksteves.com (or search for "Rick Steves Audio Tours" in iTunes).

◑ Self-Guided Tour: Start, as civilization did, in **Egypt and Mesopotamia.** Next, the Pio Clementino collection features **Greek and Roman statues.** Decorating its courtyard are some of the best Greek and Roman statues in captivity, including the *Laocoön* group (first century B.C., Hellenistic) and the *Apollo Belvedere* (a second-century Roman copy of a Greek original). The centerpiece of the next hall is the *Belvedere Torso* (just a 2,000-year-old torso, but one that had a great impact on the art of Michelangelo). Finishing off the classical statuary are two fine fourth-century porphyry sarcophagi. These royal purple tombs were made (though not used) for the Roman emperor Constantine's mother and daughter. They were Christians—and therefore outlaws—until Constantine made Christianity legal in A.D. 312. Both sarcophagi were quarried and worked in Egypt. The technique for working this extremely hard stone (a special tempering of metal was required) was lost after this, and porphyry was not chiseled again until Renaissance times in Florence.

Overachievers may first choose to pop into the **Etruscan wing**—labeled Museo Etrusco—located a few steps up from this level. Others have permission to save their aesthetic energy for the Sistine.

After long halls of tapestries, old maps, broken penises, and fig leaves, you'll come to what most people are looking for: the Raphael Rooms (or *stanza*) and Michelangelo's Sistine Chapel.

These outstanding works are frescoes. A fresco (meaning "fresh" in Italian) is technically not a painting. The color is mixed into wet plaster, and, when the plaster dries, the painting is actually part of the wall. This is a durable but difficult medium, requiring speed and accuracy, as the work is built one patch at a time.

After fancy rooms illustrating the "Immaculate Conception of Mary" (in the 19th century, the Vatican codified this hard-to-sell doctrine, making it a formal part of the Catholic faith) and the triumph of Constantine (with divine guidance, which led to his conversion to Christianity), you enter rooms frescoed by **Raphael** and his assistants. The highlight is the restored *School of Athens*. This is remarkable for its blatant pre-Christian classical orientation, especially since it originally wallpapered the apartments of Pope Julius II. Raphael honors the great pre-Christian thinkers—Aristotle, Plato, and company—who are portrayed as the leading artists of Raphael's day. The bearded figure of Plato is Leonardo da Vinci. Diogenes, history's first hippie, sprawls alone in bright blue on the stairs, while Michelangelo broods in the foreground—supposedly added later. Apparently, Raphael snuck a peek at the Sistine Chapel and decided that his arch-competitor was so good

ROME

Benedict XVI

When Josef Ratzinger became the 265th pope, he introduced himself as "a simple, humble worker in the vineyard of the Lord." But the man has a complex history, a reputation for intellectual brilliance, a flair for the piano, and a penchant for controversy for his unbending devotion to traditional Catholic doctrine.

Born in small-town Bavaria in 1927, he lived life under Nazi rule as many Germans did—outwardly obeying leaders while inwardly conflicted. Like all 14-year-old boys, he joined the Hitler Youth and, like most German men, was drafted into the army. During World War II, he trained to spray flak from anti-aircraft guns, saw Jews transported to death camps, and, like many Germans in the final days of the war, he deserted his post.

After the war, he completed his studies in theology and became a rising voice of liberal Catholicism, serving as an advisor at the Second Vatican Council (1962–1965). But after the May 1968 student revolts rocked Europe's Establishment, he became increasingly convinced that Church tradition was needed to offset the growing chaos of the world.

Pope John Paul II appointed him to several positions, and

that he had to put their personal differences aside and include him in this tribute to the artists of his generation. Today's St. Peter's was under construction as Raphael was working. In the *School of Athens*, he gives us a sneak preview of the unfinished church.

Next is the brilliantly restored **Sistine Chapel.** This is the pope's personal chapel and also the place where, upon the death of the ruling pope, a new pope is elected (as in April 2005).

The Sistine Chapel is famous for Michelangelo's pictorial culmination of the Renaissance, showing the story of creation, with a powerful God weaving in and out of each scene through that busy first week. This is an optimistic and positive expression of the High Renaissance and a stirring example of the artistic and theological maturity of the 33-year-old Michelangelo, who spent four years on this work.

Later, after the Reformation wars had begun and after the Catholic army of Spain had sacked the Vatican, the reeling Church began to fight back. As part of its Counter-Reformation, a much older Michelangelo was commissioned to paint the *Last Judgment* (behind the altar). Beautifully restored, the message is as clear as

Ratzinger became John Paul II's closest advisor and good friend. Every Friday afternoon for two decades, they met for lunch, intellectual sparring, and friendly conversation.

Under John Paul II, Ratzinger served as the Church's "enforcer" of doctrine, earning the nickname "God's Rottweiler." He spoke out against ordaining women, chastised Latin American priests for fomenting class warfare (Liberation theology), reassigned bishops who were soft on homosexuality, reaffirmed opposition to birth control, and wrote thoughtful papers challenging the secular world's moral relativism. He also punished pedophile priests, though critics charged him with glossing over the issue to preserve the Church's image.

Ratzinger chose the name of "Benedict" to recall both Pope Benedict XV (who tried to bring Europeans together after World War I) and the original St. Benedict (c. 480–543), the monk who symbolizes Europe's Christian roots. A true pan-European who speaks many languages, Ratzinger heads a Church that thrives everywhere except Europe, which is becoming increasingly secular (with the notable exception of an increasing Muslim population). In 2006, Benedict stirred controversy among many Muslims with some unguarded remarks. In 2010, he was criticized for not dealing forcefully enough with pedophile priests. Generally, Benedict XVI has continued John Paul II's two priorities: defending Catholic doctrine in a changing world and building bridges with fellow Christians.

the day Michelangelo finished it: Christ is returning, some will go to hell and some to heaven, and some will be saved by the power of the rosary.

In the controversial restoration project, no paint was added. Centuries of dust, soot (from candles used for lighting and Mass), and glue (added to make the art shine) were removed, revealing the bright original colors of Michelangelo. Photos are allowed (without a flash) elsewhere in the museum, but as part of the deal with the company who did the restoration, no photos are allowed in the Sistine Chapel.

For a **shortcut,** a small door at the far-right corner of the Sistine Chapel allows groups and individuals (without an audioguide) to escape directly to St. Peter's Basilica. If you exit here, you're done with the museum. The Pinacoteca is the only important part left. Consider doing it at the start. Otherwise it's a 15-minute heel-to-toe slalom through tourists from the Sistine Chapel to the entry/exit. Be prepared for the odd chance that the shortcut is simply closed (which sometimes happens).

If you take the long march back, you'll find the **Pinacoteca**

Is the Pope Catholic?

Rome's tour guides, who introduce tourists to the city's great art and Christian history, field a lot of interesting questions and comments from their groups. Here are a few of their favorites:

- Oh, to be here in Rome...where our Lord Jesus walked.
- Is this where Christ fought the lions?
- Who's the guy on the cross?
- This guy who made so many nice things, Rene Sance, who is he? (Say it fast, and you'll get the gist.)

- Was John Paul II the son of John Paul I?
- What's the Sistine Chapel worth in US dollars?
- How did Michelangelo get Moses to pose for him?
- What's Michelangelo doing now?
- (Upon seeing the arrow-pierced St. Sebastian) Oh, you Italians had problems with the Indians, too.

(the Vatican's small but fine collection of paintings, with Raphael's *Transfiguration*, Leonardo's unfinished *St. Jerome*, and Caravaggio's *Deposition*), a cafeteria (long lines, uninspired food), and the under-rated early Christian art section, before you exit via the souvenir shop.

▲▲▲St. Peter's Basilica (Basilica San Pietro)

There is no doubt: This is the richest and grandest church on earth. To call it vast is like calling Einstein smart. Plaques on the floor show where other, smaller churches would end if they were placed inside. The ornamental cherubs would dwarf a large man. Birds roost inside, and thousands of people wander about, heads craned heavenward, hardly noticing each other. Don't miss Michelangelo's *Pietà* (behind bulletproof glass) to the right of the entrance. Bernini's altar work and seven-story-tall bronze canopy are brilliant.

Dress Code: No shorts or bare shoulders (applies to men, women, and children), and no miniskirts. This dress code is strictly enforced.

Hours: Daily April–Sept 7:00–19:00, Oct–March 7:00–18:00. The church closes on Wednesday mornings during papal audiences. The best time to visit the church is early or late; at 17:00, when the church is fairly empty, sunbeams can work their

ROME

magic, and the late-afternoon Mass fills the place with spiritual music.

Tours: The Vatican TI conducts free 1.5-hour tours of **St. Peter's** (depart Mon–Fri from TI, generally at 9:45 and 14:15, confirm schedule at TI, tel. 06-6988-1662). Audioguides can be rented near the checkroom (€5 plus ID, daily 9:00–17:00). You can download a free audio tour at www.ricksteves.com (or search for "Rick Steves Audio Tours" in iTunes).

If you want to see the **Vatican Gardens,** you must book a tour online at least a week in advance at http://biglietteriamusei .vatican.va. No response means they're booked up (€31, 2 hours, usually daily except Wed and Sat, includes entry to Vatican Museum; tours start at 9:30 or 10:00 at Vatican Museum tour desk).

To see St. Peter's original grave, you can take a **Scavi "Excavations"** tour into the Necropolis (€12, 1.5 hours, ages 15 and older only, no photos). Book at least a month in advance by email (scavi@fsp.va) or fax (06-6987-3017), following the detailed instructions at www.vatican.va; no response means they're booked up.

Dome Climb (Cupola): Daily April–Sept 8:00–18:00, Oct–March 8:00–17:00. Allow one hour for the round-trip to the top of the dome (or a half-hour to the roof). You can take the elevator or stairs to the roof (231 steps up), then climb another 323 steps to the top of the dome. The entry to the elevator is just outside the basilica on the north side of St. Peter's (near the secret exit from the Sistine Chapel). Look for signs to the cupola.

○ Self-Guided Tour: For a quick walk through the basilica, follow these points:

❶ The atrium is itself bigger than most churches. The huge white columns on the portico date from the first church (fourth century). Notice the historic doors (the Holy Door, on the right, won't be opened until the next Jubilee Year, in 2025).

❷ The purple, circular porphyry stone marks the site of Charlemagne's coronation in A.D. 800 (in the first St. Peter's church that stood on this site). From here, get a sense of the immensity of the church, which can accommodate 60,000 worshippers standing on its six acres.

❸ Michelangelo planned a Greek-cross floor plan, rather than the Latin-cross standard in medieval churches. A Greek cross, symbolizing the perfection of God, and by association the goodness of man, was important to the humanist Michelangelo. But accommodating large crowds was important to the Church in the fancy Baroque age, which followed Michelangelo, so the original nave length was doubled. Stand halfway up the nave and imagine the stubbier design that Michelangelo had in mind.

❹ View the magnificent dome from the statue of St. Andrew. See the vision of heaven above the windows: Jesus, Mary, a ring of

St. Peter's Basilica

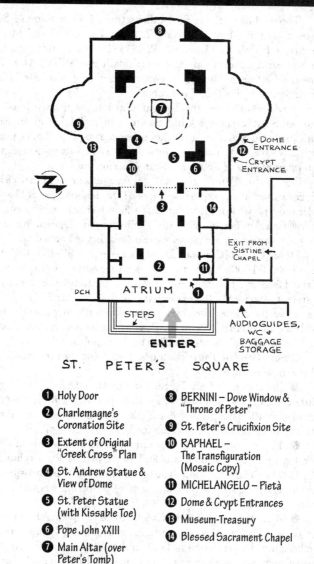

1. Holy Door
2. Charlemagne's Coronation Site
3. Extent of Original "Greek Cross" Plan
4. St. Andrew Statue & View of Dome
5. St. Peter Statue (with Kissable Toe)
6. Pope John XXIII
7. Main Altar (over Peter's Tomb)
8. BERNINI – Dove Window & "Throne of Peter"
9. St. Peter's Crucifixion Site
10. RAPHAEL – The Transfiguration (Mosaic Copy)
11. MICHELANGELO – Pietà
12. Dome & Crypt Entrances
13. Museum-Treasury
14. Blessed Sacrament Chapel

saints, rings of angels, and, on the very top, God the Father.

❺ The statue of St. Peter, with an irresistibly kissable toe, is one of the few pieces of art that predate this church. It adorned the first St. Peter's church.

❻ Circle to the right around the statue of Peter to find the lighted glass niche with the red-robed body of Pope John XXIII (r. 1958–1963), who oversaw major reforms in the Vatican II conference.

❼ The main altar sits directly over St. Peter's tomb and under Bernini's seven-story bronze canopy.

❽ St. Peter's throne and Bernini's starburst dove window is the site of a daily Mass (Mon–Sat at 17:00, Sun at 17:45—after vespers at 17:00).

❾ St. Peter was crucified here when this location was simply "the Vatican Hill." The obelisk now standing in the center of St. Peter's square marked the center of a Roman racecourse long before a church stood here.

❿ The church is filled with mosaics, not paintings. Notice the mosaic version of Raphael's *Transfiguration*.

⓫ Michelangelo sculpted his *Pietà* when he was 24 years old. (A *pietà* is a work that represents Mary with the body of Christ taken down from the cross.) Michelangelo's mastery of the body is obvious in this powerfully beautiful masterpiece. Jesus is believably dead, and Mary, the eternally youthful "handmaiden" of the Lord, accepts God's will...even if it means giving up her son.

The Holy Door (to the right of the *Pietà*, covered in gray concrete with a gold cross) won't be reopened until Christmas Eve, 2024, the dawn of the next Jubilee Year. Every 25 years, the Church celebrates an especially festive year derived from the Old Testament idea of the Jubilee Year (originally every 50 years), which encourages new beginnings and the forgiveness of sins and debts.

⓬ Visitors can go down to the Crypt within the foundations of Old St. Peter's, containing tombs of popes and memorial chapels. Exit the basilica and turn left to head down the steps (back out the way you entered, unless you took the Vatican Museum shortcut). You'll see people here lined up to visit the Crypt, and to ride up to the roof.

An elevator leads to the roof and the stairway up the dome (€7, allow an hour to go up and down). The dome, Michelangelo's last work, is (you guessed it) the biggest anywhere. Taller than a football field is long, it's well worth the sweaty climb for a great view of Rome, the Vatican grounds, and the inside of the basilica— particularly heavenly while there is singing. Look around—Rome has no modern skyline. No building in Rome is allowed to exceed the height of St. Peter's. The elevator takes you to the rooftop of the nave. From there, a few steps take you to a balcony at the base of the dome looking down into the church interior. After that, the one-way, 323-step climb (for some people, it's claustrophobic) to the cupola begins. The rooftop level (below the dome) has a gift shop, WC, drinking fountain, and a commanding view.

🔞 For most, the museum (in the sacristy) is not worth the admission.

🔞 Blessed Sacrament Chapel. You're welcome to step through the metalwork gates into this oasis of peace reserved for prayer and meditation.

Near Vatican City

▲**Castel Sant'Angelo**—Built as a tomb for the emperor, used through the Middle Ages as a castle, prison, and place of last refuge for popes under attack, and today a museum, this giant pile of ancient bricks is packed with history.

Ancient Rome allowed no tombs—not even the emperor's—within its walls. So Emperor Hadrian grabbed the most commanding position just outside the walls and across the river and built a towering tomb (c. A.D. 139) well within view of the city. His mausoleum was a huge cylinder (210 by 70 feet) topped by a cypress grove and crowned by a huge statue of Hadrian himself riding a chariot. For nearly a hundred years, Roman emperors (from Hadrian to Caracalla, in A.D. 217) were buried here.

In the year 590, the Archangel Michael appeared above the mausoleum to Pope Gregory the Great. Sheathing his sword, the angel signaled the end of a plague. The fortress that was Hadrian's mausoleum eventually became a fortified palace, renamed for the "holy angel."

Castel Sant'Angelo spent centuries of the Dark Ages as a fortress and prison, but was eventually connected to the Vatican via an elevated corridor at the pope's request (1277). Since Rome was repeatedly plundered by invaders, Castel Sant'Angelo was a handy place of last refuge for threatened popes. In anticipation of long sieges, rooms were decorated with papal splendor (you'll see paintings by Carlo Crivelli, Luca Signorelli, and Andrea Mantegna). In 1527, during a sack of Rome by troops of Charles V of Spain, the pope lived inside the castle for months with his entourage of hundreds (an unimaginable ordeal, considering the food service at the top-floor bar).

ROME

Touring the place is a stair-stepping workout. After you walk around the entire base of the castle, take the small staircase down to the original Roman floor (following the route of Hadrian's funeral procession). In the atrium, study the model of the mausoleum as it was in Roman times. Imagine being surrounded by a veneer of marble, and the niche in the wall filled with a towering "welcome to my tomb" statue of Hadrian. From here, a ramp leads to the right, spiraling 400 feet. While some of the fine original brickwork and bits of mosaic survive, the marble veneer is long gone (notice the holes in the wall that held it in place). At the end of the ramp, a bridge crosses over the room where the ashes of the emperors were kept. From here, the stairs continue out of the ancient section and into the medieval structure (built atop the mausoleum) that housed the papal apartments. Don't miss the Sala del Tesoro (Treasury), where the wealth of the Vatican was locked up in a huge chest. (*Do* miss the 58 rooms of the military museum.) From the pope's piggy bank, a narrow flight of stairs leads to the rooftop and perhaps the finest view of Rome anywhere (pick out landmarks as you stroll around). From the safety of this dramatic vantage point, the pope surveyed the city in times of siege. Look down at the bend of the Tiber, which for 2,700 years has cradled the Eternal City.

Cost and Hours: €5, more for special exhibits, Tue–Sun 9:00–19:30, closed Mon, last entry one hour before closing, near Vatican City, Metro: Lepanto or bus #64, tel. 06-681-9111.

Ponte Sant'Angelo—The bridge leading to Castel Sant'Angelo was built by Hadrian for quick and regal access from downtown to his tomb. The three middle arches are actually Roman origi-

nals, and a fine example of the empire's engineering expertise. The statues of angels (each bearing a symbol of the passion of Christ—nail, sponge, shroud, and so on) are Bernini-designed and textbook Baroque. In the Middle Ages, this was the only bridge in the area that connected St. Peter's and the Vatican with downtown Rome. Nearly all pilgrims passed this bridge to and from the church. Its shoulder-high banisters recall a tragedy: During a Jubilee Year festival in 1450, the crowd got so huge that the mob pushed out the original banisters, causing nearly 200 to fall to their deaths.

Trastevere

Trastevere is the colorful neighborhood across *(tras)* the Tiber *(Tevere)* River. Trastevere (trahs-TAY-veh-ray) offers the best look

ROME

Trastevere

Hotel/Restaurants

1. Hotel Santa Maria
2. Residenza Arco dei Tolomei & Arco del Lauro B&B
3. Relais le Clarisse
4. Casa San Giuseppe
5. Trattoria da Lucia
6. Trattoria da Olindo
7. Dar Poeta Pizzeria
8. Osteria Ponte Sisto da Oliviero
9. Ristorante Checco er Carettiere
10. Pizzeria "Ai Marmi"
11. To Cantina Paradiso
12. Gelateria alla Scala

ROME

at medieval-village Rome. The action unwinds to the chime of the church bells. Go there and wander. Wonder. Be a poet. This is Rome's Left Bank.

This proud neighborhood was long a working-class area. Now that it's becoming trendy, high rents are driving out the source of so much color. Still, it's a great people scene, especially at night. Stroll the back streets (for restaurant recommendations, see page 807).

To reach Trastevere by foot from Capitol Hill, cross the Tiber on Ponte Cestio (over Isola Tiberina). You can also take tram #8 from Largo Argentina, or bus #H from Termini and Via Nazionale

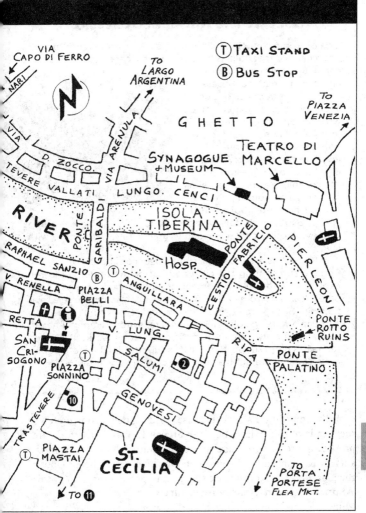

(get off at Piazza Belli). From the Vatican (Piazza Risorgimento), it's bus #23 or #271.

Linking Trastevere with my "Night Walk Across Rome": You can walk from Trastevere to Campo de' Fiori to link up with the beginning of my "Night Walk Across Rome" (see page 720): From Trastevere's church square (Piazza di Santa Maria), take Via del Moro to the river and cross at Ponte Sisto, a pedestrian bridge that has a good view of St. Peter's dome. Continue straight ahead for one block. Take the first left, which leads down Via di Capo di Ferro through the scary and narrow darkness to Piazza Farnese,

Soccer: The National Obsession

One of Rome's most local "sights" is a soccer match. Winston Churchill said that Italians lose wars like soccer matches and soccer matches like wars; soccer, or *calcio,* is the national obsession. Everyone, regardless of age or social class, is an expert, quick with an opinion on a coach's lousy decision or a referee's unprofessional conduct. Fans love to insult officials: A favorite is *"arbitro cornuto!"*—the referee is a cuckold (i.e., his wife sleeps around). The country's obsession turned into jubilation on

July 9, 2006, when Italy won the World Cup, and Rome—along with every other city, town, and village in Italy—went crazy with joy.

Rome has a special passion for soccer. It has two teams, Roma (representing the city) and Lazio (the region), and the rivalry is fanatic. When Romans are introduced, they ask each other, *"Laziale o romanista?"* The answer can compromise a relationship. Both Roma (jersey: yellow and red; symbol: she-wolf) and Lazio (jersey: light blue and white; symbol: imperial eagle) claim to be truly Roman. Lazio is older (founded in 1900), but Roma has more supporters. Lazio is supposed to be more upper-class, Roma more popular, but the social division is blurred.

with the imposing Palazzo Farnese. Michelangelo contributed to the facade of this palace, now the French Embassy. The fountains on the square feature huge one-piece granite hot tubs from the ancient Roman Baths of Caracalla. One block from there (opposite the palace) is the atmospheric square Campo de' Fiori.

▲**Santa Maria in Trastevere Church**—
One of Rome's oldest churches, this was made a basilica in the fourth century, when Christianity was legalized (free, daily 7:30–21:00). It was the first church dedicated to the Virgin Mary. Its portico (covered area just outside the door) is decorated with fascinating fragments of stone—many of them lids from catacomb burial niches—and filled with early Christian symbolism. The church is on Piazza di Santa Maria, the Trastevere neighborhood's most important meeting

The most eagerly awaited sporting event of the year is the derby, when the two teams fight it out at the Olympic Stadium. All of Italy acknowledges that team spirit is most fervent in Rome. Fans prepare months in advance, and on the day of the match they fill the entire stadium with team colors, flags, banners, and flares.

Witty slogans on banners work like dialogues: A Roma banner proclaimed, "Roma: Only the sky is higher than you." The Lazio banner replied, "In fact, the sky is blue and white" (like its team colors). The exchange revealed that there had been a Lazio informer on the Roma side, which traumatized Roma fans for weeks. Tourists go to a match more for the action in the stands than the action on the field—it's one of the most Roman of all experiences.

Both teams call the Stadio Olimpico home, so you can catch a game most weekends from September to May (Metro line A to Flaminio, then catch tram #2 to the end of the line, Piazza Mancini, and cross the bridge to the stadium). If you're coming from Termini train station, take bus #910; from the Vatican, take bus #32 from Piazza Risorgimento.

place. During major soccer games, a large screen is set up here so that everybody can share in the tension and excitement. At other times, children gather here with a ball and improvise matches of their own. For more information on the Italian passion for soccer, see sidebar above.

▲**Villa Farnesina**—Here's a unique opportunity to see a sumptuous Renaissance villa in Rome decorated with Raphael paintings. It was built in the early 1500s for the richest man in Renaissance Europe, Siennese banker Agostino Chigi. Architect Baldassare Peruzzi's design—a U-shaped building with wings enfolding what used to be a vast garden—successfully blended architecture and nature in a way that both ancient and Renaissance Romans loved. Orchards and flower beds flowed down in terraces from the palace to the riverbanks. Later construction of modern embankments and avenues robbed the garden of its grandeur, leaving it with a more melancholy charm.

In the **Loggia of Galatea,** find Raphael's painting of the nymph Galatea (on the wall by the entrance door). Galatea is

ROME

considered Raphael's vision of female perfection—not a portrait of an individual woman, but a composite of his many lovers in an idealized vision. Raphael and his assistants also painted the subtly erotic **Loggia of Psyche.**

Cost and Hours: €5; April–June and mid-Sept–Oct Mon–Sat 9:00–16:00, closed Sun; July–mid-Sept and Nov–March Mon–Sat 9:00–13:00, closed Sun; across the river from Campo de' Fiori, a short walk from Ponte Sisto on Via della Lungara, tel. 06-6802-7268.

Gianicolo Hill Viewpoint—From this park atop a hill, the city views are superb, and the walk to the top holds a treat for architecture buffs. Start at Trastevere's Piazza di San Cosimato, and follow Via Luciano Manara to Via Garibaldi, at the base of the hill. Via Garibaldi winds its way up the side of the hill to the church of San Pietro in Montorio. To the right of the church, in a small courtyard, is the Tempietto by Donato Bramante. This tiny church, built to commemorate the martyrdom of St. Peter, is considered a jewel of Italian Renaissance architecture.

Continuing up the hill, Via Garibaldi connects to Passeggiata del Gianicolo. From here, you'll find a pleasant park with panoramic city views. Ponder the many Victorian-era statues, including that of baby-carrying, gun-wielding, horse-riding Anita Garibaldi. She was the Brazilian wife of the revolutionary General Giuseppe Garibaldi, who helped forge a united Italy in the late 19th century.

Near Trastevere: Jewish Quarter

From the 16th through the 19th centuries, Rome's Jewish population was forced to live in a cramped ghetto at an often-flooded bend of the Tiber River. While the medieval Jewish ghetto is long gone, this area—just across the river and toward Capitol Hill from Trastevere—is still home to Rome's synagogue and fragments of its Jewish heritage. If you'd like more background on this neighborhood and have an iPod or other MP3 player, download my free audio tour at www.ricksteves.com (or search for "Rick Steves Audio Tours" in iTunes).

Synagogue (Sinagoga) and Jewish Museum (Museo Ebraico)—Rome's modern synagogue stands proudly on the spot where the medieval Jewish community lived in squalor for more than 300 years. The site of a historic visit by Pope John Paul II, this synagogue features a fine interior and a museum filled with artifacts of Rome's Jewish community. The only way to visit the synagogue—unless you're here for daily prayer service—is with a tour.

Cost and Hours: €7.50 ticket includes museum and guided hourly tour of synagogue; June–Sept Sun–Thu 10:00–19:00, Fri 10:00–16:00, closed Sat; Oct–May Sun–Thu 10:00–17:00, Fri 9:00–14:00, closed Sat; last entry 45 minutes before closing, modest dress required, English tours usually at :15 past the hour, 30 minutes, check schedule at ticket counter; on Lungotevere dei Cenci, tel. 06-6840-0661, www.museoebraico.roma.it. Walking tours of the Jewish Ghetto are conducted at least once a day except Saturday (€8, usually at 13:15, sign up at museum 30 minutes before departure, minimum of 3 required).

South Rome

Testaccio

In the gritty Testaccio neighborhood, several fascinating but lesser sights cluster at the Piramide Metro stop between the Colosseum and E.U.R. (This is a quick and easy stop as you return from E.U.R., or when changing trains en route to Ostia Antica.)

Working-class since ancient times, the Testaccio neighborhood has recently gone trendy-bohemian. Visitors wander through an awkward mix of yuppie and proletarian worlds, not noticing—but perhaps sensing—the "Keep Testaccio for the Testaccians" graffiti. This has long been the neighborhood of slaughterhouses, and its restaurants are renowned for their ability to cook up the least palatable part of the animals...the "fifth quarter." High-end shoe and clothing boutiques have moved into the market and the neighborhood nearby, and this is now one of the best areas in Rome to have shoes custom-made. The covered **Mercato di Testaccio** (on Piazza Testaccio, two blocks west of Via Marmarata) dominates the center of the neighborhood. This is hands-down the best, most authentic food market in Rome (Mon–Sat until 13:00). It's where Romans shop while tourists flock to Campo de' Fiori.

Pyramid of Gaius Cestius—An Egyptian-style pyramid from ancient Rome stands next to the Piramide Metro stop. The Mark Antony/ Cleopatra scandal (c. 30 B.C.) brought exotic Egyptian styles into vogue. A rich Roman magistrate, Gaius Cestius, had this pyramid built as his tomb, complete with a burial chamber inside. Made of brick covered in marble, the 90-foot structure was completed in just 330 days (as stated in its Latin inscription). While

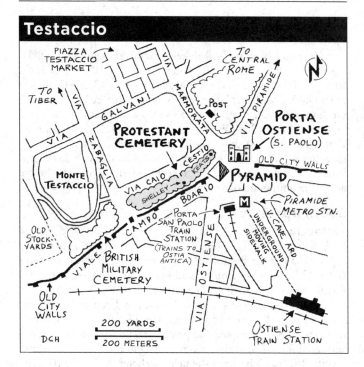

Testaccio

smaller than actual Egyptian pyramids, its proportions are correct. It was later incorporated into the Aurelian Wall, and it now stands as a marker to the entrance of Testaccio.

Porta Ostiense and Museo della Via Ostiense—This formidable gate (also next to the Piramide Metro stop) is from the Aurelian Wall, begun in the third century A.D. under Emperor Aurelian. The wall, which encircled the city, was 12 miles long and averaged about 26 feet high, with 14 main gates and 380 72-foot-tall towers. Most of what you'll see today is circa A.D. 400, but the barbarians reconstructed the gate later, in the sixth century.

Inside the gate is a tiny free museum (find entrance near pyramid; open Tue–Sat and first Sun of month 9:00–13:30, closed Mon and most Sun). The museum offers a free ramble along the ramparts, plus exhibits on Ostia Antica, Rome's ancient port (for more information, see page 790). You'll see models of the ancient city and its famed hexagonal harbor, and of the Ostian Way—the straight Roman road that paralleled the curvy Tiber for 15 miles from Rome to the sea. (For more on the Aurelian Wall, visit the San Sebastiano Gate and Museum of the Walls; see page 789.)

Protestant Cemetery—The Cemetery for the Burial of Non-Catholic Foreigners (Cimitero Acattolico per gli Stranieri al Testaccio) is a tomb-filled park, running along the wall just beyond the pyramid. The cemetery is also the only English-style landscape (rolling hills, calculated vistas) in Rome, and a favorite spot for quiet picnics and strolls. From the Piramide Metro stop, walk between the pyramid and the Roman gate on Via Persichetti, then go left on Caio Cestio to the gate of the cemetery. If it's locked, ring the bell to get inside.

Originally, none of the Protestant epitaphs were allowed to make any mention of heaven. Signs direct visitors to the graves of notable non-Catholics who died in Rome since 1738. Many of the buried were diplomats. And many, such as the poets Percy Shelley (1792–1822) and John Keats (1795–1821), were from the Romantic Age. They came on the Grand Tour and—"captivated by the fatal charms of Rome," as Shelley wrote—never left.

Head 90 degrees left to find Keats' tomb, in the far corner. Keats died in his twenties, unrecognized. He wanted to be unnamed on a tomb that read, "Young English Poet, 1821. Here lies one whose name was writ in water." (To see Keats' tomb if the cemetery is closed, look through the tiny peephole on Via Caio Cestio, 10 yards off Via Marmarata.) Shelley's tomb is straight ahead from the entrance, up the hill, at the base of the stubby tower.

Cost and Hours: €2 suggested donation—leave in box by entrance, Mon–Sat 9:00–17:00, Sun 9:00–13:00, last entry 30 minutes before closing, staff at info office can help you find specific graves, www.protestantcemetery.it.

Monte Testaccio—This small hill is a popular nightlife spot near the Protestant Cemetery (as you leave the cemetery, turn left and continue two blocks down Caio Cestio). The hill, actually a 115-foot-tall ancient trash pile, is made of broken *testae*—earthenware jars mostly used to haul oil 2,000 years ago, when this was a gritty port warehouse district. For 500 years, rancid oil vessels were discarded here. Slowly, Rome's lowly eighth hill was built. Because the caves dug into the hill stay cool, trendy bars, clubs, and restaurants compete with gritty car-repair places for a spot. The neighborhood was once known for a huge slaughterhouse and a Roma (Gypsy) camp that squatted inside an old military base. Now it's home to the Testaccio Village, a site for concerts and techno raves. To do the full monty, arrive after 21:00, when the restaurant-and-club scene is youthful and lively (Metro: Piramide).

South of Testaccio
▲Montemartini Museum (Musei Capitolini Centrale Montemartini)—This museum houses a dreamy collection of 400 ancient statues, set evocatively in a classic 1932 electric power plant, among generators and *Metropolis*-type cast-iron machinery. While the art is not as famous as the collections you'll see downtown, the effect is fun and memorable—and you'll encounter absolutely no

South of Testaccio

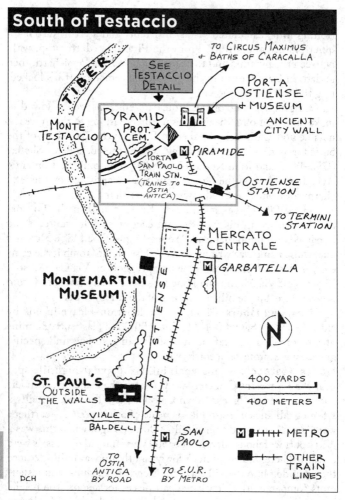

tourists. If you're tackling Rome with kids, this museum is ideal: it's uncrowded and cool, immersed in an old power plant, with art placed at kid-level.

Cost and Hours: €4.50, often €6.50–9 with special exhibits, €8.50–13 combo-ticket with Capitoline Museums, Tue–Sun 9:00–19:00, closed Mon, last entry 30 minutes before closing, Via Ostiense 106, a short walk from Metro: Garbatella, tel. 06-574-8042, www.centralemontemartini.org.

▲**St. Paul's Outside the Walls (Basilica San Paolo Fuori le Mura)**—This was the last major construction project of Imperial Rome (c. A.D. 380) and the largest church in Christendom until

St. Peter's. After a tragic 19th-century fire, St. Paul's was rebuilt in the same general style and size as the original. The column-lined courtyard leading up to the church is typical of early Christian churches—the first version of St. Peter's Basilica also had this kind of welcoming zone.

Step inside and feel as close as you'll get in the 21st century to experiencing a monumental Roman basilica. Marvel at the ceiling, and imagine building it with those massive wood beams in A.D. 380.

Alabaster windows light the vast interior. It feels sterile, but in a good way—like you're already in heaven. Along with St. Peter's Basilica, San Giovanni in Laterano, and Santa Maria Maggiore, this church is part of the Vatican rather than Italy. The triumphal arch leading to the altar has a fifth-century mosaic of Christ raising his hand in blessing. The church is built upon the supposed grave of St. Paul. According to tradition, Paul was decapitated two miles from this spot. His head was preserved at San Giovanni in Laterano, and his body was buried here under the altar. In 2006, archaeologists unearthed a sarcophagus which had early inscriptions identifying it as Paul's.

Ringing the upper part of the church are round mosaic portraits of 265 popes, from St. Peter (the first one in the right transept) to the present. Find the recent popes to the right of the altar—not in the nave, but farther to the right, under the arches of the dim right aisle. You'll see globetrotting John Paul II *(Jo Paulus II)* and progressive John XXIII, who oversaw the Vatican II changes of the 1960s. A portrait of Pope #265—Benedict XVI—was recently installed, alongside blank medallions for future popes.

The peaceful 13th-century cloister (€3) has elegant Romanesque columns and arches, and fragments of early Christian/Roman sarcophagi.

Cost and Hours: Free, daily 7:00–18:30, modest dress code enforced, dry audioguide €5 plus ID, Via Ostiense 186, Metro: San Paolo, exit the Metro station and look for the church's round tower, www.basilicasanpaolo.org.

ROME

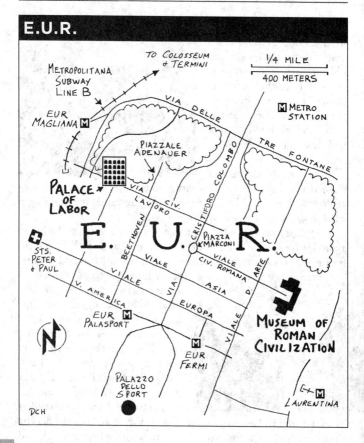

E.U.R.

In the late 1930s, Italy's dictator, Benito Mussolini, planned an international exhibition to show off the wonders of his fascist society. But these wonders brought us World War II, and Il Duce's

celebration never happened. The unfinished mega-project was completed in the 1950s, and today it houses government offices and big, obscure museums filled with important, rarely visited relics.

If Hitler and Mussolini had won the war, our world might look like E.U.R. (AY-oor). Hike down E.U.R.'s wide, pedestrian-mean boulevards. Patriotic murals, aren't-you-proud-to-be-an-extreme-right-winger pillars, and stern squares decorate the soulless planned grid and stark office blocks. Boulevards named for Astronomy, Electronics, Social Security, and Beethoven are more exhausting than inspirational. Today, E.U.R. is worth a trip for its Museum of Roman Civilization (described below). And because a few landmark buildings of Italian modernism are located here and there, E.U.R. has become an important destination for architecture buffs.

The Metro skirts E.U.R. with three stops (10 minutes from the Colosseum). Use E.U.R. Magliana for the "Square Colosseum" and E.U.R. Fermi for the Museum of Roman Civilization. Consider walking 30 minutes from the palace to the museum through the center of E.U.R.

Palace of the Civilization of Labor (Palazzo della Civiltà del Lavoro)—From the Magliana Metro stop, stairs lead uphill to this epitome of fascist architecture. With its giant no-questions-asked patriotic statues and its black-and-white simplicity, this is E.U.R.'s tallest building and key landmark. It's understandably nicknamed the "Square Colosseum." Around the corner, Caffè Palombini is still decorated in a 1930s style and is quite popular with young Romans (daily 7:00–22:00; good gelato, pastries, and snacks; Piazzale Adenauer 12, tel. 06-591-1700).

▲**Museum of Roman Civilization (Museo della Civiltà Romana)**—With 59 rooms of plaster casts and models illustrat-

ing the greatness of classical Rome, this vast and heavy museum gives a strangely lifeless, close-up look at Rome. Each room has a theme, from military tricks to musical instruments. One long hall is filled with casts of the reliefs of Trajan's Column. The highlight is the 1:250-scale model of Constantine's Rome, circa A.D. 300. The Planetarium and Astrological Museum are mostly of interest to children—so don't bother with the €8.50 combo-ticket unless you have kids.

ROME

Cost and Hours: €6.50, sometimes €9 with special exhibits, Tue–Sat 9:00–14:00, Sun 9:00–13:30, closed Mon, last entry one hour before closing, Piazza G. Agnelli; leave the E.U.R. Fermi Metro station on Via America, head toward McDonald's, and at T-intersection, turn left and go uphill three blocks to Via dell'Arte—you'll see its colonnade on the right; to return to the city center, access the Metro entrance across the street, tel. 06-5422-0919, www.museociviltaromana.it.

Ancient Appian Way and Southeast Rome

Baths of Caracalla (Terme di Caracalla)—Inaugurated by Emperor Caracalla in A.D. 216, this massive bath complex could accommodate 1,600 visitors at a time. Today it's just a shell—a

huge shell—with all of its sculptures and most of its mosaics moved to museums. You'll see a two-story roofless brick building surrounded by a garden, bordered by ruined walls. The two large rooms at either end of the building were used for exercise. In between the exercise rooms was a pool flanked by two small mosaic-floored dressing rooms. Niches in the walls once held statues. (The statues are displayed elsewhere: for example, the immense *Toro Farnese*—a marble sculpture of a bull surrounded by people—snorts in Naples' Archaeological Museum.)

In its day, this was a remarkable place to hang out. For ancient Romans, bathing was a social experience. The Baths of Caracalla functioned until Goths severed the aqueducts in the sixth century. In modern times, grand operas are performed here.

Cost and Hours: €6; Tue–Sun 9:00 until one hour before sunset: 19:00 in summer, 16:30 in winter; Mon 9:00–14:00, last entry one hour before closing.

Information: Audioguide-€4, free downloadable audio tour at www.pierreci.it—choose English and search for "terme di caracalla," good €8 guidebook can be read in shaded garden while sitting on a chunk of column.

Getting There: Take the Metro to Circus Maximus, then walk five minutes south along Via delle Terme di Caracalla; bus #714 from Termini Station or bus #118 from the Appian Way—see "Getting There" under next listing; tel. 06-3996-7700.

▲**Appian Way**—For a taste of the countryside around Rome and more wonders of Roman engineering, take the four-mile trip

from the Colosseum out past the wall to a stretch of the ancient Appian Way, where the original pavement stones are lined by several interesting sights. Ancient Rome's first and greatest highway, the Appian Way once ran from Rome to the Adriatic port of Brindisi, the gateway to Greece. Today you can walk (or bike) some stretches of the road, rattling over original paving stones, past crumbling monuments that once lined the sides.

The wonder of its day, the Appian Way (named after Appius Claudius Caecus, a Roman official) was the largest, widest, fastest

The Ancient Appian Way

TO
SAN SEBASTIANO GATE,
MUSEUM OF THE WALLS
& DOWNTOWN ROME

Ⓐ Bus #660 Stop
Ⓑ Bus #118 Stops
Ⓒ Bus #118 (Southbound Stop Only)
Ⓓ Bus #218 Stop
Ⓔ Archeobus Stops

DOMINE QUO VADIS CHURCH

VIA · APPIA

ARDEATINA

PEDESTRIAN WALKWAY (CLOSED WED)

COLUMBARIUM
SECOND MILESTONE

VICOLO DELLA BASILICA

CATACOMBS OF SAN CALLISTO & WC

FOSSE ARDEANTINE

VIA D. SETTE CHIESE

VILLA OF MAXENTIUS

CIRCUS OF MAXENTIUS

CATACOMBS OF SAN SEBASTIANO & WC

VIA DI SAN SEB.

VIA · ANTICA ·

TOMB OF CECILIA METELLA

THIRD MILESTONE

VIA CECILIA METELLA

TO AQUEDUCT PARK

APPIA ANTICA CAFFÈ & BIKE RENTAL

ALIMENTARI

TORRE DI CAPO DI BOVE

SCENIC SECTION

N

¼ MILE
.5 KM

VIA CAPO DI BOVE

TO
4TH THROUGH 11TH MILESTONES & BRINDISI

DCH

ROME

Catacombs

The catacombs are burial places for (mostly) Christians who died in ancient Roman times. By law, no one was allowed to be buried within the walls of Rome. While pagan Romans were into cremation, Christians preferred to be buried (so that they could be resurrected when the time came). But land was expensive, and most Christians were poor. A few wealthy, landowning Christians allowed their properties to be used as burial places.

The 40 or so known catacombs are scattered outside the ancient walls of Rome. From the first through the fifth centuries, Christians dug an estimated 375 miles of tomb-lined tunnels, with networks of galleries as many as five layers deep. The volcanic tuff that Rome sits atop—which is soft and easy to cut, but hardens when exposed to air—was perfect for the job. The Christians burrowed many layers deep for two reasons: to get more mileage out of the donated land, and to be near martyrs and saints already buried there. Bodies were wrapped in linen (like Christ's). Since they figured the Second Coming was imminent, there was no interest in embalming the body.

When Emperor Constantine legalized Christianity in A.D. 313, Christians had a new, interesting problem: There would be no more recently persecuted martyrs to bind them together and inspire them. Instead, the early martyrs and popes assumed more importance, and Christians began making pilgrimages to their burial places in the catacombs.

In the 800s, when barbarian invaders started ransacking the tombs, Christians moved the relics of saints and martyrs to the safety of churches in the city center. For a thousand years, the catacombs were forgotten. In early modern times, they were excavated and became part of the Romantic Age's Grand Tour of Europe.

ROME

road ever, called the "Queen of Roads." Built in 312 B.C., it connected Rome with Capua (near Naples), running in a straight line for much of the way, ignoring the natural contour of the land. Eventually, this most important of Roman roads stretched 430 miles to the port of Brindisi—the gateway to the East—where boats sailed for Greece and Egypt. Twenty-nine such roads fanned out from Rome. Just as Hitler built the Autobahn system in anticipation of empire maintenance, the expansion-minded Roman government realized the military and political value of a good road system.

Today the road and the landscape around it are preserved as a cultural park. For the tourist, the ancient Appian Way offers three attractions: the road itself, with its ruined monuments; the two major Christian catacombs open to visitors; and the peaceful atmosphere, which provides a respite from the city. Be aware, however, that the road today is busy with traffic—and actually

When abandoned plates and utensils from ritual meals were found, 18th- and 19th-century Romantics guessed that persecuted Christians hid out in these candlelit galleries. The popularity of this legend grew—even though it was untrue. By the second century, more than a million people lived in Rome, and the 10,000 early Christians didn't need to camp out in the catacombs. They hid in plain view, melting into obscurity within the city itself.

The underground tunnels, while empty of bones, are rich in early Christian symbolism, which functioned as a secret language. The dove represented the soul. You'll see it quenching its thirst (worshipping), with an olive branch (at rest), or happily perched (in paradise). Peacocks, known for their purportedly "incorruptible flesh," embodied immortality. The shepherd with

a lamb on his shoulders was the "good shepherd," the first portrayal of Christ as a kindly leader of his flock. The fish was used because the first letters of these words—"Jesus Christ, Son of God, Savior"—spelled "fish" in Greek. And the anchor is a cross in disguise. A second-century bishop had written on his tomb, "All who understand these things, pray for me." You'll see pictures of people praying with their hands raised—the custom at the time.

quite treacherous in spots.

The road starts at the massive **San Sebastiano Gate and Museum of the Walls,** about two miles south of the Colosseum (€3, Tue–Sun 9:00–14:00, closed Mon, last entry 30 minutes before closing, tel. 06-7047-5284). The stretch that's of most interest to tourists starts another two miles south of the gate. I like to begin near the Tomb of Cecilia Metella, at the far (southern) end of the key sights, and work northward (mostly downhill) toward central Rome.

Getting There: To get to the Tomb of Cecilia Metella on **public bus #660,** take Metro line A from central Rome to the Colli Albani stop, where you catch bus #660 (along Via Appia Nuova) and ride 10 minutes to the last stop—Cecilia Metella/Via Appia Antica. This drops you off right at the intersection of Via Appia Antica and Via Cecilia Metella. As it can be frustrating to buy a bus ticket on the Appian Way, have one in hand for your return trip.

A **taxi** will get you from Rome to the Tomb of Cecilia Metella for about €20. However, to return by taxi, you'll have to phone for one, as there are no taxi stands on the Appian Way (or just take handy bus #118 back to Rome).

If you want to visit just a few sights, consider **bus #118.** In Rome, catch #118 from either the Piramide or Circo Massimo Metro stops; going away from the city center, it stops at the San Sebastiano Gate, Domine Quo Vadis Church, Catacombs of San Callisto, and Catacombs of San Sebastiano. Although bus #118 does not stop at the Tomb of Cecilia Metella, the Tomb is only 500 yards away from the bus stop at the Catacombs of San Sebastiano. Going back to Rome, bus #118 takes a somewhat different route (skipping the Catacombs of San Sebastiano); catch this northbound bus just up the road at the Catacombs of San Callisto.

Bus #218 goes from San Giovanni in Laterano to Domine Quo Vadis Church and the west entrance of the Catacombs of San Callisto, but isn't handy for other Appian Way sights.

The handy, but much more expensive, **Archeobus** runs from Termini train station to the Appian Way sights (see "Tours in Rome," page 707). It stops at all the key attractions—you can hop off, tour the sights, and pick up a later bus (officially runs hourly, but service can be spotty).

Getting Back: No matter how you arrive at the Appian Way, **bus #118** is the easiest and cheapest way to return to Rome (get off at the end of the line, the Piramide Metro stop).

▲▲**Catacombs of San Sebastiano**—A guide leads you underground through the tunnels where early Christians were buried. You'll see faded frescoes and graffiti by early Christian tag artists. Besides the catacombs themselves, there's a historic fourth-century basilica with holy relics.

Cost and Hours: €8, includes 25-minute tour, 2/hour, Mon–Sat 9:00–12:00 & 14:00–17:00, last tour leaves at 17:00, closed Sun and mid-Nov–mid-Dec, Via Appia Antica 136, tel. 06-785-0350, www.catacombe.org.

▲▲**Catacombs of San Callisto**—The larger of the two sets of catacombs, San Callisto also is the more prestigious, having been the burial site for several early popes.

Cost and Hours: €8, includes 30-minute tour, at least 2/hour, Thu–Tue 9:00–12:00 & 14:00–17:00, closed Wed and Feb, Via Appia Antica 110, tel. 06-5130-1580 or 06-5130-151, www.catacombe.roma.it.

Near Rome

▲▲**Ostia Antica**—For an exciting day trip, pop down to the Roman port of Ostia, which is similar to Pompeii but a lot closer and, in some ways, more interesting. Because Ostia was a working port town, it shows a more complete and gritty look at Roman life than wealthier Pompeii. Wandering around today, you'll see warehouses, apartment flats, mansions, shopping arcades, and baths that served a once-thriving port of 60,000 people. Later, Ostia became a ghost town, and it's now excavated. Buy a map, then explore the town, including the 2,000-year-old theater. Finish with its fine little museum.

Getting There: Getting to Ostia Antica from downtown Rome is a snap—it's a 45-minute combination Metro/train ride. (Since the train is part of the Metro system, it only costs one Metro ticket each way—€2 total round-trip.)

From Rome, take Metro line B to the Piramide stop, which is also the Roma Porta San Paolo train station, so the train tracks are just a few steps from the Metro tracks. Follow signs to *Lido*—go up the escalator, turn left, and go down the steps into the Roma-Lido station. All trains depart in the direction of *Lido*, leave every 15 minutes, and stop at Ostia Antica along the way. The lighted schedule reads something like, "*Treno in partenza alle ore 13.25, bin 3*," meaning, "Train departing at 13:25 from track 3." Look for the next train, hop on, ride for about 30 minutes (keep your Metro ticket handy), and get off at the Ostia Antica stop. (If you don't have a ticket to get back, purchase one at the ticket window at the station, or from the nearby snack bar.)

Leaving the train station in Ostia Antica, cross the road via the blue skybridge and walk straight down Via della Stazione di Ostia Antica, continuing straight until you reach the parking lot. The entrance is to your left.

Cost and Hours: €6.50 for the site and museum, Tue–Sun April–Oct 8:30–19:00, Nov–Feb 8:30–17:00, March 8:30–18:00, last entry one hour before closing, closed Mon. The museum closes from 13:30 to 14:15 for lunch. Tel. 06-5635-8099; www.itnw.roma .it/ostia/scavi (Italian website), www.ostiaantica.info (English summary), or www.ostia-antica.org. A map of the site with suggested itineraries is available for €2 from the ticket office. Although you'll see little audioguide markers throughout the site, there are no audioguides. However, you can download a free Rick Steves audio tour of the site at www.ricksteves.com or from iTunes (search for "Rick Steves Audio Tours").

Sleeping in Rome

Double rooms listed in this chapter will range from about €65 (very simple, toilet and shower down the hall) to €480 (maximum plumbing and more), with most clustering around €150 (with private bathrooms). I've favored these pricier options, because intense

Sleep Code

(€1 = about $1.25, country code: 39)
S = Single, **D** = Double/Twin, **T** = Triple, **Q** = Quad, **b** = bathroom, **s** = shower only. Unless otherwise noted, breakfast is included, hotel staff speak basic English, and credit cards are accepted.

To help you sort easily through these listings, I've divided the rooms into three categories based on the price for a standard double room with bath (or for a bunk at a hostel):

$$$ Higher Priced—Most rooms €180 or more.
$$ Moderately Priced—Most rooms between €130–180.
$ Lower Priced—Most rooms €130 or less.

Prices can change without notice; verify the hotel's current rates online or by email. For other updates, see www.ricksteves.com/update.

and grinding Rome is easier to enjoy with a welcoming oasis to call home.

It's common for hotels in Rome to lower their prices 10–35 percent off-season, although prices at hostels and the cheaper hotels won't fluctuate much. Room rates are lowest in sweltering August. Easter, September, and Christmas are the most crowded and expensive (see list of holidays on page 981). Particularly on Easter (April 24 in 2011) and Saint Peter and Paul's Day (June 29), the entire city gets booked up.

Traffic in Rome roars. With the arrival of double-paned windows and air-conditioning, night noise is not the problem it once was. Even so, light sleepers who ask for a *tranquillo* room will likely get a room in the back...and sleep better.

Most hotels are eager to connect you with a shuttle service to the airport. It's reasonable and easy for departure, but upon arrival, I just catch a cab or the train into the city.

Almost no hotels have parking, but nearly all have a line on spots in a nearby garage (about €24/day).

Convents: Although I list only four, Rome has many convents that rent out rooms. At convents, the beds are twins and English is often in short supply, but the price is right. Consider these nun-run places, all listed in this chapter: the expensive but divine **Casa di Santa Brigida** (near Campo de' Fiori), the **Suore di Santa Elisabetta** (near Santa Maria Maggiore), the **Casa Il Rosario** (near Piazza Venezia), and the user-friendly **Casa per Ferie Santa Maria alle Fornaci** (near the Vatican). For more options, see the Church of Santa Susanna's website for a list (www.santasusanna.org, select "Coming to Rome").

Hostels and Dorms: For easy communication with young, friendly entrepreneurs, €20–30 dorm beds, and some inexpensive doubles—within a 10-minute hike of Termini train station—consider the various hostels I've listed, or check www.backpackers.it for more listings.

Near Termini Train Station

While not as atmospheric as other areas of Rome, the hotels near Termini train station are less expensive, restaurants are plentiful, and the many public-transportation options link it easily with the entire city. The city's two Metro lines intersect at the station, and most buses leave from here. Piazza Venezia is a 20-minute walk down Via Nazionale.

Via Firenze

Via Firenze is safe, handy, central, and relatively quiet. It's a 10-minute walk from Termini Station and the airport train, and two blocks beyond Piazza della Repubblica and the TI. The Defense Ministry is nearby, so you've got heavily armed guards watching over you all night.

The neighborhood is well-connected by public transportation (with the Repubblica Metro stop nearby). Virtually all the city buses that rumble down Via Nazionale (#64, #70, #115, #640, and the #40 express) take you to Piazza Venezia (Forum) and Largo Argentina (Pantheon). From Largo Argentina, both the #64 bus (jammed with people and thieves) and the #40 express bus continue to the Vatican. Or, at Largo Argentina, you can transfer to electric trolley #8 to Trastevere (get off at first stop after crossing the river).

Phone and Internet Center is a cute and handy little hole-in-the-wall cybercafé within a block or so of several recommended hotels (€3/hour, daily 8:30–20:30, Via Modena 48, tel. 06-482-8850). To stock your closet pantry, pop over to **Despar Supermarket** (daily 8:00–21:00, Via Nazionale 211, at the corner of Via Venezia). A 24-hour **pharmacy** near the recommended hotels is Farmacia Piram (Via Nazionale 228, tel. 06-488-4437).

$$$ Residenza Cellini feels like the guest wing of a gorgeous Neoclassical palace. It offers 11 rooms, "ortho/anti-allergy beds," four-star comforts and service, and a breezy breakfast terrace (Db-€185, larger Db-€205, extra bed-€25, prices good through 2011 with this book and cash, air-con, elevator, Internet access and Wi-Fi, Via Modena 5, tel. 06-4782-5204, fax 06-4788-1806, www.residenzacellini.it, residenzacellini@tin.it, Barbara, Gaetano, and Donato).

$$$ Hotel Modigliani, a delightful 23-room place, is energetically run in a clean, bright, minimalist yet in-love-with-life style that its artist namesake would appreciate. There's a very generous lounge, a garden, and a newsletter introducing you to each of the staff (Db-€195, but check website for deals and ask for a 10 percent Rick Steves discount; air-con, Wi-Fi; northwest of Via Firenze—from Tritone Fountain on Piazza Barberini, go 2 blocks up Via della Purificazione to #42; tel. 06-4281-5226, www.hotel modigliani.com, info@hotelmodigliani.com, Giulia and Marco).

$$ Hotel Oceania is a peaceful slice of air-conditioned heaven. This 23-room manor house–type hotel is spacious and quiet, with spotless, tastefully decorated rooms, run by Stefano, who still maintains his father Armando's tradition of serving delicious "world-famous" coffee. He works hard to maintain a caring family atmosphere with a fine staff, and provides lots of thoughtful extra touches (Sb-€125, Db-€158, Tb-€190, Qb-€212, these prices good through 2011 with this book and cash, large roof terrace, family suite, Internet access and Wi-Fi, videos in the TV lounge, Via Firenze 38, third floor, tel. 06-482-4696, fax 06-488-5586, www.hoteloceania.it, info@hoteloceania.it, Anna and Radu round out the staff).

$$ Hotel Aberdeen, which perfectly combines high quality and friendliness, is warmly run by Annamaria, with support from cousins Sabrina and Cinzia and sister Laura. The 37 comfy, modern, air-conditioned rooms are a terrific value. Enjoy the frescoed breakfast room (Sb-€102, Db-€160, Tb-€170, Qb-€200, for these rates—or better—book direct via email or use the "Rick Steves reader reservations" link on their website, much cheaper rates off-season, Internet access and Wi-Fi, Via Firenze 48, tel. 06-482-3920, fax 06-482-1092, www.hotelaberdeen.it, info@hotel aberdeen.it).

$ Hotel Adler, which serves breakfast on its garden patio, has wide halls and eight quiet, simple rooms in a good location (plus six more rooms in their slightly pricier Bellesuite wing). It's run the old-fashioned way by a charming family (Db-€130, Tb-€170, Qb-€195, Quint/b-€220, 5 percent off these prices through 2011 with this book, air-con, elevator, Internet access and Wi-Fi, Via Modena 5, second floor, tel. 06-484-466, fax 06-488-0940, www .hoteladler-roma.com, info@hoteladler-roma.com, Alessandro).

$ Hotel Nardizzi Americana, with 33 pleasant, air-conditioned rooms and a delightful rooftop terrace, is an excellent value (Sb-€95, Db-€125, Tb-€155, Qb-€175, email them or use "Rick Steves readers reservations" link on their website to get these special rates in 2011, normal website sometimes has even lower rates, additional 10 percent off any time with cash, air-con, elevator, Internet access and Wi-Fi, Via Firenze 38, fourth floor,

ROME

Hotels near Termini Train Station

1/4 MILE
400 METERS

Ⓣ TAXI STAND
Ⓜ METRO STATION
Ⓑ BUS STOP

❶ Residenza Cellini, Hotel Adler & Internet Center

❷ Hotel Modigliani

❸ Hotels Oceania & Nardizzi Americana

❹ Hotel Aberdeen

❺ Hotel Margaret

❻ Hotel Opera Roma

❼ Hotel Sonya

❽ Hotel Selene

❾ Hotel Montreal

❿ Hotel Italia Roma

⓫ Suore di Sta. Elisabetta

⓬ Gulliver's Lodge B&B

⓭ The Beehive

⓮ Hotel Select Garden

⓯ Hotel Sileo & Fawlty Towers Hostel

⓰ Funny Palace Hostel, Launderette & Internet Café

⓱ Yellow Hostel

ROME

tel. 06-488-0035, fax 06-488-0368, www.hotelnardizzi.it, info @hotelnardizzi.it, Stefano, Fabrizio, Mario, and Samy).

$ Hotel Margaret, basic but welcoming, fills its walls with Impressionist prints and offers 12 decent rooms at a good price (Db-€95, big Db-€120, Tb-€140, Qb-€170, mention this book for their best rate, air-con, elevator, Wi-Fi, northeast of Via Firenze at Via Antonio Salandra 6, fourth floor, tel. 06-482-4285, fax 06-482-4277, www.hotelmargaretrome.com, info@hotelmargaret .net, friendly Monica).

Between Via Nazionale and Santa Maria Maggiore

$$ Hotel Opera Roma, with contemporary furnishings and marble accents, boasts 15 fresh and spacious but somewhat dark rooms. It's located a stone's throw from the Opera House (Db-€165, Tb-€190, these prices good through 2011 with this book, 5 percent less with cash, air-con, elevator, Internet access and loaner laptop on request, Via Firenze 11, tel. 06-487-1787, www.hoteloperaroma .com, info@hoteloperaroma.com, Rezza and Federica).

$$ Hotel Sonya offers 28 well-equipped, high-tech rooms, a central location, and decent prices. Farhad, a member of the multi-talented staff, bakes cakes and other goodies daily for the better-than-usual breakfast (Sb-€90, Db-€150, Tb-€165, Qb-€185, Quint/b-€200, 5 percent discount with this book and cash, air-con, elevator, loaner laptops in room and Wi-Fi, faces the Opera House at Via Viminale 58, Metro: Repubblica or Termini, tel. 06-481-9911, fax 06-488-5678, www.hotelsonya.it, info@hotel sonya.it, Francesca and Ivan).

$$ Hotel Selene spreads its rooms out on a few floors of a big palazzo. With elegant furnishings and room to breathe, its 40 rooms are a good value (Db-€145, Tb-€165, €10 less with cash, air-con, elevator, Via del Viminale 8, tel. 06-482-4460, www.hotel seleneroma.it, reception@hotelseleneroma.it).

$ Hotel Montreal, run with care, is a bright, solid business-class place with 27 rooms on a big street a block southeast of Santa Maria Maggiore (Sb-€95, Db-€120, Tb-€150, may be less if you email direct and ask for a Rick Steves discount, air-con, elevator, Internet access, communal garden terrace, good security, Via Carlo Alberto 4, 1 block from Metro: Vittorio Emanuele, 3 blocks west of Termini train station, tel. 06-445-7797, fax 06-446-5522, www.hotelmontrealroma.com, info@hotelmontrealroma.com, Pasquale).

$ Hotel Italia Roma, in a busy, interesting, and handy locale, is located safely on a quiet street next to the Ministry of the Interior. Thoughtfully run by Andrea, Sabrina, Nadine, and Gabriel, it has 35 comfortable, clean, and bright rooms (Sb-€80, Db-€120, Tb-€160, Qb-€180, 30 percent cheaper July–Aug, air-con-€10 extra per day, elevator, Internet access and Wi-Fi, Via Venezia 18, just off Via Nazionale, Metro: Repubblica, tel. 06-482-8355, fax 06-474-5550, www.hotelitaliaroma.it, info@hotelitaliaroma.com). Request one of the four "residenza" rooms upstairs on the third floor, which are newer, quiet, and the same price. They also have eight decent annex rooms across the street.

$ Suore di Santa Elisabetta is a heavenly Polish-run convent with a peaceful garden and 70 beds in tidy twin-bedded (only) rooms. Often booked long in advance, with such tranquility it's a super value (S-€40, Sb-€48, D-€66, Db-€85, Tb-€106, Qb-€128,

Quint/b-€142, no air-con, elevator serves top floors only, fine view roof terrace and breakfast hall, 23:00 curfew, a block southwest of Santa Maria Maggiore at Via dell'Olmata 9, Metro: Termini or Vittorio Emanuele, tel. 06-488-8271, fax 06-488-4066, www .elzbietanki-roma.eu, ist.it.s.elisabetta@libero.it).

$ Gulliver's Lodge B&B has four fun, colorful rooms on the ground floor of a large, secure building. Well-located on a busy street, the rooms are nevertheless quiet. Although the public spaces are few, in-room extras like DVD players (and DVDs, including my Italy shows) make it a nice home base (Db-€110, Tb-€120, cash only, air-con, Internet access and Wi-Fi, a 15-minute walk southwest of Termini train station at Via Cavour 101, Metro: Cavour, tel. 06-9727-3789, www.gulliverslodge.com, stay@gulliverslodge .com, Sara and Mary).

Sleeping Cheaply, Northeast of Termini Train Station

The cheapest beds in town are northeast of Termini train station (Metro: Termini). Some travelers feel this area is weird and spooky after dark, but these hotels feel plenty safe. With your back to the train tracks, turn right and walk two blocks out of the station. **Splashnet** launderette/Internet café is handy if you're staying in this area (€6 full-serve wash and dry, Internet access-€1.50/hour, €2 luggage storage per day—or free if you wash and go online, daily 8:30–24:00, just off Via Milazzo at Via Varese 33, tel. 06-4470-3523).

$ The Beehive gives vagabonds—old and young—a cheap, clean, and comfy home in Rome, thoughtfully and creatively run by Steve and Linda, a friendly young American couple. They offer six great-value artsy-mod double rooms (D-€80, T-€105) and an eight-bed dorm (€25 bunks, Internet access and Wi-Fi, private garden terrace, 2 blocks north of Termini train station at Via Marghera 8, tel. 06-4470-4553, www.the-beehive.com, info@the -beehive.com).

$ Hotel Select Garden, a modern and comfortable 19-room hotel run by the cheery Picca family, boasts lively modern art adorning the walls and a beautiful lemon-tree garden. It's a welcome refuge from the bustling Eternal City, located on a quiet street just a couple of blocks from the train station (Sb-€85, Db-€100, Tb-€120, these prices good through 2011 with this book, air-con, Wi-Fi, Via V. Bachelet 6, tel. 06-445-6383, fax 06-444-1086, www.hotelselectgarden.com, info@hotelselectgarden.com, Armando).

$ Hotel Sileo, with shiny chandeliers in dim rooms, has a contract to house train conductors who work the night shift—so two of its doubles are rentable only from 18:30 to 9:00 for €60.

The rest of their 10 rooms are available any time of day (Db-€75, Tb-€90, air-con, elevator, Via Magenta 39, fourth floor, tel. & fax 06-445-0246, www.hotelsileo.com, info@hotelsileo.com). Friendly Alessandro and Maria Savioli don't speak English, but daughter Anna does.

$ **Funny Palace Hostel,** adjacent to Splashnet and run by its entrepreneurial owner Mabri, rents dorm beds in quiet four-person rooms and 18 stark-but-clean private rooms (dorm beds-€30, Db-€100, cash only, reception in the launderette—described earlier, Via Varese 33/31, tel. 06-4470-3523, www.hostelfunny .com).

$ **Yellow Hostel** rents 130 beds in 4-, 6-, and 12-bed coed dorms to 18- through 39-year-olds only. Hip yet sane, it's well-run with fine facilities, including lockers. There's no curfew, and a late-night bar is next door (€24–34 per bed depending on plumbing, size, and season; reserve via email—no telephone reservations accepted, no breakfast, Wi-Fi and laptop rental available, 6 blocks from station, just past Via Vicenza at Via Palestro 44, tel. 06-493-82682, www.the-yellow.com).

$ **Fawlty Towers Hostel** is all right, and works for backpackers arriving by train. It offers 50 beds and lots of fun, games, and extras (4-bed dorms-€25 per person, S-€55, D-€65, Db-€80, Q-€90, includes sheets, elevator, free Internet access, kitchenette, peaceful sun terrace, from station walk a block down Via Marghera and turn right to Via Magenta 39, tel. 06-445-0374, fax 06-4543-5942, www.fawltytowers.org, info@fawltytowers.org). Their nearby annex, **Bubbles,** offers similar beds and rates and shares the same reception desk.

Near Ancient Rome

Stretching from the Colosseum to Piazza Venezia, this area is central. Sightseers are a short walk from the Colosseum, Roman Forum, and Trajan's Column.

Near the Colosseum

$$$ **Hotel Lancelot** is a comfortable yet elegant refuge—a 60-room hotel with the ambience of a B&B. It's quiet and safe, with a shady courtyard, restaurant, bar, and tiny communal sixth-floor terrace. Well-run by Faris and Lubna Khan, it's popular with returning guests (Sb-€125, Db-€196, Tb-€222, Qb-€260, €20 extra for sixth-floor terrace room with a Colosseum view, 5 percent off these rates with this book, air-con, elevator, wheelchair-accessible, Wi-Fi, parking-€10/day, 10-minute walk behind Colosseum near San Clemente Church at Via Capo d'Africa 47, tel. 06-7045-0615, fax 06-7045-0640, www.lancelothotel.com, info@lancelot hotel.com). Faris and Lubna speak the Queen's English.

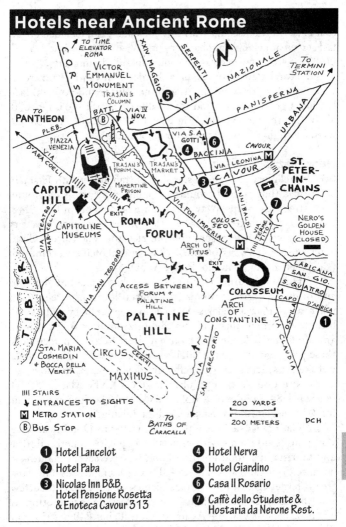

Hotels near Ancient Rome

KEY:
- |||| STAIRS
- ↓ ENTRANCES TO SIGHTS
- Ⓜ METRO STATION
- Ⓑ BUS STOP

DCH

❶ Hotel Lancelot

❷ Hotel Paba

❸ Nicolas Inn B&B, Hotel Pensione Rosetta & Enoteca Cavour 313

❹ Hotel Nerva

❺ Hotel Giardino

❻ Casa Il Rosario

❼ Caffè dello Studente & Hostaria da Nerone Rest.

$$ Hotel Paba has seven fresh rooms, chocolate box–tidy and lovingly cared for by Alberta Castelli. Though it overlooks busy Via Cavour just two blocks from the Colosseum, it's quiet enough (Db–€135, extra bed–€40, 5 percent cash discount, huge beds, breakfast served in room, air-con, elevator, Wi-Fi, Via Cavour 266, Metro: Cavour, tel. 06-4782-4902, fax 06-4788-1225, www.hotelpaba.com, info@hotelpaba.com).

$$ Nicolas Inn Bed & Breakfast, a delightful little four-room place with thoughtful touches, is spacious and bright. It's run by François and American expat Melissa, who make you feel like you have caring friends in Rome (Db-€100–170, extra bed-€30, 10 percent Rick Steves discount with this book and cash, included breakfast served at neighboring bar, air-con, Wi-Fi, Via Cavour 295, tel. 06-976-18483, www.nicolasinn.com, info@nicolasinn.com).

$ Hotel Pensione Rosetta, homey and family-run, rents 20 rooms. It's pretty minimal, with no lounge and no breakfast, but has a good location and reasonable prices (Sb-€65, Db-€90, Tb-€105, air-con, Wi-Fi, Via Cavour 295, tel. 06-478-23069, www.rosettahotel.com, info@rosettahotel.com).

Near Piazza Venezia

$$$ Hotel Nerva is a three-star slice of tranquility with 19 small, overpriced (but often discounted) rooms on a surprisingly quiet back street just steps away from the Roman Forum (Sb-€140, Db-€190, extra bed-€45, ask for Rick Steves discount, rates very soft—especially off-season, air-con, elevator, Via Tor de' Conti 3, tel. 06-678-1835, fax 06-6992-2204, www.hotelnerva.com, info @hotelnerva.com, Antonio, Paolo, Anna).

$ Hotel Giardino, true to its name, has a small garden area and offers 11 pleasant rooms in a central location three blocks northeast of Piazza Venezia. With a tiny central lobby and a small breakfast room, it suits travelers who prize location over big-hotel amenities (Sb-€85, Db-€130, one smaller Db for 15 percent less; these prices good through 2011 with this book, cash only, check website for specials, air-con, effective double-paned windows, on a busy street off Piazza di Quirinale at Via XXIV Maggio 51, tel. 06-679-4584, fax 06-679-5155, www.hotel-giardino-roma.com, info@hotel-giardino-roma.com, helpful Gianluca).

$ Casa Il Rosario is a peaceful, well-run Dominican convent renting 40 rooms with monastic simplicity to both pilgrims and tourists in a good neighborhood (reserve several months in advance, S-€42, Sb-€54, Db-€94, Tb-€120, single beds only, fans, free Internet access, roof-terrace picnics welcome, 23:00 curfew, midway between the Quirinale and Colosseum near bottom of Via Nazionale at Via Sant'Agata dei Goti 10, bus #40 or #170 from Termini, tel. 06-679-2346, fax 06-6994-1106, irodopre@tin.it).

In the Pantheon Neighborhood

Winding, narrow lanes filled with foot traffic and lined with boutique shops and tiny trattorias...this is village Rome at its best. You'll pay for the atmosphere, but this is where you want to be—especially at night, when Romans and tourists gather in the flood-lit piazzas for the evening stroll, the *passeggiata.*

Near Campo de' Fiori

You'll pay a premium (and endure a little extra night noise) to stay

Hotels in the Pantheon Neighborhood

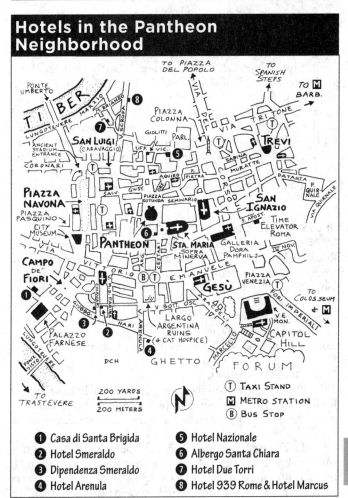

TO PIAZZA DEL POPOLO
TO SPANISH STEPS
TO M BARB.

PONTE UMBERTO
TIBER
LUNGOTEVERE MARZIO
BRIANZO
SCROFA
8
PIAZZA COLONNA
VIA DEL
VIA TRITONE
T
7
GIOLITTI
PARL.
UFF. V. VIC.
5
TREVI
SAN LUIGI (CARAVAGGIO)
ANCIENT STADIUM ENTRANCE
CORONARI
T
SABINA
MURATTE
DATARIA
P. QUIRINALE
AQUIRO
P. PIETRA
SALV.
GIUST.
PIAZZA ROTUNDA SEMINARIO
SAN IGNAZIO
VIA QUIRINALE
PIAZZA NAVONA
PIAZZA PASQUINO
CITY MUSEUM
T
6
PANTHEON
STA. MARIA SOPRA MINERVA
S. APOST.
TIME ELEVATOR ROMA
GALLERIA DORA PAMPHILJ
IV NOV.
CAMPO DE' FIORI
VITTORIO
B T
EMANUELE
GESÙ
PIAZZA VENEZIA
T
TO COLOSSEUM
FORI IMPERIALI
M
1
GIUBBO
V BOTT. OSC.
LARGO ARGENTINA RUINS (+ CAT HOSPICE)
RACCELA
V.E. MON.
CAPITOL HILL
3
NARI
2
ARENULA
PALAZZO FARNESE
4
MARCELLO
PONTE SISTO
LUNGOTEVERE SISTO
DCH
GHETTO
FORUM
TO TRASTEVERE

200 YARDS
200 METERS

N

T TAXI STAND
M METRO STATION
B BUS STOP

1 Casa di Santa Brigida
2 Hotel Smeraldo
3 Dipendenza Smeraldo
4 Hotel Arenula
5 Hotel Nazionale
6 Albergo Santa Chiara
7 Hotel Due Torri
8 Hotel 939 Rome & Hotel Marcus

in the old center. But each of these places is romantically set deep in the tangled back streets near the idyllic Campo de' Fiori and, for many, worth the extra money.

$$$ Casa di Santa Brigida overlooks the elegant Piazza Farnese. With soft-spoken sisters gliding down polished hallways and pearly gates instead of doors, this lavish 20-room convent makes exhaust-stained Roman tourists feel like they've died and gone to heaven. If you don't need a double bed, it's worth the splurge (Sb-€110, twin Db-€190, 3 percent extra if you pay with credit card, can pay with personal check for no extra charge, book well in advance, air-con, elevator, Internet access, tasty €25 dinners, roof garden, plush library, Monserrato 54, tel. 06-6889-2596, fax 06-6889-1573, piazzafarnese@brigidine.org, many of the sisters are from India and speak English). If you get no response to your fax or email within three days, consider that a "no."

$ Hotel Smeraldo, with 50 rooms, is strictly run, clean, and a great deal (Sb-€100, Db-€130, Tb-€160, rooms €30 less off-season, buffet breakfast free with this book in 2011, air-con, elevator, flowery roof terrace, midway between Campo de' Fiori and Largo Argentina at Vicolo dei Chiodaroli 9, tel. 06-687-5929, fax 06-6880-5495, www.smeraldoroma.com, albergosmeraldoroma @tin.it, Massimo and Walter). Their **Dipendenza Smeraldo,** 10 yards around the corner at Via dei Chiavari 32, has 16 similar rooms (same price and free breakfast, same reception and contact info).

In the Jewish Ghetto

$$ Hotel Arenula, with 50 decent rooms, is the only hotel in Rome's old Jewish ghetto. While it has the ambience of a gym and attracts lots of students, it's a good value in the thick of old Rome (Sb-€75–98, Db-€133, €100 July–Aug, 5 percent off with this book in high season of 2011, extra bed-€21, air-con, no elevator, Wi-Fi, opposite the fountain in the park on Via Arenula at Via Santa Maria de' Calderari 47, tel. 06-687-9454, fax 06-689-6188, www .hotelarenula.com, info@hotelarenula.com, Rosanna).

Close to the Pantheon

These places are buried in the pedestrian-friendly heart of ancient Rome, each within a four-minute walk of the Pantheon. You'll pay more here—but you'll save time and money by being exactly where you want to be for your early and late wandering.

$$$ Hotel Nazionale, a four-star landmark, is a 16th-century palace that shares a well-policed square with the Parliament building. Its 100 rooms are accentuated by lush public spaces, fancy bars, a uniformed staff, and a marble-floored restaurant. It's a big, stuffy hotel with a revolving front door, but it's a worthy splurge if you want security, comfort, and ancient Rome at your doorstep (Sb-€220, Db-€350, giant deluxe Db-€480, extra person-€70, ask for 10 percent Rick Steves discount, check online for summer and weekend discounts, air-con, elevator, Piazza Montecitorio 131, tel. 06-695-001, fax 06-678-6677, www.hotelnazionale.it, info@hotel nazionale.it).

$$$ Albergo Santa Chiara is big, solid, and hotelesque. Flavia, Silvio, and their fine staff offer marbled elegance (but basic furniture) and all the hotel services in the old center. Its ample public lounges are dressy and professional, and its 99 rooms are quiet and spacious (Sb-€138, Db-€190, Db-€215 April–June and Oct, Tb-€262, check website for discounts, book online direct and request special Rick Steves rates, elevator, behind Pantheon at Via di Santa Chiara 21, tel. 06-687-2979, fax 06-687-3144, www.albergo santachiara.com, info@albergosantachiara.com).

$$$ Hotel Due Torri, hiding out on a tiny quiet street, is beautifully located. It feels professional yet homey, with an accommodating staff, generous public spaces, and 26 small rooms. While the location and lounge are great, the rooms are overpriced (Sb-€125, Db-€195, family apartment-€230 for 3 and €260 for 4, check website for frequent discounts, air-con, elevator, pay Internet access, a block off Via della Scrofa at Vicolo del Leonetto 23, tel. 06-6880-6956, fax 06-686-5442, www.hotelduetorriroma.com, hotelduetorri@mclink.it, Cinzia).

$Hotel 939 Rome and **Hotel Marcus** are two hotels that seem like one (same entrance, lobby, and contact info). The 939 has renovated rooms, while the Marcus is more utilitarian. Together they offer 17 rooms on the second floor in the old center of Rome above noisy Via della Scrofa (Db-€100–140, extra bed-€30, check website for frequent discounts, air-con, elevator; from Via della Scrofa, turn right at Piazza Nicosia and head to Via del Clementino 94; tel. 06-6830-0312, www.hotel939.com, hotel939@hotmail.it, helpful Aurora).

In Trastevere

Colorful and genuine in a gritty sort of way, Trastevere is a treat for travelers looking for a less touristy and more bohemian atmosphere. Choices are few here, but by trekking across the Tiber, you can have the experience of being comfortably immersed in old Rome. To locate the following places, see the map on page 774.

$$$ Hotel Santa Maria sits like a lazy hacienda in the midst of Trastevere. Surrounded by a medieval skyline, you'll feel as if you're on some romantic stage set. Its 18 small but well-equipped, air-conditioned rooms—former cells in a cloister—are all on the ground floor, as are a few suites for up to six people. The rooms circle a gravelly courtyard of orange trees and stay-awhile patio furniture (Db-€180, Tb-€220; prices good through 2011 with this book, cash, and minimum stay of three nights; family rooms, free loaner bikes, Internet access and Wi-Fi, face church on Piazza Maria Trastevere and go right down Via della Fonte d'Olio 50 yards to Vicolo del Piede 2, tel. 06-589-4626, fax 06-589-4815, www.hotelsantamaria.info, info@hotelsantamaria.info, Stefano). Some rooms come with family-friendly fold-down bunks for €30 extra per person. Their freshly renovated six-room **Residenza Santa Maria** is a couple of blocks away (same prices and contact info).

$$$ Residenza Arco dei Tolomei has six small, unique, antique-filled rooms in a quiet and elegant setting—you can

ROME

pretend you're visiting aristocratic relatives (Db-€200, discounts for cash and for stays of 3 days or more, reserve well in advance, Internet access and Wi-Fi, from Piazza Piscinula a block up Via dell'Arco de' Tolomei at #27, tel. 06-5832-0819, www.bbarcodei tolomei.com, info@bbarcodeitolomei.com, Marco, Gianna Paola, and dog Pixel).

$$$ Relais le Clarisse retains the tranquil feel of its former life as a convent. Its five tastefully furnished rooms, which vary in size and amenities, surround a leafy courtyard—a little slice of the countryside in the city (Db-€205, Db suite-€195–220, Tb suite-€220–250, Qb suite-€260–290, prices vary with season, just off Viale Trastevere at Via Cardinale Merry del Val 20, tel. & fax 06-5833-4437, www.leclarisse.com, info@leclarisse.com, Maria and Toy).

$$ Casa San Giuseppe is down a characteristic laundry-strewn lane with views of Aurelian Walls. While convent-owned, it's a secular place renting 29 plain but peaceful, spacious, and spotless rooms (Sb-€115, Db-€155, Tb-€185, Qb-€215, garden-facing rooms are quiet, air-con, elevator, Internet access, parking-€15, just north of Piazza Trilussa at Vicolo Moroni 22, tel. 06-5833-3490, fax 06-5833-5754, www.casasangiuseppe.it, info @casasangiuseppe.it, Germano).

$$ Arco del Lauro B&B rents six white, minimalist rooms in a good location. Facing a courtyard (no views but little noise), the friendly welcome and good value make up for the lack of public spaces (Db-€135, Qb-€185, prices good if booked direct, cash only, included breakfast served in a café, Internet access and Wi-Fi, from Piazza Piscinula a block up Via dell'Arco de' Tolomei at #27, tel. 06-9784-0350, www.arcodellauro.it, info@arcodellauro.it, Lorenza and Daniela).

Near Vatican City

Sleeping near the Vatican is expensive, but some enjoy calling this neighborhood home. Even though it's handy to the Vatican (when the rapture hits, you're right there), everything else is a long way away.

$$$ Hotel Alimandi Vaticano, facing the Vatican Museum, is beautifully designed. Run by the Alimandi family (Enrico, Irene, Germano), it features four stars, 24 spacious rooms, and all the modern comforts you can imagine (Sb-€170, standard Db-€170–200, big Db with 2 double beds-€240–260, Tb-€230–260, 5 percent less with cash, air-con, elevator, Viale Vaticano 99, Metro: Cipro, tel. 06-397-45562, fax 06-397-30132, www.alimandi .it, alimandivaticano@alimandi.com).

$$ Hotel Alimandi Tunisi is a good value, run by other members of the friendly and entrepreneurial Alimandi family—

Hotels & Restaurants near Vatican City

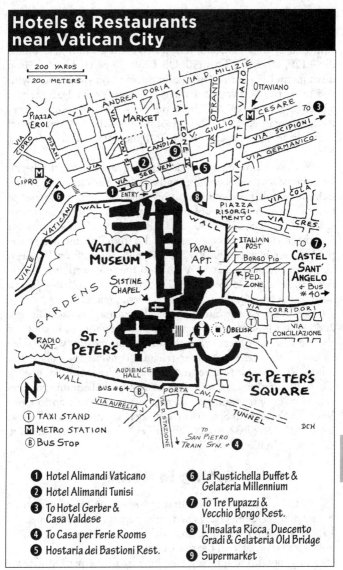

200 YARDS
200 METERS

- **T** TAXI STAND
- **M** METRO STATION
- **B** BUS STOP

- ❶ Hotel Alimandi Vaticano
- ❷ Hotel Alimandi Tunisi
- ❸ To Hotel Gerber & Casa Valdese
- ❹ To Casa per Ferie Rooms
- ❺ Hostaria dei Bastioni Rest.
- ❻ La Rustichella Buffet & Gelateria Millennium
- ❼ To Tre Pupazzi & Vecchio Borgo Rest.
- ❽ L'Insalata Ricca, Duecento Gradi & Gelateria Old Bridge
- ❾ Supermarket

Paolo, Grazia, Luigi, Marta, and Barbara. Their 27 perfumed rooms are air-conditioned, modern, and marbled in white (Sb-€90, Db-€130–175, 5 percent less with cash, grand buffet breakfast served in great roof garden, elevator, small gym, pool table, piano lounge, down the stairs directly in front of Vatican Museum, Via Tunisi 8, Metro: Cipro, reserve by phone at tel. 06-3972-3941, fax 06-3972-3943, www.alimandi.it, alimandi@tin.it).

They offer a €15/person airport shuttle.

$$ Hotel Gerber, set in a quiet residential area, is family-run with 27 well-polished, businesslike, air-conditioned rooms (Sb-€120, Db-€170, Tb-€190, Qb-€200, 10 percent high-season discount and 15 percent low-season discount off these prices with this book in 2011 if you book direct, elevator, Wi-Fi, leafy terrace, Via degli Scipioni 241, at intersection with Via Ezio, a block from Metro: Lepanto, tel. 06-321-6485, fax 06-321-7048, www.hotel gerber.it, info@hotelgerber.it, Peter, Simonetta, and friendly dog Kira).

$ Casa Valdese is an efficient, well-managed church-run hotel just over the Tiber River and near the Vatican, with 35 big, quiet rooms. It feels safe if a bit institutional, with the bonus of two breezy communal roof terraces with incredible views (two external Sb-€58, Db-€130, Tb-€180, Qb-€210, discounts for 3-night stays, Internet access and Wi-Fi; from Lepanto Metro station, go one block down Via M. Colonna, turn left on Via degli Scipioni, then continue for a block to the intersection with Via Alessandro Farnese 18; tel. 06-321-5362, fax 06-321-1843, www .casavaldeseroma.it, reception@casavaldeseroma.it).

$ Casa per Ferie Santa Maria alle Fornaci houses pilgrims and secular tourists with simple class just a short walk south of the Vatican in 54 identical stark, utilitarian, mostly twin-bedded rooms. This is the most user-friendly convent-type place I've found. Reserve at least three months in advance (Sb-€70, Db-€98, Tb-€130, air-con, elevator; take bus #64 from Termini train station to San Pietro train station, then walk 100 yards north along Via della Stazione di San Pietro to Piazza Santa Maria alle Fornaci 27; tel. 06-393-67632, fax 06-393-66795, www.trinitaridematha.it, cffornaci@tin.it).

Eating in Rome

I've listed a number of restaurants I enjoy. While most are in quaint and therefore pricey and touristy areas (Piazza Navona, the Pantheon neighborhood, Campo de' Fiori, and Trastevere), many are tucked away just off the tourist crush.

In general, I'm impressed by how small the price difference is from a mediocre restaurant to a fine one. You can pay about 20 percent more for double the quality. If I had $90 for three meals in Rome, I'd spend $50 for one and $20 each for the other two, rather than $30 on all three. For splurge meals, I'd consider Gabriello, Fortunato, and Al Bric (in that order).

Rome's fabled nightspots (most notably Piazza Navona, near the Pantheon, and Campo de' Fiori) are lined with the outdoor tables of touristy restaurants with enticing menus and formal-vested waiters. The atmosphere is super-romantic: I, too, like the idea of dining under floodlit monuments, amid a constantly flowing parade of people. But you'll likely be surrounded by tourists, and noisy English-speakers can kill the ambience of the spot...leaving you with just a forgettable and overpriced meal. Restaurants in these areas are notorious for surprise charges, forgettable food, microwaved ravioli, and bad service.

I enjoy the view by savoring just a drink or dessert on a famous square, but I dine with locals on nearby low-rent streets, where the proprietor needs to serve a good-value meal and nurture a local following to stay in business. If you're set on eating—or just drinking and snacking—on a famous piazza, you don't need a guidebook listing to choose a spot; enjoy the ritual of slowly circling the square, observing both the food and the people eating it, and just sit where the view and menu appeals to you.

Note that Rome discourages people from picnicking or drinking at historic monuments (such as on the Spanish Steps) in the old center. Technically violators can be fined, though it rarely happens. You'll be fine if you eat *with* a view rather than *on* the view.

In Trastevere

Colorful Trastevere is now pretty touristy. Still, Romans join the tourists to eat on the rustic side of the Tiber River. Start at the central square (Piazza Santa Maria). Then choose: Eat with tourists enjoying the ambience of the famous square, or wander the back streets in search of a mom-and-pop place with barely a menu. My recommendations are within a few minutes' walk of each other (between Piazza Santa Maria Trastevere and Ponte Sisto; see map on page 774).

Trattoria da Lucia lets you enjoy simple, traditional food at a good price in a great scene. It's the quintessential rustic, 100 percent Roman Trastevere dining experience, and has been family-run since World War II. You'll meet four generations of the family, including Giuliano and Renato, their uncle Ennio, and Ennio's mom—pictured on the menu in the 1950s. The family specialty is *spaghetti alla Gricia*, with pancetta (€9 pastas, €11 *secondi*, Tue–Sun 12:30–15:00 & 19:30–23:00, closed Mon, cash only, comfy indoor or evocative outdoor seating, just off Via del Mattonato on Vicolo del Mattonato 2, tel. 06-580-3601, some English spoken).

Trattoria da Olindo takes homey to extremes. You really feel like you dropped in on a family that cooks for the neighborhood to supplement their income. Don't expect any smiles here (€7 pastas, €9 *secondi*, Mon–Sat dinner served 20:00–22:30, closed Sun, cash only, indoor and funky outdoor seating, on the corner of Vicolo della Scala and Via del Mattonato at #8, tel. 06-581-8835).

Dar Poeta Pizzeria, tucked in a back alley, cranks out

some of the best wood-fired pizza I've had in Rome. It's run by four friends—Marco, Paolo, Enrico, and another Marco—who welcome you into the informal restaurant beneath exposed brick arches. If you're in a spicy mood, order *lingua di fuoco* (tongue of fire). If you're extra hungry, pay an extra euro for *pizza alto* (thicker crust). Choose between their classic, cramped interior and lively tables outside on the cobblestones. Their chocolate dessert calzone is a favorite (€6–9 pizzas, daily 12:00–24:00, Vicolo del Bologna 45, tel. 06-588-0516).

Osteria Ponte Sisto da Oliviero, small and Mediterranean, specializes in traditional Roman cuisine, but has frequent Neapolitan specials as well. Just outside the tourist zone, it caters mostly to Romans and offers beautiful desserts and a fine value (€10 pastas, €14 *secondi*, Thu–Tue 12:30–15:30 & 19:30–24:00, closed Wed, Via Ponte Sisto 80, tel. 06-588-3411, Oliviero). Crossing Ponte Sisto (pedestrian bridge) toward Trastevere, continue across the little square (Piazza Trilussa) and you'll see it on the right.

Ristorante Checco er Carettiere is a big family-run place that's been a Trastevere fixture for four generations. With white tablecloths, well-presented food, and dressy local diners, this is *the* place for a special meal in Trastevere. While it's overpriced, you'll eat well amidst lots of fun commotion. Reservations are smart, especially on weekends (€16 pastas, €22 *secondi*, daily 12:30–15:00 & 19:30–23:15, Via Benedetta 10, tel. 06-580-0985). Their *osteria* next door (#13) shares the same kitchen and offers less ambience, lower prices, and a more basic menu that changes daily (€11 pastas). Romans consider their *gelateria* (next door at #7) to be among the best on this side of the river.

Pizzeria "Ai Marmi" is a bright and noisy festival of pizza, where the oven and pizza-assembly line are surrounded by marble-slab tables (hence the nickname "the Morgue"). It's a classic Roman scene, with famously good €8 pizzas and very tight seating. Expect a long line between 20:00 and 22:00 (Thu–Tue 18:30–24:00, closed Wed, cash only, outdoor seating on busy Viale Trastevere, tram #8 from Largo Argentina to first stop over bridge, just beyond Piazza Sonnino at Viale Trastevere 53, tel. 06-580-0919).

Cantina Paradiso Wine and Cocktail Bar, a block over Viale Trastevere from the touristy action, has a simple romantic charm. During happy hour (18:00–21:00), the €6 drinks come with a well-made little buffet that can turn into a cheap, light dinner (€8 pastas, daily 12:00–24:00, lunch buffet, vegetarian options, Via San Francesco a Ripa 73, tel. 06-5899-799, Kiki).

And for Dessert: **Gelateria alla Scala** is a terrific little ice-cream shop that dishes up delightful cinnamon *(cannella)* and oh-wow pistachio (daily 12:00–24:00, Piazza della Scala 51, across from church on Piazza della Scala).

In the Jewish Ghetto

The Jewish Ghetto sits just across the river from Trastevere.

Sora Margherita, hiding without a sign on a cluttered square, has been a rustic neighborhood favorite since 1927. Amid a picturesque commotion, families chow down on old-time Roman and Jewish dishes for a decent price. As it's technically not a real restaurant (it avoids red tape by being officially designated as an *associazione culturale*), you'll need to sign a card to join the "cultural association" when you order (don't worry; membership has no obligations except that you enjoy your meal). The menu's crude term for the fettuccini gives you some idea of the mood of this place: *nazzica culo* ("shaky ass"—what happens while it's made). Reservations are almost always necessary (June–Aug Mon–Fri 12:30–15:00, dinner seatings on Thu and Fri only at 20:00 and 21:30, closed Sat–Sun; Sept–May Mon–Sat 12:30–15:00, dinner seatings on Fri and Sat at 20:00 and 21:30, closed Sun; just south of Via del Portico d'Ottavia at Piazza delle Cinque Scole 30—look for the red curtain, tel. 06-687-4216, Ivan doesn't speak English).

In the Pantheon Neighborhood

For the restaurants in this central area, I've listed them based on which landmark they're closest to: Campo de' Fiori, Piazza Navona, the Trevi Fountain, or the Pantheon itself.

On and near Campo de' Fiori

While it is touristy, Campo de' Fiori offers a sublimely romantic setting. And, since it's so close to the collective heart of Rome, it remains popular with locals, even though its restaurants offer greater atmosphere than food value. The square is lined with popular and interesting bars, pizzerias, and small restaurants—all great for people-watching over a glass of wine. Later at night it's taken over by a younger clubbing crowd.

Osteria da Giovanni ar Galletto is nearby, on the more elegant and peaceful Piazza Farnese. Angelo entertains an upscale Roman crowd and has magical outdoor seating. Regrettably, service can be horrible, you need to double-check the bill, and single diners aren't treated very well. Still, if you're in no hurry and ready to savor my favorite al fresco setting in Rome (while humoring the waiters), this is a good bet (€10 pastas, €15 *secondi,* Mon–Sat 12:15–15:00 & 19:30–23:00, closed Sun, reservations smart for outdoor seating, tucked in corner of Piazza Farnese at #102, tel. 06-686-1714).

Osteria Enoteca al Bric is a mod bistro-type place run by Roberto and Barbara, who love to cook, serve good wine, and listen to jazz. With only the finest ingredients, and an ambience elegant in its simplicity, they've created the perfect package for a romantic

Restaurants in the

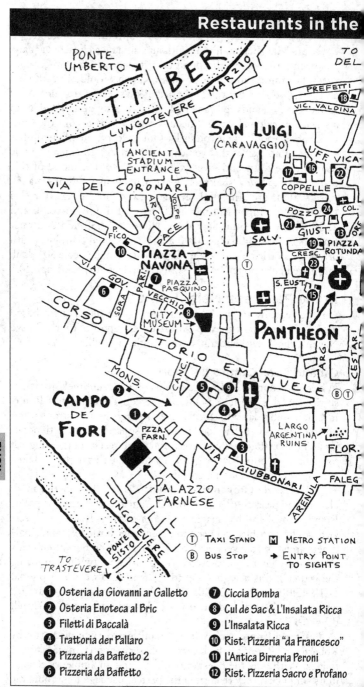

T TAXI STAND   **M** METRO STATION
B BUS STOP   ➔ ENTRY POINT TO SIGHTS

1 Osteria da Giovanni ar Galletto
2 Osteria Enoteca al Bric
3 Filetti di Baccalà
4 Trattoria der Pallaro
5 Pizzeria da Baffetto 2
6 Pizzeria da Baffetto

7 Ciccia Bomba
8 Cul de Sac & L'Insalata Ricca
9 L'Insalata Ricca
10 Rist. Pizzeria "da Francesco"
11 L'Antica Birreria Peroni
12 Rist. Pizzeria Sacro e Profano

ROME

Pantheon Neighborhood

13. Ristorante da Fortunato
14. Ristorante Enoteca Corsi
15. Miscellanea
16. Osteria da Mario
17. Le Coppelle Taverna
18. Trattoria dal Cav. Gino

19. Antica Salumeria
20. Super Market Di per Di
21. Supermercato Despar
22. Gelateria Caffè Pasticceria Giolitti
23. Crèmeria Monteforte
24. Gelateria San Crispino

ROME

night out. Wine-case lids decorate the wall like happy memories. With candlelit grace, it's perfect for the wine snob in the mood for pasta and fine cheese. Aficionados choose their bottle from the huge selection lining the walls near the entrance. Beginners order fine wine by the glass with help from the waiter when they order their meal (daily from 19:30 for dinner, closed Mon, reserve if dining after 20:30, 100 yards off Campo de' Fiori at Via del Pellegrino 51, tel. 06-687-9533). While Al Bric can be pricey, feel free to establish a price limit (e.g., €40 per person without wine) and trust them to feed you royally within that price.

Filetti di Baccalà is a cheap and basic Roman classic, where nostalgic regulars cram into wooden tables savoring their old-school favorites—fried cod finger-food fillets (€5 each) and raw *puntarelle* greens (slathered with anchovy sauce in spring and winter). Study what others are eating, and order from your grease-stained server by pointing at what you want. Sit in the fluorescently lit interior or try to grab a seat out on the little square, a quiet haven a block east of Campo de' Fiori (Mon–Sat 17:30–23:00, closed Sun, cash only, Largo dei Librari 88, tel. 06-686-4018).

Trattoria der Pallaro, an eccentric and well-worn eatery that has no menu, has a slogan: "Here, you'll eat what we want to feed you." Paola Fazi—with a towel wrapped around her head turban-style—and her gang dish up a rustic five-course meal of typically Roman food for €25, including wine and coffee, and capped with a thimble of mandarin juice. While the service is odd and the food is forgettable, the experience can be fun (Tue–Sun 12:00–15:30 & 19:00–24:00, closed Mon, cash only, indoor/outdoor seating on quiet square, a block south of Corso Vittorio Emanuele, down Largo del Chiavari to Largo del Pallaro 15, tel. 06-6880-1488).

Pizzeria da Baffetto 2 makes pizza Roman-style: thin crust, crispy, and wood-fired. Eat in the cramped informal interior, or outside on the busy square (€7–9 pizzas, Wed–Mon 12:00–15:30 & 18:30–24:00, closed Tue, a block north of Campo de' Fiori at Piazza del Teatro di Pompeo 18, tel. 06-6821-0807).

Near Piazza Navona

Piazza Navona is the most quintessential setting for dining on a Roman square. Whether you eat here or not, you'll want to stroll the piazza before or after your evening meal. This is where many people fall in love with Rome. The tangled streets just to the west are lined with popular eateries of many stripes.

Pizzeria da Baffetto, buried deep in the old quarter behind Piazza Navona, is a Roman favorite, famous for its rustic charm and tasty pizza. Its tables are tightly arranged amid the commotion of photos and sketches littering the walls. The pizza-assembly kitchen keeps things energetic, and the pizza oven keeps the main room warm (you can opt for a table on the cobbled street). Come early or late, or be prepared to wait (€7 pizzas, cash only, daily from 18:30, order "P," "M," or "D"—small, medium, or large; west of Piazza Navona on the corner of Via Sora at Via del Governo Vecchio 114, tel. 06-686-1617).

Ciccia Bomba is a traditional trattoria where Gianpaolo and crew serve up well-priced homemade pasta, wood-fired pizza, and other Roman specialties. With a name like "Fatso," this place had better have good food...and it does (€7 pastas, €9 *secondi*, Mon–Sat 12:00–15:00 & 19:00–24:00, closed Sun, off-season open Sun and closed Wed, Via del Governo Vecchio 76, a block west of Piazza Navona, just north from Piazza Pasquino, tel. 06-6880-2108).

Cul de Sac is a corridor-wide trattoria lined with wine bottles and packed with enthusiastic locals. Come early for an excellent tasting plate of salami and one of their many bottles of wine (they've got more than 1,000), or come later for a full meal of nicely cooked Roman dishes (daily 12:00–16:00 & 18:00–24:00, tel. 06-6880-1094, a block off Piazza Navona on Piazza Pasquino).

L'Insalata Ricca is a popular chain that specializes in hearty and healthy €8 salads and less-healthy pastas (daily 12:00–15:45 & 18:45–24:00). They have a handy branch on Piazza Pasquino (next to Cul de Sac, tel. 06-6830-7881), and a more spacious and enjoyable location a few blocks away, on a bigger square next to busy Corso Vittorio Emanuele (near Campo de' Fiori at Largo dei Chiavari 85, tel. 06-6880-3656).

Ristorante Pizzeria "da Francesco" is a bustling, unpretentious place with hardworking young waitstaff, great indoor seating, and classic outdoor seating on a cluttered little square that makes you want to break out a sketch pad. Their blackboard explains the daily specials (€7 pizzas, €8 pastas, €10 *secondi*, open daily, 3 blocks west of Piazza Navona at Piazza del Fico 29, tel. 06-686-4009).

Near the Trevi Fountain

L'Antica Birreria Peroni is Rome's answer to a German beer hall. Serving hearty mugs of the local Peroni beer and lots of just plain fun beer-hall food and Italian classics, the place is a hit with Romans for a cheap night out (Mon–Sat 12:00–24:00, closed Sun, midway between Trevi Fountain and Capitol Hill, a block off Via del Corso at Via di San Marcello 19, tel. 06-679-5310).

Ristorante Pizzeria Sacro e Profano fills an old church with spicy southern Italian (Calabrian) cuisine and satisfied tourists. Run with enthusiasm by Francesco and friends, this is just far enough away from the Trevi mobs. Their pizza oven is wood-fired, and their hearty €15 *antipasti* plate is a filling montage of Calabrian taste treats (daily 12:00–15:00 & 18:00–24:00, a block off Via del Tritone at Via dei Maroniti 29, tel. 06-679-1836).

Close to the Pantheon

Eating on the square facing the Pantheon is a temptation (there's even a McDonald's that offers some of the best outdoor seating in town), and I'd consider it just to relax and enjoy the Roman scene. But if you walk a block or two away, you'll get less view and better value. Here are some suggestions.

Ristorante da Fortunato is an Italian classic, with fresh flowers on the tables and waiters in white coats and black ties politely serving good meat and fish to politicians, foreign dignitaries, and tourists with good taste. Don't leave without perusing the photos of their famous visitors—everyone from former Iraqi Foreign Minister Tariq Aziz to Bill Clinton seems to have eaten here. All are pictured with the boss, Fortunato, who, since 1975, has been a master of simple edible elegance. The outdoor seating is fine for watching the river of Roman street life flow by, but the atmosphere is inside. For a dressy night out, this is a reliable and surprisingly reasonable choice—but be sure to reserve ahead (plan to spend €45 per person, Mon–Sat 12:30–15:00 & 19:30–23:30, closed Sun, a block in front of the Pantheon at Via del Pantheon 55, tel. 06-679-2788).

Ristorante Enoteca Corsi is a wine shop that grew into a thriving lunch-only restaurant. The Paiella family serves straightforward, traditional cuisine at great prices to an appreciative crowd of office workers. Check the blackboard for daily specials (gnocchi on Thursday, fish on Friday, and so on). Friendly Giuliana and Manuela welcome eaters to step into their wine shop and pick out a bottle. For the cheap take-away price, plus €2–4 (depending on the wine), they'll uncork it at your table. With €8 pastas, €11 main dishes, and fine wine at a third of the price you'd pay in normal restaurants, this can be a superb value. Consider finishing with a glass of the family's homemade *limoncello* (Mon–Sat 12:00–15:00, closed Sun, a block toward the Pantheon from the Gesù Church at Via del Gesù 87, no reservations possible, tel. 06-679-0821).

Miscellanea is run by much-loved Mikki, who's on a mission to keep foreign students well-fed. You'll find hearty and fresh €4 sandwiches and a long list of €6 salads, along with pasta and other staples. Mikki (and his son, Romero) often tosses in a fun little extra, including—if you have this book on the table—a free glass of Mikki's "sexy wine" (homemade from *fragoline*—strawberry-flavored grapes). This place is popular with American students on foreign-study programs (daily 8:00–24:00, indoor/outdoor seating, facing the rear of the Pantheon at Via della Palombella 34, tel. 06-6813-5318).

Osteria da Mario, a homey little mom-and-pop joint with a no-stress menu, serves traditional favorites in a fun dining room or on tables spilling out onto a picturesque old Roman square (€8 pastas, €10 *secondi*, Mon–Sat 13:00–15:30 & 19:00–23:00, closed Sun, from the Pantheon walk 2 blocks up Via Pantheon, go left on Via delle Coppelle, take first right to Piazza delle Coppelle 51, tel. 06-6880-6349, Marco).

Le Coppelle Taverna is simple, basic, family-friendly, and inexpensive—especially for pizza—with a checkered-tablecloth ambience (€9 pizzas, daily 12:30–15:00 & 19:30–23:30, Via delle Coppelle 39, tel. 06-6880-6557, Alfonso).

Trattoria dal Cav. Gino, tucked away on a tiny street behind the Parliament, has been a favorite since 1963. Photos on the wall recall the days when it was the haunt of big-time politicians. Grandpa Gino shuffles around grating the parmesan cheese while his sister and son serve up traditional Roman favorites and make sure things run smoothly. Reserve ahead, even for lunch (€8 pastas, €11 *secondi*, cash only, Mon–Sat 13:00–14:45 & 20:00–22:30, closed Sun, fish on Friday, behind Piazza del Parlamento and just off Via di Campo Marzio at Vicolo Rosini 4, tel. 06-687-3434, Fabrizio and Carla—Gino's son and daughter—both speak English).

Picnicking Close to the Pantheon

It's fun to munch a picnic with a view of the Pantheon. (Remember to be discreet.) Here are some options.

Antica Salumeria is an old-time *alimentari* (grocery store) on the Pantheon square. Eduardo speaks English and will help you assemble your picnic: artichokes, mixed olives, bread, cheese, meat (they're proud of their Norcia prosciutto), and wine (with plastic glasses). Just set a price (figure €10 per person), and Eduardo will assemble it. Their pastries are fresh from their own bakery. While you can create your own sandwiches (sold by the weight, more fun, and cheaper), they also sell quality ready-made sandwiches for around €5 (daily 8:00–21:00, mobile 334-340-9014).

Supermarkets near the Pantheon: Food is relatively cheap at Italian supermarkets. **Super Market Di per Di** is a convenient place for groceries a block from Gesù Church (Mon–Sat 8:00–21:00, Sun 9:00–19:30, 50 yards off Via del Plebiscito at Via del Gesù 59). Another place, **Supermercato Despar,** is a half a block from the Pantheon toward Piazza Navona (daily 9:00–22:00, Via Giustiniani 18).

Gelato Close to the Pantheon

Three fine *gelaterie* are within a two-minute walk of the Pantheon.

Gelateria Caffè Pasticceria Giolitti, Rome's most famous and venerable ice-cream joint, has reasonable take-away prices and elegant Old World seating (daily 7:00–24:00, just off Piazza Colonna and Piazza Monte Citorio at Via Uffici del Vicario 40, tel. 06-699-1243).

Crèmeria Monteforte is known for its traditional, quality gelato and super-creamy sorbets *(cremolati).* The fruit flavors are especially refreshing—think gourmet slushies (Tue–Sun 10:00–24:00, off-season closes earlier, closed Mon and Dec, faces the west side of the Pantheon at Via della Rotonda 22, tel. 06-686-7720).

Gelateria San Crispino, well-respected by Romans, serves small portions of particularly tasty gourmet gelato using creative ingredients. Because of their commitment to natural ingredients, the colors are muted; gelato purists consider bright colors a sign of unnatural chemicals used to attract children. They serve cups, but no cones (daily 12:00–24:00, a block in front of the Pantheon on Piazza della Maddalena, tel. 06-6889-1310).

In North Rome:
Near the Ara Pacis and Spanish Steps

To locate these restaurants, see the "Dolce Vita Stroll" map on page 719.

Ristorante il Gabriello is inviting and small—modern under medieval arches—and provides a peaceful and local-feeling respite from all the top-end fashion shops in the area. Claudio serves with charisma, while his brother Gabriello cooks creative Roman cuisine using fresh, organic products from his wife's farm. Italians normally just trust the waiter and say, "Bring it on." Tourists are understandably more cautious, but you can be trusting here. Simply close your eyes and point to anything on the menu. Or invest €45 in "Claudio's Extravaganza" (not including wine), and he'll shower you with edible kindness. Specify whether you'd prefer fish, meat, or both. (Note that Romans think raw shellfish is the ultimate in fine dining. If you disagree, make that clear.) When finished, I stand up, hold my belly, and say, *"Ahhh, la vita è bella"* (€10 pastas, €15 *secondi,* dinner only, Mon–Sat 19:00–23:00, closed Sun, reservations smart, air-con, dress respectfully—no shorts please, 3 blocks from Spanish Steps at Via Vittoria 51, tel. 06-6994-0810).

Osteria Gusto is thriving with trendy locals. While pricey, it's untouristy, gives a glimpse of today's Roman scene, and is fine for a glass of good wine over an artisanal cheese plate or a complete dinner (€13 pastas, €20 *secondi,* daily 12:30–15:30 & 19:00–24:00, opens at 18:30 for drinks and appetizers only, reservations recommended after 20:00 and on weekends, on the corner of Via Soderini at Via della Frezza 16, tel. 06-3211-1482).

L'EnotecAntica, an upbeat, atmospheric 200-plus-year-old *enoteca,* has around 60 Italian-only wines by the glass (€4 to €10), and a fresh €14 *antipasti* plate of veggies, salami, and cheese. It's very crowded on summer evenings (daily 11:00–24:00, Via della Croce 76b, tel. 06-679-0896).

In Ancient Rome: Eating Cheaply near the Colosseum

You'll find good views but poor value at the restaurants directly behind the Colosseum. To get your money's worth, eat at least a block away. Here are three handy eateries, all shown on the map on page 799: one at the foot of Via Cavour, and two at the top of Terme di Tito (a long block uphill from the Colosseum, near St. Peter-in-Chains church—of Michelangelo's *Moses* fame; for directions, see page 734).

Enoteca Cavour 313 is a wine bar with a mission: to offer good wine and quality food with an old-fashioned commitment to value and friendly service. It's also a convenient place for a good lunch near the Forum and Colosseum. Angelo and his three partners enjoy creating a mellow ambience under lofts of wine bottles (daily specials and fine wines by the glass, daily 12:30–14:45 & 19:30–24:00, 100 yards off Via dei Fori Imperiali at Via Cavour 313, tel. 06-6785-496).

Caffè dello Studente is popular with engineering students attending the nearby University of Rome. Pina, Mauro, and their perky daughter Simona (speaks English) give my readers a royal welcome and serve typical *bar gastronomia* fare—toasted sandwiches, salads, and pizzas (stick to any of the aforementioned fare to avoid frozen dishes). If they have a "Rick Steves menu," give it a miss. You can get your food to go *(da portar via)*, eat standing at the crowded bar, or wait for table service outside. If it's not busy, show this book when you order at the bar and sit without paying extra at a table (Mon–Sat 7:30–22:30, April–Oct Sun 9:00–22:30, Nov–March closed Sun, Via delle Terme di Tito, tel. 06-488-3240).

Hostaria da Nerone, next door, is a more formal restaurant with much better food and homemade pasta dishes. Their €9 *antipasti* plate—with a variety of veggies, fish, and meat—is a good value for a quick lunch. While the *antipasti* menu indicates specifics, you can have a plate of whatever's out—just direct the waiter to assemble the €9 *antipasti* plate of your lunchtime dreams (Mon–Sat 12:00–15:00 & 19:00–23:00, closed Sun, indoor/outdoor seating, Via delle Terme di Tito 96, tel. 06-481-7952, run by Teo and Eugenio).

Near Termini Train Station

You have several eating options near my recommended hotels on Via Firenze.

Dining

Ristorante del Giglio is an elegant circa-1900 place with a long tradition of serving traditional Roman dishes. You'll eat pricey dishes in a big hall of about 20 tables with dressy locals and

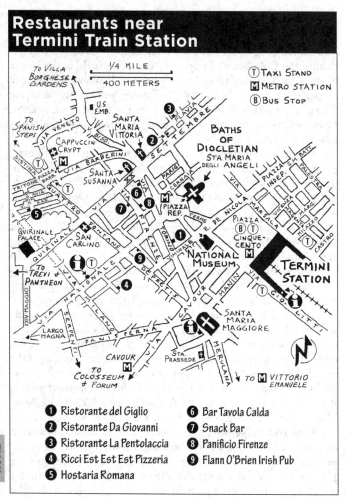

Restaurants near Termini Train Station

To VILLA BORGHESE GARDENS

¼ MILE
400 METERS

(T) TAXI STAND
(M) METRO STATION
(B) BUS STOP

TO SPANISH STEPS

U.S. EMB.

SANTA MARIA VITTORIA

CAPPUCCIN CRYPT

BATHS OF DIOCLETIAN

STA. MARIA DEGLI ANGELI

SANTA SUSANNA

QUIRINALE PALACE

SAN CARLINO

PIAZZA REP.

PIAZZA CINQUE-CENTO

TERMINI STATION

TO TREVI & PANTHEON

NATIONAL MUSEUM

LARGO MAGNA

SANTA MARIA MAGGIORE

CAVOUR

STA. PRASSEDE

TO COLOSSEUM & FORUM

TO VITTORIO EMANUELE

1 Ristorante del Giglio
2 Ristorante Da Giovanni
3 Ristorante La Pentolaccia
4 Ricci Est Est Est Pizzeria
5 Hostaria Romana

6 Bar Tavola Calda
7 Snack Bar
8 Panificio Firenze
9 Flann O'Brien Irish Pub

ROME

tourists following the recommendations of nearby hotels. While not a particularly good value, the space is nice and it's stress-free (€12 pastas, €15 *secondi,* Mon 19:00–23:00, Tue–Sat 12:15–15:00 & 19:00–23:00, closed Sun, alluring dessert cart, Via Torino 137, tel. 06-488-1606, Fiorella).

Ristorante Da Giovanni is a well-worn old-time eatery that makes no concessions to tourism or the modern world—just hardworking cooks and waiters serving standard dishes at great prices to a committed clientele. It's simply fun to eat in the middle of this high-energy, old-school diner (€6–9 pastas and *secondi,* daily specials, Mon–Sat 12:00–15:00 & 19:00–22:00, closed Sun and Aug, corner of Via XX Settembre at Via Antonio

Salandra 1, tel. 06-485-950).

Ristorante La Pentolaccia, pricier and more romantic than the nearby Da Giovanni, is a dressy, tourist-friendly place with tight seating and classic Roman cooking (Mon–Sat 12:00–15:00 & 17:30–23:00, Sun 17:30–23:00, a block off Via XX Settembre at Via Flavia 38, tel. 06-483-477).

Ricci Est Est Est Pizzeria, a venerable family-run pizzeria, has plenty of historical ambience, good €8 pizzas, and dangerously tasty *fritti*, such as fried *baccalà* (cod) and zucchini flowers (Tue–Sun 19:00–24:00, closed Mon and Aug, Via Genova 32, tel. 06-488-1107).

Hostaria Romana is a busy bistro with a hustling and fun-loving gang of waiters and noisy walls graffitied by happy eaters. While they specialize in fish and traditional Roman dishes, their €10 *antipasti* plate can make a good meal in itself (Mon–Sat 12:15–15:00 & 19:15–23:00, closed Sun, a block up the lane just past the entrance to the big tunnel near the Trevi Fountain at Via de Boccaccio 1, tel. 06-474-5284).

Fast, Simple Meals near Termini Train Station

Bar Tavola Calda is a workers' favorite for a quick, cheap lunch. They have good, fresh hot dishes ready to go for a fine price. Head back past the bar to peruse their enticing display, point at what you want, then grab a seat and the young waitstaff will serve you (Mon–Fri 6:00–18:00, closed Sat–Sun, Via Torino 40).

Snack Bar puts out a lunchtime display of inexpensive pastas, colorful sandwiches, fresh fruit, and salad. Their loyal customers love the *caffè con crema* whipped with sugar (daily 6:00–24:00, Via Firenze 33, mobile 339-393-1356, Enrica).

Panificio Firenze has take-out pizza, sandwiches, and an old-fashioned *alimentari* (grocery) with everything you'd need for a picnic (Mon–Fri 7:00–19:00, Sat 7:00–14:00, closed Sun, Via Firenze 51–52, tel. 06-488-5035).

Flann O'Brien Irish Pub is an entertaining place for a light meal of pasta...or something *other* than pasta, such as grilled meats and giant salads, served early and late, when other places are closed. They have Irish beer, live sporting events on TV, and perhaps the most Italian crowd of all. Walk way back before choosing a table (daily 7:00–24:00, Via Nazionale 17, at intersection with Via Napoli, tel. 06-488-0418).

Near Vatican City

Avoid the restaurant-pushers handing out fliers near the Vatican: bad food and expensive menu tricks. Try any of these instead (see map on page 805).

Hostaria dei Bastioni, run by Emilio, is conveniently located midway on your hike from St. Peter's to the Vatican Museum, with noisy street-side seating and a quiet interior (€7 pastas, €12 *secondi*, no cover charge, Mon–Sat 12:00–15:30 & 19:00–23:00, closed Sun, Via Leone IV 29, at corner of Vatican wall, tel. 06-3972-3034).

La Rustichella serves tasty wood-fired pizza and the usual pasta in addition to their famous and sprawling *antipasti* buffet (€8 for a single plate). Arrive when it opens at 19:30 to avoid a line and have the pristine buffet to yourself. Do like the Romans do—take a moderate amount and make one trip only (Tue–Sun 12:30–15:00 & 19:30–24:00, closed Mon, near Metro: Cipro, opposite church at end of Via Candia, Via Angelo Emo 1, tel. 06-3972-0649). Consider the fun and fruity **Gelateria Millennium** next door.

L'Insalata Ricca is another branch of the popular chain that serves salads and pastas (daily 12:30–15:30 & 18:30–23:45, across from Vatican walls at Piazza Risorgimento 5, tel. 06-3973-0387).

Duecento Gradi is a good bet for fresh and creative €5 sandwiches (daily 12:00–23:00, Piazza Risorgimento 3, tel. 06-3975-4239).

Viale Giulio Cesare: This street is lined with cheap *pizza rustica* shops, self-serve places, and inviting eateries.

Along Borgo Pio: The pedestrian-only Borgo Pio—a block from Piazza San Pietro—has restaurants worth a look, such as **Tre Pupazzi** (Mon–Sat 12:00–15:00 & 19:00–23:00, closed Sun, at corner of Via Tre Pupazzi and Borgo Pio, tel. 06-686-8371). At **Vecchio Borgo,** across the street, you can get pasta, pizza slices, and veggies to go (Mon–Sat 9:00–21:00, closed Sun, Borgo Pio 27a, tel. 06-8117-3585).

Picnic Supplies: Turn your nose loose in the wonderful **Mercato Trionfale** covered market, one of the best in the city, three blocks north of the Vatican Museum (Mon–Sat roughly 7:00–14:00, closed Sun, corner of Via Tunisi and Via Andrea Doria). If the market is closed, try several nearby supermarkets; the most convenient is **GS Di per Di** (Mon–Sat 8:00–20:00, Sun 9:00–20:00, Via Sebastiano Veniero 16).

Gelato: **Gelateria Old Bridge** scoops up hearty portions of fresh gelato for tourists and nuns alike. The quality, quantity, and value can't be beat (daily 10:00–23:00, just off Piazza Risorgimento across from Vatican walls at Via Bastioni 3).

Rome Connections

Rome is well-connected with the rest of the planet, by train, bus, plane, and cruise ship. This section addresses your arrival and departure from the city. It explains the various options and gives a rundown on their points of departure.

By Train

Rome's main train station is the centrally located **Termini** Station, which has connections to the airport. Rome's other major station is **Tiburtina** bus/train station, which is starting to get a few high-speed rail connections. For in-depth descriptions of both Termini and Tiburtina stations, see page 691. Smaller stations include **Ostiense** (useful for going to South Rome and Testaccio) and its neighbor, **Porta San Paolo** (with connections to Ostia Antica). If you're staying near the Vatican and taking a regional train, it saves time to get off at **San Pietro** Station rather than at Termini.

Since virtually all of the most convenient connections for travelers depart from Termini, I've listed those below. In 30 years of visits, I've never had occasion to use Tiburtina, but that may change—Tiburtina is currently being redeveloped for high-speed rail. At least one Eurostar Italia train stops here already, and a new company—Nuovo Trasporto Viaggiatori (NTV)—is expected to start running its Italo high-speed trains from Tiburtina sometime in 2011 (for details, see www.ntvspa.it). As a precaution, it's always smart to confirm whether your train departs from Termini or Tiburtina.

From Rome's Termini Station by Train to: Venice (roughly hourly, 3.5 hours, overnight possible), **Florence** (at least hourly, 1.5 hours, some stop at Orvieto en route), **Orvieto** (hourly, 1.25 hours), **Assisi** (hourly, 2–3.5 hours, 5 direct, most others change in Foligno), **Pisa** (hourly, 3–4 hours, many change in Florence), **La Spezia** (8/day direct, more with transfers in Pisa, 4 hours), **Milan** (hourly, 3.5–8 hours, overnight possible), **Naples** (at least hourly, 1.25 hours on Frecciarossa trains, otherwise 2–2.5 hours), **Civitavecchia** cruise-ship port (2/hour, 1.25 hours), **Brindisi** (6/day, 3 direct, 6–9 hours, overnight possible), **Amsterdam** (6/day, 20 hours), **Bern** (6/day, 9 hours, several overnight options), **Frankfurt** (7/day, 12 hours, several overnight options), **Munich** (4/day, 11 hours, several overnight options), **Nice** (6/day, 10 hours), **Paris** (3/day, 12–15 hours, several overnight options, important to reserve ahead, 19:00 railpass rule works for 18:20 night train), **Vienna** (3/day, 12 hours, several overnight options).

By Bus

Long-distance buses (such as from Siena and Assisi) use Rome's **Tiburtina Station** (described on page 692).

From Rome by Bus to: Assisi (2/day, 3 hours—the train makes much more sense), **Siena** (8/day, 3 hours), **Sorrento** (1–2/day, 4 hours; this is the quickest and easiest way to go straight to Sorrento, see page 891 for ticket details).

By Plane

Rome's two airports—**Fiumicino** (a.k.a. Leonardo da Vinci) and the small **Ciampino**—share the same website (www.adr.it). For budget flights within Europe, easyJet uses both airports, while Ryanair only uses Ciampino. Vueling and Blue Express only use Fiumicino.

Fiumicino Airport

Rome's major airport has a TI (in terminal 3, daily 8:00–19:00), ATMs, banks, luggage storage, shops, and bars. The Rome Walks website (www.romewalks.com) has a useful video on options for getting into the city from the airport.

A slick, direct **"Leonardo Express" train** connects the airport and Rome's central Termini train station in 30 minutes for €15. Trains run twice hourly in both directions from roughly 6:00 to 23:00 (leaving the airport at :06 and :36). From the airport's arrival gate, follow signs to *Stazione/Railway Station*. Buy your ticket from a machine, the Biglietteria office, or a newsstand at the platform, then validate it in a yellow machine near the track. Make sure the train you board is going to the central "Roma Termini" station, not "Roma Orte" or others.

Going from Termini train station to the airport, trains depart at about :22 and :52 past the hour, from track 25 (located way down at the far end of track 24; allow 10 minutes for the hike, moving walkways downstairs). Check the departure boards for "Fiumicino Aeroporto"—the local name for the airport—and confirm with an official or a local on the platform that the train is indeed going to the airport (€15, buy ticket from any *tabacchi* or newsstand in the station, or at the self-service machines, Termini–Fiumicino trains run 5:52–22:52). Read your ticket: If it requires validation, stamp it in the yellow machine near the platform before boarding. From the train station at the airport, you can access all of the terminals—1, 2, 3, or 5.

Allow lots of time going in either direction; there's a fair amount of transportation involved, including moving walkways, escalators, and walking (e.g., getting from your hotel to Termini, from Termini to the train platform, the ride to the airport, getting from the airport train station to check-in, etc.). Flying to the US involves an extra level of security—plan on getting to the airport even earlier (I like to arrive 2.5 hours ahead of my flight).

Shuttle van services run to and from the airport and can be economical for one or two people. Consider Rome Airport Shuttle (€25/1 person, extra people-€6 each, by reservation only, tel. 06-4201-4507 or 06-4201-3469, www.airportshuttle.it).

A **taxi** between Fiumicino and downtown Rome takes 45

ROME

minutes in normal traffic (for tips on taxis, see page 705). If you're catching a taxi at the airport, be sure to wait at the taxi stand. Avoid unmarked, unmetered taxis; these guys will try to tempt you away from the taxi-stand lineup by offering an immediate (rip-off) ride. Rome's official taxis have a fixed rate to and from the airport (€45 for up to four people with bags). If your cab driver tries to charge you more than €45 from the airport into town, say, *"Quarantacinque euro—È la legge"* (kwah-RAHN-tah CHEENG-kway AY-oo-roh—ay lah LEJ-jay; which means, "Forty-five euros—It's the law"), and they should back off.

A new law allows cabbies not based in Rome to charge €60 for the ride. That sign is posted next to the €45-fare sign—confusing many tourists and allowing dishonest cabbies to overcharge. Only use a Rome city cab (with the "SPQR" shield on the door). They can only charge €45 for the ride to anywhere in the historic center (within the old city walls, where most of my recommended hotels are located).

To get from the airport into town cheaply by taxi, try teaming up with any tourist also just arriving (most are heading for hotels near yours in the center). When you're departing Rome, your hotel can arrange a taxi to the airport at any hour.

For **airport information,** call 06-65951. To inquire about flights, call 06-6595-3640 (Alitalia: tel. 06-2222; British Airways: tel. 199-712-266; Continental: tel. 06-6605-3030; Delta: tel. 848-780-376; Swiss International: tel. 848-868-120; United: tel. 848-800-692).

Ciampino Airport

Rome's smaller airport (tel. 06-6595-9515) handles charter flights and some budget airlines (including all Ryanair and some easyJet flights).

To get to downtown Rome from the airport, you can take the Cotral bus, which leaves every 40 minutes (€1.20, 20-minute ride, toll-free tel. 800-174-471, www.cotralspa.it), to the Anagnina Metro stop, where you can connect by Metro to the stop nearest your hotel. Rome Airport Shuttle (listed earlier) also offers service to and from Ciampino. The Terravision Express Shuttle connects Ciampino and Termini, leaving every 20 minutes (€4 one-way, €8 round-trip, www.terravision.eu). The SIT Bus Shuttle also connects Termini train station to Ciampino (€6, about 2/hour, 30–60 minutes, runs 7:45–23:15 Ciampino to Termini, 4:30–21:30 Termini to Ciampino, pickup on Via Marsala just outside the train exit closest to track 1, tel. 06-591-7844, www.sitbusshuttle.it). A taxi should cost €35 to downtown (within the old city walls, including most of my recommended hotels).

By Cruise Ship

Hundreds of cruise chips—including Carnival, Royal Caribbean, Princess, and Celebrity lines—dock each year at the Port of **Civitavecchia,** about 45 miles northwest of Rome. Port facilities include a waiting room, ATMs, bag storage, and snack bar.

Getting Between Civitavecchia and Downtown Rome

Twice-hourly **trains** connect Civitavecchia and Rome's Termini Station (€5–9, 1–1.25 hours, regional and pricier IC options, get tickets at ticket window). The best deal: ask for the €9 BIRG ticket, which covers all-day, unlimited travel on regional trains in second class and on the Metro and bus system in Rome. Be sure to write your name on the back and validate it in the yellow box before getting on train.

To reach Civitavecchia's train station from the ship, take the free shuttle bus to the port entrance, and walk about 10–15 minutes straight along the seaside road. Some shuttle buses may take you all the way to the station—ask. The Rome Walks website (www.romewalks.com) has a useful video on taking the train from the port into the city.

To reach the port from Civitavecchia train station, turn right after you exit and walk 10–15 minutes along the waterfront road. Or you can take either bus #C or #F from in front of the train station; buy your ticket at the *tabacchi* shop before you board. Local taxis also run between the port and the train station (often meeting the ship, or call 076-626-121).

The road traffic between Civitavecchia and Rome is terrible, making trains faster and more economical than any of your other options. **Taxis** can run €200–400 between Civitavecchia and Rome. A slightly less expensive option is to hire a **private limousine** (figure €150 for up to three people).

Getting Between Civitavecchia and Fiumicino Airport

You'll need to take two **trains** to link Civitavecchia and Fiumicino Airport: one between the airport and Rome's Termini Station, and another between Termini and Civitavecchia. See "By Plane," earlier.

Shuttle van services run between the port and Rome's Fiumicino Airport. Try **Rome Airport Shuttle** (€90/1–2 people, €15 each additional person up to 8, share with others and save, much more for pickup between 21:00 and 7:00, tel. 06-4201-4507 or 06-4201-3469, www.airportshuttle.it).

Day Trips to Rome from Civitavecchia

Do-it-yourselfers will find it easy to visit Rome for a day using the **train** (see details earlier). Consider disembarking the train at Rome's San Pietro Station instead of more-central Termini Station, in order to start your sightseeing with St. Peter's Basilica and the Vatican. (Most regional, but not InterCity, trains stop at San Pietro; be sure you take the right train.) Then take the Metro to the Spanish Steps to explore Rome's other sights. If you return to the port from Rome's Termini Station, note that Civitavecchia trains generally leave from tracks 27–30, a 10-minute walk from the station entrance.

If your cruise ship stops in Civitavecchia for the day, you may be offered a **shore excursion** to Rome. Many of Civitavecchia's private limousine companies and the Rome Airport Shuttle also offer Rome **tours.** Look for a tour that is a minimum eight hours in length: six hours for sightseeing and two-plus hours of travel time. On shorter tours you'll see most of Rome from the bus window. Plan to spend about €200 per person.

NAPLES

Napoli

If you like Italy as far south as Rome, go farther south. It gets better. If Italy is getting on your nerves, don't go farther. Italy intensifies as you plunge deeper. Naples is Italy in the extreme—its best (birthplace of pizza and Sophia Loren) and its worst (home of the Camorra, Naples' "family" of organized crime). Just beyond Naples you'll find the impressive ruins of Pompeii and Herculaneum...and the brooding volcano that did them both in, Mount Vesuvius.

Neapolis ("new city") was a thriving Greek commercial center 2,500 years ago. Today, it remains southern Italy's leading city, offering a fascinating collection of museums, churches, and eclectic architecture. Walking through its colorful Old Town is one of my favorite sightseeing experiences anywhere in Italy.

Naples—Italy's third-largest city, with more than one million people—has almost no open spaces or parks, which makes its position as Europe's most densely populated city plenty evident. Watching the police try to enforce traffic sanity is almost comical in Italy's grittiest, most polluted, and most crime-ridden city. But Naples surprises the observant traveler with its impressive knack

for living, eating, and raising children in the streets with good humor and decency. Overcome your fear of being run down or ripped off long enough to talk with people. Enjoy a few smiles

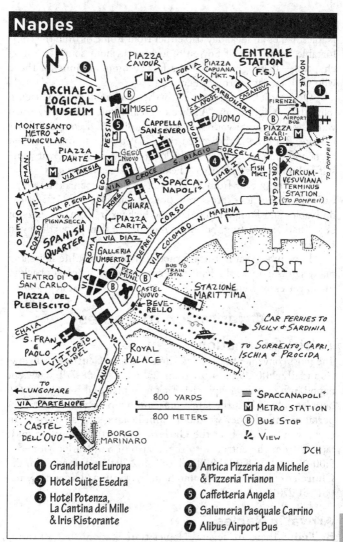

Naples

Map labels (from the figure):

PIAZZA CAVOUR · CENTRALE STATION (F.S.) · NOVARA · VIA FORIA · PIAZZA CAPUANA MKT. · VIA CARBONARA · VIA APOST. SS. · CASANOVA · FIRENZE · AIRPORT BUS · ARCHAEOLOGICAL MUSEUM · PESSINA · MUSEO · Cappella SanSevero · DUOMO · VIA DUOMO · PIAZZA GARIBALDI · MONTESANTO METRO & FUNICULAR · PIAZZA DANTE · Gesù Nuovo · S. BIAGIO · FORCELLA · CIRCUM-VESUVIANA TERMINUS STATION (to POMPEII) · TO POMPEII · E. MAN. · VIA TARSIA · TOLEDO · VIA B. CROCE · "SPACCA-NAPOLI" · Fish MKT. · CORSO GARIB. · VOMERO · VIT. CORSO · VIA P. SCURA · MORG. · S. CHIARA · CORSO · UMB. · VIA PIGNASECCA · PIAZZA CARITA · VIA DIAZ · VIA COLOMBO N. MARINA · PORT · SPANISH QUARTER · VIA ROMA · VIA DEPRETIS · GALLERIA UMBERTO I · BUS TO TRAIN STN. · VIA MUNI. · Teatro di San Carlo · CASTEL NUOVO · STAZIONE MARITTIMA · PIAZZA DEL PLEBISCITO · BEVE-RELLO · CAR FERRIES TO SICILY & SARDINIA · CHAIA · S. FRAN E PAOLO · VITTORIO TUNNEL · N. SAURO · ROYAL PALACE · TO SORRENTO, CAPRI, ISCHIA & PROCIDA · TO LUNGOMARE · VIA PARTENOPE · CASTEL DELL'OVO · BORGO MARINARO

800 YARDS · 800 METERS

"SPACCANAPOLI" · **M** METRO STATION · **B** BUS STOP · ☆ VIEW

DCH

① Grand Hotel Europa
② Hotel Suite Esedra
③ Hotel Potenza, La Cantina dei Mille & Iris Ristorante
④ Antica Pizzeria da Michele & Pizzeria Trianon
⑤ Caffetteria Angela
⑥ Salumeria Pasquale Carrino
⑦ Alibus Airport Bus

NAPLES

and jokes with the man running the neighborhood tripe shop, or the woman taking her day-care class on a walk through the traffic.

The pulse of Italy throbs in Naples. Like Cairo or Mumbai, it's appalling and captivating at the same time, the closest thing to "reality travel" that you'll find in Western Europe. But this tangled mess still somehow manages to breathe, laugh, and sing—with a captivating Italian accent.

Planning Your Time

Naples makes an ideal day trip either from Rome or from the comfortable home base of Sorrento, located an hour south (see next chapter)—although I've listed a few accommodations for those who want to stay overnight here.

On a quick visit, start with the Archaeological Museum (closed Tue), follow my "A Slice of Neapolitan Life" self-guided walk, and celebrate your survival with pizza. Of course, Naples is huge. But even with limited time, if you stick to the described route and grab a cab when you're lost or tired, it's fun. Treat yourself well in Naples; the city is cheap by Italian standards.

For a blitz tour from Rome, you could have breakfast on an early Rome–Naples express train (for example, Mon–Fri 7:35–8:45), do Naples and Pompeii in a day, and be back in Rome in time for bed. That's exhausting, but more memorable than a fourth day in Rome.

Remember that in the afternoon, Naples' street life slows and many sights close as the temperature soars. The city comes back to life in the early evening.

Orientation to Naples

Tourist Information

The most convenient of Naples' three TIs is in **Centrale train station** (daily 9:00–19:00, near track 23, tel. 081-268-779, www.ept napoli.info or www.inaples.it). Pick up a map and the *Qui Napoli* booklet, which lists the latest museum hours, events, and transportation info. If they say they're "finished," ask for an old one. In town, you'll find TIs at the **Galleria Umberto I shopping mall** (across from the entrance to the Teatro di San Carlo; Mon–Sat 9:00–19:00, Sun 9:00–14:00, tel. 081-402-394) and across from the **Church of Gesù Nuovo** (same hours as Galleria Umberto I, tel. 081-551-2701).

Arrival in Naples

By Train: There are several Naples train stations, but all trains coming into town stop at either Napoli Centrale or Garibaldi—essentially the same stop, one on top of the other.

Centrale is the busiest, facing Naples' main square, Piazza Garibaldi. You'll find all the administrative facilities in Centrale, including a TI, the Circumvesuviana stop (in the basement) for commuter trains to Sorrento and Pompeii, an ATM (at Banco di Napoli near track 24), and a baggage check (€4/5 hours, then €0.60/hour, daily 7:00–23:00, near track 5, marked *deposito bagagli*). Warning: Services in this station tend to change location frequently.

Planning Your Time in the Region

Naples, the Amalfi Coast, and Paestum

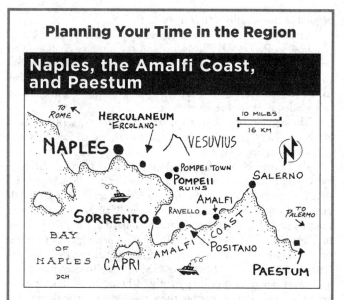

On a quick trip, give the entire area—including Sorrento and Naples—a minimum of three days. With Sorrento as your sunny springboard (see next chapter), spend a day in Naples, a day exploring the Amalfi Coast, and a day split between Pompeii and the town of Sorrento. While Paestum (Greek temples), Mount Vesuvius, Herculaneum (an ancient Roman site like Pompeii), and the island of Capri are decent destinations, they are worthwhile only if you have more time.

A regional pass, the **Campania ArteCard,** covers most sights and public transportation in the area but isn't always accepted at transit stations, making it more trouble than it's worth (€27 three-day pass covers free entry to two sights and 50 percent off others, www.campaniaartecard.it).

Garibaldi is a subway station used by trains to make a quick stop as they barrel through. It's connected to Centrale by escalators.

By Boat: Naples is a ferry hub with great boat connections to Sorrento, Capri, and other nearby ports.

If you're arriving at Naples' Port Beverello, you can get to the center by taxi, bus, or on foot; a shuttle bus runs to the airport. The **taxi stand** is in front of the port; figure €12 to get to the train station. **Buses** #152 and #601 head to Piazza Garibaldi and the train station (4/hour, 15 minutes, buy €1.10 ticket at *tabacchi,* validate ticket in yellow box on the bus as you board; with your back to the boats, head right toward the traffic lights—the bus stop is just beyond in the middle of the busy street).

On foot, it's a seven-minute **walk**—past the gigantic Castel Nuovo—to Piazza del Plebiscito and the old city center: After crossing the busy street in front of the port, walk to the left toward the overpass. The elevator beneath the overpass will take you up to the street in front of Piazza del Plebiscito. You could start my self-guided walk in reverse from here.

The stop for the Alibus **airport** shuttle buses (described below) is a couple of blocks inland from the port, between Castel Nuovo and Teatro di San Carlo.

By Plane: Naples International Airport (Capodichino) is located four miles northeast of the city center (tel. 081-789-6111 for operator, tel. 848-888-777 for info, www.gesac.it). Alibus shuttle buses zip you from the airport to Naples' Centrale train station/ Piazza Garibaldi in 15 minutes, and then head to the port for boats to Capri and Sorrento (daily 6:00–24:00, 3/hour, less frequent early and late, 30 minutes to the port, €3, pay driver, stops at train station and port only). Local bus #3S, which also goes into town, is cheaper but stops more frequently (2/hour, €1.10). It's tough to get a taxi to use the meter from the airport, but the trip should cost about €20.

To reach **Sorrento** from Naples Airport, take the direct Curreri bus (daily at 9:00, 11:00, 13:00, 14:30, 16:30, and 19:30; 1.25 hours, €10, pay driver, tel. 081-801-5420, www.curreriviaggi.it).

Helpful Hints

Theft Alert: Err on the side of caution. Don't venture into neighborhoods that make you uncomfortable. Walk with confidence, as if you know where you're going and what you're doing. Assume able-bodied beggars are thieves.

Stick to busy streets and beware of gangs of hoodlums. A third of the city is unemployed, and past local governments have set an example that the Mafia would be proud of. Assume con artists are more clever than you. Any jostle or commotion is probably a thief-team smokescreen. To keep bags safe, it's probably best to store them at Centrale Station.

Perhaps your biggest risk of theft is while catching or riding the Circumvesuviana commuter train. Remember, if you're connecting from a major train, you'll be stepping from a relatively secure compartment into a crowded Naples subway filled with thieves hunting disoriented tourists with luggage. While I ride the Circumvesuviana comfortably and safely, each year I hear of many who get ripped off on this ride. You won't be mugged—just conned or pickpocketed. Especially late at night, the Circumvesuviana train is plagued by intimidating ruffians. For maximum safety and peace of mind, sit in the front car, where the driver will double as your protector.

Con artists may say you need to "transfer" by taxi to catch the Circumvesuviana; you don't. Anyone offering to help you with your bags is likely a thief, despite displayed credentials. There are no porters at Centrale Station or in the basement where the Circumvesuviana station is located. Wear your money belt, hang on to your bag, and don't display any valuables.

Traffic: In Naples, red lights are discretionary, and pedestrians need to be wary, particularly of motor scooters. Smart tourists jaywalk in the shadow of bold and confident locals, who generally ignore crosswalks. Wait for a break in traffic, cross with confidence, and make eye contact with approaching drivers. The traffic will stop.

Local Guides: Roberta Mazzarella, who sorts through the wonders of Naples as only a local can, is excellent for a city walk (about €50/hour depending on itinerary, private tours only, mobile 339-135-7619, robertamazzarella@yahoo.it). **Pina Esposito** specializes in art and archaeology, and does fine tours of Naples' excellent but somewhat hard-to-appreciate Archaeological Museum (€120/2 hours, 10 percent off with this book, confirm one week in advance, sometimes available on shorter notice, mobile 349-596-8251, annamariaesposito1 @virgilio.it). Both are flexible and also lead tours of Capri, Pompeii, and the surrounding area.

Getting Around Naples

By Subway: Naples' subway, the Metropolitana, has two lines. Line 2, the main line, runs from Centrale Station (catch it downstairs at the Garibaldi stop) through the center of town (direction: Pozzuoli), stopping at Piazza Cavour (a 5-minute walk from the Archaeological Museum) and Montesanto (top of Spanish Quarter and Spaccanapoli street). Line 1 runs from Piscinola/Scampia (suburbs) into the city center, stopping at the Museo station, near the Archaeological Museum (connects to Line 2's Piazza Cavour subway stop). Tickets cost €1.10 and are good for 1.5 hours. All-day tickets cost €3.10. Validate tickets either at the turnstile (if there is one), or in the small yellow boxes you'll see before you reach the track.

By Taxi: If you can afford a taxi, don't mess with the buses. A short taxi ride costs about €10 (insist on the meter—*tassametro*, €2 supplement after 22:00, €1.50 supplement on Sun, extra for baggage and holidays).

On a Hop-on, Hop-off Bus Tour: The "Sightseeing Napoli" tour bus makes three loops through the city, allowing ticket-holders to get on and off as they lace the city's sights together (€22,

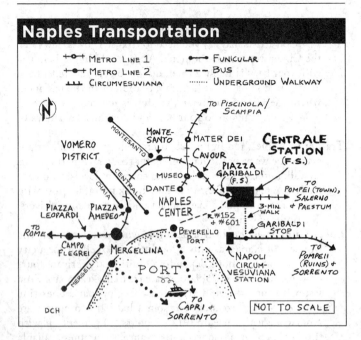

Naples Transportation

●+●+ Metro Line 1	●+● Funicular
●+●+ Metro Line 2	- - - Bus
⊥⊥⊥ Circumvesuviana	.... Underground Walkway

NOT TO SCALE

tickets good for 24 hours, buy from driver or from kiosk in front of Castel Nuovo near the port, scant recorded narration; for details, see the brochure at hotels and TI).

Self-Guided Tour

▲▲▲Archaeological Museum (Museo Archeologico)

For lovers of antiquity, this museum alone makes Naples a worthwhile stop. Considering its popularity and the importance of the collection, it's remarkable how ramshackle, unkempt, and dumpy its displays are. Still, if you can overlook the dust bunnies, this museum offers the best possible peek into the artistic jewelry boxes of Pompeii and Herculaneum. When Pompeii was excavated in the early 1800s, Naples' Bourbon king bellowed, "Bring me the best of what you find!" The actual sites are impressive but barren; the finest art and artifacts ended up here.

Cost and Hours: €6.50, but often €10 with mandatory charge for special exhibits, cash only, Wed–Mon 9:00–19:30, closed Tue.

Getting There: To take the subway from Centrale Station, follow signs to the Metro, called *Metropolitana* (near track 14, downstairs). Buy your ticket at the kiosk or a *tabacchi* and ask which track—*"Quale binario?"* (KWAH-lay bee-NAH-ree-oh)—to Piazza Cavour (direction: Pozzuoli, usually track 4). Validate your ticket in the small yellow boxes near the escalator going down to the tracks. Ride the subway one stop. As you leave the Metro, you can exit and hike uphill, or follow *Linea 1 Museo* signs through a long series of underground moving sidewalks to the *Museo* stop (on a different line), where you'll exit a bit closer to the museum. No matter where you emerge, look for a grand old red building located up a flight of stairs at the top of the block.

Figure on €10 for a taxi from the train station to the museum—insist on the meter *(tassametro)*.

Secret Room Appointment: Depending on how packed the museum is, you may need to make an appointment on arrival to visit the Secret Room (Gabinetto Segreto), which contains erotic art from Pompeii (included in admission, you get a 15-minute window; to schedule a time, go to the information counter—on your immediate right as you enter). When it's not crowded, an appointment is unnecessary.

Information: Tel. 081-442-2149. For the basics, you can follow my self-guided tour (below). If you want a **guided tour,** look for Pina Esposito at the museum (see "Helpful Hints," earlier; €120/2-hour tour, 10 percent less with this book; help her assemble a group of up to 10 to split the fee). **Audioguides,** which haven't been updated for years, cost €4 (at ticket desk). The shop sells a worthwhile *National Archaeological Museum of Naples* guidebook—at €12, it's still a better value than the audioguide. Bag check is obligatory and free. Photos are allowed without a flash.

The museum seems to be in constant chaos due to ongoing renovations. If you can't find a particular work, ask a museum custodian, *"Dov'è?"* (DOH-vay, meaning "Where is?"), followed by the item's name.

Overview

Entering the museum, stand at the base of the grand staircase. To your right, on the ground floor, are larger-than-life statues from the Farnese Collection, star-ring the *Toro Farnese*. Up the stairs on the mezzanine level (turn left at the lion) are mosaics and frescoes from Pompeii, including the *Battle of Alexander* and the Secret Room of erotic art. On the top floor is a scale model of Pompeii and bronze statues from Herculaneum (a nearby town destroyed in the same eruption that devastated Pompeii). You'll find WCs by circling behind the staircase.

• From the base of the grand staircase, turn right and head to the far end.

Ground Floor: The Farnese Collection

The museum's ground floor alone has enough Greek and Roman art to put any museum on the map. Its highlight is the Farnese Collection, a grand hall of huge, bright, and wonderfully restored statues excavated from Rome's Baths of Caracalla.

The tangled *Toro Farnese* depicts a woman being tied to a bull. At 13 feet, it's the tallest ancient marble group ever found,

and the largest intact statue from antiquity. A third-century A.D. copy of a lost bronze Hellenistic original, it was carved out of one piece of marble. Michelangelo and others "restored" it at the pope's request—meaning that they integrated surviving bits into a new work. Panels on the wall show which pieces were actually carved by Michelangelo (in blue on the chart): the head of the woman in back, the torso of the aunt under the bull, and the dog. (Imagine how the statue would stand out if it was thoughtfully lit and not surrounded by white walls.)

Here's the story behind the statue: Once upon an ancient Greek time, King Lycus was bewitched by Dirce. He abandoned his pregnant wife, Antiope (standing regally in the background). The single mom gave birth to twin boys (shown here). When they grew up, they killed their deadbeat dad and tied Dirce to the horns of a bull to be bashed against a mountain. Captured in marble, the action is thrilling: cape flailing, dog snarling, hooves in the air. You can almost hear the bull snorting. And in the back, Antiope oversees this harsh ancient justice with satisfaction.

At the far end of the hall stands **Hercules.** In a small room behind him is a glass case with the sumptuous **Farnese Cup** *(Tazza Farnese,* second century B.C., from Egypt). This large, ancient cameo made of agates looks less like a cup than a cereal bowl. Its decorations are both Egyptian (the Nile toting a lush cornucopia) and, on the flip side, Greek (Medusa's head).

• Backtrack a bit, then head up to the mezzanine level.

Mezzanine: Pompeiian Mosaics and the Secret Room

Most of these mosaics—of animals, musicians, and geometric designs—were taken from Pompeii's House of the Faun (see page 863). The house's delightful centerpiece is a 20-inch-high statue of the ***Dancing Faun.*** This rare surviving Greek bronze statue (from the fourth century B.C.) is surrounded by some of the best mosaics of that age.

A highlight is the grand ***Battle of Alexander,*** a second-century B.C. copy of the original Greek fresco, done a century earlier. It dec-

orated a floor in the House of the Faun and was found intact; the damage you see occurred as this treasure was moved from Pompeii to the king's collection here. The painting (on left, made before it was moved) shows how it once looked. Alexander (left side of the scene, with curly hair and sideburns) is about to defeat the Persians under Darius (central figure, in chariot with turban and beard). This pivotal victory allowed Alexander to quickly overrun much of Asia (331 B.C.). Alexander is the only one without a helmet...a con-fident master of the battlefield while everyone else is fight-ing for their lives, eyes bulg-ing with fear. Notice how the horses, already in retreat, add to the scene's propaganda value. Notice also the shading and

perspective, which Renaissance artists would later work so hard to accomplish. (A modern reproduction of the mosaic is now back in the House of the Faun.)

The **Secret Room** *(Gabinetto Segreto)* contains a sizable assortment of erotic frescoes, well-hung pottery, and perky stat-ues that once decorated bedrooms, meeting rooms, brothels, and even shops at Pompeii and Herculaneum. (On crowded days, you may have to make an appointment on arrival to view the room, though this is rare—see "Secret Room Appointment," page 833.) These bawdy statues and frescoes—many of them displayed in Pompeii's grandest houses—were entertainment for guests. (By the time they made it to this museum, in 1819, the frescoes could be viewed only with permission from the king—see the let-ters in the glass case just outside the door.) The Roman nobles commissioned the wildest scenes imaginable. Think of them as ancient dirty jokes.

Circulating counterclockwise through this section, look for: 1) a faun playfully pulling the sheet off a beautiful woman, only to be grossed out by the plumbing of a hermaphrodite (perhaps the original *"Mamma mia!"*); 2) horny pygmies from Africa in action; 3) Venus, the patron goddess of Pompeii, a favorite pin-up girl; 4) a particularly high-quality statue of a goat and a satyr illustrating the act of sodomy; and 5) a toga with an embarrassing bulge.

The next room is furnished and decorated the way an ancient brothel might have been. The 10 frescoes on the wall functioned as both a menu of services offered and as a kind of *Kama Sutra* of sex positions. The walls feature big stone penises that once projected over Pompeii's doorways. A massive phallus was not necessarily a sexual symbol, but a magical amulet used against the "evil eye." It symbolized fertility, happiness, good luck, riches, straight A's, and general well-being. The glass cases contain more phallic art.

• *So, now that your travel buddy is finally showing a little interest in art...finish up your visit by climbing the stairs to the top floor.*

Top Floor: Statues, Artifacts, and a Model of Pompeii

At the top of the stairs, you'll enter a grand, empty hall. This was the great hall of the university (17th and 18th centuries) until the building became the royal museum in 1777. The sundial (from 1791) still works. At noon, a sunray strikes the spot, indicating today's date...if you know your zodiac.

To your right are rooms containing **bronze statues** from Herculaneum—of racers, dancers, and fauns (first-century B.C. copies of fourth-century B.C. originals). They once decorated the holiday home (Villa dei Papyri in Herculaneum) of Julius Caesar's father-in-law. Look into the lifelike blue eyes of the intense *atleta* (athletes), bent on doing their best. The *Five Dancers*, with their inlaid-ivory eyes and graceful

poses, decorated a portico. *Resting Hermes* (with his tired little heel wings) is taking a break. The *Drunken Faun* (singing and snapping his fingers to the beat, a wineskin at his side) is clearly living for today—true to the *carpe diem* preaching of the Epicurean philosophy. Caesar's father-in-law was an Epicurean philosopher, and his library—containing 2,000 papyrus scrolls—supported his outlook.

Return to the grand hall and continue to the other side, passing through several rooms of vases, statuettes, spoons, glassware, and other objects found at Pompeii. Keep going to the far end, where you'll find a **scale model** of the archaeological site of Pompeii, circa 1879 *(plastico di Pompeii)*. Belly up to the railing and find the Porta Marina entrance and the large rectangle of the town's Forum. Another model on the wall shows the site in 2004, after more excavations.

The Rest of the Museum

After years in restoration, the museum's large collection of **frescoes** taken from the walls of Pompeii villas is back (in Rooms LXVI to LXXVIII). Pompeiians loved to decorate their homes with scenes from mythology (Hercules' Labors, Venus and Mars in love), landscapes, everyday market scenes, and faux architecture. The display is roughly chronological.

For extra credit, visit ***Doriforo***. (Ask a guard, *"Dov'è il Doriforo?"* He was last spotted on the ground floor, in the hall to the left, as you face the staircase.) This seven-foot-tall "spear-carrier" (the literal translation of *doriforo*) just stands there, as if holding a spear. What's the big deal about this statue, which looks like so many others? It's a marble replica made by the Romans of one of the most-copied statues of antiquity, a fifth-century B.C. bronze Greek original by Polyclitus. This copy once stood in a Pompeii gym, where it inspired ancient athletes with the ideal proportions of Greek beauty. So full of motion, and so realistic in its *contrapposto* pose (weight on one foot), the *Doriforo* would later inspire Donatello and Michelangelo, triggering the Renaissance. And so the glories of ancient Pompeii, once buried and forgotten, live on today.

Self-Guided Walk

▲▲▲A Slice of Neapolitan Life

Walk from the Archaeological Museum through the heart of town and back to Centrale Station. Allow at least three hours, plus pizza and sightseeing stops. If you have limited time, do a shorter, hour-long version by walking briskly and skipping the sights south of Spaccanapoli (including the Royal Palace, Teatro di San Carlo, and Galleria Umberto I).

Naples, a living medieval city, is its own best sight. Couples artfully make love on Vespas surrounded by more fights and smiles per cobblestone than anywhere else in Italy. Rather than seeing

Naples as a list of sights, visit its one great museum and then capture its essence by taking this walk through the core of the city. Should you become overwhelmed or lost, step into a store and ask for directions: "Where is the central station?" in Italian is *"Dov'è la stazione centrale?"* (DOH-vay lah staht-zee-OH-nay chen-TRAH-lay). Or point to the next sight in this book.

Part 1: Via Pessina, Via Toledo, and the Spanish Quarter

The first part of this walk is a straight one-mile ramble down a boulevard to Galleria Umberto I, near the Royal Palace. Ideally, begin by touring the Archaeological Museum (at the top of Piazza Cavour, Metro: Cavour or Museo).

• *Leaving the Archaeological Museum, turn right and go one block, to the head of Via Pessina. Follow this busy street downhill to Piazza Dante—see his statue in the distance.*

Piazza Dante: This square is marked by a statue of Dante, the medieval poet. Here you can feel Italy...but many Neapolitans merely feel the repression of the central state. When Napoleon was defeated, Naples became its own independent kingdom. But with Italian unification in 1861, Naples went from being a thriving cultural and political capital to a provincial town, its money used to help establish the industrial strength of the north. Originally, a statue of a Spanish Bourbon king stood here. The grand red-and-gray building is typical of Bourbon structures from that period. With the unification of Italy, the king, symbolic of Italy's colonial subjugation, was replaced by Dante—considered the father of the Italian language and a strong symbol of nationalism.

Old Dante looks out over an urban area that was once grand, then chaotic, and is now slowly becoming grand again. Behind Dante's right shoulder is the Port'Alba, part of Naples' old wall and the entrance to a small street lined with book vendors. Via Pessina, the long, straight street that you're walking, originated as a military road built by Spain in the 16th century. It skirted the old town wall to connect the Spanish military headquarters (now the museum) with the Royal Palace (down by the bay). A subway station called Dante (with a modern-art flair) was recently built here on Piazza Dante. Construction was slowed by the city's rich underground history: 13 feet down—Roman ruins; 23 feet down—Greek ruins; and every inch of the way—big headaches for construction workers.

Across the street, **Caffè Mexico** (at #86) is an institution known for its espresso, which is served already sweetened—ask for *senza zucchero* if you don't want sugar (pay first, then take receipt to the counter; locals tip €0.10). Most Italians agree that Neapolitan coffee is the best anywhere.

NAPLES

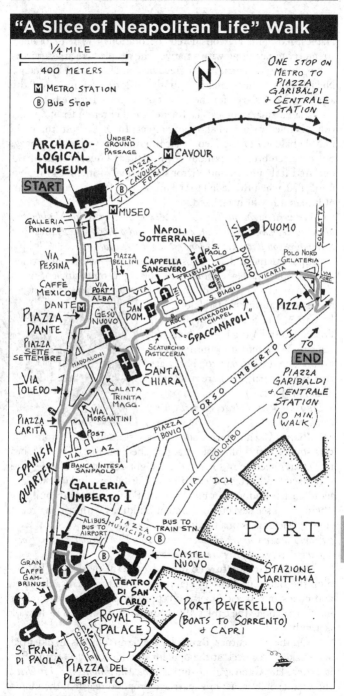

"A Slice of Neapolitan Life" Walk

¼ MILE

400 METERS

Ⓜ METRO STATION
Ⓑ BUS STOP

N

ONE STOP ON METRO TO PIAZZA GARIBALDI & CENTRALE STATION

ARCHAEO-LOGICAL MUSEUM

START

UNDER-GROUND PASSAGE

Ⓜ CAVOUR

PIAZZA CAVOUR
Ⓑ VIA FORIA

Ⓜ MUSEO

GALLERIA PRINCIPE

VIA PESSINA

NAPOLI SOTTERRANEA

S. PAOLO

VIA DUOMO

✝ DUOMO

COLLETTA

CAPPELLA SANSEVERO

TRIBUNALI

POLO NORD GELATERIA

VICARIA

VIA FORC.

CAFFÈ MEXICO

PIAZZA BELLINI

VIA PORT' ALBA

VIA

NILO

S. BIAGIO

DANTE

Ⓜ

GESÙ NUOVO

SAN DOM.

CROCE

PIAZZA DANTE

PIAZZA SETTE SETTEMBRE

MADDALONI

SCATURCHIO PASTICCERIA

MARADONA CHAPEL

"SPACCANAPOLI"

PIZZA

TO

END

VIA TOLEDO

SANTA CHIARA

CORSO UMBERTO

PIAZZA GARIBALDI & CENTRALE STATION (10 MIN. WALK)

PIAZZA CARITÀ

CALATA TRINITA MAGG.

VIA MORGANTINI

POST

PIAZZA BOVIO

COLOMBO

SPANISH QUARTER

VIA DIAZ

BANCA INTESA SANPAOLO

VIA

DCH

GALLERIA UMBERTO I

PIAZZA MUNICIPIO

ALIBUS BUS TO AIRPORT

BUS TO TRAIN STN.
Ⓑ

PORT

Ⓑ

CASTEL NUOVO

STAZIONE MARITTIMA

GRAN CAFFÈ GAMBRINUS

ⓘ

TEATRO DI SAN CARLO

PORT BEVERELLO (BOATS TO SORRENTO) & CAPRI

ⓘ

ROYAL PALACE

CONSOLE

S. FRAN. DI PAOLA

PIAZZA DEL PLEBISCITO

Continue walking downhill, remembering that here in Naples, red lights are considered "decorations." When crossing a street, try to tag along with a native. The people here are survivors: A long history of corrupt and greedy colonial overlords has taught Neapolitans to deal creatively with authority. Many credit this aspect of Naples' past for the advent of organized crime here.

Via Pessina becomes Via Toledo (another reminder of Spanish rule), Naples' principal shopping street. In 1860, from the white marble balcony of the Neoclassical building overlooking Piazza Sette Settembre, the famous revolutionary Giuseppe Garibaldi declared Italy united and Victor Emmanuel II its first king. Not until 1870, when Rome fell to the unification forces, was the dream of Italian unity fully realized.

• *Continue straight on Via Toledo. At the next left (Via Maddaloni), about three blocks below Piazza Dante and a block past Piazza Sette Settembre, you'll come to the long, straight street called...*

Spaccanapoli: Before crossing the street—whose name translates as "split Naples"—look left. Look right. Since ancient times, this thin street (which changes names several times: Maddaloni, Via B. Croce, Via S. Biagio dei Librai, Forecella, and Vicaria) has bisected the city. We'll return to this intersection later. (If you want to abbreviate this walk, turn left here and skip ahead to "Part 2.")

• *Stay on Via Toledo, which runs through...*

Piazza Carità: Surrounded by fascist architecture from 1938, this square is full of stern, straight, obedient lines. (For the best fascist architecture in town, take a slight detour from here—with your back to Via Toledo, leave Piazza Carità downhill on the right-hand corner and walk a block to the Poste e Telegrafi building. There you'll see several government buildings with stirring reliefs singing the praises of a totalitarian society.)

• *From Piazza Carità, wander south down Via Toledo for a few blocks, looking to your left for more examples of...*

Fascist Architecture (Banks): Notice the two banks. Try robbing the Banco di Napoli (Via Toledo 178). Step across the street and check out its architecture: typical fascist arches and reliefs, built to celebrate the bank's 400th anniversary (est. 1539—how old is *your* bank?).

On the next corner, **Banca Intesa Sanpaolo** fills an older palace—take a free peek at the opulent interior. On the second floor is a great late Caravaggio painting. *The Martyrdom of Saint Ursula* shows a terrible scene: His marriage proposal rejected, the king of the Huns flings an arrow into Ursula's chest. Blood spurts, Ursula is stunned but accepts her destiny sweetly, and Caravaggio himself (far right, his last self-portrait) screams to symbolize the rejection of evil (€3, Mon–Sat 10:00–18:00, closed Sun; includes 40-minute audioguide, a look at old Naples paintings, and a fine WC).

• *From here, side-trip uphill three blocks into the...*

Spanish Quarter: This is a classic world of *basso* (low) living. In such tight quarters, families generally do it in the road.

This is *the* cliché of life in Naples, as shown in so many movies. The Spanish Quarter is Naples at its rawest, poorest, and most characteristic. The only predictable things about this Neapolitan tide pool are the ancient grid plan of its streets (which survives from Greek times), the friendliness of its shopkeepers, and the boldness of its mopeds. Concerned locals will tug on their lower eyelids, warning you to be wary. Hungry? Pop into a grocery shop and ask the man to make you his best prosciutto and mozzarella sandwich (the price should be about €4).

• *Return to Via Toledo (clogged with more people than cars) and work your way down to the immense...*

Piazza del Plebiscito: This square celebrates the 1861 vote (*plebiscito,* plebiscite), when Naples chose to join Italy. Walk to the middle of the square. From here, you'll see the Church of San Francesco di Paola, with its Pantheon-inspired dome and broad, arcing colonnades.

• *Opposite is the...*

Royal Palace *(Palazzo Reale)***:** Having housed Spanish, French, and even Italian royalty, this building displays statues of all those who stayed here. Look for eight kings in the niches, each from a different dynasty (left to right): Norman, German, French, Spanish, Spanish, Spanish, French (Napoleon's brother-in-law), and, finally, Italian—Victor Emmanuel II, King of Savoy. The statues were done at the request of V. E. II's son, so his dad is the most dashing of the group. This huge, lavish palace welcomes the public (€4, more with special exhibits, Thu–Tue 9:00–20:00, closed Wed, last entry one hour before closing, audioguide-€4, or €5/2 people, tel. 848-800-288).

The palace's grand Neoclassical staircase leads up to a floor with 30 plush rooms. You'll follow a one-way route (with some English descriptions) featuring paintings by "the Caravaggio Imitators," Neapolitan tapestries, fine inlaid-stone tabletops, and more. Don't miss the huge Hercules room and the chapel with a fantastic nativity scene (a commotion of 18th-century ceramic figurines).

The **Gran Caffè Gambrinus,** facing the piazza, takes you back to the elegance of 1860. It's a classic place to sample a unique Neapolitan treat called *sfogliatella* (crispy scallop shell–shaped pastry filled with sweet ricotta cheese). Or you might prefer the mushroom-shaped, rum-soaked bread-like cakes called *babà,* which come in a huge variety. Stand at the bar *(banco),* pay double to sit *(tavola),* or just wander around as you imagine the café buzzing with the ritzy intellectuals, journalists, and artsy bohemian types who munched on *babà* here during Naples' 19th-century heyday (daily 7:00–24:00, Piazza del Plebiscito 1, tel. 081-417-582).

• *Continue 50 yards past the Royal Palace to enjoy a...*

Fine Harbor View: While boats busily serve Capri and Sorrento, Mount Vesuvius smolders ominously in the distance. Look back to see the vast "Bourbon red" palace—its color inspired by Pompeii. On the hilltop above Piazza del Plebiscito is Naples' Carthusian Monastery and the Castle of St. Elmo. This street continues to Naples' romantic harborfront—the fishermen's quarters or Borgo Marinaro—a fortified island connected to the mainland by a stout causeway, with its fanciful Castel dell'Ovo (castle of the egg) and trendy harborside restaurants. Farther along the harborfront stretches the Lungomare promenade and Santa Lucia district. (The long harborfront promenade, Via Francesco Caracciolo, is a delightful people-watching scene on balmy nights.)

• *Head back to the piazza and go behind the palace, where you can peek inside the Neoclassical...*

Teatro di San Carlo: Built in 1737, 41 years before Milan's La Scala, this is Europe's oldest opera house and Italy's second-most-respected (after La Scala). The theater burned down in 1816, and was rebuilt within the year. Guided 40-minute visits basically just show you the fine auditorium with its 184 boxes—each with a big mirror to reflect the candlelight (€5, Mon–Sat 10:00–17:30, tours every 40 minutes, closed Sun, tel. 081-553-4565, www.teatrosancarlo.it).

Beyond Teatro di San Carlo and the Royal Palace is the huge, harborfront Castel Nuovo, which houses government bureaucrats and the **Civic Museum,** featuring 14th- to 16th-century art (€5, Mon–Sat 9:00–19:00, closed Sun, last entry one hour before closing, tel. 081-795-5877).

Across the street from Teatro di San Carlo, go through the tall yellow arch into the Victorian iron and glass of the 100-year-old shopping mall, **Galleria Umberto I.** Gawk up.

• *For Part 2 of this walk, double back*

up Via Toledo to Piazza Carità, veering right on Via Morgantini to Via Maddaloni (to avoid the backtracking and uphill walk, catch an €8 taxi to the Church of Gesù Nuovo—JAY-zoo noo-OH-voh).

Part 2: Spaccanapoli Back to the Station

You're back at the straight-as-a-Greek-arrow Spaccanapoli, formerly the main thoroughfare of the Greek city of Neapolis.

• *Stop at...*

Piazza Gesù Nuovo: This square is marked by a towering 18th-century Baroque monument to the Counter-Reformation. Although the Jesuit order was powerful in Naples because of its Spanish heritage, locals never attacked Protestants here with the full fury of the Spanish Inquisition. The square also has a handy little TI and is the starting point for electric bus #E1, which makes a 40-minute loop through the characteristic old quarter and ends up back here (€1.10, buy ticket at nearby newsstand before boarding, 2/hour, daily 7:00–24:00).

• *Now visit two bulky old churches, starting with the austere, fortress-like 17th-century...*

Church of Gesù Nuovo: The unique pyramid-grill facade survives from a fortified 15th-century noble palace. Step inside for a brilliant Neapolitan Baroque interior. The second chapel on the right features a much-adored statue of Giuseppe Moscati (1880–1927), a Christian doctor famous for helping the poor. In 1987, Moscati became the first modern doctor to be canonized.

Continue on to the third chapel and enter the **Sale Moscati.** This huge room is filled with "Ex Votos"—tiny red-and-silver plaques of thanksgiving for prayers answered with the help of St. Moscati (each has a symbol of the ailment cured). Naples' practice of using Ex Votos, while incorporated into its Catholic rituals, goes back to its pagan Greek roots. Rooms from Moscati's nearby apartment are on display, and a glass case shows possessions and photos of the great doctor. As you leave the Sale Moscati, notice the big bomb casing that hangs in the left corner. It fell through the church's dome in 1943, but caused almost no damage...yet another miracle (daily 7:00–12:30 & 16:00–19:30).

• *Head across the street, to the simpler...*

Church of Santa Chiara: Dating from the 14th century, this church is from a period of French royal rule under the Angevin dynasty. Consider the stark contrast between this church (Gothic) and the Gesù Nuovo (Baroque). Notice the huge inlaid-marble Angevin coat of arms on the floor. The faded Trinity on the back wall, to the left of the entry, shows a dove representing the Holy Spirit between the heads of God the Father and Christ (c. 1414). This is an example of the fine frescoes that once covered the walls. Most were stuccoed over during Baroque times or destroyed in

1943 by World War II bombs. The altar is adorned with four finely carved Gothic tombs of Angevin kings. A chapel stacked with Bourbon royalty is just to the right (daily 7:00–12:30 & 16:30–20:00).

• *Leaving the church, take a right and head to the back of the building. Continue through the archway straight ahead, and pass all the parked cars to reach the farthest door on the right. Here you'll find the bright, ornate majolica-tiled...*

Cloistered Courtyard of Santa Chiara: Note the sprawling nativity scene immediately on your right as you enter—a cartoon-ish 3-D snapshot of Old World Napoli. Stop in at its museum (€5, Mon–Sat 9:30–17:30, Sun 9:30–14:30, last entry 30 minutes before closing).

• *Now return to the main drag, turn right, and continue straight down traffic-free Via B. Croce. A good little lunch spot, **Trattoria da Titina e Gennaro**, is just down the street across from the church (Via Santa Chiara 6).*

Since this is a university district, you'll see lots of students and bookstores. This neighborhood is also extremely superstitious. Look for incense-burning women with carts full of good-luck charms for sale.

• *Farther down Spaccanapoli, you'll see the next square...*

Piazza San Domenico Maggiore: This square is marked by an ornate 17th-century monument built to thank God for ending the plague. But more important is the well-loved **Scaturchio Pasticceria,** another good place to try *sfogliatella* (€1.50 to go, costs double at a table in the square, daily 7:20–20:40, tel. 081-551-7031).

• *From this square, detour left along the right side of the castle-like church, then follow yellow signs, taking the first right and walking one block to...*

Cappella Sansevero: This small chapel is a Baroque explosion mourning the body of Christ, who lies on a soft pillow under an incredibly realistic veil. It's also the personal chapel of Raimondo de Sangro, an eccentric Freemason. The monuments to his relatives have a second purpose: to share the Freemason philosophy of freedom through enlightenment (€6, Mon and Wed–Sat 10:00–18:00, Sun 10:00–13:30, closed Tue, last entry 20 minutes before closing, no photos but postcards are sold in gift shop, Via de Sanctis 19, tel. 081-551-8470).

Study the incredible *Veiled Christ* in the center. Carved out of marble, it's like no other statue I've seen (by Giuseppe "Howdee-doodat" Sammartino, 1753). The Christian message (Jesus died for our salvation) is accompanied by a Freemason message (the veil represents how the body and ego are obstacles to real spiritual freedom). As you walk from Christ's feet to his head, notice how the expression on Jesus' face goes from suffering to peace.

Raimondo de Sangro lies buried at the far (altar) end. An inventor, he created the deep-green pigment used on the ceiling fresco. The inlaid M. C. Escher–esque maze on the floor around de Sangro's tomb is another Freemason reminder of how the quest for knowledge gets you out of the maze of life.

To the right of the altar, the statue *Despair* struggles with a marble rope net (carved out of a single piece of stone), symbolic of a troubled mind. The Freemason symbolism shows how knowledge—in the guise of an angel—frees the human mind. On the opposite side of the altar from *Despair*, a veiled woman fingers a broken plaque, symbolizing...something.

Your Sansevero finale is downstairs: two mysterious...skeletons. Perhaps another of the mad inventor's fancies: Inject a corpse with a fluid to fossilize the veins so that they'll survive the body's decomposition. While that's the legend, it was most likely created to illustrate how the circulatory system works.

• *Return to Via B. Croce (a.k.a. Spaccanapoli), turn left, and continue your cultural scavenger hunt. At the intersection of Via Nilo, find the...*

Statue of the Nile (on the left): A reminder of the multiethnic make-up of Greek Neapolis, this statue is in what was the Egyptian quarter. Locals like to call this statue *The Body of Naples*, with the overflowing cornucopia symbolizing the abundance of their fine city. (I once asked a Neapolitan man to describe the local women, who are famous for their beauty, in one word. He replied simply, "Abundant.") This intersection is considered the center of old Naples.

A few blocks farther, at the tiny square, Via San Gregorio Armeno leads left into a colorful district (and also to the underground Napoli Sotterranea archaeological site). You'll see many shops that sell tiny components of fantastic *presepi* (nativity scenes), including figurines caricaturing local politicians and celebrities. Just as many Americans keep an eye out year-round for Christmas-tree ornaments, Italians regularly add pieces to the family *presepe*, the centerpiece of their holiday celebrations.

• *As Via B. Croce becomes Via S. Biagio dei Librai, notice the...*

Gold and Silver Shops: Some say stolen jewelry ends up here, is melted down immediately, and gets resold in some other form as soon as it cools. The inimitable Sr. Grassi runs the Ospedale delle Bambole (doll hospital) at #81.

• *Cross busy Via Duomo.*

Here, the street and side-street scenes along Via Vicaria intensify. This is known as a center of the Camorra (organized crime).

Paint a picture with these thoughts: Naples has the most intact street plan of any ancient Roman city. Imagine this city during those times (and retain these images as you visit Pompeii), with streetside shop fronts that close up after dark, turning into private homes. Today, it's just one more page in a 2,000-year-old story of a city: all kinds of meetings, beatings, and cheatings; kisses, near misses, and little-boy pisses.

You name it, it occurs right on the streets today, as it has since ancient times. People ooze from crusty corners. Black-and-white death announcements add to the clutter on the walls. Widows sell cigarettes from buckets. For a peek behind the scenes in the shade of wet laundry, venture down a few side streets. Buy two carrots as a gift for the woman  on the fifth floor if she'll lower her bucket to pick them up. The neighborhood action seems best at about 18:00.

A few blocks on, at the tiny fenced-in triangle of greenery, hang out for a few minutes to just observe the crazy motorbike action and teen scene.

• *From here, veer right onto Via Forcella (which leads to the busy boulevard that takes you to Centrale Station). A tiny, round traffic island protects a chunk of the ancient Greek wall of Neapolis (fourth century B.C.). But first, turn right on busy Via Pietro Colletta, walk 50 yards, and step into the North Pole, at the...*

Polo Nord Gelateria: The oldest *gelateria* in Naples has had four generations of family working here since 1931. Before you order, sample a few flavors, including their *bacio* or "kiss" flavor (chocolate and hazelnut)—all are made fresh daily (Mon–Sat 10:00–24:00, Sun 10:00–14:00 & 17:00–24:00, Via Pietro Colletta 41, tel. 081-205-431). Via Pietro Colletta leads past Napoli's two most competitive **pizzerias** (see "Eating in Naples," later) to Corso Umberto I.

• *Turn left on the grand boulevard–like Corso Umberto I. From here to Centrale Station, it's at least a 10-minute walk (if you're tired, hop on a bus; they all go to the station). To finish the walk, continue on Corso Umberto I—past a gauntlet of purse/CD/sunglasses salesmen and shady characters hawking stolen camcorders—to the vast, ugly Piazza Garibaldi. On the far side is the station. You made it.*

More Sights in Naples

▲▲**Napoli Sotterranea**—This archaeological site, a manmade underground maze of passageways and ruins from Greek and Roman times, can only be toured with a guide. You'll descend 121 steps under the modern city to explore. The first stop is the old Greek tuff quarry used to build the city of Neapolis, and later converted into an immense aqueduct by the Romans. Next is an excavated portion of the Greco-Roman theater. The tour involves a lot of stairs, as well as a long, narrow 20-inch-wide walkway that uses an ancient water channel (a heavyset person could not comfortably fit through this). Although there's not much to actually see, the experience is fascinating, and includes a little WWII history.

Cost and Hours: €9.30; includes 1.5-hour tour. Visits in English are offered daily at 12:00, 14:00, and 16:00; also at 10:00 and 18:00 Sat–Sun. Bring a light sweater. Tel. 081-296-944, www .napolisotterranea.org.

The site is a 10-minute walk from the Archaeological Museum, just west of Via Duomo, next to the church of San Paolo off Via dei Tribunali, at Piazza Gaetano 68. From Spaccanapoli, it's just a couple blocks uphill from the Statue of the Nile (ask for Piazza Gaetano, and look for the *Sotterranea* signs).

Open-Air Fish Market—Naples' fish market squirts and stinks as it has for centuries under the Porta Nolana (gate in the city wall) just four blocks from Centrale train station. Of the town's many boisterous outdoor markets, this will net you the most photos and memories. From Piazza Nolana, wander under the medieval gate and take your first left down Vico Sopramuro, enjoying this

wild and entirely edible cultural scavenger hunt (Tue–Sun 8:00– 14:00, closed Mon).

Two other markets with more clothing and less fish are at Piazza Capuana (several blocks northwest of Centrale Station and tumbling down Via Sant'Antonio Abate, Mon–Sat 8:00–18:00, Sun 9:00–13:00) and a similar cobbled shopping zone along Via Pignasecca (just off Via Toledo, west of Piazza Carità).

Grand View from Certosa San Martino—This ultimate view overlooking Naples, its bay, and a volcano comes with a €6 price tag. The monastery, founded in 1325 and dissolved in the early 1800s, is popular today for its dramatic view gardens, church, and museum, which features a history of the kingdoms of southern Italy and the city's best collection of *presepi* manger scenes (Thu–Tue 8:30–19:00, closed Wed, last entry one hour before closing, Metro: Montesanto, well-posted 10-minute walk from top of Montesanto funicular at Largo San Martino 5, tel. 081-558-6408).

Lungomare *Passeggiata*—Each evening, relaxed and romantic Neapolitans in the mood for a scenic harborside stroll do their *vasche* (laps) along the inviting Lungomare promenade. To join in this elegant people-watching scene (best after 19:00), stroll about

15 minutes from Piazza del Plebiscito along Via Nazario Sauro (in Santa Lucia district).

Detour out along the fortified causeway to poke around Borgo Marinaro ("fishermen's quarters"), with its striking Castel dell'Ovo and a trendy restaurant scene where you can dine amidst yachts with a view of Vesuvius. This is also known as the Santa Lucia district because this is where the song "Santa Lucia" was first performed. (The song is probably so famous in America because immigrants from Naples sang it to remember the old country.) Beyond that stretches the Lungomare, along Via Francesco Caracciolo. Taxi home or retrace your steps back to the old center.

Sleeping in Naples

With Sorrento just an hour away (see next chapter), I can't imagine why you'd sleep in Naples. But, if needed, here are a few options. These hotels are within a few blocks of the train station, but be forewarned: The area can feel unnerving, especially after dark. In this business-oriented (rather than tourist-oriented) city, summer (July–Sept) is low season, when prices are particularly soft.

$$ Grand Hotel Europa, a gem set in the seedy neighborhood around the train station, has 89 modern rooms decorated with not-quite-right reproductions of famous paintings (Sb-€65, Db-€85, Tb-€109, book directly and ask for 15 percent Rick Steves discount off these prices, also check website for special deals, air-con, Wi-Fi, cheery breakfast room, elegant restaurant; from the station, exit through gate near track 5, then head past the farmacia and police station to Corso Meridionale 14; tel. 081-267-511,

---

Sleep Code

(€1 = about $1.25, country code: 39)
S = Single, **D** = Double/Twin, **T** = Triple, **Q** = Quad, **b** = bathroom, **s** = shower only. Unless otherwise noted, credit cards are accepted, English is spoken, and breakfast is included.

To help you sort easily through these listings, I've divided the rooms into three categories based on the price for a standard double room with bath:

$$$ Higher Priced—Most rooms €140 or more.
$$ Moderately Priced—Most rooms between €80-140.
$ Lower Priced—Most rooms €80 or less.

Prices can change without notice; verify the hotel's current rates online or by email. For other updates, see www.ricksteves.com/update.

NAPLES

www.grandhoteleuropa.com, info@grandhoteleuropa.com, well-run by Claudio).

$$ Hotel Suite Esedra, run by the same people as the Grand Hotel Europa, is a four-star charmer on a tiny square just off busy Corso Umberto I. With 19 small-but-decent rooms, the hotel is located just outside of the station-neighborhood sleaze. As it may be temporarily closed for renovation, call first (Sb-€70, Db-€90, 15 percent discount if you book direct and mention Rick Steves, air-con, elevator, Wi-Fi, 10-minute walk from the station at Via Arnaldo Cantani 12, tel. & fax 081-287-451, www.sea-hotels.com, esedra@sea-hotels.com).

$ Hotel Potenza offers 26 rooms, along with a rare bit of security and peace on Piazza Garibaldi (Sb-€55, Db-€75, air-con, no elevator, 100 yards in front of the station at Piazza Garibaldi 120, tel. 081-286-330, www.hotelpotenza.com, info@hotelpotenza .com, Valenzano family).

Eating in Naples

Cheap and Famous Pizza

Naples—whose pizzerias bake just the right combination of fresh dough, mozzarella, and tomatoes in traditional wood-burning ovens—is the birthplace of pizza. Drop by one of the two most venerable pizzerias in town (both a few long blocks from the station, at the end of my "A Slice of Neapolitan Life" self-guided walk).

Antica Pizzeria da Michele is for pizza purists. Filled with locals (and tourists), it serves just two varieties: *margherita* (tomato sauce and mozzarella) and *marinara* (tomato sauce, oregano, and garlic, no cheese). Come early to sit and watch the pizza artists in action. A pizza with beer costs €6 (Mon–Sat 10:00–24:00, closed Sun; look for the vertical red *Antica Pizzeria* sign at the intersection of Via Pietro Colletta and Via Cesare Sersale at #1; tel. 081-553-9204).

Pizzeria Trianon, across the street, has been da Michele's archrival since 1923. It offers more choices, slightly higher prices (€5–7), air-conditioning, and a cozier atmosphere. For less chaos, head upstairs. While waiting for your meal, you can survey the evolution of a humble wad of dough into a smoldering bubbly feast in their entryway pizza kitchen (daily 11:00–15:30 & 19:00–23:00, Via Pietro Colletta 42, tel. 081-553-9426, Giuseppe).

Near the Archaeological Museum

Caffetteria Angela is a fun little eating complex: coffee bar; *tavola calda* with hot ready-to-eat dishes (€3–4); and a tiny meat, cheese, and bread shop with all you need for a cheap meal to go. It offers

NAPLES

Getting Around the Region

To connect Naples, Sorrento, and the Amalfi Coast, you can travel on land by train, bus, and taxi. Whenever possible, consider taking a boat—it's faster, cooler, and more scenic, and you can take coastline photos that you can't get from land. For specific travel times and costs, check the "Connections" sections of the Naples, Sorrento, and Amalfi Coast chapters. It's always a good idea to confirm schedules and prices with the TI or your hotel.

By Circumvesuviana Train: This useful commuter train—popular with locals, tourists, and pickpockets—links Naples, Herculaneum, Pompeii, and Sorrento. At Naples' Centrale Station, follow the signs to the Circumvesuviana (across from track 14, downstairs), where you'll find the ticket office and info booth. When you buy your ticket, ask which track your train will depart from (*"Quale binario?"*; KWAH-lay bee-NAH-ree-oh). Just beyond, you'll find the gate where you insert your ticket. The train platforms are downstairs. The Circumvesuviana also has its own terminal (one Metro stop or a 10-minute walk beyond Centrale Station), but there's no reason to use it unless you're nearby.

Trains marked *Sorrento,* which depart twice hourly, take you to Herculaneum/Ercolano (about 25 minutes, €1.80 one-way), Pompeii (about 35 minutes, €2.40 one-way), and Sorrento, the end of the line (70 minutes, €3.40 one-way). Though not covered by railpasses, Circumvesuviana tickets are covered by the Campania ArteCard (see page 829). Not all of the trains go as far as Sorrento; check the schedule or confirm with a local before boarding to make sure the train goes where you want. Express trains marked *DD* (6/day) get you to Sorrento 20 minutes sooner. When returning to Naples' Centrale Station on the Circumvesuviana, get off at Garibaldi—the next-to-the-last stop (Centrale Station is just up the escalator). Bonus: When returning from Sorrento, your Circumvesuviana ticket includes a ride anywhere on the Naples Metro system within three hours of validation. Be on guard: Though I haven't had problems, many readers report being ripped off on the Circumvesuviana (see "Theft Alert," page 830). For information, see www.vesuviana.it.

If you're coming **from Rome,** note that a different (non-Circumvesuviana) train—run by the national rail company—goes from Rome to Naples, then continues to the ugly modern city of Pompei. There is almost no reason to go to Pompei city, where you'll face a long walk to the actual site. Therefore, from Rome, it's better to simply get off at Naples' Centrale Station and transfer to the Circumvesuviana (to the *Pompei Scavi* stop). The Pompei city train station is useful only for connecting to Salerno or Paestum (not quite hourly, 30 minutes to Salerno, 1 hour to Paestum, direction: Sapri).

By Bus: SITA buses (often blue or green-and-white) connect the towns. Buses that travel along the highly touristed Amalfi Coast can be crowded—for tips, see "Getting Around the Amalfi Coast—By Bus" on page 904.

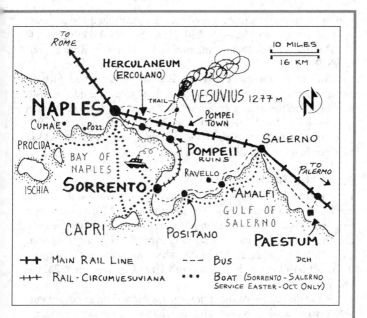

By Taxi: For €80–100, you can take a 30-mile taxi ride from Naples directly to your Sorrento hotel; agree on a set price without the meter and pay upon arrival. You can hire a cab on Capri for about €70/hour. Taxis in the Amalfi Coast are generally expensive, and more than willing to overcharge you, but they can be convenient, especially with a larger group. See "Getting Around the Amalfi Coast—By Taxi" on page 906.

By Boat: Four primary ferry companies service the Naples, Sorrento, and Amalfi Coast areas: Caremar (www.caremar.it), SNAV (www.snav.it), Metro del Mare (www.metrodelmare.com), and Alilauro (a.k.a. LMP or Gescab; www.gescab.it). Many of the schedules can be found together on www.capritourism.com; click "Shipping Timetable." Each company has different destinations and prices; some compete for the same trips. The quicker the trip, the higher the price. A hydrofoil skims between Naples and Sorrento—it's faster, safer from pickpockets, more scenic, and more expensive than the Circumvesuviana train (5/day, departs roughly every 2 hours starting at 9:00, 35 minutes, €10). A taxi from Naples' Centrale Station to its port costs about €12 (extra charge for bags, Sundays, holidays, and nighttime after 22:00).

Otherwise, check schedules at any TI or at the Port Beverello boat dock. Ticket windows clearly display the next available departure. The number of boats that run per day depends on the season. Trips are canceled in bad weather. Most boats charge an extra fee for luggage (about €2).

If you plan to arrive and leave a destination by boat, make note upon your arrival of the return times—the last boat usually leaves before 19:00.

honest pricing and simple, peaceful, air-conditioned indoor seating (no cover, open Mon–Sat 7:00–21:00, Sun 9:00–14:00, just off Via Pessina, 3 blocks below museum at Via Conte di Ruvo 21, tel. 081-549-9660).

Salumeria Pasquale Carrino is a tiny salami shop with an exuberant owner—the fun-loving and flamboyant Pasquale—who turns sandwich-making into a show (€6 sandwich good for two people, Mon–Sat 8:00–15:00 & 16:30–20:00, closed Sun, 100 yards from museum—as you leave take two rights and a left to Via Salvator Rosa 10, tel. 081-564-0889).

Near the Station

La Cantina dei Mille, a block in front of the train station, is a traditional family-style place serving good, basic Neapolitan food to good, basic Neapolitans indoors and out. It's about the only charming place I found on Piazza Garibaldi (€5 pizza and pasta, daily 12:00–16:00 & 17:00–24:00; with your back to the station, it's about halfway up the left side of Piazza Garibaldi at #126; tel. 081-283-448).

Next door, **Iris'** cadre of bow-tied waiters sling good, reasonably priced seafood, pastas, and pizzas in a comfortable *ristorante* with an outdoor patio (Sun–Fri 12:00–15:30 & 18:30–23:00, closed Sat, Piazza Garibaldi 121, tel. 081-269-988).

Grand Hotel Europa (see "Sleeping in Naples," earlier) has a restaurant peacefully buried in its basement, offering friendly service and a fine value (daily, light lunches anytime, dinner 19:00–23:00).

Naples Connections

From Naples by Boat to: Sorrento (5/day, leaves roughly every 2 hours starting at 9:00, 35 minutes, €10), **Capri** (roughly 2/hour, 45 minutes, €16), **Amalfi** (late April–Oct only, 4/day, 1.5–2 hours, €15, LMP tel. 081-807-1812). For a map showing boat connections, see page 851.

By Train to: Rome (at least hourly, 1.25 hours on Frecciarossa express trains, otherwise 2–2.5 hours), **Florence** (hourly, 3–5 hours, some change in Rome), **Salerno** (2/hour, 45–75 minutes, avoid slow *diretto* train), **Paestum** (almost hourly, 1.5 hours, direction: Sapri), **Brindisi** (8/day, 5–8 hours, overnight possible; from Brindisi, ferries sail to Greece), **Milan** (direct trains hourly, 5 hours, more with change in Rome, overnight possible), **Venice** (almost hourly, 5.5–7 hours with changes in Bologna or Rome, overnight possible), **Palermo** (5/day, 10 hours), **Nice** (2/day, 12 hours with change in Genoa), **Paris** (3/day, 13–15 hours with change in Rome or Milan). Any train listed on the schedule as leaving *Napoli PG* or *Napoli-*

Garibaldi departs not from the actual station, but from the Piazza Garibaldi subway station below.

To Pompeii: To visit the ancient site of Pompeii, don't use national train connections to the city of Pompei (which might seem convenient, especially if you're coming from Rome). Because the Pompei national train station is far from the archaeological site, you're better off transferring in Naples to the Circumvesuviana train (below)—which takes you to the *Pompei Scavi* stop near the actual site.

By Circumvesuviana Train: See "Getting Around the Region" sidebar, earlier, for information on getting to Herculaneum, Pompeii, and Sorrento.

Pompeii, Herculaneum, and Vesuvius

Stopped in their tracks by the eruption of Mount Vesuvius in A.D. 79, Pompeii and Herculaneum offer the best look anywhere at what life in Rome must have been like 2,000 years ago. These two cities of well-preserved ruins are yours to explore. Of the two sites, Pompeii is grander, while Herculaneum is smaller and more intimate. Vesuvius, still smoldering ominously, rises up on the horizon. It last erupted in 1944, and while still an active volcano, it's considered safe to visit. Shuttle buses drop you a short hike from the summit.

Pompeii

A once-thriving commercial port of 20,000, Pompeii (worth ▲▲▲) grew from Greek and Etruscan roots to become an important Roman city. Then, at about noon on August 24, A.D. 79, everything changed as the city became buried under 30 feet of hot volcanic ash. For archaeologists, this was a shake-and-bake windfall, teaching them volumes about daily Roman life. Pompeii was rediscovered in the 1600s; excavations began in 1748.

Orientation to Pompeii

Cost: €11, €20 combo-ticket includes Herculaneum (called Ercolano) and three lesser sites (valid 3 days).

Hours: Daily April–Oct 8:30–19:30, Nov–March 8:30–17:00 (last entry 1.5 hours before closing).

Getting There: Pompeii is roughly midway between Naples and Sorrento on the Circumvesuviana train line (2/hour, €2.40 and 35 minutes from Naples, €1.90 and 30 minutes from Sorrento, one-way, not covered by railpasses, www.vesuviana.it). Get off at the *Pompei Scavi, Villa dei Misteri* stop (from Naples, it's the stop after *Torre Annunziata;* from Sorrento, it's the one after *Moregine*). You can store your bag at the train station's bar for a small fee (€2, confirm last pickup time—bar often closes early), or, better yet, use the free baggage check at the site. From the Pompei Scavi train station, turn right and walk down the road about a block to the entrance (first left turn). The TI is farther down the street, but it's not a necessary stop for your visit. Parking is available at Camping Zeus near the Circumvesuviana train station (€2.50/hour).

Information: A good map and a helpful information booklet (which describes the most important stops within the site), when available, are included with your admission, but you must pick them up at the information window (to the left of the WCs). Tel. 081-857-5347, www.pompeiisites.org.

The bookshop sells the small Pompeii and Herculaneum *Past and Present* book. Its helpful text and plastic overlays allow you to re-create the ruins (€12 in bookstores, pay no more than that if you buy from a street vendor; look for the current year's edition).

Tours: My self-guided tour covers the basics. **Live guides** (around €115/2 hours) of varying quality can be risky—there really is no guarantee of what you're getting. They cluster near the ticket booth and may try to herd you into a group with other travelers, which makes the price more reasonable for you. For a private tour, hire the knowledgeable **Gaetano Manfredi,** who brings energy, intensity, and theatricality to his tours. He's a joy to follow for two hours as he brings the dusty ruins to life. Avoid impersonators. The real Gaetano takes bookings only in advance, preferably by email (rates vary with season and group size, tel. 338-725-5620, www.pompeiitourguide.com, gaetanoguide@hotmail.it). Parents, note that some sexually explicit frescoes are included on tours.

For evening visitors, Pompeii offers a "Moons of Pompeii" **sound-and-light show** that's partly a walking tour, with video footage projected onto the ruins (€20, summers only, check website for schedule, tel. 081-1930-3885, www.lelunedipompei.it).

Audioguide Tours: These are available from a kiosk near the ticket booth at the Porta Marina entrance (€6.50, €10/2 people,

Pompeii

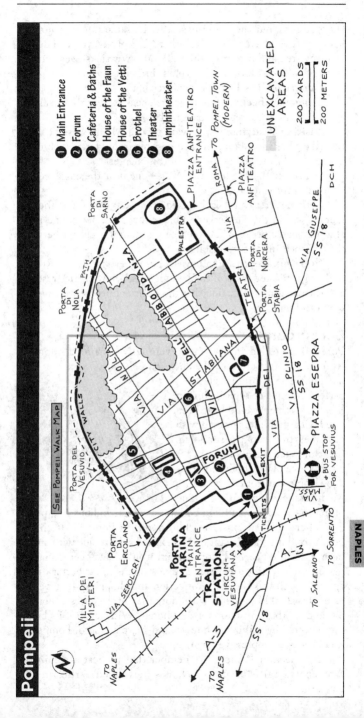

- ❶ Main Entrance
- ❷ Forum
- ❸ Cafeteria & Baths
- ❹ House of the Faun
- ❺ House of the Vetti
- ❻ Brothel
- ❼ Theater
- ❽ Amphitheater

UNEXCAVATED AREAS

200 YARDS
200 METERS

See Pompeii Walk Map

NAPLES

ID required), but they offer basically the same info as your free booklet. If you have an iPod or other MP3 player, you can download my free audio tour of this walk at www.ricksteves.com (or search for "Rick Steves Audio Tours" in iTunes).

Length of This Tour: Allow three hours.

Baggage Check: A free baggage check is near the turnstiles at the site entrance (retrieve bags by 19:00).

Visiting Vesuvius: If you want to visit Mount Vesuvius, you can take a bus from Pompeii (also possible from Herculaneum; for details, see "Vesuvius" at the end of this chapter).

Services: The site has two WCs—one near the entrance and another in the cafeteria.

Cuisine Art: Your best bet is to bring your own food. The restaurant within the site serves edible sandwiches, pizza, and pasta at a reasonable price. A few mediocre restaurants cluster between the entrance and the train station.

Starring: Roofless (collapsed) but otherwise intact Roman buildings, plaster casts of hapless victims, a few erotic frescoes, and the dawning realization that these ancient people were no different from us.

Background

Pompeii, founded in 600 B.C., eventually became a booming Roman trading city. Not rich, not poor, it was middle class—a perfect example of typical Roman life. Most streets would have been lined with stalls and jammed with customers from sunup to sundown. Chariots vied with shoppers for street space. Two thousand years ago, Rome controlled the entire Mediterranean—making it a kind

of free-trade zone—and Pompeii was a central and bustling port.

There were no posh neighborhoods in Pompeii. Rich and poor mixed it up as elegant houses existed side by side with simple homes. While nearby Herculaneum would have been a classier place to live (traffic-free streets, fancier houses, far better drainage), Pompeii was the place for action and shopping. It served an estimated 20,000 residents with more than 40 bakeries, 30 brothels, and 130 bars, restaurants, and hotels. With most of its buildings covered by brilliant white ground-marble stucco, Pompeii in A.D. 79 was an impressive town.

As you tour Pompeii, remember that its best art is in the Archaeological Museum in Naples (described earlier in this chapter).

Self-Guided Tour

• *Just past the ticket-taker, start your approach up to the...*

❶ Porta Marina

The city of Pompeii was born on the hill ahead of you. This was
the original town gate.
Before Vesuvius blew, the
sea came nearly to here.
Look to the left in the
distance to see the stone
rings where ships were
tied to the dock. Also
notice the two openings
in the gate (ahead, up
the ramp). Both were left

open by day to admit major traffic. At night, the larger one was
closed for better security.

• *Pass through the Porta Marina and continue up the street, pausing at
the three large stepping-stones in the middle.*

❷ Pompeii's Streets

Every day, Pompeiians flooded the streets with gushing water
to clean them. These stepping-stones let pedestrians cross with-

out getting their sandals wet.
Chariots traveling in either direction could straddle the stones (all
had standard-size axles). A single
stepping-stone in a road means it
was a one-way street, a pair indicates an ordinary two-way, and
three (like this) signifies a major

thoroughfare. The basalt stones are the original Roman pavement.
The sidewalks (elevated to hide the plumbing) were paved with
bits of broken pots (an ancient form of recycling) and studded with
reflective bits of white marble. These "cats' eyes" helped people get
around after dark, either by moonlight or with the help of lamps.

• *Continue straight ahead, don your mental toga, and enter the city as
the Romans once did. The road opens up into the spacious main square:
the Forum. Stand at the end of this rectangular space and look toward
Mount Vesuvius.*

❸ The Forum (Foro)

Pompeii's commercial, religious, and political center stands at
the intersection of the city's two main streets. While it's the most
ruined part of Pompeii, it's grand nonetheless. Picture the piazza

surrounded by two-story buildings on all sides. The pedestals
that line the square once held
statues (now safely displayed in
the museum in Naples). In its
heyday, Pompeii's citizens gathered here in the main square to
shop, talk politics, and socialize. Business took place in the
important buildings that lined the piazza.

The Forum was dominated by the **Temple of Jupiter,** at the
far end (marked by a half-dozen ruined columns atop a stair-step
base). Jupiter was the supreme god of the Roman pantheon—you
might be able to make out his little white marble head at the cen-
ter-rear of the temple.

At the near end of the Forum (where you're standing) is the
curia, or city hall. Like many Roman buildings, it was built with
brick and mortar, then covered with marble walls and floors. To
your left (as you face Vesuvius and the Temple of Jupiter) is the
basilica, or courthouse.

Since Pompeii was a typical town, it has the same layout and
components that you'll find in any Roman city—main square,
curia, basilica, temples, axis of roads, and so on. All power con-
verged at the Forum: religious (the temple), political (the curia),
judicial (the basilica), and commercial (this piazza was the main
marketplace). Even the power of the people was expressed here,
since this where they gathered to vote. Imagine the hubbub of this
town square.

Look beyond the Temple of Jupiter. Five miles to the north
looms the ominous backstory to this site: **Mount Vesuvius.**
Mentally draw a triangle up from the two remaining peaks to
reconstruct the mountain before the eruption. When it blew,
Pompeiians had no idea that they were living under a volcano,
since Vesuvius hadn't erupted for 1,200 years. (Still active, its last
eruption was in 1944.) Imagine the wonder—then the horror—as
the column of smoke roared upward, and then began to fall like
hail, rain, and snow, collapsing roofs and burying everything in a
blanket of ash.

• *As you face Vesuvius, the basilica is to your left, lined with stumps of
columns. Step inside and see the layout.*

❹ Basilica

Pompeii's basilica was a first-century palace of justice. This ancient
law court has the same floor plan later adopted by many Christian
churches (which are also called basilicas). The big central hall (or
nave) is flanked by rows of columns marking off narrower side

Pompeii Walk

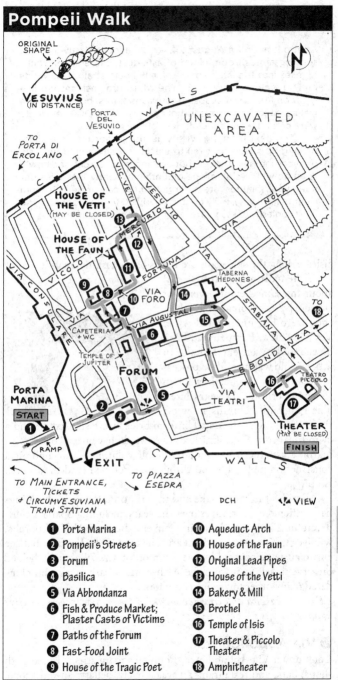

ORIGINAL SHAPE

VESUVIUS (IN DISTANCE)

Porta del Vesuvio

TO PORTA DI ERCOLANO

UNEXCAVATED AREA

WALLS

CITY

HOUSE OF THE VETTI (MAY BE CLOSED)

HOUSE OF THE FAUN

VIA VETTI

VIA VESUVIO

VIA NOLA

VIA MERCURIO

VIA FORTUNA

TABERNA HEDONES

VICOLO

VIA CONSULARE

VIA FORO

VIA STABIANA

TO 18

CAFETERIA + WC

VIA AUGUSTALI

TEMPLE OF JUPITER

Forum

VIA ABBONDANZA

TEATRO PICCOLO

PORTA MARINA

START

VIA TEATRI

THEATER (MAY BE CLOSED)

FINISH

RAMP

EXIT

CITY WALLS

TO MAIN ENTRANCE, TICKETS & CIRCUMVESUVIANA TRAIN STATION

TO PIAZZA ESEDRA

DCH

VIEW

1 Porta Marina
2 Pompeii's Streets
3 Forum
4 Basilica
5 Via Abbondanza
6 Fish & Produce Market; Plaster Casts of Victims
7 Baths of the Forum
8 Fast-Food Joint
9 House of the Tragic Poet
10 Aqueduct Arch
11 House of the Faun
12 Original Lead Pipes
13 House of the Vetti
14 Bakery & Mill
15 Brothel
16 Temple of Isis
17 Theater & Piccolo Theater
18 Amphitheater

The Eruption of Vesuvius

At about noon on August 24, A.D. 79, Mount Vesuvius blew, sending a mushroom cloud of ash, dust, cinders, and rocks 12 miles into the air. It spewed for 18 hours straight, as winds blew the cloud southward. The white-gray ash settled like snow on Pompeii, collapsing roofs and floors, but leaving the walls intact. Two thousand of the town's 20,000 residents were entombed under eight feet of fine powder.

The next morning, Vesuvius' upper portion collapsed, picking up speed as it fell to earth, creating a cloud of ash, pumice, and gas. The red-hot avalanche (a "pyroclastic flow") sped down the side of the mountain at nearly 100 miles per hour. Four minutes later, it engulfed the city of Herculaneum (four miles away), burying it in nearly 60 feet of hot mud. The mud cooled into stone, freezing the moment in time.

aisles. Along the side walls are traces of the original marble.

The column stumps—all about the same height—were not ruined by the volcano. Rather, they were left unfinished when Vesuvius blew. Pompeii had been devastated by an earthquake in A.D. 62, and was just in the process of rebuilding the basilica when Vesuvius erupted 17 years later. The half-built columns show off the technology of the day. Uniform bricks were stacked around a cylindrical core. Once finished, they would have been coated with marble dust stucco to simulate marble columns—an economical construction method found throughout Pompeii (and the Roman Empire).

Besides the earthquake and the eruption, Pompeii's buildings have suffered other ravages over the years, including Spanish plunderers (c. 1800), 19th-century souvenir hunters, WWII bombs, wild vegetation, and another earthquake in 1980. The fact that the entire city was covered by the eruption of A.D. 79 actually helped preserve it, saving it from the sixth-century barbarians who plundered many other towns into oblivion.

• *Exit the basilica and cross the square to the far side, where the city's main street hits the Forum.*

❺ Via Abbondanza

Look down Via Abbondanza, Pompeii's main street. Lined with shops, bars, and restaurants, it was a lively, pedestrian-only zone.

NAPLES

The three "beaver-teeth" stones are traffic barriers that kept chariots out. On the corner (just to the left), take a close look at the dark travertine column standing next to a white one. Notice that the marble drums of the white column are not chiseled entirely round—another construction project left unfinished when Vesuvius erupted.

• *Head toward Vesuvius, walking along the right side of the Forum. Immediately to the right of the Temple of Jupiter, a door leads into the market hall, where you'll find two glass cases.*

❻ Fish and Produce Market— Plaster Casts of Victims

As the frescoes on the wall (just inside on the left) indicate, this is where Pompeiians came to buy their food—fish, bread, chickens, and so on. These fine examples of Roman art—with their glimpses of everyday life and mastery of depth and illusion—would not be matched until the Renaissance, a thousand years after the fall of Rome.

The glass cases hold casts of Pompeiians, eerily captured in their last moments. When Vesuvius erupted, 2,000 Pompeii citizens suffocated under the ash, their bodies buried in volcanic debris. While excavating, modern archaeologists detected hollow spaces underfoot, created when the victims' bodies decomposed. By gently filling the holes with plaster, the archaeologists were able to create molds of the Pompeiians who were caught in the disaster. You're looking at modern plaster mixed with ancient bones.

• *Continue on, leaving the Forum through an arch behind the Temple of Jupiter. Here you'll find a pedestrians-only road sign (ahead on the right corner, above the* REG VII INS IV *sign) and more "beaver-teeth" traffic blocks. The modern cafeteria is the only eatery inside the archaeological site (with a coffee bar and WC). Twenty yards past the cafeteria, on the left-hand side at #24, is the entrance to the...*

❼ Baths of the Forum (Terme del Foro)

Pompeii had six public baths, each with a men's and a women's section. You're in the men's zone. The leafy courtyard at the entrance was the gymnasium. After working out, clients could relax with a hot bath *(caldarium)*, warm bath *(tepidarium)*, or cold plunge *(frigidarium)*.

The first big, plain room you enter served as the **dressing**

room. Holes on the walls were for pegs to hang clothing. The window (with Neptune underneath) was originally covered with a less-translucent Roman glass. Walk over the non-slip mosaics into the next room.

The *tepidarium* is ringed by mini-statues or *telamones* (male caryatids, figures used as supporting pillars), which divided the lockers. Clients would undress and warm up here, perhaps stretching out on one of the bronze benches near the bronze heater for a massage. Look at the ceiling—half crushed by the eruption and half intact, with its fine blue-and-white stucco work.

Next, admire the engineering in the steam-bath room, or *caldarium*. The double floor was heated from below—so nice with bare feet (look into the grate to see the brick support towers). The double walls with brown terra-cotta tiles held the heat. Romans soaked in the big tub, which was filled with hot water. Opposite the big tub is a fountain, which spouted water onto the hot floor, creating steam. The lettering on the fountain reminded those enjoying the room which two politicians paid for it...and how much it cost them (5,250 *sestertii*). To keep condensation from dripping annoyingly from the ceiling, fluting (ribbing) was added to carry water down the walls.

• *Today's visitors exit the baths through the original entry. If you're a bit hungry, immediately across the street is an ancient...*

❽ Fast-Food Joint

After a bath, it was only natural to want a little snack. So, just across the street is a fast-food joint, marked by a series of rectangular marble counters. Most ancient Romans didn't cook for themselves in their tiny apartments, so to-go places like this were commonplace. The holes in the counters held the pots for food. Each container was like a thermos, with a wooden lid to keep the soup hot, the wine cool, and so on. Notice the groove in  the front doorstep and the holes out on the curb. The holes likely accommodated cords for stretching awnings over the sidewalk to shield the clientele from the hot sun, while the grooves were for the shop's folding accordion doors. Look at the wheel grooves in the pavement, worn down through centuries of use. There are also more stepping-stones for pedestrians to cross the flooded streets.

• *Just a few steps uphill from the fast-food joint is the...*

❾ House of the Tragic Poet (Casa de Poeta Tragico)

This house is typical Roman style. The entry is flanked by two family-owned shops (each with a track for a collapsing accordion door). The home is like a train running straight away from the street: atrium (with skylight and pool to catch the rain), den (where deals were made by the shopkeeper), and garden (with rooms facing it and a shrine to remember both the gods and family ancestors). In the entryway is the famous "Beware of Dog" *(Cave Canem)* mosaic.

Today's visitors enter the home by the back door (circle around to the left). The modern pipe exposed across the lane is the same as ones used in the ancient plumbing system, hidden beneath the raised sidewalk. Inside the house, the grooves on the marble well head were formed by generations of dragging the bucket up by rope. The richly frescoed dining room is off the garden. Diners lounged on their couches (the Roman custom) and enjoyed frescoes with fake "windows," giving the illusion of a bigger and airier room. Just to the right is a humble BBQ-style kitchen with a little closet for the toilet (the kitchen and bathroom shared the same plumbing).

• *Return to the fast-food place and continue about 10 yards downhill to the big intersection. From the center of the intersection, look left to see a giant arch, framing a nice view of Mount Vesuvius.*

❿ Aqueduct Arch—Running Water

Water was critical for this city of 20,000 people, and this arch was part of Pompeii's water-delivery system. A 100-mile-long aqueduct carried fresh water down from the hillsides to a big reservoir perched at the highest point of the city wall. Since overall water pressure was disappointing, Pompeiians built arches like the brick one you see here (originally covered in marble) with hidden water tanks at the top. Located just below the altitude of the main tank, these smaller tanks were filled by gravity, and provided each neighborhood with reliable pressure.

• *If you're thirsty, fill your water bottle from the modern fountain. Then continue straight downhill one block (50 yards) to #2 on the left.*

⓫ House of the Faun (Casa del Founo)

Stand across the street and marvel at the grand entry with *"HAVE"* (hail to you) as a welcome mat. Go in. Notice the two shrines above the entryway—one dedicated to the gods, the other to this wealthy family's ancestors.

You are standing in Pompeii's largest home, where you're greeted by the delightful small bronze statue of the *Dancing Faun*, famed for its realistic movement and fine proportion.

(The original, described on page 835, is in Naples' Archaeological Museum.) With 40 rooms and 27,000 square feet, the House of the Faun covers an entire city block. The next floor mosaic, with an intricate diamond-like design, decorates the homeowner's office. Beyond that is the famous floor mosaic of the *Battle of Alexander*. (The original is also at the museum in Naples.) In 333 B.C., Alexander the Great beat Darius and the Persians. Romans had great respect for Alexander, the first great emperor before Rome. While most of Pompeii's nouveau riche had notoriously bad taste and stuffed their palaces with over-the-top, mismatched decor, this guy had class. Both the faun (an ancient copy of a famous Greek statue) and the Alexander mosaic show an appreciation for history.

The house's back courtyard leads to the exit in the far-right corner. It's lined with pillars rebuilt after the A.D. 62 earthquake. Take a close look at the brick, mortar, and fake marble stucco veneer.

• *Sneak out of the House of the Faun through its back door and turn right. (If this exit is closed, return to the entrance and make a U-turn left, around to the back of the house.) Thirty yards down, along the right-hand side of the street are metal cages protecting...*

⑫ Original Lead Pipes

These 2,000-year-old pipes (made of lead imported from Britannia) were part of the city's elaborate water system. From the aqueduct-fed water tank at the high end of town, three independent pipe systems supplied water to the city: one for baths, one for private homes, and one for public water fountains. If there was a water shortage, democratic priorities prevailed: First the baths were cut off, then the private homes. The last water supply to go was the public fountains, where all citizens could get drinking and cooking water.

• *If the street's not closed off, take your first left (on Vicolo dei Vetti), walk about 20 yards, and find the entrance (on the left) to the...*

⑬ House of the Vetti (Casa dei Vetti)

Pompeii's best-preserved home has been completely blocked off for years; unfortunately it's unlikely to reopen in time for your visit. The House of the Vetti was the bachelor pad of two wealthy merchant brothers. If you can see the entryway, you may spot the huge erection. This is not pornography. There's a meaning here: The penis and the sack of money balance each other on the goldsmith scale above a fine bowl of fruit. Translation: Only with a balance of fertility and money can you have abundance.

If it's open, step into the atrium with its ceiling open to the sky to collect light and rainwater. The pool, while decorative, was a functional water-supply tank. It's flanked by large money boxes anchored to the floor. The brothers were certainly successful merchants, and possibly money-lenders, too.

Exit on the right, passing the tight servant quarters, and go into the kitchen, with its bronze cooking pots (and an exposed lead pipe on the back wall). The passage dead-ends in the little Venus Room, which features erotic frescoes behind glass.

Return to the atrium and pass into the big colonnaded garden. It was replanted according to the plan indicated by traces of roots excavated in the volcanic ash. Richly frescoed entertainment rooms ring this courtyard. Circle counterclockwise. The dining room is finely decorated in black and "Pompeiian red" (from iron rust). Study the detail. Notice the lead humidity seal between the wall and the floor, designed to keep the moisture-sensitive frescoes dry. (Had Leonardo da Vinci taken this clever step, his *Last Supper* in Milan might be in better shape today.) Continuing around, you'll see more of the square white stones inlaid in the floor. Imagine them reflecting like cats' eyes as the brothers and their friends wandered around by oil lamp late at night. Frescoes in the Yellow Room (near the exit) show off the ancient mastery of perspective,

which would not be matched elsewhere in Europe for nearly 1,500 years.

• *Facing the entrance to the House of the Vetti, turn left and walk downhill one long block (along Vicolo dei Vetti) to a T-intersection (Via della Fortuna), marked by a stone fountain with a bull's head for a spout. Intersections like this were busy neighborhood centers, where the rent was highest and people gathered. With the fountain at your back, turn left, then immediately right, walking along a gently curving road (Vicolo Storto). On the left side of the street, at #22, find four big stone cylinders.*

⓮ Bakery and Mill (Forno e Mulini)

The brick oven looks like a modern-day pizza oven. The stubby stone towers are flour grinders. Grain was poured into the top, and donkeys or slaves pushed wooden bars that turned the stones.

The powdered grain dropped out of the bottom as flour—flavored with tiny bits of rock. Each neighborhood had a bakery like this.

Continue to the next intersection (Via degli Augustali, where there's another fast-food joint) and turn left. As you walk, look at the destructive power of all the vines, and notice how deeply the chariot grooves have worn into the pavement. Deep grooves could break wagon wheels. The suddenly ungroovy stretch indicates that this road was in the process of being repaved when the big shake shut everything down.

• *Head about 50 yards down this (obviously one-way) street to #44 (on the left). Here you'll find the Taberna Hedones (with a small atrium, den, and garden). This bar still has its original floor and, deeper in, the mosaic arch of a grotto fountain. Just past the tavern, turn right and walk downhill to #18, on the right.*

⓯ Brothel (Lupanare)

You'll find the biggest crowds in Pompeii at a place that was likely popular 2,000 ago, too—the brothel. Prostitutes were nicknamed *lupe* (she-wolves), alluding to the call they made when trying to attract business. The brothel was a simple place, with beds and pillows made of stone. The ancient graffiti includes tallies and exotic names of the women, indicating the prostitutes came from all corners of the Mediterranean (it also served as feedback from satisfied customers). The faded frescoes above the cells may have been a kind of menu for services offered. Note the idealized women (white, which was considered beautiful; one wears an early bra) and the rougher men (dark, considered horny). The bed legs came with little disk-like barriers to keep critters from crawling up.

• *Leaving the brothel, go right, then take the first left, and continue going downhill two blocks to the intersection with Pompeii's main drag, Via dell'Abbondanza. The Forum—and exit—are to the right, for those who may wish to opt out from here.*

The huge amphitheater—which is certainly skippable—is 10 minutes to your left. But for now, go left for 60 yards, then turn right just beyond the fountain, and walk down Via dei Teatri. Turn left before the columns (about 50 yards away), and head downhill another 60 yards to #28, which marks the...

⓰ Temple of Isis

This Egyptian temple served Pompeii's Egyptian community. The little white stucco shrine with the plastic roof housed holy water from the Nile. Isis, from Egyptian myth, was one of many foreign gods adopted by the eclectic Romans. Pompeii must have had a synagogue, too, but it has yet to be excavated.

• *Exit the temple where you entered, and go right. At the next intersection, turn right again, and head downhill to the adjacent theaters. Your goal is the large theater, but if it's closed for renovation, look at the smaller but similar theater (Piccolo Theater).*

❼ Theater

Originally a Greek theater (Greeks built theirs with the help of a hillside), this was the birthplace of the Greek port here in 470 B.C. During Roman times, the theater sat 5,000 people in three sets of

seats, all with different prices: the five marble terraces up close (filled with romantic wooden seats for two), the main section, and the cheap nosebleed section (surviving only on the right). The square stones above the cheap seats once supported a canvas rooftop. Take note of the high-profile boxes, flanking the stage, for guests of

honor. From this perch, you can see the gladiator barracks—the colonnaded courtyard beyond the theater. They lived in tiny rooms, trained in the courtyard, and fought in the nearby amphitheater.

• *You've seen Pompeii's highlights. When you're ready to leave, backtrack to the main road and turn left, going uphill to the Forum, where you'll find the main entrance/exit.*

However, there's much more to see—three-quarters of Pompeii's 164 acres have been excavated, but this tour has covered only a third of the site. After the theater—if you still have energy to see more—go back to the main road, and take a right toward the eastern part of the site, where the crowds thin out. Go straight for about 10 minutes, then turn right down a dirt path (about 75 yards from the wall at the edge of the site), which leads to the...

❽ Amphitheater

Climb to the upper level of the amphitheater (if the external stairs are blocked, try the entrance to the left). With Vesuvius looming in the background, mentally replace the tourists below with gladiators and wild animals locked in combat. Walk along the top of the amphitheater and look down into the grassy rectangular area surrounded by columns. This is the **Palaestra,** an area once used for athletic training. Facing the other way, look for the bell tower that tops the roofline of the modern city of Pompei, where locals go about their daily lives in the shadow of the volcano, just as their ancestors did 2,000 years ago. *HAVE!*

Herculaneum (Ercolano)

Smaller, less crowded, and not as ruined as its famous big sister, Herculaneum (worth ▲▲) offers a closer, more intimate peek into

ancient Roman life but lacks the grandeur of Pompeii (there's barely a colonnade).

Cost and Hours: €11, €20 combo-ticket includes Pompeii and three lesser sites (valid 3 days). Open daily April–Oct 8:30–19:30, Nov–March 8:30–17:00, ticket office closes 1.5 hours earlier (tel. 081-732-4311, www.pompeiisites .org).

Getting There: Herculaneum (Ercolano) is about 25 minutes from Naples and roughly 45 minutes from Sorrento on the same Circumvesuviana train that goes to Pompeii. For details on the Circumvesuviana, see page 891. Get off at the *Ercolano Scavi* train stop. To walk to the ruins, leave the Ercolano station and turn right, then left; go eight blocks straight downhill from the station to the end of the road, where you'll see the entrance marked by a grand arch. Pass through and continue down the path, taking in the bird's-eye first impression of the site. The ticket office, baggage storage (pick up bags 30 minutes prior to site closing), and WCs are located in the modern building, 200 yards ahead.

Information: Pick up a free detailed map and excellent booklet (with numbered explanations of each building) at the info desk next to the ticket window. The informative and interesting audioguide sheds light on the ruins and life in Herculaneum in the first century A.D. (€6.50, €10/2 people, ID required, pick up 100 yards after the ticket turnstiles). There is no bookstore or café at the site.

Length of This Tour: Allow one hour.

❻ **Self-Guided Tour:** Caked and baked by the same A.D. 79 eruption that pummeled Pompeii, Herculaneum is a small community of intact buildings with plenty of surviving detail. While Pompeii was initially smothered in ash and pumice, Herculaneum was buried under nearly 60 feet of boiling mud, which hardened into tuff *(tufa)*, perfectly preserving the city until excavations began in 1738.

After leaving the ticket window, walk the long path around the site to the entrance. From here, you can get a sense of just how much lava piled up. The present-day city of Ercolano looms just above, and the modern buildings don't look much different from their ancient counterparts.

After crossing the modern bridge into the excavation site, stroll straight to the end of the street and find the **Seat of the Augustali** (Sede degli Augustali). Decorated with frescoes of Hercules (for whom this city was named), it was a forum for freed slaves climbing their way up the ladder of Roman society.

Leave the building and go to the right, down a lane. The adjacent *thermopolium* was the Roman equivalent to fast food, with giant tubs for wine, oil, and snacks. Most of the buildings along here were shops, with apartments above. Look around doorways for ancient bits of lava-charred wood. Most buildings were made of stone, but the floors and beams were wood (which doesn't survive at any other ancient site).

The **Bottega ad Cucumas** wine shop still has charred remains of beams, and its drink list remains frescoed on the outside wall.

Down the street to the right, **The House of Neptune and Amphitrite** (Casa di Nettuno e Anfitrite) has colorful mosaics and an intact shell frame.

At the far end of the site is the don't-miss-it **gymnasium** *(palestra)* complex with its Hydra of Lerna. This sculpted bronze fountain features the seven-headed monster defeated by Hercules as one of his 12 labors. Find the Hydra by walking through the triangular-shaped entrances carved in the tuff wall. To light up this cavernous space, go to the second doorway on the left wall and press the switch. Just outside, take a close look at the "marble" columns, which are actually made of rounded bricks covered with a thick layer of plaster, shaped to look like carved marble. While important buildings in Rome had solid marble columns, these are typical of ordinary buildings.

Downhill, the **House of the Deer** (Casa dei Cervi) is also worth seeking out. It's named for the statues of deer being attacked by dogs in the garden courtyard (these are copies; the originals are in the Archaeological Museum in Naples). As you wander through the rooms, notice the colorfully frescoed walls. Ancient Herculaneum, like all Roman cities of that age, was filled with color, rather than the stark white we often imagine (even the statues were painted).

Continuing downhill, the **baths** (Terme Suburbane, sometimes closed) illustrate the city's devastation. After you descend into the baths, look back at the steps. You'll see the original wood charred in the disaster, protected by the wooden planks you just walked on. At the bottom of the stairs, in the waiting room to the right, notice where the floor collapsed under the sheer weight of the volcanic mud. (The sunken pavement reveals the baths' heating system: hot air generated by wood-burning furnaces and circulated between the different levels of the floor.) A doorway in front of the stairs is still filled with solidified mud. Despite the damage, elements of refinement remain intact, such as the delicate stuccoes in the *caldarium* (hot bath).

Back outside, make your way down the steps to the sunken area just below. As you descend, you're walking across what was formerly Herculaneum's beach. Looking back, the **arches** that you see were boat storage areas. During excavations in 1981, hundreds of bodies were found here, between the wall of volcanic stone behind you and the city in front of you. Some of Herculaneum's 4,000 citizens had a little more time than the people of Pompeii to flee the eruption. They tried to escape to the sea, but never made it out of Herculaneum.

Thankfully, your escape is easier. Either follow the sounds of the water and continue through the tunnel; or, more scenically, backtrack and exit the same way you entered.

Vesuvius

The 4,000-foot-high Vesuvius, mainland Europe's only active volcano, has been sleeping restlessly since 1944.

Getting to Vesuvius: The summit is accessible year-round by car (just drive to the end of the road and pay €2.50 to park), by taxi (€80 round-trip from Naples), or by bus or van.

From **Pompeii,** you have two options: the (usually blue or gray) Vesuviana Mobilità bus (10/day, 1.5 hours there, 1 hour back, departs from Piazza Anfiteatro and Piazza Esedra in front of TI, €9 round-trip plus summit admission, weather-permitting in winter, tel. 081-963-4420), or Busvia del Vesuvio's off-road "vans" (daily 8:30–16:00 depending on demand, leaves from Camping Zeus near *Pompei Scavi* Circumvesuviana station, €18.50 includes admission and guide, tel. 081-877-3436, www.busviadelvesuvio .com).

From **Herculaneum,** your best bet is the Vesuvio Express, which makes the trip in small vans from Herculaneum's *Ercolano Scavi* Circumvesuviana station (daily from 9:00, 2/hour based on demand, €10 round-trip plus summit admission, tel. 081-739-3666, www.vesuvioexpress.it). You can also take the Vesuviana Mobilità bus, but it doesn't run as predictably (when running, daily at 8:25 and 14:25, €7.80 round-trip plus summit admission, see contact info above).

At Vesuvius: Admission, with a mandatory guide, costs €6.50 (daily 9:00–17:00, until 18:00 in summer, Nov–March until 15:00, tel. 081-865-3911, www.parconazionaledelvesuvio.it). From the parking lot, it's a steep 30-minute hike to the top for a sweeping view of the Bay of Naples (often cold and windy, bring a coat, especially Oct–April). Up here,

it's desolate and lunar-like, and the rocks are newly minted. Walk the entire crater lip for the most interesting views; the far end overlooks Pompeii. Be still and alone to hear the wind and occasional cascades of rocks tumbling into the crater. Any steam? Closed when erupting.

SORRENTO AND CAPRI

Without a hint of big-city Naples and just an hour to the south, serene Sorrento makes an ideal home base for exploring all the fascinating sights in the region, from Naples to the Amalfi Coast to Paestum. And the jet-setting island of Capri is just a short cruise from Sorrento, offering more charm and fun (outside of the crowded months of July and August) than its glitzy reputation would lead you to believe.

Sorrento

Wedged on a ledge under the mountains and over the Mediterranean, spritzed by lemon and olive groves, Sorrento is an attractive resort of 20,000 residents and, in summer, just as many tourists. It's as well-located for regional sightseeing as it is a fine place to stay and stroll. The Sorrentines have gone out of their way to create a completely safe and relaxed place for tourists to come and spend money. Everyone seems to speak fluent English and work for the Chamber of Commerce. This gateway to the Amalfi Coast has an unspoiled old quarter, a lively main shopping street, and a spectacular cliff-side setting. Residents are proud of the many world-class romantics who've vacationed here, such as the famed tenor Enrico Caruso, who chose Sorrento as the place to spend his last weeks in 1921.

Planning Your Time

With Sorrento as your home base, spend a minimum of three days and nights in the region. On your way to or from Sorrento, visit

Naples as a day trip. After settling in Sorrento, spend a day touring the Amalfi Coast by bus, and another day split between Sorrento and Pompeii (accessible by Circumvesuviana train—see page 891). With more time, catch a quick boat ride to the nearby island of Capri or linger on the Amalfi Coast (see next chapter), heading as far south as Paestum's Greek temples.

Orientation to Sorrento

Sorrento is long and narrow. The main drag, Corso Italia (50 yards in front of the Circumvesuviana train station), runs paral-

lel to the sea from the station through the town center and out to the cape, where the road's name becomes Via Capo. Piazza Tasso marks the town's center. Everything mentioned here (except the hotels on Via Capo) is within a 10-minute walk of the train station. Sorrento hibernates in January and February, when many places close down.

Tourist Information

The TI (labeled *Soggiorno e Turismo*)—located inside the Foreigners' Club—hands out the free monthly *Surrentum* magazine, with a great city map and schedules of boats, buses, concerts, and festivals (Mon–Sat 8:45–18:15, Sun 8:45–16:00, shorter hours off-season, Via Luigi de Maio 35, tel. 081-807-4033, www.sorrentotourism.com). If you arrive after the TI closes, look for their useful handouts in the lobby of the Foreigners' Club (open until midnight).

To get from the train station to the TI, head straight out to Corso Italia and turn left. Walk five minutes to Piazza Tasso, turn right at the end of the square, and go down Via Luigi de Maio through Piazza Sant'Antonino, bearing right downhill about 30 yards to the Foreigners' Club mansion at #35.

If you just need quick advice, the fake tourist office—located in a green caboose just outside the train station—can be of help. While they're a private business with hopes that you'll purchase one of their overpriced excursions, they're willing to give basic information on directions, buses, and ferries.

Arrival in Sorrento

By Train: Those arriving by train (Sorrento is the last stop on the Circumvesuviana train line) will see the Amalfi bus stop, as well as taxis waiting to overcharge them. All recommended hotels—except those on Via Capo—are within a 10-minute walk (a much cheaper mode of transport than the €15 fare taxi drivers will gouge you). For details on taking the bus to hotels on Via Capo, see page 886.

By Boat: Passenger boats dock at Marina Piccola, Sorrento's little harbor. To get to Piazza Tasso, it's a 15-minute uphill hike or a short ride on a small blue bus (4/hour, €1, buy ticket from driver, day passes not valid) or a red-and-white bus (3/hour, buy €1 tickets at the *tabacchi* or adjacent Metro del Mar kiosk).

Helpful Hints

Church Services: The **cathedral** hosts an English-language Anglican service at 17:00 most Sundays mid-April–July and Sept–Oct. At **Santa Maria delle Grazie** (perhaps the most beautiful Baroque church in town), cloistered nuns sing from above and out of sight during a Mass each morning at 7:30 (on Via delle Grazie).

Bookstore: Libreria Tasso has a decent selection of books in English, including this one (Mon–Sat 10:00–13:20 & 16:30–21:30, Sun 11:30–13:15 & 19:00–22:00, shorter hours off-season, closed Sun Nov–March, Via San Cesareo 96, one block north of cathedral, near Sorrento Men's Club, tel. 081-807-1639).

Laundry: Sorrento has two handy launderettes. One is at Corso Italia 30 (daily May–Sept 7:00–24:00, Oct–April 8:00–23:00; full-service—€12/load, drop off: 8:00–13:00 & 16:00–19:30, drop before 9:30 for same-day turnaround; self-service—€6/load wash and dry, bring coins, includes soap; for self-service, enter through alley; tel. 081-878-1185). The other launderette is at the corner of Corso Italia and Via degli Aranci (daily 8:00–22:00, self-service-€8/load, includes soap).

Local Guides: Giovanna Donadio is a good tour guide for Sorrento, Amalfi, and Capri (€100/half-day, €160/day, same price for any size of group, mobile 338-466-0114, giovanna _dona@hotmail.com). **Giovanni Visetti** is a nature-lover who organizes hikes (www.giovistravels.com).

Where It's At: The **Foreigners' Club** provides reasonably priced snacks and drinks, music, dancing, and magnificent vistas from its cliffside terrace—drop in for the view overlooking the harbor and the Bay of Naples (daily 9:30–24:00, behind TI, public WC, Via Luigi de Maio 35, tel. 081-877-3263). Also see "Nightlife in Sorrento" and "Eating in Sorrento," later in this chapter.

Getting Around Sorrento

By Bus: City buses (either orange or red-and-white) all stop in the main square, Piazza Tasso. There's only one stop—under the flags closest to the sea. Bus #A runs to Meta beach or the hotels on Via Capo, buses #B and #C go to the port (Marina Piccola), and bus #D heads to the fishing village (Marina Grande). Tickets for a ride between just the port and Piazza Tasso cost €1 (see "Arrival in Sorrento," earlier); other tickets cost €2.40 and are good for 45 minutes (purchase at *tabacchi* shops and newsstands). Stamp your ticket upon entering the bus. The one-day pass (€7.20) and three-day pass (€18) are also valid for the entire Amalfi Coast.

By Rental Wheels: Many places rent motor scooters for about €40 per day, including **Europcar** (Mon–Sat 9:00–13:00 & 16:00–19:30, closed Sun, Corso Italia 210p, tel. 081-878-4956, www.sorrento.it) and **Penisola Rent,** a half-block away (daily 9:00–13:30 & 16:00–20:30, located in Hotel Nice, tel. 081-877-4664, www.penisolarent.com). Don't rent a car in summer unless you enjoy traffic jams.

By Taxi: Taxis are expensive, charging at least €15 for the short ride from the station to hotels. Because of heavy traffic and the complex one-way road system, you can often walk faster than you can ride. If you do use a taxi, even if you agree to a set price, be sure it has a meter. All official taxis have one. I think taxis are a huge rip-off, since city officials don't have the nerve to regulate them, and hotels are afraid to alienate them. Take the bus instead.

Self-Guided Walk

Welcome to Sorrento

Get to know Sorrento with this lazy self-guided town stroll.

• *Begin on the main square. Stand under the flags with your back to the sea, and face...*

Piazza Tasso: As in any southern Italian town, this "piazza" is Sorrento's living room. It may be noisy and congested, but locals want to be where the action is...and be part of the scene. The most expensive apartments and top cafés are on or near this square. Buses stop here on their way to Marina Piccola (where boats depart from the harbor for Naples and Capri, a 10-minute hike below you), to the train station (left), and to Via Capo (right).

This square spans a gorge that divided the town until the 19th century. The old town (on your right) still has some surviving ancient Greek streets. The new town (to your left) was farm country just two centuries ago. A statue of St. Anthony, patron of Sorrento, faces north as if greeting those coming from Naples (often equipped with an armload of fresh lemons and oranges). If you walk a block inland, go right up to the green railing, and look

Sorrento

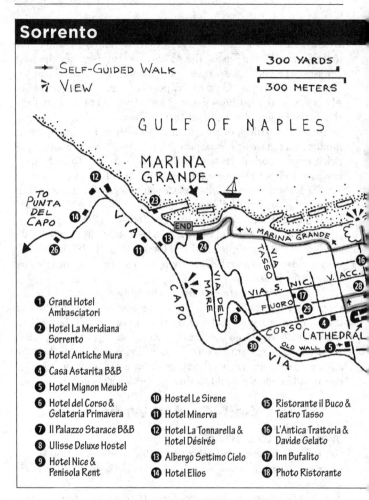

→ SELF-GUIDED WALK
↗ VIEW

300 YARDS
300 METERS

GULF OF NAPLES

MARINA GRANDE

TO PUNTA DEL CAPO

VIA CAPO

END

V. MARINA GRANDE

VIA TASSO

VIA DEL MARE

VIA S. NIC.

V. ACC.

FUORO

CORSO

OLD WALL

VIA

CATHEDRAL

1 Grand Hotel Ambasciatori
2 Hotel La Meridiana Sorrento
3 Hotel Antiche Mura
4 Casa Astarita B&B
5 Hotel Mignon Meublè
6 Hotel del Corso & Gelateria Primavera
7 Il Palazzo Starace B&B
8 Ulisse Deluxe Hostel
9 Hotel Nice & Penisola Rent
10 Hostel Le Sirene
11 Hotel Minerva
12 Hotel La Tonnarella & Hotel Désirée
13 Albergo Settimo Cielo
14 Hotel Elios
15 Ristorante il Buco & Teatro Tasso
16 L'Antica Trattoria & Davide Gelato
17 Inn Bufalito
18 Photo Ristorante

down, you'll see steps carved in the fifth century B.C.

Sorrento's name came from the Greek word for "siren," the legendary half-bird, half-woman who sang an intoxicating lullaby. According to Homer, the sirens lived on an island near here. No one had ever sailed by the sirens without succumbing to their incredible musical charms...and to death. But Homer's hero Ulysses was determined to hear the song. He put wax in his oarsmen's ears and had himself lashed to the mast of his ship. Oh, it was nice. The sirens, thinking they had lost their powers, threw themselves into the sea, and the place became safe to inhabit. Ulysses' odyssey was all about the westward expansion of Greek culture, and to the ancient Greeks, places like Sorrento were the wild, wild west.

• *With your back still to the sea, head to the far-right corner of the square,*

- ⑲ Rist. Pizzeria da Gigino
- ⑳ Rist. Pizzeria Lanterna Due
- ㉑ Pizzeria da Franco
- ㉒ Standa Supermarket
- ㉓ Ristorante Delfino
- ㉔ Trattoria da Emilia
- ㉕ Foreigners' Club Rest.
- ㉖ Verde Mare
- ㉗ Lemon Grove Garden
- ㉘ Sorrento Men's Club
- ㉙ The English Inn & Launderette
- ㉚ Launderette
- ㉛ Europcar
- ㉜ City Bus Stop
- ㉝ SITA Bus Stop

behind the statue of Torquato Tasso, the square's namesake. (A Sorrento native, he was a lively Renaissance poet.) Peek into the big courtyard of Palazzo Correale (#18, behind the statue in the right corner) to get a feel for an 18th-century aristocratic palace's courtyard, lined with characteristic tiles. Next door, a fun shop sells regional products and offers free biscuits and tastes of liqueurs. As you're leaving the courtyard, on your immediate left you'll see the narrow...

Via Santa Maria della Pietà: Here, just a few yards off the noisy main drag, is a street that goes back centuries before Christ. About 100 yards down the lane, at #24, find a 13th-century palace (no balconies back then...for security reasons). Continuing on for 10 yards, you'll see a tiny shrine across the street. Typical of southern Italy, it's where the faithful pray to their saint, who contacts

Mary, who contacts Jesus, who contacts God. This shrine is a bit more direct—it starts right with Mary.

• *Continue down the lane, which ends at the...*

Cathedral: This is the seat of the local bishop. Pop in for a cool stroll around the ambulatory, checking out the impressive *intarsio* (inlaid-wood) doors. Two sets, inlaid on both sides, show many scenes of the town and its industry. The doors facing the main street include an old town map. These were made to celebrate the pope's visit in 1992. Also notice the intricate inlaid Stations of the Cross, which describe Jesus' last hours.

• *Backtrack 10 yards down Via Santa Maria della Pietà, turn left, cross busy Corso Italia (look back at the bell tower, with its ancient Roman columns at the base), and go straight on Via P. Reginaldo Giuliani, following the...*

Old Greek Street Plan: Notice here how streets are laid out— east–west for the most sunlight and north–south for the prevailing and cooling breeze.

• *One block ahead is a fine old portico, the...*

Sorrento Men's Club: Once the meeting place of the town's nobles, this club has been a retreat for retired working-class men for generations. Strictly no women— and no phones.

Italian men venerate their mothers. (Italians joke that Jesus must have been a southern Italian because his mother believed her son was God, he believed his mom was a virgin, and he lived at home with her until he was 30.) But Italian men have also built into their culture ways to be on their own. Here, men play cards and gossip under a historic emblem of the city and a finely frescoed 16th-century dome, with its marvelous 3-D scenes.

• *At the Men's Club, turn right onto...*

Via San Cesareo: This touristy pedestrian-only shopping street leads four or five blocks back to Piazza Tasso. All along the way, you can peruse (and sample) lemon products in the very competitive shops. Notice the huge ancient doorways with their tiny doors—to carefully let in people during a dangerous age.

• *At the noisy street on the edge of Piazza Tasso, turn left and fight the traffic downhill to the next square, with another...*

Statue of St. Anthony (Antonino): Sorrento's town saint humbly looms among the palms, facing the basilica where his reliquary lies (under the altar in the crypt, surrounded by lots of votives). From here, you can quit the walk and stay in the city center, or continue to the village-like waterfront (if it's before 20:00, you can catch a bus to get back).

• *Exit the square diagonally to the left and gradually wind your way downhill toward Marina Grande (not down the street that leads to the Foreigners' Club and port). After a block or so, on the right you'll see the trees in front of the Imperial Hotel Tramontano and to their right, a path leading to a...*

Cliffside Square: This fine public square, the Villa Communale, overlooks the harbor. Belly up to the banister to enjoy the view of the little harbor and the Bay of Naples. From here, steps zigzag down to Marina Piccola, where lounge chairs, filled by vacationers working on tans, line the sundecks. The Franciscan church fronting this square has a great little cloister (pop in to see Sicilian Gothic—a 13th-century mix of Norman, Gothic, and Arabic styles).

• *Return to the road and continue downhill, walking through the next square (Piazza della Vittoria), which offers another grand view. Stay on the road closest to the water—it eventually leads to stairs that zigzag down to Marina Grande, Sorrento's big harbor. Just before reaching the harbor, you pass under an...*

Ancient Greek Gate: This gate is a reminder that Marina Grande is a separate town from Sorrento, with its own proud residents. It's said that even their cats look different. Because Marina Grande dwellers lived outside the wall and were more susceptible to rape, pillage, and plunder, Sorrentines believe that they come from Saracen (Turkish pirate) stock. Sorrentines still scare their children by saying, "Behave—or the Turks will take you away."

Marina Grande's economy is still based on its fishing fleet. People respect old traditions. Women wear black when a relative dies (one year for an uncle, aunt, or sibling; 2–3 years for a husband or parent). Men get off easy, just wearing a black button if their loved one dies.

There are two recommended restaurants on the harbor. **Trattoria da Emilia** has an old newspaper clipping, tacked near the door, about Sophia Loren filming here. On the far side of the harbor, **Ristorante Delfino** boasts a sundeck for a lazy drink before or after lunch. (See "Eating in Sorrento" later in this chapter for more details on these places.)

From here, buses return to the center at Piazza Tasso every hour (usually at :25 past the hour, note schedule, €2.40 ticket purchased from *tabacchi* shop).

Sights in Sorrento

▲▲**Strolling**—Take time to explore the surprisingly pleasant old city between Corso Italia and the sea. Views from the public park next to Imperial Hotel Tramontano are worth the detour.

Lemons

Around here, *limoni* are ubiquitous: screaming yellow painted on ceramics, dainty bottles of *limoncello,* and lemons the size of softballs at the fruit stand. The Amalfi Coast and Sorrento area produces several different kinds of lemons.

The gigantic bumpy lemons are actually citrons, called *cedri,* and are more for show—they're pulpier than they are juicy, and make a good marmalade. The juicy *sfusato sorrentino,* grown only in Sorrento, is shaped like an American football, while the *sfusato amalfitano,* with knobby points on both ends, is less juicy but equally aromatic. These two kinds of luscious lemons are used in sweets such as *granita* (shaved ice doused in lemonade), *limoncello* (a candy-like liqueur with a big kick, called *limoncino* on the Cinque Terre), *delizia* (a dome of fluffy cake filled and slathered with a thick whipped lemon cream), *spremuta di limone* (fresh-squeezed lemon juice), and, of course, gelato or *sorbetto alla limone.*

Each night in summer (May–Oct at 19:30; Nov–April weekends only), the police close off the Corso Italia to traffic, and Sorrento's main drag becomes a thriving people scene. The *passeggiata* peaks at about 22:00. (When Piazza Tasso and the main thoroughfare are closed to traffic, buses for Via Capo leave from up on Via degli Aranci, a short walk from Piazza Tasso along Via Fuorimura.)

▲**Lemon Products Galore**—Via San Cesareo is lined with hardworking rival shops selling a mind-boggling array of lemon products and offering samples of lots of sour goodies. Poke around for a pungent experience.

▲**Lemon Grove Garden (Giardini di Cataldo)**—This small park consists of an inviting organic lemon and orange grove lined with shady, welcoming paths. The owners of the grove are seasoned green thumbs, working the orchard through many generations. You'll see that they've even grafted orange-tree branches onto a lemon tree so that both fruits now grow on the same tree. The garden is dotted with benches, tables, and an inviting little tasting (and buying) stand. You'll get a chance to sniff and taste the varieties of lemons, and enjoy free samples of chilled *limoncello* along with various other homemade liqueurs made from basil, mandarins, or fennel (enthusiastically free, daily April–Sept 10:00–20:00, Oct–March 10:00–16:30, tel. 081-807-4040). The main shop selling their organic homemade products and tasty gelato is across from the Corso Italia entrance at #267; a smaller stand is inside. Enter the garden either on Corso Italia (100 yards north of the train station—where painted tiles show lemon fantasies), or at the intersection of Via Capasso and Via Rota (next to the Hotel La Meridiana Sorrento).

▲**Swimming near Sorrento**—If you require immediate tanning, you can rent a chair on the pier by the port. There are no great beaches in Sorrento—the gravelly, jam-packed private beaches of **Marina Piccola** are more for partying than pampering, and there's just a tiny spot for public use.

A sandy beach is two miles away at **Meta.** While the Meta Circumvesuviana stop is a very long walk from the beach (or a €25 cab ride), the orange or red-and-white bus #A goes directly from Piazza Tasso to the Meta beach (last stop, schedule posted for hourly returns). At Meta, you'll find pizzerias, snack bars, and a little free section of beach, but it's mostly dominated by several sprawling private-beach complexes—if you go, pay for a spot in one of these. Lido Metamare seems best (open May–Sept, €2.50 entry; also available are lockable changing cabins, lounge chairs, etc.). It's a very Italian scene—locals complain that it's "too local" (i.e., inundated with Naples' riffraff)—with light lunches, a playground, a manicured beach, loud pop music...and no international tourists.

Tarzan might take Jane to the wild and stony beach at **Punta del Capo,** a 15-minute bus ride from Piazza Tasso (2/hour, get off at stop in front of the American Bar, then walk 10 minutes past ruined Roman Villa di Pollio). From the American Bar bus stop, you can also walk to **Marina di Puolo,** a tiny fishing town popular in the summer for its sandy beach, surfside restaurants, and beachfront disco (15-minute walk, follow signs).

Tennis—The Sorrento Sport Snack Bar has two fine courts open to the public (daily 9:30–23:00, until 20:00 in winter, €12/hour including rackets and balls for two people, call for reservation, across from recommended Grand Hotel Ambasciatori at Via Califano 5, tel. 081-807-1616).

Scuba Diving—To escape the shops, dive deep into the Mediterranean. PADI-certified Futuro Mare offers a one-hour boat ride out to the protected marine zone that lies between

Sorrento and Capri, where you can try the beginners' dive (€90, includes instruction and complete supervision, April–Oct usually daily at 9:30). The boat also takes experienced certified divers (1 dive-€60, 2 dives-€95, April–Oct daily at 9:30 and 14:00). The whole experience takes about three hours, and the prices include all equipment, transportation, and the dive itself, which lasts about 40 minutes for both novices and experts (tel. 081-877-1472, mobile 349-653-6323, call a day or two in advance to reserve, www.sorrentodiving.it).

Boat Rental—You can rent motor boats big enough for four people (€150/day, plus gas—figure about €30 for a trip to Capri; "office" is in souvenir store on eastern part of Marina Piccola—with your back to the ferry-ticket offices, it's to the left at Via Marina Piccola 43, tel. 081-807-2283, www.nauticasicsic.com).

Nightlife in Sorrento

English vacationers come here in droves. Many have holidayed here annually for decades. The town is filled with pubs that try to help British guests feel right at home.

Pubs and Clubs

The English Inn offers both a street-side pub and a more refined-feeling garden out back—at least until the evening, when the stereo starts blaring. Order up baked beans on toast, fish-and-chips, or just a draft beer (daily, 8:30 until after midnight, Corso Italia 55, tel. 081-807-4357).

Photo offers a snapshot of contemporary Italy with a creative food and drink menu, DJ music, and people-watching among stylish Italians on vacation (described later, under "Eating in Sorrento").

The **Foreigners' Club** offers live Neapolitan songs, Sinatra-style classics, and jazzy elevator-type music nightly at 20:00 throughout the summer. It's just right for old-timers feeling frisky (in the center; described earlier under "Helpful Hints").

Theater Show

At **Teatro Tasso,** a hardworking troupe puts on *The Sorrento Musical,* a folk-music show that treats visitors to a schmaltzy dose of Neapolitan Tarantella music and dance—complete with "Funiculì Funiculà" and "Santa Loo-chee-yee-yah." The 75-minute Italian-language extravaganza features a cast of 14 playing guitar, violin, mandolin, and tambourines, and singing operatically from Neapolitan balconies...with Vesuvius erupting in the background. Your ticket includes a drink before and after the show. While tickets normally cost €25, Maurizio promises my readers tickets for

€20 in 2011. He also offers readers a €40 dinner package (normally €50) that includes a four-course meal, drinks, and a seat at the show (discounts good only if you buy tickets directly from their box office and show this book, maximum 2 tickets or dinner packages per book; nightly April–Oct at 21:30, box office and bar open 45 minutes before show, dinner starts at 20:00 and must be reserved in advance, theater seats 350, facing Piazza Sant'Antonino in the old town, tel. 081-807-5525, info@teatrotasso.com).

Sleeping in Sorrento

Hotels here often charge the same for a room whether it has a view, balcony, or neither. At hotels that offer sea views, ask for a room *"con balcone, con vista sul mare"* (with a balcony, with a sea view). *"Tranquillo"* is taken as a request for a quieter room off the street. Hotels listed are either near the train station and city center or along the way to Punta del Capo, a 20-minute walk—or short bus ride—from the station (for locations, see the map on pages 876–877). While many hotels close for the winter, you should have no trouble finding a room any time except in August, when the town is jammed and many hotel prices go way up. Most hotels have two rates: high season (April–Oct) and low. Outside of summer, prices can be soft—it doesn't hurt to ask for a discount (always show this book). Splurge for a hotel with air-conditioning if you wilt in the heat, but be aware that it often costs extra. Note: The spindly, more exotic, and more tranquil Amalfi Coast town of Positano (see next chapter) is also a good place to spend the night.

East of the Center

To reach these hotels, head a block in front of the train station, turn right onto Corso Italia, then left down Via Capasso (which eventually winds right and becomes Via Califano).

$$$ Grand Hotel Ambasciatori is a sumptuous four-star hotel with 100 rooms, a cliffside setting, a sprawling garden, and a pool. This is Humphrey Bogart land, with plush public spaces, a relaxing stay-a-while ambience, and a free elevator to its "private beach"—actually a sundeck built out over the water (viewless Db-€150, sea-view Db-€350, 10 percent discount with this book, prices vary wildly, check website for specials, closed Nov–March, air-con in summer, balconies, Internet access, parking-€18/day, Via Califano 18, tel. 081-878-2025, fax 081-807-1021, www.ambasciatorisorrento.com, ambasciatori@manniellohotels.com).

$$$ Hotel La Meridiana Sorrento, a fine three-star option with everything but character, offers business-class public spaces and 45 soulless rooms (Db-€160, Tb-€190, Qb-€240, discounts often available, air-con, elevator, big rooftop terrace with grand

Sleep Code

(€1 = about $1.25, country code: 39)
S = Single, **D** = Double/Twin, **T** = Triple, **Q** = Quad, **b** = bathroom,
s = shower only. Unless otherwise noted, credit cards are
accepted, English is spoken, and breakfast is included.

To help you sort easily through these listings, I've divided
the rooms into three categories based on the price for a
standard double room with bath:

$$$ **Higher Priced**—Most rooms €140 or more.
$$ **Moderately Priced**—Most rooms between €80–140.
$ **Lower Priced**—Most rooms €80 or less.

Prices can change without notice; verify the hotel's
current rates online or by email. For other updates, see www
.ricksteves.com/update.

views, next door to public Lemon Grove Garden, Via Rota 1, tel.
081-807-3535, fax 081-807-3484, www.lameridianasorrento.com,
info@lameridianasorrento.com).

In the Town Center

$$$ Hotel Antiche Mura, with 50 rooms and four stars, is
sophisticated, elegant, and plush, offering all the amenities you
could need in a hotel. Surrounded by lemon trees, the pool and
sundeck are an oasis. Just a block off the main square, it's cheaper
than other hotels nearby, and quieter too because it faces a ravine
(high-windowed Db-€150, Db-€189, balcony Db-€250, Michele
promises 15 percent off in 2011 if you reserve directly, mention
this book, and pay with cash, about a third cheaper Nov–March,
opulent buffet breakfast, air-con, elevator, Internet access and
Wi-Fi, parking-€10/day, a block inland from Piazza Tasso at
Via Fuorimura 7, tel. 081-807-3523, fax 081-807-1323, www.hotel
antichemura.com, info@hotelantichemura.com).

$$ Casa Astarita B&B is a shining gem in the middle of
town, with a crazy-quilt-tiled entryway. You'll find six bright,
tranquil air-conditioned rooms (three with little balconies) and
a fully stocked communal fridge and sideboard for help-yourself
breakfasts. Despite double-paned windows, pub noise can seep into
some of the rooms (Db-€95–105, Tb-€130, mention this book for
these rates, free Internet access in rustic-yet-elegant common room
and cable Internet in rooms, just past Ristorante Parrucchiano as
you're coming from the station on Corso Italia at #67, tel. 081-
877-4906, fax 081-807-1146, www.casastarita.com, info@casa
starita.com). Reception is open only from March through October

(7:00–19:00). If you visit off-season, check in at their shop next door, "Leaving Astarita," or at Hotel Mignon Meublè (described below)—the same family runs both hotels.

$$ Hotel Mignon Meublè rents 24 elegant, soothing blue rooms in a central location a block off Corso Italia (Sb-€90, Db-€105, Tb-€130, rates good with this book when reserving directly, air-con, free Internet access, rooftop sundeck, some balconies but no views; from station, turn left on Corso Italia—it's a 10-minute walk to Via Sersale 9; tel. 081-807-3824, fax 081-877-4348, www.sorrentohotelmignon.com, info@sorrentohotelmignon .com, sisters Annamaria and Rita, and Annamaria's son Paolo).

$$ Hotel del Corso is a funky Old World three-star hotel with 26 decent rooms. Family-run with few frills, it doesn't get any more central than this (Db-€120, Tb-€160, Qb-€180, email for specials or €10/day discount off these rates if you mention this book and pay with cash, nice breakfast, air-con, rooftop sun terrace, near Piazza Tasso at Corso Italia 134, tel. 081-807-1016, fax 081-807-3157, www.hoteldelcorso.com, info@hoteldelcorso.com, Luca and Imma).

$$ Il Palazzo Starace B&B, a lesser value than other hotels in this price range, offers seven tidy rooms in a little alley off Corso Italia (opposite Hotel del Corso, listed earlier), one block from Piazza Tasso (Db-€95, family room-€150, 10 percent off with cash and this book in 2011, includes small breakfast at a bar around the corner, air-con, no elevator but a luggage dumbwaiter, ring bell at Via Santa Maria della Pietà 9, then climb 3 floors, tel. 081-878-4031, mobile 338-276-1418, fax 081-532-9344, www.palazzostarace .com, info@palazzostarace.com, Giovanna).

$ Ulisse Deluxe Hostel is the best budget deal in town, with public areas that feel more like an elegant hotel than a hostel. The 56 marble-tiled rooms have big private bathrooms, so unless you choose to sleep in its dorm, the only thing hostel-like about this place is the price. It's a great value (Db-€70, Tb-€105, Qb-€140, €25/bunk in 2- to 8-bed single-sex dorm, get these rates by mentioning this book when reserving, breakfast-€5, air-con, Wi-Fi in lobby, spa and pool use extra, hostel membership not required, a 5-minute walk from the old-town action at Via del Mare 22, tel. 081-877-4753, fax 081-877-4093, www.ulissedeluxe.com, info @ulissedeluxe.com).

$ Hotel Nice rents 29 simple, cramped rooms with high ceilings 100 yards in front of the train station on the noisy main drag. Alfonso promises that you can have a quiet room—critical at this busy location—if you request it with your booking email (Db-€75, €85 in Aug; extra bed-€20; 10 percent discount if you book directly, mention this book, and pay with cash; air-con, elevator, rooftop terrace, Corso Italia 257, tel. 081-878-1650, fax

081-878-3086, www.hotelnice.it, info@hotelnice.it).

$ Hostel Le Sirene, a tiny hostel four blocks from the train station, offers 50 of the cheapest beds in town (€18/bunk in 8- to 10-bed dorms with bath, Db-€60; includes tiny breakfast, linens, and towels; cash only, hostel membership not required, no curfew, open year-round, elevator, Internet access, free pass to nearby disco, luggage storage, Via degli Aranci 160, tel. 081-807-2925, fax 081-877-1371, www.hostellesirene.com, info@hostellesirene.com).

With a View on Via Capo

These hotels are outside of town, near the cape (straight out Corso Italia, which turns into Via Capo). Once you're set up, commuting into town on the bus is easy. Hotel Minerva and Albergo Settimo Cielo are my favorite Sorrento splurges, while Hotel Désirée and Hotel Elios are better budget bets. If you're in Sorrento to stay put and luxuriate, these accommodations are perfect (although I'd rather luxuriate in Positano—see next chapter).

Getting to Via Capo: From the city center, it's a 15-minute walk (20 minutes from train station, last part is uphill), a €20 taxi ride, or a cheap bus ride. An occasional Via Capo–bound bus leaves from the train station itself (about every 40 minutes, usually blue or green-and-white SITA buses, direction: Massa, don't take one heading for Positano/Amalfi). Many more buses leave from Piazza Tasso in the city center, a five-minute walk from the station (go down a block and turn left on Corso Italia; look for orange or red-and-white bus #A, under flags, about 3/hour). Tickets for either bus are sold at the station newsstand and *tabacchi* shops (€2.40). Most Via Capo hotels are near the Hotel Belair bus stop. If you're headed to Via Capo after 19:30, when the center (and Piazza Tasso bus stop) is closed to traffic, catch the bus instead on Via degli Aranci (with your back to the station, wind left, up and around it; the bus stop is near the Blue Paradise Bar).

Getting from Via Capo into Town: Buses work great once you get the hang of them (and it's particularly gratifying to avoid the taxi racket). To reach downtown Sorrento from Via Capo, catch any bus heading downhill from Hotel Belair (buses depart at :14, :34, and :54 past the hour, all day and evening).

$$$ Hotel Minerva is like a sun-worshipper's temple. Catch the elevator at Via Capo 32. Getting off on the fifth floor, you'll step onto a spectacular terrace with outrageous Mediterranean views and a small cliff-hanging swimming pool and a cold-water Jacuzzi *con vista*—all complementing 60 large tiled *limoncello* rooms (Db-€160, Tb-€185, Qb-€210, these discounted prices promised with this book through 2011 only if claimed at time of inquiry, air-con, Wi-Fi, parking-€15/day, Via Capo 30, tel. 081-878-1011, fax 081-878-1949, www.minervasorrento.com, minerva@acampora.it).

$$$ Hotel La Tonnarella is an old-time Sorrentine villa with several terraces, stylish tiles, and a dreamy, chandeliered dining room. Eighteen of its 24 rooms have views of the sea (non-view Db-€126, sea-view or balcony Db-€162, Db with view terrace-€203, exotic view suite with terrace-€315, check website for rates, €30/person half-pension available, closed Dec–Feb, air-con, Internet access and free Wi-Fi, small beach with elevator access, Via Capo 31, tel. 081-878-1153, fax 081-878-2169, www .latonnarella.it, info@latonnarella.it).

$$ Albergo Settimo Cielo, the aptly named "Seventh Heaven," offers all the views and lazy resort trappings you could want, and is run by a family that really hustles to provide a fine value. At this old-fashioned cliff-hanger sitting 300 steps above Marina Grande, the reception is just off the waterfront side of the road, and the elevator passes down through four floors with 50 rooms—all with grand views, and many with balconies (Sb-€120, Db-€140, Tb-€180, Qb-€215, check website for specials or ask for 5 percent discount on these rates in 2011 when you mention this book when reserving, air-con in summer, Wi-Fi, free parking, inviting pool and sun terrace, Via Capo 27, tel. 081-878-1012, fax 081-807-3290, www.hotelsettimocielo.com, info@hotelsettimo cielo.com, Giuseppe and sons Stefano and Massimo).

$$ Hotel Désirée is a modest affair, with humbler vistas but no traffic noise. The 22 basic rooms have high ravine-facing or partial sea views, half come with balconies (all same price). Most rooms have fans, and there's a fine rooftop sunning terrace and lovable cats. Eco-friendly Corinna, daughter Cassandra, and staff—Antonio, Aldo, and Enzo—are hugely helpful with tips on exploring the peninsula (Sb-€60, small Db-€75, Db-€85, Tb-€105, Qb-€115, laundry-€8, free parking, shares driveway and beach access with La Tonnarella, Via Capo 31, tel. & fax 081-878-1563, www.desireehotelsorrento.com, info@desireehotelsorrento.com).

$ Hotel Elios, warmly run by Gianna, is humble...much like a Sorrentine *nonna*'s house. It offers 14 simple but spacious rooms—12 with balconies and views—a panoramic sun terrace, and a quiet atmosphere. They don't serve breakfast, but you're welcome to use the kitchen and dining room (Sb-€50, Db-€75, Tb-€95, extra bed-€20, family rooms, cheaper off-season but closed Dec–March, cash only, free parking, Via Capo 33, tel. 081-878-1812, www.hotelelios .it, info@hotelelios.it).

Eating in Sorrento

Gourmet Splurges Downtown

In a town proud to have no McDonald's, consider eating well for a few extra bucks. Both of these places are worthwhile splurges run by a hands-on boss with a passion for good food and exacting service. Be prepared to relax and stay a while.

Ristorante il Buco, once the cellar of an old monastery, is now a small, dressy restaurant that serves delightfully presented, playful, and creative modern dishes under a grand, rustic arch. Peppe and his staff love to explain exactly what's on the plate. The dashing team of cooks builds sophisticated dishes in a state-of-the-art kitchen, while a plasma-screen TV shows all the action. Peppe, who holds the only Michelin star in town, designs his menu around whatever's fresh, and travels in the winter to assemble a wine list sure to offer connoisseurs something new and memorable. Reservations are usually necessary to sit inside under their elegant vault (€18 pastas, €25 *secondi*, dinners run from about €50 plus wine, 10 percent discount when you show this book in 2011, always a good vegetarian selection, extravagant tasting *menù*, Thu–Tue 12:00–15:00 & 19:00–23:00, closed Wed and Jan; just off Piazza Sant'Antonino—facing the basilica, go under the grand arch on the left and immediately enter the restaurant at II Rampa Marina Piccola 5; tel. 081-878-2354).

L'Antica Trattoria serves more traditional cuisine from an inviting menu in a *romantico* candlelit ambience. Run by the same family since 1930, the restaurant has a trellised garden outside and intimate nooks inside (ideal for small groups). Walk around the labyrinthine interior before you select a place to sit. Aldo and sons will take good care of you, while the Joe Cocker–esque resident mandolin player entertains. Their wine list features well-known wines from the region. While there's a €40 four-course meal, you're welcome to eat lighter and save money by choosing only three courses for €35 (€14 for lunch). Or you can order à la carte (€16 pastas, €28 *secondi*, 10 percent discount when you show this book in 2011, always vegetarian options, daily 12:00–23:30, closed Mon Nov–Feb, air-con, reservations smart, Via Padre R. Giuliani 33, tel. 081-807-1082).

Eating Well and Cheaply Downtown

Inn Bufalito, which focuses on regional specialties, backs up its motto: "Eating well is for everyone." In an informal setting, Franco and his staff serve up a changing menu of pizza, pasta, and all things buffalo, including a delicious selection of *mozzarella di bufala* (€7 salads, €8 pasta, no cover charge, daily 12:00–16:00 & 18:00–24:00, closed Mon off-season and all of Jan–Feb, Vico I Fuoro 21, tel. 081-365-6975).

Photo, a sleek and modern place, has a creative menu, secluded garden, and DJ music. Less traditional and more expensive, it's fun for a drink or a unique meal (May–Nov daily 18:00–late, Dec–April open Fri–Sat only, reservations smart, Via Correale 19,

4-minute walk from Piazza Tasso, tel. 081-877-3686).

Ristorante Pizzeria da Gigino, lively and congested, makes huge, tasty Neapolitan-style pizzas in their wood-burning oven (pizza, pasta, and *secondi* all €8–10 each; no cover charge, daily 12:00–24:00, closed Jan–Feb; just off Piazza Sant'Antonino—take first road to the left of Sant'Antonino as you face him, pass under the archway, and take the first left to Via degli Archi 15; tel. 081-878-1927, Antonino).

Ristorante Pizzeria Lanterna Due offers an agreeable family-run atmosphere celebrating the "food, art, and music of Italian cooking," a fun staff, and decent food. Join the other tourists at the long line of tables along the alley, or in the air-conditioned interior (€8 pastas, €9 *secondi*, €2 cover, double-check your bill, daily 12:00–22:00, Via Santa Maria delle Grazie 28, tel. 081-807-4521).

Pizzeria da Franco seems to be Sorrento's favorite place for basic, casual pizza in a fun, untouristy atmosphere. There's nothing fancy about this place—just locals on benches eating hot sandwiches and great pizzas served on waxed paper in a square tin. It's packed to the rafters with a youthful crowd that doesn't mind the plastic cups (€7 pizzas, €5 salads, daily 12:00–2:00 in the morning, just across from Lemon Grove Garden on busy Corso Italia at #265, tel. 081-877-2066).

Picnics: You'll find many markets and take-out pizzerias in the old town. If you fancy a picnic dinner on your balcony, on the hotel terrace, or in the Lemon Grove Garden, get a pizza to go at Pizzeria da Franco (listed above) or groceries at the **Standa supermarket** (Mon–Sat 8:30–13:20 & 16:30–20:15, Sun 9:30–13:00 & 17:00–20:30, Corso Italia 223).

Gelato: A few doors downhill from L'Antica Trattoria, **Davide Gelato** has many repeat customers (so many flavors, so little time). In 1957, Augusto Davide opened the shop, and his grandson, Giovanni, proudly carries on the tradition today (look toward the back, where the gelato is made on-site). Walk the most enticing chorus line in Italy before ordering. Sample *Profumi di Sorrento* (an explosive sorbet of mixed fruits) and lemon crème. They also serve simple meals at fair prices (daily 9:30–24:00, shorter hours and closed Wed off-season, 2 blocks off Corso Italia at Via Padre R. Giuliani 39, tel. 081-878-1337).

At **Gelateria Primavera,** another neighborhood favorite, Antonio and Alberta whip up 70 flavors fresh daily—and still have time to make pastries for the pope (and everybody else—check out the photos). Try the *noce* (walnut, pronounced no-CHAY) or pistacchio in a homemade waffle cone (€3 for up to three flavors, daily 9:00–2:00 in the morning, tel. 081-807-3252, two-minute walk west of Piazza Tasso at Corso Italia 142).

Dinner with Sea Views

For a decent dinner *con vista,* head for a view terrace at one of these restaurants. To get to Marina Grande, where the first two are located, follow the directions from the cliffside square on the "Welcome to Sorrento" walk (described earlier). For a less scenic route, walk down Via del Mare, past the recommended Ulisse Deluxe Hostel, to the harbor. Either way, it's about a 15-minute stroll from downtown. You can also take bus #D from Piazza Tasso (3/hour, €2.40).

Ristorante Delfino gets their seafood right off the fishermen's boats at Marina Grande, and serves it up in big portions to hungry locals in a quiet and bright pier restaurant. The cooking, service, and setting are all top-notch, and the prices are good. The restaurant is lovingly run by effervescent Luisa, her brothers Andrea and Roberto, and her husband Antonio. They take good care of their guests and give travelers who carry this book a little glass of *limoncello* to cap the experience. If you're here for lunch, take advantage of the wonderful sundeck—show this book to get an hour of relaxation and digestion on the lounge chairs (daily 11:30–15:30 & 18:30–23:00, closed Nov–March; at Marina Grande, facing the water, go all the way to the left and follow signs; tel. 081-878-2038).

Trattoria da Emilia, on the tranquil Marina Grande waterfront, is considerably more rustic, less expensive, and good for straightforward, typical Sorrentine home-cooking, including fresh fish and *gnocchi di mamma*—potato dumplings with meat sauce, basil, and mozzarella (daily 12:15–15:00 & 19:30–22:30, closed Tue Nov–Feb, no reservations, indoor and outdoor pier seating, cash only, tel. 081-807-2720).

The **Foreigners' Club Restaurant** has the best sea views in town (under breezy palms), live music nightly at 20:00 (April–Oct), and passable meals. It's a good spot for dessert or an after-dinner *limoncello* (daily, bar opens at 9:30, snacks served all day, dinner 19:00–23:00, Via Luigi de Maio 35, tel. 081-877-3263).

On Via Capo

Hotel Restaurant La Tonnarella takes pride in its kitchen and service. While its dining hall is elegant, its incredible view terrace is where you'll want to be on balmy evenings (reservations smart). This is a good bet for those staying on Via Capo (€18 pastas, €25 *secondi*, good wine list, daily 19:00–22:00 only, Via Capo 31, tel. 081-878-1153).

Verde Mare is the locals' pick for a cheaper place (Thu–Tue 12:30–14:45 & 19:00–23:30, closed Wed, 300 yards uphill from La Tonnarella and other recommended hotels, tel. 081-878-2589).

Sorrento Connections

It's impressively fast to zip by boat from Sorrento to most coastal towns and islands during the summer, when there are many more departures. In fact, it's quicker and easier for residents to get around by fast boat than by car or train (see "By Boat," next page, and the map on page 851).

By Train and Bus

From Sorrento to Naples, Pompeii, and Herculaneum by Circumvesuviana Train: This commuter train runs about every 30 minutes between Naples and Sorrento (less frequently on holidays, www.vesuviana.it). From Sorrento, it's about 30 minutes to Pompeii, 45 minutes to Herculaneum (€1.90 one-way for either trip), and 70 minutes to Naples (€3.40 one-way). When returning to Naples' Centrale Station on the Circumvesuviana, get off at the next-to-the-last station, Garibaldi (Centrale station is just up the escalator). Bonus: When returning from Sorrento, your Circumvesuviana ticket includes a ride anywhere on the Naples Metro system within three hours of validation. The trip is also covered by the Campania ArteCard—see page 829. The schedule is printed in the free *Surrentum* magazine (available at TI). See "Getting Around the Region" in the Naples chapter, page 850, for more information on the Circumvesuviana and theft precautions. Note that the risk of theft is mostly limited to suburban Naples, but can be a problem anywhere. Going between Sorrento and Pompeii or Herculaneum is generally safer.

From Sorrento to the Naples Airport: Six Curreri buses run daily to and from the airport; confirm the schedule at the TI (€10, pay driver, daily at 6:30, 8:30, 10:30, 12:00, 14:00, and 16:30, maybe more in summer—double-check the schedule, 1.25 hours, departs from in front of train station, tel. 081-801-5420, www.curreri viaggi.it).

To the Amalfi Coast: See page 904.

To Rome: Most people ride the Circumvesuviana 70 minutes to Naples, then catch the express train to Rome. However, the direct Sorrento–Rome bus is cheaper, and can actually be more convenient. Marozzi buses leave Sorrento's train station daily for Rome's Tiburtina station (€17.50, Mon–Sat at 6:00 and 17:00, Sun at 17:00, off-season at 17:00 only, 4 hours; buy tickets by phone, at some travel agencies, or on board for a €4 surcharge; also stops at Pompei Scavi and Naples' Port Beverello, tel. 080-579-0111, www.marozzivt.it). A Curreri bus makes the trip as well (€16, departs Mon–Sat at 6:30, 4 hours, tel. 081-801-5420, www.curreri viaggi.it).

By Boat

The number of boats that run per day varies according to the season. The frequency indicated here is for roughly mid-May through September, with a few more boats per day in summer and less off-season. Check all schedules with the TI, your hotel, or online (visit the individual boat company websites—see below—or try www.capritourism.com and click on "Shipping timetable"). The Caremar line, a subsidized state-run ferry company, takes cars, offers fewer departures, and is just a bit slower—but cheaper—than the other boat. All of the boats take about 500 people each—and frequently fill up.

From Sorrento to Capri: Boats run at least hourly. Your options include a **ferry** (*traghetto* or *nave veloce*, 4/day, 25 minutes, €9.80, run by Caremar, tel. 081-807-3077, www.caremar.it) or a faster but pricier **jet boat** (*aliscafi*, 18/day, 20 minutes, €14, run by Gescab, tel. 081-807-1812, www.gescab.it). To avoid the crowds on Capri, it's best to buy your ticket at 8:00 and take the 8:25 jet boat (if you miss it, try to depart by 9:30 at the very latest). These early boats can be jammed, but it's worth it once you reach the island.

From Sorrento to Other Points: Naples (5/day, departs roughly every 2 hours, 35 minutes, €10; for more info, see page 852), **Positano** (4/day, late April–mid-Oct only, 30 minutes, €9), **Amalfi** (4/day, late April–mid-Oct only, 1.25 hours, €11, www.metrodelmare.com). For a slightly less touristy alternative to Capri, consider the nearby island of **Ischia** (1/day, Easter–Nov only, departure usually around 9:30; more frequent from Naples, 55 minutes, €35 round-trip).

Getting to Sorrento's Port: To get from Sorrento's Piazza Tasso to Marina Piccola (the port), walk down the stairs near the statue's left side (about 10 minutes). Or you can catch a red-and-white bus #B or #C (3/hour, €1, buy ticket at *tabacchi*) or the little blue bus (4/hour, €1, buy ticket from driver). Boat tickets are sold only at the port.

Capri

Capri was made famous as the vacation hideaway of Roman emperors Augustus and Tiberius. In the 19th century, it was the haunt of Romantic Age aristocrats on their Grand Tour of Europe. But these days, the island is a world-class tourist trap, packed with gawky name tag–wearing visitors searching for the rich and famous, and finding only their prices.

The "Island of Dreams" is a zoo in July and August—overrun with tacky, low-grade group tourism at its worst. Other times of

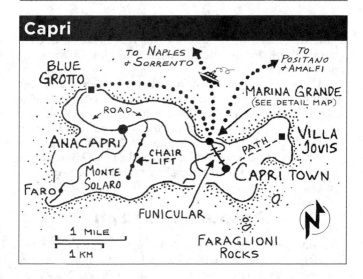

Capri

BLUE GROTTO

TO NAPLES & SORRENTO

TO POSITANO & AMALFI

MARINA GRANDE (SEE DETAIL MAP)

ROAD

ANACAPRI

CHAIR LIFT

Monte Solaro

FARO

FUNICULAR

PATH

VILLA JOVIS

CAPRI TOWN

N

1 MILE
1 KM

FARAGLIONI ROCKS

year, while still crowded, it can provide a relaxing and scenic break from the cultural gauntlet of Italy.

Planning Your Time

This is the best day-trip plan from Sorrento: Take an early jet boat to Capri (buy ticket at 8:00, boat leaves at 8:25 and arrives at 8:45—smart). Go directly to the Blue Grotto, then catch a

bus from the grotto to Anacapri and ride the chairlift to Monte Solaro. From the summit, return by chairlift (or hike down). Stroll out from the base of the chairlift to Villa San Michele for the view, then catch a bus to Capri town for the rest of your stay. At the end of the day, ride the funicular down to Marina Grande (kill time lazing on the free beach or wandering the yacht harbor) to catch the boat back to Sorrento.

Efficient travelers can make a quick trip here between destinations: Sail from Sorrento, check your bag at the harbor, see Capri, and boat directly from here to Naples.

If you buy a one-way ticket to Capri (there's no round-trip discount), you'll have maximum schedule flexibility and can take either the ferry or the jet boat back. (Check times for the last return crossing upon arrival; on Capri, get a schedule from the TI or check at boat-ticket kiosk or automated boat-departure board.) During July and August, however, it's wise to get a round-trip boat ticket with a late return (improving your odds of getting a spot on a boat when they're most crowded)—and you can use the ticket to return earlier if you like. Be 20 minutes early for the boat, or you can be bumped.

Day-trippers come down from Rome, creating a daily rush hour in each direction (arriving between 10:00–11:00, leaving around 17:00). The trip to the Blue Grotto is just a 20-minute boat ride from the arrival dock, but the commotion there can amount to a two-hour delay (described later, under "Sights in Capri"). If you're heading to Capri specifically to see the Blue Grotto, be sure to check that the tide isn't too high or the water too rough—ask the TI or your hotelier before heading over.

Orientation to Capri

First thing—pronounce it right: KAH-pree, not kah-PREE like the song or the pants. The island is small—just four miles by two miles—and is separated from the Sorrento Peninsula by a narrow strait. There are only two towns to speak of: Capri and Anacapri. The island also has some scant Roman ruins and a few interesting churches and villas. But its chief attraction is its famous Blue Grotto, and its best activity is a chairlift up the island's Monte Solaro.

Arrival in Capri

For instructions on getting from Sorrento to Capri, see page 892. Get oriented on the boat before you dock. As you near the harbor, Capri spreads out before you: The port is called **Marina Grande** (TI, boats to Blue Grotto, buses to anywhere, funicular to the town of Capri). **Capri town** fills the ridge high above the harbor. The ruins of Emperor Tiberius' palace, **Villa Jovis,** cap the peak on the left. The dramatic *"Mamma mia!"* road arcs around the highest mountain on the island **(Monte Solaro)** on the right, leading up to **Anacapri** (the island's second town, just out of sight). Notice the old zigzag steps below that road. Until 1874, this was the only connection between Capri and Anacapri. (Though it's quite old, it's nowhere near as old as its nickname, "The Phoenician Stairway," implies.) The white house on the ridge above the zigzags is **Villa San Michele** (where you'll go later for a grand view of boats like the one you're on now).

Upon arrival, get your bearings. Boats dock in two places: on the long pier and directly by the main street. If your boat arrives on the main street, take a right to get to the long pier. Stand with your back to the pier: The **funicular** is across the street. The fourth little shop to the right of the funicular (no sign, sells clothes and souvenirs) provides **baggage storage** in the back of the store (€3/day

Capri Harbor

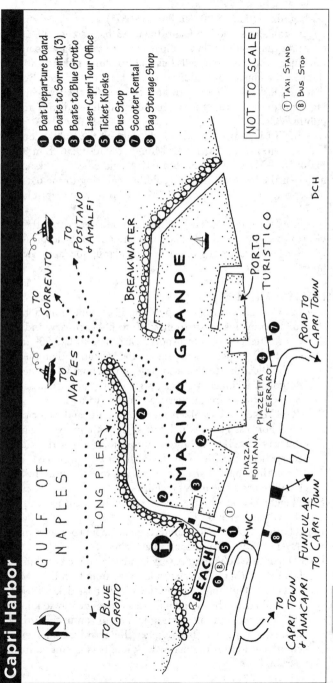

1 Boat Departure Board
2 Boats to Sorrento (3)
3 Boats to Blue Grotto
4 Laser Capri Tour Office
5 Ticket Kiosks
6 Bus Stop
7 Scooter Rental
8 Bag Storage Shop

NOT TO SCALE

T TAXI STAND
B BUS STOP

GULF OF NAPLES

TO BLUE GROTTO

TO NAPLES

TO SORRENTO

TO POSITANO + AMALFI

LONG PIER

MARINA GRANDE

BREAKWATER

PORTO TURISTICO

PIAZZA FONTANA

PIAZZETTA A. FERRARO

ROAD TO CAPRI TOWN

BEACH

WC

FUNICULAR TO CAPRI TOWN

TO CAPRI TOWN + ANACAPRI

DCH

per bag, daily 9:00–18:00, tel. 081-837-4575). If it's closed, try the upper funicular station in Capri town (€3/bag, daily 7:00–20:00; be aware that you may have to pay extra to take big bags up the funicular). The kiosk that sells **bus and funicular tickets** is to your right in the cluster of buildings at the start of the pier. Behind that are kiosks that sell return **boat tickets** (for the two competing companies). Across the street and uphill from all this are the **public WCs.**

The **TI** is near the ticket kiosk, right by the stubby dock for Blue Grotto boats (April–Oct Mon–Sat 8:30–19:30, Sun 9:00–15:00; Nov–March Mon–Sat 9:00–15:00, closed Sun; pick up free map—or the better €1 map if you'll be venturing to the outskirts of Capri town or Anacapri, tel. 081-837-0634, www.capritourism .com).

From the port, you have three transit options: boat to the Blue Grotto (best early—ideally upon arrival), bus to Anacapri (often with long and frustrating lines), or funicular up to Capri town (4/hour, 5 minutes).

Helpful Hints

Cheap Tricks: A cheap day trip to Capri is tough. From Sorrento to Capri by boat costs from €9.80 to €14 each way, and Blue Grotto tickets (plus transportation) come to €22.50—that's about €40–55 per person. Taking the bus rather than the boat to the Blue Grotto (see next page) saves about €8 per person. Although technically illegal, after 18:00, anyone can see the Blue Grotto for free, if you're willing to swim in.

Best Real Hike: Serious hikers love the peaceful and scenic three-hour Fortress Hike, which takes you entirely away from the tourists. You'll walk under ruined forts along the rugged coast, from the Blue Grotto to the *faro* (lighthouse). From there, three buses per hour return you to Anacapri. The tourist office has a fine map/brochure.

Free Beach: Marina Grande has a free pebbly beach. You can get a shower at the bar for €1.

Local Guide: Roberta Mazzarella is good (about €50/hour, mobile 339-135-7619, robertamazzarella@yahoo.it).

Boat Departure Schedule: A very handy electronic board lists all boats departing in the next hour or so from Capri. It's on the end of the building between the TI and boat-ticket kiosk (on the wall facing the mainland). This is the one way to know all the departure options coming up and to confirm your boat's departure time and dock number. The board includes a small chart that locates the many dock numbers in this confusing harbor.

Getting Around Capri

The buses and funicular are covered by the same ticket options: €1.40 per ride (two single tickets are the easiest option if going straight to Blue Grotto by public bus—one to get to Anacapri, then one to get to the Blue Grotto), €2.20 for one hour of unlimited use (even better for the Blue Grotto), or €7.90 for an all-day pass (includes deposit, turn it in at the end of the day to get €1 back). Single-ride tickets are often available at newsstands, tobacco shops *(tabacchi)*, or from the driver. Unlimited use and all-day passes are usually sold only at official ticket offices. Consider an all-day pass if you plan to take more than five rides on the buses and funicular (possible if you go by bus to the Blue Grotto and spend some time in each town). Schedules are clearly posted at all bus stations. Taxis have steep and fixed rates (Marina Grande to Capri-€15; Marina Grande to Anacapri-€20). You can hire a taxi for about €70 per hour—negotiate.

Buses and Funicular from the Port at Marina Grande: Buses pick up just uphill from where you bought your ticket. Get in line under the appropriate sign: either under *San Costanzo* for going up to the town of **Capri** (at least 4/hour), where you could then transfer to Anacapri (4/hour, 10 minutes, there's routinely a long queue for this Capri–Anacapri bus); or direct to **Anacapri** (sporadic schedule, but about every 40 minutes). For most people, the best way from the port to Anacapri is to take the funicular to Capri (4/hour, on the quarter-hour, takes 5 minutes), and then bus from there to Anacapri.

Buses from Anacapri: To use the buses smartly in Anacapri, you need to know that there are two stops: the town center (Piazza Vittoria) and the cemetery stop (Piazza della Pace—pronounced "PAH-chay"—just 200 yards farther down the main road; residents may refer to it by its former name, Piazza del Cimitero). Buses to **Capri town** (at least 4/hour) can be packed. Guarantee a seat by catching the bus from the Piazza della Pace stop, one stop before most people get on. Anacapri–Blue Grotto buses depart only from this stop (not from the town center). If you're coming from the town of Capri and want to transfer to the **Blue Grotto** buses, don't get off when the driver announces "Anacapri." Instead, ride one more stop, then transfer to the Grotta Azzurra (Blue Grotto) buses. If in doubt, ask the driver or a local.

Boat Trips Around the Island: Laser Capri runs quick trips around the island, passing stunning cliffs, caves, and views that most miss when they go only to the Blue Grotto. If you have an hour, it's well worth the extra €3. Their tiny ticket window faces dock #23 at Marina Grande, from where its boats offer three excursions: circle of the island without grotto stop (1 hour, €14), circle the island with a grotto stop (2 hours, €14), and just to the grotto and back (1 hour, €11). The €11.50 grotto admission is always extra (boats leave 9:30–16:30, Via Don Giobbe Ruocco 45, tel. 081-837-5208, www.lasercapri.com). Another company, Motoscafisti Capri, offers the trip for the same price (see listings under the "Blue Grotto," page 899).

Scooter Rental: If you like riding a scooter, this is the perfect way to have the run of the island, although the steep and narrow roads aren't ideal for novice riders. Ciro proudly rents 40 bright-yellow scooters with 50cc engines—strong enough to haul couples. Rental includes a map and instructions with parking tips and other helpful information (€15/hour, €55/day, €5 discount with this book for 2 hours or more in 2011; includes helmet, gas, and insurance; daily 9:00–19:00, Via Don Giobbe Ruocco 55, Marina Grande, tel. 081-837-8018, mobile 338-360-6918, www.capriscooter.com).

Sights in Capri

Capri Town

This is a cute but extremely touristy shopping town. The *funiculare* drops you just around the corner from Piazza Umberto, the

town's main square. The **TI** fills a closet under the bell tower on Piazza Umberto (less crowded than its sister on the port and with longer hours: Mon–Sat 8:30–20:30, Sun 9:00–15:00, tel. 081-837-0686, WC and bag storage downstairs behind TI). With your back to the funicular, the bus stop is 50 yards down Via Roma.

Capri's multi-domed Baroque **cathedral,** which faces the square, is worth a quick look. (Its multicolored marble floor at the altar was scavenged from the Roman Emperor's villa in the 19th century.)

To the left of City Hall (Municipio, lowest corner), a lane leads into the medieval part of town, which has plenty of eateries. The lane to the left of the cathedral (past Bar Tiberio, under the wide arch) has been dubbed "Rodeo Drive" by residents because it's the fashion shopping strip. Walk down Rodeo Drive (past Gelateria Buonocore at #35, famous for its fresh waffle cones) to Quisisana Hotel, the island's top old-time hotel. From there, head left for fancy shops and villas, and right for gardens and views. Downhill and to the right, a five-minute walk leads to a lovely public garden, Giardini Augusto (free, daily 9:00–18:30).

Villa Jovis and the Emperor's Capri

Even before becoming emperor, Augustus loved Capri so much he traded the family-owned Isle of Ischia to the (then-independent) Neapolitans in exchange for making Capri his personal property. Emperor Tiberius spent a decade here, 26–37 A.D. (Some figure he did so in order to escape being assassinated in Rome.)

Emperor Tiberius' ruined villa, Villa Jovis, is a scenic 45-minute hike from Capri town (€2, daily 9:00–19:00, closes earlier off-season, tel. 081-837-4549). You won't find any statues or mosaics here—just an evocative, ruined complex of terraces fitting a rocky perch over a sheer drop to the sea...and a lovely view. You can make out a large water reservoir for baths, the foundations of servants' quarters, and Tiberius' private apartments (fragments of marble flooring still survive). The ruined lighthouse dates from the Middle Ages.

▲▲Blue Grotto

Three thousand tourists a day spend a couple of hours visiting Capri's Blue Grotto *(Grotta Azzurra)*. I did—early (when the light is best), without the frustration of crowds, and with choppy waves nearly making entrance impossible...and it was great.

The actual cave experience isn't much: a five-minute dinghy ride through a three-foot-high entry hole to reach a 60-yard-long cave, where the sun reflects brilliantly blue on its limestone bot-

tom. But the experience—getting there, getting in, and getting back—is a scenic hoot. You get a fast ride on a 30-foot boat partway around the gorgeous island; along the way you see bird life and dramatic limestone cliffs with scant narration. You'll understand why Roman emperors appreciated the invulnerability of the island—it's surrounded by cliffs, with only one access point, and therefore easy to defend.

At the grotto's "distribution center," you pile into eight-foot dinghies with other tourists; from there, ruffian rowers elbow their way to the tiny hole and pull fast and hard on the cable at the low point of the swells to squeeze you into the grotto. Then your man rows you around, spouting off a few descriptive lines and singing "O Sole Mio." Depending upon the strength of the sunshine that day, the blue light inside is brilliant.

The grotto was actually an ancient Roman *nymphaeum*—a retreat for romantic hanky-panky. Many believe that, in its day, a tunnel led here directly from a palace, and that the grotto experience was enlivened by statues of Poseidon and company, placed half-underwater as if emerging from the sea. It was ancient Romans who smoothed out the entry hole used to this day.

Typically, your boatman will extort an extra tip out of you before taking you back outside to your big boat (€2 is more than enough, but you don't need to pay a penny...you've already paid plenty).

Cost and Logistics: Two companies make the boat trip from Marina Grande—Motoscafisti Capri and Laser Capri (€11 round-trip, no discount for one-way, daily from 9:00 until an hour before sunset, closes earlier off-season, boats don't run in stormy weather or during high tides—check this out *before* you purchase boat tickets; Motoscafista Capri—tel. 081-837-7714, www.motoscafisticapri.com; Laser Capri—tel. 081-837-5208, www.lasercapri.com).

Once you reach the grotto, you pay €7.50 for a rowboat to take you in for the five-minute row around the inside of the grotto (after your rower jockeys for position for at least 20 minutes), plus €4 to cover the admission to the grotto (€11.50 total for grotto visit, not counting €11 round-trip ride from port; again, tip entirely optional). While technically against the rules, some people dive in for free after 18:00, when the boats stop running—a magical experience and a favorite among locals.

When the waves or high tide make entering dangerous, the boats don't go in—the grotto can close with no notice, sending tourists (flush with anticipation) home without a chance to squeeze through the little hole. (If this happens to you, consider a one-hour €14 boat ride around the island—including a look at the Faraglioni Rocks—offered by both companies.)

You can take the boat back, or request to be dropped off on a small dock next to the grotto to return by bus to Anacapri (no discount for one-way boat ticket, stairs lead to bus stop, schedule posted at the stop, roughly 3/hour, buy ticket from driver). If you're on a budget, you can take the bus from Anacapri directly to the grotto (rather than a boat from Marina Grande). You'll save about €8, and see a beautiful, calmer side of the island (every 20 minutes from Piazza della Pace, a 200-yard walk on the main road beyond the Piazza Vittoria bus stop in Anacapri; €2.20 ticket valid one hour, usually enough time to visit the grotto and take the bus back to town).

If you're coming from Capri's port, allow 1–3 hours for the entire visit, depending on the chaos at the caves (an early trip will get you there at the same time as the boatmen in their dinghies—who hitch a ride behind your boat—resulting in less chaos and a shorter wait at the entry point).

Anacapri

Capri's second town has no sea views but some fun and interesting activities. From the busy Piazza Vittoria, where the bus drops you, head 40 yards down the pedestrian street to reach the tiny **TI** (Mon–Sat 8:30–17:30, Sun 9:00–15:00, often closed Nov–Easter, Via Orlandi 59, tel. 081-837-1524).

For a sweeping island view, go to the top of the stairs in Piazza Vittoria, and take the pedestrian path that heads left, past the deluxe Capri Palace Hotel (venture in if you can get past the treacherously eye-catching swimming pool windows), and below the Villa San Michele. (The view is even better from the villa—see below.)

Villa San Michele—The 19th-century mansion of Capri's grand personality, Axel Munthe, offers an insight into the scene here when this was the only comfortable refuge for Europe's artsy gay community. Oscar Wilde, D. H. Lawrence, and company hung out here back when being gay could land you in jail...or worse. Munthe, a Swedish doctor who lived here until 1949, left this impressive mansion littered with Roman statues, the Olivetum (museum of native birds and bugs), and a delightful garden. From the sphinx, you'll enjoy one of Capri's best views.

Cost and Hours: €6, daily 9:00–18:00, tel. 081-837-1401.

▲St. Michael's Church—This church has a remarkable majolica floor showing paradise on earth in a classic 18th-century Neapolitan style. The entire floor is ornately tiled, featuring an angel (with flaming sword) driving Adam and Eve from paradise. The devil is wrapped around the trunk of a beautiful tree. The animals—happily ignoring this momentous event—all have human expressions. For the best view, climb the spiral stairs from the postcard desk.

Cost and Hours: €2, daily April–Oct 9:00–19:00, Nov–March 10:00–14:00, in town center—after the TI continue walking 5 minutes and take a right to the church, tel. 081-837-2396.

Faro—The lighthouse is a favorite place to enjoy the sunset, with a private beach, pool, small restaurants, and a few fishermen. Reach it by bus from Anacapri (3/hour, departs from Piazza della Pace stop).

▲▲Chairlift up to Monte Solaro—From Anacapri, ride the

chairlift to the 1,900-foot summit of Monte Solaro for a commanding view of the Bay of Naples. Work on your tan as you float over hazelnut, walnut, chestnut, apricot, peach, kiwi, and fig trees and past a montage of tourists (mostly cruise-ship types; when the grotto is closed—as it often is—they bring passengers here instead). As you ascend, consider how real estate has been priced out of the locals' reach. The ride takes 15 minutes each way, and you'll want at least 30 minutes on top.

At the summit, you'll enjoy the best panorama possible: lush cliffs busy with seagulls enjoying the ideal nesting spot. The Faraglioni Rocks—with tour boats squeezing through every few minutes—are an icon of the island. The pink building nearest the rocks was an American R&R base during World War II. Eisenhower and Churchill met here. On the peak closest to Cape Sorrento, you can see the distant ruins of the Emperor Tiberius' palace, Villa Jovis. Pipes from the Sorrento Peninsula bring water to Capri (demand for fresh water here long ago exceeded the supply provided by the island's three natural springs). The Galli Islands mark the Amalfi Coast in the distance. Cross the bar terrace for views of Mount Vesuvius and Naples (€9 round-trip, €7 one-way, daily June–Oct 9:30–17:00, last run down at 17:30, closes earlier Nov–May, confirm schedule with TI, departs from top of the steps in Piazza Vittoria—the first Anacapri bus stop, tel. 081-837-1428).

A highlight for hardy walkers (provided you have strong knees and good shoes) is the 40-minute downhill hike from the top of Monte Solaro, through lush vegetation and ever-changing views, past the 14th-century Chapel of Santa Maria Cetrella (at the trail's only intersection, it's a 10-minute detour to the right), and back into Anacapri. The trail starts downstairs, past the WCs (last chance). Down two more flights of stairs, look for the sign to *Anacapri e Cetrella*—you're on your way. While the trail is well-established, you'll encounter plenty of uneven steps, loose rocks, and few signs.

Capri Connections

From Capri's Marina Grande by Boat to: Positano (mid-April–Sept only; 2–4/day, 35–50 minutes, €16), **Amalfi** (mid-April–Sept only; 2–4/day, 50–75 minutes, €15–17), **Sorrento** (fast ferry: 4/day, 25 minutes, €9.80, jet boat: 18/day, 20 minutes, €14), **Naples** (roughly 2/hour, 45 minutes, €16), **Salerno** (2/day, 2 hours, €16). Confirm the schedule carefully—last boats usually leave between 18:00 and 20:10. All departing boats are listed at the port on a handy lighted schedule board, which notes exact dock locations for each departure (facing the taxis, the board is just around the corner from the TI).

AMALFI COAST AND PAESTUM

With its stunning scenery, hill- and harbor-hugging towns, and historic ruins, Amalfi is Italy's coast with the most. The bus trip from Sorrento to Salerno along the breathtaking Amalfi Coast is one of the world's great bus rides. It will leave your mouth open and your camera's memory full. You'll gain respect for the Italian engineers who built the roads in the 1800s—and even more respect for the bus drivers who drive it today. Cantilevered garages, hotels, and villas cling to the vertical terrain, and beautiful sandy coves tease from far below and out of reach. As you hyperventilate, notice how the Mediterranean, a sheer 500-foot drop below, really twinkles. All this beautiful scenery apparently inspires local Romeos and Juliets, with the evidence of late-night romantic encounters littering the roadside turnouts. Over the centuries, the spectacular scenery and climate have been a siren call for the rich and famous, luring Roman emperor Tiberius, Richard Wagner, Sophia Loren, Gore Vidal, and others to the Amalfi Coast's special brand of *la dolce vita*.

Planning Your Time

On a quick trip, use Sorrento as your home base and do the Amalfi Coast as a day trip. But for a small-town vacation from your vacation, spend a few more days on the coast, perhaps sleeping in Positano or Amalfi town.

Trying to decide between staying in Sorrento, Positano, or Amalfi? Sorrento is the largest of the three, with the best transportation connections. Positano is the most chic and picturesque, with a decent beach. The town of Amalfi has the most actual sights and the best hiking opportunities.

Getting Around the Amalfi Coast

Amalfi Coast towns are pretty but are generally touristy, congested, overpriced, and a long hike above tiny, pebbly beaches. Most beaches are private, and access is expensive. Check and understand your bills in this greedy region. The real thrill here is the scenic Amalfi drive. This is treacherous stuff—even if you have a car, you may want to take the bus or hire a taxi. Some enjoy seeing the coast by scooter or motorbike (rent in Sorrento). The most logical springboard for this trip is Sorrento (see previous chapter), but Positano and Amalfi work, too.

Many travelers do the Amalfi Coast as a round-trip by bus, but a good strategy is to go one way by bus and return by boat. For example, instead of busing from Sorrento to Salerno (end of the line) and back, consider taking the bus to Salerno, then catching the ferry back to Amalfi or Positano, and from either town, hop a ferry to Sorrento.

Perhaps the simplest option is to take the bus to Positano and boat from there back to Sorrento (or vice-versa). Note that ferry service for this trip decreases off-season to only weekends (mid-Oct–May), and that boats don't run in stormy weather.

Looking for exercise? Consider an Amalfi Coast hike (see "Hikes" on page 924). Numerous trails connect the main towns along the coast with villages on the hills. Get a good map and/or book before you venture out.

By Bus

From Sorrento: SITA buses depart from Sorrento's train station nearly hourly (in peak season, 20/day, marked *Amalfi via Positano*) and stop at all Amalfi Coast towns (Positano in 50 minutes; Amalfi in another 50 minutes), ending up in Salerno at the far end of the coast in about three hours (easy transfer in Amalfi; return trips might also transfer in Positano). Ticket prices vary with trip length (45-minute ride, good for trips within the city-€2.40, 90-minute ride, good to Positano-€3.60, 24-hour All Amalfi Coast ticket, good to Amalfi and beyond-€7.20, 3-day ticket-€18). For most trips, you'll want the 24-hour All Amalfi Coast ticket. Buses start running as early as 6:30 and run as late as 22:00 in summer. Buy tickets at the tobacco shop nearest any bus stop before boarding.

A ticket booth is across from the bus stop (April–Oct daily 8:30–13:30), but the *tabacchi*/newsstand at street level in the train station is more reliable (daily 7:00–13:30 & 14:30–20:00, also sells

Getting Around the Amalfi Coast

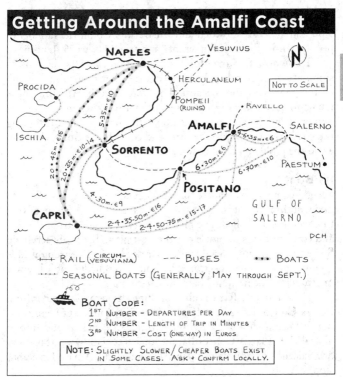

- ┼┼┼ RAIL (CIRCUM-VESUVIANA)
- ––– BUSES
- ••• BOATS
- ···· SEASONAL BOATS (GENERALLY MAY THROUGH SEPT.)

BOAT CODE:
1ST NUMBER – DEPARTURES PER DAY
2ND NUMBER – LENGTH OF TRIP IN MINUTES
3RD NUMBER – COST (ONE-WAY) IN EUROS

NOTE: SLIGHTLY SLOWER / CHEAPER BOATS EXIST IN SOME CASES. ASK + CONFIRM LOCALLY.

train tickets). If both are closed, try Bar Frisby, just down the hill.

Line up under the *Bus Stop SITA* sign (where a schedule is posted on the wall) across from the Sorrento train station (10 steps down). Carefully note the lettered codes that differentiate daily buses from weekend-only buses. *Giornaliero* means daily; *Feriale* notes Monday–Saturday departures; and *Festivo* is for Sundays and holidays. After 19:30 (and sometimes on Sundays—check the sign at the main bus stop), buses leave from Via degli Aranci (with your back to the station, go left and wind around it; the bus stop is near the Blue Paradise Bar).

Leaving Sorrento, grab a seat on the right for the best views. If you return by bus, it's fun to sit directly behind the driver for a box seat with a view over the twisting hairpin action. Sitting toward the front will also minimize carsickness.

Avoiding Crowds on the Bus: Buses are routinely unable to handle the demand during summer months and holidays. Occasionally, an extra bus is added to handle the overflow. Generally, if you don't get on, you're well-positioned to catch the next bus (bring a book). Try to arrive early in the morning. Remember that buses start taking off as early as 6:30; beginning at 8:30, they depart about every 30 minutes. Departures between 9:00 and 11:00 are crowded and frustrating. Count the number of people in line: Buses pull in empty and seat 48 (plus 25 standing).

Returning to Sorrento: The congestion can be so bad in the summer—particularly July and August—that return buses don't even stop in Positano (because they were filled in Amalfi). Those trying to get back to Sorrento are stuck with taking an extortionist taxi or, if in Positano, hopping a boat...if one's running. If touring the coast by bus, do Positano first and come home from Amalfi to avoid the problem of full buses.

By Boat

Several companies compete for passengers, and generally claim to know nothing about their rivals' services. It's wise any time of year to check posted schedules, pick up ferry schedules from the TI, and confirm times to figure out the best plan. The boats servicing Sorrento, Positano, and Amalfi operate late April through mid-October (4/day, buy ticket on dock, pick up schedule at TI, www.metrodelmare.com). No boats run off-season.

From Salerno, ferries run from June through September from Piazza Concordia to Amalfi (4–6/day, 35 minutes, €6), continuing to Positano (6/day, 70 minutes total, €10; tickets and info at TravelMar, Piazza Concordia, tel. 089-872-950, www.travelmar.it). Salerno's dock is conveniently located at the Amalfi Coast bus stop.

By Taxi

Given the hairy driving, impossible parking, congested buses, and potential fun, you might consider splurging to hire your own car and driver for the Amalfi day. (Don't bother for Pompeii, as the Circumvesuviana train serves it conveniently and only licensed guides can take you into the site.)

Fun-loving **Carmello Monetti** (a jolly, singing, in-love-with-life grandfatherly type who speaks non-stop "inventive English"), his son **Raffaele** (much better English, fewer smiles, more information), and brother-in-law **Tony** (similar to Raffaele) have long taken excellent care of my readers' transportation needs from Sorrento.

Sample trips and rates for their comfortable Mercedes or Jaguar taxis: Amalfi Coast Day (Positano–Amalfi with time for lunch in Ravello), eight hours, €240; Amalfi Coast and Paestum, 10 hours, €330; transfer to Naples airport or train station, one hour, €110. To get these special prices (promised for up to three people through 2011), mention this book.

The Monettis also do other excursions and can take up to eight passengers—at a higher rate schedule—in their air-conditioned Mercedes van. Payment is by cash only. Their reservation system is simple and reliable (Raffaele's mobile 335-602-9158 or 338-946-2860, "office" run by Raffaele's English-speaking wife, Susanna, fax 081-807-4531, www.monettitaxi17.it, monettitaxi17@libero.it).

Be careful: Many cabbies claim to be the Monettis. The real Monettis (Raffaele and Carmello are pictured on the previous page) drive Mercedes vantaxi #17, usually found at Sorrento's Piazza Tasso. Carmello's specialty is helping Italian Americans find their families in southern Italy. Email him in advance if you want to find your long-lost relatives, and he can put together a meeting and transportation package. If in any kind of a jam, call Raffaele's mobile phone for information.

Umberto and Giovanni Benvenuto offer transport and narrated excursions throughout the Amalfi Coast, as well as to Rome, Naples, Pompeii, and more. While as friendly as the Monettis, they're more up-market and formal, with steeper rates explained on their website (tel. 089-874-024, mobile 346-684-0226, US tel. 310-424-5640, www.benvenutolimos.com, info@benvenutolimos.com).

Sorrento Silver Star is a car service recommended by readers for their punctuality, professionalism, and pricing (tel. 081-877-1224, www.sorrentosilverstar.com).

Anthony Buonocore is based in Amalfi but does excursions and transfers throughout the region in his more basic but air-conditioned six-person van (rates vary depending on trip, tel. 349-441-0336, www.amalfitransfer.com, buonocoreanthony@yahoo.it).

Rides Only: If you're hiring a cabbie off the street for a ride and not a tour, here are sample fares from Sorrento to Positano: up to four people one-way for about €80 in a car, or up to six people for €90 in a minibus. Figure on paying 50 percent more to Amalfi. While taxis must use a meter within a city, a fixed rate is OK otherwise. Negotiate—ask about a round-trip.

Self-Guided Bus Tour

Hugging the Amalfi Coast

The trip from Sorrento to Salerno is one of the all-time great white-knuckle rides. Gasp from the right side of the bus as you go out and from the left as you return to Sorrento. (Those on the wrong side really miss out.) Traffic is so heavy that private tour buses are only allowed to go in one direction (southbound from Sorrento)—summer traffic is infuriating. Fluorescent-vested policemen are posted at tough bends during peak hours to help

Amalfi Coast

GULF OF NAPLES

TO NAPLES

A-3

POMPEI TOWN

TORRE ANNUNCIATA

CASTELLAMARE DI STABIA

POMPEII RUINS

TO NAPLES

VICO EQUENSE

S-366

MONTE

AGEROLA

PUNTA DEL CAPO

META

MARINA DI PRAINO

SORRENTO

S-145

S-163

ST. PETERS HOTEL

PR

SANT' AGATA

POSITANO

TERMINI

MARINA DEL CANTONE

GALLI ISLANDS

MOST

TO CAPRI

fold in side-view mirrors and keep things moving.

Here's a loosely guided tour of what you're seeing, from west to east (note that many of the towns are described in greater detail later in this chapter):

Leaving Sorrento, the road winds up into the hills past lemon groves and hidden houses. Traveling the coast, you'll see several watchtowers placed within sight of each other, so that a relay of rooftop bonfires could spread word of a Saracen (Turkish pirate) attack. The gray-green trees are olives. Dark, green-leafed trees planted in dense groves are the

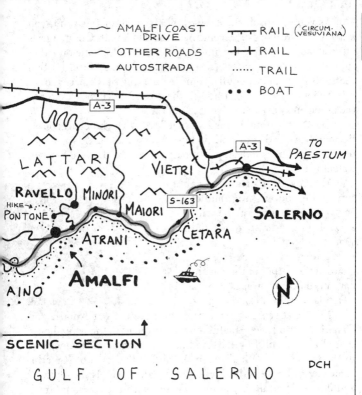

source of the region's lemons—many destined to become *limoncello* liqueur. The black nets over the orange and lemon groves create a greenhouse effect, trapping warmth and humidity for maximum tastiness.

Atop the ridge outside of Sorrento, look to your right: The two small islands after Sorrento are the **Galli Islands;** the bigger one, on the left, is Ulysses Island (see page 876 for the ancient connection). These islands, once owned by the famed ballet dancer Rudolf Nureyev, mark the boundary between the Bay of Naples and the Bay of Salerno. Technically, the Amalfi Coast drive begins here.

The limestone cliffs, plunging into the sea, were traversed by an ancient trail that became a modern road in the mid-19th century. Fruit stands sell produce from farms and orchards just over the hill. Limestone absorbs the heat, making this south-facing coastline a suntrap, with temperatures as much as 10 degrees higher than in nearby Sorrento. Bougainvillea and geraniums grow like weeds in the summer.

As you approach the exotic-looking town of **Positano,** you know you've reached the scenic heart of the Amalfi Coast. Views of Positano, the main stop along the coast, are dramatic on either side of town. Just south of Positano, **St. Peter's Hotel** (Il San Pietro di Positano, camouflaged below the tiny St. Peter's church) is just about the most posh stop on the coast. Notice the elevator to the beach and dock. Bring your credit card.

Praiano is notable for its cathedral, with the characteristic majolica-tiled roof and dome—a reminder of this region's respected ceramics industry. Just past the tunnel stands a Saracen watchtower.

Marina di Praiano is a tiny and unique fishing hamlet wedged into a tight ravine with a couple of good restaurants and some small hotels.

The next Saracen tower guarded the harbor of the Amalfi navy until the fleet was destroyed by a tidal wave in 1343.

The most striking stretch of coastline ends at **Amalfi** and **Atrani.** As you leave Amalfi, look up to the left. The white house that clings to a cliff (Villa Rondinaia) was home for many years to the writer Gore Vidal. Atop the cliff is the town of **Ravello.** From here, the western half of the Amalfi Coast is mostly wild and unpopulated until you hit **Salerno,** with the striking Greek temples at **Paestum.**

Positano

According to legend, the Greek god Poseidon created Positano for Pasitea, a nymph he lusted after. History says the town was founded when ancient Greeks at Paestum decided to move out of the swamp (to escape malaria). Specializing in scenery and sand, Positano hangs halfway between Sorrento and Amalfi town on the most spectacular stretch of the coast.

The village, a ▲▲▲ sight from a distance, is a pleasant gathering of cafés and expensive women's clothing stores, with a good but pebbly beach. Positano is famous for its fashions—90 percent of its shops are clothing boutiques.

The "skyline" looks like it did a century ago. Notice the town's characteristic Saracen-inspired rooftop domes. Filled with sand, these provide low-tech insulation—cool in summer and hot in  winter. It's been practically impossible to get a building permit in Positano for 25 years now, and landowners who want to renovate can't make external changes. The steep stairs are a way of life for the 4,000 hardy locals. Only one street in Positano allows motorized traffic; the rest are steep pedestrian lanes. Because hotels don't take large groups (bus access is too difficult), the town—unlike Sorrento—has been spared the ravages of big-bus tourism.

Consider seeing Positano as a day trip from Sorrento: Take the bus out and the afternoon ferry home, but be sure to check the boat schedules when you arrive—the last ferry often leaves before 18:00. Or spend the night to enjoy the magic of Positano. The town has a local flavor at night, when the grown-ups stroll and the kids play soccer on the church porch.

Orientation to Positano

Squished into a ravine, with narrow alleys that cascade down to the harbor, Positano requires you to stroll, whether you're going up or heading down. The center of town has no main square (unless you count the beach). There's little to do here but eat, window-shop, and enjoy the beach and views...hence the town's popularity.

Tourist Information

The **TI** is a half-block from the beach, in a small building at the bottom of the church steps (April–Sept Mon–Sat 8:30–19:30, Sun 8:30–14:30, Oct–March generally Mon–Sat 9:00–14:30, tel. 089-875-067, www.aziendaturismopositano.it).

Arrival in Positano

The main coast highway winds above the town. Regional SITA buses (blue or green-and-white) stop at two scheduled bus stops located at either end of town: Chiesa Nuova (at Bar Internazionale, nearer Sorrento, use only if you're staying at Brikette Hostel) and Sponda (nearer Amalfi town). From either stop, roads lead downhill through the town to the beach (though Chiesa Nuova is farther away). To minimize your descent, use the Sponda stop (the second Positano stop, if you're coming from

Positano

- **——— MAIN COASTAL HIGHWAY**
- **—— OTHER ROADS (FOR CARS)**
- **– – PEDESTRIAN STREETS**
- **Ⓑ BUS STOP**
- **Ⓟ PARKING**
- **🔭 VIEW**

200 YARDS
200 METERS

CHIESA NUOVA BUS STOP

🔭 Ⓑ

VIALE PASITEA

Ⓟ

Ⓟ

N

MARCONI

VIA

VIA FORNILLO

VIEWPOINT

VIA

TO SORRENTO

VIA MARCONI SS-163

FORNILLO BEACH

MEDITER

Sorrento). It's a 20-minute stroll/shop/munch from here to the beach (and TI).

If you're catching the SITA bus back to Sorrento, be aware that it may leave from the Sponda stop five minutes before the printed departure. There's no room for the bus to wait, so in case the driver is early, you should be, too (€3.60, departures about hourly, daily 7:00–22:00, until 20:00 off-season). Buy tickets from the *tabacchi* next to Bar Mulino Verde, at Positour Agency (near Piazza dei Mulini on Via Colombo), or just below the bus stop at the Total gas station (across from Hotel Marincanto). If the walk up to the stop is too tough, take the dizzy little local orange bus (marked

❶ Hotel Marincanto
❷ Hotel Savoia
❸ Albergo California
❹ Hotel Bougainville
❺ Residence la Tavolozza
❻ Villa Maria Antonietta
❼ Brikette Hostel
❽ Bar Mulino Verde (Bus Tickets)
❾ Music on the Rocks Club
❿ La Zagara Café

Interno Positano), which constantly loops through Positano, connecting the lower town with the highway's two bus stops (2/hour, €1.10 at *tabacchi* or €1.50 on board, catch it at convenient stop at the corner of Via Colombo and Via dei Mulini, heads up to Sponda). Bar Mulino Verde, located off Piazza dei Mulini (as close as cars, taxis, and the shuttle bus can get to the beach), is just across from the stop for the little orange bus, with a fine, breezy terrace you can enjoy if you're waiting.

Drivers must go with the one-way flow, entering the town only at the Chiesa Nuova bus stop (closest to Sorrento) and exiting at Sponda. Driving is a headache here. Parking is worse.

Helpful Hints

Internet Access: Your best bet is at **La Brezza Internet,** on the west side of the beach (to the right as you face the water, €5/30 minutes).

Local Guide: Christine Ornelas, an Australian lawyer who fell for a local and married into the Positano scene, has become the town historian. She weaves her interests into an interesting two-hour walk through town. Christine's tour gives the town context and brings meaning to fun hidden history, while offering an overview of the local scene, tastings of local products, and tips on shopping, beaches, restaurants, and excursions (€20, 2 people-€35 with this book, April–Oct Mon–Sat at 10:30, call to confirm—she'll do the tour for even just a couple of people, mobile 334-232-2096, www.discoverpositano .it, christineornelas@gmail.com). Christine's walk starts at Piazza dei Mulini (outside the church, Chiesa del Rosario).

Self-Guided Walk

Welcome to Positano

While there's no real sightseeing in Positano, this short downhill guided stroll will help you get your bearings from top to bottom.

• *Start at...*

Piazza dei Mulini: This is the upper town meeting point, as close to the beach as vehicles can get and the lower stop of the little orange bus (2/hour, departs on the half-hour). Bar Mulino Verde is *the* local hangout—older people gather inside while the young crowd congregates on the wisteria-draped terrace across the street. In this small town, gossip is a big pastime.

Positano's ceramic and linen industries boomed when tourists discovered the place in the 1970s. The beach-inspired Moda Positano fashion label was first created as a break from the rigid dress code of the '50s. On this piazza, and throughout town, you'll find lots of ceramic and linen shops along with galleries featuring the work of local artists (and an abundance of ATMs).

• *Wander downhill to the stepped fork in the road. You've reached...*

Midtown: At Enoteca Cuomo (#3), butcher Vincenzo stocks fine local red wines and is happy to explain their virtues. He also makes homemade sausages, salami, and *panini*—good for a quick lunch. The small set of stairs leads to the wonderful, recommended Delikatessen, where Emilia can fix you a good picnic. Their downstairs café (past the stairs, on the left at #15) sells an array of tempting edible souvenirs.

La Zagara (across the lane at #10) is a pastry shop by day and a piano bar by night. Tempting pastries such as the rum-drenched *babà* (a local favorite) fill the window display. After-hours, it's filled with traditional Neapolitan music and dancing. A bit farther downhill, Brunella (#24) is respected for traditional, quality, and locally made linen.

Across the street, Hotel Palazzo Murat fills what was a grand Benedictine monastery. Step into the plush courtyard to enjoy the scene. Continuing on, under a fragrant bougainvillea trellis, you'll come to "street merchants' gulch," where artisans display their goodies.

• *Continue to Piazza Flavio Gioia, with the big...*

Church of Santa Maria Assunta: This church originated as the abbey of Positano's 12th-century Benedictine monastery. Originally Romanesque, it was eventually abandoned along with the entire lower town out of fear of pirate attacks. When the coast was clear in the 18th century, the church was given an extreme Baroque makeover. Its dome is covered in colorful majolica tiles.

Inside (first chapel on left) is a fine manger scene *(presepe)*. Its original 18th-century figurines give you an idea of the folk costumes of the age. The Black Madonna, an icon-like Byzantine painting (above the altar), was likely brought here in the 12th century by Benedictine monks. But locals prefer the romantic legend: Saracen pirates had it on their ship as plunder. A violent storm hit—sure to sink the evil ship. The painting of Mary spoke, saying, *"Posa posa"* (lay me down), and the ship glided safely to this harbor. The pirates were so stricken they became Christians. Locals kept the painting, and the town became known as *Posa-tano* (recalling Mary's command). To the right of the altar, a small chapel holds a silver and copper bust of St. Vitus—the town patron who brought Christianity here in about A.D. 300. In the adjacent niche is a rare painting of baby Jesus being circumcised (by Fabrizio Santafede, 1599), considered the finest historic painting in town.

Back outside, you'll see the bell tower, dating from 1707. Above the door, it sports a Romanesque relief scavenged from the original church. The scene—a wolf mermaid with seven little fish—was a reminder to worshippers of how integral the sea was to their livelihood.

• *Backtrack a few steps, circling the church around to the left.*

Around the Church: You'll pass a chapel now used by local artists to show their paintings—fun because they're mostly local scenes. Farther around the side of the church, find the plaque describing in English how this spot once held a Roman villa, buried when Mount Vesuvius erupted in A.D. 79. Only a few minor rooms have been excavated (a photograph shows one of the preserved frescoes). The rest await discovery—digging has been stopped until there are enough funds to do it properly. The stairs lead down to a glass door that offers a peek into the church's crypt—originally the early church's altar. According to local legend, the Benedictines sat their dead brothers on the stone choir chairs here to decompose and remind all of their mortality.

• *Continue climbing down the steps arcing to the right. You'll eventually come to the little square facing the beach.*

Piazzetta: This is the local gathering point in the evening, as local boys hustle tourist girls into the nearby nightclub. Residents traded their historic baptistery font with Amalfi town for the two iron lions you see facing the beach. From here, you can look up and admire the colorful majolica tiles so typical of church domes in this region. Positano was once a notable naval power, with many shipyards along this beach. These eventually became fishermen's quarters and storehouses, and later, today's tourist restaurants. The Positano **beach,** called Spiaggia Grande, is half public (no shower) and half private (see prices below).

• *On the far left side of the beach is...*

Music on the Rocks: This chic club is all that's left of the 1970s scene when Positano really rocked. While it's dead until about 23:00, you're welcome to wander into the cool troglo-disco interior for a drink (see listing on next page for details).

• *Wander across the beach. Beyond the kiosks that sell boat tickets, a path climbs up and over, past a 13th-century lookout fort from Saracen pirate days, to the next beach. It's a worthwhile little five-minute walk to...*

Fornillo Beach: This is where locals go for better swimming and to escape some of the tourist crowds. The beach is lined by humble snack bars and lunch eateries.

• *Our walk is over. Time to relax.*

Sights in Positano

Beaches—Positano's pebbly and sandy primary beach, **Spiaggia Grande,** is colorful with umbrellas as it stretches wide around the cove. It's mostly private (€10–15/person, April–Oct, cost includes drink service and use of lounge chair and umbrella), with a free section near the middle, close to where the boats take off. The nearest WC is beneath the steps to the right (as you face the water).

Fornillo Beach, a less-crowded option just around the bend (to the west) of Spiaggia Grande, is favored by residents, with more affordable chair and umbrella rentals.

Boat Trips—At the west side of Spiaggia Grande (to the right as you face the sea), a series of booths sell boat tickets to a number of destinations.

Consider renting a rowboat or taking various boat tours to a nearby cave (La Grotta dello Smeraldo—Emerald Cave), fishing village (Nerano), or small islands.

Ferries run to Amalfi, Capri, and Sorrento; see "Positano Connections," page 919.

Sleep Code

(€1 = about $1.25, country code: 39)
S = Single, **D** = Double/Twin, **T** = Triple, **Q** = Quad, **b** = bathroom, **s** = shower only. Unless otherwise noted, credit cards are accepted, English is spoken, and breakfast is included.

To help you sort easily through these listings, I've divided the rooms into three categories based on the price for a standard double room with bath:

$$$ Higher Priced—Most rooms €180 or more.
  $$ Moderately Priced—Most rooms between €120–180.
    $ Lower Priced—Most rooms €120 or less.

Prices can change without notice; verify the hotel's current rates online or by email. For other updates, see www.ricksteves.com/update.

Shopping—Locally produced linen and ceramics can be found at shops and galleries throughout town. **Ceramica Assunta,** one of the oldest ceramics stores in Positano, carries colorful Solimene dinnerware and more at two locations (Via Colombo 97 and Via Colombo 137, tel. 089-875-008). The young owner-artisan couple at **Sunflower Bottega d'Arte** make and paint their own ceramic designs. Two popular (and pricey) fashion boutiques are **Brunella** (Via Pasitea 72, tel. 089-875-228) and **Pepito's** (Via Pasitea 39, tel. 089-875-446).

Nightlife—The big-time action in the old town center is the impressive club **Music on the Rocks,** literally carved into the rocks on the beach (party starts about 23:30, cover charge on weekends, just buy a drink and dance or watch the scene, Via Grotte Dell'Incanto 51, tel. 089-875-874, www.musicontherocks.it). For a more low-key atmosphere, café/pastry shop **La Zagara** hosts music nightly in summer (June–Sept) and sometimes on weekends the rest of the year (starts around 21:00, Via dei Mulini 10, tel. 089-875-964).

Sleeping in Positano

These hotels (but not the hostel) are all on Via Colombo, which leads from the Sponda SITA bus stop down into the village. Prices given are for the highest season (June–Sept)—at other times, they become soft. Expect to pay more than €20 a day to park.

$$$ Hotel Marincanto is a newly restored four-star hotel with a bright breakfast terrace practically teetering on a cliff. Suites seem to be designed for a *luna di miele*—honeymoon (Db-€210 mid-April–mid-Oct, €170 off-season, more expensive superior rooms and suites, elevator, pool, private stairs to beach, parking-€23/day, 50 yards below the Sponda bus stop at Via Colombo 50, tel. 089-875-130, fax 089-875-595, www.marincanto.it, info @marincanto.it).

$$ Hotel Savoia is family-run, with 39 sizeable, breezy, bright air-conditioned rooms (viewless Db-€130, view Db-€180, deluxe Db-€200, at least €10/day off with this book in 2011, elevator, Via Colombo 73, tel. 089-875-003, fax 089-811-844, www .savoiapositano.it, info@savoiapositano.it, Regina and daughters Mechy, Piera, and Cristina).

$$ Albergo California has lofty views, 15 spacious rooms, and a grand terrace draped with vines. The Cinque family—Maria, Frank, John, and Antonio—will welcome you (view Db-€160 June–Sept, €10 less Oct and April–May, closed Dec–March; prices promised with this book through 2011, air-con, free parking, Via Colombo 141, tel. 089-875-382, fax 089-812-154, www.hotel californiapositano.it, info@hotelcaliforniapositano.it).

$$ Hotel Bougainville rents 16 comfortable rooms, half with balconies. After a recent renovation, everything's bright, modern, and tasteful (viewless Db-€119–140, view Db-€175, 5 percent discount off these rates with this book in 2011, check website for specials, air-con, Via Colombo 25, tel. 089-875-047, www .bougainville.it, info@bougainville.it, friendly Marella).

$ Residence la Tavolozza is an attractive eight-room hotel, warmly run by Celeste (cheh-LEHS-tay) and family (daughters Francesca and Paola). Each cheerily tiled room comes with a view, a balcony, and silence. This is a good value (Db-€90–120 depending on size, these prices promised through 2011 with this book, families can ask for "Royal Apartment," cash only, must call to confirm if arriving late, lavish breakfast extra, air-con, closed Dec–Feb, Via Colombo 10, tel. & fax 089-875-040, celeste.dileva @tiscali.it).

$ Villa Maria Antonietta is a humble, no-frills place with seven backpacker rooms, all with a distant view of the sea. Head down a grungy lane off the elegant main drag and then up a few big flights of stairs (Db-€80–120 depending on season, follow signs from Via Colombo 41; tel. 089-875-071, www.villamaria antonietta.com, Maria).

$ Brikette Hostel offers your best cheap dorm-bed option in this otherwise ritzy town. Renting 25 beds and offering a great sun and breakfast terrace, it's bright and clean with the normal hostel rules: 11:00–14:30 lockout, cushy curfew at 2:00 in the morning, and no membership required. Friendly Cristiana is full of energy, organizes parties several times a week, and offers discounted prices for excursions (bed in 4- to 8-bed dorms-€23, D-€65, Db-€75, bigger family rooms, these prices with cash; hearty breakfast extra but cheap, €5 dinners; free Wi-Fi, may be closed Dec–Feb, leave bus at Chiesa Nuova/Bar Internazionale stop and backtrack uphill 500 feet to Via G. Marconi 358, tel. & fax 089-875-857, www.brikette .com, info@brikette.com).

Eating in Positano

Waterfront Dining: The pizzerias and restaurants facing the beach, while overpriced, are pleasant and convenient. At the waterfront, I like **La Cambusa** (at the top of the steps), but neighboring places also leave people fat and happy.

"*Uptown*": The unassuming **Restaurant Bruno** is a better-than-average value for Positano, near the top of Via Colombo—handy if you don't want to hike down into the town center for dinner.

Picnics: If a picnic dinner on your balcony or the beach sounds good, sunny Emilia at **Delikatessen** can supply the ingredients (*antipasto misto* to go at €1.40/100 grams, pasta for €1/100 grams, sandwiches made and sold by weight—about €3.50, she microwaves food and includes all the picnic ware, best selection early; daily

March–Oct 7:00–22:00, Nov–Feb 8:00–20:00, just below car park at Via del Mulini 5, tel. 089-875-489). **Vini e Panini,** another small grocery, is a block from the beach a few steps above the TI. Daniela, the fifth-generation owner, speaks English and happily makes sandwiches to order. Choose from the "Caprese" (mozzarella and tomato), the "Positano" (mozzarella, tomato, and ham), or create your own (priced by weight, around €3.50 each). They also have a nice selection of well-priced regional wines (daily 8:00–22:00, off-season closes 14:00–16:00, tel. 089-875-175, just off church steps).

Positano Connections

Always check boat schedules, since the last boats often leave Positano before 18:00. The schedule varies drastically according to time of year. It's more reliable in summer than off-season, but be sure to check it with the TI. There's no real dock, so stormy weather can disrupt schedules. If you're thinking of taking a Capri trip from Positano, consider a boat that goes directly to the Blue Grotto (rather than dropping you in the port to catch another boat from there).

From Positano by Boat to: Amalfi (6/day, 30 minutes,

€6), **Capri** (mid-April–Sept only; 2–4/day, 35–50 minutes, €16), **Sorrento** (4/day, late April–mid-Oct only, 30 minutes, €9), **Salerno** (6/day, 70 minutes, €10). For the most part, these boats run only in season—roughly late April to mid-October (see www .metrodelmare.com for schedules). Direct boats to **Naples** run four times a day in the summer (check with the TI); you can also change boats in Sorrento or Capri.

By Bus: See "The Amalfi Coast by Bus," at the beginning of this chapter.

Near Positano: Marina di Praiano

Wedged into a tight ravine just before Amalfi town, this tiny fishing hamlet has a pint-sized beach (half free, half pay), a couple of restaurants, and a few small hotels. All Sorrento–Positano buses stop at the top of the village. Parking is pricey (blue spots-€3/hour, pay and display).

Sleeping in Marina di Praiano: Consider **$ La Conchiglia da Antonio,** a bar that rents nine rooms across the ravine (Db-€60, €80 in July, €100 in Aug, extra bed-€20, mention this book when reserving; includes small breakfast, tel. 089-874-313, www.la conchigliapraiano.it, info@laconchigliapraiano.it). **$$ Hotel Alfonso a Mare** rents 15 rooms (Db-€140, €200 in Aug when it includes obligatory dinner, tel. 089-874-091, www.alfonsoamare .it, info@alfonsoamare.it).

Amalfi Town

The Amalfi Coast is named for this town. It was founded (according to legend) when the girlfriend of Hercules was buried here. After Rome fell, Amalfi was one of the first cities to trade goods—

coffee, carpets, and paper— between Europe and points east. Its heyday was the 10th and 11th centuries, when it was a powerful maritime republic—a trading power with a fleet that controlled this region and rivaled Genoa and Venice. The Republic of Amalfi founded a hospital in Jerusalem and claims to have founded the Knights of Malta order—even giving them the Amalfi cross, which became the

Flavio Gioia

You'll see a statue of Flavio Gioia towering above the chaos of cars and buses on the seaside piazza. Amalfi residents credit this hometown boy with the invention of the magnetic compass back in 1302, but historians can't verify that he actually existed. While an improvement to the compass did occur in Amalfi during that time period, the Chinese and Arabs had been using rudimentary compasses for years. In Gioia's time, seamen used a needle bobbing around in water as a kind of medieval GPS. If Gioia existed at all, he probably just figured out how to secure that needle inside a little box. Locals, however, have no doubts that Flavio Gioia was an inventor extraordinaire.

famous Maltese cross. Amalfi minted its own coins and established "rules of the sea"—the basics of which survive today. Paper has been a vital industry here since the glory days in the Middle Ages. They'd pound rags into pulp in a big vat, pull it up using a screen, and air-dry it to create paper (the same technique used to make paper still sold in Amalfi shops). For a demonstration of this ancient technique, check out the Paper Museum (see "Sights in Amalfi Town," later in this section).

In 1343, this little powerhouse was destroyed by a freak tidal wave caused by an undersea earthquake. That disaster, compounded by devastating plagues, left Amalfi a humble backwater. Today, its 7,000 residents live off tourism (and paper). Amalfi is not as picturesque as Positano or as well-connected as Sorrento, but take some time to explore the town. Amalfi's charms will reveal themselves, especially early and late in the day, when tourist crowds dissipate.

Orientation to Amalfi Town

The waterfront of this town is dominated by a bus station, a parking lot, two gas stations, a statue of local boy Flavio Gioia—the inventor of the compass (see sidebar)—and a TI.

Amalfi, the most big-bus accessible of the towns along the coast, is a classic tourist trap. It's packed during the day with big-bus tours (whose drivers pay €50 an hour to park while their groups shop for *limoncello* and ceramics).

Before you enter the town, notice the colorful tile above the Porta della Marina gateway, showing off the domain of the maritime Republic of Amalfi. Just to the left, along the busy road, are a series of arches that indicate the long, narrow, vaulted halls of its arsenal—where ships were built in the 11th century.

Venture into the town, and you find its once rich and formidable medieval shell is filled with trendy shops, a main square sporting a springwater-spewing statue of St. Andrew, and a cathedral—the town's most important sight.

The farther you get away from the water, the more local Amalfi gets. The Paper Museum is a 10-minute walk up Via Lorenzo d'Amalfi, the main drag. From here, the road narrows and you can turn off onto a path leading to the shaded Valle dei Mulini; it's full of paper-mill ruins that recall this once proud and prosperous industry. The ruined castle clinging to the rocky ridge above Amalfi is Torre dello Ziro, a good lookout point for intrepid hikers (see "Hikes" on page 924).

Tourist Information

The TI is about 100 yards south of the center, next to the post office; facing the sea it's to the left (generally Mon–Sat 9:00–13:00 & 14:00–18:00, closed Sun, Corso della Repubbliche Marinare 27, tel. 089-871-107, www.amalfitouristoffice.it, info@amalfitourist office.it).

Helpful Hints

Don't Get Stranded: Be warned—the last bus back to Sorrento leaves at 20:00 (at 22:00 April–Sept) and can be full. Without a public bus, your only option is a €100 taxi ride.

Internet Access: L'Altra Costiera, on the main drag a block up from the church, looks more like a travel agency but has Internet service (€3/30 minutes, daily 9:00–21:00, 4 terminals, Via Lorenzo d'Amalfi 34, tel. 089-873-6082).

Hiking Guidebook: The best book on hiking is *Sorrento Amalfi Capri Car Tours and Walks,* on sale at many local bookstores. It has useful color-coded maps and info on public transportation to the trailheads.

Baggage Storage: You can store your bag safely for €3 at the Divina Costiera Travel Office facing the waterfront square, across from the bus parking area (daily 8:00–13:00 & 14:00–19:30, tel. 089-872-467).

Laundry: The full-service **Lavalampo** offers same-day service (€5/kilo—2.2 pounds—wash and dry, Mon–Sat 8:30–13:00 & 16:30–20:00, closed Thu afternoon and Sun; drop off before 9:30 and pick up same day). It's a four-minute walk up the main drag (#51) from the cathedral.

Speedboat Charters: To hire your own boat for a tour of the coastline from Amalfi (or to Capri), consider **Charter La Dolce Vita** (mobile 329-460-3771, www.amalficoastyacht.it).

Sights in Amalfi Town

Cathedral—This church is "Amalfi Romanesque" (a mix of Moorish and Byzantine flavors, built c. 1000–1300) with a fanciful Neo-Byzantine facade from the 19th century. Climb the imposing stairway—which functions as a handy outdoor theater for town events. The 1,000-year-old bronze door at the top was given to Amalfi by a wealthy local merchant who had it made in Constantinople.

Cost and Hours: €3, daily 7:00–19:00, shorter off-season, closed Jan–Feb, from 10:00–17:00 access church through cloister, pick up English flier, tel. 089-871-324. There's a fine, free WC at the top of the steps (through unmarked green door, just a few steps before ticket booth).

❷ **Self-Guided Tour:** Visitors are directed on a one-way circuit through the cathedral complex with these four stops:

"Cloister of Paradise": This courtyard of 120 graceful columns was the cemetery for local nobles in the 13th century (note their stone sarcophagi). Don't miss the fine view of the bell tower and its majolica tiles.

Basilica of the Crucifix: The original ninth-century church is now a museum filled with the art treasures of the cathedral. The Angevin Mitre (Mitra Angioina), with a "pavement of tiny pearls" setting off its gold and gems, has been worn by bishops since the 14th century. On the far wall is a plank from a Saracen pirate ship that wrecked just outside of town in 1544 during another freak storm. This storm was caused by a saint, rather than an earthquake—and saved the town, rather than destroyed it. The plank reminds locals how St. Andrew (see below) rescued the town from certain Turkish pillage and plunder.

Crypt of St. Andrew: Just as Venice needed Mark to get on the pilgrimage map, Amalfi needed St. Andrew—one of the apostles who left his nets to become the original "fishers of men." What are believed to be his remains (under the huge bronze statue) were brought here from Constantinople in 1206 during the Crusades—an indication of the wealth and importance of Amalfi back then.

Cathedral: The interior is notable for its fine 13th-century wooden crucifix. The painting behind it shows St. Andrew martyred on an X-shaped cross flanked by two Egyptian granite columns supporting a triumphal arch. Before leaving, check out the delicate mother-of-pearl crucifix (right of door in back).

▲**Paper Museum**—At this cavernous, cool 13th-century paper mill–turned-museum, a multilingual guide collects groups at the entrance (no particular times) for a 25-minute tour that recounts the history and process of papermaking, a long-time industry for the town of Amalfi (€4, March–Oct daily 10:00–18:30, sporadic hours Nov–Feb, a 10-minute walk up the main street from the cathedral, look for signs to *Museo della Carta*, tel. 089-830-4561, www.museodellacarta.it).

Hikes

Amalfi is the starting point for several fine hikes (see "Hiking Guidebook" on page 922). Here are two:

Hike #1—This loop trail leads up the valley past paper-mill ruins, ending in the tiny town of **Pontone;** you can get lunch there, and head back down to the town of Amalfi (allow 3 hours total). Bring a good map, since it's easy to veer off the main route. Start your hike by following the main road (Via Lorenzo d'Amalfi) away from the sea.

After the Paper Museum, jog right, then left to join the trail, leading through the shaded woods along a babbling stream. Heed the signs to stay away from the ruins of paper mills (no matter how tempting), since many are ready to collapse on unwary hikers. Continue up to Pontone, where Trattoria l'Antico Borgo offers wonderful cuisine and a great view (Via Noce 4, tel. 089-871-469). After lunch, return to Amalfi via a steep stairway.

If you're feeling ambitious, before you head back to Amalfi, add a one-hour detour (30 minutes each way) to visit the ridge-hugging **Torre dello Ziro** (ask a local how to find the trail to this tower). You'll be rewarded with a spectacular view.

Hike #2—For an easier hike (more of a stroll), head to the nearby town of **Atrani.** This village, just a 15-minute stroll beyond Amalfi town, is a world apart; its 1,500 residents consider themselves definitely *not* from Amalfi. Leave Amalfi via the main road, and stay on the water side until the sidewalk ends. Cross the street and head up the stairs; the paved route takes you over the hill, and drops you into Atrani in about 15 minutes. Piazza Umberto is the core of town, with cafés and a little grocery store that makes sandwiches. Amazingly, Atrani has none of the trendy resort feel of Amalfi, with relatively few tourists, a delightful town square, and a free, sandy beach (if you drive here, pay for parking at harbor). This town also has some accommodations (see "Sleeping in Amalfi Town," next page).

From Atrani, you can continue up to **Ravello** (see page 926). But be warned: Unless you're part mountain goat, you'll probably prefer catching the bus to Ravello from Amalfi town instead.

Sleeping in Amalfi Town

(€1 = about $1.25, country code: 39)

Sleeps are better in Positano, but if you're marooned in Amalfi, here are some options. High season on the Amalfi Coast (especially July–Sept) demands the highest prices; prices listed here are peak-season rates (roughly April–Oct).

$$ Hotel Amalfi, with 40 rooms and a garden, is lacking in warmth, but is a fine choice (Db-€80–120, peaks at €160 Aug–Sept, air-con, Wi-Fi, roof-terrace breakfast, no sea views, 50 yards from cathedral, head up the pedestrian street and take staircase to the left before underpass, Via dei Pastai 3, tel. 089-872-440, fax 089-872-250, www.hamalfi.it, info@hamalfi.it).

$$ Hotel Bussola, a five-minute walk north along the harbor, rises above the ocean with 60 adequate, sunny rooms, most boasting terraces with a breezy ocean view (Sb-€90, Db-€140, Signore Dilieto offers a 10 percent Rick Steves discount in 2011 if you book direct—but not valid July–Aug, air-con, Wi-Fi, parking-€15/day, Lungomare dei Cavalieri 16, tel. 089-871-533, www.labussolahotel .it, info@labussolahotel.it).

$ Residenza del Duca is a fancy little seven-room boutique B&B taking advantage of its wonderful location in the heart of this touristy enclave (minuscule Sb-€60, Db-€90, €130 Aug–Sept, €10 less per day with this book and cash, air-con, glimpses of ocean through the rooftops; 25 yards uphill from Piazza Duomo, take the first left, up the stairs and follow the signs, then up more stairs, Via Mastalo II Duca 3; tel. 089-873-6365, www.residencedelduca .it, info@residencedelduca.it, Andrea).

Nearby in Atrani

Accommodation options are limited in Atrani, a small-town Amalfi hideaway without the glitz and hill-climbing of Positano (described under "Hike #2" on the previous page).

$ A'Scalinatella is a dingy, informal backpackers' hostel, with a honeycomb of cramped 3- to 10-bed dorms, way-overpriced private rooms, and a communal kitchen. It's run by English-speaking owners Filippo and Gabriele (dorm bed-€25, D-€60, Db-€90, prices very soft, cash only, no hostel membership required, 100 yards up from main square at Scalinatella Piazza Umberto I 5, tel. 089-871-492, www.hostelscalinatella.com, info@hostelscalinatella .com). They also rent rooms scattered all over town.

$ L'Argine Fiorito B&B, which stands like a little castle overlooking a ravine at the top of town, rents five tidy and tiled rooms (Db-€105, extra bed-€35; tel. 089-873-6309, mobile 347-531-1158, www.larginefiorito.it, info@larginefiorito.it).

Ravello

Ravello sits atop a lofty perch 1,000 feet above the sea and offers an interesting church, two villas, and a chance to catch a glimpse of celebrities. American author Gore Vidal, who lived here for decades, is one of a sizable group of rich and famous artists—including Richard Wagner, D. H. Lawrence, Henry Wadsworth Longfellow, and Greta Garbo—who have succumbed to Ravello's charms.

To see the sights listed here, start at the bus stop and walk through the tunnel to the main square, where you'll find the church on the right, Villa Rufolo on the left, and the **TI** (daily 9:00–13:00 & 14:00–18:00, 100 yards from the square—follow the signs to Via Roma 18, tel. 089-857-096, www.ravellotime .com; ask for the color-coded trail map called *Passeggiata/Walks*). A 10-minute walk through the town (follow the signs) leads to Villa Cimbrone.

Sights in Ravello

Duomo—You can't miss Ravello's cathedral, located right on the main square. The two main features of this church are the bronze doors, with 54 scenes of the life of Christ, the carved marble pulpit supported by six lions, and a chance to climb behind the altar for a close-up look at the relic of holy blood. The geometric designs show Arabic influence. The humble cathedral museum (€2) is two rooms of well-described carved marble evoking the historical importance of the town.

Cost and Hours: Church free, open daily May–Oct 9:00–12:30 & 17:30–19:00, shorter off-season, museum open daily 9:00–19:00; you can generally get into the church all day long via the museum, entrance on the right, tel. 089-858-311.

Villa Rufolo—The villa, built in the 13th century, is only a barren ruin today. It has pleasant Arabic/Norman gardens, which provide a delightful frame for the commanding coastline view (you can enjoy the same view, without the entry fee, from the bus parking lot just below the villa). It's also one of the venues for Ravello's annual arts festival, which runs from July to the end of September (www.ravellofestival.com). During the concert season (March–Oct), locals perch a bandstand on the edge of the cliff, giving concert attendees the combination of wonderful music and a dizzying view. Wagner visited here and was impressed enough to set the second act of his opera *Parsifal* in the villa's magical gardens. A concert on the cliff is a sublime experience (villa entry-€5, daily May–Sept 9:00–20:00, Oct–April 9:00 until sunset, may close earlier if hosting a concert, tel. 089-857-621, concert information tel. 089-858-149, www.ravelloarts.org).

Villa Cimbrone—This villa, located at the other end of Ravello, was built in the 20th century by Englishman William Beckett. It offers extensive gardens and a killer view from the "Terrace of Infinity." Consider buying a picnic in town and munching it here discreetly with magnificent Italian panoramas at your feet. A wander through the gardens will reveal reproductions of famous sculptures and lots of great views.

  Cost and Hours: €6, daily 9:00 until 30 minutes before sunset, tel. 089-858-072.

▲Hike to Amalfi Town from Villa Cimbrone—To walk downhill from Ravello's Villa Cimbrone to the town of Amalfi (a path for hardy hikers only—follow the TI's *Passeggiata/Walks* brochure), retrace your steps back toward town. Take the first left that turns into a stepped path winding its way below the cliff. Pause here to look back up at the rock with a big white mansion—Villa La Rondinaia, where Gore Vidal lived for many years. Continue down the fairly steep path about 40 minutes to the town of Atrani, where several bars on the main square offer well-deserved refreshment. From here, it's about a 15-minute walk back to Amalfi (see "Hike #2" on page 924).

Eating & Sleeping in Ravello

Ristorante Garden clings to the hillside and serves up unbeatable views of the coastline below—and delicious homemade pasta. Savor a relaxing lunch on their terrace. Make sure to save room for the local favorite, *delizia al limone*—calling it a "lemon cream puff" doesn't begin to do it justice (€13 pastas, €16 *secondi*, daily 12:00–15:00 & 19:30–22:00, closed Jan, facing the church walk to the right through the tunnel, next to Villa Rufolo, Via Boccaccio 4, tel. 089-857-226). They also rent nine basic but comfortable rooms, all with balconies, with the same sweeping views (Db-€100–125, air-con, Wi-Fi, www.gardenravello.com, info@gardenravello.com, Anna).

Ravello Connections

Ravello and the town of Amalfi are connected by a winding road and a bus. Coming from Amalfi town, buy your ticket at the bar on the waterfront, and ask where the bus stop is (buses usually stop to the left as you face the water, near the inventor statue on the waterfront Piazza Flavio Gioia). In Ravello, line up early, since the buses are often crowded (hourly, 25 minutes, €2.40, buy ticket in *tabacchi;* catch bus 100 yards off main square, just past tunnel).

Paestum

Paestum (PASTE-oom) has one of the best collections of Greek temples anywhere—and certainly the most accessible to Western Europe. Serenely situated, it's surrounded by fields and wildflowers, and has a sandy beach and only a modest commercial strip.

This town was founded as Poseidonia by Greeks in the sixth century B.C., and became a key stop on an important trade route. In the fifth century B.C., the Lucanians, a barbarous inland tribe, conquered Poseidonia, changed its name to Paistom, and tried to adopt the cultured ways of the Greeks. The Romans, who took over in the third century B.C., gave Paestum the name it bears today. The final conquerors of Paestum, malaria-carrying mosquitoes, kept the site wonderfully deserted for nearly a thousand years. Rediscovered in the 18th century, Paestum today offers the only well-preserved Greek ruins north of Sicily.

Planning Your Time

Allow two hours, including the museum. Depending on your interest and the heat, start with either the site or the museum. You'll enjoy the best light and smallest crowds late in the day.

Orientation to Paestum

Tourist Information: At the **TI**, next to the Paestum Archaeological Museum, pick up a free info booklet of the site (TI open daily 9:00–19:00, hours vary off-season, tel. 082-881-1016, www.infopaestum.it, info@infopaestum.it).

Arrival at Paestum: Buses from Salerno (see "Paestum Connections," at the end of this chapter) stop near a corner of the ruins (at a little bar/café). Or, if you're arriving by train, exit the station and walk through the old city gate; the ruins are an eight-minute walk straight ahead.

Cost: €4 for the museum, €4 for the site, €6.50 for a combo-ticket.

Hours: Both museum and site open daily at 9:00 (except the first and third Mon of each month, when the museum is closed). Year-round, the museum closes at 18:45 (last ticket sold at 18:15). The site closes one hour before sunset (as late as 19:30 June–July, as early as 15:30 in winter, last site ticket sold one hour before closing, tel. 082-872-2654).

Information: There's little English information at the site itself. Several mediocre guidebooks are offered at the museum's bookshop, including a €13 past-and-present guide. Dull €5 audioguides are available to rent at the site entrance and cover both museum and site (ID required). Or you can follow my self-guided tours, below.

Local Guide: Silvia Braggio is a good guide who gives a fine two-hour walk of the site and museum (special rate with this book-€100, mobile 347-643-2307, www.silviaguide.it, silvia@silvia guide.it).

Eating: A couple of typical, touristy eateries flank the TI and site entrance. Your best lunch option is **Ristorante Nettuno** (quality food, reasonable prices, great setting, good temple views from tables, located at south entrance).

Entry: The site and museum have separate entrances. The museum, just outside the ruins, is in a cluster with the TI and a small paleo-Christian basilica.

Self-Guided Tours

Paestum Archaeological Site

This tour begins at the Temple of Ceres, goes through the center of the Roman town past the Greek Memorial Tomb, circles around the other two Greek temples, then leaves the site to walk down the modern road to the Ekklesiasterion (which faces the museum). With this information, most visitors will not need to rent the audioguide or buy a book.

Background: While Paestum is famous for its marvelous Greek temples, much of what you see is Roman. Five elements of Greek Paestum survive: three misnamed temples, a memorial tomb, and a circular meeting place (or Ekklesiasterion). The rest, including the wall that defines the site, is Roman.

Paestum was once a seaport (the ocean has since retreated about a mile away—the wall in the distance, which stretches about three miles, is about halfway to today's coastline). Only about a fifth of the site has been excavated. The Greek city, which archaeologists figure had a population of about 13,000, was first conquered by Lucanians (who were pretty crude and made almost

Paestum

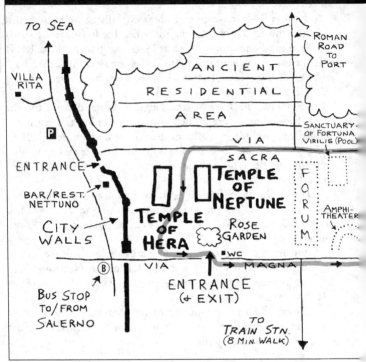

no changes in the physical city), and then by the Romans (who completely made it over).

The remaining Greek structures survive because the Romans were superstitious—they respected sacred areas, and didn't mess with temples and tombs. While most old Christian churches are built upon Roman temples (it's just what people do when they conquer another culture), no Roman temple is built upon a Greek temple. Romans appreciated how religion could function as the opiate of the masses. As long as people paid their taxes and obeyed the emperor's dictates, the practical Romans had no problem with any religion. The three Greek temples that you'll see here today have stood for about 2,500 years.

• Buy your ticket, enter the site, and stand in front of the...

Temple of Ceres: All three Paestum temples have inaccurate names, coined by 19th-century archaeologists who based their "discoveries" on wishful thinking. (While the Romans made things easy by leaving lots of inscriptions, the Greeks did not.) Those 1800s archaeologists wanted this temple to be devoted to Ceres, the goddess of agriculture. However, all the little votive

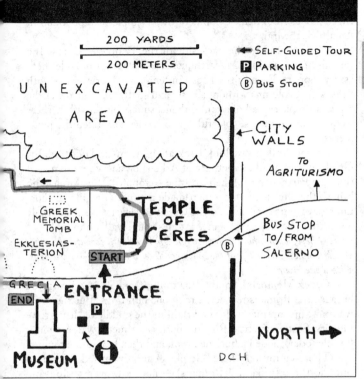

statues found later, when modern archaeologists dug here, instead depicted a woman with a big helmet: Athena, goddess of wisdom

and war. (The Greeks' female war goddess was also the goddess of wisdom—thinking... strategy...female. The Romans' masculine war god was Mars— just fighting.) Each temple is part of a sanctuary—an open, sacred space around the temple. Because regular people couldn't go into the temple, the altar logically stood outside.

The Temple of Ceres dates from 500 B.C. It's made of locally quarried limestone block. Good roads and shipping didn't come along until the Romans, so the Greeks' buildings were limited to local materials. The wooden roof is long gone. Like the other two temples, this one was once painted white, black, and red, and has an east–west orientation—facing the rising sun. This temple's *cella* (interior room) is gone, cleared out when it was used as a Christian church in the sixth century. In medieval times, Normans scavenged stones from here. Chunks of these temples can be found in Amalfi's cathedral.

Walk around to the back side of the Temple of Ceres. The capitals broke in a modern earthquake, so a steel bar provides necessary support. Each of the Paestum temples is Doric style—with three stairs, columns without a base, and shafts that narrow at the top to a simple capital of a round then a square block. While there were no carved reliefs, colorful frescoes once decorated the pediments.

As you walk away, look back at the temple. Traditionally, Greeks would build a sanctuary of Athena on a city's highest spot (like the Parthenon in Athens, on the Acropolis). Paestum had no hill, so the Greeks created a man-made mound. The hill was more impressive in its time because the Greek city level was substantially lower than the Roman pavement stones you'll walk on today.

• *From here, walk about 100 yards down Via Sacra toward the other Greek temples. To the left of the road, you'll see a little half-buried house with a tiled roof.*

Greek Memorial Tomb: This tomb (from 500 B.C.) survived because the Romans respected religious buildings. But the tomb was most inconveniently located right in the middle of their growing city. So the practical Romans built a perimeter wall around it (visible today), added a fine tiled roof, and then buried the tomb.

There's a mystery here. Greeks generally buried their dead outside the city (as did Romans)—there are over a thousand ancient tombs outside Paestum's walls—yet this tomb was parked smack-dab in the center of town. When it was uncovered in 1952, no bodies were found inside. The tomb instead held nine perfectly preserved vases (now in the museum). Archaeologists aren't sure of the tomb's purpose. Perhaps it was a memorial dedicated to some great hero (like a city founder). Or perhaps it was a memorial to those lost when a neighboring community had to evacuate and settle as refugees here.

• *Continue walking down Via Sacra, the main drag of...*

Roman Paestum: Roman towns were garrison towns: rectangular with a grid street plan and two main streets cutting north–south and east–west, dividing the town into four equal sections. They were built by military engineers with a no-nonsense standard design. New excavations (on the left) have uncovered Roman-era lead piping. City administration buildings were on the left, and residential buildings were on the right.

You'll come to a big Roman pool that archaeologists believe was a sanctuary dedicated to Fortuna Virilis, goddess of luck and fertility. The strange stones likely supported a wooden platform for priests and statues of gods. Imagine young women walking down the ramp at the far end and through the pool, hoping to conceive a child.

The next big square is the Roman Forum and ancient Paestum's main intersection. The road on the right led directly (and very practically) to the port. It made sense to have a direct connection to move freight between the sea and the market (Forum).

Until 2007, the vast field of ruins between the Forum and the next temple (on the right) was covered in vegetation. It's recently been cleared, and cleaned of harmful lichen, which eats the calcium limestone. Study the rocks: Yellow lichen is alive, black is dead. Even the great temples of Paestum were covered in this destructive lichen until 2000, when they were cleaned for the first time in a two-year-long project.

· *Ahead on the left are the so-called...*

Temples of Neptune and Hera: The **Temple of Neptune** dates from 450 B.C. and employs the Greek architectural trick where the base line is curved up just a tad, to overcome the illusion of sagging caused by a straight base. The Athenians built their Parthenon (with a similar bowed-up base line) just 30 years after this. Many think this temple could have been their inspiration.

The adjacent Temple of Hera, dating from 550 B.C., is the oldest of Paestum's three temples and one of the oldest Greek temples still standing anywhere. Notice the change 100 years makes in the architectural styles: Archaic Doric in 550 B.C. versus Classic Doric in 450 B.C.

Archaeologists now believe the "Temple of Neptune" was actually devoted to a different god. Votive statues uncovered here indicate that Hera was the focus (perhaps a new and improved version of the adjacent, simpler, and older Temple of Hera). Or perhaps it was a temple to Zeus, Hera's husband, to honor the couple together.

Together, the two temples formed a single huge sanctuary with altars on the far (east) side. Walk around to the front. Notice how overbuilt the Temple of Hera appears. Its columns and capitals are closer together than necessary, as if the builders lacked confidence in their ability to span the distance between supports. Square pillars mark the corners of the *cella* inside. Temples with an odd number of columns (nine) had a single colonnade crossing in the center inside to support the wooden roof. More modern temples had six columns, with two colonnades passing through the *cella*. This left a line of vision open through the middle so that worshippers could see the big statue of the god.

By the way, in 1943, Allied paratroopers dropped in near here during the famous "Landing of Salerno." The Temple of Hera served as an Allied military tent hospital. From here the Allies pushed back the Nazis, marching to Naples, Cassino, and finally to Rome.

• *Leave the site and turn left on the modern road, Via Magna Grecia. The king of Naples built this Naples-to-Paestum road in 1829 to inspire his people with ancient temples. While he was modern in his appreciation of antiquity, his road project destroyed a swath of the ancient city. Just past the amphitheater, you'll find the...*

Ekklesiasterion: Immediately across the street from the museum is what looks like a sunken circular theater. This rare bit of ancient Greek ruins was the Ekklesiasterion, a meeting place where the Greeks would get together to discuss things and vote. Archaeologists believe that the Agora, or market, would also have been located here.

• *Across the street is the...*

Paestum Archaeological Museum

Paestum's museum offers the rare opportunity to see artifacts—dating from prehistoric to Greek to Roman times—at the site where they were discovered. These beautifully crafted works (with good English descriptions throughout) help bring Paestum to life.

Before stepping into the museum, notice the proud fascist architecture. While the building dates from 1954, the design is pre-WWII fascist. It seems to command that you *will* enjoy this history lesson.

The exhibit is on two levels: pre-Roman on the ground floor (Greek artifacts from the Temple of Hera in front, frescoes from tombs in the back) and Roman art upstairs (statues, busts, and inscriptions dating from the time of the Roman occupation). While Roman art is not unique to Paestum, the Greek collection is—so that's what you should focus on. Here are the highlights:

Temple Reliefs: Wrapping around the first room, the large carvings overhead once adorned a sanctuary of the goddess Hera (wife of Zeus) five miles outside the city. Some of the carvings show scenes from the life of Hercules.

• *In the back of this room are glass cases holding nine perfectly preserved...*

Vases: One ceramic and eight bronze, with artistic handles, these vases were found in Paestum's Greek Memorial Tomb (described earlier). Greek bronzes are rare because Romans often melted them down to make armor. These were discovered in 1952, filled with still-liquid honey and sealed with beeswax. The honey (as you can see in the display cases below) has since crystallized. Honey was a standard part of a funeral because, to ancient Greeks, honey symbolized immortality...it lasts forever.

• *The next room is filled with ancient Greek...*

Votive Offerings: These were dug up around the Temple of Hera. Such offerings are a huge help to modern archaeologists, since the figures worshippers brought to a temple are clues as to which god the temple honored. These votives depict a woman with a crown on a throne—clearly Hera. The clay votives were simple, affordable, and accessible to regular people.

• *The next room holds...*

Temple Ornaments: The temples were once adorned with decorations, such as these ornamental spouts that spurted rainwater out of lions' mouths. Notice the bits of the surviving black, red, and white paint, and the reconstructions showing archaeologists' best guesses as to how the original decorations might have looked.

• *In a glass case nearby, find the statue of...*

Zeus: This painted clay statue of Zeus dates from 520 B.C. The king of the gods was so lusty with his antics, he's still smirking.

• *Look out the museum's back window for a good...*

View of Ancient Paestum: The walls of ancient Paestum reach halfway to the mountain—a reminder that most of the site is still private property and yet to be excavated. The town up on the mountainside is Capaccio, established in the eighth century when inhabitants of the original city of Paestum were driven out by malaria and the city was abandoned.

• *Along the corridor are...*

Objects from Tombs: Over 1,000 tombs have been identified outside of the ancient city's wall. About 100 were found decorated with frescoes or containing objects such as these.

• *At the end of the corridor is...*

The Tomb of the Diver: This is the museum's treasure and the most precious Paestum find. Dating from 480 B.C., it's the only Greek tomb fresco ever found in southern Italy. Discovered in

1968, it has five frescoed slabs (four sides and a lid; the bottom wasn't decorated). The Greeks saw death as a passage: diving from mortality into immortality...into an unknown world. Archaeologists believe that the pillars shown on the fresco are actually the Pillars

of Hercules at Gibraltar, which in ancient times defined the known world. The ocean beyond the Mediterranean was the great unknown...like the afterlife. The Greek banquet makes it clear that this was an aristocratic man. This is the only ancient Greek tomb fresco in the museum.

• *After the Tomb of the Diver, a room displays...*

Lucanian Tomb Frescoes: The many other painted slabs in the museum date from a later time, around 350 B.C., when Paestum fell under Lucanian rule. These frescoes are cruder than their earlier Greek counterpart. The people who conquered the Greeks tried to appropriate their art and style, but lacked the Greeks' distinct, light touch. Still, these offer fascinating glimpses into ancient life here at Paestum.

Sleeping in Paestum

(€1 = about $1.25, country code: 39)
Paestum at night, with views of the floodlit ruins, is magic.

$$ Il Granaio dei Casabella, a converted old granary, is close to the action and reasonably priced. It has a beautiful garden, and views of one of the ancient temples from a corner of the property (Sb-€80–100, Db-€100–120, tel. 082-872-1014, fax 082-881-1893, Via Tavernelle 84, www.ilgranaiodeicasabella.com, info@ilgranaiodeicasabella.com, hospitable owners Angelo and Laura, manager Regina).

$ Hotel Villa Rita is a tidy, quiet country hotel set on two acres within walking distance of the beach and the temples. It has 19 bright, modern air-conditioned rooms, a kid-friendly swimming pool, and free parking (Db-€90–100, €130 in Aug, third bed-€30, lunch or dinner-€15, Luigi promises a 10 percent discount with this book and cash in 2011, Wi-Fi, Via Principe di Piemonte—a.k.a. Via Nettuno—9; tel. 082-881-1081, fax-082-872-2555, www.hotelvillarita.it, info@hotelvillarita.it). The hotel is a 10-minute walk west of the Hera entrance and public bus stop, and a 15-minute walk from the train station.

Nearby

$$ Agriturismo Seliano offers 14 spacious, spotless rooms on a peaceful ramshackle, once-elegant farm estate with plush public spaces and a pool (Db-€115 in Aug, €95 in July, €75 Sept–June, air-con, serves a fine €20 lunch or dinner with produce fresh from the garden and all your drinks, one mile north of ruins on main road—Via Magna Grecia—a small sign directs you down long dirt driveway, best for drivers, tel. 082-872-3634, www.agriturismoseliano.it, seliano@agriturismoseliano.it, run by Cecilia, an English-speaking baroness).

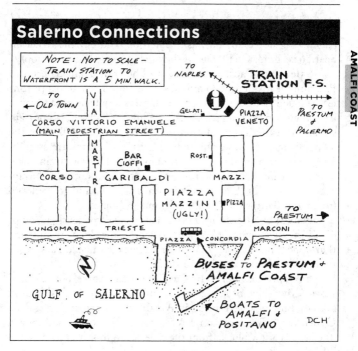

Paestum Connections

Salerno and Paestum

Salerno, the big city just north of Paestum, is the nearest transportation hub. From Naples or Sorrento, you'll change buses in
Salerno to reach Paestum; from Naples or Pompeii, the train is
easiest. Salerno's **TI** has bus, ferry, and train schedules (Mon–Sat
9:00–13:00 & 16:30–19:30, Sun 9:00–13:00, shorter hours and
closed Sun off-season, on Piazza Veneto, just outside train station,
tel. 089-231-432, toll-free 800-213-289, www.turismoinsalerno.it).

Salerno to Paestum by Bus: Four companies (CSTP, SCAT,
Giuliano, and Lettieri) offer a Salerno–Paestum bus service, all
conveniently leaving from the same stop at Piazza della Concordia
on the waterfront (2–3/hour, 80 minutes, schedules extremely
sparse on Sun—better by train). Buy the €3 round-trip ticket on
the bus, except on CSTP buses (buy these from the nearby *tabacchi*). No clear schedule is posted at the Salerno stop. Simply ask a
local or a bus representative at the stop for the next bus to Paestum;
otherwise, get a schedule at the TI (more impartial, since they
don't represent a particular company and their schedule shows all
companies and times). Note that orange city buses use the same
stop; ignore these.

When leaving Paestum, catch a northbound bus from either

of the intersections that flank the ruins (see map on the previous page). Flag down any bus, ask "Salerno?" and buy the ticket on board (except for CSTP buses—buy ticket at bar closest to stop).

Salerno to Paestum by Train: The train from Salerno to Paestum (nearly hourly, 35 minutes, direction: Paola or Sapri) runs less frequently than the buses, though it's a quicker ride because it's immune to traffic jams; check schedules at Salerno's TI or train station. Paestum's train station is an eight-minute walk from the ruins (from station, go through old city wall, ruins are straight ahead). If you plan to leave Paestum by train, buy your train ticket at the bar-café near the TI, because the station is not staffed (train schedules at TI). Leaving Paestum, trains bound for Salerno (direction: Battipaglia) usually continue to Naples.

Naples to Salerno by Train: Trains run frequently (2/hour, 45–75 minutes), but don't board the extra-slow *diretto* train. Note that some trains stop at Pompeii, and some continue to Paestum— ideal if you want to avoid a transfer.

Sorrento to Salerno by Bus: The scenic three-hour Amalfi Coast drive (blue or green-and-white SITA bus, in peak season 20/day, 3 hours, easy transfer in Amalfi) drops you at Piazza della Concordia (where you can catch a bus to Paestum—see above). The stop is a few blocks from the Salerno train station, where the TI is located.

Buses from Salerno to Sorrento (and points in between) stop directly in front of Salerno's train station exit, on the median strip under the *Fermata SITA* sign. Buy your bus ticket at the newsstand inside the train station and tell the vendor your destination (prices vary). If it's closed, try the ticket windows in the train station or walk two blocks to Bar Cioffi (CHOH-fee), across the square from Piazza della Concordia (see map above). Ticket vendors change periodically; if Bar Cioffi no longer sells tickets, ask anyone, such as a clerk at a *tabacchi* or magazine shop, "Who sells bus tickets to ?" by saying, *"Chi vende i biglietti dell'autobus per ?"* (kee VEHN-dee ee beel-YET-tee del-OW-toh-boos pehr).

Sorrento to Salerno by Train: Ride the Circumvesuviana to Naples' Centrale station (2/hour, 70 minutes) and catch the Salerno train (2/hour, 45 minutes).

Salerno by Ferry to: **Amalfi** (4–6/day, 35 minutes, €6), **Positano** (6/day, 70 minutes, €10), **Capri** (2/day, 2 hours, €16). Boats run May–Sept with fewer boats off-season. Most ferries depart from Salerno's Piazza della Concordia, shown on the map on the previous page (tickets and info at TravelMar, Piazza della Concordia, tel. 089-872-950, www.travelmar.it).

Drivers: While the Amalfi Coast is a thrill to drive off-season, summer traffic is miserable. From Sorrento, Paestum is 60 miles and three hours via the coast and a much smoother two hours by autostrada. To reach Paestum from Sorrento via the autostrada, drive toward Naples, catch the autostrada (direction: Salerno), skirt Salerno (direction: Reggio), exit at Battipaglia, and drive straight through the roundabout. During your ride, you'll see many signs for *mozzarella di bufala*, cheese made from the milk of water buffalo. Try it here—it can't be any fresher.

ITALIAN HISTORY

Italy has a lot of history, so let's get started.

Origins of Rome (c. 753 B.C.–450 B.C.)

A she-wolf breastfed two human babies, Romulus and Remus, who grew to build the city of Rome in 753 B.C.—you buy that? Closer to fact, farmers and shepherds of the Latin tribe settled near the mouth of the Tiber River, a convenient trading location. The crude settlement was sandwiched between two sophisticated civilizations—Greek colonists to the south (Magna Grecia, or greater Greece), and the Etruscans of Tuscany, whose origins and language are largely still a mystery to historians (for more on the Etruscans, see page 616). Baby Rome was both dominated and nourished by these societies.

When an Etruscan king raped a Roman woman (509 B.C.), her husband led a revolt, driving out the Etruscan kings and replacing them with elected Roman senators and (eventually) a code of law ("Laws of the Twelve Tables," 450 B.C.). The Roman Republic was born.

The Roman Republic Expands (c. 509 B.C.–A.D. 1)

Located in the center of the peninsula, Rome was perfectly situated for trading salt and wine. Roman businessmen, backed by a disciplined army, expanded through the Italian peninsula, establishing a Roman infrastructure as they went. Rome soon swallowed up its northern Etruscan neighbors, conquering them by force and absorbing their culture.

Next came Magna Grecia, with Rome's legions defeating the Greek general Pyrrhus after several costly "Pyrrhic" victories (c. 275 B.C.). Rome now ruled a united federation stretching from

Tuscany to the toe, with a standard currency, a system of roads (including the Via Appia), and a standing army of a half-million soldiers ready for the next challenge: Carthage.

Carthage (modern-day Tunisia) and Rome fought the three bitter Punic Wars for control of the Mediterranean (264–201 B.C. and 146 B.C.). The balance of power hung precariously in the Second Punic War (218–201 B.C.), when Hannibal of Carthage crossed the sea to Spain with a huge army of men and elephants. He marched 1,200 miles overland, crossed the Alps, and forcefully penetrated Italy from the rear. Almost at the gates of the city of Rome, he was finally turned back. The Romans prevailed and, in the mismatched Third Punic War, they burned the city of Carthage to the ground (146 B.C.).

The well-tuned Roman legions easily subdued sophisticated Greece in three Macedonian Wars (215–146 B.C.). Though Rome conquered Greece, Greek culture dominated the Romans. From hairstyles to statues to temples to the evening's entertainment, Rome was forever "Hellenized," becoming the curators of Greek culture, passing it down to future generations.

By the first century B.C., Rome was master of the Mediterranean. Booty, cheap grain, and thousands of captured slaves poured in, transforming the economic model from small farmers to unemployed city dwellers living off tribute from conquered lands. The Republic had changed.

Civil Wars and the Transition to Empire (First Century B.C.)

With easy money streaming in and traditional roles obsolete, Romans bickered among themselves over their slice of the pie. Wealthy landowners (patricians, the ruling Senate) wrangled with the middle and working classes (plebeians) and with the growing population of slaves, who demanded greater say-so in government. In 73 B.C., Spartacus—a Greek-born soldier-turned–Roman slave who'd been forced to fight as a gladiator—escaped to the slopes of Mount Vesuvius, where he amassed an army of 70,000 angry slaves. After two years of fierce fighting across Italy, the Roman legions crushed the revolt and crucified 6,000 rebels along the Via Appia as a warning.

Amid the chaos of class war and civil war, charismatic generals who could provide wealth and security became dictators—men such as Sulla, Crassus, Pompey...and Caesar. Julius Caesar (100–44 B.C.) was a cunning politician, riveting speaker, conqueror of Gaul, author of *The Gallic Wars,* and lover of Cleopatra, Queen of Egypt. In his four-year reign, he reformed and centralized the government around himself. Disgruntled Republicans feared that he would make himself king. At his peak of power, they surrounded

THE
ROMAN EMPIRE
AT ITS PEAK:
PAX ROMANA A.D. 120

Caesar in the Senate on the "Ides of March" (March 15, 44 B.C.) and stabbed him to death.

Julius Caesar died, but the concept of one-man rule lived on in his adopted son. Named Octavian at birth, he defeated rival Mark Antony (another lover of Cleopatra, 31 B.C.) and was proclaimed Emperor Augustus (27 B.C.). Augustus outwardly followed the traditions of the Republic, while in practice he acted as a dictator with the backing of Rome's legions and the rubber-stamp approval of the Senate. He established his family to succeed him (making the family name "Caesar" a title), and set the pattern of rule by emperors for the next 500 years.

The Roman Empire (c. A.D. 1–500)

In his 40-year reign, Augustus ended Rome's civil wars and ushered in 200 years of prosperity and relative peace called the Pax Romana. Rome ruled an empire of 54 million people, stretching from Scotland to Africa, from Spain to the "Cradle of Civilization" (modern-day Iraq). Conquered peoples were welcomed into the fold of prosperity, linked by roads, common laws, common gods, education, and the Latin language. The city of Rome, with more than a million inhabitants, was decorated with Greek-style statues and monumental structures faced with marble. It was the marvel of the known world.

The empire prospered on a (false) economy of booty, slaves, and cheap imports. On the Italian peninsula, traditional small farms were swallowed up by large farming and herding estates. In this "global economy," the Italian peninsula became just one province of many in a worldwide Latin-speaking empire, ruled by an emperor who was likely born elsewhere. The empire even survived the often turbulent and naughty behavior of emperors such as Caligula (r. 37–41) and Nero (r. 54–68).

Decline and Fall (A.D. 200–500)

Rome peaked in the second century A.D. under the capable emperors Trajan (r. 98–117), Hadrian (r. 117–138), and Marcus Aurelius (r. 161–180). For the next three centuries, the Roman Empire declined, shrinking in size and wealth, a victim of corruption, disease, an overextended army, a false economy, and the constant pressure of "barbarian" tribes pecking away at the borders. By the third century, the army had become the real power, handpicking figurehead emperors to do its bidding—in a 40-year span, 15 emperors were saluted then assassinated by fickle generals.

Trying to stall the disintegration, Emperor Diocletian (r. 284–305) split the empire into two administrative halves under two equal emperors. Constantine (r. 306–337) solidified the divide by moving the capital of the empire from decaying Rome to the new city of Constantinople (330, present-day Istanbul). Almost instantly, the once-great city of Rome became a minor player in imperial affairs. (The eastern "Byzantine" half of the empire would thrive and live on for another thousand years.) Constantine also legalized Christianity (313), and the once-persecuted cult soon became virtually the state religion, the backbone of Rome's fading hierarchy.

By 410, "Rome" had shrunk to the city itself, surrounded by a protective wall. Barbarian tribes from the north and east poured in to loot and plunder. The city was sacked by Visigoths (410), vandalized by Vandals (455), and the pope had to plead with Attila the Hun for mercy (451). The peninsula's population fell to six million, trade and agriculture were disrupted, schools closed, and the infrastructure collapsed. Peasants huddled near powerful lords for protection from bandits, planting the seeds of medieval feudalism.

In 476, the last emperor sold his title for a comfy pension, and Rome fell like a huge column, kicking up dust that would plunge Europe into a thousand years of darkness. For the next 13 centuries, there would be no "Italy," just a patchwork of rural dukedoms and towns, victimized by foreign powers. Italy lay in shambles, helpless.

Invasions (A.D. 500–1000)

In 500 years, Italy suffered through a full paragraph of invasions: Lombards (568) and Byzantines (under Justinian, 536) occupied the north. In the south, Muslim Saracens (827) and Normans (1061) established thriving kingdoms. Charlemagne, King of the Franks (a Germanic tribe), defeated the Lombards, and on Christmas Day A.D. 800, he knelt before the pope in St. Peter's in Rome to be crowned "Holy Roman Emperor." For the next thousand years, Italians would pledge nominal allegiance to weak, distant German kings as their "Holy Roman Emperor," an empty title meant to resurrect the glory of ancient Rome united with medieval Christianity.

Through all of the invasions and chaos, the glory of ancient Rome was preserved in the pomp, knowledge, hierarchy, and wealth of the Christian Church. Strong popes (Leo I, 440–461, and Gregory the Great, 590–604) ruled like small-time emperors, governing territories in central Italy called the Papal States.

Prosperity and Politics (A.D. 1000–1300)

Italy survived Y1K, and the economy picked up. Sea-trading cities like Venice, Genoa, Pisa, Naples, and Amalfi grew wealthy as middlemen between Europe and the Orient. During the Crusades (e.g., First Crusade 1097–1130), Italian ships ferried Europe's Christian soldiers eastward, then returned laden with spices and highly marked-up luxury goods from the Orient. Trade spawned banking, and Italians became capitalists, loaning money at interest to Europe's royalty. Italy pioneered a new phenomenon in Europe—cities *(comuni)* that were self-governing commercial centers. The medieval prosperity of the cities laid the foundation of the future Renaissance.

Politically, the Italian peninsula was dominated by two rulers—the pope in Rome and the German "Holy Roman Emperor" (with holdings in the north). It split Italy into two warring political parties: supporters of the popes (called Guelphs, centered in urban areas) and those of the emperors (Ghibellines, popular with the rural nobility).

The Unlucky 1300s

In 1309, the pope—enticed by Europe's fast-rising power, France—moved from Rome to Avignon, France. At one point, two rival popes reigned, one in Avignon and the other in Rome, and they excommunicated each other. The papacy eventually returned to Rome (1377), but the schism had created a breakdown in central authority that was exacerbated by an outbreak of bubonic plague (Black Death, 1347–1348) that killed a third of Italians.

In the power vacuum, new powers emerged in the independent cities. Venice, Florence, Milan, and Naples were under the protection and leadership of local noble families *(signoria)* such as the Medici in Florence. Florence thrived in the wool and dyeing trade, which led to international banking, with branches in all of

Church Architecture

History comes to life when you visit a centuries-old church. Even if you wouldn't know your apse from a hole in the ground, learning a few simple terms will enrich your experience. Note that not every church has every feature, and that a "cathedral" isn't a type of church architecture, but rather a designation for a church that's a governing center for a local bishop.

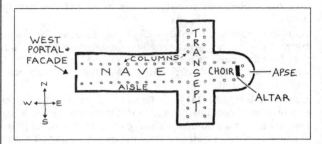

Aisles: The long, generally low-ceilinged arcades that flank the nave.

Altar: The raised area with a ceremonial table (often adorned with candles or a crucifix), where the priest prepares and serves the bread and wine for Communion.

Apse: The space beyond the altar, generally bordered with small chapels.

Choir: A cozy area, often screened off, located within the church nave and near the high altar, where services are sung in a more intimate setting.

Cloister: A square-shaped series of hallways surrounding an open-air courtyard, traditionally where monks and nuns got fresh air.

Facade: The outer wall of the church's main (west) entrance, viewable from outside and generally highly decorated.

Groin Vault: An arched ceiling formed where two equal barrel vaults meet at right angles. Less common usage: term for a medieval jock strap.

Narthex: The area (portico or foyer) between the main entry and the nave.

Nave: The long, central section of the church (running west to east, from the entrance to the altar) where, in medieval times, the congregation stood through the service.

Transept: The north–south part of the church, which crosses (perpendicularly) the east–west nave. In a traditional Latin cross-shaped floor plan, the transept forms the "arms" of the cross.

West Portal: The main entry to the church (on the west end, opposite the main altar).

Top 10 Italians

Romulus: Breastfed on wolf milk, this legendary orphan grew to found the city of Rome (traditionally in 753 B.C.). Over the next seven centuries, his descendants dominated the Italian peninsula, ruling from Rome as a Republic.

Julius Caesar (100–44 B.C.): After conquering Gaul (France), subduing Egypt, and winning Cleopatra's heart, Caesar ruled Rome with king-like powers. In an attempt to preserve the Republic, senators stabbed him to death, but the concept of one-man rule lived on.

Augustus (born Octavian, 63 B.C.–A.D. 14): Julius's adopted son became the first of the Caesars that ruled Rome during its 500 years as a Europe-wide power. He set the tone for emperors both good (Trajan, Hadrian, Marcus Aurelius) and bad (Caligula, Nero, and dozens of others).

Constantine (c. 280–337 A.D.): Raised in a Christian home, this emperor legalized Christianity, almost instantly turning a persecuted sect into a Europe-wide religion. With the Fall of Rome, the Church was directed by strong popes and so guided Italians through the next thousand years of invasions, plagues, political decentralization, and darkness.

Lorenzo the Magnificent (1449–1492): Soldier, poet, lover, and ruler of Florence in the 1400s, this Renaissance Man embodied the "rebirth" of ancient enlightenment. Lorenzo's wealthy Medici family funded Florentine artists who pioneered a realistic 3-D style.

Michelangelo Buonarroti (1475–1564): His statue of *David*—slaying an ignorant brute—stands as a monumental symbol of Italian enlightenment. Along with fellow geniuses Leonardo da Vinci and Raphael, Michelangelo spread the Italian Renaissance (painting, sculpture, architecture, literature, and ideas) to a worldwide audience.

Europe's capitals. A positive side effect of the terrible Black Death was that the now-smaller population got a bigger share of the land, jobs, and infrastructure. By century's end, Italy was poised to enter its most glorious era since antiquity.

The Renaissance (1400s)

The Renaissance *(Rinascimento)*—the "rebirth" of ancient Greek and Roman art styles, knowledge, and humanism—began in Italy (c. 1400), and spread through Europe over the next two centuries. Many of Europe's most famous painters, sculptors, and thinkers—Michelangelo, Leonardo, Raphael, etc.—were Italian.

It was a cultural boom that changed people's thinking about

Giovanni Lorenzo Bernini (1598–1680): The "Michelangelo of Baroque" kept Italy a major exporter of sophisticated trends. Bernini's ornate statues and architecture decorated palaces of the rising power in France, even as Italy was reverting to an economically stagnant patchwork of foreign-ruled states.

Victor Emmanuel II (1820–1878): As the only Italian-born ruler on the peninsula, this King of Sardinia became the rallying point for Italian unification. Aided by the general Garibaldi, writer Mazzini, and politician Cavour (with a soundtrack by Verdi), he became the first ruler of a united, democratic Italy in September 1870. (The preceding proper nouns have since come to adorn streets and piazzas throughout Italy.)

Benito Mussolini (1883–1945): A kinder, gentler Hitler, he derailed Italy's fledgling democracy, becoming dictator of a fascist state, leading the country into defeat in World War II. No public places honor Mussolini, but many streets and piazzas throughout Italy bear the name of Giacomo Matteotti (1885–1924), a politician whose outspoken opposition to Mussolini got him killed by Fascists.

Federico Fellini (1920–1993): Fellini's films (*La Strada, La Dolce Vita, 8½*) chronicle Italy's postwar years in gritty black and white—the poverty, destruction, and disillusionment of the war followed by the optimism, decadence, and materialism of the economic boom. He captured the surreal chaos of Italy's abrupt social change from traditional Catholic to a secular, urban world presided over by Mafia bosses and weak government.

Top Italian Number 11 (?): Has Italy produced another recent citizen who's dominant enough to make his or her mark on the world? Could it be Prime Minister Silvio Berlusconi, Italy's richest man? Opera singer Luciano Pavarotti? Or big-pec'd model "Fabio" Lanzoni, named "Sexiest Man on Earth" by *Cosmopolitan* magazine? The world awaits.

every aspect of life. In politics, it meant democracy. In religion, it meant a move away from Church dominance and toward the assertion of man (humanism) and a more personal faith. Science and secular learning were revived after centuries of superstition and ignorance. In architecture, it was a return to the balanced columns and domes of Greece and Rome. In painting, the Renaissance meant 3-D realism.

Italians dotted their cities with publicly financed art—Greek gods, Roman-style domed buildings. They preached Greek-style democracy and explored the natural world. The cultural boom was financed by booming trade and lucrative banking. In the Renaissance, the peninsula once again became the trendsetting cultural center of Europe.

End of the Renaissance, France and Spain Invade (1500s)

In May 1498, Vasco da Gama of Portugal landed in India, having found a sea route around Africa. Italy's monopoly on trade with the East was broken. Portugal, France, Spain, England, and Holland—nation-states under strong central rule—began to overtake decentralized Italy. Italy's once-great maritime cities now traded in an economic backwater, just as Italy's bankers (such as the Medici in Florence) were going bankrupt. While the Italian Renaissance was all the rage throughout Europe, it declined in its birthplace. Italy—culturally sophisticated but weak and decentralized—was ripe for the picking by Europe's rising powers.

France and Spain invaded (1494 and 1495)—initially invited by Italian lords to attack their rivals—and began divvying up territory for their noble families. Italy also became a battleground in religious conflicts between Catholics and the new Protestant movement. In the chaos, the city of Rome was brutally sacked by foreign mercenary warriors (1527).

Foreign Rule (1600–1800)

For the next two centuries, most of Italy's states were ruled by foreign nobles, serving as prizes for the winners of Europe's dynastic wars. Italy ceased to be a major player in Europe, politically or economically. Italian intellectual life was often cropped short by a conservative Catholic Church trying to fight Protestantism. Galileo, for example, was forced by the Inquisition to renounce his belief that the earth orbited the sun (1633). But Italy did export Baroque art (Giovanni Lorenzo Bernini) and the budding new medium of opera.

The War of the Spanish Succession (1713)—a war in which Italy did not participate—gave much of northern Italy to Austria's ruling family, the Habsburgs (who now wore the crown of "Holy Roman Emperor"). In the south, Spain's Bourbon family ruled the Kingdom of Naples (known after 1816 as the Kingdom of the Two Sicilies), making it a culturally sophisticated but economically backward area, preserving a medieval, feudal caste system.

In 1720, a minor war (the War of Austrian Succession) created a new state at the foot of the Alps, called the Kingdom of Sardinia (a.k.a. the Kingdom of Piedmont, or Savoy). Ruled by the Savoy family, this was the only major state on the peninsula that was actually ruled by Italians. It proved to be a toehold to the future.

Italy Unites—The Risorgimento (1800s)

In 1796, Napoleon Bonaparte swept through Italy and changed everything. He ousted Austrian and Spanish dukes, confiscated Church lands, united scattered states, and crowned himself "King

Italian Unification

Note: Dates indicate the year of annexation to the Kingdom of Sardinia. After 1861, this became the Kingdom of Italy.

SWITZ.

AUSTRIA

VENETIA (1866)

LOMBARDY (1859)

PIEDMONT

PARMA

MOD.

• Venice

STATES OF THE CHURCH (1870)

• Florence

FRANCE

TUSCANY (1860)

KINGDOM OF SARDINIA

ADRIATIC SEA

SARDINIA

Rome •

Naples

KINGDOM OF THE TWO SICILIES

MEDITERRANEAN

SICILY

DCH

SEA

of Italy" (1805). After his defeat (1815), Italy's old ruling order (namely, Austria and Spain) was restored. But Napoleon had planted a seed: What if Italians could unite and rule themselves like Europe's other modern nations?

For the next 50 years, a movement to unite Italy slowly grew. Called the Risorgimento—a word that means "rising again"— the movement promised a revival of Italy's glory. It started as a revolutionary, liberal movement—taking part was punishable by death. Members of a secret society called the Carbonari (led by a professional revolutionary named Giuseppe Mazzini) exchanged secret handshakes, printed fliers, planted bombs, and assassinated conservative rulers. Their small revolutions (1820–1821, 1831, 1848) were easily and brutally slapped down, but the cause wouldn't die.

Gradually, Italians of all stripes warmed to the idea of unification. Whether it was a united dictatorship, a united papal state, a united kingdom, or a united democracy, most Italians could agree that it was time for Spain, Austria, and France to leave.

The movement coalesced around the Italian-ruled Kingdom of Sardinia and its king, Victor Emmanuel II. In 1859, Sardinia's prime minister, Camillo Cavour, cleverly persuaded France to drive Austria out of northern Italy, leaving the region in Italian hands. A plebiscite (vote) was held, and several central Italian states (including some of the pope's) rejected their feudal lords and chose to join the growing Kingdom of Sardinia.

After victory in the north, Italy's most renowned Carbonari general, Giuseppe Garibaldi (1807–1882), steamed south with a thousand of his best soldiers *(I Mille)* and marched on the Spanish-ruled city of Naples (1860). The old order simply collapsed. In two short months, Garibaldi had achieved a seemingly impossible victory against a far superior army. Garibaldi sent a one-word telegram to the king of Sardinia: *"Obbedisco"* (I obey). The following year, an assembly of deputies from throughout Italy met in Turin and crowned Victor Emmanuel II "King of Italy." Only the pope in Rome held out, protected by French troops. When the city finally fell easily to the unification forces on September 20, 1870, the Risorgimento was complete. Italy went ape.

The Risorgimento was largely the work of four men: Garibaldi (the sword), Mazzini (the spark), Cavour (the diplomat), and Victor Emmanuel II (the rallying point). Today, street signs throughout Italy honor them and the dates of their great victories.

Mussolini and War (1900–1950)

Italy—now an actual nation-state, not just a linguistic region—entered the 20th century with a progressive government (a constitutional monarchy), a collection of colonies, and a flourishing northern half of the country. In the economically backward south (the Mezzogiorno), millions of poor peasants emigrated to the Americas. World War I (1915–1918) left 650,000 Italians dead, but being on the winning Allied side, survivors were granted possession of the alpine regions. In the postwar cynicism and anarchy, many radical political parties rose up—Communist, Socialist, Popular, and Fascist.

Benito Mussolini (1883–1945), a popular writer for socialist and labor-union newspapers, led the Fascists. ("Fascism" comes from Latin *fasci*, the bundles of rods that symbolized unity in ancient Rome.) Though only a minority (6 percent of the parliament in 1921), they intimidated the disorganized majority with organized violence by black-shirted Fascist gangs. In 1922, Mussolini seized the government (see "The March on Rome" sidebar) and began his rule as dictator for the next two decades.

Mussolini solidified his reign among Catholics by striking an agreement with the pope (Concordato, 1929), giving Vatican City to the pope, while Mussolini ruled Italy with the implied bless-

The March on Rome

In October 1922, Benito Mussolini, head of the newly formed Fascist Party, boldly proposed a coup d'état, saying: "Either the government will be given to us, or we will take it by marching on Rome." Throughout Italy, black-shirted Fascists occupied government buildings in their hometowns. Others grabbed guns, farming hoes, and kitchen knives and set off to converge on the outskirts of Rome. (Estimates of the size of the Fascist band range from 300 to the 300,000 of Fascist legend.) Mussolini sent the government an ultimatum to surrender. Though the Fascists were easily outmanned and outgunned by government forces, the show of force intimidated the king, Victor Emmanuel III, into avoiding a nasty confrontation. He invited Mussolini to Rome. Mussolini arrived the next day (by first-class train), was made prime minister, then marched his black-shirted troops triumphantly through the streets of Rome.

ing of the Catholic Church. Italy responded to the great worldwide Depression (1930s) with big public works projects (including Rome's subway), government investment in industry, and an expanded army.

Mussolini allied his country with Hitler's Nazi regime, drawing an unprepared Italy into World War II (1940). Italy's lame army was never a factor in the war, and when Allied forces landed in Sicily (1943), Italians welcomed them as liberators. The Italians toppled Mussolini's government and surrendered to the Allies, but Nazi Germany sent troops to rescue Mussolini. The war raged on as Allied troops inched their way north against German resistance. Italians were reduced to dire poverty. In the last days of the war (April 1945), Mussolini was captured by the Italian resistance. They shot him and his girlfriend and hung their bodies upside down in a public square in Milan.

Postwar Italy

At war's end, Italy was physically ruined and extremely poor. The nation rebuilt in the 1950s and 1960s (the "economic miracle") with Marshall Plan aid from the United States. Many Italian men moved to northern Europe to find work; many others left the farm and flocked to cities. Italy regained its standing among nations, joining the United Nations, NATO, and, eventually, the European Union.

However, the government remained weak, changing on average once a year, shifting from right to left to centrist coalitions (it's had 61 governments since World War II). All Italians acknowledged that the real power lay in the hands of backroom politicians and organized crime—a phenomenon called *Tangentopoli*, or "Bribe City." The country remained strongly divided between the rich, industrial north and the poor, rural south.

Italian society changed greatly in the 1960s and 1970s, spurred by the liberal reforms of the Catholic Church at the Vatican II conference (1962–1965). The once-conservative Catholic country legalized divorce and contraception, and the birth rate plummeted. In the 1970s, the economy slowed thanks to inflation, strikes, and the worldwide energy crisis. Italy suffered a wave of violence from left- and right-wing domestic terrorists and organized crime, punctuated by the assassination of Prime Minister Aldo Moro (1978). A series of coalition governments in the 1980s brought some stability to the economy.

Italy Today

In the early 1990s, the judiciary launched a campaign to rid politics of corruption and Mafia ties. Though still ongoing, the investigation sent a message that Italy would no longer tolerate evils that were considered necessary just a generation earlier. As home to the Vatican, Italy keeps a close watch on the Catholic church's ongoing scandal of pedophile priests.

In 2001, controverisal billionaire Silvio Berlusconi, the owner of many of Italy's media outlets and Italy's richest person, became prime minister, heading a center-right coalition. In 2003, Berlusconi backed the US invasion of Iraq, a policy that polarized Italy—and three years later, he lost a close election to former Prime Minister Romano Prodi, who opposed the Iraq war. But in 2008, the 74-year-old Berlusconi was re-elected after promising to keep Italy out of Iraq. Berlusconi's personal life makes him a polarizing figure, a role he seems to relish. Whether he's being accused of corruption or of consorting with women three-fourths his age, Berlusconi appeals to a populist base while eliciting shudders of disgust from others. The next elections are in 2013.

The Greek debt crisis of 2010 that threatened Europe's economic stability forced Italy to tighten its belt. Though not in the same situation as Greece, Italy has run up big deficits providing comfy social security to a populace that has come to expect generous public benefits as a right.

As you travel through Italy today, you'll encounter a thriving country with a rich history and a per capita income that rivals its neighbors to the north. Italy is enthusiastically part of Europe...yet it's as wonderfully Italian as ever.

APPENDIX

Contents

Tourist Information

The Italian national tourist offices **in the US** are a wealth of information. Before your trip, scan their website (www.italiantourism .com) or contact the nearest branch to briefly describe your trip and request information. They'll mail you a general interest brochure and you can download many other brochures free of charge. If you have a specific problem, they're a good source of sympathy.

In New York: tel. 212/245-5618, brochure hotline tel. 212/245-4822, fax 212/586-9249, newyork@enit.it; 630 Fifth Ave. #1565, New York, NY 10111.

In Illinois: tel. 312/644-0996, brochure hotline tel. 312/644-0990, fax 312/644-3019, chicago@enit.it; 500 N. Michigan Ave. #506, Chicago, IL 60611.

In California: tel. 310/820-1898, brochure hotline tel. 310/820-0098, fax 310/820-6357, losangeles@enit.it; 12400 Wilshire Blvd. #550, Los Angeles, CA 90025.

In **Italy,** your best first stop is generally the tourist information office (abbreviated **TI** in this book, and marked *i, turismo,* and *APT* in Italy). While Italian TIs are about half as helpful as those in other countries, their information is twice as important. Prepare a list of questions and a proposed plan to double-check.

TIs are good places to get a city map, advice on public transportation (including bus and train schedules), walking-tour information, tips on special events, and recommendations for nightlife. Many TIs have information on the entire country or at least the region, so try to pick up maps for destinations you'll be visiting later in your trip. If you're arriving in town after the TI closes, call ahead or pick up a map in a neighboring town. Since Italy is ever-changing, ask the local TI for a current list of the city's sights, hours, and prices.

Be wary of the travel agencies or special information services that masquerade as TIs but serve fancy hotels and tour companies. They're in the business of selling things you don't need.

While the TI is eager to book you a room, use its room-finding service only as a last resort. They are unable to give hard opinions on the relative value of one place over another. The accommodations stakes are too high to go potluck through the TI. Even if there's no "fee," you'll save yourself and your host money by going direct with the listings in this book.

Communicating

Hurdling the Language Barrier

Many Italians—especially those in the tourist trade and in big cities—speak some English. Still, you'll get more smiles and results by using at least the Italian pleasantries. In smaller, nontouristy towns, Italian is the norm. For a list of survival phrases, see page 989.

Note that Italian is pronounced much like English, with a few exceptions, such as: c followed by e or i is pronounced ch (to ask, *"Per centro?"*—To the center?—you say, pehr CHEHN-troh). In Italian, ch is pronounced like the hard c in Chianti (*chiesa*—church—is pronounced kee-AY-zah). Give it your best shot. Italians appreciate your efforts.

Telephones

Smart travelers use the telephone to reserve or reconfirm rooms, get tourist information, reserve restaurants, confirm tour times, or phone home. Generally the easiest, cheapest way to call home is to use an international phone card purchased in Italy. This section covers dialing instructions, phone cards, and types of phones (for more in-depth information, see www.ricksteves.com/phoning).

APPENDIX

How to Dial

Calling from the US to Italy, or vice versa, is simple—once you break the code. The European calling chart later in this chapter will walk you through it.

Dialing Domestically Within Italy

Italy has a direct-dial phone system (no area codes). To call anywhere within Italy, just dial the number. For example, the number of one of my recommended Florence hotels is 055-289-592. That's the number you dial whether you're calling it from Florence's train station or from Rome.

Land lines start with 0; mobile lines start with 3; toll-free lines start with 80; and expensive toll lines begin with 8 followed by any number other than 0. Keep in mind that Italian phone numbers vary in length; a hotel can have, say, an eight-digit phone number and a nine-digit fax number.

Dialing Internationally to or from Italy

If you want to make an international call, follow these steps:

1. Dial the international access code (00 if you're calling from Europe, 011 from the US or Canada).

2. Dial the country code of the country you're calling (39 for Italy, or 1 for the US or Canada).

3. Dial the local number. Note that in most European countries, you have to drop the zero at the beginning of the local number—but in Italy, you dial it. (The European calling chart lists specifics per country.)

Calling from the US to Italy: To call the Florence hotel from the US, dial 011 (the US international access code), 39 (Italy's country code), then 055-289-592.

Calling from any European country to the US: To call my office in Edmonds, Washington, from anywhere in Europe, I dial 00 (Europe's international access code), 1 (the US country code), 425 (Edmonds' area code), and 771-8303.

Note: You might see a + in front of a European number. When dialing the number, replace the + with the international access code of the country you're calling from (00 from Europe, 011 from the US or Canada).

Public Phones and Hotel-Room Phones

To make calls from public phones, you'll need a prepaid phone card. There are two different kinds of phone cards: insertable and international. (Both types of phone cards work only in Italy. If you have a live card at the end of your trip, give it to another traveler to use up.) Coin-op phones are virtually extinct.

Insertable Phone Cards: This type of card can only be used at a pay phone. These Telecom cards, considered "official" since they're sold by Italy's phone company, give you the best deal for calls within Italy and are reasonable for international calls. You can buy Telecom cards in denominations of €5 or €10 at *tabacchi* (tobacco) shops, post offices, and machines near phone booths (many phone booths have signs indicating where the nearest phone-card sales outlet is located).

Rip off the perforated corner to "activate" the card, and then physically insert it into a slot in the pay phone. It displays how much money you have remaining on the card. Then just dial away. The price of the call is automatically deducted while you talk.

International Phone Cards: These are the cheapest way to make international calls from Europe—with the best cards, it costs literally pennies a minute. They can also be used to make local calls, and work from any type of phone, including your hotel-room phone. To use the card, you'll dial a toll-free access number, then type in your scratch-to-reveal PIN code. If you're calling from a hotel, be sure to dial the *freephone* number (starts with "80") provided on your card rather than the "local access" number (which would incur a charge).

You can buy the cards at small newsstand kiosks, *tabacchi* shops, Internet cafés, hostels, and hole-in-the-wall long-distance phone shops. Because there are so many brand names, simply ask for an international phone card (*carta telefonica prepagata internazionale*, KAR-tah teh-leh-FOHN-ee-kah pray-pah-GAH-tah inter-naht-zee-oh-NAH-lay). Tell the vendor where you'll be calling the most (*"per Stati Uniti"*—to America), and he'll select the brand with the best deal.

Buy a lower denomination in case the card is a dud. I've had good luck with the Europa card, which offers up to 350 minutes from Italy to the US for €5.

Hotel-Room Phones: Calling from your hotel room can be cheap for local calls (ask for the rates at the front desk first), but is often a rip-off for long-distance calls, unless you use an international phone card (explained above). Incoming calls are free, making this a cheap way for friends and family to stay in touch (provided they have a good long-distance plan for calls to Europe—and a list of your hotels' phone numbers).

US Calling Cards: These cards, such as the ones offered by AT&T, Verizon, or Sprint, are the worst option. You'll nearly always save a lot of money by using a locally purchased phone card instead.

Metered Phones: In Italy, some call shops have phones with meters. You can talk all you want, then pay the bill when you leave—but be sure you know the rates before you have a lengthy conversation. Note that charges can be "per unit" rather than per minute; find out the length of a unit.

Mobile Phones

Many travelers enjoy the convenience of traveling with a mobile phone.

Using Your Mobile Phone: Your US mobile phone works in Europe if it's GSM-enabled, tri-band or quad-band, and on a calling plan that includes international calls. Phones from T-Mobile and AT&T, which use the same GSM technology that Europe does, are more likely to work overseas than Verizon or Sprint phones (if you're not sure, ask your service provider). Most US providers charge $1.29 per minute while roaming internationally to make or receive calls, and 20–50 cents to send or receive text messages.

You'll pay cheaper rates if your phone is electronically "unlocked" (ask your provider about this); then in Europe, you can simply buy a tiny **SIM card,** which gives you a European phone number. SIM cards are sold at mobile-phone stores and some newsstand kiosks for about $5–10, and generally include several minutes' worth of prepaid domestic calling time. When you buy a SIM card, you may need to show ID, such as your passport. Insert the SIM card in your phone (usually in a slot behind the battery), and it'll work like a European mobile phone. When buying a SIM card, always ask about fees for domestic and international calls, roaming charges, and how to check your credit balance and buy more time.

Many **smartphones,** such as the iPhone or BlackBerry, work in Europe—but beware of sky-high fees, especially for data downloading (checking email, browsing the Internet, watching videos, and so on). Ask your provider in advance how to avoid unwittingly "roaming" your way to a huge bill. Some applications allow for cheap or free smartphone calls over a Wi-Fi connection.

Using a European Mobile Phone: Mobile-phone shops all over Europe sell basic phones. Phones that are "locked" to work with a single provider start around $20; "unlocked" phones (which allow you to switch out SIM cards to use your choice of provider) start around $60. You'll also need to buy a SIM card and prepaid credit for making calls. (My Italian friends tell me that TIM is a reliable Italian mobile-phone company.) When you're in the phone's home country, domestic calls are reasonable, and incoming calls are free. You'll pay more if you're "roaming" in another country.

Calling over the Internet

Some things that seem too good to be true...actually are true. If you're traveling with a laptop, you can make calls using VoIP (Voice over Internet Protocol). With VoIP, two computers act as the phones, and the Internet-based calls are free (or you can pay a

European Calling Chart

Just smile and dial, using this key:
AC = Area Code, LN = Local Number.

European Country	Calling long distance within ...	Calling from the US or Canada to ...	Calling from a European country to ...
Austria	AC + LN	011 + 43 + AC (without the initial zero) + LN	00 + 43 + AC (without the initial zero) + LN
Belgium	LN	011 + 32 + LN (without initial zero)	00 + 32 + LN (without initial zero)
Bosnia-Herzegovina	AC + LN	011 + 387 + AC (without initial zero) + LN	00 + 387 + AC (without initial zero) + LN
Britain	AC + LN	011 + 44 + AC (without initial zero) + LN	00 + 44 + AC (without initial zero) + LN
Croatia	AC + LN	011 + 385 + AC (without initial zero) + LN	00 + 385 + AC (without initial zero) + LN
Czech Republic	LN	011 + 420 + LN	00 + 420 + LN
Denmark	LN	011 + 45 + LN	00 + 45 + LN
Estonia	LN	011 + 372 + LN	00 + 372 + LN
Finland	AC + LN	011 + 358 + AC (without initial zero) + LN	999 (or other 900 number) + 358 + AC (without initial zero) + LN
France	LN	011 + 33 + LN (without initial zero)	00 + 33 + LN (without initial zero)
Germany	AC + LN	011 + 49 + AC (without initial zero) + LN	00 + 49 + AC (without initial zero) + LN
Gibraltar	LN	011 + 350 + LN	00 + 350 + LN
Greece	LN	011 + 30 + LN	00 + 30 + LN
Hungary	06 + AC + LN	011 + 36 + AC + LN	00 + 36 + AC + LN
Ireland	AC + LN	011 + 353 + AC (without initial zero) + LN	00 + 353 + AC (without initial zero) + LN

European Country	Calling long distance within ...	Calling from the US or Canada to ...	Calling from a European country to ...
Italy	LN	011 + 39 + LN	00 + 39 + LN
Montenegro	AC + LN	011 + 382 + AC (without initial zero) + LN	00 + 382 + AC (without initial zero) + LN
Morocco	LN	011 + 212 + LN (without initial zero)	00 + 212 + LN (without initial zero)
Netherlands	AC + LN	011 + 31 + AC (without initial zero) + LN	00 + 31 + AC (without initial zero) + LN
Norway	LN	011 + 47 + LN	00 + 47 + LN
Poland	LN	011 + 48 + LN (without initial zero)	00 + 48 + LN (without initial zero)
Portugal	LN	011 + 351 + LN	00 + 351 + LN
Slovakia	AC + LN	011 + 421 + AC (without initial zero) + LN	00 + 421 + AC (without initial zero) + LN
Slovenia	AC + LN	011 + 386 + AC (without initial zero) + LN	00 + 386 + AC (without initial zero) + LN
Spain	LN	011 + 34 + LN	00 + 34 + LN
Sweden	AC + LN	011 + 46 + AC (without initial zero) + LN	00 + 46 + AC (without initial zero) + LN
Switzerland	LN	011 + 41 + LN (without initial zero)	00 + 41 + LN (without initial zero)
Turkey	AC (if there's no initial zero, add one) + LN	011 + 90 + AC (without initial zero) + LN	00 + 90 + AC (without initial zero) + LN

- The instructions above apply whether you're calling a land line or mobile phone.
- The international access codes (the first numbers you dial when making an international call) are 011 if you're calling from the US or Canada, or 00 if you're calling from virtually anywhere in Europe (except Finland, where it's 999 or another 900 number, depending on the phone service you're using).
- To call the US or Canada from Europe, dial 00, then 1 (the country code for the US and Canada), then the area code and number. In short, 00 + 1 + AC + LN = Hi, Mom!

few cents to call from your computer to a telephone). If both computers have webcams, you can even see each other while you chat. The major providers are Skype (www.skype.com) and Google Talk (www.google.com/talk).

Useful Phone Numbers

Italy's toll-free numbers start with "80." These numbers—called *freephone* or *numero verde* (green number)—can be dialed free from any phone without using a phone card. Note that you can't call Italy's toll-free numbers from America, nor can you count on reaching America's toll-free numbers from Italy.

Any Italian phone number that starts with "8" but isn't followed by a "0" is a toll call, generally costing €0.10–0.50 per minute.

Emergency Needs
English-Speaking Police Help: 113
Ambulance: 118
Road Service: 116

Embassies and Consulates
US Embassy in Rome: 24-hour emergency line—tel. 06-46741, non-emergency—tel. 06-4674-2406 (Mon–Fri 8:30–12:30, closed Sat–Sun, Via Vittorio Veneto 121, www.usembassy.it)
US Consulates: Milan—tel. 02-290-351 (Via Principe Amedeo 2/10, http://milan.usconsulate.gov), **Florence**—tel. 055-266-951 (Lungarno Vespucci 38, http://florence.usconsulate.gov), **Naples**—tel. 081-583-8111 (Piazza della Repubblica, http://naples.usconsulate.gov)
Canadian Embassy in Rome: tel. 06-854-441 (Mon–Fri 9:00–12:00, closed Sat–Sun, Via Zara 30, Rome, www.italy.gc.ca)
Canadian Consulates: Naples—tel. 081-401-338 (Via Carducci 29), **Padua**—tel. 049-876-4833 (Riviera Ruzzante 25). The website for all locations is www.italy.gc.ca.

Travel Advisories
US Department of State: tel. 202/647-5225, www.travel.state.gov
Canadian Department of Foreign Affairs: Canadian tel. 800-267-6788, www.dfait-maeci.gc.ca
US Centers for Disease Control and Prevention: tel. 800-CDC-INFO (800-232-4636), www.cdc.gov/travel

Directory Assistance
Telephone Help (in English; free directory assistance): 170
Directory Assistance (for €0.50, an Italian-speaking robot gives the number twice, very clearly): 12

Internet Access

It's useful to get online periodically as you travel—to confirm trip plans, check train or bus schedules, get weather forecasts, catch up on email, blog or post photos from your trip, or call folks back home (explained earlier, under "Calling over the Internet").

Many hotels offer a computer in the lobby with Internet access for guests. Smaller places may sometimes let you sit at their desk for a few minutes just to check your email, if you ask politely. If your hotel doesn't have access, ask your hotelier to direct you to the nearest place to get online. Because of an anti-terrorism law in Italy, you may be asked to show your passport (carry it in your money belt) when using a public Internet terminal at an Internet café or in a hotel lobby. The proprietor will likely make a copy of your passport.

Traveling with a Laptop: With a laptop or netbook, it's easy to get online if your hotel has Wi-Fi (wireless Internet access) or a port in your room for plugging in a cable. Most hotels offer Wi-Fi for free; others charge by the minute or hour. A cellular modem—which lets your laptop access the Internet over a mobile phone network—provides more extensive coverage, but is much more expensive than Wi-Fi (in Italy, www.wind.it and www.tim.it offer pay-as-you-go mobile broadband).

Mail

While you can arrange for mail delivery to your hotel (allow 10 days for a letter to arrive), phoning and emailing are so easy that I've dispensed with mail stops altogether. Mail service in Italy has improved over the last few years, but even so, mail nothing precious from an Italian post office. Federal Express makes pricey two-day deliveries.

Transportation

By Car or Public Transportation?

Each has pros and cons. Public transportation is one of the few bargains in Italy. Trains give you the convenience and economy of doing long stretches overnight. By train, I arrive relaxed and well-rested—not so by car.

Cars are best for three or more traveling together (especially families with small kids), those packing heavy, and those scouring the countryside. Trains and buses are best for solo travelers, blitz tourists, and city-to-city travelers; those with an ambitious, multi-country itinerary; and those who don't want to drive.

While a car gives you more freedom—enabling you to search for hotels more easily and carrying your bags for you—trains and buses zip you scenically from city to city, usually dropping you in the center, often near a TI.

Considering how handy and affordable Italy's trains and buses are (and that you're likely to go both broke and crazy driving in Italian cities), I'd do most of Italy by public transportation. If you want to drive, consider doing the big, intense stuff (Rome, Naples area, Milan, Florence, and Venice) by train or bus and renting a car for the hill towns of central Italy and for the Dolomites. A car is a worthless headache on the Riviera and in the Lake Como area.

In this section, I'll cover specifics on traveling by train, bus, and car in Italy.

Trains

To travel cheaply in Italy, you can simply buy tickets as you go. Though train-station lines can be long, ticket machines work well and are easy to use (see "Buying Tickets," later). Pay all ticket costs in the station before you board or pay a penalty on the train.

Types of Trains: You'll encounter several types of trains in Italy: pokey *regionali,* slow *diretto* and IR *(interregionali),* medium-speed *espresso,* fast EC (EuroCity), IC (InterCity), and the super-fast ES (Eurostar Italia train, including Alta Velocità and Frecciarossa). If you're traveling with a railpass (covered below), note that reservations are optional for IC trains, but required for EC and international trains (€5) and ES trains (€10). Regional trains don't require reservations. A new high-speed rail service—Nuovo Trasporto Viaggiatori (NTV)—is expected to launch its Italo trains sometime in 2011 (www.ntvspa.it).

For point-to-point tickets, you'll pay more the faster you go, but even the fastest trains are affordable (for example, a second-class ticket on a Venice–Rome express train costs about €70).

Schedules: At the train station, the easiest way to check schedules is at a handy automated ticket machine (described later, under "Buying Tickets"). Enter the desired date, time, and destination to view all your options. Printed schedules are also posted at the station (departure posters are always yellow).

Newsstands sell up-to-date regional and all-Italy timetables (€5, ask for the *orario ferroviario*). On the Web, check http://bahn.hafas.de/bin/query.exe/en (Germany's excellent all-Europe website), or www.trenitalia.com. There is a single all-Italy telephone number for train information (24 hours daily, toll tel. 892-021, Italian only, consider having your hotelier call for you).

Point-to-Point Tickets

Train tickets may be a better value than railpasses for traveling in Italy. Fares are shown on the map on page 964, though fares can vary for the same journey depending on the time of day, the speed

Italy's Public Transportation

APPENDIX

SICILY

— RAIL   ✈ PRIVATE RAIL   ···· SHIP   --- BUS

✈ AIRPORT (NOT ALL SHOWN)

NOT TO SCALE

Train Costs in Italy

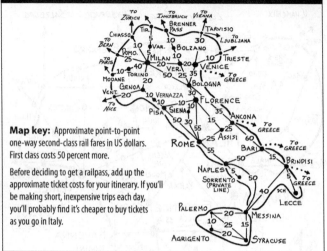

Map key: Approximate point-to-point one-way second-class rail fares in US dollars. First class costs 50 percent more.

Before deciding to get a railpass, add up the approximate ticket costs for your itinerary. If you'll be making short, inexpensive trips each day, you'll probably find it's cheaper to buy tickets as you go in Italy.

of the train, and more. **First-class** tickets cost 50 percent more than **second-class.** While second-class cars go as fast as their first-class neighbors, Italy is one country where I would consider the splurge of first class. The easiest way to "upgrade" a second-class ticket once on board a crowded train is to nurse a drink in the snack car.

Discounts: Families with young children can get price breaks—kids ages 4 and under travel free; ages 4–11 at half-price. Sometimes the parents get a 20 percent price break. Ask for the "Offerta Familia" deal when buying tickets at a counter (or, at a ticket machine, choose "Yes" at the "Do you want ticket issue?" prompt, then choose "Familia"). The deal doesn't apply to all trains at all times, but it's worth checking out.

Discounts for youths and seniors require purchase of a separate card (Carta Verde for ages 12–26 costs €40; Carta Argento for ages 60 and over is €30), but the discount on tickets is so minor (10–15 percent respectively for domestic travel), it's not worth it for most.

Buying Tickets: Avoid big-city train-station ticket lines whenever possible by using automated ticket machines (in train stations) or going to local travel agencies. You'll be able to easily purchase tickets, make seat reservations, and even book a *cuccetta* (koo-CHEHT-tah; overnight berth).

Automated ticket machines (marked *Biglietto Veloce/Fast Ticket*) are user-friendly and found in all but the tiniest stations in Italy. You can pay by cash (they give change) or by debit or credit

Anatomy of an Italian Train Ticket

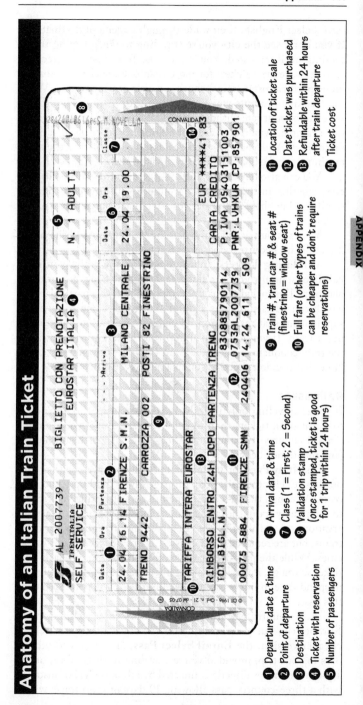

1. Departure date & time
2. Point of departure
3. Destination
4. Ticket with reservation
5. Number of passengers
6. Arrival date & time
7. Class (1 = First; 2 = Second)
8. Validation stamp (once stamped, ticket is good for 1 trip within 24 hours)
9. Train #, train car # & seat # (finestrino = window seat)
10. Full fare (other types of trains can be cheaper and don't require reservations)
11. Location of ticket sale
12. Date ticket was purchased
13. Refundable within 24 hours after train departure
14. Ticket cost

card. Select English, then wade through a menu of destinations. If you don't see the city you're traveling to, keep keying in the spelling until it's listed. You can choose from first- and second-class seats, request tickets for more than one traveler, and (on the high-speed Eurostar trains) choose an aisle or window seat. When the machine prompts you—"Fidelity Card?"—choose no. Don't select a discount rate without being sure that you meet the criteria (for example, Americans are not eligible for any EU or resident discounts). And you can even validate your ticket in the same machine if you're boarding your train right away.

You can also buy tickets and make reservations at **travel agencies,** whether in the station or around town. Agencies charge a small fee, but there's often less of a language barrier than at the station.

You can't buy tickets online on the Italian train website (www .trenitalia.it), because it does not accept US credit cards.

Validating Tickets: Before boarding the train, you must **validate** (stamp) your train documents in the yellow box near the platform. This includes whatever you need to take a particular trip, which can be as simple as a single ticket, but can also involve a supplement, seat reservation, or *cuccetta* reservation on an overnight train. If you forget to stamp your ticket, go right away to the train conductor—before he comes to you—or you'll pay a fine. Note that you don't need to stamp a railpass or e-ticket.

Railpasses

If you're traveling only in Italy, it may be cheaper to buy point-to-point train tickets than to get a railpass. But if you're taking a multi-country trip, the Eurail Select Pass is worth considering (and mentioned below).

The **Italy Pass** for Italian State Railways saves neither time nor hassle. Use the price map on page 964 to add up your ticket costs. Although the pass covers the full cost of getting you from A to B on many trains in Italy, it doesn't include the price of seat reservations or overnight berths. Reservations are optional for many trains, but are required for the fastest trains between major Italian cities. While the pass does save you from having to buy each train ticket as you go, if you'll be taking a few fast trains, you'll still have to spend time in line—essentially eliminating the point of buying this pass.

A 21-country **Eurail Global Pass** can work well for an all-Europe trip, but is a bad value for travel exclusively in Italy. A cheaper version, the **Eurail Select Pass,** allows you to tailor a pass to your trip, provided you're traveling in three, four, or five adjacent countries directly connected by rail or ferry. For instance, with a three-country pass allowing 10 days of train travel within

Railpasses

Prices listed are for 2010 and are subject to change. For the latest prices, details, and train schedules (and easy online ordering), see my comprehensive *Guide to Eurail Passes* at www.ricksteves.com/rail.

"Saver" prices are per person for two or more people traveling together. "Youth" means under age 26. The fare for children 4–11 is half the adult individual fare or Saver fare. Kids under age 4 travel free.

ITALY PASS

	Individual 1st Class	Individual 2nd Class	Saver 1st Class	Saver 2nd Class	Youth 2nd Class
3 days in 2 months	$230	$188	$196	$160	$152
Extra rail days (max 7)	$27-30	$21-24	$22-26	$18-21	$18-20

ITALY RAIL & DRIVE PASS

Any 3 rail days and 2 car days in 2 months.

Car Category	1st Class	2nd Class	Extra Car Day
Economy	$360	$306	$68
Compact	390	336	98
Intermediate	419	365	126
Extra rail days (max 7)	35	26	

Prices are per person, two traveling together. Solo travelers pay about 20 percent more. To order a Rail & Drive pass, call your travel agent or Rail Europe at 800-438-7245. *This pass is not sold by Europe Through the Back Door.*

FRANCE–ITALY PASS

	Individual 1st Class	Individual 2nd Class	Saver 1st Class	Saver 2nd Class	Youth 2nd Class
4 days in 2 months	$338	$288	$288	$245	$220
Extra rail days (max 6)	39-41	33-35	33-35	28-30	25-27

Be aware of your route. Many daytime connections from Paris to Italy pass through Switzerland (an additional $60 2nd class or $90 1st class if not covered by your pass). Routes via Nice, Torino, or Modane will bypass Switzerland. Direct Paris–Italy day or night trains are covered by the pass, regardless of their route.

GREECE–ITALY PASS

	Individual 1st Class	Individual 2nd Class	Saver 1st Class	Saver 2nd Class	Youth 2nd Class
4 days in 2 months	$322	$257	$273	$219	$210
Extra rail days (max 6)	33	27	29	23	21

Covers deck passage on overnight Superfast Ferries between Patras, Greece and Bari or Ancona, Italy (starts use of one travel day). Or 30-50% discount on Hellenic Mediterranean Line ferry with basic cabin Patras-Corfu-Brindisi (does not use a travel day). Does not cover travel to or on Greek islands, except a 30% discount on Blue Star Ferries.

SELECTPASS

This pass covers travel in three adjacent countries. Please visit **www.ricksteves.com/rail** for four- and five-country options.

	Individual 1st Class	Saver 1st Class	Youth 2nd Class
5 days in 2 months	$411	$349	$268
6 days in 2 months	454	387	297
8 days in 2 months	538	460	349
10 days in 2 months	624	528	404

APPENDIX

Deciphering Italian Train Schedules

At the station, look for the big yellow posters labeled *Partenze*—Departures (ignore the white posters, which show arrivals).

Schedules are listed chronologically, hour by hour, showing the trains leaving the station throughout the day. Each schedule has columns:

- The first column *(Ora)* lists the time of departure.
- The next column *(Treno)* shows the type of train.
- The third column *(Classi Servizi)* lists the services available (first- and second-class cars, dining car, *cuccetta* berths, etc.) and, more important, whether you need reservations (usually denoted by an *R* in a box). Note that all Eurostar (ES) and Alta Velocita (AV) trains, many InterCity (IC) and EuroCity (EC) trains, and most international trains require reservations.
- The next column lists the destination of the train *(Principali Fermate Destinazioni)*, often showing intermediate stops, followed by the final destination, with arrival times listed throughout in parentheses. Note that *your* final destination may be listed in fine print as an intermediate destination. If you're going from Milan to Florence, scan the schedule and you'll notice that virtually all trains that terminate in Rome stop in Florence en route. Travelers who read the fine print end up with a far greater choice of trains.
- The next column *(Servizi Diretti e Annotazioni)* has pertinent notes about the train, such as "also stops in..." *(ferma anche a...)*, "doesn't stop in..." *(non ferma a...)*, "stops in every station" *(ferma in tutte le stazioni)*, "delayed..." *(ritardo...)*, and so on.
- The last column lists the track *(Binario)* the train departs from. Confirm the *binario* with an additional source: a ticket seller, the electronic board that lists immediate departures, TV monitors on the platform, or the railway officials who are usually standing by the train unless you really need them.

For any odd symbols on the poster, look at the key at the end. Some of the phrasing can be deciphered easily, such as *servizio periodico* (periodic service—doesn't always run). For the trickier ones, ask a local or railway official, try your *Rick Steves' Italian Phrase Book & Dictionary,* or simply take a different train.

You can also check schedules—for trains anywhere in Italy, not just from the station you're currently in—at the handy ticket machines. Enter the date and time of your departure (to or from any Italian station), and you can view all your options.

a two-month period ($700 for a single adult in 2010), you could choose France–Italy–Greece or Germany–Austria–Italy. A **France and Italy Pass** combines just those two countries and covers night trains to and from Paris via Switzerland (but if your route crosses Switzerland by day, you'll pay extra—so the Select Pass is a better choice if you want to see the Alps). Before you buy a Select Pass or France and Italy Pass, think carefully how many travel days you'll really need. Use the pass only for travel days that involve long hauls or several trips. Pay out of pocket for tickets on days you're taking only short, cheap rides.

For a summary of railpass deals and the latest prices, check my Guide to Eurail Passes at www.ricksteves.com/rail. If you decide to get a railpass, this guide will help you know you're getting the right one for your trip.

Train Tips

This section contains information on making seat reservations, storing baggage, avoiding theft, and dealing with strikes.

Seat Reservations: Trains can fill up, even in first class. If you're on a tight schedule, you'll want to reserve a few days ahead for fast trains (see "Types of Trains," earlier). Purchasing required seat reservations onboard a train comes with a nasty penalty. Buying them at the station can be a time-waster unless you use the automatic ticket machines.

If you don't need a reservation, and if your train originates at your departure point (e.g., you're catching the Milan–Venice train in Milan), arriving at least 15 minutes before the departure time will help you snare a seat.

Some major stations have train composition posters on the platforms showing where first- and second-class cars are located when the trains arrive (letters on the poster are supposed to correspond to letters posted over the platform—but they don't always). Since most trains now allow you to make reservations up to the time of departure, conductors no longer mark reserved seats with a card—instead, they simply post a list of the reservable and non-reservable seat rows (sometimes in English) in each train car's vestibule. This means that if you board a crowded train and get one of the last seats, you may be ousted when the reservation holder comes along.

Baggage Storage: Many stations have *deposito bagagli* where you can safely leave your bag for €8 per 12-hour period (payable when you pick up the bag, double-check closing hours). Due to security concerns, no Italian stations have lockers.

Theft Concerns: Italian trains are famous for their thieves. Never leave a bag unattended. I've noticed that police now ride the trains, and things seem more controlled. Still, for an overnight trip, I'd feel safe only in a *cuccetta* (a bunk in a special sleeping car with an attendant who keeps track of who comes and goes while you sleep—approximately €20 in a 6-bed compartment, €25 in a less-cramped four-bed compartment).

Strikes: Strikes, which are common, generally last a day. Train employees will simply explain, *"Sciopero"* (strike). But in actuality, sporadic trains, following no particular schedule, lumber down the tracks during most strikes. When a strike is pending, travel agencies (and Web-savvy hoteliers) can check the Internet for you to see when the strike goes into effect and which trains will continue to run. If I need to get somewhere and know a strike is imminent, I leave early (heading off the strike, which often begins at 9:00), or I just go to the station with extra patience in tow and hop on anything rolling in the direction I want to go.

Buses

You can usually get anywhere you want to in Italy by bus, as long as you're not in a hurry, and plan ahead using bus schedules (pick up at local TIs). For reaching small towns, buses are sometimes the only option if you don't have a car.

Buy bus tickets at newsstands or *tabacchi* shops (with the big *T* signs). Confirm the departure point *("Dov'è la fermata?")*—some piazzas have more than one bus stop, so double-check that the posted schedule lists your destination and departure time. In general, orange buses are local city buses, and blue buses are for long distances.

Once the bus arrives, confirm the destination with the driver. You are expected to stow big backpacks underneath the bus (open the luggage compartment yourself if it's closed).

Sundays and holidays are problematic; even from large cities schedules are sparse, departing buses are jam-packed, and ticket offices are often closed. Plan ahead and buy your ticket in advance. Most travel agencies book bus (and train) tickets for just a small fee.

Renting a Car

If you're renting a car in Italy, bring your driver's license. You're also technically required to have an International Driving Permit—a translation of your driver's license (sold at your local AAA office for $15 plus the cost of two passport-type photos; see www.aaa.com). While that's the letter of the law, I've often rented cars in Italy without having—or being asked to show—this permit.

Rental companies require you to be at least 18 years old and to have held your license for one year. Drivers under the age of 25 may incur a young-driver surcharge, and some rental companies do not rent to anyone 75 and over. If you're considered too young or old, look into leasing, which has less-stringent age restrictions.

Research car rentals before you go. It's cheaper to arrange most car rentals from the US. Call several companies and look online to compare rates, or arrange a rental through your home-town travel agent.

Most of the major US rental agencies (such as Alamo/National, Avis, Budget, Dollar, Hertz, and Thrifty) have offices in Italy. It can be cheaper to use a consolidator, such as Auto Europe (www.autoeurope.com) or Europe by Car (www.ebctravel.com), but by using a middleman, you risk trading customer service for lower prices; if you have a problem with the rental company, you can't count on a consolidator to intervene on your behalf.

For the best rental deal, rent by the week with unlimited mileage. I normally rent the smallest, least-expensive model with a stick shift (cheaper than an automatic). Roads and parking spaces are narrow in Italy, so you'll do yourself a favor by renting the smallest car that meets your needs.

For a three-week rental, allow $900 per person (based on two people sharing a car), including insurance, tolls, gas, and parking. For trips of this length, look into leasing (see next page); you'll save money on insurance and taxes. Compare pick-up costs (downtown can be cheaper than the airport) and explore drop-off options (south of Rome can be a problem).

You can sometimes get a GPS unit with your rental car or leased vehicle for an additional fee (around $15/day; be sure it's set to English and has all the maps you need before you drive off). Or, if you have a portable GPS device at home, consider taking it with you to Europe (buy and upload European maps before your trip).

When you pick up the rental car, check it thoroughly and make sure any damage is noted on your rental agreement. Find out how your car's lights, turn signals, wipers, and gas cap function, and know what kind of gas the car takes.

Returning a car at a big-city train station can be tricky; get precise details on the car drop-off location and hours. Note that rental offices usually close from midday Saturday until Monday. When you return the car, make sure the agent verifies its condition with you.

If you want a car for only a couple of days, a **rail-and-drive pass** (such as a EurailDrive, Select Pass Drive, or Italy Rail and Drive) can be put to thoughtful use. Certain areas are great by car, such as the Dolomites and the hill towns of Tuscany and Umbria, while most of Italy (including the Cinque Terre) is best by train. The basic Italy Rail and Drive Pass, which includes theft insurance and CDW (CDW described below), comes with two days of car rental and three days of rail in two months. While rail-and-drive passes are convenient, they're also pricey, particularly for solo travelers.

Car Insurance Options

Accidents can happen anywhere, but when you're on vacation, the last thing you need is stress over car insurance. When you rent a car, you're liable for a very high deductible, sometimes equal to the entire value of the car. Limit your financial risk in case of an accident by choosing one of these two options: Buy Collision Damage Waiver (CDW) coverage from the car-rental company (figure roughly 25 percent extra), or get coverage through your credit card (free, but more complicated).

In Italy, most car-rental companies' rates automatically include CDW coverage. Even if you try to decline CDW when you reserve your Italian car, you may find when you show up at the counter that you must buy it after all.

While each rental company has its own variation, basic CDW costs $15–35 a day and reduces your liability, but does not eliminate it. When you pick up the car, you'll be offered the chance to "buy down" the deductible to zero (for an additional $15–30/day; this is sometimes called "super CDW").

If you opt for credit-card coverage, there's a catch. You'll technically have to decline all coverage offered by the car-rental company, which means they can place a hold on your card for up to the full value of the car. In case of damage, it can be time-consuming to resolve the charges with your credit-card company. Before you decide on this option, quiz your credit-card company about how it works.

For more on car-rental insurance, see www.ricksteves.com /cdw.

Theft Insurance: Note that theft insurance (separate from CDW insurance) is mandatory in Italy. The insurance usually costs about $15–20 a day, payable when you pick up the car.

Leasing

For trips of three weeks or more, consider leasing (which automatically includes zero-deductible collision and theft insurance). By technically buying and then selling back the car, you save lots of money on tax and insurance. Leasing provides you a brand-new car with unlimited mileage and a 24-hour emergency assistance program. You can lease for as little as 17 days to as long as six months. Car leases must be arranged from the US. One of many companies offering affordable lease packages is Europe by Car (US tel. 800-223-1516, www.ebctravel.com).

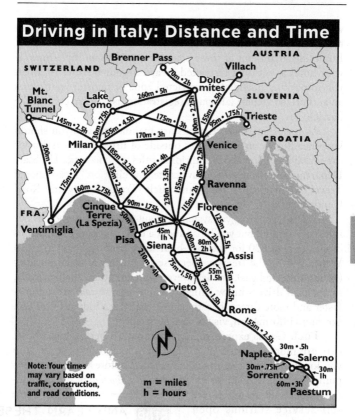

Driving in Italy: Distance and Time

Note: Your times may vary based on traffic, construction, and road conditions.

m = miles
h = hours

Driving

Driving in Italy can be scary—a video game for keeps, and you only get one quarter. Italian drivers can be aggressive. They drive fast and tailgate as if it were required. They pass where Americans are taught not to—on blind corners and just before tunnels. Roads have narrow shoulders or none at all. Driving in the countryside is less stressful than driving through urban areas, but stay alert. On one-lane roads, larger vehicles have the right-of-way. If you're on a

ZONA
TRAFFICO
LIMITATO

red↗

truckers' route, stifle your Good Samaritan impulse when you see provocatively dressed women standing by camper-vans at the side of the road; they're not having car trouble.

Road Rules: Stay out of restricted traffic zones or you'll risk huge fines. Car traffic is restricted in many city centers. Don't drive or park in any area that has a sign reading Zona Traffico Limitato (ZTL, often shown above a red circle, see image). If you do, your license plate can be photographed and a hefty (€100-plus) ticket mailed to your home without your ever having met a cop. Bumbling in and out of these zones can net you multiple fines. If your hotel is within a restricted area, ask your hotelier to direct you to parking outside the restricted zone or register your car as an authorized vehicle (although registration usually isn't worth the hassle).

As for other rules, seatbelts are mandatory, and you should keep headlights on at all times outside of urban areas. Ask your car-rental company about additional rules, or check the US State Department website (www.travel.state.gov, click on "International Travel," then specify "Italy" and click "Traffic Safety and Road Conditions").

Tolls: Italy's freeway system, the autostrada, is as good as our interstate system, but you'll pay about a dollar for every 10 minutes of use. (I paid €20 for the four-hour drive from Bolzano to Pisa.) While I favor the freeways because I feel they're safer, cheaper (saving time and gas), and less nerve-wracking than smaller roads, savvy local drivers know which toll-free *superstradas* are actually faster and more direct than the autostrada (e.g., Florence to Pisa). For more information, visit www.autostrade.it.

Fuel: Gas is expensive—often about $6 per gallon. Diesel cars are more common in Europe than back home, so be sure you know what type of gas your car takes before you fill up. Gas pumps are color-coded for unleaded *(senza piombo)* or diesel *(gaso-lio)*. Autostrada rest stops are self-service stations open daily without a siesta break. Many 24-hour-a-day stations are entirely automated. Small-town stations are usually cheaper and offer full service but shorter hours.

Maps and Signage: A good map is essential. Learn the universal road signs (explained in charts in most road atlases and at service stations). Although roads are numbered on maps, actual road signs don't list route numbers. Instead, roads are indicated by blue signs with a city name on them (for example, if you want to take a road heading east out of

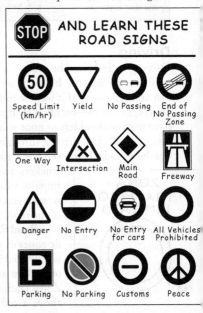

STOP **AND LEARN THESE ROAD SIGNS**

(50) Speed Limit (km/hr)	▽ Yield	No Passing	End of No Passing Zone
⇒ One Way	⊗ Intersection	◆ Main Road	Freeway
⚠ Danger	No Entry	No Entry for cars	All Vehicles Prohibited
P Parking	No Parking	⊖ Customs	Peace

Venice—marked route S-11 on your map—you'd follow signs to Padua, the next town along this road). The signs are inconsistent: They may direct you to the nearest big city or simply the next town along the route.

Theft: Cars are routinely vandalized and stolen. Thieves easily recognize rental cars and assume they are filled with a tourist's gear. Try to make your car look locally owned by hiding the "tourist-owned" rental-company decals and putting an Italian newspaper in your back window. Be sure all of your valuables are out of sight and locked in the trunk, or even better, with you or in your room.

Parking: White lines generally mean parking is free. Blue lines mean you'll have to pay—usually €1 per hour (use machine, leave time-stamped receipt on dashboard). If there's no meter, there's probably a roving attendant who will take your money. Study the signs. Often the free zones have a 30- or 60-minute time limit. Signs showing a street cleaner and a day of the week indicate which day the street is cleaned; there's a €100 tow-fee incentive to learn the days of the week in Italian.

Zona disco has nothing to do with dancing. Italian cars come equipped with a time disk (a cardboard clock), which you set at your arrival time and lay on the dashboard so the attendant knows how long you've parked. This is a fine system that all drivers should take advantage of. (If your rental car doesn't come with a *zona disco,* pick one up at a tobacco shop or just write your arrival time on a piece of paper and place it on the dashboard.)

Garages are safe, save time, and help you avoid the stress of parking tickets. Take the parking voucher with you to pay the cashier before you leave.

Cheap Flights

If you're visiting one or more cities on a longer European trip, or linking up far-flung Italian cities (such as Rome and Venice) consider the affordable intra-European airlines. While trains are still the best way to connect places that are close together, a flight can save both time and money on long journeys. When comparing a flight versus a train trip, consider the time it takes to get to the airport and how early you'll need to arrive to check in before the flight. Most flights make sense only as an alternate to a train ride five or more hours in length.

One of the best websites for comparing inexpensive flights is www.skyscanner.net. Other comparison search engines include www.wegolo.com and www.whichbudget.com.

Well-known cheapo airlines include easyJet (www.easyjet .com) and Ryanair (www.ryanair.com). Other budget airlines that touch down in Italy include Belle Air (www.belleair.it) and

Begin Your Trip at www.ricksteves.com

At our travel website, you'll find a wealth of free information on European destinations, including fresh monthly news and helpful tips from thousands of fellow travelers. You'll also find my latest guidebook updates (www.ricksteves.com/update) and my travel blog.

Our **online Travel Store** offers travel bags and accessories specially designed by me to help you travel smarter and lighter. These include my popular carry-on bags (roll-aboard and rucksack versions), money belts, totes, toiletries kits, adapters, other accessories, and a wide selection of guidebooks, planning maps, and DVDs.

Choosing the right **railpass** for your trip—amid hundreds of options—can drive you nutty. We'll help you choose the best pass for your needs, plus give you a bunch of free extras.

Rick Steves' Europe Through the Back Door travel company offers **tours** with more than three dozen itineraries and about 400 departures reaching the best destinations in this book...and beyond. Our Italy tours include "the best of" in 17 days, Village Italy in 14 days, South Italy in 13 days, Venice–Florence–Rome in 10 days, the Heart of Italy in 9 days, Sicily in 9 days, and a week-long Rome tour. You'll enjoy great guides, a fun bunch of travel partners (with small groups of generally around 28), and plenty of room to spread out in a big, comfy bus. You'll find European adventures to fit every vacation length. For all the details, and to get our Tour Catalog and a free Rick Steves Tour Experience DVD (filmed on location during an actual tour), visit www.ricksteves.com or call us at 425/608-4217.

Baboo (www.flybaboo.com). Italy-based discount airlines include Air One (www.flyairone.it), Meridiana (www.meridiana.it), and Windjet (http://w1.volawindjet.it). Airport websites may list small airlines that serve your destination.

Be aware of the potential drawbacks of flying on the cheap: nonrefundable and nonchangeable tickets, minimal or nonexistent customer service, treks to airports far outside town, and pricey baggage fees. If you're traveling with lots of luggage, a cheap flight can quickly become a bad deal. To avoid unpleasant surprises, read the small print before you book.

Resources

Resources from Rick Steves

Rick Steves' Italy 2011 is one of many books in my series on European travel, which includes country guidebooks, city guide-

books (Rome, Florence, Paris, London, etc.), Snapshot guides (excerpted chapters from my country guides), Pocket guides (full-color little books on big cities), and my budget-travel skills handbook, *Rick Steves' Europe Through the Back Door.* My phrase books—for Italian, French, German, Spanish, and Portuguese—are practical and budget-oriented. My other books include *Europe 101* (a crash course on art and history) and *Travel as a Political Act* (a travelogue sprinkled with tips for bringing home a global perspective). For a list of my books, see the inside of the last page of this book.

Video: My public television series, *Rick Steves' Europe,* covers European destinations in 100 shows, with 14 episodes on Italy. To watch episodes, visit www.hulu.com/rick-steves-europe; for scripts and other details, see www.ricksteves.com/tv.

Audio: My weekly public radio show, *Travel with Rick Steves,* features interviews with travel experts from around the world. I've also produced free self-guided audio tours of the top sights and neighborhoods in Florence, Rome, Venice, and more. All of this audio content is available for free at Rick Steves Audio Europe, an extensive online library organized by destination. Choose whatever interests you, and download it to your iPod, smartphone, or computer at www.ricksteves.com or iTunes.

Maps

The black-and-white maps in this book, designed by my well-traveled staff, are concise and simple. The maps are intended to help you locate recommended places and get to local TIs, where you can pick up more in-depth maps of cities and regions (usually free). Better maps are sold at newsstands and bookstores. Before you buy a map, look at it to be sure it has the level of detail you want. Drivers will want to pick up a good, detailed map in Europe (I'd recommend a 1:200,000- or 1:300,000-scale map).

Other Guidebooks

For most travelers, this book has more than enough information. But if you're heading beyond my recommended destinations, $40 for extra maps and books can be money well-spent. If you'll be spending a lot of time in Italian cities, consider these books in the Rick Steves series: *Florence, Rome,* and *Venice.*

The following books are worthwhile, though are not updated annually; check the publication date before you buy. Lonely Planet's *Italy* is thorough, well-researched, and packed with travel information, maps, and hotel recommendations for various budgets. The similar *Rough Guide to Italy* is also good and more insightful, updated by British researchers. The highly opinionated *Let's Go: Italy,* researched by Harvard students, is great for students and vagabonds. If you're a low-budget train traveler interested in hosteling and the youth and nightlife scene (which I have largely ignored), get *Let's Go: Italy.* The Italy section in the bigger *Let's Go: Europe* is sparse.

Cultural and Sightseeing Guides: The colorful Eyewitness series, which focuses mainly on sights, has editions on Italy, its various regions, and the major cities. They're fun for their great graphics and photos, but they're relatively skimpy on content and weigh a ton. You can buy them in Italy (no more expensive than in the US) or simply borrow a book for a minute from other travelers at certain sights to make sure that you're aware of that place's highlights. The tall, green Michelin guides to Italy and Rome have minimal information on room and board, but include great maps for drivers and lots of solid, encyclopedic coverage of sights, customs, and culture (sold in English in Italy). The Cadogan guides to various parts of Italy offer a thoughtful look at the rich and confusing local culture, as does *Culture Shock: Italy.*

Recommended Books and Movies

To learn more about Italy past and present, check out a few of these books or films.

Non-Fiction

For the classics of Italian history, look to Machiavelli's *The Prince* and *Florentine Histories*. Written in the 18th century, Edward Gibbon's *Decline and Fall of the Roman Empire* is the landmark history of ancient Rome.

Travelers' Tales Italy (Calcagno) is an excellent compilation of travel writing. Susan Cahill collected travelogues by female authors in *Desiring Italy*. In *Italian Days*, Barbara Grizzuti Harrison crafts travel essays on destinations ranging from Milan to Naples.

Italian Neighbors (Parks) describes life as an Englishman in a small Italian town, while *The Italians* (Barzini), written by an Italian, sheds light on the national character of this fascinating country.

Florence history buffs would enjoy reading the story of the Renaissance city's first family, *The House of Medici* (Hibbert). *Brunelleschi's Dome* (King) describes the trials involved with building Florence's magnificent Duomo. *Under the Tuscan Sun* was a bestseller for Frances Mayes (and is better than the movie of the same name).

Out of Paul Hofmann's multiple books about Italy, *The Seasons of Rome* is the favorite among readers. Elizabeth Gilbert's eloquent *Eat, Pray, Love* describes her time in Rome (in the "Eat" section). David Macaulay's illustrated books about the Eternal City—*Rome Antics* and *City: A Story of Roman Planning and Construction*—please both kids and adults.

For a solid overview of Venice, try *A History of Venice* (Norwich). Mary McCarthy's *Venice Observed* is a well-written memoir. In *The City of Falling Angels*, John Berendt tells the real-life mystery of the La Fenice Opera House fire.

For a true story about the Sicilian Mafia, consider *Excellent Cadavers* (Stille). *Midnight in Sicily* (Robb) offers a good general history of the Mob. In the memoir *Christ Stopped at Eboli: The Story of a Year*, Carlo Levi describes his banishment to southern Italy.

Pomp and Sustenance: Twenty-Five Centuries of Sicilian Food (Simeti) is both a cookbook and an historical overview. Gourmets also like *The Marling Menu-Master for Italy*.

Fiction

Fans of classical literature will want to read Dante's *Divine Comedy* and Boccaccio's *Decameron*. Among the Shakespeare plays set in Italy are *Romeo and Juliet* (Verona), *The Merchant of Venice, Much Ado About Nothing* (Sicily), *The Two Gentlemen of Verona*, and *The Taming of the Shrew* (Padua).

In his 18th-century collection of writings titled *Italian Journey*, Goethe describes his travels to Rome, Sicily, and Naples. Henry James often wrote stories with an Italian theme, and three recommended books—*The Wings of the Dove, Italian Hours,* and *The Aspern Papers and Other Stories*—use Venice as their backdrop. Another classic tale is Thomas Mann's *Death in Venice.*

For historical fiction that brings ancient Rome to life, try *The First Man in Rome* (McCullough) and *I, Claudius* (Graves). *Pompeii* (Harris), set in the ancient doomed city, tells of a young man's rescue attempt.

In the 19th and early 20th centuries, great European writers fell in love with Florence. Two great books from this time are George Eliot's *Romola* and E. M. Forster's *A Room with a View.* Modern novels with Florence as the setting include *The Passion of Artemisia* (Vreeland), *The Sixteen Pleasures* (Hellenga), *Birth of Venus* (Dunant), and *Galileo's Daughter* (Sobel).

If Venice is on your itinerary, consider reading *Invisible Cities* (Calvino), set in the city during Marco Polo's time; *The Passion* (Winterson), a complex tale of love; and *In the Company of the Courtesan* (Dunant), a chronicle of romantic intrigue in Renaissance Venice.

Regarded as one of the most important works of Italian literature, *The Leopard* (di Lampedusa) describes Sicilian life during the Risorgimento. *A Bell for Adano,* set in Sicily, won John Hersey the Pulitzer Prize in 1945. *A Soldier of the Great War* (Helprin)—which takes place partially in the Italian Alps and partially in Sicily—is a brutal tale set in World War I. *A Thread of Grace* (Russell) follows a group of Jews trying to find a safe haven in WWII Italy.

One of the best (and bestselling) murder mysteries is Umberto Eco's *The Name of the Rose,* set in a 14th-century Italian monastery. Mystery fans should also consider the books by Michael Dibdin, including *Ratking* (set in Umbria) and *Cabal* (Rome), *A Full Rich Death* (Florence), and *Dead Lagoon* (Venice). Dan Brown, the author of *The Da Vinci Code,* used Rome as the backdrop for his earlier murder mystery, *Angels and Demons.* Two Florentine-based mysteries are *The Dante Game* (Langton) and *Bella Donna* (Cherne). Donna Leon's detective stories often take place in Venice; *Death at La Fenice* is one of her most popular.

Films

Roberto Rossellini's *Open City* (1945) and Vittorio de Sica's *Bicycle Thieves* (1949), both classics of Italian Neorealism, continue to inspire audiences today.

In *Roman Holiday* (1953), Audrey Hepburn and Gregory Peck sightsee the city on his scooter. Two campy big-budget Hollywood flicks bring ancient Rome to life: *Ben-Hur* (1959) and *Spartacus* (1960). In *La Dolce Vita* (1961), Fellini captures the Roman character, while *Gladiator* (2000) was a crowd-pleaser and an Academy Award winner.

1900 (1977) is Bernardo Bertolucci's epic tale of life under fascism; it stars Robert De Niro and Gérard Depardieu.

A Room with a View (1986), a close adaptation of the classic novel, captures Florence's appeal to turn-of-the-century English travelers. Oscar-winning *Life Is Beautiful* (1997) has sections set in a Tuscan town.

Cinema Paradiso (1990), about a film projectionist and a little boy in post-WWII Sicily, won the Oscar for Best Foreign Picture. In *Enchanted April* (1991), filmed in Portofino, an all-star British cast fall in love, discuss relationships, eat well, and take naps in the sun. *Ciao, Professore!* (1994) shows the influence of a grade-school teacher in Southern Italy. In *Il Postino* (1995), poet Pablo Neruda befriends his Italian postman.

In *Bread and Tulips* (2000), a harassed Italian housewife discovers beauty, love, and her true self in Venice. For an adrenaline-laced chase scene through Venice's canals, see *The Italian Job* (2003).

The warm-hearted epic *Best of Youth* (2003), a story of two brothers, takes place in several Italian locations and gives you a good feel for the last several decades of Italian history. *Nuovomondo* (2006, also called *The Golden Door*) tells the story of Sicilian immigrants leaving home for Ellis Island.

Gorgeous Italian backdrops star in two 2010 movies: *Letters to Juliet*, shot in Verona and Siena, and the film adaptation of *Eat, Pray, Love*, with scenes in Naples and Rome.

Holidays and Festivals

Italy celebrates many holidays, which close sights and bring crowds.

Note that the following list (for 2011) isn't complete. In Italy, holidays seem to strike without warning. For instance, every town has a festival honoring its patron saint. Your best source for general information is the tourist information office in each town. You can also check with Italy's national tourist offices (www.italiantourism.com), listed at the beginning of this chapter. Be warned that the Vatican closes for many lesser-known Catholic holidays—confirm their schedule at http://mv.vatican.va. Before planning your trip around a festival, make sure that you verify the dates via the website for the festival or the national TI.

Jan	Fashion convention, Florence
Jan 1	New Year's Day
Jan 6	Epiphany
Feb 26–March 8	Carnevale (Mardi Gras, www.carnevale.venezia.it), Venice

2011

JANUARY						
S	M	T	W	T	F	S
						1
2	3	4	5	6	7	8
9	10	11	12	13	14	15
16	17	18	19	20	21	22
23/30	24/31	25	26	27	28	29

FEBRUARY						
S	M	T	W	T	F	S
		1	2	3	4	5
6	7	8	9	10	11	12
13	14	15	16	17	18	19
20	21	22	23	24	25	26
27	28					

MARCH						
S	M	T	W	T	F	S
		1	2	3	4	5
6	7	8	9	10	11	12
13	14	15	16	17	18	19
20	21	22	23	24	25	26
27	28	29	30	31		

APRIL						
S	M	T	W	T	F	S
					1	2
3	4	5	6	7	8	9
10	11	12	13	14	15	16
17	18	19	20	21	22	23
24	25	26	27	28	29	30

MAY						
S	M	T	W	T	F	S
1	2	3	4	5	6	7
8	9	10	11	12	13	14
15	16	17	18	19	20	21
22	23	24	25	26	27	28
29	30	31				

JUNE						
S	M	T	W	T	F	S
			1	2	3	4
5	6	7	8	9	10	11
12	13	14	15	16	17	18
19	20	21	22	23	24	25
26	27	28	29	30		

JULY						
S	M	T	W	T	F	S
					1	2
3	4	5	6	7	8	9
10	11	12	13	14	15	16
17	18	19	20	21	22	23
24/31	25	26	27	28	29	30

AUGUST						
S	M	T	W	T	F	S
	1	2	3	4	5	6
7	8	9	10	11	12	13
14	15	16	17	18	19	20
21	22	23	24	25	26	27
28	29	30	31			

SEPTEMBER						
S	M	T	W	T	F	S
				1	2	3
4	5	6	7	8	9	10
11	12	13	14	15	16	17
18	19	20	21	22	23	24
25	26	27	28	29	30	

OCTOBER						
S	M	T	W	T	F	S
						1
2	3	4	5	6	7	8
9	10	11	12	13	14	15
16	17	18	19	20	21	22
23/30	24/31	25	26	27	28	29

NOVEMBER						
S	M	T	W	T	F	S
		1	2	3	4	5
6	7	8	9	10	11	12
13	14	15	16	17	18	19
20	21	22	23	24	25	26
27	28	29	30			

DECEMBER						
S	M	T	W	T	F	S
				1	2	3
4	5	6	7	8	9	10
11	12	13	14	15	16	17
18	19	20	21	22	23	24
25	26	27	28	29	30	31

Mid-Feb	Carnevale Celebrations/Mardi Gras in Florence (costumed parades, street water fights, jousting competitions)
First week of April	Vinitaly (wine festival), Verona
April/May	Italy's Cultural Heritage Week (check www.beniculturali.it)
April 21	City Birthday, Rome
April 24	Easter Sunday (and Scoppio del Carro fireworks in Florence)
April 25	Easter Monday
April 25	Italian Liberation Day, St. Mark's Day, Venice
May 1	Labor Day
Mid-May	Cricket Festival, Florence (music, entertainment, food, crickets sold in cages)
Late May–Early June	Vogalonga Regatta, Venice
June	Fashion convention, Florence

APPENDIX

June 1–30	Annual Flower Display, Florence (carpet of flowers on the main square, Piazza della Signoria)
June 2	Anniversary of the Republic, Feast of the Ascension Day
June 16–17	Festival of St. Ranieri, Pisa
Mid-June–Aug	Verona Opera season
June 24	St. John the Baptist Day, Rome; Festival of St. John, Florence (parades, dances, boat races); and Calcio Fiorentino (costumed soccer game on Florence's Piazza Santa Croce)
June 29	Sts. Peter and Paul Day, most fervently celebrated in Rome
Late June–Early Sept	Florence's annual outdoor cinema season (contemporary films)
July 2	Palio horse race, Siena
Early July	Murano Regatta
July 16–17	Feast and Regatta of the Redeemer (third Sun in July and the preceding evening—parade, fireworks), Venice
Aug	Musical Weeks, Lake Maggiore
Aug 10	St. Lawrence Day, Rome
Aug 15	Assumption of Mary (Ferragosto)
Aug 16	Palio horse race, Siena
Sept	Chestnut Festivals (festivals, chestnut roasts), most towns, mainly north of Rome
First week of Sept	Festa della Rificolona, Florence (children's procession with lanterns, street performances, parade)
Sept 3–4	Historical Regatta, Venice
Sept 13–14	Volto Santo (procession and fair), Lucca
Mid-Sept	Burano Regatta
Oct	Musica dei Popoli Festival, Florence (ethnic and folk music and dances)
Oct 8–9	Castelrotto Festival (second weekend in Oct), Dolomites
Nov 1	All Saints' Day
Nov 21	Feast of Our Lady of Good Health, Venice
Dec	Christmas Market, Rome, Piazza Navona, and crèches in churches throughout Italy
Dec 8	Feast of the Immaculate Conception
Dec 25	Christmas
Dec 26	St. Stephen's Day

Conversions and Climate

Numbers and Stumblers

- Europeans write a few of their numbers differently than we do. 1 = 1, 4 = 4, 7 = 7.
- In Europe, dates appear as day/month/year, so Christmas is 25/12/11.
- Commas are decimal points and decimals commas. A dollar and a half is 1,50, and there are 5.280 feet in a mile.
- When pointing, use your whole hand, palm down.
- When counting with fingers, start with your thumb. If you hold up your first finger to request one item, you'll probably get two.
- What Americans call the second floor of a building is the first floor in Europe.
- On escalators and moving sidewalks, Europeans keep the left "lane" open for passing. Keep to the right.

Metric Conversions (approximate)

A kilogram is 2.2 pounds, and 1 liter is about a quart, or almost four to a gallon. A kilometer is six-tenths of a mile. I figure kilometers to miles by cutting them in half and adding back 10 percent of the original (120 km: 60 + 12 = 72 miles, 300 km: 150 + 30 = 180 miles).

1 foot = 0.3 meter	1 square yard = 0.8 square meter
1 yard = 0.9 meter	1 square mile = 2.6 square kilometers
1 mile = 1.6 kilometers	1 ounce = 28 grams
1 centimeter = 0.4 inch	1 quart = 0.95 liter
1 meter = 39.4 inches	1 kilogram = 2.2 pounds
1 kilometer = 0.62 mile	32°F = 0°C

Roman Numerals

In the US, you'll see Roman numerals—which originated in ancient Rome—used for copyright dates, clocks, and the Super Bowl. In Italy, you're likely to observe these numbers chiseled on statues and buildings. If you want to do some numeric detective work, here's how: In Roman numerals, as in ours, the highest numbers (thousands, hundreds) come first, followed by smaller numbers. Many numbers are made by combining numerals into sets: V = 5, so VIII = 8 (5 plus 3). Roman numerals follow a subtraction principle for multiples of fours (4, 40, 400, etc.) and nines (9, 90, 900, etc.); the number four, for example, is written as IV (1 subtracted from 5), rather than IIII. The number nine is IX (1 subtracted from 10).

   Rick Steves' Italy 2011—written in Italian with Roman numerals—would translate as *Rick Steves' Italia MMXI*. Big numbers such as dates can look daunting at first. The easiest way to handle them is to read the numbers in discrete chunks. For example, Michelangelo was born in MCDLXXV. Break it down: M (1,000) + CD (100 subtracted from 500, or 400) + LXX (50 + 10 + 10, or 70) + V (5) = 1475. It was a very good year.

M = 1000	XL = 40
CM = 900	X = 10
D = 500	IX = 9
CD = 400	V = 5
C = 100	IV = 4
XC = 90	I = duh
L = 50	

Clothing Sizes

When shopping for clothing, use these US-to-European comparisons as general guidelines (but note that no conversion is perfect).

- Women's dresses and blouses: Add 30
  (US size 10 = European size 40)
- Men's suits and jackets: Add 10
  (US size 40 regular = European size 50)
- Men's shirts: Multiply by 2 and add about 8
  (US size 15 collar = European size 38)
- Women's shoes: Add about 30
  (US size 8 = European size 38–39)
- Men's shoes: Add 32–34
  (US size 9 = European size 41; US size 11 = European size 45)

Italy's Climate

First line, average daily temperature; second line, average daily low; third line, average days without rain. For more detailed weather statistics for destinations in this book (as well as the rest of the world), check www.worldclimate.com.

J	F	M	A	M	J	J	A	S	O	N	D
Rome											
52°	55°	59°	66°	74°	82°	87°	86°	79°	71°	61°	55°
40°	42°	45°	50°	56°	63°	67°	67°	62°	55°	49°	44°
13	19	23	24	26	26	30	29	25	23	19	21
Milan and Florence											
40°	46°	56°	65°	74°	80°	84°	82°	75°	63°	51°	43°
32°	35°	43°	49°	57°	63°	67°	66°	61°	52°	43°	35°
25	21	24	22	23	21	25	24	25	23	20	24
Venice											
42°	46°	53°	62°	70°	76°	81°	80°	75°	65°	53°	46°
33°	35°	41°	49°	56°	63°	66°	65°	61°	53°	44°	37°
25	21	24	21	23	22	24	24	25	24	21	23

Temperature Conversion:
Fahrenheit and Celsius

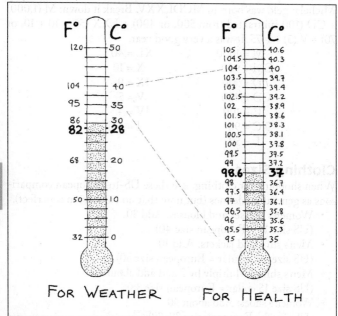

FOR WEATHER   FOR HEALTH

Europe takes its temperature using the Celsius scale, while we opt for Fahrenheit. For a rough conversion from Celsius to Fahrenheit, double the number and add 30. For weather, remember that 28°C is 82°F—perfect. For health, 37°C is just right.

Essential Packing Checklist

Whether you're traveling for five days or five weeks, here's what you'll need to bring. Remember to pack light to enjoy the sweet freedom of true mobility. Happy travels!

- ❑ 5 shirts
- ❑ 1 sweater or lightweight fleece jacket
- ❑ 2 pairs pants
- ❑ 1 pair shorts
- ❑ 1 swimsuit (women only—men can use shorts)
- ❑ 5 pairs underwear and socks
- ❑ 1 pair shoes
- ❑ 1 rain-proof jacket
- ❑ Tie or scarf
- ❑ Money belt
- ❑ Money—your mix of:
  - ❑ Debit card for ATM withdrawals
  - ❑ Credit card
  - ❑ Hard cash in US dollars ($20 bills)
- ❑ Documents (and back-up photocopies):
  - ❑ Passport
  - ❑ Printout of airline e-ticket
  - ❑ Driver's license
  - ❑ Student ID and hostel card
  - ❑ Railpass/car rental voucher
  - ❑ Insurance details
- ❑ Daypack
- ❑ Sealable plastic baggies
- ❑ Camera and related gear
- ❑ Empty water bottle
- ❑ Wristwatch and alarm clock
- ❑ Earplugs
- ❑ First-aid kit
- ❑ Medicine (labeled)
- ❑ Extra glasses/contacts and prescriptions
- ❑ Sunscreen and sunglasses
- ❑ Toiletries kit
- ❑ Soap
- ❑ Laundry soap
- ❑ Clothesline
- ❑ Small towel
- ❑ Sewing kit
- ❑ Travel information
- ❑ Necessary map(s)
- ❑ Address list (email and mailing addresses)
- ❑ Postcards and photos from home
- ❑ Notepad and pen
- ❑ Journal

If you plan to carry on your luggage, note that all liquids must be in three-ounce or smaller containers and fit within a single quart-size baggie. For details, see www.tsa.gov/travelers.

Hotel Reservation

To: _____   _____
          hotel   *email or fax*

From: _____   _____
            name   *email or fax*

Today's date: _____ /_____ /_____
                    day   *month*   *year*

Dear Hotel _____ ,

Please make this reservation for me:

Name: _____

Total # of people: _____   # of rooms: _____   # of nights: _____

Arriving: _____ /_____ /_____   My time of arrival (24-hr clock): _____
              day *month* *year*   (I will telephone if I will be late)

Departing: ____ /____ /____
                day *month* *year*

Room(s): Single____   Double ____   Twin ____   Triple ____   Quad____

With: Toilet _____   Shower _____   Bath _____   Sink only ____

Special needs: View____   Quiet ____   Cheapest ____   Ground Floor____

Please email or fax confirmation of my reservation, along with the type of room reserved and the price. Please also inform me of your cancellation policy. After I hear from you, I will quickly send my credit-card information as a deposit to hold the room. Thank you.

_____
Name

_____
Address

_____
City   *State*   *Zip Code*   *Country*

Before hoteliers can make your reservation, they want to know the information listed above. You can use this form as the basis for your email, or you can photocopy this page, fill in the information, and send it as a fax (also available online at www.ricksteves.com/reservation).

Italian Survival Phrases

Good day.	**Buon giorno.**	bwohn JOR-noh
Do you speak English?	**Parla inglese?**	PAR-lah een-GLAY-zay
Yes. / No.	**Sì. / No.**	see / noh
I (don't) understand.	**(Non) capisco.**	(nohn) kah-PEES-koh
Please.	**Per favore.**	pehr fah-VOH-ray
Thank you.	**Grazie.**	GRAHT-seeay
You're welcome.	**Prego.**	PRAY-go
I'm sorry.	**Mi dispiace.**	mee dee-speeAH-chay
Excuse me.	**Mi scusi.**	mee SKOO-zee
(No) problem.	**(Non) c'è un problema.**	(nohn) cheh oon proh-BLAY-mah
Good.	**Va bene.**	vah BEHN-ay
Goodbye.	**Arrivederci.**	ah-ree-vay-DEHR-chee
one / two	**uno / due**	OO-noh / DOO-ay
three / four	**tre / quattro**	tray / KWAH-troh
five / six	**cinque / sei**	CHEENG-kway / SEHee
seven / eight	**sette / otto**	SEHT-tay / OT-toh
nine / ten	**nove / dieci**	NOV-ay / deeAY-chee
How much is it?	**Quanto costa?**	KWAHN-toh KOS-tah
Write it?	**Me lo scrive?**	may loh SKREE-vay
Is it free?	**È gratis?**	eh GRAH-tees
Is it included?	**È incluso?**	eh een-KLOO-zoh
Where can I buy / find...?	**Dove posso comprare / trovare...?**	DOH-vay POS-soh kohm-PRAH-ray / troh-VAH-ray
I'd like / We'd like...	**Vorrei / Vorremmo...**	vor-REHee / vor-RAY-moh
...a room.	**...una camera.**	OO-nah KAH-meh-rah
...a ticket to ___.	**...un biglietto per ___.**	oon beel-YEHT-toh pehr
Is it possible?	**È possibile?**	eh poh-SEE-bee-lay
Where is...?	**Dov'è...?**	DOH-veh
...the train station	**...la stazione**	lah staht-seeOH-nay
...the bus station	**...la stazione degli autobus**	lah staht-seeOH-nay DAYL-yee OW-toh-boos
...tourist information	**...informazioni per turisti**	een-for-maht-seeOH-nee pehr too-REE-stee
...the toilet	**...la toilette**	lah twah-LEHT-tay
men	**uomini, signori**	WOH-mee-nee, seen-YOH-ree
women	**donne, signore**	DON-nay, seen-YOH-ray
left / right	**sinistra / destra**	see-NEE-strah / DEHS-trah
straight	**sempre diritto**	SEHM-pray dee-REE-toh
When do you open / close?	**A che ora aprite / chiudete?**	ah kay OH-rah ah-PREE-tay / keeoo-DAY-tay
At what time?	**A che ora?**	ah kay OH-rah
Just a moment.	**Un momento.**	oon moh-MAYN-toh
now / soon / later	**adesso / presto / tardi**	ah-DEHS-soh / PREHS-toh / TAR-dee
today / tomorrow	**oggi / domani**	OH-jee / doh-MAH-nee

In the Restaurant

I'd like...	Vorrei...	vor-REHee
We'd like...	Vorremmo...	vor-RAY-moh
...to reserve...	...prenotare...	pray-noh-TAH-ray
...a table for one / two.	...un tavolo per uno / due.	oon TAH-voh-loh pehr OO-noh / DOO-ay
Non-smoking.	Non fumare.	nohn foo-MAH-ray
Is this seat free?	È libero questo posto?	eh LEE-bay-roh KWEHS-toh POH-stoh
The menu (in English), please.	Il menù (in inglese), per favore.	eel may-NOO (een een-GLAY-zay) pehr fah-VOH-ray
service (not) included	servizio (non) incluso	sehr-VEET-seeoh (nohn) een-KLOO-zoh
cover charge	pane e coperto	PAH-nay ay koh-PEHR-toh
to go	da portar via	dah POR-tar VEE-ah
with / without	con / senza	kohn / SEHN-sah
and / or	e / o	ay / oh
menu (of the day)	menù (del giorno)	may-NOO (dayl JOR-noh)
specialty of the house	specialità della casa	spay-chah-lee-TAH DEHL-lah KAH-zah
first course (pasta, soup)	primo piatto	PREE-moh peeAH-toh
main course (meat, fish)	secondo piatto	say-KOHN-doh peeAH-toh
side dishes	contorni	kohn-TOR-nee
bread	pane	PAH-nay
cheese	formaggio	for-MAH-joh
sandwich	panino	pah-NEE-noh
soup	minestra, zuppa	mee-NEHS-trah, TSOO-pah
salad	insalata	een-sah-LAH-tah
meat	carne	KAR-nay
chicken	pollo	POH-loh
fish	pesce	PEH-shay
seafood	frutti di mare	FROO-tee dee MAH-ray
fruit / vegetables	frutta / legumi	FROO-tah / lay-GOO-mee
dessert	dolci	DOHL-chee
tap water	acqua del rubinetto	AH-kwah dayl roo-bee-NAY-toh
mineral water	acqua minerale	AH-kwah mee-nay-RAH-lay
milk	latte	LAH-tay
(orange) juice	succo (d'arancia)	SOO-koh (dah-RAHN-chah)
coffee / tea	caffè / tè	kah-FEH / teh
wine	vino	VEE-noh
red / white	rosso / bianco	ROH-soh / beeAHN-koh
glass / bottle	bicchiere / bottiglia	bee-keeAY-ray / boh-TEEL-yah
beer	birra	BEE-rah
Cheers!	Cin cin!	cheen cheen
More. / Another.	Ancora un po.' / Un altro.	ahn-KOH-rah oon poh / oon AHL-troh
The same.	Lo stesso.	loh STEHS-soh
The bill, please.	Il conto, per favore.	eel KOHN-toh pehr fah-VOH-ray
tip	mancia	MAHN-chah
Delicious!	Delizioso!	day-leet-seeOH-zoh

For more user-friendly Italian phrases, check out *Rick Steves' Italian Phrase Book & Dictionary* or *Rick Steves' French, Italian, and German Phrase Book*.

INDEX

INDEX

INDEX

INDEX

MAP INDEX

Audio Europe

Free mobile app (and podcast)

With the **Rick Steves Audio Europe** app, your iPhone or smartphone becomes a powerful travel tool.

This exciting app organizes Rick's entire audio library by country— giving you a playlist of all his audio walking tours, radio interviews, and travel tips for wherever you're going in Europe.

Let the experts Rick interviews enrich your understanding. Let Rick's self-guided tours amplify your guidebook. With Rick in your ear, Europe gets even better.

Thanks Facebook fans for submitting photos while on location! From top: John Kuijper in Florence, Brenda Mamer with her mother in Rome, Angel Capobianco in London, and Alyssa Passey with her friend in Paris.

▶ Plan Your Trip

Browse thousands of articles and a wealth of money-saving tips for planning your dream trip. You'll find up-to-date information on Europe's best destinations, packing smart, getting around, finding rooms, staying healthy, avoiding scams and more.

▶ Eurail Passes

Find out, step-by-step, if a railpass makes sense for your trip—and how to avoid buying more than you need. Get a bunch of free extras!

▶ Graffiti Wall & Travelers' Helpline

Learn, ask, share—our online community of savvy travelers is a great resource for first-time travelers to Europe, as well as seasoned pros.

Rick Steves®

www.ricksteves.com

EUROPE GUIDES

Best of Europe
Eastern Europe
Europe Through the Back Door

COUNTRY GUIDES

Croatia & Slovenia
England
France
Germany
Great Britain
Ireland
Italy
Portugal
Scandinavia
Spain
Switzerland

CITY & REGIONAL GUIDES

Amsterdam, Bruges & Brussels
Athens & the Peloponnese
Budapest
Florence & Tuscany
Istanbul
London
Paris
Prague & the Czech Republic
Provence & the French Riviera
Rome
Venice
Vienna, Salzburg & Tirol

SNAPSHOT GUIDES

Barcelona
Berlin
Bruges & Brussels
Copenhagen & the Best of
    Denmark
Dublin
Dubrovnik
Hill Towns of Central Italy
Italy's Cinque Terre
Krakow, Warsaw & Gdansk
Lisbon
Madrid & Toledo
Munich, Bavaria & Salzburg
Naples & the Amalfi Coast
Northern Ireland
Norway
Scotland
Sevilla, Granada & Southern Spain
Stockholm

TRAVEL CULTURE

Europe 101
European Christmas
Postcards from Europe
Travel as a Political Act

Rick Steves guidebooks are published by Avalon Travel,
a member of the Perseus Books Group.

NOW AVAILABLE: eBOOKS, APPS, DVDs, & BLU-RAY

eBOOKS

Most guides available as eBooks from Amazon, Barnes & Noble, Borders, Apple iBook and Sony eReader, beginning January 2011

RICK STEVES' EUROPE DVDs

Austria & the Alps
Eastern Europe, Israel & Egypt
England & Wales
European Travel Skills & Specials
France
Germany, Benelux & More
Greece & Turkey
Iran
Ireland & Scotland
Italy's Cities
Italy's Countryside
Rick Steves' European Christmas
Scandinavia
Spain & Portugal

BLU-RAY

Celtic Charms
Eastern Europe Favorites
European Christmas
Italy Through the Back Door
Surprising Cities of Europe

PHRASE BOOKS & DICTIONARIES

French
French, Italian & German
German
Italian
Portuguese
Spanish

JOURNALS

Rick Steves' Pocket Travel Journal
Rick Steves' Travel Journal

APPS

Rick Steves' Ancient Rome Tour
Rick Steves' Historic Paris Walk
Rick Steves' Louvre Tour
Rick Steves' Orsay Museum Tour
Rick Steves' St. Peter's Basilica Tour
Rick Steves' Versailles

PLANNING MAPS

Britain, Ireland & London
Europe
France & Paris
Germany, Austria & Switzerland
Ireland
Italy
Spain & Portugal

Credits

Researchers

To update his four books on Italy, Rick relied on the help of...

Helen Inman

After graduating with a law degree, Helen left England for the Mediterranean, finding sunshine, vibrant energy, and Latin culture and languages. Currently working as a guide for Rick Steves tours and as a guidebook researcher, she enjoyed five years in *bella* Roma before moving to Spain, where she thrives on a diet of dancing, laughter, *cava,* and seafood.

Ben Cameron

Ben experienced his first taste of European travel when he was three, exploring medieval castles with his parents. Returning after graduation, he was hooked and has spent much of his time since exploring Europe independently and leading tours for Rick Steves. When not living out of his backpack, he splits his time between Rome and Seattle.

Amanda Scotese

Amanda Scotese freelances as a journalist and editor in Chicago. Her travels in Italy include a stint selling leather jackets in Florence's San Lorenzo Market, basking in the Sicilian sun, and of course, helping out with Rick Steves' guidebooks and tours.

Contributor

Gene Openshaw

Gene is the co-author of seven Rick Steves' books. For this book, he wrote material on Italy's art, history, and contemporary culture. When not traveling, Gene enjoys composing music, recovering from his 1973 trip to Europe with Rick, and living everyday life with his daughter.

Images

Location	Photographer
Front color matter, title page: Varenna	David C. Hoerlein
Front color matter: Venice	Mike Potter
Front color matter: Venice	Laura VanDeventer
Venice: Church of San Giorgio Maggiore	David C. Hoerlein
Towns Near Venice: Verona's Roman Arena	David C. Hoerlein
The Dolomites: Alpe di Siusi	Julie Coen
The Lakes: Bellagio	Rick Steves
Milan: Cathedral (Duomo)	David C. Hoerlein
Cinque Terre: Corniglia	Rick Steves
Riviera Towns near the Cinque Terre: Portofino	David C. Hoerlein
Florence: View from Piazzale Michelangelo	Rick Steves
Pisa and Lucca: Pisa's Field of Miracles	Rick Steves
Siena: Il Campo	David C. Hoerlein
Assisi: Basilica of St. Francis	Rick Steves
Hill Towns of Central Italy: Civita di Bagnoregio	David C. Hoerlein
Rome: Piazza Navona	Rick Steves
Naples: Mt. Vesuvius	David C. Hoerlein
Sorrento and Capri: Capri	David C. Hoerlein
Amalfi Coast and Paestum: Positano	David C. Hoerlein

Images

Rick Steves' Guidebook Series

Country Guides

Rick Steves' Best of Europe

Rick Steves' Croatia &
  Slovenia

Rick Steves' Eastern Europe

Rick Steves' England

Rick Steves' France

Rick Steves' Germany

Rick Steves' Great Britain

Rick Steves' Ireland

Rick Steves' Italy

Rick Steves' Portugal

Rick Steves' Scandinavia

Rick Steves' Spain

Rick Steves' Switzerland

City and Regional Guides

Rick Steves' Amsterdam,
  Bruges & Brussels

Rick Steves' Athens &
  the Peloponnese

Rick Steves' Budapest

Rick Steves' Florence &
  Tuscany

Rick Steves' Istanbul

Rick Steves' London

Rick Steves' Paris

Rick Steves' Prague &
  the Czech Republic

Rick Steves' Provence &
  the French Riviera

Rick Steves' Rome

Rick Steves' Venice

Rick Steves' Vienna,
  Salzburg & Tirol

Rick Steves' Phrase Books

French

French/Italian/German

German

Italian

Portuguese

Spanish

Snapshot Guides

Excerpted chapters from country guides, such as *Rick Steves'
Snapshot Barcelona, Rick Steves' Snapshot Scotland,* and
Rick Steves' Snapshot Hill Towns of Central Italy.

Pocket Guides (new in 2011)

Condensed, pocket-size, full-color guides to Europe's top
cities: Paris, London, and Rome.

Other Books

Rick Steves' Europe 101: History and Art for the Traveler

Rick Steves' Europe Through the Back Door

Rick Steves' European Christmas

Rick Steves' Postcards from Europe

Rick Steves' Travel as a Political Act

Avalon Travel
a member of the Perseus Books Group
1700 Fourth Street
Berkeley, CA 94710

Printed in the U.S.A. by Worzalla. First printing September 2010.

ISBN 978-1-59880-660-1
ISSN 1084-4422

For the latest on Rick's lectures, guidebooks, tours, public radio show, and public television
series, contact Europe Through the Back Door, Box 2009, Edmonds, WA 98020, tel.
425/771-8303, fax 425/771-0833, www.ricksteves.com, rick@ricksteves.com.

Europe Through the Back Door Reviewing Editor: Cameron Hewitt
ETBD Editors: Jennifer Madison Davis, Tom Griffin, Gretchen Strauch,
    Sarah McCormic, Cathy McDonald, Cathy Lu
ETBD Managing Editor: Risa Laib
Research Assistance: Helen Inman, Ben Cameron, Amanda Scotese, Trina Kudlacek,
    Cathy McDonald, Cathy Lu
Avalon Travel Senior Editor and Series Manager: Madhu Prasher
Avalon Travel Project Editor: Kelly Lydick
Copy Editor: Amy Scott
Proofreader: Patrick Collins
Indexer: Stephen Callahan
Production and Typesetting: McGuire Barber Design
Cover Design: Kimberly Glyder Design
Graphic Content Director: Laura VanDeventer
Maps & Graphics: David C. Hoerlein, Laura VanDeventer, Lauren Mills, Barb Geisler,
    Mike Morgenfeld, Brice Ticen
Photography: Rick Steves, Gene Openshaw, David C. Hoerlein, Laura VanDeventer,
    Jennifer Hauseman, Dominic Bonuccelli, Mike Potter, Les Wahlstrom, Robyn Cronin,
    Bruce VanDeventer, Anne Jenkins Steves
Cover Photo: Varenna, Italy © David C. Hoerlein

Foldout Color Map ▶

The foldout map on the opposite page includes:
• **A map of Italy on one side**
• **City maps, including Rome, Florence, Venice,
  and Siena on the other side**